Encyclopedia of

Women's

Associations

Worldwide

ENCYCLOPEDIA OF
Women's
Associations
Worldwide

A Guide to Over 3,400 National and Multinational Nonprofit Women's
and Women-Related Organizations

Jacqueline K. Barrett, Editor
Jane A. Malonis, Associate Editor

 Gale Research International Ltd.

LONDON   DETROIT   WASHINGTON D. C.

Donald P. Boyden, *Senior Editor*
Jacqueline K. Barrett, *Editor*
Deborah M. Burek, Lee Ripley Greenfield, Karin E. Koek,
and Susan B. Martin, *Contributing Editors*

Editorial Staff

Jane A. Malonis, *Associate Editor*
Yolanda A. Johnson, Jeffrey Lehman, Julie A. Synkonis,
Linda Thurn, and Melissa Walsh, *Assistant Editors*

Contributors

Mike Kroll, *Associate Editor*
Kelly M. Cross, and Carolyn A. Fischer, *Assistant Editors*

Research Staff

Victoria B. Cariappa, *Research Manager*
Gary J. Oudersluys, *Research Supervisor*
Tracie A. Wade, *Editorial Associate*
Melissa E. Brown, Andreia Earley, Charles Jewell,
Kim Klaty, Colin C. McDonald, Michele McRobert,
Michele D. Pica, Phyllis Shepherd, and
Barbara J. Thornton, *Editorial Assistants*

Production Staff

Mary Beth Trimper, *Production Manager*
Mary Kelley, *External Production Assistant*

Cynthia D. Baldwin, *Art Director*
Barbara Yarrow, *Graphic Services Supervisor*
Nicholas Jakubiak, *Map Illustrator*
Yolanda Y. Latham, *Desktop Publisher*

Benita L. Spight, *Data Entry Supervisor*
Gwendolyn S. Tucker, *Data Entry Group Leader*
Kenneth D. Benson, Jr., *Data Entry Associate*

Theresa Rocklin, *Supervisor of Systems and Programming*
Dan Bono, *Programmer*

The paper used in this publication meets the minimum requirements of American National Standard for Information Sciences --
Permanence Paper for Printed Library Materials, ANSI Z39.48-1984. ∞™

Copyright © 1993
Gale Research International Ltd.
Cheriton House
North Way
Andover, Hants. SP10 5YE, United Kingdom
Library of Congress Catalog Number
ISBN 1-8734-77-25-2
CIP 93-13702

Printed in the United States of America
Published in the United Kingdom by Gale Research International Ltd.
Published simultaneously in the United States
by Gale Research Inc.
(An affiliated company of Gale Research International Ltd.)

The trademark **ITP** is used under license.

Contents

Descriptive Listings

Highlights

The *Encyclopedia of Women's Associations Worldwide (EWAW)* is a comprehensive guide to women's and women-related nonprofit, national and multinational organizations worldwide. *EWAW* provides current, detailed information on organizations concerned with a wide range of subject areas, including:

- Women's Business and Professional Associations
- Women's Sports Associations
- Women's Social Clubs and Organizations
- Women's Health Issues
- Divorce
- Domestic Violence
- Reproductive Rights and Right-to-Life
- AIDS

Detailed Information In a Convenient Arrangement

The first edition of *EWAW* offers:

▶ A convenient one-stop source of information for the international women's community.

▶ Over 3,400 descriptive listings organized into 8 separate chapters by regions, and by country within chapters.

▶ Listings that typically contain complete contact data, including addresses, telephone/fax numbers, and names of individuals to be contacted, information describing the activities/objectives of the organization, information on any publications the organization may produce, and information outlining any conventions/meetings the organization may hold.

Easy Access to Information Resources

The Alphabetic Name Index provides quick and easy access to the descriptive listings through a single alphabetic arrangement of all the official organization names, national language name translations, and former/alternate names of organizations.

The Organizations' Activities Index groups organizations alphabetically under subject categories, including topics such as:

- Abortion
- Breast Cancer
- Family Planning
- Lesbianism
- National Women's Umbrella Organizations
- Political Action
- Sexual Harassment
- Women's Studies
- and more...

Aperçu

Encyclopedia of Women's Associations Worldwide (EWAW) est un guide mondial complet des organismes caritatifs, nationaux et internationaux pour les femmes ou touchant à elles. *EWAW* comporte des informations détaillées mises à jour sur les organismes touchant à une large gamme de domaines, tels que:

- Associations commerciales et professionnelles pour femmes
- Associations sportives pour femmes
- Clubs et associations sociales pour femmes
- Associations consacrées aux problèmes médicaux des femmes
- Divorce
- Violence domestique
- Droits reproductifs, et droit-à-la-vie
- SIDA

Des informations détaillées dans un format commode

Cette première édition de *EWAW* apporte:

▶ Une source unique d'informations commodes pour la communauté internationale des femmes.

▶ Plus de 3,400 références descriptives organisées en 8 chapitres, séparés par région puis par pays à l'intérieur de chaque chapitre.

▶ Les références contiennent généralement des informations complètes sur les modalités de contact: adresses, numéros de téléphone/téléfax, noms des personnes à contacter, activités et objectifs de l'organisme, informations sur les publication de chaque organisme et indication des congrès et réunions organisés par l'organisme.

Un accès facile aux ressources d'information

L'index alphabétique par nom permet un accès facile et rapide aux références descriptives, grâce à sa liste alphabétique contenant tous les noms d'organismes officiels, les traductions de ces noms dans la (les) langue(s) du pays, d'éventuels anciens noms ainsi que d'autres noms qui puissent exister.

L'index par activité regroupe les organismes par ordre alphabétique sous des rubriques par domaine, tels que:

- Avortement
- Cancer du sein
- Planning familial
- Lesbianisme
- Organismes nationaux de regroupement
- Action politique
- Harcèlement sexuel
- Enseignement sur la condition féminine
- et plus...

Höhepunkte

Das *Encyclopedia of Women's Asociations Worldwide (EWAW)*, ist ein umfassender Führer für gemeinnützige Frauenorganisationen und verbundene Organisationen, die weltweit auf einer nationalen oder internationalen Ebene tätig sind. Das *EWAW* bietet aktuelle, detaillierte Informationen über Organisationen, die sich mit einer Vielzahl von verschiedenen Themen befassen, wie zum Beispiel:

- Geschäfts- und Berufsverbände für Frauen
- Sportverbände für Frauen
- Geselligkeitsvereine für Frauen
- Frauenspezifische Gesundheitsfragen
- Scheidung
- Gewalttätigkeit im Heim
- Rechtsfragen zur Fortpflanzung und das Recht zum Leben
- AIDS

Detaillierte Praktische Angeordnete Informationen

Die erste Auflage des *EWAW* bietet:

▶ Eine praktische, umfassende Informationsquelle für die internationale Frauengemeinde in einem Band.

▶ Eintragungen über mehr als 3,400 beschriebene Organisationen, die in 8 einzelne Kapitel nach Region, und innerhalb der Kapitel, nach Land geordnet sind.

▶ Eintragungen, die im typischen Fall alle zur Kontaktaufnahme notwendigen Daten enthalten, einschließlich der Adresse, Telefon-/Telefaxnummern, und Namen der Kontaktpersonen, sowohl Information bezüglich der Tätigkeit/Ziele, Veröffentlichungen, und Tagungen/Veranstaltungen der Organisationen.

Zugang zu den Informationsmitteln

Das alphabetische Namensregister bietet durch die Aufführung aller offiziellen Namen der Organisationen, Übersetzungen der Namen in der jeweiligen Landessprache, und ehemalige und alternative Namen der Organisationen in alphabetischer Reihenfolge raschen und mühelosen Zugang zu den Eintragungen.

Im Index der Aktivitäten der Organisationen werden die Organisationen in alphabetischer Reihenfolge innerhalb von Schlagwortgruppen, mit Schlagwörtern aufgeführt. Beispiele von Schlagwörtern sind unter anderem:

- Abtreibung
- Brustkrebs
- Familienplanung
- Lesbiertum
- Nationale Dachorganisationen für Frauen
- Politische Aktion
- Sexuelle Belästigung
- Femministik
- und so weiter ...

Puntos sobresalientes

La *Encyclopedia of Women's Associations Worldwide (EWAW)* es una guía mundial completa de las organizaciones no gananciales nacionales y multinacionales de mujeres y de asuntos de mujeres. La *EWAW* contiene información actual y detallada sobre organizaciones que tratan una amplia gama de áreas de interés, incluyendo:

- Asociaciones comerciales y profesionales de mujeres
- Asociaciones deportivas de mujeres
- Clubs y organizaciones sociales de mujeres
- Temas de la salud de la mujer
- Divorcio
- Violencia doméstica
- Derechos reproductivos y derecho a la vida
- SIDA

Información detallada organizada cómodamente

La primera edición de *EWAW* ofrece:

▶ Una fuente de información única para la comunidad femenina internacional.

▶ Más de 3,400 listados descriptivos organizados en 8 capítulos separados por región y por país dentro de los capítulos.

▶ Listados que típicamente contienen datos de contacto completos, incluyendo direcciones, números de teléfono/fax, y los nombres de los individuos a ser contactados, información descriptiva sobre las actividades/objetivos de la organización, información sobre las publicaciones que la organización produzca e información resumida sobre posibles congresos/reuniones de la organización.

Fácil acceso a los recursos de información

El Índice alfabético de nombres da acceso rápido y fácil a los listados descriptivos por medio de una sola disposición alfabética de todos los nombres de organizaciones oficiales, traducciones del idioma nacional de los nombres, y nombres anteriores/alternativos de las organizaciones.

El Índice de actividades de organizaciones agrupa las organizaciones en orden alfabético bajo categorías temáticas, incluyendo las siguientes materias:

- Aborto
- Cáncer de la mama
- Planificación familiar
- Lesbianismo
- Organizaciones de coalición nacional de la mujer
- Acción política
- Acoso sexual
- Estudios sobre la mujer
- y más...

Acknowledgments

The editor would like to thank the following members of the "Friends of *EWAW*" group for their time and cooperation in reviewing the coverage, content, and arrangement of this volume:

- Joan Ariel, Women's Studies Librarian, University of California, Irvine

- Deirdre Coleman, Librarian, International Planned Parenthood Federation

- Salma Ginwalla, Librarian, Zambia Association for Research and Development

- Sarah M. Pritchard, Director of Libraries, Smith College

- Cathy Shepherd, Documentalist, Caribbean Association for Feminist Research and Action

- Lucinda Zoe, Information Officer, International Women's Tribune Center

Foreword

The United Nations Decade for Women 1976-1985, along with the burgeoning women's movement, brought forth an abundance of new information, data, and scholarship on women and women's concerns. The world's women recognized and learned quickly that knowledge is, indeed, power, and that access to accurate and timely information was necessary if they were to succeed in their efforts at social change. As the movement has grown, there has been a parallel growth and interest in women's organizations and information and documentation centers in all parts of the world. These women's organizations that have developed over the past two decades have grown up in the post-industrial society of a new age of information. Often underfunded and operating on a shoestring budget, these centers have continued to flourish, providing technical assistance and training, support services, and documentation and research services. They have been collecting information on project design and activities, teaching aids, education kits, planning documents, conference materials, unpublished papers and reports, training opportunities, sources of financial support, mailing lists, small local newsletters, and statistical data on women in their regions. By setting up regional networks, groups have worked together to discuss training, computerization and new technologies, and strategies for change.

The International Women and Development community emerged in the 1970s as a result of the concerns of both the feminist and development communities. Numerous studies demonstrated that although women were often the primary contributors to the productivity of their communities, their economic contribution was not reflected in either national statistics or in the planning or implementation of development projects. Findings indicated that the status of women was declining in developing countries under the dominant approaches to development. The need for timely and reliable information on women's lives and situations for use by policy makers, planners, and grass-roots organizations was identified as essential to ensure that an equitable share of benefits would be given to women. The successful participation of women in the development process depends largely on access to information through the building of effective organizations and information mechanisms at national, sub-regional, and regional levels. It became imperative that regional and local women's organizations begin to work together to provide the services needed to better influence and affect social change.

The need for specific programs to address the struggle of women in their efforts to achieve equality and play a more significant role in the development process, and the insufficiency of information on women, became evident at the World Conference of the International Women's Year in 1975. Information collection, analysis, and dissemination was identified as a primary goal at the beginning of the United Nations' Decade for Women and was recognized as a clear need in the Programme of Action for the Second Half of the United Nations' Decade for Women adopted at the World Conference for Women in Copenhagen in 1980, and then again in the Forward-Looking Strategies for the Advancement of Women adopted at the World Conference for Women in Nairobi in 1985.

Women's organizations have continued to emerge over the past two decades throughout Africa, Asia, the Caribbean, Europe, Latin America, the Middle East, and North America. The need to communicate with one another and disseminate information has also continued to increase. Directories such as the *Encyclopedia of Women's Associations Worldwide* will be useful tools to those working in the international community to stay better informed and keep up with emerging issues. Now in the 1990s, as in the beginnings of the women and development movement when the first International Tribunal on Crimes Against Women was held in Brussels in 1976, violence against women is one of the most critical issues facing the world's women. Women's human rights are a major concern as women worldwide come together at the 1993 United Nations World Conference on Human Rights to demand that violations against women's human rights be placed high on the world's agenda. As we move toward the year 2000, and more specifically toward the United Nations Fourth World Conference on Women in 1995, the areas of interest and concern in the international women's community remain those of equality, development, and peace.

Additional themes identified for the coming years include legal literacy, equality in economic decision-making, nutrition and health issues, particularly women and AIDS, as well as women and the peace process and the growing role women must play in international decision-making. An increasing interest in information processing and exchange, especially with regard to electronic communications, is also an area of growth. The focus will be to keep the improvement of women's status high on the global agenda. A key to doing this is better communication and networking. Contact, communication, networking. To do this, any of this, we must be able to find one another. Information is Power...Use it, Share it.

Lucinda Rhea Zoe, Information Officer
International Women's Tribune Center, New York, NY
April 1993

Prologue

La Décennie de la Femme déclarée par l'ONU (1976-85) et le mouvement grandissant pour l'amélioration de la condition féminine ont fourni de nombreux renseignements, données, et études sur les femmes et leurs problèmes. Les femmes du monde ont très vite compris et appris que le savoir rend puissant, et que des informations à jour et d'accès facile sont nécessaires à la réussite de leur effort de renouvellement social. Parallèlement au mouvement pour la condition féminine, les organismes pour femmes ainsi que les centres d'information et de documentation pour femmes ont joui d'une forte croissance en effectifs et en renommée partout dans le monde. Les organismes pour femmes apparus pendant les deux dernières décennies ont grandi dans une société post-industrielle où l'information est reine. Ces centres, dont beaucoup fonctionnent sur un budget réduit, ont continué à grandir et à fournir leurs services d'assistance et de formation technique, de soutien, de documentation, et de recherche. Ils ont amassé des données sur la conception et l'exécution des projets, des matériels et kits éducatifs, des documents de planification, des documents conférenciers, des articles, rapports, et compte-rendus non-publiés, des informations sur des stages et sur des soutiens financiers, des listes d'adresses pour correspondance, des petits bulletins locaux, et des données statistiques sur les femmes sur leur territoire d'action. Au moyen de réseaux régionaux, les groupes ont travaillé ensemble pour discuter de la formation, de l'informatisation, et de nouvelles technologies et stratégies pour le changement.

La communauté Internationale Femme et Développement est apparue pendant les années 1970 à la suite de constations par les mouvements pour la condition féminine et pour le développement. De nombreuses études ont montré que malgré leur contribution souvent prépondérante à la productivité de leur communauté, la contribution économique des femmes était souvent absente des statistiques nationales ainsi que de la conception et de la mise en oeuvre des projets de développement. Il s'est avéré que les approches actuelles dominantes pour le développement ont dégradé la condition féminine dans les pays en voie de développement. Le besoin en informations fiables et à jour sur la vie et la condition des femmes s'est avéré vital pour que les gouvernements, les planificateurs, et les associations publiques puissent assurer aux femmes une part équitable des avantages apportés par le développement. La participation efficace des femmes au processus de développement dépend de la dissémination d'informations les concernant par l'intermédiaire d'organismes et de réseaux nationaux, sous-régionaux, et régionaux. Il s'est avéré nécessaire que les organismes régionaux et locaux travaillent ensemble pour apporter les services nécessaires pour influencer et changer la société.

La nécessité de programmes spécifiques pour adresser la lutte de femmes pour l'égalité et leur participation accrue dans le processus de développement, ainsi que la pénurie d'informations sur elles sont devenues évidentes lors de la Conférence Mondiale de l'Année Internationale de la Femme en 1975. La collection, l'analyse, et la dissémination des informations ont été déclarées objectifs principaux au début de la Décennie Internationale de la Femme de l'ONU, et ont été déclarées de première nécessité, à la fois dans le programme d'action pour la seconde moitié de la décennie de la femme adopté à Copenhague en 1980 pendant la Conférence Mondiale pour les Femmes, et dans les Stratégies pour l'Avenir pour l'Avancement des Femmes adoptées pendant la conférence Mondiale pour les Femmes à Nairobi en 1985.

Les organismes pour les femmes ont continué apparaître pendant les deux dernières décennies en Afrique, en Asie, dans les Caraïbes, en Europe, en Amérique Latine, au Moyen-Orient, et en Amérique du Nord. La nécessité de communiquer et de partager les informations a aussi continué à grandir. Les annuaires tels que l'*Encyclopedia of Women's Associations Worldwide* serviront d'outils pour celles et ceux qui travaillent dans la communauté internationale pour s'informer et rester au courant. Pendant les années 90, tout comme au début du mouvement Femmes et Développement lorsque le Tribunal International sur les Crimes envers les Femmes a siégé pour la première fois en 1976, la violence contre les femmes est une des grandes causes à laquelle sont confrontées les femmes du monde. Les violations des droits fondamentaux des femmes constituent une question pressante, que les femmes du monde s'efforcent de mettre au premier plan lors de la Conférence Mondiale sur les Droits de l'Homme de l'ONU en 1993. Au fur et à mesure de l'approche de l'an 2000, et surtout de la Quatrième Conférence Mondiale des Femmes de l'ONU en 1995, les domaines attirant l'intérêt et l'inquiétude de la communauté internationale des femmes demeurent l'égalité, le développement, et la paix. Les années à venir devront aussi toucher à l'éducation juridique, l'égalité dans la prise de décisions économiques, la nutrition, la santé (surtout le SIDA), ainsi que les rôles à jouer par les femmes dans le maintien de la paix et dans les décisions internationales. L'intérêt grandit dans le domaine du traitement et de l'échange des informations, surtout au moyen des communications électroniques. La tâche principale sera de garder l'amélioration de la condition des femmes en tête de l'agenda international. Pour ce faire, il faudra communiquer mieux. Contacter, communiquer, s'étendre. Pour réussir, nous devons pouvoir nous trouver... Utilisez-le, partagez-le.

Lucinda Rhea Zoe, Information Officer
International Women's Tribune Center, New York, NY
April 1993

Vorwort

Das Vereinte Nationen Jahrzehnt der Frau von 1976 - 1985 hat zusammen mit der wachsenden Frauenbewegung eine Fülle von neuen Informationen, Daten und neuer Forschung über Frauen und den Angelegenheiten von Frauen hervorgebracht. Die Frauen der Welt haben erkannt, und rasch gelernt, daß Wissen wirklich doch gleich Macht ist, und daß der Zugriff auf genaue und aktuelle Informationen unentbehrlich ist, wenn sie mit ihrem Bemühen um soziale Änderungen erfolgreich sein wollen. Mit dem Wachstum der Bewegung ergab sich ein paralleler Zuwachs und Interesse an Frauenorganisationen, Informationen über Frauen, und Dokumentationsstellen in allen Teilen der Welt. Diese Frauenorganisationen, die sich in den letzten zwei Jahrzehnten entwickelt haben, sind in der post-industriellen Gesellschaft eines neuen Zeitalters der Information aufgewachsen. Diese Stellen, die oft unzureichend fundiert sind und mit einem Minibudget betrieben werden, waren mit ihrem Angebot an technischer Unterstützung und technischer Schulung, Unterstützungsdienstleistungen, und Dokumentations- und Forschungsdienstleistungen fortlaufend erfolgreich. Sie haben Informationen über die Entwicklung von Projekten und Veranstaltungen, Lehrmittel, Erziehungsmittel, Planungsdokumente, Tagungsmaterialien, unveröffentlichte Arbeiten und Berichte, Ausbildungsgelegenheiten, Quellen finanzieller Unterstützung, Anschriftenlisten, kleine, lokale Mitteilungsblätter, und statistische Daten über Frauen in ihren Gebieten angesammelt. Durch die Aufstellung von regionalen Netzen haben Gruppen zusammengearbeitet, um die Schulung, Computerisierung und neue Technologien und Strategien zur Änderung zu diskutieren.

Die internationale Frauen- und Entwicklungsgemeinde entstand in den 1970er Jahren als Ergebnis der Interessen der femministischen Gemeinde sowohl wie der Entwicklungsgemeinde. Eine Vielzahl von Untersuchungen haben belegt, daß der wirtschaftlicher Beitrag der Frauen weder in nationalen Statistiken noch in der Planung oder Durchführung von Entwicklungsprojekten wiedergespiegelt ist, obwohl Frauen oft die Hauptbeitragleistenden in der Produktivität ihrer jeweiligen Gemeinden sind. Die Befunde haben angedeutet, daß das Ansehen der Frauen in entwickelnden Ländern unter den dominierenden Ansätzen zur Entwicklung abfiel. Die Notwendigkeit aktueller und zuverlässiger Informationen über das Leben und der Situationen von Frauen zum Gebrauch von leitenden politischen Beratern, Planern, und Bürgerinitiativen wurde als unbedingt notwendig erkannt, um sicherzustellen, daß ein gerechter Anteil der Vergünstigungen Frauen zukommen würde. Die erfolgreiche Beteiligung von Frauen im Entwicklungsvorgang hängt zum größten Teil vom Zugang zu Informationen durch den Aufbau von effektiven Organisationen und Informationsmechanismen auf den nationalen, sub-regionalen und regionalen Ebenen ab. Es wurde dringend erforderlich, daß regionale und lokale Frauenorganisationen anfangen zusammenzuarbeiten, um die Dienstleistungen bieten zu können, die benötigt werden, um einen besseren Einfluß auf die sozialen Änderungen zu haben.

Der Bedarf an spezifischen Programmen, um den Kampf der Frauen in ihrem Bemühen zur Erreichung der Gleichberechtigung anzusprechen, um eine wichtigere Rolle im Entwicklungsprozeß zu spielen, und die Unzulänglichkeit der Informationen über Frauen wurde bei der Weltkonferenz des Internationalen Jahres der Frau in 1975 deutlich. Die Sammlung, Analyse und Verteilung von Informationen wurde als Hauptziel am Anfang des Vereinte Nationen Jahrzehnt der Frau erkannt, und wurde im Aktionsprogramm für die zweite Hälfte des Vereinte Nationen Jahrzehnts der Frau, das bei der Weltkonferenz der Frau in Kopenhagen in 1980 übernommen wurde, sowohl wie in den vorwärtsblickenden Strategien für die Förderung der Frau, die bei der Weltkonferenz der Frau in Nairobi in 1985 übernommen wurden, als dringende Notwendigkeit erkannt.

Frauenorganisationen sind in den letzten zwei Jahrzehnten anhaltend überall in Afrika, Asien, der Karibik, Europa, Südamerika, im Mittleren Osten und in Nordamerika aufgetaucht. Der Bedarf miteinander zu kommunizieren und Informationen zu verbreiten hat auch anhaltend zugenommen. Verzeichnisse wie das *Encyclopedia of Women's Associations Worldwide* werden nutzvolle Werkzeuge für diejenigen sein, die in der internationalen Gemeinde arbeiten, um besser informiert zu bleiben und mit neuen Fragen und Angelegenheiten aufrechtzuerhalten. Heute in den 1990er Jahren, wie am Anfang der Frauen- und Entwicklungsbewegungen, als das erste internationale Tribunal für Verbrechen gegen Frauen 1976 in Brüssel stattfand, sind Gewalttaten gegen Frauen eines der kritischsten Angelegenheiten, die die Frauen der welt Konfroutiert. Die Menschenrechte der Frauen sind eine wichtige Angelegenheit, wenn sich Frauen aus aller Welt bei der Vereinte Nationen

Weltkonferenz über Menschenrechte in 1993 versammeln, um zu fordern, daß die Verletzung der Menschenrechte der Frauen eine hohe Stelle bei den Verhandlungsgegenständen der Welt einnimmt. Als wir uns dem Jahr 2000, und besonders der Vereinten Nationen Vierten Welt Konferenz der Frauen im Jahre 1995 annähern, bleiben die Gebiete, für die sich die internationale Frauengemeinde interessiert und mit denen sie sich befaßt, also die der Gleichberechtigung, der Entwicklung, und des Friedens. Weitere Themen, die für die kommenden Jahre erkannt worden sind, umfassen die Fähigkeit, sich mit rechtlichen Fragen zu befassen, Gleichheit bei den wirtschaftlichen Entscheidungsprozessen, Fragen der Ernährung und Gesundheit, insbesondere Frauen und AIDS, sowohl wie die Rolle der Frauen bei den internationalen Entscheidungsprozessen. Das steigende Interesse an Datenverarbeitung und -austausch, insbesonders mit Hinsicht auf die elektronische Kommunikation, ist auch ein Wachstumsgebiet. Der Brennpunkt ist, die Verbesserung des Frauenansehens oben auf der Liste der Verhandlungsgegenstände der Welt zuer halten. Ein Schlüssel hierzu ist bessere Kommunikation und die Aufstellung von Netzwerken. Kontakt, Kommunikation, Netzwerke. Um dies, oder auch nur ein Teil hiervon, zu erreichen, müssen wir uns einander finden können. Information ist Macht .. Wendet sie an, Verbreitet sie!

Lucinda Rhea Zoe, Information Officer
International Women's Tribune Center, New York, NY
April 1993

Prefacio

La Década de la mujer de las Naciones Unidas (1976-1985), junto con el floreciente movimiento de la mujer, trajo consigo una gran abundancia de información, datos, y estudios nuevos sobre la mujer y sus problemas. Las mujeres del mundo reconocieron y aprendieron rápidamente que tener conocimiento es, en efecto, tener poder, y que es necesario el acceso a la información precisa y oportuna para tener éxito en sus esfuerzos para cambiar la sociedad. Mientras que ha crecido el movimiento, ha habido un crecimiento e interés paralelos en organizaciones de mujeres y en centros de información y documentación por todo el mundo. Estas organizaciones de mujeres que se han desarrollado durante las últimas dos décadas han crecido en la sociedad post-industrial de una nueva era de información. A menudo con muy pocos fondos y operando con un presupuesto sumamente pequeño, estos centros han continuado prosperando, proporcionando asistencia técnica y entrenamiento, servicios de apoyo, y servicios de documentación y investigación. Ellos han recolectado información sobre diseños y actividades de proyectos, dispositivos pedagógicos, juegos educacionales, documentos de planificación, materiales para conferencias, documentos e informes no publicados, oportunidades de entrenamiento, fuentes de apoyo financiero, listas de direcciones, pequeños boletines locales, y estadísticas sobre mujeres en sus respectivas regiones. Al organizar redes regionales, estos grupos han cooperado para tratar temas como la capacitación, computarización y nuevas tecnologías, y estrategias para efectuar cambios.

La Comunidad de mujeres y desarrollo internacional comenzó en la década de 1970 como resultado de las preocupaciones de la comunidad feminista y de la comunidad de desarrollo. Numerosos estudios han demostrado que, aunque las mujeres eran muchas veces las mayores contribuidoras a la productividad de su comunidad, su contribución económica no había sido reflejada en estadísticas nacionales ni en la planificación o ejecución de proyectos de desarrollo. Las conclusiones demostraron que la situación de las mujeres era declinante en algunos países en desarrollo bajo las estrategias de desarrollo dominantes. La necesidad de información oportuna y confiable sobre las vidas y las situaciones de las mujeres para el uso de políticos, planificadores, y organizaciones comunales ha sido identificada como esencial para asegurar que una parte equitativa de los beneficios vayan a las mujeres. La exitosa participación de las mujeres en el proceso de desarrollo depende en gran parte del acceso a la información por medio de la creación de organizaciones y mecanismos de información eficaces a nivel nacional, sub regional, y regional. Era esencial que las organizaciones de mujeres regionales y locales trabajaran juntas para proporcionar los servicios necesarios y para mejor influir y efectuar cambios sociales.

La necesidad de programas específicos para tratar la lucha de la mujer para alcanzar la igualdad y desempeñar un papel más significativo en el proceso de desarrollo, y la insuficiencia de información sobre la mujer, se hicieron evidentes en la Conferencia mundial del Año internacional de la mujer en 1975. La recolección, el análisis, y la diseminación de la información fueron identificados como una meta principal al principio de la Década de la mujer de las Naciones Unidas (1976-1985) y fueron reconocidos como una necesidad básica en el Programa de acción para la segunda mitad de la Década de la mujer de las Naciones Unidas, adoptado en la Conferencia mundial de la mujer en Copenhague en 1980, y luego de nuevo en las Estrategias para el futuro del Progreso de la mujer, adoptado en la Conferencia mundial de la mujer en Nairobi en 1985.

Las organizaciones de mujeres han seguido surgiendo durante las últimas dos décadas por toda Africa, Asia, Caribe, Europa, Latinoamérica, Medio Oriente, y Norteamérica. La necesidad de comunicarnos unos con los otros y de diseminar información también ha continuado a crecer. Los directorios, como la *Encyclopedia of Women's Associations Worldwide* serán herramientas útiles para los que trabajan en la comunidad internacional, para que éstos puedan mantenerse mejor informados y al día sobre nuevos temas. Ahora, en la década de 1990, como al principio del movimiento de la mujer y del movimiento del desarrollo, cuando el primer Tribunal internacional sobre crímenes contra la mujer fue celebrado en Bruselas en 1976, la violencia contra las mujeres es uno de los temas más críticos de los que se enfrentan las mujeres del mundo. Los derechos humanos de la mujer son una gran preocupación, y las mujeres de todo el mundo se juntarán en la Conferencia mundial sobre los derechos humanos de las Naciones Unidas de 1993 para exigir que las violaciones de los derechos humanos de las mujeres ocupen una posición destacada en la agenda internacional. Mientras nos acercamos al año 2000, y más específicamente a la Cuarta conferencia mundial sobre la mujer de las Naciones Unidas en 1995, las áreas de interés y atención de la comunidad internacional de mujeres continúan siendo las de igualdad, desarrollo, y paz. Otros temas identificados para los años que se aproximan incluyen el entendimiento legal, la igualdad en el proceso de decisiones económicas, temas de nutrición y salud, particularmente la mujer y el SIDA, así como la mujer y el proceso de paz, y el creciente papel que debe desempeñar la mujer en el proceso de decisiones a nivel internacional. Un creciente interés en el procesamiento e intercambio de información, especialmente en lo que concierne las comunicaciones electrónicas, también es un área de crecimiento. El enfoque será él de mantener la mejoría de la situación de la mujer como una alta prioridad en la agenda internacional. Una clave para realizar esto se encuentra en una mejor comunicación y en redes de información. El contacto, la comunicación, las redes de información. Para realizar esto, o cualquier parte de esto, debemos poder encontrarnos. Tener la información es tener el Poder... Úselo, compártalo.

Lucinda Rhea Zoe, Information Officer
International Women's Tribune Center, New York, NY
April 1993

Introduction

The first edition of *Encyclopedia of Women's Associations Worldwide (EWAW)* provides contact information and descriptions for national and multinational women's and women-related organizations worldwide. *EWAW's* coverage spans a wide variety of issues concerning women including women in business, women's education, breast cancer, divorce, reproductive rights and right-to-life, AIDS, domestic violence, women's sports organizations, professional and social sororities, women's labor issues, and more.

Organizations listed in *EWAW* offer significant benefits to the international women's community. These include:

▶ Serving as vehicles through which individuals, organizations, and governments address the special concerns and advance the interests of women.

▶ Acting as clearinghouses for the exchange of information on women's issues.

▶ Promoting dialogue and fostering communication.

Compiled With the Help of Experts

EWAW comprises more than 3,400 listings of organizations carefully selected for inclusion based on their direct relevance to women or women's issues in such areas as education, health, equal rights, business, religion, and politics. *EWAW's* international scope, comprehensive coverage, and convenient single volume format eliminates the need to consult multiple, often hard-to-locate specialized sources.

Convenient Arrangement and Thorough Indexing
Speed Access to Information Sources

EWAW consists of a main body of descriptive listings and two convenient indexes: the Alphabetic Name Index and the Organizations' Activities Index.

The descriptive listings are arranged into 8 separate chapters according to the geographic region in which the organization is located, as outlined on the "Contents" page. Entries typically contain complete contact data, descriptive information outlining the organization's activities/objectives, and additional information on publications produced and conventions/meetings held.

The Alphabetic Name Index provides quick access to all organizations included in the descriptive listings section by the official names of organizations and by national language name translations. Citations to former/alternate names mentioned within the descriptive listings are also included in this index.

The Organizations' Activities Index provides thorough access to all organizations by subject terms relevant to the organizations' activities. Cross-references are included to facilitate users accessing related subject terms.

For more information on the content, arrangement, and indexing of *EWAW*, consult the "User's Guide" following this Introduction.

Method of Compilation

EWAW was compiled from a variety of sources. Relevant entries were carefully selected from other Gale Research Inc. directories such as *Encyclopedia of Associations* and *Encyclopedia of Associations, International Organizations*, and lists and directories supplied by numerous organizations located throughout the world. Questionnaire mailings were used to contact organizations directly.

Research efforts were directed equally to all regional areas, but due to social and political situations in geographic regions such as the Middle East, and in countries such as Somalia, information on women's organizations was either limited or unobtainable.

Acknowledgments

The editor thanks the following individuals and organizations for their continued assistance and provision of materials for listings:

> Jackie Chang - U.N. Center for the Advancement of Women
> Doris C. Chargualaf - Guam Bureau of Women's Affairs
> Jill Emberson - Pacific Women's Resource Bureau
> Fundacion Arias para la Paz y el Progreso Humano
> Colette Guilder - Women's National Commission, United Kingdom
> Kim Holden - Australia Office of the Status of Women
> Fran Hosken - Women's International Network
> Cheng Kexiong - Xinhua Publishing House
> Albert Makovoz - AIM Marketing Services
> Bernard Ntegeye - U.N. Development Programme, Lome, Togo
> Linda Poole - Organization of American States, Inter-American Commission of Women
> Women's International Tribune Center

Thanks also to the following Gale editors for their valuable contributions to this directory: Deborah M. Burek, Lee Ripley Greenfield, Karin E. Koek, and Susan B. Martin.

Available in Electronic Formats

Diskette/Magnetic Tape. *EWAW* is available for licensing on magnetic tape or diskette in a fielded format. Either the complete database or a custom selection of entries may be ordered. The database is available for internal data processing and nonpublishing purposes only. For more information, call 800-877-GALE.

Comments Welcome

We encourage users to bring new or unlisted organizations to our attention. Every effort will be made to provide information about them in subsequent editions of the Directory. Comments and suggestions for improving the Directory are also welcome. Please contact:

Encyclopedia of Women's Associations Worldwide
Gale Research Inc.
835 Penobscot Bldg.
Detroit, MI, USA 48226-4094
Telephone: (313)961-2242
Toll-Free: 800-347-GALE
Fax: (313)961-6815

Introduction

La première édition de l'*Encyclopedia of Women's Associations Worldwide (EWAW)* comporte des informations de contact et des descriptions pour les organismes nationaux et multinationaux pour les femmes ou les touchant fortement. L'*EWAW* recouvre de nombreux domaines relatifs aux femmes, y compris les femmes dans l'entreprise, l'éducation des femmes, le cancer du sein, le divorce, les droits reproductifs et le droit à la vie, le SIDA, la violence domestique, les associations sportives féminines, les groupes professionnels et sociaux, le travail des femmes, et d'autres.

Les organismes indiqués dans *EWAW* apportent beaucoup à la collectivité féminine mondiale. Par exemple, ils peuvent servir:

▶ de véhicule permettant aux personnes, aux organismes, et aux gouvernements d'adresser les problèmes spécifiques et d'améliorer les conditions des femmes.

▶ d'intermédiaire pour l'échange de l'information sur les questions intéressant les femmes

▶ de promoteur de dialogue et de communication.

Compilé avec l'aide d'experts

L'*EWAW* comprend plus de 3,400 références d'organismes soigneusement sélectionnés en fonction de leur pertinence envers les femmes ou les questions qui leurs sont importantes, dans les domaines de l'enseignement, de la santé, de l'égalité juridique, de l'entreprise, de la religion, et de la politique. Le caractère international de l'*EWAW*, sa couverture compréhensive, et son format en un seul volume facile d'emploi évite d'avoir à consulter des sources spécialisées multiples souvent difficiles à trouver.

Une disposition commode et un répertoriage complet accélèrent l'accès aux informations.

L'*EWAW* comporte une partie principale contenant des références descriptives et deux index commodes: l'Index Alphabétique par Nom et l'Index par Domaine d'activité de l'Organisme.

Les références descriptives sont disposées en 8 chapitres séparés selon la région géographique où l'organisme est situé, comme indiqué à la page «Table des Matières». Les références contiennent généralement des informations de contact complètes, des informations descriptives décrivant les activités et les objectifs de l'organisme, et des renseignements supplémentaires sur les publications et les congrès et réunions organisés.

L'Index Alphabétique par Nom permet un accès rapide à tous les organismes compris dans la partie des références descriptives, à partir de leur nom officiel ou de la traduction du nom en langue(s) nationale(s). Cet index comprend aussi les anciens noms cités dans la référence descriptive et d'autres noms utilisés pour cet organisme.

L'index par Domaines d'activité de l'Organisme permet l'accès à tous les organismes recouvrant un domaine correspondant à l'activité de l'organisme. Des références croisées permettent de passer facilement d'un sujet donné à des sujets proches.

Pour plus de renseignements sur le contenu, la disposition, et le répertoriage de l'*EWAW*, reportez-vous au «Mode d'emploi» qui suit cette introduction.

Méthode de compilation

EWAW a été compilé à partir de nombreuses ressources. Les références sélectionnées ont été soigneusement choisies à partir de références présentes dans d'autres répertoires produits par Gale Research Inc., tels que l'*Encyclopedia of Associations* et l'*Encyclopedia of Associations, International Organizations*, et les listes et répertoires fournis par de nombreux organismes situés partout dans le monde. Des questionnaires ont été envoyés pour entrer en contact directement avec chaque organisme.

Les efforts de recherche ont été répartis de façon égale dans toutes les régions, mais à cause des situations socio-politiques dans certaines zones tels que le Moyen-Orient et certains pays tels que la Somalie, l'information sur les organismes pour les femmes était limitée ou impossible à obtenir.

Remerciements

La rédaction tient à remercier les personnes et les organismes qui suivent pour leur assistance continue et les documents qui nous ont été fournis par eux pour établir la liste:

> Jackie Chang - U.N. Center for the Advancement of Women
> Doris C. Chargualaf - Guam Bureau of Women's Affairs
> Jill Emberson - Pacific Women's Resource Bureau
> Fundacion Arias para la Paz y el Progreso Humano
> Colette Guilder - Women's National Commission, United Kingdom
> Kim Holden - Australia Office of the Status of Women
> Fran Hosken - Women's International Network
> Cheng Kexiong - Xinhua Publishing House
> Albert Makovoz - AIM Marketing Services
> Bernard Ntegeye - U.N. Development Programme, Lome, Togo
> Linda Poole - Organization of American States, Inter-American Commission of Women
> Women's International Tribune Center

Nous remercions aussi les rédactrices de chez Gale qui ont beaucoup contribué à ce répertoire: Deborah M.Burek, Lee Ripley Greenfield, Karin E. Koek, et Susan B. Martin.

Disponible sous formats électroniques

Disquette/Bande Magnétique: l'*EWAW* est disponible pour l'attribution de licence sur bande magnétique, ou sur disquette en format à champs. Il est possible de commander la base de données entière ou une portion quelconque de celle-ci. La base de données est disponible pour l'emploi informatique à usage interne sans publication. Pour plus de renseignements, appelez le (313) 961-2242.

Si vous avez un commentaire

Nous encourageons nos usagers à nous communiquer le nom d'organismes nouveaux ou non-répertoriés. Nous ferons de notre mieux pour indiquer des renseignements sur eux dans des éditions suivantes du répertoire.

Nous serions aussi contents de recevoir des suggestions et des commentaires en vue de l'amélioration de ce répertoire. Veuillez contacter:

Encyclopedia of Women's Associations Worldwide
Gale Research Inc.
835 Penobscot Bldg.
Detroit, MI, USA 48226-4094
Téléphone: (313) 961-2242
Gratuit: 800-347-GALE
Téléfax: (313) 961-6815

Einleitung

Die erste Ausgabe des *Encyclopedia of Women's Associations Worldwide (EWAW)* bietet Kontaktinformationen für, und Beschreibungen von, Frauenorganisationen und verbundene Organisationen, die weltweit auf einer nationalen oder internationalen Ebene tätig sind. Das *EWAW* deckt eine breite Auswahl von Themen, die für Frauen vom Interesse sind, darunter Frauen im Geschäftsleben, die Bildung von Frauen, Brustkrebs, Scheidung, Rechtsfragen zur Fortpflanzung und das Recht zum Leben, AIDS, Gewalttätigkeit im Heim, Sportverbände für Frauen, berufliche und gesellige Studentinnenvereinigungen, frauenspezifische Arbeiterfragen, und so weiter.

Die im *EWAW* aufgeführten Organisationen sind Organisationen, aus denen die internationale Frauengemeinde großen Nutzen ziehen kann. Wie zum Beispiel:

▶ Es dient als Medium, mit dem Einzelpersonen, Organisationen und Regierungen die besonderen Interessen der Frauen ansprechen und fördern.

▶ Es dient als Zentralen zum Austausch von Informationen über Angelegenheiten, die für Frauen vom Interesse sind.

▶ Es fördert den Dialog und die Kommunikation.

Mit der Hilfe von Experten kompiliert

Das *EWAW* enthält über 3,400 Eintragungen von Organisationen, die aufgrund ihrer direkten Relevanz auf Frauen oder Frauenfragen in Bereichen wie Bildung, Gesundheit, Gleichberechtigung, Geschäftsleben, Religion und Politik für ihren Einschluß in das *EWAW* sorgfältig ausgewählt wurden. Durch den internationalen Rahmen, die umfassende Deckung und den praktischen Einbandformat wird durch das *EWAW* das Nachschlagen in mehreren, oft schwer auffindbaren, spezialisierten Quellen überflüssig.

Rascher Zugang Zuden auf Informationsquellen durch praktische Anordnung und konsequenten Index

Das *EWAW* besteht aus einem Hauptteil mit den beschriebenen Eintragungen und zwei praktischen Verzeichnissen: das alphabetische Namensregister und der Index der Aktivitäten der Organisationen.

Wie auf der "Inhalts-"Seite beschrieben, werden die beschriebenen Eintragungen in 8 einzelne Kapitel gemäß der geographischen Region, in der sich die Organisation befindet, geordnet. Die Eintragungen enthalten im typischen Fall alle zur Kontaktaufnahme notwendigen Daten, Informationen bezüglich der Tätigkeit/Ziele der Organisation, und zusätzliche Informationen bezüglich der Veröffentlichungen und Tagungen/Veranstaltungen der Organisationen.

Das alphabetische Namensregister bietet durch die offiziellen Namen der Organisationen und die Übersetzung der Namen in der jeweiligen Landessprache raschen Zugang zu allen im Abschnitt mit den beschreibenden Eintragungen enthaltenen Organisationen. Dieses Register enthält auch Verweise auf die in den beschreibenden Eintragungen erwähnten ehemaligen/alternativen Namen.

Der Index der Aktivitäten der Organisation bietet durch Schlagwörter, die sich auf die Tätigkeit der Organisation beziehen, umfassenden Zugang zu allen Organisationen. Dieses Register enthält auch Querverweise, um den Zugang zu verbundenen Schlagwörtern zu erleichtern.

Nähere Informationen zum Inhalt, der Anordnung und der Verzeichnisse des *EWAW* befinden sich in der dieser Einführung angeschlossenen "Benutzerführung."

Kompilationsmethode

Das *EWAW* wurde aus verschiedenen Quellen kompiliert. Die entsprechenden Eintragungen wurden sorgfältig aus anderen Verzeichnissen von Gale Research Inc., wie zum Beispiel das *Encyclopedia of Associations* und das *Encyclopedia of Associations, International Organizations* sowohl wie von Listen und Verzeichnissen von einer Vielzahl von Organisationen überall in der Welt ausgewählt. Fragebögen wurden auch versandt, um direkt mit den Organisationen Kontakt aufzunehmen.

Nachforschungen wurden gleichermaßen für alle regionalen Gebiete angestellt, jedoch waren in Gebiete wie der Mittlerer Osten oder Länder wie Somalia Informationen über Frauenorganisationen aus sozialen oder politischen Gründen entweder nur beschränkt oder überhaupt nicht erhältlich.

Danksagungen

Die Redaktion möchte sich bei den folgenden Einzelpersonen und Organisationen für Ihre anhaltende Unterstützung und Bereitstellung von Materialien für die Eintragungen bedanken:

Jackie Chang - U.N. Center for the Advancement of Women
Doris C. Chargualaf - Guam Bureau of Women's Affairs
Jill Emberson - Pacific Women's Resource Bureau
Fundacion Arias para la Paz y el Progreso Humano
Colette Guilder - Women's National Commission, United Kingdom
Kim Holden - Australia Office of the Status of Women
Fran Hosken - Women's International Network
Cheng Kexiong - Xinhua Publishing House
Albert Makovoz - AIM Marketing Services
Bernard Ntegeye - U.N. Development Programme, Lome, Togo
Linda Poole - Organization of American States, Inter-American Commission of Women
Women's International Tribune Center

Wir möchten uns auch bei den folgenden Gale Redakteure für Ihre wertvollen Beiträge zu diesem Führer bedanken: Deborah M. Burek, Lee Ripley Greenfield, Karin E. Koek, und Susan B. Martin.

In elektronischen Formaten erhältlich

Diskette/Magnetband. Das *EWAW* ist zur Lizenzerteilung mit einem Datenfeldformat auf Magnetband oder Diskette erhältlich. Es kann entweder die vollständige Datenbank, oder eine Ihren Anforderungen angepassten Auswahl der Eintragungen bestellt werden. Die Datenbank ist nur für Zwecke der internen Datenverarbeitung erhältlich, und nicht zur Veröffentlichung bestimmt. Nähere Informationen sind unter Rufnr. 800-877-GALE erhältlich.

Bemerkungen sind immer Willkommen

Wir möchten unsere Benutzer bitten, uns auf neue oder nicht in den Eintragungen enthaltenen Organisationen aufmerksam zu machen. Wir werden alle Anstrengungen machen, Informationen über diese Organisationen in nachfolgenden Auflagen des Führers aufzunehmen. Kommentare und Vorschläge zur Verbesserung des Führers sind auch willkommen. Setzen Sie sich bitte in Verbindung mit:

Encyclopedia of Women's Associations Worldwide
Gale Research Inc.
835 Penobscot Bldg.
Detroit, MI, USA 48226-4094
Telefon: (313) 961-2242
Gebührenfrei: 800-347-GALE
Telefax: (313) 961-6815

Introducción

La primera edición de la *Encyclopedia of Women's Associations Worldwide (EWAW)* proporciona información de contacto y descripciones para organizaciones nacionales y multinacionales de mujeres y de temas de mujeres en todo el mundo. La *EWAW* contiene información acerca de una gran variedad de temas de la mujer, incluyendo la mujer en el mundo de los negocios, la educación de la mujer, el cáncer de la mama, el divorcio, los derechos reproductivos y el derecho a la vida, el SIDA, la violencia doméstica, organizaciones deportivas de la mujer, asociaciones profesionales y sociales de mujeres, temas laborales de la mujer, y más.

Las organizaciones listadas en la *EWAW* ofrecen beneficios importantes a la comunidad femenina internacional. Estos incluyen los siguientes:

▶ Servir como vehículos a través de los cuales individuos, organizaciones, y gobiernos puedan dirigirse para tratar las preocupaciones especiales y avanzar los intereses de la mujer.

▶ Hacer el papel de una agencia de información para el intercambio de noticias sobre los temas de la mujer.

▶ Promover el diálogo y fomentar la comunicación.

Recopilada con la ayuda de expertos

La *EWAW* está compuesta de más de 3,400 listados de organizaciones cuidadosamente seleccionadas para inclusión en base a su relación directa a la mujer o a temas de la mujer en áreas como la educación, la salud, la igualdad de derechos, el negocio, la religión y la política. El enfoque internacional de la *EWAW*, su cobertura completa, y su cómodo formato de un solo volumen elimina la necesidad de consultar múltiples fuentes especializadas que a veces son muy difíciles de localizar.

Organización cómoda e índice completo agilitan su acceso a las fuentes de información

La *EWAW* está compuesta de una parte principal de listados descriptivos y dos cómodos índices: el Índice por nombre alfabético y el Índice por actividad de organización.

Los listados descriptivos están organizados en 8 capítulos separados de acuerdo a la región geográfica en que está ubicada la organización, como se explica en la página de "Contenido". Las entradas típicamente contienen datos de contacto completos, información descriptiva que traza las actividades/objetivos de la organización, e información adicional sobre publicaciones producidas y congresos/reuniones celebradas.

El Índice por nombre alfabético proporciona un acceso rápido a todas las organizaciones incluidas en la sección de listado descriptivo por el nombre oficial de las organizaciones y por traducciones del idioma nacional de los nombres. También se incluyen nombres anteriores/alternativos de las organizaciones mencionadas dentro del listado descriptivo en este índice.

El Índice por actividad de organización proporciona un acceso completo a todas las organizaciones por medio de temas pertinentes a las actividades de las organizaciones. También se incluyen referencias cruzadas para facilitar el acceso por parte del usuario a términos relacionados a los sujetos.

Para más información sobre el contenido, organización, y organización de índice de la *EWAW*, véase el "Guía de usuario" que sigue esta Introducción.

Método de recopilación

La *EWAW* fue recopilada de una variedad de fuentes. Las entradas importantes fueron cuidadosamente seleccionadas de otros directorios de Gale Research, Inc., como *Encyclopedia of Associations* y *Encyclopedia of Associations, International Organizations*, y listas y directorios suministrados por numerosas organizaciones mundiales. Se utilizaron cuestionarios enviados por correo para comunicarse con las organizaciones de forma directa.

Los esfuerzos de investigación fueron dirigidos de igual forma a todas las regiones, pero debido a problemas sociales y políticos en zonas geográficas como el Medio Oriente y en países como Somalia, la información sobre las organizaciones de mujeres fue limitada o no pudo ser obtenida.

Agradecimientos

La editora desea agradecer a los siguientes individuos y organizaciones por su continuada asistencia y el proporcionamiento de materiales para los listados:

    Jackie Chang - U.N. Center for the Advancement of Women
    Doris C. Chargualaf - Guam Bureau of Women's Affairs
    Jill Emberson - Pacific Women's Resource Bureau
    Fundación Arias para la Paz y el Progreso Humano
    Colette Guilder - Women's National Commission, United Kingdom
    Kim Holden - Australia Office of the Status of Women
    Fran Hosken - Women's International Network
    Cheng Kexiong - Xinhua Publishing House
    Albert Makovoz - AIM Marketing Services
    Bernard Ntegeye - U.N. Development Programme, Lome, Togo
    Linda Poole - Organization of American States, Inter-American Comission of Women
    Women's International Tribune Center

Gracias también a las siguientes editoras de Gale por sus valiosas contribuciones a este directorio: Deborah M. Burek, Lee Ripley Greenfield, Kerin E. Koek, y Susan B. Martin.

Disponible en formato electrónico

Disquete/cinta magnética. La *EWAW* está disponible para ser licenciada en cinta magnética o en disquete en un formato de campos. Se puede pedir la base de datos completa o una selección de entradas personalizada pueden ser pedidas. La base de datos está disponible para un procesamiento de datos interno y para propósitos que no sean de publicación. Para obtener más información, llame al 800-877-GALE.

Envíenos sus comentarios

Nos complace que nuestros usuarios nos hagan saber de nuevas organizaciones u organizaciones no listadas. Se hará todo el esfuerzo posible para proporcionar información acerca de estas organizaciones en ediciones subsiguientes del Directorio. Comentarios acerca de como mejorar el Directorio también son bienvenidos. Por favor, comuníquese con:

Encyclopedia of Women's Associations Worldwide
Gale Research Inc.
835 Penobscot Bldg.
Detroit, MI, USA 48226-4094
Teléfono: (313) 961-2242
Gratis: 800-347-GALE
Fax: (313) 961-6815

User's Guide

Encyclopedia of Women's Associations Worldwide (EWAW) consists of a main body of descriptive listings arranged into 8 separate chapters by geographic region in which the organization is located, and two convenient indexes. The Alphabetic Name Index lists organizations alphabetically by the official names of the organizations and by any national language name translations. The Organizations' Activities Index lists organizations alphabetically under subject terms relevant to the organizations' activities. Each of these parts is described below.

Descriptive Listings

Each regional chapter is divided into subheadings arranged alphabetically by country. Within each subheading, entries are listed alphabetically by organization name. A sample entry illustrating the types of information typically provided in an entry is shown below.

Sample Entry

The boldfaced number preceding each portion of the sample entry designates an item of information that might be included in an entry. Each numbered item is explained in the paragraph of the same number following the diagram.

---

1 France

---

2 ★138★ **3** Association for the Advancement of Women in France
4 AAWF
5 (Association pour l'Amelioration des Femmes en France - AAFF)
6 42, ave. de la Liberation
F-75016 Paris, France
7 Monique Devreaux, Pres.

8 PH: 1 44563777
FX: 1 44993721
TX: 123456
CB: AAWFCBLE

9 Founded: 1984. **10** Members: 50,000. **11** Membership Dues: 60 Fr/year. **12** Staff: 7. **13** Budget: 75,000 Fr. **14** Local Groups: 5. **15** Languages: English, French. **16** National. **17** Individuals and organizations united to represent and promote the interests of women in France. Lobbies the French government. Fosters networking and communication among members. **18** Library: Reference. Holdings: 20,000; books, periodicals, and newspaper clippings. Subjects: women's issues such as abortion, domestic violence, and reproductive rights. **19** Awards: Annual scholarship. **20** Computerized Services: Data base, pending legislation. **21** Telecommunications Services: Electronic bulletin board. **22** Committees: Women in Government; Women in Medicine. **23** Sections: Traditional Roles. **24** Also Known As: Vive les Femmes. **25** Formerly: (1986) French Women's Society. **26** Publications: AAWF Journal (in English and French), monthly. **27** Price: 25 Fr. **28** ISSN: 1234–5678. **29** Circulation: 35,000. **30** Advertising: accepted. **31** Alternate Formats: microfilm. **32** Also Cited As: AAWF Review. ● Membership Directory, annual. ● Brochures, pamphlets. **33** Convention/Meeting: annual (with exhibits) - 1993 Nov. 7-14, Nancy, France; 1994 Sept. 9-16, Geneva, Switzerland; 1995 October, Germany.

1   **COUNTRY SUBHEADING.** In each of the chapters, country names are given as subheadings and listed alphabetically. Organizations are listed in alphabetical order within the country subheading in which the organization is located. The first country subheading on each left-hand page and the last country subheading on each right-hand page are typeset next to the entry numbers at the top outer corners of the pages.

2   **SEQUENTIAL ENTRY NUMBER.** The entries in this volume are numbered sequentially, and the entry numbers (rather than the page numbers) are used in the index to refer to entries. To facilitate location of the entries in the text, the first entry number on each left-hand page and the last entry number on each right-hand page are typeset at the top outer corners of the pages.

3   **NAME OF ORGANIZATION.** The official English version is given. In cases where the organization is not officially referred to by an English name, the principal national language name is used. (See paragraph 5.) "The" and "Inc." are omitted from most listings, unless they are an integral part of the acronym used by the association.

4   **ACRONYM.** The short form or abbreviation of the organization's name is usually composed of the initial letter or syllable of each word in it. **NOTE:** Some organizations use only one acronym regardless of the number of translations of their name or the languages used. The acronym used here may be that of the principal national language name.

5   **PRINCIPAL NATIONAL LANGUAGE NAME AND ACRONYM.** Most international organizations use official versions of their names in several languages. Additional national language names can be found under the boldfaced rubric "**Also Known As:**" (See paragraph 24.)

6   **ADDRESS.** The address is that of the permanent headquarters or of the executive officer if there is no permanent address.

7   **CHIEF OFFICIAL AND TITLE.** Many organizations employ full-time executives to handle their affairs. If the association does not employ a full-time executive, the name of an elected officer has been provided.

8   **PHONE, FAX, TELEX, CABLE, AND ELECTRONIC MAIL.** Telephone and fax numbers include the city routing code before the local number. Consult the "Table of International Country Access Codes" for country code information.

9   **FOUNDING DATE.** Indicates the year in which the organization was formed. If the group has changed its name, the founding date is for the earliest name by which it was known. If, however, the group was formed by a merger or supersedes another group, the founding date refers to the year in which this action took place; an attempt is also made to give the founding dates for the predecessor organizations.

10   **NUMBER OF MEMBERS.** This figure may represent individuals, firms, institutions, other associations, or a combination of these categories. Since membership constantly fluctuates, the figure listed should be considered an approximation. If an organization describes itself as nonmembership, such notation is made in the entry, preceding the descriptive text.

11   **MEMBERSHIP DUES.** Often listed are the amount (including currency type), frequency of renewal, and type of membership.

12   **STAFF.** Many associations employ a small permanent paid staff. The fact that an organization has no paid staff does not mean it has a limited program. Many groups carry on extensive activities through volunteer workers and committees.

13   **BUDGET.** This figure represents the approximate annual budget for all activities, as reported by the organization. Consult the "Currency Abbreviations and Definitions Tables" for explanations of symbols and currency units by abbreviation and by country.

14   **REGIONAL, NATIONAL, STATE, AND LOCAL GROUPS.** Indicates the number of regional (continental or multinational), national, state, and local sections, chapters, clubs, councils, and branches comprising the organization.

15   **LANGUAGES.** The official and/or working languages of the organization are listed. If the organization does not correspond in English, the message "*does not correspond in English.*" will appear. **NOTE:** The languages in which publications are available, listed following the boldfaced rubric "**Publications**," do not necessarily indicate languages of correspondence.

16   **GEOGRAPHIC SCOPE.** The boldfaced words **Multinational** and **National** indicate the scope of each organization.

17   **DESCRIPTION.** Briefly outlines the types of membership, the purpose, and the activities of the association.

18   **LIBRARY.** Includes type of collection, holdings, and subjects of resources, as indicated by the organization.

19   **AWARDS.** If the group offers awards, the names, types, and recipients are noted here.

20   **COMPUTERIZED SERVICES.** Lists computer-based services offered by the organization, including online services and data bases, bibliographic or other search services, automated mailing list services, and electronic publishing capabilities.

21   **TELECOMMUNICATIONS SERVICES.** Lists special communications services sponsored by the organization. Services included are electronic bulletin boards, teleconferencing capabilities, phone referral systems, teletypes, and TDDs. Consult the "Table of International Country Access Codes" for country code information.

22   **COMMITTEES.** Notes those committees that give an indication of the activities of the group, as distinguished from administrative committees such as membership, finance, and convention. This information often supplements the **Description** (paragraph 17) by providing details about the organization's programs and fields of interest.

23   **SECTIONS AND DIVISIONS.** As in the listing of committees, only those sections or divisions related to definitive activities are included. Geographic divisions are omitted. Other titles used by some associations are Commissions, Councils, Departments, and Task Forces.

24   **ALSO KNOWN AS.** If the group is also known by another name, legally doing business under another name, or otherwise operates under a name different than its official title, that name is provided here. Additional foreign language names are also listed here.

25   **SUPERSESSIONS, ABSORPTIONS, MERGERS, AND CHANGES OF NAME.** If the group superseded or absorbed another organization or was formed by a merger, the original organization name(s) and founding date(s) are listed. Former names and the date(s) of change to a new name are also indicated.

26 **PUBLICATIONS.** The official publication(s) -- including magazines, bulletins, journals, proceedings, directories, and similar periodicals -- are listed alphabetically, with frequency of publication noted. Monographs, pamphlets, handbooks, and similar publications are listed following the official publications, but the listing of such materials is not necessarily complete. Languages in which the publications are available are noted when provided by the organization. If the organization does not issue publications, this is noted at the end of the **Description**. (See paragraph 17.)

27 **PRICE.** Lists the figure(s) provided by the organization. Consult the "Currency Abbreviations and Definitions Tables" for explanations of symbols and currency units by abbreviation and by country.

28 **ISSN**. The International Standard Serial Number is a unique code for the purpose of identifying a specific serial publication. It is listed when provided by the organization; not all publications have been assigned ISSNs.

29 **CIRCULATION.** Provides the figure reported by the organization.

30 **ADVERTISING.** Indicates whether or not the association accepts advertising in the publication.

31 **ALTERNATE FORMATS.** Notes online and microform (microfiche and microfilm) availability.

32 **ALSO CITED AS.** Lists any alternate or former names of the publication.

33 **CONVENTION/MEETING.** Gives the frequency, the date, and the location (city and state or country) of the association's conventions, meetings, or conferences. Also noted is the presence of commercial exhibits. If the organization does not hold conventions or meetings, this is stated at the end of the **Description**. (See paragraph 17.)

Alphabetic Name Index

The Alphabetic Name Index provides access to all entries included in *EWAW* by the official name of the organization and by any national language name translations. Former/alternate names of organizations that appear within entry texts are also included.

Citations for an official name of an organization are followed in parentheses by the city and country in which the organization is located.

Index references are to book entry numbers rather than page numbers. Entry numbers preceded by a star (★) signify that the organization is not listed separately, but is mentioned or described within the entry indicated by the entry number.

Sample entries that could appear in the index follow:

Action Education des Femmes en France .... ★**721**
Afghan Orgn. for the Rights of Women (Kabul, Afghanistan) **2549**
Albanian Fed. of Women Against Domestic Violence (Tirana, Albania) **1049**
Amer. Assn. of Pro-Life Physicians (Boston, USA) **3675**
Bahamas Fed. of Family Planning Clinics .... ★**2160**
Christian Women United in Fellowship (Utrecht, Netherlands) **2773**
Dominica Comm. on Sexual Harassment .... ★**1214**
Equal Rights Fed. of Zimbabwe (Harare, Zimbabwe) **342**
Family Planning Assn. of Equatorial Guinea (Malabo, Equatorial Guinea) **2005**

Organizations' Activities Index

The Organizations' Activities Index provides access to all entries included in *EWAW* by subject term(s) relevant to the organizations' activities. Official organization names appear alphabetically under subject term headings for quick access by topics. Citations are followed in parenthesis by the city, state (if applicable), and country in which the organization is located. National language name translations and former/alternate names are not cited in this index. The terms "woman" and "women" have not been used as subject headings in the index since, as a general category, they cover all the entries in the book.

"See" and "See Also" italicized citations refer the user to related bolded subject terms appearing in the index.

Index references are to book entry numbers rather than page numbers.

Sample entries that could appear in the index follow:

Abortion - *See* Reproductive Rights; Right-to-Life
Abuse - *See* Domestic Violence; Sexual Abuse; Substance Abuse
African American
African Amer. Women in Defense of Ourselves (Chicago, IL, USA) 3021
Black Women's Professional Musicians Soc. (St. Louis, MO, USA) 2940
Black Women's Intl. Medical Assn. (New York, NY, USA) 3176
AIDS
Positively Women (London, England) 1700
Women and AIDS (New York, NY, USA) 3200
Battered Women - *See* Domestic Violence; Sexual Abuse
Breastfeeding
Breastfeeding Support Group of Thailand (Bangkok, Thailand) 903
La Leche League of Canada (Montreal, PQ, Canada) 1875
Career Development
Women in Careers (Lome, Togo) 539

Mode d'emploi

L'*Encyclopedia of Women's Associations Worldwide* comporte une partie principale contenant des références descriptives disposées en 8 chapitres séparés selon la région géographique où l'organisme est situé, et deux index commodes. L'Index Alphabétique par Nom répertorie les organismes par leur nom officiel et par la traduction de leur nom en langue(s) nationale(s). L'index par Domaines d'activité de l'Organisme répertorie par ordre alphabétique les organismes recouvrant un domaine donné.

Références descriptives

Chaque chapitre régional est divisé en rubriques disposées alphabétiquement par pays. Dans chaque rubrique, les références sont disposées alphabétiquement par nom de l'organisme. Un exemple de référence illustrant les types d'informations fournies est indiqué ci-dessous.

Exemple de référence

Le nombre en caractères gras au début de chaque partie de la référence indique une information qui pourrait être comprise dans une référence. Chaque information numérotée est expliquée dans le paragraphe du même numéro, après le diagramme.

---

1 France

2 ★138★   **3** Association for the Advancement of Women in France
4 AAWF
5 (Association pour l'Amelioration des Femmes en France - AAFF)
6 42, ave. de la Liberation
F-75016 Paris, France
7 Monique Devreaux, Pres.

8 PH: 1 44563777
FX: 1 44993721
TX: 123456
CB: AAWFCBLE

9 Founded: 1984. **10** Members: 50,000. **11** Membership Dues: 60 Fr/year. **12** Staff: 7. **13** Budget: 75,000 Fr. **14** Local Groups: 5. **15** Languages: English, French. **16** National. **17** Individuals and organizations united to represent and promote the interests of women in France. Lobbies the French government. Fosters networking and communication among members. **18** Library: Reference. Holdings: 20,000; books, periodicals, and newspaper clippings. Subjects: women's issues such as abortion, domestic violence, and reproductive rights. **19** Awards: Annual scholarship. **20** Computerized Services: Data base, pending legislation. **21** Telecommunications Services: Electronic bulletin board. **22** Committees: Women in Government; Women in Medicine. **23** Sections: Traditional Roles. **24** Also Known As: Vive les Femmes. **25** Formerly: (1986) French Women's Society. **26** Publications: AAWF Journal (in English and French), monthly. **27** Price: 25 Fr. **28** ISSN: 1234–5678. **29** Circulation: 35,000. **30** Advertising: accepted. **31** Alternate Formats: microfilm. **32** Also Cited As: AAWF Review. ● Membership Directory, annual. ● Brochures, pamphlets. **33** Convention/Meeting: annual (with exhibits) - 1993 Nov. 7-14, Nancy, France; 1994 Sept. 9-16, Geneva, Switzerland; 1995 October, Germany.

---

1 **SOUS-TITRE DE PAYS.** Dans chacun de ces chapitres, les noms de pays sont indiqués en rubrique et listés alphabétiquement. Les organismes sont indiqués par ordre alphabétique à l'intérieur de la rubrique du pays où se trouve l'organisme souhaité. La première rubrique de pays à la gauche de la page et la dernière rubrique de pays à la droite de la page sont imprimés à côté des numéros de référence, sur le coin extérieurs en haut de chaque page.

2 **NUMERO SEQUENTIEL DE LA REFERENCE.** Les références de ce volume sont numérotées en ordre croissant; l'index emploie le numéro de référence pour se reporter au texte, non pas le numéro de page. Afin de faciliter la recherche des références, le premier numéro de référence de la page de gauche et le dernier numéro de référence de la page de droite sont imprimés sur les bords supérieurs externes des pages.

3 **NOM DE L'ORGANISME.** La version officielle en anglais est indiquée. Lorsque la désignation officielle de l'organisme n'est pas en anglais, la principale langue du pays est employée. (Reportez-vous au paragraphe 5). «The» et «Inc.» sont généralement omis, sauf s'ils font partie du sigle de l'association.

4 **ACRONYME.** Cette forme abrégée du nom de l'organisme contient généralement la première lettre ou la première syllabe de chaque mot. **REMARQUE:** Certains organismes n'emploient qu'un acronyme, sans considération du nombre de traductions différentes de leur nom ou de la langue employée. L'acronyme indiqué ici peut être celui obtenu avec la langue nationale principale.

5 **NOM ET ACRONYME DANS LA LANGUE NATIONALE PRINCIPALE.** La plupart des organismes internationaux emploient des versions officielles de leur nom en plusieurs langues. Vous pouvez trouver les autres noms en langue nationale dans la rubrique en caractères gras «**Aussi Appele:**» (Voir paragraphe 24).

6 **ADRESSE.** L'adresse donnée est celle du siège permanent ou celle du directeur s'il n'y a pas d'adresse permanente.

7 **DIRECTEUR ET TITRE.** La plupart des organismes emploient des personnels de direction à temps complet pour assurer les tâches. Si l'association n'emploie pas de directeur à temps complet, le nom d'un des officiers élus sera indiqué.

8 **TELEPHONE, TELEFAX, TELEX, TELEGRAPHE, ET MESSAGERIE ELECTRONIQUE.** Les numéros de téléphone et de téléfax comprennent l'indicatif interurbain, puis le numéro local. Reportez-vous au «Table of International Country Access Codes» pour téléphoner un pays donné.

9 **DATE DE FONDATION.** Indique l'année pendant laquelle l'organisme a été formé. Si l'organisme a changé de nom, la date donnée se rapporte au premier nom connu. Par contre, si l'organisme a été formé par fusion de plusieurs groupes ou en remplacement d'un autre groupe, la date de fondation se rapporte à cette action; nous avons aussi essayé de donner les dates de fondation des organismes précédents.

10 **NOMBRE D'ADHERENTS.** Ce nombre peut représenter des individus, des entreprises, des collectivités, d'autres associations, ou une combinaison de ceux-ci. Comme le nombre d'adhérents varie sans cesse, le nombre indiqué n'est qu'une approximation. Si un organisme ne sollicite pas d'adhérents, ce fait est indiqué dans la référence, avant le texte descriptif.

11 **COTISATIONS.** Généralement, le montant de la cotisation (y compris la monnaie), la fréquence de renouvellement, et le type d'adhésion sont indiqués.

12 **EFFECTIF SALARIE.** De nombreuses associations emploient un petit nombre de salariés. L'absence de salariés ne signifie pas que le programme de l'association soit limité. De nombreuses associations accomplissent beaucoup au moyen de bénévoles et de comités.

13 **BUDGET.** Ce nombre représente le budget annuel approximatif indiqué par l'organisme pour l'ensemble des activités. Reportez-vous au «Currency Abbreviations and Definitions Tables» pour les explications des symboles et des unités de monnaie par abréviation et par pays.

14 **GROUPES NATIONAUX, REGIONAUX ET LOCAUX.** Indique le nombre de sections, chapitres, clubs, conseils, ou branches régionaux (continentaux ou multinationaux), nationaux, provinciaux/départementaux, et locaux.

15 **LANGUES.** Les langues officielles et/ou de travail de l'organisme sont indiquées. Si l'organisme ne correspond pas en anglais, le message «*does not correspond in English*» sera indiqué. **REMARQUE:** Les langues dans lesquelles les publications sont disponibles sont indiquées en caractères gras sous la rubrique «**Publications**»; elles ne sont pas nécessairement le langues employées pour la correspondance.

16 **TERRITOIRE D'ACTION GEOGRAPHIQUE.** Les mots «**Multinational**» et «**National**» en caractères gras indiquent le territoire d'action.

17 **DESCRIPTION.** Donne un aperçu des différentes modalités d'adhésion, du but et des activités de l'association.

18 **BIBLIOTHEQUE.** Comprend le type de collection, d'inventaire, et de sujets couverts, conformément aux indications de l'organisme.

19 **PRIX ATTRIBUES.** Si le groupe attribue des prix, les noms, types de prix, et les personnes les ayant reçus sont indiqués ici.

20 **SERVICES INFORMATIQUES.** Indique les services informatiques offerts par l'organisme, y compris des services informatiques en direct et des services de recherche bibliographique ou sur bases de données, des listes de correspondance, et des systèmes de publication assistée par ordinateur.

21 **SERVICES DE TELECOMMUNICATIONS.** Indique les services de communications organisés par l'organisme. Ils peuvent comprendre des bulletins électroniques, des téléconférences, des listes de consultants accessibles par téléphone et des télétypes ordinaires et pour malentendants. Reportez-vous au «Table of International Country Access Codes» pour connaître ceux-ci.

22 **COMITES.** Indique les comités liés aux activités du groupe, non pas les comités administratifs tels que la gestion des adhérents, les finances, et les congrès. Ces informations sont souvent un complément de la **Description** (paragraphe 17) en apportant des détails sur les programmes et les domaines d'intérêt de l'organisme.

23 **SECTIONS ET DIVISIONS.** Comme dans la liste des comités, seules les sections et divisions liées au but final de l'organisme sont citées. Les divisions géographiques ne sont pas indiquées. Certains associations emploient les mots de «Commission», «Conseil», «Service», et «Groupe de travail» pour recouvrir la même idée.

24 **AUSSI APPELE.** Si le groupe est aussi connu sous un autre nom, agit juridiquement sur un autre nom, ou fonctionne de façon générale en partie sous un autre nom que son nom officiel, ce nom est indiqué ici. Les versions du nom en autres langues étrangères sont aussi indiquées ici.

25 **REMPLACEMENTS, FUSIONS, ET CHANGEMENTS DE NOM.** Si le groupe a remplacé ou fusionné avec un autre organisme, le nom de celui-ci et sa date de fondation sont indiqués. En cas de changement de nom, les anciens noms et les dates de changement sont indiqués.

26 **PUBLICATIONS.** Les publications officielles -- y compris revues, bulletins, compte-rendus de travaux, annuaires, et autres périodiques -- sont données par ordre alphabétique avec indication de la fréquence de parution. Les monographies, pamphlets, manuels, et autres publications semblables sont données après les publications officielles, mais cette liste n'est pas forcément complète. Les langues de ces publications sont données conformément aux informations fournies par l'organisme. Si l'organisme ne publie rien, ce fait est noté à la fin de la **Description** (Voir paragraphe 17).

27 **PRIX.** Indique les prix communiqués par l'organisme. Reportez-vous au «Currency Abbreviations and Definitions Tables» pour les explications des symboles et des unités de monnaie par abréviation et par pays.

28 **ISSN.** Le numéro de série standard international (International Standard Serial Number) est un code permettant d'identifier une publication spécifique de façon unique. Il est indiqué lorsque l'organisme le communique; certaines publications n'ont pas reçu de numéro.

29 **TIRAGE.** Indique le nombre communiqué par l'organisme.

30 **PUBLICITE.** Indique si l'organisme accepte les publicités dans sa publication.

31 **AUTRES FORMATS.** Indique la disponibilité sur liaison informatique en temps réel, microfiche, et microfilm.

32 **AUSSI CITE SOUS LE NOM DE.** Indique d'anciens noms ou d'autres noms employés par la revue.

33 **CONGRES/REUNION.** Indique la fréquence, la date, et l'emplacement (ville et province/état/département ou pays) des congrès, réunions, ou conférences de l'association. Si l'organisme organise des salons, ce fait sera indiqué. Si l'organisme ne tient pas de des congrès ou réunions, ce fait sera indiqué à la fin de la **Description**. (Voir paragraphe 17.)

Index alphabétique par nom

L'Index Alphabétique par Nom permet l'accès à toutes les références du *EWAW* par le nom officiel de l'organisme et toute autre traduction en langue nationale. Les anciens noms et autres noms de chaque organisme sont aussi compris, du moment qu'ils soient dans le paragraphe 24 de la référence.

Les indications du nom officiel d'un organisme sont suivies de la ville, de l'état (ou province, département, etc...) le cas échéant, puis du pays où l'organisme est situé, le tout entre parenthèses.

Les numéros indiqués dans l'index sont des numéros de référence, pas des numéros de page. Les numéros de référence précédés d'une étoile (★) signifient que l'organisme n'est pas répertoriée séparément, mais qu'elle est citée ou décrite dans la référence désignée par le numéro donné.

Voici des exemples possibles du contenu de l'index:

Index des organismes par domaine d'activité

L'Index des Organismes par domaine d'activité permet l'accès à toutes les références de l'encyclopédie *EWAW* par l'intermédiaire du (des) domaine(s) d'activité de l'organisme. Le nom officiel de chaque organisme apparaît par ordre alphabétique sous chaque domaine d'activité. Les traductions en langues nationales et les anciens/ autre noms ne sont pas employés ici. Les mots «woman» et «women» ne sont pas employés ici, puisqu'ils recouvrent toutes les références contenues dans ce volume.

Les mentions «See» et «See Also» en italiques reportent le lecteur aux domaines apparentés indiqués en caractères gras dans l'index.

Les références de l'index se rapportent aux numéros de référence du volume plutôt que numéros de la page.

Voici des exemples possibles du contenu de l'index:

Abortion - *See* **Reproductive Rights; Right-to-Life**
Abuse - *See* **Domestic Violence; Sexual Abuse; Substance Abuse**
African American
African Amer. Women in Defense of Ourselves (Chicago, IL, USA) 3021
Black Women's Professional Musicians Soc. (St. Louis, MO, USA) 2940
Black Women's Intl. Medical Assn. (New York, NY, USA) 3176
AIDS
Positively Women (London, England) 1700
Women and AIDS (New York, NY, USA) 3200
Battered Women - *See* **Domestic Violence; Sexual Abuse**
Breastfeeding
Breastfeeding Support Group of Thailand (Bangkok, Thailand) 903
La Leche League of Canada (Montreal, PQ, Canada) 1875
Career Development
Women in Careers (Lome, Togo) 539

Benutzerführung

Das *Encyclopedia of Women's Associations Worldwide (EWAW)* besteht aus einem Hauptteil mit beschriebenen Eintragungen, das in 8 einzelne Kapitel nach der geographischen Region, in der sich die Organisation befindet, angeordnet ist, und zwei praktische Verzeichnisse. Im alphabetischen Namensregister werden die Organisationen in alphabetischer Reihenfolge mit ihren offiziellen Namen sowohl wie jeglicher Übersetzungen der Namen in der jeweiligen Landessprache aufgeführt. Im Index der Aktivitäten der Organisationen werden die Organisationen in alphabetischer Reihenfolge innerhalb von Schlagwortgruppen, die sich auf die Tätigkeit der jeweiligen Organisation beziehen, aufgeführt. Jeder dieser einzelnen Teile wird nachstehend beschrieben.

Beschriebene Eintragungen

Jedes regionale Kapitel ist in Unterabteilungen, die in alphabetischer Reihenfolge nach Land geordnet sind, unterteilt. Innerhalb jeder Unterabteilung sind die Eintragungen, in alphabetischer Reihenfolge nach dem Namen der Organisation geordnet, aufgeführt. Ein Beispiel einer Eintragung, mit der die Art der Informationen dargestellt wird, die üblicherweise in einer Eintragung enthalten sind, ist unten aufgeführt.

Eintragungsbeispiel

Information, die in einer Eintragung enthalten sein könnte, wird mit der mit Fettdruck gedruckten Nummer vor jedem Teil des Eintragungsbeispiels angegeben. Jeder numerierter Posten wird im Absatz mit der entsprechenden Nummer nach dem Diagramm erläutert.

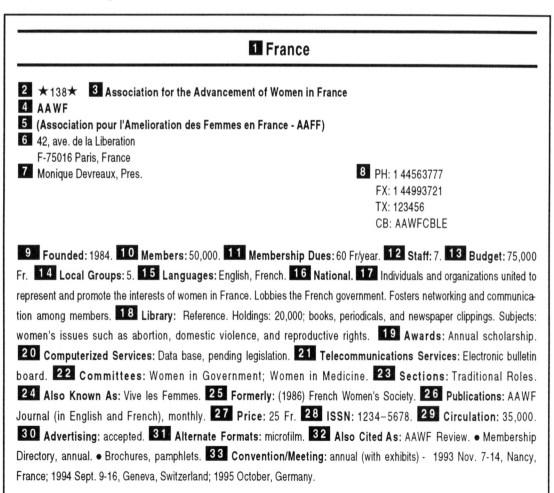

1 **UNTERABSCHNITT FÜR JEDES LAND.** In jedem der Kapitel werden die Namen von Länder als Unterabschnitte angegeben und in alphabetischer Reihenfolge aufgeführt. Organisationen werden in alphabetischer Reihenfolge innerhalb des Unterabschnittes des Landes, in dem sie sich befinden, aufgeführt. Der erste Landesunterabschnitt auf jeder linken Seite und der letzte Landesunterabschnitt auf jeder rechten Seite wird neben der Eintragungsnummer auf den äußeren Ecken oben auf der Seite gedruckt.

2 **LAUFENDE EINTRAGUNGSNUMMER.** Jeder Eintragung in diesem Band wird eine laufende Nummer zugeordnet, und diese Eintragungsnummern werden im Verzeichnis (anstelle der Seitennummern) verwendet, um auf die Eintragungen zu verweisen. Die erste Eintragungsnummer auf jeder linken Seite sowohl wie die letzte Eintragungsnummer auf jeder rechten Seite wird auf den äußeren Ecken oben auf der Seite gedruckt, um die Eintragungen im Text leichter auffinden zu können.

3 **NAME DER ORGANISATION.** Die offizielle englische Version wird angegeben. In den Fällen, in denen die Organisation nicht offiziell bei einem englischen Namen genannt wird, wird der Name bei dem die Organisation in der jeweiligen Landessprache üblicherweise genannt ist, verwendet (Siehe Absatz 5). "The" und "Inc." wird üblicherweise in den Eintragungen ausgelassen, es sei denn, sie sind ein fester Bestandteil des von der Organisation verwendeten Akronyms.

4 **AKRONYM.** Die Kurzform oder Abkürzung des Namens der Organisation, das üblicherweise aus den Anfangsbuchstaben oder der Anfangssylben von jedem Wort im Namen gebildet wird. **HINWEIS:** Einige Organisationen verwenden trotz der Anzahl der Übersetzungen ihres Namens oder der verwendeten Sprache nur einen Akronym. Der hier angegebene Akronym könnte von einem Namen der Hauptlandessprache der Organisation stammen.

5 **NAME UND AKRONYM IN DER HAUPTLANDESSPRACHE.** Die meisten internationalen Organisationen verwenden offizielle Versionen ihres Namens in mehrere Sprachen. Weitere Namen in der jeweiligen Landessprache können auch unter der mit Fettdruck gedruckten Rubrik **"Auch Bekannt Unter Dem Namen:"** (Siehe Abschnitt 24) gefunden werden.

6 **ADRESSE.** Die Adresse ist die des ständigen Hauptsitzes, oder falls kein ständiger Hauptsitz existiert, die der leitenden Führungskraft.

7 **LEITENDE FÜHRUNGSKRAFT UND TITEL.** Viele Organisationen stellen ganztägig beschäftigte Führungskräfte an, um die Geschäfte der Organisation zu führen. Falls die Organisation keine ganztägig beschäftigten Führungskräfte anstellt, wird der Name eines gewählten Vorstandsmitgliedes angegeben.

8 **TELEFON, TELEFAX, TELEX, TELEGRAMM, UND ELEKTRONISCHE POST.** Die Telefon- und Telefaxnummern enthalten die Ortsvorwahl vor der Ortsnummer. Für nähere Angaben zur Landesvorwahl, siehe die "Table of International Country Access Codes."

9 **DATUM DER GRÜNDUNG.** Das Jahr in dem die Organisation gegründet wurde wird angegeben. Bei Gruppen die ihren Namen geändert haben ist das Datum der Gründung für den ersten Namen, unter dem die Gruppe bekannt war, angegeben. Falls die Gruppe jedoch durch den Zusammenschluß zweier Gruppen geformt wurde, oder eine andere Gruppe ersetzt, wird mit dem Datum das Jahr, in dem dies geschehen ist, angegeben; ein Versuch wird auch gemacht, die Gründungsdaten der Vorgangsorganisationen anzugeben.

10   **ANZAHL DER MITGLIEDER.** Mit diesen Angaben können Einzelpersonen, Firmen, Gesellschaften, andere Verbände, oder eine Kombination dieser Kategorien dargestellt werden. Da die Mitgliedschaft sich ständig ändert, verstehen sich die Angaben als Schätzwerte. Falls sich eine Organisation als Nichtmitglied bezeichnet, wird dies in der Eintragung vor dem beschriebenen Text angegeben.

11   **MITGLIEDSCHAFTSBEITRÄGE.** Oft angegeben werden die Höhe des Beitrags (inclusive Währung), der Erneuerungsintervall, und die Mitgliedschaftskategorien.

12   **PERSONAL.** Viele Vereinigungen haben eine kleine, ständige, bezahlte Belegschaft. Falls eine Organisation kein bezahltes Personal hat, ist nicht anzunehmen, daß sie ein beschränktes Programm hat. Viele Gruppen betreiben ein umfangreiches Programm mit freiwilligen Hilfskräften und Ausschüssen.

13   **HAUSHALT.** Mit dieser Zahl wird der von der Organisation angegebene, ungefähre Jahreshaushalt für alle Aktivitäten dargestellt. Eine Erklärung der Symbole und Währungseinheiten nach Abkürzung und Land geordnet kann der "Currency Abbreviations and Definitions Tables" entnommen werden.

14   **REGIONALE, NATIONALE, LANDESWEITE, UND LOKALE GRUPPEN.** Hiermit wird die Anzahl der einzelnen Abteilungen, Gruppen, Verbände, Räte und Zweiggruppen, die auf regionaler (kontinentaler oder internationaler), nationaler, landesweiter oder lokaler Ebene tätig sind, und aus der die Organisation besteht, angegeben.

15   **SPRACHEN.** Die offizielle und/oder die gebräuchliche Sprachen der Organisation werden aufgeführt. Falls die Organisation nicht auf Englisch korrespondiert, wird die Meldung *"does not correspond in English"* erscheinen. **HINWEIS:** Die Sprachen in denen die erhältlichen Veröffentlichungen gedruckt sind, und die nach der in Fettdruck gedruckten Rubrik **"Veröffentlichungen"** aufgeführt sind, entsprechen nicht unbedingt die Sprachen in denen die Organisation korrespondiert.

16   **GEOGRAPHISCHER AKTIONSBEREICH.** Der Aktionsbereich der Organisation wird mit den in Fettdruck gedruckten Wörtern **"Multinational"** und **"National"** angedeutet.

17   **BESCHREIBUNG.** Die verschiedenen Sorten der Mitgliedschaft, der Zweck, und die Tätigkeiten der Organisation werden kurz zusammengefaßt.

18   **BIBLIOTHEK.** Diese Eintragung enthält, gemäß den Angaben der Organisation, die Art und den Umfang der Sammlung, sowohl wie die Sachgebiete der Materialien.

19   **AUSZEICHNUNGEN.** Falls Preise von der Gruppe verliehen werden, werden die Namen, die Art und die Empfänger der Auszeichnungen an dieser Stelle angegeben.

20   **COMPUTERISIERTE DIENSTLEISTUNGEN.** Hier werden jegliche von der Organisation angebotenen computerisierten Dienstleistungen, wie zum Beispiel on-line Dienstleistungen und Datenbanken, bibliographische oder andere Suchdienste, automatisierte Anschriftenlistendienste, und Fähigkeiten zur elektronischen Veröffentlichung aufgeführt.

21   **TELEKOMMUNIKATIONSDIENSTLEISTUNGEN.** An dieser Stelle werden besondere Kommunikationsdienstleistungen, die von der Organisation gefördert werden, aufgeführt. Diese Dienstleistungen schließen unter anderem elektronische Anschlagtafeln, Telekonferenzfähigkeiten, Telefonvermittlungsdienste, Fernschreiber und TDDs um. Für Angaben zur Landesvorwahl, siehe die "Table of International Country Access Codes."

22 **AUSSCHÜßE.** Hier werden, im Gegensatz zu solchen Verwaltungsausschüßen wie diejenigen für die Mitgliedschaft, die Finanzen und der Tagungen, diejenigen Ausschüße aufgeführt, die einen Hinweis auf die Tätigkeiten der Gruppe geben. Diese Informationen ergänzen oft die **Beschreibung** (Absatz 17), indem sie Aufschluß über die Programme und Interessenbereiche der Organisation geben.

23 **ABTEILUNGEN UND GRUPPEN.** Hier werden, wie bei der Aufführung der Ausschüße, nur diejenigen Abteilungen und Gruppen aufgeführt, die direkt mit den maßgeblichen Aktivitäten der Gruppe verbunden sind. Geographische Abteilungen werden nicht aufgeführt. Andere Titel, die von einigen Organisationen verwendet werden, sind Kommissionen, Räte, Ressorts, und Sondereinheiten.

24 **AUCH BEKANNT UNTER DEM NAMEN.** Falls die Gruppe auch unter einem anderen Namen bekannt ist, rechtskräftige Geschäfte unter einem anderen Namen betreibt, oder in einer sonstigen Weise einen anderen Namen als den offiziellen Namen verwendet, wird dieser Name hier angegeben. Zusätzliche Namen in Fremdsprachen werden auch hier angegeben.

25 **ABLÖSUNGEN, FUSIONEN, ZUSAMMENSCHLÜSSE UND NAMENSÄNDERUNGEN.** Falls die Gruppe eine andere Organisation ersetzt oder durch Fusion übernommen hat, oder durch den Zusammenschluß zweier Gruppen geformt wurde, werden die Namen und das Gründungsdatum der jeweiligen Gruppe hier angegeben. Die ehemaligen Namen und das jeweilige Datum, an der die organisatorische Änderung stattgefunden hat, wird auch angegeben.

26 **VERÖFFENTLICHUNGEN.** Die offiziellen Veröffentlichungen -- wie zum Beispiel Zeitschriften, Nachrichtenblätter, Fachzeitschriften, Protokolle, Verzeichnisse und ähnliche Veröffentlichungen -- werden in alphabetischer Reihenfolge, mit einem Hinweis darauf, wie oft die Zeitschrift veröffentlicht wird, aufgeführt. Monographien, Broschüren, Handbücher und ähnliche Veröffentlichungen werden nach den offiziellen Veröffentlichungen aufgeführt. Diese Auflistung jedoch erhebt keinen Anspruch auf Vollständigkeit. Die Sprachen, in denen die Veröffentlichungen erhältlich sind, werden, wenn sie uns von der Organisation bekanntgegeben wurden, auch vermerkt. Falls die Organisation keine Veröffentlichungen herausgibt, wird dies am Ende der **Beischreibung** angegeben (Siehe Abschnitt 17).

27 **PREIS.** An dieser Stelle werden die von der Organisation mitgeteilten Angaben aufgeführt. Eine Erklärung der Symbole und Währungseinheiten nach Abkürzung und Land geordnet kann der "Currency Abbreviations and Definitions Tables" entnommen werden.

28 **ISSN.** Die Internationale Standardseriennummer (International Standard Serial Number) ist ein einzigartiger Kode zur Identifizierung einer bestimmten periodisch erschienenen Zeitschrift. Sie wird, wenn sie von der Organisation angegeben wurde, an dieser Stelle aufgeführt; nicht alle Veröffentlichungen haben eine ISSN.

29 **AUFLAGE.** Die von der Organisation mitgeteilten Angaben werden hier aufgeführt.

30 **WERBUNG.** Hier wird angedeutet, ob die Organisation in der Veröffentlichung Werbung annimmt.

31 **ALTERNATIVE FORMATE.** An dieser Stelle wird angedeutet, ob die Veröffentlichung auch on-line oder in Mikroformaten (Mikrofiche und Mikrofilm) erhältlich ist.

32 **AUCH AUFGEFÜHRT ALS.** Jegliche alternative oder ehemalige Namen der Veröffentlichung werden aufgeführt.

TAGUNGEN/VERANSTALTUNGEN. An dieser Stelle werden die Häufigkeit, das Datum und den Ort (Stadt und Staat oder Land) der Tagungen, Veranstaltungen und Kongresse der Organisation angegeben. Die Anwesenheit von kommerziellen Ausstellungen wird auch angedeutet. Wenn die Organisation keine Tagungen/Veranstaltungen veranstaltet, wird dies am Ende der **Beschreibung** (Siehe Absatz 17) angegeben.

Alphabetisches Namensregister

Das alphabetische Namensregister bietet durch die Aufführung der offiziellen Namen der Organisationen und der Übersetzungen der Namen in der jeweiligen Landessprache Zugang zu allen Eintragungen im *EWAW*. Ehemalige/alternative Namen der Organisationen, die im Text der Eintragungen erscheinen, werden auch aufgeführt.

Nach der Eintragung des offiziellen Namens einer Organisation wird die Stadt, den Staat (falls zutreffend), und das Land, in dem sich die Organisation befindet, in Klammern eingeschlossen, angegeben.

Die Verweise im Register beziehen sich auf die Eintragungsnummern im Buch, und nicht auf die Seitennummer. Wird einer Eintragungsnummer ein Sternchen (★) vorangestellt, wird die entsprechende Organisation nicht einzeln aufgeführt, sondern sie wird in der Eintragung, die der Nummer entspricht, erwähnt oder beschrieben.

Nachstehend ist ein Beispiel einer Eintragung, die im Register erscheinen könnte.

Action Education des Femmes en France	★721
Afghan Orgn. for the Rights of Women (Kabul, Afghanistan)	2549
Albanian Fed. of Women Against Domestic Violence (Tirana, Albania)	1049
Amer. Assn. of Pro-Life Physicians (Boston, USA)	3675
Bahamas Fed. of Family Planning Clinics	★2160
Christian Women United in Fellowship (Utrecht, Netherlands)	2773
Dominica Comm. on Sexual Harassment	★1214
Equal Rights Fed. of Zimbabwe (Harare, Zimbabwe)	342
Family Planning Assn. of Equatorial Guinea (Malabo, Equatorial Guinea)	2005
Federacion Argentina de Mujeres	★1672
Ghana Assembly of Women's Feds. (Accra, Ghana)	434
Housewives' League of Sweden (Stockholm, Sweden)	3000
Iceland Feminists for Equality (Reykjavik, Iceland)	2879
Iniciativa de Mujeres Feministas (San Jose, Costa Rica)	1226

Index der Aktivitäten der Organisationen

Der Index der Aktivitäten der Organisationen bietet durch Schlagwortgruppen, die sich auf die Tätigkeit der Organisationen beziehen, Zugang zu allen im *EWAW* enthaltenen Eintragungen. Rascher Zugang nach Thema wird durch die Aufführung der offiziellen Namen der Organisationen in alphabetischer Reihenfolge innerhalb der Schlagwortgruppen geboten. In diesem Index werden Übersetzungen der Namen in der jeweiligen Landessprache und ehemalige/alternative Namen nicht angegeben. Die Ausdrücke "woman" und "women" wurden in diesem Index nicht als Schlagwörter verwendet, da sie als allgemeine Kategorien alle Eintragungen in diesem Buch enthalten würden.

Die Verweise "See" und "See also," die im Kursivdruck gedruckt sind, verweisen den Benutzer die Benuzerin auf die in Fettdruck gedruckten Schlagwörter, die im Index erscheinen.

Die Verweise im Index beziehen sich auf die Eintragungsnummer im Buch, und nicht auf die Seitennummer.

Nachstehend ist ein Beispiel einer Eintragung, die im Index erscheinen könnte.

Abortion - *See* **Reproductive Rights; Right-to-Life**
Abuse - *See* **Domestic Violence; Sexual Abuse; Substance Abuse**
African American
African Amer. Women in Defense of Ourselves (Chicago, IL, USA) **3021**
Black Women's Professional Musicians Soc. (St. Louis, MO, USA).................... **2940**
Black Women's Intl. Medical Assn. (New York, NY, USA) **3176**
AIDS
Positively Women (London, England) **1700**
Women and AIDS (New York, NY, USA) **3200**
Battered Women - *See* **Domestic Violence; Sexual Abuse**
Breastfeeding
Breastfeeding Support Group of Thailand (Bangkok, Thailand) **903**
La Leche League of Canada (Montreal, PQ, Canada) **1875**
Career Development
Women in Careers (Lome, Togo) **539**

Guía del usuario

La *Encyclopedia of Women's Associations Worldwide* se compone de una parte principal de listados descriptivos organizados en 8 capítulos individuales por región geográfica donde se ubica la organización, y dos cómodos índices. El Índice de nombre alfabético lista las organizaciones en forma alfabética por los nombres oficiales de las organizaciones y por las traducciones del idioma nacional de los nombres. El Índice por actividad de organización lista las organizaciones en forma alfabética bajo temas relacionados con las actividades de las organizaciones. Cada una de estas partes se describen a continuación.

Listados descriptivos

Cada capítulo regional está dividido en subtítulos organizados alfabéticamente por país. Dentro de cada subtítulo, las entradas son listadas alfabéticamente por el nombre de la organización. Un ejemplo de una entrada que muestra los tipos de información típicamente proporcionados en una entrada se muestra a continuación.

Ejemplo de entrada

El número en negrilla que viene antes de cada porción del ejemplo de entrada asigna un artículo de información que puede ser incluido en una entrada. Cada artículo numerado se explica en el párrafo del mismo número que sigue el diagrama.

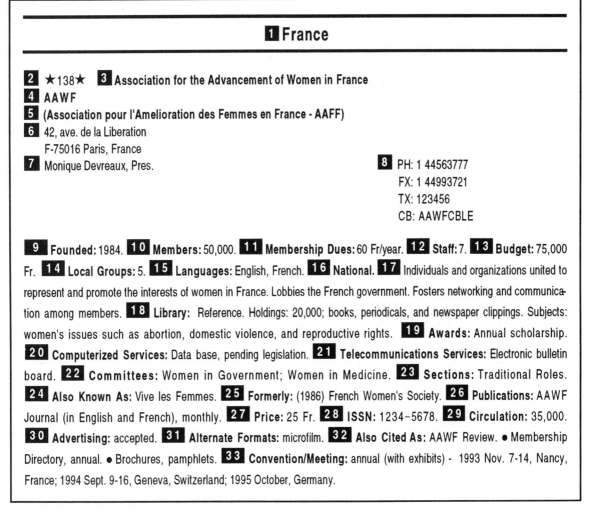

1 **SUBTÍTULO DE PAÍS**. En cada uno de los capítulos, los nombres de los países se proporcionan como subtítulos y son listados alfabéticamente. Las organizaciones son listadas en orden alfabético dentro del subtítulo de país donde se ubica la organización. El primer subtítulo de país en cada página a mano izquierda y el último subtítulo de país en cada página a mano derecha son puestos al lado de los números de entrada en las esquinas superiores externas de las páginas.

2 **NÚMERO DE ENTRADA SECUENCIAL**. Las entradas de este volumen son numeradas secuencialmente, y los números de entrada (en vez de los números de página) se utilizan en el índice para referirse a las entradas. Para facilitar la ubicación de las entradas en el texto, el primer número de entrada en cada página a mano izquierda y el último número de entrada en cada página a mano derecha son puestos en las esquinas superiores externas de las páginas.

3 **NOMBRE DE LA ORGANIZACIÓN**. Se proporciona la versión oficial en inglés. En los casos donde no se refiere a la organización por un nombre en inglés, se utiliza el nombre principal en el idioma nacional. (Véase el párrafo 5.) El artículo "The" e "Inc." se omiten de la mayoría de los listados, a menos que sean una parte integrante de las siglas utilizadas por la asociación.

4 **SIGLAS**. La forma corta o abreviatura del nombre de la organización generalmente se compone de la letra o sílaba inicial de cada palabra constituyente. **NOTA:** Algunas organizaciones sólo usan un tipo de siglas, aunque hayan múltiples traducciones de su nombre en muchos idiomas. Las siglas utilizadas aquí pueden ser aquellas del nombre principal en el idioma nacional.

5 **NOMBRE PRINCIPAL EN EL IDIOMA NACIONAL Y SIGLAS**. La mayoría de las organizaciones internacionales usan varias versiones oficiales de su nombres en varios idiomas. Los nombres adicionales en el idioma nacional se pueden encontrar bajo la rúbrica en negrilla **"También Llamado:"** (Véase el párrafo 24.)

6 **DIRECCIÓN**. La dirección es la de la oficina central permanente o la del director ejecutivo si no hay una dirección permanente.

7 **EJECUTIVO ENCARGADO Y TITULO**. Muchas organizaciones emplean a ejecutivos de jornada completa para manejar sus asuntos. Si la asociación no emplea un ejecutivo de jornada completa, se proporciona el nombre de un director elegido.

8 **TELÉFONO, FAX, TELEX, CABLE, Y CORREO ELECTRÓNICO**. Los números de teléfono y fax incluyen el código de ciudad antes del número local. Consulte la "Table of International Country Access Codes" para información sobre los códigos de países.

9 **FECHA DE FUNDACIÓN:** Indica el año en que fue fundada la organización. Si el grupo ha cambiado su nombre, la fecha de fundación es para el primer nombre por el cual la organización fue conocida. Sin embargo, si el grupo fue el resultado de una fusión o suplanta otro grupo, la fecha de fundación se refiere al año en el cual está acción se desarrolló; también se intenta dar fechas de fundación para las organizaciones anteriores.

10 **NÚMERO DE MIEMBROS**. Esta figura puede representar individuos, empresas, instituciones, otras asociaciones, o una combinación de estas categorías. Ya que el número de miembros fluctúa constantemente, la cifra listada debe ser considerada como una aproximación. Si una organización se describe como una organización que no tiene una lista de miembros, se hace una anotación al respecto en la entrada, antes del texto descriptivo.

11 **CUOTA DE MIEMBRO**. A veces se lista la cantidad (incluyendo el tipo de moneda), la frecuencia con que se tiene que renovar, y el tipo de miembro.

12 **PERSONAL.** Muchas asociaciones emplean un pequeño personal asalariado permanente. El hecho que una organización no tenga personal asalariado no significa que tenga un programa limitado. Muchos grupos realizan extensas actividades por medio de trabajadores voluntarios y comités.

13 **PRESUPUESTO.** Esta figura representa una aproximación del presupuesto anual para todas las actividades, según la organización. Véase la "Currency Abbreviations and Definitions Tables" para obtener explicaciones de símbolos y unidades de moneda por abreviatura y por país.

14 **GRUPOS REGIONALES, NACIONALES, ESTATALES Y LOCALES.** Indica el número de sectores, secciones, partes, clubs, concilios, y ramas regionales (continentales o multinacionales), nacionales, estatales, y locales que consisten de la organización.

15 **IDIOMAS.** Se lista el idioma oficial y/o de trabajo de la organización. Si la organización no contesta su correspondencia en inglés, aparecerá el mensaje "*does not correspond in English*." **NOTA:** Los idiomas en que están disponibles las publicaciones, listados bajo la rúbrica en negrilla **Publicaciones**," no indican necesariamente los idiomas en que la publicación contesta su correspondencia.

16 **ALCANCE GEOGRÁFICO.** Las palabras en negrilla **Multinacional** y **Nacional** indican el alcance de la organización.

17 **DESCRIPCIÓN.** Traza brevemente los tipos de miembros, el propósito, y las actividades de la asociación.

18 **BIBLIOTECA.** Incluye el tipo de colección, libros, y temas de los recursos, según la organización.

19 **PREMIOS.** Si el grupo ofrece premios, los nombres, tipos, y receptores se anotan aquí.

20 **SERVICIOS COMPUTARIZADOS.** Lista los servicios computarizados ofrecidos por la organización, incluyendo servicios en línea y bases de datos, servicios bibilográficos u otros servicios de investigación, servicios de lista postal automatizada, y capacidades de impresión electrónica.

21 **SERVICIOS DE TELECOMUNICACIONES.** Lista los servicios de comunicaciones especiales patrocinados por la organización. Los servicios incluyen tablero de avisos electrónico, capacidades de teleconferencia, sistemas de referencia de otros teléfonos, teletipos, y TTD. Consulte la "Table of International Country Access Codes" para obtener información sobre los códigos de países.

22 **COMITÉS.** Señala aquellos comités que dan una indicación de las actividades del grupo, a diferencia de comités administrativos, como son los comités de miembros, finanzas, y de congresos. Esta información puede suplementar la **Descripción** (párrafo 17) proporcionando detalles acerca de los programas de la organización y de sus áreas de interés.

23 **SECCIONES Y DIVISIONES.** Como en el listado de comités, solo se incluyen aquellas secciones o divisiones relacionadas con actividades específicas. Se omiten las divisiones geográficas. Otros títulos usados por algunas asociaciones son Comisiones, Concilios, Departamentos y Grupos de trabajo especiales.

24 **TAMBIÉN LLAMADO.** Si el grupo también es conocido por otro nombre, hace negocios legalmente bajo otro nombre, o de alguna otra forma opera bajo algún otro nombre fuera de su título oficial, ese nombre es proporcionado aquí. Nombres adicionales en otros idiomas también se proporcionan aquí.

25 **SUPLANTACIONES, ABSORCIONES, FUSIONES Y CAMBIOS DE NOMBRES.** Si el grupo suplantó o absorbió otra organización o fue formado por una fusión, se proporcionan el(los) nombre(s) original(es) de la(s) organización(es) y su(s) fecha(s) de fundación. También se indican los nombres anteriores y la(s) fecha(s) de cambio al nuevo nombre.

26 **PUBLICACIONES.** La(s) publicación(es) oficial(es), incluyendo revistas, boletines, periódicos, actas, directorios, y publicaciones similares, se listan alfabéticamente, con la frecuencia de publicación señalada. Las monografías, panfletos, manuales, y publicaciones similares se enumeran después de las publicaciones oficiales, pero el listado de estos materiales no está necesariamente completo. Los idiomas en los cuales están disponibles dichas publicaciones se notan cuando estos son proporcionados por la organización. Si la organización no edita publicaciones, esto se nota al final de la **Descripción**. (Véase el párrafo 17.)

27 **PRECIO.** Lista el(los) precio(s) dados por la organización. Consulte la "Currency Abbreviations and Definitions Tables" para obtener explicaciones de símbolos y unidades de moneda por abreviatura y por país.

28 **ISSN.** El Número de serie estándar internacional (International Standard Serial Number) es un código único que sirve para identificar un publicación en serie específica. Se lista cuando es proporcionado por la organización; no todas las publicaciones han sido asignadas ISSN.

29 **TIRADA.** Proporciona las cifras proporcionadas por la organización.

30 **PUBLICIDAD.** Indica si la asociación acepta publicidad en la publicación.

31 **FORMATOS ALTERNATIVOS.** Nota la disponibilidad en línea y de microformato (microficha y microfilme).

32 **TAMBIÉN LLAMADO.** Lista cualquier otro nombre o nombre anterior de la publicación.

33 **CONGRESO/REUNIÓN.** Da la frecuencia, la fecha, y la ubicación (ciudad, estado o país) de los congresos, reuniones y conferencias de la asociación. También se nota la presencia de exposiciones comerciales. Si la organización no celebra congresos o reuniones, esto se indica al final de la **Descripción**. (Véase el párrafo 17.)

Índice de nombre alfabético

El Índice de nombre alfabético le proporciona acceso a todas las entradas incluidas en la *EWAW* por el nombre oficial de la organización y por cualquier traducción del idioma nacional de los nombres. Los nombres alternativos/anteriores de las organizaciones que aparezcan dentro de los textos de entrada también son incluidos.

Las citas de un nombre oficial de una organización vienen seguidas de la ciudad, el estado (si aplicable), y el país en que está ubicada la organización, todo en paréntesis.

Las referencias del índice son a números de entrada de libro en vez de a números de página. Los números de entrada precedidos de una estrella (★) significan que la organización no se lista separadamente, pero se menciona o describe dentro de la entrada indicada por el número de entrada.

Las siguientes son ejemplos de entradas que podrían aparecer en el índice:

Action Education des Femmes en France .... **★721**
Afghan Orgn. for the Rights of Women (Kabul, Afghanistan) **2549**
Albanian Fed. of Women Against Domestic Violence (Tirana, Albania) **1049**
Amer. Assn. of Pro-Life Physicians (Boston, USA) **3675**
Bahamas Fed. of Family Planning Clinics .... **★2160**
Christian Women United in Fellowship (Utrecht, Netherlands) **2773**

Índice por actividad de organización

El Índice por actividad de organización proporciona acceso a todas las entradas incluidas de la *EWAW* por tema(s) relacionado(s) con las actividades de la organización. Los nombres oficiales de la organización aparecen alfabéticamente bajo títulos temáticos para rápido acceso por tópicos. Las traducciones del idioma nacional de los nombres y nombres alternativos/anteriores no se citan en este índice. Los términos "mujer" y "mujeres" no se han utilizado como títulos temáticos en el índice, ya que, como categoría general, cubren todas las entradas del libro.

Las citas "See" and "See Also" en letra cursiva refieren el usuario a temas relacionados en negrilla que aparecen en el índice.

Las referencias del índice son a números de entrada de libro y no a números de página.

Ejemplos de entradas que podrían aparecer en el índice siguen a continuación:

Abortion - *See* Reproductive Rights; Right-to-Life
Abuse - *See* Domestic Violence; Sexual Abuse; Substance Abuse
African American
African Amer. Women in Defense of Ourselves (Chicago, IL, USA) 3021
Black Women's Professional Musicians Soc. (St. Louis, MO, USA) 2940
Black Women's Intl. Medical Assn. (New York, NY, USA) 3176
AIDS
Positively Women (London, England) 1700
Women and AIDS (New York, NY, USA) 3200
Battered Women - *See* Domestic Violence; Sexual Abuse
Breastfeeding
Breastfeeding Support Group of Thailand (Bangkok, Thailand) 903
La Leche League of Canada (Montreal, PQ, Canada) 1875
Career Development
Women in Careers (Lome, Togo) 539

Address Abbreviations

Table of Australian State and Territory Postal Codes

ACT .... Australian Capital Territory
NSW .... New South Wales
NT .... Northern Territory
QLD .... Queensland

SA .... South Australia
TAS .... Tasmania
VIC .... Victoria
WA .... Western Australia

Table of Canadian Province and Territory Postal Codes

AB .... Alberta
BC .... British Columbia
MB .... Manitoba
NB .... New Brunswick
NF .... Newfoundland
NS .... Nova Scotia

NT .... Northwest Territories
ON .... Ontario
PE .... Prince Edward Island
PQ .... Quebec
SK .... Saskatchewan
YT .... Yukon Territory

Table of United Kingdom Postal Abbreviations
(England, Scotland, Northern Ireland, Wales)

Beds .... Bedfordshire
Berks .... Berkshire
Bucks .... Buckinghamshire
Cambs .... Cambridgeshire
E.Sussex .... East Sussex
Glos .... Gloucestershire
Hants .... Hampshire
Herts .... Hertfordshire
Lancs .... Lancashire
Leics .... Leicestershire
Lincs .... Lincolnshire
M.Glam .... Mid Glamorgan
N.Humberside .... North Humberside

N.Yorkshire .... North Yorkshire
Northants .... Northamptonshire
Northd .... Northumberland
Notts .... Nottinghamshire
Oxon .... Oxfordshire
S.Glam .... South Glamorgan
S.Humberside .... South Humberside
S.Yorkshire .... South Yorkshire
Staffs .... Staffordshire
W.Glam .... West Glamorgan
W.Midlands .... West Midlands
W.Sussex .... West Sussex
W.Yorkshire .... West Yorkshire
Wilts .... Wiltshire

Table of United States State and Territory Codes

AK .... Alaska
AL .... Alabama
AR .... Arkansas
AZ .... Arizona
CA .... California
CO .... Colorado
CT .... Connecticut
DC .... District of Columbia
DE .... Delaware
FL .... Florida
GA .... Georgia

GU .... Guam
HI .... Hawaii
IA .... Iowa
ID .... Idaho
IL .... Illinois
IN .... Indiana
KS .... Kansas
KY .... Kentucky
LA .... Louisiana
MA .... Massachusetts
MD .... Maryland

ME	Maine	OR	Oregon
MI	Michigan	PA.	Pennsylvania
MN	Minnesota	PR	Puerto Rico
MO	Missouri	RI	Rhode Island
MS	Mississippi	SC	South Carolina
MT	Montana	SD	South Dakota
NC	North Carolina	TN	Tennessee
ND	North Dakota	TX	Texas
NE	Nebraska	UT	Utah
NH	New Hampshire	VA	Virginia
NJ	New Jersey	VI	Virgin Islands
NM	New Mexico	VT	Vermont
NV	Nevada	WA	Washington
NY	New York	WI	Wisconsin
OH	Ohio	WV	West Virginia
OK	Oklahoma	WY	Wyoming

Table of Abbreviations Used in Addresses and the Index

Acad	Academy	Ln	Lane
AFB	Air Force Base	Ltd	Limited
Amer	American	Mfrs	Manufacturers
APO	Army Post Office	Mgmt	Management
Apt	Apartment	Mt	Mount
Assn	Association	N	North
Ave	Avenue	Natl	National
Bd	Board	NE	Northeast
Bldg	Building	No	Number
Blvd	Boulevard	NW	Northwest
Br	Branch	Pkwy	Parkway
Bur	Bureau	Pl	Place
c/o	Care of	PO	Post Office
Co	Company	Prof	Professor
Coll	College	Rd	Road
Comm	Committee	RD	Rural Delivery
Commn	Commission	RFD	Rural Free Delivery
Conf	Conference	Rm	Room
Confed	Confederation	RR	Rural Route
Cong	Congress	Rte	Route
Corp	Corporation	S	South
Coun	Council	SE	Southeast
Ct	Court	Sect	Section
Dept	Department	Soc	Society
Div	Division	Sq	Square
Dr	Drive	St	Saint, Street
E	East	Sta	Station
Expy	Expressway	Ste	Sainte, Suite
Fed	Federation	Subcomm	Subcommittee
Fl	Floor	Subcommn	Subcommission
Found	Foundation	SW	Southwest
FPO	Fleet Post Office	Terr	Terrace, Territory
Ft	Fort	Tpke	Turnpike
Fwy	Freeway	T.V	Television
Govt	Government	U.N	United Nations
GPO	General Post Office	Univ	University
Hwy	Highway	U.S	United States
Inc	Incorporated	U.S.A	United States of America
Inst	Institute	W	West
Intl	International		

Table of International Country Access Codes

When contacting an organization by telephone or fax, you will need to use that country's international access code.

Listings in the mainbody of *EWAW* provide the city access code and the local telephone or fax number. International access codes, which should be dialed or pressed before the city access codes and local numbers, are listed below.

Country names followed by "**" indicate that direct-dial access is not available in that country. An international operator must be contacted to reach organizations in these countries.

Afghanistan (**)
Albania (355)
Algeria (213)
American Samoa (684)
Andorra (33)
Angola (244)
Antigua-Barbuda (1)
Argentina (54)
Armenia (7)
Aruba (297)
Australia (61)
Austria (43)
Azerbaijan (7)
Bahamas (1)
Bahrain (973)
Bangladesh (880)
Barbados (1)
Belarus (7)
Belgium (32)
Belize (501)
Benin (229)
Bermuda (1)
Bhutan (975)
Bolivia (591)
Bosnia-Hercegovina (38)
Botswana (267)
Brazil (55)
British Virgin Islands (1)
Brunei Darussalam (673)
Bulgaria (359)
Burkina Faso (226)
Burundi (257)
Cameroon (237)
Canada (1)
Cape Verde (238)
Cayman Islands (1)
Central African Republic (236)
Chad (235)
Chile (56)

China, People's Republic of (86)
Colombia (57)
Comoros (269)
Congo (242)
Cook Islands (682)
Costa Rica (506)
Cote d'Ivoire (225)
Croatia (38)
Cuba (**)
Cyprus (357)
Czech Republic (42)
Denmark (45)
Djibouti (253)
Dominica (1)
Dominican Republic (1)
Ecuador (593)
Egypt (20)
El Salvador (503)
England (44)
Equatorial Guinea (240)
Estonia (7)
Ethiopia (251)
Faroe Islands (298)
Fiji (679)
Finland (358)
France (33)
French Antilles (596)
French Guinea (594)
Gabon (241)
Gambia (220)
Georgia (7)
Germany (49)
Ghana (233)
Gibraltar (350)
Greece (30)
Greenland (299)
Grenada (1)
Guadeloupe (590)
Guam (671)

Guatemala (502)
Guinea (224)
Guinea-Bissau (245)
Guyana (592)
Haiti (509)
Honduras (504)
Hong Kong (852)
Hungary (36)
Iceland (354)
India (91)
Indonesia (62)
Iran (98)
Iraq (964)
Ireland, Republic of (353)
Israel (972)
Italy (39)
Jamaica (1)
Japan (81)
Jordan (962)
Kazakhstan (7)
Kenya (254)
Kirgizstan (1)
Kiribati (686)
Korea, Democratic People's
  Republic of (82)
Korea, Republic of (82)
Kuwait (965)
Laos (**)
Latvia (7)
Lebanon (961)
Lesotho (266)
Liberia (231)
Libya (218)
Liechtenstein (41)
Lithuania (7)
Luxembourg (352)
Macao (853)
Macedonia (38)
Madagascar (261)

Malawi (265)
Malaysia (60)
Maldives (960)
Mali (223)
Malta (356)
Marshall Islands (692)
Martinique (596)
Mauritania (222)
Mauritius (230)
Mexico (52)
Micronesia, Federated States of (691)
Moldova (7)
Monaco (33)
Mongolia (976)
Montserrat (1)
Morocco (212)
Mozambique (258)
Myanmar (Burma) (**)
Namibia (264)
Nauru (674)
Nepal (977)
Netherlands (31)
Netherlands Antilles (599)
New Caledonia (687)
New Zealand (64)
Nicaragua (505)
Niger (227)
Nigeria (234)
Niue (683)
Norfolk Island (672)
Northern Ireland (44)
Norway (47)

Oman (968)
Pakistan (92)
Panama (507)
Papua New Guinea (675)
Paraguay (595)
Peru (51)
Philippines (63)
Poland (48)
Portugal (351)
Qatar (974)
Reunion Island (262)
Romania (40)
Russia (7)
Rwanda (250)
St. Kitts and Nevis (1)
St. Lucia (1)
St. Pierre and Miquelon (508)
St. Vincent and the Grenadines (1)
San Marino (39)
Sao Tome and Principe (239)
Saudi Arabia (966)
Scotland (44)
Senegal (221)
Seychelles (248)
Sierra Leone (232)
Singapore (65)
Slovakia (42)
Slovenia (38)
Solomon Islands (677)
Somalia (**)
South Africa, Republic of (27)
Spain (34)

Sri Lanka (94)
Sudan (**)
Suriname (597)
Swaziland (268)
Sweden (46)
Switzerland (41)
Syria (963)
Taiwan (886)
Tajikistan (7)
Tanzania (255)
Thailand (66)
Togo (228)
Tonga (676)
Trinidad and Tobago (1)
Tunisia (216)
Turkey (90)
Turkmenistan (7)
Tuvalu (688)
Uganda (256)
Ukraine (7)
United States (1)
Uruguay (598)
Uzbekistan (7)
Vanuatu (678)
Venezuela (58)
Vietnam (84)
Wales (44)
Yemen (967)
Yugoslavia (38)
Zaire (243)
Zambia (260)
Zimbabwe (263)

Currency Abbreviations and Definitions Table
Arranged by Country Name

Country	Currency Unit	Abbreviation
Afghanistan	afghani	Af
Albania	lek	Lk
Algeria	dinar	DA
American Samoa	U.S. dollar	$
Andorra	French franc	Fr
Angola	kwanza	Kz
Antigua-Barbuda	East Caribbean dollar	EC$
Argentina	Argentinian austral	A
Armenia	ruble	Rb
Aruba	Aruban florin	AF
Australia	Australian dollar	$A
Austria	Austrian Schilling	AS
Azerbaijan	ruble	Rb
Bahamas	Bahamian dollar	B$
Bahrain	Bahraini dinar	BD
Bangladesh	taka	Tk
Barbados	Barbados dollar	BD$
Belarus	ruble	Rb
Belgium	Belgian franc	BFr
Belize	Belizean dollar	$B
Benin	Communaute Financiere Africaine franc	Fr CFA
Bermuda	Bermuda dollar	Bm$
Bhutan	ngultrum	Ng
Bolivia	boliviano	$b
Bosnia-Hercegovina	dinar	Din
Botswana	pula	P
Brazil	cruzado	Cr$
British Virgin Islands	U.S. dollar	$
Brunei Darussalam	Brunei dollar	Br$
Bulgaria	leva	Lv
Burkina Faso	Communaute Financiere Africaine franc	Fr CFA
Burundi	Burundi franc	FrB
Cambodia	riel	riel
Cameroon	Communaute Financiere Africaine franc	Fr CFA
Canada	Canadian dollar	C$
Cape Verde	escudo	Ec
Cayman Islands	Cayman Island dollar	CI$
Central African Republic	Communaute Financiere Africaine franc	Fr CFA
Chad	Communaute Financiere Africaine franc	Fr CFA

Country	Currency Unit	Abbreviation
Chile	Chilean peso	ChP
China, People's Republic of	yuan	Yu
Colombia	Colombian peso	CoP
Comoros	Communaute Financiere Africaine franc	Fr CFA
Congo	Communaute Financiere Africaine franc	Fr CFA
Cook Islands	New Zealand dollar	NZ$
Costa Rica	colon	C
Cote d'Ivoire	Communaute Financiere Africaine franc	Fr CFA
Croatia	dinar	Din
Cuba	Cuban peso	CuP
Cyprus	Cyprus pound	£C
Czech Republic	koruna	Kcs
Denmark	Danish krone	DKr
Djibouti	Djibouti franc	DFr
Dominica	East Caribbean dollar	EC$
Dominican Republic	Dominican peso	DP
Ecuador	sucre	S
Egypt	Egyptian pound	£E
El Salvador	colone	C
England	pound sterling	£
Equatorial Guinea	Communaute Financiere Africaine franc	Fr CFA
Estonia	ruble	Rb
Ethiopia	Ethiopian birr	E$
European Economic Community	European currency units	ECU
Faroe Islands	Danish krone	DKr
Fiji	Fijian dollar	$F
Finland	Finnish mark	FM
France	franc	Fr
French Guiana	French franc	Fr
Gabon	Communaute Financiere Africaine franc	Fr CFA
Gambia	dalasi	D
Georgia	ruble	Rb
Germany	Deutsche Mark	DM
Ghana	cedi	Cd
Gibraltar	Gibraltar pound	£G
Greece	drachma	Dr
Greenland	Danish krone	DKr
Grenada	East Caribbean dollar	EC$
Guadeloupe	French franc	Fr
Guam	U.S. dollar	$
Guatemala	quetzal	Q
Guinea	Guinea franc	GFr
Guinea-Bissau	Guinea-Bissau peso	GBP
Guyana	Guyana dollar	G$
Haiti	gourde	G
Honduras	lempira	Lp
Hong Kong	Hong Kong dollar	HK$
Hungary	forint	Ft

Country	Currency Unit	Abbreviation
Iceland	Icelandic krona	IKr
India	rupee	Rs
Indonesia	rupiah	Rp
Iran	Iranian rial	RI
Iraq	Iraqi dinar	ID
Ireland, Republic of	Irish pound	IR£
Israel	Israel shekel	IS
Italy	lira	Lr
Jamaica	Jamaican dollar	J$
Japan	yen	Y
Jordan	Jordanian dinar	JD
Kazakhstan	ruble	Rb
Kenya	Kenyan shilling	KSh
Kirgizstan	ruble	Rb
Kiribati	Australian dollar	A$
Korea, Democratic People's Republic of	won	W
Korea, Republic of	won	W
Kuwait	Kuwaiti dinar	KD
Laos	new kip	K
Latvia	ruble	Rb
Lebanon	Lebanese pound	L£
Lesotho	maloti	Ml
Liberia	Liberian dollar	L$
Libya	Libyan dinar	LD
Liechtenstein	Swiss franc	SFr
Lithuania	ruble	Rb
Luxembourg	Luxembourg franc	LFr
Macao	pataca	Ptcs
Macedonia	dinar	Din
Madagascar	Malagasy franc	MFr
Malawi	Malawi kwacha	MKw
Malaysia	Malaysian dollar	M$
Maldives	Maldivian rufiya	MRu
Mali	Communaute Financiere Africaine franc	Fr CFA
Malta	Maltese lira	ML
Marshall Islands	U.S. dollar	$
Martinique	French franc	Fr
Mauritania	ouguiya	Og
Mauritius	Mauritius rupee	MRs
Mexico	Mexican peso	MP
Micronesia, Federated States of	U.S. dollar	$
Moldova	ruble	Rb
Monaco	French franc	Fr
Mongolia	tugrik	Tg
Montserrat	East Caribbean dollar	EC$
Morocco	dirham	Dh
Mozambique	metical	Mt
Myanmar (Burma)	kyat	Ky
Namibia	South African rand	R
Nauru	Australian dollar	$A
Nepal	Nepalese rupee	NRs

Country	Currency Unit	Abbreviation
Netherlands	florin	f
Netherlands Antilles	Antillean florin	NAf
New Caledonia	Colonial Francs Pacifique	CFP
New Zealand	New Zealand dollar	NZ$
Nicaragua	new cordoba	c$
Niger	Communaute Financiere Africaine franc	Fr CFA
Nigeria	naira	N
Niue	New Zealand dollar	NZ$
Norfolk Island	Australian dollar	A$
Northern Ireland	pound sterling	£
Norway	Norwegian krone	NKr
Oman	rial Omani	Rlo
Pakistan	Pakistan rupee	PRs
Panama	balboa	B
Papua New Guinea	kina	K
Paraguay	guarani	Gs
Peru	inti	It
Philippines	Philippine peso	PP
Poland	zloty	Zl
Portugal	escudo	Esc
Qatar	riyal	QRl
Reunion Island	French franc	Fr
Romania	leu	L
Russia	ruble	Rb
Rwanda	Rwandan franc	RFr
St. Kitts and Nevis	East Caribbean dollar	EC$
St. Lucia	East Caribbean dollar	EC$
St. Pierre and Miquelon	French franc	Fr
St. Vincent and the Grenadines	East Caribbean dollar	EC$
San Marino	Italian lira	Lr
Sao Tome and Principe	dobra	Db
Saudi Arabia	Saudi riyal	SRl
Scotland	pound sterling	£
Senegal	Communaute Financiere Africaine franc	Fr CFA
Seychelles	Seychelles rupee	SRs
Sierra Leone	leone	Le
Singapore	Singapore dollar	S$
Slovakia	koruna	Kcs
Slovenia	dinar	Din
Solomon Islands	Solomon Island dollar	SI$
Somalia	Somali shilling	SSh
South Africa	rand	R
Spain	peseta	Ptas
Sri Lanka	Ceylon rupee	CRs
Sudan	Sudanese pound	£S
Suriname	Suriname florin	Sf
Swaziland	emalangeni	Eg
Sweden	Swedish krona	SKr
Switzerland	Swiss franc	SFr
Syria	Syrian pound	£Syr
Taiwan	New Taiwanese dollar	NTs

Country	Currency Unit	Abbreviation
Tajikistan	ruble	Rb
Tanzania	Tanzanian shilling	TSh
Thailand	baht	Bht
Togo	Communaute Financiere Africaine franc	Fr CFA
Tonga	pa'anga	T$
Trinidad and Tobago	Trindad and Tobagoan dollar	TT$
Tunisia	Tunisian dinar	TD
Turkey	Turkish lira	TL
Turkmenistan	ruble	Rb
Tuvalu	Australian dollar	$A
Uganda	Ugandan shilling	USh
Ukraine	ruble	Rb
Uruguay	nuevo peso	NP
Uzbekistan	ruble	Rb
Vanuatu	vatu	V
Venezuela	bolivar	Bs
Vietnam	dong	Dg
Wales	pound sterling	L
Yemen	Yemen rial	YRl
Yugoslavia	dinar	Din
Zaire	Zaire	Z
Zambia	Zambian kwacha	ZKw
Zimbabwe	Zimbabwe dollar	Z$

Currency Abbreviations and Definitions Table
Arranged by Currency Abbreviation

Abbreviation	Currency Unit	Country
$	U.S. dollar	American Samoa, British Virgin Islands, Guam, Marshall Islands, Federated States of Micronesia
$A	Australian dollar	Australia, Kiribati, Nauru, Norfolk Island, Tuvalu
$B	Belizean dollar	Belize
$b	boliviano	Bolivia
$F	Fijian dollar	Fiji
£	pound sterling	England, Northern Ireland, Scotland, Wales
£C	Cyprus pound	Cyprus
£E	Egyptian pound	Egypt
£G	Gibraltar pound	Gibraltar
£S	Sudanese pound	Sudan
£Syr	Syrian pound	Syria
A	Argentinian austral	Argentina
Af	afghani	Afghanistan
AF	Aruban florin	Aruba
AS	Austrian Schilling	Austria
B	balboa	Panama
B$	Bahamian dollar	Bahamas
BD	Bahraini dinar	Bahrain
BD$	Barbados dollar	Barbados
BFr	Belgian franc	Belgium
Bht	baht	Thailand
Bm$	Bermuda dollar	Bermuda
Br$	Brunei dollar	Brunei Darussalam
Bs	bolivar	Venezuela
C	colon	Costa Rica, El Salvador
Cd	cedi	Ghana
C$	Canadian dollar	Canada
C$	new cordoba	Nicaragua
CFP	Colonial Francs Pacifique	New Caledonia
ChP	Chilean peso	Chile
CI$	Cayman Island dollar	Cayman Islands
CoP	Colombian peso	Colombia
Cr$	cruzado	Brazil
CRs	Ceylon rupee	Sri Lanka
CuP	Cuban peso	Cuba
D	dalasi	Gambia
DA	dinar	Algeria
Db	dobra	Sao Tome and Principe
DFr	Djibouti franc	Djibouti

Abbreviation	Currency Unit	Country
Dg	dong	Vietnam
Dh	dirham	Morocco
Din	dinar	Bosnia-Hercegovina, Croatia, Macedonia, Slovenia, Yugoslavia
DKr	Danish krone	Denmark, Faroe Islands, Greenland
DM	Deutsche Mark	Germany
DP	Dominican peso	Dominican Republic
Dr	drachma	Greece
Ec	escudo	Cape Verde
EC$	East Caribbean dollar	Antigua-Barbuda, Dominica, Grenada, Montserrat, St. Kitts and, St. Lucia, St. Vincent and the Grenadines
ECU	European currency unit	European Economic Community
E$	Ethiopian birr	Ethiopia
Eg	emalangeni	Swaziland
Esc	escudo	Portugal
f	florin	Netherlands
FM	Finnish mark	Finland
Fr	franc	Andorra, France, French Guiana, Guadeloupe, Martinique, Monaco, Reunion, Island, St. Pierre and Miquelon
FrB	Burundi franc	Burundi
Fr CFA	Communaute Financiere Africaine franc	Benin, Burkina Faso, Cameroon, Central African Republic, Chad, Comoros, Congo, Cote d'Ivoire, Equatorial Guinea, Gabon, Mali, Niger, Senegal, Togo
Ft	forint	Hungary
G	gourde	Haiti
GBP	Guinea-Bissau peso	Guinea-Bissau
G$	Guyana dollar	Guyana
GFr	Guinea franc	Guinea
Gs	guarani	Paraguay
HK$	Hong Kong dollar	Hong Kong
ID	Iraqi dinar	Iraq
IKr	Icelandic krona	Iceland
IR£	Irish pound	Republic of Ireland
IS	Israel shekel	Israel
It	inti	Peru
J$	Jamaican dollar	Jamaica
JD	Jordanian dinar	Jordan
K	kina	Papua New Guinea
K	new kip	Laos
Kcs	koruna	Czech Republic, Slovakia
KD	Kuwaiti dinar	Kuwait
KSh	Kenyan shilling	Kenya
Ky	kyat	Myanmar (Burma)

Abbreviation	Currency Unit	Country
Kz	kwanza	Angola
L	leu	Romania
L$	Liberian dollar	Liberia
LD	Libyan dinar	Libya
Le	leone	Sierra Leone
LFr	Luxembourg franc	Luxembourg
Lk	lek	Albania
Lp	lempira	Honduras
L£	Lebanese pound	Lebanon
Lr	lira	Italy, San Marino
Lv	leva	Bulgaria
M$	Malaysian dollar	Malaysia
MFr	Malagasy franc	Madagascar
MKw	Malawi kwacha	Malawi
Ml	maloti	Lesotho
ML	Maltese lira	Malta
MP	Mexican peso	Mexico
MRs	Mauritius rupee	Mauritius
MRu	Maldivian rufiya	Maldives
Mt	metical	Mozambique
N	naira	Nigeria
NAf	Antillean florin	Netherlands Antilles
Ng	ngultrum	Bhutan
NKr	Norwegian krone	Norway
NP	nuevo peso	Uruguay
NRs	Nepalese rupee	Nepal
NTs	New Taiwanese dollar	Taiwan
NZ$	New Zealand dollar	Cook Islands, New Zealand Niue
Og	ouguiya	Mauritania
P	pula	Botswana
PP	Philippine peso	Philippines
PRs	Pakistan rupee	Pakistan
Ptas	peseta	Spain
Ptcs	pataca	Macao
Q	quetzal	Guatemala
QRl	riyal	Qatar
R	rand	South Africa, Namibia
Rb	ruble	Armenia, Azerbaijan, Belarus, Estonia, Georgia, Kazakhstan, Kirgizstan, Latvia, Lithuania, Moldova, Russia, Tajikstan, Turkmenistan, Ukraine, Uzbekistan
RFr	Rwandan franc	Rwanda
riel	riel	Cambodia
Rl	Iranian rial	Iran
Rlo	rial Omani	Oman
Rp	rupiah	Indonesia
Rs	rupee	India
S	sucre	Ecuador
S$	Singapore dollar	Singapore

Abbreviation	Currency Unit	Country
Sf	Suriname florin	Suriname
SFr	Swiss franc	Switzerland, Liechtenstein
SI$	Solomon Island dollar	Soloman Islands
SKr	Swedish krona	Sweden
SRl	Saudi riyal	Saudi Arabia
SRs	Seychelles rupee	Seychelles
SSh	Somali shilling	Somalia
T$	pa'anga	Tonga
TD	Tunisian dinar	Tunisia
Tg	tugrik	Mongolia
Tk	taka	Bangladesh
TL	Turkish lira	Turkey
TSh	Tanzanian shilling	Tanzania
TT$	Trinidad and Tobagoan dollar	Trinidad and Tobago
USh	Ugandan shilling	Uganda
V	vatu	Vanuatu
W	won	Democratic People's Republic of Korea, Republic of Korea
Y	yen	Japan
YRl	Yemen rial	Yemen
Yu	yuan	People's Republic of China
Z	Zaire	Zaire
Z$	Zimbabwe dollar	Zimbabwe
ZKw	Zambian kwacha	Zambia
Zl	zloty	Poland

ENCYCLOPEDIA OF
Women's
Associations
Worldwide

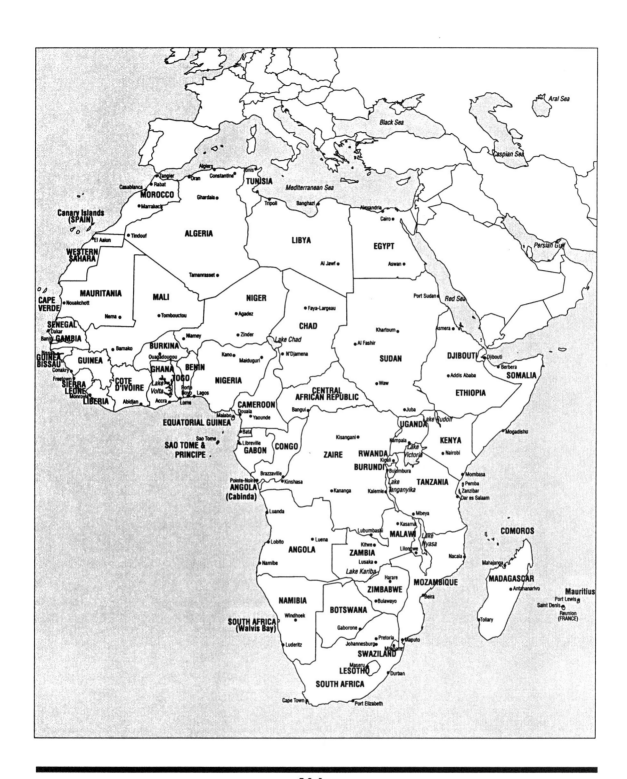

Africa

Algeria	Egypt	Mali	Somalia
Angola	Ethiopia	Mauritania	South Africa,
Benin	Gabon	Mauritius	Republic of
Botswana	Gambia	Morocco	Sudan
Burkina Faso	Ghana	Mozambique	Swaziland
Burundi	Guinea	Namibia	Tanzania, United
Cameroon	Guinea-Bissau	Niger	Republic of
Cape Verde	Kenya	Nigeria	Togo
Central African Republic	Lesotho	Rwanda	Tunisia
Chad	Liberia	Sao Tome and Principe	Uganda
Comoros	Madagascar	Senegal	Zaire
Congo	Malawi	Seychelles	Zambia
Cote d'Ivoire		Sierra Leone	Zimbabwe

Africa

Algeria

★1★ ASSOCIATION ALGERIENNE POUR LA PLANIFICATION FAMILIALE (AAPF)
14, ave. Ridha Houhou
Alger, Algeria
Mr. Latreche Bouteldja Rabah, Exec. Dir.
PH: 2 636019
FX: 2 610783
TX: 040855257 AAPF DZ

Languages: Arabic, French. **National**. Promotes responsible parenthood and family planning as a basic human right. Works to reduce the number of unwanted pregnancies and abortions. Sponsors educational programs in health, family planning, and sexually transmitted diseases. Provides contraceptive and basic health care services.

Angola

★2★ ORGANIZATION OF ANGOLAN WOMEN (OMA)
(Organizacao des Mulheres Angolanas)
Rua Comondauta Jica
Luanda, Angola

National. Supports and promotes the rights of Angolan women. Works to achieve political, economic, and social equality. Organizes activities. Disseminates information.

★3★ PAN-AFRICAN WOMEN'S ORGANIZATION (PAWO)
(Organization Panafricaine des Femmes)
37/39, Rua dos Cogneiros
Luanda, Angola
Maria Ruth Neto, Sec.Gen.
PH: 2 391935
TX: 3194 OPMAN

Members: 52. **Staff:** 27. **Languages:** French, English, Portuguese, Arabic. **Multinational**. Umbrella organization of women's organizations and liberation movements in Africa. Promotes women's rights in regions of Africa. Encourages women's organizations to unite to work for a common goal. Works to integrate women into the development process. Sponsors programs to protect children's rights. **Awards:** Periodic (scholarship).

Benin

★4★ ALLIANCE DES FEMMES POUR LA DEMOCRATIE ET LE DEVELOPPEMENT DU BENIN
BP 378
Porto-Novo, Benin

Languages: French. **National**. Women interested in Benin's development and democratization. Sponsors social affairs. Promotes issues of particular concern to women.

★5★ ANIMATION PARMI LES FEMMES POUR LA PROMOTION DE LA FAMILLE (AFPF)
BP 77
Dassa-Zoume, Benin
Agathe Okounde, President

Founded: 1987. **Members:** 2,000. **Staff:** 9. **Budget:** 3,000,000 Fr CFA. **Languages:** French. **National**. Seeks to raise the status of women. Works for the full recognition of the importance of women's roles in society. Encourages women to become actively involved in the development process in Benin. Offers training in agriculture and crafts to augment women's income. Provides health, educational, and literacy programs to improve women's well-being. Promotes family planning. Conducts research.

Conventions/Meetings: annual general assembly - Dassa-Zoume, Benin.

★6★ ASSOCIATION BENINOISE POUR LA PROMOTION DE LA FAMILLE (ABPF)
PO Box 1486
Cotonou, Benin
Mr. Roger Danlodji, Exec. Dir.
PH: 320049
TX: 5111

Languages: French. **National**. Seeks to enhance the quality of life for people living in Benin by promoting responsible parenthood and family planning. Attempts to stop the spread of sexually transmitted diseases, especially AIDS. Provides contraceptive and health care services. Sponsors programs in sex education, family planning, and health. Acts as an advocate for family planning on national level.

★7★ ASSOCIATION DES FEMMES D'AFFAIRES ET ENTREPRENEURS DU BENIN (AFACED)
BP 1226
Cotonou, Benin

Languages: French. **National**. Women in business and management in Benin. Promotes the entrepreneurial spirit of women, and works to defend their rights.

★8★ ASSOCIATION DES FEMMES BENINOISES POUR LE DEVELOPPEMENT (AFBD)
BP 1
Cotonou, Benin

Languages: French. **National**. Promotes the development and interests of women in Benin.

★9★ ASSOCIATION DES FEMMES JURISTES DU BENIN (AFJB)
BP 2753
Cotonou, Benin
Grace d'Almeida Adamon, President
PH: 321711
FX: 321711

Founded: 1990. **Members:** 40. **Staff:** 4. **Languages:** French. **National**. Female lawyers united to defend the rights of women. Promotes the legal profession for women. Seeks to make legal representation accessible to rural and urban women. Works to eliminate sexism and defend human rights.

Publications: *Guide Juridique de la Femme Beninoise* (in French). Book.

★10★ ASSOCIATION DES FEMMES EN LUTTE
BP 34
Bohican, Benin
Samuel Orounla, Contact

National. Participates in the women's struggle to secure recognition of women's rights and interests. Encourages political participation working to express feminist concerns on issues affecting women.

★11★ ASSOCIATION DES FEMMES DE TCHAKALOKE (AFT)
BP 15
Sokpunta
Dassa-Zoume, Benin

Languages: French. **National**. Women involved in charitable activities in Benin. Provides food to the aged and to orphaned children. Involved in agriculture and food production.

★12★ BUREAU DIOCESAIN DU BORGOU POUR LE
DEVELOPPEMENT - COMMISSION FEMMES
BP 226
Pakakou, Benin   PH: 611116
Mme. Zenabou Gado   611117

Founded: 1988. **Members:** 12. **Staff:** 1. **Languages:** French. **National**. Feminists working to improve the status of African women. Conducts research; disseminates information. Coordinates activities for members.

★13★ CONGREGATION NOTRE-DAME DES APOTRES
BP 29
Tanguita, Benin

Languages: French. **National**. Promotes women's development through Catholic evangelistic activities.

★14★ CONSEIL NATIONAL DES FEMMES INDEPENDANTES DU
BENIN (CONAFIB)
BP 232
Cotonou, Benin
Anne Z. Koutimy, President

Founded: 1990. **Members:** 450,000. **Staff:** 145. **Budget:** 10,000,000 Fr CFA. **Regional Groups:** 67. **Local Groups:** 1,356. **Languages:** French. **National**. Women's organizations and individual women. Works to improve the quality of life for women living in Benin. Encourages women to establish economic independence. Offers programs in conservation, health, parenting, and vocational training. Sponsors social welfare programs in the areas of drug rehabilitation, homelessness, illiteracy, and children's rights. Encourages public awareness of women's rights and recognition of women's abilities. Conducts research in agriculture and rural development.

Conventions/Meetings: periodic meeting (exhibits).

★15★ FEDERATION NATIONALE DES ASSOCIATIONS DES FEMMES
DU BENIN
BP 1331
Cotonou, Benin

Languages: French. **National**. Umbrella organization of women's associations throughout Benin. Unites members to promote the development of women. Seeks to raise consciousness about issues affecting women.

★16★ GROUPE D'ACTION POUR LA JUSTICE ET L'EGALITE
SOCIALE (GAJES)
BP 03-2156
Cotonou, Benin

Languages: French. **National**. Promotes social equality and legal justice for women, in Benin.

★17★ GROUPE DE RECHERCHE-ACTION FEMME ET
DEVELOPPEMENT (GRAFD)
BP 329
Porto-Novo, Benin

Languages: French. **National**. Seeks to promote the research and development of women's issues in Benin. Conducts research and educational programs.

★18★ JEUNESSE PAN-AFRICAINE ESPOIR POUR LE
DEVELOPPEMENT
BP 03-2010
Cotonou, Benin

Languages: French. **Multinational**. Seeks to unite young women throughout Africa to focus on women's issues and the development of women's lives across the African continent.

★19★ MOUVEMENT NATIONALE DES FEMMES BENIN
Directrice d'Ecole Mixte des Houeyiho
BP 1535
Dahomey
Cotonou, Benin
Therese Madode, Director

Languages: French. **National**. Promotes equal rights for women and men. Encourages women to involve themselves in political and public life.

★20★ ORGANISATION DES FEMMES HANDICAPEES DU BENIN
(OFHB)
BP 03-0803
Cotonou, Benin
Mme. Albertine Vignon, President   PH: 314947

Founded: 1988. **Members:** 40. **Languages:** French. **National**. Women with disabilities and interested others in Benin. Promotes the social integration of disabled women into Benin's society. Offers support and programs to improve the economic conditions of disabled women, and to promote financial independence. Sponsors sex education programs.

★21★ UNION DES FEMMES MUSULMANES DU BENIN (UFMUB)
BP 1331
Cotonou, Benin

Languages: French. **National**. Women Muslims in Benin. Promotes the role of Muslim women in Benin's society. Supports the Muslim religion and its practics.

Botswana

★22★ ASSOCIATION OF BOTSWANA WOMEN
Private Bag 0045
Gaborone, Botswana
Mrs. G. Sethokge-Sechele, President

Languages: Setswana, English. **National**. Promotes the interests of women in Botswana. Works to enhance the social and financial status of women.

★23★ BOTSWANA COUNCIL FOR WOMEN (BCW)
PO Box 339
Gaborone, Botswana
Lady R. Khama, President

National. Umbrella organization supporting and defending women's equal rights in Botswana society. Coordinates activities for women and women's organizations. Investigates women's status and disseminates findings.

★24★ BOTSWANA FAMILY WELFARE ASSOCIATION (BOFWA)
Private Bag 00100
Gaborone, Botswana   PH: 31 335615
Mrs. Cally Ramalefo, Exec. Dir.   TX: 2345 BOOTH BD

Languages: English, Setswana. National. Works to improve the quality of life for individuals living in Botswana by promoting family planning and responsible parenthood. Acts as an advocate for family planning on a national level. Sponsors programs in family planning, sex education, and sexually transmitted diseases, especially AIDS. Provides contraceptive services.

★25★ BOTSWANA YOUNG WOMEN'S CHRISTIAN ASSOCIATION
(BYWCA)
PO Box 359
Gaborone, Botswana
Mrs. Mandisi Vanqa, Sec.Gen.   PH: 31 353681

Founded: 1962. Members: 3,000. Staff: 35. Regional Groups: 6. Local Groups: 65. Languages: English, Setswana. National. Women and girls interested in building fellowships, encouraging Christian-living principles, and serving the community without facing race, nationality, class, political, or religious discrimination. Provides opportunities for prayer and bible study, informal education, and recreation. Offers leadership training seminars and workshops, and commercial classes. Hosts panel discussions. Committees: Employment Creation. Programs: Commercial Classes; Counselling; Day Care Centre; Energy and Environment Education; Home Economics; HIV AIDS Education; Rural Projects in Agriculture; Youth Activities and Development Programs. Subcommittees: Cafeteria; Education; Health; Hostel; Projects and Activities; Refugee.

Publications: Newsletter (in English), annual. ● Five Year Development Plan.

Conventions/Meetings: annual conference - always August.

★26★ EMANG BASADI WOMEN'S ASSOCIATION
PO Box 1829
Gaborone, Botswana

Founded: 1986. National. Works to improve the social, political, and economic status of women. Seeks to increase women's awareness of their rights. Provides legal counseling. Investigates women's status. Disseminates information.

★27★ WOMEN IN DEVELOPMENT (WID)
PO Box 0022
Gaborone, Botswana

Founded: 1981. National. Works to improve rural women's standard of living. Assists rural women in finding aid and projects that benefit them. Trains and educates rural women in income generating fields. Coordinates activities. Disseminates information.

Burkina Faso

★28★ ASSOCIATION AMITIE AFRICAINE
BP 378
Ouaga, Burkina Faso

Languages: French. Multinational. Works to abolish illiteracy among women in Africa. Promotes women's development projects.

★29★ ASSOCIATION BURKINABE POUR LE BIEN-ETRE FAMILIAL
(ABBEF)
BP 535
Ouagadougou, Burkina Faso   PH: 310598
Mr. Andre D. Gnoumou, Exec. Dir.   TX: 1111

Languages: French. National. Promotes family planning as a basic human right. Works to reduce the number of unwanted pregnancies and abortions. Attempts to stop the spread of AIDS and other sexually transmitted diseases through education and contraceptive services. Sponsors programs in family planning and health care. Conducts research.

★30★ ASSOCIATION POUR LE DEVELOPPEMENT DELWENDE
(DELWENDE)
BP 5178
Ouaga, Burkina Faso   PH: 308258

Languages: French. National. Seeks the development of women in conjunction with the following areas: rural development; water provision; environmental issues; reforestation; agriculture; health; education.

★31★ ASSOCIATION DE L'EGLISE EVANGELIQUE REFORMEE DU
BURKINA (AEERB)
BP 3946
Ouagadougou 01, Burkina Faso   PH: 340378
Rev. S. Lazare Kinda, President   FX: 310648

Founded: 1986. Members: 3,600. Budget: 12,000,000 Fr CFA. Languages: French. National. Christian evangelistic charity organization working to improve the living conditions of women and children. Offers training and educational programs in agriculture, handicrafts, and the environment.

Conventions/Meetings: periodic meeting. ● annual convention.

★32★ ASSOCIATION VIVE LE PAYSAN (AVLP)
BP 6274
Ouaga, Burkina Faso   PH: 304035

Languages: French. National. Women's development organization in Burkina Faso active in the following areas: agriculture, health; education.

★33★ FEDERATION DES FEMMES BURKINABE
BP 1059
Ouaga, Burkina Faso

Languages: French. National. Umbrella organization of women in Burkina Faso. Promotes the development of women's issues. Promotes women's health through sanitation education. Provides assistance to children; works to abolish illiteracy.

★34★ GROUPE DE RECHERCHE ET D'ACTION POUR UN
DEVELOPPEMENT ENGOGENE RURALE (GRADE FRB)
BP 3656
Ouaga, Burkina Faso

Languages: French. National. Promotes the development of rural women in Burkina Faso. Conducts research and educational programs.

★35★ PROMO-FEMMES/DEVELOPPEMENT SPORT
BP 2532
Ouagadougou 01, Burkina Faso   PH: 313052
                                     313052

Founded: 1982. Members: 38. Budget: 15,000,000 Fr CFA. Languages: French. National. Professional women in Burkina Faso. Promotes women's cultural development through involvement in sports. Supports programs in areas of women's health, economic status, rights of women, and the environment.

Conventions/Meetings: semiannual general assembly.

Burundi

★36★ ASSOCIATION POUR LA PROMOTION ECONOMIQUE DE LA
FEMME (APEF)
BP 2690
Bujumbura, Burundi   PH: 26862

Languages: French. **National.** Promotes the economic development of
women in Burundi. Supports programs that provide financial assistance to
women for small business ventures.

Cameroon

★37★ ASSOCIATION DES FEMMES CAMEROUNAISES
BP 1004
Yaounde, Cameroon
Suzanne Ekollo, President

Languages: French, English. **National.** Promotes the interests of women in
Cameroon. Works to improve the status of women. Promotes solidarity
among women.

★38★ ASSOCIATION DE VEUVES DE CAMEROUN
Centre de Nutrition
PO Box 6163
Yaounde, Cameroon
Veronique Ada, Contact

Languages: French. **National.** Promotes the interests of and offers support
to widows in Cameroon. Fosters communication among widows. Offers
emotional and financial counseling.

★39★ CAMEROON NATIONAL ASSOCIATION FOR FAMILY WELFARE
(ABURBEF)
BP 11994
Yaounde, Cameroon   PH: 231473
Mrs. Grace F. Walla, Exec. Dir.   TX: 8512 CAMNAFAW

Languages: French. **National.** Encourages public awareness of family
planning and responsible parenthood in Cameroon. Works to reduce the
number of unwanted pregnancies and abortions. Advocates family planning
as a basic human right. Sponsors programs in sex education, family planning,
and health. Provides contraceptive services.

★40★ CENTRE RURAL D'APPUI TECHNIQUE (CRAT)
BP 71   PH: 285828
Sa'a, Cameroon   TX: 2858218

Founded: 1975. **Members:** 25. **Languages:** French. **National.** Encourages
advancement of rural women. Provides social, agricultural, and economic
development programs to communities. Encourages religious influence in
rural communities; conducts research on education; offers management
support of programs implemented for the amerlioration and support of the
peasant. Believes that the welfare of humanity can be furthered through
improved health care, education, and the status of women. Maintains
information center.

★41★ MEDICAL WOMEN'S INTERNATIONAL ASSOCIATION -
CAMEROON (MWIA-C)
Hopital General de Yaounde
BP 5408
Yaounde, Cameroon
Barbara Boulet Abeng Yomo, President

Languages: French, English. **National.** Cameroon branch of the Medical
Women's International Association (see separate entry). Women physicians.

Provides a forum for discussion of women's health care issues. Encourages
women to enter the field of medicine. Works to overcome discrimination
against female physicians. Sponsors research and educational programs.

Cape Verde

★42★ ORGANIZATION OF WOMEN OF CAPE VERDE (OMCV)
(Organizacao das Mulheres de Cabo Verde)
BP 213
S. Tiago
Praia, Cape Verde   PH: 612539
Maria Helena, Contact   612455

Founded: 1981. **Members:** 8,000. **Staff:** 15. **Budget:** 36,000 Ec. **Local
Groups:** 15. **Languages:** Portuguese, French. **National.** Umbrella organization promoting the interests of women in Cape Verde. Supports the
emancipation of women and the eradication of discriminatory and exploitive
practices against women. Promotes the development of a new society where
women's worth and rights are fully recognized. Encourages the participation
and integration of women in political and economic processes. Works to
improve welfare of rural women. Offers programs in the areas of: con-
sciouness-raising, literacy, health awareness, handicraft making, agriculture
enhancement, and vocational training.

Conventions/Meetings: monthly executive committee meeting. ● monthly
regional meeting. ● annual general assembly. ● triennial congress.

Central African Republic

★43★ ASSOCIATION CENTRAFRICAINE POUR LE BIEN-ETRE
FAMILIAL (ACABEF)
BP 1366
Bangui, Central African Republic   PH: 615435

Languages: English. **National.** Promotes and supports the use of family
planning techniques for citizens of the Central African Republic. Fosters
family welfare through educational programs and counseling.

★44★ ASSOCIATION EDUCATION A LA MAITRISE DE LA
FECONDITE (EMF-RCA)
BP 335
Bangui, Central African Republic
Micheline Quetier, Pres.

Founded: 1984. **Languages:** French. **National.** Works to educate women in
the Central African Republic about natural methods of contraception
especially the "rhythm method." Provides information on health and family
issues. Develops training programs for mothers on prenatal and child care.
Disseminates literature on sexuality, fertility, nutrition, and preventative
health care.

★45★ CENTRE EVANGELIQUE DE FORMATION ET DE PRODUCTION
ARTISANALE (CEFPA)
Point Kilometrique 12
BP 1067
Bangui, Central African Republic   PH: 615741

Languages: English. **National.** Promotes the economic independence of
women in the Central African Republic. Offers two-year educational programs focusing on home craft subjects such as sewing and knitting.

★46★ COMITE INTERNATIONAL DES FEMMES AFRICAINES POUR
LE DEVELOPPEMENT - CENTRAL AFRICAN REPUBLIC (CIFAD)
BP 379
Bangui, Central African Republic   PH: 614437

Languages: French. **National.** Women working to promote personal and economic development programs for women in the Central African Republic.

Chad

★47★ ASSOCIATION TCHADIENNE POUR LE BIEN-ETRE FAMILIAL
(ATCHBEF)
BP 4064
N'djamena-Moursal, Chad   PH: 51 4337
Achta Tone Gossingar, President   TX: CAB PU 5248 KD

Languages: French. **National.** Promotes responsible parenthood and family planning as a basic human right. Works to reduce the number of unwanted pregnancies and abortions. Attempts to stop the spread of AIDS and other sexually transmitted diseases through education and contraceptive services. Conducts research.

Comoros

★48★ UNION DES FEMMES COMORIENNES
BP 694
Moroni, Comoros

Languages: French. **National.** Umbrella organization promoting the interests of women in Comoros. Fosters solidarity among women through the dissemination of information.

Congo

★49★ ASSOCIATION CONGOLAISE POUR LE BIEN-ETRE FAMILIAL
(ACBEF)
BP 13112
Brazzaville, Congo
Mr. Philippe Nzaba, Exec. Dir.   PH: 836331

Languages: French. **National.** Promotes family planning as a basic human right. Works to reduce the number of unwanted pregnancies and abortions. Attempts to stop the spread of AIDS and other sexually transmitted diseases through education and contraceptive services. Provides contraceptive and health care services. Conducts research.

★50★ ASSOCIATION CONGOLAISE DES FEMMES CHERCHEURS
(ACFC)
BP 2499
Brazzaville, Congo   PH: 810780

Languages: French. **National.** Women researchers in the Congo. Represents the role of women researchers in academic and government environments.

★51★ ASSOCIATION FEMININE POUR LE SAUVETAGE DES JEUNES
ET ENFANTS DE RUE (AFSJER)
BP 2043
Brazzaville, Congo   PH: 814215

Languages: French. **National.** Women in the Congo. Provides aid and assistance to youths and children of the street. Seeks to integrate these children into stabilized environments.

★52★ ASSOCIATION DES FEMMES MANAGERS DU CONGO (AFMC)
University Marien Ngouabi/Rectorat
BP 13060
Brazzaville, Congo   PH: 812436

Languages: French. **National.** Women managers. Promotes the interests of women in managerial positions in the Congo. Encourages women to excel in the workplace. Supports community development programs and the use of technology in business.

★53★ COMITE INTERNATIONAL DES FEMMES AFRICAINES POUR
LE DEVELOPPEMENT - CONGO (CIFAD)
BP 94
Brazzaville, Congo   PH: 826937

Languages: French. **National.** Promotes the active participation and effective integration of African women into the socio-economic development processes of Africa. Works to support personal development programs among African women.

★54★ DYNAMIQUE ENTREPRENARIALE FEMININE POUR LE
DEVELOPPEMENT (DEFD)
P13-257V-Semico/Moukondo
BP 14082
Brazzaville, Congo

Languages: French. **National.** Encourages women in entrepreneurial endeavors. Provides expertise in infrastructure, small business development, project financing, and appropriate technology. Promotes communication and cooperation among groups of women engaged in productive experimental activities.

Cote d'Ivoire

★55★ AMIS DU FOYER CLAIR LOGIS DE BOUAKE
Rue de l'Amitie
BP 818
Bouake, Cote d'Ivoire   PH: 632451

Languages: French. **National.** Promotes women's development in the home and community through training and activities.

★56★ ASSOCIATION POUR L'AMELIORATION ET L'AMENAGEMENT
DU CADRE DE VIE (AMCAV)
BP 66
Boundiali, Cote d'Ivoire
Konate Moujja Soma, Sec.   PH: 820062

Founded: 1986. **Members:** 10. **Budget:** 500,000 Fr CFA. **Languages:** French. **National.** Promotes economic idependence for women. Encourages cattle breeding and agriculture as means for women to achieve economic stability. Offers programs in agriculture, health, and cattle breeding.

★57★ ASSOCIATION DES FEMMES IVOIRIENNES
BP 2005
Abidjan, Cote d'Ivoire
Hortense Aka Anguih, President

National. Umbrella organization promoting the interests of women. Coordinates activities; disseminates information.

★58★ ASSOCIATION IVOIRIENNE POUR LE BIEN-ETRE FAMILIAL
BP 5315
Abidjan 01, Cote d'Ivoire   PH: 224171
Mrs. Yvette Koue-Lou, Exec. Dir.   TX: 23930 CABINC CI

Languages: French. **National.** Promotes family planning as a basic human right. Works to reduce the number of unwanted pregnancies and abortions. Attempts to stop the spread of AIDS and other sexually transmitted diseases through education and contraceptive services. Sponsors programs in family planning and health care. Conducts research.

★59★ COMITE INTERNATIONAL DES FEMMES AFRICAINES POUR LE DEVELOPPEMENT - COTE D'IVOIRE (CIFAD)
BP 5147   PH: 229384
Abidjan 01, Cote d'Ivoire   FX: 329322

Languages: French. **National.** Women interested in the formation of development programs in Africa. Areas of interest include: craft industry; small business development; training; women's concerns; agriculture; irrigation; breeding; rural development; business management; research.

Egypt

★60★ ARAB WOMEN SOLIDARITY ASSOCIATION (AWSA)
25 Murad St.
Giza, Egypt
Dr. Nawal el Saadawi, President   PH: 2 723976

Founded: 1982. **Members:** 3,000. **Staff:** 4. **Budget:** £E 2,000. **Languages:** Arabic, English. **Multinational.** Women in Arab countries. Supports and promotes the interests and rights of Arab women. Works to empower and raise the consciousness of Arab women. Organizes and coordinates activities among member groups. Disseminates information.

Conventions/Meetings: biennial conference.

★61★ ASSOCIATION FOR WOMEN SOLIDARITY
25 Murad St.
Giza, Egypt   PH: 2 723976

Languages: Arabic, English. **National.** Works for the equal rights of women in Egypt. Develops cultural and educational activities designed to improve the role of women in Egypt. Provides a forum for communication among members.

★62★ EGYPTIAN FAMILY PLANNING ASSOCIATION (EFPA)
6 Gazirat Al Arab St.   PH: 2 3488445
Al Mohandisseen   2 3607328
El Giza, Egypt   FX: 2 3607328
Mr. Mohamed Mahmoud Hassan, Exec.   TX: 22950 EFPA UN
    Dir.   CBL: GEFPLAN CAIRO

Languages: Arabic, English. **National.** Promotes family planning as a basic human right. Encourages public awareness of family planning and responsible parenthood. Works to reduce the number of unwanted pregnancies and abortions. Acts as an advocate for family planning on the national level. Sponsors educational programs on family planning, health care, and sexually transmitted diseases. Provides contraceptive services. Conducts research.

★63★ EGYPTIAN WOMEN'S ASSOCIATION
4 el Awhady St.
Menshiet el Bakri
Cairo, Egypt
Siadate Ahmed Maher, President   PH: 2 835271

Languages: Arabic. **National.** Provides a forum for information exchange on women's issues. Works to unify women.

★64★ FEMALE CIRCUMCISION PROJECT
c/o Cairo Family Planning Association
50 Goumhouria St.
Cairo, Egypt

National. Works to eradicate the practice of female circumcision. Promotes sexual health and awareness. Disseminates information.

★65★ FRIENDS OF THE PEOPLE ASSOCIATION
6A Ismail Mohamed St.
Zamalek
Cairo, Egypt   PH: 2 841119
Mrs. Awatef Wali, President   2 3406295

Languages: Arabic. **National.** Promotes women's rights in Egypt.

★66★ HODA CHARAWAY ASSOCIATION
22 Kasr el Ainy
Cairo, Egypt
Mrs. Munira Assem, President   PH: 2 847682

Languages: Arabic. **National.** Works to raise awareness of women's issues. Fosters friendly relations among women.

★67★ MEDICAL WOMEN'S INTERNATIONAL ASSOCIATION - EGYPT (MWIA-G)
Faculty of Medicine
Cairo University
Cairo, Egypt
Mervat El Ratie, Contact

Languages: Arabic, French, English. **National.** Egypt branch of the Medical Women's International Association (see separate entry). Women physicians. Provides a forum for discussion of women's health care issues. Encourages women to enter the field of medicine. Works to overcome discrimination against female physicians. Sponsors research and educational programs.

★68★ NATIONAL WOMEN'S ORGANIZATION
c/o Arab Socialist Union (Women's Section)
Cornish el Nil
Cairo, Egypt
Dr. Soad Aboul Seoud, President

National. Umbrella organization for women's groups in Egypt. Promotes women's interests. Coordinates activities. Disseminates information on women's issues.

★69★ REGIONAL INFORMATION NETWORK ON ARAB WOMEN
c/o Social Research Center
American University in Cairo
PO Box 2511
113 Sharia Kasr El-Aini
Cairo, Egypt

Multinational. Provides a forum for information exchange and discussion of issues affecting Arab women. Compiles and disseminates information on the status, role, culture, and achievements of Arab women.

★70★ YOUNG WOMEN'S CHRISTIAN ASSOCIATION - EGYPT
11 Sharia Emad el Din
Cairo, Egypt   PH: 2 913466
Ellen Sourial, Gen.Sec.   2 913932

National. Promotes the development of young women in Egypt. Upholds Christian beliefs and values in its programs. Works to instill self worth and self-esteem in young women.

Ethiopia

★71★ AFRICAN TRAINING AND RESEARCH CENTRE FOR WOMEN
(ATRCW)
PO Box 3001
Addis Ababa, Ethiopia

Languages: Amharic. **National**. Encourages women's participation in development activities. Seeks to increase women's access to such resources as raw materials, credit and loans, education, training, appropriate technology, and land.

Publications: *African Women in Development: Annotated Bibliography*. Book.

★72★ FAMILY GUIDANCE ASSOCIATION OF ETHIOPIA (FGAE)
PH: 1 518909
PO Box 5716   FX: 1 512192
Addis Ababa, Ethiopia   TX: 21473 FGAE
Mr. Ato Wondayehu Kassa, Exec. Dir.   CBL: BETESEB

Languages: Amharic, English. **National**. Promotes family planning and responsible parenthood as a means to enhance the quality of life for people living in Ethiopia. Works to stop the spread of AIDS and other sexually transmitted diseases. Provides contraceptive services. Sponsors programs in family planning, sex education, and health. Conducts research.

★73★ INTER-AFRICAN COMMITTEE ON TRADITIONAL PRACTICES
AFFECTING THE HEALTH OF WOMEN AND CHILDREN (ECA/
ATRCW)
PO Box 30001
Addis Ababa, Ethiopia

Multinational. Works to eradicate the practice of female genital mutilation. Conducts educational programs to sensitize people to the importance of this issue. Organizes informational seminars for school girls, child care workers, clergy, mothers, nurses, and doctors. Lobbies governmental organizations. Researches and compiles surveys. Broadcasts information via television and radio. **Committees:** Training and Information Campaign (TIC); Training of Trainers (TOT). **Projects:** Mother and Child Health Education. **Programs:** Alternative Employment Opportunities. **Commissions:** Law Reform.

Publications: *IAC Newsletter*.

Gabon

★74★ ASSOCIATION GABONAISE DES FEMMES D'AFFAIRES ET DE
DEVELOPPEMENT (AGFAD)
BP 246   PH: 742022
Libreville, Gabon   FX: 742018

Languages: French. **National**. Women's business and career development organization involved in areas such as agriculture, savings, credit, housing, and training.

★75★ GABONESE ASSOCIATION OF BUSINESS WOMEN
PO Box 246
Lebreville, Gabon
Jacqueline Sita, President

Languages: French. **National**. Executives and other business women in Gabon. Provides a forum for members to create business ties. Supports the goals and objectives of professional women.

Gambia

★76★ GAMBIA FAMILY PLANNING ASSOCIATION (GFPA)
PO Box 325   PH: 91743
Banjul, Gambia   CBL: FAMPLANASS:
J. Tunde Taylor-Thomas, Exec.Dir.   BANJUL

Founded: 1968. **Members:** 5,000. **Staff:** 80. **Budget:** 4,000,000 D. **Local Groups:** 25. **Languages:** English. **National**. Strives to improve maternal and child health care and to reduce infant mortality rates through family planning education programs. Distributes contraceptives; sponsors educational and developmental programs. Conducts research; organizes seminars and workshops. **Libraries:** Type: reference. Holdings: 1,500. **Computer Services:** Data base.

Publications: *Newsletter* (in English), periodic.

Conventions/Meetings: annual - always May/June.

★77★ GAMBIA NATIONAL WOMEN'S BUREAU
c/o Vice President's Office
7 Lasso Wharf
Banjul, Gambia   PH: 28730
Mrs. Isatore Njie-Saidy, Exec. Secty.   28733

Founded: 1980. **Languages:** English. **National**. Women's umbrella organization in Gambia. Seeks to enhance awareness of women's issues. Strives to improve women's rights and standard of living. Conducts research on women in development and the fishing industries. Coordinates and supports educational programs. **Libraries:** Type: reference. Holdings: books. Subjects: women's issues.

Publications: *AWA Magazine* (in English), quarterly.

Conventions/Meetings: periodic workshop. ● periodic seminar.

★78★ GAMBIA WOMEN'S FEDERATION
PO Box 83
Banjul, Gambia
Cecilia M. R. Cole, President

National. Umbrella organization for women's groups in Gambia. Promotes the interests of women. Coordinates women's activities. Disseminates information on women's concerns.

★79★ WOMEN IN SERVICE DEVELOPMENT ORGANISATION AND
MANAGEMENT (WISDOM)
214 Tasfir Demba Mbaye
PO Box 108
Banjul, Gambia   PH: 226051

Languages: French. **National**. Women's social service organization active in the following areas: nutrition and food processing; children's needs; health/ sanitation; enterprise development for women; credit and savings support for women; education and literacy; group and leader training.

★80★ YOUNG WOMEN'S CHRISTIAN ASSOCIATION - GAMBIA
PO Box 974
Banjul, Gambia
Iris Casel, Gen.Sec.   PH: 27940

National. Promotes the development of young women in Gambia. Upholds Christian values and beliefs in its programs. Works to instill self worth and self-esteem in young women.

Ghana

★81★ ABOKOBI RURAL WOMEN'S DEVELOPMENT ASSOCIATION
Box 138
Accra, Ghana

Languages: French. **National.** Women's development organization. Works in areas as such as family planning and health. Participates in environmental protection programs.

★82★ FEDERATION OF GHANA BUSINESS AND PROFESSIONAL
WOMEN (FGBPW)
Box 16892
North Kanda E
Accra, Ghana

Languages: English. **National.** Women active in business and professional fields in Ghana. Promotes women's development in Ghana's professional industries. Seeks the elevation of the economic status of women.

★83★ GHANA ASSEMBLY OF WOMEN
Box 459
Accra, Ghana

Languages: English. **National.** Umbrella organization of women in Ghana. Promotes the interests of women. Offers training and educational programs.

★84★ GHANA ASSOCIATION FOR RESEARCH ON WOMEN (GAFRO)
Institute of African Studies
University of Ghana
Legon, Ghana
Takywaa Manuh, Contact

National. Promotes awareness and study of women's issues. Conducts research on the women of Ghana. Disseminates information.

★85★ MEDICAL WOMEN'S INTERNATIONAL ASSOCIATION - GHANA
(MWIA-G)
PO Box 18
Korle-Bu
Accra, Ghana
Dr. Rhoda Shash Manu, Contact

Languages: English. **National.** Ghana national branch of the Medical Women's International Association (see separate entry). Women physicians. Provides a forum for discussion of women's health care issues. Encourages women to enter the field of medicine. Works to overcome discrimination against female physicians. Sponsors research and educational programs.

★86★ METHODIST WOMEN'S FELLOWSHIP - GHANA (MWF)
c/o Mrs. Adwowa Godwyll
PO Box 30
Sunyani, Ghana
Mrs. Adwowa Godwyll, Contact   PH: 3415

Founded: 1931. **Members:** 35,285. **Budget:** Cd 2,500,000. **Regional Groups:** 10. **Languages:** English, Ewe, Ga. **National.** Methodist women. Conducts leadership training and evangelism courses; maintains Sunday school for girls. Offers children's placement and rehabilitation services; organizes prison visits. Sponsors competitions, rallies, and retreats.

Publications: *Working Hand Book*, annual. ● Also publishes cookbooks and manuals (in Ewe, Fanti, Ga, and Twi).

Conventions/Meetings: annual - always Ghana. 1993 Sept. 9, Kumasi, Ghana; 1994 Sept. 8, Cape Coast, Ghana. ● weekly regional meeting.

★87★ PLANNED PARENTHOOD ASSOCIATION OF GHANA (PPAG)
                                                PH: 21 226992
PO Box 5756   21 227073
Accra, Ghana   TX: 2113 HOTEL GHANA
Mr. Isaac K. Boateng, Exec. Dir.   CBL: PPAGHANA

Languages: English. **National.** Promotes family planning as a basic human right. Works to reduce the number of unwanted pregnancies and abortions. Attempts to stop the spread of AIDS and other sexually transmitted diseases through education and contraceptive services. Offers programs in family planning and health care. Acts as an advocate for family planning on a national level.

★88★ RURAL WOMEN'S ASSOCIATION
Box 260
Bolgatanga, Ghana

Languages: English. **National.** Rural women in Ghana. Promotes women's development programs. Participates in environmental protection projects.

★89★ TELANIA WOMEN'S ASSOCIATION
Box 1
Navrongo, Ghana

Languages: English. **National.** Rural women in Ghana. Promotes women's interests in Ghana's agricultural system. Areas of interest include poultry and livestock farming, and new agricultural processes.

★90★ YOUNG WOMEN'S CHRISTIAN ASSOCIATION - GHANA
(YWCA)
Adabraka near Holy Spirit Cathedral
Box 1504   PH: 21 221944
Accra, Ghana   21 220567
Kate Parkes, Gen.Sec.   CBL: YWCA ACCRA

Languages: English. **National.** Ghana branch of international young women's Christian fellowship organization. Works for social justice and the building of a world community. Provides training programs for women.

Guinea

★91★ ASSOCIATION DES ANCIENNES NORMALIENNES DE GUINEES
(AANG)
BP 1960
Boulbinet
Conakry, Guinea

Languages: French. **National.** Promotes women and infant health programs through education and social projects.

★92★ ASSOCIATION FEMININE D'INFORMATION AND D'AIDE A
CREATION D'ENTERPRISE (CFIACE)
BP 3210
Conakry, Guinea

Languages: French. **National.** Women's development organization involved in the creation of small business, cooperatives, training, and community development. Provides technical assistance and information to women's groups. Conducts financial research and offers expert counseling.

★93★ ASSOCIATION DES FEMMES GUINEENNES POUR LA
RECHERCHE ET LE DEVELOPMENT (AFGRED)
BP 945
Conakry, Guinea
Aminatou Diallo, Contact

Languages: French. **National.** Promotes research development into the economic and social concerns of women. Conducts socio-economic research programs.

★94★ ASSOCIATION GUINEENNE POUR LE BIEN-ETRE FAMILIAL
(AGBEF)
BP 1471
Camayenne, Guinea   PH: 465627

Languages: French. **National.** Promotes family planning in Guinea. Supports women's health and social programs. Disseminates information; sponsors educational programs.

★95★ COMMISSION NATIONALE DES FEMMES TRAVAILLEUSES DE
GUINEE (COFETRAG)
Bourse du Travail
Conakry, Guinea

Languages: French. **National.** Working women in Guinea. Promotes the interests and rights of working women. Provides training programs.

★96★ GFAG WOMEN BUSINESS ASSOCIATION OF GUINEA
PO Box 3009   PH: 4 441892
Conakry, Guinea   FX: 4 442491
Hadja F. Tete Nabe Diallo, Pres.   TX: 23358 BONAG GE

Founded: 1989. **Languages:** French. **National.** Women in executive and middle management positions and women business owners. Promotes the interests of women in business. Encourages women in Guinea to become actively involved in business. Lobbies government on issues affecting women in business. Offers a forum for interaction among women with similar interests and concerns. Disseminates information on business in Guinea.

★97★ SOCIETE GUINEENNE DE GYNECOLOGIE ET OBSTETRIQUE
(SOGGO)
BP 1209
Conakry, Guinea

Languages: French. **National.** Gynecologists and obstetricians concerned with maternal health, infant health, and neonatology. Promotes the profession of gynecology and obstetrics in Guinea. Engages in exchange of scientific information.

Guinea-Bissau

★98★ ASSOCIACAO DE GUINE-BISSAU PARA A EDUCACAO E
PROMOCAO DA SAUDE FAMILIAR
Rua Eduardo
Mondlane 1160
Apartado 2
Bissau, Guinea-Bissau   PH: 213582
Mr. J.C. Rodrigues, Secretary   FX: 201400

Languages: Portuguese. **National.** Promotes family planning and responsible parenthood as a means to improve the quality of life for individuals living in Guinea Bissau. Works to stop the spread of AIDS and other sexually transmitted diseases. Offers programs in sex education, family planning, and health. Provides contraceptive services. Conducts research.

Kenya

★99★ AFRICAN WOMEN'S FEATURES SERVICE
PO Box 74536
Nairobi, Kenya

Languages: English, Swahili. **National.** Works to raise women's status in Africa. Promotes the portrayal of women in the media. Fosters communication among members.

★100★ AFRICAN WOMEN'S TASK FORCE (FEMNET)
Africa Women's Development and
Communications Network
PO Box 54562
Nairobi, Kenya
Dr. Eddah Gachukia, Chairperson   PH: 2 15441555

Languages: English. **Multinational.** Works to increase public awareness of women's needs and to provide a network of information and contacts for women in Central Africa. **Sections:** Women in Development; Communications.

★101★ ASSOCIATION OF AFRICAN WOMEN FOR RESEARCH AND
DEVELOPMENT - KENYA (AAWORD)
University of Nairobi
Dept. of Literature
PO Box 30197
Nairobi, Kenya
Kavetsa Adagala, Contact

Multinational. Promotes the study of women and women's issues throughout Africa. Conducts research on issues affecting women in developing nations; identifies resources to assist members' research; provides networking opportunities for African women researchers. Addresses labor, demographic, educational, political, professional, and ideological issues.

★102★ ASSOCIATION FOR VOLUNTARY SURGICAL
CONTRACEPTION - KENYA (AVSC)
Box 57964
Nairobi, Kenya

Languages: English. **National.** Promotes family planning options in Kenya. Supports surgical methods for contraception.

★103★ CENTRE FOR AFRICAN FAMILY STUDIES (CAFS)
(CAFS Centre d'Etudes de la Famille Africaine)
Pamstech House
Woodvale Grove
Westlands   PH: 2 448618
PO Box 60054   FX: 2 448621
Nairobi, Kenya   TX: 22792 CAFS KE
Prof. H.W. Okoth-Ogendo, Dir. CBL: CAFS

Founded: 1975. **Staff:** 36. **Languages:** English, French. **Multinational.** Works to raise public awareness about family planning; promotes the significance of family planning in national development. Provides technical assistance to family planning associations; organizes training courses for managers, supervisors, and other personnel employed in family planning programs and organizations. Conducts research; disseminates information; compiles statistics. Sponsors seminars and workshops on family planning issues. **Libraries:** Type: reference. Holdings: 4,000. **Computer Services:** Data base. **Divisions:** Research, Information and Documentation; Training.

Publications: *CAFS News* (in English and French), semiannual. Newsletter. **Circulation:** 1,500. **Advertising:** not accepted. ● *CAFS Information Brochure* (in English and French), annual. **Circulation:** 2,000. **Advertising:** not accepted. ● *CAFS Prospectus* (in English and French), annual. ● *Programme of Activities* (in English and French), annual. ● *Introduction to Family Life*

Education in Africa (in English and French). Research report. ● *Family Life Education Curriculum Guidelines* (in English and French). Research report.

Conventions/Meetings: biennial conference.

★104★ CHURCH WOMEN IN KENYA
PO Box 21360
Nairobi, Kenya

Languages: Swahili, English. **National**. Women's religious organization. Conducts lectures on religious topics. Promotes missionary work.

★105★ CPK MOTHERS' UNION (CPKMU)
Box 40502
Nairobi, Kenya

Languages: English. Mothers in Kenya. Promotes issues that affect the welfare of women and their children.

★106★ EAST AFRICA WOMEN'S LEAGUE (EAWL)
Box 40308
Nairobi, Kenya

Languages: English. **Multinational**. Promotes the interests of women in Eastern Africa.

★107★ FAMILY LIFE COUNSELING ASSOCIATION OF KENYA (FLCAK)
Box 30325
Nairobi, Kenya

Languages: English. **National**. Promotes family issues in Kenya. Supports the role of the family in Kenya's society.

★108★ FAMILY PLANNING ASSOCIATION OF KENYA (FPAK)
PO Box 30581
Nairobi, Kenya   PH: 2 215676

Founded: 1961. **Budget:** 864,800 KSh. **Languages:** English. **National**. Encourages the use of more effective methods of birth control and family planning. Establishes family planning clinics; provides educational services for rural citizens. Conducts seminars and film presentations.

Conventions/Meetings: annual - always April.

★109★ FAMILY PLANNING INTERNATIONAL ASSISTANCE (FPIS)
Box 53538
Nairobi, Kenya

Languages: English. **Multinational**. Family planning organization that works for worldwide involvement in family planning programs.

★110★ FEDERATION OF AFRICAN MEDIA WOMEN - KENYA
PO Box 50795
Nairobi, Kenya

Languages: Swahili, English. **National**. Women working in television, radio, and print media. Promotes positive portrayals of women in the media. Represents members' interests.

★111★ FEMNET
c/o Njoki Wainana
PO Box 54562   PH: 2 440299
Nairobi, Kenya   FX: 2 443868
Njoki Wainana, Contact   TX: 23137

Multinational. Women's organizations in Kenya and Zambia striving to empower women. Works to increase public awareness of women's needs. Coordinates activities among groups. Encourages and assists interaction among women's organizations. Disseminates information and investigates women's issues.

Publications: *Newsletter*.

★112★ HABITAT INTERNATIONAL COALITION - WOMEN AND SHELTER NETWORK
c/o Mazingira International
PO Box 14564
Nairobi, Kenya   PH: 2 443219
Diana Lee-Smith, SEC   FX: 2 444643

Founded: 1988. **Members:** 500. **Staff:** 2. **Budget:** US$40,000. **Languages:** English, French. **Multinational**. Individuals and nongovernmental organizations working toward the provision of adequate shelter for women in developing regions of Africa. Acts as a forum for the exchange of information on housing issues for women worldwide. Conducts research on the connections between housing and gender issues.

Publications: *Newsletter* (in English, French, Spanish, and Portuguese), periodic.

Conventions/Meetings: periodic workshop.

★113★ HUMA MULTIPURPOSE WOMENS' GROUP (HMWG)
Via Homa Bay
PO Box 70
Kandiege, Kenya   PH: 2 749747
Achoka Awori, Coord.   TX: 25222 KENGO KE

Languages: Swahili. **National**. Works to unite women living in developing areas of Kenya. Offers programs in primary education, health care, and parenting. Sponsors special programs for the aged to insure adequate housing and food provision. Promotes the interests of women and children's rights.

★114★ INTERNATIONAL PLANNED PARENTHOOD FEDERATION - AFRICA REGIONAL OFFICE
                                  PH: 2 720280
PO Box 30234   FX: 2 726596
Nairobi, Kenya   TX: 22703 INFED
Dr. Richard Turkson, Regional Dir. CBL: INFED NAIROBI

Languages: English. **Multinational**. Co-ordinates activities of Planned Parenthood member offices operating in Africa. Advocates family planning as a basic human right. Works to heighten governmental and public awareness of the population problems of local communities in Africa. Seeks to extend and improve family planning services. Conducts research on human fertility and contraception.

★115★ INTERNATIONAL PLANNED PARENTHOOD FEDERATION - KENYA (IPPF)
Box 30234
Nairobi, Kenya

Languages: English. **National**. Promotes family planning programs in Kenya.

★116★ KENYA THIRSTY CHILD AND WOMEN AID ORGANISATION (KTCWAO)
Box 44126
Nairobi, Kenya

Languages: English. **National**. Works to aid women and children in Kenya with food, welfare, and health programs.

★117★ KENYA WOMEN FELLOWSHIP ASSOCIATION (KWFA)
Box 74197
Nairobi, Kenya

Languages: English. **National.** Encourages fellowship among women in Kenya. Promotes the interests of women in Kenya.

★118★ KENYA WOMEN FINANCE TRUST (KWFT)
Gateway House, 6th Fl.
PO Box 55919
Nairobi, Kenya
Mary Okello, Chair

National. Promotes the advancement of Kenyan women in business and economics. Makes available loans.

★119★ KENYA WOMEN'S SOCIETY
Box 49838
Nairobi, Kenya

Languages: English. **National.** Promotes the interests of women in Kenya.

★120★ LUMI WOMEN GROUP
c/o CCFA Church Lumi
PO Box 93
Taveta, Kenya

Languages: Swahili. **National.** Women concerned about the environment. Works to protect natural resources and the environment in Kenya. Encourages appreciation of nature.

★121★ MEDICAL MISSION SISTERS - KENYA (SCMM-K)
PO Box 25162
Nairobi, Kenya
Rita Syron, District Superior   PH: 2 48892

Staff: 6. **Languages:** Swahili, English. **Multinational.** Women working to improve health care services to people living in developing areas of Kenya and Uganda, representing the interests of women and children. Sponsors programs in all areas of medical treatment, parenting, public health, nutrition, and midwife training.

★122★ MEDICAL WOMEN'S INTERNATIONAL ASSOCIATION - KENYA
KMWA
PO Box 49877
Nairobi, Kenya
Evelyn Wagaiyu, Contact

Languages: Swahili, English. **National.** Kenya national branch of the Medical Women's International Association (see separate entry). Women physicians. Provides a forum for discussion of women's health care issues. Encourages women to enter the field of medicine. Works to overcome discrimination against female physicians. Sponsors research and educational programs.

★123★ MUSLIM WOMEN'S ASSOCIATION (MWA)
PO Box 58171
Nairobi, Kenya   PH: 2 566602
Qamar Jehan, Chair   2 765799

Founded: 1948. **Members:** 200. **Staff:** 4. **Languages:** English. **National.** Muslim women 18 years of age and older. Seeks to improve the quality of life for Muslim women living in Kenya. Encourages public awareness of women's rights and an understanding of women's role in the Muslim religion. Works to improve relations with other women's organizations and communication among women of different cultures. Sponsors social welfare programs. Offers educational programs for women, including literacy and library services. Conducts charity bazaars and festivals. **Libraries:** Type:. Holdings: books, periodicals. Subjects: women's issues; issues relating to the

Islamic faith. **Awards:** Periodic (scholarship). **Committees:** Education; Social; Welfare.

Conventions/Meetings: annual (exhibits) - Nairobi, Kenya.

★124★ NATIONAL COUNCIL OF WOMEN OF KENYA (NCWK)
(Kiswahili)
PO Box 43741
Nairobi, Kenya   PH: 2 24634

Founded: 1964. **Members:** 60. **Staff:** 35. **Local Groups:** 45. **Languages:** English. **National.** Umbrella organization for women's groups in Kenya involved in community development projects. Promotes environmental awareness through activities such as tree planting. Conducts charitable and educational programs; bestows awards to individuals active in community improvement projects.

Publications: *On Traditional Practices*, monthly. Reports from workshops detailing harmful traditional health practices.

Conventions/Meetings: semiannual.

★125★ SOCIETY FOR THE ADVANCEMENT OF WOMEN STUDIES (SACWS)
Box 61510
Nairobi, Kenya

Languages: English. **National.** Promotes women's studies in Kenya.

★126★ TOTOTO HOME INDUSTRIES
Jubilee Bldg., Moi Ave.
Mombasa, Kenya   PH: 11 312853

National. Women who promote local business and financial self-sufficiency. Provides economic support and job training for women interested in starting businesses. Encourages women to enter non-traditional careers.

★127★ UNITED WOMEN'S MUSLIM ASSOCIATION (UWMA)
Box 45107
Nairobi, Kenya

Languages: English. **National.** Promotes the interests and concerns of Muslim women in Kenya.

★128★ WOMEN FOR WOMEN
                                        PH: 2 224591
PO Box 48611   2 332188
Nairobi, Kenya   FX: 2 210664
Dr. Pamela Nereah Kola, Chairperson   TX: 2 22670

Founded: 1993. **Members:** 100. **Budget:** 2,000,000 KSh. **Languages:** English. **National.** Women managers and professionals in Kenya. Provides a forum whereby women with similar pursuits, interests, and concerns can meet to exchange information, opinions, and expertise. Works to heighten awareness on issues of exploitation and discrimination of women, and to provide a means of securing the improvement of the status of women and the recognition of women's rights. Promotes women's reproductive rights. **Committees:** Education; Health; Gender; Development.

★129★ WOMEN'S ENTERPRISES DEVELOPMENT (WED)
Box 67833
Nairobi, Kenya

Languages: English. **National.** Promotes development of women's business enterprises in Kenya.

★130★ WOMEN'S RESOURCE CENTRE
PO Box 7631
Nairobi, Kenya

National. Provides resources and opportunities for women's self development. Offers counseling, educational programs, and economic assistance. Guides women's careers. Organizes and coordinates women's activities.

★131★ YOUNG WOMEN'S CHRISTIAN ASSOCIATION - KENYA
PO Box 40710   PH: 2 724789
Nairobi, Kenya   2 724699
Louisa Owiti, Gen.Sec   FX: 2 710519

Founded: 1912. **Members:** 10,000. **Staff:** 130. **Languages:** English. **National**. Women and girls interested in encouraging Christian living principles. Supports individual and community development. Promotes fellowship among members. Offers educational programs in areas such as: health; environment; income generation; leadership skills.

Conventions/Meetings: quarterly conference.

Lesotho

★132★ BASALI ITEKENG WOMEN'S SOCIETY
Box 955
Maseru, Lesotho

Languages: English. **National**. Promotes the interests of women in Lesotho.

★133★ BOITEKO WOMEN'S ASSOCIATION
Box 840
Maseru, Lesotho

Languages: English. **National**. Promotes interests of women in Lesotho.

★134★ HOUSEWIVES LEAGUE OF LESOTHO
Box 604
Maseru, Lesotho

Languages: English. **National**. Promotes the interests and concerns of housewives in Lesotho.

★135★ LESOTHO ALLIANCE OF WOMEN
Box 582
Maseru, Lesotho

Languages: English. **National**. Umbrella organization promoting the interests and concerns of women in Lesotho.

★136★ LESOTHO BUSINESS AND PROFESSIONAL WOMEN'S COOPERATIVE
Box 844
Maseru, Lesotho

Languages: English. **National**. Promotes the interests of business women in Lesotho.

★137★ LESOTHO FEDERATION OF WOMEN LAWYERS
PO Box 0534
Maseru 105, Lesotho
Ms. Masebelu Makliobole, Contact   PH: 322088

Founded: 1988. **Staff:** 3. **Languages:** English. **National**. Women lawyers and other women professionals. Promotes the status and development of women in Lesotho through human rights and legal education programs. Advocates law reforms and the inclusion of women in the democratization process. Conducts research on the minority status of women.

Publications: *Women and Law in Lesotho.* ● Series of pamphlets on women's legal issues.

Conventions/Meetings: weekly executive committee meeting - Maseru, Lesotho. ● annual meeting - Maseru, Lesotho.

★138★ LESOTHO GIRL GUIDES ASSOCIATION
c/o LOIC
Box 2542
Maseru, Lesotho

Languages: English. **National**. Lesotho branch of international organization. Seeks to develop skills such as self-reliance and leadership in girls while preparing them to contribute to community service. Encourages unity and belief in principles common to the Girl Scout/Girl Guide movement throughout the world.

★139★ LESOTHO HOMEMAKERS' ASSOCIATION
Box 1280
Maseru, Lesotho

Languages: English. **National**. Women working in the home in Lesotho. Promotes the interests of members.

★140★ LESOTHO NATIONAL COUNCIL OF WOMEN
PO Box MS 1340
Maseru, Lesotho
Malerato Motseta, President   PH: 325482

National. Women and women's organizations. Supports and promotes the development of women in Lesotho. Coordinates programs and activities.

Conventions/Meetings: monthly workshop - Maseru, Lesotho. ● annual seminar - Maseru, Lesotho.

★141★ LESOTHO PLANNED PARENTHOOD ASSOCIATION
Box 340
Maseru, Lesotho

Languages: English. **National**. Works to extend the practice of voluntary family planning by providing information, education, and services. Conducts research. Sponsors specialized educational programs.

★142★ WOMEN IN BUSINESS
P/Bag A197
Maseru, Lesotho

Languages: English. **National**. Promotes the interests of business women in Lesotho.

★143★ WOMEN'S RESEARCH COLLEGE
c/o NUL
PO Roma 180
Lesotho, Lesotho

Languages: English. **National**. Promotes the study of the interests and concerns of women in Lesotho. Sponsors research programs.

Liberia

★144★ FAMILY PLANNING ASSOCIATION OF LIBERIA (FPAL)
PO Box 938
Monrovia, Liberia
Wokie T. Stewart, Exec.Dir.   PH: 224649

Founded: 1956. **Staff:** 71. **Budget:** L$550,000. **Local Groups:** 2. **Languages:** English. **National**. Promotes enhanced awareness of family planning services. Believes that planned parenthood is a basic human right. Sponsors educational programs. Conducts research. **Libraries:** Type: reference.

Publications: *Directory*, periodic. ● *FPAL Informer Magazine*, annual.

★145★ NATIONAL FEDERATION OF LIBERIAN WOMEN
PO Box 2703
Monrovia, Liberia
Mrs. C. Leona Chesson, President

National. Promotes and supports women and women's interests. Coordinates activities for women. Disseminates information on women's issues.

★146★ NATIONAL FEDERATION OF WOMEN'S ORGANIZATIONS OF LIBERIA
PO Box 2703
Monrovia, Liberia

Languages: English. **National.** Umbrella organization of women's groups promoting equal rights for women. Provides a forum for collaboration among members.

★147★ YOUNG WOMEN'S CHRISTIAN ASSOCIATION - LIBERIA
PO Box 10-0118
Sinkor
Monrovia, Liberia   PH: 261285
Elizabeth G.S. Williams, Sec.   CBL: NAYCAL MONROVIA

Languages: English. **National.** Liberian branch of international women's Christian fellowship organization. Works for social justice and the building of a world community. Provides training programs for women.

Madagascar

★148★ ASSOCIATION ANAKANY AMIN-DRENY (AAR)
BP 42
Vohipeno 321, Madagascar

Founded: 1975. **Languages:** French. **National.** Women of Madagascar working in areas such as maternal and infant health, environmental concerns, agricultural development, and literacy. Promotes the interests of women.

★149★ EQUIPE FEMININE D'EDUCATION NUTRITIONELLE (EFEN)
SESMES, Ministere de la Sante
BP 866
Antananarivo, Madagascar   PH: 2 25132

Languages: French. **National.** Women volunteers working to develop nutritional programs in Madagascar. Conducts educational programs on nutrition.

★150★ FIANAKAVIANA SAMBATRA (FISA)
23 ter, rue Lenine, Lot IVD
BP 730
Antananarivo 101, Madagascar   PH: 224498

Languages: French. **National.** Promotes family planning and responsible parenthood programs in Madagascar. Provides family planning services, information, and education to women in rural and urban communities.

★151★ NATIONAL COUNCIL OF ASSOCIATIONS OF WOMEN IN MADAGASCAR
(Conseil National des Associations de Femmes de Madagascar)
BP 17-37
Antananarivo 101, Madagascar
Mrs. Zaveline Ramarosoona, President   PH: 2 21116

Languages: Malagasy. **National.** Umbrella organization for women's groups in Madagascar. Supports and promotes women's interests. Coordinates women's activities. Disseminates information on women's issues.

★152★ YOUNG WOMEN'S CHRISTIAN ASSOCIATION - MADAGASCAR
(Fikambanana Kristiana ho an'ny Zatovovavy eto Madagasikara)
BP 1140
Antananarivo 101, Madagascar
Felicienne Bernadette Bairtoa, Sec.Gen.   PH: 2 24062

National. Promotes the development of young women in Madagascar. Upholds Christian beliefs and values in its programs. Works to instill self worth and self-esteem in young women.

Malawi

★153★ NATIONAL COMMITTEE ON WOMEN IN DEVELOPMENT (NCWID)
Private Bag 330
Capital City   PH: 780411
Lilongwe 3, Malawi   FX: 732796
Mrs. E.J. Kalyati, Chairperson   TX: 44361

Founded: 1984. **Languages:** English. **National.** Malawian organizations interested in assisting women. Seeks to improve the educational, economic, and political status of women. Investigates and advocates legislators on legal, employment, and economic issues as they affect women. Researches family and maternal health; food and nutrition needs; fuel and energy alternatives; and drop-out rates for primary school girls. Proposes educational and research programs. Plans to establish a documentation center. **Committees:** Employment; Family Health and Welfare; Agriculture and Natural Resources; Planning Research and Evaluation; Education and Training; Small- and Medium-Scale Industries. **Programs:** Girls Attainment of Basic Literacy and Education. **Alternate name:** Steering Commission of Women in Development.

Publications: *Women and the Law in Malawi* (in English).

Mali

★154★ ASSOCIATION D'ENTRAIDE ET DE DEVELOPPEMENT (AED)
BP 153
N'Tomikoro
Bamako, Mali   PH: 223142

Languages: French. **National.** Supports rural women's groups involved in income generating activities. Active in training and literacy programs.

★155★ ASSOCIATION POUR LE DEVELOPPEMENT DES ACTIVITES DE PRODUCT ET DE FORMAT (ADAF/GALLE)
Rue 8 X 37 Missira Bamako
BP 2436
Bamako, Mali   TX: 1200 CABPUB

Languages: French. **National.** Promotes the development of revenue generating activities for women. Works to improve women and children's quality of life and state of health. Participates in studies of women and their socio-cultural environment.

★156★ ASSOCIATION POUR UNE ENTRAIDE AVEC LES TOUAREG DE GOSSI (AETG)
BP 8031
Gossi
Bamako, Mali

Languages: French. **National.** Seeks improved understanding of the women of Mali and of the traditional therapeutic resources of that country with the goal of promoting health for its population.

★157★ ASSOCIATION MALIENNE POUR LA PROTECTION ET LA PROMOTION DE LA FAMILLE (AMPPF)
BP 105
Niarela Bamako
Bamako, Mali   PH: 224494

Languages: French. **National.** Seeks to improve the quality of family life for the people of Mali. Creates conditions that will assist in safeguarding physical, mental, and moral health. Encourages family planning. Aids sterile couples in finding counseling. Provides educational programs in contraception methods and family life.

Mauritania

★158★ ASSOCIATION MAURITANIENNE POUR LA PROMOTION DE LA FAMILLE (AMPF)
PO Box 3127
Nouakchott, Mauritania
Mr. Alioune Ould Ahmed, Exec. Dir.   PH: 55803

Languages: French. **National.** Promotes family planning and responsible parenthood as a means to enhance the quality of life for people in Mauritania. Works to reduce the number of unwanted pregnancies and abortions. Advocates family planning as a basic human right. Offers programs in sex education, family planning, and health. Acts as an advocate for family planning on a national level.

★159★ BUREAU D'ASSISTANCE ET DE COORDINATION DE LA FEMME MAURITANIENNE (BAC/PFM)
BP 1017   PH: 53755
Nouakchott, Mauritania   52194

Languages: French. **National.** Identifies and promotes community development projects initiated by women in Mauritania. Seeks to impvove the living conditions of individuals in Mauritania.

★160★ INTERNATIONAL ASSOCIATION OF FRANCOPHONE WOMEN (AIFF)
BP 71
Nouakchott, Mauritania
Mme. Aissata Kane, President

Founded: 1987. **Languages:** French. **Multinational.** African women promoting cultural exchange and unity among French speaking women. Seeks to improve the social, economic, and political status of women. Strives to increase public awareness of women's values and abilities and to organize women in defense of their rights. Emphasizes the cultural role of women. Represents women at international conferences.

Mauritius

★161★ ACTION FAMILIALE
Royal Rd.   PH: 43512
Rose Hill, Mauritius   547903

Languages: English. Promotes the welfare of families in Mauritius. Fosters the concepts of harmonious married life, responsible parenthood, and natural contraception methods.

★162★ MATERNITY AND CHILD WELFARE SOCIETY
Remono St.
Curepipe, Mauritius

Languages: English. **National.** Promotes the health and well-being of mothers and young children in Mauritius. Sponsors programs that provide: physician consultations; milk distribution; medicine; pre- and post-natal care.

★163★ MAURITIAN ACTION FOR PROMOTION OF BREAST-FEEDING AND INFANT NUTRITION (MAPBIN)
4 Cattlewalk St.
PO Box 1134   PH: 20892
Port Louis, Mauritius   24436

Languages: English. **National.** Promotes maternal and child health. Provides counseling and information on infant nutrition and the benefits of breast-feeding. Conducts research.

★164★ MAURITIUS ALLIANCE OF WOMEN (MAW)
Corner Murphy & St. Jean Rd.
Quatre-Bornes, Mauritius
Mrs. G. Ghoorah, Vice President   PH: 4243489

Founded: 1978. **Staff:** 2. **Budget:** MRs 120,000. **Languages:** French, English. **National.** Umbrella organization of women's groups and interested individuals. Promotes the social, political, and economic development of women. Represents women's issues and raises consciousness about laws affecting women. Seeks to institute equality between men and women. Encourages women to accept civil responsibilities in local, national, and international issues. Strives to eliminate obstacles preventing women from full participation in the development of Mauritius. Advocates and prepares women to acquire access to decision-making bodies. Sponsors educational programs, counseling, pre-primary and nursery school for children, and seminars. Maintains resource center.

Publications: *MAW in Action* (in English). ● *The Quarterly Booklet.* ● *Souvenir Magazine.* ● Series of booklets on cookery, energy, and women and food production.

Conventions/Meetings: monthly. ● annual (exhibits) - Quatre-Bornes, Mauritius.

★165★ MAURITIUS CHILD CARE SOCIETY
Nalletamby Rd.
Phoenix, Mauritius   PH: 6964381

Languages: English. **National.** Promotes the skills of motherhood and child care among women of Mauritius. Provides health- related educational programs.

★166★ MAURITIUS FAMILY PLANNING ASSOCIATION
PO Box 1166   PH: 82784
Port Louis, Mauritius   TX: 4364 IW

Languages: French. **National.** Promotes enhanced awareness of family planning services. Encourages the use of more effective methods of birth control and family planning.

★167★ MOTHERS' UNION
Bishop's House
Phoenix, Mauritius   PH: 6865158

Languages: English. **National.** Mothers working to strengthen and preserve marriage and Christian family life in Mauritius.

★168★ WOMEN SELF-HELP ASSOCIATION
Self-Help Boutique
Royal Rd.
Curepipe, Mauritius   PH: 6766111

Languages: English. **National.** Promotes women's development through programs fostering self-help principles. Has developed programs concerned with: home economics; adult education/literacy; hygiene; dental care; family planning.

Morocco

★169★ ASSOCIATION MAROCAINE DE PLANIFICATION FAMILIALE
(AMPF)
6, rue Ibn El Kadi   PH: 7 720362
PO Box 1217   7 721224
Les Orangers   FX: 7 720362
Rabat, Morocco   TX: 32833 AMPF
Mr. Abdellah El-Madhi, Exec. Dir.   CBL: FAMPLAN RABAT

Languages: Arabic, French. **National.** Advocates family planning as a basic human right and as a means to improve life. Works to reduce the number of unwanted pregnancies and abortions. Attempts to stop the spread of AIDS and other sexually transmitted diseases. Offers programs in sex education, family planning, and health. Provides contraceptive and health care services. Conducts research.

★170★ NATIONAL UNION OF MOROCCAN WOMEN
(Union Nationale des Femmes Marocaines)
3, rue El Afghani
BP 30
Rabat, Morocco
Hafida Guessous   PH: 7 727937

Founded: 1968. **Members:** 55,000. **Budget:** 800,000 Dh. **Languages:** French, Arabic. **National.** Umbrella organization of women professionals and housewives. Offers material and psychological support to Morrocan women. Works to elevate the status of women. Offers educational programs in home management, professional development, small business establishment, sanitation, and family planning. Conducts agricultural research; plans to establish a library. **Commissions:** Public Relations; Education/Training. **Committees:** International Affairs; Research; Development; Information.

Publications: *Aicha*, quarterly. Journal.

Conventions/Meetings: annual convention - Morocco.

Mozambique

★171★ ASSOCIACAO MOZAMBICANA PARA O DESENVOLIMENTO
DA FAMILIA (AMODEFA)
Rua Armando Tivane
50-Amodefa   PH: 1 492287
PO Box 1535   FX: 1 32103
Maputo, Mozambique   TX: 6239 MISAU MO

Languages: Portuguese. **National.** Works to improve the quality of life for individuals living in Mozambique by promoting responsible parenthood and family planning. Attempts to stop the spread of AIDS and other sexually transmitted diseases. Offers programs in family planning, sex education, and health. Provides contraceptive and health care services. Acts as an advocate for family planning on a national level. Conducts research.

Namibia

★172★ NAMIBIA NATIONAL WOMEN'S ORGANISATION (NANAWO)
PO Box 24301
Windhoek, Namibia
Netumbo Nandi-Ndaitwah, President

Founded: 1991. **National.** Namibian women organized to improve their standard of living. Seeks to organize women in their struggle for equality. Strives to increase public awareness among women of their legal rights. Works to eradicate discriminatory practices in law, school, and employment. Encourages women to become active as leaders and to obtain careers in traditionally male fields. Educates women about AIDS and other sexually transmitted diseases. Investigates drop-out rates, teenage pregnancy, and teenage sexual behavior. Disseminates information.

★173★ NAMIBIA WOMEN'S VOICE
PO Box 7256
Katatura 9000, Namibia

National. Namibian women working to achieve political, economic, and social equality. Provides a forum for exchanging information and ideas. Encourages Namibian women to participate in the struggle for their rights. Conducts research and disseminates information on women's status.

★174★ NAMIBIAN WOMEN'S ASSOCIATION (NAWA)
PO Box 3370
Windhoek, Namibia   PH: 61 62461
Ms. Ottlie Abrahams, Chairperson   61 622021

National. Promotes interests of women in Namibia.

★175★ SISTER NAMIBIA COLLECTIVE
PO Box 40092
Windhoek, Namibia
Estelle Coetzee, Admin.   PH: 61 36371

Founded: 1989. **Members:** 15. **Staff:** 4. **Budget:** US$70,000. **Languages:** English. **National.** Women involved in educational and media professions in Namibia. Promotes and supports the development of women in Namibia regardless of race or political affiliation. Seeks to increase the role of women in Namibia's government. Disseminates information on gender issues. Encourages women to participate in workshops and to publish writings focusing on women's lives. Is establishing a resource center to act as a clearinghouse for information on gender issues. **Computer Services:** Electronic publishing, desk top. **Alternate name:** Sisters.

Publications: *Sister Namibia* (in English and Afrikaans), bimonthly. Magazine.

Conventions/Meetings: weekly meeting.

★176★ SWA NATIONAL UNION WOMEN'S LEAGUE
PO Box 24301
Windhoek, Namibia   PH: 61 2982390
Ms. Ripanga Muundjua, Contact   61 298111

National. Promotes unity among women in Namibia.

★177★ WOMEN'S SOLIDARITY
PO Box 23941
Windhoek, Namibia
Ms. Diane Hubbard, Contact   PH: 61 220077

National. Works to create solidarity among Namibian women to advance their social, cultural, and educational rights.

★178★ WORKS AND PEASANT WOMEN'S ASSOCIATION
PO Box 1231
Khomasdal
Windhoek, Namibia
Ms. Erica Beukes, Contact   PH: 61 62915

National. Represents the rights and interests of rural women workers in Namibia.

★179★ YOUNG WOMEN'S CHRISTIAN ASSOCIATION - NAMIBIA
PO Box 21445
Windhoek 9000, Namibia   PH: 61 63484
Nelago Kindombolo, Gen.Sec.   FX: 61 63484

Founded: 1985. **Members:** 200. **Staff:** 8. **Budget:** R 200,000. **Languages:** English. **National.** Women of all races, religions, political ideologies, ages, and income levels. Seeks to bring women and girls of different Christian traditions into a worldwide fellowship. Works for social justice and the building of a world community. Provides training programs for women. Offers assistance to rural communities. Operates day care centers.

Conventions/Meetings: triennial general assembly. ● annual regional meeting.

Niger

★180★ ASSOCIATION DES FEMMES DU NIGER
BP 28-18
Niamey, Niger
Mrs. Fatoumata Diallo, President   PH: 733730

National. Umbrella organization for women's groups in Niger. Supports and promotes women's interests. Coordinates activities. Disseminates information.

★181★ CENTRE NATIONAL DE LA SANTE FAMILIALE
Ministere de la Sante Publique et des
   Affaires Sociales
Immeuble Sonara II
BP 11286   PH: 734538
Niamey, Niger   734666
Dr. Halima Maidouka, Director   TX: 5270 OMS NI

Languages: French. **National.** Works to improve the quality of life for people living in Niger by promoting responsible parenthood and family planning. Attempts to reduce the number of unwanted pregnancies and abortions. Offers programs in sex education, family planning, and health. Provides contraceptive and health care services. Conducts research.

Nigeria

★182★ ANTI-EARLY MARRIAGE WOMEN ASSOCIATION
c/o Ikot Ntot
PO Box 2677
Calabar, Cross River, Nigeria
Ikot Ntot, Contact

National. Works to decrease the traditional practice of arranged marriages, especially the marrying of girls and very young women in Nigeria.

★183★ COMMITTEE ON WOMEN AND DEVELOPMENT
Bodija Estate
82 Adiyi Ave.
Ibadan, Oyo, Nigeria
M.A. Feyisayo, Contact

Languages: English. **National.** Promotes the interests of women in developing areas. Works to increase women's role in the development process.

★184★ COUNTRY WOMEN ASSOCIATION OF NIGERIA (COWAN)
2 Afunbiowo St.
PMB 809
Akure, Ondo, Nigeria   PH: 231945

Languages: English. **National.** Provides broad range of assistance and support to rural women in Nigeria. Active in areas such as: family planning; small business development; technical and financial assistance, including revolving loans; education and services.

★185★ CRUSADE FOR LIFE (CRULIFE)
PO Box 942
Akwa Ibom
Uyo, Cross River, Nigeria
Pastor John Michael

Founded: 1986. **Members:** 250. **Staff:** 5. **Budget:** N 47,000. **Languages:** English. **National.** Promotes the right to life for the unborn. Opposes abortion and programs that support its occurrence. Offers counseling, housing accommodation, and training to promote self-sufficiency among women with crisis pregnancies. Sponsors educational programs and vocational training. Conducts lectures and essay competitions. **Libraries:** Type:. Holdings: books, periodicals. Subjects: Abortion and child development. **Committees:** Educational. **Alternate name:** Crulife.

Publications: *Life News* (in English), monthly. Newsletter.

Conventions/Meetings: annual - 1993 Nov. 1 - 14, Uyo, CR, Nigeria.

★186★ DEVELOPMENT ALTERNATIVES WITH WOMEN FOR A NEW ERA - NIGERIA (DAWN)
Women's Research and Documentation
   Centre
Institute of African Studies
University of Ibadan
Ibadan, Nigeria
Prof. Bolanle Awe, Chair

Languages: English. **National.** Works to reduce the negative impact of development activities on women and the environment. Conducts research, training, and advocacy programs to eliminate inequalities of gender, class, and race. Facilitates communication and networking among women's movements. Protects and defends women's reproductive rights.

★187★ ENU-ANI LADIES PACESSETTER CLUB OF NIGERIA
University of Lagos Staff School
Akoka, Lagos, Nigeria

Languages: English. **National.** Women of Nigeria. Promotes social interests of members through activities and programs.

★188★ FEDERATION OF MUSLIM WOMEN'S ASSOCIATION OF NIGERIA (FOMWAN)
c/o Islamic Education Trust
105 Tokunbo St.
PO Box 637
Lagos, Nigeria

Languages: English. **National.** Muslim women of Nigeria. Promotes the interests of Muslim women through activities and programs. Supports the practices of the Muslim religion.

★189★ GIRL GUIDES AND BUSINESS AND PROFESSIONAL WOMEN
PO Box 1625
Ibadan, Oyo, Nigeria

National. Professional women of Nigeria working in concert with the Girl Guides Association (see separate entry). Supports the goals of the Girl Guides Association. Seeks to develop in young girls such skills and qualities as self-reliance, self-respect, leadership, and teamwork while preparing them to contribute to community service.

★190★ GIRLS BRIGADE OF NIGERIA - METHODIST CHURCH
Wesley House
21/22 Marina
PO Box 2011
Lagos, Nigeria

Languages: English. **National.** Methodist women and girls. Promotes and supports the concerns of women and girls in Nigeria through the Methodist church. Sponsors activities.

★191★ IMOLITE SISTERS CLUB
PO Box 149   PH: 234 963983
Ikeja, Lagos, Nigeria   234 960409

Languages: English. **National.** Women of Nigeria. Social interaction among women.

★192★ JAMIYYAR MATAN AREWA
12 Dendo Rd.
PO Box 9163
Kaduna, Nigeria

Languages: English. **National.** Promotes the interests and concerns of women in Nigeria. Sponsors activities.

★193★ LIGHT OF SALVATION WOMEN'S FELLOWSHIP (LSWF)
(UE Unwana ke Edinyanga)
28 E. Yellow Duke St.
PO Box 851
Calabar, Cross River, Nigeria
Hannah Sunday Obot, Sec.

Founded: 1982. **Members:** 320. **Staff:** 15. **Languages:** English. **National.** Women involved in missionary work. Encourages religious unity among women in Nigeria. Provides charitable assistance to orphanages and underprivileged individuals. Organizes training programs for women on preaching methods.

Conventions/Meetings: annual - always Feb. 10.

★194★ MEDICAL WOMEN ASSOCIATION OF NIGERIA
PO Box 1136
Calabar, Cross River, Nigeria
Ufok Samsonakan, Contact

Languages: English. **National.** Nigerian national branch of the Medical Women's International Association (see separate entry). Women physicians. Provides a forum for discussion of women's health care issues. Encourages women to enter the field of medicine. Works to overcome discrimination against female physicians. Sponsors research and educational programs.

★195★ METHODIST WOMEN ASSOCIATION
Methodist Church Nigeria
1 New Town Rd.
Ebute-Metta West, Lagos, Nigeria   PH: 1 612091

Languages: English. **National.** Women of the Methodist faith in Nigeria. Sponsors programs and activities of interest to women that support Methodist principles.

★196★ NATIONAL COMMISSION FOR WOMEN
Block 65, Area 2, Section I
PMB 229
Garki
Abuja, Nigeria
Victoria N. Okobi, Contact

Languages: English. **National.** Promotes and supports the interests of Nigerian women. Organizes and coordinates activities for the promotion of women's rights. Investigates women's concerns. Disseminates information.

★197★ NATIONAL COUNCIL OF WOMEN'S SOCIETIES (NCWS)
Plot PC 14 Ahmed Onibudo St.
Off Idowu Taylor St.
Victoria Island
Lagos, Nigeria
Emily Aig-Imokhuede, Pres.

Languages: English. **National.** Investigates and promotes the interests and concerns of women. Supports the interests of women living in developing regions of Nigeria. Works to educate the public about women's issues. Conducts research.

★198★ NIGERIAN ASSOCIATION FOR FAMILY DEVELOPMENT (NAFD)
PO Box 941
Surulere, Nigeria

Languages: English. **National.** Promotes family planning options in Nigeria. Sponsors programs.

★199★ NIGERIAN ASSOCIATION FOR THE WELFARE AND DEVELOPMENT OF WOMEN
PO Box 1337
Abeokuta, Ogun, Nigeria
Ester Uduhei, President

Languages: English. **National.** Seeks to enhance the well-being of women through development programs. Works to improve women's health, employment conditions, and education.

★200★ NIGERIAN GIRL GUIDES ASSOCIATION
25 Obalende Rd.
PO Box 640   PH: 1 680135
Ikoyi, Lagos, Nigeria   FX: 1 521084

Founded: 1919. **Members:** 62,000. **Staff:** 30. **Regional Groups:** 2. **Languages:** English. **National.** Young women. Supports and promotes programs of benefit to girls in Nigeria. Seeks to develop girls and young women into leaders of tomorrow. Conducts educational programs, seminars, training sessions, and research. Sponsors activities. Maintains vocational centers for handicapped girls, and a day care center for working mothers. **Libraries:** Type: reference.   **Committees:** Management; Training; Day Care Center; Building; Guide Shop.

Publications: *Girl Guides Magazine for the Youth*, quarterly.

Conventions/Meetings: semiannual National Training Camps - Nigeria. ● semiannual seminar (exhibits) - Nigeria.

★201★ NNEWI/BETTER LIFE WOMEN COOPERATIVE SOCIETY
PO Box 578
Nnewi, Anambra, Nigeria

Languages: English. **National.** Seeks to enhance the roles of women in rural development. Supports the growth of small business enterprises. Sponsors programs to encourage productive activity in areas such as farming, weaving, basketry, oil production, and animal husbandry.

★202★ PLANNED PARENTHOOD FEDERATION OF NIGERIA (PPFN)
224 Ikorodu Rd.
Palmgrove
Somolu
PMB 12657
Lagos, Nigeria
Dr. A.B. Sulaiman, Exec. Dir.

PH: 1 820945
FX: 1 820526
TX: 27604 NG
CBL: PLANFED LAGOS

Languages: English. **National.** Works to improve the quality of life for individuals living in Nigeria by promoting responsible parenthood and family planning. Advocates family planning as a basic human right. Attempts to stop the spread of AIDS and other sexually transmitted diseases. Offers programs in sex education, family planning, and health. Provides contraceptive and health care services.

★203★ RURAL WOMEN HEALTH ASSOCIATION
44A Etuk St.
Akwa Ibom
Uyo, Cross River, Nigeria

Languages: English. **National.** Provides support for rural women's health services and related educational efforts in Nigeria. Seeks to enhance the state of women's health in rural communities.

★204★ ST. ANDREW'S WOMEN'S ORGANIZATION
PO Box 312
Okigwe, Imo, Nigeria

Languages: English. **National.** Promotes women's development through programs and activities focusing on women's issues.

★205★ STEERING COMMITTEE OF WOMEN IN NIGERIA
Ahmadu Ballo University
Dept. of Sociology
Zaria, Nigeria

Languages: English. **National.** Promotes the study of women's issues in Nigeria. Encourages women's development through activities and programs.

★206★ WOMEN COOPERATIVE BUSINESS ASSOCIATION (WCBA)
Umudimkwa
Umudim
PO Box 1092
Nnewi, Anambra, Nigeria   PH: 1 684876

Languages: English. **National.** Local and village craft cooperative societies in Nigeria. Provides business support for women producers of traditional crafts in Nigeria. Fosters appreciation for traditional crafts in Africa. Works to improve the market and supply of traditional African crafts. Works to establish a system of stable income for women in local communities. Offers business and management training programs. Disseminates information on government regulations and policies affecting cooperative businesses. Sponsors seminars and exhibitions.

★207★ WOMEN IN DEVELOPMENT LINK
18 Boyle St.
Lagos, Nigeria

Languages: English. **National.** Promotes the development of women in Nigeria through sponsorship of programs and activities focusing on women's issues.

★208★ WOMEN IN NIGERIA
University of Calabar
PO Box 3663
Calabar, Cross River, Nigeria

Languages: English. **National.** Promotes the interests of women in Nigeria.

★209★ WOMEN WELFARE ASSOCIATION OF NIGERIA
33 Goodwill St. & College Rd.
Benin-City, Bendel, Nigeria

Languages: English. **National.** Promotes women's welfare in Nigerian societies through sponsored programs, activities, and educational efforts focusing on women's issues.

★210★ WOMEN'S CENTRE OF NIGERIA (WCN)
(Centro de Mujeres de Nigeria)
c/o Hannah Edemikpong
Box 185
Eket, Rivers, Nigeria
Hannah Edemikpong, Contact

Founded: 1980. **Members:** 190. **Staff:** 5. **Budget:** US$39,000. **Regional Groups:** 5. **Languages:** English. **National.** Low- and middle-income women; concerned men. Volunteer organization that seeks to: campaign against female circumcision, AIDS, and sexually transmitted diseases; offer shelter and care to abused women, abandoned and orphaned children, the aged, and the homeless; increase public awareness of factors affecting the health of women and children in Africa through research and education programs. Provide counseling on women's health and sexuality. Conducts studies on female circumcision and AIDS. **Libraries:** Type: reference. Holdings: 1,000. **Committees:** Research and Documentation.

Publications: *Newsletter* (in English), quarterly.

Conventions/Meetings: annual - always Nov. 25. ● quarterly meeting.

★211★ WOMEN'S HEALTH AND ECONOMIC DEVELOPMENT
    ASSOCIATION (WHEDA)
44A Etuk St.
Akwa Ibom
Uyo, Cross River, Nigeria   PH: 85 20427

Languages: English. **National.** Works to prevent health problems of women in rural Nigerian communities. Provides education and counseling on nutritional and family planning issues. Encourages economic independence for women through supportive programs and activities.

★212★ WOMEN'S HEALTH RESEARCH NETWORK IN NIGERIA
    (WHERNIN)
Ahmadu Bello University
Dept. of Sociology
Zaria, Kaduna, Nigeria
Prof. M.N. Kisekka, Coord.

Languages: English. **National.** Promotes the health of women in Nigeria through action-oriented advocacy, research, and coordination of grassroots projects. Works in close collaboration with health professionals and women's organizations.

★213★ WOMEN'S IMPROVEMENT SOCIETY
SW8/1246 Ogundipe St.
Oke Ado
Ibadan, Oyo, Nigeria
Tayo Ogundipe, President

Languages: English. **National.** Works to raise the status of women in Nigeria. Encourages women's pursuit of higher education.

★214★ WORKING GROUP ON WOMEN AND WORK
University of Ibadan
Ibadan, Oyo, Nigeria

Languages: English. **National.** Promotes the development and study of women in the workplace and issues affecting women laborers.

★215★ YOUNG WOMEN'S CHRISTIAN ASSOCIATION - NIGERIA
PO Box 449
Lagos, Nigeria
Grace N. Onyekwere, Gen.Sec.   PH: 1 630950

Languages: English. **National.** Nigerian branch of international women's fellowship organization. Works to encourage Christian living principles and promotes involvement in community service. Provides opportunities for informal education and recreation through programs and activities.

Rwanda

★216★ ASSOCIATION RWANDAISE POUR LE BIEN-ETRE FAMILIAL
  (ARBEF)
BP 1580
Kigali, Rwanda   PH: 76127

Languages: French. **National.** Promotes maternal and infant health through educational efforts. Encourages the practice of family planning in Rwanda.

★217★ DUTERIMBERE
BP 758
Kigali, Rwanda   PH: 73598

Languages: French. **National.** Seeks to integrate women into Rwanda's economic development. Provides credit for revenue generating projects and businesses. Works to stimulate a spirit of enterprise and to improve the socio-economic status of women.

★218★ EGLISE METHODISTE LIBRE AU RWANDA (EMLR)
BP 1668
Kigali, Rwanda
Mme. Mukakibibi Zerda, Contact   PH: 73047

Founded: 1987. **Budget:** 20,000 RFr. **Languages:** French, English. **National.** Methodist women in Rwanda. Works to raise women's awareness of their rights, responsibilities, and social services available to them. Works to improve women's health. Conducts educational and training programs.

Conventions/Meetings: quarterly meeting.

★219★ RESEAU DES FEMMES POUR LE DEVELOPPEMENT RURAL
BP 2368   PH: 73268
Kigali, Rwanda   72310
Isabella Nibakure, Contact   FX: 72899

Founded: 1986. **Members:** 100. **Budget:** 1,000,000 RFr. **Languages:** French. **National.** Seeks to improve the status of women in rural Rwanda. Supports women's groups engaged in national development activities. Organizes regular training sessions and consults on a variety of subjects. **Libraries:** Type: reference.

Publications: *Femmes et Terre* (in French). Book. ● *Femmes et Democratie* (in French). Book. ● *Directory*, annual.

Conventions/Meetings: periodic meeting.

★220★ SERUKA
BP 1117
Kigali, Rwanda
Mukahirwa Patriwe, Contact   PH: 76127

Founded: 1991. **Members:** 500. **Languages:** French, Kingwana. Seeks to improve the status of rural women in Rwanda. Encourages women's participation in development activities. Conducts research, educational, and training programs.

Conventions/Meetings: semiannual meeting.

Sao Tome and Principe

★221★ ORGANISATION DES FEMMES DE SAO TOME ET PRINCIPE
  (OMSTEP)
2, ave. Juan N'Krumah
BP 88
Sao Tome, Sao Tome and Principe   PH: 21174

Languages: French. **National.** Umbrella organization of women and women's organizations in Sao Tome and Principe. Promotes and supports the women of Sao Tome through sponsorship of programs and activities focusing on women's issues.

Senegal

★222★ ACTION HUMAINE POUR LE DEVELOPPEMENT INTEGRE AU
  SENEGAL (AHDIS)
BP 21395
Dakar, Senegal   PH: 224820
Bambey S. Dakar, Contact   225183

Founded: 1988. **Members:** 13. **Staff:** 8. **Budget:** 20,000,000 Fr CFA. **Languages:** French, English. **National.** Promotes the personal development of women in urban and rural areas in Senegal. Aims to improve the nutritional and health status of women and children. Sponsors agricultural and business training programs. Conducts educational and research projects.

Publications: *Journal*, annual. ● *Monograph*, periodic. Sectorial studies on marketing.

Conventions/Meetings: periodic convention. ● monthly meeting.

★223★ ASSOCIATION OF AFRICAN WOMEN FOR RESEARCH AND
  DEVELOPMENT (AAWORD)
(AFARD Association des Femmes Africaines pour la Recherche sur le
  Developpement)
BP 3304   PH: 252572
Dakar, Senegal   FX: 241289
Ndeye Sow, Deputy Exec.Sec.   TX: 61339 CODES SG

Founded: 1977. **Members:** 510. **Staff:** 2. **National Groups:** 13. **Languages:** English. **Multinational.** African women in 42 countries working in the field of social science; national research groups; researchers and research groups outside of Africa. Aims to increase the participation of African women in their society; to this end, conducts research into issues affecting African women, identifies resources to assist members in such research, and provides networking among African women researchers. Addresses labor, demographic, educational, political, professional, and ideological issues. Studies the situation of women in developing countries. Sponsors seminars. Organizes training programs and specialized research workshops, such as the Working Group on Women and Reproduction in Africa, in an effort to identify research sources and develop methodologies of study. **Computer Services:** Data base.

Publications: *ECHO* (in English and French), quarterly. Newsletter. **ISSN:** 0850-8704. **Advertising:** accepted. ● Also publishes occasional papers and bibliographical series.

Conventions/Meetings: quadrennial general assembly.

★224★ ASSOCIATION SENEGALAISE POUR LE BIEN-ETRE FAMILIAL
(ASBEF)
BP 6084
Dakar, Senegal
Mr. Roger Danlodji, Exec. Dir.   PH: 320049

Languages: French. **National.** Works to improve the quality of life for individuals living in Senegal by promoting responsible parenthood and family planning. Attempts to reduce the number of unwanted pregnancies and abortions. Offers programs in sex education, family planning, and health. Conducts research.

★225★ FEDERATION DES ASSOCIATIONS FEMININES DU SENEGAL
(FAFS)
                          PH: 250872
Dakar, Senegal   252151

Languages: French. **National.** Women's associations. Works to support and promote the status and the activities of women's organizations in Senegal. Focuses efforts on the following thematic areas: agriculture; women's issues; fishing and aquaculture; education and training.

★226★ FEMMES DEVELOPPEMENT ENTREPRISE EN AFRIQUE
(FDEA)
Rue 1, F Point E
BP 3921   PH: 220240
Dakar, Senegal   230058

Languages: French. **National.** Promotes financial independence among African women through support of business enterprises. Offers educational training and expertise in agricultural areas. Provides credit to women for business ventures.

★227★ NATIONAL COUNCIL OF NEGRO WOMEN (NCNW)
Rue Tolbiac and Autoroute
Immeuble Assane Ouseynou
BP 2984
Dakar, Senegal

Languages: French. **National.** Black women working to improve the quality of life for the people of Senegal. Active in the following thematic areas: agriculture; the environment; women's issues; water supply; health; education and training; breeding.

Seychelles

★228★ SEYCHELLES FAMILY PLANNING ASSOCIATION
PO Box 590
Mahe, Seychelles

Languages: Creole, English. **National.** Advocates family planning as a basic human right. Works to reduce the number of unwanted pregnancies and abortions. Attempts to stop the spread of AIDS and other sexually transmitted diseases through education and contraceptive services. Offers programs in family planning and health. Conducts research.

★229★ SEYCHELLES WOMEN'S ASSOCIATION
PO Box 81
Victoria
Mahe, Seychelles   PH: 23967

Languages: Creole. **National.** Works for women's equality and development. Promotes the interests of women in Seychelles.

Sierra Leone

★230★ MEDICAL WOMEN'S INTERNATIONAL ASSOCIATION - SIERRA LEONE
11 Martin St.
Freetown, Sierra Leone
Fatmatta Kargbo, Contact

Languages: French, English. **National.** Sierra Leone national branch of the Medical Women's International Association (see separate entry). Women physicians. Provides a forum for discussion of women's health care issues. Encourages women to enter the field of medicine. Works to overcome discrimination against female physicians. Sponsors research and educational programs.

★231★ MUSU LAKO
c/o Neneba Jalloh
African Development Foundation
48 Rawdon St.
Freetown, Sierra Leone
Neneba Jalloh, P   PH: 22 9262

Founded: 1985. **Members:** 25. **Languages:** English. **National.** Women and non-governmental organizations working to improve the quality of life for women and children living in developing areas of Sierra Leone. Offers educational programs for young women, training for illiterate women, and employment facilities. Sponsors daycare programs.

Conventions/Meetings: annual meeting (exhibits) - Kabala, Sierra Leone.

★232★ PLANNED PARENTHOOD ASSOCIATION OF SIERRA LEONE
(PPASL)
2 Lightfoot-Boston St.
PO Box 1094
Freetown, Sierra Leone   PH: 22 22774
Dr. W.E. Taylor, Exec. Dir.   TX: 3210

Languages: English. **National.** Works to enhance the standard of living for individuals living in Sierra Leone by promoting family planning. Advocates family planning as a basic human right. Attempts to stop the spread of sexually transmitted diseases, especially AIDS. Offers programs in sex education, family planning, and health. Provides contraceptive and health care services.

★233★ SIERRA LEONE HOME ECONOMICS ASSOCIATION
c/o Family Welfare and Counselling
   Centre
19 Walpole St.
Freetown, Sierra Leone
Mrs. Lilian Adami-Davies, President

Languages: French, English. **National.** Promotes, develops, and disseminates information on women working in the home. Supports the availability of individual and family counselling services. Fosters communication among members.

★234★ SIERRA LEONE MUSLIM WOMEN'S ASSOCIATION - KANKAYLAY (SLMWAK)
15 Blackhall Rd.
PO Box 1168
Kissy
Freetown, Sierra Leone
Alhaji Ibrahim Alpha Turay II, Education
Sec.   PH: 22 50931

Founded: 1972. **Members:** 250,000. **Staff:** 10. **Budget:** US$75,000. **Local Groups:** 12. **Languages:** Arabic, English. **National.** Espouses education for Muslim women in Sierra Leone. Organizes courses for teachers; bestows scholarships and awards. Offers children's services, charitable program, and placement bureau. Conducts seminars and in-service courses. **Libraries:** Type: reference. Holdings: 7,000. **Divisions:** Primary Education; Secondary Education.

Publications: *Voice of Kankaylay* (in English), semiannual.

Conventions/Meetings: monthly meeting (exhibits).

★235★ SIERRA LEONE WOMEN'S MOVEMENT
17 Charlotte St.
Freetown, Sierra Leone
Constance Cummings John, President

Languages: English. **National.** Provides a forum for discussion of women's issues. Encourages women to become involved in public life.

★236★ WOMEN'S STUDY AND RESEARCH GROUP
PO Box 335
Freetown, Sierra Leone
Staneala Beckley, Contact

National. Works to establish information and studies on women of Sierra Leone.

★237★ YOUNG WOMEN'S CHRISTIAN ASSOCIATION - SIERRA LEONE
PO Box 511
Freetown, Sierra Leone
Bernadette Cole, Contact   PH: 22 40383

Languages: English. **National.** Works to promote the spiritual and physical development of young women in Sierra Leone. Sponsors programs and activities that encourage personal growth, civic responsibility, and participation in public service.

Somalia

★238★ INSTITUTE FOR WOMEN'S EDUCATION
PO Box 619
Mogadishu, Somalia

Languages: Somali, English. **National.** Works to provide women with equal access to educational facilities. Sponsors continuing education programs for women. Conducts research on women's issues.

★239★ SOMALIA FAMILY HEALTH CARE ASSOCIATION (SFHCA)
PO Box 3783   PH: 1 22438
Mogadishu, Somalia   1 22433
Mr. Abbi Mayde Elmi, Exec. Dir.   TX: 3785 INTERACT SM

Languages: Somali. **National.** Works to improve the quality of life by promoting responsible parenthood and family planning. Attempts to reduce the number of unwanted pregnancies and abortions. Offers programs in sex education, family planning, and health. Provides contraceptive and health care services. Acts as an advocate for family planning on a national level.

★240★ SOMALIA WOMEN'S DEMOCRATIC ORGANIZATION
PO Box 1740
Mogadishu, Somalia

Languages: Somali, English. **National.** Women united to uphold democratic principles. Supports humanistic policies with a democratic framework. Strives for women's equality and social justice.

★241★ SOMALIA WOMEN'S DEVELOPMENT ORGANIZATION
PO Box 3425
Mogadishu, Somalia

Works for women's equality and development. Provides assistance and support to impoverished women. Conducts health, educational, and training programs.

South Africa, Republic of

★242★ AFRICAN NATIONAL CONGRESS WOMEN'S LEAGUE
51 Plein St., 17th Fl.   PH: 11 3307288
Johannesburg 2000, Republic of South   11 3307136
Africa   FX: 11 3307144

Founded: 1954. **Members:** 800,000. **Staff:** 105. **Budget:** R 2,500,000. **Languages:** English. **National.** Seeks to represent women's issues within the African National Congress. Participates in the party's policy formulation. Facilitates women's development in South Africa through education and training and research programs. Sponsors workshops. Organization's operations were banned in South Africa in 1961; group was allowed to resume activities in 1990. **Committees:** Development; Media; Policy.

Publications: *The Rock* (in English), bimonthly.

Conventions/Meetings: triennial conference - 1994 May.

★243★ ANGLICAN WOMEN'S FELLOWSHIP (AWF)
The Rectory
Main Rd.
Hout Bay
Cape Town 7800, Republic of South
Africa
Mrs. Jennifer Frye, President   PH: 12 7901029

Founded: 1965. **Members:** 11,000. **Languages:** English. **Multinational.** Female members of the Anglican church in Botswana, Lesotho, Namibia, South Africa, and Swaziland. Coordinates activities among women's groups. Encourages women to form their own groups. Conducts and organizes educational programs for women. Seeks to involve women more actively in church functions.

Publications: *Contact* (in English), 3/yr.

Conventions/Meetings: biennial Provincial Council Meeting. Discusses church business, education, and fellowship projects. - next 1994. Cape Town, Republic of South Africa.

★244★ BLACK HOUSEWIVES' LEAGUE
687 Maptla
Moroka 1860, Republic of South Africa

National. Black housewives and interested individuals. Promotes and supports black housewives. Seeks to increase public awareness of their needs.

★245★ CATHOLIC WOMEN'S LEAGUE - SOUTH AFRICA
PO Box 18981
Wynberg
Cape Town 7824, Republic of South
  Africa
Prof. P. Harrison, President

Languages: English. **National**. Catholic women. Encourages women to study theology. Seeks fuller participation of women in church functions.

★246★ CO-ORDINATED ACTION FOR BATTERED WOMEN
PO Box 10034
Caledon Sq.
Cape Town 7905, Republic of South
  Africa
J. De Souza, Contact

National. Works to end violence against women. Conducts educational and sensitization classes for individuals and institutions. Supports battered women economically, psychologically, and legally. Lobbies governmental, law enforcement, and religious bodies. Plans to establish a shelter for women victims of violence. Investigates violence against women and disseminates findings.

★247★ CONCERNED WOMEN
PO Box 5355
Cape Town 8000, Republic of South
  Africa

Languages: English. **National**. Women working to eradicate violence and bring about peace in South Africa. Disseminates information.

★248★ FEDERALE VROUERAAD VOLKSBELANG
Postbus 40537
Arcadia
Pretoria 0007, Republic of South Africa
Mrs. S. van Graan, Director   PH: 12 3261571

Members: 8,000. **Languages:** Afrikaans, English. **National**. Women working to improve their health and living conditions. Coordinates health services and acts as an advisor to the government on health issues.

Conventions/Meetings: annual general assembly - always October.

★249★ FEDERATION OF WOMEN'S INSTITUTES
PO Box 153
Pietermaritzburg 3200, Republic of South
  Africa

Languages: English. **National**. Women's institutes promoting the study of women and women's issues. Defends and supports women's rights.

★250★ GIRL GUIDES ASSOCIATION OF SOUTH AFRICA
PO Box 3343
Honeydew 2040, Republic of South
  Africa

National. Promotes the emotional, intellectual, and physical development of girls and young women in South Africa. Provides training based on the fundamental principles of the Girl Guide movement. Conducts activities and educational programs.

★251★ HOUSEWIVES' LEAGUE OF SOUTH AFRICA
PO Box 4532
Randburg
Johannesburg 2125, Republic of South
  Africa

National. Housewives and individuals interested in raising housewives' status. Promotes and supports South African housewives.

★252★ IKAKENG (BUILD YOURSELVES) WOMEN'S CLUB
PO Box 61147
Marshalltown
Johannesburg 2107, Republic of South
  Africa
Marjorie Mohlala, President   PH: 11 7363332

Members: 10,800. **Languages:** Afrikaans, English. **National**. Black women organized to improve economic, social, and health conditions. Educates black communities on prevention of tuberculosis. Maintains health centers which provide medical aid and information. Plans to organize Peace Seminars and Regional Resource Centers. Offers after-school childcare; community food services; literacy courses for adults; and sewing and other income-generating classes. Associates with other women's organizations. Holds public lectures.

Conventions/Meetings: annual National Ikageng Women's Club Conference conference - always October.

★253★ KONTAK FOR BETTER RELATIONS
PO Box 3246
Johannesburg 2000, Republic of South
  Africa   PH: 11 298996
Hildegaard van Zyl, President   FX: 11 298990

Founded: 1976. **Members:** 3,000. **Membership Dues:** R 10; R 20. **Staff:** 3. **Languages:** Afrikaans, English. **National**. Women striving to increase understanding, peace, and tolerance among different peoples. Conducts educational programs to aid teachers. Organizes programs and activities for young people. Offers financial assistance to mothers seeking education degrees. Promotes economic and political responsibility through programs on bookkeeping and political literacy. Strives to increase public awareness of the negative effects of violence. Disseminates information through media and publications. **Awards:** Recognition. Recipient: distinguished non-member. ● Annual Woman of the Year.

Publications: *KONTAK*, periodic. Newsletter. ● *Nation Building-Everybody's Responsibility* (in English). ● *Contact Amongst Children* (in English).

Conventions/Meetings: annual general assembly.

★254★ MEDICAL WOMEN'S INTERNATIONAL ASSOCIATION -
  SOUTH AFRICA
PO Box 28284
Danhof 9310, Republic of South Africa
Esabe Nel, Contact

Languages: Afrikaans, English. **National**. South African national branch of the Medical Women's International Association (see separate entry). Women physicians. Provides a forum for discussion of women's health care issues. Encourages women to enter the field of medicine. Works to overcome discrimination against female physicians. Sponsors research and educational programs.

★255★ METHODIST CHURCH OF SOUTH AFRICA - WOMEN'S
  ASSOCIATIONS
107 Green Point Rd.
Buffalo Flats Ext. 4
Cape Town 5209, Republic of South
  Africa
Mrs. Sophie Adams

National. Groups of Methodist women. Promotes the development of Methodist teachings in South Africa. Conducts activities for church members. Coordinates community service projects.

★256★ METHODIST WOMEN'S AUXILIARY COMBINED CENTRAL
    COURT
15 Edmonds Rd.
Glenwood 4001, Republic of South
    Africa

National. Women members of the Methodist Church. Fosters broadening of Methodist teachings in South Africa. Encourages women to become active in church and community functions.

★257★ NATIONAL ASSEMBLY FOR WOMEN
(Nasionale Raad Vir Sakevroue)
PO Box 31792
Braamfontein
Johannesburg 2000, Republic of South
    Africa
Kotie Botha, President   PH: 11 9071085

Members: 2,000. **Membership Dues:** R 100 annual. **Languages:** Dutch, English, Afrikaans. **National**. South African business women. Encourages and assists women in business professions. Promotes networking among business women of all races and languages. Plans to establish a data base of information on women's business organizations and relevant issues. Collaborates with other women's business groups. **Awards:** Annual Entrepreneur/ Business Women of the Year.

Conventions/Meetings: annual congress. ● periodic International Business and Professional Women's Congress congress - Republic of South Africa.

★258★ NATIONAL COUNCIL FOR AFRICAN WOMEN
AME Church Centre
18 Philip St.
Johannesburg 2000, Republic of South
    Africa
Winkie Direko, President   PH: 12 8054938

Members: 4,500. **Languages:** English. **National**. Umbrella organization working to enhance women's status. Encourages women to participate in national development activities. Promotes community involvement. Organizes, initiates, and supports community groups and their projects. Helps to establish welfare and educational organizations.

Conventions/Meetings: annual conference.

★259★ NATIONAL COUNCIL OF WOMEN OF SOUTH AFRICA
(NCWSA)
(Nasionale Vroueraad Van Suid-Afrika)
The Secretary
PO Box 1242
Johannesburg 2000, Republic of South   PH: 11 8341366
    Africa   11 46126172
Mrs. Heather Tracy, President   FX: 11 46126172

Founded: 1909. **Members:** 650. **Staff:** 1. **Budget:** R 40,000. **Languages:** English. **National**. Umbrella organization of women and women's groups in South Africa. Works to remove the legal, economic, and social barriers women face. Promotes equal rights and responsibilites for all people. Seeks to keep members current on local, national, and international events. Influences government policy on education, employment, family issues, and social welfare. **Libraries:** Type: reference. Holdings: archival material.

Publications: *NCW News* (in English), quarterly. Newsletter. Contains supplements in Zulu, Xhosa, Tswana, Sotho, and Afrikaans. **Advertising:** not accepted. ● *Directory*, annual.

Conventions/Meetings: annual conference (exhibits). ● periodic workshop.

★260★ NATIONAL WOMEN'S REGISTER
21 Great Britain St.
Turffontein 2091, Republic of South
    Africa
Sandy Baggot, President   PH: 11 6835426

Members: 400. **Membership Dues:** Regular, R 30 annual; Senior citizen, R 15 annual. **Languages:** English. **National**. Women organized for social interaction. Provides a center for social gatherings. Seeks to increase women's self-esteem and desire for education. Encourages tolerance, self-education, and community involvement.

Conventions/Meetings: annual conference.

★261★ PEOPLE OPPOSING WOMEN ABUSE
PO Box 93416
Yeoville
Johannesburg 2143, Republic of South
    Africa   PH: 21 6424345

National. Works towards the eradication of abuse against women. Disseminates information bringing about public awareness and political action demanding protection of victims and prosecution of aggressors.

★262★ PLANNED PARENTHOOD ASSOCIATION OF SOUTH AFRICA
    (PPASA)
(GSA Gesinsbeplanningsvereniging van Suid-Afrika)
York House, 3rd Fl.
46 Kerk St.
Johannesburg 2001, Republic of South
    Africa   PH: 11 8381525
Lumka Funani, Natl.Dir.   FX: 11 8347549

Founded: 1930. **Members:** 180. **Staff:** 70. **Budget:** R 2,000,000. **Regional Groups:** 5. **Languages:** Afrikaans, English, Sotho, Tswana, Xhosa, Zulu. **National**. Encourages family planning activities in South Africa and promotes family planning as a basic human right. Works to: improve maternal and child health; reduce the incidence of unwanted pregnancy and abortion; address issues related to adolescent sexuality and teen pregnancy; increase public knowledge of the prevention of AIDS and other sexually transmitted diseases; increase societal awareness of the relationship between population growth, natural resource consumption, and the conservation of the environment. Coordinates information, education, and training programs on sexual responsibility and reproductive health. Conducts research. **Libraries:** Type: reference.

Publications: *Aids Scan* (in English), quarterly. ● *Responsible Teenage Sexuality*. Book.

Conventions/Meetings: annual general assembly.

★263★ PROVINCIAL MOTHERS' UNION
PO Box 61394
Marshalltown
Johannesburg 2107, Republic of South
    Africa   PH: 11 8365771
Mrs. L. Joan Beddy, President   FX: 11 8365782

Members: 60,000. **Staff:** 24. **Budget:** R 400,000. **Languages:** English. **National**. Mothers in South Africa. Promotes the development of Christian marriage and family life in South Africa. Supports Christ's teaching on marriage. Encourages parents to raise their children in the faith and life of the church. Maintains a worldwide fellowship of Christians united in prayer worship and service. Provides assistance to individuals with troubled family life. Conducts adult literacy projects and skill training. Bestows study bursaries.

★264★ SOUTH AFRICAN ASSOCIATION OF UNIVERSITY WOMEN
(SAAUW)
(SAVUV Suid-Afrikaanse Vereniging van Universiteits°Vrou)
c/o Dr. Beverly Ramstad
7 Selbourne Rd.
Grahamstown 6140, Republic of South
    Africa
Dr. Beverly Ramstad, Natl.Pres.   PH: 461 26298

Founded: 1923. **Members:** 380. **Budget:** R 4,233. **Regional Groups:** 52. **Local Groups:** 7. **Languages:** Afrikaans, English. **National**. Women involved in various aspects of academia. Works to: establish equal educational and career opportunities for women (with an emphasis on higher education); act as a unifying body for its diverse membership. Represents members' interests before governmental bodies on issues concerning education, employment, and laws of marriage, divorce, guardianship, and taxation. Operates community service such as literacy and fundraising programs and donations to local libraries. Offers career symposia. **Awards:** SAAUW Fellowship (scholarship). Recipient: female post-graduate student. ● Grant. Recipient: female post-graduate student.

Publications: *Bluestocking* (in English), annual. Journal.

Conventions/Meetings: periodic conference. ● monthly meeting.

★265★ SOUTH AFRICAN COUNCIL OF SOROPTIMIST CLUBS
161 North Ridge Rd.
Durban 4001, Republic of South Africa
Hannah Lurie, President

Multinational. Professional women. Promotes and strives for peace, environmental protection, and women's rights. Conducts educational and productive projects. Disseminates information.

★266★ SOUTH AFRICAN FEDERATION OF BUSINESS AND
PROFESSIONAL WOMEN (SAFBPW)
PO Box 9482
Pretoria 0001, Republic of South Africa   PH: 12 3415945
Miss E.E. Beecham, Secretary   FX: 12 3415945

Founded: 1948. **Members:** 800. **Languages:** English. **National**. Professional and business women. Works to improve the social, economic, and business conditions of South African women. Lobbies the government to improve taxation, divorce, and other laws that affect women. Provides opportunities for business women to interact with others in their fields. Promotes international understanding. **Awards:** Gold Award (recognition). Recipient: companies that show most progress toward equality in employment. **Committees:** Agriculture; Business, Trade & Technology; Development, Training & Employment; Health; Legislation

Publications: *Career Woman* (in English), semiannual. Magazine.

★267★ SOUTH AFRICAN UNION OF TEMPLE SISTERHOODS
16 Hastings St.
Tamboers Kloof 8001, Republic of South
    Africa   PH: 21 239624
Mrs. Shirley Robinson, President   FX: 21 4342400

Founded: 1933. **Members:** 3,000. **Languages:** English, Afrikaans. **National**. Jewish women participating in social action projects. Establishes schools and day care centers in small towns. Distributes toys to poor or hospitalized children. Programs for the elderly include Kosher Meals on Wheels and cultural acitivties. Operates soup kitchens; provides disaster relief. Conducts literacy projects. **Libraries:** Type: reference. Holdings: 0; books. **Awards:** Scholarship. Recipient: rabbinic and other students.

Conventions/Meetings: biennial congress.

★268★ SOUTH AFRICAN VROUE FEDERASIE TRANSVAAL
PO Box 40526
Arcadia
Pretoria 0007, Republic of South Africa

Languages: Afrikaans. **National**. Supports the objectives of women's organizations. Works for women's rights. Coordinates activities.

★269★ SOUTH AFRICAN WOMEN'S AGRICULTURAL UNION (SAWAU)
16 9th Ave.
Voelklip 7203, Republic of South Africa
S.S. le Roux, President   PH: 253 7705577

Founded: 1931. **Members:** 28,000. **Languages:** English, Afrikaans. **National**. Umbrella organization of women's agricultural groups in South Africa. Promotes the development of women through instruction and training in agriculture, needlework, homemaking, national and international goodwill, public affairs, education, health, arts, crafts, and culture. Acts as liaison between member organizations, the government, and other national and international groups. Encourages organization and cooperation in agriculture. **Awards:** Periodic (scholarship). Recipient: members' children.

Publications: *Magazine*, periodic.

Conventions/Meetings: triennial congress. ● annual conference. ● annual congress. ● annual executive committee meeting (exhibits).

★270★ UNION OF HOMEMAKER'S CLUBS
PO Box 4220
Cape Town 8000, Republic of South
    Africa
Mrs. A. Jansen, Chair

National. South African women working in the home and women's homemakers' groups. Offers assistance to women and families. Organizes community projects and social activities. Offers opportunities to interact with other women socially.

★271★ UNION OF JEWISH WOMEN OF SOUTH AFRICA (UJWSA)
PO Box 3622
Johannesburg 2000, Republic of South
    Africa   PH: 11 3310331
Minx Sapir, Contact   FX: 11 3316703

Founded: 1936. **Members:** 7,000. **Staff:** 5. **Local Groups:** 44. **Languages:** English. **National**. Jewish women working to promote goodwill and understanding among the people of South Africa through social welfare activities. Represents Jewish women and provides a forum for the discussion of topics of Jewish and general interest. Holds President's Table to discuss matters of common interest with women from different organizations, religions, and races. Conducts home instruction program for underprivileged children; in-service training for pre-primary teachers in Soweto (in conjunction with Tel Aviv University); socialization and skills training for domestic workers; interlingual/interracial youth group. Provides disaster relief assistance. Operates soup kitchens; collects blankets for the poor and toys for handicapped children. Conducts educational programs on Gauchers and Tay Sachs diseases; operates Hebrew nursery school; hosts Jewish festivals; assists in Jewish synagogues. Maintains fund for the Parasitology Lab at Hebrew University, Braille Fund, United Communal Fund, and Toni Saphra Bursary Fund for postgraduate educational assistance; provides for the Israeli Soldiers Education Fund. **Divisions:** Adult Education; Chaplaincy. **Projects:** Hippy; Hug a Baby; Kenmekaar; Matal; Operation School-Books; Operation Snowball. **Programs:** Kosher Mobile Meals; Friendship Clubs.

Conventions/Meetings: triennial conference - Johannesburg, Republic of South Africa. ● periodic conference.

★272★ UNITED SISTERHOOD
16 Sue Ave.
Blangowme
Randburg 2194, Republic of South
    Africa

National. Promotes interaction among women. Encourages women to actively participate in women's causes. Coordinates activities.

★273★ UNITED WOMEN'S CONGRESS
PO Box 120
Athlone
Cape Town 7700, Republic of South
    Africa

National. Women and women's organizations. Promotes and supports women's rights. Coordinates activities.

★274★ WOMEN FOR PEACE
PO Box 87233
Houghton 2041, Republic of South
    Africa
Janet Semple, Co-chair   PH: 11 4406973

Members: 1,200. **Membership Dues**: R 10 annual. **Languages**: English. **National**. Women opposed to violence. Works to achieve peace and justice through the participation of women. Maintains a center providing care for children and differently abled people. Conducts educational projects. Provides opportunities for debate and exchange of ideas. Disseminates information about the causes and effects of violence. **Awards**: Annual Women of the Year. **Projects**: Wonderbox.

Conventions/Meetings: annual conference. ● annual general assembly. ● monthly meeting.

★275★ WOMEN FOR PEACEFUL CHANGE NOW
PO Box 18281
Dalbridge
Natal 4014, Republic of South Africa   PH: 31 3055164

National. Encourages non-violent problem solving techniques. Seeks to increase public awareness of the effects of violence. **Projects**: Teacher Textbook; Training and Resources for Early Education; Youthreach.

Publications: *Newsletter*, quarterly.

Conventions/Meetings: annual general assembly - Durban, Republic of South Africa.

★276★ WOMEN FOR SOUTH AFRICA
PO Box 1996
Rustenburg 0300, Republic of South
    Africa   PH: 142 31052

Membership Dues: R 10 annual   **Languages**: English, Dutch. **National**. Women working to improve the standard of living and to achieve peace in South Africa. Conducts youth seminars and summits. **Awards**: Annual Bridgebuilder of the Year.

Conventions/Meetings: annual general assembly. ● annual Regional Goodwill Day.

★277★ WOMEN'S ASSOCIATION OF THE PRESBYTERIAN CHURCH
    OF SOUTH AFRICA
433 Fehrsen St.
Baileys Muckleneuk
Pretoria 0181, Republic of South Africa
Mrs. Val Cowie, President

National. Presbyterian women. Fosters development of groups teaching Christian doctrine. Organizes and coordinates church activities.

★278★ WOMEN'S BUREAU OF SOUTH AFRICA
PO Box 705
Pretoria 0001, Republic of South Africa
Margaret Lessing, Exec. Dir.   PH: 12 476176

Members: 24,000. **Languages**: Afrikaans, English. **National**. Works to improve women's social and economic empowerment. Investigates laws that relate to women and children. Helps define and defend women's needs and rights. Strives to eliminate violence against women. **Libraries**: Type: reference. Holdings: 0; books, archival material. Subjects: South African women's issues. **Awards**: Annual Raymond Ackerman Award. Recipient: Woman who excels in community work. **Working Groups**: Child Abuse; Disability; Retirement; Environment.

Publications: *FOCUS*, quarterly. Magazine.

Conventions/Meetings: periodic conference.

★279★ WOMEN'S CHRISTIAN TEMPERANCE UNION - REPUBLIC OF
    SOUTH AFRICA
3 Upper Wrench Rd.
Observatory
Cape Town 7925, Republic of South
    Africa
Mrs. M.E. Powell, Contact

Languages: English. **National**. Women promoting abstinence from alcohol, tobacco, and narcotic drug use in the Republic of South Africa. Upholds Christian values and beliefs in its programs. Disseminates information about the effects of drugs. Lobbies government to reduce or abolish the production and sale of alcohol, tobacco, and narcotics.

Publications: *White Ribbon* (in English), quarterly.

Conventions/Meetings: annual meeting.

★280★ WOMEN'S COALITION
PO Box 62319
Marshalltown 2107, Republic of South
    Africa

Languages: English. **National**. Umbrella group of South African women's organizations. Promotes the interests of women's organizations throughout South Africa.

★281★ WOMEN'S LEGAL STATUS COMMITTEE (WLSC)
PO Box 1974
Parklands
Johannesburg 2121, Republic of South
    Africa   PH: 11 4401973
Babette Kabak, Convenor   11 4428985

Founded: 1975. **Membership Dues**: Individual, R 10 annual; Organization, R 20 annual. **Budget**: R 3,000. **Languages**: English. **National**. Individual women and national women's organizations. Works to improve the legal status of South African women. Investigates the effects of laws on women's work, marriage, and health. Lobbies South African government regarding women's issues. Conducts research on women's legal status. Disseminates information through the media.

Publications: *Living Together Unmarried* (in English). Book. ● *WLSC* (in English), 3-4/yr. Newsletter. ● *Memorandum on Women in Employment* (in English). Booklet. ● *Survey of Working Women* (in English). Booklet.

Conventions/Meetings: annual general assembly.

★282★ THE WOMEN'S LOBBY (TWL)
PO Box 130721
Bryanston
Johannesburg 2021, Republic of South   PH: 11 4428985
Africa   11 4632068
Babette Kabak, Chairman of the Board   FX: 11 4428985

Founded: 1991. **Members:** 100. **Budget:** R 65,000. **Languages:** English. **National.** Professional, academic, and business women, and national organizations. Promotes gender equality in South Africa. Conducts government lobbying to facilitate women's entrance into the political process. Encourages and assists women's active participation in local, regional, and national levels of government. Administers educative workshops and conducts on-going research on South African women. **Libraries:** Type: not open to the public.

Conventions/Meetings: monthly general assembly (exhibits) - Johannesburg, Republic of South Africa.

★283★ WORLD ASSOCIATION OF WOMEN ENTREPRENEURS
(Les Femmes Chefs d'Enterprises Mondiales)
PO Box 55136
Northlands 2116, Republic of South
Africa
Aida Geffen, President   PH: 11 7882035

Members: 50. **Languages:** English, French. **National.** Women in business working to provide all women with economic and legal equality. Investigates and fights to maintain the rights and interests of women and families in business. Informs women entrepreneurs of available resources. Encourages members to establish and initiate international communication. Conducts workshops, management seminars, and small business week. Plans to organize a women's entrepreneurs network.

Conventions/Meetings: quarterly congress. ● periodic convention.

★284★ YOUNG WOMEN'S CHRISTIAN ASSOCIATION - SOUTH
AFRICA
PO Box 61494
Marshalltown 2107, Republic of South
Africa
Joyce N. Seroke, Gen.Sec.

Founded: 1886. **Members:** 1,200. **Staff:** 23. **Budget:** R 75,000. **Local Groups:** 6. **Languages:** English. **National.** Seeks to promote Christian beliefs and ideals among women in South Africa. Promotes spiritual, social, physical, and intellectual development in young women. Provides assistance to woman in need, danger, or distress. Conducts outreach programs to the elderly.

Publications: *Y's News and Views* (in English), quarterly.

Conventions/Meetings: monthly executive committee meeting. ● biennial conference.

Sudan

★285★ BABIKER BADRI SCIENTIFIC ASSOCIATION FOR WOMEN'S
STUDIES (BBSAWS)
PO Box 167
Omdurman, Sudan
Dr. Amna Badin, Sec.   PH: 53363

Founded: 1979. **Members:** 72. **Staff:** 3. **Languages:** Arabic, English. **National.** Sudanese women and others who seek to advance the rights of women. Studies the status of Sudanese women, and initiates projects recommended by such research. Campaigns against the Sudanese traditon of female circumcision by coordinating programs with other African associa-

tions and distributing educational materials. Trains rural women in simple food preparation and preservation, hygiene, sewing, and handicrafts, in order to increase their family income. Encourages women trainees to form local training centers and cooperative societies. Plans to improve water supplies to homes by utilizing wind power. Conducts periodic seminars, workshops, and lectures. Maintains bibliographical archives, children's services, and speaker's bureau. Organization is named after Sheikh Babiker Badri, the initiator of education for Sudanese women. **Committees:** Women's Studies Documentation.

Publications: *Women* (in Arabic and English), annual. ● Also publishes workshop proceedings and booklets (in Arabic).

Conventions/Meetings: biennial.

★286★ ISLAMIC AFRICAN RELIEF AGENCY (IARA)
PO Box 3372
Khartoum, Sudan

Languages: Arabic, English. **National.** Muslim women in the Sudan offering social welfare programs in the Sudan. Conducts educational and training programs. Operates health clinics to improve the health of women and children, prevent the spread of AIDS, and provide family planning information.

Publications: *ISRA Magazine* (in Arabic).

★287★ SUDAN FAMILY PLANNING ASSOCIATION (SFPA)
PH: 11 443460
PO Box 170   TX: 22069 SHECO SD
Khartoum, Sudan   CBL: FAMPLAN
Mr. Ahmed Mohamed Youssif, Exec. Dir.   KHARTOUM SOU

Languages: Arabic. **National.** Promotes family planning and responsible parenthood as a means to improve the quality of life for individuals living in Sudan. Works to reduce the number of unwanted pregnancies and abortions. Offers programs in family planning, sex education, and health. Acts as an advocate for family planning on a national level. Conducts research.

★288★ SUDAN FERTILITY CARE ASSOCIATION (SFCA)
PO Box 7093
Khartoum, Sudan   PH: 79748

Founded: 1975. **Members:** 150. **Staff:** 32. **Budget:** £S 755,000. **Languages:** Arabic, English. **National.** Individuals and institutions promoting family planning in Sudan. Offers educational programs for new mothers; conducts research programs on infertility and on male attitudes towards family planning. Operates family planning clinic. Maintains small library.

Publications: *Bulletin*, quarterly.

Conventions/Meetings: annual.

★289★ SUDANESE WOMEN SOLIDARITY
PO Box 970
Omduran, Sudan

National. Promotes unity among Sudanese women in striving for the recognition of women's rights and furthering the women's movement.

Swaziland

★290★ FAMILY LIFE ASSOCIATION OF SWAZILAND
PO Box 1051   PH: 4153586
Manzini, Swaziland   4153082

Languages: English. **National.** Promotes family planning programs in Swaziland. Works for the improvement of maternal, child, and family health.

★291★ NATIONAL SPIRITUAL ASSEMBLY OF THE BAHAI'S OF SWAZILAND
PO Box 298   PH: 4152689
Mbabane, Swaziland   4171115

Languages: English. National. Women in Swaziland promoting world peace and unity. Encourages social and economic development through education and activities for women and young people. Works with international peace organizations to realize objectives.

★292★ SWAZILAND ALLIANCE OF WOMEN
PO Box 377
Mbabane, Swaziland
Mary Magagula

Languages: SiSwati. National. Women united to defend women's rights as mothers, workers, and citizens.

★293★ TONGOTONGO ASSOCIATION FOR VOCATIONAL TRAINING OF RURAL WOMEN
PO Box 22
Hlatikulu, Swaziland   PH: 4176240

Languages: English. National. Works to assist rural women in attaining income generating skills through the implementation of training and small business development programs.

★294★ ZONDLE MOTHER'S ORGANISATION
PO Box 276
Manzini, Swaziland   PH: 4153768

Languages: English. National. Mothers in Swaziland. Seeks to protect the interests of the nation's children. Works to improve living conditions.

Tanzania, United Republic of

★295★ ASSOCIATION OF AFRICAN WOMEN FOR RESEARCH AND DEVELOPMENT - TANZANIA (AAWORD)
University of Dar es Salaam
PO Box 35044
Dar es Salaam, United Republic of
   Tanzania
Amandina Lihamba, Contact

National. Promotes the study of women and women's issues in Tanzania. Aims to increase African women's participation in society. Conducts research into issues affecting African women; identifies resources to assist members' research; provides networking opportunities among African women researchers. Addresses labor, demographics, educational, political, professional, and ideological issues.

★296★ AZANIA WOMAN
PO Box 2142
Dar es Salaam, United Republic of
   Tanzania

National. Women advocating the abolition of apartheid in Azania (Azania is the termk for South Africa, as used by the Pan Africanist Congress). Strives to increase public awareness of the effects of apartheid on women. Works to ensure women's freedom and equality in South Africa. Organizes and coordinates activities. Disseminates information.

★297★ CATHOLIC WOMEN ORGANIZATION OF TANZANIA
(Wanawake Wawatoliki Tanzania Wawata)
PO Box 9361
Dar es Salaam, United Republic of
   Tanzania   PH: 51 30071
Mrs. Olive Luena, President   51 34640

Founded: 1972. Members: 600,000. Budget: 76,000 TSh. Regional Groups: 29. Languages: Swahili, English. National. Women of the Catholic faith 14 years or older. Promotes the development of women in the Catholic church. Encourages Tanzanian women to contribute to the development of society and church. Conducts educational and research programs. Libraries: Type: reference.

Conventions/Meetings: annual congress (exhibits) - always September. Dar es Salaam, United Republic of Tanzania.

★298★ FAMILY PLANNING ASSOCIATION OF TANZANIA
(Chama Cha Uzazi Na Malezi Bora Tanzania)
PO Box 1372   PH: 51 28425
Dar es Salaam, United Republic of   51 28424
   Tanzania   FX: 51 28426
Mrs. Christina M.K. Nsekela, Exec. Dir. TX: 41780

Founded: 1959. Members: 500,000. Budget: US$1,000,000. Languages: English. National. Promotes family planning programs among the people of Tanzania. Trains medical and paramedical personnel in the provision of clinical services and contraceptive usage. Sponsors informational and educational programs. Libraries: Type: open to the public.

Publications: Uzazi Bora, quarterly. Newsletter. ● Adolescent Fertility in Tanzania, Knowledge, Perception and Practices (in English). Monograph.

Conventions/Meetings: annual conference (exhibits) - always July. Dar-es-Salaam, United Republic of Tanzania. ● semiannual executive committee meeting. ● periodic regional meeting.

★299★ HOME AND FAMILY ASSOCIATION
PO Box 2537
Dar es Salaam, United Republic of
   Tanzania   PH: 51 21886

Languages: English. National. Promotes and coordinates the activities of Christian women in various churches. Supports Christian education in home and family life. Works to assist women in contributing to the socio-economic improvement of Tanzania.

★300★ LEGAL AID SCHEME FOR WOMEN
PO Box 868
Dar es Salaam, United Republic of
   Tanzania

National. Promotes the availability of advocacy and legal consultancy services for women who are victims of discrimination, abuse, and oppression.

★301★ MEDICAL WOMEN'S INTERNATIONAL ASSOCIATION - TANZANIA
c/o MEWATA
PO Box 4160
Dar es Salaam, United Republic of
   Tanzania
WinniFrida Mpanju, Contact

Languages: Swahili, English. National. Tanzania national branch of the Medical Women's International Association (see separate entry). Women physicians. Provides a forum for discussion of women's health care issues. Encourages women to enter the field of medicine. Works to overcome discrimination against female physicians. Sponsors research and educational programs.

★302★ SUWATA LEGAL AID CENTRE
PO Box 868
Dar es Salaam, United Republic of
 Tanzania

National. Female attorneys. Provides legal counseling and assistance to women. Offers support services for women. Conducts educational programs to increase women's awareness of their legal rights.

★303★ TANZANIA GIRL GUIDES ASSOCIATION
PO Box 424
Dar es Salaam, United Republic of
 Tanzania   PH: 51 27056

Languages: English. **National.** Tanzanian branch of international organization. Seeks to develop in girls and young women such qualities as character, responsible citizenship, and a desire to participate in community service. Encourages members to involve themselves in all facets of family, social, cultural, economic, and political life in both Tanzania and abroad. Focuses on issues of health, intelligence, and service. Active in handicraft production.

★304★ TANZANIA MEDIA WOMEN ASSOCIATION (TAMWA)
PO Box 6143   PH: 51 29904
Dar es Salaam, United Republic of   51 23904
 Tanzania   TX: 41207

Languages: English. **National.** Women working in the media professions. Champions the positive portrayal of women in the media. Provides a forum for exchange of ideas on technical skills and resources. Promotes the concerns of professional women in all fields.

★305★ TANZANIA WOMEN DEVELOPMENT FOUNDATION
PO Box 71308
Dar es Salaam, United Republic of
 Tanzania

Languages: English. **National.** Promotes the participation of women in economic and business oriented activities. Encourages women in the establishment of business ventures. Offers expertise in technical support, while providing legal advice, as well as banking, loan, and credit assistance.

★306★ UNION OF TANZANIA WOMEN (UWT)
(Umoja Wa Wanawake Tanzania)
                                             PH: 61 22903
PO Box 825   61 21853
Dodoma, United Republic of Tanzania   TX: 53175

Languages: English. **National.** Umbrella organization of women and women's organizations in Tanzania. Works to raise the morale and status of women in Tanzania through economic, social, and political development efforts. Attempts to raise awareness of the need for women's "emancipation from man's subjection" in Tanzania. Active in literacy education.

★307★ UZAZI NA MALEZI BORA TANZANIA (UMATI)
PO Box 1372   PH: 51 28424
Dar es Salaam, United Republic of   51 23932
 Tanzania   TX: 41780 UMATI TZ
Mrs. Christina Nsekela, Exec. Dir.   CBL: UMATI

Languages: Swahili, English. **National.** Advocates family planning and responsible parenthood as a means to improve the quality of life. Promotes family planning as a basic human right. Offers programs in sex education, family planning, and health. Provides contraceptive and health care services. Acts as an advocate for family planning on the national level.

★308★ WOMEN AND COOPERATIVE
PO Box 3070
Moshi, United Republic of Tanzania
Zakiya Meghji, Contact

National. Promotes and supports the formation of women's cooperatives. Assists women in forming groups. Lobbies government to change laws concerning the formation of cooperatives.

★309★ WOMEN AND DEVELOPMENT
PO Box 828
Zanzibar, United Republic of Tanzania
Mariam Hamdani, Contact

National. Promotes and supports the improvement of women's standard of living. Conducts projects intended to improve women's economic status. Organizes educational and cultural programs. Produces television and radio programs.

★310★ WOMEN'S RESEARCH AND DEVELOPMENT PROJECT
PO Box 35544
Dar es Salaam, United Republic of
 Tanzania

National. University women, researching women's issues. Promotes and supports women in their fight for equality. Conducts educational workshops and training programs. Disseminates information to increase public awareness of women's issues. Coordinates activities.

Publications: *Newsletter* (in Kiswahili).

★311★ WOMEN'S RESEARCH AND DOCUMENTATION PROJECT
(WRDP)
University of Dar es Salaam
PO Box 35108
Dar es Salaam, United Republic of   PH: 51 49192
 Tanzania   FX: 51 48271
Dr. Zubeida Tumbo-Masabo, Convenor   TX: 41327 UNISCIETZ

Founded: 1979. **Members:** 40. **Languages:** English, French, Kiswahili. **National.** Teachers, librarians, researchers, journalists, and other professionals in the United Republic of Tanzania. Promotes the development of women. Conducts research on the role of women in Tanzania. Interests include: teenage reproductive health; women's life cycles; economy and women; language; and women's role in the workforce. Offers seminars, workshops, and panel discussions. **Libraries:** Type:. Holdings: 500; books, periodicals. Subjects: Development of women. **Committees:** Co-ordination; Documentation; Editorial; Research.

Publications: *Mwenzangu Newsletter* (in Kiswahili), semiannual.

Conventions/Meetings: monthly seminar - Dar es Salaam, United Republic of Tanzania.

★312★ WOMEN'S STUDY GROUP (WSG)
University of Dar es Salaam
Institute of Development Studies
PO Box 35169
Dar es Salaam, United Republic of   PH: 51 49160
 Tanzania   51 491920

Languages: English. **National.** Promotes the study of and research into issues of concern to women in Tanzania.

★313★ YOUNG WOMEN'S CHRISTIAN ASSOCIATION - TANZANIA
PO Box 2086
Dar es Salaam, United Republic of
 Tanzania   PH: 51 22439
Helena Fliakos, Gen.Sec.   FX: 51 25281

National. Promotes the development of young women in Tanzania. Upholds

Christian beliefs and values in its programs. Works to instill self-worth and self-esteem in young women.

Togo

★314★ ASSOCIATION POUR LA PROMOTION DE LA FEMME ET DE L'ENFANT EN MILIEU RURAL
BP 2573
Tokoin-Doumassesse
Lome, Togo   PH: 213822
Kavege K. Basile, P   FX: 213822

Founded: 1988. **Members:** 20. **Staff:** 3. **Budget:** 11,326,000 Fr CFA. **Languages:** French. **National.** Seeks to improve health and living conditions for women and children living in rural areas in Togo. Encourages cooperation among different villages to realize development projects. Works to end illiteracy among women and children. Offers programs in hygiene, maintaining pure water supplies, pisciculture, parenting, and vocational training. Sponsors education and vocational training centers in 13 regions of Togo. Conducts research on rural technology. **Alternate name:** Solidarite Humaine.

Conventions/Meetings: annual general assembly.

★315★ ASSOCIATION TOGOLAISE POUR LE BIEN-ETRE FAMILIAL (ATBEF)
Rue Dosseh Tokoin-Lycee
BP 4056
Lome, Togo   PH: 214193

Languages: French. **National.** Promotes family planning programs in Togo. Encourages use of family planning techniques. Supports programs to uphold family values. Works on projects in the following areas: water supply; sanitation; animal and vegetable production; education; handicrafts; health.

★316★ COMITE INTERNATIONAL DES FEMMES AFRICAINES POUR LE DEVELOPPEMENT - TOGO (CIFAD)
BP 369   PH: 216879
Lome, Togo   216946

Languages: French. **National.** Promotes the active participation and effective integration of African women into the socio-economic development processes of Africa.

★317★ FEDERATION DES ORGANIZATIONS FEMININES CATHOLIQUES DU TOGO
BP 8890
Lome, Togo   PH: 211339

Languages: French. **National.** Promotes the contributions of Catholic women in the ecclesiastical community in Togo.

★318★ INTERNATIONAL PLANNED PARENTHOOD FEDERATION - CENTRAL AND WEST AFRICA
                                             PH: 210716
BP 4101   FX: 215140
Lome, Togo   TX: 5046 INFED TO
Kodjo Efu, Contact   CBL: INFEDTO

Languages: French. **Multinational.** Umbrella organization coordinating activities of member offices of Planned Parenthood in Central and West Africa. Advocates family planning as a basic human right. Works to heighten government and public awareness of the population problems of local communities. Promotes effective family planning services. Seeks to extend and improve family planning programs. Conducts research on human fertility and contraception.

★319★ SOROPTIMIST INTERNATIONAL
BP 4864
Lome, Togo   PH: 215337

Languages: French. **Multinational.** Business and professional women. Encourages the establishment of international friendships and promotes issues of concern to women around the world. Active in civic projects to benefit communities, such as well drilling to establish healthy water supplies, and infrastructure development.

★320★ UNION NATIONALE DES FEMMES DU TOGO
BP 3233
Lome, Togo   PH: 212738
Ahlonkoba Aithnard, President   211908

Languages: French. **National.** Promotes the interests of women in Togo. Encourages communication and friendly relations among all women.

Tunisia

★321★ ALL OF TUNIS WOMEN FOR RESEARCH AND INFORMATION ON WOMEN
7, rue Sinan Pacha
Tunis, Tunisia

National. Promotes women's studies. Compiles and disseminates information pertaining to women's issues and the history of the women's movement.

★322★ ASSOCIATION DES FEMMES TUNISIENNES POUR LA RECHERCHE ET LE DEVELOPPEMENT (AFTURD)
Cite SPROLS
Port 9, Appart. 4
2092 Elmenzah, Tunisia   PH: 1 880837
Melika Horchani Zamiti, Pres.   FX: 1 792170

Founded: 1988. **Members:** 100. **Budget:** 70,000 TD. **Languages:** French, Arabic. **National.** Women in Tunisia promoting research into women and women's issues. Works to increase the participation of women in the Tunisienne society. Promotes the role of women in society and history. Encourages the development of women culturally, socially, and economically. Conducts research on issues affecting women in Africa. **Committees:** Women and Work; Women and Law; Women and Education; Women and History; Women and Politics.

Publications: *Ibhathi*, quarterly. Bulletin. ● *Tunisiennes en Devenir: Comment les Femmes Vivent.* Book. ● *Tunisiennes en Devenir: La Moitie Entiere.* Book.

Conventions/Meetings: semiannual meeting - Tunis, Tunisia.

★323★ ASSOCIATION TUNISIENNE DU PLANNING FAMILIAL (ATPF)
9, rue Essoyouti   PH: 1 232419
El Menzah   1 232141
1004 Tunis, Tunisia   FX: 1 767263
Mr. Lotfi Labbane, Exec. Dir.   CBL: FAMPLAN TUNIS

Languages: Arabic, French. **National.** Advocates family planning as a basic human right. Works to reduce the number of unwanted pregnancies and abortions. Attempts to stop the spread of AIDS and other sexually transmitted diseases. Offers programs in sex education, family planning, and health. Provides contraceptive and health care services. Acts as an advocate for family planning on the national level.

★324★ COMMUNICATION DROITS DES FEMMES
Ligue Tunisienne
1, rue Canada
1002 Tunis, Tunisia

National. Strives to secure women's rights to participate in decision making, to speak and write freely and frankly, and to hold responsible leadership positions in society.

★325★ INTERNATIONAL PLANNED PARENTHOOD FEDERATION - TUNIS
17, rue Mahmoud El Materi   PH: 1 284173
Le Belvedere   1 284309
1002 Tunis, Tunisia   FX: 1 789934
Mr. Tijani Chaouch-Bouraoui, Director   TX: 15106 IPPF TN

Languages: French, Arabic. **National.** Advocates family planning as a basic human right in Tunisia. Works to increase governmental and public awareness of population problems. Promotes effective family planning services. Conducts research on human fertility and contraception.

★326★ NATIONAL FAMILY AND POPULATION OFFICE (NOFPP)
(ONFP Office National Famille et Population)
                                  PH: 1 341088
42, avenue de Madrid   FX: 1 354507
Tunis, Tunisia   TX: 15164 TN
Dr. Mohamed Boukhris, Exec. Officer   CBL: ONFP

Founded: 1973. **Languages:** Arabic, French. **National.** Encourages family planning activites in Tunisia in an effort to improve the general health and well-being of the populace. Conducts population and medical research programs; sponsors professional and continuing training courses for social and medical workers; compiles statistics. Offers children's services. Maintains biographical archives. **Libraries:** Type: reference. Holdings: 1,500. **Computer Services:** Data base.

Publications: *Famille et Population*, periodic. Magazine. • *Note d'Information*, periodic. • *Statistics Bulletin*, periodic. • *Sante Familia.* • Also publishes medical news and bibliographic index.

★327★ TUNISIAN NATIONAL WOMEN'S UNION (TNWU)
(Union Nationale des Femmes de Tunisie)
c/o MME Faiza Kefi
56, blvd. Bab Bjeknat   PH: 1 260178
1002 Tunis, Tunisia   1 260181
Mme. Faiza Kefi, Contact   FX: 1 567131

Founded: 1956. **Members:** 100,000. **Staff:** 115. **Regional Groups:** 27. **Languages:** French, Arabic. **National.** Umbrella organization of women and women's organizations in Tunisia. Seeks to improve women's social, economic, and political status. Works to: eliminate discrimination against women; end violence; raise awareness of women's rights; encourage women's education; improve working conditions; and insure quality health care. Defends access to facilities for safe childbirth. Encourages environmental protection and conservation. Conducts research; disseminates information. **Libraries:** Type: reference.

Conventions/Meetings: weekly seminar (exhibits).

Uganda

★328★ ACTION FOR DEVELOPMENT (ACFODE)
PO Box 16729
Wandegeya
Kampala, Uganda
Maude Mugisha, Exec.Sec.   PH: 41 245936

Founded: 1985. **Members:** 400. **Staff:** 18. **Budget:** US$370,000. **Languages:** English. **National.** Individuals in Uganda dedicated to improving the quality of life for women and helping them realize their full potential. Seeks to widen women's professional, educational, economic, and personal opportunities by increasing public awareness of the economic contributions of rural and working women and of the problems they face. Campaigns for a more

positive portrayal of women in all areas of society and works to ensure adequate representation and participation in local and national decisions affecting their status. Strives to eliminate sexual stereotyping in education, and fosters the study of gender issues at all levels. Maintains a research center to collect, process, and disseminate data on feminist activities in Uganda and other developing countries. Conducts seminars, workshops, and educational programs on family life and law. Provides assistance and support to self-help initiatives that offer growth opportunities for women. Bestows awards. **Committees:** Research; Education; Legal and Political; Projects.

Publications: *ACFODE Newsletter* (in English), quarterly. • *Arise* (in English), quarterly. Magazine. • *Women Breaking Through*, periodic. Report. • *Women's Legal Rights*, periodic. • *House.* Booklet. • *Responsible Adulthood.* Booklet. • *Adolescent Boy and Girl.* Booklet. • *Afterdeath.* Booklet.

Conventions/Meetings: monthly meeting.

★329★ ASSOCIATION OF WOMEN MEDICAL DOCTORS
PO Box 4121
Kampala, Uganda

Languages: English. **National.** Women doctors united to promote and maintain high standards in the medical profession. Fosters understanding and information exchange among members.

★330★ CHRISTIAN WOMEN FELLOWSHIP
PO Box 335
Kampala, Uganda

Languages: English. **National.** Anglican women in Uganda. Fosters friendly relations among members.

★331★ DAUGHTERS OF CHARITY
PO Box 6885
Kampala, Uganda

Languages: English. **National.** Women working to aid orphaned children. Provides children with medical care, shelter, and counselling.

★332★ FAMILY PLANNING ASSOCIATION OF UGANDA (FPAU)
PO Box 10746
Kampala, Uganda   PH: 41 258300
Mr. Serebe Sepuya, Exec. Dir.   TX: 61301 SAMPAN

Languages: English. **National.** Advocates family planning as a basic human right. Works to stop the spread of sexually transmitted diseases and reduce the number of unwanted pregnancies and abortions. Offers programs in sex education, family planning, and health. Acts as an advocate for family planning on the national level. Conducts research.

★333★ FIDA UGANDA
PO Box 2157
Kampala, Uganda

National. Offers legal assistance for indigent women. Supports and promotes the rights of women in Uganda.

★334★ FLORENCE NIGHTINGALE WOMEN'S ASSOCIATION
PO Box 1663
Kampala, Uganda

Languages: English. **National.** Women nurses in Uganda. Provides job placement assistance for women trained in nursing. Conducts educational programs.

★335★ KYEMBE WOMEN'S CREDIT AND SAVINGS COOPERATIVE
PO Box 950
Kampala, Uganda

Languages: English. **National.** Works to improve the socio-economic status of women. Assists women in attaining credit.

★336★ MEDICAL WOMEN'S INTERNATIONAL ASSOCIATION -
UGANDA
c/o AUWMD
PO Box 10035
Kampala, Uganda
Christine Biryabarema, Contact

Languages: English. **National.** Uganda national branch of the Medical Women's International Association (see separate entry). Women physicians. Provides a forum for discussion of women's health care issues. Encourages women to enter the field of medicine. Works to overcome discrimination against female physicians. Sponsors research and educational programs.

★337★ MOTHER'S UNION
Province Church of Uganda
PO Box 14123
Kampala, Uganda

Languages: English. **National.** Anglican mothers promoting the church in Uganda. Conducts children's and community service programs.

★338★ NATIONAL ASSOCIATION OF PRIVATE MIDWIVES
PO Box 30963
Kampala, Uganda

Languages: English. **National.** Independently practicing midwives in Uganda. Works to raise the status of midwifery. Provides a forum for communication and exchange among members.

★339★ NATIONAL ASSOCIATION OF REGISTERED NURSES AND
MIDWIVES
PO Box 8322
Kampala, Uganda

Languages: English. **National.** Women nurses and midwives practicing in Uganda. Seeks to improve the care received by mothers and babies. Promotes professional research and education.

★340★ NATIONAL ASSOCIATION OF WOMEN'S ORGANIZATIONS OF
UGANDA
PO Box 1663
Kampala, Uganda
Mrs. Florence Nekyon, Secretary   PH: 41 258463

Languages: English. **National.** Umbrella organization for women's groups in Uganda. Supports activities of women's organizations to enhance the status of women. Fosters communication among members. **Formerly:** National Council of Women.

★341★ NATIONAL UNION OF EDUCATIONAL INSTITUTIONS -
WOMEN'S WING
PO Box 16086
Kampala, Uganda

Languages: English. **National.** Seeks to advance educational opportunities for women in Uganda. Coordinates cultural and educational activities.

★342★ NATIONAL WOMEN AND CHILDREN'S COMMITTEE OF THE
BAHAI'S OF UGANDA
PO Box 2662
Kampala, Uganda

Languages: English. **National.** Fosters growth of the Baha'i faith. Works to improve the health and well-being of women and children. Conducts charitable programs.

★343★ SAFE MOTHERHOOD INITIATIVE
Plot 196 Upper Mawanda Rd.
PO Box 1191
Kampala, Uganda   PH: 41 235791

Languages: English. **National.** Seeks to improve women's health and to reduce the number of women who die from complications of pregnancy and childbirth. Promotes family planning activities; conducts educational programs on teenage sexuality, sexually transmitted diseases, AIDS, and parenting.

Publications: *Africa Women and Health*, periodic. Magazine.

Conventions/Meetings: periodic seminar.

★344★ SOROPTIMIST INTERNATIONAL OF UGANDA
PO Box 9314
Kampala, Uganda

Languages: English. **National.** Professional women working to promote human rights, peace, and international understanding. Fosters communication among members.

★345★ UGANDA ADVENTIST WOMEN'S ORGANISATION
PO Box 15034
Kampala, Uganda

Languages: English. **National.** Ugandan women of the Adventist faith. Fosters friendship among members.

★346★ UGANDA ASSOCIATION OF UNIVERSITY WOMEN (UAUW)
c/o Maria Musoke
Makerere University
PO Box 7062
Kampala, Uganda   PH: 41 533475
Maria Musoke, Chwm.   TX: 62104 MAKU

Founded: 1957. **Members:** 60. **Budget:** US$10,000. **Languages:** English. **National.** Unites university and other professional women to encourage higher education for women in Uganda. Offers career guidance, counseling, and financial support to girls and young women seeking university educations. Conducts research. Sponsors debates, lectures, seminars, and workshops. **Libraries:** Type: reference.   Subjects: women and development. **Committees:** Bursary Fund; Fundraising; International Relations; Research and Publications.

Publications: *Bulletin*, annual. ● *Women in Uganda: A Bibliography*, periodic.

Conventions/Meetings: monthly.

★347★ UGANDA CATHOLIC WOMEN'S GUILD
PO Box 14009
Kampala, Uganda

Languages: English. **National.** Seeks to unite Catholic women. Disseminates information on Catholic teachings.

★348★ UGANDA DISABLED WOMEN'S ASSOCIATION
PO Box 3368
Kampala, Uganda

Languages: English. **National.** Mentally and physically disabled women, their families, and individuals interested in the empowerment of disabled people. Works to develop equal opportunities for the disabled. Encourages unity among members.

★349★ UGANDA FEDERATION OF COMMUNITY DEVELOPMENT CLUBS
PO Box 7305
Kampala, Uganda

Languages: English. **National**. Seeks to develop the leadership skills of girls and young women through involvement in community service.

★350★ UGANDA GIRL GUIDES ASSOCIATION
PO Box 696
Kampala, Uganda   PH: 41 256872

Languages: English. **National**. Girls and women in Uganda. Fosters members' self-awareness, personal development, and leadership abilities.

★351★ UGANDA HOTELS FOOD AND ALLIED WORKERS' UNION - WOMEN'S WING
PO Box 3799
Kampala, Uganda

Languages: English. **National**. Women employed in hotels, bars, and restaurants in Uganda. Works to improve women's wages, working conditions, and benefits.

★352★ UGANDA INTERNATIONAL WOMEN'S CLUBS
PO Box 30196
Kampala, Uganda

Languages: English. **National**. Works to eliminate discrimination against women and promote equal rights with men. Fosters solidarity among members.

★353★ UGANDA MEDIA WOMEN'S ASSOCIATION
PO Box 7263
Kampala, Uganda

Languages: English. **National**. Women working in television, radio, or print media. Seeks to ensure equal employment opportunities for media women.

★354★ UGANDA MUSLIM LADIES ASSOCIATION
PO Box 608
Kampala, Uganda

Languages: English. **National**. Muslim women in Uganda. Spreads knowledge of Islamic culture. Advocates women's religious development.

★355★ UGANDA MUSLIM WOMEN'S ASSOCIATION
PO Box 1146
Kampala, Uganda

Languages: English. **National**. Women united to promote Islamic teachings. Liaises with other Muslim organizations.

★356★ UGANDA POSTS AND TELECOMMUNICATIONS EMPLOYEES UNION - WOMEN'S WING
PO Box 1410
Kampala, Uganda

Languages: English. **National**. Women postal and telephone workers. Seeks to improve members' standard of living and working conditions.

★357★ UGANDA TRADITIONAL BIRTH ATTENDANTS ASSOCIATION
PO Box 31049
Kampala, Uganda

Languages: English. **National**. Promotes education concerning natural childbirth. Conducts research and educational programs regarding midwifery.

★358★ UGANDA WOMEN DOCTORS' ASSOCIATION
c/o Mulago Hospital
PO Box 7051
Kampala, Uganda

National. Women physicians and health professionals. Works to increase public awareness of women's health needs. Provides medical assistance.

★359★ UGANDA WOMEN ENTREPRENEURS ASSOCIATION
PO Box 10002
Kampala, Uganda

Languages: English. **National**. Women who manage their own businesses. Works to improve professional status of women and create friendship and business links among members.

★360★ UGANDA WOMEN FOUNDATION FUND
PO Box 4531   PH: 41 258138
Kampala, Uganda   FX: 41 245580

Languages: English. **National**. Works to improve the financial and health status of women in Uganda. Conducts community ecological programs. Offers financial assistance to needy women. Organizes and coordinates activities intended to improve living conditions.

★361★ UGANDA WOMEN'S EFFORT TO SAVE ORPHANS (UWESO)
Uganda House
Popular Garnments
Box 6885
Kampala, Uganda

Languages: English. **National**. Women in Uganda providing aid and assistance to orphaned children.

★362★ UGANDA WOMEN'S FINANCE CREDIT AND TRUST FUND
PO Box 6972
Kampala, Uganda

Languages: English. **National**. Promotes the economic development of women in Uganda. Makes available loans to women to better serve their socio-economic needs. Provides management training.

★363★ UGANDA WOMEN'S LAWYERS' ASSOCIATION
PO Box 2157
Kampala, Uganda

National. Women lawyers and individuals interested in protecting women's rights. Conducts legal aid clinics to increase women's awareness of law. Represents women and women's rights in court cases.

★364★ WEST NILE WOMEN'S ASSOCIATION
PO Box 6532
Kampala, Uganda

Languages: English. **National**. Encourages fellowship and exchange among members. Conducts activities.

★365★ WOMEN'S GLOBAL NETWORK ON REPRODUCTIVE RIGHTS - UGANDA
Box 2395
Kampala, Uganda

Languages: English. **National**. Ugandan branch of international network of women's health groups, reproductive rights campaigns, clinics, health workers, and interested individuals. Supports a woman's right to decide if and when to have children; defends the right to safe, effective contraceptives, legal abortion, and freedom from sterilization abuse. Campaigns on a variety of related topics. Seeks to raise public awareness of issues surrounding maternal mortality and illness.

★366★ YOUNG WOMEN'S CHRISTIAN ASSOCIATION - UGANDA
PO Box 2018   PH: 41 241519
Kampala, Uganda   41 242024
Joyce Mungherera, Gen.Sec.   FX: 41 241519

Languages: English. **National.** Christian women in Uganda. Offers vocational training, educational programs, and cultural exchange to girls and women.

Zaire

★367★ ASSOCIATION ZAIROISE POUR LE BIEN-ETRE FAMILIAL
   (AZBEF)
BP 15313   PH: 12 26175
Kinshasa, Zaire   TX: 21536 LASCO ZR

Languages: French. **National.** Works to improve the quality of life for individuals living in Zaire by promoting responsible parenthood and family planning. Attempts to reduce the number of unwanted pregnancies and abortions. Offers programs in sex education, family planning, and health. Provides contraceptive and health care services. Acts as an advocate for family planning on the national level.

★368★ CENTRE DE FORMATION FEMININE
BP 289
Mbuji Mayi, Zaire

Languages: French. **National.** Promotes the interests and concerns of women in Zaire. Active in areas such as education and health.

★369★ FEMMES SOLIDAIRES POUR LE DEVELOPPEMENT AU
   BUSHI (FESODEBU)
BP 1058
Bukavu, Zaire

Languages: French. **National.** Women actively involved in Zaire's rural development. Supports and sponsors activities in areas such as agriculture, breeding of livestock, literacy, cooperatives, and health.

Zambia

★370★ ASSOCIATION FOR THE ADVANCEMENT OF WOMEN IN
   AFRICA
PO Box 35500
Kabwe, Zambia
Joyce Mapoma, Contact

Languages: English. **Multinational.** Works to enhance the social and economic status of women in Africa.

★371★ BUSINESS AND PROFESSIONAL WOMEN - ZAMBIA
Box 360131
Kafue, Zambia

Languages: English. **National.** Promotes the interests of business and professional women in Zambia.

★372★ PLANNED PARENTHOOD ASSOCIATION OF SELF-HELP
   DEVELOPMENT IN ZAMBIA (PPAZ)
Box 34356
Lusaka, Zambia

Languages: English. **National.** Encourages family planning activities in Zambia and promotes family planning as a basic human right. Works to improve maternal and child health, and to decrease the incidence of unwanted pregnancy. Provides information and education on reproductive issues.

★373★ PLANNED PARENTHOOD ASSOCIATION OF ZAMBIA (PPAZ)
                          PH: 1 217613
PO Box 32221   1 217437
Lusaka, Zambia   TX: 40293 PLAPAZ ZA
Mrs. Margaret Mutambo, Exec. Dir.   CBL: PLAPAZA

Languages: English. **National.** Advocates family planning as a basic human right. Works to reduce the number of unwanted pregnancies and abortions and stop the spread of sexually transmitted diseases, especially AIDS. Offers programs in sex education, family planning, and health. Provides contraceptive services. Acts as an advocate for family planning on the national level.

★374★ SOUTH AFRICA WOMEN'S INITIATIVE PROJECT
c/o Zambia Association for Research
   and Development
PO Box 37836   PH: 1 224507
Lusaka, Zambia   FX: 1 222883

Founded: 1992. **Languages:** English. **National.** A project of the Zambia Association for Research and Development (see separate entry). Studies the progress of the women's movement in South Africa. Conducts workshops on topics such as gender issues, promotion of women's issues through publications, and networking among women and women's organizations. Plans to establish a publishing house for the publication of materials promoting women's issues in South Africa.

★375★ WOMEN'S LEAGUE (WL)
Freedom House
PO Box 30302
Lusaka, Zambia
Bernadette N. Sikanyika, Sec.   PH: 1 224107

Founded: 1958. **Members:** 500,000. **Staff:** 200. **Budget:** US$1,800,000. **Languages:** English. **National.** A political group working to organize the women of Zambia through the United Nations Independence Party. Encourages support of the party by younger generations. Cooperates with similar women's organizations in an effort to eradicate all forms of discrimination. Promotes the establishment of small-scale industry, cooperatives, and nurseries. Aims to secure increased educational scholarships for women. Conducts educational programs in family planning, literacy, and business entrepreneurship. Sponsors research on women in agriculture, politics, education, and the media. Campaigns for job opportunity awareness for women. Holds seminars and workshops. **Libraries:** Type: reference. Holdings: 300.

Publications: *Annual Report* (in English). ● *Five Year Report* (in English). ● *Women's Magazine* (in English), quarterly.

Conventions/Meetings: triennial.

★376★ WOMEN'S NGO COORDINATING COMMITTEE IN ZAMBIA
1st Fl., Bible House
PO Box 37879
Freedom Way
Lusaka, Zambia   PH: 1 21384

National. Umbrella organization coordinating the activities of women's non-governmental organizations in Zambia. Organizes programs. Maintains a documentation center. Encourages women and women's organizations to interact.

Zimbabwe

★377★ WOMENSPEAK
BAM International
Regionalal Coordinator
PO Box 35624
Lusaka, Zambia

National. Encourages women to participate in personal and community development programs. Provides a forum for women to exchange ideas. Coordinates activities.

Publications: *Womenspeak.* Newsletter.

★378★ YOUNG WOMEN'S CHRISTIAN ASSOCIATION - ZAMBIA
PO Box 50115
Lusaka, Zambia
Mary Kazunga, Gen.Sec.   PH: 1 254751

National. Promotes the develpment of young women in Zambia. Upholds Christian beliefs and values in its programs. Works to instill self worth and self-esteem in young women.

★379★ ZAMBIA ALLIANCE OF WOMEN
PO Box 51068
Lusaka, Zambia
Mrs. Fanni Chikamba, President

Languages: English. **National.** Seeks to enhance women's standard of living. Promotes awareness of women's issues.

★380★ ZAMBIA ASSOCIATION FOR RESEARCH AND DEVELOPMENT
(ZARD)
PO Box 37836
Lusaka, Zambia   PH: 1 224507
Evelyn Mwila, Exec. Secty.   FX: 1 222883

Founded: 1984. **Members:** 300. **Membership Dues:** Individuals outside Zambia., US$50; Organizations outside Zambia., US$100; Individuals in Zambia., 250 ZKw; Organizations in Zambia., 500 ZKw. **Staff:** 4. **Languages:** English. **National.** Conducts research on the role of women in Zambia. Encourages discussion on gender roles. Acts as a forum for the exchange of information for individuals and groups interested in women's issues. Works to influence government policy to improve women's place in society. Sponsors seminars and workshops. Offers computer training programs and legal education courses. Operates a resource center that collects information and documents on women. **Telecommunication Services:** Electronic mail. **Committees:** Co-ordinating; Projects.

Publications: *Newsletter*, periodic.

Conventions/Meetings: annual (exhibits) - 1993 Sept. 6 - 7, Lusaka, Zambia.
● monthly executive committee meeting.

★381★ ZAMBIA MEDIA WOMEN'S ASSOCIATION (ZAMWA)
PO Box 30007   PH: 1 251631
Lusaka, Zambia   FX: 1 251631
Rosemary Nyaywa, Contact   TX: 42120

Founded: 1990. **Members:** 170. **Languages:** English. **National.** Women employed in media fields, student journalists, and others. Seeks to raise awareness of women's issues through the media and via public forums, such as debates, marches, workshops, and seminars. Supports a more positive portrayal of women in the media. Works to improve women's health care, rights and employment. Fosters communication among members. Conducts research. **Committees:** Image Monitoring and Current Affairs; Training; Fundraising; Projects.

Conventions/Meetings: quarterly seminar.

★382★ ASSOCIATION OF WOMEN OF ZIMBABWE
c/o Mrs. Granger
24 Kirrie Close
Marlborough, Zimbabwe

Languages: English. **National.** Works to coordinate activities of women's voluntary organizations in Zimbabwe. Primary objective is to "promote the welfare of mankind, the family, and the individual." Works with women's voluntary organizations worldwide.

★383★ ASSOCIATION OF WOMEN'S CLUBS (AWC)
PO Box UA 339
Harare, Zimbabwe
Mrs. B.F. Mtero, Exec. Dir.   PH: 263 726910

Members: 20,000. **Languages:** English. **National.** Women's non-governmental organizations in Zimbabwe. Primary objective is to empower women to participate fully in the development of their communities, thus contributing to the improvement of their socio-economic status. Provides a broad range of skills training programs to member organizations. Focuses on courses in: vocational, domestic, and income-generating skills; pre-school education; nutrtition; hygiene; forestry; club management.

Publications: *AWC News.* Newsletter.

★384★ FEDERATION OF AFRICAN MEDIA WOMEN - ZIMBABWE
(FAMW)
c/o Zimbabwe Inter-Africa News Agency   PH: 4 730151
PO Box 8166   4 730153
Causeway   FX: 4 794336
Harare, Zimbabwe   TX: 26133 ZW
Henry E. Muradzikwa, Editor-in-Chief   CBL: ZIANA

Founded: 1981. **Staff:** 80. **Budget:** Z$3,000,000. **Languages:** English. **National.** Female media professionals, organizations, or institutions working for the improvement of the status of women in Zimbabwe. Promotes the development and education of media women. Provides training to enhance skills. Disseminates information on the status of women's development in Zimbabwe. Conducts regional workshops and seminars. Bestows scholarships.

Conventions/Meetings: monthly general assembly - Harare, Zimbabwe.

★385★ INTERNATIONAL RESOURCE NETWORK OF WOMEN OF
AFRICAN DESCENT (IRNWAD)
Box 648
Avondale
Harare, Zimbabwe

National. Works to increase solidarity among women of African descent. Strives to improve social and economic conditions for women of African descent.

Publications: *Network: Pan-African Women's Forum.* Book.

★386★ NATIONAL FEDERATION OF BUSINESS AND PROFESSIONAL
WOMEN OF ZIMBABWE
1 Mimosa St.   PH: 20 62429
Mutare, Zimbabwe   20 64224

Languages: English. **National.** Works to organize business and professional women in Zimbabwe, and throughout the world. Encourages members to use their combined skills and strengths to accomplish goals that will be of benefit to all women.

★387★ SOCIETY FOR THE PROTECTION OF THE UNBORN CHILD
14 Princess Dr.
Highlands
Harare, Zimbabwe   PH: 4 732429

Languages: English. **National.** Right-to-life organization in Zimbabwe. Provides counselling and assistance to women and girls dealing with unplanned pregnancies. Loans maternity clothing and baby equipment. Offers education in usage of family planning techniques.

★388★ UNION OF JEWISH WOMEN (UJW)
3 Lorna Rd.
Mt. Pleasant
Harare, Zimbabwe   PH: 4 304900
Mrs. S. Pitluck, Pres.   FX: 4 731396

Budget: Z$6,000. **Local Groups:** 2. **Languages:** English. **National.** Goodwill and service club of Jewish women dedicated to helping the needy. Visits and provides entertainment for residents of old age and children's homes; collects and distributes clothing to needy children; sponsors Annual party for underprivileged children. Conducts cultural talks and fundraising activities.

★389★ WOMEN, LAW AND DEVELOPMENT
H5 Lambtan Ct.
186 Baines Ave.
Harare, Zimbabwe

National. Women lawyers and individuals interested in improving women's standard of living. Offers legal advice and assistance for women. Conducts educational programs to increase women's awareness of their rights. Organizes and coordinates activities among women's law groups. Researches legal and women's issues; disseminates information.

★390★ WOMEN IN LAW AND DEVELOPMENT IN AFRICA (WILDAF)
PO Box 4622
Harare, Zimbabwe

Languages: English. **Multinational.** Seeks to empower women through legal education, law reform, and legal services. Operates training and educational programs on legal literacy. Conducts research and disseminates information on legal issues affecting women. Coordinates activities with other organizations concerned with women and the law.

Publications: *Newsletter*, periodic. ● *Directory*, periodic.

★391★ WOMEN AND LAW IN SOUTHERN AFRICA PROJECT (WLSA)
PO Box UA 171   PH: 4 729151
Union Ave.   4 729152
Harare, Zimbabwe   FX: 4 729152

Languages: English. **Multinational.** Works to improve the quality of life for women living in Botswana, Lesotho, Mozambique, Swaziland, Zambia, and Zimbabwe through improving their legal rights. Sponsors programs to educate women about their legal rights. Offers legal advice. Organizes campaigns to change laws that are biased against women. Offers a forum for exchange of information for international women's organizations. Conducts research on issues relevant to women and law, such as family and inheritance laws. Disseminates information; compiles statistics. **Computer Services:** Data base, research results.

Publications: *Newsletter*, quarterly.

Conventions/Meetings: periodic seminar.

★392★ WOMEN'S ACTION GROUP (WAG)
PO Box 135
Harare, Zimbabwe
Salina Rauiro Mumbengegwi, Director   PH: 4 702986

Founded: 1983. **Members:** 3,000. **Staff:** 10. **Languages:** English. **National.** Promotes the economic, social, educational, and cultural advancement of

women in Zimbabwe. Supports public education programs focusing on the basic human rights of women. Assists other organizations that provide advice and help for women. Empowers women to be directly involved in making decisions on issues regarding their lives. Lobbies the Zimbabwe government on legislation affecting women's lives. Conducts group discussions, workshops, and research surveys. Disseminates information on women's issues. **Libraries:** Type: reference.
Committees: Health Advisory.

Publications: *Speak Out* (in Shona and English), quarterly. Magazine. Information on legal, health, and societal issues pertaining to women. **Also Cited As:** *Khulumani.*

Conventions/Meetings: annual conference - Harare, Zimbabwe.

★393★ WOMEN'S ASSOCIATION OF ZIMBABWE
PO Box MR 37
Marloborough
Harare, Zimbabwe
Dr. Graham, President

Languages: English. **National.** Women working to improve the standard of living in Zimbabwe. Encourages women to actively participate in development activities.

★394★ YOUNG WOMEN'S CHRISTIAN ASSOCIATION - ZIMBABWE
PO Box AY 154
Amby
Harare, Zimbabwe   PH: 4 44124
Evelyn Shawa, Gen.Sec.   4 44191

Founded: 1957. **Members:** 2,000. **Staff:** 20. **Local Groups:** 60. **Languages:** English, Shona. **National.** Young christian women in Zimbabwe; adult women sponsors. Promotes peace and justice. Strives to develop members' leadership and self-reliance skills and increase their awareness for "total development of the body, soul, and mind." Sponsors charitable program for the needy and refugee programs. Operates nurseries and educational programs for children. Maintains speakers' bureau. Organizes competitions. Conducts workshops and seminars for leadership development. **Committees:** Building; Christian Identity; Leadership Development; Projects; Public Relations; Youth.

Publications: *Annual Report* (in English and Shona).

Conventions/Meetings: annual conference (exhibits). ● biennial Council Meeting.

★395★ ZIMBABWE NATIONAL FAMILY PLANNING COUNCIL (ZNFPC)
PO Box 220
Southerton   PH: 4 67656
Harare, Zimbabwe   4 67657
Dr. Norbert Mugwagwa, Exec. Dir.   TX: 26521 ZW

Languages: English. **National.** Promotes family planning and responsible parenthood as a means to improve the quality of life for individuals living in Zimbabwe. Advocates family planning as a basic human right. Works to reduce the number of unwanted pregnancies and abortions. Offers programs in family planning, sex education, and health. Provides contraceptive and health care services. Conducts research.

★396★ ZIMBABWE WOMEN'S BUREAU
43 Hillside Rd.
PO Cranborne
Harare, Zimbabwe   PH: 4 734205
Lydia Chikwavaire, Coordinator/Director   FX: 4 734295

Founded: 1978. **Members:** 3,000. **Staff:** 25. **Budget:** US$2,835,454. **Regional Groups:** 13. **Languages:** English. **National.** Umbrella organization promoting awareness of issues affecting women in developing regions of Zimbabwe. Works to improve the quality of life for women through the establishment of stable financial resources. Sponsors programs in food production, adult literacy, health, and nutrition. Conducts research.

Committees: Personal; Projects; Information; Fundraising.

Publications: *Newsletter* (in English), periodic. ● *Directory* (in English), periodic.

Conventions/Meetings: semiannual (exhibits) - Harare, Zimbabwe.

★397★ ZIMBABWE WOMEN'S RESOURCE CENTRE AND NETWORK
   (ZWRCN)
PO Box 2192
Harare, Zimbabwe
Sithembile Nyoni, Coord.

Founded: 1990. **Languages:** English. **National**. Works to enhance the role of women in Zimbabwean society. Conducts research on issues affecting women in Zimbabwe. Encourages public awareness of problems facing women. Acts as a forum for the exchange of information among women's associations. Serves as an information clearinghouse on women's issues. **Libraries:** Type: lending. Holdings: books, periodicals. Subjects: women's issues. **Computer Services:** Data base, organizations and individuals working on gender and development issues.

Publications: *ZWRCN News Bulletin* (in English), semiannual. **Advertising:** not accepted.

Conventions/Meetings: periodic workshop.

★398★ ZIMBIL ASSOCIATION
15 Baker Ave.
Harare, Zimbabwe   PH: 4 705067

Languages: English. **National**. Promotes and teaches the Billings method of natural family planning in which women are taught to recognize the fertile phase of their menstrual cycle by analyzing the appearance of mucus secreted from the cervix. Provides information and education to the public.

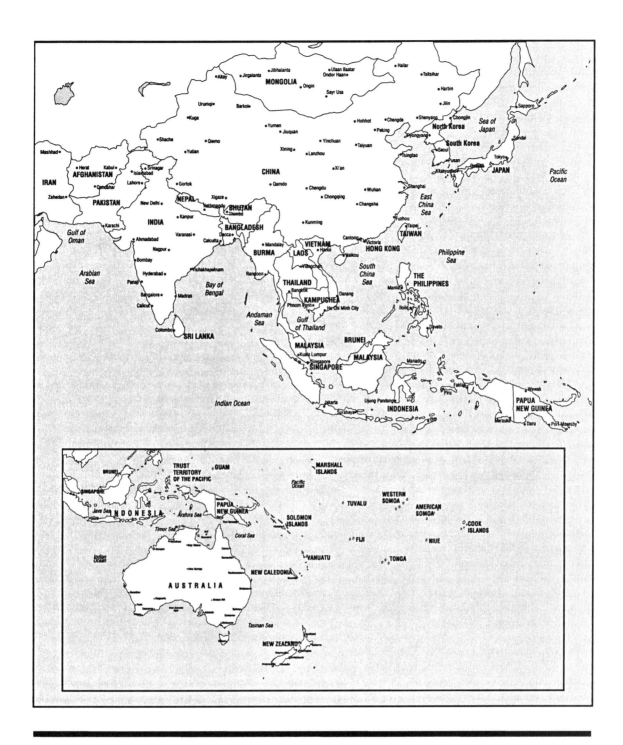

Asia and the Pacific

Afganistan
American Samoa
Australia
Bangladesh
Bhutan
Brunei Darussalam
China, People's Republic of
Cook Islands
Fiji
French Polynesia
Guam
Hong Kong

India
Indonesia
Japan
Kiribati
Korea, Democratic People's
  Republic of
Korea, Republic of
Lao People's Democratic
  Republic
Malaysia
Marshall Islands

Mongolia
Myanmar
Nepal
New Caledonia
New Zealand
Niue
Pakistan
Papua New Guinea
Philippines
Singapore

Solomon Islands
Sri Lanka
Taiwan
Thailand
Tonga
Trust Territory of the Pacific
  Islands
Tuvalu
Vanuatu
Vietnam
Western Samoa

Asia and the Pacific

Afghanistan

★399★ AFGHANISTAN FAMILY GUIDANCE ASSOCIATION (AFGA)
PO Box 545
Kartichar, Opposite General Depot of
  Medicine   PH: 22659
Kabul, Afghanistan   CBL: FAMILYGUIDE
Mr. Said Negatullah Hussaini, Exec. Dir.   KABUL

Languages: Pashto, English. **National**. Works to improve the quality of life for individuals living in Afghanistan by promoting responsible parenthood and family planning. Advocates family planning as a basic human right. Seeks to reduce the number of unwanted pregnancies and abortions. Sponsors programs in sex education, family planning, and health. Attempts to stop the spread of sexually transmitted diseases, especially AIDS. Conducts research programs.

★400★ DEMOCRATIC WOMEN'S ORGANIZATION OF AFGHANISTAN
Ministry of Foreign Affairs
Government of Democratic Republic of
  Afghanistan
Kabul, Afghanistan

National. Women advocating democratic principles in Afghanistan.

American Samoa

★401★ AMERICAN SAMOA PLANNED PARENTHOOD ASSOCIATION
PO Box 1043
Pago Pago, American Samoa

Languages: English. **National**. Promotes responsible parenthood and family planning as a means to improve the quality of life for people living in American Samoa. Advocates family planning as a basic human right. Sponsors programs in sex education, family planning, and health. Provides contraceptive and health care services.

★402★ YOUNG WOMEN'S CHRISTIAN ASSOCIATION - SAMOA
PO Box 4829
Pago Pago, American Samoa 96799
Tasi L. Petri, Gen.Sec.   FX: 6332721

National. Promotes the development of young women in American Samoa. Upholds Christian beliefs and values in its programs. Works to instill self worth and self-esteem in young women.

Australia

★403★ ASSOCIATION OF CIVILIAN WIDOWS
3 Forth St.
Kempsey, NSW 2440, Australia
Mrs. Joyce Thurgood, President

Languages: English. **National**. Fosters cooperation and friendly relations among widowed women in Australia. Coordinates social and community service activities.

★404★ ASSOCIATION OF NON-ENGLISH SPEAKING BACKGROUND
  WOMEN OF AUSTRALIA
2/133 Parramatta Rd.
Granville, NSW 2142, Australia   PH: 2 6374370
Ms. Debbie Georgopoulos, Contact   FX: 2 6376129

Founded: 1986. **Members:** 332. **Budget:** $A 85,000. **Languages:** English. **National**. Organizations and individuals. Lobbies government on issues of interest to immigrant women in Australia. Seeks to abolish racism and sexism. Assists immigrant women in job training and placement; provides access to childcare. Offers English language classes and health care. Conducts research. **Libraries:** Type: reference.

Publications: *ANESBWA Newsletter* (in English), quarterly. ● *Annual Report* (in English). ● Also publishes members' papers.

Conventions/Meetings: biennial meeting (exhibits).

★405★ ASSOCIATION OF WOMEN'S FORUM CLUBS OF AUSTRALIA
5 Skye Ct.
Sorrento, QLD 4217, Australia
Joyce Feige, Secretary   PH: 75 317163

Founded: 1941. **Members:** 450. **Budget:** $A 10,000. **Languages:** English. **National**. Women of all age groups and ethnic backgrounds. Promotes the enhancement of administrative and communication skills among women. Seeks to improve confidence and self-esteem in women by providing speech and communication training. Conducts educational programs and seminars.

Publications: *Mr. Chairman.* ● *How to Chair a Meeting.* ● *Speaking in Public.*

Conventions/Meetings: biennial conference. ● annual convention.

★406★ AUSTRALIAN CHURCH WOMEN
PO Box 44
Burnie, TAS 7320, Australia   PH: 4 312973
Mrs. A. Fitzgerald, Secretary   FX: 4 316222

Languages: English. **National**. Australian Christian women. Promotes unification, understanding, and cooperation among women in the church, the family, and in society. Provides opportunities for Christian women of varying denominations to study and interact together. **Awards:** Winifred Keil Scholarship.

Conventions/Meetings: biennial conference.

★407★ AUSTRALIAN COUNCIL OF TRADE UNION - WOMEN'S
COMMITTEE
393-397 Swanston St.
Melbourne, VIC 3000, Australia
Mr. Martin Ferguson, Contact

Languages: English. **National**. Works to improve women's working conditions, wages, and employment opportunities. Promotes solidarity among working women in Australia.

★408★ AUSTRALIAN FEDERATION OF BUSINESS AND
PROFESSIONAL WOMEN
PO Box 617
Belconnen, ACT 2616, Australia
Ms. Di Manning, President

Languages: English. **National**. Provides a forum for business women to establish personal and professional contacts. Seeks to improve the status of working women.

★409★ AUSTRALIAN FEDERATION OF UNIVERSITY WOMEN (AFUW)
PO Box 6620
Upper Mt. Gravatt
Queensland, TAS 4122, Australia   PH: 7 3457141
Mrs. H. Webb, Sec.   FX: 7 8757507

Founded: 1922. **Members:** 2,000. **Local Groups:** 8. **Languages:** English. **National**. Female university graduates. Fosters communication and exchange among members in order to advance and improve the status of women. Lobbies on women's issues. Encourages cooperation with other women's organizations. Promotes educational programs and members' active participation in program development. Sponsors lectures, conferences, discussion groups, and seminars. **Computer Services:** Data base.

Publications: *Newsletter*, quarterly.

Conventions/Meetings: triennial convention - 1994. ● bimonthly meeting.

★410★ AUSTRALIAN NATIONAL CONSULTATIVE COMMITTEE ON
REFUGEE WOMEN (ANCCORW)
69-71 Parramatta Rd.
Camperdown, NSW 2050, Australia   PH: 2 5659121
Eileen Pittaway, Contact   FX: 2 5504509

Founded: 1989. **Members:** 120. **Languages:** English. **National**. Refugee women and people working on their behalf. Lobbies and advocates for refugee women. Provides employment and training programs. **Programs:** Jobskills.

Conventions/Meetings: periodic meeting.

★411★ AUSTRALIAN NATIONAL WOMAN'S CHRISTIAN
TEMPERANCE UNION
5 Cecil St.
Gordon, NSW 2072, Australia
Joan Cocks, Treas.   PH: 2 4987937

Founded: 1891. **Members:** 5,207. **Staff:** 7. **Budget:** $A 24,522. **State Groups:** 7. **Local Groups:** 104. **Languages:** English. **National**. Individuals in Australia united to end drug and alcohol use through Christian education. Coordinates visits to educational institutions; communicates concerns to government authorities. Operates speakers' bureau and charitable programs. Conducts training programs. Sponsors contests for children and youth; bestows awards. Offers library services through state branches. **Departments:** Alcohol-Free Hospitality; Christian Outreach; Citizenship; Education; Home Protection; Promotions' Methods; Public Relations; Social Services. **Programs:** Abstaining Christians Everywhere; Recruit Australian Children Everywhere.

Publications: *White-Ribbon Signal* (in English), bimonthly. ● *Booklet*.

Conventions/Meetings: periodic meeting (exhibits) - 1995, Sydney, NW, Australia.

★412★ AUSTRALIAN WOMEN LAWYERS' FORUM
PO Box 14
Hawker, ACT 2614, Australia
Ms. Margaret Brewster, Exec. Dir.

Languages: English. **National**. Women lawyers and scholars of law. Lobbies government to improve women's rights under the law.

★413★ AUSTRALIAN WOMEN'S EDUCATION COALITION
PO Box 6267
East Perth, WA 6004, Australia

Languages: English. **National**. Works to improve the status of women through improved education. Fosters equality between the sexes.

★414★ AUSTRALIAN WOMEN'S HEALTH NETWORK
Canberra Women's Health Centre
Box 1492
Woden, ACT 2606, Australia   PH: 6 2902166
Ms. Dorothy Broom, Contact   FX: 6 2864742

Founded: 1989. **Languages:** English. **National**. Lobbies government on women's health issues. Promotes eqitable access to health care for all people; works to eliminate discrimination in health care on the basis of ethnicity, age, sexual orientation, or disability. Supports a woman's ability to control her reproductive choices. Fosters development of women's health groups and services. Provides a national forum for discussion of women's health care issues.

★415★ CATHOLIC WOMEN'S LEAGUE OF AUSTRALIA
GPO Box 889
Adelaide, SA 5001, Australia
Ms. Patricia Fitzpatrick, President

Languages: English. **National**. Women working to promote Catholic beliefs in Australia. Sponsors community service activities.

★416★ COALITION OF AUSTRALIA PARTICIPATING ORGANISATION
OF WOMEN
PO Box 4586
Kingston, ACT 2604, Australia

Languages: English. **National**. Umbrella organization for women's groups in Australia. Seeks to raise women's status. Coordinates activities for member groups.

★417★ COMMISSION FOR THE STATUS OF WOMEN - AUSTRALIAN
COUNCIL OF CHURCHES
Clarence St.
PO Box C199
Sydney, NSW 2000, Australia
Ms. J. Nelson-Clegg, Contact

National. Religious women's organization. Promotes improved status and development of women in Australia.

★418★ CONSTRUCTIVE WOMEN
PO Box 294
Cammeray, NSW 2062, Australia

Founded: 1983. **Members:** 150. **Languages:** English. **National**. Women involved in the field of architecture. Promotes women in their careers as architects. Provides a support group. Sponsors seminars and group meetings. Contacts and encourages students by giving talks. Contributes to forums on building and planning issues. Holds and participates in exhibits.

Publications: *Constructive Times* (in English), quarterly.

★419★ COUNTRY WOMEN'S ASSOCIATION - AUSTRALIA
40 Fort St.
Riverside, TAS 7250, Australia
Mrs. Ailsa Bond, President

National. Promotes and supports the interests and development of rural women.

★420★ DOMESTIC VIOLENCE TASK FORCE, WOMEN'S INTEREST
   DIVISION
197 St. Georges Terr., 2nd Fl.
Perth, WA, Australia   PH: 8 4209631

National. Offers support services to victims of domestic violence, such as: shelters, recovery programs, support groups, advocacy, and counseling. Works towards the development of legislation to firmly protect the rights of victims and enforces action against aggressors. Disseminates information.

★421★ ELISHEVA GROUP NA'AMAT (EGN)
4 Alfriston St.
Melbourne, Elwood 3184, Australia
Rachelle Banshevska, Contact   PH: 3 5311500

Languages: English. **Multinational.** Working and professional women. Works to advance the status of women by providing a variety of educational, community, and legal services. Believes that strong family relations are the foundation of a stable society. Members identify with the Zionist movement.

★422★ FAMILY PLANNING FEDERATION OF AUSTRALIA (FPFA)
LUA Bldg., Ste. 3, 1st Fl.
39 Geils Ct.
PO Box 26   PH: 62 851244
Deakin, ACT, Australia   FX: 62 825298
Ms. Dianne Proctor, Exec. Dir.   TX: AA121822 SY2840

Languages: English. **National.** Promotes family planning and responsible parenthood. Advocates family planning as a basic human right. Works to reduce the number of unwanted pregnancies and abortions. Sponsors programs to stop the spread of sexually transmitted diseases, especially AIDS. Provides contraceptive services. Conducts research.

★423★ FEDERAL WOMEN'S COMMITTEE - LIBERAL PARTY OF
   AUSTRALIA
Blackall & Macquarie Sts.
Barton, ACT 2600, Australia
Ms. Kristine Incher, Secretary

National. Women's political organization. Supports free enterprise and individual liberties.

★424★ FEMINIST INTERNATIONAL NETWORK OF RESISTANCE TO
   REPRODUCTIVE AND GENETIC ENGINEERING (FINNRAGE)
PO Box 248
East Kew, VIC 3102, Australia
Christine Ewing, Contact

Languages: English. **National.** Works to discourage the extraordinary measures taken by medical professionals to improve a woman's fertility. Aims to eliminate the practice of genetic engineering and experimentation. Conducts research; disseminates information.

Publications: *FINNRAGE* (in English), periodic. Journal.

★425★ GIRL GUIDES ASSOCIATION OF AUSTRALIA
PO Box 6
Strawberry Hills, NSW 2012, Australia   PH: 2 3197206
Mrs. Barbara Horsfield, Contact   FX: 2 3197453

Founded: 1926. **Members:** 90,000. **Budget:** $A 750,000. **Languages:** English. **National.** Girls and young women (ages 6 to 25). Provides training based on the fundamental principles of the Girl Guide movement. Conducts educational and recreational activities to prepare members for responsible citizenship. Encourages community service activities.

Publications: *Guiding in Australia* (in English), monthly. Newsletter.

★426★ INTERNATIONAL WOMEN'S DEVELOPMENT AGENCY (IWDA)
PO Box 1680
Collingwood, NSW 3066, Australia   PH: 3 4193004
Ms. Janet Hunt, Director   FX: 3 4160519

Founded: 1985. **Members:** 1,500. **Staff:** 2. **Budget:** $A 700,000. **Languages:** English. **Multinational.** Works to actively involve women in development projects. Maintains that many traditional development projects fail because they neglect to seek and consider women's input. Provides skill training programs. Fosters communication among development workers. Organizes informational forums and conducts educational courses. **Libraries:** Type: reference.

Publications: *International Women's Development Agency Report to Associates and Friends*, quarterly. Magazine.

★427★ LOCAL GOVERNMENT WOMEN'S ASSOCIATION
Forbes Shire Council
Forbes, NSW 2871, Australia
Diane Decker, President

Languages: English. **National.** Encourages women's participation in local politics throughout Australia. Seeks to advance the status of women.

★428★ MATERNITY ALLIANCE - AUSTRALIA (MA)
PO Box 314
Katoomba, NSW 2780, Australia   PH: 47 822008
Ms. Hilda Bastian, Coord.   TF: 47 825090

Founded: 1987. **Members:** 140. **Budget:** $A 15,000. **Languages:** English. **National.** Maternity consumer groups, interested consumers, and maternity professionals. Organizes consumer groups to ensure that women have an effective voice in issues relating to maternity care in Australia. Strives to improve the services offered to women during pregnancy, childbirth, and children's first years of life.

Publications: *MA News* (in English), biennial.

★429★ MEDICAL WOMEN'S INTERNATIONAL ASSOCIATION -
   AUSTRALIA (MIA-A)
38 Davenport Terr.
Wayville, SA 5034, Australia
Margret Moody, Contact

Languages: English. **National.** Australia branch of the Medical Women's International Association (see separate entry). Women physicians. Provides a forum for discussion of women's health care issues. Encourages women to enter the field of medicine. Works to overcome discrimination against female physicians. Sponsors research and educational programs.

★430★ MOVEMENT FOR THE ORDINATION OF WOMEN (MOW)
12/98 Vale St.
East Melbourne, VIC 3002, Australia
Dr. Janet Scarfe, President

National. Represents the movement of Australian women wishing to serve as ministers or priests.

★431★ NATIONAL COMMITTEE ON VIOLENCE AGAINST WOMEN
Office of the Status of Women
Prime Minister & Cabinet
3-5 National Circuit
Barton, ACT 2600, Australia
Helen L'Orange, Chair

Languages: English. **National.** Aims to erradicate violence against women. Seeks to raise public awareness of the dangers of sexism. Conducts research; disseminates infomation.

★432★ NATIONAL CONSULTATIVE GROUP OF SERVICE SPOUSES
PO Box 280
Civic Square, ACT 2608, Australia
Ms. Ula Gordon, Convenor

National. Provides advice and support to spouses of civil and military servants in Australia.

★433★ NATIONAL COUNCIL OF JEWISH WOMEN OF AUSTRALIA
    (NCJWA)
PO Box 57
Woollahra, NSW 2025, Australia
Dee Hitchings, Contact   PH: 2 3630257

Founded: 1923. **Members:** 2,000. **Local Groups:** 8. **Languages:** English. **National.** Women in Australia dedicated to improving, in the spirit of Judaism, the social welfare and status of women in the Jewish and general communities. Conducts community service and educational programs. Conducts fundraising programs for projects in Israel. Provides advocacy services; operates speaker's bureau. Offers Annual scholarship.

Publications: *Council Bulletin*, quarterly.

Conventions/Meetings: triennial conference.

★434★ NATIONAL COUNCIL FOR THE SINGLE MOTHER AND HER
    CHILD (NCSMC)
66 Johnston St.
PO Box 1399M
Collingwood   PH: 3 4151171
Melbourne, VIC 3001, Australia   3 4151172
Maree Kelly, Secretary   FX: 3 4151276

Founded: 1969. **Membership Dues:** Individual members., $A 4; Associate members., $A 8; Organizational members., $A 20. **Languages:** English. **National.** Promotes the interests of single mothers and their children. Monitors legislation affecting the lives and rights of single mothers. Disseminates information to community groups and professionals on sole parent issues. Conducts lectures, research, and consulting services. **Libraries:** Type: reference. Holdings: 0. Subjects: single parenting issues for women. **Computer Services:** Electronic publishing.

Publications: *The Scarlett Letter* (in English), bimonthly. ● *Sharing Homes Booklet.* ● *Mother Booklet.* ● *Tenant Advocacy Kit.* Directory.

★435★ NATIONAL COUNCIL OF WOMEN OF AUSTRALIA
PO Box 85
Stones Corner, QLD 4120, Australia
Yvonne Bain, President

Languages: English. **National.** Strives for the advancement of the status of women socially, economically, and legally, equal opportunity and social wefare for all, a peaceful and just society, and strong representation of the concerns and interests of women in government and business. Cooperates with governmental bodies at national and local levels. Networks with other women's and sister organizations nationally and internationally. Works with women towards the advancement of all people.

★436★ NATIONAL FOUNDATION OF AUSTRALIAN WOMEN (NFAW)
PO Box 1465
Canberra, ACT 2601, Australia   PH: 6 2472276
Ms. Mary Mortimer, Convenor   FX: 6 2472228

Founded: 1989. **Members:** 1,000. **Budget:** $A 50,000. **Languages:** English. **National.** Seeks to propagate feminist ideals. Sponsors feminist research activities; fosters communication among women's groups. Conducts educational programs. **Awards:** Grant. Recipient: individuals conducting women's research.

Publications: *Broadside* (in English), quarterly. Journal. ● *Tradeswomen's Directory* (in English), annual.

Conventions/Meetings: periodic seminar. ● periodic regional meeting.

★437★ NATIONAL STATUS OF WOMEN COMMITTEE
PO Box 553
Taralgon, VIC, Australia
Norma Ford, Contact

Languages: English. **National.** Seeks to improve the social, economic, and political status of women in Australia. Disseminates information on women' issues.

★438★ NATIONAL WOMEN'S HOUSING CAUCUS
PO Box 25   PH: 6 2473319
Hackett, ACT 2602, Australia   6 2472679
Ms. Lea Corbett, Coord.   FX: 6 2571814

Founded: 1988. **Members:** 11. **Budget:** $A 25,000. **Languages:** English. **National.** Seeks to improve housing facilities for women. Lobbies government on women's housing needs. Seeks to raise public awareness of discrimination in housing. Liaises with other women's housing action groups.

Conventions/Meetings: annual meeting.

★439★ NATIONAL WORKING PARTY II ON PORTRAYAL OF WOMEN
    IN THE MEDIA
50 Darling St.
Balmain, NSW 2041, Australia
Anne Deveson, Chair

Languages: English. **National.** Works to eliminate sexist portrayals of women in the media. Conducts research; dissemiates information.

★440★ NETWORK OF WOMEN STUDENTS
Women's Rights Area
University of Queensland
St. Lucia, QLD 4067, Australia
Ms. Fleur Yuile, Contact

Languages: English. **National.** Encourages women students' pursuit of higher education. Seeks to raise public awareness of women's issues. Conducts research; disseminates information.

★441★ NURSING MOTHERS' ASSOCIATION OF AUSTRALIA
PO Box 231
Nunawading, VIC 3131, Australia   PH: 3 8775011
Mrs. Joan Brendan, Exec. Officer   FX: 3 8943270

Founded: 1964. **Members:** 14,000. **Membership Dues:** $A 31 annual; $A 60 biennial. **Staff:** 24. **Budget:** $A 200,000. **Languages:** English. **National.** Encourages mothers in Australia to breastfeed their babies. Educates the public on the nutritional and emotional values of breastfeeding. Offers professional counselling services, 24-hour telephone helpline, and support group to mothers. Fosters communication among members. Conducts research. **Libraries:** Type: reference. Holdings: books, periodicals, clippings.

Publications: *NMAA Newsletter* (in English), bimonthly. ● *Breastfeeding Review* (in English), semiannual. Journal. ● *Talkabout* (in English). Magazine.

Conventions/Meetings: annual conference. ● monthly regional meeting.

★442★ OLDER WOMEN'S NETWORK
87 Lower Fort St.
Millers Point, NSW 2000, Australia
Ms. Joy Ross, Coord.
PH: 2 2477046
FX: 2 2474202

Founded: 1985. **Staff:** 1. **Budget:** $A 90,000. **Languages:** English. **National.** Seeks to protect older women from discrimination based on sex or age, especially in the areas of housing, health care, and social security. Raises public awareness of ageism and sexism through cabaret performance groups. Conducts self-help and educational programs. Offers bereavement and loss counselling.

Publications: *OWN Newsletter* (in English), monthly. ● *Making Known* (in English), semiannual. Magazine. ● Also publishes papers and reports.

Conventions/Meetings: biweekly seminar - Sydney, NW, Australia.

★443★ ORAH GROUP NA'AMAT (OGN)
8 Swinburne Ave.
Hawthorn, Melbourne 3122, Australia
Hava Rieder, Contact
PH: 3 8191382
FX: 3 5686290

Languages: English. **Multinational.** Working and professional women. Works to advance the status of women by providing a variety of educational, community, and legal services. Believes that strong family relations are the foundation of a stable society. Members identify with the Zionist movement.

★444★ PAN PACIFIC AND SOUTHEAST ASIA WOMEN'S
ASSOCIATION - AUSTRALIA
1 McCaw Pl.
Calwell, ACT 2905, Australia
Mrs. Val Nicholas, President

National. Women in Australia united to promote and support the development of Pacific and Southeast Asian women.

★445★ PHILIPPINE-AUSTRALIAN ALLIANCE OF WOMEN
Bononia Heights
Melbourne, VIC 3155, Australia
Mrs. Belen Mendonez, President

Languages: Filipino, English. **National.** Promotes friendly relations and understanding between women in the Philippines and Australia. Encourages cultural exchange and understanding.

★446★ QUOTA INTERNATIONAL - AUSTRALIA
2/5 Cove Ave.
Manly, NSW 2095, Australia
Ms. Julie-Rose Moffet, Director

National. Women business executives and professionals of Australia. Seek to create a network of service and friendship to improve women's quality of life. Espouses values such as the desire to serve country and community, a commitment to high ethical standards, and a belief in the worth of work and friendship.

★447★ SISTERS OF SAINT JOSEPH OF THE SACRED HEART (RSJ)
(Hermanas de San Jose del Sagrado Corazon)
11 Mount St.
North Sydney, NSW 2059, Australia
Sr. Mary Cresp RSJ, Leader
PH: 2 9297344
FX: 2 9540572

Founded: 1866. **Members:** 1,380. **Languages:** English, Spanish. **Multinational.** Sisters and volunteers in Australia, Republic of Ireland, New Zealand, and Peru. Has established 270 centers, mostly in rural areas, that offer

educational, medical, and social services. Engages in pastoral work. Offers children's services and charitable programs. Sponsors ministry conferences for members of the congregation.

Publications: *Soundings* (in English), semiannual.

Conventions/Meetings: periodic meeting.

★448★ SOCIETY OF WOMEN WRITERS OF AUSTRALIA
13B Peel Rd.
O'Connor, WA 6163, Australia
Constance M. Herbert, President
PH: 9 3312321

Languages: English. **National.** Female fiction and non-fiction writers. Offers advice on getting published. Provides a forum for exchange among members.

★449★ SOROPTIMIST INTERNATIONAL OF THE SOUTH WEST
PACIFIC (SISWP)
GPO Box 1439
Sydney, NSW 2001, Australia
Irma Reid, Exec. Officer
PH: 2 2350439
FX: 2 2350439

Founded: 1921. **Members:** 3,700. **Staff:** 1. **Languages:** English. **Multinational.** Business and professional women from 7 countries. Participates in the struggle for peace and human rights, particularly the rights of women. Compiles statistics. Bestows awards; offers scholarships; provides children's services.

Publications: *Soroptimist News*, periodic.

Conventions/Meetings: biennial conference - 1994.

★450★ UNIFEM OF AUSTRALIA
64 Lugg St.
Bardon, QLD 4065, Australia
Ms. Bev Perel, Contact

National. Promotes solidarity among women in Australia.

★451★ UNION OF AUSTRALIAN WOMEN (UAW)
Trades Hall
4 Goulburn St.
Box 24
Sidney, NSW 2000, Australia
Audrey McDonald, Secretary
PH: 2 2645283
FX: 2 2645283

Founded: 1950. **Members:** 1,000. **Budget:** $A 10,000. **State Groups:** 4. **Languages:** English. **National.** Takes action in issues of concern to women such as: consumerism, health, education, child care, and international, peace, development, aid, and solidarity. Participates in trade union campaigns. Cooperates with projects and programs of other women's organizations which support and work to further the women's movement. **Libraries:** Holdings: archival material, periodicals, books.

Publications: *UAW INK* (in English), quarterly. ● *For the Rights of Women, 30 Years of Struggle*.

Conventions/Meetings: triennial conference. ● annual executive committee meeting.

★452★ UNITED NATIONS ASSOCIATION OF AUSTRALIA - STATUS
OF WOMEN NETWORK
42 Mathouura Rd.
Toorak, VIC 3142, Australia
Ms. Diane B. Alley, Convenor
PH: 3 8272363

Founded: 1975. **State Groups:** 8. **Languages:** English. **National.** Seeks to raise public awareness of women's issues. Works to raise women's status by lobbying Australian federal and state governments. Promotes the work and goals of International Women's Year.

Conventions/Meetings: annual general assembly (exhibits). ● monthly regional meeting (exhibits).

★453★ UNITED NATIONS DEVELOPMENT FUND FOR WOMEN OF
    AUSTRALIA (UNIFEM)
64 Lugg St.
Bardon, QLD 4065, Australia
Ms. Bev Perel

Languages: English. **National.** Provides technical and financial support to educational programs in developing countries that benefit rural women or underprivileged women in urban areas. Funds numerous projects including: training in food preservation; training of child care workers; promotion and training of rural women in income-raising group activities; case studies. Organizes workshops to build skills in management of small-scale industries. Areas of interest include revolving loan funds, energy resource development, and community self-help activities for low-income women.

★454★ WAR WIDOWS GUILD OF AUSTRALIA
PO Box 398
Manuka, ACT 2603, Australia
Mrs. Marge Gilmore, President

Languages: English. **National.** Wives of men who died while performing national military service. Fosters communication among members.

★455★ WIMMIN FOR SURVIVAL (WFS)
PO Box 199
Summer Hill, NSW 2130, Australia
M. Glover, Contact

Founded: 1983. **Local Groups:** 8. **Languages:** English. **National.** Women concerned with issues regarding violence against women, animals, and the earth. Seeks to communicate with women's organizations worldwide and creatively act towards global disarmament.

Publications: *Newsletter* (in English), semiannual.

Conventions/Meetings: annual.

★456★ WOMEN AND DEVELOPMENT NETWORK - AUSTRALIA
37 Allambee St.
Reid, ACT 2601, Australia
Ms. Anne Cullen, Convenor

National. Promotes the development and improved status of women throughout Australia.

★457★ WOMEN IN MANAGEMENT (WIM)
24 Graham St.
Pascoe Vale South, VIC 3044, Australia   PH: 3 3832307
Marilyn Bowler, President   FX: 3 3841052

Founded: 1974. **Languages:** English. **National.** Professional women providing support to women in management positions. Maintains a women's management network. Encourages women to work for their goals. Fosters solidarity among women. Investigates women's interests and disseminates information. **Programs:** Women at Work.

Publications: *Newsletter* (in English), quarterly. ● *Directory* (in English), annual.

Conventions/Meetings: monthly meeting.

★458★ WOMEN IN SCIENCE ENQUIRY NETWORK
GPO Box 647
Glebe, NSW 2037, Australia
Ms. Diana Temple, Contact

National. Represents Australian women who are interested in science. Encourages young women to pursue education in scientific fields.

★459★ WOMEN'S ACTION ALLIANCE
2 Sharne Ct.
East Doncaster, VIC 3109, Australia
Mrs. Pauline Smit, President

National. Seeks to enhance women's social and political status. Works to unify women with similar interests and concerns throughout Australia.

★460★ WOMEN'S ELECTORAL LOBBY - AUSTRALIA (WEL)
3 Lobelia St.
O'Connor, ACT 2601, Australia   PH: 6 2476679
Ann Wentworth, Natl.Coord.   FX: 6 2474669

Founded: 1972. **Members:** 7,000. **Budget:** $A 40,000. **Languages:** English. **National.** Non-partisan women lobbyists in Australia. Seeks to achieve social, economic, educational, and sexual equality for women through legislative reform. Works to raise public awareness of women's rights.

Publications: *Inkwel* (in English), bimonthly. Newsletter.

★461★ WOMEN'S FEDERAL COUNCIL OF THE NATIONAL PARTY
    OF AUSTRALIA
PO Box 152
Berrigan, NSW 2712, Australia
Mrs. Helen Dickie, President

Languages: English. **National.** Women working to involve women in Australian politics. Represents members' interests.

★462★ WOMEN'S HEALTH CENTRE
PO Box 665
Spring Hill, QLD 4004, Australia

National. Provides information on women's health issues in Australia.

Publications: *Women and Media - Report from Australia.* Journal.

★463★ WOMEN'S INTERNATIONAL LEAGUE FOR PEACE AND
    FREEDOM - AUSTRALIA
PO Box 476
Glenorchy, TAS 7010, Australia   PH: 2 492487
Lesley Alcorso, Secretary   FX: 2 494903

Founded: 1925. **Members:** 350. **Budget:** $A 20,000. **Languages:** English. **National.** Australian national chapter of the Women's International League for Peace and Freedom (see separate entry). Works to abolish violence, racism, and war. Encourages peaceful forms of settling disputes and environmental conservation. Promotes economic, social, and political justice for all people.

Publications: *Peace and Freedom* (in English), quarterly. Magazine. ● Papers and tapes.

Conventions/Meetings: triennial conference.

★464★ WOMEN'S NETWORK DISABLED PEOPLES INTERNATIONAL
PO Box 169
Curtin, ACT 2605, Australia
Ms. Rae Hurrell, Contact

Multinational. Mentally or physically handicapped women and their families united to promote the rights of the disabled. Works for equality in participation and opportunity for the disabled.

★465★ WOMEN'S RURAL ACTION COMMITTEE
Koonadan
Leeton, NSW 2705, Australia
Mrs. Robyn Tiffen, Contact

Languages: English. **National.** Works to improve the economic, social, and political status of rural women. Conducts income generation programs.

★466★ WOMEN'S VIEW CLUBS OF AUSTRALIA
16 Larkin St.
Locked Bag 1000
Camperdown, NSW 2050, Australia
Mrs. Bridget Battersby, Secretary
PH: 2 5504422
FX: 2 5504235

Founded: 1960. **Members:** 30,000. **Staff:** 3. **Budget:** $A 400,000. **Languages:** English. **National.** VIEW is the acronym for Voice, Interests, and Education of Women. Provides a forum for women to develop friendships and exchange experiences. Lobbies the Australian government on issues affecting women. Seeks to create positive changes in the environment, health, law, and social welfare. Conducts debates. **Awards:** Annual Short Story. ● Annual Poetry.

Publications: *Women's View* (in English), quarterly. Magazine. Members' short stories, poems, letters, and photographs.

Conventions/Meetings: annual - always September.

★467★ WOMENSPORT AUSTRALIA (WSA)
State Association House
1 Stuart St.
Adelaide, SA 5000, Australia
Ms. Shirley Brown, President
PH: 8 2130630
FX: 8 2117115

Founded: 1991. **Members:** 125. **Membership Dues:** Member, $A 20; Member Organisation, $A 40; Concession, $A 10. **Budget:** $A 17,500. **Languages:** English. **National.** Women working for equal opportunity, funding, and media coverage of women in sport and physical recreation. Seeks to increase public awareness of the benefits of sport for women and girls. Encourages women to participate in sports. Conducts educational and informational seminars and workshops. Lobbies legislators and decision makers for women's recreational needs. Investigates quality and quantity of physical activity programs for women and girls. Nominates women to positions of importance. Provides a forum for exchange of information. Disseminates information and broadcasts opinions through media. **Telecommunication Services:** Teleconference, 8 011441. **Formerly:** Women's Sport Promotion Unit.

Publications: *Womensport Australia - Sport & Physical Recreation for Women* (in English). Newsletter. ● Also publishes and distributes promotional material.

Conventions/Meetings: annual seminar. ● annual general assembly.

★468★ WORLD'S WOMAN'S CHRISTIAN TEMPERANCE UNION -
    AUSTRALIA
12 The Avenue
Belmont, VIC 3216, Australia
Mrs. Isobel Burch, Treas.

National. Women working to educate children and adults on the "evils of alcohol, tobacco, and narcotic drugs." Conducts drug abuse seminars and workshops for youth; sponsors professional training programs for counselors.

★469★ YOUNG WOMEN'S CHRISTIAN ASSOCIATION - AUSTRALIA
156 George St., 1st Fl.
Fitzroy, VIC 3065, Australia
Annemary Doyle, Exec. Officer
PH: 3 4176099
FX: 3 4198893

Languages: English. **National.** Works to improve the lives of women through training programs, counseling, and recreational activities. Assists women in establishing social contacts, developing new skills, becoming involved in organizing community activities, and developing and maintaining personal physical fitness.

★470★ ZONTA INTERNATIONAL - AUSTRALIA
4 Burke Dr.
Attadale, WA 6156, Australia
Ms. Bobbie Porter, Contact

Languages: English. **National.** Women professionals. Works to advance the status of women through maintaining contact with the United Nations and several of its agencies. Sponsors women's development programs. Seeks to advance future leaders through mentoring and scholarship programs designed to encourage students, especially young women, to pursue nontraditional careers. Addresses women's issues including, economic self-sufficiency, equal rights, aging, educational opportunities for women, and women's health and nutrition.

Bangladesh

★471★ AIN-O-SALISH KENDRA (ASK)
55 Inner Circular Rd.
Shantinagar
Dacca 1217, Bangladesh
Salma Sobhan, Contact
FX: 2 833966

Founded: 1986. **Members:** 20. **Staff:** 12. **Languages:** English, Bangla. **National.** Lawyers, social scientists, development workers, and writers. Works to increase women's awareness of their legal rights. Offers legal aid. Provides a forum for mediation of disputes. Supports equality and human rights for all. Conducts children's programs and research. **Libraries:** Type: reference. Holdings: periodicals, books. Subjects: legal records, reports, and journals.

Publications: *Illegal Migration of Women.* Monograph.

Conventions/Meetings: periodic workshop - Dacca, Bangladesh.

★472★ BANGLADESH FEDERATION OF UNIVERSITY WOMEN
House No. 16/1
Road No. 6
Dhanmondi
Dacca, Bangladesh
PH: 2 503813

Languages: Bangla. **National.** University educated women. Promotes solidarity and the exchange of ideas and insight among women academics concerning topics of mutual interest.

★473★ BANGLADESH GIRL GUIDES ASSOCIATION
Guide House
New Bailey Rd.
Dacca 2, Bangladesh

Languages: Bangla. **National.** Promotes the welfare and development of girls. Offers recreational and developmental programs.

★474★ BANGLADESH MAHILA SAMITY
New Bailey Rd.
Dacca, Bangladesh
Mrs. Marina Chowdliwu, Exec. Officer
PH: 2 316812

Founded: 1960. **Members:** 1,000. **Staff:** 28. **Regional Groups:** 1. **Local Groups:** 12. **Languages:** Bengali, English. **National.** Works to improve the quality of life for women and children in Bangladesh. Operates schools. Sponsors training programs for women. Offers legal aid and family planning services. Conducts research and charitable programs and children's services. Sponsors competitions. Maintains speakers' bureau and library; compiles statistics.

Publications: *Status of Women in the Eye of the Law in Bangladesh*, semiannual. Magazine. **Advertising:** not accepted.

Conventions/Meetings: semiannual (exhibits).

★475★ BANGLADESH NATIONAL WOMEN LAWYERS ASSOCIATION
Chancery Chambers
Amin Court, 7th Fl.
62-63 Motijheel C/A
Dacca, Bangladesh
Sigma Huda, Director

National. Provides a forum for discussion and information exchange among women lawyers. Provides information for professional advacement.

★476★ BANGLADESH WOMEN'S ASSOCIATION
New Baily Rd.
Dacca, Bangladesh   PH: 2 401741

Languages: Bangla. **National.** Works to improve the status of women living in Bangladesh. Conducts educational programs.

★477★ BANGLADESH WOMEN'S HEALTH COALITION
7/6 Block A, Lamatia
GPO Box 2295
Dacca, Bangladesh   PH: 2 326570

Languages: Bangla. **National.** Works to increase awareness of health issues among women in Bangladesh. Promotes health education, self-help methods, and access to health care.

★478★ CONCERNED WOMEN FOR FAMILY PLANNING (CWFP)
108 Kakrail Rd.   PH: 2 406504
Dacca 1205, Bangladesh   2 401064

Languages: Bangla. Promotes reproductive rights. Defends legislation for the legalization of abortion. Offers counseling on contraceptive devices and pregnancy termination.

★479★ DEVELOPMENT ALTERNATIVES WITH WOMEN FOR A NEW
    ERA - SOUTH ASIA (DAWN)
Ain O Salish Kendra
55 Inner Circular Rd.
Shantinagar
Dacca, Bangladesh
Dr. Hameeda Hossain, Contact

Languages: Bangla. **Multinational.** Works to reduce the negative impact of development activities on women and the environment. Conducts research, training, and advocacy programs to eliminate inequalities of gender, class, and race. Facilitates communication and networking among women's movements. Protects and defends women's reproductive rights.

★480★ FAMILY PLANNING ASSOCIATION OF BANGLADESH (FPAB)
(BPPS Bangladesh Paribar Parikalpana Samitu)
2 Naya Paltan   PH: 2 416134
Dacca 2, Bangladesh   FX: 2 833008
Mizanur Rahman, Dir. Gen.   TX: 632379 IFIC BJ

Founded: 1953. **Members:** 4,000. **Staff:** 687. **Budget:** US$1,538,900. **Languages:** Bengali, English. **National.** Advocates family planning among the underpriveleged in Bangladesh, primarily in rural areas. Works to change policies affecting women such as marriage age and inheritance laws. Offers health education programs and maternal and child health services. Conducts research projects on family planning methods and their effectiveness. Collaborates with family planning organizations in India, Nepal, Pakistan, and Sri Lanka. Sponsors youth activies in community development and population education programs. Conducts workshops. **Libraries:** Type: reference. Holdings: 4,000. **Computer Services:** Data base.

Publications: *Annual Report.* ● *FPAB Highlight* (in English), quarterly. Newsletter. ● *Sukhi Paribar* (in Bengali), bimonthly. Magazine. **Also Cited As:**

Happy Family. ● *Three Year Plan,* annual. ● *Why and How to Plan a Family.* ● *Facts on Family Planning Association of Bangladesh.* ● *Child Care and Role of Mothers.*

Conventions/Meetings: annual meeting - usually December. ● quarterly executive committee meeting.

★481★ WOMEN FOR WOMEN: A RESEARCH AND STUDY GROUP
    (WFW)
63/2 Laboratory Rd.
S. Dhanmondi
Dacca 1205, Bangladesh   PH: 2 504697
Rasheda K. Choudhury, Secretary   FX: 2 813010

Founded: 1973. **Members:** 46. **Staff:** 5. **Budget:** US$29,900. **Languages:** Bangla, English. **National.** Female scholars, social scientists, professionals, activists, and others who have earned at least a master's degree. Engages in research on problems affecting the lives of Bangladeshi women. Seeks to raise awareness of women's issues, and affect public policy. Fosters communication and exchange between women's groups and the government. Conducts "Research Methodology and Women's Issues" training programs for young researchers. Encourages women's development activities. Supports educational programs for university students. Disseminates information. **Libraries:** Type: reference. Holdings: books. Subjects: gender issues. **Committees:** Library and Linkage.

Publications: *Eshon* (in Bangla), quarterly. Newsletter. ● Also publishes books and documentary videos.

Conventions/Meetings: monthly workshop. ● annual conference.

★482★ YOUNG WOMEN'S CHRISTIAN ASSOCIATION - BANGLADESH
13 Green Sq.
Green Rd.
Dacca 1205, Bangladesh   PH: 2 503600
Asrukana Das, Contact   FX: 2 813466

Languages: Bangla. **National.** Acts in accordance with the constitutional functions of the World YWCA. Promotes international understanding, improved social and economic conditions, and human rights. Accepts a responsibility to work towards development fronted by women, influenced by Christianity, and guided by an attitude that development is a fundamental human right. Seeks to address serious economic, social, cultural, and spiritual needs of women; secure the participation of women in all areas of development; adopt technologies for projects that will protect the environment. Strives to secure the dignity of every human being and a just society. Encourages self-determination and personal development of women and girls. Acts as a voice for women, a source of consultation on women's issues, and a supporter and defender of social change. Community services include: shelters for abused women; child care; advocacy on issues affecting women; leadership programs; and fitness programs.

Bhutan

★483★ NATIONAL WOMEN'S ASSOCIATION OF BHUTAN
Norzin Lam
Thimphu, Bhutan

Founded: 1981. **Languages:** Dzongkha, English. **National.** Promotes the interests of women in Bhutan. Fosters solidarity among women. Works to improve women's standard of living.

Brunei Darussalam

★484★ BRUNEI DARUSSALAM INTERNATIONAL WOMEN'S CLUB
(Kelab Wanita Antarabangsa Brunei Darussalam)
PO Box 320
Bandar Seri Begawan 1903, Brunei
    Darussalam
Ungku Datin Hajah Fanzah Osman,
    President

Founded: 1988. Members: 455. Languages: English, Malay. National. Promotes solidarity among women locally and internationally. Offers cultural activities including: singing, traditional dancing, cooking, and painting. Encourages multi-culturalism; fosters exchange and friendship among women of different nationalities. Conducts language education programs.

Publications: *Newsletter*, periodic.

★485★ BRUNEI GOVERNMENT OFFICERS' WIVES' WELFARE
    ASSOCIATION
(BISTARI Badan Kebajikan Isteri-Isteri Pegawi Kerajaan Brunei)
PO Box 2758
Bandar Seri Begawan 1927, Brunei
    Darussalam
Dayang Hajah Fatimah binti Haji Gassan,
    Gen. Sec.

Founded: 1982. Members: 170. Languages: Malay, English. National. Wives of government officers. Seeks to increase members' knowledge of husbands' professions. Offers support to women adapting to their husbands' jobs. Provides financial support for impoverished individuals. Organizes sports activities, lectures, and travel excursions.

★486★ BRUNEI MALAY TEACHERS ASSOCIATION - WOMEN
    SECTION
(Persekutuan Guru-Guru Melayu Brunei Bahagian Wanita)
160-601 Brunei Malay Teachers Bldg.
Jalan Kianggeh
Bandar Seri Begawan 2088, Brunei
    Darussalam
Penigran Hajah Mariam binti Penigran
    Haji Matarsat, Director

Founded: 1982. Members: 650. Languages: Malay, English. National. Seeks to improve the status of female teachers. Encourages women's participation in religious, welfare and social activities. Organizes goodwill visits to other countries. Presents lectures; conducts research.

★487★ BRUNEI PERTIWI ASSOCIATION
(Persatuan Pertiwi Brunei)
Taman Asuhan Pertiwi
Lot No. 19631
Jalan Jawatan Dalam
Mabohai 2092, Brunei Darussalam
Datin Hajah Tinah binti Ahmad, President

Founded: 1968. Members: 4,000. Languages: Malay, English. National. Maylay and Muslim women over 18 years of age. Seeks to improve women's social, cultural, and economic welfare. Encourages women's participation in sports, education, and cultural activities. Operates kindergarten, transportation and housing cooperatives. Fosters communication among members.

Publications: *Berbagai Jenis Anyaman Ketupat*. Book.

★488★ COUNCIL OF WOMEN OF BRUNEI DARUSSALAM
(Majlis Wanita Negara Brunei Darussalam)
PO Box 3061
Bandar Seri Begawan 1930, Brunei
    Darussalam
Datin Hajah Masni binti Hj Mohd Ali,
    President

Founded: 1985. Languages: Malay, English. National. Women's associations and individual women. Seeks to improve the economic, cultural, and social status of women. Offers educational programs for women. Fosters friendship among members. Gathers and disseminates information.

★489★ FIRST BRUNEI'S GIRLS BRIGADE
(Briged Puteri Kompeni Pertama Brunei)
PO Box 2182
Bandar Seri Begawan 1921, Brunei
    Darussalam
Mrs. Audrene Chia, Captain   PH: 2 223359

Founded: 1977. Members: 20. Languages: Malay, English. National. Christian girls over the age of 9. Educates members using Christian beliefs as a basis. Encourages ''reverence, self-control, and self-respect.''.

Publications: *Brigade*, monthly. Newsletter.

★490★ GIRL GUIDES ASSOCIATION OF BRUNEI DARUSSALAM
No. 23, Jalan Sinuai
Bandar Seri Begawan 2094, Brunei
    Darussalam
Datin Paduka Hajah Jusnani binti Haji
    Lawie, Contact

Founded: 1951. Members: 1,100. Languages: Malay, English. National. Girls from 7 to 18 years of age. Fosters personal development and sense of citizenship. Encourages interest in crafts, health, social service, nature appreciation, traditional arts, and customs. Facilitates friendship among girls from different nations. Organizes camping and sporting activities. Sponsors Peace Day and Thinking Day.

Publications: *Warta Pandu Puteri*, quarterly. Newsletter. ● *Buku Kenang-kenangan*. Book.

★491★ PETROLEUM WIVES CLUB
c/o DPP
Syarikat Minyak Shell Brunei Sdn. Bhd.
Seria 7082, Brunei Darussalam
Mrs. Lynne Keir, President

Founded: 1978. Members: 30. Languages: Malay, English. National. Women whose husbands work in the petroleum industry. Seeks to unite women to exchange ideas and skills.

Publications: *Newsletter*, monthly. Information on the group's activities.

Conventions/Meetings: monthly meeting.

★492★ POLICE WIVES AND FAMILIES WELFARE ASSOCIATION
(PEKERTI Perkumpulan Kebajikan Isteri-Isteri Dan Keluarga-Keluarga
    Polis)
Police Hdqtrs.
Gadong 2040
Bandar Seri Begawan, Brunei
    Darussalam
Datin Hajah Fatimah binti Haji Zaini,
    President   PH: 423901

Members: 1,656. Languages: Malay, English. National. Female police officers, wives and daughters of police officers. Fosters friendship among members through educational programs, sporting events, cultural activities, and religious gatherings.

★493★ UNIVERSITY BRUNEI DARUSSALAM WOMEN'S ASSOCIATION
(Persatuan Wanita Universiti Brunei Darussalam)
Universiti Brunei Darussalam
Gadong 3186, Brunei Darussalam
Jean Eggleton, Hon.Treas.

Founded: 1987. **Members:** 77. **Languages:** Malay, English. **National.**
Female staff of the University Brunei Darussalam and wives of male staff. Encourages women's participation in national development projects. Promotes cultural, athletic, educational, and welfare activities. Organizes play groups for children. Fosters communication among members.

Publications: *Newsletter*, monthly. ● *Life in Brunei*. Book.

★494★ WOMEN GRADUATES ASSOCIATION
(Persatuan Siswazah Wanita)
PO Box 2282
Bandar Seri Begawan 1922, Brunei
 Darussalam
Dy Nellie binti Dato Paduka Haji Sunny,
 President

Founded: 1990. **Members:** 50. **Languages:** Malay, English. **National.**
Female graduates, undergraduates who are nationals or permanent residents of Brunei Darussalam, and contributors to national development. Seeks to preserve professional ties among women graduates. Provides a forum for discussion of national development, women's personal and family development. Operates social and welfare programs. Conducts research and lectures.

Publications: *Newsletter*, periodic. ● *Journal*, periodic. ● *Magazine*, periodic.

★495★ WOMEN'S CORONA SOCIETY
(Persatuan Corona Wanita)
PO Box 2488
Bandar Seri Begawan 1924, Brunei
 Darussalam
Datin Vivienne Chin, President

Founded: 1965. **Members:** 75. **Languages:** Malay, English. **National.**
Women in Brunei Darussalam interested in living outside of Brunei Darussalam. Fosters communication between members and the host nation. Provides advice and information to travelling women.

Publications: *Newsletter*, monthly.

Conventions/Meetings: monthly meeting.

★496★ WOMEN'S INSTITUTE OF BRUNEI DARUSSALAM
(Pertubuhan Perkumpulan Perempuan Brunei)
PO Box 1255
Bandar Seri Begawan 1912, Brunei
 Darussalam
Dayang Hajah Marhani binti Abd Latif,
 President

Founded: 1961. **Members:** 2,500. **Languages:** Malay, English. **National.**
Women and girls over 15 years of age. Seeks to improve women's status. Works to influence government legislation regarding the domestic economy, and the welfare of women and children. Fosters communication among members.

China, People's Republic of

★497★ ALL-CHINA WOMEN'S FEDERATION (ACWF)
(Federation des Femmes Chinoises)
50 Deng Shi Kou
Beijing 100730, People's Republic of
 China   PH: 1 5134126
Chen Muhua, President   FX: 1 5136044

Founded: 1949. **Languages:** Chinese, English, French. **National.** Adult women in the Chinese Communist Party. Works to represent and protect women and women's rights and to achieve equality of the sexes. Encourages women to participate politically and productively. Seeks to empower women through education and preparation for non-traditional careers. Strives to ensure non-discriminatory laws and policies concerning women and children. Motivates private organizations to aid women and women's causes. Maintains and operates the China Women Administration Institute, the China Women's Travel Service, the China Women's Publishing House, the Institute of Chinese Women's Studies, and the Chinese Children's Activities and Development Center. Plans to establish a worldwide network for peace.
Departments: Urban and Rural Women's Work; Children's Welfare; International Liaison; Organization and Liaison; Women's Development.

Publications: *Women of China* (in English), monthly. ● *Chinese Women* (in Chinese), periodic. ● *Chinese Women's News* (in Chinese), periodic. Newspaper.

Conventions/Meetings: quinquennial general assembly.

★498★ CHINA ASSOCIATION FOR FAMILY EDUCATION
50 Dengshikou St.
Dongcheng District
Beijing 100730, People's Republic of
 China
Lu Leshan, President

Founded: 1989. **Members:** 44. **Languages:** Chinese. **National.** Researches family education and childbearing practices in urban and rural areas; disseminates information. Sponsors training and educational courses. Promotes international networking.

★499★ CHINA ASSOCIATION OF WOMEN MAYORS
Ministry of Construction
Haidian District
Beijing 100835, People's Republic of
 China   PH: 1 8319248
Wu Yi, President   1 8320606

Founded: 1991. **Members:** 250. **Languages:** Chinese. **National.** Promotes cooperation and the exchange of knowledge among women mayors in China. Sponsors inner-city exchanges. Works to safeguard the equal rights of women.

★500★ CHINA ASSOCIATION FOR WOMEN'S JOURNALS AND
 PERIODICALS
50 Dengshikou St.
Dongcheng District
Beijing 100730, People's Republic of
 China
Wang Menglan, President   PH: 1 5134956

Founded: 1992. **Members:** 5. **Languages:** Chinese. **National.** Women's information groups. Promotes the exchange of experience and knowledge among professionals affiliated with women's journals. Offers personnel training. Organizes international networking.

★501★ CHINA EXPERT CONSULTANCY COMMITTEE ON MATERNITY
1 Xixhiku St.
Xicheng District
Beijing 100034, People's Republic of
    China
Yan Renying, Chair   PH: 1 3049020

Founded: 1989. **Members:** 28. **Languages:** Chinese. **National.** Professionals in maternity and child care. Seeks to improve the quality of health care for mothers and children. Offers consultancy service to maternity and child care facilities in China.

★502★ CHINA FAMILY PLANNING ASSOCIATION (CFPA)
1 Bei Li
Shengguzhuang   PH: 1 4214624
He Ping Li   1 4219966
Beijing, People's Republic of China   FX: 1 4227612
Dr. Qui Shuhua, Secretary   TX: 211231 CFPA CN

Languages: Chinese. **National.** Works to enhance the quality of life for individuals living in China by promoting family planning. Works to reduce the number of unwanted pregnancies and abortions. Provides contraceptive and health care services. Sponsors programs in family planning, sex education, and health. Conducts research.

★503★ CHINA SOCIETY FOR THE STUDY OF MARRIAGE AND
    FAMILY
50 Dengshikou St.
Dongcheng District
Beijing 100730, People's Republic of
    China   PH: 1 5127711
Chen Muhua, President   1 5127353

Founded: 1981. **Members:** 146. **Languages:** Chinese. **National.** Individuals and groups. Conducts research on marriage and family issues. Offers advice to couples seeking to improve relationships within the marriage or family. Sponsors academic exhange; disseminates information.

★504★ CHINA WOMEN'S HEALTH CARE SOCIETY
17 Qihe Bldg.
Dongcheng District
Beijing 100006, People's Republic of
    China   PH: 1 5121620
Xiang Xiaoying, Secretary   1 5507331

Founded: 1989. **Members:** 3,000. **Languages:** Chinese. **National.** Works to improve accessibility of preventative physical and mental health care for women in China. Conducts scientific research; sponsors academic exchange and professional training in the area of women's medicine. Participates in international conventions regarding women's health care.

★505★ CHINESE ASSOCIATION FOR BIRTH PLANNING AND
    CHILDHOOD HEALTH IMPROVEMENT SCIENCES
Bldg. 12, Block 2
Anhua Xili
Chaoyang District
Beijing 100011, People's Republic of
    China   PH: 1 4213546
Qian Xinzhong, President   1 4219966

Founded: 1979. **Members:** 12. **Languages:** Chinese. **National.** Family planning and child health care consulting service to departments of central and local governments. Provides counseling and information. Conducts research; compiles data.

★506★ CHINESE ASSOCIATION FOR IMPROVING BIRTH QUALITY
    AND CHILD UPBRINGING
No. 2, 22 Taiping Rd.
Haidian District
Beijing 100036, People's Republic of
    China   PH: 1 6887029
Chen Minzhang, President   1 6887744

Founded: 1989. **Members:** 100,100. **Languages:** Chinese. **National.** Individuals and groups working to improve the quality of maternal and child care. Offers educational, informational, and social services on child rearing. Sponsors research.

★507★ CHINESE NURSING ASSOCIATION
42 Dongsi West St.
Dongcheng District
Beijing 100710, People's Republic of
    China   PH: 1 553685
Lin Juying, President   1 5133311

Founded: 1909. **Languages:** Chinese. **National.** Women nurses in China. Promotes the nursing profession; encourages application of knowledge and technology acquired through research findings. Offers training courses and seminars. Organizes networking and the sharing of knowledge and experience among nursing professionals. Sponsors academic exchange. Organizes research projects, and arranges study tours. Protects the rights of nursing professionals.

★508★ CHINESE SOCIETY OF MARRIAGE MANAGEMENT
    RESEARCH
9 Xi Huangchenggen South St.
Xicheng District
Beijing 100032, People's Republic of
    China
Zhang Ming, President   PH: 1 656061

Founded: 1989. **Members:** 140. **Languages:** Chinese. **National.** Organizes studies on women's status in marriage. Works towards the enforcement of marriage law and the development of marriage management in China.

★509★ CHINESE WOMEN'S DEVELOPMENT FUND
50 Deng Shi kou
Beijing 100730, People's Republic of
    China   PH: 1 5129909

Founded: 1989. **Languages:** Chinese, English. **National.** Works to protect and ensure women's rights. Organizes educational and training programs. Provides counseling services for women and daycare services for children. Supports economic development of disadvantaged populations. Encourage implementation of scientific and technical skills for practical gains. Bestows awards to women. Develops contacts with Chinese and international organizations with similar goals.

★510★ WOMEN OF CHINA
50 Deng Shi Kou
Beijing, People's Republic of China

Languages: Chinese. **National.** Individuals working to enhance women's status in China. Goals include: sexual equality, proportional representation of women in politics, and better education and employment opportunities for women. Formulates laws for the protection of women's rights, interests, and equality. Seeks to eliminate arranged and mercenary marriages.

Publications: *Comments on: The Law on the Protection of Women's Rights and Interests.* Book. ● *Women of China*, monthly. Newsletter.

★511★ YOUNG WOMEN'S CHRISTIAN ASSOCIATION - CHINA
123 Sitzang Rd. S
Shanghai, People's Republic of China
Cora Deng, Gen.Sec.   FX: 21 3203053

National. Promotes the development of young women in the People's Republic of China. Upholds Christian beliefs and values in its programs. Seeks to instill self worth and self-esteem in young women.

Cook Islands

★512★ COOK ISLANDS FAMILY WELFARE ASSOCIATION (CIFWA)
PO Box 296
Public Service Commission
Rarotonga, Cook Islands   PH: 23420
Ms. Tupuna Taripo, Exec. Dir.   FX: 23421

Languages: English. **National**. Works to enhance the quality of life for individuals living in the Cook Islands by promoting responsible parenthood and family planning. Advocates family planning as a basic human right. Sponsors programs in sex education, family planning, and health. Provides contraceptive and health care services.

★513★ COOK ISLANDS NATIONAL COUNCIL OF WOMEN
PO Box 733   PH: 29420
Rarotonga, Cook Islands   23540
Vereara Maeva, President   FX: 23421

Founded: 1984. **Members:** 53. **Languages:** English. **National**. Promotes the interests of women in the Cook Islands. Provides a forum for collaboration among women's groups. Fosters environmental preservation.

Conventions/Meetings: periodic meeting.

Fiji

★514★ DEVELOPMENT ALTERNATIVES WITH WOMEN FOR A NEW
   ERA - PACIFIC (DAWN)
University of South Pacific
School of Social and Economic
   Development
Department of History and Politics
PO Box 1168
Suva, Fiji
Ms. Claire Slatter, Contact

Languages: English. **Multinational**. Works to reduce the negative impact of development activities on women and the environment. Conducts research, training, and advocacy programs to eliminate inequalities of gender, class, and race. Facilitates communication and networking among women's movements. Protects and defends women's reproductive rights.

★515★ FAMILY PLANNING ASSOCIATION OF FIJI (FPAF)
PO Box 619   PH: 300355
Suva, Fiji   FX: 304953
Mr. Lasarusa Turaga, Exec. Dir.   CBL: FAMPLAN SUVA

Languages: English. **National**. Promotes family planning as a basic human right. Works to reduce the number of unwanted pregnancies and abortions. Encourages public awareness of family planning and responsible parenthood. Sponsors programs in sex education, family planning, and health. Conducts research.

★516★ FIJI NATIONAL COUNCIL OF WOMEN
PO Box 840
Suva, Fiji
Ms. Sereima Lomaloma, President   PH: 22961

National. Umbrella organization for women's groups in Fiji. Supports women and women's interests. Coordinates activities for women. Disseminates information on women's issues.

★517★ FIJI WOMEN'S RIGHTS MOVEMENT (FWRM)
PO Box 14194
Suva, Fiji   PH: 313156
Peni B. Moore, Coordinator   FX: 305033

Founded: 1986. **Members:** 300. **Staff:** 4. **Budget:** $F 80,000. **Languages:** Fijian, English. **National**. Seeks to raise the status of women. Assists women's efforts to find employment and increase their economic power. Works to influence legislation and social attitudes to benefit women. Conducts anti-rape and employment workshops. Sponsors research. **Libraries:** Type: reference.

Publications: *Balance* (in English and Fijian), monthly. Newsletter.

★518★ YOUNG WOMEN'S CHRISTIAN ASSOCIATION - FIJI
PO Box 534   PH: 315667
Suva, Fiji   304829
Amelia Rokotuivuna, Gen.Sec.   FX: 303004

National. Promotes the development of young women in Fiji. Upholds Christian beliefs and values in its programs. Works to instill self worth and self-esteem in young women.

★519★ YOUNG WOMEN'S CHRISTIAN ASSOCIATION - PACIFIC
   REGION
PO Box 3940
Samabula, Fiji   PH: 301222
Salama Fulivai, Dir.   FX: 301222

Multinational. Pacific regional branch of the international Christian organization. Promotes the development of young women in the Pacific region. Upholds Christian beliefs and values in its programs. Works to instill self worth and self-esteem in young women.

French Polynesia

★520★ MOUVEMENT POLYNESIEN POUR LE PLANNING FAMILIAL
BP 676
Papeete, Tahiti, French Polynesia

Languages: Polynesian, French. **National**. Advocates family planning as a basic human right and as a means to improve the quality of life for individuals living in Polynesia. Works to reduce the number of unwanted pregnancies and abortions. Offers programs in sex education, family planning, and health. Provides contraceptive and health care services. Conducts research.

Guam

★521★ AMERICAN ASSOCIATION OF UNIVERSITY WOMEN - GUAM
2 Calachucha St.
Barrigada Heights, Guam 96921
Ms. Francesca Remengesau, Contact

National. University educated women. Provides a forum for information exchange and fellowship among women scholars.

★522★ BAHA'I WOMEN'S ASSOCIATION OF GUAM
PO Box 20280
Agana, Guam 96921
Ms. Tahereh Gerling, Contact

National. Women followers of the Baha'i religion. Fosters religious teaching and fellowship.

★523★ CATHOLIC DAUGHTERS OF THE AMERICAS, COURT OUR
 LADY OF CAMARIN
PO Box 776   PH: 4723441
Agana, Guam 96910   4723442
Elizabeth P. Arriola, Contact   FX: 4775632

Founded: 1972. **Members:** 99. **Multinational.** Women united to advance human rights. Upholds principles of justice and peace. Fosters women's Christian fellowship.

★524★ CHRISTIAN WOMEN'S CLUB OF GUAM
PO Box 23496
Agana, Guam 96921
Phyllis Eliason, Contact   PH: 7343708

Founded: 1920. **National.** Women promoting the Christian Gospel. Fosters fellowship and sharing among members.

★525★ FILIPINO LADIES' ASSOCIATION OF GUAM
PO Box 3789
Agana, Guam 96910
Gloria D. Estampador, President   PH: 7893042

Founded: 1962. **Members:** 45. **National.** Fosters solidarity among Philippino women in an effort to preserve Philippino culture and traditions. Cooperates with governmental authorities and other women's organizations to promote women's interests.

★526★ GUAM WOMEN'S CLUB
PO Box 454
Agana, Guam 96910   PH: 6462500
Chita Blaise, Contact   FX: 6492928

Founded: 1952. **Members:** 80. **Languages:** English. **National.** Women working to improve the education, health, and standard of living in Guam. Researches health issues, economic conditions, and educational methods. Supports and promotes similar organizations. Conducts fundraising activities to assist charitable projects. **Awards:** Annual (scholarship). Recipient: students. **Projects:** Guam Women's Club History.

Conventions/Meetings: monthly meeting.

★527★ HAFA ADAI LIONS CLUB
PO Box 7927
Tamuning, Guam 96911   PH: 6469268
Lion Monina Moreno, President   FX: 6496948

Founded: 1989. **Languages:** English. **National.** Women working to improve living conditions in Guam; seeks to increase international understanding and tolerance. Promotes and supports social welfare projects. Offers assistance to social welfare organizations.

Publications: *Lions Roar!* (in English), quarterly. Newsletter.

★528★ INDIAN WIVES ASSOCIATION
PO Box 5259
Mangilao, Guam 96923
Ms. Pramila Sullivan, Contact

National. Indian women and wives of Indian men. Offers cultural and recreational acitivities to promote fellowship and solidarity among members.

★529★ INTERNATIONAL WOMEN'S CLUB
PO Box 2020
Agana, Guam 96910   PH: 6534300
June Webber, President   FX: 4774826

Founded: 1973. **Languages:** English. **National.** Works to unite the women of Guam in fellowship activities. Encourages international cultural exchange among women. Conducts community programs and social events, such as fashion shows and dances.

Publications: *Newsletter* (in English), monthly.

Conventions/Meetings: meeting - 8/year. ● monthly luncheon.

★530★ JAPAN WOMEN'S CLUB OF GUAM
PO Box 7746
Agana, Guam 96910
Ms. Hiroko Johnson, Contact

National. Japanese women living in Guam. Offers recreational and cultural activities, promoting fellowship and solidarity among members.

★531★ KOREAN WOMEN'S ASSOCIATION
PO Box 3522
Agana, Guam 96910
Ms. Hija Lee, Contact

National. Offers recreational and cultural activities, promoting fellowship and solidarity among Korean women living in Guam.

★532★ PROFESSIONAL BLACK WOMEN
PO Box 2491
Agana, Guam 96910

National. Provides a forum for information exchange and fellowship among educated and professional black women.

★533★ SOROPTIMIST INTERNATIONAL OF GUAM
PO Box 952
Agana, Guam 96910
Ms. Liz Duenas, Contact

National. Women professionals. Facilitates educational programs on the environment, health, human rights, the status of women, and economic and social development. Promotes international goodwill and understanding. Cooperates with non-governmental organizations for the advancement of peace.

Hong Kong

★534★ ASSOCIATION FOR THE ADVANCEMENT OF FEMINISM (AAF)
8A, 444 Nathan Rd.
Kowloon, Hong Kong   PH: 7871900
Tsang Gar-Yin, Exec. Secty.   FX: 3855319

Founded: 1984. **Members:** 70. **Languages:** Chinese, English. **National.** Works to eliminate discrimination against women in sexual, economic, social, cultural, legal, and political arenas. Promotes women's rights and the development of women in all sectors of society. Cooperates with local women's organizations to address problems faced by women throughout all regions in Hong Kong. Organizes coalitions and seminars; conducts research and educational programs. **Libraries:** Type: reference.

Publications: *Women's News Digest*, quarterly. Newsletter. **Advertising:** not accepted.

Conventions/Meetings: annual meeting.

★535★ COMMITTEE FOR ASIAN WOMEN (CAW)
57 Peking Rd., 4th Fl.
Kowloon, Hong Kong   PH: 7226150
Maria Rhie Chol Soon, Contact   FX: 3699895

Founded: 1981. **Staff:** 3. **Languages:** English. **Multinational.** Promotes the interests of women workers in Asia. Seeks to protect the rights of women. Offers financial support to needy local women's organizations. Organizes educational training and workshops. Proposes to research the impact of industrial restructuring on women workers. **Libraries:** Type: reference. Holdings: books. Subjects: women's issues and rights.

Publications: *Asian Women Workers Newsletter* (in English), quarterly. ● Books related to issues concerning women workers in Asia.

★536★ FAMILY PLANNING ASSOCIATION OF HONG KONG (FPAHK)
                                      PH: 754477
10th Fl., Southorn Centre   754478
130 Hennessy Rd.   FX: 8346767
Wanchai, Hong Kong   CBL: FAMPLAN
Dr. Margaret Kwan, Exec. Dir.   HOUNGKONG

Languages: English. **National.** Works to improve the quality of life for people living in Hong Kong by promoting family planning and responsible parenthood. Works to reduce the number of unwanted pregnancies and abortions. Advocates family planning as a basic human right. Sponsors programs in sex education, family planning, and health. Conducts research.

★537★ HONG KONG ASSOCIATION OF WOMEN WORKERS
Block B, 16/F
Pak Lok Manison
332 Nathan Rd.
Kowloon, Hong Kong

National. Works to unify the efforts of women workers demanding equal rights as laborers. Heightens awareness of discrimination and exploitation against them; encourages women to contribute to the women's movement.

Publications: *Hong Kong Association of Women Workers News.*

★538★ HONG KONG COUNCIL OF WOMEN (HKCW)
GPO Box 819
Hong Kong
Helen Siebers, Chair   PH: 7287760

Founded: 1947. **Membership Dues:** HK$150 annual. **National.** Works to defend women against violence, discrimination, exploitation, and oppression. Campaigns for the abolition of concubinage, elimination of pornography, and the involvement of women police officers in the investigation of rape cases. Operates a rape hotline and a shelter for battered women. Lobbies for child care services rights and the establishment of a government agency dealing with women's issues. Advocates women's equal oppotunities for professional and personal development, regardless of socio-economic status or religion. Networks with other women's groups in pursuit of similar goals. **Subcommittees:** Women's Studies Research; Legal; Education; Health; Childbirth Education.

Publications: *Newsletter*, periodic.

Conventions/Meetings: monthly meeting.

★539★ JEWISH WOMEN'S ASSOCIATION OF HONG KONG (JWAHK)
70 Robinson Rd.
Hong Kong   PH: 5 594872

Founded: 1950. **Members:** 100. **Languages:** English. **National.** Charitable organization comprised of Jewish women. Conducts fundraising activities. Sponsors lectures.

Publications: *Newsletter*, monthly.

Conventions/Meetings: monthly luncheon.

★540★ YOUNG WOMEN'S CHRISTIAN ASSOCIATION - HONG KONG
No. 1 Macdonnell Rd.
Hong Kong   PH: 5223101
Alice Yuk Tak Fun, Gen.Sec.   FX: 5244237

National. Promotes the development of young women in Hong Kong. Upholds Christian beliefs and values in its programs. Works to instill self worth and self-esteem in young women.

India

★541★ AAWAAZ-E-NISWAAN
c/o Inayat Akhtar
20 Yakub St., 2nd Fl., No. 19
Ghanchi Bldg.
Bombay 400 003, Maharashtra, India

Founded: 1987. **Languages:** Hindi, English. **National.** Muslim women in India. Fights oppression of women, communalism, and religious fundamentalism. Offers legal advice and emotional counselling to women in distress. Conducts children's programs.

★542★ ACTION INDIA
5/24 Jangpura B
New Delhi, Delhi, India

Languages: Hindi, English. **National.** Campaigns to raise public awareness of women's issues. Promotes the rights of women in India. Works to improve women's standard of living through training, skill sharing, and income generation programs.

★543★ AHMEDABAD WOMEN'S ACTION GROUP (AWAG)
5 Professors' Colony
Navrangpura
Ahmedabad 380 009, Gujarat, India
Dr. Ila Pathak, Secretary   PH: 451589

Founded: 1981. **Members:** 70. **Staff:** 58. **Languages:** English. **National.** Works to further the women's movement through consciousness raising and encouraging the participation of women in leadership within all areas of society. Promotes women's activities in labor unions. Strives to eliminate violence against women. Defends the rights of women to equal treatment and opportunity. Protests against unequal pay for women. Offers workshops in elevating awareness among women of their exploited condition. Offers literacy training. Conducts research; disseminates information. **Libraries:** Type: reference. Holdings: 4,000; books.

★544★ ALL INDIA CONGRESS COMMITTEE, WOMEN'S
   DEPARTMENT
Dept. 7, Jautar Mantar Rd.
New Delhi, Delhi, India

Languages: Hindi. **National.** Encourages women's active participation in political and public life.

★545★ ALL INDIA COUNCIL OF CHRISTIAN WOMEN
1542 5th St., H Block
11th State Rd.
Anna Nagar
Madras 600 040, Tamil Nadu, India

Languages: Hindi, English. **National.** Women united to promote Christianity. Seeks to stimulate theological dialogue. Fosters communication among members.

★546★ ALL INDIA DEMOCRATIC WOMEN'S ASSOCIATION
23 Vithal Bhai Patel House
New Delhi 110 001, Delhi, India

Founded: 1982. **Languages:** Hindi, English. **National.** Women united in India to uphold democratic principles of government. Seeks to ensure women's equality in employment, education, and social status.

★547★ ALL INDIA WOMEN'S CONFERENCE (AIWC)
6 Bhagwan Dass Rd.
New Delhi 110 001, Delhi, India   PH: 11 389680
Dr. Aparna Basu, Sec.Gen.   11 389314

Founded: 1927. **Staff:** 29. **Budget:** Rs 11,185,350. **Languages:** English, Hindi. **National.** Works to improve the self-confidence and self-reliance of women. Seeks to ensure equal rights and social justice by providing vocational training and opportunities for self-employment. Concentrates on improving efficiency of cookstoves used in rural areas, leading to less energy use and greater freedom from domestic chores for women.

★548★ ANNAPOOMA MAHILA MANDAL
Navnit Ram Maruti Rd.
Bombay 400 028, Maharashtra, India

Founded: 1976. **Languages:** Hindi, English. **National.** Works to improve the economic and social welfare of low-income women in India. Offers women educational courses in basic management skills and literacy. Assists women in attaining credit from banks.

★549★ ANTI-DOWRY FRONT VIDERBHA
9 Ramtelke Bungalow
Tilak Nagar
Nagpur 440 016, Madhya Pradesh, India

Languages: Hindi, English. **National.** Women united to end the dowry tradition in India. Seeks to eliminate oppression and discrimination against women.

★550★ ANTI-RAPE CAMPAIGN, A WOMEN'S COLLECTIVE
304 Prema Bldg.
Rua de Ourem
Panaji 403 001, Goa Daman and Diu,
   India

National. Strives to: bring about public awareness of the prevalence of rape and of the facts related to rape; protect the rights of the victims of rape; set in motion firmer legislative and judiciary action against criminal aggressors of rape.

★551★ ANVESHI RESEARCH CENTRE FOR WOMEN'S STUDIES
Osmania University Campus
Hyderabad 500 007, Andhra Pradesh,
   India

Languages: Hindi, English. **National.** Encourages and evaluates research into the history, condition, and rights of women. Seeks to advance the status of women.

★552★ ASSOCIATION FOR IMPROVING THE DOWNTRODDEN (AID)
Thogapadi
Kondengi
South Arcot 605 301, Tamil Nadu, India
C.M. Anandan, President

Founded: 1984. **Staff:** 10. **Budget:** Rs 80,000. **Local Groups:** 15. **Languages:** English, Hindi. **National.** Works to improve the well-being of oppressed and exploited people, especially women and children. Provides education programs to the general public. Conducts programs in literacy, job training, health, and family planning. Implements income generation programs. **Formerly:** AID Development Centre.

Publications: *Bulletin*, periodic. ● *Newsletter*, periodic. Includes progress reports on group projects.

★553★ ASSOCIATION OF THEOLOGICALLY TRAINED WOMEN OF INDIA
c/o Mrs. K.K. George
Kanichukattil House
Eraviperoor
Kerala 689 542, India

Languages: Hindi, English. **National.** Women engaged in theological studies. Stimulates the production of scholarly works and teaching materials in theology. Fosters communication among members.

★554★ AVEHI
c/o Chondita
Nehru Science Centre Planetarium
Discovery of India Project Worli
Bombay 400 039, Maharashtra, India

Languages: Hindi, English. **National.** Conducts programs in India to improve women's health. Creates and displays posters to raise public awareness.

★555★ BANWASI SEVA ASHRAM (BSA)
Govindur
Via Turra
Sonbhadra 231 221, Uttar Pradesh, India
Mr. Prembhai, Gen.Sec.   CBL: BANWASI ASHRAM

Founded: 1956. **Staff:** 295. **Budget:** Rs 20,000,000. **Languages:** English, Hindi. **National.** Seeks to improve society by promoting equality for women, refugees, and lower castes. Programs include: education, resettlement, and forestry. Seeks to raise public awareness regarding entitlements for underpriveleged classes. Compiles narrative progress reports. **Awards:** Periodic (scholarship).

★556★ BHARATHA SEVA TRUST (BST)
Avvaiyr Eco-Farm & Training Centre
Paulo Friere Village
PO Box 72
Pudukkottai 622 001, Tamil Nadu, India
V.R. Ganeshan, Exec. Dir.   CBL: BEEYESTEE

Founded: 1984. **Staff:** 9. **Budget:** Rs 325,000. **Languages:** Hindi, English. **National.** Seeks to improve the status of rural women in India by creating social mobility. Women's programs include: literacy, library service, skill training in carpentry and tailoring, and envirnomental activities. Provides shelter for rural children.

★557★ BHARATIYA GRAMEEN MAHILA SABHA
9/104 Jamnagar Hutment, Block 11
Mansingh Rd.
New Delhi 110 001, Delhi, India

Languages: Hindi, English. **National.** Seeks to raise awareness of women's issues, especially in rural areas. Conducts women's development programs to improve housing, training, and education. Lobbies government.

★558★ BHARATIYA GRAMEEN MAHILA SANGH
Malyili Begum Haveli
Shahali Banda
Hyderabad 500 002, Andhra Pradesh,
   India

Founded: 1973. **Languages:** Hindi, English. **National.** Seeks to raise the status of women. Conducts vocational training and educational programs to encourage women to become self-sufficient. Operates agricultural projects and exchange programs between states. Works to improve women's health facilities.

★559★ CENTRE FOR DOCUMENTATION AND RESEARCH ON WOMEN (AALOCHANA)
'KEDAR'
86/11-B Kanchangalli
Erandavana
Poona 411 004, Maharashtra, India
Simrita Gopal Singh, Coordinator   PH: 212 343563

Founded: 1989. **Members:** 6. **Languages:** Marathi, English. Women artists, journalists, students, researchers, and women's groups. Acts as a clearinghouse of information on women's social, political, economic, and legal issues. Holds lectures; offers a forum for discussion among members. Networks with other women's groups. Maintains research centers locally, nationally, and abroad. Compiles statistics. **Libraries:** Type: reference.

★560★ CENTRE FOR HEALTH EDUCATION, TRAINING AND NUTRITION AWARENESS (CHETNA)
Drive-in Cinema Bldg.   PH: 272 490378
Thaltej Rd.   272 496325
Ahmedabad 380 054, Gujarat, India   TX: 1216779
Indu Capoor, Director   CBL: CHETNESS

Staff: 23. **Languages:** Hindi, English. **National.** Collaborates with other nongovernmental organizations to contribute to the empowerment of women. Seeks to enable women to have self-determination over their health, family, and education. Operates the Child Resource Centre. Raises public awareness of women's and children's rights.

★561★ CENTRE FOR WOMEN'S DEVELOPMENT STUDIES (CWDS)
                                       PH: 11 6438428
B-43 Panscheel Enclave   TX: CARE: 3162395 NKSG
New Delhi 110 017, Delhi, India   I
Dr. Kumud Sharma, Dir.   CBL: W OMENDEVS

Founded: 1980. **Members:** 58. **Staff:** 35. **Languages:** English. **National.** Individuals and organizations. Works for women's equality and development in all areas of society. Strives to assist women in realizing their full potential and in exercising their influence. Promotes and develops knowledge, and disseminates information on the evolution of women's role in society. Conducts research on topics such as women's employment, available child care facilities, strategies for advancement, and the role of rural women's organizations in development. Organizes educational courses on women's issues; sponsors training programs for underprivileged women. Collaborates with academic institutions to create women's programs. Provides a clearinghouse for exchange of information among women's group. Maintains library.

Publications: CWDS Bulletin, biennial. ● Journal of Women's Studies, annual.

Conventions/Meetings: annual workshop.

★562★ CENTRE FOR WOMEN'S STUDIES
Department of Adult and Continuing
   Education
University of Rajasthan
Jaipur 302 004, Rajasthan, India

Languages: Hindi, English. **National.** Seeks to raise awareness of women's issues. Conducts research; disseminates information.

★563★ CENTRE FOR WOMEN'S STUDIES AND DEVELOPMENT
Isabella Thoburn College
Lucknow 226 007, Uttar Pradesh, India

Languages: Hindi. **National.** Works for women's equality and development in India through study and research programs. Disseminates information.

★564★ CHATTISGARH MAHILA JAGRITI SANGATHAN
Gramin Shilp Shaka Mahasundara
PO Mahasmudi
Raipur 493 445, Madhya Pradesh, India

Languages: Hindi, English. **National.** Seeks to raise the status of rural women. Conducts campaigns to raise awareness of women's rights.

★565★ CHATTRA YUVA SANGHARSH VAHINI
12 Rajindra Nagar
Patna 800 016, Bihar, India

Founded: 1975. **Languages:** Hindi, English. **National.** Works to raise public consciousness of women's issues. Seeks to improve women's well-being through camps and educational programs.

★566★ CITU WORKING WOMEN'S ASSOCIATION
6 Talkatora Rd.
New Delhi 110 001, Delhi, India

Languages: Hindi, English. **National.** Seeks to advance the status of working women. Encourages women's increased participation in the workplace. Organizes women workers' unions to improve working conditons.

Publications: Voice of the Working Woman, bimonthly.

★567★ COMMITTEE ON THE PORTRAYAL OF WOMEN IN THE MEDIA
4 Bhagwandas Rd.
New Delhi 110 001, Delhi, India

Languages: Hindi, English. **National.** Works to eliminate exploitation of women. Protests negative images of women in all media.

★568★ COMMUNITY AID AND SPONSORSHIP PROGRAMME (CASP)
A-2 Rasadhara Cooperative Housing
   Society Ltd.
385 SVP Rd.   PH: 22 368002
Bombay 400 004, Maharashtra, India   22 381496
Surendra R. Apte, Exec. Dir.   CBL: PRATIPALAN

Staff: 70. **Budget:** Rs 3,667,117. **Languages:** Hindi, English. **National.** Assists impoverished and oppressed women. Seeks to diminish the influx of people from villages to cities by improving village infrastructure, health, education, and economy. Conducts programs in: vocational training for women, water availability, and housing. Raises public awareness of oppression of women, drug abuse, health hazards, and education through slide shows and films.

★569★ CONGREGATION OF MOTHER OF CARMEL (CMC)
(Congregation de la Mere du Carmel)
Mount Carmel Generalate
Alwaye 683 106, Kerala, India
Sr. Prima CMC, Superior Gen.   PH: 4854 4270

Founded: 1866. **Members:** 4,910. **Languages:** Hindi, Malayalam, English. **Multinational.** Roman Catholic women religious in 8 countries. Promotes religious and educational teaching. Provides medical and social assistance.

★570★ CONGREGATION OF THE SISTERS OF THE ADORATION OF THE BLESSED SACRAMENT (SABS)
Adoration Generalate
Cenacle
Alwaye 683 102, Kerala, India
Mother Mary Delphine SABS, Superior
Gen.   PH: 4854 3866

Founded: 1908. **Members:** 3,281. **Languages:** English, Malay. **Multinational**. Religious women living in communal homes and following rules approved by the Vatican; members reside in Australia, Germany, Kenya, India, and Italy. Seeks to inspire worldwide devotion to the Holy Eucharist through pastoral activities such as teaching, working in hospitals, and running orphanages, hostels, and homes for the aged and the handicapped. Provides teacher training; conducts seminars for women and young girls. Sponsors competitions and bestows awards. Maintains museum and 3800 volume library.

Publications: *Directory of the Adoration Congregation* (in Malay). every 6 years. ● *Voice of the Cenacle* (in Malay), quarterly ● *Roma Yathra*. Book. ● *Muthumanical*. Book. ● *Dheera Vanitha*. Book.

Conventions/Meetings: annual conference - always Nov. or Dec.

★571★ COUNTRY WOMEN'S ASSOCIATION OF INDIA
6/1 Durusaday Rd.
Calcutta 700 019, W. Bengal, India

Languages: Hindi. **National**. Examines the welfare of rural women and works for their development. Works to improve rural women's status.

★572★ CYRIAC ELIAS VOLUNTARY ASSOCIATION (CEVA)
CEVA Bhavan
Prior General's House
Ernakulam, Chochin
Karikkamuri 682 011, Karnataka, India
Rev. Fr. Paul Ben Nettikadan, Secretary   PH: 363990

Founded: 1987. **Staff:** 5. **Budget:** Rs 925,390. **Languages:** Hindi, English. **National**. Coordinates women's and children's programs and development activities in India. Programs implemented include: public health, housing, dairy development, and water sanitation.

★573★ DALIT RANGABHOOMI
c/o Shilpa Mumbiskar 307
Mangalwar Peth Bhimnagar
Poona 411 004, Maharashtra, India

Languages: Hindi, English. **National**. Individuals working to raise the status of Dalit women. (Dalit, meaning one who has been oppressed, refers to the lowest of the Hindu castes, sometimes called the "untouchables.") Seeks to abolish the caste system in India.

★574★ FAMILY PLANNING ASSOCIATION OF INDIA (FPAI)
                                           PH: 22 2029080
                                               22 2025174
Bajaj Bhavan   FX: 22 2029038
Nariman Point   TX: 114428 CBCO IN
Bombay 400 021, Maharashtra, India   CBL: FAMPLAN BOMBAY
E.S. Lala, Secretary   INDIA

Languages: Hindi Suriname Hindustanti, English. **National**. Works to improve the quality of life for people living in India by promoting family planning and responsible parenthood. Works to reduce the number of unwanted pregnancies and abortions. Advocates family planning as a basic human right. Offers programs in sex education, family planning, and health. Provides contraceptive and health care services. Conducts research.

★575★ FAMILY PLANNING FOUNDATION
198 Golf Links
New Delhi 110 003, Delhi, India
J. Tata, Chair

Languages: Hindi, English. **National**. Provides information, education, and services to women and their partners regarding family planning. Conducts research; disseminates information.

★576★ FORUM AGAINST THE OPPRESSION OF WOMEN
We Ourselves
Kunda Kadam 120
Safalaya Bldg. 2, 1st Fl.
Curry Rd.
Bombay 400 012, Maharashtra, India

Founded: 1979. **Languages:** Hindi, English. **National**. Organizes demonstrations to raise awareness of opppression of women. Investigates cases of rape. Offers support, counselling, and legal advice to women.

★577★ GITANJALI
Luz Ginza
140 Royapettah High Rd.
Madras 600 004, Tamil Nadu, India
Ms. Vimala Menon, Contact   PH: 44 73507

Founded: 1983. **Staff:** 3. **Languages:** English. **National**. Women and women's organizations throughout India. Promotes the awareness of women's rights and interests. Sponsors book exhibitions.

★578★ IDARA JAIPUR WOMEN'S DEVELOPMENT PROGRAMME
C-85 Ramdas Marg
Tilak Nagar
Jaipur 302 004, Rajasthan, India

Languages: Hindi, English. **National**. Seeks to organize and raise the consciousness of rural women in India. Conducts training and educational programs on health and women's rights. Disseminates information.

★579★ INDIA SINGLES FELLOWSHIP
D-1/189 Chanakyapuri
New Delhi 110 021, Delhi, India
N.M. Balasubrahmanyam, Vice President

Languages: Hindi. **National**. Organizes support groups for widowed and divorced women. Offers legal and financial advice.

★580★ INDIAN FEDERATION OF UNIVERSITY WOMEN'S ASSOCIATIONS (IFUWA)
10 Phayre Rd.
Poona 411 040, Maharashtra, India
Dr. Goolcheher D. Coyaji, President   PH: 212 671726

Founded: 1921. **Members:** 700. **Languages:** English, Hindi. **National**. Promotes advanced education of women and girls. Operates pre-schools and working women's hostels. Fosters edcuational programs and members' active participation in their development. **Awards:** Periodic (scholarship). Recipient: female students.

Conventions/Meetings: quarterly regional meeting. ● biennial conference - 1993 Sept., Poona, MH, India. ● triennial conference

★581★ INSTITUTE OF SOCIAL STUDIES TRUST
5 Deen Dayal
Upadhyaya Marg
New Delhi 110 002, Delhi, India

Languages: Hindi, English. **National**. Promotes the interests of women in India. Conducts research on issues of concern to women. Provides forum for discussion among researchers. **Libraries:** Type: reference.

Conventions/Meetings: periodic seminar.

★582★ JAGRUT MAHILA KENDRA
Morgachiwadi
Pathras
PO Karjat Taluka
Raigad, Maharashtra, India

Founded: 1984. **Languages:** Hindi, English. **National.** Works to improve the socio-economic status of tribal women. Participates in rural development programs. Lobbies government on tribal and women's issues.

★583★ JANVADI MAHILA SAMITI
14 Vithal Bahi Patel House
New Delhi 110 001, Delhi, India

Languages: Hindi, English. **National.** Works to improve the status of women. Campaigns against social oppression and violence against women.

★584★ JANWADI MAHILA SABHA
All India Janwadi Mahila Sabha
Janpath
New Delhi 110 001, Delhi, India

Founded: 1981. **Languages:** Hindi, English. **National.** Works to raise the status of women in India. Aims to: liberate women from the traditions of dowry and suttee; eliminate wage discrimination; fight inflation; encourage improved nutrition; and provide health facilities for women.

★585★ JOINT ACTION FORUM FOR WOMEN
55 Chamiers Rd.
Madras, Tamil Nadu, India

Languages: Hindi, English. **National.** Women's rights activists in India united to advance the social, educational, and economic status of women. Conducts consciousness raising campaigns.

★586★ JOINT WOMEN'S PROGRAMME (JWP)
CISRS House
14 Jangpura B   PH: 11 619821
Mathura Rd.   FX: 11 4623681
New Delhi 110 013, Delhi, India   TX: 74016 IRIS IN

Founded: 1977. **Members:** 10,000. **Local Groups:** 329. **Languages:** Bengali, English, Hindustani, Kannada, Tamil. **National.** Seeks freedom and equality for women in India. Believes that India's present social system is exploitive and oppressive of women. Promotes grassroots organization in urban and rural areas and networking at the regional and national levels among womens's groups and others. Conducts educational and research programs. Maintains library.

Publications: *Ankush* (in Bengali), semiannual. Newsletter. ● *Banhi* (in English and Hindi), semiannual. Newsletter. ● *Kahale* (in Kannada), periodic. Newsletter.

★587★ KARMIKA
B-26 Gulmohar Park
New Delhi 110 049, Delhi, India

Founded: 1982. **Languages:** Hindi, English. **National.** Seeks to raise awareness of women's issues. Offers counselling and legal advice to women in need. Lobbies government for improvement in the status and condition of women.

★588★ KASTURBA GANDHI NATIONAL MEMORIAL TRUST
Kasturbagram
Indore 452 020, Madhya Pradesh, India   PH: 66193
Dr. Sushila Nayar, Chairman   60182

Founded: 1944. **Staff:** 1,390. **Local Groups:** 900. **Languages:** Hindi, English. **National.** Works to improve the standard of living of rural Indian women. Encourages rural women to become self-reliant through increased agricultural and khadi (spun cotton cloth) production. Conducts programs to improve family welfare and health. Trains women as health workers, bookbinders, printers, and other practical and leadership roles. Provides short-term shelter for needy women and children; offers rehabilitation. Coordinates and organizes community and group activities. Disseminates information on women's health, financial, and social status. **Libraries:** Type: reference; open to the public.   Subjects: information relevant to residents of Kasturbagram.

Publications: *Kasturba Darshan* (in Hindi), quarterly. Magazine. ● Also publishes books and other informational works in Hindi.

Conventions/Meetings: semiannual executive committee meeting.

★589★ KASTURBA VANVASI KANYA ASHRAM
Nivali
Nimad, Madhya Pradesh, India

Founded: 1953. **Languages:** Hindi, English. **National.** Works to raise the status of women in India. Conducts programs in: health; education; vocational training; and adult literacy. Operates children's welfare programs.

★590★ LEKHIKA SANGH
G-13 Maharani Bagh
New Delhi 110 065, Delhi, India

Founded: 1959. **Languages:** Hindi, English. **National.** Encourages women to participate in creative writing. Fosters communication among members.

★591★ MADHU KISHWAR
C-202 Lajpat Nagar, 1st Fl.   PH: 11 6833022
New Delhi 110 024, Delhi, India   11 6839158

Founded: 1978. **Staff:** 3. **Languages:** English, Hindi. **National.** Campaigns for equal rights for women and men. Creates street plays and songs to raise public awareness. Coordinates activities to increase communication between various women's groups. Conducts research.

Publications: *Manushi* (in Hindi and English). Journal.

★592★ MAHILA DAKSHATA SAMITI
2 Telegraph Ln.
New Delhi 110 001, Delhi, India

Founded: 1978. **Languages:** Hindi, English. **National.** Promotes issues of interest to women through campaigns, discussion groups, and demonstrations. Defends consumers' rights.

★593★ MAHILA HAKKA SAURAKSHAN SAMITI
Gole Colony
Opp. Gadre Mangal Karyalaya
Nasik 422 001, Maharashtra, India
Mahila Hakka Saurakshan Samiti,
  President   PH: 72813

Founded: 1982. **Members:** 425. **Staff:** 14. **Languages:** Gujarati, Hindi, Marathi, English. **National.** Seeks to raise public awareness of domestic violence, especially that directed toward women, such as ''dowry death''. Conducts demonstrations. Operates counselling center; assists husbands and wives in reconciling differences. Provides women with shelter and legal advice. Offers literacy programs, job training programs, street plays, and seminars. Gathers and disseminates information. **Libraries:** Type: reference. Subjects: women's rights.

Conventions/Meetings: monthly regional meeting.

★594★ MAHILA JAGAN SANGATANA
c/o Samta Gram Sewa Sanghatana
Purbi
Lohanipur
Patna 800 003, Bihar, India
Shree Rabindra

Staff: 10. **Languages:** English, Hindi. **National.** Seeks to enhance public awareness of the problems facing women. Provides public service and educational programs. Engages in research. **Libraries:** Type: reference.

★595★ MAHILA MUKTI MORCHA
c/o Sagjam Shetra Vikas Samiti
Sevapuri
Varanasi 221 403, Uttar Pradesh, India
Rama Kaut Rai, Contact   PH: 21 53470

Founded: 1955. **Members:** 16. **Budget:** Rs 2,500,000. **Languages:** Hindi, English. **National.** Works to: raise the status of women and poor people; eradicate child labor; improve health and sanitation. Conducts educational programs and research on issues of interest to women. **Libraries:** Type: reference. Holdings: 0; books. **Subcommittees:** Health; Literacy; Women's issues.

Publications: *Newsletter* (in Hindi), periodic.

Conventions/Meetings: quarterly workshop (exhibits) - Varanasi, UP, India.

★596★ MAITHRI
c/o Kalpana Kannabiran 606
Amrit Apartments
Kapadia Ln.
Somajiguda
Hyderabad 500 482, Andhra Pradesh,
    India

Languages: Hindi, English. **National.** Conducts discussions and campaigns to raise awareness of women's issues. Disseminates information.

★597★ MAITRINI
c/o Granthali
IES Girls High School
Babrekar Marg, Gokhale Rd.
Dadar (W)
Bombay 400 028, Maharashtra, India

Languages: Hindi. **National.** Aims to raise public consciousness of women's issues. Provides a forum for women to exchange information and experiences. Encourages friendships among members.

★598★ MANASWINI WOMEN'S PROJECT
c/o Manavlok
Dhadpad Office
PO Box 23
Ambajogai 431 517, Maharashtra, India
Mrs. Shaila Lohiya, Contact

Founded: 1984. **Members:** 40. **Staff:** 11. **Budget:** Rs 500,000. **Languages:** Hindi, Marathi, English. **National.** Seeks to raise public awareness of the violations of Asian women's human rights. Works to raise the social, religious, and economic status of women. Provides shelter to destitute women; operates a girls' hostel and education center. Encourages production and sale of handicrafts and agricultural products for women's economic

emancipation; makes available credit to women. Organizes demonstrations. Conducts research surveys. **Libraries:** Type: reference.

Conventions/Meetings: periodic seminar (exhibits).

★599★ MANINI
15-4th N. Block
Rajajinagar
Bangalore 560 010, Karnataka, India
Dr. Meera Chakravorty, Contact   PH: 812 358127

Founded: 1978. **Members:** 60. **Budget:** Rs 12,000. **Languages:** Hindi, Kannada, English. **National.** Works to promote egalitarianism; upholds democratic values. Seeks to raise public awareness of women's issues, environmental problems, and human rights violations. Organizes camps, seminars, and debates. Conducts research; publishes articles. **Libraries:** Type: reference.

Publications: *Kambani* (in Kannada). Book. ● *Mahileyara Munnade* (in Kannada). Book.

Conventions/Meetings: periodic conference.

★600★ MANUSHI
C-1/202 Lajpat Nagar
New Delhi 110 024, Delhi, India

Founded: 1979. **Languages:** Hindi, English. **National.** Conducts group discussions and campaigns in defense of women's rights. Offers legal assistance to women in need. Conducts research.

Publications: *Manushi* (in English). Magazine. Information from a feminist perspective.

★601★ MEDICAL WOMEN'S INTERNATIONAL ASSOCIATION - INDIA
    (MWIA-I)
A-64 Flower Queen
18 Veera Desai Rd.
Andheri (West)
Bombay 400 027, Maharashtra, India
Manju V. Mataliya, Contact

Languages: Hindi. **National.** India national branch of the Medical Women's International Association (see separate entry). Women physicians. Provides a forum for discussion of women's health care issues. Encourages women to enter the field of medicine. Works to overcome discrimination against female physicians. Sponsors research and educational programs.

★602★ NATIONAL COUNCIL OF WOMEN OF INDIA
Newal Kishore Residence
Hazratganj
Lucknow 226 001, Uttar Pradesh, India   PH: 522 243432
Rani Lila Ramkumar Bhargava, President   522 243376

National. Umbrella organization for women's groups in India. Promotes women's interests. Disseminates information on women's issues.

★603★ NATIONAL FEDERATION OF INDIAN WOMEN
1002 Ansal Bhavan
Kasturba Gandhi Marg
New Delhi 110 001, Delhi, India

Founded: 1954. **Languages:** Hindi, English. **National.** Seeks to improve the status of women. Represents and defends the interests of working women. Organizes campaigns and discussions to raise public awareness of women's issues. Lobbies government.

★604★ NISHANT NATYA MANCH
Neelima Sharma
A/2-15 Model Town
New Delhi 110 009, Delhi, India   PH: 11 7248242
Neelima Sharma, Secretary   11 2222145
Founded: 1971. **Members:** 30. **Staff:** 3. **Budget:** Rs 100,000. **Languages:**
Hindi, Punjabi, Bhojpuri, Urdu, English. **National.** Seeks to raise awareness
of women's issues, communalism, health and education, and workers' rights
through street theatre. Members perform songs, distribute literature, orga-
nize marches, and present plays. Focus areas are low-income and working
class villages, and educational institutions. **Libraries:** Type: reference.

★605★ ORGANIZATION FOR WOMEN'S LIBERATION
No. 12/970-A, 1st Mile
Devarshola Rd.
Gudalur, Tamil Nadu, India
Ms. B. Mythily, President   PH: 4269557
Founded: 1984. **Members:** 16. **Budget:** Rs 100,000. **Languages:** English.
Works toward the advancement of the position and status of women and the
protection of women against exploitation and oppression. Provides women's
development programs: formal education, preventative health awareness,
women and community development, and leadership training. Also offers
daycare and preschool services.

Conventions/Meetings: monthly meeting - Gudalur, India.

★606★ PENNURAMAI IYAKKAM
13 New Colony
Josier St.
Nungambakkam
Madras 600 034, Tamil Nadu, India
Founded: 1979. **Languages:** Hindi, English. **National.** Works to raise public
awareness of women's issues in India. Offers legal counselling to women.

★607★ POONA MAHILA MANDAL
17 Parvati
Poona 411 009, Maharashtra, India
Founded: 1927. **Languages:** Hindi, English. **National.** Works to raise
women's awareness of their legal rights. Conducts lectures and research on
issues of women and the law.

★608★ RAIGARH AMBIKAPUR HEALTH ASSOCIATION
c/o Bishop's House
PO Kunkuri
Raigarh, Madhya Pradesh, India
Founded: 1969. **Languages:** Hindi, English. **National.** Works to improve
women's standard of living in India. Conducts health and educational
programs.

★609★ SABHLA SANGH
G Block, Jehangirpuri
New Delhi 110 033, Delhi, India
Languages: Hindi, English. **National.** Works to improve the well-being of
women and increase public awareness of women's issues. Conducts income
generation programs.

★610★ SACHETANA
31 Mahanirban Rd.
Calcutta 700 029, W. Bengal, India
Languages: Hindi, English, Bengali. **National.** Represents the political, legal,
and social interests of women in India. Seeks to enhance public awareness of
women's rights.

Publications: *Newsletter* (in Bengali), periodic.

★611★ SAHELI-WOMEN'S RESOURCE CENTRE
105-108 Shopping Centre
Defence Colony Flyover
New Delhi 110 024, Delhi, India
Founded: 1981. **Languages:** Hindi, English. **National.** Conducts activities to
improve women's well-being. Offers emotional and legal counselling to
women; provides women's health facilities.

Conventions/Meetings: periodic workshop (exhibits).

★612★ SAMAJWADI MAHILA SABHA
250-K Shanivar Peth
Pune 411 030, Maharashtra, India
Founded: 1959. **Languages:** Hindi, English. **National.** Seeks to raise
women's awareness of politics and legal issues. Provides vocational training
and part-time employment for women. Disseminates information.

★613★ SARVAHARA MAHILA AGHADI
c/o Kala Rathod
Naik Nagar
Banjara Colony
Aurangabad 431 001, Maharashtra, India
Founded: 1979. **Languages:** Hindi, English. **National.** Organizes nomadic
tribal women in India to improve their living conditions. Concerns include:
water sanitation; peace; employment; and equal wages.

★614★ SELF EMPLOYED WOMEN'S ASSOCIATION (SEWA)
SEWA Reception Centre
OPPI-Victoria Garden
Bhandra
Ahmedabad 380 001, Gujarat, India   PH: 272 390577
Pratibha Pandya, Admin.   FX: 272 469101
Founded: 1980. **Members:** 46,000. **Staff:** 125. **Languages:** English, Gujara-
ti, Hindi. **National.** Self-employed women united to achieve equal status in
social, economic, political, and cultural matters. Encourages formation of
cooperatives; conducts educational and research programs; offers children's
services. SEWA was formerly a section of the Textile Labour Association of
India.

Publications: *Anasuya* (in Gujarati), biweekly. ● *Annual Activities Report* (in
English). ● *SEWA Annual Report* (in English, Gujarati, and Hindi). **Circulation:**
1,200. ● *We the Self-Employed* (in English), periodic. ● Also publishes
booklets.

Conventions/Meetings: monthly (exhibits).

★615★ SHRAMIK STREE MUKTI SANGATHANA
Shahada
Monde Rd.
Dhulia, Maharashtra, India
Languages: Hindi, English. **National.** Seeks to raise awareness of women's
rights. Conducts social welfare programs, especially among tribal women.

★616★ STREE ADHAR KENDRA (SAK)
Anand Clinic
Satawwadi Hadapsar
Pune 411 028, Maharashtra, India
Dr. Neelam Gorhe, Chairman of the   PH: 212 342172
   Board   212 672278
Founded: 1984. **Members:** 1,000. **Staff:** 6. **Budget:** Rs 10,000. **Languages:**
Hindi, English, Marathi. **National.** Seeks to change attitudes and laws
regarding dowries, domestic violence, rape, child marriage, sexual discrimina-

tion, and other activities that oppress women. Believes that men exploit women through the agencies of religion, superstition, customs, and casteism. Conducts activities to raise public awareness of women's issues through educational programs, think tanks, cultural programs, and dialogue with other women's groups. Encourages women to develop sustainable livelihoods and participate in politics. Provides women with econmic aid, moral support, and legal and medical advice. **Committees:** Women and Law; Women and Health; Income Generation for Women; Counselling and Atrocities against Women.

Publications: *Amhi Streya* (in Marathi), monthly. Magazine. ● *TARA* (in English), quarterly. Magazine.

★617★ STREE ATYACHAR VIRODHI PARISHAD
Plot No. 17, Ganesh Colony
Ring Rd.
Rana Pratap Nagar Sq.
Nagpur 440 022, Maharashtra, India

Languages: Hindi, English. **National.** Seeks to raise public awareness of women's issues through exhibtions and poster creation and display. Disseminates information.

★618★ STREE KAMGAR KARMACHARI SANGATHANA
174 Shukrawar Peth
Bhinde Alley
Poona 411 002, Maharashtra, India

Languages: Hindi, English. **National.** Works to influence trade unions to take account of women's interests in their policies.

★619★ STREE MUKTI SANGATHANA
c/o Sharda Sathe
Shramik
Vincent Sq., Ln. No. 3
Dadar
Bombay 400 014, Maharashtra, India

Languages: Hindi, English. **National.** Organizes demonstrations and produces plays to raise women's consciousnesss of events affecting their lives. Disseminates information.

★620★ STREEVANI - VOICE OF WOMEN
c/o Ishvani Kendra
Dhole Patel Rd.
Vinay Vikas Bldg.
Poona 411 001, Maharashtra, India   PH: 212 660761

Founded: 1982. **Staff:** 3. **Languages:** Hindi, English. **National.** Activists, scholars, and other interested individuals. Studies women's self-perception through their oral histories, religious beliefs, and myths. Encourages women to gain the self-confidence necessary for personal growth and development. Networks with other women's organizations to facilitate social change. Conducts research and sponsors educational programs. Operates a drop-in counselling center for women in distress. Plans to establish a library.

Conventions/Meetings: periodic seminar.

★621★ U.T. WOMEN'S WELFARE ASSOCIATION
Physics Laboratory
Govt. College for Women, Sector 11
Chandigarh, Punjab, India
Ms. Harjinder Jawanda, Contact

Languages: Hindi, English. **National.** Seeks to raise women's standard of living. Represents women's interests to trade unions.

★622★ VASUKI SEVA NILAYAM (VSN)
13A Vandipathai
K. Pudur
Madurai 625 014, Tamil Nadu, India   PH: 44500
Dr. P.N. Narayana Raja, Secretary   42312

Founded: 1982. **Members:** 120. **Staff:** 6. **Budget:** US$7,500. **Languages:** Hindi, English. **National.** Works to improve women's well being in India. Provides shelter and food for widows, orphans, and victims of domestic violence. Conducts vocational training programs in tailoring, nursing, and small scale industry. Offers counselling services and legal assistance. Operates children's programs and educational services for college students. Encourages AIDS awareness and prevention. **Libraries:** Type: reference. Holdings: 100; books.

Conventions/Meetings: annual (exhibits) - Madurai, TN, India.

★623★ VIGIL INDIA MOVEMENT
13 Charles Campbell Rd.
Bangalore 560 005, Karnataka, India

Founded: 1977. **Members:** 3,000. **Languages:** Hindi, English. **National.** Women fighting against oppression and exploitation. Aims to educate the public on women's issues. Disseminates information.

★624★ VIMOCHANA
7 Balaji Layout
Wheeler Rd. Extension
Bangalore 560 005, Karnataka, India

Founded: 1980. **Languages:** English, Hindi, Kannada. **National.** Works to raise awareness of women's issues in India through campaigns and demonstrations. Represents women in sexual harassment cases. Conducts research.

Publications: *Newsletter* (in Kannada and English), periodic.

★625★ WOMEN AND CHILD DEVELOPMENT ASSOCIATION (WCDA)
PO Box 63
Churachandpur 795 128, Manipur, India
S. Singson, Secretary

Languages: Hindi. **National.** Works for women's equality and development. Sponsors training programs in traditional and commercial skills. Provides educational and children's programs. Conducts research; disseminates information.

★626★ WOMEN LAWYERS COLLECTIVE
818 Stock Exchange Towers
Dalal St.
Bombay 39, Maharashtra, India   PH: 22 272794
Indira Jaising, Director   22 276637

National. Provides a forum for discussion and information exchange among women lawyers. Provides information for professional advancement. Promotes women's interests in legal development and decision making.

★627★ WOMEN AND MEDIA GROUP
c/o B.U.J.
Prospect Chambers, 2nd Fl.
D.N. Rd.
Bombay 400 001, Maharashtra, India

Languages: Hindi, English. **National.** Works to raise public awareness of exploitation of women in the media. Conducts research on participation and portrayal of women in the media, and its impact on their lives.

★628★ WOMEN'S CENTRE (WC)
(NKM Nari Kendra Mumbai)
104-B Sunrise Apartments
Nehru Rd.
Vakola
Santacruz, East
Bombay 400 055, Maharashtra, India
Ammu Abraham, Contact   PH: 22 6140403

Founded: 1982. **Members:** 40. **Staff:** 4. **Budget:** Rs 200,000. **Regional Groups:** 1. **Local Groups:** 1. **Languages:** Bengali, English, Gujarati, Hindi, Malayalam, Marathi. **National.** Women united to give mutual support. Seeks to enhance awareness of women's issues. Offers financial, medical, legal, and employment search assistance to women. Participates in demonstrations and campaigns. Operates placement service, counseling service, and charitable program. Conducts research; sponsors conferences, lectures, meetings, seminars, and workshops. Organizes essay and music competitions; maintains library.

Publications: *Womennews* (in English, Gujarati, Hindi, and Marathi), periodic. Newsletter. includes articles and songs. **Circulation:** 1,000. **Advertising:** not accepted. ● *Women's Centre Newsletter* (in English and Marathi), bimonthly. Contains information on the activities of the Women's Centre. **Advertising:** not accepted. ● Also publishes research monographs on violence in the family and regional language booklets on violence against women.

Conventions/Meetings: annual - always Bombay, India.

★629★ WOMEN'S CO-ORDINATION COUNCIL (WCC)
5/1 Red Cross Pl.
Calcutta 700 062, W. Bengal, India
Mrs. Renuka Ray, President   PH: 33 289732

Founded: 1960. **Members:** 222. **Languages:** English, Bengali. **National.** Women's organizations and interested individuals. Assists needy communities through the provision of welfare programs. Offers disaster relief programs for communities affected by natural disasters. Operates adult education, drug counseling, and legal aid centers. Maintains homes for children and the aged. Conducts awareness programs on women's rights, health, hygiene, and sanitation. **Libraries:** Type: reference.

Publications: *Directory of WCC* (in English and Bengali). List of coordinated organizations.

Conventions/Meetings: semimonthly meeting. ● bimonthly general assembly. ● WCC Annual Exhibition (exhibits) - Calcutta, WB, India.

★630★ WOMEN'S DEVELOPMENT ASSOCIATION
(Nari Bikash Sangha)
Post Office
Jhilimili
Bankura 722 135, W. Bengal, India
Malati Mandi, Secretary

Founded: 1986. **Members:** 19. **Languages:** English, Bengali. **Multinational.** Rural women and organizations striving to increase the standard of living for women and children. Coordinates the projects of local affiliates. Provides child care, adult education, training, and raw materials. Helps to market local groups' products. Distributes food, clothes, and kerosene oil to the needy. Offers legal help to female victims of violence. Communicates with development groups. Conducts workshops and seminars. Encourages women to become self-sufficient. Participates in research.

Conventions/Meetings: annual general assembly. ● executive committee meeting - 3/year.

★631★ WOMEN'S EQUAL RIGHTS GROUP
D/3 Akashdeep Apartments
Ellis Bridge
Ahmedabad 380 006, Gujarat, India

Languages: Hindi, English. **National.** Works to eliminate sexism. Promotes equal opportunity for women's employment, education, and social status.

★632★ WOMEN'S FEATURE SERVICE

49 Golf Links
New Delhi 110 003, Delhi, India
Anita Anand, Director

PH: 11 4629886
FX: 11 4629886
TX: 3161922 RAJAINN
E-Mail: TCN1850

Founded: 1978. **Staff:** 16. **Languages:** English. **Multinational.** Promotes the interests of women on international, national, and local levels. Disseminates information on women's development. Works to change discrimination in the media's portrayal or women.

Conventions/Meetings: periodic workshop.

★633★ WOMEN'S FORUM FOR ACTION
Institute for Development Education
18 Ormes Rd.
Kilpauk
Madras 600 010, Tamil Nadu, India
Sarah Mathew, Contact

Languages: Hindi, English. **National.** Inidividuals organized to seek solutions to discrimination and inequity facing women in India. Represents and defends the rights of women.

★634★ WOMEN'S INSTITUTE FOR NEW AWARENESS (WINA)
John's Hill
Nandigudda Rd.
Attavar
Mangalore 575 001, Karnataka, India
Dr. Jessie B. Tellis-Nayak, Coord.

Founded: 1982. **Members:** 110. **Staff:** 1. **Budget:** Rs 50,000. **Languages:** Hindi, Kannada, English. **National.** Aims to build solidarity among women. Fosters communication and exchange with women worldwide. Conducts research and educational programs on feminist theology and literature. Seeks to raise consciousness regarding women's issues and disseminate positive, non-traditional information. Encourages women to write and publish articles and books. Trains women's development workers. **Libraries:** Type: reference. Holdings: books. Subjects: feminist literature. **Formerly:** Women in India, Asia, and Africa.

Publications: *WINA VANI*, periodic. Newsletter.

Conventions/Meetings: periodic executive committee meeting.

★635★ WOMEN'S PROTECTION LEAGUE
(NRS Nari Raksha Samiti)
Rajeniwas Marg
Civil Lines
New Delhi 110 054, Delhi, India
Mrs. Usha Ahuja, President   PH: 11 2523949

Founded: 1949. **Members:** 400. **Staff:** 6. **Languages:** Hindi, English. **National.** Works to assist the development of women and children who have been abused, neglected, or victimized by their families or by society. Denounces India's dowry system; offers legal assistance to women opposing dowry laws. Opposes trafficking in women; seeks the rehabilitation of women victimized by trafficking rings. Supports the maintenance of shelters for women and children. Conducts educational programs that focus on women's self-employment. Distributes supplies to underpriveleged women.

Conventions/Meetings: monthly meeting, Zone organizers. (exhibits) - New

Delhi, DH, India. ● quarterly meeting, Area meetings. (exhibits) - New Delhi, DH, India.

★636★ WORKING WOMEN'S COORDINATION COMMITTEE
F-156 Rajpura Colony
Patiala, Punjab, India
Ms. Ravinderjeet Kaur, Contact

Languages: Hindi, English. **National.** Represents and defends the interests of working women in trade unions.

★637★ WORKING WOMEN'S FORUM - INDIA
c/o Ms. Jaya Arunachalam
55 Bhimsena Garden Rd.
Madras 600 004, Tamil Nadu, India   PH: 44 74553
Ms. Jaya Arunachalam, Pres.   FX: 44 944444

Founded: 1978. **Members:** 160,000. **Budget:** US$200,000. **Local Groups:** 9. **Languages:** English, Hindi, Kannada, Tamil, Telugu. **National.** Women working in the "informal sector" of the Indian economy includng small-scale traders, vendors of produce and handicrafts, and hand launderers and other service providers. (Women in the informal sector traditionally come from lower castes and have very low incomes.) Works to: enable women to influence public policy through collective action; advance the legal rights and social standing of women; oppose traditional definitions of dowry, rape, and divorce which WWFI believes increase women's susceptibility to economic and social domination. Facilitates economic independence of members through credit program providing low-interest loans to neighborhood groups of women. Conducts health care projects which: provide members with health care, nutrition education, and family planning assistance; train women to perform marketable skills in the health care field; disseminate information on existing health care programs. Maintains services to enhance members' entrepreneurial skills and support the economic role of women including day care centers, night classes for children of informal workers, and training courses. Sponsors rallies and demand marches. Conducts research programs. Bestows awards. Compiles statistics.

Publications: *Directory* (in English), periodic. ● *SEEDS*, periodic. Pamphlet series. ● *Decade of the Forum.* Book. ● *Empowering Women Workers.* Book. ● *Credit Needs of Women Workers in the Informal Sector.* Bulletin. ● *Towards Sustainable Development: Empowerment of Poor Women.* Bulletin. ● *Working Women's Forum: A Counter-Culture by Poor Women.* Bulletin.

Conventions/Meetings: semiannual meeting.

★638★ YOUNG WOMEN'S CHRISTIAN ASSOCIATION - INDIA
                                        PH: 11 310294
10 Parliament St.   11 311561
New Delhi 110 001, Delhi, India   CBL: EMISSARIUS NEW
Sadhona Ganguli, Gen.Sec.   DELHI

Founded: 1961. **Languages:** Hindi, English. **National.** Women seeking to develop young women in India emotionally, spiritually, and physically through Christian beliefs. Strives to develop young women's leadership skills. Conducts educational and training programs. Operates a handicraft cooperative. Supports children's health improvement programs.

Indonesia

★639★ ASSOCIATION OF WOMEN OF THE REPUBLIC OF
    INDONESIA (PERWARI)
JL Mentrng Raya 35
Pusat
Jakarta, Indonesia
Mrs. E. Maria Abdul Karim, President   PH: 21 56996

Languages: Indonesian. **National.** Aims to foster solidarity among women. Encourages awareness of women's issues.

★640★ INDONESIAN PLANNED PARENTHOOD ASSOCIATION (IPPA)
                                        PH: 21 715905
Jalan Hang Jebat III/F3   21 713904
PO Box 6017   FX: 21 7394088
Kebayoran Baru   TX: 46024 PUBLIC IA
12060 Jakarta, Indonesia   INDO
Dr. Kus Hardjanti, Exec. Dir.   CBL: IPPA JAKARTA

Languages: Indonesian, English. **National.** Works to improve the quality of life for individuals living in Indonesia through responsible parenthood and family planning. Advocates family planning as a basic human right. Offers programs in family planning, sex education, and health care. Provides contraceptive and health care services. Conducts research.

★641★ INDONESIAN SOCIETY FOR PERINATOLOGY (PERINASIA)
(PERINASIA Perkumpulan Perinatologi Indonesia)
Jalan Tebet Utara IA/22
12820 Jakarta, Indonesia   PH: 21 8281243
Gulardi H. Wiknjosastro M.D., Contact   FX: 21 8300074

Founded: 1981. **Members:** 300. **Budget:** 200,000,000 Rp. **Local Groups:** 17. **Languages:** English, Indonesian. **National.** Obstetricians, gynecologists, pediatricians, midwives, and interested others. Strives to reduce the perinatal mortality rate; works to improve prenatal, natal, and postnatal health care; seeks improved medical facilities. Holds workshops, congresses, seminars, and symposia on perinatal health care and related subjects. Advocates research in safe birth practices; promotes the use of preventive medicine in prenatal care. Encourages community participation in health care improvement programs. Offers technical assistance to government authorities. Cooperates with similar international organizations. Conducts surveys. Disseminates information.

Publications: *Perinasia B* (in Indonesian), quarterly. Bulletin. **ISSN:** 0215-9422. **Circulation:** 1,000. **Advertising:** accepted. ● Also publishes congress proceedings and books.

Conventions/Meetings: triennial congress - 1994.

★642★ INDONESIAN WOMEN'S CONGRESS
(Kongres Wanita Indonesia)
Jalan Imam Bonjol 58
10310 Jakarta, Indonesia   PH: 21 364921
Endang Abimanyu, Secretary   21 364679

Founded: 1928. **Members:** 64. **National.** An umbrella organization consisting of 64 social, professional, functional, and religious women's organizations. Promotes the total development of women in a just and prosperous society based on the Pancasila State Philosophy and the 1945 Constitution. The Pancasila sets out: "Belief in the One and Supreme God; Just and Civilized Humanity; Unity of Indonesia; Democracy guided by the wisdom of Consultation among Representations; Social Justice for all of the Indonesian people". Aims to coordinate women's efforts for full implementation of women's equal rights in Indonesia. Establishes a communication and information network. Seeks to: empower women; enhances women's role in the family and society; fully integrate women in all fields of development. Promotes education and professionalism of women in Indonesia. Conducts vocational skill training and job placement. **Libraries:** Type: open to the public.   Subjects: women's development issues. **Awards:** Periodic (scholarship). **Subcommittees:** Organizations, Structures, Procedures and Cadreforming; Education, Science and Technology; Mental Enrichment and Culture; Health, Family and Social Welfare; Population and Environment; Economy and Cooperatives; Employment; Laws; International Relations; Humanitarian Foundations; Communication, Information and Documentation.

★643★ INTERNATIONAL FEDERATION FOR FAMILY HEALTH (IFFH)
(Federasi Keschatan Keluarga Internasional)
Jalan Makmur 24
Bandung, Indonesia   PH: 22 52902
Prof. Sulaiman Bandung, Pres.   CBL: IFFH BANDUNG

Founded: 1977. **Members:** 17. **Staff:** 2. **Multinational.** National fertility research programs engaged in the evaluation of family planning projects designed to improve the quality of life in the Third World. Primary objectives are: to promote family health care; to exchange ideas, problems, and experiences resulting from project activities within member countries. Efforts are aimed at reducing maternal and perinatal mortality and encouraging acceptance of postpartum family planning counseling. Encourages autonomous national fertility research programs; maintains library. **Committees:** Scientific.

Publications: *Family Health Programs*, annual. ● *Membership Roster*, periodic. ● Also publishes brochure and activities report; plans to publish newsletter.

Conventions/Meetings: annual general assembly.

★644★ KALYANAMITRA WOMEN'S COMMUNICATION AND INFORMATION CENTRE (WCIC)
(YKM Kalyanamitra - Pusat Komunikasi dan Informasi Wanita)
Jl. Sebret 10A
Ps. Minggu
12540 Jakarta, Indonesia   PH: 21 7806683
Sita Aripurnami, Program Coord.   FX: 21 4899706

Founded: 1985. **Members:** 10. **Staff:** 7. **Budget:** 150,000,000 Rp. **Languages:** English, Indonesian. **National.** Provides aid to all women disadvantaged by lack of access to information and minimal opportunity for communication with other women. Seeks to create strong networks among women's groups and provide effective channels for communication. Conducts research. Offers educational programs which include training sessions. Maintains 2500 volume library including working papers, serials, and clippings. **Computer Services:** Data base, bibliographies and abstracts; mailing lists. **Sections:** Library and Documentation; Research; Training and Discussion.

Publications: *DONGBRET: Internal* (in English and Indonesian), semiannual. Bulletin. Kalyanamitra foundation. ● *Newsletter* (in English and Indonesian), quarterly. ● Also publishes periodic reports.

Conventions/Meetings: bimonthly, External and internal discussion. (exhibits).

★645★ KANTOR MENTERI NEGARA URUSAN PERANAN WANITA
Jalan Medan Merdeka Barat 15
10110 Jakarta, Indonesia   PH: 21 3805558
Ms. Achie Sudiarti Luhulima, Contact   21 3805562

National. Promotes and supports the interests of Indonesian women. Investigates women's concerns; disseminates information.

Japan

★646★ ASIAN WOMEN WORKERS CENTER
2-3-18-34 Nishi-Waseda
Shinjuku-ku
Tokyo 169, Japan
Miyoko Shiozawa, Director

National. Protects the rights of Asian women workers. Disseminate information on health care, education, and other issues related to women laborers in Japan.

Publications: *Newsletter*, periodic. Issues on women's labor in Japan.

★647★ ASIAN WOMEN'S ASSOCIATION
c/o Nishihara Church
76 Aza Goya
Nishihara-cho
Okinawa 903-01, Japan

Languages: Japanese. **Multinational.** Works to advance the status of Asian women by providing a variety of educational, community, and legal services.

★648★ FAMILY PLANNING FEDERATION OF JAPAN (FPFJ)
Hoken Kaikan Bekkan
1-1 Sadohara-cho   PH: 3 332694738
Ichigaya   FX: 3 332672658
Shinjuku-ku   TX: 2324584 JOICFP
Tokyo 162, Japan   CBL: JOICFPJAPAN
Mr. Yasuo Kon, Secretary   TOKYO

Languages: Japanese. **National.** Works to improve the quality of life for individuals living in Japan by promoting family planning and responsible parenthood. Works to reduce the number of unwanted pregnancies and abortions. Offers programs in family planning, sex education, and health. Provides contraceptive services. Acts as an advocate for family planning on a national level. Conducts research.

★649★ FEDERATION OF JAPANESE WOMEN'S ORGANIZATIONS (FUDANREN)
303, 4-11-9 Sendagaya
Shibuya-ku   PH: 3 34016147
Tokyo 151, Japan   FX: 3 354745585
Masako Shirai, Gen.Sec.   CBL: FUJINRENGO

Founded: 1953. **Members:** 700,000. **Languages:** English, Japanese. **National.** Women's organizations. Seeks to improve the lives of women and promote the interests of member groups. Encourages communication and cooperation among members.

Publications: *Women's Newsletter* (in Japanese), monthly.

★650★ INTERNATIONAL FEDERATION OF CERVICAL PATHOLOGY AND COLPOSCOPY (IFCPC)
(Federacion Internacional de Patologia Cervical y Colposcopia)
c/o Dr. H. Sugimori
Dept. of Gynecology and Obstetrics
Saga Medical School
Nabeshima
Saga 849, Japan   PH: 952 316511
Dr. H. Sugimori, Sec.Gen.   FX: 952 316543

Founded: 1972. **Members:** 22. **Languages:** English, French, German, Spanish. **Multinational.** National societies encouraging basic and applied research and the dissemination of information concerning uterine cervical pathology and colposcopy.

Conventions/Meetings: triennial world congress (exhibits) - 1996, Sydney, Australia.

★651★ JAPAN INSTITUTE OF WOMEN'S EMPLOYMENT
3F Kono Bldg.
1-23-9 Nishi-Shimbashi
Minato-ku
Tokyo 105, Japan
Ryoko Akamatsu, President

National. Promotes the development and social status of women workers in Japan.

Publications: *Japanese Women.* Book. Issues on women's development from the past to the present.

★652★ JAPANESE ASSOCIATION OF UNIVERSITY WOMEN (JAUW)
Toyama Mansion, No. 241
7-17-8 Shinjuku
Shinjuku-ku
Tokyo, Japan   PH: 3 32020572
Reiko Aoki, President   FX: 3 32020830

Founded: 1946. **Members:** 2,020. **Staff:** 2. **Budget:** 21,700,000¥. **Regional Groups:** 32. **Languages:** Japanese, English. **National.** Female college graduates united to elevate the status of women. Works to improve social welfare; promotes international understanding and friendship. Conducts research; disseminates information. **Awards:** National (scholarship). ● International (scholarship). ● Dr. Holmes (scholarship).

Publications: *JAUW* (in Japanese), quarterly. Magazine. ● *Seminar Report* (in Japanese), annual. Bulletin.

Conventions/Meetings: annual general assembly - always April 1. Tokyo, Japan. ● monthly board meeting. ● annual congress - always March 31. Tokyo, Japan.

★653★ JAPANESE WOMEN SPEAK OUT
c/o PARC
PO Box 5250
Tokyo International
Tokyo, Japan

National. Works towards full public recognition of women's rights through information dissemination, political activity, and meetings and lectures.

★654★ LEAGUE OF WOMEN VOTERS OF JAPAN
21-11, Yoyogi chome
Shibuya-ku
Tokyo 151, Japan   PH: 3 3702727
Michiko Mastuure, President   3 3705650

Languages: Japanese. **National.** Encourages participation of women in politics. Conducts voter education campaigns. Disseminates information.

★655★ MEDICAL WOMEN'S INTERNATIONAL ASSOCIATION - JAPAN
Ichigaya House 604
39 Yakojimachi, Ichigaya
Shinjuku-ku
Tokyo 162, Japan
Teruko Nomoto, Contact

Languages: Japanese. **National.** Japanese national branch of the Medical Women's International Association (see separate entry). Women physicians. Provides a forum for discussion of women's health care issues. Encourages women to enter the field of medicine. Works to overcome discrimination against female physicians. Sponsors research and educational programs.

★656★ NATIONAL WOMEN'S EDUCATION CENTRE OF JAPAN
(Kokuritsu Fujin Kuyoiku Kaikan)
728 Sugaya
Ranzan-machi
Hiki-gun
Saitama 355, Japan   PH: 493 626711
Mizue Maeda, Director   FX: 493 626721

Founded: 1977. **Staff:** 31. **Languages:** Japanese, English. **National.** Promotes continuing education for women. Sponsors women's history studies, family studies, and international exchange. Provides a forum for exchange among members. Collects and disseminates information; conducts research. Operates training and educational programs for women. **Libraries:** Type: reference. Holdings: 35,750; books, periodicals. **Computer Services:** Online services, WINET (Women's Information Network System); bibliographic search, monographs and periodicals on women's issues; data base, information on women's centers and educational programs in Japan.

Publications: *NWEC Newsletter* (in English), semiannual. **ISSN:** 0910-4623.

Advertising: not accepted. ● *Fujin Kyoiku Joho* (in Japanese), semiannual. Journal. Women's education. ● *Kokuritsu Fujin Kyoiku Kaikan Nyusu* (in Japanese), quarterly. Newsletter. Women's education. ● *Directory*, periodic. Register of women's studies courses offered at educational institutions in Japan.

Conventions/Meetings: periodic National Exchange Meeting for Women meeting. ● periodic International Forum on Intercultural Exchange convention.

★657★ WORLD'S WOMAN'S CHRISTIAN TEMPERANCE UNION - JAPAN
4-29, Kuhgahara
4-chome, Ohta-ku
Tokyo 146, Japan
Mrs. Eiko Nagano, V.Pres.

National. Women working to educate children and adults on the "evils of alcohol, tobacco, and narcotic drugs." Conducts drug abuse seminars and workshops for youth; sponsors professional training programs for counselors.

★658★ YOUNG WOMEN'S CHRISTIAN ASSOCIATION - JAPAN
8-8 Kudan Minami, 4-chome
Chiyodakyu
Tokyo 102, Japan
Reiko Suzuki, Gen.Sec.   PH: 3 32640661

National. Promotes the development of young women in Japan. Upholds Christian beliefs and values in its programs. Works to instill self worth and self-esteem in young women.

Kiribati

★659★ KIRIBATI WOMEN'S FEDERATION
(AMAK Aia Maea Ainen Kiribati)
Division of Community Development
Ministry of Home Affairs and
   Decentralisation
PO Box 75
Bairiki
Tarawa, Kiribati

Founded: 1982. **Languages:** English. **National.** Promotes the interests of women in Kiribati. Encourages friendly relations among women. Liaises with other women's organizations to improve the status of women.

Korea, Democratic People's Republic of

★660★ FAMILY PLANNING & MCH ASSOCIATION OF THE
   DEMOCRATIC PEOPLE'S REPUBLIC OF KOREA (FPMCHA-DPRK)
Puksong-2-Dong
Pyongchon District
Pyong Yang City, Democratic People's
   Republic of Korea   CBL: POP CENTRE
Prof. M.D. Hong Sun Won, Chairman   PYONGYANG

Languages: Korean. **National.** Advocates family planning and responsible parenthood as a means to enhance the quality of life. Promotes family planning as a basic human right. Works to reduce the number of unwanted pregnancies and abortions. Offers programs in sex education, family planning, and health. Provides contraceptive services. Conducts research.

Korea, Republic of

★661★ CATHOLIC WOMEN'S CENTER
Seok Joun Dong 224-7
Masan City, Republic of Korea

Languages: Korean. **National.** Promotes principles of Catholicism among women in Korea. Supports missionary activities.

★662★ KOREA RAPE CRISIS CENTER
1595-2, Socho-dong
Century-2 Bldg., Room 802
Socho-ku
Seoul 137-070, Republic of Korea   PH: 2 5221040

Languages: Korean. **National.** Provides support services to victims of rape, such as counseling, support groups, and legal advice. Promotes efforts towards firmer legal prosecution of aggressors.

★663★ KOREA WOMEN'S ASSOCIATIONS UNITED (KWAU)
1-23 Chung-dong
Choong-ku   PH: 2 7382883
Seoul 100-120, Republic of Korea   2 7376891
Mrs. Han Myung-Sook, Contact   FX: 2 7229244

Founded: 1987. **Members:** 25. **Staff:** 6. **Languages:** English. **National.** Umbrella organization of 25 women's movement groups. Aims to build solidarity and unity among members to accomplish democratization, national autonomy, and reunification of Korea. Seeks to liberate women on the basis of unity with the national democratic minjung (people) movement. Advocates the improvement of women's rights. Opposes gender oppression and military rule. Conducts forums, seminars, training programs, and workshops. **Committees:** Peace and Reunification; International Cooperation; Legislation of Special Sexual Violence Act; Labour.

Publications: *Democratic Women* (in Korean), semiannual. Bulletin. ● Research reports and information booklets on related issues.

★664★ KOREAN FEDERATION OF BUSINESS AND PROFESSIONAL
      WOMEN'S CLUBS
Cho Oryon Bldg., 2nd Fl.
85-1 Shinsa-dong
Kangnam-gu   PH: 2 5145200
Seoul, Republic of Korea   2 5169608
Dr. Yunsook Hong, Pres.   FX: 2 515 2187

Founded: 1969. **Members:** 500. **Staff:** 2. **Budget:** US$27,500. **Local Groups:** 16. **Languages:** Korean, English. **National.** Seeks to promote women's rights, improve occupational opportunity, and consolidate affiliations with women of other countries. Conducts educational programs for career women as well as high school and college girls. **Awards:** Distinguished Career Woman of the Year (recognition). **Telecommunication Services:** Phone referral system.

Publications: *Annual Report.* ● *Business and Professional Women*, biennial. Newsletter. Includes summaries of symposia; reports on group activities and events. **Circulation:** 500.

Conventions/Meetings: monthly meeting. ● annual meeting - 1993, Seoul, Republic of Korea. ● triennial congress - always Seoul, Korea.

★665★ KOREAN NATIONAL COUNCIL OF WOMEN
40-427 The 3rd St.
Han River
Yongsan-ku   PH: 2 7935196
Seoul 140-013, Republic of Korea   2 7944560
Mrs. Kyung-O Kim, President   FX: 2 7964995

Founded: 1959. **Members:** 27. **Languages:** English, Korean. **National.** Organizations of Korean women working to improve public welfare, to develop cooperation among Korean women's groups, and to support and promote the interests of women. Conducts educational and training programs for the leaders of member organizations. Conducts research and lobbies government on: sexual discrimination against working women; media's representation of women; public opinion of women's issues. Implements consumer education programs. Fosters international relations among women's organizations.

Publications: *Women* (in Korean), monthly. Magazine. Group activities and voicing opinions. ● *The Women* (in English), monthly. Magazine.

Conventions/Meetings: periodic board meeting.

★666★ KOREAN WOMEN DEVELOPMENT INSTITUTE (KWDI)
1-363 Bulkwang-dong   PH: 2 3560070
Eunpyung-ku   FX: 2 3561467
Seoul 122-040, Republic of Korea   TX: MOHSAS K23230
Ms. Young-Ja Kwon, President   (KWDI)

Founded: 1983. **Members:** 164. **Budget:** US$5,600,000. **Languages:** English, Korean. **National.** Works to guarantee the rights of women in Korea and to aid in women's development. Researches legal issues relevant to women; women and education; women and culture; family welfare; women's health; and women's studies. Provides leadership training and vocational education for women; operates speakers' bureau. Encourages women to participate in volunteer work. Offers guidance and counseling services. Coordinates activities among women's groups. Maintains day care center, dormitory for students, and educational facilities. Lobbies government regarding the status of women. Disseminates information via media sources. **Libraries:** Type: reference. Holdings: 20,200; monographs, periodicals, audio recordings, video recordings, books. Subjects: academic materials on women's studies and related topics. **Computer Services:** Bibliographic search; data base; mailing lists. **Divisions:** Research; Education and Training; Resource Development; Information and Publication.

Publications: *Women's Development News* (in Korean), monthly. Newsletter. **Circulation:** 60,000. ● *Korean Women Today* (in English), quarterly. Newsletter. ● *Women's Studies* (in Korean). Journal. Academic periodical. ● *Women's Studies Forum* (in English), annual. Journal. ● *Annotated Bibliography in Women's Studies: 1945-March 1984.* Book. ● *Abstracts of Dissertations on Women in Korea 1975-1985.* Book. ● *Index to Periodical Articles on Women.* Book. ● *Videos.*

★667★ KOREAN WOMEN WORKERS ASSOCIATION (KWWA)
409-54 Guro Bon Dong
Guro-ku
Seoul, Republic of Korea

Founded: 1987. **National.** Promotes the concerns of women workers within the male-dominated labor movement. Organizes educational programs and activities.

Publications: *When the Hen Crows.* Book.

★668★ KOREAN WOMEN'S INSTITUTE
c/o Ewha Womans University   PH: 2 3603225
Seoul 120-750, Republic of Korea   2 3603226
Prof. Pilwha Chang, Director   FX: 2 3123625

Founded: 1977. **Staff:** 4. **Budget:** 50,000 W. **Languages:** Korean, English. **National.** Works to raise the consciousness about women's issues through research, teaching, outreach programs to communities, and national and international exchange of knowledge and information. Investigates and identifies problems facing Korean women in the past and present, and ways to promote social change. Provides educational programs and workshops for disadvantaged women and children. Researches the history of women from a feminist point of view. Maintains a social welfare center for urban poor women and children.

Publications: *Women's Studies Review* (in Korean), annual. ● *Challenges for*

Women: Women Studies in Korea (in English). ● *Gender Division of Labor in Korea* (in English).

Conventions/Meetings: annual conference - Seoul, Republic of Korea. ● Women's Studies Meeting (exhibits) - 3/year. Seoul, Republic of Korea.

★669★ MEDICAL WOMEN'S INTERNATIONAL ASSOCIATION - KOREA
201 Jinhung Villa Zol
54, Samsung Dong
Kangnam-Ku
Seoul 135-090, Republic of Korea
Shinae Yoo, Contact

Languages: Korean. **National.** Korean national branch of the Medical Women's International Association (see separate entry). Women physicians. Provides a forum for discussion of women's health care issues. Encourages women to enter the field of medicine. Works to overcome discrimination against female physicians. Sponsors research and educational programs.

★670★ NATIONAL COMMITTEE ON WOMEN'S POLICIES
Ministry of Political Affairs
Government Bldg.
77-6 Sejong-ro
Chongro-ku
Seoul 110-760, Republic of Korea

Founded: 1983. **Languages:** Korean. **National.** Promotes the interests of women in the Republic of Korea. Works to improve living and working conditions for women.

★671★ PLANNED PARENTHOOD FEDERATION OF KOREA (PPFK)
CPO Box 3360
Seoul, Republic of Korea   PH: 2 6348212
Mr. Il-Sang Park, Exec.Dir.   FX: 2 6718212

Founded: 1961. **Staff:** 557. **Budget:** US$8,740,000. **Local Groups:** 12. **Languages:** English, Korean. **National.** Family planning professionals in the Republic of Korea. Seeks to enhance the quality of life of Koreans by promoting family planning and improving maternal and infant health care. Encourages ''culturally, economically, and socially healthy'' families. Conducts educational programs for military personnel, industrial workers, students, and other groups; disseminates family planning information through mass media. Operates clinics, audio visual materials development center, and 10 sections. **Libraries:** Type:. Holdings: 3,500. Subjects: family planning, sex education, and health.

Publications: *Happy Home* (in Korean), monthly. Magazine. ● *PPFK Annual Report* (in English and Korean).

Conventions/Meetings: annual general assembly.

★672★ WORLD'S WOMAN'S CHRISTIAN TEMPERANCE UNION - KOREA
103-3, Ka Dong So Moon Dong
Sung Puk Ku
Seoul, Republic of Korea
Dr. Jung Joo Kim, V.Pres.

National. Women working to educate children and adults on the ''evils of alcohol, tobacco, and narcotic drugs.'' Conducts drug abuse seminars and workshops for youth; sponsors professional training programs for counselors.

★673★ YOUNG WOMEN'S CHRISTIAN ASSOCIATION - KOREA
1-3 First St.
Myung Dong
Seoul 100-21, Republic of Korea   PH: 2 7749702
Chong Kyung Lee, Gen.Sec.   FX: 2 7749724

National. Promotes the development of young women in the Republic of Korea. Upholds Christian beliefs and values in its programs. Works to instill self worth and self-esteem in young women.

Lao People's Democratic Republic

★674★ LAO WOMEN'S UNION
PO Box 59
Vientiane, Lao People's Democratic
    Republic

Founded: 1955. **Languages:** Laotian, French. **National.** Promotes the interests of women in the Lao People's Democratic Republic. Fosters solidarity among women through the dissemination of information.

★675★ WOMEN AND CHILDCARE DEPARTMENT, UNION DES FEMMES LAO
BP 59
Vientiane, Lao People's Democratic
    Republic   PH: 2057

Languages: Laotian. **National.** Provides health care awareness information and counselling for women and children. Promotes increased accessibility to health services and the furthering of preventative health care programs.

Malaysia

★676★ ALL WOMEN'S ACTION SOCIETY (AWAM)
43C Rd., SS 6/12
Kelana Jaya
47301 Selangor, Malaysia   PH: 3 7037334
Rosalind Leong, Coord.   FX: 3 7039266

Founded: 1988. **Members:** 45. **Staff:** 3. **Budget:** M$120,000. **Languages:** English. **National.** Promotes the development of women in Malaysia. Seeks to create a national awareness about domestic violence; lobbies the government on legislation relating to domestic violence. Works to change the negative portrayal of women in the media. Collects documentation on issues affecting women. Conducts discussion groups and educational programs. Offers health and legal referral programs; operates a counselling service for women in distress. **Libraries:** Type: reference. Holdings: 0; books, clippings, video recordings, audio recordings. **Committees:** Training and Education; Services; Media Watch; Resources; Violence Against Women.

Publications: *Come Together: An Action Pack for Campaign on Legal Reforms for Women in Malaysia*. ● *Going to Court: A Guide for Victims of Domestic Violence*. ● *How to Lobby Your Member of Parliment (A Case Study of Lobbying for the Domestic Violence Bill)*.

Conventions/Meetings: monthly meeting (exhibits).

★677★ ASIA PACIFIC FORUM ON WOMEN, LAW AND DEVELOPMENT (APWLD)
    PH: 3 2550648
PO Box 12224   3 2550649
50770 Kuala Lumpur, Malaysia   FX: 3 2541371
Salbiah Ahmad, Contact   TX: MA 31655 MPS

Founded: 1988. **Members:** 55. **Staff:** 4. **Budget:** US$500,000. **Languages:**

English. **Multinational**. Women's organizations comprised of women's activists, lawyers, human rights activists, and interested individuals. Seeks to enable women in the Asia Pacific region to utilize the law as an effective instrument to empower them in struggles for justice and equality. Promotes women's development in family, society, economics, politics, and national development. Fosters exchange of information among members. Seeks to establish a Women's Rights Charter. Lobbies Asian Pacific governments to ratify the U.N. Convention on the Elimination of All Forms of Discrimination Against Women. Advocates the basic concept of human rights. **Libraries:** Type: not open to the public. Holdings: 0. **Task Forces:** Women and Religion; Women and Economical Rights; Women and Democratization; Violence Against Women.

Publications: *Forum News* (in English), quarterly. ● Workshop papers, task force reports, and consultation results.

Conventions/Meetings: periodic regional meeting, Meetings involving consultations, trainings, research, and strategic planning..

★678★ ASIAN AND PACIFIC DEVELOPMENT CENTRE (APDC)
Persiaran Duta
PO Box 12224
50770 Kuala Lumpur, Malaysia   PH: 3 2548088
Noeleen Heyzer, Director   FX: 603 2550316

A program of Women in Development. Overseas development projects in Asia and the Pacific. Offers educational and informational services.

★679★ ASIAN-PACIFIC RESEARCH CENTRE FOR WOMEN (ARROW)
APDC Bldg., Rm. 608   PH: 3 2531130
Pesiaran Duta   FX: 3 2531130
50480 Kuala Lumpur, Malaysia E-Mail: WOMEN
Rita Raj-Hashim, Contact   ARROW.MY

Founded: 1993. **Languages:** English. **National**. Researches and analyzes women's issues, such as reproductive health; advises governmental and legislative organizations on women's issues. Investigates and evaluates media coverage of women's health issues. Conducts programs to increase public awareness of population growth and reproductive health. Offers consultancy and counseling services on women's development. Encourages and promotes networking among women and women's organizations.
Computer Services: Data base, women and health; bibliographic search; information services; online services, CD-ROM.

★680★ DEVELOPMENT ALTERNATIVES WITH WOMEN FOR A NEW
ERA - SOUTHEAST ASIA (DAWN)
Asia and Pacific Development Centre
Pesiaran Duta
PO Box 12224
50770 Kuala Lumpur, Malaysia
Dr. Noeleen Heyzer, Contact

Languages: Malay. **Multinational**. Works to reduce the negative impact of development activities on women and the environment. Conducts research, training, and advocacy programs to eliminate inequalities of gender, class, and race. Facilitates communication and networking among women's movements. Protects and defends women's reproductive rights.

★681★ FEDERATION OF FAMILY PLANNING ASSOCIATIONS OF
MALAYSIA (FFPAM)
81-B Jalan SS 15/5A   PH: 3 7337516
Subang Jaya   3 7337514
47500 Petaling Jaya, Malaysia FX: 3 7346638
Mrs. Cheng Yin Mooi, Exec. Dir. TX: 30638 MA IPESEA

Languages: Malay. **National**. Works to improve the quality of life for individuals living in Malaysia by promoting responsible parenthood and family planning. Attempts to stop the spread of AIDS and other sexually transmitted

diseases. Offers programs in sex education, family planning and health. Provides contraceptive and health care services. Conducts research.

★682★ FRIENDS OF WOMEN - MALAYSIA
(Pestuan Sahabat Wanita)
No. 17, Rd. 17, Sungei Way
47300 Petaling Jaya, Selangor, Malaysia

Languages: Malay. **National**. Women's organizations, individual women, and others interested in promoting awareness of women's issues.

★683★ NATIONAL COUNCIL OF WOMEN'S ORGANIZATIONS
MALAYSIA
157 Jalan Tun
Razak
50400 Kuala Lumpur, Malaysia
Dr. Fatimah Bte Haji Hashim, President   PH: 3 2989251

National. Umbrella organization for women's groups in Malaysia. Promotes and supports women's interests. Coordinates activities for women. Disseminates information on women's issues.

★684★ PLANNED PARENTHOOD FEDERATION - MALAYSIA
                              PH: 3 4566122
                                  3 4566246
246 Jalan Ampang   FX: 3 4566386
50450 Kuala Lumpur, Malaysia TX: 30638 MA IPESEA

Languages: Malay. **Multinational**. Works to co-ordinate activities for Planned Parenthood offices operating in the Asia and Oceania region. Advocates family planning as a basic human right. Works to increase governmental and public awareness of population problems in local regions. Promotes effective family planning programs. Conducts research on human fertility and contraception.

★685★ SARAWAK WOMEN FOR WOMEN SOCIETY (SWWS)
PO Box 551
93175 Kuching, Malaysia   PH: 82 416053
Margaret Bedus, President   82 422660

Founded: 1985. **Members:** 60. **Membership Dues:** M$2 annual. **Budget:** M$5,000. **Languages:** English, Malay. **National**. Women over 15 years of age. Seeks to raise public awareness of women's issues. Fosters women's personal development. Provides legal, financial, and employment advice. Works to erradicate exploitation of women in advertising and pornography. Operates a women's drop-in center, workshops on women's health, rape survivors' support group, and a women's crisis phoneline. Conducts educational and research programs. **Libraries:** Type: reference.

Publications: *Newsletter*, quarterly.

Conventions/Meetings: annual meeting (exhibits).

★686★ WOMENFORCE
29 Jalan SS15/5D
Subang Jaya
Petaling
47500 Kuala Lumpur, Malaysia

Languages: Malay. **National**. Works to empower women. Encourages women's participation in political and social matters. Active in social assistance efforts.

★687★ WOMEN'S AID ORGANIZATION (WAO)
(PPW Pertubhan Pertolongan Wanita)
Jalan Sultan
PO Box 493
Petaling Jaya   PH: 3 7554426
46760 Selangor, Malaysia   3 7563467
Ivy N. Josiah, Contact   FX: 3 7563237

Founded: 1982. **Members:** 150. **Staff:** 8. **Budget:** M$150,000. **Languages:** Malay, English, Mandarin, Tamil. **National**. Seeks to raise public awareness of the prevalence of domestic violence. Provides services to abused women including: access to shelter, day care center for children, 24-hour helpline, and professional counselling. Works to influence legislation against domestic violence. Participates in International Day Against Violence Against Women. **Libraries:** Type: reference.

Publications: *Annual Review*. Magazine.

Conventions/Meetings: annual general assembly.

★688★ WOMEN'S DEVELOPMENT COLLECTIVE
43C Jalan SS 6/12
47301 Petaling Jaya, Malaysia   PH: 7037334

Works towards the advancement of women from developing nations. Organizes development projects. Conducts educational and training programs. Disseminates information and offers consulting services on agriculture, educational opportunities, and health care.

★689★ YOUNG WOMEN'S CHRISTIAN ASSOCIATION - MALAYSIA
(Persatuan Wanita Keristian Malaysia)
PO Box 10064
50704 Kuala Lumpur, Malaysia   PH: 3 7563959
Rolla Lee Joe Joe, Gen.Sec.   FX: 3 2306102

National. Promotes the development of young women in Malaysia. Upholds Christian beliefs and values in its programs. Works to instill self worth and self-esteem in young women.

Marshall Islands

★690★ WOMEN UNITED TOGETHER IN THE MARSHALL ISLANDS
PO Box 1258
Majuro, Marshall Islands 96960   PH: 9 3236
Marie Madison, President   FX: 9 3538

Founded: 1987. **Members:** 1,400. **National**. Seeks to raise the status of women in the Marshall Islands. Works to improve women's health care, education, and employment. Fosters women's positive sense of self-worth and autonomy.

Publications: *Wutumi Nuuj Leta*, periodic. Newsletter.

Mongolia

★691★ MONGOLIAN WOMEN'S FEDERATION
Central Council of Mongolian Women's
  Federation
Ulaan Baator
Mongolia, Mongolia   PH: 1 67204
B. Uranchimeg, Contact   1 67170

Founded: 1924. **Staff:** 80. **Budget:** US$500,000. **Languages:** Khalkha Mongol, English. **National**. Women over 16 years of age. Seeks to promote and protect women's interests and equal rights. Formulates and influences government policy regarding women's welfare. Provides information and

training for women in: family planning, income generation, health, and nutrition.

Publications: *Goo Maral* (in Khalkha Mongol), bimonthly. Journal. ● *Mongoljin Goo* (in Khalkha Mongol), biweekly. Newsletter.

Conventions/Meetings: semiannual seminar. ● quinquennial congress.

Myanmar

★692★ COUNCIL OF WOMEN'S ASSOCIATIONS
280A U Wishara Rd.
Rangoon, Myanmar

National. Umbrella organization for women's groups in Myanmar. Promotes and supports women and women's interests. Conducts and coordinates activities. Disseminates information to increase public awareness of women's concerns.

★693★ YOUNG WOMEN'S CHRISTIAN ASSOCIATION - MYANMAR
119 Bogalay Zay St.
Yangon, Myanmar   PH: 86371
Katherine Khin Khin, Gen.Sec.   CBL: MAIDENS YANGON

National. Promotes the development of young women in Myanmar. Upholds Christian beliefs and values in its programs. Works to instill self worth and self-esteem in young women.

Nepal

★694★ CENTRE FOR WOMEN AND DEVELOPMENT (CWD)
(Manila Tatna Vikas Kendra)
PO Box 2682
Kamladi
Kathmandu, Nepal   PH: 225801
Prabha Thacker, Chairperson   TX: 2464 RAUNIAR NP

Founded: 1983. **Members:** 7. **Budget:** US$30,000. **Languages:** English. **National**. Seeks to change current assumptions, values, and beliefs regarding women and their role in Nepal's society. Seeks to create an environment in which the potential of women will be effectively recognized and exercised. Offers courses on communications, young women's development, gender training, and gender analysis. Conducts evaluations and socio-economic studies on women and development. Supports welfare programs that focus on development for poor women, skill improvement, and entrepreneurship. Disseminates information on women and development. Fosters information exchange with other women's organizations. Holds seminars and workshops. **Libraries:** Type: reference.   Subjects: women and development. **Awards:** Scholarship. Recipient: young women seeking higher education. **Committees:** Research and Training; Documentation; Computer.

Publications: *CWD Networker* (in English), 3/year. Bulletin. Information about women and issues that affect their development. **Price:** NRs 150 institutions within Nepal.; NRs 75 individuals within Nepal.; US$30 institutions outside Nepal.; US$20 individuals outside Nepal..

Conventions/Meetings: periodic CHETNA Forum, Discussions on current topics concerning Nepali women. (exhibits) - Kathmandu, Nepal.

★695★ FAMILY PLANNING ASSOCIATION OF NEPAL (FPAN)
Central Office   PH: 1 524648
PO Box 486   1 524440
Harihar Bhavan   FX: 1 524211
Pulchowk   TX: 2307 FPAN NP
Kathmandu, Nepal   CBL: NEPFAPLANS
Mr. R.K. Neupane, Exec. Dir.   KATHMANDU

Languages: Nepali. **National.** Works to improve the quality of life for individuals living in Nepal by promoting responsible parenthood and family planning. Attempts to reduce the number of unwanted pregnancies and abortions. Offers programs in family planning, sex education, and health. Provides contraceptive and health care services. Conducts research.

★696★ NEPAL WOMEN'S ORGANIZATION
PO Box 106
Pulchok
Lalitpur, Nepal
Mrs. Indira Shrestha, President   PH: 5 21904

National. Umbrella organization for women's groups in Nepal. Supports the interests of women. Coordinates activities. Disseminates information on women's issues.

★697★ WOMEN ACTING TOGETHER FOR CHANGE (WATCH)
GPO Box 5723
Kathmandu, Nepal
Meena Poudel, Chair   PH: 416518

Founded: 1992. **Languages:** English. **National.** Works to increase women's awareness of the physical and psychological problems involved in prostitution. Seeks to increase public awareness of sexually transmitted diseases and AIDS and their relationship to prostitution. Plans to establish counseling, training, and financial support services for women with AIDS.

★698★ WOMEN AWARENESS CENTRE NEPAL (WACN)
PO Box 2245
Kathmandu, Nepal

National. Works to advance the status of women in all spheres of society; discourage religious, cultural, and traditional practices that hinder the advancement and development of women; eradicate the media's negative influences on women and children. Seeks to achieve public recognition of women's potential and achievements. Offers training and development programs. Conducts research on women's and children's studies. Provides a forum for exchange among women.

★699★ WOMEN'S SERVICES CO-ORDINATION COMMITTEE
Vrikutinandap
PO Box 373
Kathmandu, Nepal
Mrs. Prativa Rana, President

Languages: Nepali. **National.** Offers social services to improve women's living conditions.

New Caledonia

★700★ PACIFIC WOMEN'S RESOURCE BUREAU (PWRB)
(Bureau Technique des Femmes du Pacifique)
                                         PH: 262000
                                         FX: 263818
c/o South Pacific Commission   TX: 3139 NMSOPACOM
BP D5   CBL: SOUTHPACOM
Noumea Cedex, New Caledonia   NOUMEA

Founded: 1982. **Staff:** 3. **Languages:** English, French. **Multinational.** Pacific island women. Promotes the study of women and women's issues. Supports and offers assistance to national women's organizations to help with women's development issues in the Pacific region. Disseminates information to women throughout the Pacific isles. Conducts conferences, meetings, training, and workshops. **Libraries:** Type: reference; open to the public.

Publications: *Women's News* (in English and French), quarterly. Newsletter. **ISSN:** 1017-3900. **Also Cited As:** *L'Actualite au Feminin.* ● UPDATE (in English and French), monthly. **Also Cited As:** *Nouvelles.* ● *Directory of Pacific Women's Organizations.* ● *Working with Women.* Book. ● *Resource Kit for Pacific Women.*

Conventions/Meetings: triennial Regional Conference of Pacific Women.

New Zealand

★701★ ABORTION LAW REFORM ASSOCIATION OF NEW ZEALAND
(ALRANZ)
PO Box 28-008
Kelburn
Wellington, New Zealand
Dr. Margaret Sparrow, President   PH: 4 4769070

Founded: 1970. **Members:** 500. **Languages:** English. **National.** Promotes the availability of safe, legal abortion services. Counsels women dealing with unwanted pregnancy; encourages the provision and accessibility of contraceptive services and responsible sex education.

Publications: *Newsletter* (in English), 3/year.

Conventions/Meetings: annual meeting.

★702★ AOTEAROA BIRTHMOTHERS SUPPORT GROUP
Wellesley St.
PO Box 5479
Auckland, New Zealand   PH: 9 3660752
Janice Hamilton, Contact   9 3602204

Founded: 1985. **Members:** 900. **Languages:** English. **Multinational.** Women who have given up children for adoption. Works to reunite adopted children with their biological parents. Offers emotional support to grieving mothers who have given up children for adoption. Conducts searches of public records at the request of parents or children in order to reunite families. Lobbies government to change laws that seal birth and adoption records. Sponsors lectures.

Publications: *Newsletter* (in English), periodic.

Conventions/Meetings: periodic workshop.

★703★ AOTEAROA - NEW ZEALAND WOMEN AND POLITICS
NETWORK
Dept. of Parks, Recreation, and Tourism
Lincoln University   PH: 3 325811
PO Box 84   FX: 3 3252944
Canterbury, New Zealand   E-Mail: HAYWARD
Bronwyn Hayward   @KEA.LINCOLN.AC.NZ

Founded: 1989. **Members:** 270. **Budget:** NZ$1,000. **Languages:** English. **National.** Academics, researchers, community activists, politicians, and community members. Promotes communication between women academics and researchers, or those interested or involved in politics and public policy. Includes women outside of New Zealand on its mailing list. Organized 1993 women's suffrage commemoration in celebration of the centennial in New Zealand. Also plans a variety of exhibitions, conferences, theatre and fine arts events, and other activities.

Publications: *Aotearoa - New Zealand Women and Politics Network*

Newsletter (in English), 3/year. **ISSN:** 1171-9273. ● *New Zealand Women and Politics Network Mailing List* (in English). Directory.

Conventions/Meetings: annual conference, Academic, in conjunction with the New Zealand Political Science Association.

★704★ ASSOCIATION OF ANGLICAN WOMEN
229 Ruahine St.
Palmerston North, New Zealand
Mrs. Anne Carpenter, President   PH: 63 589134

Founded: 1969. **Members:** 9,000. **Budget:** NZ$13,000. **Languages:** English. **National**. Anglican women united to promote Christian family life in New Zealand, Fiji, Samoa, and Tonga. Conducts educational and research programs. Lobbies government on issues affecting Christian women. Offers community service programs in New Zealand, Africa, and Asia; provides relief from natural disasters. Sponsors festivals and workshops. **Libraries:** Type: reference.

Publications: *Circle* (in English), quarterly. Magazine.

Conventions/Meetings: biennial conference - always August. ● annual general assembly.

★705★ ASSOCIATION OF PRESBYTERIAN WOMEN
35 Vernon Terr.
Christchurch 2, New Zealand   PH: 3 3326150
Mrs. Margaret McLean, President   3 3321660

National. New Zealand women of the Presbyterian church. Promotes Christian beliefs and supports the interests of Presbyterian women in New Zealand.

★706★ ASSOCIATION FOR WOMEN IN THE SCIENCES
PO Box 184
Wellington, New Zealand   PH: 4 4286089
Jean Fleming, Contact   4 4730875

Languages: English. **National**. Women scientists in New Zealand. Promotes research and development in physics, biology, energy, ecology, and geology. Encourages fellowship among members.

★707★ BAHA'I WOMEN'S COMMITTEE
49 Collingwood St.
Palmerston North, New Zealand   PH: 6 3550873
Mary Day, Chairperson   6 3458872

National. Promotes the interests of New Zealand women who believe in Baha'ism. Baha'ism is a religious movement, orginating from Iran in the 19th century, that stresses the spiritual unity of mankind.

★708★ BAPTIST WOMEN'S MINISTRIES
61 Frame St.
Opoho
Dunedin, New Zealand   PH: 3 4738438
Mrs. Nola Myles, President   3 4738236

National. Representatives from New Zealand Baptist churches. Promotes the interests and development of Christian women in New Zealand.

★709★ BREAST CANCER SUPPORT SERVICE
c/o Marjorie Davidson
8 Birdwood Crescent
Parnell
Auckland, New Zealand   PH: 4 3798494

Regional Groups: 23. **Languages:** English. **National**. Works directly with breast cancer patients. Provides counselling and support. Disseminates information.

★710★ CATHOLIC WOMEN'S LEAGUE OF NEW ZEALAND
2/5 Johanna Ln.
Christchurch 6, New Zealand
Mary Caldwell, Secretary   PH: 3 3890893

National. Catholic women in New Zealand. Promotes the values of Christianity among women in New Zealand. Supports the development of women's spiritual beliefs.

★711★ CHILDBIRTH EDUCATORS - NEW ZEALAND
26 Bell Rd.
Remuera
Auckland 5, New Zealand

Languages: English. **National**. Promotes education concerning the principles of natural childbirth; facilitates communication and cooperation among parents and medical professionals. Provides educational opportunities to parents and parents-to-be.

★712★ CHRISTIAN WOMEN'S FELLOWSHIP OF THE ASSOCIATED
    CHURCHES OF CHRIST
c/o Melva Sutcliffe
29 Elnma Rd.
Gonville
Wanganui, New Zealand
Miss Beth Overend, President

National. New Zealand Christian women. Works to promote Christian fellowship and service among women in New Zealand.

★713★ COUNCIL OF JEWISH WOMEN OF NEW ZEALAND
C-11 Parnell St.
Lower Hutt 6009, New Zealand   PH: 4 5671679
Mrs. Ann Benda, Secretary   FX: 4 5660133

Founded: 1929. **Members:** 400. **Languages:** English. **National**. Jewish women working to support Israel and to better the community through education and fellowhip. Encourages women to take part in established Jewish organizations usually run by men. Seeks to raise public awareness of Judaism by conducting synagogue tours. Coordinates activities with other Jewish womens' organizations. **Committees:** Social Welfare; Status of Women. **Formerly:** Union of Jewish Women.

Publications: *Newsletter*, periodic.

Conventions/Meetings: biennial conference.

★714★ DISABLED PERSONS ASSEMBLY WOMEN'S CAUCUS (DPA)
PO Box 10-138
The Terrace
Wellington, New Zealand   PH: 4 4722626
Carolyn Weston, Contact   FX: 4 4722626

Languages: English. **National**. Disabled individuals and related agencies addressing and serving the needs of disabled women. Seeks to empower women with disabilities by monitoring available services, disseminating information, and addressing their unique concerns. Provides self-advocacy and employment education. Intends to re-establish a national network of women with disabilities. Lobbies for government support. Conducts conferences, seminars, and public awareness programs. **Awards:** Disability Pride. Recipient: employers of disabled people.

Publications: *Able Update* (in English), 4-6/year. Newsletter.

Conventions/Meetings: annual general assembly - Wellington, New Zealand. ● semimonthly executive committee meeting - Wellington, New Zealand. ● monthly regional meeting - Wellington, New Zealand.

★715★ FEDERATION OF WOMEN'S HEALTH COUNCILS - NEW ZEALAND
CPO Box 853
Auckland, New Zealand   PH: 9 5205175
Judi Strid, Contact   FX: 9 5204152

Founded: 1990. **Staff:** 2. **Budget:** NZ$65,000. **Languages:** English. **National**. Women's health councils united to develop a national health policy for women. Coordinates information sharing and networking among member organizations. Monitors the provision of women's health care services to ensure that doctors and health professionals are accountable to consumers. Defends women's rights to control their bodies; supports access to free abortions. Fosters research activities. **Libraries:** Type: reference.

Publications: *Accident Compensation: A Women's Issue* (in English). Monograph. ● *Ensuring the Cervical Screening Programme Survives the Health Changes* (in English). Monograph. ● *Consumer Consultation, Representation and Participation* (in English). Monograph. ● *Newsletter* (in English), bimonthly.

Conventions/Meetings: annual conference. ● semiannual regional meeting (exhibits).

★716★ FEMINIST NURSES NETWORK
55 Churchill Rd.
Murray's Bay
Auckland, New Zealand
Barbara Austin, Contact

Languages: English. **National**. Feminist nurses in New Zealand. Works to influence and improve national health care policy. Promotes advancement of the nursing profession. Fosters coordination and cooperation among similar associations.

★717★ FERTILITY ACTION
16 McEntee Rd.
Waitakere
Auckland, New Zealand

Languages: English. **National**. Promotes the awareness of infertility studies. Seeks to reduce rates of human infertility. Conducts research; disseminates information.

★718★ GIRL GUIDES ASSOCIATION OF NEW ZEALAND
c/o Chief Commissioner
National Hdqtrs.
PO Box 13-143
Christchurch, New Zealand   PH: 3 3668409
Susan Gallagher, Contact   FX: 3 3668413

Founded: 1908. **Members:** 52,254. **Languages:** English. **National**. Fosters personal growth and development of girls (6-19 years of age) in New Zealand. Encourages members to be responsive to others' needs through community service activities. Educational programs include life skills, conservation, and technology. **Committees:** Training; Voluntary Personnel; Public Relations; Trading; Sponsorship and Fundraising.

Publications: *Te Rama* (in English), bimonthly. Magazine. ● *Directory* (in English), annual. Register of office holders.

Conventions/Meetings: biennial Jamboree - always January. New Zealand. ● biennial conference.

★719★ GIRLS' BRIGADE NEW ZEALAND
PO Box 68-547
Newton
Auckland, New Zealand
Philippa Pedersen, Exec. Dir.   PH: 9 3600204

National. Local groups of girls age 5 and older in New Zealand that are affiliated with a church or mission of a Christian denomination. Helps girls to become followers of Jesus Christ and to find true enrichment through reverence, self-control, and a sense of responsibility. Provides activities designed to help members attain physical, mental, and spiritual maturity. Encourages girls to express what they learn through practical service to home, community, and church.

★720★ HOME BIRTH ASSOCIATION
PO Box 7093
Wellesley St.
Auckland, New Zealand

Languages: English. **National**. Encourages natural childbirth methods. Disseminates information.

★721★ HOME LEAGUE
c/o The Salvation Army Territorial
  Hdqtrs.
PO Box 6015
Te Aro
Wellington, New Zealand   PH: 4 3845649
Mrs. Karen Thompson, Colonel   FX: 4 3845644

Founded: 1911. **Members:** 4,909. **Staff:** 5. **Languages:** English. **National**. Women over fifteen years of age. Promotes worship, education, fellowship, and public service. Seeks to provide women with the knowledge and skills they may need as homemakers and parents. Encourages women in the development of Christian faith. Conducts annual training camps for local leaders. Holds branch history competitions and arts/crafts exhibitions.

Publications: *Home League Highlights* (in English), semiannual. Bulletin.

Conventions/Meetings: weekly meeting.

★722★ INTERNATIONAL WOMEN'S CRICKET COUNCIL (IWCC)
(Conseil International de Cricket Feminin)
45 Reynolds Ave.
Christchurch 5, New Zealand   PH: 3 3596651
Thelma Macdonald, Exec. Officer   FX: 3 657491

Founded: 1958. **Members:** 8. **Languages:** English. **Multinational**. Women's national cricket associations. Serves as international liaison between members; promotes women's cricket. Holds discussions on pertinent topics.

Conventions/Meetings: periodic meeting.

★723★ LA LECHE LEAGUE OF NEW ZEALAND
14 Dr. Taylor Terr.
PO Box 13-393
Johnsonville
Wellington, New Zealand   PH: 4 4785213

Regional Groups: 100. **Languages:** English. **National**. Seeks to foster good mothering and close family relationships through breastfeeding. Disseminates information; offers counselling services.

★724★ LABOUR WOMEN'S COUNCIL
PO Box 784
Wellington, New Zealand
Jo Fitzpatrick, Secretary   PH: 4 3847649

National. Women who are employed in New Zealand. Promotes and supports the interest of women laborers in New Zealand.

★725★ LEAGUE OF MOTHERS AND HOMEMAKERS OF NEW
ZEALAND
Kern Rd.
RD3
D3
Drury, New Zealand
Mrs. Margaret Hunkin, Contact

Regional Groups: 20. **Languages:** English. **National.** Women working at home. Fosters communication among members. Encourages women's involvement in community service activities.

★726★ MAORI WOMEN'S WELFARE LEAGUE
PO Box 12-072   PH: 4 4736451
Wellington 1, New Zealand   4 4710767
Aroha Reriti-Crofts, President   FX: 4 4996802

National. Maori (Polynesian) women native to New Zealand. Supports the interests and development of Maori women.

★727★ MATERNITY ACTION ALLIANCE
PO Box 884
Christchurch, New Zealand
Rhea Daellenbach, Contact

Languages: English. **National.** Works to improve services for mothers, fathers, and babies, through the first year of life. Disseminates information on maternity benefits and rights; advises midwives and health visitors. Offers post-natal support to parents with disabilities. Campaigns for policies designed to meet the needs of users of healthcare services; provides a forum for discussion between users and service providers.

★728★ MEDIAWOMEN
c/o Ruth Nichol
PO Box 275
Wellington, New Zealand   PH: 4 4753513

Languages: English. **National.** Women professionals working in television, radio, and print media in New Zealand. Represents members' interests. Provides career development and networking opportunities.

★729★ MEDICAL WOMEN'S INTERNATIONAL ASSOCIATION - NEW
ZEALAND
66B Volga St.
Wellington 2, New Zealand
D. Read, Contact

Languages: English. **National.** New Zealand national branch of the Medical Women's International Association (see separate entry). Women physicians. Provides a forum for discussion of women's health care issues. Encourages women to enter the field of medicine. Works to overcome discrimination against female physicians. Sponsors research and educational programs.

★730★ METHODIST WOMEN'S FELLOWSHIP OF NEW ZEALAND OF
THE WORLD FEDERATION OF METHODIST WOMEN
564 Main Rd., Flat 1
Stoke
Nelson, New Zealand
Ruth Dolejs, Contact   PH: 54 79168

Members: 5,240. **Languages:** English. **National.** Methodist women. Works to spread the teachings of Christ.

Publications: *Tree of Life*, quarterly.

★731★ NATIONAL ADVISORY COUNCIL ON THE EMPLOYMENT OF
WOMEN (NACEW)
Department of Labour
PO Box 3705
Wellington, New Zealand   PH: 4 4954045
Ms. Judith Byrne, Secretary   FX: 4 4954040

Founded: 1967. **Members:** 16. **Budget:** NZ$50,000. **Languages:** English. **National.** Investigates the needs and concerns of working women in New Zealand. Conducts research on sexual discrimination, pay equity, maternity leave provisions, employment of disabled women, and educational equality. Encourages the dissemination of information on women's employment issues. Recommends policies and procedures to governmental bodies. Organizes and coordinates forums on working women's interests. **Working Groups:** Women and Self Employment.

Publications: *Beyond the Barriers - The State, the Economy and Women's Employment 1984-1990* (in English). Book. ● *Forward Report* (in English). Book. Update of forums on employment and training of women with disabilities.

★732★ NATIONAL COLLECTIVE OF INDEPENDENT WOMEN'S
REFUGES
85 The Terrace
PO Box 5136
Wellington, New Zealand   PH: 4 4991881

Languages: English. **National.** Organizations providing shelter and counselling for underprivileged and abused women. Works to raise awareness of women's rights.

★733★ NATIONAL COLLECTIVE OF RAPE CRISIS AND RELATED
GROUPS OF AOTEAROA
PO Box 6181
Palmerston North, New Zealand   PH: 4 3847028
Fran Alexander, National Admin.   FX: 4 3847202

Founded: 1986. **Members:** 300. **Languages:** English. **National.** Organizations and individuals in New Zealand working to eliminate rape and sexual abuse against women and children. Seeks to improve facilities and increase the number of trained professionals in this field. Strives to increase public awareness of sexual violence and its effects on women. Conducts educational programs for companies and individuals. Offers psychological and legal counseling to women.

Conventions/Meetings: bimonthly meeting.

★734★ NATIONAL COUNCIL OF WOMEN OF NEW ZEALAND
(NCWNZ)
10 Park St.
PO Box 12117
Thorndon
Wellington, New Zealand   PH: 4 4737623
Alison Roxburgh, President   FX: 4 4737623

Founded: 1896. **Members:** 250,000. **Languages:** English. **National.** Umbrella organization of women's organizations and individuals. Promotes the social, economic, legal, and political advancement of women in New Zealand. Works to improve the spiritual, moral, civil, and social welfare of New Zealand's society. Seeks to improve women's access to education, health care, housing, and employment. Collaborates with women's organizations and governments worldwide to advance women's causes. Conducts research, educational, and children's programs. **Libraries:** Type: reference. Holdings: books. **Committees:** Child and Family; Cultural; Economics; Education; Environment; Habitat; Health; Home Economics and Consumer Affairs; International Relations and Peace; Laws and the Status of Women; Mass Media; Migration; Social Welfare; Women in Employment.

Publications: *Circular* (in English), monthly. Newsletter. ● *My Ancestry: My Country.* Monograph.

Conventions/Meetings: biennial conference. ● annual executive committee meeting.

★735★ NATIONAL LEAGUE OF MOTHERS AND HOMEMAKERS
161 Waimumu Rd.
Massey
Auckland, New Zealand   PH: 9 8337336
Mrs. Zita Kay, President   9 2948059

National. New Zealand mothers and homemakers. Promotes the interests and development of mothers and homemakers in New Zealand.

★736★ NATIONAL NETWORK OF NEW MOTHER SUPPORT GROUPS
PO Box 9600
Te Aro
Wellington, New Zealand   PH: 4 3847103

Regional Groups: 23. **Languages:** English. **National.** Offers advice and counselling to new mothers. Promotes improved maternal and neonatal health care. Operates support groups; fosters exchange and friendship among mothers.

★737★ NATIONAL NETWORK OF WOMEN WITH DISABILITIES
68 Heretaunga St.
Petone, New Zealand
Robyn Hunt, Contact

Languages: English. **National.** Encourages physically disabled women to explore new interests and develop friendships. Seeks to integrate members into mainstream life. Works to achieve equal opportunities for disabled people.

★738★ NATIONAL WOMEN'S COMMITTEE OF THE NEW ZEALAND COUNCIL OF TRADE UNIONS (NZCTU)
PO Box 6645
Wellington, New Zealand   PH: 4 3851334
Angela Foulkes, Secretary   FX: 4 3856051

Founded: 1987. **Members:** 344,083. **Budget:** NZ$1,500,000. **Languages:** English. **National.** Employed women belonging to public and private sector unions. Conducts seminars, public relations, campaigns, and research promoting women's interests. Fosters communication among members.

Conventions/Meetings: biennial National Women's Conference conference.

★739★ NEW ZEALAND ASSOCIATION OF NATURAL FAMILY PLANNING
PO Box 1019
Hamilton, New Zealand
Mrs. Ann Griffin, President   PH: 7 8564331

National. Promotes and supports natural family planning in New Zealand. Disseminates information.

★740★ NEW ZEALAND CHILD CARE ASSOCIATION
(Te Tari Puna Ora o Aotearo)
PO Box 11-863
Wellington, New Zealand   PH: 4 3846947
Ellen Ilalio, Secretary   4 2376711

National. Promotes and supports accessibility to quality child care in New Zealand.

★741★ NEW ZEALAND COLLEGE OF MIDWIVES
PO Box 21106
Christchurch, New Zealand   PH: 3 3772732
Karen Guilliland, Coord.   FX: 3 3772732

Founded: 1990. **Members:** 1,300. **Staff:** 1. **Budget:** NZ$100,000. **Regional**

Groups: 10. **Languages:** English. **National.** Midwives, consumer groups, and interested individuals. Promotes midwifery services and education, and represents the interests of midwives to governmental bodies and the public. Prescribes and monitors standards for the practice and education of midwifery. Encourages women to become involved in the development and maintenance of midwifery. Acts as a consultant for governmental agencies; engages in the negotiation and dispensing of government funding for midwifery services at home deliveries. Offers courses jointly with colleges and universities. **Libraries:** Type: reference.

Publications: *New Zealand College of Midwives* (in English), semiannual. Journal. ● *Newsletter*, bimonthly.

Conventions/Meetings: biennial conference - always August. New Zealand.

★742★ NEW ZEALAND DENTAL THERAPISTS ASSOCIATION
49 Austin St.
Mt. Victoria
Wellington 1, New Zealand
Maggie Morgan, Contact   PH: 4 3857969

Founded: 1921. **Members:** 400. **Budget:** NZ$12,000. **Languages:** English. **National.** Women dental therapists of New Zealand. Promotes the professional interests of members. Works to ensure the provision of dental services to children and adults in New Zealand. Establishes industry standards. **Libraries:** Type: reference. Holdings: archival material. Subjects: oral histories.

Publications: *Dental Therapist Journal*, annual.

Conventions/Meetings: monthly meeting. ● executive committee meeting - 3/year.

★743★ NEW ZEALAND EDUCATIONAL INSTITUTE - WOMEN'S NETWORK (NZEI)
Education House - West Block, 12th Fl.
178-182 Willis St.
Wellington, New Zealand   PH: 4 3849689
Lynn Middleton, Secretary   FX: 4 3851772

Founded: 1883. **Members:** 24,000. **Staff:** 48. **Budget:** NZ$6,000,000. **Languages:** English. **National.** Seeks to improve working conditions, salary, and status of female teachers. Encourages women's active participation in teachers' associations. Promotes childcare availability for working teachers. Offers counselling and support for victims of sexual harrassment. Provides professional training programs for members. Encourages affirmative action programs in upper level teaching and administrative positions. Conducts research on equal education opportunities for boys and girls. **Libraries:** Type: reference. Holdings: books. Subjects: education and industrial relations. **Awards:** Educational Excellence Award. **Committees:** Women and Girls; Professional Practices; Special Education Advisory Services; School Support Staff.

Publications: *Rourou*, semiweekly. Newsletter.

Conventions/Meetings: biennial conference.

★744★ NEW ZEALAND ENDOMETRIOSIS FOUNDATION
PO Box 1683
Palmerston North, New Zealand
Margaret McAffer, Coord.

Founded: 1986. **Members:** 400. **Budget:** NZ$4,000. **Languages:** English. **National.** Works to educate the public on the symptoms and treatments for endometriosis. Provides information kits and conducts lectures. Encourages women to seek proper treatment and emotional support. Fosters friendship among sufferers of endometriosis. Operates a 24-hour hotline. **Libraries:** Type: reference. Holdings: books.

Publications: *Newsletter* (in English), quarterly.

★745★ NEW ZEALAND FAMILY PLANNING ASSOCIATION (NZFPA)
PO Box 11-515
Manners St.
Wellington, New Zealand
Ms. Joan Mirkin, Exec. Dir.

PH: 4 3844349
FX: 4 3828356
CBL: FAMPLAN

Languages: English. **National.** Promotes family planning and responsible parenthood on a national level. Works to reduce the number of unwanted pregnancies and abortions. Attempts to stop the spread of AIDS and other sexually transmitted diseases through education and contraceptive services. Offers programs in family planning and health. Conducts research.

★746★ NEW ZEALAND FEDERATION OF BUSINESS AND
PROFESSIONAL WOMEN'S CLUBS
20 Lakewood Ave.
Wellington 4, New Zealand
Anne Knowles, President

PH: 4 4783590
9 4245339

National. A collective group of New Zealand business and professional clubs for women. Promotes the development and interests of professional women in New Zealand.

★747★ NEW ZEALAND FEDERATION OF COUNTRY WOMEN'S
INSTITUTES
1 Collin Terr.
PO Box 12007
Wellington North, New Zealand
Mrs. Brenda Harden, Secretary

PH: 4 476666

Founded: 1921. **Members:** 19,600. **Staff:** 2. **Languages:** English. **National.** Encourages rural women's participation in community affairs, handicrafts, choir, drama, and other cultural activities. Promotes communication among members and women around the world. Provides adult education opportunities for members. **Awards:** Gold Honours Badge for Outstanding Service (recognition). ● World Role of Honour (recognition). ● Medical Research (scholarship).

Publications: *Home and Country* (in English), bimonthly. Magazine.

Conventions/Meetings: annual general assembly.

★748★ NEW ZEALAND FEDERATION OF UNIVERSITY WOMEN
Box 6334
Dunedin, New Zealand
Lorraine Isaacs, President

PH: 3 4798434
3 4793032
FX: 3 4775003

Founded: 1921. **Members:** 1,900. **Regional Groups:** 17. **Languages:** English. **National.** Advocates women's pursuit of higher education. Promotes understanding, cooperation, and friendship among university women worldwide. Encourages women to apply their studies to ease problems occurring locally, nationally, and internationally. Conducts research on women's roles in education, health, politics, and economics. Maintains speakers' bureau. **Awards:** Grant. Recipient: female scholars. ● Scholarship. Recipient: postgraduate students.

Publications: *National Bulletin* (in English), bimonthly.

Conventions/Meetings: triennial conference - 1994 Sept., Dunedin, New Zealand.

★749★ NEW ZEALAND MEDICAL WOMEN'S ASSOCIATION
46 Park Rd.
Miramar
Wellington, New Zealand
Dr. Aine M.C. McCoy, Pres.

PH: 4 3887018
4 3855833
FX: 4 3883503

Founded: 1921. **Members:** 250. **Budget:** NZ$3,500. **State Groups:** 5. **Languages:** English. **National.** Women physicians. Promotes the interests of New Zealand women in the medical profession. Fosters fellowship between members. Represents members in various matters affecting women's roles in the medical profession. Promotes understanding and friendship among women in the medical field throughout the world. Conducts educational programs. **Awards:** Imigran Young Investigators Award.

Publications: *Newsletter* (in English), monthly. ● *Women Doctors in New Zealand: An Historical Perspective 1921-1986* (in English). Book.

★750★ NEW ZEALAND METHODIST WOMEN'S FELLOWSHIP
52 Acacia Ave.
Christchurch, New Zealand
Lynne Scott, National Sec.

PH: 3 3484378

Founded: 1964. **Members:** 6,000. **National.** Women involved in the Methodist church in New Zealand. Promotes prayer, study, fellowship, and service among members. Seeks to incorporate Christianity in the home, church, and community. Supports the work of the Methodist church. Encourages interest in worldwide missions and evangelism.

Conventions/Meetings: biennial meeting, Focuses on business topics, personal growth workshops, seminars, and mission work. - always October. ● biennial meeting - always October.

★751★ NEW ZEALAND PROSTITUTES COLLECTIVE
PO Box 11-412
Manners St.
Wellington, New Zealand

PH: 4 3828791

Languages: English. **National.** Works to prevent exploitation of prostitutes. Supports improved health and safety programs for prostitutes.

★752★ NEW ZEALAND WOMEN'S CHRISTIAN TEMPERANCE UNION
PO Box 243
Cambridge, New Zealand
Mrs. Margaret Jackson, President

PH: 7 8274131

National. Christian women in New Zealand. Promotes elimination of alcohol and drug use through Christian education.

★753★ NEW ZEALAND WOMEN'S HEALTH NETWORK (NZWHN)
PO Box 2312
Tauranga, New Zealand
Sarah Calvert, Contact

PH: 75 81643

Founded: 1977. **Members:** 200. **Languages:** English. **National.** Individuals and organizations interested in women's health. Disseminates information; conducts seminars. Coordinates members' activities. Operates speaker's bureau.

Publications: *Newsletter*, quarterly. ● *Women's Mental Health: the Report of the Tauranga's Women's Mental Health Project.* ● *Coping with Menstruation: a Handbook for Disabled Women.*

Conventions/Meetings: periodic conference.

★754★ NEW ZEALAND WOMEN'S STUDIES ASSOCIATION
PO Box 5067
Wellington, New Zealand

Languages: English. **National.** Promotes research on women's issues. Works to improve the status of women in New Zealand.

★755★ PAN PACIFIC AND SOUTH EAST ASIA WOMEN'S
ASSOCIATION - NEW ZEALAND (PPSEAWA)
33 Hawker St.
Wellington 1, New Zealand
Mrs. May Spoor, President

PH: 4 3844628

National. New Zealand women. Supports the interests and development of women throughout the Pacific and South East Asia.

★756★ PERINATAL SOCIETY OF NEW ZEALAND (PSNZ)
Wellington Hospital
Dept. of Obstetrics and Gynecology
Wellington, New Zealand
Dr. P. Store, Pres.   PH: 4 3855943

Founded: 1979. Members: 240. Budget: NZ$2,000. Local Groups: 12.
Languages: English. National. Pediatricians, obstetricians, neo-natal and
obstetric nurses, and midwives in New Zealand. Aims to foster continued
improvement in the standards of perinatal medicine and nursing. Works to
increase public understanding of the activities in and the objectives of
perinatology. Sponsors continuing education programs in perinatology.
Promotes collaboration and open discussion among members. Formerly:
(1990) New Zealand Perinatal Society.

Conventions/Meetings: annual meeting (exhibits).

★757★ RAPE CRISIS NATIONAL OFFICE
PO Box 6181
Te Aro
Wellington, New Zealand   PH: 4 847028

National. Offers counseling and support services to victims of rape.
Maintains support groups, and rape prevention and recovery programs.
Disseminates information.

★758★ SALVATION ARMY WOMEN'S ORGANISATION
PO Box 6015
Wellington 1, New Zealand   PH: 4 3845649
Mrs. W. Maxwell, President   FX: 4 3845644

National. Women donating time to religious and social welfare activities in
New Zealand. Encourages Christian ideals and high moral standards; seeks
to minister to the physical, spiritual, and emotional needs of mankind. Serves
to propagate Christianity, provide education, relieve poverty, and establish
charitable projects in New Zealand.

**★759★ SOCIETY FOR THE PROTECTION OF THE UNBORN CHILD-
NEW ZEALAND**
Box 12-286
Thorndon
Wellington, New Zealand   PH: 4 4721451
P. Lynch, Secretary   3 6848388

National. Individuals who oppose abortion in New Zealand. Advocates fetal
rights from fertilization onwards. Promotes right to life issues.

**★760★ SOCIETY FOR RESEARCH ON WOMEN IN NEW ZEALAND
(SROW)**
PO Box 13-078
Johnsonville
Wellington, New Zealand   PH: 4 3854803
A. Horsfield, Treasurer   4 3895227

Founded: 1966. Members: 140. Languages: English. National. Women and
men interested in women's research dealing with social issues, such as
unemployment and living conditions. Provides a forum for discussion of
women's political and social issues.

Publications: Newsletter (in English), bimonthly. ● Career Development in the
Public Service. Book. ● Motherhood After 30. Book. ● Women and Trade
Unions. Book. ● What Has Happened. Book.

Conventions/Meetings: monthly conference.

★761★ SOLO PARENTS NEW ZEALAND
62 Bledisloe Cres
Wainuiomata, New Zealand
Mrs. Diana Gratton, President

National. Single parents in New Zealand. Promotes and supports the
interests of single parents throughout New Zealand.

★762★ SOROPTIMIST INTERNATIONAL OF NEW ZEALAND
PO Box 2127
Wellington, New Zealand
Betty Loughhead, Spokesperson   PH: 4 4793021

National. Business and professional women in New Zealand. Promotes high
ethical standards, peace, and human rights, particularly the rights of women.
Seeks to elevate the status of women in New Zealand.

★763★ VICTIMS ADVOCATES
PO Box 5227
Christchurch, New Zealand   PH: 3 3520173
Doris Church, Founder   FX: 3 3524489

Founded: 1989. Staff: 1. Budget: NZ$20,000. Languages: English. National. Represents the interests and defends the rights of victims, such as
women who have been battered, raped, and molested. Lobbies the New
Zealand government on issues and legislation that affect women. Sponsors
informational media programs to inform the public about victims' rights.
Operates national hotline. Conducts research.

Publications: How to Get Out of Your Marriage Alive. Book. Advice to all
victims of domestic violence. ● Violence Against Women: Its Causes and
Effects. Book. Key events in the lives of 101 battered women. ● Listen to Me
Please!. ● The Police and You.

★764★ VISUALLY IMPAIRED EMPOWERING WOMEN (VIEW)
National Office, RNZABPB
PO Box 37-414
Parnell
Auckland, New Zealand
Rosemary Wilkinson, Contact   PH: 9 779215

Languages: English. National. Strives to improve social and medical
services available to visually impaired women. Conducts advocacy activities;
offers information and advice.

**★765★ WIDOWS' AND WIDOWERS' ASSOCIATION OF NEW
ZEALAND (WWANZ)**
Box 11-595
Wellington, New Zealand   PH: 4 3828777
Mrs. Margaret Doe, Secretary   4 4768108

National. New Zealand widows and widowers. Promotes the interests of
widows and widowers in New Zealand. Provides opportunities for fellowship
among members.

★766★ WOMEN CLIMBING
12 Darwin St.
Wellington 5, New Zealand
Jay Davidson, Contact   PH: 4 4764673

Founded: 1985. Members: 160. Budget: NZ$5,000. Languages: English.
National. Women interested in mountain climbing, rock climbing, and skiing.
Encourages women to assume leadership roles at climbing activities. Fosters
women's appreciation of the outdoors. Facilitates communication among
members. Provides climbing training courses.

Publications: Women Climbing (in English), bimonthly. Newsletter.

Conventions/Meetings: annual general assembly. ● monthly regional meeting.

★767★ WOMEN FOR LIFE
11A Hamilton Parade
Hamilton, New Zealand
Mrs. Ruth Van der Sluis, President

National. New Zealand women opposed to abortion. Promotes recognition of the right to life of all human beings from conception to natural death.

★768★ WOMEN OUTDOORS NEW ZEALAND (WONZ)
National Collective
PO Box 68-296
Newton
Auckland, New Zealand

Languages: English. **National**. Encourages women's particpation in outdoor activities. Sponsors athletic events and nature appreciation programs.

★769★ WOMEN AND POLITICS NETWORK
c/o Bronwyn Hayward
Lincoln University
Dept. of Parks, Recreation, & Tourism
PO Box 84
Canterbury, New Zealand

Languages: English. **National**. Seeks to raise public awareness of women's issues. Encourages women to voice their concerns to political leaders. Promotes women's participation in all decision making processes.

★770★ WOMEN FOR SOBRIETY
PO Box 6399
Dunedin, New Zealand
Mary Benson, Contact   PH: 3 4737896

Languages: English. **National**. Women united to prevent alcohol abuse and assist in rehabilitation. Disseminates information.

★771★ WOMEN ON WATER (WOW)
c/o Wellington Yachting Association
PO Box 860
Wellington, New Zealand   PH: 4 2331056
Mrs. Kate Spackman, Chair   FX: 4 3857366

Founded: 1985. **Members:** 150. **Membership Dues:** women only., NZ$5 annual. **Budget:** NZ$600. **Regional Groups:** 1. **Languages:** English. **National**. Women interested in the sport of sailing. Organizes training courses for sailing and boat racing. Sponsors community "Try-a-Boat" days.

Publications: *Have a Go-Sailing* (in English). Book. ● *Newsletter* (in English). Informs members of sailing events and training courses.

Conventions/Meetings: Summer, every third week.

★772★ WOMENS DIVISION - FEDERATED FARMERS OF NEW
      ZEALAND (WDFF)
PO Box 12021
Thorndon   PH: 4 4735524
Wellington, New Zealand   3 2071833
Josephine Gravit, Exec. Officer   FX: 4 4728946

Founded: 1925. **Members:** 7,500. **Staff:** 3. **Budget:** NZ$258,000. **Languages:** English. **National**. Women working in agriculture and others interested in the role of women in New Zealand's agriculture industry. Seeks to strengthen rural communities through education, fellowship, and community involvement. Offers courses in personal skills development. Conducts research programs on the status of rural women. **Awards:** New Zealand Education Bursaries (grant).

Publications: *Rural Women* (in English), bimonthly. Newsletter.

Conventions/Meetings: annual conference.

★773★ WOMEN'S ELECTORAL LOBBY
PO Box 11-285
Wellington, New Zealand
Louise Ryan, Secretary   PH: 4 5628992

National. Politically involved women of New Zealand. Supports candidates and campaigns on behalf of issues of importance to women.

★774★ WOMEN'S INTERNATIONAL MOTORCYCLE ASSOCIATION
      (WIMA)
PO Box 48-085
Silverstream
Upper Hutt, New Zealand   PH: 4 5678680
Karen Stansfield, Contact   FX: 4 5670881

Founded: 1986. **Members:** 90. **Membership Dues:** NZ$25. **Languages:** English. **Multinational**. Women interested in international motorcycling competition. Encourages activities that promote the sport of motorcycle racing among women. Conducts fundraisers for the blind and for women's refuge centers.

Publications: *WIMA NZ Newsletter* (in English), bimonthly.

Conventions/Meetings: annual (exhibits) - always September.

★775★ WOMEN'S INTERNATIONAL ZIONIST ORGANIZATION-NEW
      ZEALAND (WIZO)
4 Lethenty Wayy
Karori
Wellington 5, New Zealand   PH: 4 767296
Doris Lewis, President   FX: 4 3846542

Founded: 1920. **Members:** 365. **Budget:** NZ$35,000. **Languages:** English. **National**. Non-political, voluntary movement of Zionist women in New Zealand. Promotes the interests of Jewish women. Provides for the welfare of infants, children, the umemployed, and elderly. Conducts educational courses in tailoring, chiropody, and cosmetology. Operates counselling center and clothing distribution station. Offers cultural programs.

Publications: *Annual Report* (in English).

Conventions/Meetings: biennial conference - New Zealand. ● monthly regional meeting.

★776★ WOMEN'S LEGAL RESOURCE PROJECT
PO Box 24-005
Wellington, New Zealand   PH: 4 4992928
Dot Kettle, Contact   FX: 4 4722320

Founded: 1988. **Languages:** English. **National**. Lawyers, law students, and women consumers of legal services. Seeks to educate women about their legal rights, to make the law more accessible to women, and to improve the law as it relates to women. **Libraries:** Type: reference.
Committees: Lesbian; Law Reform.

Publications: *Women Know Your Legal Rights Handbook*. ● *Lesbian Will Making Kit*. Book.

★777★ WOMEN'S NATIONAL ABORTION ACTION CAMPAIGN
      (WONAAC)
PO Box 14-314
Wellington, New Zealand
Di Cleary, Contact   PH: 4 3861857

Founded: 1972. **Members:** 200. **Budget:** NZ$2,000. **Languages:** English. **National**. Women in New Zealand united to decriminalize abortion. Supports availability of free abortion services for the public. Conducts sexual education programs. Fosters communication among members.

Publications: *Newsletter* (in English), semiannual.

Conventions/Meetings: bimonthly conference.

★778★ WOMEN'S REFUGE
Town Hall
303 Queen St.
Auckland, New Zealand

Languages: English. **National**. Works for the provision of material and emotional support to women in need.

★779★ WOMEN'S WORLD BANKING
c/o Noeline Matthews
PO Box 31-367
Lower Hutt, New Zealand

Languages: English. **National**. Seeks to enhance the economic status of women. Offers financial advice.

★780★ YOUNG WOMEN'S CHRISTIAN ASSOCIATION - NEW ZEALAND
PO Box 9315
Courtenay Pl.   PH: 4 3848116
Wellington, New Zealand   4 3848117
Cathy Lythe, Co-Dir.   FX: 4 3843301

Founded: 1926. **Members:** 2,000. **Staff:** 2. **Budget:** NZ$400,000. **Languages:** English. **National**. Young women and adult women leaders. Aims to enhance the spiritual, physical, and mental well-being of women through its activities. Seeks to achieve social justice by fighting sexism, racism, and economic oppression. Conducts programs in: peace education; self-defense training; migrant integration; conservation; health; and human rights awareness. Distributes historical information about women's suffrage to New Zealand secondary schools. **Awards:** Annual Women's Welfare League Scholarship (scholarship). Recipient: female students. **Committees:** World YWCA Cooperation for Development; Maori Women; Training; Young Women; Personnel and World YWCA.

Publications: *Overview* (in English), semiannual. Magazine.

Conventions/Meetings: annual general assembly. • quarterly conference.

★781★ ZONTA INTERNATIONAL-NEW ZEALAND
184 Remeura Rd.   PH: 9 5201409
Auckland, New Zealand   9 5758477
Joan-Mary Longcroft, Sec.   FX: 9 5201409

Founded: 1965. **Members:** 980. **Budget:** NZ$19,000. **State Groups:** 31. **Languages:** English. **National**. New Zealand branch of international executive women's group. Seeks to advance the status of women through its relationship with the United Nations and its agencies. Funds programs to assist women in developing countries. Provides mentoring and scholarship programs designed to encourage young women in a variety of career paths. Local groups undertake projects concerned with such issues as economic self-sufficiency, legislative equality, aging, educational access, health, and nutrition. Sponsors programs in areas such as literacy, environmental issues, and refugee support. Conducts exhibitions. **Libraries:**
Subjects: current government and New Zealand Ministry of Women's Affairs publications. **Awards:** Amelia Earhart Award (monetary). • Young Women in Public Affairs Award. Recipient: secondary school female students. **Computer Services:** Data base, membership list. **Committees:** International Relations; Organization and Extension; Nominating; Service; Status of Women; United Nations.

Publications: *District Governor's Newsletter* (in English), quarterly. • *Who's Who in the District* (in English), biennial. Directory. • *History of District 16*. Book.

Conventions/Meetings: biennial conference, Features speakers, business meetings, United Nations issue-driven workshops, resolutions, and fellowship opportunities. - 1993 Sept. 17 - 19, New Zealand.

Niue

★782★ NIUE WOMEN'S ADVISORY COUNCIL
Alofi, Niue
Lady Patrical Tagaloa Rex, President   PH: 4027

Founded: 1982. **Members:** 500. **Staff:** 7. **National**. Women working to promote and preserve traditional culture through crafts and agriculture in Niue. Supports community development projects.

Conventions/Meetings: periodic workshop.

Pakistan

★783★ AGHS LEGAL AID CELL (ALAC)
                     PH: 42 879273
131-A E/1 Gulberg III   42 871813
Lahore, Pakistan   FX: 42 877945
Asma Jahangir, Partner   TX: 44626 HALAPK

Founded: 1980. **National**. Lawyers and individuals working in the law profession. Promotes legal awareness, education, protection from exploitation, legal research, counseling, and legal assistance to women throughout Pakistan. Provides legal aid to women involved in family disputes, as well as women and/or children in prison, bonded labor and victims of human rights violations. Advocates and campaigns for: child and women prisoners; rights of bonded labor; reforms in family laws; women victims; and other human rights cases. Maintains a home for destitute women. Conducts research and paralegal training program.

Publications: *Newsletter* (in Urdu and English), monthly. • *Simple Version of Laws in Marriage, Divorce, Custody*. Booklet. • *Penal Laws Affecting Women*. Booklet. • *Right to Vote*. Booklet. • *Family Law*. Videos. • *Strategies to Overcome Child Labor*. Booklet.

★784★ ALL PAKISTAN WOMEN'S ASSOCIATION (APWA)
67/B Garden Rd.
Karachi 3, Pakistan
Begum Jahan Ara Hai, Chairperson   PH: 21 712991

Founded: 1949. **Languages:** English. **National**. Works to improve the moral, social, and economic welfare of Pakistani women and children. Encourages the participation of women in developing Pakistan. Seeks to enhance women's legal, governmental, and economic situation. Consults with international and national organizations and advises them on women's needs. Conducts labor, educational, and recreational programs intended to help women and children gain access to more lucrative job opportunities. Maintains family welfare centers and trains workers. Conducts seminars and workshops on maternal and pre-natal health care, breast feeding, sterilization, and contraception options. Provides training in arts and crafts, dress making, carpet weaving, and job skills. Organizes national literacy programs. Lobbies governmental bodies to reform laws that affect women and children. Raises funds for charities. **Sections:** APWA Korangi and Akhtar Colony Crafts Centre. **Projects:** Rural Village Project. **Sections:** Legal Aid and Awareness Centre; Activities of UN Affairs; International Affairs.

★785★ ASIAN WOMEN'S INSTITUTE (AWI)
Assn. of Kinnaird Coll. for Women
93 Jail Rd.
Lahore, Pakistan   PH: 42 487165
Santosh Singha, Coordinator   CBL: AWINSTI

Founded: 1975. **Members:** 13. **Languages:** English. **Multinational**. Christian universities and colleges that offer baccalaureate degrees and that have developed women's studies programs. Works to assist Asian women in leading fuller lives and gaining self-confidence by promoting study and development of women and their communities through documentation, research, social action, and communication. Sponsors continuing education programs for women, career services for Asian women, and research on women's concerns. Maintains library.

Publications: *Asian Woman*, quarterly. ● *Newsletter*, quarterly.

Conventions/Meetings: triennial meeting - 1994.

★786★ BUSINESS, PROFESSIONAL AND AGRICULTURAL WOMEN'S ASSOCIATION
I-Michni Ln.
Peshawar Cantonment
Peshawar, Pakistan   PH: 521 304702

Languages: Urdu, English. **National.** Represents the interests of women employed outside of the home. Seeks to improve the economic status and working conditions of women in Pakistan.

★787★ BUSINESS AND PROFESSIONAL WOMEN'S CLUB - PAKISTAN
411 Pak Block
Allama Iqbal Town
Lahore, Pakistan

Languages: Urdu, English. **National.** Women in business and management positions. Works to enhance the status of women in Pakistan. Promotes high professional and ethical standards.

★788★ FAMILY PLANNING ASSOCIATION OF PAKISTAN (FPAP)
                                PH: 42 212999
3-A Temple Rd.   42 361583
Lahore, Pakistan   FX: 42 368692
Prof. Laeeq A. Khan, CEO   TX: 44877 PEARL PK

Languages: Urdu, English. **National.** Advocates family planning and responsible parenthood as a basic human right and as a means to improve the quality of life for individuals living in Pakistan. Works to stop the spread of AIDS and other sexually transmitted diseases. Offers programs in sex education, family planning, and health. Provides contraceptive and health care services. Conducts research.

★789★ FEDERATION OF BUSINESS AND PROFESSIONAL WOMEN'S ASSOCIATIONS
9/3 Rimpa Twin Star
Opposite Hotel Mehran
Karachi 4, Pakistan

Languages: Urdu, English. **National.** Umbrella organization for professionally employed women's groups. Provides a forum for members to make social and business contacts. Represents members' interests.

★790★ MATERNITY AND CHILD WELFARE ASSOCIATION OF PAKISTAN (MCWAP)
MCH House
29/30-F, Gulberg II
Lahore 54660, Pakistan   PH: 42 874621
Dr. A.H. Awan, Pres.   FX: 42 485645

Founded: 1961. **Staff:** 19. **Budget:** PRs 3,584,000. **Languages:** English. **National.** Promotes health care for mothers and children in Pakistan through maternal and child health education and services. Assists development of medical personnel in the areas of nutrition, medical social work, and family guidance. Offers assistance in establishing school health services. Conducts conferences, seminars, and workshops.

Publications: *Mother and Child* (in English), quarterly. **Advertising:** accepted.

Conventions/Meetings: periodic meeting.

★791★ PAKISTAN ASSOCIATION OF WOMEN ENTREPRENEURS (PAWE)
1017 UNI Plaza   PH: 21 2423964
I.I. Chundrigar Rd.   FX: 21 2412480
Karachi, Pakistan   TX: 23728

National. Promotes and protects the interests of women entrepreneurs in Pakistan. Fosters information exchange among members to advance the development of women in Pakistan's economic structure. Cooperates with other national women's entrepreneurial organizations to further the development of women in business worldwide. Organizes research and educational programs. Disseminates information.

★792★ PAKISTAN WOMEN LAWYERS ASSOCIATION (PAWLA)
Rm. 710, Kashif Centre
Shahra-e-Faisal
Karachi 2, Pakistan
Mrs. Rashida Muhammad Hussain Patel,
   President   PH: 21 518796

Founded: 1981. **Budget:** PRs 779,268. **Languages:** English. **National.** Women lawyers. Works to: advance the status of women, particularly in the legal professional field; secure women's rights within the law; eradicate discriminatory, exploitive laws and practices against women; build awareness among women of issues affecting women. Lobbies legislators and legal organizations to adopt policies designed for women and children. Cooperates with other women's organizations with similar aims. **Libraries:** Type: reference.   **Projects:** PAWLA Legal Aid Services.

Conventions/Meetings: annual convention. ● bimonthly executive committee meeting. ● periodic seminar (exhibits).

★793★ PAKISTAN WOMEN'S INSTITUTE
93 Jail Rd.
Lahore, Pakistan
Mrs. S. Singha, Contact   PH: 42 487165

Founded: 1975. **Languages:** English, Urdu. **National.** Encourages the improvement and expansion of women's roles. Seeks to arrive at creative solutions to problems of prejudice and discrimination against women. Conducts research and educational programs. Fosters communication among members; organizes debates and discussion groups. Provides career services including: job placement, field trips to job sites, continuing education courses, and leadership development. Offers legal advice. **Libraries:** Type: reference.   books, periodicals. Subjects: works by and about women.

Publications: *PWI Newsletter*, semiannual. Essays and articles on women's issues and other women's institutes.

Conventions/Meetings: periodic workshop.

★794★ PROGRESSIVE WOMEN'S ASSOCIATION
House 16B, Street 45
F 8/1
Islamabad, Pakistan   PH: 51 855545
Shahnaz Rashid, President   FX: 51 584566

Languages: English. **National.** Women working to help female victims of violence. Maintains a women's support center from which it supplies psychological and emotional counseling; legal aid and advice; job skill training; and job placement assistance. Prepares women for social work and management of small businesses.

Publications: *Women's World* (in English). Magazine. **Circulation:** 6,000.

★795★ SIMORGH WOMEN'S RESOURCE AND PUBLICATION
CENTER
PO Box 3328
Gulberg II
Lahore 54660, Pakistan

Languages: Urdu. **National.** Seeks to raise awareness of women's issues. Produces informational and literary material related to the women's movement and women's issues.

★796★ WOMEN LIVING UNDER MUSLIM LAWS
18-A Milan Mir Rd.
PO Mughalpura
Lahore 15, Pakistan   PH: 42 874951

Languages: Urdu. **National.** Provides a forum for discussion and information sharing among Muslim women. Provides educational and informational services.

★797★ WOMEN'S ACTION FORUM
F/25 A Block 9
Clifton
Karachi 75600, Pakistan

Languages: Urdu. **National.** Works to enhance the status of women. Organizes programs and activities to strengthen awareness of women's issues.

★798★ WOMEN'S RESOURCE CENTRE
(Shirkat Gah)
1 Bath Island Rd.   PH: 21 573079
Karachi 75530, Pakistan   21 573082
Meher Maeker Noshiewani, Coord.   TX: 24154 MARK PK

Founded: 1975. **Languages:** Urdu, English. **National.** Works to improve women's economic, social, and environmental standard of living. Researches women's issues and disseminates information.

Publications: *SUBHA* (in Urdu and English), quarterly. Newsletter. • *Rehnumah* (in Urdu). Book. • *Women Living under Muslim Laws.* Booklet. • *Bibliography of Women in Pakistan.* Book. • *Information Kit on Women in Quran.* Booklet.

★799★ YOUNG WOMEN'S CHRISTIAN ASSOCIATION - PAKISTAN
14 Shahrah-e-Fatima Jinnah
Lahore, Pakistan   PH: 42 304707
Merle Jivanandham, Contact   CBL: YWCA LAHORE

National. Promotes the development of young women in Pakistan. Upholds Christian beliefs and values in its programs. Works to instill self worth and self-esteem in young women.

Papua New Guinea

★800★ FAMILY PLANNING ASSOCIATION OF PAPUA NEW GUINEA
(FPAPNG)
PO Box 7123
National Capital District   PH: 255112
Boroko, Papua New Guinea   255100
Mrs. Catherine Natera, Exec. Dir.   FX: 250528

Languages: English. **National.** Works to improve the quality of life by promoting responsible parenthood and family planning. Advocates family planning as a basic human right. Offers programs in family planning, sex education, and health. Provides contraceptive and health care services. Conducts research.

★801★ INTERNATIONAL PLANNED PARENTHOOD FEDERATION -
PAPUA NEW GUINEA
PO Box 987
National Capital District   PH: 250096
Boroko, Papua New Guinea   FX: 250528

Languages: English. **Multinational.** Works to co-ordinate activities of regional Planned Parenthood offices. Advocates family planning as a basic human right. Works to increase public awareness of population problems. Promotes effective family planning programs. Conducts research on human fertility and contraception.

★802★ NATIONAL COUNCIL OF WOMEN OF PAPUA NEW GUINEA
(NCWPNG)
PO Box 154 UPNG
Port Moresby, Papua New Guinea   PH: 260375
Maria Kopkop, President   FX: 251230

National. Umbrella organization for women's groups in Papua New Guinea. Supports the interests of women. Coordinates activities for women. Disseminates information.

★803★ PACIFIC ISLANDS PLANNED PARENTHOOD AFFILIATION
(PIPPA)
c/o IPPF Papua New Guinea Field Office
PO Box 987
National Capital District   PH: 212858
Boroko, Papua New Guinea   FX: 217194

Languages: English. **National.** Umbrella group of national planned parenthood associations in the Pacific Islands. Works to improve the quality of life for individuals living in the Pacific Islands by promoting responsible parenthood and family planning. Attempts to reduce the number of unwanted pregnancies and abortions. Offers programs in sex education, family planning, and health. Provides contraceptive and health care services. Conducts research.

★804★ PAPUA NEW GUINEA NATIONAL COUNCIL OF WOMEN
PO Box 154, University
National Capitol District   PH: 261375
Port Moresby, Papua New Guinea   261720
Ms. Maria Kopkop, President   FX: 261764

Founded: 1979. **Staff:** 7. **Languages:** English. **National.** Promotes the interests of women in Papua New Guinea. Sponsors women's development programs. Lobbies government on women's issues policies. Operates a crisis center. **Awards:** International Women of the Year.

Publications: *Nius Blong Meri.*

★805★ YOUNG WOMEN'S CHRISTIAN ASSOCIATION - PAPUA NEW
GUINEA
PO Box 5884
Boroko, Papua New Guinea   PH: 250133
Au Doko Aruai, Exec.Dir.   250510

National. Promotes the development of young women in Papua New Guinea. Upholds Christian beliefs and values in its programs. Works to instill self worth and self-esteem in its programs.

Philippines

★806★ ANAK-SERVICE PROGRAM FOR ALTERNATIVE DAY CARE IN
THE PHILIPPINES
142-A Scout Rallos
Kamuning 1103
Quezon City, Metro Manila, Philippines   PH: 2 869268

Languages: Filipino. **National.** Women working to increase availability and quality of childcare facilities in the Philippines.

★807★ ASIAN CHRISTIAN CENTER FOR WOMEN STUDIES
PO Box 461
Manila, Philippines   PH: 2 982921

Languages: Filipino. **National.** Promotes research of women's roles as they relate to the Christian faith.

★808★ ASIAN WOMEN'S HUMAN RIGHTS COUNCIL (AWHRC)
PO Box 190   PH: 2 7218883
Manila 1099, Philippines   FX: 2 7218883

Founded: 1986. **Languages:** Filipino. **Multinational.** Women lawyers and feminist activists involved in the promotion and defense of basic human rights and women's rights. Encourages study of human rights. Fosters cooperation and solidarity between women's groups and individuals advocating human rights recognition. Compiles information on national policies throughout Asia which affect human rights.

Conventions/Meetings: periodic seminar. ● periodic regional meeting.

★809★ ASIAN WOMEN'S RESEARCH AND ACTION NETWORK
PO Box 208
Davao City 9501, Philippines   PH: 82 775341

Languages: Filipino. **National.** Promotes the study and development of Asian women in their communities. Conducts research on women's issues.

★810★ CENTRE FOR WOMEN'S RESOURCES (CWR)
Mar-Santos Bldg., 2nd Fl.
43 Don A Roces Ave.
Quezon City, Metro Manila, Philippines
Carol Anonuero, Contact

Languages: Filipino. **National.** Promotes women's personal development programs in the Philippines. Offers educational opportunities.

★811★ CIVIC ASSEMBLY OF WOMEN OF THE PHILIPPINES
The Philippine Women's University
1743 Taft Ave.
Manila, Philippines
Trinidad Gomez, President

Languages: Filipino, English. **National.** Encourages women to become involved in local and national politics. Lobbies government on women's issues.

★812★ DEPTHNEWS WOMEN'S SERVICE
c/o Press Foundation of Asia
PO Box 1843   PH: 2 591478
Manila, Philippines   FX: 2 5224365

Languages: Filipino. **National.** Works to improve the media's portrayal of women. Aims to enhance the status of women through educational and social service programs.

★813★ FAMILY PLANNING ORGANIZATION OF THE PHILIPPINES
(FPOP)
          PH: 2 7217302
PO Box 1279   2 7217101
Broadway   FX: 2 7214067
Quezon City, Metro Manila, Philippines   TX: 63320 ETPMO PN
Mr. Javier Gil C. Montemayor, Secretary   CBL: FPOPHIL MANILA

Languages: English, Filipino. **National.** Advocates family planning and responsible parenthood as a basic human right and a means to enhance the quality of life for individuals living in the Philippines. Attempts to stop the spread of AIDS and other sexually transmitted diseases through education and contraceptive services. Provides programs in family planning and health care. Conducts research.

★814★ FEDERATION OF ASIAN WOMEN'S ASSOCIATIONS
Centro Escolar University
Mendiola
Manila, Metro Manila, Philippines

Languages: Filipino. **Multinational.** Promotes awareness of women's issues. Sponsors educational and research programs.

★815★ GABRIELA COMMISSION ON VIOLENCE AGAINST WOMEN
(GCVAW)
20-B Florfina St.
Roxas District
Quezon City, Metro Manila, Philippines
Cecilia Hofmann, Coord.   PH: 2 991772

Founded: 1987. **Staff:** 4. **Languages:** English. **National.** Focuses on issues pertaining to rape, domestic violence, sexual harrassment, prostitution, and other issues based in violence towards women. Supports actions to protest anti-women policies and practices. Operates program to focus on the media's treatment of women. Offers research and educational programs. Provides a referral service to victimized women. **Libraries:** Type: reference. Subjects: women and violence. **Task Forces:** Amerasian Children in Base Areas; Women and Bases Conversion; Legislative Advocacy; Sex Trafficking; AIDS.

Publications: *Kamulatan* (in Tagalog), quarterly. **Also Cited As:** *Awareness*.

★816★ GENERAL ASSEMBLY BINDING WOMEN FOR REFORMS,
INTEGRITY, LEADERSHIP AND ACTION (GABRIELA)
35 Scout Delgado
Roxas District
Quezon City, Metro Manila, Philippines
Sister Mary John Mananzan, Chairperson   PH: 998034

Founded: 1984. **Members:** 48,000. **Regional Groups:** 3. **State Groups:** 3. **Local Groups:** 2. **Languages:** English. **National.** Individuals and organizations working to unite women politically. Works to eliminate economic and political discrimination; sexual violence and abuse; and denial of health and reproductive rights to women. Strives for establishment of a representative, democratic government. Conducts educational and training programs for women. Investigates the effects of militarization; women's property rights; governmental fiscal policy; and prostitution and trafficking of women. Increases public awareness of women's issues via performing group and media. **Libraries:** Type: reference. Holdings: books. Subjects: women's issues. **Commissions:** Children & Family; Women's Political Rights; Violence Against Women; Women's Health & Reproductive Rights; Women & Economic Development; International Relations; Migrant Filipinas. **Departments:** Education; Performing Group; Socio-Economics.

Publications: *Women's Update* (in English), quarterly. Newsletter. ● Also publishes resource materials.

Conventions/Meetings: quarterly National Council meeting. ● biennial National Congress. ● periodic Women's International Solidarity Affair in the Philippines.

★817★ GIRL SCOUTS OF THE PHILIPPINES
901 Padre Faura
1000 Ermita
Manila, Philippines
Milagros Villasor, President   PH: 1 8177226

Languages: Filipino, English. **National**. Girls and young women in the Philippines. Encourages responsible citizenship through community service activities.

★818★ INSTITUTE FOR SOCIAL STUDIES AND ACTION (ISSA)
QCC PO Box 1078
Quezon City, Metro Manila 1104,
   Philippines   PH: 2 997396
Ms. Alexandrina Marcelo, Exec. Dir.   FX: 2 9240717

Founded: 1983. **Languages:** English, Filipino. **National**. Filipino women and health organizations working to increase public awareness of women's health needs. Seeks to improve maternal health; fertility management and contraceptive practices; techniques for prevention of sexually transmitted diseases; and government action on violence against women. Monitors and lobbies the legislative and executive levels of government on women's issues. Organizes informational and educational activities on women's health and reproductive rights issues. Maintains clinics which offer OB/GYN, pediatric, family planning, general medicine, and counseling services for disadvantaged citizens. Trains members of like-minded organizations in health care and helps them organize clinics. Refers clients to resource, counseling, legal, and medical centers. **Libraries:** Type: open to the public; reference. Holdings: 800; books, periodicals, audio recordings, video recordings. **Computer Services:** Data base, women's health and related topics; record retrieval services; information services.

Publications: *Medium for the Advancement and Achievement of Reproductive Rights, Health Information and Advocacy*, quarterly. Bulletin. **Circulation:** 1,000. **Advertising:** accepted. **Also Cited As:** *MARHIA*.

★819★ ISIS INTERNATIONAL - PHILIPPINES
85-A East Maya St.
Philamlife Homes
Quezon City, Metro Manila 1104,
   Philippines   PH: 2 993292
La Rainne Abad-Sarmiento, Coordinator   FX: 2 990507

Founded: 1974. **Members:** 2,500. **Budget:** US$250,000. **Languages:** English, Spanish. **Multinational**. Women's information and communication service. Facilitates global communication among women and disseminates information and materials produced by women and women's groups in an effort to foster solidarity among women. Examines issues such as women's role in development, health, education, food and nutrition, media, prostitution and violence against women, employment, and theories of feminism. Provides technical assistance in communication skills and information management. Seeks to mobilize support and solidarity among women on an international scale. Is currently developing the Asia-Pacific Women's Health Network to coordinate the exchange of information between women and health organizations. Maintains biographical archives, documentation center, and library of 800 women's serials and 700 volumes on women's issues. (The group is named for Isis, the Egyptian goddess of knowledge and fertility.). **Computer Services:** Data base, audiovisual; data base, bibliographic; data base, human resources; data base, health. **Programs:** Communication and Networking; Health and Networking; Women and Audiovisual. **Alternate name:** Women's International Information and Communication Service.

Publications: *ISIS International Women's Book Series*, semiannual. Monograph. ● *Powerful Images: A Woman's Guide to Audiovisual Resources*, periodic. Directory. ● *Women in Action*, quarterly. Journal. ● *Directory of Third World's Women's Publications*. ● *Women's Actions for the Environment Information Pack*. Booklet. ● *Women in Development Resource Guide*. Booklet.

★820★ KAHAYAG FOUNDATION
121 University Ave.
Matina
Davao City, Philippines   PH: 82 63949
Patricia Mangrobang Sarenas, Exec. Dir.   FX: 82 64393

Founded: 1977. **Staff:** 15. **Budget:** 60,000 PP. **Languages:** English, Filipino. **National**. Liaises with other non-governmental organizations to provide training and education for poor women. Works to improve women's health, child care, and education. Represents and defends women's interests.

Conventions/Meetings: semiannual Gender and Development Training seminar - Davao City, Philippines.

★821★ KANLUNGAN CENTER FOUNDATION
77 K-10th St.
Kamias
Quezon City, Metro Manila, Philippines   PH: 2 9217849
Gina Alunan Melgar, Exec. Dir.   FX: 2 9217849

Founded: 1989. **Staff:** 11. **Budget:** 1,500,000 PP. **Languages:** Filipino, English. **National**. Aims to protect the dignity, rights, and well-being of Filipino migrant women from abuses encountered while working abroad. Offers legal assistance for victims of illegal recruitment, violations of job contracts, and unjust working terms. Conducts educational and training programs for returning and prospective migrant workers regarding their rights; lobbies asnd advocates for such individuals. Liaises with nongovernmental and grassroots organizations to provide crisis intervention services to migrant working women. **Computer Services:** Data base, legal cases.

Publications: *Kanlungan ng Migrante* (in Filipino), semiannual. Newsletter. Practical and legal information on working and living abroad. ● *Trends, News, and Tidbits*, quarterly. Newsletter.

★822★ LEAGUE OF WOMEN VOTERS OF THE PHILIPPINES
12J Abad Santos
Heroes Hills
Quezon City, Metro Manila, Philippines
Felicidad Singson Calip, President   PH: 2 997938

Languages: Filipino. **National**. Encourages women's participation in politics. Conducts voter education campaigns. Disseminates information.

★823★ MATERNAL AND CHILD HEALTH ASSOCIATION OF THE
   PHILIPPINES (MCHAP)
NFP Bldg.
107 E. Rodriguez Sr. Blvd.
Quezon City, Metro Manila 1102,
   Philippines
Carmelita B. Cuyugan M.D., Pres.   PH: 2 7121474

Founded: 1972. **Members:** 513. **Staff:** 1. **Regional Groups:** 2. **Local Groups:** 4. **Languages:** English. **National**. Physicians, nurses, midwives, and other professionals interested in promoting maternal and child health in the Philippines. Fosters increased awareness of the health and medical care needs of mothers and children. Encourages up-to-date methods of research and data collection and evaluation. Seeks the integration of maternal and child health topics into all levels of medical education curricula. Sponsors conferences, seminars, and symposia. Offers children's services. Maintains speakers' bureau. Bestows awards. **Committees:** Awards; Continuing Education; Domestic Affairs; International Affairs; Legislation and Amendments; Service Program and Projects. **Projects:** Involving Children in Selected Aspects of Primary Health Care.

Publications: *Newsletter* (in English), semiannual.

Conventions/Meetings: annual.

★824★ METRO MANILA COUNCIL OF WOMEN - BALIKATAN
MOVEMENT
215 Regency Park
207 Santolan Rd.
Quezon City, Metro Manila, Philippines
Rexie Constantino, Gen.Sec.   PH: 2 797230

Founded: 1980. **Members:** 16,700. **Staff:** 2. **Budget:** 300,000 PP. **Regional Groups:** 4. **State Groups:** 7. **Local Groups:** 13. **Languages:** English, Filipino. **National.** Seeks to raise the socio-economic status of women. Provides members with educational opportunities as a means to employment. Conducts training programs and study tours. Participates in environmental research. **Awards:** Annual International Women's Day Award.

Publications: *Ang Pilipina* (in Filipino and English), quarterly. Magazine.

Conventions/Meetings: monthly regional meeting. ● annual conference (exhibits) - always November. Metro Manilia, Philippines.

★825★ NATIONAL COMMISSION ON THE ROLE OF FILIPINO
WOMEN (NCRFW)
1145 J.P. Laurel St.   PH: 2 7415028
San Miguel, Metro Manila, Philippines   2 7417208
Remedios I. Rikken, Exec. Dir.   FX: 2 7125267

Founded: 1975. **Staff:** 65. **Budget:** 7,000,000 PP. **Languages:** English, Filipino. **National.** Advocates equal rights for women in the Philippines. Conducts educational and training programs. Engages in research and policy studies; acts as a clearinghouse of information on women's issues. **Computer Services:** Information services, CDS-ISIS; bibliographic search.

Publications: *Philippine Development Plan for Women (1989-1992)* (in English). Monograph. ● *Usapang Babae* (in Tagalog), periodic. Newsletter. ● *Women's Resource Directory.*

★826★ NATIONAL COMMISSION ON WOMEN
1145 J.P. Laurel St.
San Miguel
Manila, Philippines   PH: 2 7415093
Remedios Rikken, Exec. Dir.   2 7415028

Languages: Filipino. **National.** Works for public recognition of women's rights. Compiles and disseminates information on women's issues and the national women's movement.

★827★ NATIONAL COUNCIL OF WOMEN OF THE PHILIPPINES
c/o Philippine Women's University
1743 Taft Ave.
Manila, Philippines
Justice Leonor I. Luciano, President   PH: 2 588201

Languages: Filipino. **National.** Umbrella organization for women's groups in the Philippines. Promotes and supports women's interests. Coordinates activities; disseminates information.

★828★ NATIONAL FEDERATION OF PEASANT WOMEN (AMIHAN)
PO Box 4386
Manila 2800, Philippines

Languages: English, Tagalog. **National.** Represents the interests and seeks the development of Filipino peasant and rural women.

Publications: *Pagsibol*, 3/year. Newsletter.

Conventions/Meetings: semiannual convention.

★829★ NATIONAL FEDERATION OF WOMEN'S CLUBS OF THE
PHILIPPINES (NFWC)
962 Josefa Escoda
Corner of Leon Guinto
Ermita, Metro Manila, Philippines   PH: 2 595758
Josefina Manio, Contact   2 593950

Founded: 1921. **Members:** 300,000. **Staff:** 9. **Budget:** 2,500,000 PP. **Languages:** English. **National.** Women in both urban and rural areas in the Philippines. Promotes the unification of Filipino women through the enhancement of general welfare, mutual understanding, and cooperation. Assists women to become more effective participants in national development efforts. Organizes study clubs, nursery classes, seminars, and forums. **Awards:** Annual Outstanding Mothers' Award (recognition). ● Biennial Outstanding Club Women (recognition). ● Scholarship. Recipient: yung women seeking higher education.

Publications: *Newsletter*, quarterly. Articles of interest to women; organization news. **Circulation:** 1,000.

Conventions/Meetings: biennial meeting - Manila, Philippines.

★830★ PHILIPPINE MEDICAL WOMEN'S ASSOCIATION (PMWA)
PMWA Bldg., No. 70
V. Luna Rd., Cor. Malakas St.
Quezon City, Metro Manila, Philippines
Lorie A. Lanuzo, Contact   PH: 2 9213947

Founded: 1949. **Members:** 3,500. **Staff:** 7. **Local Groups:** 56. **Languages:** English. **National.** Filipino women physicians. Works to increase public awareness of the medical profession. Promotes unity among members. Encourages women in the medical profession to participate in national issues affecting women and children. Operates medical and dental clinics and laboratories and the PMWA Learning Center, a kindergarten and daycare center. Conducts charitable activities; offers scholarships and grants. Maintains library.

Publications: *PMWA Newsette*, quarterly. ● *Philippine Medical World*, 1-2/year. Journal. Journal includes research papers. **Circulation:** 1,000. **Advertising:** not accepted.

Conventions/Meetings: semiannual workshop (exhibits).

★831★ PHILIPPINE WOMAN'S CHRISTIAN TEMPERANCE UNION
(PCWTU)
21 Santolan Rd.
Quezon City, Metro Manila, Philippines
Mrs. Villa Granada de Guia, Pres.   PH: 2 703969

Founded: 1929. **Members:** 1,000. **Staff:** 2. **Languages:** English, Tagalog. **National.** Christian women in the Philippines. Seeks to prohibit the manufacture, sale, and advertising of alcoholic beverages. Works to: unite members in collecting and disseminating scientific information; cooperate with government agencies in enforcing laws against the use of narcotics. Maintains speaker's bureau and Abiertas House of Friendship for unwed mothers and abandoned infants; provides charitable and children's services. Sponsors educational and research programs; bestows awards. **Committees:** Public Relations. **Departments:** Alcohol-Free Hospitality; Christian Outreach; Citizenship; Education; Home Protection; Loyal Temperance Legion; Promotion Methods; Social Service; Young People; Promotion Methods.

Publications: *Alcohol Free Beverages* (in English and Tagalog), semiannual. ● *PCWTU Newsletter* (in English and Tagalog), quarterly. ● *Temperance Devotional Booklet* (in English and Tagalog), semiannual. ● *White Ribbon Bulletin* (in English and Tagalog), semiannual.

Conventions/Meetings: semiannual conference. ● quarterly seminar. ● monthly board meeting.

★832★ THIRD WORLD MOVEMENT AGAINST THE EXPLOITATION
OF WOMEN (TW-MAE-W)
41 Rajah Matanda
Project 4
Quezon City, Metro Manila 1109,
  Philippines   PH: 2 786469
Sr. Mary Soledad Perpinan, Coordinator   FX: 2 9215662

Founded: 1980. **Staff:** 6. **Multinational.** Women's groups and individuals in
45 countries concerned with organizing action against what the TW-MAE-W
views as female sexual slavery and exploitation. Seeks a transnational
approach to women's issues as an effective means for women to liberate
themselves. Serves as a networking organization focusing attention on
phenomena affecting women such as marriage bureaus, migrant labor,
international beauty contests, child prostitution, Islamic oppression of
women, and the importation of Third World entertainers. Has staged a
protest against organized Japanese sex tours and launched CAMP International, the Campaign Against Military Prostitution; draws attention to
prostitution occurring near military bases. Runs centers for prostitutes and a
transition home for those prostitutes seeking an alternative livelihood;
conducts AIDS prevention and care programs among sex workers. Maintains
speakers' bureau. Conducts research on issues concerning women, such as
labor, self-determination, and the role of the media and sex tourism in
prostitution. Conducts workshops and charitable and educational programs.
Libraries: Type: reference.   **Computer Services:** Data base.

Publications: *TW-MAE Action Bulletin*, bimonthly. ● *Women's Diary and
Directory*, periodic.

★833★ WOMANHEALTH PHILIPPINES
25-A B Gonzales St.
1108 Loyola Hts.
Quezon City, Metro Manila 1108,
  Philippines
Ana Maria Ronquillo-Nemenzo,   PH: 2 975896
  Nat.Coord.   2 987643

Founded: 1987. **Languages:** English. **National.** Non-governmental organizations, women's groups, health workers, researchers, and individual women.
Works to promote and protect women's health and reproductive rights.
Seeks to: establish governmental policies and programs designed to benefit
women; increase women's awareness of their medical rights and needs;
promote and support institutions with similar objectives; organize support
groups; coordinate social interaction among women.

★834★ WOMEN IN DEVELOPMENT FOUNDATION (WIDF)
Agricultural Training Institute, Rm. 109
Quezon City, Metro Manila, Philippines   PH: 2 978541

Founded: 1987. **Languages:** Filipino, English. **National.** Encourages Filipino
women's economic and political participation in society. Strives to empower
women financially and intellectually. Lobbies legislators and governmental
organizations on women's issues. Organizes and conducts training in
community organization skills, project management, media, small-business
operation, leadership, and political awareness. Assists and promotes wom-
en's organizations. Conducts research; provides counseling and consultancy
services.

Conventions/Meetings: periodic seminar.

★835★ WOMEN LAWYER'S ASSOCIATION OF THE PHILIPPINES
4 New Jersey
New Manila
Quezon City, Metro Manila, Philippines
Adoracion Angeles, President

Languages: Filipino. **National.** Female lawyers in the Philippines. Works to
improve the status of women; advises women of their legal rights. Promotes
the legal profession for women. Supports the career goals and objectives of
members.

★836★ WOMEN FOR WOMEN FOUNDATION (ASIA), INC. (WOW)
Development Academy of the Philippines
  Bldg., 2nd Fl. lower   PH: 2 6320806
San Miguel Ave.   2 6312119
Pasig, Metro Manila, Philippines   FX: 2 6312123

Founded: 1987. **Languages:** Filipino, English. **Multinational.** Support network for women managers and professionals. Provides a forum for women
with similar pursuits, interests, and concerns to meet and exhange information, opinions, and expertise. Offers services such as: training, counseling,
placement, and research. Maintains that the female population is "an under-
utilized human resource which ought to be nurtured, harnessed and
moblilized, both for women's own personal and professional advancement
and for national progress."

★837★ WOMEN'S LEGAL BUREAU
Augustin Bldg., Rm. 309
139 Malakas St., Central Dist.
Diliman
Quezon City, Metro Manila, Philippines   PH: 2 9213893

Languages: Filipino. **National.** Offers advocacy and legal counseling and
referral services to women whose civil rights have been violated.

★838★ WOMEN'S RIGHTS MOVEMENT OF THE PHILIPPINES
73 Ermine Garcia
Quezon City, Metro Manila, Philippines
Josefina S. Alberacia, President

Languages: Filipino. **National.** Defends and protects the rights of women.
Provides counselling to women who have experienced sexism.

★839★ YOUNG WOMEN'S CHRISTIAN ASSOCIATION - PHILIPPINES
                       PH: 2 501926
880 United Nations Ave.   2 599658
Manila 2801, Philippines   CBL: EMISSARIUS
Nilda B. Chua, Exec.Dir.   MANILA

National. Promotes the development of young women in Philippines.
Upholds Christian beliefs and values in its programs. Works to instill self
worth and self-esteem in young women.

Singapore

★840★ ASSOCIATION OF WOMEN FOR ACTION AND RESEARCH
  (AWARE)
PO Box 244
Tanglin 9124, Singapore

National. Works to raise awareness of women's issues through studies.
Conducts research; disseminates information.

★841★ CHRISTIAN CONFERENCE OF ASIA - WOMEN'S DIVISION
10 New Industrial Rd., No. 05-00
Singapore 1953, Singapore

Multinational. Women members of Christian churches throughout Asia.
Encourages fellowship among women. Promotes studies in evangelism,
international relations, and human development.

★842★ INTERNATIONAL BUSINESS WOMEN'S ASSOCIATION (IBWA)
PO Box 23, Orchard Point Post Office
Singapore 9123, Singapore   PH: 4675357
Shantha Farris, Contact   FX: 4675357

Founded: 1984. **Members:** 150. **Languages:** English. **Multinational.** Professional women. Promotes and supports women in business; seeks to assist

women in professional and personal growth. Coordinates a business women's network; organizes social and informational activities for members.

Publications: *Newsletter* (in English), bimonthly. ● *Directory* (in English), annual.

★843★ NATIONAL COUNCIL OF WOMEN - SINGAPORE
9 Balmoral Rd.
Singapore 1025, Singapore
Mrs. Gracia Tay Chee, President   PH: 7322064

Founded: 1975. **Languages:** English. **National.** Seeks to improve living conditions for women. Promotes women's rights, education, and literacy. Encourages communication and cooperation among women. Works in cooperation with the United Nations.

★844★ SINGAPORE ASSOCIATION OF WOMEN LAWYERS (SAWL)
14 Robinson Rd.
No. 09-02 Far East Finance Bldg.   PH: 2255822
Singapore 0104, Singapore   FX: 2241515

Founded: 1974. **Members:** 100. **Staff:** 1. **Languages:** English, Mandarin. **National.** Women lawyers in Singapore. Works to increase public knowledge of the law. Cooperates with women's organizations on projects addressing women's issues. Sponsors seminars and legal clinics. Maintains Tan Ah Tah Fund, an education fund for the handicapped, and speakers' bureau.

Publications: *SAWL Newsletter*, quarterly. **Advertising:** not accepted.

★845★ SINGAPORE COUNCIL OF WOMEN'S ORGANIZATIONS
(SCWO)
Block 24, No. 03-115
Outram Pk.
Singapore 0316, Singapore   PH: 3366641
Mrs. Anamah Tan, President   FX: 3365276

Founded: 1980. **Members:** 94,000. **Languages:** English. **National.** Women's organizations and individuals dedicated to improving women's educational, economic, social, and cultural status. Seeks to empower women to achieve equality. Provides a forum for social and intellectual interaction among women. Offers research, informational, and educational services for women. Coordinates activities among women's organizations and women leaders. Conducts fund raisers for women's causes. **Committees:** Education & Personal Development; Research & Legislation; International Affairs; Editorial & Publication.

Publications: *One Voice*, quarterly. Newsletter. Informs members of events, activities, and news relevant to women.

Conventions/Meetings: monthly board meeting.

★846★ SINGAPORE PLANNED PARENTHOOD ASSOCIATION (SPPA)
03-04 Pek Chuan Bldg.
116 Lavender St.   PH: 2942691
Singapore 1233, Singapore   2952693
Mrs. Amy Tan, Exec. Dir.   FX: 2938719

Languages: English. **National.** Promotes family planning as a basic human right and as a means to improve the quality of life for people living in Singapore. Works to reduce the number of unwanted pregnancies and abortions. Offers programs in sex education, family planning, and health. Provides contraceptive services. Acts as an advocate for family planning on a national level.

★847★ WOMEN'S SOCIETY OF CHRISTIAN SERVICE GENERAL
CONFERENCE
10 Mount Sophia   PH: 3375155
Singapore 0922, Singapore   FX: 3389575
Kathleen Beng-Leong Tan, Pres.   CBL: Methodist

Founded: 1887. **Members:** 1,764. **Staff:** 1. **Languages:** English, Mandarin,

Tamil. **National.** Women united to help each other grow in Christian knowledge and make Christ known throughout the world. Maintains center for the training of educationally disadvantaged girls; conducts visits to old-age homes and women's prisons; provides tuition assistance to children of blind and partially-sighted parents; ministers to women suffering health or marital problems. Conducts workshops, seminars, retreats, and leadership training.

Publications: *Sophia Blackmore in Singapore* (in English). Book.

Conventions/Meetings: quadrennial conference - 1996.

★848★ YOUNG WOMEN'S CHRISTIAN ASSOCIATION - SINGAPORE
150 Orchard Rd.
08-08 Orchard Plaza
Singapore 0923, Singapore
Lucy Tan, Exec.Dir.   PH: 2358822

National. Promotes the development of young women in Singapore. Upholds Christian beliefs and values in its programs. Works to instill self worth and self-esteem in young women.

Solomon Islands

★849★ SOLOMON ISLANDS NATIONAL COUNCIL OF WOMEN
PO Box 494
Honiara, Solomon Islands   PH: 23166

National. Umbrella organization for women's groups in the Solomon Islands. Supports and promotes women's interests. Coordinates activities. Disseminates information on women's concerns.

★850★ SOLOMON ISLANDS PLANNED PARENTHOOD ASSOCIATION
(SIPPA)
PO Box 554
Lombi Cress   PH: 22991
Honiara, Solomon Islands   23007
Mr. Cherry Galo, Exec. Dir.   FX: 23653

Languages: English. **National.** Advocates family planning as a basic human right and as a means to enhance the standard of living for individuals living in the Solomon Islands. Work to stop the spread of sexually transmitted diseases such as AIDS. Offers programs in sex education, family planning, and health. Provides contraceptive services. Conducts research.

★851★ YOUNG WOMEN'S CHRISTIAN ASSOCIATION - SOLOMON
ISLANDS
PO Box 494
Honiara, Solomon Islands   PH: 22661
Annie Homelo, Gen.Sec.   23371

National. Promotes the development of young women in the Solomon Islands. Upholds Christian beliefs and values in its programs. Work to instill self worth and self-esteem in young women.

Sri Lanka

★852★ ALL CEYLON MUSLIM WOMEN'S ASSOCIATION
191/50 Mangala Uyana
Thimbirigasyaya Rd.
Colombo, Sri Lanka   PH: 1 695706

National. Muslim women in Sri Lanka. Works to promote the interests of women while upholding Muslim principles and beliefs.

★853★ BAPTIST WOMEN'S LEAGUE OF SRI LANKA
19/2 Sri Saranankara Rd.   PH: 564745
Dehiwela, Sri Lanka   28559

National. Baptist women in Sri Lanka. Promotes the interest of women in Sri Lanka while upholding Christian Baptist beliefs and values.

★854★ CENTRE FOR WOMEN'S RESEARCH (CENWOR)
12 1/1, Ascot Ave.   PH: 1 502153
Colombo 5, Sri Lanka   FX: 1 580721
Dr. Swarna Jayaweera, Contact   TX: 21537 METALIX CE

Founded: 1984. **Members:** 10. **Staff:** 11. **Languages:** English, Tamil, Sinhalese. **National**. Members of research institutions focusing on issues affecting women. Disseminates and exchanges information and research findings. Advocates for women and women's issues. Provides training in areas such as literacy and gender sensitization. Conducts pilot projects intended to bring about improvements in women's conditions nationwide. Evaluates and promotes policies, projects, and research relating to women. Offers help and guidance for individuals and groups interested in studying or helping women. Sponsors and conducts public seminars and workshops. Acts as information center. **Libraries:** Type: reference.

Publications: *Newsletter* (in English, Sinhalese, and Tamil). Free. ● *The Hidden Face of Development*. Book. ● *Gender and Education in Sri Lanka*. Book.

Conventions/Meetings: periodic National Conference on Women conference, Research-oriented. - Colombo, Sri Lanka.

★855★ FAMILY PLANNING ASSOCIATION OF SRI LANKA (FPASL)
                                       PH: 1 584153
                                          1 584157
PO Box 365   FX: 1 580915
37/27 Bullers Ln.   TX: 22238 TRUST CE
Colombo 7, Sri Lanka   CBL: FAMPLAN
Mr. Daya Abeywickrema, Exec. Dir.   COLOMBO

Languages: Sinhalese. **National**. Advocates family planning as a basic human right and as a means to enhance the quality of life for individuals living in Sri Lanka. Works to reduce the number of unwanted pregnancies and abortions. Offers programs in sex education, family planning, and health. Provides contraceptive and health care services. Conducts research.

★856★ GIRLS FRIENDLY SOCIETY - SRI LANKA
58 Green Path
Colombo 3, Sri Lanka

Languages: Sinhalese, English. **National**. Fosters healthy emotional, physical, and intellectual development in girls and young women. Conducts recreational activities.

★857★ HINDU WOMEN'S SOCIETY
9 Castle Ln.
Colombo 4, Sri Lanka

National. Hindu women in Sri Lanka. Promotes the interests of women practicing Hindusim.

★858★ INSTITUTE OF AGRICULTURE AND WOMEN IN
   DEVELOPMENT (IAWID)
                                       PH: 1 685487
41-2/1 Gregory's Rd.   1 692998
Colombo 7, Sri Lanka   FX: 1 685040
Dr. C.P. Pillai, President   TX: 22154 HPTCE

Founded: 1990. **Staff:** 6. **Budget:** US$13,570. **Languages:** Sinhalese, English. **National**. Aims to enable rural women to have an equal role to men in Sri Lankan society. Encourages rural women to participate in agriculture as a means to social and economic emancipation. Coordinates rural development

programs with governments, colleges, and agricultural organizations. Collects and disseminates information. **Libraries:** Type: reference.

★859★ LANKA JATHIKA SARVODAYA SHRAMADANA SANGAMAYA
   (WOMEN'S GROUP)
97 Sarvodaya Headquarters
32 Rawatawatta Rd.
Moratuwa, Sri Lanka
Mrs. Sita Rajasuriya, Contact   PH: 507843

Founded: 1987. **Members:** 503. **Budget:** CRs 3,500,000. **Languages:** English. **National**. Women professionals. Works to empower women through education and increased public awareness of their needs. Provides courses for women in literacy; health; nutrition; moral, cultural, social, and legal awareness; and job skills and self-employment. **Alternate name:** Sarvodaya Women's Movement.

Publications: *Annual Report* (in English and Sinhalese). ● Also publishes reports on program events and progress.

Conventions/Meetings: quarterly executive committee meeting.

★860★ METHODIST WOMEN'S FRIENDSHIP OF SRI LANKA
c/o Methodist Hdqtrs.
Galle Rd.
Colombo 3, Sri Lanka   PH: 1 717641

National. Methodist women in Sri Lanka. Promotes the interests of members. Upholds Christian beliefs and values in its programs.

★861★ MUSLIM WOMEN'S RESEARCH AND ACTION FRONT
   (MWRAF)
17 Park Ave.
Colombo 5, Sri Lanka   PH: 1 582798
Ms. Faizun Zackariya, Coord.   FX: 1 574917

Founded: 1986. **Members:** 10. **Staff:** 1. **Budget:** CRs 200,000. **Languages:** English. **National**. Promotes Muslim women's total development and represents issues affecting Muslim women in Sri Lanka. Conducts social awareness programs on family law, fundamentalism, and human rights. Coordinates research programs involving women in law, religion, and culture. Seeking to establish a resource center. **Committees:** Project and General Coordinator; Correspondence and Studies; Documentation and Publication; Project and Planning.

Publications: *Challenge for Change* (in English). ● *Women and Media* (in Tamil). ● *Resource Directory*.

★862★ SINHALA, TAMIL RURAL WOMEN'S NETWORK
72 Shanthi Pura
Nuwara-Eliya, Sri Lanka
Wimali Karunaratne, President   PH: 52 2777

Founded: 1988. **Members:** 6,000. **Staff:** 16. **Budget:** CRs 60,000. **Languages:** English, Tamil, Sinhalese. **National**. Promotes rural women's development. Works to protect the natural environment. Encourages communication and cooperation between linguistic communities. Conducts leadership seminars and projects.

Conventions/Meetings: biweekly regional meeting - Nuwara-Eliya, Sri Lanka.

★863★ SINHALA WOMEN'S ORGANIZATION
G 6-7 National Housing Complex
Vipulasena Mawatha
Colombo 10, Sri Lanka   PH: 1 533695

National. Promotes the interests of Sinhalese-speaking women in Sri Lanka.

★864★ SOCIAL SERVICE LADIES LEAGUE
Mt. Lavinia
357 Galle Rd.   PH: 716424
Dehiwela, Sri Lanka   716657

National. Women in Sri Lanka sponsoring social service programs to help the disadvantaged and disabled.

★865★ SRI LANKA FEDERATION OF UNIVERSITY WOMEN (SLFUW)
Vidya Mandiraya
Vidya Mawatha
Colombo 7, Sri Lanka

Languages: Sinhalese, English. National. Women involved in various aspects of academia. Works to establish equal educational and career opportunities for women.

★866★ SRI LANKA GIRL GUIDES ASSOCIATION
10 Sir Marcus Fernando Mawatha
Colombo 7, Sri Lanka   PH: 1 695720

National. Promotes the development of girls and young women in Sri Lanka. Sponsors programs that foster personal achievement. Conducts educational projects.

★867★ SRI LANKA HOUSEWIVES ASSOCIATION
179 Sir James Peiris Mawatha   PH: 1 449715
Colombo 7, Sri Lanka   1 637687

National. Women working in the home in Sri Lanka. Promotes the interests of members.

★868★ SRI LANKA WOMEN'S CONFERENCE
19 Greenlands Ln.
Colombo 5, Sri Lanka
Mrs. Dorothy Abeywickrama, President

Languages: Sinhalese. National. Seeks to enhance awareness of women's issues.

★869★ VOICE OF WOMEN
(Kantha Handa)
25 Kirula Rd.
Colombo 5, Sri Lanka   PH: 1 500530

Languages: Sinhalese. National. Strives to: facilitate cooperation and information exchange among women in an effort to mobilize action towards peace; encourage the mutual cooperation and understanding necessary for peaceful negotiations among nations; communicate with national leaders; provide opportunity for women to exercise responsibility in the world.

★870★ WOMEN FOR PEACE
58 Green Path
Colombo 3, Sri Lanka
Sunila Abeysekera, Coord.   PH: 1 573223

Founded: 1984. Members: 45. Staff: 1. Languages: English. National. Promotes the unification of Sri Lankan women to object all forms of societal violence, including ethnic and religious disorders, external aggression, and nuclear threat. Establishes ethnic harmony on the basis of inter-communal justice and equality. Opposes racial prejudice and discrimination. Advocates equality, democratic and human rights, and civil liberties for individuals in Sri Lanka. Administers trauma counseling, refugee relief, and peace education programs. Committees: Coordinating.

Conventions/Meetings: monthly meeting (exhibits) - Colombo, Sri Lanka.

★871★ WOMEN'S BUREAU OF SRI LANKA
Inland Revenue Bldg.
Sir Chittampalam A
Gardiner Mawatha
Colombo 2, Sri Lanka   PH: 1 423878
Miss Manel Chandrasekera, Contact   1 437407

Founded: 1978. Staff: 32. Budget: US$479,021. Languages: Tamil. National. Umbrella organization promoting the interests of women in Sri Lanka. Represents the interests of women in public and government areas. Disseminates information. Conducts research and educational programs. Libraries: Type: reference.

Publications: Kantha Siviya, quarterly. Journal. ● Kantha Puwath, periodic. Newsletter.

★872★ WOMEN'S CHAMBER OF COMMERCE AND INDUSTRY
10 1/1 Sir Marcus Fernando Mawatha
Colombo 7, Sri Lanka   PH: 1 585759

National. Women promoting and involved in business and industry in Sri Lanka. Works to support programs to develop Sri Lanka's businesses and industries.

★873★ WOMEN'S EDUCATION AND RESEARCH CENTRE (WERC)
17 Park Ave.
Colombo 5, Sri Lanka
Ms. N. Selvy Thiruchandran, Exec. Dir.   PH: 1 582798

Founded: 1982. Members: 7. Staff: 5. Languages: English, Sinhalese, Tamil. National. Feminist researchers and activists. Promotes study and research on various aspects of women's subordination in Sri Lanka in order to create awareness and increase consciousness on feminist issues. Organizes a forum for women to express themselves as writers, researchers, poets, and novelists. Disseminates information about women through conferences, lecturers, seminars, and workshops. Libraries: Type: open to the public; reference. Holdings: books. Subjects: social sciences, women's studies, contemporary novels, and short stories. Committees: Women's Studies; Media Monitoring. Formerly: Women's Education Centre.

Publications: On the Foot Steps of Women (in Tamil). ● Women and Mass Media (in Tamil). ● Literary Women. ● Newsletter, semiannual. ● Journal, annual.

★874★ WOMEN'S TEMPERANCE UNION OF SRI LANKA (WTUSL)
22/15 Kalyani Rd.
Colombo 6, Sri Lanka
Doreen Perema, Pres.   PH: 1 588211

Founded: 1886. Members: 50. Languages: English, Sinhalese, Tamil. National. Works to educate children and adults in Sri Lanka on the "evils of alcohol, tobacco, and narcotic drugs." Conducts drug abuse seminars and workshops for youth; sponsors professional training program for counselors. Maintains speakers' bureau; organizes contests; bestows awards and certificates. Cooperates with similar nongovernmental organizations in Sri Lanka and abroad.

Publications: Magazine, monthly.

Conventions/Meetings: monthly (exhibits).

★875★ YOUNG WOMEN'S CHRISTIAN ASSOCIATION - SRI LANKA
                                   PH: 1 28589
7 Rotunda Gardens   1 23498
Colombo 3, Sri Lanka   CBL: KANTHAVO
Manel Nanayakkara, Gen.Sec.   COLOMBO

National. Promotes the development of young women in Sri Lanka. Upholds Christian beliefs and values in its programs. Works to instill self worth and self-esteem in young women.

Taiwan

★876★ AWAKENING FOUNDATION
1 Po-Ai Rd., Ln. 1, 3rd Fl.
Taipei, Taiwan   PH: 2 3110333

Languages: Mandarin. **National.** Works towards the advancement of the status of women through providing educational and cultural programs and activities.

★877★ CHINESE WOMEN'S ANTI-AGGRESSION LEAGUE (CWAAL)
27 Changsha St., Section 1
Taipei 10001, Taiwan   PH: 2 3114974
Ms. Cecilia Yen Koo, Sec.Gen.   FX: 2 3751671

Founded: 1950. **Members:** 252,546. **Languages:** Chinese, English. **Multinational.** Operates in 12 countries. Encourages Chinese women to improve their status through participation in political movements. Works to improve human relations among all people. Operates Women's Development Centers for hearing impaired women and children. Provides services for children; compiles statistics. **Programs:** Housing for Military Dependants; Pre-School Day Care; Relief Work; Morale-Boosting.

Publications: *China's Women* (in Chinese), bimonthly. **Circulation:** 4,000. **Advertising:** not accepted. ● *Madame Chiang's Paintings* (in Chinese and English). Book. ● *Pictorial of CWAAL* (in Chinese and English). Book. ● *Madame Chiang Kai-Shek Selected Speeches* (in Chinese and English). Book.

Conventions/Meetings: annual conference.

★878★ FAMILY PLANNING ASSOCIATION - TAIWAN
No. 1 Ln.
160 Fu Hsin South Rd., Sec. 2
Taipei, Taiwan

Languages: Mandarin. **National.** Works to improve the quality of life for individuals living in Taiwan by promoting family planning and responsible parenthood. Works to stop the spread of AIDS and other sexually transmitted diseases through education and contraceptive services. Offers programs in family planning and health. Conducts research.

★879★ GRASSROOTS WOMEN WORKERS CENTER
No. 208, Chienkang Rd., 4th Fl.
Taipei 10577, Taiwan   PH: 2 7621006
Miss Yvonne Lin Mei-jung, Contact   FX: 2 7621006

Founded: 1988. **Members:** 11. **Staff:** 1. **Budget:** US$8,000. **Languages:** English, Chinese. **National.** Women human rights activists, feminists, women workers, and other interested women. Seeks to: abolish patriarchal ideology; reform the male-dominated labor market; and develop unions for women workers. Seeks to protect women from being forced into prostitution. Offers female workers legal assistance. Conducts training and educational programs for factory workers. **Libraries:** Type: reference.

Publications: *Asian Women Workers* (in Chinese), bimonthly. Newsletter. ● *Female Workers in Taiwan* (in English), quarterly. Newsletter. Information on working conditions for women.

★880★ MEDICAL WOMEN'S INTERNATIONAL ASSOCIATION -
    TAIWAN
Department of Radiology
Veterans General Hospital
Taipei 11217, Taiwan
Chui-Mei Tiu, Contact

Languages: Mandarin, English. **National.** Taiwan national branch of the Medical Women's International Association (see separate entry). Women physicians. Provides a forum for discussion of women's health care issues. Encourages women to enter the field of medicine. Works to overcome discrimination against female physicians. Sponsors research and educational programs.

★881★ WOMEN'S RESEARCH PROGRAM
National Taiwan University
Population Studies Center
Taipei, Taiwan   PH: 2 3630197
Dr. Chueh Chang, Coord.   FX: 2 3639565

Founded: 1965. **Budget:** NTs 50,000. **Languages:** Chinese, English. **National.** Promotes the status of women in Taiwan society. Conducts and promotes interdisciplinary research on women in Taiwan. Develops collaborative research and exchange programs with other women's research programs and scholars abroad. Disseminates information to researchers, practitioners, and the public. Offers courses on gender relations; sponsors lectures and research conferences. **Libraries:** Type: open to the public. Subjects: women's research. **Awards:** Grant. Recipient: graduate students in women's studies.

Publications: *Research on Women in Taiwan.* ● *Journal of Women and Gender Studies* (in Chinese and English). ● *Bulletin,* quarterly. ● Journals, reports, monographs, and newsletters on women's research in Taiwan.

Conventions/Meetings: semiannual seminar - Taipei, Taiwan.

★882★ YOUNG WOMEN'S CHRISTIAN ASSOCIATION - TAIWAN
No. 7 Ching Tao W Rd., 6th Fl.
Taipei 100, Taiwan   PH: 2 3140408
Ping Lee, Gen.Sec.   FX: 2 3831340

Founded: 1977. **Members:** 11,000. **Staff:** 3. **Local Groups:** 5. **Languages:** Mandarin. **National.** Promotes physical, mental, and spiritual growth of members. Provides social services including: free medical examinations for aboriginal women; programs for young adults, senior citizens, the blind, and women; religious services, classes, and celebrations; rehabilitation programs for juvenile delinquents and teenage prostitutes. Maintains daycare center. Offers lectures, workshops, training programs, and environment protection camp. Operates library; compiles statistics. **Computer Services:** Data base. **Committees:** Religious Education; Volunteer Training; Women's; Youth.

Publications: *Annual Report* (in English and Mandarin). **Advertising:** not accepted. ● *Association Membership List* (in Mandarin), biennial. **Advertising:** not accepted. ● *Bulletin,* quarterly.

Conventions/Meetings: annual meeting.

Thailand

★883★ ASEAN CONFEDERATION OF WOMEN'S ORGANIZATIONS
127/1 Sukumvit 79
Bangkok 10250, Thailand
Ruankeo Brandt, President

Languages: Thai, English. **National.** Women's groups in Brunei, Indonesia, Malaysia, Philippines, Singapore, and Thailand. Fosters collaboration among women's groups. Disseminates information.

★884★ ASSOCIATION FOR THE PROMOTION OF THE STATUS OF
    WOMEN (APSN)
501/1 MU3 Dechatungka Rd.
Sikan
Donmuane
Bangkok 10210, Thailand   PH: 2 5661774
Khunying Kanitha Wichiencharoen,   2 5662288
    Contact   FX: 2 5663481

Founded: 1980. **Staff:** 70. **Languages:** English, Thai. **National.** Promotes women and women's interests. Seeks to stop the trafficking of women and alleviate the conditions that cause women to enter prostitution. Maintains a shelter for disadvantaged women and victims of violence. Provides job skills training and general education programs. Researches gender relations and women's issues; encourages women to participate in development projects; educates private and governmental leaders on women's needs. Disseminates information designed to increase public and media awareness of the status of women.

★885★ BUSINESS AND PROFESSIONAL WOMEN'S ASSOCIATION OF
    THAILAND (BPWT)
Phrakaruna Nivas Bldg.
6/2 Pichai Rd.
Dusit
Bangkok 10300, Thailand
Lalida Chandraprasert, President   PH: 2 2415768

Founded: 1954. **Members:** 30. **Staff:** 1. **Languages:** Thai, English. **National.** Promotes friendship, and the exchange of views and experiences, among business and professioanl women worldwide. Seeks to advance the status of business and professional women. Encourages women's participation in national and international politics to benefit humanity. Conducts educational programs.

Publications: *Journal* (in Thai), annual.

Conventions/Meetings: monthly board meeting - Bangkok, Thailand.

★886★ EDUCATION MEANS PROTECTION OF WOMEN ENGAGED IN
    RE-CREATION (EMPOWER)
359/3 Soi Surasena, Silom Rd.
Bangkok 10500, Thailand   PH: 2 233444

Languages: Thai, English. **National.** Promotes the availability of family planning services and reproductive rights for women in Thailand.

★887★ FOUNDATION FOR WOMEN (FFW)
35/267 Charansanitwong 62
Bangkok 10700, Thailand   PH: 2 4335149
Ms. Siriporn Skrobanek, Secretary   FX: 2 4346774

Founded: 1987. **Members:** 300. **Staff:** 16. **Budget:** US$80,000. **Languages:** Thai, English. **National.** Rural and urban women. Works to: prevent violence against women; raise the status of poor women; end prostitution and exploitation of women. Collaborates with primary school teachers to eliminate child prostitution. Encourges women to instigate social change. Provides a home and telephone counseling service for abused women. Conducts eductional programs. Produces videos, slides, and posters to sensitize women and others to the exploitation women face. Plans to implement a program to protect migrant women. **Libraries:** Type: reference.

Publications: *Newsletter* (in Thai), quarterly. ● *Voices of Thai Women* (in English), semiannual. Newsletter.

Conventions/Meetings: annual executive committee meeting.

★888★ FRIENDS OF WOMEN FOUNDATION (FOW)
1379/30 Soi Praditchai Samsennai
Payathai   PH: 2 2700928
Bangkok 10400, Thailand   2 2700929
Ampiwal Sakmuang, Contact   FX: 2 2700929

Founded: 1980. **Languages:** Thai, English. **National.** Seeks to enhance public awareness of the unfair treatment of women. Works to defend women against sexual discrimination and sexual violence. Educates women on herbal remedies, yoga, and natural family planning through a community health center. Collaborates with other women's groups to fight male chauvenism. Plans to establish a women's labor movement. **Libraries:** Type: reference. Holdings: books, periodicals. Subjects: women's issues.

Publications: *Women's Views* (in Thai), bimonthly. Magazine. ● *Progressive*

Women (in Thai), bimonthly. Newsletter. ● *FOW Newsletter* (in English), semiannual. ● *The Understanding of Sexual Crimes.* Booklet. ● *Basic Family Laws for Women.* Booklet. ● *Women's Rights According to the Laws.* Booklet.

★889★ FRIENDS OF WOMEN - THAILAND
49 Phra-athit Rd.
Bangkok 10200, Thailand   PH: 2 2800429

Languages: Thai. **National.** Women's organizations, individual women, and others interested in promoting awareness of women's issues.

Publications: *Newsletter*, semiannual.

★890★ MEDICAL WOMEN'S INTERNATIONAL ASSOCIATION -
    THAILAND
Armed Forces Research Institute of
    Medical Science
Rajvithi Rd.
Bangkok 10400, Thailand
Kyunying Ananda Nisalak, Contact

Languages: Thai. **National.** Thailand national branch of the Medical Women's International Association (see separate entry). Women physicians. Provides a forum for discussion of women's health care issues. Encourages women to enter the field of medicine. Works to overcome discrimination against female physicians. Sponsors research and educational programs.

★891★ NATIONAL COMMISSION ON WOMEN'S AFFAIRS
Office of the Prime Minister
Government House
Bangkok 10300, Thailand

Founded: 1983. **Languages:** Thai. **National.** Promotes the interests of women in Thailand. Works to improve the financial and economic status of women.

★892★ NATIONAL COUNCIL OF WOMEN OF THAILAND
Manangkasilla Mansion
Larnluang Rd.
Bangkok, Thailand   PH: 2 2810081
Prof. Khunying Duangduen Bisalputra,   2 2810206
    President   FX: 2 2812189

National. Umbrella organization for women's groups in Thailand. Promotes and supports women's interests. Coordinates activities. Disseminates information.

★893★ PAN PACIFIC AND SOUTH-EAST ASIA WOMEN'S
    ASSOCIATION (PPSEAWA)
Office of the President
2234 New Petchburi Rd.
Bangkok 10310, Thailand
Sumalee Chartikavanij, Pres.   PH: 2 3144316

Founded: 1928. **Regional Groups:** 2. **National Groups:** 23. **Languages:** English. **Multinational.** Women from 18 countries united for the purpose of strengthening the bonds of peace by fostering better understanding and friendship among Pacific and Southeast Asian women. Promotes cooperation among women in these regions for the study and improvement of social conditions. **Councils:** International.

Publications: *Conference Proceedings*, triennial. ● *International Bulletin* (in English), semiannual.

Conventions/Meetings: triennial conference (exhibits) - 1994, Tonga.

★894★ PLANNED PARENTHOOD ASSOCIATION OF THAILAND
(PPAT)
8 Soi Dai Dee
Vibhavadi-Rangsit Super Hwy.   PH: 2 5790084
Lard-Yao, Bangkhen   2 5790086
Bangkok 9, Thailand   FX: 2 5799559
Mr. Sombhong Pattawichaiporn, Exec.   CBL: PATTAIBANGKOK
    Dir.   10900

Languages: Thai. National. Works to improve the quality of life for people
living in Thailand by promoting responsible parenthood and family planning.
Attempts to reduce the number of unwanted pregnancies and abortions.
Offers programs in sex education, family planning, and health. Provides
contraceptive and health care services. Conducts research.

★895★ POPULATION AND COMMUNITY DEVELOPMENT
ASSOCIATION (PDA)
                                      PH: 2 2560080
8 Sukhumvit Rd., SOI-12   FX: 2 2558804
Bangkok 10110, Thailand   TX: 82603 PDA TH
Mechai Viravaidya, Contact   CBL: COMBAT:BANGKOK

Founded: 1974. Members: 485. Budget: US$4,800,000. Languages:
English, Thai. National. Seeks to improve the quality of life and increase
economic levels in rural areas of Thailand. Coordinates development projects
focusing on family planning, primary health care, and rural development.
Offers training courses on the management of community-based develop-
ment programs; conducts population research; educates communities on
AIDS prevention. Maintains the Asian Center for Population and Community
Development. Worked to popularize birth control practices through socially
entertaining programs such as condom-blowing contests and the Cops and
Rubbers Project. Over the past 15 years Thailand's population growth has
been cut in half through these types of programs. Departments: Community-
Based Integrated Rural Development; Community Development and Health.
Formerly: (1977) Community-Based Family Planning Services.

Publications: Family Planning Bulletin, 3/year. ● Mechai Newsletter, monthly.

★896★ THAI MEDICAL WOMEN ASSOCIATION
980/2 Sukhumvit Rd.
Opp. Wat Dhat Thong
Phrakanong
Bangkok 10110, Thailand
Prof. Sudsakhon Tuchinda, President   PH: 2 3910400

Languages: Thai, English. National. Works to enhance the status of women
in the health care professions. Supports research on women's health.
Disseminates information.

★897★ THAI WOMEN'S ASSOCIATION
Kiatnakin Bldg.
Bush Ln.
New Rd.
Bangkok 5, Thailand
Mrs. Chansarmurn Wattanevkin,
    President   PH: 2 2345555

Languages: Thai. National. Encourages collective action to raise the social
standing of women.

★898★ VOICES OF THAI WOMEN
PO Box 7-47
Bangkok 10700, Thailand

National. Works to achieve greater public respect towards women and their
contributions to society. Supports the eradication of commercialized sex,
such as prostitution and pornography, maintaining that it contributes to
exploitation of women.

★899★ WOMEN LAWYERS ASSOCIATION OF THAILAND
6 Sukhothai Rd.
Dusit
Bangkok 10300, Thailand
Ms. Varee Naskul, President   PH: 2 2410737

Languages: Thai, English. National. Women lawyers working to increase
public awareness of the law. Seeks to raise the status of women lawyers.
Cooperates with women's organizations addressing women's issues.

★900★ WOMEN SECRETARIES' ASSOCIATION OF THAILAND
6/2 Pichai Rd.
Dusit
Bangkok 10300, Thailand
Ms. Penpan Visuddhi Na Ayudhya,
    President   PH: 2 2415555

Languages: Thai, English. National. Women secretaries united to raise the
status of the secretarial profession. Fosters friendly relations among
members.

★901★ WOMEN'S EDUCATION FOR ADVANCEMENT AND
EMPOWERMENT
Chaing Mai University
PO Box 58
Chiang Mai 50002, Thailand

Languages: Thai. National. Provides informational and educational services
and programs pertaining to women's issues, including, status rights, and
advancement. Supports women's studies and exchange programs.

★902★ YOUNG WOMEN'S CHRISTIAN ASSOCIATION - THAILAND
13 Sathorn Tai Rd.   PH: 2 2865764
Bangkok 10120, Thailand   2 2860216
Chanthanee Molee, Exec.Dir.   FX: 2 2873016

National. Promotes the development of young women in Thailand. Upholds
Christian beliefs and values in its programs. Works to instill self worth and
self-esteem in young women.

Tonga

★903★ PAN PACIFIC AND SOUTH EAST ASIA WOMEN'S
ASSOCIATION - TONGA (PPSEAWA)
PO Box 642
Nuku'alofa, Tonga

National. Promotes and supports the interests and development of women in
Tonga.

★904★ TONGO FAMILY PLANNING ASSOCIATION (TFPA)
PO Box 1142
Nuku'Alofa, Tonga   PH: 21209
Mr. Sione Kengike, Exec. Dir.   FX: 23766

Languages: English, Tongan. National. Advocates family planning and
responsible parenthood as a means to enhance the quality of life for
individuals living in Tonga. Promotes family planning as a basic human right.
Works to stop the spread of AIDS and other sexually transmitted diseases.
Offers programs in sex education, family planning, and health. Provides
contraceptive and health care services. Conducts research.

★905★ YOUNG WOMEN'S CHRISTIAN ASSOCIATION - TONGA
c/o FWC Education Office
PO Box 57
Nuku'alofa, Tonga
Sela Tu'ipulotu, Sec.   PH: 21033

National. Promotes the development of young women in Tonga. Upholds Christian beliefs and values in its programs. Works to instill self worth and self-esteem in young women.

Trust Territory of the Pacific Islands

★906★ DIDIL BELAU
PO Box 966
Koror, Trust Territory of the Pacific
  Islands 96940
Lorenza Olkeriil, Contact   PH: 4882680

Founded: 1989. **Members:** 22. **National.** Promotes the interests of women in the Trust Territory of the Pacific Islands. Fosters awareness of women's issues. Sponsors educational and children's programs.

Tuvalu

★907★ TUVALU FAMILY HEALTH ASSOCIATION (TUFHA)
c/o Medical Division
PO Box 41
Funafuti, Tuvalu
Ms. Penieli Metia, Program Co-ord.   TX: GOVT TV 4803

Languages: English. **National.** Works to improve the quality of life for individuals living in Tuvalu by advocating family planning and responsible parenthood. Attempts to stop the spread of sexually transmitted diseases and reduce the number of unwanted pregnancies and abortions. Offers educational programs in family planning and health. Provides contraceptive and health care services. Conducts research.

Vanuatu

★908★ VANUATU FAMILY HEALTH ASSOCIATION (VFHA)
Private Mail Bag 0065
Port Vila, Vanuatu   PH: 22140
Mme. Blandine Boulekone, Exec. Dir.   FX: 24627

Languages: English. **National.** Advocates family planning as a basic human right. Works to stop the spread of sexually transmitted diseases and reduce the number of unwanted pregnancies and abortions. Offers educational programs in family planning and health. Provides contraceptive and health care services. Conducts research.

★909★ VANUATU NATIONAL COUNCIL OF WOMEN
PO Box 975
Port Vila, Vanuatu
Mrs. Rolenas Lolo, Director   PH: 23108

Founded: 1980. **Staff:** 11. **Languages:** English. **National.** Promotes the interests of women in Vanuatu. Seeks to unite women to achieve development projects. Provides a forum for women to meet and exchange knowledge and skills. Offers training programs. Broadcasts radio programs; operates women's programs.

Vietnam

★910★ VIETNAM FAMILY PLANNING ASSOCIATION (VINAFPA)
43 Trang Thi 9   PH: 4 252161
Hanoi, Vietnam   FX: 4 254638
Dr. Pham Xuan Tieu, Exec. Dir.   CBL: VINAGOFPA

Languages: Vietnamese. **National.** Works to improve the quality of life for people living in Vietnam by promoting responsible parenthood and family planning. Attempts to stop the spread of AIDS and other sexually transmitted diseases through education and contraceptive services. Offers programs in family planning and health care. Acts as an advocate for family planning on the national level.

★911★ VIETNAM WOMEN'S UNION
39 Hang Chuoi
Hanoi, Vietnam

Founded: 1930. **Languages:** Vietnamese. **National.** Promotes the interests of women in Vietnam. Works to strengthen ties among women in Vietnam.

Western Samoa

★912★ FATUPAEPAE TOKELAU
Tokelau Affairs Office
PO Box 865   PH: 20822
Apia, Western Samoa   20823
Juliana Perez, Director   FX: 21761

Founded: 1986. **Languages:** English. **National.** Promotes the interests of women in Western Samoa. Liaises with other women's groups to enhance the status of women in Western Samoa. Fosters solidarity among women.

Publications: *Newsletter*, periodic.

★913★ NATIONAL COUNCIL OF WOMEN OF WESTERN SAMOA
PO Box 1162
Apia, Western Samoa
Mrs. Mata'afa, Secretary

National. Umbrella organization for women's groups in Western Samoa. Supports women's interests. Coordinates activities; disseminates information.

★914★ WESTERN SAMOA FAMILY HEALTH ASSOCIATION (WSFHA)
PO Box 3029   PH: 24560
Apia, Western Samoa   FX: 24560
Mr. Faumuina Lemalu, CEO   TX: 219 GOLDSTAR SX

Languages: English. **National.** Advocates family planning and responsible parenthood as a means to improve the quality of life for individuals in Western Samoa. Works to reduce the number of unwanted pregnancies and abortion. Attempts to stop the spread of AIDS and other sexually transmitted diseases. Offers programs in family planning, health, and sex education. Acts as an advocate for family planning on a national level.

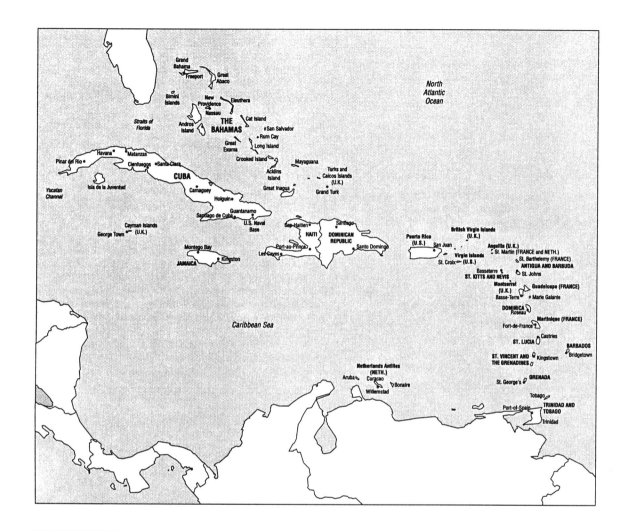

Caribbean

Anguilla	British Virgin Islands	Haiti	St. Kitts & Nevis
Antigua-Barbuda	Cuba	Jamaica	St. Lucia
Aruba	Dominica	Martinique	St. Vincent &
Bahamas	Dominican Republic	Montserrat	the Grenadines
Barbados	Grenada	Netherlands Antilles	Trinidad & Tobago
Bermuda	Guadeloupe	Puerto Rico	Virgin Islands of the
			United States

Caribbean

Anguilla

★915★ ANGUILLA FAMILY PLANNING ASSOCIATION (AFPA)
PO Box 168
The Valley, Anguilla
Mrs. Susan Harrigan, President
PH: (809)497-2391
FX: (809)497-2050
TX: 3179329 IDMITCH LA

Languages: English. **National.** Works to improve the quality of life for people living in Anguilla through the promotion of family planning and maternal and infant health care. Seeks to reduce the number of unwanted pregnancies and abortions. Provides educational programs, information, and health care services. Encourages public awareness of family planning and views family planning as a basic human right. Acts as an advocate for family planning on the national level.

Antigua-Barbuda

★916★ ANTIGUA PLANNED PARENTHOOD ASSOCIATION (APPA)
Bishopgate St.
PO Box 419
St. John's, Antigua-Barbuda
Dr. Marlene Joseph, President
PH: (809)462-0947
FX: (809)462-1187
CBL: FAMPLAN

Languages: English. **National.** Promotes family planning and maternal and infant health care as a way to improve the quality of life for individuals living in Antigua Barbuda. Seeks to reduce the number of unwanted pregnancies and abortions. Provides contraceptive services for men and women. Sponsors programs on family plannng and sex education. Acts as an advocate for family planning on the national level. Conducts research.

★917★ ANTIGUA TRADES AND LABOR UNION - WOMEN'S
  AUXILIARY
46 Morth St.
St. John's, Antigua-Barbuda
Ethlyn Wynter, President
PH: (809)462-0090

Founded: 1965. **Members:** 15. **Languages:** English. **National.** Works to enhance the status of working women. Seeks to improve working conditions and health care facilities for women. Offers educational and training programs.

★918★ CARIBBEAN CHURCH WOMEN - ANTIGUA
PO Box 911
St. John's, Antigua-Barbuda

Languages: English. **National.** Promotes fellowship among Christian women. Conducts community service activities.

★919★ CARIBBEAN FAMILY PLANNING AFFILIATION (CFPA)
PO Box 419
Factory and Airport Rds.
St. Johns, Antigua-Barbuda
Dr. Tirbani P. Jagdeo, CEO
PH: (809)462-4171

Founded: 1971. **Members:** 21. **Staff:** 11. **Languages:** English. **Multinational.** Family planning associations in Caribbean countries. Works to increase awareness and acceptance of family planning in the region. Advocates family planning as a basic human right and assists member governments in incorporating family planning into maternal and child health care services. Develops training programs for adolescents and young mothers. Studies demographic, sociological, and health issues. Offers training to teachers, family planning workers, and clinic workers. Produces and distributes audiovisual educational materials. Compiles statistics. Offers research programs; sponsors competitions. Operates documentation centre for students, teachers, and researchers. **Computer Services:** Data base.

Publications: *Annual Report.* ● *Current Awareness Bulletin* (in English), semiannual. Lists current data on population and health issues in the Caribbean. ● *Selected Bibliographies* (in English), annual. ● Also publishes pamphlets.

Conventions/Meetings: annual.

★920★ NAZERENE WOMEN'S OUTREACH
Amy Buyer Street Villa
PO Box 487
St. John's, Antigua-Barbuda
Mrs. Eileen Charles, President
PH: (809)461-0729

Founded: 1976. **Members:** 49. **Languages:** English. **National.** Women in Antigua-Barbuda united to enhance the public's spiritual awareness. Offers bible study courses to elderly sectors of the population.

★921★ WOMEN OF THE CHURCH OF GOD (WCG)
Horth St.
PO Box 963
St. John's, Antigua-Barbuda
Ms. Cicily Jones, President
PH: (809)461-1399
(809)462-1300

Founded: 1970. **Members:** 29. **Languages:** English. **National.** Women members of the Church of God engaged in public service activities with a Christian influence, including: visits to people confined to their homes; delivery of provisions for the needy; and organization of activities for underpriveleged children. Arranges concerts, religious programs, and other social and cultural events.

★922★ WOMEN'S ACTION GROUP OF THE ANTIGUA LABOUR
  PARTY
c/o Mrs. Millicent Percival
PO Box 598
St. John's, Antigua-Barbuda
Mrs. Millicent Percival, President

Founded: 1973. **Members:** 500. **Budget:** EC$5,000. **Languages:** English. **National.** Women interested in campaigning for the Antigua Labor Party. Conducts community service activities; encourages adult education for students who did not complete their schooling. Conducts skill training programs in shorthand, typing, and dress making.

Conventions/Meetings: annual conference - always October. St. John's, Antigua-Barbuda.

★923★ YOUNG WOMEN'S CHRISTIAN ASSOCIATION - ANTIGUA
Nugent Ave.
St. John's, Antigua-Barbuda

National. Promotes the development of young women in Antigua. Fosters Christian ideals in young women's development. Provides a forum for personal development and the instilling of self-esteem among young women.

Aruba

★924★ FOUNDATION FOR PROMOTION OF RESPONSIBLE
   PARENTHOOD (FPRP)
PO Box 2256
Bernhardstraat 75   PH: 8 48833
San Nicolas, Aruba   FX: 8 41107
Mrs. Jennifer Ritveld, President   CBL: FAMIA PLANEA

Languages: Dutch. **National.** Works to improve the quality of life of people living in Aruba through promotion of family planning and maternal and infant health care. Sponsors programs in family planning, sex education, and basic health care. Offers contraceptive services. Conducts research.

Bahamas

★925★ ANGLICAN CHURCH WOMEN
St. Stephen's Parish
Fresh Creek
Andros, Bahamas   PH: (809)368-2056
Mabel Stubbs, President   (809)368-2514

Founded: 1981. **Members:** 32. **Languages:** English. **National.** Women members of the Anglican church. Promotes the spiritual growth of women. Seeks to strengthen the family structure. Conducts community service programs for impoverished and sick people.

★926★ BAHAMAS FAMILY PLANNING ASSOCIATION (Bah.FPA)
PO Box N-9071   PH: (809)325-1663
Nassau, Bahamas   (809)323-6338
Dr. Baldwin Carey, President   FX: (809)325-4886

Languages: English. **National.** Works to improve the quality of life for individuals through promotion of family planning and basic health care services. Promotes family planning as a basic human right. Sponsors programs in family planning, health care, and sex education. Offers contraceptive services.

★927★ COUNCIL OF WOMEN IN THE BAHAMAS
PO Box 1145
Nassau, Bahamas
Mrs. Dorothy Wilson, President

National. Umbrella organization for women's groups in the Bahamas. Promotes and supports women and women's interests. Conducts and coordinates women's activities. Disseminates information to increase public awareness of women's concerns.

★928★ DEVELOPMENT ALTERNATIVES FOR WOMEN NOW -
   BAHAMAS (DAWN)
PO Box N-1147
Nassau, Bahamas   PH: (809)393-6241

Languages: English. **National.** Supports the advancement of women's personal and economic development. Conducts research, training, and advocacy programs to eliminate inequalities of gender, class, and race. Facilitates communication and networking among women's movements.

★929★ NATIONAL WOMEN'S MOVEMENT
PO Box F1267
Freeport, Bahamas
Genevieve Bethel, President

Languages: English. **National.** Promotes the interests of women in the Bahamas.

★930★ YOUNG WOMEN'S CHRISTIAN ASSOCIATION - BAHAMAS
PO Box 1269
Nassau, Bahamas
Marion Bethel-Sears, Sec.

National. Promotes the development of young women in the Bahamas. Upholds Christian principles and values in its programs. Seeks to instill personal worth and self-esteem among young women.

Barbados

★931★ BARBADOS CONFERENCE OF MORAVIAN WOMEN'S
   FELLOWSHIP
c/o Gloria Skeete
Near Sharon
St. Thomas, Barbados
Gloria Skeete, President   PH: (809)433-1688

Founded: 1959. **Members:** 250. **Languages:** English. **National.** Women united to promote Christian teachings. Works to strengthen families through prayer, worship, and service. Seeks to establish a worldwide fellowship of Christians. Conducts educational programs against drug abuse.

★932★ BARBADOS FAMILY PLANNING ASSOCIATION (BFPA)
                                     PH: (809)426-2027
Bay St.   (809)426-2226
Bridgetown, Barbados   FX: (809)427-6611
Mr. Keith Yearwood, President   CBL: FAMPLAN

Languages: English. **National.** Promotes family planning as a basic human right. Encourages family planning activities in Barbados. Offers educational programs in family planning, sexually transmitted diseases, and health care. Provides contraceptive services. Acts as an advocate for family planning on a national level.

★933★ BARBADOS WOMEN'S MOVEMENT
Wavell Ave.
Black Rock
St. Michael, Barbados
Octavia Braithwaite, President

Languages: English. **National.** Promotes the interests of women in Barbados.

★934★ BRITISH WOMEN'S CLUB OF BARBADOS
c/o Mrs. June Rochell
Chance Hall
Brittons Hill
St. Michaels, Barbados   PH: (809)427-0171
Mrs. June Rochell, Contact   (809)432-7359

Founded: 1977. **Members:** 150. **Languages:** English. **National.** British women living in Barbados. Sponsors social interaction programs and activities. Conducts fund raising programs for elderly people and children.

★935★ CARIBBEAN WOMEN'S FEATURE SYNDICATE
PO Box 159
Bridgetown, Barbados

Languages: English. **Multinational.** Promotes positive media portrayals of women. Fosters solidarity among women through the dissemination of information. Works to improve women's welfare.

★936★ DEMOCRATIC LEAGUE OF WOMEN
Kennington George St.
St. Michael, Barbados
Marjorie Lashley, Chair   PH: (809)427-2478

Founded: 1966. **Members:** 80. **Languages:** English. **National.** Women promoting democratic principles in Barbados. Works to improve public health, insurance coverage, and community development activities. Operates children's home. Offers educational programs.

★937★ DEVELOPMENT ALTERNATIVES WITH WOMEN FOR A NEW
      ERA - BARBADOS (DAWN)
Women & Development Unit
School of Continuing Studies
Pinelands
St. Michael, Barbados   PH: (809)426-9288
Peggy Antrobus, Coord.   FX: (809)426-3006

Founded: 1984. **Staff:** 4. **Languages:** English. **National.** Promotes women's personal and economic development in Barbados. Works to reduce the negative impact of development activities on women and the environment. Conducts research, training, and advocacy programs to eliminate inequalities of gender, class, and race. Facilitates communication and networking among women's movements. Protects and defends women's reproductive rights.

Publications: *DAWN Informs* (in English), 3/year. Newsletter. ● *Environment and Development: Grass Roots Women's Perspective*. Book. ● *Report of the Meeting of the Steering Committee* (in English), annual.

Conventions/Meetings: annual Steering Committee Meeting.

★938★ GIRL GUIDE ASSOCIATION OF BARBADOS
Pax Hill
Belmont Rd.
St. Michael, Barbados
Mrs. Hazel Farmer, President   PH: (809)426-2202

Founded: 1918. **Members:** 3,508. **Languages:** English. **National.** Fosters personal growth and development of girls. Conducts activities to encourage interest in the arts, homemaking, nature, education, and health.

★939★ METHODIST WOMEN'S LEAGUE - BARBADOS
Eastbourne
St. Philip, Barbados
Norma Roach, President   PH: (809)423-6576

Members: 600. **Languages:** English. **National.** Women of the Methodist faith in Barbados. Conducts development activities for low-income women. Seeks to enhance women's personal development and Christian growth. Offers educational, skill training, income-generation, and family counselling programs.

★940★ NATIONAL ORGANIZATION OF WOMEN - BARBADOS (NOW)
PO Box 962
Bridgetown, Barbados
Ms. Milroy Reece, President

Founded: 1970. **Members:** 30. **Languages:** English. **National.** Umbrella organization of women's groups and individuals. Provides training for entrepreneurial women in small business development. Offers educational programs in: agricultue, English, journalism, home management, food preparation, government, and citizenship.

★941★ SALVATION ARMY HOME LEAGUE
Reed St.
PO Box 57
Bridgetown, Barbados
Major Murphy John, President   PH: (809)426-2467

Founded: 1962. **Members:** 400. **Languages:** English. **National.** Encourages women to expand their understanding of the Bible and Christianity. Offers educational courses in homemaking skills. Conducts community service programs.

Conventions/Meetings: weekly meeting.

★942★ WOMEN IN DEVELOPMENT (WID)
Meltourne Belmont Rd.   PH: (809)427-8154
St. Michael, Barbados   (809)426-0045

Languages: English. **National.** Promotes improvement in the standard of living of rural women. Organizes and conducts educational, training, and cultural programs. Produces television and radio programs. Coordinates activities. Disseminates information.

★943★ WOMEN AND DEVELOPMENT STUDIES GROUP (WAND)
University of the West Indies
School of Continuing Studies   PH: (809)436-6312
The Pine   (809)436-6313
St. Michael, Barbados   FX: (809)426-3006
Ms. Peggy Antrobus, Coord.   TX: UNIVADOS

Founded: 1978. **Staff:** 15. **Languages:** English. **National.** Seeks to empower women by raising feminist consciousness. Supports the study of women and women's issues. Promotes activities for the development of women and their communities. Provides training for women, technical assistance, communications expertise, and advocacy of women's rights. **Libraries:** Type: reference.

Publications: *Womanspeak* (in English), annual. Magazine.

★944★ WOMEN'S FORUM
PO Box 332
Bridgetown, Barbados

National. Provides a forum for women organizations to network and discuss issues affecting them, focusing on the welfare of women and children. Disseminates information. Organizes seminars and lectures. Conducts research.

★945★ WOMEN'S SELF-HELP ASSOCIATION
Broad St.
Bridgetown, Barbados
Marianne Manning, President   PH: (809)426-2570

Founded: 1907. **Members:** 300. **Languages:** English. **National.** Promotes personal development programs for women in Barbados. Assists women in becoming independent through the marketing and sale of their handicrafts. Members' works include: needle work, paintings, floral wreaths, stamp and china collections. Fosters communication among members.

★946★ YOUNG WOMEN'S CHRISTIAN ASSOCIATION - BARBADOS
PO Box 657
General Post Office
Bridgetown, Barbados
Katrina Taylor, Gen.Sec.

Founded: 1950. **Members:** 250. **Languages:** English. **National.** Promotes the development of young women in Barbados. Upholds Christian beliefs and values in its programs. Seeks to instill self-worth and self-esteem in young women.

Bermuda

★947★ WORLD'S WOMAN'S CHRISTIAN TEMPERANCE UNION -
BERMUDA
c/o Mrs. Marguerite Place
PO Box 1217
HMFX
Hamilton 29, Bermuda
Mrs. Marguerite Place, V.Pres.

National. Women working to educate children and adults on the "evils of alcohol, tobacco, and narcotic drugs." Conducts drug abuse seminars and workshops for youth; sponsors professional training programs for counselors.

★948★ Y.H.E.D. TEEN SERVICES
Tencer House
PO Box HM1324
Hamilton HM FX, Bermuda
Mrs. H.G. Hill, President   PH: (809)292-4598

Languages: English. **National**. Promotes the availability of family planning services to teens in Bermuda. Sponsors programs in family planning and sex education. Works to reduce the number of unwanted pregnancies and abortions in the teen population. Acts as an advocate for family planning issues.

British Virgin Islands

★949★ BRITISH VIRGIN ISLANDS FAMILY LIFE ASSOCIATION
(BVIFLA)
PO Box 1064
West End   PH: (809)494-3426
Tortola, British Virgin Islands   FX: (809)494-4435
Mrs. Nadine Battle, President   TX: 3187959

Languages: English. **National**. Works to enhance the quality of life through the promotion of family planning and maternal and infant health care. Encourages responsible parenthood and family planning. Seeks to reduce the number of unwanted pregnancies and abortions. Offers programs in family planning, sex education, sexually transmitted diseases, especially AIDS, and basic health care. Provides contraceptive services.

Cuba

★950★ FEDERATION OF CUBAN WOMEN (FMC)
(Federacion de Mujeres Cubanas)
Paseo 260   PH: 39932
Vedado   39933
Havana, Cuba   FX: 33019
Vilma Espin Guillois, President   TX: 511270 FMC CU

Founded: 1960. **Staff:** 300. **Languages:** Spanish, Castilian, French, German, English. **National**. Umbrella organization of women and women's organizations in Cuba. Works to obtain full equality for women in all areas of Cuban society. Maintains the Casa de la Mujer y la Familia which provides educational programs for parents, children, and teachers; legal help for women; non-traditional jobskills training for women; sex education talks and debates; exercise and general health programs; forums for female artists; and workshops on women's themes, self-esteem, and the concept of equality. Conducts research. **Libraries:** Type: reference. **Programs:** Mujer y Empleo; Mujer y Salud; Mujer y Educacion; Promocion de la Mujer.

Publications: *Newspaper* (in Spanish), semimonthly.

★951★ SOCIEDAD CINETIFICA CUBANA PARA EL DESARROLLO DE
LA FAMILIA (SOCUDEF)
5ta Avenida 3207, Esquina 34
Miramar
Havana, Cuba

Languages: Spanish. **National**. Promotes responsible parenthood and family planning as a means to enhance the quality of life for individuals living in Cuba. Advocates family planning as a basic human right. Provides contraceptive and health care services. Sponsors educational programs.

Dominica

★952★ DOMINICA NATIONAL COUNCIL OF WOMEN (DNCW)
18 King George V St.
PO Box 145
Roseau, Dominica
Mrs. Neva Edwards, President   PH: (809)448-3935

Founded: 1986. **Members:** 5,000. **Staff:** 2. **Budget:** EC$100,000. **Languages:** English. **National**. Women's umbrella organization in Dominica. Aims to unite and empower women through education, training, and research. Works to increase the role of women in Dominica's development. Seeks to enhance public awareness of AIDS, child abuse, violence against women, and women's rights. Offers counseling to victims of abuse. Represents views of Dominican women at national, regional, and international forums. Participates in International Women's Day (March 8). **Telecommunication Services:** Phone referral system, (809)448-7546.

Publications: *In Touch* (in English), quarterly. Newsletter. ● *Annual Report* (in English).

Conventions/Meetings: annual general assembly - always July. ● annual Rally. ● quarterly meeting.

★953★ DOMINICA PLANNED PARENTHOOD ASSOCIATION (DPPA)
37 Cork St.
PO Box 247
Roseau, Dominica   PH: (809)448-4043
Mrs. Dorothy James, President   FX: (809)448-1111

Languages: English. **National**. Works to improve the quality of life of individuals living in Dominica by promoting responsible parenthood and family planning. Offers educational programs on family planning and contraception to teens and adults. Encourages public awareness of AIDS and other sexually transmitted diseases. Seeks to decrease the number of unwanted pregnancies and abortions.

★954★ SISTERS IN SOLIDARITY
c/o Movement for Cultural Awareness
PO Box 268
Roseau, Dominica

National. Women united against discriminatory practices and attitudes. Promotes women's rights in the community, local and national government, and in the workplace.

★955★ SPAT WOMEN'S ASSOCIATION FOR PROGRESS (SWAP)
PO Box 268
6 Fort Ln.   PH: (809)448-2377
Roseau, Dominica   (809)448-2308

National. Pursues action to bring about the advancement of women and the eradication of violations of women's rights in all spheres of society. Promotes improvement of the economic status and educational level of urban and rural women.

★956★ WOMEN IN COMPUTER SERVICES
5 Gt. Mariborough St.   PH: (809)448-8798
Roseau, Dominica   (809)448-6988

National. Women with careers in the computer industry. Promotes the professional advancement of women and the training and education of young women for careers in technological and computer-related industries.

★957★ WOMEN'S DESK
Bath Rd.
Roseau, Dominica   PH: (809)448-2401

National. Women's groups and other non-governmental organizations seeking to empower women. Works to: improve health and nutrition; decrease violence against women; and provide child care.

Dominican Republic

★958★ ASOCIACION DOMINICANA PRO-BIENESTAR DE LA FAMILIA
(PROFAMILIA)
       PH: (809)688-3566
Socorro Sanchez 64, Zona 1   (809)689-4209
Apartado 1053   FX: (809)686-8276
Santo Domingo, Dominican Republic   TX: 3264112 SDGTXDR
Mu-Yein Sang de Suarez, President   CBL: DOMBIEFA

Languages: Spanish. **National**. Advocates responsible parenthood and family planning. Seeks to educate the public on methods of family planning, contraception, and sexually transmitted diseases, especially AIDS. Promotes family planning as a basic human right. Provides contraceptive and basic health care services. Conducts research.

★959★ CENTRO DE INVESTIGACION PARA LA ACCION FEMENINA
(CIPAF)
Apartado Postal 1744   PH: (809)567-0120
Santo Domingo, Dominican Republic   (809)563-1159

Languages: Spanish. **National**. Promotes the advancement of women. Conducts studies on the status of women and on the women's movement. Disseminates information.

★960★ CENTRO DE SERVICIOS LEGALES PARA LA MUJER
Beningno del Castillo No. 28
Santo Domingo, Dominican Republic

Languages: Spanish. **National**. Promotes the availability of legal aid to women in the Dominican Republic. Provides legal advocacy services to women. Offers consultation and information on legal issues.

★961★ CENTRO DE SOLIDARIDAD PARA EL DESARROLLO DE LA
MUJER
Apartado 21880
Santo Domingo, Dominican Republic   PH: (809)686-7474

Languages: Spanish. **National**. Promotes the study of women and women's issues in the Dominican Republic. Works to enhance women's economic and social development. Promotes solidarity among women.

★962★ CIRCULO DE ESTUDIO FEMINISTA (CEF)
Apartado Postal 2793
Santo Domingo, Dominican Republic   PH: (809)687-1831

Languages: Spanish. **National**. Promotes the study of women and women's

issues in the Dominican Republic. Fosters awareness of women's issues. Provides a forum for exchange of ideas and discussion. Conducts feminist research.

★963★ COLECTIVO MUJER Y SALUD
Paseo de los Profesores No. 14
Mirardor Sur
Apartado Postal 482-9
Los Jardines
Santo Domingo, Dominican Republic
J. Garcia, Contact   FX: (809)562-6893

Languages: Spanish. **National**. Works to bring about public awareness of women's health issues. Supports means of preventative health care. Disseminates information.

★964★ CONSEJO NACIONAL DE MUJERES DE LA REPUBLICA
DOMINICANA
Calle 9, No. 13
Urbanizacion Fernandez
Santo Domingo, Dominican Republic   PH: (809)566-2672
Gladys Nivar de Scaroina, President   (809)689-5087

Languages: Spanish. **National**. Umbrella organization for women's groups in the Dominican Republic. Promotes women's interests. Coordinates activities. Disseminates information to increase public awareness of women's concerns.

★965★ EQUIPO DE MUJERES DE LA ASOCIACION POR LOS
DERECHOS BARRIALES
Santa Ana 20, Barrio Altagracia
Herrera
Santo Domingo, Dominican Republic   PH: (809)530-8829

Languages: Spanish. **National**. Works to protect and further women's rights through public awareness programs, lectures, and the dissemination of information.

★966★ IDENTIDAD: MOVIMIENTO POR LA IDENTIDAD DE LA MUJER
NEGRA
Casimiro de Moya 104
Gazoue   PH: (809)686-6744
Santo Domingo, Dominican Republic   (809)686-7474

Languages: Spanish. Organizes and supports heritage awareness projects for black women. Sponsors lectures and other speaking engagements. Disseminates information.

★967★ INTERNATIONAL RESEARCH AND TRAINING INSTITUTE FOR
THE ADVANCEMENT OF WOMEN (INSTRAW)
Cesar Nicolas Penson 102-A
Apartado Postal 21747   PH: (809)685-2111
Santo Domingo, Dominican Republic   FX: (809)685-2117
Dunja Pastizzi Ferencic, Dir.   TX: 3264280 WRASD

Languages: Spanish, English. **Multinational**. Works to create networks of individuals and organizations concerned with women's issues in the Caribbean. Distributes training materials produced by the United Nations International Institute for Research and Training for the Promotion of Women; conducts research programs to trace trends in programs working to empower women in the region.

Publications: *INSTRAW News* (in Spanish and English), periodic. Newsletter.

★968★ MUJERES EN DESARROLLO DOMINICANA (MUDE)
Leopoldo Navarro 61
Apartado 325   PH: (809)685-8111
Santo Domingo, Dominican Republic   (809)685-8113

Languages: Spanish. **National.** Works to further the national women's movement and improve the status of urban and rural women. Disseminates information.

★969★ NUCLEO DE APOYO A LA MUJER
Calle General Lopez 90
PO Box 288
Santiago, Dominican Republic   PH: (809)581-7311

Languages: Spanish. **National.** Supports and furthers the economic, political, and social interests of womem. Works to advance the professional and personal development of women. Disseminates information.

★970★ WOMEN'S LEGAL AID AND SUPPORT
Arzobispo Novel 55
Zona Colon
Santo Domingo 2270, Dominican
   Republic

Languages: Spanish. **National.** Provides legal advocacy, counseling and referral services to women. Investigates civil rights violations.

★971★ YOU, WOMAN
(Tu, Mujer)
PO Box 21040   PH: (809)685-8634
Santo Domingo, Dominican Republic   (809)597-8088
Cristina Sanchez Martinez, Contact   FX: (809)682-9927

Founded: 1986. **Members:** 31. **Staff:** 13. **Budget:** US$110,000. **Languages:** English, Spanish. **National.** Professionals, scholars, and other individuals interested in improving women's equal participation in society. Provides educational and training programs in health, nutrition, and natural medicine; literacy; income generation; vocational skills; and horticulture. Offers legal counseling. Coordinates activities of women's organizations. **Formerly:** Casa de la Mujer.

Grenada

★972★ AGENCY FOR RURAL TRANSFORMATION (ART)
Women's Resource Centre
Albert St.
Grenville
St. Andrew's, Grenada   PH: (809)442-6125

National. Works towards the development and advancement of rural women. Offers training and health awareness programs. Disseminates information.

★973★ GRENADA PLANNED PARENTHOOD ASSOCIATION (GPPA)
Scott St.   PH: (809)440-3341
PO Box 127   (809)440-2636
St. George's, Grenada   FX: (809)440-4100
Dr. Bernard Gittens, President   CBL: GPPA

Languages: English. **National.** Advocates responsible parenthood and family planning. Promotes family planning as a basic human right. Encourages public awareness of contraception, family planning, and sexually transmitted diseases. Provides contraceptive health care services. Sponsors educational programs. Conducts research.

★974★ GROUP OF CONCERNED WOMEN
PO Box 697
St. George's, Grenada

National. Strives to improve women's personal development through counseling, training, fund-raising, and personal assistance. Sponsors and supports development projects.

★975★ YOUNG WOMEN'S CHRISTIAN ASSOCIATION - GRENADA
Corner of Scott and Tyrell Sts.
St. George's, Grenada
Dawne Cyrus, Gen.Sec.   PH: (809)440-1647

National. Promotes the development of young women in Grenada. Upholds Christian beliefs and values in its programs. Works to instill self worth and self-esteem in young women.

Guadeloupe

★976★ CENTRE ADMINISTRATIF DU PLANNING FAMILIAL (CAPF)
39, rue Nassau
BP 677
97169 Pointe-a-Pitre Cedex, Guadeloupe   PH: 822978
Mr. Arthur Groevius, Exec. Dir.   821712

Languages: French. **National.** Works to enhance the quality of life for people living in Guadeloupe through the promotion of responsible parenthood and family planning. Advocates family planning as a basic human right. Offers contraceptive and health care services. Sponsors programs in family planning, sex education, and health care to adults and teens.

Haiti

★977★ ASSOCIATION POUR LA PROMOTION DE LA FAMILLE HAITIENNE (PROFAMIL)
86, rue du Champs de Mars
BP 1493   PH: 1 239085
Port-au-Prince, Haiti   1 239147
Mrs. Maggy de Catalogne, President   FX: 1 239147

Languages: French. **National.** Promotes responsible parenthood and family planning for adults and teens. Encourages public awareness of family planning, contraception, and sexually transmitted diseases, especially AIDS. Works to reduce the number of unwanted pregnancies and abortions. Provides contraceptive and health care services. Acts as an advocate for family planning on a national level.

★978★ CENTRE DE PROMOTION DES FEMMES OUVRIERES (CPFO)
PO Box 1329   PH: 462858
Port-au-Prince, Haiti   1220110

Languages: French. **National.** Promotes the advancement of women workers. Provides a forum for discussion and information exchange among members. Offers consulting. Disseminates information.

★979★ MERES ET ENFANTS D'HAITI (MEH)
c/o Prof. Jean Boisrond
Angle de Rues St. Honore et
   Monseigneur Guilloux
Port-au-Prince, Haiti
Prof. Jean Boisrond, President   PH: 1 222760

Founded: 1987. **Members:** 71. **Staff:** 8. **Budget:** US$9,000. **Languages:** English, French. **National.** Obstetricians, gynecologists, pediatricians, nurses, and medical and nursing students in Haiti. Strives to improve maternal and child health. Encourages advancements in the fields of obstetrics, gynecology, and pediatrics. Promotes research on human reproduction and women's and child health. Organizes courses and programs aimed at improving maternal and child health; communicates with directors of educational institutions. Operates family planning program; offers consulting services. Sponsors seminars and training programs. **Councils:** Scientifique. **Projects:** Pilote.

Publications: *Bulletin*, periodic. ● *MCI Bulletin*, quarterly.

Conventions/Meetings: annual congress - Port-au-Prince, Haiti. ● annual general assembly. ● quarterly conference.

★980★ SOLIDARITE FANM AYISYEN
87, Martin Luther King
Port-au-Prince, Haiti

Languages: French. **National.** Promotes the interests of women in Haiti.

Jamaica

★981★ ASSOCIATION OF WOMEN'S ORGANIZATIONS IN JAMAICA
(AWOJA)
c/o The Women's Centre
42 Trafalger Rd.
Kingston 10, Jamaica   PH: (809)929-8911

National. Umbrella organization of women's groups in Jamaica. Provides a network for communication and cooperation among women's organizations. Organizes seminars and meetings.

★982★ CARIBBEAN CHURCH WOMEN - JAMAICA
PO Box 527
Kingston 10, Jamaica

Languages: English. **National.** Promotes fellowship among Christian women. Conducts community service activities.

★983★ CARRIBEAN WOMEN FOR DEMOCRACY (CWD)
11 Worthington Ave.
PO Box 281
Kingston 5, Jamaica

National. Promotes equal rights for women. Works towards the development of legislation and policies that support and protect democracy and equal treatment of all people.

★984★ JAMAICA FAMILY PLANNING ASSOCIATION (JFPA)
32 1/2 Duke St.   PH: (809)922-8157
Kingston, Jamaica   FX: (809)922-8156
Mr. H. Peter Meyers, President   CBL: JFPA

Languages: English. **National.** Works to improve the quality of life for Jamaicans through the promotion of family planning and contraception. Encourages public knowledge of family planning, contraception, and sexually transmitted diseases, especially AIDS. Provides contraceptive and health care services.

★985★ JAMAICA FEDERATION OF WOMEN
74 Arnold Rd.
Cross Roads Post Office
Kingston 5, Jamaica
Mrs. Carole Diaz, Chair

Languages: English. **National.** Seeks to enhance the status of women. Fosters collaboration among women's groups to achieve equality.

★986★ WOMAN A-FIRE CREATIVE WRITERS' GROUP
20 Kensington Crescent
Kingston 5, Jamaica   PH: (809)929-2457
A. Folashade, Coord.   (809)929-6171

Founded: 1987. **Languages:** English. **National.** Seeks to raise consciousness of women's issues through creative expression. Objectives include: assisting women writers to realize and develop their potential of persuasion through writing; developing a united forum for women writers; increasing the possibility of writing to become an economically viable career. Networks with other groups. **Formerly:** Sistren Creative Writing Group.

Conventions/Meetings: monthly meeting.

★987★ WOMEN'S MEDIA WATCH (WMW)
PO Box 344
Stony Hill   PH: (809)978-0096
Kingston 9, Jamaica   (809)942-2203

Founded: 1987. **Languages:** English. **Multinational.** Jamaican women's organizations concerned with the societal increase in sexual violence. Works to increase public awareness of sexual violence and its causes. Seeks to create a new media image for women. Conducts public lectures, discussions, and drama workshops. Screens films and videos. Lobbies through letters to the press and private companies. Broadcasts opinions on radio programs. Meets and coordinates activities with other women's groups.

★988★ WOMEN'S RESOURCE AND OUTREACH CENTRE
47 Beechwood Ave.
Kingston 5, Jamaica   PH: (809)929-6954

Languages: English. **National.** Offers assistance to women in crisis. Maintains training and community outreach programs.

★989★ YOUNG WOMEN'S CHRISTIAN ASSOCIATION - JAMAICA
2H Camp Rd.   PH: (809)928-3023
Kingston 5, Jamaica   CBL: EMISSARIUS
Minna McLeod, Gen.Sec.   JAMAICA

National. Promotes the development of young women in Jamaica. Upholds Christian beliefs and values in its programs. Works to instill self-worth and self-esteem in young women.

Martinique

★990★ ASSOCIATION MARTINIQUAISE POUR L'INFORMATION ET
L'ORIENTATION FAMILIALES (AMIOF)
125-127, rue Moreau de Joanes
Fort de France, Martinique
Dr. Roger Boucher, Exec. Dir.   PH: 714601

Languages: French. **National.** Promotes responsible parenthood and family planning for teens and adults. Works to reduce the number of unwanted pregnancies and abortions. Offers educational programs. Provides contraceptive and health care services.

★991★ COMITE PERMANENT DE SOUTIEN AUX FEMMES
AGRESSEES (CPSFA)
Grosse-Roche 186, Voie 1
97200 Fort de France, Martinique

Languages: French. **National.** Supports the efforts of women activists within the women's movement. Fosters public awareness of issues affecting women. Furthers mobilization of women for the advancement of women's rights. Disseminates information.

★992★ UNION DES FEMMES DE LA MARTINIQUE
Ex Hospital Civil
Rue Carlos Finlay
BP 367
97258 Fort de France, Martinique
Solange Fitte-Duval, President   PH: 734412

Founded: 1944. **Members:** 350. **Languages:** French. **National**. Umbrella organization of women in Martinique. Strives to achieve the following goals: defense of rights for women and children; social progress; peace; and the establishment of social and cultural activities. Seeks to affect the lives of women of modest means, such as: farming women; single mothers; and the underemployed. Assists individual women of low economic status; strives to enhance society's perception of women's worth. Commemorates the "International Day of Women" annually in accordance with other women's organizations.

Publications: *Femmes Martiniquaises* (in French). Journal.

Conventions/Meetings: monthly meeting.

Montserrat

★993★ FAMILY LIFE SERVICES (FLS)
Upper Dagenham
PO Box 118
Pylmouth, Montserrat   PH: (809)491-2736
Mrs. Dorothy Greenway, President   FX: (809)491-3599

Languages: English. **National**. Encourages family planning activities in Montserrat and promotes family planning as a basic human right. Works to reduce the number of unwanted pregnancies and abortions. Offers educational programs to teens and adults. Seeks to limit the spread of sexually transmitted diseases, especially AIDS. Provides contraceptive and health care services.

★994★ YOUNG WOMEN'S CHRISTIAN ASSOCIATION -
    MONTSERRAT
PO Box 476
Plymouth, Montserrat
Carol White, Contact

National. Promotes the develoment of young women in Montserrat. Upholds Christian beliefs and values in its programs. Works to instill self-worth and self-esteem in young women.

Netherlands Antilles

★995★ DEVLELOPMENT ALTERNATIVES WITH WOMEN FOR A NEW
    ERA - CARIBBEAN (DAWN)
PO Box 4395
Willemstead
Curacao, Netherlands Antilles
Dr. Sonia Cuales, Contact

Multinational. Works to reduce the negative impact of development activities on women and the environment. Conducts research, training, and advocacy programs to eliminate inequalities of gender, class, and race. Facilitates communication and networking among women's movements. Protects and defends women's reproductive rights.

★996★ FOUNDATION FOR THE PROMOTION OF RESPONSIBLE
    PARENTHOOD (FPRP)
Parallelweg 38   PH: 9 611323
Julianadorp   FX: 9 611024
Curacao, Netherlands Antilles   TX: 3841492 LRNA OPR
Dr. Sergio Leon, President   CBL: PLANFAM

Languages: Dutch. **National**. Advocates responsible parenthood and family planning. Seeks to reduce the number of unwanted pregnancies and abortions. Encourages public knowledge of AIDS and other sexually transmitted diseases. Offers educational programs on family planning and maternal and infant health care.

Puerto Rico

★997★ ASOCIACION PUERTORRIQUENA PRO BIENESTAR DE LA
    FAMILIA (APPBF)
Calle Padre las Casas 117
Urbanizacion El Vedado
Hato Rey, Puerto Rico 00919
Idalia Colon Rondon, Contact   PH: (809)765-7373

National. Offers educational and medical services for family planning. Emphasizes education as a means to prevent unwanted pregnancies. Sponsors peer-counseling program on sexually transmitted diseases and AIDS. Conducts periodic seminars and workshops. Maintains library.

★998★ CENTRO DE AYUDA A VICTIMAS DE VIOLACION
PO Box 40798
San Juan, Puerto Rico 00657   PH: (809)765-2285

Languages: Spanish. **National**. Offers counseling and recovery programs to women victims of violence. Disseminates information on violence awareness and prevention.

★999★ CENTRO DE ESTUDIOS, RECURSOS Y SERVICIOS A LA
    MUJER
Centro de Investigaciones Sociales
Universidad de Puerto Rico
Rio Piedras, Puerto Rico 00931   PH: (809)764-0000

Languages: Spanish. **National**. Promotes the study of women and women's issues in Puerto Rico. Offers training and informational services to women. Conducts research; disseminates information.

★1000★ COMISION PARA LOS ASUNTOS DE LA MUJER (CAM)
151-153 San Francisco St.
Old San Juan
San Juan, Puerto Rico 00905
Yolanda Zayas, Exec.Dir.

National. Seeks to increase public awareness of women's issues and rights. Provides crisis intervention; offers legal counseling. Maintains library. Organizes discussion groups and workshops.

Conventions/Meetings: periodic conference.

★1001★ COORDINADORA DE ORGANIZACIONES FEMINISTAS (COF)
Apartado 21939, Estacion UPR
Rio Piedras, Puerto Rico 00931   PH: (809)751-7833

National. Coordinates efforts of feminist activist organizations, especially for the International Day of the Working Woman (Mar. 8) and the International Day of No More Violence Against Women (Nov. 25).

★1002★ FEDERACION DE ENFERMERIA PRACTICA DE PUERTO RICO (FEPPR)
Apartado Postal 7745
Bo. Obrero
Santurce, Puerto Rico 00916   PH: (809)726-3938

National. Seeks to improve working conditions for women in health care professions. Operates continuing education courses. Offers legal services. Supports workers in labor disputes.

★1003★ FEMINISTS ON THE MARCH (FEM)
(Feministas en Marcha)
Apartado 21939, Estacion UPR
Rio Piedras, Puerto Rico 00931   PH: (809)751-7833

Founded: 1983. **Members:** 30. **Languages:** Spanish. **National.** Is concerned with legal processes and political work affecting women. Conducts periodic discussion groups. Bestows biennial Golden Pig Award honoring individuals who work to improve the image of women in the media.

Publications: *Luna Nueva*, quarterly.

★1004★ INSTITUTO PUERTORRIQUENO DE DERECHOS CIVILES (IPDC)
Julian Blanco 11
Rio Piedras, Puerto Rico 00925   PH: (809)754-7390
Marilucy Gonzalez Baez, Contact   FX: (809)753-9829

National. Offers legal consulting and representation service. Operates educational programs concerning sexual harassment, sexual and pregnancy related discrimination, and domestic violence. Conducts conferences and seminars.

★1005★ LEAGUE OF WOMEN VOTERS OF PUERTO RICO (LWVPR)
(Liga de Mujeres Votantes de Puerto Rico)
PO Box 13485, Santurce Sta.
Santurce, Puerto Rico 00908
Marianne Maldonado, Pres.   PH: (809)722-3924

Founded: 1962. **Members:** 175. **Languages:** English, Spanish. **National.** Encourages the participation of women in politics. Conducts voter education campaigns. Disseminates information.

Publications: *Informa*, bimonthly. Newsletter. Profiles educational, environmental and elctoral matters. **Circulation:** 350. **Advertising:** accepted.

★1006★ MUJERES UNIDAS EN ACCION (MUA)
Calle Artico 611
Puerto Nuevo, Puerto Rico   PH: (809)781-5208

National. Coordinates conferences and workshops on various issues of concern to women.

★1007★ ORGANIZACION PRO DERECHOS DE LA MUJER (ODM)
c/o Comision de las Elecciones
PO Box 2353
Old San Juan
San Juan, Puerto Rico 00902   PH: (809)724-4979
Olga Colon, Pres.   FX: (809)725-6732

National. Advocates increased legislation addressing women's rights issues. Offers legal consulting service. Organizes conferences and workshops.

★1008★ ORGANIZACION PRO DESARROLLO DE LOS DERECHOS DE LA MUJER (ODDM)
Escuela de Derecho
Estacion 6
Ponce, Puerto Rico 00732   PH: (809)844-4150

Languages: English, Spanish. **National.** Seeks legislation addressing women's rights issues. Operates legal consulting service. Organizes conferences and workshops.

★1009★ ORGANIZACION PUERTORRIQUENA DE LA MUJER TRABAJADORA (OPMT)
Apartado 23136, Estacion UPR
Rio Piedras, Puerto Rico 00931   PH: (809)764-9639

Founded: 1982. **National.** Seeks to enhance awaresess of working women's issues. Organizes conferences, discussions, and workshops.

Publications: *Mujeres en Marcha* (in Spanish), bimonthly. Newsletter.

★1010★ PROYECTO SOBRE DERECHOS DE LA MUJER
Instituto Puertorriqueno de Derechos
   Civiles
Calle Julian Blanco No. 11   PH: (809)754-7390
Rio Piedras, Puerto Rico 00925   (809)753-9829

Languages: Spanish. **National.** Organizes programs and activites to strengthen women's rights at all levels of society. Disseminates information.

★1011★ PROYECTO DE ESTUDIOS DE LA MUJER (PROMUJER)
Colegio Universitario de Cayey
Universidad de Puerto Rico
Cayay, Puerto Rico 00633   PH: (809)738-2161

Languages: Spanish. **National.** Encourages and supports studies on the development of the women's movement and current issues affecting women.

★1012★ WOMEN'S INFORMATION AND SERVICE CENTER
Box 22025
VPR Sta.
Rio Piedras, Puerto Rico 00931

National. Provides information on the women's movement, women's issues, women's health, and women's services. Compiles and maintains various resource material. Offers referral service.

★1013★ YOUNG WOMEN'S CHRISTIAN ASSOCIATION - PUERTO RICO
(Asociacion Cristiana de Mujeres Jovenes de Puerto Rico)
PO Box 10111
Santurce, Puerto Rico 00908
Alicia Lopez de Mestey, Contact   PH: (809)724-1037

National. Promotes the development of young women in Puerto Rico. Upholds Christian beliefs and values in its programs. Works to instill self worth and self-esteem in young women.

St. Kitts and Nevis

★1014★ BUSINESS AND PROFESSIONAL WOMEN - ST. KITTS AND NEVIS
PO Box 305
Basseterre, St. Kitts and Nevis
Mrs. Cecile Jacobs, Contact   PH: (809)465-8195

Languages: English. **National.** Promotes and supports the interests of working women. Strives to achieve economic equality. Provides a forum for interaction.

★1015★ CARIBBEAN WOMEN'S ASSOCIATION - ST. KITTS (CARIWA)
PO Box 49
Basseterre, St. Kitts and Nevis
Anne Liourd, Contact

Languages: English. **National.** Supports women's rights. Encourages friendly relations among women.

★1016★ METHODIST WOMEN'S LEAGUE - ST. KITTS AND NEVIS
PO Box 141
Methodist Manse
Basseterre, St. Kitts and Nevis   PH: (809)465-2391

Founded: 1945. **Members:** 141. **Regional Groups:** 8. **Languages:** English. **National.** Women members of the Methodist church in St. Kitts and Nevis. Conducts community sevice programs focusing on children, sick, and elderly people. Sponsors educational, recreational, and religious activities. Conducts fundraising for the Methodist church.

★1017★ NEVIS FAMILY PLANNING ASSOCIATION (NFPA)
PO Box 88
Charlestown, St. Kitts and Nevis
Mr. Cecil Wilkes Jr., Secty. & Treasurer   PH: (809)469-5521

Languages: English. **National.** Encourages family planning and responsible parenthood. Promotes awareness of family planning, contraception, and sexually transmitted diseases. Offers educational programs. Provides contraceptive and health care services. Conducts research.

★1018★ PRESIDENT MOTHERS' UNION
PO Box 55
Basseterre, St. Kitts and Nevis   PH: (809)465-2167

National. Anglican women who are mothers. Encourages women to participate in church and social activities. Conducts and coordinates community aid programs.

★1019★ ST. KITTS INTERNATIONAL WOMEN
PO Box 123
Basseterre, St. Kitts and Nevis
Mae Pertha, Contact

Multinational. Supports and promotes the interests of women. Encourages women to work toward their goals. Coordinates activities.

★1020★ ST. KITTS-NEVIS FAMILY PLANNING ASSOCIATION (SKFPA)
Cayon St.
PO Box 358
Basseterre, St. Kitts and Nevis   PH: (809)465-2918
Mr. Eustace John, President   FX: (809)465-1106

Languages: English. **National.** Promotes responsible parenthood and family planning as a means to improve the quality of life. Works to reduce the number of unwanted pregnancies and abortions. Encourages public knowledge of family planning, contraception, and sexually transmitted diseases. Provides contraceptive and health care services. Conducts research.

★1021★ ST. KITTS AND NEVIS TRADES AND LABOUR UNION
    WOMEN'S GROUP
c/o Brenda Clarke
Masses House
Church St.
Basseterre, St. Kitts and Nevis   PH: (809)465-2229
Ms. Brenda Clarke, President   FX: (809)465-5519

Founded: 1988. **Members:** 100. **Languages:** English. **National.** Working women united to make the public aware of women's issues. Lobbies government on issues concerning employed women and the cost of living.

Members engage in voluntary social work. Conducts research. Sponsors seminars and workshops.

★1022★ SALVATION ARMY HOME LEAGUE
c/o The Salvation Army
PO Box 56
Basseterre, St. Kitts and Nevis
Marcia Morria, President   PH: (809)465-2106

Founded: 1939. **Members:** 58. **Languages:** English. **National.** Women united to uphold Christian beliefs. Participates in community service programs, focusing on senior citizens. Offers educational programs in homemaking skills.

Conventions/Meetings: annual competition - always October. ● annual banquet.

★1023★ WESLEY WOMEN'S LEAGUE
PO Box 141
Basseterre, St. Kitts and Nevis   PH: (809)465-2346

National. Methodist women. Coordinates social and productive programs for women. Encourages women to become active in church activities.

St. Lucia

★1024★ ST. LUCIA GIRL GUIDES ASSOCIATION
PO Box 327
Castries, St. Lucia   PH: (809)452-5763

Founded: 1925. **Members:** 1,500. **Languages:** English. **National.** Seeks to develop self-reliance and leadership in girls through community service programs. Works to improve conditions for people in hospitals, nursing homes, and other institutions. Offers educational, skill training, and athletic programs.

★1025★ ST. LUCIA PLANNED PARENTHOOD ASSOCIATION (SLPPA)
                              PH: (809)452-4335
83 Chaussee Rd.   (809)453-7284
Castries, St. Lucia   FX: (809)452-5313
Mr. George Compton, President   CBL: PARENTHOOD

Languages: English. **National.** Encourages responsible parenthood and family planning as a means to improve quality of life for people in St. Lucia. Advocates family planning as a basic human right. Provides health care and contraceptive services. Conducts research.

★1026★ WOMEN'S ACTION COUNCIL
c/o A.F. Valmont & Co.   PH: (809)452-3817
Castries, St. Lucia   FX: (809)452-4225

National. Encourages and facilitates programs furthering full recognition of women's rights in all spheres of society. Organizes meetings and seminars. Disseminates information.

St. Vincent

★1027★ COMMITTEE FOR THE DEVELOPMENT OF WOMEN (CDW)
PO Box 1343
Kingstown, St. Vincent   PH: (809)446-2341

National. Facilitates and supports projects to advance the development of rural women. Offers training and health awareness programs. Promotes women's rights in developing regions. Diseminates information.

★1028★ NATIONAL COUNCIL OF WOMEN
PO Box 1157
Kingstown, St. Vincent   PH: (809)457-2058

National. Umbrella organization of women and women's issues in St. Vincent. Provides a forum for sharing of information regarding women's issues. Pursues means of attaining full recognition of women's rights.

★1029★ ST. VINCENT PLANNED PARENTHOOD ASSOCIATION
SVPPA
Victoria Park W   PH: (809)456-1793
PO Box 99   (809)456-1185
Kingstown, St. Vincent   FX: (809)456-1648
Mr. Monty Eustace, President   CBL: VINPLAM

Languages: English. **National.** Works to improve the quality of life for people living in St. Vincent by promoting responsible parenthood and family planning. Advocates family planning as a basic human right. Sponsors programs in family planning, sex education, and health. Provides contraceptive and basic health care services. Acts as an advocate for family planning on a national level.

★1030★ YOUNG WOMEN'S CHRISTIAN ASSOCIATION - ST. VINCENT AND THE GRENADINES
Murray Rd.
Kingstown, St. Vincent
Norissa Cruickshank, Gen.Sec.   PH: (809)457-2769

Founded: 1958. **Members:** 106. **Languages:** English. **National.** Promotes the development of young women in St. Vincent and the Grenadines. Upholds Christian values and beliefs in its programs. Works to instill self worth and self-esteem in young women.

Trinidad and Tobago

★1031★ AMERICAN WOMEN'S CLUB - TRINIDAD AND TOBAGO
c/o American Embassy
15 Queen's Park W
Port of Spain, Trinidad and Tobago

Languages: English. **National.** American women living in Trinidad and Tobago. Conducts educational and cultural programs. Fosters communication among members.

★1032★ BUSINESS AND PROFESSIONAL WOMEN'S CLUB
PO Box 221
St. James Post Office
St. James, Trinidad and Tobago
Deborah Thomas-Felix, President

Languages: English. **National.** Seeks to advance status of business and professional women in Trinidad and Tobago. Promotes high business and professional standards. Fosters communication among members.

★1033★ CANADIAN WOMEN'S CLUB
c/o Canadian High Commission
71 S. Quay
Port of Spain, Trinidad and Tobago

Languages: English. **National.** Canadian women living in Trinidad and Tobago. Promotes multi-cultural awareness and social programs. Conducts community service activities.

★1034★ CARIBBEAN ASSOCIATION FOR FEMINIST RESEARCH AND ACTION (CAFRA)
PO Bag 442
Tunapuna Post Office   PH: (809)633-8670
Tunapuna, Trinidad and Tobago   (809)662-1231
Gemma Tang Nain   FX: (809)663-6482

Founded: 1985. **Members:** 280. **Staff:** 8. **Budget:** US$300,000. **Languages:** English, Spanish. **Multinational.** Caribbean feminist researchers, activists, and women's organizations. Researches women's issues, disseminates information, and works collectively for improvement in the ways women are perceived and treated both individually and as a whole. Provides educational opportunities for women to increase their practical, creative, financial, and political knowledge. Maintains a documentation center. **Libraries:** Type: reference.   **Programs:** Women in Caribbean Agriculture; Women's History and Creative Expression; Debt and Structure Adjustment; Health, Sexuality, and Reproductive Rights; Gender Consciousness and Relations Among Young People; Women and the Law; Health, Sexuality & Reproductive Rights.

Publications: *CAFRA News* (in English and Spanish), quarterly. **Also Cited As:** *Novedades CAFRA.* ● *Creation Fire.* Book. Anthology of Caribbean women's poetry.

Conventions/Meetings: triennial general assembly. ● annual regional meeting. ● annual Continuation Committee.

★1035★ CARIBBEAN CHURCH WOMEN - TRINIDAD AND TOBAGO
PO Box 876
Port of Spain, Trinidad and Tobago

Languages: English. **National.** Promotes fellowship among Christian women. Conducts community service activities.

★1036★ CARIBBEAN WOMEN'S ASSOCIATION - TRINIDAD AND TOBAGO (CARIWA)
15 Sheriff St.
Tunapuna, Trinidad and Tobago
Ruth Antoine, Secretary   PH: (809)622-5965

Founded: 1970. **Members:** 6. **Languages:** English. **National.** Women's organizations in Anguilla, Antigua and Barbuda, Barbados, Guyana, and St. Vincent and the Grenadines. Seeks to increase the independence of women through improving their job skills and educate women about health and political matters. Conducts training courses in managerial skills and cottage industries such as production of dried fruit, sausage-making, and the manufacture of tableware. Conducts seminars and lectures in cooperation with local government agencies.

Conventions/Meetings: annual CARIWA Conference conference.

★1037★ CHURCH WOMEN UNITED - TRINIDAD AND TOBAGO
7 1st Ave.
Mount Lambert, Trinidad and Tobago
Ms. D. Sampath, Contact   PH: (809)638-3313

Languages: English. **National.** Promotes fellowship for Christian women. Conducts community service activities.

★1038★ CONCERNED WOMEN FOR PROGRESS
31 Eastern Main Rd.
Laventille, Trinidad and Tobago

Languages: English. **National.** Women involved in community development programs in Trinidad and Tobago.

★1039★ DEMOCRATIC WOMEN'S ASSOCIATION
PO Box 3692
Port of Spain, Trinidad and Tobago

Languages: English. **National.** Women in Trinidad and Tobago united to uphold democratic principles. Fosters communication among members.

★1040★ ELECTRICAL ASSOCIATION OF WOMEN
c/o TTEC
63 Frederick St.
Port of Spain, Trinidad and Tobago

Languages: English. **National.** Women working in the electrical supply industry. Aims to improve quality of service. Encourages exchange of information; represents members' interests.

★1041★ FAMILY PLANNING ASSOCIATION OF TRINIDAD AND
TOBAGO (FPATT)
79 Oxford St.   PH: (809)623-4764
Port of Spain, Trinidad and Tobago   (809)625-6533
Mr. Emile Elias, President FX: (809)625-2256
                            CBL: PLANFAM

Languages: English. **National.** Works to improve quality of life by promoting responsible parenthood and family planning. Advocates family planning as a basic human right. Seeks to reduce the number of unwanted pregnancies and abortions. Sponsors programs in family planning, sex education, and health. Provides basic health care and contraceptive services.

★1042★ GIRL GUIDES ASSOCIATION OF TRINIDAD AND TOBAGO
8 Rust St.
St. Clair, Trinidad and Tobago   PH: (809)628-7966

Languages: English. **National.** Promotes the healthy mental, spiritual, and physical development of girls. Teaches teamwork and leadership skills.

★1043★ GROUP
4 Starboard Dr.
Schooner Ct.
Westmoorings by the Sea
Carenage, Trinidad and Tobago   PH: (809)632-2250

National. Works to enhance the economic, social, and political status of women. Disseminates information.

★1044★ HINDU WOMEN'S ORGANIZATION OF TRINIDAD AND
TOBAGO
1 Gallus St.
Woodbrook, Trinidad and Tobago   PH: (809)625-3652
Mrs. Brenda Goppeesingh, Contact FX: (809)645-0330

Founded: 1987. **Members:** 127. **Budget:** TT$6,000. **National.** Hindu women of Trinidad and Tobago. Supports and promotes the ideals of dharma (righteous actions) and the tradition of Hinduism. Works to enhance and project a positive image of Hindu women. Disseminates information and educates the public on relevant issues. Seeks to create an understanding and awareness of the role Hindu women play in local and national arenas. Co-sponsors a literacy program. Bestows awards.

Conventions/Meetings: monthly general assembly.

★1045★ INFORMATIVE BREASTFEEDING SERVICE
13 Rust St.
St. Clair
Port of Spain, Trinidad and Tobago   PH: (809)622-7273

National. Provides education and information regarding the physical and emotional benefits of breastfeeding.

★1046★ ISLAMIC LADIES' RELIGIOUS SOCIAL AND CULTURAL
ORGANIZATION
17 Valleton Ave.
Maraval, Trinidad and Tobago

Languages: English. **National.** Fosters fellowship and cooperation among Islamic women. Maintains educational programs.

★1047★ JAYCEES WOMEN'S LEAGUE
3 Melville Ln.
Port of Spain, Trinidad and Tobago

Languages: English. **National.** Seeks to strengthen women's leadership skills through community development activities. Sponsors educational programs.

★1048★ LADIES' ASSOCIATION OF THE AGE OF ENLIGHTENMENT
8 Fondes Amandes Rd.
St. Ann's, Trinidad and Tobago

Languages: English. **National.** Fosters solidarity among women. Offers lectures on education, drug rehabilitation, and health care.

★1049★ METHODIST WOMEN'S LEAGUE - TRINIDAD AND TOBAGO
3 Victoria Ave.
Port of Spain, Trinidad and Tobago   PH: (809)624-2820

Languages: English. **National.** Women of the Methodist faith working to further the development of the Methodist church. Supports mission work.

★1050★ MOTHERS' UNION COURT
Mt. Paran Spiritual Baptist Church
Pond St.
La Romain, Trinidad and Tobago

National. Mothers in Trinidad and Tobago. Works to influence national policies affecting the welfare and education of children. Supports the observance of Christian teaching and ethics in policy making and education.

★1051★ MOTHERS' UNION OF TRINIDAD AND TOBAGO
Diocesan Office
Hayes Ct.
Port of Spain, Trinidad and Tobago

National. Mothers working to improve the welfare and education of children.

★1052★ NATIONAL COUNCIL OF WOMEN OF TRINIDAD AND
TOBAGO
118 Saddle Rd.
Gor. Lynch Dr.
Maraval, Trinidad and Tobago

National. Umbrella organization for women's groups in Trinidad and Tobago. Supports women's interests. Coordinates activities for women. Disseminates information.

★1053★ NATIONAL EXECUTIVE CHURCH WOMEN UNITED OF
TRINIDAD AND TOBAGO
28 Roy Ave.
Marabella, Trinidad and Tobago
Jessie Kesraj, Contact

National. Provides a forum for discussion and fellowship among Christian women. Supports the observance of Christian teachings and ethics in policy making and education.

★1054★ NATIONAL ORGANISATION OF WOMEN - TRINIDAD AND
  TOBAGO
10 Albion St.   PH: (809)623-2583
Port of Spain, Trinidad and Tobago   (809)627-2804

Languages: English. **National**. Works for the rights and increased influence
of women. Seeks to enhance public awareness of women's issues.

★1055★ NATIONAL SECRETARIES' ASSOCIATION
PO Box 1241
Port of Spain, Trinidad and Tobago

Languages: English. **National**. Women united to improve working conditions
in the secretarial field. Advances the economic and social interests of
secretaries.

★1056★ NATIONAL UNION OF DOMESTIC EMPLOYEES - TRINIDAD
  AND TOBAGO (NUDE)
c/o Clotil Walcott
Mt. Pleasant Rd.
Arima, Trinidad and Tobago
Clotil Walcott, Contact   PH: (809)667-5247

Languages: English. **National**. Works to improve the social and economic
status of domestic workers. Provides a forum for discussion of professional
problems and concerns.

★1057★ NATIONAL WOMEN'S ACTION COMMITTEE - TRINIDAD AND
  TOBAGO (NWAC)
40 Duke St.
Port of Spain, Trinidad and Tobago   PH: (809)623-5662

Languages: English. **National**. Works for equal rights for women in political,
social, and economic life. Liaises with other women's organizations.

★1058★ PEOPLE'S NATIONAL MOVEMENT WOMEN'S LEAGUE
c/o Balisier House
Tranquility St.
Port of Spain, Trinidad and Tobago

National. Works to secure women's rights nationally. Active in legislative
development and policy making to further equal opportunity.

★1059★ POLICE WIVES ASSOCIATION
41 New St.
Port of Spain, Trinidad and Tobago

National. Provides a forum for discussion, mutual support, the exchange of
information and experiences, and fellowship among wives of police officers.

★1060★ POPULATION PROGRAMME UNIT
Gordon Grant Bldg.
8 Saint Vincent St.
Port of Spain, Trinidad and Tobago
Joan Bishop, Director   PH: (809)623-4373

Languages: English. **National**. Seeks to heighten public awareness of
overpopulation issues. Works to improve family planning and primary health
care programs. Disseminates information.

★1061★ PRESBYTERIAN CHURCH WOMEN UNITED
20A Warner St.
St. Augustine, Trinidad and Tobago

National. Provides a forum for discussion and fellowship among women
sharing membership in the Presbyterian church. Promotes the observance of
Christian teachings and ethics in policy making and education.

★1062★ PSYCHIATRIC NURSES ASSOCIATION OF TRINIDAD AND
  TOBAGO
St. Ann's Hospital
PO Box 65
Port of Spain, Trinidad and Tobago

Languages: English. **National**. Women in the psychiatriac nursing profession. Promotes the advancement of the profession. Encourages further
education of psychiatric nurses.

★1063★ PUBLIC SERIVICES ASSOCIATION - WOMEN'S ADVISORY
  COMMITTEE
89-91 Abercromby St.
Port of Spain, Trinidad and Tobago   PH: (809)623-7987
Jennifer Baptiste, Contact   (809)623-5472

Languages: English. **National**. Women employed in public service. Coordinates training and education for members.

★1064★ RAPE CRISIS SOCIETY OF TRINIDAD AND TOBAGO
40 Woodford St.
Newtown
Port of Spain, Trinidad and Tobago
Claire Eunice Gittens, President   PH: (809)622-7273

Founded: 1984. **Members:** 30. **Languages:** English. **National**. Seeks to
raise public awareness of violence against women and children; conducts
preventative and educational programs on sexual violence and AIDS. Works
to achieve social, political, and legal changes regarding sexual violence.
Offers walk-in and telephone counselling services.

★1065★ ST. MARY'S WOMEN'S HANDICRAFT GROUP
St. Mary's Village
Moruga, Trinidad and Tobago

Languages: English. **National**. Works to improve women's economic
development through marketing and sale of handicrafts. Seeks to promote,
study, and expand the creation of traditional handicrafts in Trinidad and
Tobago.

★1066★ SALVATION ARMY - TRINIDAD AND TOBAGO
PO Box 248
27 Edward St.
Port of Spain, Trinidad and Tobago
Major Carol Ganot, Secretary   PH: (809)625-4120

Founded: 1901. **Members:** 400. **Languages:** English. **National**. Women
engaged in social and religious work based in Christian values and beliefs.
Conducts community service activities for senior citizens and children.
Operates hostels and low-cost housing.

★1067★ SOROPTIMIST CLUB - TRINIDAD AND TOBAGO
76 Ellerslie Park
St. Clair, Trinidad and Tobago
Ms. Bernice Dolly, Contact

National. Women professionals. Promotes international goodwill and understanding. Conducts educational and research programs on: the environment;
health; human rights; the status of women; and economic and social
development. Cooperates with non-governmental organizations for the
advancement of peace; encourages interaction among local and international
clubs. **Alternate name::** National Council of Soroptimist International.

★1068★ SYRIAN LEBANESE WOMEN'S ASSOCIATION
6 Devan
Les Efforts W
San Fernando, Trinidad and Tobago

Languages: English. **National**. Syrian and Lebanese women living in Trinidad and Tobago. Provides a forum for discussion, fellowship, and cultural exchange among members. Offers assistance and support.

★1069★ TASK FORCE FOR WOMEN IN DEVELOPMENT
3 Little Rd.
Cascade, Trinidad and Tobago

National. Organizes and supports projects and activities which further the development of rural women. Offers training and health care programs.

★1070★ TASK FORCE FOR WOMEN IN DEVELOPMENT-WOMEN'S RESOURCE AND RESEARCH CENTRE
008F & 009F Charford Ct.
Charlotte St.
Port of Spain, Trinidad and Tobago
Karen Bart-Alexander, Director   PH: (809)623-8830

Founded: 1988. **Members:** 60. **Membership Dues:** individual, TT$10 annual; organization, TT$25 annual. **Staff:** 1. **Budget:** TT$250,000. **Languages:** English. **National**. Facilitates the participation of women in development activities to enable them "to become the predominant creative force in their own lives." Conducts training, educational, and literacy programs. Promotes women's businesses at a commercial display outlet; provides career guidance. Offers confidential and professional legal, medical, and family counselling. Conducts research. **Libraries:** Type: reference. Holdings: books, periodicals, audio recordings, video recordings. **Formerly:** First Resource Centre for Women in Trinidad and Tobago.

Conventions/Meetings: annual meeting. ● monthly board meeting.

★1071★ TRINIDAD AND TOBAGO COALITION AGAINST DOMESTIC VIOLENCE
c/o Queensway Store
62 Queen St.
Port of Spain, Trinidad and Tobago
Diana Mahabir, Chair   PH: (809)623-5052

Founded: 1988. **Languages:** English. **National**. Seeks to raise public awareness of domestic violence. Works to enact legislation to discipline perpetrators of domestic violence. Offers counselling to victims of domestic violence. Conducts fund-raising activities to support member organizations and shelters.

★1072★ TRINIDAD AND TOBAGO FEDERATION OF WOMEN'S INSTITUTES
15 Dunlop Dr.
Cocorite, Trinidad and Tobago   PH: (809)637-5359

National. Promotes the study of women and women's issues in Trinidad and Tobago. Provides a networking forum for national women's institutes. Fosters women's solidarity.

★1073★ TRINIDAD AND TOBAGO LEAGUE OF WOMEN VOTERS
7 4th St.
Mt. Lambert
San Juan, Trinidad and Tobago
Nesta Patrick, President   PH: (809)638-3851

Languages: English. **National**. Encourages women's participation in politics. Conducts voter education campaigns. Disseminates information.

★1074★ TRINIDAD AND TOBAGO NETWORK OF NGOS FOR THE ADVANCEMENT OF WOMEN
7 Chandie Ln.
Mausica Rd.
D'Abadie, Trinidad and Tobago
Mrs. Manswell-St. Louis, Contact

National. Umbrella organization. Provides a forum for discussion, negotia-

tion, and information exchange among non governmental organizations to achieve improvement of the status of women and full public recognition of women's rights.

★1075★ TRINIDAD AND TOBAGO TEACHERS' UNION, WOMEN'S AUXILIARY BRANCH
70 Christian Dr.
Plaisance Park
Pointe-a-Pierre, Trinidad and Tobago

National. Works towards the preservation and improvement of the working conditions of women teachers.

★1076★ UNION OF WOMEN CITIZENS OF TRINIDAD AND TOBAGO
15 Sheriff St.
Tunapuna, Trinidad and Tobago

National. Women active in policy making in Trinidad and Tobago. Promotes the improvement of the status of women in all spheres of society. Encourages the involvement of women in political affairs.

★1077★ WOMEN MISSIONARY COUNCIL
7 Althazar St.
Tunapuna, Trinidad and Tobago
Inez Sterling, President

National. Provides a forum for fellowship and discussion related to the experiences and circumstances of women missionaries.

★1078★ WOMEN WORKING FOR SOCIAL PROGRESS
8 Niles St.
Tunapuna, Trinidad and Tobago   PH: (809)663-9509

Founded: 1985. **Members:** 30. **Membership Dues:** Women, TT$10 monthly; Women, TT$100 annual; Students and unemployed., TT$5 monthly; Students and unemployed, TT$50 annual; Overseas members and men., TT$20 annual. **Languages:** English. **National**. Seeks to enable women to overcome obstacles and develop their full potential. Arranges theatre productions to create awareness of women's issues. Encourages women to become involved in national politics. Supports efforts to establish the Caribbean's cultural sovereignty. Conducts educational programs.

Publications: *Working Women* (in English), periodic. Newsletter.

Conventions/Meetings: monthly meeting. ● quarterly meeting. ● monthly Potluck Dinner - Third Friday each month.

★1079★ WOMEN'S CORONA SOCIETY OF TRINIDAD AND TOBAGO
7 Pomme Rose Ave.
Cascade, Trinidad and Tobago

National. Promotes international cultural exchange among women. Coordinates members' activities.

★1080★ YOUNG WOMEN'S CHRISTIAN ASSOCIATION - TRINIDAD AND TOBAGO
8A Cipriani Blvd.
Port of Spain, Trinidad and Tobago
Lystra Nicholas, Gen.Sec.   PH: (809)627-6388

National. Promotes the development of young women in Trinidad and Tobago. Upholds Christian values and beliefs in its programs. Works to instill self worth and self-esteem in young women.

Virgin Islands of the United States

★1081★ VIRGIN ISLANDS FAMILY PLANNING ASSOCIATION (VIFPA)
49-50 Kogens-Gade
PO Box 9816
St. Thomas, Virgin Islands of the United
   States   PH: (809)774-2150
Mr. Sylvester Edwards, President   (809)774-2652

Languages: English. **National.** Promotes responsible parenthood and family planning. Advocates family planning as a basic human right. Works to reduce the number of unwanted pregnancies and abortions. Sponsors programs in sex education, family planning, and health. Seeks to stop the spread of AIDS and other sexually transmitted diseases. Provides contraceptive and health care services.

★1082★ WOMEN'S COALITION
7 East St.
PO Box 2734
Christiansted
St. Croix, Virgin Islands of the United   PH: (809)773-9272
   States 00822-2734   (809)773-WCSC

National. Works towards recognition of women's rights and public awareness of the concerns of women relating to current issues and policies. Provides a forum for discussion and information exchange.

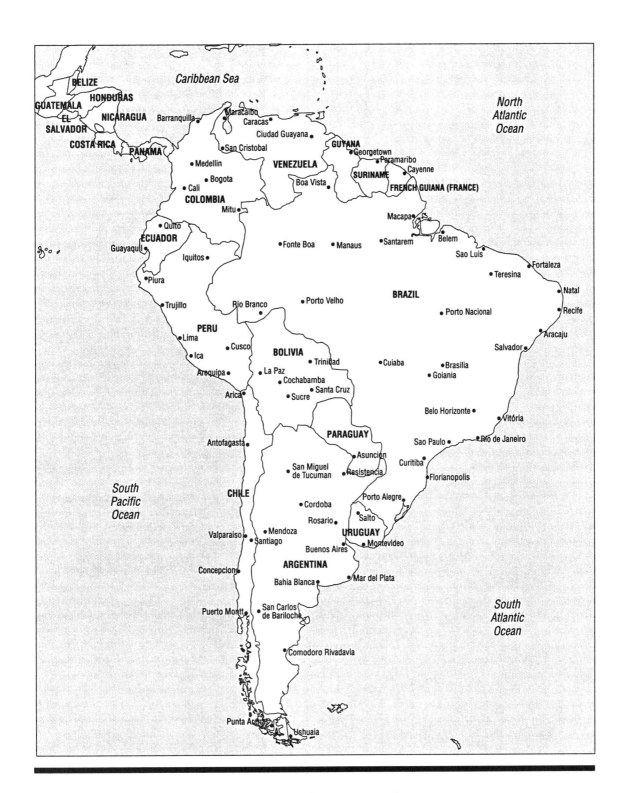

Central and South America

Argentina	Chile	Guatemala	Paraguay
Belize	Colombia	Guyana	Peru
Bolivia	Costa Rica	Honduras	Suriname
Brazil	Ecuador	Nicaragua	Uruguay
	El Salvador	Panama	Venezuela

Central and South America

Argentina

★1083★ ALTERNATIVA FEMINISTA
Catamarca 970
1231 Buenos Aires, Argentina

Languages: Spanish. **National.** Feminist women in Argentina. Works to increase awareness of women's issues.

★1084★ AMERICAN WOMEN'S CLUB - ARGENTINA (AWC)
(Asociacion de Mujeres Americans)
Avenida Cordoba 632, Piso 11
1054 Buenos Aires, Argentina
Simone Verniki, Pres.   PH: 1 3225707

Founded: 1917. **Members:** 160. **Staff:** 2. **Budget:** US$15,000. **National Groups:** 1. **Languages:** English, Spanish. **National.** Central, North, and South American women in Argentina. Works to strengthen ties between women in the Americas through social programs and activities. Provides assistance to organizations that support women and their needs; supports Argentine charities that provide aid to women, children, and the elderly. Conducts seminars and lectures on educational and cultural topics; sponsors monthly luncheon with speakers. **Libraries:** Type: reference.
   Subjects: novels in English.

Publications: *AWC Membership Directory* (in English), annual. ● *AWC Newsletter* (in English), monthly. ● *Benefit Program* (in English and Spanish), annual. Booklet. ● *American Women's Club Cookbook.*

Conventions/Meetings: annual dinner.

★1085★ AMIGAS SEFARADIES DE NA'AMAT (ASN)
Presidente Peron 1878
1040 Buenos Aires, Argentina   PH: 1 454707

Languages: Spanish. **Multinational.** Working and professional women. Works to advance the status of women by providing a variety of educational, community, and legal services. Believes that strong family relations are the foundation of a stable society. Members identify with the Zionist movement.

★1086★ ASOCIACION ARGENTINA DE PROTECCION FAMILIAR
   (AAPF)
Aguero 1355/59
1425 Buenos Aires, Argentina   PH: 1 8248419
Dr. Oswaldo Bottiroli, President   FX: 1 8248416

Languages: Spanish. **National.** Promotes family planning as a basic human right. Seeks to reduce the number of unwanted pregnancies and abortions in Argentina. Offers programs in family planning, sex education, and basic health care. Provides contraceptive services. Acts as an advocate for family planning on the national level.

★1087★ ASOCIACION CRISTIANA FEMENINA - ARGENTINA
Tucuman 844
Buenos Aires, Argentina   PH: 1 3221550
Maria Dove de Dardie, President   1 3225027

Languages: Spanish. **National.** Christian women in Argentina. Disseminates information on Christianity. Supports missionary activities.

★1088★ ASOCIACION DE TRABAJO Y ESTUDIOS DE LA MUJER
   (ATEM)
Combate de los Pozos 185
Buenos Aires, Argentina

Languages: Spanish. **National.** Fosters research on women in Argentina. Works to improve women's standard of living. Provides a forum for communication and exchange among members.

★1089★ ASSOCIATION OF WOMEN JUANA MANSO
(Asociacion de Mujeres Juana Manso - Casa de las Mujeres)
La Rioja 590, Piso 1, Local 13
5000 Cordoba, Argentina
Isabel Donato, President   PH: 51 803898

Founded: 1986. **Members:** 200. **Budget:** US$50,000. **Languages:** Spanish. **National.** Women working to improve their social, political, economic, and personal status. Strives to increase public awareness of women's concerns, to organize women in action, and to make government more accessible and responsive to women. Maintains a center for women which provides legal, medical, and psychological assistance; self-help and group therapy; educational programs on women's issues; family planning and other health related services; and aid to battered women. **Libraries:** Type: reference. Holdings: archival material, periodicals.

Publications: *Violencia Domestica-La Mujer Maltratada.* Booklet. **Circulation:** 5,000.

Conventions/Meetings: semiannual seminar.

★1090★ CASA DE LA MUJER - ARGENTINA
Cochabamba 971
2000 Rosario, Argentina   PH: 41 813283

Languages: Spanish. **National.** Offers charitable programs for needy women.

★1091★ CENTRO DE APOYO A LA MUJER MALTRATADA (CAMM)
25 de Mayo e H. Yrigoyen
Mar del Plata 7600
Buenos Aires, Argentina

Founded: 1988. **Members:** 27. **Languages:** English, Spanish. **National.** Works to educate about and eliminate violence against women. Provides personal and group assistance to victims of physical, sexual, or mental abuse. Organizes lectures; conducts debates; sponsors workshops in schools and other places of learning. Investigates the effects and causes of violence against women. Disseminates information. **Libraries:** Type: reference.

★1092★ COLECTIVO REVISTA FEMINARIA
Casilla de Correo 402
1000 Buenos Aires, Argentina   PH: 1 8553472

Languages: Spanish. **National.** Promotes awareness of women's issues through information dissemination. Fosters friendly relations among women.

★1093★ COMISION DE LA MUJER Y SUS DERECHOS
Avenida Callao 569, 1 piso, No. 15
1022 Buenos Aires, Argentina

Languages: Spanish. **National.** Promotes public awareness of issues affecting women and full recognition of women's rights to equal opportunities and treatment in all spheres of society.

★1094★ CONSEJO DE MUJERES DE LA REPUBLICA ARGENTINA
French 2727 Pta. Baja D
1425 Buenos Aires, Argentina
Hilda M. Gorrini Caprile, President

Founded: 1900. **Members:** 24. **Languages:** English, French, Spanish. **National.** Umbrella organization for women's groups in Argentina. Promotes and intensifies public and private activities of women working in the sciences, arts, education, and cultural professions. Seeks to empower women politically and spiritually. Works for peace and the improvement of society. Offers legal counseling services, literacy programs, and training for parents. Provides health and child care services. **Commissions:** Escuelas Ahijadas; Ayuda Socio-Cultura.

Conventions/Meetings: periodic Reunion Hemisferica congress - 1993 Nov. 14 - 15, Buenos Aires, Argentina.

★1095★ ECUMENICAL WOMEN'S GROUP
(Grupo Ecumenico de Mujeres)
Fundacion Ecumenica de Cuyo
Casilla de Correo 60
San Jose
5519 Mendoza, Argentina
Alieda Verhoeven, President

Founded: 1970. **Members:** 44. **Staff:** 38. **Languages:** English, Spanish. **National.** Women members of Fundacion Ecumenica de Cuyo. Focuses efforts on women's concerns such as achieving social, political, and employment equality. Investigates women's concerns such as domestic violenc, pay inequity, and family law. Conducts programs designed to increase public awareness of women's needs. **Libraries:** Type: reference. Holdings: 0; archival material.

Publications: El Diario de las Chicas (in Spanish), bimonthly. Journal.

★1096★ EMERGER FUNDACION
Dorrego 2381/73   PH: 1 7716155
1425 Buenos Aires, Argentina   1 7738431
Maria Cristina Ravazzola M.D., Contact   FX: 1 7711251

Founded: 1991. **Members:** 2. **Budget:** US$2,000. **Languages:** English, French, Italian, Spanish. **National.** Psychotherapists assisting women. Conducts training and educational programs. Provides assistance with development activities. Investigates women's concerns.

★1097★ EQUAL RIGHTS FOR ARGENTINE WOMEN
(DIMA Derechos Iguales para la Mujer Argentina)
Luis Maria Campos 1616, Planta Baja B
1426 Buenos Aires, Argentina
Sara Riojo Medrano, President   PH: 1 7838520

Founded: 1976. **Members:** 150. **Budget:** US$3,000. **Languages:** English, French, Portuguese, Spanish. **National.** Seeks to improve the standard of living of Argentine women through education. Conducts investigational, educational, and health care programs for women. Organizes activities. Disseminates information. **Libraries:** Type: reference. Holdings: books, archival material, periodicals, audio recordings.

Publications: El Largo Camino (in Spanish), semiannual. Bulletin. activities updates. **Circulation:** 1,000. **Advertising:** not accepted.

Conventions/Meetings: annual La Mujer en el Mundo de Hoy congress. ● monthly seminar.

★1098★ EQUIPO DE INVESTIGACION Y ASISTENCIA PARA LA MUJER
Beruti 3032
1425 Buenos Aires, Argentina

Languages: Spanish. **National.** Offers social services to women in need. Works to raise the status of women in Argentina.

★1099★ FEDERACION ARGENTINA DE MUJERES UNIVERSITARIAS
Sarmiento 1848 4E
Buenos Aires, Argentina
Susana Galtieri, Secretary

Languages: Spanish. **National.** Female university graduates. Conducts research and disseminates information on the status of women in Argentina. Addresses problems encountered by women in higher education.

★1100★ FEDERACION FEMENINA EVANGELICA METODISTA ARGENTINA (FFEMA)
c/o Alicia P. de Fernandez
Rivadavia 4044
1205 Buenos Aires, Argentina
Alicia P. de Fernandez, Contact   PH: 1 9826288

Founded: 1930. **Members:** 1,000. **Languages:** English, Spanish. **National.** Promotes the spiritual, moral, and intellectual interests of women.

★1101★ LATIN AMERICAN COUNCIL OF CATHOLIC WOMEN
(CLAMUC)
(Consejo Latinoamericano de Mujeres Catolicas)
c/o Dr. Elena Cumella
Gelly y Obes 2213
1425 Buenos Aires, Argentina
Dr. Elena Cumella, Sec.Gen.   PH: 1 8034901

Founded: 1975. **Members:** 544. **Budget:** US$44,000. **Languages:** English, French, Spanish. **Multinational.** Catholic women's organizations in 23 Latin American countries. Works to: advance women in Latin America and Latin American societies; strengthen the family unit through the woman; promote Catholicism; communicate with women religious and Christian organizations. Operates the Centro de Estudios para la Promocion Integral, offering programs on family and women's issues, adult education, and Christian faith. Maintains training centers in underdeveloped communities. Monitors international events; conducts religious discussion groups; holds seminars. Works in conjunction with Catholic church authorities; maintains liaisons with the United Nations, the U.N. Educational, Scientific and Cultural Organization, and the Food and Agriculture Organization of the U.N.

Publications: La Persona Humana, periodic. Newsletter.

Conventions/Meetings: periodic meeting.

★1102★ LEGAL AND SOCIAL WOMEN'S STUDIES INSTITUTE
(INDESO Instituto de Estudios Juridico Sociales de la Mujer)
Balcarce 357
2000 Rosario, Argentina   PH: 41 42369
Susana Chiaro, Co-coord.   FX: 41 423369

Founded: 1984. **Members:** 20. **Staff:** 12. **Budget:** US$60,000. **Languages:** English, Spanish. **National.** Works to: eliminate all forms of discrimination against women; increase public awareness of women's concerns; improve the status of women. Investigates the legal and social conditions that generate and perpetuate discriminatory practices and laws; disseminates findings; and establishes programs to rectify the situation. Provides legal access, counseling, and services for battered women, homeless women, victims of sexual abuse, and women with other legal problems. Offers job skills training. Organizes and coordinates activities and programs with similar organizations. **Libraries:** Type: reference. Holdings: 500; books, periodicals.

Publications: La Chancleta (in Spanish), 3/yr. Booklet. **Circulation:** 2,000.

Conventions/Meetings: periodic workshop. ● periodic seminar.

★1103★ LUGAR DE LA MUJER
2 Sanchez de Bustamante 515
1173 Buenos Aires, Argentina   PH: 1 937223

Languages: Spanish. **National.** Provides a forum and meeting place for women to discuss and share information on issues affecting them.

★1104★ NA'AMAT PIONERAS
NP
Larrea 266, Piso 1   PH: 1 9514157
1030 Buenos Aires, Argentina   1 9529604

Languages: Spanish. **Multinational.** Working and professional women. Works to advance the status of women by providing a variety of educational, community, and legal services. Believes that strong family relations are the foundation for a stable society. Members identify with the Zionist movement.

★1105★ NEW DIMENSION
(Nueva Dimension)
Olavarria y Gascon
Mar del Plata 7600
Buenos Aires, Argentina   PH: 1 515795

Founded: 1984. **Members:** 25. **Languages:** English, Spanish. **National.** Women social activists and interested individuals. Works to end discrimination against women. Organizes lectures, debates, educational courses, and other informational gatherings. Participates in conferences. Provides assistance to battered women. Works on the community level to encourage women to become active. Investigates women's issues; disseminates results.

Publications: *Nueva Dimension* (in Spanish), quarterly. Magazine. **Circulation:** 200. **Advertising:** not accepted.

Conventions/Meetings: annual meeting.

★1106★ TRABAJO, INVESTIGACION, DESARROLLO Y
  ORGANIZACION DE LA MUJER (TIDO)
Casilla de Correo 91, Suc. 25
1425 Buenos Aires, Argentina
Olga Marin de Hammar, Director   PH: 1 7718901

Founded: 1985. **Staff:** 2. **Budget:** US$60,000. **Languages:** Spanish. **National.** Promotes the study of women and women's issues in Argentina. Organizes and coordinates activities of women's organizations. Trains women in small business management, self-management, and health. Provides emergency assistance for women in need. Conducts training programs on health and development issues. Offers workshops and informational projects. Disseminates information to increase public awareness of women's issues. **Sections:** Urban Development; Health; Women and Development; Employment.

★1107★ WOMEN'S STUDIES CENTER
(Centro de Estudios de la Mujer)
Olleros 2554
1426 Buenos Aires, Argentina

Languages: Spanish. **National.** Promotes the study of women and women's issues in Argentina.

★1108★ YOUNG WOMEN'S CHRISTIAN ASSOCIATION - ARGENTINA
(YWCA)
(Federacion de las Asociaciones Cristianas Femeninas de la Republica
  Argentina)
Humberto 1, 2360
1229 Buenos Aires, Argentina   PH: 1 9413775
Leonor Stok de Llovet, Gen.Sec.   FX: 1 9527987

Founded: 1890. **Members:** 400. **Staff:** 14. **Languages:** English, Spanish. **National.** Strives to assist young women in developing physically, mentally, and spiritually. Maintains a center for mammography and gynecological exams. Provides school supplies to disadvantaged girls and women returning to school. Conducts educational programs on vocational skills, English, and public speaking. Offers housing to young women. Networks with other women's groups.

Conventions/Meetings: semiannual workshop.

Belize

★1109★ BELIZE FAMILY LIFE ASSOCIATION (BFLA)
127 Barracks Rd.
PO Box 529   PH: 2 31018
Belize City, Belize   2 44399
Mrs. Phyllis Cayetano, President   FX: 2 32667

Languages: English. **National.** Works to enhance the quality of life in Belize through promotion of family planning and maternal and infant health care. Encourages public awareness of methods of contraception. Offers educational programs in family planning, sex education, and health care. Provides contraceptive services.

★1110★ BELIZE NATIONAL WOMEN'S COMMISSION
PO Box 1598
Belize City, Belize   PH: 2 75592
Dorla Bowman, President   2 74275

Founded: 1982. **Budget:** $B 25,000. **Languages:** English. **National.** Investigates the economic, social, civil, and political situation of women in Belize. Works with governmental and private women's institutions. Promotes recognition of women's accomplishments. Seeks to influence legislators through exchange of information relevant to women's issues and needs. Advocates revision of labor policies; ratification of the UN Convention on the Elimination of Discrimination Against Women; and improvement of government services for women. Researches and publishes information on women's issues. **Alternate name:** Commission on the Status of Women in Belize.

Publications: *Mothers of Modern Belize* (in English). Booklet.

★1111★ BELIZE ORGANIZATION FOR WOMEN AND DEVELOPMENT
  (BOWAND)
87 Freetown Rd.
PO Box 1243
Belize City, Belize   PH: 2 45196

National. Promotes improvement in the standard of living and economic status of women. Offers training programs. Disseminates information.

★1112★ BELIZE RURAL WOMEN'S ASSOCIATION
PO Box 1190   PH: 8 22664
Belmopan, Belize   8 23383

National. Works to improve the standard of living for rural women. Offers assistance in locating financial aid and projects that benefit rural women. Conducts training programs. Disseminates information.

★1113★ BELIZE WOMEN AGAINST VIOLENCE MOVEMENT (BWAV)
PO Box 1190   PH: 2 74845
Belize City, Belize   FX: 2 77236

Founded: 1985. **Membership Dues:** $B 5 annual. **Regional Groups:** 6.
Languages: English. **National**. Women concerned about domestic and
neighborhood violence. Offers services to victims of violence; researches
violence and its causes; provides results of studies to law making bodies.
Works to create an increased public awareness of the problems associated
with violence. Sponsors educational programs. Conducts workshops on
rape, domestic violence, and personal safety awareness. Provides counseling, support, and shelter location assistance for spouse abuse, rape, incest,
and sexual harassment victims. **Programs:** Education/Advocacy; Neighbourhood Watch.

Publications: *Newsletter* (in English), quarterly.

★1114★ BREAST IS BEST LEAGUE
18 Eve St.
PO Box 1203
Belize City, Belize   PH: 2 77398

National. Promotes breast-feeding, stressing the health benefits to both
mother and child. Fosters public awareness of proper prenatal, neonatal, and
maternal health care. Disseminates information.

★1115★ YOUNG WOMEN'S CHRISTIAN ASSOCIATION - BELIZE
PO Box 158
Belize City, Belize
Sonia Lenares, Gen.Sec.   PH: 2 44971

National. Promotes the development of young women in Belize. Upholds
Christian beliefs and values in its programs. Works to instill self worth and
self-esteem in young women.

Bolivia

★1116★ BOLIVIAN FOUNDATION FOR THE PROMOTION AND
    DEVELOPMENT OF THE MICRO-ENTERPRISE SECTOR
(Fundacion para la Promocion y Desarrollo de la Micro°empresa)
Calle Buenos Aires, No. 36
Casilla de Correo 1904   PH: 33 60136
Santa Cruz, Bolivia   33 60137
Francisco Otero, Dir.   FX: 33 26379

Founded: 1985. **Languages:** Spanish. **National**. Provides small businesses
and entrepreneurs in Bolivia, mainly women, with affordable credit and basic
business skills. Eighty percent of loan recipients are women. Works in the
following sectors: appropriate technology; women's development; employment; micro-economies. Offers expertise and training in administration,
management, and merchandising.

★1117★ CARITAS BOLIVIANA - INSTITUCION DE PROMOCION,
    ACCION SOCIAL Y ASISTENCIA
Calle Ingavi, esq. Pichincha 780, casilla
    475
La Paz, Bolivia
Lilia Rojas, Contact   PH: 2 342402

Languages: Spanish. **National**. Encourages and promotes women and
women's organizations. Organizes community development projects for
women. Coordinates a national food donation program for women.

★1118★ CASA DE LA MUJER - BOLIVIA
Calle Ingavi, casilla 672
Santa Cruz, Bolivia
Alcira Penafiel, Contact

Founded: 1990. **Languages:** Spanish. **National**. Works to increase public
awareness of women's concerns and to increase public participation in
activities designed to assist women. Conducts lectures and conferences on
women's issues. Provides opportunities for interaction among women
interested in participating in community and social development programs.

★1119★ CENTRO DE CAPACITACION E INVESTIGACION DE LA
    MUJER CAMPESINA TARIJENA (CCIMCAT)
Calle Suipacha 974, Casilla 164
Tarija, Bolivia   PH: 66 25658

Founded: 1987. **Languages:** Spanish. **National**. Seeks to increase rural
women's awareness of their social and economic status; enhance their self-
esteem; improve their participation in development. Conducts skills training in
craft work for income generation. Organizes productive agricultural and
cattle raising projects. Investigates women's issues. Disseminates information.

★1120★ CENTRO COMUNAL VILLA EL CARMEN
Calle Canonigo Ayllon 1271
Casilla 4235
La Paz, Bolivia
Maria Amparo Carvajal, Contact   PH: 2 343901

Languages: Spanish. **National**. Promotes and defends women and women's
rights. Works to improve women's social and legal status. Provides legal
assistance to women. Encourages women to participate in the struggle for
equality.

★1121★ CENTRO DE ESTUDIOS Y TRABAJOS DE LA MUJER
    (CETM)
Calle Junin 246
Cochabamba, Bolivia
Maria Lourdes Zabala Canedo, Contact   PH: 42 22719

Founded: 1987. **Members:** 4. **Staff:** 7. **Budget:** US$30,000. **Languages:**
Spanish. **National**. Promotes the study of women and women's issues.
Supports women in their struggle for equality. Provides opportunities for
social and intellectual interaction among women. Offers technical training
workshops for rural women and sensitization workshops in local schools.
Investigates women's concerns, such as domestic violence and homelessness. **Libraries:** Type: reference. Holdings: 0.

Publications: *Nosotras y Lawray*, monthly. Newsletter. Women's issues.
Circulation: 4,000. **Advertising:** not accepted.

★1122★ CENTRO DE INFORMACION Y DESARROLLO DE LA MUJER
    (CIDEM)
Sacilla 14036
Calle Aspiazu 736
La Paz, Bolivia
Sonia Virreira, Contact

Languages: French, Spanish. **National**. Works to improve the status of
women in Bolivia. Organizes and coordinates informational and educational
programs designed to assist women in development. Researches drug
trafficking and its effects on women.

★1123★ CENTRO INTEGRAL DE LA MUJER
Tarija
Instituto Cochabambine de Apoyo Social
Casilla No. 2196
Cochabamba, Bolivia

Languages: Spanish. **National**. Provides information on the objectives of the women's movement. Strives to promote awareness of and participation in women's issues.

★1124★ CONFEDERACION DE INSTITUCIONES FEMENINAS (CONIF)
Edificio El Condor, Oficina 907
Casilla 4471
La Paz, Bolivia
Lucinda Rossel, Contact   PH: 2 343426

Founded: 1958. **Members:** 13. **Languages:** Spanish. **National.** Women's organizations. Promotes and supports the interests of Bolivian women. Encourages women to become politically and socially active. Conducts educational and training programs for women. Maintains and fosters interaction among women's groups nationally and internationally.

★1125★ CONFEDERACION NACIONAL DE CLUBES DE MADRES DE BOLIVIA
Avenida Busch 1234
La Paz, Bolivia
Gladys Mayorga de Cox, Contact

Founded: 1980. **Languages:** Spanish. **National.** Bolivian mothers and women's groups working to improve women's standard of living. Coordinates a national food distribution campaign. Conducts social and productive projects designed to assist women in development. Offers training and educational programs in job skills and women's health issues. Conducts programs to improve sanitation, consumer awareness, and social organization.

★1126★ CONSEJO NACIONAL DE MUJERES DE BOLIVIA
PO Box 4579
La Paz, Bolivia
Elsa Paredes de Salazar, President   PH: 2 785022

Languages: Spanish. **National.** Umbrella organization for women's groups in Bolivia. Promotes and supports women and women's interests. Conducts and coordinates activities. Disseminates information to increase public awareness of women's concerns.

★1127★ FEDERACION DEMOCRATICA DE MUJERES DE BOLIVIA
Ed. Satenia, 40 piso
La Paz, Bolivia
Ana Quitoga Morales, Contact

Languages: Spanish. **National.** Women's political organization. Promotes the participation of women in Bolivian politics and government. Works for human rights, equality, and peace.

★1128★ FEDERACION NACIONAL DE MUJERES CAMPESINAS DE BOLIVIA
Casilla 22108
La Paz, Bolivia
Camila Choqueticilla, Exec. Secty.

Languages: Spanish. **National.** Works to improve the economic and working status of rural Bolivian women. Supports and promotes women's employment concerns. Investigates women's issues. Disseminates information.

★1129★ FEDERATION OF METHODIST WOMEN IN BOLIVIA (FMWB)
(FEFEME Federacion Feminina Metodista)
Evangelical Methodist Church of Bolivia
Casilla 356
La Paz, Bolivia
Eugenia Carita de Mamani, Coordinator   PH: 2 352732

Members: 630. **Staff:** 1. **Budget:** $b 5,000. **Regional Groups:** 10. **Local Groups:** 63. **Languages:** Spanish. **National.** Furthers the development of the Methodist religion in Bolivia. Conducts Bible study meetings and workshops on health and handicrafts.

Conventions/Meetings: annual meeting.

★1130★ FUNDACION SAN GABRIEL
Avenida Tito Yupanqui 1205
Casilla 4093
La Paz, Bolivia
Maritza Jimenez, Contact   PH: 2 332276

Languages: Spanish. **National.** Works to improve the status of women. Seeks to: increase public awareness of women's issues and concerns; incorporate women in political, labor, and cultural areas; promote and implement a national women's movement. Maintains women's centers, providing general educational courses, technical training, credit assistance for small businesses, aid for women's political causes, and health services for mothers and children.

★1131★ GROGORIO APAZA - CENTRO DE PROMOCION SOCIAL DE LA MUJER
Calle Eulert 115
Casilla 12571
La Paz, Bolivia
Carmen Beatriz Ruiz, Contact   PH: 2 389351

Languages: Spanish. **National.** Works to improve the standard of living of Bolivian women. Seeks to strengthen women's participation in development activities through organization of women, promotion of women leaders, and distribution of labor among women. Investigates women's issues; documents materials on women's concerns; disseminates information.

★1132★ MEDICAL WOMEN'S INTERNATIONAL ASSOCIATION - BOLIVIA (MWIA-B)
Casilla 10302
Miraflores
La Paz, Bolivia
Dr. Amparo Irihuela Nicolau, Contact

Languages: Spanish. **National.** Bolivia branch of the Medical Women's International Association (see separate entry). Women physicians. Provides a forum for discussion of women's health care issues. Encourages women to enter the field of medicine. Works to overcome discrimination against female physicians. Sponsors research and educational programs.

★1133★ OFICINA JURIDICA PARA LA MUJER
Calle Jordan 388
Casilla 2287
Cochabamba, Bolivia
Julieta Montano, Director   PH: 42 28928

National. Works towards developing legislation which protects and guarantees women's rights. Provides advocacy and legal counseling services.

★1134★ PROMOCION DE LA MUJER PASTORAL SOCIAL (PROMUTAR)
Calle Hugo Lopez Holz 0-03998
Casilla 1247
Tarija, Bolivia
Elbina Mendoza, Contact   PH: 6 25211

Languages: Spanish. **National.** Promotes and supports women's interests. Organizes and trains women to provide social and health services to small communities.

★1135★ WOMEN'S DEVELOPMENT AND INFORMATION CENTER
(WDIC)
Aspiazu 736
Casilla Postal 14036
La Paz, Bolivia   PH: 2 374961
Maria Isabel Caero, Dir.   FX: 2 392111

Founded: 1984. **Members:** 18. **Staff:** 17. **Languages:** Spanish. **National.**
Provides assistance and support to women in impoverished urban areas of
Bolivia. Develops cultural and educational activities designed to improve the
role of women in Bolivian society. Offers health, legal, and job placement
services; conducts research; maintains documentation center. **Libraries:**
Type: reference. Holdings: 1,500; archival material, books. **Computer
Services:** Data base. **Divisions:** Documentation; Economic Participation;
Health; Legal.

Publications: *Boletin Centro Document* (in Spanish), 3/year. Bulletin. ●
Cartillas de Educacion (in Spanish), periodic. Newsletter. ● *Guia Util* (in
Spanish), periodic. Directory. Women's organizations. ● *Informe de Activi-
dades* (in Spanish), annual. Directory.

Conventions/Meetings: annual meeting.

★1136★ YOUNG WOMEN'S CHRISTIAN ASSOCIATION - BOLIVIA
(Asociacion Cristiana Femenina National - Bolivia)
Casilla Postal 13676
La Paz, Bolivia
Isabel Prado Palma, Gen.Sec.

National. Promotes the development of young women in Bolivia. Upholds
Christian beliefs and values. Works to instill self worth and self-esteem in
young women.

**★1137★ YOUNG WOMEN'S CHRISTIAN ASSOCIATION - LATIN
AMERICA REGION**
(Asociaciones Cristianas Femeninas de America Latina)
PO Box 5262
Santa Cruz, Bolivia   PH: 3 324011
Alicia Tejada de Torrico, Contact   FX: 3 351336

Multinational. Latin American regional branch of the international Christian
organization. Promotes the development of young women throughout Latin
America. Upholds Christian beliefs and values in its programs. Works to instill
self worth and self-esteem in young women.

Brazil

★1138★ ACAO DEMOCRATICA FEMININA GAUCHA (ADFG)
Rua Miguel Tostes 694
90420 Porto Alegre, Rio Grande do Sul,
  Brazil
Magda Renner, Contact   PH: 512 328884

Languages: Spanish, Portuguese. **National.** Women's group active in
environmental concerns, conservation, and development.

★1139★ BLACK WOMEN'S HOUSE OF CULTURE
(Casa de Cultura da Mulher Negra)
Av. Cons. Nebias 651
11050 Santos, SP, Brazil   PH: 132 349976
Alzira Rufino, Director   FX: 132 349976

Founded: 1986. **Members:** 22. **Staff:** 5. **Budget:** US$30,000. **Languages:**
English, French, Portuguese, Spanish. **National.** Black women in support of
women's human rights. Works to eliminate racial and sexual discrimination.
Seeks to empower Black women and to increase their political and social
status. Strives to increase public awareness of Black women's concerns.
Provides legal and psychological counseling. Offers cultural, educational, and

support programs to Black children. Dispenses food and health care to
homeless girls. Conducts research and educational programs on women's
rights. Organizes income generating projects, including a restaurant, bookstore, and crafts and clothing boutique.Maintains exhibits of: women's and
Blacks' art work. **Libraries:** Type: reference.

Publications: *I, Black Woman, Resist* (in Portuguese). Book. Poems. ●
Muriquinho Piquininho (in Portuguese). Book. ● *The Black Woman Has
History* (in Portuguese). Booklet. History of 28 Black Brazilian women. ●
Black Women in Brazil: A Historical Perspective (in English and Portuguese).
Booklet. Roles of Black women in Brazil. ● *Articulating* (in Portuguese). Book.
Collection of news articles.

Conventions/Meetings: periodic general assembly.

★1140★ CASA DE PASAGEM
Rua Paissanou 200/301
Boa Vista
Recife, Pernambuco, Brazil
Ana Maria Pachecho de Vasconcelos,
  Contact   PH: 81 2223985

Founded: 1989. **Languages:** Spanish, English. **National.** Community development organization with special interest in helping young Brazilian girls who
live on the street. Provides health care, nutrition, counseling, AIDS education,
and shelter. Seeks to raise community awareness of the problems associated with raising female children in poverty. Works to prevent such vulnerable
individuals from experiencing abuse or entering prostitution, and assists their
integration back into productive society.

★1141★ CEMINA - CENTRO DE PROJETOS DA MULHER (CEMINA)
Rua Barao do Flamengo 22/304   PH: 21 2056297
CEP 22.226   21 2857510
22220 Rio de Janeiro, RJ, Brazil   FX: 21 5563383
Thais Corral, Coord.   E-Mail: ax:REDEH

Founded: 1989. **Members:** 8. **Staff:** 3. **Languages:** English, French,
Portuguese, Spanish. **National.** A project of Rede de Defesa da Especie
Humana. Works to increase awareness of women's issues in Brazil and Latin
America. Conducts and promotes workshops, conferences, and speeches on
women's health issues, population, genetic engineering, and the environ-
ment. Researches women's issues such as contraceptive techniques and
health. Maintains a documentation center. **Libraries:** Type: reference.
Committees: Environment; Health.

Publications: *Gente* (in Portuguese and Spanish), quarterly. Bulletin. ●
Cadernos de REDEH (in Portuguese), semiannual. Magazine. ● *Terra Femina*
(in English and Portuguese), annual. Journal.

★1142★ CENTRO INFORMACAO MULHER
Leoncio Gurgel, 11-Luz
Caixa Postal 11399
CEP 054990 Sao Paulo, SP, Brazil   PH: 11 2294818

Languages: Portuguese. **National.** Promotes the study of women and
women's issues in Brazil. Seeks to increase public awareness of women's
rights in Brazil. Fosters solidarity among women.

★1143★ COLECTIVO DE ENTIDADES FEMINISTAS
Rua Bartolomeu Nunega, 49-Pinheiros
05426 Sao Paulo, SP, Brazil

Languages: English, Portuguese, French. **National.** Feminist groups in
Brazil. Works to improve economic and social status of women. Fosters
solidarity among members.

★1144★ COLECTIVO DE MULHERES NEGRAS DA BAIXASA
   SANTISTA
Av. Conselheiro Nebias 651
11050 Santos, SP, Brazil   PH: 132 349976

Languages: Portuguese. **National.** Provides a forum for discussion and fellowship among black women in Brazil. Fosters awareness of issues affecting black women.

★1145★ COMISSAO ORGANIZADORA DO VIII ENCONTRA NATIONAL
   FEMINISTA
Av. Franklin Roosevelt, 39 S/713
Caixa Edificio Postal 20021
Rio de Janeiro, RJ, Brazil   PH: 21 2205128

Languages: Portuguese. **National.** Feminst women's organizations in Brazil. Works to protect women's rights.

★1146★ CONSEJO NACIONAL DE LOS DERECHOS DE LA MUJER
   (CNDM)
Sede do Ministerio da Justica 5o
Andar, Sala 509
Esplanada do Ministerios
70064 Brasilia, DF, Brazil

National. Works to secure full public recognition of women's rights. Develops and supports legislation aimed towards guaranteeing equal rights and opportunities for women.

★1147★ CONSELHO NACIONAL DOS DIREITOS DA MULHER (CNDM)
Edificio Sede do Ministerio da Justica, 5
   Andar, Sala 509
Esplanada dos Ministerios
70064 Brasilia, DF, Brazil
Ms. Catia Maria Soares de Vasconcelos,
   President   PH: 61 2267710

Languages: Portuguese. **National.** Promotes and defends Brazilian women's rights. Works to increase public awareness of women's concerns. Investigates women's legal and political status. Disseminates information.

★1148★ CONSELHO NACIONAL DE MULHERES DO BRAZIL
Rue Baratra, Ribeiro 539, Apt. 201
720000 Copacabana, RJ, Brazil
Romy M. Madeiros de Fonseca,   PH: 21 2579043
   President   21 46773600

Languages: Portuguese. **National.** Umbrella organization for women's groups in Brazil. Promotes and supports women and women's interests. Conducts and coordinates activities. Disseminates information to increase public awareness of women's concerns.

★1149★ COORDENADORIA ESPECIAL DA MULHER
Pav. Pe. Manoel da Nobrega, sala 13-
   terreo
Parque Ibirapuera
0498 Sao Paulo, SP, Brazil

Languages: Portuguese. **National.** Promotes and supports the objectives of the women's movement. Provides a forum for discussion of women's issues.

★1150★ DEVELOPMENT ALTERNATIVES WITH WOMEN FOR A NEW
   ERA - BRAZIL (DAWN)
(MUDAR Mulheres por um Desenvolvimento Alternativo - Brazil)
Rua Paulino Fernandes 32
22270 Rio de Janeiro, RJ, Brazil   PH: 21 2461830
Neuma Aguiar, Gen.Coord.   TX: 2137842 DAWNBR

Founded: 1984. **Staff:** 3. **Regional Groups:** 6. **Multinational.** Individuals and organizations interested in women's issues. Assesses current development

debates as they relate to the women's movement. Focuses on global problems such as food, energy, and debt crises as they affect women in developing countries. Advocates alternatives to current development policies; works to influence policy making. Facilitates communication and networking among women's movements. Sponsors training programs on alternative visions of development for women. **Working Groups:** Advocacy; Communications; International Relations; Research; Training.

Publications: *DAWN Directory* (in English), annual. ● *DAWN Informs* (in English, Portuguese, and Spanish), quarterly. Newsletter. ● *Development, Crisis, and Alternative Visions*. Book.

Conventions/Meetings: biennial International congress.

★1151★ DEVELOPMENT ALTERNATIVES WITH WOMEN FOR A NEW
   ERA - LATIN AMERICA (DAWN)
c/o IUPERJ
Rua da Matriz
82 Botafogo
22260 Rio de Janeiro, RJ, Brazil
Dr. Neuma Aguiar, Contact

Languages: Portuguese. **National.** Works to reduce the negative impact of development activities on women and the environment. Conducts research, training, and advocacy programs to eliminate inequalities of gender, class, and race. Facilitates communication and networking among women's movements. Protects and defends women's reproductive rights.

★1152★ LESBIAN INFORMATION NETWORK
(Um Outro Olhar Rede de Informacao Lesbica)
Caixa Postal 51540
01495 Sao Paulo, SP, Brazil   PH: 11 2598132
Miriam Martinho, Contact   FX: 11 9620369

Founded: 1990. **Members:** 60. **Languages:** English, Spanish, Portuguese. **National.** Women between the ages of 20 and 50 years old. Strives to create a network of contacts for lesbians; minimize marginalization and isolation of lesbians; provide venues for interaction and expression of opinions, feelings, and creativity; increase public awareness of the causes and effects of discrimination against women, especially lesbians. Maintains speakers' bureau. Disseminates information. **Libraries:** Type: reference. Holdings: 2,000; books, periodicals, archival material, video recordings. Subjects: homosexuality.

Publications: *Um Outro Olhar* (in Portuguese), quarterly. Bulletin. **Circulation:** 200. **Advertising:** accepted.

Conventions/Meetings: semiannual meeting.

★1153★ MEDICAL WOMEN'S INTERNATIONAL ASSOCIATION -
   BRAZIL (MWIA-B)
Rua Sergipe 686, 8 andar
CEP 01243
Sao Paulo, SP, Brazil
Nadyr Valverde Bardato de Prates,   PH: 11 2589396
   President   FX: 11 2879437

Languages: Portuguese. **National.** Brazil branch of the Medical Women's International Association (see separate entry). Women physicians. Provides a forum for discussion of women's health care issues. Encourages women to enter the field of medicine. Works to overcome discrimination against women physicians. Sponsors research and educational programs.

★1154★ NA'AMAT PIONEIRAS (NP)
Rua Sao Martinho 48   PH: 11 675247
01202 Sao Paolo, SP, Brazil   FX: 11 668761

Languages: Portuguese. **Multinational.** Working and professional women. Works to advance the status of women by providing a variety of educational, community, and legal services. Believes that strong family relations are the foundation of a stable society. Members identify with the Zionist movement.

★1155★ SOCIEDADE CIVIL BEM ESTAR FAMILIAR NO BRASIL
(BEMFAM)
Avenida Republica do Chile 230, Andar
  17
Caixa Edificio Postal 20 031 Centro
Rio de Janeiro, RJ, Brazil   PH: 21 2102448
Olimpia V. Resende, Contact   TX: 30634

Founded: 1965. **Members:** 584. **Staff:** 396. **Budget:** Cr$240,000,000. **Local Groups:** 11. **Languages:** English, Portuguese, Spanish. **National.** Gynecologists and obstetricians dedicated to improving family planning services in Brazil. Promotes family planning as a human right, a health movement, a necessary factor in social development, and as a contributor to the well-being of the family as the basic cell of society. Seeks to eliminate the socioeconomic and cultural barriers that obstruct the access of impoverished people to family planning, and instead, works to improve it through strong political, institutional, and community leadership. Offers group study, group discussion, and home visits on family planning, health, social development, sex education, human reproduction, and the relationship between family well-being and that of the community; disseminates information on the advantages and disadvantages of various forms of contraception. Trains health agents, educators, and community leaders to provide services and give educational lectures in their own communities. Undertakes medical, psychological, behavioral, social, economic, and demographic research, as well as specialized research into the health and social problems of prostitution. Coordinates activities with other public and private institutions. Maintains documentation center. **Libraries:** Type: reference. Holdings: 10,000. Subjects: population, family planning, and related materials. **Computer Services:** Data base. **Programs:** Women's and Maternal-Infant Health. **Projects:** National Research on Maternal-Infant Health and Family Planning; Reproductive Health.

Publications: *Jornal do Rio* (in Portuguese), monthly. Journal. ● *Populacao e Desenvolvimento* (in Portuguese), bimonthly. Bulletin.

★1156★ SOS CORPO - GRUPO DE SAUDE DA MULHER
Rua do Hospicio
859/4 andar
50050 Recife, Pernambuco, Brazil   PH: 81 2213018

Languages: Portuguese. **National.** Works towards raising awareness of women's health issues. Disseminates information and provides education on women's health care and health risks.

★1157★ SOUTHERN WOMEN DEMOCRATIC REACTION (SWDR)
Rua Miguel Tostes 694   PH: 512 328884
90420 Porto Alegre, Rio Grande do Sul,   FX: 512 328884
  Brazil   TX: 512527 MKPA BR TO
Giselda Castro, V.Pres.   AD

Founded: 1985. **Members:** 393. **Budget:** US$2,000. **Languages:** English, French, German, Portuguese. **National.** Women interested in maintaining and expanding Brazilian laws ensuring public participation in the political process. Works to safeguard the social and environmental well-being of the people of Brazil. Drafts proposals and popular amendments on subjects including the rights of indigenous peoples and environmental health. Monitors the programs of and advises international agencies working in Brazil, including the International Organization of Consumers Unions, Oxfam, Food and Agriculture Organization of the United Nations, and Environment Liaison International. Conducts surveys of farmers and agricultural workers, government agricultural officials, and officers of companies producing agrotoxic chemicals and pesticides. Participates in public forums discussing environmental and social welfare matters. **Committees:** Education; Environment; Public Relations; Social Work.

Publications: *Newsletter* (in Portuguese), monthly.

Conventions/Meetings: semiannual meeting.

★1158★ YOUNG WOMEN'S CHRISTIAN ASSOCIATION - BRAZIL
(Associacao Crista Feminina do Brasil)
Caixa Postal 51568
01495-970 Sao Paulo, SP, Brazil
Edelmira Castillo Carvacho, Gen.Sec.   PH: 11 2833715

National. Promotes the development of young women in Brazil. Upholds Christian beliefs and values in its programs. Works to instill self worth and self-esteem in young women.

Chile

★1159★ ACCION FEMENINA
Av. Ricardo Cumming 59
Santiago, Chile   PH: 2 6994355

Languages: Spanish. **National.** Supports improved living conditions of Chilean women. Promotes womens rights. Organizes and coordinates activities designed to create social change.

★1160★ ASOCIACION CHILENA DE PROTECCION DE LA FAMILIA
(APROFA)
                                           PH: 2 7370478
Avenida Santa Maria 0494   2 7371909
Casilla 16504, Correo 9   FX: 2 7371384
Santiago, Chile   TX: 352340436 PBVTR CK
Dr. Carlos Justiniano, President   CBL: APROFA

Languages: Spanish. **National.** Works to improve the quality of life in Chile by promoting family planning and basic health care. Encourages public awareness of contraception and family planning. Sponsors programs in sex education, family planning, and awareness of sexually transmitted diseases, especially AIDS. Provides contraceptive services. Conducts research.

★1161★ CASA MALEN
Las Encinas 966
Lo Prado
Santiago, Chile   PH: 2 7775243

Languages: Spanish. **National.** Provides temporary housing and medical services to women in Chile and their children. Seeks to improve women's standard of living.

★1162★ CASA DE LA MUJER - CHILE
Huamachuco 2
Santiago, Chile   PH: 2 6415680

Languages: Spanish. **National.** Provides shelter and other services to needy women. Conducts community outreach programs.

★1163★ CASA DE LA MUJER SUR PROFESIONALES
Manutara 8791
Villa O'Higgins, Sector 5
La Florida
Santiago, Chile

Languages: Spanish. **National.** Promotes the needs of professional women. Provides opportunities for social and professional interaction among women. Offers educational programs on business topics.

★1164★ CASA SOFIA
Sofanor Parra 1363
J.J. Perez y Neptuno
Cerro Navia
Santiago, Chile   PH: 2 7734775

Languages: Spanish. **National**. Maintains housing and medical facilities for women in need. Provides educational and training programs designed to assist women in development.

★1165★ CENTRO DE DESARROLLO DE LA MUJER (DOMOS)
Chile Espana 485
Casilla 322-II
Nunoa
Santiago, Chile   PH: 2 2041377

Languages: Spanish. **National**. Promotes and supports women's participation in development. Seeks to improve women's standard of living. Organizes and coordinates development projects for women. Disseminates information.

★1166★ CENTRO DE ESTUDIA Y ATENCION DEL NINO Y LA
     MUJER
Enrique Foster Sur 24, Dpto. 10
Santiago, Chile

Languages: Spanish. **National**. Works to improve living and health conditions for women and children in Chile. Offers educational and training programs. Conducts research.

★1167★ CENTRO DE ESTUDIOS PARA EL DESARROLLO DE LA
     MUJER (CEDEM)
Purisima 305
Barrio Bellavista
Santiago, Chile   PH: 2 7772297
Angelica Willson, Director   FX: 2 7772297

Languages: Spanish. **National**. Seeks to improve women's educational access, and thereby improve their standard of living. Conducts workshops and educational courses on women's issues, personal development, and income generation skills. Provides technical training and organizational help. Investigates women's interests; disseminates information. **Libraries:** Type: reference. Holdings: audio recordings, video recordings. Subjects: women's issues.

★1168★ CENTRO DE PROMOCION HUMANA TIERRA NUESTRA
Ceylan 6268
Casilla 64, Correo 14
La Cisterna   PH: 2 5251481
Santiago, Chile   FX: 2 5515331

Languages: Spanish. **National**. Supports and promotes women and women's rights. Works to improve women's status and participation in development. Disseminates information.

★1169★ CIRCULO DE ESTUDIOS DE LA MUJER
Bellavista 0547
Santiago, Chile

Languages: Spanish. **National**. Fosters awareness of women's issues. Provides a forum for exchange of ideas and discussion. Conducts research.

★1170★ COMISION CHILENA DE DERECHOS HUMANOS
(Chilean Commission of Human Rights)
Huerfanos 1805   PH: 2 6987287
Santiago, Chile   FX: 2 6990841

Languages: Spanish. **National**. Promotes and investigates the human rights of women in Chile. Encourages personal development and organizational support. Offers legal advice.

★1171★ COMITE DE DEFENSA DE LOS DERECHOS DE LA MUJER
     (CODEM)
Ricardo Cumming 59
Casilla 13279, Correo 21
Santiago, Chile   PH: 2 6994355

Languages: Spanish. **National**. Defends the rights of women. Offers legal counseling and educational programs for women. Works to increase public awareness of women's legal concerns.

★1172★ COORDINADORA ORGANIZACIONES DE MUJERES MEMCH
     '83
Ricardo Cumming 59
Casilla 13751, Correo 21
Santiago, Chile   PH: 2 6994355

Languages: Spanish. **National**. Works to improve women's standard of living. Supports and promotes Chilean and international women's organizations. Coordinates and organizes women's programs and activities. Disseminates information.

★1173★ COORDINATING OFFICE OF ASSISTANCE FOR COUNTRY
     WOMEN (OCAC)
(Oficina Coordinadora de Asistencia Campesina)
Av. Providencia 175, Depto. 31   PH: 2 2740315
Santiago, Chile   FX: 2 2255946

Languages: Spanish. **National**. Promotes the development and interests of rural women in Chile. Disseminates labor advice to women. Supports small businesses and organizations involving women. Conducts training programs.

★1174★ EDUCATION PROJECT FOR DEMOCRACY (PRED)
(Proyecto Educacion para la Democracia)
                                   PH: 2 342302
Alameda 292, Depto. 42   2 2226166
Santiago, Chile   FX: 2 2225039

Languages: Spanish. **National**. Promotes educational opportunities for women in Chile. Supports women's rights. **Awards:** Periodic (monetary).

★1175★ FEMPRESS
Box 16-637
Santiago 9, Chile   PH: 2 2322557
Adriana Santa Cruz, Director   FX: 2 2325000

Founded: 1981. **Languages:** English, Spanish. **National**. Seeks to establish a network of Latin American feminists. Investigates women's issues, politics, race, and culture. Works to increase public and media awareness of women's issues and abilities. Provides forums for women to address topics of interest. Disseminates information.

Publications: *MUJER-fempress* (in Spanish), monthly. Magazine. ● *Special Dossier* (in Spanish), periodic. Bulletin. ● *Directory* (in Spanish), periodic. **Circulation:** 4,000. ● *Press Service* (in Spanish). Booklet.

★1176★ FUNDACION EMERGER
Las Violetas 2055, Depto. 51
Providencia
Santiago, Chile   PH: 2 2749665

Languages: Spanish. **National**. Promotes and supports women's participation in development. Organizes activities. Conducts informational and educational programs. Disseminates information on women's issues.

★1177★ GROUPS OF AGRARIAN INVESTIGATIONS (GIA)
(Grupo de Investigaciones Agrarias)
Ricardo Matte Perez 0342   PH: 2 2255636
Santiago, Chile   FX: 2 2235249

Languages: Spanish. **National**. Promotes the interests of rural women in

Chile. Assists women with a methodological approach. Disseminates labor advice. Encourages personal development and group support.

★1178★ INSTITUTO DE LA MUJER
Claudio Arrau 0211
Providencia
Santiago, Chile   PH: 2 2220784

Languages: Spanish. **National.** Promotes and supports women and women's organizations. Conducts educational programs on women's issues. Provides opportunities for social and intellectual interaction among women. Disseminates information.

★1179★ ISIS INTERNACIONAL - CHILE
Casilla 2067
Carreo Central
Santiago, Chile
Amparo Claro, Coord.   PH: 2 334582

Founded: 1984. **Members:** 1,800. **Languages:** English, Spanish. **Multinational.** Chilean branch of ISIS International (see separate entry). Facilitates global networking and information sharing among women. Fosters solidarity among women through the dissemination of information and materials produced by women and women's groups. Examines women's welfare issues at urban, rural, regional, and national levels. Places special emphasis on women's health issues in developing countries. Administers the Latin American and Caribbean Women's Health Network to coordinate the exchange of information between women and health organizations. **Libraries:** Type: reference. Holdings: 1,800. **Computer Services:** Data base.

Publications: *Revista* (in Spanish), quarterly. Newsletter. ● *Latin American and Caribbean Women's Health Network Journal*, bimonthly. Magazine. ● *Women's Health Journal* (in English), quarterly. ● *Violence Against Women* (in English and Spanish). Booklet. Report. ● *Mujer Ansente (Derechos Humanos en el Mundo)* (in Spanish). Booklet.

★1180★ LATIN AMERICAN ASSOCIATION FOR THE DEVELOPMENT AND INTEGRATION OF WOMEN (LAADIW)
(ALADIM Asociacion Latinoamericana para el Desarollo y la Integracion de la Mujer)
Estado 115, Oficina 703
Casilla 9540
Santiago, Chile
Felicitas Klimpel J.D., Pres.   PH: 2 332491

Founded: 1984. **Members:** 360. **Local Groups:** 7. **Languages:** Spanish. **Multinational.** Individuals interested in the defense of women's rights. Aims to: disseminate legal information related to the rights of women; advise and help protect women who have been physically or psychologically abused; work against all discrimination; improve the status of women for mental and economic independence. Works to establish a home for abused women. Produces films and radio programs. Conducts research, and fosters educational programs. Compiles statistics on women in the workforce, female delinquency, and domestic violence. Sponsors lectures and seminars. **Libraries:** Type: reference. Holdings: 200.

Publications: *Information Bulletin* (in English and Spanish), semiannual. ● *The Chilean Women: Their Cooperation in the Social Development.* Book.

Conventions/Meetings: biennial - 1994.

★1181★ LATIN-AMERICAN ASSOCIATION FOR HUMAN RIGHTS - WOMEN'S RIGHTS AREA
(ALDHU Asociacion Latinoamericana para los Derechos Humanos - Area Derechos de la Mujer)
Concha y Toro 17, Segundo Piso
Santiago, Chile   PH: 2 6716815
Maria Isabel Matamala M.D., Contact   FX: 2 6723038

Founded: 1986. **Staff:** 4. **Languages:** Spanish. **Multinational.** Promotes and

defends women's human rights. Researches women's social, cultural, sexual, reproductive, and political rights. Conducts workshops to educate women about their rights. Develops programs and policies to recommend to politicians on domestic violence; sexual and reproductive rights; and socio-political participation of women.

Publications: *Adolescencias y Maternidades* (in Spanish). Book. **Circulation:** 3,000. **Alternate Formats:** online.

Conventions/Meetings: annual conference.

★1182★ LATIN AMERICAN AND CARIBBEAN WOMEN'S HEALTH NETWORK
Casilla 2067
Correo Central   PH: 2 44150
Santiago, Chile   2 490271
Ampara Claro, Director   FX: 2 490271

Founded: 1984. **Members:** 1,700. **Languages:** Spanish, English. **Multinational.** Members include groups and organizations working directly or indirectly in fields related to women's health. Seeks to establish contacts among women and organizations active in women's health issues at the local, regional, and national levels. Promotes the sharing of information, experiences, and ideas through the development of communication networks. Coordinates common activities. Encourages informational campaigns on such subjects as reproductive rights, medicine, the environment, and other health topics of interest to women. Participates in conferences, seminars, and meetings. **Computer Services:** Data base, bibliographic information on health-related groups and organizations in Latin America, the Caribbean, and other regions.

Publications: *Revista de Salud* (in Spanish), quarterly. Magazine. ● *Women's Health Journal*, quarterly. Magazine.

★1183★ LA MORADA
Purisima 251   PH: 2 7771453
Casilla 51510, Correo Central   2 7353465
Santiago, Chile   FX: 2 7377419

Languages: Spanish. **National.** Seeks to increase public awareness of women' issues. Provides temporary housing. Conducts educational courses. Disseminates information.

★1184★ MUJERES DE CHILE (MUDECHI)
Av. Ricardo Cumming 59
Santiago, Chile   PH: 2 6994355

Languages: Spanish. **National.** Promotes and supports interests of Chilean women. Organizes activities for women. Disseminates information in order to increase public awareness of women's concerns.

★1185★ NATIONAL FEDERATION OF SYNDICATES OF WOMEN WORKERS OF A PARTICULAR HOME
(Federacion Nacional de Sindicatos de Trabajadoras de Casa Particular)
Moneda 2314
Santiago, Chile   PH: 2 6991413

Languages: Spanish. **National.** Promotes the interests and development of women workers. Provides organizational support. Encourages women workers to become involved in politics.

★1186★ NATIONAL SERVICE FOR WOMEN
(SERNAM Servicio Nacional de la Mujer)
Rosa Rodriguez 1375
Casilla 319, Correo 22   PH: 2 6973021
Santiago, Chile   FX: 2 6971082

Languages: Spanish. **National.** Promotes and support the interests of woman who are the heads of households in Chile. Offers training for personal development. Operates information centers concerning the rights of women.

★1187★ OFICINA LEGAL DE LA MUJER
Casilla 51985
Correo Central
Santiago, Chile   PH: 2 382665
Nelly Gonzalez, Director   FX: 2 395072

Makes available advocacy and counseling services to women whose rights have been violated. Participates in legal action securing recognition of women's rights.

★1188★ PARTICIPA
Almirante Simpson 014   PH: 2 2225384
Santiago, Chile   2 341564
Monica Jimenez, Contact   FX: 2 2221374

Founded: 1989. **Staff:** 21. **Languages:** English, Spanish. **National.** Works to increase women's participation in political and social activities. Promotes the democratic system in Panama. Sponsors educational programs. Researches legal and political issues.

Publications: *Documentos de Estudio* (in Spanish), 8/yr. **Advertising:** accepted.

★1189★ RED DE INFORMACION DE LOS DERECHOS DE LA MUJER
   (RIDEM)
Padre Mariano 70
Providencia
Santiago, Chile   PH: 2 2352845

Languages: Spanish. **National.** Works to improve the legal and political status of Chilean women. Investigates women's rights and human rights abuses against women; informs the public and governmental organizations of findings. Makes recommendations on legislation.

★1190★ REGIONAL CENTER OF WOMEN'S INFORMATION (CRIM)
(Centro Regional de Informatica de la Mujer)
Triana 820
Casilla 10015
Santiago, Chile   PH: 2 2742526

Languages: Spanish. **Multinational.** Promotes the study of women and women's issues in Latin America. Disseminates information on women's issues. **Libraries:** Type: reference.   **Computer Services:** Data base.

★1191★ SECRETARIA NACIONAL DE LA MUJER
Villavicencio 346
Santiago, Chile
Maria Isabel Saenz Hernadez, Secretary

Languages: Spanish. **National.** Umbrella organization for women's groups in Chile. Promotes and supports women and women's interests. Conducts and coordinates activities. Disseminates information to increase public awareness of women's concerns.

★1192★ EL TELAR
Purisima 160-A
Casilla 321, Correeo 22
Recoleta
Santiago, Chile   PH: 2 7378769

Languages: Spanish. **National.** Works to improve the employment and economic conditions of women working in the textile industry. Investigates wage and sex discrimination. Lobbies industry and government regarding women's concerns. Disseminates information.

★1193★ WOMEN'S STUDIES CENTER
(Centro de Estudios de la Mujer)
Purisima 353
Recoleta
Santiago 0547, Chile   PH: 2 7771194
Rosalba Todaro, Director   FX: 2 7351230

Founded: 1984. **Staff:** 15. **Budget:** US$300,000. **Languages:** English, French, Italian, Portuguese, Spanish. **National.** Strives to eliminate sex discrimination and to achieve gender equality. Works to increase public awareness of women's conditions, gender relations, and sexual discrimination; seeks to improve women's standard of living. Investigates women's work conditions and political participation and sex discrimination. Trains women as political and labor leaders.

Publications: *Mujer: Salud y Trabajo* (in Spanish). Book. ● *Yo Trabajo Asi.En Casa Particular* (in Spanish). Book.

Conventions/Meetings: periodic seminar.

★1194★ YOUNG WOMEN'S CHRISTIAN ASSOCIATION - CHILE
(Asociacion Cristiana Femenina de Chile)
Casilla Postal 2071
Valparaiso, Chile   PH: 32 253761
Vinka Montero, Contact   FX: 32 216341

National. Promotes the development of young women in Chile. Upholds Christian beliefs and values in its programs. Works to instill self worth and self-esteem in young women.

Colombia

★1195★ ASOCIACION PRO-BIENESTAR DE LA FAMILIA
   COLOMBIANA (PROFAMILIA)
Calle 34, Numero 14-52   PH: 1 2872100
Bogota, Colombia   FX: 1 28755 30
Miguel Trias M.D., Exec.Dir.   CBL: PROFAMILIA

Founded: 1965. **Staff:** 750. **Budget:** US$10,000,000. **Languages:** English, Spanish. **National.** Promotes and protects the right to family planning in Colombia. Seeks to improve maternal and child health by increasing the time between pregnancies and foster awareness of the possible effects of population on the socio-economic development of Colombia. Operates family planning clinics in Colombia offering legal, medical, and educational services. Has established the Population Management Training Centre for staff employed at the clinics. Provides continuing education programs for gynecologists, obstetricians, and other doctors. Conducts studies and surveys; sponsors lectures, seminars, and workshops. **Libraries:** Type: reference. Holdings: 2,000. **Computer Services:** Data base; mailing lists. **Divisions:** Planning and Research.

Publications: *Annual Report* (in English and Spanish). Journal. ● *Profamilia, Planificacion, Poblacion y Desarrollo* (in Spanish), semiannual.

Conventions/Meetings: annual general assembly - Bogota, Colombia.

★1196★ CENTRO DE ESTUDIOS E INVESTIGACIONES DE LA MUJER
Apartado Aereo 49105
Medellin, Colombia

Languages: Spanish. **National.** Fosters enhanced study and awareness of women and women's issues in Colombia. Conducts research; disseminates information.

★1197★ CENTRO DE INFORMACION Y RECURSOS PARA LA MUJER
Calle 36, No. 17-44
Bogota, Colombia   PH: 1 2872319

Languages: Spanish. **National**. Promotes the study of women and women's interests in Colombia. Aims to enhance women's status. Conducts research.

★1198★ CONSEJO NACIONAL DE MUJERES DE COLOMBIA
Calle 107A, No. 9A-47
Zona Postal 8
Bogota, Colombia   PH: 1 2145870
Ines Barrera Estevez, President   FX: 1 2119307

Founded: 1959. **Members:** 60. **Staff:** 1. **Budget:** 1,000,000 CoP. **Languages:** English, Spanish. **National**. Umbrella organization for women's groups in Colombia. Promotes and supports women and women's interests through training and educational programs. Conducts and coordinates activities. Develops legislative strategies for achieving equality for women. Conducts children's programs. Disseminates information to increase public awareness of women's concerns. Compiles statistics. **Libraries:** Type: reference. Holdings: archival material. Subjects: health, work, social security, and violence against women.

Publications: *Dona Productiva* (in Spanish), periodic. Magazine. women's health and work issues. **Circulation:** 2,000.

Conventions/Meetings: annual meeting.

★1199★ DIALOGO MUJER FOUNDATION (DMF)
Apartado Aereo 43061
Bogota, Colombia
Sara Gomez, Gen.Dir.   PH: 1 2472273

Founded: 1993. **Staff:** 15. **Budget:** US$148,000. **Languages:** Spanish. **National**. Colombian women. Promotes and supports women's participation in development. Provides educational and training programs on management and practical skills. Conducts research on young women and sexuality. Organizes and coordinates activities for members. **Libraries:** Type: reference. Holdings: archival material, books. Subjects: gender issues. **Programs:** Maternal and Infant Health.

Publications: *Dialogo Mujer* (in Spanish), semiannual. Journal. **Circulation:** 1,500.

★1200★ FUNDACION CINE MUJER
Avenida 25C, Numero 4-A-24
Oficina 202
Bogota, Colombia   PH: 1 3426184
Patricia Alvear, Contact   FX: 1 2867586

Founded: 1978. **Members:** 3. **Languages:** Spanish. **National**. Women working to promote women's development. Supports the creation of films and videos on women and women's issues. Conducts training programs for women in various areas. **Libraries:** Type: reference. Holdings: books, video recordings. Subjects: women, development, and health.

Publications: *Directory*, periodic. Films about Spanish women.

★1201★ FUNDACION MUNDO MUJER (FMM)
(Women of the World Foundation)
Calle 5 No. 3-18, Popayan
Cauca, Colombia   PH: 928 241734
Leonor Melo de Valasco, President   FX: 928 232631

Founded: 1985. **Staff:** 13. **Budget:** US$39,000. **Languages:** Spanish. **National**. Works to improve the socio-economic status of disadvantaged women and their families. Conducts training programs for women in technical and job skills, legal rights, and credit assessment. Organizes and coordinates productive development projects. Provides legal, financial, and technical assistance to women and women's groups.

★1202★ MEDICAL WOMEN'S INTERNATIONAL ASSOCIATION - COLOMBIA (MWIA-C)
Apartado Aero 89771
Bogata, Colombia
Silenia Cabanzo, President

Languages: Spanish. **National**. Columbia branch of the Medical Women's International Association (see separate entry). Women physicians. Provides a forum for discussion of women's health care issues. Encourages women to enter the field of medicine. Works to overcome discrimination against female physicians. Sponsors research and educational programs.

★1203★ RED DE EDUCACION POPURAR ENTRE MUJERES (REPEM)
Apartado Aereo 51372
Bogota, Colombia   PH: 1 867426
Amparo Parra, Gen.Coord.   FX: 1 867426

Founded: 1981. **Members:** 400. **Budget:** US$80,000. **Languages:** English, French, Spanish. **Multinational**. Non-governmental women's organizations. Seeks to eliminate sex-discrimination in education. Works to improve women's leadership and communication skills. Offers courses to educators and adult women. **Computer Services:** Mailing lists, members' addresses; data base. **Programs:** Campana Latinoamericana de Educacion No-Sexista; Leadership; Communication; Popular Economy.

Publications: *Tejiendo Nuestra Red* (in Spanish), 3/yr. Magazine. ● *Aportes para el Debate* (in Spanish), periodic. Monograph.

Conventions/Meetings: annual conference.

★1204★ SERVICIO COLOMBIANO DE COMUNICACION - SOCIAL CIRCULO DE MUJERES (SCC)
Carrera 16, 39A-78
Apartado Aereo 24910   PH: 1 2871287
Bogota, Colombia   1 2856740
Camilo Moncada, Exec. Dir.   FX: 1 2881581

Founded: 1972. **Members:** 18. **Staff:** 11. **Languages:** English, Spanish. **National**. Works to educate and prepare women for political leadership positions. Seeks to establish autonomous and self-organized groups able to work productively on local levels. Conducts workshops and educational courses on economics, politics, teaching, and productivity. **Libraries:** Type: reference. Holdings: archival material, books. **Programs:** Communication.

Publications: *Materiales de Trabajo* (in Spanish), semiannual. Newsletter. Updates organizational activities. **Circulation:** 1,000. **Advertising:** accepted.

Conventions/Meetings: biweekly workshop.

★1205★ YOUNG WOMEN'S CHRISTIAN ASSOCIATION - COLOMBIA (Asociacion Cristiana Femenina de Colombia)
          PH: 1 2127998
Calle 67, No. 6-11   CBL: EMISSARIUS
Bogota 2, Colombia   BOGOTA

National. Promotes the development of young women in Colombia. Upholds Christian beliefs and values in its programs. Works to instill self worth and self-esteem in young women.

Costa Rica

★1206★ AGENCIA CANADIENSE PARA EL DESARROLLO INTERNACIONAL - INTEGRACION DE LA MUJER EN DESARROLLO (ACDI-IMD)
Apartado Postal 10303-1000   PH: 553522
San Jose, Costa Rica   FX: 552395
Lucy Bazinet, Contact   TX: 2179 DOMCAN

Founded: 1984. **Staff:** 35. **Languages:** Spanish. **Multinational**. Women in

Canada and women of Canadian descent working in Costa Rica for the development of Costa Rican women. Aids in development of women by providing opportunities for participation in projects and programs that address their unique concerns. Seeks to understand the roles of women in developing countries. Cooperates with government organizations to alleviate wage discrepancies. Emphasizes programs designed to generate and maintain equitable wages. Conducts projects and programs with other agencies and institutions that focus on women's issues. **Projects:** Recuperacion y Ajuste Economico; Desarrollo Sostenido y Recursos Naturales; Alivio de la Pobreza.

★1207★ ALIANZA DE MUJERES COSTARRICENSES (AMC)
Calle 5, Avenida 12
Casa 363
Apartado Postal 6851-1000
San Jose, Costa Rica
Ana Hernandez, Coordinator   PH: 335769

Founded: 1952. **Staff:** 14. **Languages:** Spanish. **National**. Strives to organize women in the struggle for their rights, for children, and for peace. Provides legal advice, psychological aid, and job skill training. Teaches health-care workers how to conduct workshops and educational courses on women's health issues. Organizes and mobilizes programs to improve the standard of living. Interacts with affiliated groups. Maintains documentation center. **Projects:** Centro Popular de Asesoria Legal para la Mujer. **Programs:** Programa de Promotoras para la Salud.

Publications: *Nuestra Voz* (in Spanish), bimonthly. Bulletin. ● *AMPREC* (in Spanish), monthly. Newsletter.

★1208★ ARIAS FOUNDATION FOR PEACE AND HUMAN PROGRESS
(Fundacion Arias para la Paz y el Progresso Humano)
Toyota Pasen Colon 125 mts Norte
Avenidas 1/3 119 de la, Calle 36
Apartado Postal 8-6410
San Jose 1000, Costa Rica   PH: 552955
Maria Eugenia Penon de Cotter,   552885
    Exec.Dir.   FX: 552244

Founded: 1988. **Staff:** 14. **Budget:** US$150,000. **Languages:** Spanish. **National**. Works to improve the social and economic position of disadvantaged women and children in Costa Rica through special projects. Supports efforts to increase freedom, social justice, and democracy.

★1209★ ASOCIACION ANDAR COSTA RICA
San Pedro de Montes de Oca
San Jose, Costa Rica   PH: 242788
Vanda Melendez, Exec. Dir.   243903

Founded: 1990. **Staff:** 7. **Budget:** US$100,000. **Languages:** Spanish. **Multinational**. Works to strengthen the role of local organizations, particularly women's groups, in developmental decision making in Costa Rica, Guatemala, and Honduras. Conducts projects to better enable local groups to administer development programs instituted by international development bodies.

★1210★ ASOCIACION DEMOGRAFICA COSTARRICENSE (ADC)
La Uruca 300 metros al Norte y 100
    metros al   PH: 314211
Este de la Fabrica de Galletas Pozuelo   314361
Apartado Postal 10203   FX: 314430
San Jose, Costa Rica   TX: 3032604 ASDECO
Virginia Beckles, President   CBL: ASDECO

Languages: Spanish. **National**. Advocates responsible parenthood and family planning in Costa Rica. Seeks to reduce the number of unwanted pregnancies and abortions. Encourages public awareness of contraception and methods of family planning. Offers contraceptive services. Sponsors

programs in family planning, sex education, and awareness of sexually transmitted diseases, especially AIDS. Conducts research.

★1211★ ASOCIACION DE DESARROLLO ECONOMICO LABORAL
    FEMENINO INTEGRAL (ASODELFI)
Apartado Postal 49-1007
Centro Colon, Costa Rica   PH: 246517
Elizabeth Chaves Alfaro, Exec. Dir.   259383

Founded: 1974. **Staff:** 16. **Languages:** Spanish. **National**. Works to improve women's standard of living and economic development through proper education and training. Offers educational, social, and legal help for women. Conducts courses in small business management and vocational training programs for adolescent mothers. Provides financial and technical help. Apportions resources such as machinery and other materials. Maintains a documentation center specializing in women's issues. **Programs:** Servicio de Enlace Laboral. **Projects:** Proyecto de Asistentes Domiciliarios para Ancianos.

Publications: *ASODELFI Informa* (in Spanish), quarterly. Bulletin.

★1212★ ASOCIACION FEMENINA TRABAJO Y CULTURA (WWCA)
Apartado 7-1540
San Jose, Costa Rica   PH: 2339933
Dr. Clara Lieberman, Exec. Dir.   FX: 330461

Founded: 1967. **Members:** 15. **Staff:** 3. **Budget:** US$10,000. **Languages:** Spanish. **National**. Seeks to educate working women in Costa Rica. Conducts educational programs and disseminates information. Organizes productive projects and coordinates cultural activities. Seeks to aid in women's development.

Publications: *Protagonista La Mujer* (in Spanish), semiannual. Newspaper. **Circulation:** 3,000. **Advertising:** accepted.

★1213★ ASOCIACION DE MUJERES, TRABAJO Y CULTURA
Apartado 7-1540
San Jose, Costa Rica   PH: 570734

Languages: Spanish. **National**. Works to improve Costa Rican women's standard of living. Encourages the preservation of traditional central American arts and crafts.

★1214★ ASOCIACION NACIONAL DE GRUPOS ASOCIATIVOS
    FEMENINOS (ASONAGAF)
Apartado Postal 235-1350
San Jose, Costa Rica
Leda Marenco, Contact   PH: 266203

Founded: 1987. **Languages:** Spanish. **National**. Helps form groups of women that work in associated projects. Provides technical assistance and financial aid for productive programs. Conducts workshops on empowerment, formation of groups, and promotion of women's status. Aids women's groups.

Publications: *ASONAGAF en Accion* (in Spanish), quarterly. Bulletin.

★1215★ ASOCIACION PROGRAMA NACIONAL DE ASESORIA Y
    CAPACITACION PARA LA MUJER COOPERATIVISTA (APROMUJER)
Edificio Cooperativo
Apartado Postal 4849-1000
San Jose, Costa Rica   PH: 346943
Marta Campos Mendez, President   FX: 254903

Founded: 1987. **Staff:** 4. **Languages:** Spanish. **National**. Urges women to participate in the development of their country and communities. Helps create and improve cooperatives so that women can incorporate themselves in decision making positions. Organizes services of community responsibilities to help alleviate women's domestic work. Contributes to increasing women's levels of self-esteem. Aids transfer of technological knowledge. Offers courses in women's history and technical training for administrative positions. Provides direct access to and researches progress of other women's groups.

Publications: *APROMUJER* (in Spanish), periodic. Newspaper.

★1216★ CENTRO NACIONAL PARA EL DESARROLLO DE LA MUJER
Y LA FAMILIA (CMF)
Del ICE San Pedro 100   PH: 537841
San Jose, Costa Rica   539624
Mary Alban, Director   FX: 538823

Founded: 1974. **Staff:** 35. **Languages:** Spanish. **National.** Works to improve the standard of living of Costa Rican women. Offers training in technical and organizational skills. Provides legal assistance. Investigates women's issues and compiles statistics. Organizes and coordinates activities. Offers aid to groups that help women. **Libraries:** Type: reference.

Publications: *Mujer y Familia* (in Spanish), bimonthly. Bulletin. ● *La Gaceta* (in Spanish). Newsletter.

★1217★ CENTRO DE ORIENTACION FAMILIAR (COF)
Calle 19, Ave. 1 y 3
Apartado 6808-1000
San Jose, Costa Rica
Marina de Solano, Director   PH: 214776

Founded: 1988. **Languages:** Spanish. **National.** Works to improve the standard of living of disadvantaged women in Costa Rica. Organizes employment and income generating programs for women. Provides training in administration and production. Conducts educational courses on health, sexuality, and reproduction. Researches women's issues and disseminates information.

★1218★ CENTRO PRO-MUJER
(Asociacion Colmena)
Apartado San Pedro de Montes de Oca
San Jose, Costa Rica   PH: 539662
Sonya Mayela Rodriguez, Contact   404870

Founded: 1980. **Languages:** Spanish. **National.** Works to improve women's status and standard of living. Conducts educational programs on topics of interest to women and women's groups. Organizes and coordinates activities. Disseminates information.

★1219★ COLECTIVO PANCHA CARRASCO (CPC)
Calle 24 y 26, Avenida 3
Apartado Postal 7-3200
San Jose, Costa Rica
Liliana Quesada, Contact   PH: 215755

Founded: 1986. **Staff:** 3. **Languages:** Spanish. **National.** Promotes the participation, organization, and empowerment of women. Seeks to strengthen women's social movement for development of a better society. Supports self-management in projects that improve the standard of living. Conducts courses that stress empowerment through education. Disseminates information through publications, radio programs, and theater productions. Promotes projects to develop the local infrastructure and generate wages. Maintains a documentation center. **Projects:** Aprendiendo a ser Mujer; Fomentando la Creatividad Productiva; No violencia contra la Mujer; Autocuidado de la Salud.

Publications: *Nuestras Vidas en lucha* (in Spanish), periodic. Bulletin. ●
Infomujer (in Spanish), periodic. Bulletin.

★1220★ COMISION PARA LA DEFENSA DE LOS DERECHOS
HUMANOS EN CENTROAMERICANA - PROGRAMA LOS
DERECHOS DE LAS HUMANAS (CODEHUCA)
Barrio Escalante
Apartado 189-1002 Paseo Los   PH: 250634
  Estudiantes   245970
San Jose, Costa Rica   FX: 342935
Ana Virginia Duarte, Contact   TX: 3286

Founded: 1990. **Languages:** Spanish. **National.** Implements and coordinates a network of women's organizations working to eliminate human rights violations against women in Central America.

Publications: *Brecha* (in Spanish), monthly. Bulletin.

★1221★ COMISION INTERAMERICANA DE MUJERES (CIM)
Departamento Consular y Servicio
  Exterior
Apartado 10027-1000   PH: 237555
San Jose, Costa Rica   FX: 239328
Eida Fonseca de Munoz, Contact   TX: 2107 REECR

Founded: 1928. **Languages:** Spanish. **National.** Works to assist women in achieving equality. Supports their dual roles as mother and worker. Strives to ensure education. Solicits the Costa Rican government for aid to women and reforms in law. Acts as a consultant.

★1222★ COMISION PERMANENTE DE COOPERATIVAS DE
AUTOGESTION - PROGRAMA MUJER EN AUTOGESTION (CPCA)
Edificio Cooperativo, piso 3
Apartado 17-1009   PH: 346223
San Jose, Costa Rica   346221
Yamileth Salas, Coord.   FX: 212907

Languages: Spanish. **National.** Works to help women in self-management cooperatives. Offers training in organization, administration, and gender issues. Conducts workshops on self-management, interpersonal relations, and group organization. Organizes and coordinates group activities.

★1223★ COMITE INTERCONFEDERAL FEMENINO
Apartado Postal 6534-1000
San Jose, Costa Rica   PH: 258740
Vilma Meza, Contact   336430

Founded: 1985. **Languages:** Spanish. **National.** Encourages women to promote, assume responsibility for, and work toward the defense of their rights as workers. Examines the problems facing pregnant women and corn-mill workers. Informs women of labor and family law. Conducts middle management training. Receives and takes legal action in response to complaints. Organizes cultural and sporting activities.

★1224★ COMITE LATINAMERICANO DE DEFENSA DE LOS
DERECHOS DE LA MUJER - COSTA RICA (CLADEM)
Apartado Postal 841-2050
San Jose, Costa Rica
Lidiethe Madden, President   PH: 211635

Founded: 1988. **Staff:** 2. **Languages:** Spanish. **National.** Works to defend women's rights. Seeks to change stereotypes of women at all levels of society. Lobbies Latin American governments regarding the needs and concerns of women. Provides legal assistance regarding domestic violence, ownership of land, and worker's rights. Disseminates information via radio program, "Dona Justa," and educational brochures. Conducts seminars on self-esteem.

Publications: *Boletin Regional* (in Spanish), periodic. Bulletin. ● *CLADEM* (in Spanish), periodic. Bulletin.

★1225★ COMITE NACIONAL POR LA NO VIOLENCIA CONTRA LA
MUJER Y LA FAMILIA
Barrio Los Yoses
Apartado 5355-1000
San Jose, Costa Rica
Ana Carcedo, President   PH: 244620

Founded: 1988. **Languages:** Spanish. **National.** Assists women victims of
domestic violence. Investigates the causes and effects of violence against
women. Provides temporary shelter. Offers legal and psychological counseling and assistance. Coordinates activities and services with other women's
organizations.

★1226★ CREDIMUJER - BANCO DE LA MUJER
Barrio Los Yoses
Apartado 2553-1000
San Jose, Costa Rica   PH: 246095

Seeks to improve the economic status of Costa Rican women. Provides
credit assistance. Offers training and technical assistance for women
beginning small businesses.

★1227★ FACULTAD LATINOAMERICANA DE CIENCIAS SOCIALES -
AREA DE LA MUJER (FLACSO)
Iglesia Santa Teresita
Apartado 5429-1000   PH: 570533
San Jose, Costa Rica   FX: 215671
Miriam Abramovay, Coordinator   TX: 2846 FLACSOCR

Founded: 1989. **Staff:** 33. **Languages:** Spanish. **Multinational.** Seeks to
make public and private institutions aware of women's problems and issues.
Works to develop planned activities by and for women based on investigation
of their needs. Conducts inventories of organizations working with women
and demographic studies of women. Plans projects on reproductive health,
nutrition, rural women, and public policy. Maintains the Asociacion Andar to
train women leaders. **Projects:** Mujeres Latinoamericanas en Cifras.

Conventions/Meetings: periodic Mujer, Genero y Desarrollo workshop.

★1228★ FEMINIST CENTER FOR INFORMATION AND ACTION
(CEFEMINA)
(Centro Feminista de Informacion y Accion)
PO Box 5355   PH: 225860
San Jose 1000, Costa Rica   244620
Marta Trejos, Exec. Dir.   FX: 346875

Founded: 1981. **Members:** 400. **Staff:** 15. **Budget:** US$100,000. **Lan-
guages:** English, French, Spanish. **Multinational.** Works to: improve the
standard of living for women; eliminate obstacles to women's development;
increase public awareness of women's issues. Provides education and
training in home construction; organizes groups of women to design, plan,
and construct new communities. Instructs women in health, legal, and
economic issues. Offers support and assistance in cases of abuse. Seeks to
inform people in legal professions of problems facing women; assesses and
pursues women's legal cases. Conducts environmental reconstruction and
preservation projects. Promotes and organizes sports and other activities for
women. Monitors and investigates housing, baby food, medical supplies,
sexually transmitted diseases, and legal and governmental programs designed to help women. Coordinates efforts with women's organizations
internationally. **Libraries:** Type: reference.   Subjects: women's
health. **Telecommunication Services:** Phone referral system. **Programs:**
Healthy Living; Women and Sustainable Development in Central America.

Publications: *Hasta me da miedo decirlo* (in Spanish). Book. Poetry. **Also
Cited As:** *Until it Frightens Me to Say It.* ● *Mujer* (in Spanish), quarterly.
Magazine. Women's issues. **Circulation:** 5,000. **Advertising:** accepted. **Also
Cited As:** *Woman.*

★1229★ FEMINIST INTERNATIONAL RADIO ENDEAVOUR (FIRE)
c/o Radio for Peace International
Apartado 88   PH: 491821
Santa Ana, Costa Rica   FX: 491929

Languages: Spanish. **National.** Works to raise awareness of women's
issues through radio broadcasts. Sponsors media training programs.

★1230★ FONDO DE LAS NACIONES UNIDAS PARA EL
DESARROLLO DE LA MUJER (UNIFEM)
Apartado Postal 4540-1000   PH: 553311
San Jose, Costa Rica   FX: 553778
Maria Luisa Silva, Contact   TX: 2339

Founded: 1976. **Staff:** 4. **Languages:** Spanish. **Multinational.** Strives to
ensure the integration of women into development activities and to support
experimental projects that could benefit women. Promotes development of
rural women through workshops on gender and sponsorship of productive
projects. Conducts educational workshops in conjunction with institutions.
Helps women initiate and complete group activities. Offers information about
women's health issues and domestic violence.

★1231★ FORMACION Y PARTICIPACION DE LA MUJER EN EL
AUTODESARROLLO COMUNITARIO
Diagonal Tribunales de Justicia
Apartado 292-4050   PH: 415526
Alajuela, Costa Rica   417644
Olga Quesada, Coord.   FX: 421152

Founded: 1988. **Languages:** Spanish. **National.** Assists Christian and
indigent women in community development. Conducts workshops and
training courses on self-esteem, management, technical skills, and organization. Organizes community development programs. Offers opportunities for
interaction among women. Fosters participation of children and elderly
people in development projects. Disseminates information.

Publications: *Mujeres* (in Spanish), quarterly. Magazine.

★1232★ FUNDACION ACCION YA
San Rafael de Escazu
Apartado 1009
Centro Colon
San Jose, Costa Rica   PH: 282766
Cristina Zeledon, Exec. Dir.   FX: 289829

Founded: 1981. **Languages:** Spanish. **National.** Seeks to help women with
families and adolescent mothers. Offers social, psychological, and economic
assistance. Maintains centers for medical services and personal counseling.
Conducts training and educational courses to increase women's earning
potential. **Programs:** Atencion del Menor de la Calle. **Working Groups:** Maria
Chiquita. **Divisions:** Centro de Capacitacion y Produccion Artesenal.

★1233★ GRUPO LESBICO FEMINISTA COSTARRICENSE - LAS
ENTENDIDAS (GLFC)
Calle 15, Avenida 6
Apartamentos Blancas Umana 1
Apartado 1057
San Jose, Costa Rica   PH: 513849

Founded: 1986. **Languages:** Spanish. **National.** Women defending the
lesbian identity by fighting socio-cultural stereotypes. Seeks to provide
opportunities for lesbians to interact and communicate. Conducts support
groups for victims of incest and alcohol abuse. Organizes workshops and
recreation activities. Offers medical, legal, and psychological help. Maintains
a specialized documentation center.

Publications: *Boletina* (in Spanish), quarterly. Bulletin.

★1234★ GRUPO NEFTA - MUJER LIBRE
Avenida 14, Calle 5, Casa 355
Apartado 1307-1000   PH: 225038
San Jose, Costa Rica   584450
Carmen Hutchinson, Coordinator   FX: 331018

Founded: 1987. **Languages:** Spanish. **National.** Women working to raise consciousness of the political, social, economic, religious, and cultural situation of Afro-Costa Rican women. Seeks to change the biased history being taught in Costa Rican schools. Works with Afro-Costa Rican churches to help alleviate the suffering caused by racial alienation and oppression. Conducts workshops on women's rights, women and culture, and the mission of women. Organizes round table discussions and expositions on Afro-Costa Rican issues.

★1235★ INSTITUTO CENTROAMERICANO DE ESTUDIOS DE LA
    MUJER (ICEMU)
Calle 5, Avenida 14
Apartado 1260
San Jose, Costa Rica   PH: 251322
Dr. Yolanda Ingianna Mainieri, Exec. Dir.   FX: 251322

Founded: 1991. **Languages:** Spanish. **Multinational.** Promotes and disseminates knowledge, theory, and practices relative to women's social reality. Seeks to create and expand social conditions under which all people will work toward equality for women. Encourages new forms of interaction, study, and teaching. Studies epidemiology of diseases affecting women. Conducts research and educational programs on women and health; women and communication; feminist theory; women and the economy; and women and politics. Investigates women's lives and history.

★1236★ INSTITUTO COSTARRICENSE DE ACUEDUCTORS Y
    ALCANTARRILLADOS - OFICINA DE LA MUJER Y LA FAMILIA
    PARA EL DESARROLLO
Calle 5 avenida central y 1
Edificio La Llacuna
Apartado 5120-1000   PH: 332155
San Jose, Costa Rica   FX: 222259
Laura Chen, Contact   TX: 2724

Founded: 1990. **Languages:** Spanish. **National.** Works to educate Costa Rican women on sanitation, nutrition, health, and development. Investigates the social, legal, and employment status of women. Provides educational and training programs on legal issues, community leadership, and job skills. Coordinates activities with similar organizations. Disseminates research findings in order to increase public awareness of women's concerns.

Publications: *Mujer, Agua y Salud* (in Spanish), quarterly. Bulletin.

★1237★ INSTITUTO INTERAMERICANO DE DERECHOS HUMANOS -
    PROGRAMA MUJER Y DERECHOS HUMANOS
Barrio Los Yoses   PH: 340404
Apartado 10081-1000   340405
San Jose, Costa Rica   FX: 340955
Laura Guzman, Prog.Coord.   TX: 2233 CORTE CR

Founded: 1990. **Languages:** Spanish. **Multinational.** Works to improve the human rights conditions of women in Central America. Investigates human rights abuses; disseminates results. Promotes and supports women and women's issues. Conducts training, education, and sensitization programs for women, women's organizations, and other interested parties.

★1238★ MOVIMENTO SALVADORENO DE MUJERES (MSM)
Apartado 70-10009
San Jose, Costa Rica
Angeles Marroquin de Huezo, Contact   PH: 210435

Languages: Spanish. **National.** Promotes increased independence and improved social status for Costa Rican women. Seeks to combat sexism and traditional views of the place of women in society; works to increase the role of women in the workforce.

★1239★ MUJERES UNIDAD EN SALUD Y DESARROLLO (MUSADE)
Apartado 141-San Ramon
Alajuela, Costa Rica
Etelvina Alvarado, President   PH: 455310

Founded: 1986. **Languages:** Spanish. **National.** Supports the efforts of women seeking to improve their standard of living, health and attain full, social participation. Helps alert women to their rights and their potential for impacting the growth of gender equality. Works to eradicate violence against women. Educates men and women in order to eliminate discrimination in employment. Provides doctors, social workers, and lawyers for battered women. Conducts workshops, seminars, and courses in women's issues. **Libraries:** Type: reference.

Publications: *Dialogo Comunal* (in Spanish), quarterly. Bulletin.

★1240★ MUJERES UNIDAS DE SARAPIQUI (MUSA)
Salon Comunal de Horquetas de
    Sarapiqui
Apartado 952
Heredia, Costa Rica   PH: 590408
Ana Lorena Camacho, President   764094

Founded: 1984. **Languages:** Spanish. **National.** Works to improve the standard of living of rural women. Provides training in organization, production, and leadership skills; conducts educational courses on gender issues. Organizes community projects on bamboo home construction and natural medicine use. Conducts research; disseminates information.

★1241★ OFICINA PANAMERICANA DE LA SALUD - ORGANIZACION
    MUNDIAL DE LA SALUD - PROGRAMA REGIONAL MUJER, SALUD
    Y DESARROLLO (OPS/OMS-MSD)
Ministerio de Salud, piso 3
Apartado 3745-1000   PH: 337354
San Jose, Costa Rica   231686
Lea Guido, Coord.   FX: 338061

Languages: Spanish. **Multinational.** Promotes and supports the improvement of women's health status in Central America. Coordinates and organizes activities with like-minded organizations. Researches women's health legislation and social, political, and economic status. Conducts campaigns to increase public awareness of women's concerns. Provides assistance and education for women on health care. Encourages women to organize and participate in community development and health projects.

★1242★ ORGANIZACION DE MUJERES CARMEN LYRA (OMCAL)
Apartado Postal 6613-1000
San Jose, Costa Rica   PH: 350124
Alicia Albertazzi, President   262972

Founded: 1985. **Languages:** Spanish. **National.** Defends women and seeks to improve their social status. Organizes and executes educational projects, community development activities, and courses in women's self-esteem. Investigates women's working conditions. Promotes self-help groups and organizes rural women's groups. Provides financial, technical, and professional aid to women. **Programs:** Defensa Derechos de la Mujer Trabajadora de la Maquila. **Projects:** Hablemos; Unidades a Distancia.

Publications: *Hablemos* (in Spanish), monthly. Bulletin. ● Also publishes documents, pamphlets, and booklets on topics of interest to women.

★1243★ ORGANIZACION PANAMERICANA DE LA SALUD -
PROGRAMA MUJER, SALUD Y DESARROLLO (OPS-MSD)
Ministerio de Salud, Piso 3
Apartado 3745-1000
San Jose, Costa Rica   PH: 337354
Lea Guido, Contact   FX: 338061

Founded: 1986. **Staff:** 3. **Languages:** Spanish. **Multinational.** Advises
government and private organizations on women's health issues. Works to
change laws relating to women and health. Supports more integrated health
services for women. Researches the legal and medical situation of women.
Trains workers for the Health Ministry. Conducts workshops on self-help
medical procedures. Disseminates information about women's health issues.
Encourages formation of women's groups. **Programs:** Sistema de Informacion e Investigacion para Centroamerica (SIMUS).

★1244★ RED DE MUJERES TRABAJANDO CON MUJERES
Apartado Postal 6851-1000
San Jose, Costa Rica
FYolanda Bertozzi, Contact   PH: 552813

Founded: 1987. **Languages:** Spanish. **National.** Works to abolish patriarchal
biases and to develop communication among women's organizations. Seeks
to coordinate efforts with similar international and national groups. Promotes
cooperation and solidarity among women striving to expand their opportunities. Plans to reshape church and community organizations in an attempt to
eradicate sexism. Shares and develops research projects on women's
educational, work, social, legal, health, and spiritual needs. Helps groups
fighting for women's rights. Disseminates plans for and results of programs.
Projects: Comunicacion; Capacitacion; Relaciones Internacionales; Finanzas
y Coordinacion General.

★1245★ WOMEN'S FOUNDATION
(Fundacion Mujer)
Montes de Oca
Central San Pedro
Apartado 841
San Jose 2050, Costa Rica   PH: 531661
Patricia Rodriguez Canossa, Exec.Dir.   FX: 243903

Founded: 1947. **Staff:** 12. **Budget:** US$112,500. **Languages:** Spanish.
National. Works to increase self-sufficiency of women in Costa Rica,
particularly with regard to the planning and implementation of development
projects. Provides financial assistance to development projects of benefit to
women; offers technical support to women owning or operating small
businesses.

★1246★ WOMEN'S INTERNATIONAL LEAGUE FOR PEACE AND
FREEDOM - COSTA RICA
(LIMPAL Liga Internacional de Mujeres pro Paz y Libertad - Costa
Rica)
Apartado 1507
San Jose 1000, Costa Rica   PH: 244376
Erna Castro, Exec. Officer   FX: 686470

Founded: 1982. **Members:** 30. **Languages:** Spanish. **National.** Costa Rica
national chapter of the Women's International League for Peace and
Freedom (see separate entry). Works to abolish violence, racism, and war.
Encourages peaceful forms of settling disputes and environmental conservation. Promotes economic, social, and political justice for all people.

Publications: *Limpal*, monthly. Bulletin.

Conventions/Meetings: periodic congress.

Ecuador

★1247★ ASOCIACION PRO-BIENESTAR DE LA FAMILIA
ECUATORIANA (APROFE)
Noguchi 1516 y Letamendi   PH: 4 400386
Apartado Postal 5954   4 402991
Guayaquil, Ecuador   FX: 4 441952
Sr. Felipe Costa, President   CBL: APROFE

Languages: Spanish. **National.** Works to enhance the quality of life for
people living in Ecuador through the promotion of responsible parenthood
and family planning. Encourages public knowledge of family planning,
contraception, AIDS, and other sexually transmitted diseases. Provides
contraceptive and health care services. Sponsors educational programs.
Conducts research.

★1248★ CENTER ECUATORIANO PARA LA PROMOCION Y ACCION
DE LA MUJER (CEPAM)
Calle Los Rios 2238, Gandara
Quito, Ecuador

Languages: Spanish. **National.** Promotes educational opportunities for
women in Ecuador. Seeks to raise awareness of women's issues. Disseminates information.

★1249★ CENTRO DE ACCION DE LAS MUJERES (CAM)
Bogota 400 y Tegucigalpa
Casilla Postal 10201
Guayaquil, Ecuador   PH: 441893

Languages: Spanish. **National.** Promotes equality for women in Ecuador.
Seeks to raise awareness of women's issues.

★1250★ CENTRO ECUATORIANO PARA LA PROMOCION Y ACCION
DE LA MUJER (CEPAM)
Rios 2238 y Gandara
Apartado 182-C, Sucursal 15
Quito, Ecuador

Languages: Spanish. **National.** Promotes the study of women and women's
issues in Ecuador. Fosters solidarity and feminism among women. Collaborates with other women's organizations to enhance women's status.

★1251★ INSTITUTO ECUATORIANO DE INVESTIGACIONES Y
CAPACITACION DE LA MUJER (IECAIM)
Luis Felipe Borja 217
Quito, Ecuador
Fabiola Cuvi Ortiz, Contact   PH: 2 563232

Founded: 1986. **Members:** 16. **Staff:** 3. **Budget:** US$10,000. **Languages:**
Spanish. **National.** Works to improve women's standard of living and involve
them in development activities. Conducts training and educational programs
on topics of interest to women. Investigates women's issues and disseminates findings in order to increase public awareness of women's needs.
Libraries: Type: reference. Holdings: 1,000; archival material, books.

Publications: *Magazine* (in Spanish), annual. **Circulation:** 500. **Advertising:**
accepted. ● *Journal* (in Spanish), annual. **Circulation:** 500. **Advertising:**
accepted. ● *Revistas Informativas* (in Spanish), annual. Magazine.

★1252★ MEDICAL WOMEN'S INTERNATIONAL ASSOCIATION -
ECUADOR (MWIA-E)
PO Box 3602
Guayaquil, Ecuador
Isabel Araus de Palcios, President

Languages: Spanish. **National.** Ecuador branch of the Medical Women's
International Association (see separate entry). Women physicians. Provides a
forum for discussion of women's health care issues. Encourages women to

enter the field of medicine. Works to overcome discrimination against female physicians. Sponsors research and educational programs.

★1253★ NATIONAL COUNCIL OF JEWISH WOMEN (NCJW)
(SFIE Sociedad Feminina Israelita de Ecuador)
Casilla Postal 8779, Sucursal 7
Quito, Ecuador
Suse Tugendhat, Pres.

Members: 220. **Languages:** English, Spanish. **National.** Jewish women in Ecuador united to provide social services through voluntary action. Offers first aid and other medical supplies such as wheel chairs and oxygen tanks to individuals suffering from non-curable diseases. Provides clothes, food, and financial aid to individuals in need. Offers assistance to elementary school children.

★1254★ UNION NACIONAL DE MUJERES DEL ECUADOR
Versales 1103 y Carrion
Quito, Ecuador   PH: 2 455447

National. Umbrella organization for women's groups in Ecuador. Promotes women's interests. Coordinates activities. Disseminates information on women's issues.

★1255★ WOMEN'S NETWORK OF THE COUNCIL FOR ADULT
     EDUCATION IN LATIN AMERICA (WN-CAELA)
(REPEM-CEAAL Red de Educacion Popular entre Mujeres Afiliada al
     Consejo de Educacion de Adultos de America Latin)
Casilla 17-15-0123-C
Quito, Ecuador   PH: 2 571315
Rocio Rosero, Coordinator   FX: 2 580112

Founded: 1981. **Members:** 400. **Staff:** 5. **Budget:** US$100,000. **Languages:** Portuguese, Spanish. **Multinational.** Women's organizations and institutions. Promotes public education for women and seeks to develop a systematized educational theory and methodology for the education of women in Latin America. Coordinates members' activities; participates in research; conducts seminars, training programs, and educational courses. **Libraries:** Type:. Holdings: 3,500; books, archival material. Subjects: education in Latin America. **Computer Services:** Electronic publishing; mailing lists. **Sections:** Communication; Leadership; Popular Economy; Systemization; Training for Educators and Trainers.

Publications: *Tejiendo Nuestra Red* (in Spanish), 3/year. Magazine. **Advertising:** accepted. ● *Las Mujeres Oreando Nuevos Saberes*. Book. ● *Liderazgo y Participacions de las Mujeres en la Construccion de la Demogracia en America Latina*. Book.

Conventions/Meetings: annual.

El Salvador

★1256★ ASOCIACION DEMOGRAFICA SALVADORENA (ADS)
Avda. Olimpica y 65 Avda. Sur
Colonia Escalon   PH: 234874
Apartado Postal 1338   245705
San Salvador, El Salvador   FX: 242270
Dr. Oscar Rodriguez, President   CBL: DEMOSAL

Languages: Spanish. **National.** Promotes responsible parenthood and family planning. Encourages public knowledge of contraception, family planning, AIDS, and other sexually transmitted diseases. Promotes family planning as a basic human right. Sponsors educational programs on family planning for teens and adults. Conducts research.

★1257★ ASOCIACION DE MUJERES SALVADORENAS (ADEMUSA)
Calle San Antonio Abad 2214
San Salvador, El Salvador
Zoila Quijada, Contact   PH: 252790

Founded: 1988. **Staff:** 17. **Languages:** Spanish. **National.** Promotes the interests of women in El Salvador. Women promoting the basic principles of human rights. Sponsors programs to help the needy. Provides training for health practitioners and establishes reading groups for communities. Teaches subsistence farming and harvesting of basic grains. Works with political prisoners.

★1258★ ASOCIACION PARA LA ORGANIZACION Y EDUCACION
     EMPRESARIAL FEMENINA
Calle San Antonio Abad 2321
Colonia Centroamericana
San Salvador, El Salvador
Emma Dinora Mendez de Sanchez,   PH: 253750
     Contact   FX: 233750

Founded: 1988. **Staff:** 14. **Languages:** Spanish. **National.** Facilitates development of women through organization and through community and socio-economic participation. Provides women in rural areas with the skills to attain a better standard of living and to initiate their own small-business ideas. Helps to establish community banks and credit unions. Educates women in technical fields. Interacts with community leaders to improve wages.

★1259★ CENTRO DE ESTUDIOS DE LA MUJER "NORMA VIRGINIA
     GUIROLA DE HERRERA" (CEMUJER)
Centro de Gobierno
Apartado Postal 3159
San Salvador, El Salvador   PH: 264334
Alba Guirola, Contact   259037

Founded: 1990. **Languages:** Spanish. **National.** Works to increase public awareness of women's issues through studies and research. Generates new methodologies for organizations that assist women. Supports the establishment of community leaders. Strives to create new ways for women to enter previously unavailable job markets. Trains rural leaders, prostitutes, and the infirm. Publishes and distributes primer books, bulletins about group activities, and articles for news media.

Conventions/Meetings: periodic convention.

★1260★ CENTRO DE ORIENTACION RADIAL PARA LA MUJER
     SALVADORENA (COMARS)
1 Calle Poniente Colonia Escalon
San Salvador, El Salvador
Silvia Sanchez, Contact   PH: 782706

Founded: 1989. **Staff:** 6. **Languages:** Spanish. **National.** Promotes the participation of women in all socio-economic activities and awareness of gender politics. Improves interaction with other women's organizations. Broadcasts health, educational, and news information through a series of forums and radio programs. Provides training in health, management, and gender issues. Offers technical assistance for women working in orchards and aviaries.

★1261★ COORDINADORA NACIONAL DE LA MUJER SALVADORENA
     (CONAMUS)
Pasaje Las Palmeras 130
Urbanizacion Florida
San Salvador, El Salvador   PH: 262080
Isabel Ramirez, Contact   FX: 262080

Founded: 1986. **Staff:** 14. **Languages:** Spanish. **National.** Strives to increase women's participation in society in order to initiate changes, to unify forces and groups that can aid women, and to establish a working relationship with other groups struggling for women's rights. Implements informational campaigns on hygiene and gynecology. Offers workshops on women's issues; conducts literacy groups and other forms of cooperative education. Provides work opportunities so that women can gain experience and eventually form their own groups. Lends money to groups of organized women and allows them to manage it. Operates a clinic that offers legal, medical, psychological, and social attention to victims of domestic and sexual violence; provides shelter for women in crisis. Conducts education campaigns designed to sensitize the community to women's issues.

★1262★ FEDERACION NACIONAL DE ASOCIACIONES
    COOPERATIVAS AGROPECUARIAS (FENACOA de RL)
5 Ave. Norte y 5
Calle Poniente 340
San Salvador, El Salvador   PH: 213038
Mario Eduardo Espinoza, Contact   FX: 213038

Founded: 1984. **Staff:** 30. **Languages:** Spanish. **National.** Network of women striving for women's rural and agricultural development. Works to: promote effective participation of women in education, law, society, economics, and politics. Seeks to: help others understand the problems women face; identify and organize projects intended to aid women financially and otherwise; facilitate access to official and private organizations offering help for women. Provides technical instruction for affiliated groups, math and language literacy programs, and hands-on agricultural training.

★1263★ FUNDACION SALVADORENA PARA EL DESARROLLO DE LA
    MUJER Y EL NINO (FUNDEMUN)
Ave. Santa Monica y Calle Aurora
Edificio Carisma 4
Apartado Postal 0583
San Salvador, El Salvador   PH: 253518
Sara Ventura, Contact   FX: 269194

Founded: 1989. **Staff:** 14. **Languages:** Spanish. **National.** Seeks to: safeguard the rights of women, families, and communities; promote development based on belief in equality; achieve full access of women to the land, water, and other natural resources. Provides educational programs such as: literacy, preventive medicine, dress making, and money management. Maintains a center for research and documentation.

★1264★ INICIATIVA DE MUJERES CRISTIANAS (IMC)
Urbanizacion Venezuela
Ave. Carracas 7A
San Salvador, El Salvador
Margarita Marroquin, Contact   PH: 230062

Founded: 1990. **Languages:** Spanish. **National.** Women seeking to strengthen church, family, and society by promoting women's groups. Coordinates activities among autonomous organizations with similar goals. Plans to create an assistance center for homemakers. Conducts workshops and educational programs dealing with job training, racial issues, and role of women in the church. Promotes importance of feminism and feminist theory.

★1265★ INSTITUTO DE INVESTIGACION, CAPACITACION Y
    DESARROLLO DE LA MUJER "NORMA VIRGINIA GUIROLA DE
    HERRERA" (IMU)
27 Ave. Norte 1411
San Salvador, El Salvador   PH: 260543
Nora Garcia, Contact   FX: 260543

Founded: 1988. **Members:** 25. **Staff:** 20. **Budget:** C 360,000. **Languages:** Castilian, Spanish. **National.** Promotes the study of women and women's issues in El Salvador. Works to realize a situation in which Salvadoran women can discover their role in solving their problems through active participation. Encourages women to participate in the areas of investigation, analysis, and resolution of their political, ideological, and labor problems. Teaches women about their rights and responsibilities concerning legal

protection for single mothers and victims of domestic violence and war. Acts as advisor in creating a non-discriminatory education system and in making education more accessible. Propitiates programs developing women's abilities to conserve cultural values and traditions. Maintains a health care facility for children with medical, nutritional, and psychological help. Conducts research and training projects. **Programs:** Centro de Asistencia Legal para la Mujer Salvadorena. **Projects:** CELEDAN Proyecto de Comunicaciones.

★1266★ ORGANIZACION DE MUJERES SALVADORENAS PARA LA
    PAZ (ORMUSA)
12 Calle Poniente 1720
Colonia Flor Blanca
Apartado Postal 1294
San Salvador, El Salvador
Angelica Batres, Contact   PH: 229718

Founded: 1985. **Staff:** 8. **Languages:** Spanish. **National.** Women in El Salvador working for peace. Works to eliminate all forms of political, social, and economic discrimination against women and spread knowledge of their specific problems. Encourages complete participation of women in the fight for peace and human rights. Promotes programs that help women with health, education, living, domestic, and legal difficulties. Offers seven courses in job skills such as dress making, embroidery, cultivation of fruit gardens, etc. Studies communities to find out what needs there are and organizes women into committees to meet those needs.

Publications: *Sihuat* (in Spanish). Bulletin.

★1267★ PROGRAMA DE LAS NACIONES UNIDAS PARA EL
    DESARROLLO (PNUD)
Apartado Postal 114
San Salvador, El Salvador   PH: 234466
Walter Franco, Contact   FX: 240957

Founded: 1949. **Languages:** Spanish. **Multinational.** Works to improve the quality of life for families by involving women in development projects. Seeks to make women aware that they can overcome the problems of poverty through organization. Helps to develop productive projects through a combination of available resources and application of suitable technology. Prepares women in organization and administration duties to carry out projects themselves. Provides technical assistance and training. Investigates and documents activities of Salvadoran women. Provides technical assistance to other women-oriented organizations.

Guatemala

★1268★ AGRUPACION DE MUJERES TIERRA VIVA (AMTV)
4 Avenida, 12-07, Zona 1
Edificio Shaffer 301
Guatemala City, Guatemala   PH: 2 23089
Carmen Pellecer, Contact   FX: 2 23089

Founded: 1988. **Staff:** 2. **Languages:** Spanish. **National.** Promotes the defense of women's rights and works to eliminate inequality in areas such as poverty, hunger, disease, and lack of education. Fosters personal development and growth among members. Maintains a document center for health, law, feminist, cultural, ecological, and religious materials. Provides legal and individual counseling. Conducts workshops for pregnant women in prenatal and pediatric care. Offers use of and access to professional, communication, and natural resources. Occasionally conducts studies of target populations.

★1269★ ALIANZA CIVICA DE ASOCIACIONES FEMENINAS (ACAF)
3 Avenida A, 0-09 Zona 3
Colonia Bran
Guatemala City, Guatemala
Sofia Castillo, President & Chairman of
the Board   PH: 2 81035

Founded: 1962. **Languages:** Spanish. **National.** Promotes national civic action programs for the development of women in Guatemalan society. Works to further the democratic development of Guatemala and to reshape the educational system at all levels. Stimulates the organization and creation of new groups. Helps civic officials prepare for their duties. Disseminates public information and studies problems that can be solved locally. Major projects include workshops for women on how to make clothing and crafts. Conducts forums intended to encourage women to participate in government.

★1270★ ASOCIACION PARA EL DESARROLLO INTEGRAL DE LA MUJER Y LA FAMILIA (ADIMYF)
12 Avenida, 9-69, Zona 2
Guatemala City, Guatemala
Blanca Mendoza de Sanchez, Contact   PH: 2 522674

Founded: 1990. **Languages:** Spanish. **National.** Investigates the causes of problems affecting women while implementing programs of empowerment, access, techno-financial assistance, and other services that offer solutions. Encourages educational and social mobilization aimed at improving the standard of living. Assists groups with related goals and establishes contacts with similar national and international organizations. Provides legal access and aid as well as technical and professional assessment of problems.

★1271★ ASOCIACION GUATEMALTECA DE MUJERES UNIVERSITARIAS (AGMU)
4 Calle A 1-68, Zona 1
Guatemala City, Guatemala
Consuelo Ruiz Lecheel, Contact   PH: 2 84482

Founded: 1959. **Languages:** Spanish. **National.** Women graduates from Guatemalan universities. Participates in studies of women's problems and their causes. Strives to improve the social, economic, and legal conditions of women and children. Issues opinions in support of the public interest, and advises entities that request counsel. Sees that the government carries out international resolutions about women. Participates in studies of women's problems and their causes. Conducts seminars, workshops, and other educational gatherings.

★1272★ ASOCIACION PRO-BIENESTAR DE LA FAMILIA DE GUATEMALA (APROFAM)
                              PH: 2 514001
9a Calle 0-57, Zona 1   2 537842
Apartado Postal 1004   FX: 2 514017
Guatemala City, Guatemala   TX: 3059336 APROFA GU
Dr. Luis Carrillo, President   CBL: ASOFAMGUA

Staff: 457. **Languages:** Spanish. **National.** Educators, doctors, social workers, and others interested in improving the quality of life through the promotion of family planning. Advocates family planning as a basic human right. Conducts family development program that stresses self-sufficiency and offers help in how to improve family income and health. Works to educate the public on family planning, contraception, AIDS, and other sexually transmitted diseases. Operates a clinic for women from which it provides contraceptive and health care services such as instruction in pre- and post-natal care; tests and treatment for infertility; tests to detect cervical and uterine cancer; coloscopies; and ultrasound. Conducts research.

★1273★ CENTRO PARA LA FORMACION INTEGRAL DE LA MUJER (CEFIM)
4 Avenida 13-69, Zona 9
Guatemala City, Guatemala   PH: 2 319968
Patricia Guillermo de Chea, President   FX: 2 367719

Founded: 1989. **Staff:** 4. **Languages:** Spanish. **National.** Seeks to promote, increase awareness of, and support women in their political lives via informal, educational programs. Promotes activities that allow women introduction into the political process. Conducts a sereies of conferences on presidential candidates designed to facilitate a representative voter turnout. Works to improve the infrastructure in semi-urban and rural areas.

★1274★ CLUB ALTRUSA DE GUATEMALA
4 Calle 0-21, Zona 1
Guatemala City, Guatemala   PH: 2 21650
Maria Lopez de Vasquez, President   2 27926

Founded: 1947. **Languages:** Spanish. **National.** Prepares women of limited resources for better income generating careers. Coordinates and promotes activities among groups trying to solve the social problems of Guatemala. Encourages women in their business and professional lives. Seeks to improve the standard of professional ethics as it relates to women. Prompts women to become active in community affairs. Maintains a social club which acts as an educational center training women in such skill areas as: textiles; dress cutting and crafting; sewing; pastry and bread making; beauty.

★1275★ CONSEJO NACIONAL DE MUJERES DE GUATEMALA (CNMG)
15 Avenida 20-40, Zona 13
Guatemala City, Guatemala
Ane Marie de Sandoval, President   PH: 2 335775

Founded: 1964. **Languages:** Spanish. **National.** Seeks to join all Guatemalan women in solidarity with the goal of improving the overall well-being of the country's people. Works to free women of all obstacles preventing them total access to their legal rights. Encourages women to gain access to and utilize fully all rights presently granted to them. Offers jobskill classes in dressmaking, cooking, and manual labor. Maintains a public clinic for women and children and gives courses in child care. Supplies technical resources, financial help, and informational activities. Presents speakers and follow-up training. Cooperates in national studies and disseminates findings. **Awards:** Scholarship. Recipient: students.

★1276★ COOPERATIVA AMERICANA DE REMESAS AL EXTERIOR - MUJERES EN DESARROLLO (CARE-MED)
15 Avenida 3-66, Zona 13
Guatemala City, Guatemala   PH: 2 345625
Telma Perez, Contact   2 345627

Founded: 1959. **Staff:** 150. **Languages:** Spanish. **National.** Strives to incorporate women into the forestry and cattle industries on an equal level with men so that they may improve their incomes, learn new skills, and gain access to expanding services. Works to create the proper conditions under which women can initiate and carry out organized activities. Assists in the development of community banks from which credit may be granted to aid small-businesses and other productive enterprises. Enables women to access educational and health facilities through financial aid and counseling. Organizes local groups.

★1277★ FUNDACION PARA EL DESARROLLO DE LA MUJER
Avenida Reforma 3-48, Zona 9
Edificio Anel 107
Guatemala City, Guatemala
Maria Marta de Brolo, President   PH: 2 3664715

Founded: 1982. **Staff:** 10. **Languages:** Spanish. **National.** Strives to extend female participation in productive enterprises through credit, technical, and preparatory assistance. Helps to develop women's projects. Provides training as well as financial and technical assessment. Conducts courses in craftsmanship, cattle farming, and continuation of industrial skills. Receives and evaluates women's business proposals. Initiates necessary steps for enaction and completion of approved proposals.

★1278★ GRUPO FEMENINO PRO MEJORAMIENTO FAMILIAR
(GRUFEPROMEFAM)
11 Calle 8-4, Zona 1
Edificio Tecun 35
Guatemala City, Guatemala
Olga Rivas Arriaga, Contact   PH: 2 22801

Founded: 1986. **Languages:** Spanish. **National.** Promotes the rights of women in Guatemalan society. Promotes the need for all people to participate in solving societal problems that affect women. Urges women to become more active in overcoming their specific obstacles. Educates women about their legal rights and the defense of them. Activities include: technically oriented projects to improve work capability; collaboration with the popular media in order to promote better working conditions; and provision of child care, as well as medical and psychological treatment, for working women and their children. **Libraries:** Type:. Holdings: archival material, video recordings.

★1279★ INSTITUTO DE LA MUJER "MARIA CHINCHILLA"
11 Avenida 11-21, Zona 1
Guatemala City, Guatemala   PH: 2 27059
Dinora Gosseth Perez Valdez, Contact   FX: 2 534641

Founded: 1988. **Staff:** 2. **Languages:** Spanish. **National.** Seeks to defend and increase public awareness of women's rights through responsible methods. Works with related groups to design and enact educational activities. Conducts workshops on subjects such as women and family, women and health, and women and work. Aids in workshops and forums of other organizations. Coordinates forums and conferences on women's issues. Investigates problems specific to women.

★1280★ MEDICAL WOMEN'S INTERNATIONAL ASSOCIATION -
GUATEMALA (MWIA-G)
17 Calle 1-61, Zona 1
CP 01001
Guatemala City, Guatemala
Gina de Dios R. de Cordon, Contact

Languages: Spanish. **National.** Guatemala national branch of the Medical Women's International Association (see separate entry). Women physicians. Provides a forum for discussion of women's health care issues. Encourages women to enter the field of medicine. Works to overcome discrimination against female physicians. Sponsors research and educational programs.

★1281★ PROYECTO DE APOYO PARA LA SALUD MATERNO
INFANTIL (PAMI)
15 Calle A, Numero A 14-40, Zona 10   PH: 2 680383
01010 Guatemala City, Guatemala   2 335459
Susan Hewes de Calderon, Director   FX: 2 680383

Languages: Spanish. **National.** Seeks to improve health and nutrition for women and children. Works to improve technological, financial, and administrative resources of health institutions. Investigates and implements new methods for the improvement of health education, disease prevention, and cures. Promotes ethical practices in medicine, human rights, and the right to quality health care.

Guyana

★1282★ CARIBBEAN WOMEN'S ASSOCIATION - GUYANA (CARIWA)
284 Forshaw St.
Queenstown
Georgetown, Guyana
Olga Byrne, Contact

Languages: English. **National.** Supports women's rights in Guyana. Encourages friendly relations among women.

★1283★ GUYANA ASSOCIATION OF WOMEN LAWYERS
Lot 9 Croal St.
Stabroek   PH: 2 62671
Georgetown, Guyana   2 63892
Pearlene Roach, President   FX: 2 61819

Founded: 1987. **Members:** 40. **Budget:** 200,000 G$. **Languages:** English, Spanish. **National.** Women lawyers working to improve legal protection of women and women's rights. Strives to increase public awareness of the law. Provides assistance to women in prison. Conducts educational workshops and lectures on topics of interest to women. Researches domestic violence and ownership laws. Disseminates information through radio and television broadcasts. **Committees:** Education; Legal Reform.

Conventions/Meetings: monthly meeting.

★1284★ GUYANA RESPONSIBLE PARENTHOOD ASSOCIATION
(GRPA)
70 Quamina St.   PH: 2 53286
S. Cummingsburg   2 53278
Georgetown, Guyana   FX: 2 60061
Mrs. Sybil Wilshire, President   CBL: GUYRESPAR

Languages: English. **National.** Promotes family planning as a basic human right. Works to educate the public on family planning, sex education, AIDS, and other sexually transmitted diseases. Seeks to reduce the number of unwanted pregnancies and abortions. Provides contraceptive and health care services.

★1285★ GUYANA WOMEN'S LEAGUE OF SOCIAL SERVICE
339 East St.
S. Cummingsburg
Georgetown, Guyana
Sylvia Agard, President   PH: 2 63142

Languages: English. **National.** Provides assistance and support to women. Works to improve women's economic, educational, and social status.

★1286★ RED THREAD WOMEN'S DEVELOPMENT PROJECT
294 Quamina St.   PH: 2 68179
Georgetown, Guyana   2 58504

National. Works to further the advancement of rural women, offering vocational training, personal development workshops, and health awareness programs. Disseminates information.

★1287★ YOUNG WOMEN'S CHRISTIAN ASSOCIATION - GUYANA
PO Box 12112
Georgetown, Guyana
Audrey Whyte, Gen.Sec.   PH: 2 65610

National. Promotes the development of young women in Guyana. Upholds Christian beliefs and values in its programs. Works to instill self worth and self-esteem in young women.

Honduras

★1288★ ASOCIACION HONDURENA DE PLANIFICACION DE FAMILIA
(ASHONPLAFA)
Calle Principal, entre: Colonias Alameda
  y Ruben Dario
Apartado Postal 625
Tegucigalpa, Honduras
Yolanda P. de Vargas, President

PH: 323225
     322178
FX: 325140
TX: 3111395 APLAFAM
HO
CBL: ASHONPLAFA

Languages: Spanish. **National.** Works to enhance the quality of life of people living in Honduras through the promotion of responsible parenthood and family planning. Advocates family planning as a basic human right. Seeks to reduce the number of unwanted pregnancies and abortions. Provides programs in family planning, sex education, and health.

★1289★ ASOCIACION NACIONAL DE MUJERES CAMPESINAS
(ANAMUC)
Barrio La Hoya, Avenida Juan Ramon
  Molina
Calle Salvador Corleto 1002
Tegucigalpa, Honduras
Juana Sanchez, Contact   PH: 226714

Founded: 1972. **Languages:** Spanish. **National.** Strives to organize rural women in the struggle for agricultural reform. Provides programs offering access to technical supplies, finances, and training. Conducts programs helping women with credit, organizational skills, formation of cooperatives, and community development as well as job skill training in aviary and apiary work.

★1290★ CENTRO DE DERECHOS DE MUJERES
Bo. San Rafael, Ave. Terencio
Sierra 525 B, Contg. Rest.
Pekin
Tegucigalpa, Honduras   PH: 390747
Gilda Maria Rivera Sierra, Contact   FX: 390747

Founded: 1988. **Members:** 13. **Staff:** 9. **Budget:** US$100,000. **Languages:** Spanish. **National.** Legal and other professionals working to promote and defend women's rights. Seeks to improve the social and legal status of women, and thereby eliminate threats of violence against them. Develops educational activities on legal rights for women. Conducts a training program for legal teachers on how to instruct women about their rights and how to use them. **Libraries:** Type: reference.   Subjects: law, society, and gender.

Publications: *Hoja Informativa* (in Spanish), monthly. Bulletin. **Circulation:** 1,500.

★1291★ CENTRO DE ESTUDIOS DE LA MUJER (CEM-H)
Edificio de COPEM, 2 piso
Tegucigalpa, Honduras   PH: 327153
Maria Mendez, Contact   315006

Founded: 1988. **Languages:** Spanish. **National.** Promotes the study of women and women's issues in Honduras. Strives to strengthen women's position in society and aid them in defending their rights. Improves access to women's organizations. Provides training in gender issues. Carries out campaigns on specific themes in defense of women. Researches and disseminates information aboutviolence against women. Conducts campaigns to defend the rights of women.

Publications: *Bulletin* (in Spanish), periodic.

★1292★ COMITE HONDURENO DE MUJERES POR LA PAZ -
''VISITACION PADILLA''
Barrio Abajo 1338
Tegucigalpa, Honduras
Alba de Mejia, Contact   PH: 383704

Founded: 1984. **Staff:** 3. **Languages:** Spanish. **National.** Works toward peace, justice, and safety for women. Investigates women's lives and histories. Conducts programs of political empowerment. Provides technical and job skills training. Offers a shelter for battered women that provides medical, psychological, and legal aid. Disseminates information about women's issues.

★1293★ COMITE LATINOAMERICANO PARA LA DEFENSA DE LOS
DERECHOS DE LAS MUJERES DE HONDURAS (CLADEM-H)
Barrio San Rafael, 1 Calle 1416
Tegucigalpa, Honduras   PH: 220674
Gilda Rivera, Contact   FX: 317073

Founded: 1989. **Staff:** 3. **Languages:** Spanish. **National.** Works to: re-evaluate women's role in order to support the promotion and defense of their legal and social rights; prompt women's groups to implement educational programs; eradicate all types of violence against women. Investigates legal processes relavent to women, such as divorce and custody procedings. Disseminates information through mass media. Celebrates el Dia de la Mujer and el Dia de la Madre.

★1294★ CONSEJO PARA EL DESARROLLO INTEGRAL DE LA
MUJER CAMPESINA (CODIMCA)
Barrio La Rayuela
Ave. Paz 10
Apartado Postal 1884
Tegucigalpa, Honduras   PH: 222664
Rosa Dilia Rivera, Contact   FX: 222664

Founded: 1988. **Staff:** 8. **Languages:** Spanish. **National.** Promotes the development of rural women. Provides technical, financial, and professional help and training. Enacts programs in health and finance education. Aids in formation of worker's guilds. Conducts information and communication activities. **Programs:** Salud y Medicina Natural; Alfabetizacion de Adultos.

★1295★ COORDINADORA PARA EL DESARROLLO DE LA MUJER
HONDURENA (CODEMUH)
Apartado Postal 2615
Tegucigalpa, Honduras
Zoila Madrid, Contact

Founded: 1989. **Languages:** Spanish. **National.** Women seeking to organize women in the struggle for equality and equal wages. Supplies manuals for, and conducts courses in: health; natural medicine; alternative food sources; and women, marginality, and oppression. Seeks help from women's organizations.

★1296★ FEDERACION DE ASOCIACIONES FEMENINAS DE
HONDURAS (FAFH)
Ave Juan Lindo
Colonia Palmira
Tegucigalpa, Honduras
Gabriela Gonzales de Herrera, President   PH: 323595

Founded: 1951. **Staff:** 1. **Languages:** Spanish. **National.** Strives to understand the national situation of women in order to promote total participation in all activities necessary for the improvement of women's conditions internationally. Conducts political empowerment programs and educational courses. Creates legal instruments that aid women. Organizes social and educational activities aimed at redefining women's social image. Encourages spreading of women's rights and responsibilities. **Projects:** Corte y Confeccion; Mejoramiento de la Vivienda.

★1297★ FEDERACION HONDURENA DE MUJERES CAMPESINAS
(FEHMUC)
Barrio El Manchen
Tegucigalpa, Honduras
Maria Concepcion Betanco, Contact   PH: 370613

Founded: 1969. **Languages:** Spanish. **National**. Seeks to integrate women in the process of developing their country through organizations that value their needs. Fights for women's right to contribute in community plans and decisions. Provides needed technical and organizational education and training. Helps to form health care and first aid stations. Conducts community projects in adult literacy, child care, legal rights, and harvesting and animal rearing.

★1298★ ORGANIZACION DE DESARROLLO EMPRESARIAL
FEMENINO (ODEF)
Apartado Postal 357
San Pedro Sula, Honduras   PH: 523571
Francisca de Escoto, Exec. Dir.   FX: 528349

Founded: 1984. **Languages:** Spanish. **National**. Works to improve women's socio-economic condition and to increase their earning opportunities. Provides technical and financial help. Seeks to educate women in areas such as politics and the solution of economic problems. **Programs:** Mujeres de Negocios; Bancos Comunales; Microempresa; Estufas Solares; Mejoramiento de la Vivienda Rural.

★1299★ PROGRAMA MUJER, SALUD, Y DESARROLLO -
ORGANIZACION PANAMERICANA DE LA SALUD (MSD-OPS)
Ministerio de Salud Publica, 2 Piso
Apartado 728
Tegucigalpa, Honduras   PH: 380358
Maribel Lozano, Contact   FX: 380598

Founded: 1983. **Staff:** 1. **Languages:** Spanish. **National**. Works to design policies and programs that address the problems of Honduran women. Researches socio-legal and gender issues. Stimulates and promotes education on the effects of discrimination and inequality on women's health. Facilitates, and urges women to participate in, activities intended to bring about change. Trains health-care workers on women's needs; supplies technical and professional training. Disseminates information.

★1300★ UNIDAD DE SERVICIOS PARA FOMENTAR LA
PARTICIPACION DE LA MUJER HONDURENA (UNISA)
Subida a la Leona 1414, 2 Piso
Apartado Postal 1003
Tegucigalpa, Honduras
Melba Zuniga, Contact

Founded: 1985. **Staff:** 6. **Languages:** Spanish. **National**. Works to involve women's in community development programs in Honduras. Supplies technical support as well as legal, financial, and business expertise. Maintains child health-care centers. **Programs:** Banco Comunal; Centros de Produccion; Pequena Industria.

★1301★ UNO MAS UNO CONSULTORES
Barrio San Rafael, 1 Calle
Casa 1514
Tegucigalpa, Honduras   PH: 324093
Elsa Lily Caballero, Contact   323189

Founded: 1990. **Languages:** Spanish. **National**. Aids organizations and institutions that work with women in areas such as health and community welfare. Conducts women's nutrition workshops for health-care workers. Researches reproductive rights; investigates and assesses women's health. Conducts conferences on women's themes.

Nicaragua

★1302★ ASOCIACION PARA EL APOYO DE LA NUEVA FAMILIA EN
NICARAGUA - CENTROS IXCHEN (ANFAN)
Apartado Postal 2273
Managua, Nicaragua
Maria de Lourdes Bolanos, Contact   PH: 2 43189

Founded: 1988. **Staff:** 70. **Languages:** Spanish. **National**. Supplies legal access, training, and information to women. Offers clinical health services such as pap smears, treatment for sexually transmitted diseases, prenatal care, and family planning. Conducts talks and workshops on sexuality and birth control methods. Provides legal help in rape, abuse, and divorce cases. Disseminates information.

★1303★ ASOCIACION NICARAGUENSE PRO DEFENSA DE LA
MUJER (ASONICMU)
Managua, Nicaragua
Silvia Carrasco, Contact   PH: 2 660169

Founded: 1990. **Languages:** Spanish. **National**. Promotes the interests and rights of women in Nicaragua. Works to provide women with needed services that will enable them to withstand and overcome social stereotypes. Maintains women's care facilities providing preventive medicine, pap smear testing, education about breast feeding, and other basic gynecological aid. Offers psychological counseling for women, adolescents, and families. Conducts training courses in sewing, beauty, nutrition, and women's issues.

★1304★ ASOCIACION PRO-BIENESTAR DE LA FAMILIA
NICARAGUENSE (PROFAMILIA)
Apartado Postal 4220   PH: 2 780841
Managua, Nicaragua   2 785629
Guillermo Arostegui, President   FX: 2 70802

Languages: Spanish. **National**. Encourages family planning activities in Nicaragua and promotes family planning as a basic human right. Sponsors educational programs in family planning, contraception, and sexually transmitted diseases, especially AIDS. Works to reduce the number of unwanted pregnancies and abortions. Provides contraceptive and health care services.

★1305★ ASOCIACION DE TRABAJADORES DEL CAMPO -
SECRETARIA DE LA MUJER (ATC)
Busto Jose Marti, Piso 3
Managua, Nicaragua   PH: 2 23221
Alba Palacios Benavides, Contact   FX: 2 23221

Founded: 1979. **Languages:** Spanish. **National**. Organizes and encourages women to participate in union activities. Seeks to realize a political labor ideology that will help develop fuller consciousness of the female worker's socio-economic situation. Conducts training and educational programs in sex education, law, and collective bargaining. Maintains mobile health clinics for women that provide basic gynecological care. Offers financial assistance and health services for rural infants. Works with labor groups to develop new work methods. Aids projects that work to solve women's problems.

★1306★ ASSOCIATION OF NICARAGUAN WOMEN LUISA AMANDA
ESPINOZA (AMNLAE)
(Asociacion de Mujeres Nicaraguenses Luisa Amanda Espinoza)
Casa de la Mujer
Apartado A
Managua, Nicaragua
B. Stewart, Libn.   PH: 2 71661

Founded: 1977. **Staff:** 50. **Local Groups:** 1,000. **Languages:** English, Spanish. **National**. Individuals organized to seek solutions to the problems of discrimination and inequality facing Nicaraguan women. Represents the political, legal, and social interests of women; encourages international cooperation on women's development projects; organizes skills training programs; sponsors workshops. Operates legal aid offices, childcare centers, and maternity homes. Conducts research; maintains library and Center for Information and Publications About Women. **Divisions:** Capacitacion; Centro de Informacion; Movilizacion; Propaganda; Relaciones Internacionales.

★1307★ CENTRAL SANDINISTA DE TRABAJADORES - SECRETARIA
DE LA MUJER (CST)
Iglesia El Carmen
Managua, Nicaragua   PH: 2 24121
Sandra Ramos Lopez, Contact   2 26484

Founded: 1987. **Languages:** Spanish. **National.** Seeks to make possible the unionization of women. Works to facilitate women's participation in the struggle for their rights. Strives for the peace and economic survival of women laborers. Provides training for leaders and workers in non-traditional skills. Offers help with labor related legal problems. Conducts workshops for women on family planning, sex education, legal rights, and gender issues. **Programs:** Centro de Desarrollo Infantil.

★1308★ CENTRO DE ASESORIA Y SERVICIOS MUJER Y FAMILIA
Avenida Universitaria 598
Managua, Nicaragua   PH: 2 75088

Founded: 1990. **Staff:** 2. **Languages:** Spanish. **National.** Strives to increase awareness of women's issues. Provides guidance for children of broken homes. Offers legal, medical, and psychological help for female victims of violence. Conducts workshops and training in breast feeding, nutrition, and sex education. Aids in the organization of small businesses and productive projects. Maintains a health center providing gynecological, obstetric, and nutritional care. Researches labor law and women's social situation. Disseminates information to the public.

★1309★ CENTRO DE INVESTIGACION Y ACCION DE LA MUJER
LATINOAMERICANA (CIAM-LA)
Hospital de Especialidades
Managua, Nicaragua
Pilar Jaime, Contact   PH: 2 664981

Founded: 1988. **Staff:** 4. **Languages:** Spanish. **Multinational.** Promotes the study of women and women's issues. Works for understanding, development, participation, and emancipation of Latin American women. Seeks to reform laws regarding repatriation and female refugees. Provides legal help and informs women of their rights. Participates in forums and assemblies by advocating women's needs. Conducts research and disseminates information. **Projects:** Propuesta de un marco Juridico sobre los Derechos de las Mujeres Refugiadas y Repatriadas.

★1310★ CENTRO DE MUJER
Contiguo al cine Salinas
Managua, Nicaragua   PH: 2 43189

Languages: Spanish. **National.** Provides information on women's issues and the women's movement. Encourages women's studies.

★1311★ CENTRO MUJER JOVEN
La Plaza Espana
Managua, Nicaragua   PH: 2 666601
Haydee Castillo Flores, Contact   FX: 2 662891

Founded: 1990. **Languages:** Spanish. **National.** Strives to create productive and enjoyable activities and projects for young women. Offers workshops on sex education, health, and law from a feminist perspective. Works to involve young women in struggle for rights currently denied to women and children. Offers classes in drama, dance, and art. Screens educational films and distributes informational pamphlets. Aids community, cultural groups. Provides job listings.

★1312★ COMITE EVANGELICO PRO-AYUDA AL DESARROLLO -
PROGRAMA PASTORAL DE LA MUJER (CEPAD)
Cementerio General
Apartado 3091
Managua, Nicaragua
Isabel Rios Rivas, Coordinator   PH: 2 664236

Founded: 1974. **Staff:** 2. **Languages:** Spanish. **National.** Female evangelists working to improve society by attaining peace and equality for all. Organizes and conducts technical and agricultural projects designed to give women new employment and nutritional options. Trains church leaders in theology and psychological counseling. Provides technical, financial, and administrative assistance to regional and local projects. Maintains a support center to help families deal with economic and psychological problems.

★1313★ CONFEDERACION NICARAGUENSE DE ASOCIACIONES DE
PROFESIONALES "HEROES Y MARTIRES" - SECRETARIA DE LA
MUJER (CONAPRO-H y M)
Editorial Vanguardia
Managua, Nicaragua   PH: 2 22701
Zoila Guadamuz, Contact   2 24448

Founded: 1988. **Staff:** 5. **Languages:** Spanish. **National.** Works to organize and train professionals about the inequalities and problems that female professionals face. Strives to organize women in defense of their rights. Conducts workshops in feminist theory and gender issues. Manages informational, fundraising, and training activities. Offers training in legislation and political participation.

Conventions/Meetings: periodic Asamblea de Constitucion de la Secretaria general assembly.

★1314★ FRENTE CONTINENTAL DE MUJERES
Apartado Postal 847
Managua, Nicaragua   PH: 71095

Languages: Spanish. **National.** Works to ensure women's rights in Nicaragua.

★1315★ FUNDACION PUNTOS DE ENCUENTRO
Central Sandinista
Managua, Nicaragua   PH: 2 662643
Olga Maria Espinoza, Contact   FX: 2 662643

Founded: 1990. **Staff:** 18. **Languages:** Spanish. **National.** Works to educate people about the effects of sexual, class, and ethnic discrimination. Plans to develop a center for reflection, interaction, analysis, and debate on women's issues. Trains people to recognize sexist attitudes and practices in the educational system. Studies and issues reports on political actions important to women. Provides technical and professional assistance to organizations operating programs for women. Conducts art workshops for young people. Disseminates information on subjects such as maternal fatality and violence against women.

★1316★ INSTITUTO DE INVESTIGACIONES ITZTANI - DIRECCION DE
ESTUDIOS DE LA MUJER
Antojitos Intercontinental
Casa 1004
Managua, Nicaragua
Ada Julia Pena, Contact   PH: 2 24044

Founded: 1988. **Staff:** 14. **Languages:** Spanish. **National.** Contributes to the campaign to involve women in development projects and the struggle for rights. Works to foster an academic atmosphere more responsive to women's needs. Seeks to develop solidarity among women. Conducts research on the socio-economic situation of Managuan women, rural development projects, and the women's movement in Nicaragua. Provides technical and professional assistance to women's groups. Conducts workshops and seminars for women. Disseminates information.

★1317★ UNION NACIONAL DE AGRICULTORES Y GANADORES - SECRETARIA DE LA MUJER (UNAG)
Parque Las Palmas
Apartado 4563
Managua, Nicaragua   PH: 2 660632
Benigna Mendiola, Contact   2 664110

Founded: 1987. **Staff:** 3. **Languages:** Spanish. **National.** Works to integrate rural women in organizational and development projects. Seeks to empower women through training. Encourages women and men to initiate projects of benefit to women. Trains leaders in organizational skills. Provides legal access for women seeking property rights and productive work. **Projects:** Proyecto Cooperativa Luis Hernandez; Proyecto Cooperativa Luisa Amanda Espinoza; Proyecto Cooperativa Blanca Arauz.

Panama

★1318★ ASOCIACION DE MUJERES DE PANAMA-ESTE (ADEMUPE)
San Miguelito
Panama 5, Panama   PH: 350443

Languages: Spanish. **National.** Promotes the unity of Panamanian women in defense of their rights and in their struggle for equality. Coordinates activities for women.

★1319★ ASOCIACION NACIONAL CONTRA EL CANCER (ANCEC)
C1-40 cerca del Edificio de los Casinos
   Nacionales   PH: 254322
Panama, Panama   258404

Languages: Spanish. **National.** Works to educate Panamanian women on prevention and detect of breast cancer. Helps treat women with breast or uterine cancer. Informs women on prevention, self-testing, and importance of regular gynecological examinations. Maintains clinics offering mammograms and Pap smears.

★1320★ ASOCIACION PANAMENA PARA EL PLANEAMIENTO DE LA FAMILIA (APLAFA)
                                       PH: 362102
                                           364428
Apartado Postal 4637
Panama City 5, Panama   FX: 362979
Jorge Riba, President   CBL: APLAFA

Languages: Spanish. **National.** Works to enhance the quality of life for Panamanians through the promotion of responsible parenthood and family planning. Advocates family planning as a basic human right. Sponsors educational programs in family planning, contraception, and sexually transmitted diseases. Conducts research.

★1321★ CENTRO PARA EL DESARROLLO DE LA MUJER (CEDEM)
Apartado 6339
32 Avenida Mejico   PH: 272061
Panama 5, Panama   250579
Amelia Marquez de Perez, Exec. Dir.   FX: 256158

Founded: 1988. **Languages:** Spanish. **National.** Supports women's rights. Seeks to improve women's social, economic, and political status. Strives to increase public awareness of women's issues and problems; promotes studies of projects and policies designed to alleviate women's problems. Conducts educational programs on gender and legal rights. Organizes and coordinates income-generating work programs for women. Offers medical, nutritional, legal, and psychological assistance to women in need.

★1322★ CENTRO DE LA MUJER CONTRA EL MALTRATO
Ave. Ecuador y Justo Arosemena
Edificio ARCIA   PH: 250828
Sagundo piso 205   251515
Panama 9A, Panama   FX: 233665

Languages: Spanish. **National.** Provides assistance to female victims of domestic violence. Offers legal, psychological, and social counseling services; self help groups and group therapy; and temporary shelter. Investigates the effects and causes of violence against women and children.

★1323★ CENTRO DE LA MUJER PANAMENA
San Miguelito C1-I, #1783
Apartado Postal 7433
Panama 5, Panama   PH: 671558

Languages: Spanish. **National.** Promotes the study of women and women's issues in Panama. Seeks to improve the standard of living of Panamanian women. Strives to increase women's socio-economic status through educational and training programs on self-management and gender awareness.

★1324★ COMISION DE ESTUDIO DE LA MUJER
Universidad de Panama
Vicerectoria de Docencia e Investigacion
Apartado Postal 9256   PH: 239985
Panama 6, Panama   613245

Languages: Spanish. **National.** Promotes and supports women and women's issues. Conducts educational programs on gender issues. Organizes academic and social projects about women and women's issues. Researches themes of interest to women; disseminates information.

★1325★ COMISION NACIONAL PARA LA DEFENSA DE LOS DERECHOS DE LA MUJER
Apartado 6-3093
El Dorada, Panama

Languages: Spanish. **National.** Fosters public awareness of discrimination against and exploitation of women; supports and develops legislation and policies aimed towards achieving full public recognition of women's rights. Disseminates information.

★1326★ COORDINADORA NACIONAL DE LA MUJER (CAM)
San Miguelito (Auto-Motor)
Apartado Postal 2521
Panama 3, Panama   PH: 677313

Languages: Spanish. **National.** Works to improve the status of women in Panama. Strives to achieve women's equality and their acceptance as full members of society. Promotes and supports women and women's organizations. Encourages women to participate in development projects and to acquire skills necessary for effective contribution to women's groups and humanitarian causes. Offers training and educational programs on communication and organizational skills. Conducts research on women and women's issues.

★1327★ FEDERACION DE MUJERES CATOLICAS
C1-86 Carrasquilla
Apartado Postal 8714
Panama 5, Panama   PH: 261658

Languages: Spanish. **National.** Catholic women supporting and promoting the development of Panamanian women. Encourages women to work toward improving the standard of living in Panama.

★1328★ FEDERACION DE MUJERES METODISTAS
Calle 86
Apartado Postal 8714
Carrasquilla
Panama 5, Panama   PH: 261658

Languages: Spanish. **National.** Women members of the Methodist church in Panama. Works to improve the living conditions of Panamanian women and children. Seeks to improve women's self-worth and dignity through instruction in Christianity. Encourages women to participate in community development with the objective of ensuring a better life for future generations.

★1329★ FEDERACION NACIONAL DE MUJERES DE NEGOCIOS Y
    PROFESIONALES
Edificio UNICENTRO
Bella Vista
Apartado Postal 8778   PH: 270053
Panama 5, Panama   FX: 270053

Languages: Spanish. **National.** Business and professional women. Encourages members' participation in business and community activities. Organizes and coordinates activities designed to assist indigent and impoverished women in Panama.

★1330★ FUNDACION PARA LA PROMOCION DE LA MUJER
Ave. Justo Arosemena, calle 39, #436
Apartado Postal 8926   PH: 254187
Bella Vista   254194
Panama 5, Panama   FX: 251698

Languages: Spanish. **National.** Works to increase and improve women's status in Panama. Conducts educational and informational courses for women on legal issues, self-management, and business operation. Promotes awareness of laws and supports legislation beneficial to women.

★1331★ GRUPO NACIONAL MUJER, SALUD Y DESARROLLO
Ministerio de Salud
Ave. 5, calle 35
Apartado Postal 2048   PH: 233450
Panama 1, Panama   604167

Languages: Spanish. **National.** Works to improve the health and development conditions of women in Panama. Coordinates and evaluates women's health and development programs. Coordinates efforts with similar organizations.

★1332★ INSTITUTO DE CAPACITACION Y PROMOCION DE LA
    MUJER PANAMENA (ICAPROMUPA)
Ave. de los Martires, Edificio Esmeralda
Apartado Postal 6-5950
El Dorado   PH: 623662
Panama, Panama   682144

Languages: Spanish. **National.** Promotes and supports women in development. Implements projects designed to improve women's social, economic, and political status. Conducts research on women's issues; offers vocational training programs.

★1333★ PAN AMERICAN MEDICAL WOMEN'S ALLIANCE (PAMWA)
c/o Dr. Juana Diaz de Ruiz
Apartado Postal 6-9414
Panama, Panama
Dr. Juana Diaz de Ruiz, Contact   PH: 604518

Founded: 1947. **Members:** 1,700. **Languages:** English. **Multinational.** Women doctors in the Caribbean and North, South, and Central America. Promotes friendship among women physicians and encourages the exchange of ideas and information on improved methods of treatment and social and economic services related to women in medicine. Provides assistance to physicians in obtaining residencies in specialties. Maintains travel fund to help members attend congresses.

Publications: *Newsletter*, periodic.

Conventions/Meetings: biennial congress

★1334★ UNION NACIONAL DE MUJERES PANAMENAS (UNAMUP)
C1-37 Oeste
Edificio Pastor 3
Apartamento 5 Planta Baja
Panama, Panama

Languages: Spanish. **National.** Panamanian women working to increase women's awareness of their capacity to create social change. Seeks to incorporate women more actively in politics and developmental programs. Strives to improve women's employment and social status so that they may attain equal rights, responsibilities, and pay. Contributes to programs designed to benefit women, children, and families.

Paraguay

★1335★ CENTRO PARAGUAYO DE ESTUDIOS DE LA MUJER
    (CEPEM)
C.C. 1718, Independencia Nacional y
    Comuneros
Asuncion, Paraguay
Olga Aquino, Director   PH: 21 497926

Languages: Spanish. **National.** Seeks to increase public awareness of women's interests; conducts public educational and informational courses. Investigates women's issues and disseminates information.

★1336★ CENTRO PARAGUAYO DE ESTUDIOS DE POBLACION
    (CEPEP)
Edificio "El Dorado", 8vo. Piso   PH: 21 44842
Juan E. O'Leary y Manduvira   21 91627
Asuncion, Paraguay   FX: 21 444842
Dr. Ruben Molinas, President   CBL: CEPEP

Languages: Spanish. **National.** Encourages responsible parenthood and family planning activities in Paraguay. Promotes family planning as a basic human right. Works to reduce the number of unwanted pregnancies and abortions. Sponsors educational programs in family planning, contraception, and sexually transmitted diseases. Conducts research.

★1337★ CONSEJO NACIONAL DE MUJERES DEL PARAGUAY
    (CNMP)
Venezuela 842
Asuncion, Paraguay
Gloria Espana de Gutierrez, President   PH: 21 200508

Languages: Spanish. **National.** Works to improve the status of women. Organizes and coordinates educational, developmental, and income generation projects for women. Organizes cultural and social activities.

★1338★ GRUPO DE ESTUDIOS DE LA MUJER PARAGUAYA
    (GEMPA)
C.C. 2157
Eligio Ayala 973
Asuncion, Paraguay   PH: 21 443734
Graziella Corvalan, Coord.   FX: 21 447127

Languages: Spanish. **National.** Promotes the study of women and women's issues. Seeks to improve women's standard of living. Conducts educational programs for women. Investigates women's issues and publishes results. Organizes cultural activities for women.

★1339★ LIGA PARAGUAYA DE LOS DERECHOS DE LA MUJER
(LPDM)
Ayolas 1136 e/Igatimi y Avenida Gaspar
R. de Francia
Asuncion, Paraguay
Maria Elina Olmedo de Pereira, President   PH: 21 491953

Languages: Spanish. **National.** Supports and promotes the human rights of Paraguayan women. Organizes educational programs on women's rights. Provides training to assist women in development.

Publications: *Memoria de la Comision Ejecutiva Central* (in Spanish). Bulletin.
• *Newsletter*, periodic.

★1340★ MUJERES POR LA DEMOCRACIA (MXD)
Eligio Ayala 877
Asuncion, Paraguay
Greta Gustafson de Marcos, Gen.Sec.   PH: 21 490433

Languages: Spanish. **National.** Supports and defends women and women's human rights. Conducts training and educational courses. Works to increase public awareness of women's interests and human rights.

Publications: *La Residentia* (in Spanish).

★1341★ UNION DE MUJERES PARAGUAYAS (UMPA)
Pitiantuta 923
Asuncion, Paraguay   PH: 22539

Founded: 1982. **Members:** 567. **Languages:** Spanish. **National.** Women seeking to improve the standard of living and status of women. Participates in the fight to reevaluate and empower the working class. Conducts community training and social promotion campaigns on education, politics, and health. Encourages women to fight for human rights. Organizes agrarian programs for land rights and improved production.

Peru

★1342★ ASOCIACION PARA EL DESARROLLO E INTEGRACION DE
LA MUJER (ADIM)
Calle Sevilla 250
Higuereta-Surco
Lima, Peru   PH: 14 484355
Gabriela Perez -Albela, Exec. Dir.   FX: 14 421498

Languages: Spanish. **National.** Seeks to improve the status and participation of women in development. Conducts educational programs on technology, human rights, small business operations, and personal health care. Investigates population and women's rights issues. Disseminates information.

★1343★ ASOCIACION MUJER Y TRABAJO
Calle Miguel Iglesias 2589-A
Lima 14, Peru
Rosario Leon, Contact   PH: 14 221120

Languages: Spanish. **National.** Promotes and supports women in development. Offers employment assistance. Organizes and coordinates informational activities.

★1344★ ASOCIACION PERU MUJER
Apartado Postal 11-0206
Almiranate Guisse 2550, Lince
Lima 14, Peru   PH: 14 223655
Rosa Chavarri, Director   14 415187

Founded: 1979. **Staff:** 25. **Budget:** US$400,000. **Languages:** Spanish. **National.** Women promoting women's equal rights and opportunities. Seeks

to increase women's participation in development. Conducts community based programs on maternal and infant health; technical skills; small business management and development; consumer issues; and legal rights. Researches women's issues and disseminates results.

★1345★ AURORA VIVAR ASSOCIATION (AVA)
(AAV Asociacion Aurora Vivar)
Jr. Nazca 179, Jesus Maria
Apartado Postal 11-0422
Lima 11, Peru
Ana Maria Diaz, Coordinator   PH: 14 311183

Founded: 1985. **Members:** 5. **Languages:** English, Spanish. **National.** Promotes women's rights, especially those of laboratory and clothing industry workers. Seeks to enhance awareness of violations of women's rights and to establish equal rights for all. Offers legal advice for women and women's unions. Investigates the standards of living and the working conditions of women as well as their participation in professional organizations. Holds discussions, roundtables, and union workshops. **Programs:** Autoconciencia; Promocion y Capacitacion; Salud y Gimnasia.

Publications: *El Derecho de Sala-Cuna*. Book. • *La Lucha Tiene que Continuar*. Book. • *La Menopausa: Mitos y Realidades*. Book. • *La Secretarie de Asuntos Femeninos*. Book. • *Nostras y la Mate*. Book.

Conventions/Meetings: quarterly Day of Reflection and Action meeting. • periodic meeting.

★1346★ CENTRO DE LA MUJER PERUANA FLORA TRISTAN
(CMPFT)
    PH: 14 330694
Parque Hernan Velarde 42   14 332765
Lima 1, Peru   FX: 14 339060
Mariella Sala, Gen.Dir.   E-Mail: GEONET

Founded: 1979. **Members:** 60. **Languages:** Spanish. **National.** Individuals, organizations, and representatives of government bodies. Promotes women's rights in Peru. Follows the teachings of Flora Tristan, a pioneer of the women's rights movement in Peru. Strives to: fulfill women's needs in rural development programs; establish a permanent training program for workers in development projects; encourage the founding of regional development organizations. Investigates women's working conditions and the status of women in the areas of legislation, health, and sexuality; examines women's roles throughout history. Has established research, methodology, and project evaluation standards for project workers. Offers legal assistance. Conducts educational programs on health and reproductive rights; sponsors seminars, workshops, and radio program. Disseminates information; compiles bibliographic guides. **Libraries:** Type: reference. Holdings: 4,000. **Computer Services:** Data base.

Publications: *Chacarera*. Magazine. 3/year. • *Viva!*, quarterly. Magazine.

Conventions/Meetings: periodic meeting.

★1347★ CENTRO DE PROMOCION DE LA MUJER DEL NORTE
(CEPROMUN)
Gamarra 452, Of. 206
Apartado 1060
Trujillo, Peru
Carmen Salazar Cortegana, Contact   PH: 44 241164

Founded: 1989. **Members:** 10. **Staff:** 5. **Budget:** 10,000 It. **Languages:** Spanish. **National.** Works to organize women for self-development and improvement in their standard of living. Seeks to increase public awareness of women's status. Conducts educational, informational, and training courses for women and children on various development related topics. Encourages women to participate in community development projects. Organizes and coordinates economic, social, and cultural development activities. Offers medical assistance to women and their children. Disseminates information on the living conditions of impoverished women and children. **Libraries:** Type: reference. **Programs:** Servicio Infantil.

Publications: *Newsletter* (in Spanish), quarterly. Organizational activities. **Advertising:** accepted.

Conventions/Meetings: annual regional meeting.

★1348★ CONSEJO NACIONAL DE MUJERES DEL PERU
Calle 1-397
Corpac
San Isidro
Lima 27, Peru
Carmen Barionuevo de Pacheco,
President

National. Umbrella organization for women's groups in Peru. Promotes the interests of women. Coordinates activities; disseminates information.

★1349★ INSTITUTO PERUANO DE PATERNIDAD RESPONSABLE
(INPPARES)
Gregorio Escobedo 115
Casilla Postal 2191   PH: 14 633152
Lima 11, Peru   14 635965
Sra. Martha Triveno de Quintana,   FX: 14 635965
President   TX: 39420339 PECP

Languages: Spanish. **National.** Works to improve the quality of life for people living in Peru through the promotion of family planning and responsible parenthood. Advocates family planning as a basic human right. Sponsors programs on family planning, contraception, and sexually transmitted diseases. Conducts research.

★1350★ LA VOZ DE LA MUJER
Villa Maria del Perpetuo Socorro
Conde de la Vega Baja 809
Lima 50, Peru

Languages: Spanish. **National.** Promotes the concerns and interests of women. Monitors development of legislation concerning policies affecting women. Disseminates information to foster public awareness of discrimination against and exploitation of women.

★1351★ LATIN AMERICAN COMMITTEE FOR THE DEFENSE OF THE
RIGHTS OF THE WOMAN
(CLADEM Comite Latinoamericano para la Defensa de los Derechos de
la Mujer)
Apartado Postal 11-0470
Lima 11, Peru
Roxana Vasquez, Regional Coord.   PH: 14 615670

Founded: 1987. **Members:** 16. **Staff:** 4. **Languages:** Spanish. **National.** Individuals and organizations. Promotes and defends the rights of women in Latin America. Sponsors women's development programs. Facilitates the interchange of information on women's rights. Conducts research on violence in equal relations, rape, abortion, prostitution, sterilization, and incest.

Publications: *Boletin* (in Spanish), semiannual. Bulletin. ● *Guia Bibliographica* (in Spanish), quarterly. Book. ● *Capacitarion Legal a Mujeres* (in Spanish). Book. ● *Mujer y Derechos Humanos* (in Spanish). Book. ● *Directory*, periodic. Regional.

Conventions/Meetings: biennial regional meeting. ● periodic workshop.

★1352★ MEDICAL WOMEN'S INTERNATIONAL ASSOCIATION - PERU
c/o Herminia Guerrero de Bernuy
6 de Agosto 1260
Jesus Maria
Lima 11, Peru
Lila Ravello de Cabini, Contact

Languages: Spanish. **National.** Peru national branch of the Medical Women's International Association (see separate entry). Women physicians. Provides a forum for discussion of women's health care issues. Encourages women to enter the field of medicine. Works to overcome discrimination against female physicians. Sponsors research and educational programs.

★1353★ NA'AMAT PIONERAS GRUPO SHALOM MANE PRUTZCHI
(NPGMP)
Comandante Jimenez 415
Lima 17, Peru   PH: 14 617993

Languages: Spanish. **Multinational.** Working and professional women. Works to advance the status of women by providing a variety of educational, community, and legal services. Believes that strong family relations are the foundation of a stable society. Members identify with the Zionist movement.

★1354★ WOMEN AND SOCIETY
(Centro de Comunicacion e Investigacion Aplicado Mujer y Sociedad)
Parque Hernan Velarde 93
Lima 1, Peru
Zoila Hernandez, President   PH: 14 246627

Staff: 25. **Budget:** US$305,000. **Languages:** Spanish. **National.** Assists and promotes women's organizations. Seeks to improve women's standard of living; women's access to natural resources and political positions; public perception and awareness of women's issues. Organizes activities designed to gain social, economic, and political equality for women. Strives to develop new models of leadership better suited to women's needs. Conducts programs on: income generation; socio-cultural development; job and leadership skills; and women's health. Coordinates social and cultural events for women. Organizes and coordinates activities among women's groups. Monitors governmental and private organizations whose actions affect women.

★1355★ YOUNG WOMEN'S CHRISTIAN ASSOCIATION - PERU
(Asociacion Cristiana Femenina - Peru)
Apartado Postal 110343
Lima 11, Peru   PH: 14 326694
Carmen Gushiken, Gen.Sec.   FX: 14 300607

National. Promotes the development of young women in Peru. Upholds Christian beliefs and values in its programs. Works to instill self worth and self-esteem in young women.

Suriname

★1356★ ASA FOUNDATION FOR WOMEN
c/o Solonstraat 22   PH: 470284
Ma Retraite, Suriname   472586

National. Supports activities and programs that further the women's movement.

★1357★ NATIONAL COUNCIL OF WOMEN OF SURINAME
Rust en Vredestraat 64B
PO Box 1574
Paramaribo, Suriname
Dr. Lilian Komproe, President   PH: 471692

Founded: 1970. **Members:** 18. **Staff:** 5. **Languages:** English. **National.**

Umbrella organization for women's organizations in Suriname. Promotes women's development. Asserts views on social, political, and governmental issues affecting women. Maintains a women's bureau for documentation and the dissemination of information.

★1358★ NATIONAL WOMEN'S MOVEMENT
Sommelsdikstraat 8
PO Box 129
Paramaribo, Suriname   PH: 410784

National. Pursues means of achieving full public and governmental recognition of women's rights. Works towards furthering the interests of women in matters of public policy, legislation, and social code. Disseminates information.

★1359★ STICHTING LOBI
Fajalobiestraat 13
PO Box 9267   PH: 497111
Paramaribo, Suriname   465714
Mrs. Monique Essed-Fernandes,   FX: 465714
    President   CBL: LOBI

Languages: Dutch, English. **National.** Promotes responsible parenthood and family planning as a means to enhance the quality of life for individuals living in Suriname. Works to reduce the number of unwanted pregnancies and abortions. Sponsors programs in sex education, family planning, and sexually transmitted diseases, especially AIDS. Provides contraceptive and health care services. Conducts research.

★1360★ YOUNG WOMEN'S CHRISTIAN ASSOCIATION - SURINAME
PO Box 1404
Paramaribo, Suriname   PH: 72089
Cynthia Karijodinomo, Gen.Sec.   76981

National. Promotes the development of young women in Suriname. Upholds Christian beliefs and values in its programs. Works to instill self worth and self-esteem in young women.

Uruguay

★1361★ ASOCIACION DE MUJERES URUGUAYAS LOURDES PINTO
    (AMULP)
Martin C. Martinez 1604, Primer Piso
Montevideo, Uruguay   PH: 2 402012

Languages: Spanish. **National.** Women in Uruguay united to improve their living and working conditions.

★1362★ CATOLICAS POR EL DERECHO A DECIDIR (CDD)
Avenida Rivera 2160, Apt. 01   PH: 2 485005
Montevideo, Uruguay   2 499398
Dr. Gristina Grela, Coord.   FX: 2 485005

Founded: 1987. **Members:** 2,500. **Staff:** 11. **Budget:** US$50,000. **Languages:** English, Portuguese, Spanish. **Multinational.** Catholics interested in reforming women's reproductive rights in Latin America. Investigates women's issues such as sexuality and maternity as they relate to Catholic women. Conducts educational programs, workshops, forums, and seminars. **Libraries:** Type: reference. Holdings: archival material, books, clippings. Subjects: sexuality, women, religion, and reproductive rights.

Publications: *Videos.*

★1363★ CENTRO DE INVESTIGACION SOCIAL, FORMACION Y
    ESTUDIOS DE LA MUJER (CISFEM)
Avenida Vollmer, Esquina Andres Bello
Edificio Noimendie
San Bernardino
Caracas, Uruguay   PH: 2 5754165
Virginia Olivio de Celli, Gen.Dir.   2 5754558

Languages: Spanish. **National.** Promotes the study of women and women's issues in Suriname. Supports the needs and interests of disadvantaged women. Promotes activities to improve women's standard of living. Provides socio-economic and legal assistance. Monitors women's rights. Fosters improvement of educational opportunities for women.

★1364★ CONSEJO NACIONAL DE MUJERES DEL URUGUAY
Solano Antuna 2749
Apartado 202
Montevideo, Uruguay   PH: 2 702975
Silvia Tron, President   2 70886

Languages: Spanish. **National.** Umbrella organization for women's groups in Uruguay. Supports and promotes women's interests. Coordinates activities for women. Disseminates information.

★1365★ FUNDACION PLENARIO DE MUJERES DEL URUGUAY
    (PLEMUU)
Ave. Uruguay 1555
11200 Montevideo, Uruguay   PH: 2 417470

Languages: Spanish. **National.** Works towards full public recognition of women's rights. Disseminates infomation to raise public awareness of discrimination against and exploitation of women.

★1366★ GRUPO DE ESTUDIOS SOBRE LA CONDICION DE LA
    MUJER EN EL URUGUAY (GRECMU)
Caxila Postal 11200
Miguel del Corro 1474
Montevideo, Uruguay   PH: 2 416415

Languages: Spanish. **National.** Researches the interests of business and professional women. Conducts workshops on topics of interest to women, small business management, and employment opportunities. Disseminates information.

Publications: *De la Mar a la Mesa.* Videos.

★1367★ INSTITO MUJER Y SOCIEDAD
Juan Manuel Blanes 1231
Montevideo, Uruguay   PH: 2 493631

Languages: Spanish. **National.** Conducts and supports research on women's roles. Provides information on the history and current state of the women's movement and women's contributions to society.

★1368★ MUJER AHORA
Rivera 2160, Apartado 2
Montevideo, Uruguay   PH: 2 409641

Languages: Spanish. **National.** Fosters the union and mobilization of women to achieve equal rights. Disseminates information aimed towards raising public consciousness of discrimination against women.

★1369★ NA'AMAT PIONERAS (NP)
Canelones 1084, Piso 3
11100 Montevideo, Uruguay

Languages: Spanish. **Multinational.** Working and professional women. Works to advance the status of women by providing a variety of educational, community, and legal services. Believes that strong family relations are the foundation of a stable society. Members identify with the Zionist movement.

★1370★ S.O.S. MUJER
Daniel Fernandaz Crespo 1813 esq.
Cerro Largo
11800 Montevideo, Uruguay

Languages: Spanish. **National.** Promotes the advancement of women's equal rights; works towards the eradication of discrimination against women.

★1371★ URUGUAYAN FAMILY PLANNING ASSOCIATION
(AUPFIRH Asociacion Uruguaya de Planification Familiar)

	PH: 2 420051
PO Box 10634, Dist.1	2 498916
11200 Montevideo, Uruguay	FX: 2 487515
Renee Pietracaprina, President	CBL: AUPFIRH

Founded: 1967. **Members:** 40. **Staff:** 47. **Budget:** US$306,000. **Languages:** English, Spanish. **National.** Promotes family planning and responsible parenthood as a means to enhance the quality of life for individuals living in Uruguay. Works to reduce the number of unwanted pregnancies and abortions. Provides contraceptive and health care services. Offers programs in family planning, sex education, and sexually transmitted diseases, especially AIDS. Acts as an advocate for family planning on a national level. **Libraries:** Type: reference; open to the public. Holdings: archival material. Subjects: gynecology and family planning.

Publications: *La Carta* (in Spanish), bimonthly. Bulletin. Information for professionals in family planning. **Circulation:** 600.

★1372★ YOUNG WOMEN'S CHRISTIAN ASSOCIATION - URUGUAY
(Asociacion Cristiana Femenina - Uruguay)
Calle Paraguay 1438

Montevideo, Uruguay	PH: 2 908196
Nelida Algare Faraut, Gen.Sec.	2 910434

National. Promotes the development of young women in Uruguay. Upholds Christian beliefs and values in its programs. Works to instill self worth and self-esteem in young women.

Venezuela

★1373★ ASOCIACION VENEZOLANA DE MUJERES (AVM)
Avenida Presidente Medina, con Maria,
  Teresa Toro
Las Acacias
Caracas, Venezuela
Nelly de Masroa, President   PH: 2 612955

Languages: Spanish. **National.** Seeks to improve the social, economic, and health status of women in Venezuela. Works with women in development. Provides medical and educational assistance to single mothers and their children. Conducts courses in dress making; and maternal and child health care.

★1374★ THE BAD LIFE (TBL)
(LMV La Mala Vida)
Edificio la Colina
Calle la Colina
Apartado 24
Las Acacias
Caracas 104, Venezuela
Giovanna Merola, Dir.   PH: 2 618769

Founded: 1978. **Members:** 5. **Budget:** US$1,200. **Languages:** Spanish. **National.** Draws attention to women's disadvantaged position in Venezuelan society and strives to improve their political and civil rights. Seeks to unify Venezuelan women and help them attain proper education, adequate health care and working conditions, secure role within the family, and fair political

representation. Organizes public forums, symposia, and seminars; conducts radio and television interviews.

Publications: *La Mala Vida* (in Spanish), quarterly. Newsletter.

Conventions/Meetings: annual workshop (exhibits).

★1375★ CIRCULOS FEMENINOS POPULARES
Apartado 4240
Caracas 1010-A, Venezuela

Languages: Spanish. **National.** Disseminates information on issues concerning women. Offers a forum for discussion among members.

★1376★ COORDINADORA DE ORGANIZACIONES NO
  GUBERNAMENTALES DE MUJERES (CONG)
Apartado 4491
Caracas 1010-A, Venezuela
Helena Salcedo, Coord.   PH: 2 4627014

Languages: Spanish. **National.** Non-governmental women's organizations in Venezuela. Works to: improve women's standard of living; increase public awareness of women's issues; and promote interaction among women's organizations. Organizes and coordinates activities among women's groups. Disseminates information.

Publications: *De las Mujeres* (in Spanish). Bulletin. Activities of member organizations.

★1377★ FEDERACION VENEZOLANA DE ABROGADAS TODOS
  JUNTAS (FEVA)
Apartado 4240
San Jose del Avila
Caracas 1010-A, Venezuela

Languages: Spanish. **National.** Works to defend the rights of women. Advocates the development of legislation securing equal opportunity and treatment of women in all spheres of society.

★1378★ GRUPO DE ESTUDIOS SOBRE MUJER Y AMBIENTE (GEMA)
Avenida Andres Eloy Blanco (Este 2)
Torre Los Caobos, piso 17, Apartado
  171-B
Los Caobos
Caracas, Venezuela   PH: 2 5717648
Flor Isabel Tur, Gen.Coordinator   25717648

Languages: Spanish. **National.** Seeks to increase public awareness of women's interests, and to improve health care for women. Conducts educational and informational programs for women. Provides training for women and children. Researches maternal and general health standards. Organizes and coordinates activities for women and women's groups. **Libraries:** Type: reference.

★1379★ RED DE APOYO DE ORGANIZACIONES POPULARES DE
  MUJERES
Apartado Postal 4438
San Jose del Avila
Caracas 1010-A, Venezuela   PH: 2 2853385
Inocencia Orellano, Coord.   FX: 2 4516596

Founded: 1981. **Members:** 150. **Languages:** Spanish. **National.** Works with women's organizations in Latin America. Provides opportunities for women and groups to interact, reflect, and act on issues of interest and importance to women. Organizes and coordinates activities for women's organizations. Helps women's groups develop assistance programs. Trains women's organizations in organizational and technical skills. Conducts research on women leaders.

Conventions/Meetings: annual general assembly. ● bimonthly meeting.

★1380★ SOCIEDAD DE PLANIFICACION FAMILIAR (PLAFAM)

Apartado Postal 69592
Las Mercedes 1063-A
Caracas, Venezuela
Dr. Walter Baumgartner, President

PH: 2 6612269
    2 6622461
FX: 2 6612269
TX: 39527427
    CAFIVCBAUM

Languages: Spanish. **National**. Works to enhance the quality of life for individuals living in Venezuela by promoting responsible parenthood and family planning. Advocates family planning as a basic human right. Seeks to reduce the number of unwanted pregnancies and abortions. Provides contraceptive and health care services. Attempts to stop the spread of AIDS and other sexually transmitted diseases. Conducts research.

★1381★ WORLD UNION OF CHRISTIAN DEMOCRATIC WOMEN
  (WUCDU)
(UMFDC Union Mundial de Mujeres Democratas Cristianas)
Avenida Aristides Calvani
Villa San Remo
Los Chorros
Caracas 1071, Venezuela
Maria Bello de Guzman, Contact

PH: 2 360598
FX: 2 348368
TX: 27214 FUHIN VC

Founded: 1979. **Members:** 58. **Staff:** 4. **Languages:** English, German, Italian, Spanish. **Multinational**. Womens' Christian Democrat organizations. Fosters the political participation of women in Christian Democrat activities. Organizes political and social activities; sponsors seminars.

Publications: *Informe de la IDC* (in English, German, Italian, and Spanish), monthly.

Conventions/Meetings: semiannual conference.

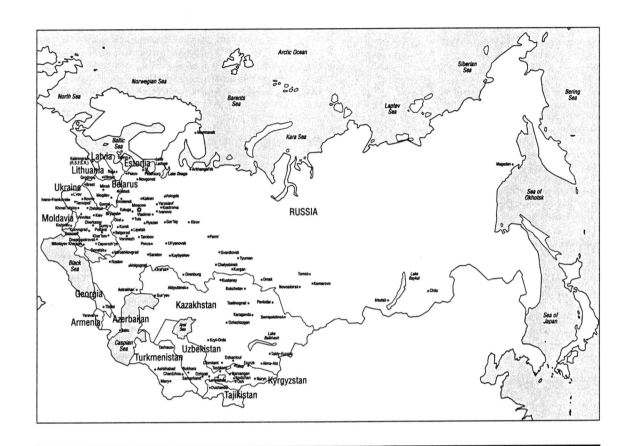

C.I.S. and the Baltic States

Belarus	Kazakhstan	Lithuania
Estonia	Latvia	Russia
Georgia		Ukraine

C.I.S. and the Baltic States

Belarus

★1382★ VERA, NADEZHDA, LYUBOV
Karbysheva str. 1
220000 Minsk, Belarus
Antonina Demeshko, Director   PH: 172 232270

Founded: 1992. **National.** Women providing humanitarian aid to underprivileged individuals in Belarus.

★1383★ WOMEN UNION OF THE REPUBLIC OF BELORUSSIA
Kommunisticheskaya str. 2
220029 Minsk, Belarus   PH: 172 366362
Lyudmila Tolkachova, Vice-Chairwoman   172 366443

Founded: 1991. **Members:** 8,000. **National.** Women and women's organizations in Belarus. Promotes the improvement of the economic, social, legal, and political aspects of women's lives. Provides counseling services. Conducts charitable programs; offers legal assistance.

Estonia

★1384★ WOMEN CENTRE
Pikka str. 9, Apt. 43
200036 Tallinn, Estonia
Olga Gromova, Director   PH: 142 3223830

Founded: 1989. **National.** Promotes the interests of women in Estonia. Conducts educational and charitable programs.

★1385★ YOUNG WOMEN'S CHRISTIAN ASSOCIATION - ESTONIA
Mai 20
200016 Tallinn, Estonia   PH: 142510295
Lagle Suurorg, Contact   FX: 142237243

National. Promotes the development of young women in Estonia. Upholds Christian beliefs and values in its programs. Works to instill self worth and self-esteem in young women.

Georgia

★1386★ MEDICAL WOMEN'S INTERNATIONAL ASSOCIATION -
    GEORGIA (MWIA-G)
Zhordania Institute of Human
    Reproduction
43 Lenin St.
380009 Tbilisi, Georgia
Nana G. Sichinava, Contact

National. Georgia national branch of the Medical Women's International Association (see separate entry). Women physicians. Provides a forum for discussion of women's health care issues. Encourages women to enter the field of medicine. Works to overcome discrimination against female physicians. Sponsors research and educational programs.

Kazakhstan

★1387★ SOLDIERS' MOTHERS COMMITTEE
14th District 33-43
Manghyshlak Region
466200 Shevchenko, Kazakhstan
Vera Tishinskaya, Chairwoman   PH: 3292232728

Founded: 1989. **National.** Women whose sons are currently serving in the unified military of the independent nations of the former Soviet Union. Provides support to mothers whose sons are away from home during their military service. Offers legal assistance.

Latvia

★1388★ WOMEN'S LEAGUE OF LATVIA (WLL)
(LSL Latuijas Sieviesu Liga)
Vecpilsetas 13/15
Riga, Latvia   PH: 132 210376
Anita Stankevich, Chair   TX: 161177 LTF SU

Founded: 1989. **Members:** 500. **Staff:** 4. **Local Groups:** 20. **Languages:** Latvian, Russian. **National.** Women's division of the Popular Front of Latvia (see separate entry). Renders aid to citizens of Latvia. Supports parents of small children with material and medical assistance. Provides placement service; compiles statistics; maintains speakers' bureau. **Libraries:** Type: reference. **Computer Services:** Data base.

Publications: *All Our Sons*, periodic. Newsletter. ● *Riga in Barricades*. Book. ● *Latvian Chronicle*. Book.

Conventions/Meetings: periodic conference.

★1389★ YOUNG WOMEN'S CHRISTIAN ASSOCIATION - LATVIA
(Jauna Sieviesu Kristiga Savieniba)
J. Alunana iela 7   PH: 132332131
226010 Riga, Latvia   FX: 132225039
Gunta Kelle, Contact   TX: 161172 YWCA

National. Promotes the development of young women in Latvia. Upholds Christian beliefs and values in its programs. Works to instill self worth and self-esteem in young women.

Lithuania

★1390★ CARITAS - CATHOLIC WOMEN'S CHARITABLE
ORGANIZATION
(Katallkiskas Moteru Samburis - Caritas)
4-11A Vliniaus
233000 Kaunas, Lithuania
Albina Pajarskaite, Contact   PH: 127221869

Founded: 1989. **Members:** 4,000. **National.** Women working for Christian reform in Lithuania. Supports orphanages and libraries; provides medical aid.

Publications: *Caritas*, monthly. Magazine.

Russia

★1391★ ALL-RUSSIAN CHARITY FOUNDATION OF THE INSTITUTE
OF NOBLE VIRGINS
Chernomorskiy boulvard 11-1, Apt. 61
113452 Moscow, Russia
Aleksey Smorchkov, Director   PH: 95 3180056

Founded: 1991. **National.** Seeks to assist underprivileged and orphaned girls and young women in Russia. Conducts educational programs.

★1392★ ALL-UNION COMMITTEE OF SOLDIERS' MOTHERS
Tsuryupy str. 15-2, No. 80
117418 Moscow, Russia   PH: 95 3313841
Maria Kirbasova, Chairwoman   95 1824685

Founded: 1989. **Members:** 1,400. **National.** Women in Russia whose sons in the military were killed during peace times. Offers legal assistance.

★1393★ "ANIKA" - COMMITTEE OF DISABLED WOMEN AND
WOMEN SERVED IN AFGHANISTAN
Khachaturyana str. 2, Apt. 370
127562 Moscow, Russia   PH: 95 4018753
Lyubov Yakovleva, Chairwoman   95 3140834

Founded: 1991. **Members:** 500. **National.** Disabled women who have served in the Russian military in Afghanistan. Provides welfare assistance and legal advice.

★1394★ ASSOCIATION OF BUSINESS WOMEN
Chaykovskogo str. 35, Apt. 96
170000 Tver, Russia
Klavdiya Stepanova, President   PH: 822233443

Founded: 1992. **National.** Promotes women in business and management in Russia. Offers legal and financial support to women in the development of businesses.

★1395★ ASSOCIATION OF DISABLED WOMEN
Dimitrova str. 12
191000 St. Petersburg, Russia
Aleksandra Kachanova, President   PH: 812 3509131

Founded: 1990. **Members:** 200. **National.** Disabled women. Promotes the interests of disabled women in Russia. Conducts charitable programs.

★1396★ ASSOCIATION OF LARGE FAMILIES
Slavyanskaya Sq. 4
121352 Moscow, Russia
Anna Antonenko, Chairwoman   PH: 95 2200086

Founded: 1993. **Members:** 220. **National.** Women promoting issues that affect large families. Provides support to members of large families.

★1397★ ASSOCIATION OF SOLDIERS' MOTHERS
60 Years of October str. 8, Apt. 7
454047 Chelyabinsk, Russia   PH: 3512240866
Lyudmila Zinchenko, Chairwoman   3512338363

Founded: 1989. **Members:** 436. **National.** Mothers whose sons serving in the Russian military were killed during peace times. Conducts charitable programs.

★1398★ ASSOCIATION OF WOMEN ENTREPRENEURS
Biryusinka str. 4
107241 Moscow, Russia   PH: 95 2421963
Tatyana Malyutina, President   95 2455553

Founded: 1991. **National.** Promotes the development of women in business and management in Russia. Offers legal and financial support to women in the formation of women-owned businesses.

★1399★ ASSOCIATION OF WOMEN INITIATIVES
Shishkinskiy blvd. 8
423834 Naberezhnye Chelny, Russia
Ekaterina Lyamina, Chairwoman   PH: 4392531405

Founded: 1991. **Members:** 270. **National.** Promotes women's business initiatives in Russia. Provides legal and financial support to women in the development of new businesses. Acts as a resource center for women in business.

★1400★ BASHKIRIAN ASSOCIATION OF WOMEN ENTREPRENEURS
Tukaeva str. 46, Apt. 211
450101 Ufa, Russia   PH: 3472 251050
Alla Troitskaya, President   3472 233981

Founded: 1991. **National.** Promotes the involvement of women in Russian business and industry. Provides support to women entrepreneurs seeking to develop businesses. Offers legal and financial support to women.

★1401★ BEAUTY WILL SAVE THE WORLD
Millionnaya str. 10, Apt. 48
107564 Moscow, Russia
Lidia Rogojina-toom, President   PH: 95 1607915

Founded: 1990. **National.** Feminist organization. Promotes the interests of women in Russia.

★1402★ BIG FAMILY
Svobody str. 8/4, Apt. 176
123362 Moscow, Russia
Tatyana Daurova, President   PH: 95 4914689

Founded: 1991. **Members:** 78. **National.** Women providing support to large families and their special interests in Russia. Conducts charitable programs.

★1403★ BUSINESS WOMAN
Bardina str. 32-1, Apt. 152
620146 Ekaterinbourg, Russia   PH: 3432573122
Zoya Korshunova, President   3432 732444

Founded: 1992. **National.** Promotes women in business and management in Russia. Provides assistance to women-owned businesses.

★1404★ BUSINESS WOMAN - C.I.S.
Merzlyakovsky ln. 8-5, Rm. 7   PH: 95 2483419
121814 Moscow, Russia   95 2906325
Lyudmila Konareva, President   FX: 95 2001207

Founded: 1992. **Multinational.** Encourages the involvement of women in international business. Promotes women's economic independence. Offers legal and financial assistance to women in business ventures. Fosters networking and communication between members.

★1405★ CENTER OF WOMEN RESEARCHERS
Elizarovoy str. 10
103064 Moscow, Russia
Irina Jurna, Director
PH: 95 9210219
95 2383641
FX: 95 9752190

Founded: 1992. **Multinational.** Women scientists and researchers. Promotes the involvement of women in the sciences throughout the independent nations of the former Soviet Union.

★1406★ CENTRE FOR BUSINESS ACTIVITY OF WOMEN UNDER
CONDITIONS OF UNEMPLOYMENT
Pobedy Sq. 1a, Apt. 192
121293 Moscow, Russia
Marina Pavlova, Director
PH: 95 1480324
FX: 95 4341204

Founded: 1991. **Members:** 710. **National.** Works to assist unemployed women pursue career development programs.

★1407★ CENTRE OF GENDER RESEARCHERS
Krasikova str. 27, 9th Fl.
117218 Moscow, Russia
Anastasiya Passadskaya, Director
PH: 95 1246185

Founded: 1990. **Members:** 19. **National.** Works to study issues affecting women's lives in Russia, such as gender concerns and equal rights.

★1408★ CENTRE OF SOCIAL PROBLEMS AND HUMANITARIAN
DEVELOPMENT OF WOMEN AND YOUTH
District 2 - No. 67
Tyumen Region
626310 Uray, Russia
Galina Egorova, President
PH: 3547631473
3547632914

Founded: 1992. **National.** Assists women and their children, and young women, in the development of their social and personal lives. Promotes the interests of women and children in Russia. Offers legal assistance, counseling services, and educational programs.

★1409★ CENTRE OF WOMAN'S CULTURE - "IDIOMA"
Marii Ulyanovoy str. 14, Apt. 81
117331 Moscow, Russia
Natalia Kamenetskaya, Director
PH: 95 1334149

Founded: 1989. **National.** Feminist organization promoting the development of women in Russian society and culture. Studies the role of women in Russian culture and the philosophy of the women's movement.

★1410★ CENTRE OF WOMEN'S INITIATIVES
Bumazhny dr. 14
101458 Moscow, Russia
Elvira Novikova, President
PH: 95 2505738
FX: 95 2926511

Founded: 1992. **National.** Promotes the interests of women in Russia. Offers counseling services; conducts charitable programs.

★1411★ CLUB OF BUSINESS WOMEN
c/o Economy and Life Newspaper
Bumazhny dr. 14
101462 Moscow, Russia
Eleonora Luchnikova, Director
PH: 95 5222451

Founded: 1992. **Multinational.** Women directors of large industrial enterprises. Promotes the involvement of women in Russian business and industry. Fosters communication among members. Offers consulting services to members. Provides financial and legal assistance to members.

★1412★ CLUB OF FLIGHT PERSONNEL WOMEN - AVIATRISSA
Krasnoarmeyskaya str. 4
125167 Moscow, Russia
Galina Korchuganova, President
PH: 95 4762369

Founded: 1992. **Members:** 80. **National.** Women who have been involved in the flight industry. Promotes social events and fellowship among members. Conducts charitable programs.

★1413★ FAMILY AND HEALTH
Vesnina str. 24
121000 Moscow, Russia
Irina Manuilova, Gen.Dir.
PH: 95 2411436
95 2410306

Founded: 1991. **Multinational.** Promotes improved health conditions for women and their families. Conducts educational programs on health. Offers counseling services.

★1414★ FELINA
Altufievskoe Hwy. 78, Entrance No. 1,
Ground Fl.
127349 Moscow, Russia
Valentina Kutuzova, Director

Founded: 1992. **National.** Women homemakers. Promotes the interests of women who work at home. Conducts charitable programs.

★1415★ FEMINISTIC ORIENTATION CENTRE
M. Djalil str. 5-1, Apt. 397
115580 Moscow, Russia
Marina Libarakina, Contact
PH: 95 3955864
FX: 95 1868903

Founded: 1992. **Members:** 21. **National.** Feminist organizations in Russia. Promotes the interests of women. Conducts charitable programs.

★1416★ FOUNDATION FOR HELP AND ASSISTANCE TO WOMEN-
VICTIMS OF STALIN'S REPRESSIONS
Bumazhny dr. 14
101458 Moscow, Russia
Zoya Krylova, President
PH: 95 2503886
FX: 95 9569004

Founded: 1990. **National.** Seeks to assist women who suffered oppression and human rights abuses during the Stalin government of the former U.S.S.R. Provides welfare assistance programs.

★1417★ FREE ASSOCIATION OF FEMINISTIC ORGANIZATIONS
Leninskiy ave. 123-1, Apt. 706
117513 Moscow, Russia
Natalya Stepanova, Contact
PH: 95 4386115

Founded: 1992. **National.** Feminist organizations in Russia. Promotes the interests of women in Russian public and government arenas.

★1418★ GAIA WOMEN'S CENTER
Institute of the USA and Canada Studies
2/3 Klebny per.
121814 Moscow, Russia

National. Provides training, educational, counseling, and informational services to women. Supports the worldwide women's movement and women's development.

★1419★ GEYA - INTERNATIONAL WOMEN FORUM
Leninskiy ave. 43, Apt. 45
117334 Moscow, Russia
Elena Ershova, President
PH: 95 1353207
FX: 95 2001207

Founded: 1991. **Multinational.** Feminist organization. Promotes the interests of women in Russia. Works for the advancement of women in legal, social, political, and economic areas.

★1420★ GRANDMOTHERS AND GRANDCHILDREN
Altufievskoe Highway 20 b, Apt. 25
127562 Moscow, Russia
Serafima Lapteva, Secretary   PH: 95 4014748

Founded: 1991. **National**. Grandmothers in Russia promoting the role of grandmothers in the lives of their grandchildren. Conducts charitable programs.

★1421★ INDEPENDENT ASSOCIATION OF WOMEN INITIATIVES - "NOZHI"
Vishnevskogo str. 15, Apt. 4
248007 Kaluga, Russia
Lyubov Mikhailova, President   PH: 842247189

Founded: 1992. **Members:** 120. **National**. Promotes the interests of women in Russia. Works toward the attainment of equal rights for women in social, economic, legal, and political areas. Assists women in the development of their careers. Lobbies governments and organizations to create an increased number of jobs for women in the economic restructuring of Russia. Conducts vocational courses.

★1422★ INDEPENDENT BROADCASTING FOR WOMEN
Pyatnitskaya str. 25
113326 Moscow, Russia   PH: 95 2336588
Irina Korolyova, Gen.Dir.   FX: 95 2302828

Founded: 1992. **Members:** 10. **National**. Women broadcasters in Russia. Promotes the interests of members. Fosters communication among women broadcasters throughout Russia. Conducts charitable programs.

★1423★ INDEPENDENT WOMEN CENTRE OF THE FOUNDATION TRANSFORMATION
Lermontova str. 321a, Apt. 29
664033 Irkutsk, Russia   PH: 3952462745
Valentina Kazimirovskaya, Chairwoman   3952 463574

Founded: 1992. **National**. Feminist organization promoting the interests of women in Russia. Studies issues affecting women's lives. Offers educational programs, counseling, and legal assistance.

★1424★ INTERNATIONAL ASSOCIATION OF RUSSIAN MOTHERS
Verhnyaya Maslovka str. 21
125083 Moscow, Russia
Larisa Podgorbunskaya, President   PH: 95 3931492

Founded: 1992. **Multinational**. Promotes the interests of mothers in the independent nations of the former Soviet Union. Provides welfare assistance and charitable programs. Offers legal assistance.

★1425★ INTERNATIONAL ASSOCIATION OF UNIVERSITIES WOMEN
Nauki ave. 6/1, Apt. 61
195257 St. Petersburg, Russia   PH: 812 5551260
Marina Akimova, President   812 2714700

Founded: 1992. **Members:** 177. **Multinational**. Women who have earned university degrees throughout the independent nations of the former Soviet Union. Promotes university education among women. Represents the interests of women throughout the C.I.S. Offers legal assistance.

★1426★ INTERNATIONAL INDEPENDENT INFORMATION AND ADVERTISING AGENCY OF WOMEN IN RUSSIA - INTERFAM
Suvorovsky blvd. 6   PH: 95 2919595
121019 Moscow, Russia   95 2919885
Tatyana Kostygova, President   FX: 95 2076284

Founded: 1992. **Multinational**. Women in the advertising and public relations industries. Advances the interests of women working in promotional industries. Fosters communication among members. Disseminates information.

★1427★ INTERNATIONAL LEAGUE OF LADY WRITERS
Vorovskogo str. 52
121825 Moscow, Russia
Larisa Vasilieva, President   PH: 95 2029920

Founded: 1992. **Multinational**. Women writers worldwide. Promotes the writings of members. Assists members in having works published. Sponsors programs to promote young women's writings. Conducts charitable programs.

★1428★ INTERNATIONAL WOMEN CENTRE - FUTURE OF THE WOMAN
Sadovaya Kudrinskaya str. 18
103001 Moscow, Russia   PH: 95 2901798
Aleksandra Momdzhan, President   FX: 95 2003262

Founded: 1990. **Members:** 230. **Multinational**. Individuals and organizations supporting the equal rights of women in political, social, and economic arenas. Disseminates information. Offers educational courses; provides legal assistance.

★1429★ INTERREPUBLICAN ASSOCIATION - WOMAN AND BUSINESS
Profsoyuznaya str. 3
117036 Moscow, Russia
Lyudmila Lineva, President   PH: 95 1247202

Founded: 1991. **Multinational**. Promotes the involvement of women in Russian business and industry. Conducts programs to assist women in the development of their business and management skills. Offers legal and financial assistance to members.

★1430★ JEWISH WOMEN ORGANIZATION - HAVA
Domodedovskaya str. 5-2, No. 438
115551 Moscow, Russia   PH: 95 3915035
Valeriya Babaeva, President   FX: 95 2199662

Founded: 1991. **Multinational**. Umbrella organization of Jewish women's organizations throughout the independent nations of the former Soviet Union. Represents the interests of Jewish women. Conducts educational programs. Offers charitable services.

★1431★ KRESTYANKA
Bumazhny dr. 14   PH: 95 2121239
101460 Moscow, Russia   95 2573773
Anastasiya Kupriyanova, Contact   FX: 95 2500884

Founded: 1922. **Members:** 137. **National**. Promotes the interests of rural women in Russia. Works to develop grass-roots local organizations to assist the development of women in rural areas. Produces publications.

★1432★ MIRBIS
Stremyanny ln. 28   PH: 95 2378277
113054 Moscow, Russia   95 2379220
Tatyana Komissarova, Director   FX: 95 2373430

Founded: 1991. **Multinational**. Promotes career development among women in business and industry. Conducts academic and vocational education programs.

★1433★ MISSION
Box 25
117513 Moscow, Russia   PH: 95 1100821
Tatyana Lukyanenko, President   FX: 95 1134020

Founded: 1989. **Members:** 800. **Multinational**. Promotes the entrance of women into the workforce. Works with business and government in the creation of jobs for women. Sponsors programs to assist women in personal career development.

★1434★ MOLLY ORGANIZATION
Dubininskaya str. 42-2, Apt. 100
127951 Moscow, Russia
Lyudmila Ugolkova, Chairwoman   PH: 95 1521657

Founded: 1991. **National.** Lesbians in Russia interested in the arts. Promotes the involvement of lesbians in the arts.

★1435★ MOSCOW INTERNATIONAL WOMEN CLUB
Sadovo-Kudrinskaya str. 21a
103001 Moscow, Russia   PH: 95 2542111
Rehana Syed, President   95 9763533

Multinational. Non-Russian women living in Russia. Promotes the exchange of non-Russian and Russian cultures. Fosters fellowship and communication between members.

★1436★ MOTHER'S RIGHT FOUNDATION
c/o Yunost
1st Tverskaya-Yamskaya str. 2/1   PH: 95 2060581
101524 Moscow, Russia   95 4932637
Veronika Marchenko, Director   FX: 95 2017139

Founded: 1990. **National.** Mothers whose sons serving in the Russian military were killed during peace times.

★1437★ ONLY MAMA
Mostovyh str. 3a
111555 Moscow, Russia
Marina Kienya, President   PH: 95 1336574

Founded: 1990. **Members:** 100. **National.** Single mothers in Russia. Provides support and encouragement to women who have sole responsibility for the care of their children. Offers legal and welfare assistance programs.

★1438★ ORTHODOX CHURCH CHARITY SISTERHOOD
Leninskiy ave. 8-2
Hospital Church
117049 Moscow, Russia   PH: 95 2369263
Andrey Efimov, Contact   95 2316141

Founded: 1992. **National.** Women of the Russian Orthodox church working to aid orphaned girls in Russia. Conducts charitable programs. Sponsors orphanages.

★1439★ RABOTNITSA
Bumazhny dr. 14
101458 Moscow, Russia
Zoya Krylova, Contact   PH: 95 2122039

Founded: 1922. **National.** Promotes the interests of women workers in Russia. Assists women in career development programs. Produces publications.

★1440★ RAINBOW
Box 356
103064 Moscow, Russia   PH: 95 2702809
Larisa Babuh, President   FX: 95 4651740

Founded: 1992. **Members:** 130. **National.** Women in business. Promotes women's ownership of businesses in Russia. Offers legal and financial assistance.

★1441★ RUSSIAN ASSOCIATION OF WOMEN MATHEMATICIANS
Architecter Vlasov str. 51
117393 Moscow, Russia   PH: 95 1280592
Irina Yaroshevskaya, Chairwoman   FX: 95 1280590

Founded: 1993. **National.** Women mathematicians in Russia. Promotes

women's roles in the field of mathematics. Conducts educational courses. Sponsors charitable programs.

★1442★ RUSSIAN ASSOCIATION OF WOMEN WITH UNIVERSITY
EDUCATION
Mishina str. 12, Apt. 75
125083 Moscow, Russia   PH: 95 1837214
Olga Romashko, President   95 1936015

Founded: 1992. **Members:** 420. **National.** Women in Russia who have attained a university education. Promotes the educational status of women in Russia. Conducts charitable programs.

★1443★ RUSSIAN FAMILY PLANNING ASSOCIATION
18/20 Vadkovsky Per.   PH: 95 2892323
101479 Moscow, Russia   95 2892216
Inga Grebesheva, President   FX: 95 2893023

Languages: Russian. **National.** Advocates family planning and responsible parenthood as a basic human right and as a means to enhance the quality of life. Works to reduce the number of unwanted pregnancies and abortions. Attempts to stop the spread of AIDS and other sexually transmitted diseases. Offers programs in sex education, family planning, and health. Provides contraceptive and health care services. Conducts research.

★1444★ SANTA - ASSOCIATION OF THE WOMEN WORKING AT
LAW PROTECTING ORGANIZATIONS
Holzunov ln. 6, Apt. 39
119021 Moscow, Russia
Tatyana Zernova, President   PH: 95 2467501

Founded: 1991. **Members:** 400. **National.** Women working for law enforcement agencies in Russia. Promotes the interests of women. Fosters networking among members. Conducts charitable programs; offers legal assistance to members.

★1445★ SCHOOL OF WOMEN LEADERSHIP
Kominterna str. 50, Apt. 6
140160 Moscow, Russia
Larisa Fyodorova, Director   PH: 95 5564254

Founded: 1991. **National.** Feminist organization promoting the interests of women in Russia. Conducts research and educational programs on the role of women in Russian society. Offers legal assistance.

★1446★ SERVICE OF WOMEN OF THE 7TH DAY ADVENTISTS
CHURCH
Isakovskogo str. 4-1
123181 Moscow, Russia   PH: 95 9447467
Lyudmila Krushenitskaya, Contact   FX: 95 9447465

Founded: 1991. **Members:** 320. **Multinational.** Umbrella organization of women's Seventh Day Adventist organizations throughout the independent nations of the former Soviet Union. Upholds the beliefs and principles of the Seventh Day Adventist faith. Promotes Christian fellowship and activities among members. Conducts educational programs. Provides charitable services to the needy.

★1447★ SOCIETY OF FRIENDSHIP OF KOREAN WOMEN OF
MOSCOW WITH WOMEN OF SOUTH KOREA
Nagornaya str. 14-2, Apt. 46
113186 Moscow, Russia   PH: 95 1278376
Lidiya Pak, Chairwoman   FX: 95 2411491

Founded: 1990. **Members:** 150. **Multinational.** Promotes friendship and cultural exchange between women in Russia and the Republic of Korea. Sponsors exchange programs. Conducts educational programs.

★1448★ SOCIETY OF HUMANITARIAN INITIATIVES
Zhukovsky str. 1
Moscow Region
140160 Zhukovsky, Russia   PH: 95 5564566
Olga Bessolova, President   FX: 95 5564428

Founded: 1989. **Members:** 213. **National.** Women promoting the involvement of women in Russian politics and government.

★1449★ SOCIETY FOR PROTECTION OF MOTHERHOOD AND
     CHILDHOOD
Krasnopolyanskaya str. 6-2, Apt. 63
127599 Moscow, Russia
Olga Popova, Co-Chairwoman   PH: 95 4862379

Founded: 1989. **Members:** 11. **National.** Promotes the quality of maternal and infant healthcare in Russia. Conducts charitable programs.

★1450★ SOGLASIE
Krasnoy Armii str. 169, Rm. 404
Moscow Region
141300 Sergiev Pasad, Russia
Lidiya Gorbatova, Chairwoman   PH: 965445383

Founded: 1992. **National.** Promotes career development among women in Russia. Conducts educational courses to assist women in the exploration of new careers.

★1451★ SOLDIER'S MOTHER
Liteyniy ave. 20, No. 21
190000 St. Petersburg, Russia
Mariya Averkina, Chairwoman

Founded: 1989. **National.** Women whose sons are currently serving in the Russian military. Provides support to mothers whose sons are away from home during their military service. Offers legal assistance.

★1452★ SOVIET WOMEN'S COMMITTEE
(Komitet Sovetskikh Zhenshchin)
ulitsa Nemirovicha-Danchenko 6
103832 Moscow, Russia   PH: 95 2097433
Zoya Pavlovna Pukhova, Chair   95 2294062

Founded: 1941. **Members:** 3,000,000. **Staff:** 60. **National.** Works for equal rights for women in political, social, and economic life. Protects the social rights of families and mothers of small children; works for protection of women in the work force. Supports and organizes educational programs. **Libraries:** Type: reference. Holdings: 9,000. **Computer Services:** Data base, publications on women's issues.

Publications: *Soviet Woman* (in Russian), monthly.

★1453★ STORK NEST
Simonovskiy Val str. 24-1, Apt. 30
109088 Moscow, Russia
Galiya Morozova, Director   PH: 95 2477001

Founded: 1992. **National.** Provides support to women during the last month of pregnancy. Offers counselling services.

★1454★ STUDENT-GIRLS ORGANIZATION - EVA
Sadovaya str. 57, Apt. 51
Bryansk Region
243000 Novozybkov, Russia
Natalya Nehaychik, Chairwoman   PH: 834320376

Founded: 1991. **Members:** 780. **National.** Provides support to girls and young women in Russia. Sponsors educational and charitable programs.

★1455★ TVORCHESTVO
Kosygina str. 5, Apt.328
117334 Moscow, Russia
Tatyana Ryabikina, President   PH: 95 1374343

Founded: 1989. **Members:** 1,500. **National.** Promotes the interests of women in Russia. Conducts educational programs to assist women in their economic, social, legal, and political development. Sponsors charitable projects.

★1456★ UNION OF BIG FAMILIES
Volodarskogo str. 80, Apt. 34
440000 Penza, Russia
Lyubov Borodina, Director   PH: 8412551934

Founded: 1992. **National.** Offers support to women raising large families. Works to represent the concerns faced by large families in Russia. Conducts charitable programs. Offers legal assistance.

★1457★ UNION OF SINGLE MOTHERS AND MOTHERS WITH
     DISABLED CHILDREN
Strastnoy blvd. 12
125592 Moscow, Russia
Augusta Plekhova, Chairwoman   PH: 95 4989427

Founded: 1992. **Members:** 35. **National.** Provides support and assistance to single mothers and mothers who are responsible for raising disabled children in Russia.

★1458★ UNION OF WOMEN FROM NAVY
Bolshoy Kozlovskiy ln. 6
103175 Moscow, Russia
Marina Dobrovolskaya, Chairwoman   PH: 95 2042722

Founded: 1992. **Members:** 340. **National.** Women who have served, or are currently serving, in the Russian navy. Promotes the interests of members. Conducts charitable programs.

★1459★ UNION OF WOMEN ORGANIZATIONS
Stolyarny ln. 16
123022 Moscow, Russia
Natalya Andrianova, Chairman of the
     Board   PH: 95 2521844

Founded: 1991. **Members:** 100. **National.** Umbrella organization of women's organizations in Russia. Promotes women's interests; defends the rights of women in government. Conducts charitable and educational programs. Offers legal assistance to members.

★1460★ URAL INDEPENDENT ASSOCIATION OF BUSINESS WOMEN
Yurovskoy str. 18, Apt. 166
620040 Ekaterinbourg, Russia
Ella Vorobyova, Chairwoman   PH: 3432589387

Founded: 1992. **Members:** 210. **National.** Promotes the interests of women in business and management in Russia. Offers financial and legal assistance to members.

★1461★ URAL INDEPENDENT WOMEN ASSOCIATION
Karl Libknecht str. 3
620219 Ekaterinbourg, Russia   PH: 3432518758
Ella Vorobyova, Chairwoman   3432 514158

Founded: 1991. **National.** Promotes the interests of women in Russia. Works toward achieving equal rights for women in economic, social, legal, and political areas. Conducts educational programs. Offers legal assistance.

★1462★ WOMAN AND BUSINESS
Pervomayskaya str. 51, Apt. 69
Republic of Komi
181000 Syktyvkar, Russia   PH: 8212220690
Valentina Kutuzova, President   8212222442

Founded: 1992. Members: 340. National. Promotes the involvement of women in business and management in Russia. Conducts programs to assist women in the development of their business and management skills. Offers legal and financial assistance to women seeking to develop a business.

★1463★ WOMAN AND BUSINESS IN RUSSIA
Zaozyornaya str. 8
191000 St. Petersburg, Russia   PH: 812 1101347
Irina Fyodorova, President   812 5206078

Founded: 1992. National. Promotes the involvement of women in Russian business. Sponsors research programs focusing on the development of women-owned businesses in Russia. Offers legal assistance to women in the development of businesses.

★1464★ WOMAN AND REALITY
Kachalova str. 14, Apt. 32
121069 Moscow, Russia   PH: 95 4711324
Eugeniya Smetannikova, Chairwoman   95 1809292

Founded: 1990. National. Promotes the interests of women in Russia. Conducts educational courses to help women improve their social and economic situations. Offers legal assistance.

★1465★ WOMAN THEME
Leninskiy ave. 83, Apt. 183
423826 Naberezhnye Chelny, Russia
Elena Kobzeva, Chairwoman   PH: 4392562244

Founded: 1992. Members: 210. National. Promotes the interests of women in Russia. Conducts charitable projects. Offers educational programs, legal assistance, and counseling.

★1466★ WOMAN'S WORLD
Miusskaya sq. 6
125267 Moscow, Russia
Valentina Fiodorova, Contact   PH: 95 2506731

Founded: 1991. Members: 100. Multinational. Promotes the interests of women throughout the independent nations of the former Soviet Union. Produces publications.

★1467★ WOMEN AGAINST VIOLENCE
Bestuzhevyh str. 7b, No. 176
127577 Moscow, Russia
Olga Sarofanova, Chairwoman   PH: 95 4018010

Founded: 1989. Members: 350. National. Women promoting peace and an end to violence in public and military life in Russia.

★1468★ WOMEN ALLIANCE
Pilyugina str. 14-2, Apt. 302
117331 Moscow, Russia
Tatyana Ivanova, President   PH: 95 1327171

Founded: 1991. Members: 170. National. Promotes the interests of women in Russia.

★1469★ WOMEN CENTRE
Box 83
198097 St. Petersburg, Russia   PH: 812 3067438
Olga Lipovskaya, President   812 5281830

Founded: 1991. Members: 332. National. Umbrella organization of women's organizations in Russia. Promotes the interests of women in Russian society.

★1470★ WOMEN CENTRE OF INNOVATIONS - "EAST-WEST"
Box 375
12819 Moscow, Russia
Steffie Engert, President   PH: 95 2971813

Founded: 1990. Multinational. Women throughout the Commonwealth of Independent States and Europe. Promotes feminism. Fosters cultural exchange between women in all member movements.

★1471★ WOMEN FOR CONVERSION
Vorontsovskiy ln. 2
109044 Moscow, Russia   PH: 95 9211074
Tamara Leontieva, President   FX: 95 2740090

Founded: 1992. Multinational. Provides assistance to women-owned businesses involved in the economic conversion process throughout the Commonwealth of Independent States. Sponsors educational courses.

★1472★ WOMEN-ENTREPRENEURS
Korneychuka str. 48a, Apt. 136
123481 Moscow, Russia
Lyubov Slovesnova, Chairwoman   PH: 95 4055354

Founded: 1992. National. Promotes the role of women in business and management throughout the independent nations of the former Soviet Union. Offers legal and financial assistance to women in the development of businesses.

★1473★ WOMEN ENTREPRENEURS CLUB
Gamarnika str. 19-3, Apt. 54
681028 Komsomolsk-on-Amur, Russia
Natalya Tetyueva, President   PH: 4213136431

Founded: 1991. National. Women business owners in Russia. Promotes the development of women-owned businesses. Provides legal advice to women seeking to develop businesses. Conducts charitable programs.

★1474★ WOMEN INITIATIVES SUPPORT FOUNDATION
Sovetskiy ave. 62
650099 Kemerovo, Russia
Natalya Saptsyna, Director   PH: 3842231380

Founded: 1991. Members: 112. Multinational. Promotes women's roles in business; conducts programs that assist women in developing their business and management skills. Provides legal advice for women exploring the development of new businesses.

★1475★ WOMEN MOVEMENT AGAINST ABORTION - RIGHT TO LIFE
Svobody str. 17
Economy Centre
123362 Moscow, Russia   PH: 95 4938037
Galina Seryakova, President   FX: 95 1291237

Founded: 1991. Members: 200. National. Women united opposing abortion. Conducts educational programs to inform women and the public about abortion. Offers medical and counselling assistance to women in crisis pregnancies.

★1476★ WOMEN AND PROGRESS
Malaya Filyovskaya sr. 66, Apt. 105
121433 Moscow, Russia   PH: 95 1441517
Galina Silaste, President   FX: 95 2926030

Founded: 1992. **Members:** 140. **Multinational.** Promotes the rights of women. Seeks to abolish discrimination against women. Conducts research programs in gender studies.

★1477★ WOMEN FOR SOCIAL DEMOCRACY
Shtahanovskogo str. 7, Apt. 21
344095 Rostov-on-don, Russia
Galina Kruth, President   PH: 8632336585

Founded: 1992. **Members:** 318. **National.** Feminist organization working towards the democratization of Russia. Promotes the interests of women and the need for equal rights for women in Russian society. Seeks to improve the social, legal, economic, and political status of women.

★1478★ WOMEN FOR SOCIAL DEMOCRACY
1st Dubrovskaya str. 1, Apt. 17
109044 Moscow, Russia
Galina Venediktova, Chairwoman   PH: 95 1267792

Founded: 1993. **Members:** 710. **Multinational.** Promotes equal rights for women and works against discrimination throughout the Commonwealth of Independent States.

★1479★ WOMEN FOR SOCIAL INNOVATION
1st Cheriomushkinskiy dr. 5
117037 Moscow, Russia
Natalya Kubetskaya, Chairwoman   PH: 95 1370733

Founded: 1991. **Members:** 132. **National.** Works to improve the social status of women. Offers assistance with food, shelter, clothing, and other welfare programs. Provides legal aid to women in need.

★1480★ WOMEN SOCIETY FOR MUTUAL AID
Zatsepa str. 41, Room No. 27
113162 Moscow, Russia
Margarita Gromova, President   PH: 95 2378651

Founded: 1991. **Members:** 437. **National.** Women in Russia working to assist underprivileged individuals. Offers financial and legal assistance.

★1481★ WOMEN IN SUPPORT FOR ECOLOGICAL PROJECTS -
   "ECOFAM"
Nemirovicha-Danchenko str. 6
103832 Moscow, Russia   PH: 95 1700930
Tatyana Popova, President   FX: 95 2097727

Founded: 1992. **Members:** 180. **National.** Women in Russia dedicated to the improvement of the environment. Sponsors programs to increase environmental awareness. Disseminates information.

★1482★ WOMEN OF THE WORLD AGAINST DRUGS
Gilyarovskogo str. 65
129110 Moscow, Russia   PH: 95 2811587
Galina Silaste, Coordinator   FX: 95 9716835

Founded: 1992. **Members:** 34. **Multinational.** Works to abolish drug abuse among women. Conducts educational programs. Offers medical assistance.

★1483★ WOMEN'S CHRISTIAN UNION
Sheremetievskaya str. 25, Apt. 339
127521 Moscow, Russia
Tatyana Latysheva, Exec.Dir.   PH: 95 1444794

Founded: 1992. **National.** Christian women in Russia. Upholds Christian

beliefs, ideals, and values. Conducts religious programs to share the Christian faith with the Russian public. Sponsors charitable programs.

★1484★ WOMEN'S INITIATIVE FOUNDATION
Tverskaya str. 22a
103050 Moscow, Russia
Lyudmila Shvetsova, President   PH: 95 1881111

Founded: 1992. **National.** Promotes women's careers in business and management in the formation of the new Russian economic structure. Seeks the creation of new jobs that involve women more directly in Russian business and industry. Conducts educational programs.

★1485★ WOMEN'S UNION
Kommunisticheskaya str. 8, No. 610
Republic of Komi
181000 Syktyvkar, Russia
Angelina Belyaeva, Chairwoman   PH: 8212223143

Founded: 1992. **Members:** 9,500. **National.** Promotes the interests of women; defends women's rights. Provides welfare assistance programs to women in need. Offers educational courses and legal services.

★1486★ WOMEN'S UNION OF RUSSIA
Nemirovich-Danchenko str. 6
103832 Moscow, Russia   PH: 95 2293223
Alevtina Fedulova, President   FX: 95 2097727

Founded: 1992. **Members:** 12,000. **National.** Umbrella organization of women's organizations in Russia. Promotes the interests of women in Russia. Offers legal and counseling services.

Ukraine

★1487★ COMMITTEE OF THE INDEPENDENT WOMEN CENTRE
Vinogradovskaya str. 20/12
334270 Alushta, Ukraine
Nina Karpacheva, Chairwoman   PH: 656035303

Founded: 1992. **Members:** 92. **National.** Promotes the interests of women in the Ukraine. Organizes programs that research and study issues affecting women. Conducts educational courses. Offers legal assistance to women.

★1488★ UKRAINIAN ASSOCIATION OF WOMEN MOVIE-MAKERS
Saksaganskogo str. 5
252033 Kiev, Ukraine
Silviya Sergeychikova, Chairwoman   PH: 44 2273130

Founded: 1967. **Members:** 87. **National.** Women filmmakers in Russia. Promotes the work of members. Offers support and assistance.

★1489★ WOMAN AND BUSINESS - CENTRE OF SOCIAL
   PROGRAMMES
Box 3139
290054 Lvov, Ukraine
Viktoriya Logvinenko, President

Founded: 1992. **National.** Promotes the career development of women in business and management industries. Conducts educational and developmental programs. Supports the development of jobs for women within the Ukraine's new economic structure.

★1490★ WOMEN UNION OF UKRAINE
Saksaganskogo str. 129, Apt. 22
252033 Kiev, Ukraine
Elena Suslova, Vice-Chairwoman   PH: 44 2209750

Founded: 1992. **National**. Promotes the involvement of women in economic, legal, political, and social arenas of Ukrainian society. Studies women and their role in the Ukraine. Conducts research and educational programs.

Europe

Austria	England	Luxembourg	Romania
Belgium	Finland	Malta	Scotland
Bulgaria	France	Netherlands	Spain
Croatia	Germany	Northern Ireland	Sweden
Cyprus	Greece	Norway	Switzerland
Czech Republic	Hungary	Poland	Turkey
Denmark	Iceland	Portugal	Wales
	Ireland, Republic of		
	Italy		

Europe

Austria

★1491★ AUF-EINE FRAUENZEITSCHRIFT
Postfach 817
A-1011 Vienna, Austria
Sonja Rotter, Contact   PH: 1 639164

Founded: 1974. **Members:** 5. **Budget:** 300,000 AS. **Languages:** German. **Multinational.** Autonomous women. Addresses issues such as: feminism; homosexuality; the economy; health; and socialism. Supports the following views: women's reasonable retirement age; non-discriminatory employment practices; legal rights of both parents to work part-time until children are 6 years of age; the opening of more quality childcare facilities as an essential ingredient to equal treatment; and an adequate salary minimum. Offers programs in political education.

Publications: *Newsletter* (in German), quarterly. ● *Die Frauen Wiens* (in German). Book.

Conventions/Meetings: monthly meeting - Vienna, Austria.

★1492★ BUND OSTERREICHISCHER FRAUENVEREINE
Wilhelm-Exner-Gasse 34-36
A-1090 Vienna IX, Austria   PH: 222 3484493
Mrs. Friedl Corcoran, President   222 5126330

National. Umbrella organization for women's groups in Austria. Promotes and supports women and women's interests. Conducts and coordinates activities. Disseminates information to increase public awareness of women's concerns.

★1493★ CENTRE FOR SOCIAL DEVELOPMENT AND HUMANITARIAN
    AFFAIRS - DIVISION FOR THE ADVANCEMENT OF WOMEN
United Nations Office at Vienna   PH: 1 211315284
Postfach 500   1 211314270
A-1400 Vienna, Austria   FX: 1 237495
Ms. Chafika Meslem, Director   TX: 135612 UNOA

Staff: 27. **Languages:** French, Spanish, English. **Multinational.** Monitors and appraises advances in women's struggle for equality. Seeks to eliminate all forms of discrimination against women. Undertakes research on women's economic, social, and educational status. Prepares reports and makes recommendations on women's issues. **Computer Services:** Bibliographic search, WIS (Women's Information Service) in French, Spanish, and English. United Nation's documents on women's issues since 1985.

Publications: *Women 2000* (in French, Spanish, and English), 5 issues/year. Magazine. ● *World Survey on the Role of women in Development*, quinquennial. Monograph. ● *WIS Accessions List*, 3 or 4 issues/year. Directory. Bibliographic references of recent United Nations documents. ● *National Machinery for the Advancement of Women: United Nations and UN Organizations Focal Points for the Advancement of Women*, periodic. Directory.

Conventions/Meetings: annual Commission on the Status of Women meeting - always March. ● annual Committee on the Elimination of Discrimination Against Women meeting - always February.

★1494★ COMMISSION ON THE STATUS OF WOMEN (CSW)
United Nations Vienna International
    Centre   PH: 1 211315284
Postfach 500   FX: 1 232156
A-1400 Vienna, Austria   TX: 135612 UNO A
Mrs. C. Meslem, Dir.   CBL: UNATIONS VIENNA

Founded: 1946. **Members:** 45. **Budget:** US$196,400. **Regional Groups:** 6. **Languages:** Arabic, Chinese, English, French, Russian, Spanish. **Multinational.** Established by the Economic and Social Council. Consists of representatives from United Nations member countries. Promotes women's rights in political, economic, civil, social, and educational fields. Encourages cooperation between organizations seeking to advance the status of women, and advises the U.N. and member bodies on situations requiring immediate attention. **Working Groups:** Communications on the Status of Women.

Conventions/Meetings: annual meeting (exhibits).

★1495★ COMMITTEE ON ELIMINATION OF DISCRIMINATION
    AGAINST WOMEN (CEDAW)
Division for the Advancement of Women
Vienna International Centre
PO Box 500
A-1400 Vienna, Austria

National. Provides information to the United Nations regarding discrimination against women. Promotes the development and status of women. Monitors implementation of the 1979 Convention on the Elimination of All Forms of Discrimination Against Women. Examines articles of the convention related to violence, sexual harassment, and exploitation of women. Fights to eliminate all types of discrimination toward women.

★1496★ FEDERATION OF AMERICAN WOMEN'S CLUBS OVERSEAS
    (FAWCO)
c/o Ann Day
Wambachergasse 1
A-1130 Vienna, Austria   PH: 1 8047176
Ann Day, Pres.   FX: 1 8047176

Founded: 1931. **Members:** 49. **Multinational.** American women's clubs or associations based in Europe, the Far East, and Africa; represents over 15,000 individuals. Serves as a link among American women abroad, and promotes better understanding between the U.S. and other nations. Studies cultural heritage, multi- and bilingualism, citizenship status, including legislation pertaining to Americans married to nationals of other countries, and methods of improving voter registration for Americans abroad. Conducts research and educational programs on culture shock and women's legal status abroad; compiles statistics. Maintains a relief fund and resource center. **Committees:** Citizenship; Education; Environment; International Social Problems.

Publications: *Conference Reports*, biennial. Booklet. ● *Directory*, periodic. ● *Presidential Newsletter*, 2-3/year. ● *Social Security Benefits Overseas*. Booklet. ● *University Education in the United States: A College Planning Guide*. Book. ● *Handbook for the American Family Abroad*. Booklet.

Conventions/Meetings: biennial conference, Seminars and workshops - always odd-numbered years. ● periodic regional meeting.

★1497★ FRAUENZIRKEL OF AUSTRIA
Veithgasse 9/6
A-1031 Vienna, Austria
Rosy Weiss, President   PH: 222 71158

Languages: German. **National**. Works to advance the status of women. Fosters communication among members.

★1498★ KOMMUNIKTIONS ZENTRUM FUR FRAUEN -
    FRAUENZENTRUM
Wahringerstr. 59/6
A-1090 Vienna, Austria   PH: 1 4085057

Founded: 1981. **Members:** 350. **Budget:** 1,000,000 AS. **Languages:** German. **National**. Individual women and women's groups. Defends women against oppression and discrimination. Creates communication opportunities for women. Strives to promote and support the interests of women in all spheres of life, especially in the areas of science, culture, society, and labor. Special committees work with: female immigrants; female craft workers; the organization newspaper; a feminist girls' school; and self defense groups. Extends events, courses, a meeting place, and speeches to the public. **Libraries:** Type: reference.

Publications: *Frauenachtrichten/Lesbennachrichten* (in German). Magazine.
● *Anschlage* (in German). Newspaper.

Conventions/Meetings: bimonthly meeting - Vienna, Austria. ● annual general assembly - Vienna, Austria.

★1499★ MEDICAL WOMEN'S INTERNATIONAL ASSOCIATION -
    AUSTRIA
Canisiusgasse 3-5
A-1090 Vienna, Austria
Judith Volkert, Contact   PH: 1 347685

Languages: German. **National**. Austria branch of the Medical Women's International Association (see separate entry). Women physicians. Provides a forum for discussion of women's health care issues. Encourages women to enter the field of medicine. Works to overcome discrimination against female physicians. Sponsors research and educational programs.

★1500★ OSTERREICHISCHE GESELLSCHAFT FUR
    FAMILIENPLANUNG (OGF)
II Universitatsfrauenklinik
Skpitalgasse 23
A-1090 Vienna, Austria   PH: 1 404002924
Ms. Elisabeth Pracht, Secretary   FX: 1 3105854

Languages: German. **National**. Works to imiprove the quality of life for individuals living in Austria by promoting family planning and responsible parenthood. Works to reduce the number of unwanted pregnancies and abortions and stop the spread of sexually transmitted diseases, especially AIDS. Provides programs in family planning, sex education, and health. Provides contraceptive services.

★1501★ SOCIALIST WOMEN OF AUSTRIA
Loewlstr. 18
A-1014 Vienna, Austria
Solanda Offenbeck, President

Languages: German. **National**. Women advocating the principles of democratic socialism in Austria. Fosters women's involvement in public life.

★1502★ YOUNG WOMEN'S CHRISTIAN ASSOCIATION-AUSTRIA
    (YWCA)
Neubaugurtel 28/5
A-1070 Vienna, Austria
Christa Gartner, Contact   PH: 222 9339363

National. Works to promote Christian fellowship and service among young women in Austria. Advocates peace and justice.

Belgium

★1503★ AAF
21, rue de la Science
B-1040 Brussels, Belgium   PH: 2 2307295

Languages: French. **National**. French-speaking Catholic women farmers. Promotes improved farming conditions and supports the development of rural women.

★1504★ ABBV/FGTB - WOMEN
Hoogstraat 42
B-1000 Brussels, Belgium   PH: 2 5116466

Languages: French, Dutch. **National**. Socialist women members of trade unions. Works to improve women's employment opportunities and working conditions.

★1505★ ASSOCIATION DES FEMMES AU FOYER (AFF)
49, ave. Eudore Pirmez
B-1040 Brussels, Belgium
Nicole Janssens, Contact   PH: 2 6403500

Founded: 1976. **Members:** 3,000. **Budget:** 425,000 BFr. **National**. Works to improve the status of women who work in the home. Offers support groups and a forum for communication among women working in the home. Promotes working in the home as of equal value to working outside the home. Supports paying housewives a salary for the work they do in the home. Sponsors programs to protect the rights of children.

Publications: *Association des Femmes au Foyer* (in French), quarterly. Bulletin. ● *Femmes au Foyer, Que Veulent-Elle?*. Booklet.

Conventions/Meetings: annual general assembly (exhibits) - Belgium.

★1506★ ASSOCIATION DES MAISONS D'ACCEUIL (AMA)
78, rue Rempart des Moines
B-1000 Brussels, Belgium   PH: 2 5136225
Francoise Lassaux, Sec.   2 5136225

Founded: 1968. **Members:** 51. **Staff:** 1. **Languages:** French, English. **National**. Umbrella organization for homeless women's shelters. Special interest is paid to unwed mothers. Sponsors educational and vocational training programs. Works to eliminate poverty in Belgium. Offers referral services for women with financial difficulties. Works to protect the rights of women and children living in poverty. Conducts research on causes of poverty and homelessness and its effects on women.

Publications: *Amascopie* (in French), annual. Journal. ● *Directory* (in French), periodic. Homeless shelters in Belgium.

★1507★ ATOL-VROUWENGROEP (STUDIE-EN
    DOCUMENTATIECENTRUM VOOR AANGEPASTE TECHNOLOGIE IN
    ONTWIKKELINGSLANDEN)
Blijde Inkomststraat 9
B-3000 Louvain, Belgium   PH: 16 224517
Rob Buisten   FX: 16 222256

Founded: 1976. **Staff:** 8. **Languages:** French, Flemish, English. **National**.

Promotes entrepreneurship and advancement of women in technological industries. Conducts research of technology and industry.

★1508★ BELGIAN CORP. OF FLIGHT HOSTESSES (BCFH)
65, rue Edouard Stuckens
B-1140 Brussels, Belgium

Founded: 1971. **Languages:** French, Flemish, English. **National.** Women civil aviation flight personnel. Defends the rights and social and professional interests of national commercial flight personnel, especially that of flight attendants.

Conventions/Meetings: periodic congress, In conjuction with the International Flight Attendants Association. - Brussels, Belgium.

★1509★ BOND VAN VORMINGS - EN ONTWIKKELINGSORGANISTIES
   - INVENTARISATIE VORMINGSWERK MET VROUWEN (BVVO)
Tiensevest 142
B-3000 Louvain, Belgium   PH: 16 223419
Bea Elskens, Contact   FX: 16 295112

Founded: 1971. **Members:** 80. **Staff:** 5. **Languages:** Dutch, French, English. **National.** Umbrella organization for international women's development programs. Works to influence governmental policies on women's issues. Conducts social, educational, and cultural programs for women. Fosters communication and exchange among members. **Libraries:** Type: reference.

Publications: *Koepel 5* (in Dutch), quarterly. Newsletter.

★1510★ CENTRE FEMININ D'EDUCATION PERMANENTE
11, ave. de Mercure
BP 4
B-1011 Brussels, Belgium
Jacqline DeGroote, Contact

Languages: French. **National.** Promotes women's educational opportunities in Belgium. Works to eliminate sexual discrimination.

★1511★ CENTRE FOR RESEARCH ON EUROPEAN WOMEN (CREW)
(CRFE Centre de Recherches sur les Femmes Europeennes)
21, rue de la Tourelle   PH: 2 2305158
B-1040 Brussels, Belgium   FX: 2 2306230
Rebecca Franceskides, Co-Dir.   E-Mail: MCRI:CREW

Founded: 1980. **Staff:** 11. **Multinational.** Promotes the study of women's issues. Supports women's cooperatives and self-managed businesses in the European Community. Provides information on women's employment issues and training programs. **Computer Services:** Data base.

Publications: *CREW Reports* (in English and French), monthly. Bulletin.

Conventions/Meetings: annual meeting.

★1512★ CMBV
Spastraat 8, bus 2
B-1040 Brussels, Belgium   PH: 2 2303384

Languages: French, Dutch. **National.** Women entrepreneurs and business-women in Belgium. Seeks to enhance the status of women professionals.

★1513★ COLLECTIVE FOR BATTERED WOMEN
(Collectif pour Femmes Battues)
29, rue Blanche
B-1050 Brussels, Belgium
Odette Simon, Director   PH: 2 5392744

Founded: 1977. **Staff:** 10. **Languages:** French. **National.** Offers counseling and therapy for victims and aggressors of domestic violence. Involved in educational activities to sensitize society to domestic violence. Provides

confidential refuge for victims which includes: counseling services; relaxation workshops; and personalized assistance in establishing independence.

★1514★ COMITE DES ORGANIZATIONS PROFESSIONELLES
   AGRICOLES - COMMISSION FEMININE (COPA)
23-25, rue de la Science   PH: 2 2872711
B-1040 Brussels, Belgium   FX: 2 2871700
Mr. V. Desantis, Sec.   TX: 25816

Founded: 1960. **Members:** 5,000,000. **Staff:** 50. **Languages:** French, English, German, Italian, Spanish. **Multinational.** Women living in rural areas of Europe with interests in farming. Acts as a forum for the exchange of information among women. Promotes women's rights. Works to protect the interests of female farmers. Disseminates information on political and economic conditions relevant to women working in agriculture.

Conventions/Meetings: triennial meeting.

★1515★ COMMISSION FEMMES DE L'ACTION CATHOLIQUE DES
   MILIEUX INDEPENDANTS (ACI)
19, rue du Manteau
B-1040 Brussels, Belgium   PH: 2 2185447
Francoise Capart, Secretary   FX: 2 2231393

Founded: 1985. **Members:** 15. **Languages:** French. **National.** Women ages 40 to 65. Promotes Catholic ideals and the Christian way of life. Studies the relation between women's roles in society and the scriptures. Strives to improve the women's status in the Catholic church. Supports ideas of ACI and encourages the involvement of women in the organization. Aims to support and spread the organization views on life, morals, and thought.

Conventions/Meetings: annual meeting.

★1516★ COMMISSION INTERFEDERALE DES FEMMES DU PARTI
   SOCIALISTE
13, blvd. de l'Empereur
B-1000 Brussels, Belgium   PH: 2 5138270
Anne Marie Lizin, President   2 5132019

Founded: 1983. **Members:** 500. **Budget:** 200,000 BFr. **Languages:** French. **National.** Women who support the ideals of the Socialist party. Acts as a forum for the exchange of information among women in Belgium. Promotes the interests of women in the economy, law, politics, and culture.

Publications: *Bulletin*, periodic.

Conventions/Meetings: weekly meeting - Brussels, Belgium.

★1517★ COMMISSION DU TRAVAIL DES FEMMES
(Commissie Vrouwenarbeid)
                                            PH: 2 2334016
Belliardstraat 51   2 2334020
B-1040 Brussels, Belgium   FX: 2 2334032

Languages: Dutch, French. **National.** Union members and employers in Belgium. Seeks to achieve equal employment opportunities for women. Conducts research.

★1518★ CONSEIL DES FEMMES FRANCOPHONES DE BELGIQUE
c/o Jacqueline Alixin
28, square de Meeus
B-1040 Brussels, Belgium
Jacqueline Alixin, President   PH: 2 5144949

Founded: 1905. **Members:** 371. **Staff:** 3. **Budget:** 6,000,000 BFr. **Languages:** French. **National.** Individual women and women's groups from varying ideological and philosophical orientations. Promotes women's social, political, and economic independence. Areas of concern include: children's welfare, economics, family finances, education, environmental awareness, women in society, law, women immigrants, politics, media, health, work, and elderly women. **Awards:** Annual Femme de l'Annee. **Committees:** Arts and

Letters; Development; Economy. **Formerly:** Conseil National des Femmes Belges.

Publications: *Objectif* (in French), monthly. Bulletin. ● *Objectif* (in French), quarterly. Booklet.

★1519★ CONSEIL NATIONAL DES FEMMES BELGES (CNFB)
(Nationale Vrouwenraad)
Square de Meeus 28   PH: 2 5144949
B-1040 Brussels, Belgium   2 5118243
Alixin Jaequeline, President   FX: 2 5024492

Founded: 1905. **Members:** 371. **Membership Dues:** Individual., 600 BFr annual. **Staff:** 3. **Budget:** 600,000 BFr. **Languages:** French. **National.** Women and women's organizations. Works to increase women's rights politically, economically, socially, and culturally. Lobbies government to adopt laws that provide equal rights to women. Offers programs in economics, education, conservation, law, immigration issues, health, and children's rights. Sponsors seminars; conducts research on women's issues. **Libraries:** Type: reference. **Awards:** Annual Femme de l'Annee.

Publications: *Bulletin* (in French), quarterly. ● *Newsletter* (in French), monthly.

Conventions/Meetings: periodic meeting (exhibits) - Brussels, Belgium.

★1520★ COORDINATION DES GROUPES CONTRE LES VIOLENCES
   FAITES AUX FEMMES
29, rue Blanche
B-1050 Brussels, Belgium
Mme. de Vinck, Contact   PH: 2 5392744

Founded: 1987. **Members:** 8. **Languages:** French. **National.** Offers support services and referrals to women who are victims of violence. Operates shelters and recovery programs for battered women. Represents concerns of women victims of violence in legislation and policy development.

Publications: *Information et Formation de Policies sur les Violences Faites aux Femmes* (in French). Book.

Conventions/Meetings: monthly meeting.

★1521★ EUROPEAN ASSOCIATION FOR THE DEVELOPMENT OF
   INFORMATION AND TRAINING OF WOMEN (EUDIFF)
(Association Europeene pour le Developpement de l'Information et de la
   Formation des Femmes)
73, ave. 1
Geyskens
B-1160 Brussels, Belgium   PH: 2 4132311
Marie-Therese Destercke, Secretary   FX: 2 4133090

Multinational. Parent organization of European women's organizations working to make information on women and women's issues available. Circulates information on women's rights and achievments throughout Europe. Networks with organizations that also champion women's advancement. Demands that EC nations fully recognize women's rights. Supports women's development and equality; encourages women's participation in leadership roles. Facilitates exchange among members.

★1522★ EUROPEAN ASSOCIATION FOR THE DEVELOPMENT OF
   INFORMATION AND TRAINING OF WOMEN - BELGIUM (EUDIFF)
(Association Europeene pour le Developppment de l'Information et de la
   Formation des Femenes - Belgium)
12 St. Goriksplein, bus 20
B-1000 Brussels, Belgium
Anne-Sophie Van Neste, Contact   PH: 2 5117695

Languages: Flemish, French. **National.** Circulates information on women and women's issues throughout Belgium. Networks with organizations that also champion women's advancement. Demands that EC nations fully recognize women's rights. Supports women's development and equality;

encourages women's participation in leadership roles. Facilitates exchange among members.

★1523★ EUROPEAN COMMUNITY WOMEN IN DECISION-MAKING
   NETWORK
33A, rue Mercelis
B-1050 Brussels, Belgium
Sabine de Bethune, Contact

Languages: French, Dutch. **Multinational.** Seeks to "achieve a balanced distribution of public and political power between men and women" in the European Community. Encourages women's increased participation in political decision-making. Liaises with trade unions and other women's organizations to achieve women's equality.

★1524★ EUROPEAN COUNCIL OF WOMEN (ECW)
139, ave. Brand-Whitlock
B-1200 Brussels, Belgium   PH: 2 7337410
M. Blanke, V.Pres.   FX: 2 7323523

Multinational. Promotes the interests of women in the European Community. Fosters communication and cooperation among members; upholds the cooperative ideals of the EC.

★1525★ EUROPEAN NETWORK OF WOMEN (ENW)
29, rue Blanche
B-1050 Brussels, Belgium
M. Harst, Contact   PH: 2 5384773

Founded: 1983. **Multinational.** Analyzes and reviews European Community policies on women's issues. Lobbies for women's rights and issues that affect the status of women in the EC.

★1526★ EUROPEAN WOMEN'S LOBBY (EWL)
(LEF Lobby Europeen des Femmes)
22, rue du Meridien
B-1030 Brussels, Belgium   PH: 2 2179020
Ana Vale, Pres.   FX: 2 2179020

Staff: 4. **Budget:** 300,000 BFr. **Multinational.** Seeks the fair and equal representation of women's rights and women's issues in the formation of the European Community. Cooperates with other European women's organizations.

Publications: *Newsletter*, quarterly.

Conventions/Meetings: annual general assembly.

★1527★ EUROPEAN WOMEN'S MANAGEMENT DEVELOPMENT
   NETWORK (EWMD)
40, rue Washington
B-1050 Brussels, Belgium   PH: 2 6480385
Ariane Berthoin Antal, Pres.   FX: 2 6460768

Founded: 1984. **Members:** 1,000. **Staff:** 1. **Languages:** English. **Multinational.** Women in 30 countries with professional interests in management development. Strives to improve management in Europe by developing women's managerial skills.

Publications: *EWMD* (in English), annual. Directory. ● *EWMD Newsletter* (in English), quarterly.

Conventions/Meetings: annual conference.

★1528★ EUROPEAN YOUNG WOMEN'S CHRISTIAN ASSOCIATIONS
94, ave. Brugmann
B-1060 Brussels, Belgium   PH: 2 3449861
Denise Siegrist-Rey, Coord.   2 3465946

Founded: 1971. **Members:** 17. **Staff:** 1. **Budget:** 1,200,000 BFr. **Languages:** English. **Multinational.** Umbrella organization of national YWCA organizations. Upholds the beliefs and principles of the World Young Women's Christian Association (see separate entry). Works to promote Christian fellowship and service among young women in Europe. Enables networking between YWCAs throughout Europe. Conducts educational and exchange programs, leadership training, and seminars for women and youth with a Christian perspective.

Publications: *Newsletter*, 3/year.

Conventions/Meetings: semiannual European Liaison Group Meetings. ● annual European Regional Meetings. ● quadrennial East/West Seminars.

★1529★ FEDERATIE VROUWEN IN DE MIDDENLEEFTIJD - VROUWEN ANDERE LEEFTIJD (VIM - VAL)
Breughelstraat 31-33
B-2018 Antwerp, Belgium
Ludgarde Van Parys, Contact   PH: 3 2393049

Founded: 1985. **Members:** 66. **Budget:** 250,000 BFr. **Languages:** Flemish. **National.** Middle-aged and older women. Addresses older women's issues. Promotes the importance of self-esteem and self-awareness for older women. Assists women in finding positive direction for their lives. Provides cultural and recreational activities, seminars, and educational programs.

Publications: *Newsletter* (in Flemish), quarterly.

★1530★ FEDERATION FRANCOPHONE BELGE POUR LE PLANNING FAMILIAL ET L'EDUCATION SEXUELLE (FFBPFLES)
(Federatie Centra voor Greboortenregling en Sexuelle Opvoeding)
34, rue de la Tulipe   PH: 2 5028203
B-1050 Brussels, Belgium   2 5026800
Ms. Clare Gavroy, Exec. Dir.   FX: 2 5025613

Languages: French. **National.** Advocates family planning as a basic human right. Works to reduce the number of unwanted pregnancies and abortions. Attempts to stop the spread of AIDS and other sexually transmitted diseases through education and contraceptive services. Sponsors programs in family planning and health. Acts as an advocate for family planning on a national level.

★1531★ GRIF AVEC LA COMMISSION EUROPEENE (GRACE)
c/o GRIF
29, rue Blanche
B-1050 Brussels, Belgium   PH: 2 5388487
Geraldine H. Wooley, Coord.   FX: 2 5375596

Founded: 1987. **Budget:** 100,000 BFr. **Languages:** French, English. **Multinational.** A European women's studies project created and managed by Groupe de Recherche et d'Information Feministe (GRIF). Promotes the interests of researchers, students, and teachers of women's studies. Provides information on teaching and research issues in women's studies. **Computer Services:** Data base, information on individual researchers and women's studies centres; courses and bibliographies in Europe.

Publications: *Power, Empowerment, and Politics* (in French and English). Book. **Also Cited As:** *Pouvoir, Feminisation du Pouvoir et Politique.* ● *Feminist Research* (in French and English). Book. **Also Cited As:** *Recherches Feministes.* ● *Women and Work* (in French and English). Book. **Also Cited As:** *Femmes et Travail.* ● *Student Guide* (in English and French). Book. **Also Cited As:** *Guide Etudiant.*

★1532★ GROUP FOR FEMINIST RESEARCH AND INFORMATION
(GRIF Groupe de Recherche et d'Information Feministe)
29, rue Blanche
B-1050 Brussels, Belgium   PH: 2 5388487
Maria France Joly, Coord.   FX: 2 5375596

Founded: 1973. **Staff:** 3. **Languages:** French, English, Dutch. **Multinational.**

Studies the "feminine condition" and women's changing roles in Belgium and France. Disseminates information. **Computer Services:** Data base.

Publications: *Les Cahiers du Grif* (in French), periodic. Journal.

Conventions/Meetings: periodic conference.

★1533★ HOUSE OF HOPE
(DAA Dar Al Amal)
De Ribaucourt Straat 51
B-1080 Brussels, Belgium   PH: 2 4267495
Lorendi Marchi, Contact   FX: 2 4257439

Founded: 1978. **Languages:** Dutch, French, English. **National.** Assists in the integration of migrant women into Belgian society. Provides shelter for migrants in homes of volunteer hosts. Offers language, cooking, and sewing courses. Fosters communication and exchange among migrant women.

★1534★ IMPULS - CENTRUM VOOR VORMING, TRAINING EN GROEPSONTWIKKELING
Albertlaan 27
B-3200 Aarschot, Belgium
Mips Meyntiens   PH: 16 569568

Founded: 1977. **Staff:** 5. **Budget:** 6,000,000 BFr. **Languages:** Flemish. **National.** Offers education and personal growth courses for women relating to: assertiveness; self-defense; feminist help groups; homosexuality; and exercise. **Programs:** Organization Development; Team Building; Counseling Training.

★1535★ INTERNATIONAL ASSOCIATION OF WOMEN AND HOME PAGE JOURNALISTS (AIJPF)
(Association Internationale des Journalistes de la Presse Feminine et Familiale)
c/o IPC
1, blvd. Charlemagne, boite 54
B-1040 Brussels, Belgium
Brigitte Soyer, Pres.

Founded: 1964. **Members:** 400. **Budget:** US$145,750. **Languages:** English, French. **Multinational.** Professional press, radio, and television journalists in 25 countries whose material is intended for women and families. Exchanges news and attempts to ensure a better knowledge of problems which concern women; promotes the advancement of women in all countries and fields. Examines personal, family, civic, cultural, consumer, and artistic topics. Conducts surveys, study trips, and seminars with international bodies.

Publications: *Directory*, biennial. ● *Newsletter* (in English and French), quarterly.

Conventions/Meetings: biennial congress - 1994.

★1536★ INTERNATIONAL LESBIAN AND GAY ASSOCIATION (ILGA)
c/o Antenne Rose & FWH
81, rue Marche-au-Charbon
B-1000 Brussels 1, Belgium   PH: 2 5022471
Micha Ramakers, Information Sec.   FX: 2 5022471

Founded: 1978. **Members:** 300. **Staff:** 1. **Budget:** 28,000 BFr. **Languages:** English, Spanish. **Multinational.** Gay and lesbian groups in 50 countries. Fights discrimination against homosexuals and promotes the recognition of lesbian and gay rights by applying pressure on governments, international groups, and the media. Serves as information clearinghouse on gay oppression and liberation issues. Maintains archives. **Computer Services:** Data base; mailing lists. **Projects:** Council of Europe/CSCE; European Community; Homosexual Prisoners; Iceberg-Project on Discrimination of Lesbians and Gays; ILGA Pink Book Project; ILGA Project on Amnesty International; Twinning. **Committees:** Action; Women. **Study Groups:** Ableism; Africa; Asia; Community Centres; Christian Churches; Culture;

Eastern Europe; Gays and Lesbians in Military; Immigration; Latin America; Youth.

Publications: *Conference Report*, annual. Booklet. ● *ILGA Bulletin*, 5/year. ISSN: 0281-6270. Advertising: not accepted.

Conventions/Meetings: annual conference - 1994 June, New York, NY, United States.

★1537★ KATHOLIEK VORMINGSWERK VOOR LANDELIJKE
  VROUWEN (KVLV)
Schapenstr. 34
B-3000 Louvain, Belgium   PH: 16 243999
Nieke Rutten   16 243909

Founded: 1911. Members: 162,000. Staff: 80. Languages: Flemish. National. Catholic female farmers and naturalists. A socio-cultural organization for women from the countryside. Promotes personal, social, and relational growth and development of rural women. Pursues the professional advancement and interests of female farmers. Strives to bring women together in the pursuit of influencing the political realm. Structured to allow members to participate in its organization.

Publications: *Eipen Aard* (in Flemish), monthly. Newsletter. ● *Daheim* (in German), monthly. Newsletter. ● *Contact* (in Flemish), quarterly. Bulletin. ● *Beschursblad* (in Flemish), monthly. Newsletter.

★1538★ KAV
Poststraat 111
B-1210 Brussels, Belgium   PH: 2 2203081

Languages: Flemish. National. Flemish Catholic women. Promotes principles of Catholicism.

★1539★ KONTAKTSTATTE FUR FRAUEN
Neustr. 63
B-4700 Eupen, Belgium
Doris Malmendier, Clerk   PH: 87 744241

Founded: 1984. Members: 22. Staff: 1. Budget: 78,000,000 BFr. Languages: German. National. Women of the German-speaking region of Belgium. Works to promote social and cultural exchange programs. Offers development seminars for women addressing different women's issues. Provides counseling and legal services for women in crisis situations. Libraries: Type: reference.   Subjects: women's literature.

Conventions/Meetings: semiannual general assembly.

★1540★ KVLV
Schapenstraat 34
B-3000 Louvain, Belgium   PH: 2 243999

Languages: Flemish. National. Flemish-speaking Catholic women farmers. Promotes improved farming conditions and supports the development of rural women.

★1541★ LESBISCH DOE FRONT (LDF)
Postbus 621
B-9000 Ghent, Belgium   PH: 91 216331

Founded: 1986. Budget: 2,000,000 BFr. Languages: English. National. Provides information to individuals and the public regarding lesbian issues.

Conventions/Meetings: annual Lesbian day event. - Belgium.

★1542★ MEDICAL WOMEN'S ASSOCIATION OF BELGIUM (MWABE)
Nachtegalenlaan 21
B-2070 Zwijndrecht, Belgium   PH: 3 2526688
Dr. Christiane Ponliart, President   FX: 3 2320680

Founded: 1989. Members: 200. Budget: 750,000 BFr. Languages: Flem-
ish, French, English. National. Promotes medical research by women for women in the areas of: osteoporosis, breast cancer, heart disease, endometriosis, infertility, and premenstrual syndrome. Active in improving social respect for women doctors through: bestowing grants; and lobbying. Educates women on health issues.

Conventions/Meetings: quarterly regional meeting. ● board meeting - 9/year. ● annual congress (exhibits). ● annual general assembly. ● Generale Bank Meir - 1993 Nov. 11, Antwerp, Belgium.

★1543★ MENOPAUZE: PROBLEEMOPVANG
University Hospital Sasthuisberg-St.
  Rafael
Dept. of Obstetrics and Gynecology
Capucienenvoer 33
B-3000 Louvain, Belgium
Prof. P. Nijs, Contact   PH: 16 332632

Founded: 1968. Members: 8. Staff: 6. Languages: English, French, Dutch. National. Promotes the study of menopause. Supports theories of psychosomatic menopause. Conducts clinical training and teaching programs in psychosomatic gynecology. Offers marriage and family therapy sessions. Conducts sexological research. Libraries: Type: reference. Holdings: books. Subjects: biomedical science.

Conventions/Meetings: triennial European Symposium on Psychosomatic Obstetrics and Gynecology. ● biennial International Symposium on Psychosomatic Gynecology - Montpelier, France.

★1544★ MOUVEMENT DU NID
14, rue Hydraulique
B-1040 Brussels, Belgium   PH: 2 2178472
Robert Roelens, Secretary   FX: 2 2685078

Founded: 1982. Members: 40. Staff: 9. Budget: 8,300,000 BFr. Languages: French. Multinational. Works to increase awareness through political action and media exposure of the situations of impoverished women and others in crisis. Maintains assistance program for women coming out of prostitution.

Publications: *Nouvelles du Nid* (in French), quarterly. Newsletter.

Conventions/Meetings: annual Journee Internationale de l'Abolition de l'Esclavage sous Toutes ses Formes conference (exhibits) - Belgium.

★1545★ NA'AMAT UNION DES FEMMES PIONIERES (NUFP)
22, ave. d'Overhem   PH: 2 3743880
B-1050 Brussels, Belgium   FX: 2 3749271

Languages: Dutch, French. Multinational. Working and professional women. Works to advance the status of women by providing a variety of educational, community, and legal services. Believes that strong family relations are the foundation of a stable society. Members identify with the Zionist movement.

★1546★ NATIONAAL CENTRUM ONTRIKKELINGS SAMENVERKIG
(NCOS-Vrouwengroep)
Vlasfabriekstraat 11   PH: 2 5392620
B-1060 Brussels, Belgium   FX: 2 5391343

Founded: 1985. Members: 70. Budget: 145,000 BFr. Languages: Flemish, French. National. Coordinates activities of nongovernmental organizations on issues of concern to women in developing nations. Supports and participates in the activities of member groups, such as development projects, volunteer recruitment, and educational programs. Organizes training workshops and seminars; strives to heighten public awareness of the concerns of women in developing countries through the dissemination of information; conducts studies on population. Computer Services: Data base, women's organizations and movements in developing countries.

Publications: *Bulletin* (in Flemish), quarterly.

Conventions/Meetings: monthly meeting - Brussels, Belgium.

★1547★ NATIONALE COORDINATIE "ABORTUS UIT HET STRAFRECHT"
Lesbroussartstr. 28
B-1050 Brussels, Belgium
Arlette Bordage   PH: 2 6419373

Founded: 1975. **Languages:** French. **National.** Abortion clinics in Belgium. Makes available abortion procedure that is safe for women. Involved in the pursuit to legalize abortion. **Alternate name:** Groupe d'Action des Centres Extra-Hospitaliers Pratiquant l'Avortement.

★1548★ NEDERLANDSTALIGE VROUWENRAAD NUR
De Meeussquare 28
B-1040 Brussels, Belgium   PH: 2 5118243
Mrs. M. Van Haegendoren, Chair   FX: 2 5024492

Founded: 1973. **Members:** 26. **Staff:** 7. **Budget:** 1,000,000 BFr. **Languages:** Flemish, French, English. **National.** Works towards: establishing proportional representation of men and women in Belgian governmental bodies at the federal, provincial, and city level; eliminating discrimination against women in the social security system; improving childcare; and improving divorce legislation. Maintains documentation center. **Committees:** Elderly; Culture; Education; Law; Immigrants; Labor; Health; Family.

Publications: *Vrouwenrad Nieuwsbrief* (in Flemish), quarterly. • *Yearbook of Women in Flanders*.

Conventions/Meetings: monthly meeting.

★1549★ OMSCHAKELEN
Uitbreidingstraat 498
B-2600 Berchem, Belgium
Rita Ruys, Contact   PH: 3 2305472

Founded: 1981. **Staff:** 4. **Budget:** 3,500,000 BFr. **Languages:** Dutch, English. **National.** Seeks to enhance women's social, economic, and political status. Encourages women's participation in professional and socio-cultural activities. Offers educational, training, and job placement programs to women. **Libraries:** Type: reference.

Conventions/Meetings: semiannual meeting.

★1550★ PARENT CARRYING OUT FAMILY DUTIES AT HOME
(Thuiswerkende ouder Gezin Samenleving)
Lange Beeldekensstraat 71
B-2060 Antwerp, Belgium
Jeanne Appels-Sterkens, Secretary   PH: 3 2358903

Founded: 1977. **Languages:** Flemish, English. **National.** Protects the interests and rights of women working at home. Works to influence legislation regarding parental leave, changing standard work hours, and wages for housework. Disseminates information. Sponsors International Day of the Housewife (October 24th). Maintains documentation center.

Publications: *Thuiswerkende Ouder Gezin Samenleving*, quarterly. Magazine.

Conventions/Meetings: semiannual general assembly.

★1551★ PARTI FEMINISTE HUMANISTE
35, ave. des Phalenes, boite 14
B-1050 Brussels, Belgium
Renee Fosseprez, Contact   PH: 2 6488738

Founded: 1972. **Languages:** French. **National.** Political organization of women of middle and low socio-economic status. Areas of concern include: ethnic strife, social and economic stratification, the environment, and human rights. Promotes the self-determination of peoples desiring independence from national or foreign occupation and oppression, and the adoption of a globally neutral language such as Esperanto. Supports educational programs and research. Maintains speakers' bureau.

Publications: *Libre* (in French), quarterly. Newsletter.

★1552★ PASOP VZW
Brabantdam 100B
B-9000 Ghent, Belgium
Dr. Mak, Chair   PH: 91 334767

Founded: 1990. **Staff:** 3. **Budget:** 4,000,000 BFr. **Languages:** French, Dutch, English. **National.** Provides prostitutes with health care. Conducts a hepatitis B vaccination campaign.

★1553★ ROL EN SAMENLEVING (ROSA)
Gallaitstraat 86
B-1210 Brussels, Belgium
R. van Mechelen, Contact   PH: 2 2162323

Founded: 1977. **Staff:** 6. **Languages:** Dutch, English. **National.** Promotes the interests of women in Belgium. Supports documentation of women's issues, especially employment, sex roles, feminism and lifestyles. **Libraries:** Type: reference. Holdings: books, clippings, periodicals, monographs. Subjects: women's issues.

Publications: *Zakboekje voor de Vrouw* (in Dutch). Book.

★1554★ SAGO - VROUWENWERKING
Lange Lozanastr. 14
B-2018 Antwerp, Belgium   PH: 3 2385181
Yvette Deploige, Coord.   FX: 3 2375562

Founded: 1970. **Members:** 12. **Staff:** 1. **Budget:** 10,000,000 BFr. **Languages:** Spanish, English. **National.** Facilitates networking, solidarity, and cultural exchange among European and Latin American women. Offers educational information on development. Coordinates activities among women's groups.

Publications: *Aqui Nosotras* (in Spanish), 3/year. Bulletin.

Conventions/Meetings: periodic meeting (exhibits).

★1555★ SISTERS OF CHARITY OF JESUS AND MARY (SCJM)
(ZLJM Zusters van Liefe Jezus en Maria)
c/o Sr. Ludo Vercammen
25, rue St.-Bernard
B-1060 Brussels, Belgium
Sr. Ludo Vercammen, Superior Gen.   PH: 2 5375065

Founded: 1803. **Members:** 1,500. **National Groups:** 9. **Languages:** English, Flemish, French. **Multinational.** Women religious who have taken vows of chastity, poverty, and obedience in 16 countries. Members perform works of charity "in the Spirit of St. Vincent de Paul.".

Publications: *Caritas-Contact* (in English, Flemish, and French), periodic.

Conventions/Meetings: annual conference.

★1556★ SOCIALISTISCHE VOOKUITZIENDE VROUWEN (SVV)
Sint-Janstraat 32-38   PH: 2 5150414
B-1000 Brussels, Belgium   2 5150411
Gisele De Block, Contact   FX: 2 5150207

Founded: 1922. **Members:** 400,000. **Staff:** 1. **Local Groups:** 500. **Languages:** Flemish, French, English. **National.** Promotes women's rights and education fostering socialistic ideology. Offers services to members, including: child daycare service; holiday events for children; consultation of preventative health care; job orientation programs; professional education programs.

Publications: *Stem der Vrouw* (in Flemish), periodic. Magazine. • *Newsletter* (in Flemish), quarterly.

Conventions/Meetings: annual meeting.

★1557★ SOPHIA
Veije Universiteit Brussel
Centrum voor Vrouwenstudies
Pleinlaan 2
B-1050 Brussels, Belgium
Micheline Sheys, President
PH: 2 6412035
FX: 2 6412282

Founded: 1990. **Members:** 80. **Languages:** French, Flemish. **National.**
Researchers, teachers, social workers, and feminist activists. Involved in
research and education regarding feminist issues. Strives for equality among
men and women through promoting women's studies.

Conventions/Meetings: annual meeting - Brussels, Belgium. ● semiannual
meeting - Brussels, Belgium.

★1558★ UNION FEMININE ARTISTIQUE ET CULTURELLE (UFACSI)
80-2, blvd. Louis Schmidt
B-1040 Brussels, Belgium
Helene Deguel, President
PH: 2 7351472

Founded: 1948. **Languages:** French, Dutch, English. **Multinational.** Goals
include: discovering talented young women; backing young female artists
and creating a bond of fellowship among them; bringing to public consciousness the value of the cultural contribution female artists make to
society; and promoting peace and understanding between cultures. Provides
a forum for female artists to reveal their work noncommercially. Organizes
international expositions of the works of UFACSI members.

★1559★ UNIVERSITE DES FEMMES
1A, pl. Quetelet
B-1030 Brussels, Belgium
Laurence Broze, President
PH: 2 2196107
FX: 2 2192943

Founded: 1979. **Staff:** 6. **Budget:** 4,000,000 BFr. **Languages:** French,
English. **National.** Conducts research on women's issues, especially sexual
harassment at the workplace, women and politics, and women and the
media. Offers a research center for public use. Disseminates information.
Sponsors educational programs.

Publications: *Chronique Feministe* (in French), 5/year. Journal.

Conventions/Meetings: periodic convention - Brussels, Belgium.

★1560★ VIE FEMININE MOUVEMENT CHRETIEN D'ACTION
CULTURELLE ET SOCIALE (VFMCACS)
111, rue de la Poste
B-1210 Brussels, Belgium
Anne Boulvin, Sec.Gen.
PH: 2 2172952

National. Christian women's social and cultural organization in Belgium.

★1561★ VLAARS INSTITUT DER BEVORDERING EN
ONDERSTEUNING VAN DE SARENLEVINGS-ODBOUEN (VIBOSO)
Handelskaai 18/3
B-1000 Brussels, Belgium
Rita L'Enfant
PH: 2 2175595
FX: 2 2230573

Founded: 1982. **Staff:** 9. **Budget:** 15,000,000 BFr. **Languages:** French.
National. Comprised mainly of women professionals concerned with the
participation of women in different phases of community life and professional
administration. In 1993 activity will be in the areas of: the role of women in
research and women in poverty.

★1562★ LA VOIX DES FEMMES
18, rue de l'Alliance
B-1040 Brussels, Belgium
Talbia Belhari, Contact
PH: 2 2187787
FX: 2 2196085

Founded: 1988. **Languages:** French. **National.** Promotes equality between
the sexes. Works to protect women's and children's rights. Sponsors literacy
programs.

Conventions/Meetings: monthly meeting (exhibits).

★1563★ VROUWELIJKE KRISTELIJKE ARBEIDERS°JEUGD (VKAJ)
Paleizenstraat 90
B-1210 Brussels, Belgium
Margriet Meyvis, Chwm.

Founded: 1925. **Members:** 4,000. **Languages:** Dutch, English. **National.**
Young Christian women's labor organization in Belgium.

Publications: *Kei-Hart*, monthly.

★1564★ VROUWEN OVERLEG KOMITEE (VOK)
Breughelstraat 31-33
B-2018 Antwerp, Belgium
Katrien Boone, President
PH: 3 2186560

Founded: 1972. **Members:** 65. **Staff:** 2. **Budget:** 2,000,000 BFr. **Languages:** Dutch, Flemish, English. **National.** Promotes awareness of and
debate on women's issues in Europe. Lobbies government on issues of
importance to women. Liaises with other feminist groups to improve
women's rights. **Committees:** Women in Politics; Women and New Legislation on Nightwork; Influence of Extreme Right Political Movements on
Women.

Publications: *V.O.K. Nieuwsbrief* (in Dutch and Flemish), monthly. Newsletter.

Conventions/Meetings: annual Women's Day meeting

★1565★ WERKGROEP PARTNER VAN EEN SLACHTOFFER VAN
SEKSUEEL GEWEID
Cumontstr. 3
B-9300 Aalst, Belgium
Mark Layten, Contact
PH: 53 787513

Founded: 1990. **Languages:** Dutch, English. **National.** Fosters communication among victims of sexual violence and friends and family members of
such victims. Encourages victims of sexual violence to come out of their
physical or emotional isolation and exchange experiences with one another.
Disseminates information.

Conventions/Meetings: workshop - 5/year. 1993 Sept. 14; 1993 Nov. 9.

★1566★ WOMEN IN THE VOLKSUNIE
(Volksunie Vrouwen)
Barrikadenplein 12
B-1000 Brussels, Belgium
Mrs. Nora Tommelein, President
PH: 2 2194930
FX: 2 2173510

Founded: 1980. **Members:** 14,000. **Languages:** Flemish. **National.** Political
women's group. Advocates autonomy for Flanders.

Publications: *Newsletter* (in Flemish), weekly.

Conventions/Meetings: annual general assembly.

★1567★ YOUNG CHRISTIAN FEMALE WORKERS (YCFW)
(JOCF Jeunesse Ouvriere Chretienne Feminine)
3, rue de Moucherons
B-1000 Brussels, Belgium
Mirkes Marina, Sec.   PH: 2 5137912

Languages: French. **National.** Labor organization for young Christian women in Belgium. Conducts educational programs.

Publications: *Face A* (in French), monthly.

★1568★ YOUNG WOMEN'S CHRISTIAN ASSOCIATION - BELGIUM
Heernislaanm 108
B-1060 Ghent, Belgium
Nadine Veys, Contact

National. Promotes the development of young women in Belgium. Upholds Christian beliefs and values in its programs. Seeks to instill self worth and self-esteem in young women.

Bulgaria

★1569★ DEMOCRATIC UNION OF WOMEN IN BULGARIA
82 P. Evtimii str.
BG-1000 Sofia, Bulgaria   PH: 2 521356
Dr. Emilia Maslarova, Chair   2 525318

Membership Dues: 5 Lv annual. **Staff:** 2. **Languages:** Bulgarian, English. **National.** Women's organizations and individual women united to improve women's status. Seeks to create a "democratic and humane" society in which women and children's rights are protected. Works to enhance recognition of the social value and importance of parenthood, family, housework, and children's rights. Lobbies government regarding policies having an effect on women, the family, and children. Liaises with women's, labor, business, youth, and political organizations to achieve social equality. **Alternate name::** Women's Democratic Union.

Publications: *Zhenata Dnes* (in Bulgarian). Magazine. Women's issues. ● *Nie Zhenite* (in Bulgarian). Newsletter.

Conventions/Meetings: triennial general assembly.

★1570★ INTERNATIONAL COORDINATION COMMITTEE FOR
    IMMUNOLOGY OF REPRODUCTION
(Comite International de Coordination d'Immunologie de la Reproduction)
73 Lenin Ave.
BG-1113 Sofia, Bulgaria
Dr. V. Dikov, Sec.Gen.   PH: 2 720046

Founded: 1967. **Members:** 46. **Languages:** English, French, Russian. **Multinational.** Conducts research on reproductive medicine. Disseminates information.

Publications: *Immunology of Reproduction* (in English, French, and Russian), triennial. Symposium proceedings.

Conventions/Meetings: triennial symposium (exhibits) - always Varna, Bulgaria.

★1571★ SOCIETY FOR PLANNED PARENTHOOD AND FAMILY
    DEVELOPMENT (SPPFD)
Zdrave Str. No. 2   PH: 2 517267
BG-1431 Sofia, Bulgaria   FX: 2 517052
Dr. Todor Chernev, President   TX: 22797 RES VITBG

Languages: Bulgarian. **National.** Promotes family planning and responsible parenthood as a means to improve the quality of life for individuals living in Bulgaria. Works to reduce the number of unwanted pregnancies and abortions. Sponsors educational programs in family planning and health.

Provides contraceptive and health care services. Acts as an advocate for family planning on a national level.

Croatia

★1572★ KARETA FEMINIST GROUP
Vlaska 91
CT-4100 Zagreb, Croatia   PH: 41 4834

Languages: Croatian. **National.** Seeks to further the women's movement and enhance recognition of women's rights. Provides a forum for discussion of issues affecting women's interests.

Cyprus

★1573★ ASSOCIATION AGAINST VIOLENCE IN THE FAMILY
PO Box 5337
Nicosia, Cyprus

National. Works to eradicate domestic violence and child abuse through development of strict legislation against aggressors. Offers support services to victims, including shelters, counseling, and support groups. Disseminates information.

★1574★ CYPRUS ASSOCIATION FOR THE PREVENTION AND
    HANDLING OF VIOLENCE IN THE FAMILY
Panikou Demetriou II
Makedonitissa
Nicosia, Cyprus
Aliki Hadjgeorgiou, President   PH: 2 365055

Founded: 1988. **Members:** 70. **Staff:** 1. **Budget:** £C 7,000. **Languages:** Greek, English. **National.** Associations and individuals. Works towards: the prevention of family violence; the provision of immediate aid to victims; access to shelters, safety, support, and counseling by victims; the recruitment of volunteers and their training; an awareness and sensitivity among society of the problem of family violence; the development and improvement of legislation dealing with family violence; recognition by police of the problem of family violence and police enforcement against aggressors; and research related to family violence. Strives to achieve goals through: a center for victims of family violence; organization seminars, lectures, and exhibits; ongoing cooperation with other services related to family violence; media publication of services the center provides; dissemination of information pertaining to family violence for individuals and institutions that professionally provide service to victims. Also provides counseling and emergency service through a 24-hour hotline. **Libraries:** Type: reference. Holdings: books, video recordings.

Publications: *Book* (in Greek). For police. ● *Book* (in Greek). For volunteers.

Conventions/Meetings: semimonthly executive committee meeting. ● periodic seminar (exhibits).

★1575★ FAMILY PLANNING ASSOCIATION OF CYPRUS (FPAC)
25 Boumboulina St.
Nicosia, Cyprus   PH: 2 442093
Ms. Kiki Patsalides, Exec. Dir.   FX: 2 367495

Languages: Greek, Turkish, English. **National.** Works to enhance the quality of life for individuals living in Cyprus by promoting responsible parenthood and family planning. Works to reduce the number of unwanted pregnancies and abortions. Advocates family planning as a basic human right. Sponsors programs in sex education, family planning, and health. Provides contraceptive and health care services.

★1576★ PANCYPRIAN FEDERATION OF WOMEN ORGANIZATIONS
(POGO)
56 Kennedy Ave.
Nicosia, Cyprus   PH: 2 494906

National. Seeks to enhance women's advancement. Provides a forum for networking and cooperation among Cyprian women's organizations.

★1577★ PANCYPRIAN MOVEMENT FOR EQUAL RIGHTS AND
EQUAL RESPONSIBILITIES
PO Box 1472   PH: 2 353222
Nicosia, Cyprus   2 455225
Sofia Georgalla, President   FX: 2 472526

Languages: Greek, Turkish, English. **National.** Seeks to advance the rights of women in Cyprus. Works to improve women's living and working conditions.

★1578★ WOMEN ORGANISATION OF DEMOCRATIC PARTY
50 Grivas Digenis Ave.
Nicosia, Cyprus
Mrs. Mary Plapadopoulou, President   PH: 2 472002

National. Women's political organization. Furthers special interests of women within the party platform.

★1579★ WOMEN'S SOCIALIST MOVEMENT
PO Box 9107
Nicosia, Cyprus   PH: 2 457293
Mrs. Marcia Alexaki, President   FX: 2 458894

National. Works to further the integration of socialist ideas into the political/economic system. Promotes the concept of gender equality prevalent in socialist ideology.

Czech Republic

★1580★ MOVEMENT FOR WOMEN'S EQUAL RIGHTS IN BOHEMIA
AND MORAVIA
(Hnuti za Rovnopravne Postaveni zen v Cechach a na Morave)
Na Pankraci 55
CS-140 00 Prague 4, Czech Republic
Eleonora Slavickova Ph.D., Chairperson   PH: 2 4339917

Founded: 1990. **Members:** 35,000. **Languages:** English. **National.** Promotes the development of women in Czechoslovakia. Represents women's interests and strives to increase the role of women in Czech society. Works to provide economic, legal, and social protection to women and children. Encourages women to participate at all levels of government in order to achieve equal rights. Conducts educational, public, and research programs. **Committees:** Social and Health Affairs; Ecology and Agriculture; Political Organizational and International Affairs; Foreign Affairs; Legislative Affairs; Education, Hobbies, and Development of Women's Personality; Economy and Business Management.

Conventions/Meetings: monthly executive committee meeting - Prague, Czech Republic.

★1581★ YOUNG WOMEN'S CHRISTIAN ASSOCIATION - CZECH
REPUBLIC
Zitna 12
CS-129 05 Prague 2, Czech Republic
Jirina Kozdorova, Gen.Sec.   PH: 2 206651

National. Works to promote Christian fellowship and service among young women in the Czech Republic. Upholds Christian values and beliefs in its programs. Seeks to instill self worth and self-esteem in young women.

Denmark

★1582★ DANISH FAMILY PLANNING ASSOCIATION (DFPA)
(FF Foreningen fur Familieplanlaegning)
Aurehojvej 2
DK-2900 Hellerup, Denmark
Marianne Sondergaard, Information   PH: 31625688
  Officer   FX: 31620282

Founded: 1956. **Members:** 17. **Staff:** 5. **Budget:** US$550,000. **Languages:** Danish. **National.** Health, social, and educational societies and institutions in Denmark. Promotes improved education and research in family planning. Provides contraceptives and contraceptive information to individuals and family planning professionals in an effort to increase family planning practices and lessen the need for abortions. Operates family planning clinics; offers counseling services. Conducts sex education classes for young students in connection with compulsory integrated sex education in Danish schools. Distributes materials on contraception, abortion, sexually transmitted diseases, and AIDS; holds demonstrations, seminars, and workshops. **Libraries:** Type: reference.

Publications: *Annual Report.* ● *Information and Debate* (in Danish), quarterly. Newsletter. ● *Sex and Health* (in Danish), semiannual. Booklet.

Conventions/Meetings: annual meeting - always April. Copenhagen, Denmark.

★1583★ DANISH NATIONAL COUNCIL OF WOMEN
(DKN Dansk Kvinders Nationalrad)
Niels Hemmingsensgade 8
DK-1153 Copenhagen K, Denmark   PH: 33128087
Aase Rieck Sorensen, Sec.   FX: 33126740

Members: 39. **Languages:** Danish. **National.** Humanitarian and religious organizations, professional organizations for women, and political parties representing over 1,000,000 individuals. Works for the rights and increased influence of women in Denmark.

★1584★ DANISH WOMEN'S SOCIETY
(Dansk Kvindesamfund)
Niels Hemmingsensgade 10,3
DK-1153 Copenhagen K, Denmark   PH: 33157837
Benthe Stig, President   FX: 33157837

Founded: 1871. **Members:** 1,500. **Staff:** 1. **Languages:** Danish, German, English, Swedish, Norwegian. **National.** Professional women, politicians, and other individuals interested in raising public awareness of women's issues. Works to achieve equal employment opportunities, salary, and social welfare for women and men. Encourages women to become involved in decision making processes in politics and the financial world. Prepares and suggests school curriculums; offers evening courses. Operates a counseling center. Maintains archives. **Awards:** Mathilde. Recipient: people who have made outstanding contributions to women's struggle for equality. **Committees:** Labor Market Questions; Education; International Cooperation; Women in Developing Countries; Women in Politics; Health Policy; Family Policy.

Publications: *Kvinden & Samfundet* (in Danish), 8/year. Newsletter. ● *Women and Influence in the E.C.* Book.

Conventions/Meetings: annual general assembly (exhibits). ● periodic seminar.

★1585★ KULU - WOMEN AND DEVELOPMENT
(KULU Kuindernes u Landsudvalg)
Landgreven 7, 3 tv.
DK-1301 Copenhagen K, Denmark   PH: 33157870
Ruth Ejdrup Olsen, Sec.   FX: 33325330

Founded: 1976. **Members:** 153. **Staff:** 2. **Multinational.** Regional organizations, women's groups, and individuals. Supports the rights of women in developing countries and attempts to influence national and international policies affecting their development. Monitors legislation dealing with feminist issues and disseminates information. Encourages the creation of women's groups in developing countries and lobbies for increased financial aid to assist in their formation.

Publications: *Kulu-bladet*, semiannual. ● *Kulu Women and Development's Directory of Women's Organizations* (in Danish and English), periodic.

★1586★ KVINFO
Nyhavn 22
Postboks 1574
DK-1051 Copenhagen K, Denmark   PH: 33135088
Elisabeth Moller Jensen, Contact   FX: 45111156

Founded: 1981. **Staff:** 5. **Budget:** 2,500,000 DKr. **Languages:** Danish, English, German, Italian, French. **National.** Works to raise public awareness of gender issues. Fosters interdisciplinary research on women and gender. Organizes cultural activities. **Libraries:** Type: lending. Holdings: 13,200; books, periodicals, archival material. **Computer Services:** Data base, Danish Research Libraries (ALBA); data base, Royal Libraries (REX); data base, Gothenburg University Library's articles and books concerning women and gender (KVINSAM); data base, DIMDI; data base, DIALOG.

Publications: *Nyt Forum for Kvindeforskning*, periodic. Journal.

★1587★ MEDICAL WOMEN'S INTERNATIONAL ASSOCIATION -
DENMARK (MWIA-D)
Baunegaardsvej 56B
DK-2900 Hellerup, Denmark
Sigbrit Christensen, Contact

Languages: Danish. **National.** Denmark branch of Medical Women's International Association (see separate entry). Women physicians. Provides a forum for discussion of women's health care issues. Encourages women to enter the field of medicine. Works to overcome discrimination against female physicians. Sponsors research and educational programs.

★1588★ NORDIC WOMEN'S PEACE NETWORK (NWPN)
(NKF Nordiske Kvinners Fredsnettverk)
Buegarden 9, st.th.
DK-2880 Bagsvaerd, Denmark
Inger B. Andersen, Contact   PH: 44440897

Founded: 1988. **Members:** 100. **Languages:** Danish, English, Finnish, Norwegian, Swedish. **Multinational.** Women in Denmark, Finland, Norway, and Sweden united in the effort to make the Nordic nations a "peace zone." Initiates and participates in non-violent action against poverty, militarization, and environmental pollution. Monitors pertinent legislation and local and international political activities.

Publications: *Fredsstikka* (in Norwegian), 7/year. Magazine.

Conventions/Meetings: annual meeting.

★1589★ WOMEN FOR PEACE
Postboks 314
DK-5700 Svendborg, Denmark
Dagny Riis, Coord.

Multinational. Women working to heighten public awareness on human conflicts and human rights violations existing worldwide. Works to stimulate a national and international public and governmental effort to development and implement means towards peaceful resolution of conflict and recognition of human rights.

★1590★ WOMEN WORKERS' UNION IN DENMARK
(KAD Kvindeligt Arbejderforbund i Danmark)
Ewaldsgade 3-9
DK-2200 Copenhagen N, Denmark   PH: 31393115
Kirsten Moller, Coordinator   FX: 31390540

Founded: 1891. **Members:** 100,000. **Staff:** 130. **Local Groups:** 61. **Languages:** Danish, English. **National.** Working women in Denmark. Works to improve working conditions and women's status in the workplace. Seeks to protect jobs, achieve wages equal to men's, and provide a safe and healthy working environment. Negotiates with employers and government on issues affecting women in the workplace. Offers educational and training programs. **Libraries:** Type: reference.

Publications: *Magazine*, 10/year.

★1591★ WOMEN'S INTERNATIONAL LEAGUE FOR PEACE AND
FREEDOM - DENMARK (WILPF)
(ILFF International Liga for Fred og Frihed)
Vesterbrogade 10
DK-1620 Copenhagen, Denmark
Ms. Hanne Norup Carlsen, Chwm.   PH: 31231097

Founded: 1915. **Members:** 400. **Budget:** 167,000 DKr. **Local Groups:** 12. **Languages:** Danish, English. **National.** Danish national chapter of the Women's International League for Peace and Freedom (see separate entry). Women of different political persuasions in Denmark. Advocates the principles of the United Nations, disarmament, and the strict observance of human rights worldwide. Conducts courses, seminars, hearings, and demonstrations.

Publications: *Fred og Frihed* (in Danish), quarterly.

Conventions/Meetings: triennial congress - 1995.

★1592★ YOUNG WOMEN'S CHRISTIAN ASSOCIATION-DENMARK
(YWCA)
Valby Langgade 19
DK-2500 Valby, Denmark   PH: 31166033
Birgit Steffensen, Sec.   FX: 31160818

National. Works to promote Christian fellowship and service among young women in Denmark. Advocates unity, justice, and peace.

England

★1593★ THE 300 GROUP
36-37 Charterhouse Sq.
London EC1M 6EA, England   PH: 71 6002390
Clare Pettitt, Administrator   FX: 71 6002391

Founded: 1980. **Members:** 830. **Budget:** £21,000. **Regional Groups:** 14. **Languages:** French, German, English. **National.** Multi-party campaign working for the greater presence of women in Parliament and the raising of women's status in all levels of public life. Offers specialist training. Participates in House of Commons debates. Sponsors fringe meetings at party conferences. Sends speakers to lecture at schools and colleges. Disseminates information. **Computer Services:** Data base.

Publications: *Newsletter* (in English), annual.

Conventions/Meetings: monthly board meeting.

★1594★ ABORTION LAW REFORM ASSOCIATION (ALRA)
27-35 Mortimer St.
London W1N 7RJ, England
Jane Roe, Coord.   PH: 71 6377264

Founded: 1936. **Members:** 1,000. **Languages:** English. **National.** Individuals and organizations in England united to liberalize the Abortion Act passed in Parliament in 1967, which permits a woman to terminate her pregnancy only if she can prove continuing it would involve a medical risk. Seeks to extend and protect a women's right to choose to terminate her pregnancy. Distributes information to schools and the public. Monitors legislation on abortion and related issues and expresses concerns to the British Parliament, Department of Health, and National Health Service. Lobbies for reversal of Northern Ireland's law which prohibits abortion regardless of circumstance. **Computer Services:** Data base.

Publications: *Chains*, quarterly. Magazine. ● *Why Discuss Abortion*. Information packet for teachers.

Conventions/Meetings: annual meeting.

★1595★ **ACTION ON SMOKING AND HEALTH - WOMEN AND SMOKING GROUP (ASH)**
109 Gloucester Pl.
London W1H 3PH, England   PH: 71 9353519
Amanda Sandford, Development Officer   FX: 71 9353463

Founded: 1985. **Members:** 18. **Budget:** £1,000. **Languages:** English. **National.** Women's health specialists. Stimulates research pertaining to the health risks of smoking for women. Promotes public awareness of the dangers associated with smoking. Disseminates information.

Publications: *Women and Smoking* (in English). Booklet. ● *Teenage Girls and Smoking* (in English). Booklet. ● *Smoke Still Gets in Her Eyes* (in English). Booklet.

Conventions/Meetings: semiannual meeting, Members only..

★1596★ **AFRICAN WOMEN'S WELFARE GROUP (AWWG)**
High Cross United Reformed Church
Colsterworth Rd.
London N15 4BD, England

National. Promotes the development and social status of women in Africa. Protects the rights of women and children. Opposes female genital mutilation.

★1597★ **ALL ENGLAND WOMEN'S HOCKEY ASSOCIATION (AEWHA)**
51 High St.
Shrewsbury, Salop SY1 1ST, England   PH: 743 233572
T. Morris, Dir.   FX: 743 233583

Founded: 1895. **Members:** 500,000. **Staff:** 9. **Regional Groups:** 5. **Local Groups:** 3,500. **Languages:** English. **National.** Associations, clubs, and schools of amateur women hockey players. Seeks to promote and develop field hockey locally and nationally. Bestows awards; provides insurance; tests umpires. **Libraries:** Type: reference. Holdings: video recordings. **Subcommittees:** Coaching; Competitions; Indoor Hockey; International Relationships; Youth; Umpiring.

Publications: *Hockey Digest*, periodic. Magazine.

Conventions/Meetings: annual convention.

★1598★ **ALL ENGLAND WOMEN'S LACROSSE ASSOCIATION (AEWLA)**
4 Western Ct.
Bromley St.
Digbeth
Birmingham, W. Midlands B9 4AN,
    England
Miss A. Nathan, Admin.   PH: 21 7734422

Founded: 1912. **Members:** 1,100. **Staff:** 3. **Local Groups:** 5. **Languages:** English. **National.** Clubs, colleges, individuals, and schools. Furthers the sport of lacrosse for women and girls in England, and fosters friendly relations between players of all countries. Organizes international matches;

examines umpires. **Committees:** Development; Fixtures; National Events; Publicity; Rules; Selection; Team Preparation.

Publications: *Annual Report* (in English). ● *Handbook* (in English), annual. ● *LacrosseTalk* (in English), 8/year. Newsletter.

★1599★ **AMARANT TRUST (AT)**
80 Lambeth Rd.
London SE1 7PW, England   PH: 71 4013855
Debbie Catt, Contact   FX: 71 9281702

Languages: English. **National.** Works to promote a better understanding of menopause through research and exchange of information. Seeks to educate women in Britain on the benefits of Hormone Replacement Therapy (HRT).

★1600★ **ANOREXIA AND BULIMIA NERVOSA ASSOCIATION (ABNA)**
Totterhan Women and Health Centre,
    Annexe
Totterham Town Hall
London N15 4ZB, England
Amanda Thornton   PH: 81 8853936

Founded: 1982. **Members:** 6. **Languages:** English. **National.** Seeks to assist women affected by eating disorders. Provides helpline service for sufferers of eating disorders and for their families and friends. Offers counseling and therapy referral assistance. Disseminates information about eating disorders. Maintains a drop-in center. **Libraries:** Type: reference. **Telecommunication Services:** Phone referral system.

★1601★ **ASSOCIATED COUNTRY WOMEN OF THE WORLD (ACWW)**
(Union Mondiale des Femmes Rurales)
Vincent House
Vincent Sq.
London SW1P 2NB, England
Jennifer Pearce, Gen.Sec.   PH: 71 8348635

Founded: 1930. **Staff:** 12. **Languages:** English. **Multinational.** Rural women's societies. Promotes friendly relations among women's organizations in 70 countries and assists in the economic, social, and cultural development of their members and countries. Maintains consultative status with the United Nations Economic and Social Council. Offers leadership training course, nutrition education, and functional literacy programs. Serves as information clearinghouse. **Committees:** Extension and Mutual Services; United Nations.

Publications: *The Countrywoman*, quarterly. Magazine.

Conventions/Meetings: triennial conference - 1995.

★1602★ **ASSOCIATION OF CATHOLIC WOMEN**
22 Surbiton Hill Park
Surbiton, Surrey KT4 8ET, England
Mrs. Real, Contact

Founded: 1989. **Members:** 650. **Languages:** English. **National.** Religious women in the service of the Catholic church. Promotes Catholicism in the United Kingdom.

★1603★ **ASSOCIATION FOR IMPROVEMENTS IN THE MATERNITY SERVICES (AIMS)**
40 Kingswood Ave.
London NW6 6LS, England
Sandar Warshal, Contact

Founded: 1960. **Members:** 1,000. **Local Groups:** 10. **Languages:** English. **National.** Parents and health care professionals. Campaigns to improve maternity services.

Publications: *AIMS Journal*, quarterly.

★1604★ ASSOCIATION OF LAWYERS FOR THE DEFENCE OF THE UNBORN (ALDU)
40 Bedford St.
London WC2E 9EN, England

Founded: 1978. **Members:** 2,200. **National.** Judges, barristers, law professors and students, solicitors, and legal executives in 25 countries united to oppose abortion and to persuade lawyers that abortion is unjust. Supports full legal protection of the fetus against abortion and advocates fetal rights from the point of conception.

Publications: *News and Comment* (in English), quarterly. Newsletter.

★1605★ ASSOCIATION OF RADICAL MIDWIVES (ARM)
62 Greetby Hill
Ormskirk, Lancs. L39 2DT, England
Ishbel Kargar, Secretary   PH: 695 572776

Founded: 1976. **Members:** 1,700. **Membership Dues:** UK and Europe., £22; Overseas., £30. **Budget:** £25,000. **Languages:** English. **National.** Midwives, mothers, health professionals, and interested individuals. Provides supportive services and information to women experiencing difficulty in securing adequate and sympathetic maternity care. **Libraries:** Type: lending.

Publications: *Midwifery Matters* (in English), quarterly. Magazine.

Conventions/Meetings: quarterly meeting.

★1606★ ASSOCIATION OF WOMEN TRAVEL EXECUTIVES
Hawaii Visitors Bureau
14 The Green
Richmond TW9 1PX, England
Valerie Arends, Chair

Founded: 1954. **Members:** 307. **Languages:** English. **National.** Female management professionals in the travel industry. Promotes improvement in the status of women employed in the travel industry. Provides career developemnt and networking opportunities for members. Conducts educational and research programs. Sponsors awards. **Committees:** Education; Travelwoman.

Publications: *Travelwoman* (in English), monthly. ● *Directory*, periodic. Membership.

Conventions/Meetings: monthly meeting. ● annual convention, International..

★1607★ BAHA'I NATIONAL WOMEN'S COMMITTEE
27 Rutland Gate
London SW7 1PD, England
Lois Hainsworth, Contact

Founded: 1979. **Members:** 2,500. **Languages:** English. **National.** Promotes the Baha'i faith in England. Works to achieve equality between women and men. Believes that only after women achieve full equality will international peace emerge. Encourages Baha'i women to involve themselves in the social, civic, and religious life of their community. Cooperates with international Baha'i women's committees.

Publications: *Newsletter*, periodic. ● *Annual Report*.

★1608★ BANGLADESH WOMEN'S ASSOCIATION
91 Highbury Hill
London N5 1SX, England
Mrs. Rumy Huque, Contact   PH: 71 3595836

Founded: 1971. **Languages:** English. **National.** Women over 16 years of age who have emigrated from Bangladesh to England. Promotes the exchange of Bengalee and British culture between women in the U.K. Works to preserve the Bengalee culture by offering weekend and evening language classes, multi-racial summer holidays, and children's programs. Provides advice on immigration, race relations, welfare rights, and education.

★1609★ BREAST CARE AND MASTECTOMY ASSOCIATION (BCMA)
15-19 Britten St.
London SW3 3TZ, England
Andrea Whalley, Director   PH: 71 8678275

Languages: English. **National.** Doctors, scientists, and other interested individuals. Provides emotional and practical support to people who have had, or think they may have, breast cancer. Operates advice line.

★1610★ BRITISH FEDERATION OF WOMEN GRADUATES (BFWG)
Crosby Hall
Cheyne Walk
London SW3 5BA, England
Christel Moor, Vice President   PH: 71 3525354

Founded: 1907. **Members:** 2,500. **Staff:** 1. **Local Groups:** 8. **Languages:** English. **National.** Women graduates from accredited colleges and universities interested and involved in education for women. Prepares women for combining career and homelife through offering networks, seminars, and conferences, addressing topics such as: health; food; education; law; and opportunities for self-advancement. Provides support and encouragement to educated/career women. **Awards:** Scholarship. Recipient: women involved in post-graduate research. **Committees:** International; European.

Publications: *BFWG News* (in English), 5/year. Newsletter. ● *BFWG Conference News*, annual. Magazine.

Conventions/Meetings: monthly meeting ● triennial conference. ● annual meeting - always July.

★1611★ BRITISH HOUSEWIVES ASSOCIATION
24 Liverpool Rd.
Kingston Hill, Surrey, England
Mrs. A.C. Horsfield, Contact   PH: 81 5463388

Founded: 1945. **Languages:** English. **National.** British women working in the home. Works to provide women with a voice in social issues. Encourages "development of personality in accordance with Christian tradition.".

Publications: *Home* (in English), monthly. Magazine.

★1612★ BRITISH NA'AMAT (BN)
11 Falkland Crescent
Leeds, W. Yorkshire LS17 6JL, England
Diana Austin, Contact   PH: 532 681934

Languages: English. **Multinational.** Working and professional women. Works to advance the status of women by providing a variety of educational, community, and legal services. Believes that strong family relations are the foundation of a stable society. Members identify with the Zionist movement.

★1613★ BRITISH ORGANIZATION OF NON-PARENTS (BON)
BM Box 5866
London WC1N 3XX, England
Root Cartwright, Chair   PH: 81 5542731

Founded: 1978. **Members:** 150. **Languages:** English. **National.** People who choose not to have children. Promotes and represents the views of those choosing not to have children. Provides advice and information to those experiencing pressure from family or peers. Works towards presenting a positive image of "non-parents." Resists media and cultural bias promoting parenthood regardless of the obstacles and sacrifice. Directs attention to the global population crisis.

Publications: *Newsletter* (in English), periodic. ● *Am I Parent Material?* (in English). Booklet. ● *You Do Have a Choice* (in English). Booklet. ● *No Regrets* (in English). Booklet.

★1614★ BRITISH SUPPORT GROUP - INTER-AFRICAN COMMITTEE AGAINST HARMFUL TRADITIONAL PRACTICES
Severn Trow Cottage
21 Dunn's Ln.
Upton-upon-Severn
Worcester, Hereford and Worcester WR8
 0HZ, England
Joan Higman Davies, Director   PH: 684 592563

Founded: 1990. **Languages:** English. **National.** Expresses solidarity with African women who struggle against traditional health practices which are harmful to their lives, health, and personal dignity. Raises funds and conducts research. Arouses public awareness through the media. Offers educational programs related to the population in Africa and African immigrants in Britain.

Publications: *Newsletter*, bimonthly.

★1615★ BRITISH WOMEN'S PILOTS ASSOCIATION
Rochester Airport
Chatham, Kent ME5 9SD, England

Founded: 1955. **Members:** 250. **Languages:** English. **National.** Women pilots united to foster a better understanding of aviation. Offers career counseling services.

Publications: *Gazette* (in English), annual. Magazine.

★1616★ BUSINESS WOMEN'S TRAVEL CLUB
520 Fulham Rd.
London SW6 5NJ, England
Trisha Cochrane, Contact   PH: 71 3841121

Founded: 1987. **Languages:** English. **National.** Business and professional women in England. Works to ensure that business women receive equal treatment from hotels, airlines, and travel agents. Plans to set up a database of recommended hotels. Fosters exchange among members.

Publications: *Travel Logue* (in English), quarterly. Newsletter.

★1617★ CAMPAIGN FOR PRESS AND BROADCASTING FREEDOM - WOMEN'S SECTION
96 Dalston Ln.
London E8 1NG, England
Teresa Stratford, Contact   PH: 71 9233671

Founded: 1979. **Languages:** English. **National.** Women in the fields of radio and television communications. Monitors television, radio, and print media. Works to achieve equality of men and women through raising public awareness of sexism in the media. Conducts research.

Publications: *Women in Focus* (in English), periodic. Newsletter.

★1618★ CATHOLIC WOMEN'S LEAGUE - UNITED KINGDOM
PO Box 621
Earls Colne
Colchester, Essex CO6 2ST, England
Mrs. J. Crossman, Contact   PH: 787 223382

Founded: 1906. **Members:** 9,500. **Languages:** English. **National.** Roman Catholic women in England. Promotes members' intellectual and religious interests. Collectively represents Catholic viewpoints to decision making bodies.

Publications: *C.W.L. News* (in English), quarterly. Newsletter.

★1619★ CATHOLIC WOMEN'S NETWORK
42 Priory Rd.
Hampton TW1 22PJ, England
Veronica Seddon, Contact   PH: 81 9795902

Founded: 1984. **Members:** 340. **Budget:** £6,000. **Local Groups:** 5. **Languages:** English. **National.** Christian women in England. Provides a support network to assist women in the development of their spiritual lives. Promotes women's participation in church activities. Encourages members to study theology and to improve methods of worship. Conducts workshops and lectures. **Committees:** Rapid Response.

Publications: *Newsletter*, quarterly.

★1620★ CHANGE - INTERNATIONAL REPORTS: WOMEN AND SOCIETY
PO Box 824
London SEZ4 9JS, England
Georgina Ashworth, Director   PH: 71 2776187

Founded: 1979. **Staff:** 2. **Languages:** English, French, Spanish. **Multinational.** Researches and publishes reports concerning the status of women worldwide. Affirms that: the suppression of women in society has been a disadvantage to economic and political processes; the central purpose of a nongovernmental organization should be to represent the need for change; reports should be written by women natives of the relevant country; and although there exist real economic inequalities, developed and underdeveloped countries should not be separated, in order to prevent patronizing attitudes. Works to: educate the public about the inequalities women struggle against in society through: dissemination of information; encouraging an international exchange of information; promotion of recognition of women's human rights; the publication of such abuse by governments, businesses, or individuals. Contributes to campaigns, networks, and conferences worldwide. Offers gender training, and lobby and advocacy training. **Libraries:** Type: reference; open to the public.

Publications: *Economic Development and Women's Place: Women in Singapore* (in English). Book. ● *Providence and Prostitution: Image and Reality for Women in Buddhist Thailand* (in English). Book. ● *Israeli Women and Men: Divisions Behind the Unity* (in English). Book. ● *Minus Lives: Women of Bangladesh* (in English). Book. ● *In Search pf Ethiopian Women* (in English). Book. ● *Sisters of the Sun: Japanese Women Today* (in English). Book. ● *Contradictions and Ironies: Women of Lesotho* (in English). Book. ● *Women in Pakistan: A New Era?* (in English). Book. ● *Unseen Phenomenon: the Rise of Industrial Homeworking* (in English). Book. ● *Sexonomics: an Introduction to the Political Economy of Sex, Time and Gender* (in English). Book. ● *When Will Democracy Include Women?* (in English). Book.

Conventions/Meetings: periodic meeting.

★1621★ CITY CENTRE
32-25 Featherstone St.
London EC1Y 8QX, England
Rohan Collier, Women's Employment
 Off.   PH: 71 6081338

Founded: 1984. **Members:** 300. **Staff:** 4. **Budget:** £80,000. **Languages:** English, French. **National.** Office workers, trade unions, and women's groups in England. Promotes the interests of women employed in England's labor force. Supports equal opportunities and women returning to the work force. Disseminates information and advice to the public. Works to eliminate sexual harrassment and racial discrimination in the workplace. Organizes training courses. Conducts research. **Libraries:** Type: open to the public.

Publications: *Newsletter*, quarterly. ● *Safer Office*, quarterly. Bulletin.

Conventions/Meetings: periodic seminar.

★1622★ CITY WOMEN'S NETWORK (CWN)
Byword
PO Box 353
London UB10 0UN, England
Jeanette Masarati, Contact   PH: 81 5692351

Founded: 1978. **Members:** 250. **Languages:** English. **National.** Senior executive and professional business women. Provides a forum for members to share common interests and experiences. Represents members' opinions to professional, governmental, and international organizations. Maintains speakers' bureau. **Committees:** Education; Employment; Special Events; Public Policy; Public Relations; Speakers.

Publications: *Connections* (in English), monthly. Newsletter. ● *Directory* (in English), annual.

Conventions/Meetings: annual dinner. ● weekly meeting.

★1623★ CLUB 2000
c/o IHC
8 Thornton Pl.
London W1H 1FG, England
Irene Harris, Contact   PH: 71 9358706

Founded: 1991. **Members:** 100. **Languages:** English. **National.** Professional businesswomen. Provides a forum for business contacts. Conducts debates on issues of interest to members.

Publications: *Bulletin* (in English), monthly.

★1624★ COMMUNIST PARTY OF GREAT BRITAIN - WOMEN'S NETWORK
6 Cynthia St.
London N1 9JF, England
Sarah Gasguoine, Contact   PH: 71 2514406

Founded: 1920. **Members:** 18,000. **Languages:** English. **National.** Promotes the involvement of women in the Communist party. Advises the Communist party on women's issues. Supports programs that advocate: human rights, peace, environmental conservation, and child care.

Publications: *Link* (in English), quarterly. Magazine.

★1625★ CONSERVATIVE WOMEN'S NATIONAL COMMITTEE
32 Smith Sq.
Westminster
London SW1P 3HH, England
Mrs. Jane Garrett, Contact   PH: 71 2229000

Founded: 1904. **Languages:** English. **National.** Women members of the Conservative party in England. Acts as an advisory to the Conservative party on matters of concern to women. Works for the election of members of the Conservative party to national and local governments.

★1626★ COOPERATIVE WOMEN'S GUILD
342 Hoe St.
Walthamstow
London E17 9PX, England
Susan Bell, Secretary   PH: 81 5204902

Founded: 1883. **Members:** 5,500. **Staff:** 1. **Languages:** English. **National.** Promotes equal opportunities for complete and free development. Educates women on principles and practices of cooperation so that they may participate in the women's movement. Works towards improving the status of women and encouraging their participation in community, national, and international affairs. Promotes world peace. Provides social, cultural, and recreational activities.

Publications: *Newsletter* (in English), bimonthly.

Conventions/Meetings: annual congress.

★1627★ CORONA WORLDWIDE
35 Belgrave Sq.
London SW1X 8BQ, England
Miss Freda Anderson, Contact   PH: 71 2351230
                                      FX: 71 2352023

Founded: 1950. **Members:** 4,000. **Budget:** £45,000. **National Groups:** 70. **Languages:** English. **Multinational.** Assists women and families who have emmigrated from their native country. Strives to spread friendship and

understanding between people. Works to make living in different cultures a stimulating and an enjoyable experience for the whole family. Disseminates practical information on resettlement. Conducts educational and research programs; operates children's programs. **Committees:** Courses and Briefing Service; Women Speakers for the Commonwealth. **Alternate name::** Women's Corona Society.

Publications: *Magazine*, annual. ● *The Women's Corona Society: 1950-1990.* Book.

Conventions/Meetings: annual meeting. ● triennial conference (exhibits) - always July. 1995 July, London, England.

★1628★ CREATIVE AND SUPPORTIVE TRUST
CAST
37-39 Kings Terr.
London NW1 0JR, England
Fiona McLean, Director   PH: 71 3835228

Founded: 1982. **Members:** 12. **Staff:** 6. **Budget:** £220,000. **Languages:** English. **National.** Assists women who have experienced any form of detention such as prison or psychiatric detention. Visits detained women who are about to be released and provides pre- and post-release counseling and support, including referrals relating to: housing; child custody; health issues; welfare benefits; and financial management. Maintains accredited education and training programs on: information technology; literacy; self-defense; confidence and communication; photography; and art and design. **Committees:** Education; Welfare.

★1629★ DAYCARE TRUST
Wesley House
4 Wild Court
London W2B 5AU, England
Marion Kozak, Contact   PH: 71 4055617
                                FX: 71 8316632

Founded: 1986. **Staff:** 3. **Languages:** English. **National.** Provides information and advice in establishing quality childcare to parents, childcare workers, employers, professionals, colleges, and trade unions. Undertakes research on issues relating to childcare. Promotes a substantial increase in affordable and accessible childcare services which will equally provide service to children, regardless of race, culture, or gender.

Publications: *ABC of Quality Childcare, The Start-Up Guide* (in English). Book. ● *ABC for Providers, Daycare and the Children Act 1989* (in English). Book. ● *ABC of Creche Training* (in English). Book. ● *The Family-Friendly Employer, Examples from Europe* (in English). Book. ● *Childcare: the European Challenge* (in English). Book. ● *Childcare Now* (in English), periodic. Magazine. ● *Babies in Daycare, an Examination of the Issues* (in English). Book. ● *Full Marks for Trying, a Survey of Childcare Providers* (in English). Book. ● *Under Five and Underfunded* (in English). Book. ● *Daycare for Kids, a Parents' Survival Guide* (in English). Book.

Conventions/Meetings: periodic conference.

★1630★ DRUGS AND ALCOHOL WOMEN'S NETWORK (DAWN)
CI-Ghaas
30-31 Great Sutton St.
London EC1R 0DX, England
Seonaid Wright, Admin.   PH: 71 2536221

Languages: English. **National.** Maintains a support network for women with alcohol or drug problems. Works to heighten awareness of specific problems women experience in relation to drugs and alcohol. Supports research progress in the area of substance abuse.

★1631★ EEC MIDWIVES LIAISON COMMITTEE (EEC-LCM)
(Comite de Liaison des Sages-Femmes de la CEE)
Royal College of Midwives
15 Mansfield St.
London W1M 0BE, England   PH: 71 5806523
Ruth M. Ashton, Sec.   FX: 71 4363951

Founded: 1968. **Members:** 22. **National Groups:** 12. **Languages:** English, French. **Multinational.** Representatives of associations of midwives in the European Economic Community. Promotes the interests of midwives; represents midwife associations before the Commission of the European Communities and other organizations.

Conventions/Meetings: annual convention.

★1632★ EUROPEAN ASSOCIATION FOR THE DEVELOPMENT OF INFORMATION AND TRAINING OF WOMEN - ENGLAND (EUDIFF)
Equal Opportunities Commission
Overseas House, Quay St.
Manchester M2 3HN, England   PH: 61 8339244
Judith Byrne-White, Contact   FX: 61 8351657

Languages: English. **National.** Circulates information on women and women's issues throughout England. Networks with organizations that also champion women's advancement. Demands that EC nations fully recognize women's rights. Supports women's development and equality; encourages women's participation in leadership roles. Facilitates exchange among members.

★1633★ EUROPEAN NETWORK FOR WOMEN'S RIGHTS TO ABORTION AND CONTRACEPTION (ENWRAC)
c/o NAC
Wesley House
4 Wild Ct.
London WC2B 5AU, England

Multinational. Promotes the rights of women to decide freely and responsibly on: giving birth; the number and spacing of their children; and choosing abortion without state interference. Offers men and women access to the whole range of contraceptives methods. Provides women with all medically approved methods of abortion. Lobbies for the payment of abortion by social insurance in the same way as other medical treatments. Sponsors sympathetic and unbiased abortion counseling. Disseminates information.

Conventions/Meetings: periodic conference.

★1634★ EUROPEAN UNION OF WOMEN - BRITISH SECTION
32 Smith Sq.
London SW1, England
Mrs. Patricia Leaver, Secretary   PH: 71 2229000

Founded: 1953. **Members:** 3,000. **Languages:** English. **National.** Women affiliated with moderate and right wing political parties in Europe. Liaises with similar women's organizations to improve the status of women in politics. Provides a forum for exchange of ideas among members. Encourages women to involve themselves in national and local politics. Supports peace efforts worldwide.

Publications: *Newsletter* (in English), annual. ● *Annual Commission Report* (in English).

★1635★ EXPLORING PARENTHOOD
Latimer Education Centre
194 Freston Rd.
London W10 6TT, England   PH: 81 9601678
Clare Mumby, Contact   FX: 81 9641827

Founded: 1982. **Languages:** English. **National.** Maintains a parent advice-line counseling service. Organizes workshops and seminars on various issues pertaining to parenting. Disseminates information to parents and organizations on a wide range of topics, such as: coping with stress in the

family; divorce; premature birth; and toddler tantrums. Provides training programs for parents and professionals in teaching, school counseling, school medical services, and education support services. **Telecommunication Services:** Phone referral system.

Publications: *Divorce and Children* (in English). Booklet. ● *Leaving Home* (in English). Booklet. ● *Being a Grandparent* (in English). Booklet. ● *Life after Birth* (in English). Booklet. ● *Parenting Alone* (in English). Booklet. ● *The Working Parent* (in English). Booklet. ● *Adolescents and Alcohol* (in English). Booklet. ● *Adolescents and Drugs* (in English). Booklet. ● *Adolescents and AIDS* (in English). Booklet. ● *Step Parenting* (in English). Booklet. ● *Stress at Christmas* (in English). Booklet.

★1636★ FAMILY PLANNING ASSOCIATION - ENGLAND (FPA)
27-35 Mortimer St.
London W1N 7RJ, England   PH: 71 6367866
Doreen Massey, Director   FX: 71 4363288

Founded: 1930. **Members:** 1,000. **Staff:** 40. **Languages:** English. **National.** Health service professionals and individuals. Promotes sexual health and family planning to the public by means of information dissemination, research, education, training, and publicity. Offers courses in sexuality and personal relationships to professionals in the health, social services, and education fields. **Libraries:** Type: open to the public.   Subjects: sexual health and family planning. **Committees:** Policy; Medical Advisory.

Publications: *Family Planning Today* (in English). Newsletter. ● *Manifesto* (in English). Booklet.

Conventions/Meetings: annual conference.

★1637★ FARM WOMEN'S CLUBS
Greenfield House
69-73 Manor Rd.
Wallington, Surrey SM6 0DE, England   PH: 81 6614930

Founded: 1948. **Members:** 3,000. **Languages:** English. **National.** Women involved in farming. Conducts charitable activities. Fosters communication among members.

Publications: *Magazine* (in English), quarterly.

★1638★ FAWCETT SOCIETY
46 Harleyford Rd.
London SE11 5AY, England   PH: 71 5871287
Prof. Dorothy Wedderburn, Pres.   FX: 71 5871287

Founded: 1866. **Members:** 470. **Staff:** 2. **Languages:** English. **National.** Campaigns for equality between the sexes; seeks to abolish all sex discrimination. Strives for new attitudes towards gender relationships in society. Conducts lobbying activities including Women to the Top, a campaign for part-time workers rights, as well as periodic women's forums. **Libraries:** Type: reference. Holdings: 40,000; books, periodicals, clippings. **Awards:** Periodic Positive Action. ● Periodic Book Prize. **Committees:** Education.

Publications: *Fawcett Information*, periodic. Newsletter.

★1639★ FEDERATION OF ARMY WIVES (FAW)
c/o FHWS UKLF
Old Sarum
Salisbury, Wilts. SP4 6BN, England
Roz Potts, Secretary   PH: 722 336222

Founded: 1982. **Languages:** English. **National.** Army wives. Channels communication between army wives and the military. Concerns itself with matters affecting army families, such as: housing; education; employment; health; and special needs of children. Acts as a liaison with other women's organizations. **Awards:** NAAF Good Neighbours Award.

Publications: *Army Wives Journal* (in English), quarterly.

Conventions/Meetings: semiannual regional meeting. ● annual conference.

★1640★ FEMINIST LIBRARY AND RESOURCE CENTRE (FLRC)
5 Westminster Bridge Rd.
London SE1 7XW, England
PH: 71 9287789

Founded: 1975. Members: 1,500. Budget: £4,000. Languages: English. National. Women interested in feminist issues. Disseminates information on women's studies and feminism. Maintains biographical archives. Formerly: (1984) Feminist Library, (1989) Women's Research and Resource Centre.

Publications: Feminist Library Newsletter (in English), quarterly. Includes calendar of events, publications list, and book reviews.

★1641★ FEMINISTS AGAINST EUGENICS (FAE)
173 Minster Ct.
Liverpool, Merseyside L7 30F, England
Pauline Conner, Research Officer   PH: 51 7090094

Founded: 1985. Members: 150. Budget: £1,500. Languages: English. National. Pro-life feminists. Opposes social policies and legislation with eugenic implications. Areas of concern include: abortion; euthanasia; genetic engineering; pre-natal screening; militarism; pornography; and reproductive experiments. Affirms the right to life and right to bodily integrity for all living persons. Studies connections between the pro-life movement, anti-feminism, and pro-family thought. Libraries: Type: reference.

Publications: Newsletter (in English), quarterly. ● Journal (in English), annual.

Conventions/Meetings: semiannual meeting.

★1642★ FOUNDATION FOR WOMEN'S HEALTH RESEARCH AND
    DEVELOPMENT (FORWARD)
Africa Centre
38 King St.
Covent Garden
London WC2E 8JT, England

Multinational. Promotes the studies of women's health research and development throughout Europe and other western countries. Supports the rights of women and children. Protects women and children from becoming victims of abuse. Opposes and fights for the elimination of the practice of gential mutilation of young girls. Disseminates information. Conducts training programs.

Publications: Another Form of Physical Abuse: Prevention of Female Genital Mutilation in the United Kingdom. Videos. ● Child Protection and Female Genital Mutilation: Advice for Health, Education, and Social Work Professionals. Book. ● Working Together: A Guide to Arrangement for Inter-Agency Protection of Children from Abuse. Book.

Conventions/Meetings: periodic conference.

★1643★ GEMMA
BM Box 5700
London WC1N 3XX, England
Elsa Beckett, Coord.   PH: 71 4854024

Founded: 1976. Members: 250. Budget: £500. Languages: English. National. Homosexual and bisexual women with and without disabilities. Works towards diminishing the isolation of homosexual and bisexual women with disabilities through a pen-, tape-, phone-, and braille-friend network. Provides information on other lesbian groups and helplines.

Publications: Newsletter (in English), quarterly. ● Facets (in English). Magazine.

Conventions/Meetings: monthly meeting - London, England.

★1644★ GENDER AND MATHEMATICS ASSOCIATION (GAMMA)
Faculty of Education
Goldsmith College
New Cross
London SE14 6NW, England   PH: 81 6927171
Lesley Jones, Contact   FX: 81 6919504

Founded: 1980. Members: 250. Languages: English. National. Math educators. Works towards redressing the imbalance of girls' participation in mathematics. Conducts educational conferences for teenage girls.

Publications: Newsletter (in English), semiannual.

Conventions/Meetings: annual conference.

★1645★ GIRLS' BRIGADE - ENGLAND
Girls' Brigade House
Foxhall Rd.
Didcot, Oxon. OX11 7BQ, England   PH: 235 510425
Miss D.M. Cosser, Secretary   FX: 235 510429

Founded: 1965. Members: 52,200. Languages: English. National. Girls affiliated with a church of the Christian denomination. Encourages members to observe the motto "seek, serve, and follow Christ" in all activities. Helps members become followers of Jesus Christ and attain self-control, a sense of responsibility, and true enrichment.

Publications: Girls' Brigade Gazette (in English), bimonthly. Newsletter.

★1646★ GIRLS FRIENDLY SOCIETY - UNITED KINGDOM (GFS)
Townsend House
126 Queens Gate
London SW7 5LQ, England   PH: 71 5899628
Hazel Compton, Secretary   FX: 71 2251458

Founded: 1875. Members: 2,000. Budget: £14,000,000. Languages: English. Multinational. Girls and women from the ages of 7 and up. Conducts creative and challenging recreational and training activities for girls. Offers low-cost, secure housing for women. Provides guidance and support to troubled young women. Provides funding to female chaplains working in commerical and industrial spheres. Libraries: Type: reference.

Publications: Newsletter (in English), semiannual. ● Mothering Sunday Pack (in English), annual. Booklet.

Conventions/Meetings: triennial meeting, World Council..

★1647★ GIRLS' VENTURE CORPS AIR CADETS
Redhill Aerodrome
Kings Mill Ln.
S. Nutfield
Redhill, Surrey RH1 5JY, England
Miss Hazel Prosper, Director   PH: 737 823345

Founded: 1964. Languages: English. National. Young women and girls between the ages of 13 and 18 years. Provides opportunities for members to develop their self-discipline and resourcefulness through community service projects. Offers leadership training programs. Conducts outdoor activities including: aviation, camping, canoeing, sailing, rifle shooting, and skiing.

Publications: GVC (in English), periodic. Newsletter.

★1648★ HOUSEWIVES IN DIALOGUE
Kings Cross Women's Centre
71 Tonbridge St.
London WC1, England

Languages: English. National. Works to raise the social and economic status of women working in the home. Conducts research and disseminates information on the relationship between racism, sexism, and women's unpaid work. Offers educational courses, counselling, and recreational activities to low-income women, housewives, and other women poorly renumerated for their work.

Publications: *The Global Kitchen* (in English). Book. ● *The UN Decade for Women: An Offer We Couldn't Refuse* (in English). Book. ● *Disarmament and Development Beginning with Women and Children* (in English). Book. ● *Women the Welfare Providers* (in English). Book. ● *Women Count Women's Work* (in English). Book.

★1649★ **HYSTERECTOMY SUPPORT GROUP**
The Venture
Green Ln.
Huntingdon, Cambs. PE17 5YE, England
Mary Fountain, Secretary

Founded: 1980. **Languages:** English. **National.** Women who have had or are considering having a hysterectomy performed. Provides a forum for members to informally exchange information and experiences. Seeks to raise women's gynecological awareness. Offers information on alternative treatments to hysterectomies.

Publications: *New Horizon* (in English). Booklet. Information on hysterectomies.

★1650★ **HYSTERECTOMY SUPPORT NETWORK**
3 Lynne Close
Green St. Green
Orpington, Kent BR6 6BS, England
Murial Jackson

Founded: 1980. **Members:** 200. **Membership Dues:** Employed., £5 annual. **Languages:** English. **National.** Disseminates information to women and their families regarding hysterectomy surgery: the operation itself, the reasons for it, and recovery from it. Encourages an informal sharing of experiences among women who will have or have had hysterectomy surgery. Strives towards a heightened awareness of the difficulties a woman struggles with when faced with the need for a hysterectomy. **Telecommunication Services:** Phone referral system.

Publications: *Hysterectomy: a New Horizon* (in English).

Conventions/Meetings: quarterly meeting.

★1651★ **ICA WOMEN'S COMMITTEE**
13 Unity Rd.
Enfield
London EN3 6PA, England
Muriel Russell, Hon.Sec.

Founded: 1965. **Members:** 59. **Multinational.** Addresses questions concerning women in the cooperative movement. Areas of interest include access to credit, educational opportunities, and right to membership and participation in cooperatives. Sponsors research programs.

★1652★ **INDEPENDENT MIDWIVES ASSOCIATION**
24 Auckland Rd.
Upper Norwood
London SE19 2DB, England
Alice Coyle, Contact

Founded: 1982. **Languages:** English. **National.** Midwives practicing in England. Promotes the involvement of midwives in childbirth. Promotes education in midwifery. Represents members' interests.

★1653★ **INTERNATIONAL BLACK WOMEN FOR WAGES FOR HOUSEWORK**
King's Cross Women's Centre
71 Tonbridge St.　　　　　　PH: 71 8377509
London WC1H 9DZ, England　FX: 71 8334817

Languages: English. **National.** Network of black women from developing and industrialized countries working towards compensation for women for housework and agricultural work. Challenges sexism and racism in order to achieve objectives. Organizes campaigns relating to: racism; immigration controls; development; welfare benefits; low wages; rape; prostitution; police priorities and illegalities; lesbian and gay rights; civil and human rights; nuclear power/weapons; military/industrial pollution; health; and ecology and peace.

Publications: *Black Women and the Peace Movement* (in English). Book. ● *Roots: Black Ghetto Ecology* (in English). Book. ● *Strangers and Sisters: Women, Race and Immigration* (in English). Book. ● *Refusing Nuclear Housework* (in English). Book. ● *No Justice, No Peace - the 1992 Los Angeles Rebellion* (in English). Book.

★1654★ **INTERNATIONAL CONFEDERATION OF MIDWIVES (ICM)**
(CISF Confederation Internationale des Sages-Femmes)
10 Barley Mow Passage
Chiswick　　　　　　　　PH: 81 9946477
London W4 4PH, England　FX: 81 9941533
Miss J. Walker, Sec.Gen.　TX: 8811418

Founded: 1949. **Members:** 54. **Staff:** 2. **Budget:** £24,000. **Regional Groups:** 4. **Languages:** English, French, Spanish. **Multinational.** National midwives' associations in 47 countries. Seeks to improve the standard of care provided to mothers, babies, and the family by promoting midwifery education and disseminating information about the art and science of midwifery. Conducts workshops and seminars on midwifery and safe motherhood.

Publications: *Congress Proceedings*, triennial. Booklet. ● *Newsletter*, quarterly. ● *Maternity Care in the World*. Booklet.

Conventions/Meetings: triennial congress. ● periodic conference.

★1655★ **INTERNATIONAL FEDERATION OF BUSINESS AND PROFESSIONAL WOMEN (IFBPW)**
(Federation Internationale des Femmes de Carrieres Liberales et Commerciales)
Cloisters House, Studio 16
Cloisters Business Centre　　PH: 71 7388323
8 Battersea Park Rd.　　　　FX: 71 6228528
London SW8 4BG, England　　CBL: PROFED LONDON
Yvette V.A. Swan, President　EC1

Founded: 1930. **Members:** 80. **Staff:** 3. **Budget:** US$245,000. **National Groups:** 91. **Languages:** English, French, Spanish. **Multinational.** National organizations of business and professional women. Promotes high business and professional standards. **Committees:** Agriculture; Business Trade and Technology; Constitution Advisory; Educational and Cultural; Employment; Health; Legislation; Trade and Commerce; Translations; United Nations.

Publications: *Circular*, quarterly. Magazine. ● *IFBPW Trade Directory*, periodic. ● *Roster*, semiannual. Directory. ● *Widening Horizons*, semiannual. Magazine.

Conventions/Meetings: biennial congress (exhibits)

★1656★ **INTERNATIONAL FEDERATION OF GYNECOLOGY AND OBSTETRICS (FIGO)**
(FIGO Federation Internationale de Gynecologie et d'Obstetrique)
27 Sussex Pl.
Regent's Park
London NW1 4RG, England　　PH: 71 7232951
Prof. D.V.I. Fairweather, Sec.Gen.　FX: 71 7247725

Founded: 1954. **Members:** 89. **Staff:** 2. **Languages:** English, French, Spanish. **Multinational.** National societies of obstetrics and gynecology. Objectives are to: promote and assist in the development of scientific and research work relating to all facets of gynecology and obstetrics; improve the physical and mental health of women, mothers, and their children; provide an exchange of information and ideas; improve teaching standards; promote international cooperation among medical bodies. Acts as liaison with World Health Organization and other international organizations. Compiles statistics. **Committees:** Education; Ethical Aspects of Human Reproduction; Gynecological Oncology; Perinatal Mortality and Morbidity; Safe Motherhood; Study of the Female Breast. **Task Forces:** WHO/FIGO.

Publications: *Annual Report.* ● *International Journal of Gynecology and Obstetrics*, monthly.

Conventions/Meetings: triennial congress (exhibits).

★1657★ INTERNATIONAL NETWORK OF WOMEN LIBERALS (INWL)
c/o Liberal International
1 Whitehall Pl.   PH: 71 8395905
London SW1A 2HE, England   FX: 71 9252685

Languages: English. **Multinational.** Women representatives of parties and groups within Liberal International.

Conventions/Meetings: annual congress.

★1658★ INTERNATIONAL PLANNED PARENTHOOD FEDERATION
(IPPF)
(IPPF Federation Internationale pour la Planification Familiale)
Regent's College
Inner Circle   PH: 71 4860741
Regent's Park   FX: 71 4877950
London NW1 4NS, England   TX: 919573
Dr. Halfdan Mahler, Sec.Gen.   CBL: IPEPEE G LONDON

Founded: 1952. **Members:** 107. **Staff:** 309. **Budget:** US$76,800,000. **Regional Groups:** 6. **National Groups:** 134. **Languages:** English. **Multinational.** National, independent, and nongovernmental family planning associations. Works to: initiate and support family planning services throughout the world; heighten governmental and public awareness of the population problems of local communities and the world. Promotes effective family planning services in order to preserve and protect the mental and physical health of parents and their children; concerns itself with the efficacy and safety of various methods of contraception. Seeks to: create strong volunteer participation; promote family planning as a basic human right; extend and improve family planning services; meet the needs of young people; improve the status of women; increase male involvement in family planning; develop human financial and material resources; stimulate research on subjects related to human fertility and disseminate the findings of such research; encourage and coordinate training of the federation's professional workers. Offers programs that concentrate on family life, population, and sex education. Sponsors workshops and seminars. **Libraries:** Type: reference. Holdings: 5,000. **Departments:** International Liaison; Medical; Policy; Programme Development; Public Affairs; Resource Development.

Publications: *AIDS Watch* (in English and French), quarterly. Newsletter. ● *Earthwatch/Eco-Monde* (in English and French), quarterly. Magazine. ● *IPPF Annual Report* (in English). ● *IPPF Directory of Contraceptives*, periodic. ● *IPPF Medical Bulletin* (in English, French, and Spanish), bimonthly. ● *Open File*, semimonthly. Magazine. ● *People/Peuple* (in English and French), quarterly. Newsletter. ● *Research in Reproduction*, quarterly. Magazine. ● *Family Planning Handbook for Doctors.*

Conventions/Meetings: triennial convention - 1995.

★1659★ INTERNATIONAL PROSTITUTES COLLECTIVE
King's Cross Women's Centre
71 Tonbridge St.   PH: 71 8377509
London WC1H 9DZ, England   FX: 71 8334817

Languages: English. **National.** Prostitutes campaigning for the legalization of prostitution. Promotes economic and civil rights for prostitutes. Seeks higher welfare benefits, wages, student grants, and housing for impoverished women who depend on prositution as a livlihood.

Publications: *Prostitutes - Our Life* (in English). Book. ● *Prostitute Women and AIDS: Resisting the Virus of Repression* (in English). Book. ● *Who's the Good Girl Then? - the Costs to Women of Anti-Porn Feminism.* Book.

★1660★ INTERNATIONAL WAGES FOR HOUSEWORK CAMPAIGN
(IWFHC)
King's Cross Women's Centre
71 Tonbridge St.
London WC1H 9DZ, England   PH: 71 8377509
Selma James, Contact   FX: 71 8334817

Founded: 1972. **Languages:** English, French, German, Spanish, Punjabi, Urdu. **Multinational.** A network of women in developing and industrialized countries campaigning for compensation for housework. Asserts that women's unpaid work is the foundation of every nation's economy and profit. Campaigns for women's wages to come from money freed up from the dismantling of the military-industrial complex. Lobbies for legislation for compensation for housework at the national level. Disseminates information regarding organization's objectives. **Libraries:** Type: reference. Holdings: archival material.

Publications: *The Power of Women and the Subversion of the Community* (in English). Book. ● *Black Women and the Peace Movement* (in English). Book. ● *The Disinherited Family* (in English). Book. ● *Sex, Race and Class* (in English). Book. ● *The Global Kitchen* (in English). Book. ● *Women, the Unions and Work* (in English). Book. ● *Marx and Feminism* (in English). Book.

Conventions/Meetings: annual Time Off for Women convention - week of October 24.

★1661★ ISSUE
St. George's Rectory
Tower St.
Birmingham, W. Midlands B19 3UY,
England   PH: 21 3594887
John R. Dickson, Director   FX: 21 3596357

Founded: 1976. **Members:** 6,000. **Staff:** 7. **Budget:** £200,000. **Languages:** English. **National.** Infertile women and men. Disseminates information and provides support and counseling to infertile individuals regarding: treatment; adoption; inter-country adoption; and coping with infertility. Finances research into infertility.

Publications: *Issue* (in English), quarterly. Magazine.

Conventions/Meetings: annual conference - always in October.

★1662★ JOSEPHINE BUTLER SOCIETY (JBS)
Candida
49 Hawkshead Ln.
North Mymms
Hatfield, Herts. AL9 7TD, England
Margaret Schwarz, Exec. Officer   PH: 707 43150

Founded: 1869. **Staff:** 1. **Budget:** £500. **Languages:** English. **National.** Espouses the principle of social justice and equality among women and men, and the need for a high and equal standard of morality and sexual responsibility. Promotes the principles of the International Abolitionist Federation in an effort to abolish state regulation of prostitution, combat traffic in persons, and prevent exploitation of prostitution by third parties. Addresses legislation concerning prostitution; opposes the lowering of the age of consent and the licensing of brothels. Sponsors charitable programs and speakers' bureau. Operates the Josephine Butler Educational Trust. The society is named for Josephine Butler (1828-1906), a British social reformer. **Libraries:** Type: reference. Holdings: 20,000.

Publications: *News and Views* (in English), annual. Newsletter.

Conventions/Meetings: annual meeting - always November.

★1663★ LABOUR PARTY WOMEN'S ORGANISATION - NEC
WOMEN'S COMMITTEE
150 Walworth Rd.
London SE17 1JT, England
Vicky Phillips, Contact   PH: 71 7011234

Founded: 1990. **Languages:** English. **National**. Women members of the British Labour party representing the labor constituency. Represents women's views within the labor party. Campaigns for the election of labor party members to office.

Publications: *Women's News* (in English), quarterly. Newsletter.

★1664★ LEAGUE OF JEWISH WOMEN
Woburn House
Upper Woburn Pl.
London WC1J 0EP, England
Gillian Gold, President   PH: 71 3877688

Founded: 1943. **Members:** 5,000. **Languages:** English. **National**. Promotes friendly relations, understanding, and mutual support among Jewish women. Seeks to: improve the status of women in the Jewish and general communities; "intensify in each Jewish woman her sense of Jewish consciousness;" and encourage solidarity among members.

Publications: *Around the League* (in English), semiannual. Newsletter.

★1665★ LIFE
Life House
Newbold Terr.
Leamington Spa, Warwickshire CV32
  4EA, England   PH: 926 421587
Nuala Scarisbrick, Hon.Admin.   FX: 926 336497

Founded: 1970. **Members:** 40,000. **Staff:** 13. **Local Groups:** 243. **Languages:** English. **National**. Individuals dedicated to the abolition of abortion in the United Kingdom. Seeks to increase knowledge of the potential health risks involved in abortion in an attempt to dissuade women from undergoing the operation. Operates pregnancy care centers offering pregnancy counseling, free testing, welfare advice, and provision of baby and maternity clothes and equipment. Maintains "Life Houses" providing shelter and aid to impoverished pregnant women. Coordinates petition drives and public information campaigns; distributes videos. Has organized the Back Alton's Bill - Yes Campaign/BABY, which sought to limit abortion to pregnancies of less than 18 weeks. Sponsored campaign to ban research on human embryos. Holds rallies; offers speaker's bureau. **Divisions:** Evangelicals for Life; Life Anglicans; Life Doctors.

Publications: *Life News* (in English), quarterly. Newsletter.

Conventions/Meetings: annual conference.

★1666★ LITTLE COMPANY OF MARY (LCM)
28 Trinity Crescent
Tooting Bec
London SW17 7AE, England   PH: 81 6820928
Sr. Marie Therese Nilon LCM, Contact   FX: 81 6820552

Founded: 1877. **Members:** 520. **Languages:** English. **Multinational**. Women religious in 10 countries. Provides spiritual and physical care for the sick and dying.

★1667★ MARIE STOPES INTERNATIONAL (MSI)
62 Grafton Way   PH: 71 3883740
London W1P 5LO, England   FX: 71 3881946
Timothy R.L. Black, Chief Exec.   TX: 94016277 PPSE G

Founded: 1971. **Members:** 6. **Staff:** 13. **Languages:** English. **Multinational**. Maintains mother and child health care services, family planning clinics, and educational programs in developing countries. Seeks to prevent unwanted births. Promotes population control policy. Cooperates with nongovernmen-

tal organizations with similar goals. Disseminates information. **Formerly:** Population Services Europe.

★1668★ MARRIED WOMEN'S ASSOCIATION
16 Hollycroft Ave.
London NW3 1QL, England
Simone Grasse, President

Founded: 1938. **Members:** 200. **Languages:** English. **National**. Seeks to raise the status of married women to that of an equal financial partner during marriage. Fosters communication among members.

Publications: *Bulletin* (in English), quarterly.

★1669★ MATERNITY ALLIANCE - ENGLAND (MA)
15 Britannia St.
London WC1X 9JP, England   PH: 71 8371265
Christine Gowdridge   FX: 71 8371273

Founded: 1980. **Members:** 120. **Languages:** English. **National**. Organizations and individuals. Works to improve services for, and defending the rights of, mothers, fathers, and babies, through the first year of life. Disseminates information on maternity benefits and rights; advises midwives and health visitors. Offers post-natal support to parents with disabilities. Campaigns for policies designed to meet the needs of users of healthcare services; provides a forum for discussion between users and service providers. **Committees:** Management; Disability. **Working Groups:** Minority Ethnic Community; Trade Union Working Party.

Publications: *Maternity Action* (in English), 5/year. Magazine.

★1670★ MEDICAL WOMEN'S FEDERATION (MWF)
Tavistock House N
Tavistock Sq.
London WC1H 9HX, England   PH: 71 3877765
Lyn Perry, Secretary   FX: 71 3877765

Founded: 1917. **Members:** 2,000. **Staff:** 2. **Budget:** £120,000. **Local Groups:** 20. **Languages:** English. **National**. Women doctors and medical students. Promotes equal opportunities for women doctors and improved choices for patients.

Publications: *Medical Woman* (in English), 3/year. Magazine. ● *Annual Report* (in English).

Conventions/Meetings: periodic meeting.

★1671★ MEDICAL WOMEN'S INTERNATIONAL ASSOCIATION -
UNITED KINGDOM
32 Aldsworth Ct.
Goring St.
Goring by Sea, W. Sussex BN12 5AG,
  England
Marjorie Semmens, Contact

Languages: English. **National**. U.K. branch of the Medical Women's International Association (see separate entry). Women physicians. Provides a forum for discussion of women's health care issues. Encourages women to enter the field of medicine. Works to overcome discrimination against female physicians. Sponsors research and educational programs.

★1672★ MIDWIVES INFORMATION AND RESOURCE SERVICE
(MIDIRS)
Institute of Child Health
Royal Hospital for Sick Children
St. Michael's Hill
Bristol, Avon BS2 8BJ, England   PH: 272 251791
Joy Rodwell, Contact   FX: 272 251792

Founded: 1983. **Staff:** 9. **Languages:** English. **Multinational**. Provides information to professional midwives concerning: research in midwifery;

midwifery education; professional and statutory developments. Acts as a clearinghouse, offering articles, books, and other information regarding midwifery. Conducts educational programs. **Computer Services:** Data base, medical journal articles focusing on midwifery.

Publications: *Directory of Maternity Organisations*, periodic. ● *How To Find Out - Information Sources in Midwifery*, periodic. Directory. ● *MIDIRS Midwifery Digest*, quarterly. Journal. **ISSN:** 0961-5555. **Circulation:** 10,000. **Advertising:** not accepted.

Conventions/Meetings: bimonthly conference (exhibits).

★1673★ MISCARRIAGE ASSOCIATION
Clayton Hospital
Northgate
Wakefield, W. Yorkshire WF1 3JS,
   England
Mrs. Kathryn Ladley, Secretary   PH: 924 200799

Founded: 1982. **Members:** 1,300. **Languages:** English. **National.** Women who have had a miscarriage. Provides support and information to members and their families.

Publications: *Newsletter* (in English), quarterly. ● *Booklet* (in English). Information on miscarriages.

★1674★ NATIONAL ABORTION CAMPAIGN (NAC)
The Print House
18 Ashwin St.
London E8 3DL, England   PH: 71 9234976
Leonora Lloyd, Contact   FX: 71 9234979

Founded: 1975. **Members:** 600. **Staff:** 2. **Budget:** £40,000. **Languages:** English. **National.** Individuals and organizations. Supports the right of women to choose abortion. Campaigns for the legalization of abortion, improved contraception, and family planning services. Disseminates information.

Publications: *Women's Choice* (in English), quarterly. Newsletter.

Conventions/Meetings: annual conference.

★1675★ NATIONAL ALLIANCE OF WOMEN'S ORGANIZATIONS
   (NAWO)
279-281 Whitechapel Rd.
London E1 1BY, England   PH: 71 2477052
Jane Grant, Director   FX: 71 2474490

Founded: 1989. **Members:** 200. **Budget:** £150,000. **Languages:** English. **National.** Umbrella organization for women's groups. Promotes the interests of women. Acts as an advocate for the consensus view of its members. Provides support and information for women's groups. **Libraries:** Type: open to the public; reference. **Committees:** Equal Opportunities. **Working Groups:** Media Action; Women Education and Training; Women in Development; World Issues; Rural Issues Advisory.

Publications: *NAWO*, bimonthly. Newsletter.

Conventions/Meetings: annual conference. ● semiannual meeting.

★1676★ NATIONAL ASSEMBLY OF WOMEN (NAW)
1 Camden Hill Rd.
London SE19 1NX, England   PH: 81 7617532
Elsie Wilson, Gen.Sec.   81 3932067

Founded: 1952. **Members:** 1,000. **Languages:** English. **National.** Women of all classes, intellectual and physical description, color, race, sexual orientation and religion. Works to raise the economic, social, and legal status of women. Campaigns for international peace and understanding. Organizes educational meetings for both members and non members.

Publications: *Sisters* (in English), quarterly. Journal.

Conventions/Meetings: biennial general assembly. ● periodic meeting.

★1677★ NATIONAL ASSOCIATION OF LADIES' CIRCLES OF GREAT
   BRITAIN AND IRELAND (NALC)
Provincial House
Cook St.
Keighley, W. Yorkshire BD21 3NN,
   England
Marlene Sharkey, Secretary   PH: 535 607617

Founded: 1936. **Languages:** English. **Multinational.** Promotes friendly relations and exchange between women in the United Kingdom and the Republic of Ireland. Conducts community service activities. Organizes social activities.

★1678★ NATIONAL ASSOCIATION FOR MATERNAL AND CHILD
   WELFARE
Strode House, Ste. 25
46/48 Osnaburgh St.
London NW1 3ND, England
Freny Kapadia, Contact   PH: 71 3834117

Founded: 1911. **Languages:** English. **National.** Health authorities, schools, and voluntary organizations concerned with improving the health and well-being of mothers and children. Offers health education programs; conducts research.

Conventions/Meetings: periodic conference.

★1679★ NATIONAL ASSOCIATION OF SCHOOLMASTERS AND
   UNION OF WOMEN TEACHERS (NASUWT)
Hillscourt Education Centre
Rose Hill
Rednal
Birmingham, W. Midlands B45 8RS,
   England   PH: 21 4536150
Barry Gandy, Asst.Sec.   FX: 21 4537224

Founded: 1919. **Members:** 170,000. **Staff:** 75. **Local Groups:** 400. **Languages:** English. **National.** Active, retired, and student female teachers. Regulates relations between members and other employees in the education field. Works to ensure competitive salary scale. Advises government and local education authorities on educational matters. Offers members insurance coverage as well as legal advice and assistance; provides housing. Conducts research. Maintains speakers' bureau. **Libraries:** Type: reference. Holdings: 0. **Computer Services:** Data base.

Publications: *Career Teacher* (in English), 9/year. Newsletter. ● *Career Teacher* (in English), quarterly. Journal.

Conventions/Meetings: annual conference (exhibits) - 1994 Apr. 4 - 8, Blackpool, LC, England; 1995 Apr. 17 - 21, Eastbourne, ES, England; 1996 Apr. 8 - 12, Glasgow, Scotland.

★1680★ NATIONAL ASSOCIATION OF WIDOWS
54-57 Allison St.
Digbeth
Birmingham, W. Midlands B5 5TH,
   England
Gill Milner, Chair.   PH: 21 6438348

Founded: 1971. **Members:** 3,000. **Staff:** 2. **Regional Groups:** 57. **Local Groups:** 13. **Languages:** English. **National.** Provides information and advice to widows on coping with grief, loneliness, and financial difficulty. Assists widows, their friends, and families in facing problems within today's society through friendly support from other widows. Offers location where widows can share their experiences. Monitors actions of local and federal government to ensure that the interests and concerns of widows are properly represented in legislation.

Publications: *Newsletter* (in English), semiannual.

Conventions/Meetings: annual meeting. ● semiannual seminar.

★1681★ NATIONAL ASSOCIATION OF WOMEN PHARMACISTS
(NAWP)
c/o Office Manager
Royal Pharmaceutical Society of Great
Britain
1 Lambeth High St.
London SE1 7JN, England
Dr. Cherrie Temple, Secretary

Founded: 1905. **Members:** 400. **Languages:** English. **National.** Women pharmacists. Promotes the careers of women in pharmacy and the role of women pharmacists in public life. Encourages continuing education and career development for women pharmacists. Works with other women's organizations. Conducts courses and lectures.

Publications: *Newsletter*, 3/year.

Conventions/Meetings: annual Weekend School.

★1682★ NATIONAL ASSOCIATION OF WOMEN'S CLUBS (NAWC)
5 Vernon Rise
Kings Cross Rd.
London WC1X 9EP, England
Mrs. Stella Nicholas, Secretary   PH: 71 8371434

Founded: 1935. **Members:** 13,800. **Membership Dues:** £2 annual. **Staff:** 1. **Budget:** £100,000. **Regional Groups:** 420. **Languages:** English. **National.** Promotes the self-development of women through education and recreation. Maintains day schools and workshops for members. Encourages community and charity work of members to enhance community spirit. Conducts competitions and social activities. Conducts research. **Committees:** Education; Promotional.

Publications: *Club News and Views*, 3/year. Newsletter.

Conventions/Meetings: annual conference (exhibits).

★1683★ NATIONAL BOARD OF CATHOLIC WOMEN (NBCW)
83 Alleyn Rd.
London E21 8AD, England
Anne Leeming, Secretary

Founded: 1938. **Members:** 32. **Budget:** £10,000. **Languages:** English. **National.** National women's Catholic organizations. Promotes and supports the development of Catholic women in England and Wales. Disseminates information about women of the Catholic faith. Encourages Catholic women to increase participation in consultation and decision making within the Church. Conducts courses, public services, and research. **Committees:** Marriage and the Family; Social Responsibility; Women in the Church.

Publications: *Do Not be Afraid.* Booklet.

Conventions/Meetings: quarterly general assembly. ● quarterly executive committee meeting.

★1684★ NATIONAL BRITISH WOMEN'S TOTAL ABSTINENCE UNION
(NBWTAU)
Rosalind Carlisle House
23 Dawson Pl.
London W2 4TH, England
Mrs. E.M. Hitcham, Pres.   PH: 71 2290804

Founded: 1876. **Members:** 900. **Staff:** 2. **Local Groups:** 70. **Languages:** English. **National.** Women teetotallers in England; men teetotallers are associate members. Encourages solidarity between women who abstain from the use of alcoholic beverages, narcotics, and other habit-forming drugs. Seeks to inspire, through personal example, "the moral and religious uplift of the nation." Promotes alcohol education, especially among children and adults. Organizes exhibitions; distributes literature; makes recommendations to church and government leaders. Also maintains biographical

archives. **Awards:** . **Departments:** Abstaining Youth Movement (ages 14 to 30); Little White Ribboners (children up to 5 years of age); White Ribbon Circle (children ages 5 to 14).

Publications: *White Ribbon* (in English), quarterly. Magazine.

Conventions/Meetings: annual meeting.

★1685★ NATIONAL CHILDBIRTH TRUST
Alexander House
Oldham Terr.
Acton
London W2 4TH, England
Eileen Hutton, President   PH: 81 9928637

Founded: 1956. **Languages:** English. **National.** Seeks to prepare couples for the experience of childbirth and the responsibilities of parenting. Offers antenatal classes, postnatal support groups, information on breastfeeding, and educational classes in schools and colleges.

Publications: *New Generation* (in English), quarterly.

★1686★ NATIONAL CHILDCARE CAMPAIGN/DAYCARE TRUST
(NCCC/DT)
Wesley House
4 Wild Ct.
London WC2B 5AU, England   PH: 71 4055617
Marion Kozak, Secretary   FX: 71 8316632

Staff: 3. **Languages:** English. **National.** Promotes the development of quality, affordable, accessible, and equitable child care. Works to improve child care nationwide through: dissemination of information; negotiations with politicians, administrators, and trade unions; and cooperation with other voluntary organizations having similar goals.

Publications: *Newsletter* (in English), quarterly. ● *Under-Five and Underfunded* (in English). ● *Babies in Daycare* (in English). ● *Daycare for Kids* (in English). ● *The ABC of Creche Training* (in English). ● *The ABC of Quality Childcare* (in English).

★1687★ NATIONAL COUNCIL OF WOMEN OF GREAT BRITAIN
36 Danbury St.
Islington
London N1 8JU, England
Sheila Green, Contact   PH: 71 3542395

Founded: 1895. **Members:** 2,590. **Languages:** English. **Multinational.** Encourages women's participation in public and political life. Promotes the establishment and maintenance of world peace, international understanding, and human rights awareness. Works to combat sexism. Promotes collaboration and exchange among women's groups worldwide.

Publications: *Council* (in English), bimonthly. Newsletter.

★1688★ NATIONAL FEDERATION OF WOMEN'S INSTITUTES (NFWI)
104 New King Rd.
London SW6 4LY, England   PH: 71 3719300
Miss Heather Mayall, Secretary   FX: 71 7363652

Founded: 1915. **Members:** 310,000. **Staff:** 40. **Budget:** £1,900,000. **Regional Groups:** 70. **Languages:** English. **National.** Women, particularly in rural areas. Provides a democratically controlled educational and social organization for women. Encourages women to work and learn together to improve the quality of life within their communities. Promotes the development of women's skills and talents through courses, social activities, sporting events, music, arts and crafts, and cooperative produce marketing. Offers a forum for women to express their concerns on matters of local, national, and international importance. Maintains Denman College, an adult educational center.

Publications: *Home and Country* (in English), monthly. Magazine. **Circulation:** 100,000.

Conventions/Meetings: annual general assembly. ● periodic conference. ● monthly convention.

★1689★ NATIONAL FREE CHURCH WOMEN'S COUNCIL
27 Tavistock Sq.
London WC1H 9HH, England   PH: 71 3878413
Pauline Butcher, Secretary   FX: 71 3830150

Founded: 1908. **Members:** 2,000. **Staff:** 1. **Regional Groups:** 18. **Languages:** English. **National.** Women members of the free church denominations. Promotes development of the elderly and disadvantage girls living in England and Wales. Provides free church women the chance to further the work and witness of Christ. Maintains homes for the elderly and hostels for single mothers.

Conventions/Meetings: semiannual general assembly (exhibits)

★1690★ NATIONAL JOINT COMMITTEE OF WORKING WOMEN'S ORGANIZATIONS
150 Walworth Rd.
London SE17 1JJ, England
Vicky Phillips, Contact   PH: 71 7011234

Founded: 1916. **Members:** 20. **Languages:** English. **National.** Umbrella organization for groups working to enhance the status of working women. Lobbies local, national and international committees and governments on issues of interest to working women.

★1691★ NATIONAL MARRIAGE GUIDANCE
Information Dept.
Little Church St.
Rugby, Warwickshire CV21 3AP,
     England   PH: 788 73241

Founded: 1938. **Languages:** English. **National.** Promotes the availability of marriage counseling and sex therapy services to couples in England. Conducts educational programs regarding personal relationships. Trains counselors through courses, workshops, and conferences. Supports research on human relationships, particularly on marital and family relationships. **Alternate name::** Relate.

★1692★ NATIONAL UNION OF CIVIL AND PUBLIC SERVANTS: WOMEN'S ADVISORY COMMITTEE (NUCPS)
124-126 Southwark St.
London SE1 QTU, England
Judy McKnight, Secretary   PH: 71 9289671

Founded: 1983. **Languages:** English. **National.** Works to improve women's employment opportunities, working conditions, and salary. Encourages women's active participation in union activities. Disseminates information on maternity leave, sexual harassment, and job sharing.

Publications: *Annual Report* (in English). ● *Action for Equality* (in English), periodic. Newsletter.

★1693★ NATIONAL UNION OF TEACHERS - WOMEN'S SECTION
NUT Hamilton House
Mabledon Pl.
London WC1H 9BD, England
Frances Migniuolo, Contact   PH: 71 3886191

Languages: English. **National.** Women teachers in England. Lobbies government to establish equal opportunity policies. Conducts research and educational programs on gender equality.

★1694★ NATIONAL WOMEN'S NETWORK FOR INTERNATIONAL SOLIDARITY (NWN)
Box 110
190 Upper St.
London N1 1RQ, England
Shirley Nelson, Coord.   PH: 71 7002800

Founded: 1985. **Members:** 250. **Membership Dues:** Individual, unwaged., £3 annual; Individual., £8 annual; Supporting., £13 annual; Local groups., £13 annual; Regional groups., £25 annual; National groups., £50 annual. **Staff:** 1. **Budget:** £12,000. **Languages:** English. **National.** Professionals, development workers, voluntary agencies, Christian women's organizations, and community groups. Promotes the rights of women and their development in society. Communicates with other women's organizations on related issues. Focuses on areas such as: violence against women; peace; justice; environmentally sustainable livelihoods. Conducts training and campaigns for improvement in policies for women. **Libraries:** Type: reference. **Alternate name:.** National Women's Network.

Publications: *NWN Newsletter* (in English), monthly.

Conventions/Meetings: annual conference (exhibits).

★1695★ NATIONAL WOMEN'S REGISTER
9 Bank Plain
Norwich, Norfolk NR2 4SL, England   PH: 603 765392

Founded: 1960. **Languages:** English. **National.** Women organized for social interaction. Provides a center for social gatherings. Seeks to increase women's self-esteem and desire for education. Encourages tolerance, self-education, and community involvement.

Publications: *Newsletter*, periodic.

★1696★ NETWORK
9 Abbotts Yard
35 King St.
Royston, Herts. GS8 9AZ, England
Celia Nex, Contact   PH: 763 242225

Founded: 1981. **Members:** 800. **Languages:** English. **National.** Professional women in England. Seeks to enhance the status of women. Provides a forum for women to develop social and professional contacts.

★1697★ NEW WAYS TO WORK
309 Upper St.   PH: 71 2264026
London N1 2TY, England   FX: 71 3542978

Founded: 1981. **Members:** 300. **Budget:** £60,000. **Languages:** English. **National.** Offers supports services to working women. Lobbies government on women's employment issues.

Publications: *Newsletter* (in English), quarterly. ● *Putting Policy into Practice, a Job Sharing Manual* (in English). Booklet.

★1698★ NEWLIFE
Kay House
51 Stonebridge Dr.
Frome, Somerset BA11 2TW, England
Kay Palmer, Coord.   PH: 373 451632

Founded: 1990. **Members:** 1,000. **Membership Dues:** Low income., £4; Low income, joint (two people living at same address)., £6; Individual., £8; Joint., £12. **Budget:** £1,000. **Languages:** English. **National.** Individuals who oppose abortion. Promotes recognition of the right to life of unborn children in England. Disseminates information on non-abortive family planning. Supports other organizations that assist women during pregnancy and beyond. Conducts lobbying for laws that protect unborn children.

Publications: *New Voice/New Life Update*, bimonthly. Newsletter.

★1699★ OPPORTUNITIES FOR WOMEN (OFW)
Centre Two
Ossian Mews
London N4 4DX, England
Dr. Clive Mira-Smith, Co-Dir.
PH: 81 3489458
FX: 81 3403975
TX: 9312130343 G

Founded: 1988. **Staff:** 4. **Languages:** English. **Multinational.** Works to improve the status of women in developing countries. Supports programs and services which promote self-dependency and personal growth among women of developing countries, including: income-generation projects, literacy and training programs, and health care counseling. Conducts research; compiles information.

★1700★ POSITIVELY WOMEN
5 Sebastion St.
London EC1V 0HE, England
Lesley Foote, Contact
PH: 71 4905501
FX: 71 4901690

Founded: 1987. **Staff:** 12. **Budget:** £310,000. **Languages:** English. **National.** Provides counseling and support to women with the HIV virus or AIDs. Maintains a facility for weekly support groups. **Libraries:** Type: reference.

★1701★ PREGNANCY ADVISORY SERVICE
11-13 Charlotte St.
London W1P 1HD, England
Jonathan Tuppeny, Mkt. Mgr.
PH: 71 6378962
FX: 71 3234215

Founded: 1968. **Staff:** 50. **Languages:** English, French, German, Spanish. **National.** Promotes improved sexual education programs in England. Disseminates information and advice on topics such as: abortion; pregnancy testing; morning after birth control; cervical smears; donor insemination; and male and female sterilization.

★1702★ PROGRESS CAMPAIGN FOR RESEARCH INTO HUMAN REPRODUCTION
27-35 Mortimer St.
London W1N 7RJ, England
Denise Servante, Contact
PH: 71 4364528

Founded: 1985. **Members:** 800. **National.** Promotes reproductive rughts and supports pre-embryo research into human reproduction. Strives to develop medical technology to eliminate infertility, miscarriage, and congenital handicap. Conducts educational activities.

Publications: *Bulletin*, quarterly.

★1703★ REEL WOMEN
57 Holmewood Gardens
Brixton
London SW2 3NB, England
M.J. Beveridge, Secretary
PH: 81 6877404

Founded: 1990. **Members:** 100. **Budget:** £5,000. **Languages:** English. **National.** Women professionals and students of the film industry. Networking organization which organizes meetings where women involved in the entertainment/media industry may share their work, knowledge, and insights. **Computer Services:** Data base. **Committees:** Management.

Publications: *Newsletter* (in English), monthly.

Conventions/Meetings: monthly meeting (exhibits) - London, England.

★1704★ RIGHTS OF WOMEN (ROW)
52-54 Featherstone St.
London EC1Y 8RT, England
Sibusiso Mavolwane, Contact
PH: 71 2516577
71 6080928

Founded: 1975. **Members:** 400. **Membership Dues:** Students and unemployed individuals., £3; Low income individuals., £5; Individuals., £10; Local groups., £15; National organizations., £30. **Staff:** 6. **Budget:** £89,000.

Languages: English. **National.** Women's organizations, companies, and individuals. Informs women of their legal rights and promotes the interests of women through legal action. Provides legal advice for women regarding: relationship breakdown; sexual and domestic violence; and employment rights. Defends the rights of children. Advocates abortion, the criminalization of rape in marriage, and lesbian parenthood. Operates an advice line offering legal advice and referrals. Organizes and sponsors talks, conferences, and training.

Publications: *ROW* (in English), 3/year. Bulletin. Trends in the law affecting women. ● *ROW* (in English), bimonthly. Newsletter. Developments in law, events, notices, and advertisements. **Advertising:** accepted.

★1705★ ROMAN CATHOLIC FEMINISTS
33 Arlow Rd.
London N21 3JS, England
Jackie Field, Contact
PH: 81 8860779

Founded: 1977. **Members:** 300. **National.** Works to unite Roman Catholic feminists in the effort to achieve full liberation within the Church. Legitimizes this aim by referring to a statement of the Vatican II: 'Every type of discrimination. . .based on sex. . .is to be overcome and eradicated as contrary to God's intent'(Gaudium et Spes:29).

Publications: *Newsletter*, periodic.

★1706★ ROYAL BRITISH LEGION WOMEN'S SECTION (RBLWS)
Haig House
48 Pall Mall
London SW1Y 5JY, England
Miss J.H. Green, Secretary
PH: 71 9730633
FX: 71 8397917

Founded: 1921. **Members:** 112,000. **Staff:** 11. **Budget:** £800,000. **Languages:** English. **National.** Wives, widows, female dependents, and relatives of service and ex-service men and women. Promotes and defends the interests of those who have served or are serving in the military or Red Cross in Britain and their dependents. Raises funds. Conducts seminars. **Committees:** Central; Widows' and Ex-Servicewomen's Allowance Scheme; Rest and Convalescence; Publicity.

Publications: *Newsletter* (in English), quarterly.

Conventions/Meetings: annual conference. ● annual general assembly.

★1707★ ROYAL COLLEGE OF MIDWIVES
15 Mansfield St.
London W1M 0BE, England
PH: 71 5806523
FX: 71 5806524

Founded: 1881. **Members:** 34,500. **Languages:** English. **National.** Promotes the practice of midwifery, and works to maintain high standards in the field. Provides educational programs to midwives in the areas of maternity, child care, and personal development. Represents worker rights of midwives to national legal and political authorities. Encourages and supports research. **Libraries:** Type: reference.

Publications: *Midwives Chronicle*. Magazine. ● *Delivery*. Newsletter. ● *Current Awareness Service*. Bulletin.

★1708★ ROYAL INSTITUTE OF BRITISH ARCHITECTS - WOMEN ARCHITECTS' GROUP
66 Portland Pl.
London W1N 4AD, England
PH: 71 5805533

Founded: 1985. **Members:** 15. **Languages:** English. **National.** Promotes the interests of women architects in England. Provides a forum for discussion and professional information exchange among women architects.

★1709★ SALVATION ARMY HOME LEAGUE (SAHL)
(Ligue de Foyer)
101 Queen Victoria St.
PO Box 249
London EC4 4EP, England
Gen. Eva Burrows, Pres.   PH: 71 2365222

Founded: 1907. **Members:** 399,846. **Languages:** English. **Multinational.** Women over the age of 16 from 94 countries. Provides for education, fellowship, service, and worship.

★1710★ SANCTUARY
PO Box 2615
London WI4 0DW, England   PH: 71 3714666
Sasha Chaudhri, Contact   71 3714333

Founded: 1991. **Staff:** 3. **Budget:** £77,000. **Languages:** English. **National.** Provides counseling and support to women survivors of sexual abuse. Educates and advises individuals, organizations, and health practitioners regarding sexual abuse. Disseminates information. **Libraries:** Type: reference. Holdings: 0; books. **Telecommunication Services:** Phone referral system. **Committees:** Training; Employment; Volunteer.

★1711★ SCOTTISH NATIONAL PARTY - WOMEN'S FORUM
6 N. Charlotte St.
Edinburgh EH2 4JH, England
Helen Davidson, Contact   PH: 31 2263661

Founded: 1987. **Languages:** English. **National.** Women members of the Scottish National Party. Ensures that women's issues are addressed within the party platform.

★1712★ SOCIALIST INTERNATIONAL WOMEN (SIW)
(Internationale Socialiste des Femmes)
Maritime House   PH: 71 6274449
Old Town   FX: 71 7204448
Clapham   TX: 261735 SISEC G
London SW4 OJW, England   CBL: INTESOCON
Maria Rodriguez-Jonas, Gen.Sec.   LONDON SW4

Founded: 1907. **Members:** 68. **Languages:** English, French, Spanish. **Multinational.** Promotes action programmes to combat sex discrimination. Works for human rights, development, and peace.

Publications: *Women and Politics*, quarterly. Magazine.

Conventions/Meetings: triennial conference - next 1995.

★1713★ SOROPTIMIST INTERNATIONAL OF GREAT BRITAIN AND
    IRELAND
127 Wellington Rd. S
Stockport, Cheshire SK1 3TS, England   PH: 61 4807686
Kay Hindley   FX: 61 4776152

Founded: 1921. **Members:** 15,000. **Staff:** 5. **Languages:** English. **Multinational.** Women professionals. Participates in the struggle for issues such as: the environment; health; human rights; the status of women; international goodwill and understanding; and economic and social development.

Publications: *The Soroptimist* (in English), quarterly. Magazine.

Conventions/Meetings: annual conference - always in October.

★1714★ SRI LANKA WOMEN'S ASSOCIATION IN THE U.K.
214 Hoppers Rd.
Winchmore Hill
London N21, England
Miss S. Situnayake, President   PH: 81 8866633

Languages: English, Sinhalese. **National.** Sri Lankan women living in England. Promotes the interests of Sri Lankan women. Fosters communication and exchange among members.

★1715★ STANDING CONFERENCE OF WOMEN'S ORGANIZATIONS
Cap d'Or
Whidborne Ave.
Marine Dr.
Torquay TQ1 2PQq, England
O.I. Jarmain, Secretary   PH: 803 296564

Founded: 1942. **Members:** 1,500. **Languages:** English. **National.** Representatives of British, local women's organizations. Fosters cooperation among women's groups. Works to further progress towards common objectives concerning women's issues.

Publications: *Newsletter* (in English), periodic.

Conventions/Meetings: monthly meeting - England.

★1716★ STEP FAMILY
72 Willesden Ln.
London NW6 7TA, England
Erica De'ath, Contact   PH: 71 3720844

Founded: 1983. **Members:** 300. **National.** Provides information and counseling and support services to step-families. Supports research. Trains professionals.

Publications: *Newsletter*, quarterly.

★1717★ TOC H
1 Forest Close
Wendover
Aylesbury, Bucks. HP22 6BT, England
Mr. Stewart Casimir, Contact   PH: 296 623911

Founded: 1915. **Members:** 5,602. **Languages:** English. **National.** Promotes friendship and the elimination of prejudicial thought and action against women. Promotes Christian love and charity. Strives to bring about a respect of human rights and mutual love among society.

Publications: *Point 3*, monthly. Magazine.

★1718★ TOWNSWOMEN'S GUILDS
Chamber of Commerce House
75 Harborne Rd.
Edgbaston
Birmingham, W. Midlands B15 3DA,
    England   PH: 21 4563435
Rosie Styles, Secretary   FX: 21 4521890

Founded: 1928. **Members:** 100,000. **Staff:** 12. **Regional Groups:** 115. **Local Groups:** 1,990. **Languages:** English. **National.** Fosters the social awareness of all women, irrespective of race, creed, or political affiliation. Members meet regularly to exchange ideas, learn new skills, and participate in recreational and educational activities. Mounts a strong political lobby nationally and regionally on a variety of issues. Supports research into: premenopausal breast cancer; AIDS education; equal rights for part-time workers; toxic waste; food safety; rationalization of the pension age. Conducted national survey of children's playgrounds; presently implementing a British Playsafe Code. **Formerly:** National Union of Townswomen's Guilds.

Publications: *Townswoman* (in English), monthly. Newsletter.

Conventions/Meetings: bimonthly executive committee meeting. ● semiannual meeting, Central Council. ● annual meeting, National Council. ● annual Royal Show

★1719★ TOXOPLASMOSIS TRUST (TTT)
61-71 Collier St.
London N1 9BE, England   PH: 71 7130663
Christine Asbury, Contact   FX: 71 7130611

Founded: 1989. **Members:** 5,000. **Staff:** 4. **Budget:** £150,000. **Languages:**

English. **National**. Health professionals, individuals affected by toxoplasmosis, and others. Strives to foster public awareness of toxoplasmosis, a serious congenital or acquired disease that affects the central nervous system of infants. Provides support for those suffering from toxoplasmosis. Maintains an up-to-date information and advising center; promotes the testing of women for toxoplasmosis during pregnancy; supports medical research. **Libraries**: Type: not open to the public. **Telecommunication Services**: Phone referral system.

Publications: *The Toxoplasmosis Trust Trust Update*, periodic. Magazine.

★1720★ TRADES UNION CONGRESS - WOMEN'S COMMITTEE
Congress House
Great Russel St.
London WC1B 3LS, England
Kay Carberry   PH: 71 6364030

Members: 3,000,000. **Languages**: English. **National**. Promotes the interests of women workers within the trade union movement. Publicational available upon request.

★1721★ UNITED KINGDOM ASIAN WOMEN'S CONFERENCE
19 Wykeham Rd.
London NW4 2TB, England
Mrs. Tara Kotheri   PH: 81 2026125

Founded: 1977. **Members**: 700. **Languages**: English. **National**. Offers informational and advising services to Asian women residing in the United Kingdom. Supports cultural exchange programs. Conducts recreational programs. Promotes principles of social justice and equality.

Publications: *Newsletter*, periodic.

★1722★ UNITED KINGDOM FEDERATION OF BUSINESS AND
     PROFESSIONAL WOMEN
23 Andsdell St.
Kensington
London W8 5BN, England
Mrs. Rita Bangle, Contact   PH: 71 9381729

Founded: 1938. **Members**: 7,000. **Languages**: English. An umbrella orgnization. Aims to enable business and professional women to achieve in their careers. Encourages women to take an active part in public life and decision making at all levels. Evaluates changing work patterns and press for development in education and training to meet them. Strives to ensure that the same opportunities and facilities are available to both men and women. Undertakes studies of problems common to business and professional women in Europe and worldwide.

Publications: *BPW News*, periodic. Newsletter. ● *Network News*, periodic. Newsletter.

★1723★ WAR WIDOWS' ASSOCIATION OF GREAT BRITAIN
81 Gargrave Rd.
Skipton-in-Craven, W. Yorkshire BD23
   1QN, England
Mrs. R. Rigby   PH: 756 793719

Founded: 1971. **Members**: 4,000. **Languages**: English. **National**. Provides assistance and referral services to war widows from World War I to present. Offers support and encouragement.

Publications: *Courage* (in English), 3/year. Magazine.

★1724★ WOMANKIND WORLDWIDE (WW)
122 Whitechapel High St.
London E1 7PT, England
Sheila Fernando, Admin.   PH: 71 2476931

Languages: English. **National**. Promotes, supports, and funds women's

initiatives in developing countries. Seeks to create a more peaceful society through social welfare programs.

★1725★ WOMEN AGAINST FUNDAMENTALISM (WAF)
BM Box 2706
London WC1 3XX, England   PH: 71 5719595

Founded: 1989. **Languages**: English. **National**. Opposes fundamentalist ideology in religious and political sectors of society. Believes that fundamentalists support the patriarchal family as a "central agent" that seeks to "control.women's minds and bodies." Defends reproductive rights and opposes enforced sterilization. Works to establish refuge centers for battered women and children. Seeks to cease government funding of religious schools. Disseminates information.

★1726★ WOMEN AGAINST RAPE - BRITAIN (WAR)
King's Cross Women' s Centre
71 Tonbridge Street   PH: 71 8377509
London WC1H 9DZ, England   FX: 71 8334817

Languages: English. **National**. Strives to eradicate women's vulnerability to violent acts. Blames not only rapists for acts of rape, but also the State. Maintains that the state government protects the aggressor and punishes the victim in the court system. Facilitated successful campaign to gain recognition of rape within marriage as a crime. Demands compensation for victims of rape.

Publications: *Ask Any Woman: a London Inquiry into Rape and Sexual Assault* (in English). Book. ● *The Rapist Who Pays the Rent* (in English). Book. ● *The Power to Refuse - Rape in the Home and Outside* (in English). Book.

★1727★ WOMEN IN BANKING
55 Bourne Vale
Bromley
Kent BR2 7NW, England
Ann Leverett, Contact

Founded: 1980. Works for the advancement of the role of women in the banking industry.

Publications: *Newsletter*, periodic.

★1728★ WOMEN IN CONSTRUCTION ADVISORY GROUP
Southbank House, Rm. 182
Black Prince Rd.
London SE1 TSJ, England   PH: 71 5875071
Pat Quirke, Contact   71 5871802

Founded: 1984. **National**. Promotes equal opportunities, training, and employement for women in the construction industry. Raises awareness among employers of the achievements of women in construction.

Publications: *Recruitment and Employing Women Guide*, annual. Booklet. ● *Resources Guide*. Booklet.

★1729★ WOMEN IN DENTISTRY
64 Wimpole St.
Dolphin Square
London W1M 8AL, England   PH: 21 4541443
Marton Press, Chair   71 4918862

Founded: 1986. **Members**: 500. **Regional Groups**: 17. **Languages**: English. **National**. Women dentists in the United Kingdom. Strives to assist women dentists in achieving professional goals through advice, practical support, and political representation. Cooperates with organizations in France, the United States, and Australia with similar aims. Disseminates information.

Publications: *Women in Dentistry* (in English), quarterly. Newsletter.

Conventions/Meetings: annual, Symposium - alway June. ● annual dinner - always November. ● periodic workshop.

★1730★ WOMEN IN ENGINEERING CENTRE (WIE)
c/o The Engineering Council
10 Maltravers St.
London WC2, England   PH: 71 2407891
Ms. Fatema Benyahya, Head   FX: 71 2407517

Founded: 1988. Staff: 2. Budget: £40,000. Languages: English. National. Women employed or interested in engineering and related fields. Works in conjunction with Women in Engineering Project. Provides support for women employed in engineering fields; encourages students, teachers, and career advisers to help increase the number of women entering engineering professions. Sponsors courses; organizes conventions, group discussions, and visits to educational institutions.

Publications: Women in Engineering Matters (in English), monthly. Newsletter.

Conventions/Meetings: periodic meeting (exhibits).

★1731★ WOMEN IN FILM AND TELEVISION - UNITED KINGDOM
(WFTV)
Garden Studios
11-15 Betterton St.
London WC2H 9BP, England   PH: 71 3790344
Janet Fielding, Contact   FX: 71 3791625

Founded: 1990. Members: 500. Staff: 2. Budget: £80,000. Languages: English. National. Women with a minimum of three years or work in the film and television industry. Provides information and professional support to members. Offers educational programs. Protects the interests of women in the film and television industry; promotes equal opportunities for members within the industry. Organizes events at major markets and festivals, aiming to facilitate sister chapters in other countries. Committees: International; Regional; Social; Screening; Reel Talks; Action

Publications: News Update and Calendar (in English), monthly. Newsletter. ● In Sync (in English), quarterly. Magazine. ● Directory (in English), annual.

Conventions/Meetings: weekly meeting. ● monthly board meeting. ● monthly executive committee meeting. ● periodic workshop.

★1732★ WOMEN LIBERAL DEMOCRAT (WLD)
4 Cowley St.
London SW1P 3NB, England   PH: 71 2227999
Susette Palmer, Exec. Officer FX: 71 7992170

National. Political organization for women in the United Kingdom. Operates under the Liberal Democrats.

★1733★ WOMEN IN MANAGEMENT (WIM)
64 Marryat Rd.
Wimbledon
London SW19 5BN, England
Janet Brady, Chair   PH: 81 9446332

Founded: 1969. Members: 1,000. National. Supports the advencement of women in management careers. Encourages the development of management knowledge among women, offering training seminars and activities. Provides a forum for the exchange of information related to management.

Publications: Newsletter, quarterly.

★1734★ WOMEN AND MANUAL TRADES (WAMT)
52-54 Featherstone St.   PH: 71 2519192
London EC1Y 8RT, England   71 2519193

Founded: 1975. National. Encourages women and girls to pursue careers in the skilled trades, construction industry. Provides information and advice to women working in the trades.

Publications: Newsletter, periodic. ● Crossing the Border. Book. ● If I Had a Hammer. Book.

★1735★ WOMEN IN MARKETING AND DESIGN
9 Greenside Rd.
London W12 9JQ, England
Kate Fishenden, Chair

Founded: 1991. National. Supports the advancement of women in marketing and design careers, and encourages women in professional and personal development. Addresses issues within the industry.

★1736★ WOMEN IN MEDICINE (WIM)
21 Wallingford Ave.
London W1O 6QA, England
Rosemary Goddard, Secretary   PH: 81 9607446

Founded: 1981. Members: 200. Budget: £4,500. Languages: English. National. Women doctors, medical students, and health professionals. Provides support and political representation for women in the medical profession. Counteracts propaganda stereotyping women medical professionals. Collects and disseminates information regarding women in the medical profession. Supports the National Health Care Service. Conducts research on sexual harassment towards female medical students.

Publications: Women in Medicine (in English), bimonthly. Newsletter. ● Careers for Women in Medicine, Planning and Pitfalls (in English). Book. ● Job Sharing and Part-Time Work in General Practice (in English). Book.

Conventions/Meetings: annual conference.

★1737★ WOMEN IN MIND
22 Harley St.
London W1N 2ED, England
Laureen Levy, Contact   PH: 71 6370741

National. Raises awareness of the underdeveloped state of mental health care for women.

Publications: Finding Our Own Solutions. Booklet. ● The Hidden Majority. Book.

★1738★ WOMEN IN PHYSICS
The Institute of Physics
47 Belgrave Sq.   PH: 71 2356111
London SW1X 8QX, England   FX: 71 2596002
Dr. Helen Agnew, Professional Serv.Mgr. E-Mail: 10P@UK.AC.ULCC

Founded: 1985. Members: 16,000. Languages: English. National. Professionals teachers and students of physics. Strives to increase the number of girls studying physics and to raise the status of professional women physicists. Promotes physics as a viable career choice for women in England. Encourages networking among members. Bestow awards. Disseminates information.

Publications: Women in Physics (in English), quarterly. Newsletter. ● A Career Break Kit for Physicists (in English). Booklet. ● Professional Training for Women (in English). Booklet. ● Directory, periodic. Women members.

Conventions/Meetings: annual meeting, includes lectures and workshops..

★1739★ WOMEN IN THE PUBLIC SECTOR NETWORK
2A Templar St.
Myatts Fields
London SE5 9JB, England
Pamela Whitford Jackson, Contact   PH: 71 7333710

Founded: 1990. Promotes increased and advanced roles for women in corporate and public leadership. Encourages women managers and leaders to work to their full potential and to overcome obstacles they face because of their gender.

Publications: *Newsletter*, periodic. ● *Directory*, periodic.

★1740★ WOMEN IN PUBLISHING
12 Dyott St.
London WC1A 1DF, England

Founded: 1979. **Members:** 700. **National**. Supports the advancement of women in the publishing industry. Provides a forum for networking and mutual support among women publishers and editors. Assists training and career development efforts.

Publications: *Wiplash* (in English), monthly. Newsletter. ● *Reviewing the Reviews* (in English). Magazine. ● *Twice as Many, Half as Powerful* (in English). Booklet.

★1741★ WOMEN RETURNERS NETWORK (WRN)
8 John Adam St.
London WC2N 6EZ, England   PH: 71 8398188
Mrs. Ruth Michaels, President   FX: 71 8395805

Founded: 1984. **Members:** 300. **Languages:** English. **National**. Women and professionals. Promotes the re-entry of women into the labor force. Disseminates information, advice, and support to women returning to work. Offers job placement assistance. Encourages the development of flexible employment and educational programs for women with families. Engages in networking on local, national, and international levels.

Publications: *Return* (in English), quarterly. Newsletter. ● *Country Choices for Women* (in English). Booklet. ● *Returning to Work*, periodic. Directory.

Conventions/Meetings: quarterly meeting. ● periodic workshop.

★1742★ WOMEN WELCOME WOMEN (WWW)
8A Chestnut Ave.
High Wycombe, Bucks. HP11 1D1,
   England
Frances Alexander, Contact   PH: 494 439481

Founded: 1984. **Members:** 1,100. **Membership Dues:** £10 annual. **Staff:** 1. **Budget:** £10,000. **Languages:** English. **Multinational**. Women of all ages interested in international cultural exchange. Fosters international friendship among women from different countries. Organizes members' travel excursions and visits with other members.

Publications: *Newsletter*, semiannual. ● *Directory*, periodic.

Conventions/Meetings: periodic general assembly.

★1743★ WOMEN TO WOMEN: WORLDWIDE LINKING FOR
   DEVELOPMENT
c/o OXFAM
274 Banbury Rd.
Oxford OX2 7DZ, England
Dimza Pityana, Coord.

Regional Groups: 6. **Multinational**. Women from Brazil, Senegal, Philippines, South Africa, Palestine, Mexico, Egypt, and India. Enables women from around the world to network with other women and women's groups to exchange information on common struggles and strategies. Aims to formulate strategies and to promote the implementation of aid policies which can help create a just world for women. **Working Groups:** Gender and Development Unit (GADU).

Conventions/Meetings: periodic workshop.

★1744★ WOMEN WORKING FOR A NUCLEAR-FREE AND
   INDEPENDENT PACIFIC
10 The Drive
New Costessy
Norwich, Norfolk, England
Diana Shanks, Contact

Languages: English. **National**. Women working to defend human rights in the Pacific. Assists indigenous peoples of the Pacific in preventing militarism, nuclearization, and colonization. Conducts educational programs.

Publications: *Videos*.

Conventions/Meetings: periodic conference.

★1745★ WOMEN WORKING WORLDWIDE (WWW)
190 Upper St.
Box 92
London N1 1RQ, England
Claire Hodgson, Contact   PH: 71 2787019

Founded: 1983. **Members:** 12. **Regional Groups:** 2. **Languages:** English. **Multinational**. Promotes the interest of women employed in the work force in the United Kingdom. Encourages the improvement of employment, wages, and working conditions for women workers. Supports women employees through information exchange, international networking, and public education. Focuses efforts on industries that employ large numbers of women, such as clothing, textiles, and electronics. Conducts research and educational programs on health and safety issues, and employment legislation. **Computer Services:** Data base.

Publications: *Common Interests: Women Organising in Global Electronics*. Book. ● *Labour Behind the Label*. Book.

Conventions/Meetings: biweekly executive committee meeting. ● annual meeting (exhibits).

★1746★ WOMEN'S AID FEDERATION ENGLAND (WAFE)
PO Box 391
Bristol, Avon BS99 7WS, England
Caroline J. McKinlay, Publicity and   PH: 272 633494
   Publications Off.   FX: 272 633712

Founded: 1987. **Members:** 120. **Staff:** 6. **Languages:** English. **National**. Umbrella organization of women's aid groups in England. Coordinates shelters for women and children escaping domestic violence. Disseminates advice and information to women. Lobbies agencies and government about violence in the home and the needs of women and children escaping violent men. Conducts educational and research programs.

★1747★ WOMEN'S AMATEUR ATHLETIC ASSOCIATION
Francis House
Francis St.
London SW1P 1DE, England
Miss M. Hartman, Secretary   PH: 71 8284731

Founded: 1922. **Members:** 600. **Languages:** English. **National**. Women's amateur athletic clubs. Organizes and monitors women's athletic activities. Stipulates rules and regulations. Maintains records. Advises on proper training and conditions for women athletes.

★1748★ WOMEN'S CAMPAIGN FOR SOVIET JEWRY
Pannell House
779/781 Finchley Rd.
London NW11 8DN, England   PH: 81 4587147
Margaret Rigal, Co-Chwm.   FX: 81 4589971

Founded: 1970. **Members:** 5,000. **Languages:** English. **Multinational**. Human rights groups, members of the media and parliament, trade unionists, religious bodies, and concerned individuals in 16 countries. Seeks to call attention to the treatment accorded to Jews in the Commonwealth of

Independent States who are imprisoned or persecuted for having tried to obtain permission to emigrate or for having observed religious or cultural conventions. Furthers public awareness of such injustices; exerts pressure on members of parliament and influential organizations; stages demonstrations and petition drives. Provides speakers; holds seminars. Offers children's services; maintains charitable program . Compiles statistics. **Libraries:** Type: reference. Subjects: biographies of Soviet Jewish prisoners on conscience.

Publications: *Newsletter*, biweekly. ● *35's Circular*, periodic. Newsletter.

Conventions/Meetings: annual conference.

★1749★ WOMEN'S CHARTER FOR TRANSPORT STEERING GROUP
c/o Greater Manchester Transport
    Resource Unit
St. Thomas Centre
Ardwick Green N
Manchester M12 6FZ, England   PH: 61 2737451
Ms. Margaret Downs, Admin.   FX: 61 2738296

Founded: 1990. **Members:** 60. **Staff:** 2. **Languages:** English. **National.** Women's groups and individual women. Promotes the interest of women who are users of public transportation. Maintains that the transport systems in England fail to meet the need of women, thereby affecting women's professional, public, and social lives. Strives to influence transport planning, legislation, and provision. Addresses topics on: access, safety, planning, information, rural transport needs, the environment, political commitment and funding, and women's involvement.

★1750★ WOMEN'S COMMITTEE
Trade Union Congress
Congress House
Great Russell St.   PH: 71 6364030
London WC1B 3LS, England   FX: 71 6360632
Kay Carberry, Secretary   TX: 268 328TUCG

Founded: 1930. **Members:** 35. **Languages:** English. **National.** Women members of trade unions in England. Works to improve services to women workers. Demands equal treatment among women and men workers and enforces equal rights legislation on trade unions. Members serve on public bodies at national and international levels. **Libraries:** Type: open to the public. **Awards:** Annual Women's Gold Badge.

Publications: *Directory* (in English), annual.

Conventions/Meetings: annual Trade Union Congress Women's Congress congress (exhibits). ● periodic seminar.

★1751★ WOMEN'S ENGINEERING SOCIETY
Imperial College of Science and
    Technology
Dept. of Civil Engineering
Imperial Rd.
London SW7 2BU, England
G. Maxwell, Contact   PH: 71 5895111

Founded: 1919. **Members:** 750. **National.** Encourages women's pursuit of careers in engineering. Promotes the admission of women into engineering programs and the employment of women into engineering positions. Provides a forum or information and experience exchange among female engineering students and professional.

Publications: *The Women Engineer*, periodic. Journal.

★1752★ WOMEN'S ENVIRONMENTAL NETWORK (WEN)
Aberdeen Studios
22 Highbury Grove
London N5 2EA, England   PH: 71 3548823
Lin Collins, Contact   FX: 71 3540464

Founded: 1988. **Members:** 2,500. **Languages:** English, French, German, Spanish. **National.** Women working to improve environmental awareness. Seeks to change governmental and private policies harmful to the environment. Researches population, use of packaging, production of clothing, and detergents. Conducts political campaigns designed to increase public awareness of environmental issues and to effect change.

Publications: *Newsletter* (in English), quarterly. ● *A Tissue of Lies? The Sanitary Protection Scandal, Chocolate Unwrapped* (in English). Book. ● *Bulletin*, periodic.

★1753★ WOMEN'S FARM AND GARDEN ASSOCIATION (WFGA)
175 Gloucester St.
Cirencester, Glos. GL7 2DP, England
Patricia McHugh, Organizer   PH: 285 658339

Founded: 1899. **Members:** 280. **Staff:** 2. **Budget:** £15,000. **Languages:** English. **National.** Women working in agriculture and horticulture in England. Promotes members' interests. Offers an employment service and career advice. Conducts research. **Awards:** Travel Bursary (grant).

Publications: *The Hidden Workforce*. Book.

Conventions/Meetings: annual conference - always autumn. ● monthly regional meeting.

★1754★ WOMEN'S FARMING UNION (WFU)
Crundalls
Matfield
Tonbridge, Kent TN12 7EA, England   PH: 892 722803
Mrs. Pat Stallwood, Secretary   FX: 892 723900

Founded: 1979. **Members:** 2,000. **Staff:** 2. **Languages:** English. **National.** Farmers' wives, women farmers, and others engaged in agriculture and food production industries. Promotes farm produce and food manufactured in England. Encourages farmers and growers to improve marketing techniques. Lobbies against unfair competition.

Publications: *Annual Review* (in English), always November. ● *Through the Farm Gate*. Videos.

Conventions/Meetings: annual meeting.

★1755★ WOMEN'S HEALTH
52-54 Featherstone St.   PH: 71 2516580
London EC1Y 8RT, England   FX: 71 6080928

Founded: 1982. **Members:** 150. **Staff:** 2. **Languages:** English. **National.** Feminist women. Works to empower women to make informed decisions about health and reproductive issues. Disseminates information. **Libraries:** Type: reference. Holdings: 4,000; books, clippings. **Computer Services:** Data base, Self-help groups.

Publications: *Women's Health* (in English), quarterly. Newsletter.

★1756★ WOMEN'S HEALTH CONCERN
83 Earl's Court Rd.
London W8 6EF, England
Joan Jenkins, Contact   PH: 71 9383932

Founded: 1972. Works to advance research aimed towards finding cures for and relief from gynecological and obstetrical disorders. Disseminates informational booklets.

★1757★ WOMEN'S HEALTH NETWORK (WHN)
c/o National Community Health Resource
57 Chalton St.
London NW1 1HU, England
Justine Pepperell, Dev. Worker   PH: 71 3833841

Founded: 1986. **Members:** 500. **Membership Dues:** nonprofit women's groups and unemployed individuals, £5; organizations and employed individuals, £12; institutions, £20. **Staff:** 2. **Budget:** £30,000. **Languages:** English. **National.** Women health care workers and women's organizations interested in women's health. Strives to improve community health initiatives in the United Kingdom. Provides support to individuals working in the field of women's health. Disseminates advice and information to community health care workers. Fosters collaboration among community health groups. Conducts training courses. **Libraries:** Type: not open to the public. Holdings: books, periodicals, clippings. Subjects: women's health. **Computer Services:** Data base, Women's health projects and organizations.

Publications: *Women's Health Network* (in English), bimonthly. Newsletter.

★1758★ WOMEN'S HEALTH AND REPRODUCTIVE RIGHTS
INFORMATION CENTRE (WHRRIC)
52 Featherstone St.
London EC1Y 8RT, England

Languages: English. **National.** Provides information on issues pertaining to health and reproductive rights to women throughout the United Kingdom. Serves as an information clearinghouse.

Publications: *Newsletter* (in English), periodic. Women's health and reproductive issues.

★1759★ WOMEN'S INTER CHURCH CONSULTATIVE COMMITTEE
FCFC/WICC
27 Tavistock Sq.
London WC1 9HH, England
Pauline Butcher, Contact   PH: 71 3878413

Founded: 1952. **Members:** 35. **Languages:** English. **National.** Provides a forum for discussion and planning among women's organizations of various church dominations. Addresses social and theological issues.

★1760★ WOMEN'S INTERNATIONAL DEMOCRATIC FEDERATION
(WIDF)
Flat 1-130 Allitsen Rd.
St. John's Wood
London NW8 7AU, England   PH: 71 7225494
Fatima Ibrahim, President   FX: 71 7225494

Founded: 1945. **Members:** 146. **Staff:** 2. **Languages:** English. **Multinational.** Women's organizations. Promotes: equal rights in decision-making; children's rights; democracy; social justice; peace; development; and solidarity against discrimination. Works to combat oppression of women.

Publications: *An Outcry* (in English). Magazine.

Conventions/Meetings: triennial congress.

★1761★ WOMEN'S INTERNATIONAL MOTORCYCLE ASSOCIATION
(WIMA)
75 West View
Taunton
Somerset, England
Cherry Selby, Contact   PH: 823 443477

Founded: 1950. **Members:** 300. Women interested in the sport of motorcycling. Encourages activities that promote the sport of motorcycle racing among women. Conducts fundraisers for the blind and for women's refugee centers.

Publications: *WIMA News*, monthly. Newsletter.

★1762★ WOMEN'S INTERNATIONAL RESOURCE CENTRE (WIRC)
173 Archway Rd.
London N6 5BL, England   PH: 81 3414403

Staff: 1. **Local Groups:** 1. **National.** Developmental education center designed to raise consciousness about issues of concern to women. Areas of interest include: the implications of European unification on the status of women; employment opportunities and trade union participation; development of training and education that take gender issues into consideration. Maintains information center. Acts as a forum for the exchange of information among women's groups. Promotes research and consultation on women's issues; disseminates information. Conducts workshops. **Libraries:** Type: reference.

Publications: *Annual Report.* ● *WIRC Links*, annual. Journal. ● *WIRC*, monthly. Newsletter. ● *Women's International Magazine*, periodic. **Also Cited As:** *W'IM*.

★1763★ WOMEN'S LEAGUE OF HEALTH AND BEAUTY (WLHB)
Walter House, 3rd Fl.
418/422 Strand
London WC2R 0PT, England
P.J.W. Hutton, Sec.   PH: 71 2408456

Founded: 1930. **Members:** 23,500. **Staff:** 4. **Languages:** English. **Multinational.** Promotes education for women in physical training, health, and fitness. Offers training courses.

★1764★ WOMEN'S MEDIA RESOURCE PROJECT
85 Kingsland High St.
London E8 2PB, England   PH: 71 2546536

Founded: 1985. **National.** Works to provide comprehensive multi-racial and multi-cultural media information for women working in television and film.

★1765★ WOMEN'S NATIONAL CANCER CONTROL CAMPAIGN
(WNCCC)
1 S. Audley St.
London W1Y 5DQ, England
Dr. Mary Buchanan, Chair   PH: 71 4997532

Languages: English. **National.** Seeks to educate women regarding the prevention and detection of cancer. Operates speakers' bureau, mobile screening units, and a telephone helpline. Fosters communication among members.

★1766★ WOMEN'S NATIONAL COMMISSION (WNC)
Government Offices, Rm. 50A/4
Horse Guards Rd.
London SW1P 3AL, England
Sam Spence, Contact   PH: 71 2705903

Founded: 1969. **Members:** 50. **Staff:** 6. **Languages:** English. **National.** Women in the United Kingdom who are the elected or appointed officials of: women's sections of major political parties; trade unions; religious groups; professional organizations; other groups representative of women. Seeks to "ensure by all possible means that the informed opinions of women are given their due weight in the deliberations of Government." Addresses such issues as: divorce law; education and training; homelessness; caring for the elderly; taxation and other financial matters; women and the health service; violence against women; social security; women and public appointments; stress and addiction among women; women and debt; single parent families; women returners. Conducts studies and submits results to government bodies.

Publications: *Annual Report.* ● *Women's Organisations in United Kingdom*, biennial. Directory. ● *Public Appointments: A Handbook for Women's Organisations*, biennial. Booklet.

★1767★ WOMEN'S NATIONWIDE CANCER CONTROL CAMPAIGN (WNCCC)
Suna House
128-130 Curtain Rd.
London EC2A 3AR, England
Ms. Sandra Cater, Information Off.
PH: 71 7294688
71 7292229
FX: 71 6130771

Founded: 1965. **Members:** 400. **Staff:** 6. **National.** Women experienced in health care and counseling. Promotes education about cancer risks for women. Disseminates information on breast and cervical cancer. Operates confidential helpline. Sponsors mobile screening units. Maintians speakers' bureau; conducts research. **Committees:** Medical Advisory; Health Education.

Publications: *National Clinic List of Well Woman/Family Planning Clinics*, periodic. Directory. ● *Breast Awareness*. Booklet. ● *Calling All Women: Smears and Breast Self-Examination* (in Gujarati, Punjabi, Bengali, Urdu, Hindi, English, Turkic Dialects, Cantonese, and Vietnamese). Book. ● *An Abnormal Smear - What Does It Mean?*. Booklet. ● *Choice for Life*. Videos. Risk factors associated with cancer. ● *Breast Self-Examination*. Videos.

Conventions/Meetings: periodic Youth Symposium.

★1768★ WOMEN'S NETWORK OF THE METHODIST CHURCH
The Methodist Church, Network Office
25 Marylebone Rd.
London NW1 5JR, England
Stella Bristow, Secretary
PH: 71 4865502

Founded: 1987. Provides a forum for communication and activity among Methodist women. Encourages and assists women in participating in church activities.

Publications: *Magnet*, 3/year. Magazine.

★1769★ WOMEN'S ROYAL VOLUNTARY SERVICE (WRVS)
234-244 Stockwell Rd.
London SW9 9SP, England
Mrs. Ethel Owens, Contact
PH: 71 4160146

Founded: 1938. **Languages:** English. **National.** Women providing welfare services to women, children, the elderly, the sick, the disabled, and victims of domestic abuse.

★1770★ WOMEN'S SPORTS FOUNDATION (WSF)
Wesley House
4 Wild Ct.
London WC2B 5AU, England
Dusty Rhodes, Off.
PH: 71 8317863
FX: 71 8315448

Founded: 1984. **Members:** 600. **Languages:** English. **National.** Promotes the interests of women and girls involved in sports. Cooperates with similar groups to challenge discrimination against women. Offers educational and training programs. Organizes career seminars. **Libraries:** Type: reference. Holdings: 0. **Awards:** Sports Awards for Girls. Recipient: girls ages 11 to 19 years old. **Committees:** Media; Press; Sponsorship; Education.

Publications: *Women in Sport* (in English), quarterly. Magazine. Careers in sports and recreation for women.

★1771★ WOMEN'S THERAPY CENTRE
6-9 Manor Gardens
London N7 6LA, England
Debbie Waluisley, Director
PH: 71 2636200
FX: 71 2817879

Founded: 1976. **Staff:** 3. **Budget:** £250,000. **Languages:** English. **National.** Promotes individual and group psychotherapy for women regardless of ability to pay, age, race, or sexual preference. Specializes in eating disorders and incest survival therapy for women. Disseminates advice and information to women and professionals. Provides training to professionals interested in women's therapy. Conducts educational programs.

★1772★ WOMENWEALTH AMBIKA (WA)
19 Cumberland Terr.
London NW1 4H5, England
Claire Weldon, Dir.
PH: 71 9359055

Founded: 1986. **Languages:** English. **Multinational.** Individuals and organizations working to improve the economic status of rural women craft producers in developing countries. Provides direct access to the market in the United Kingdom and offers technical marketing assistance. **Formerly:** (1986) Ambika.

Conventions/Meetings: biennial convention.

★1773★ WORKING MOTHERS ASSOCIATION (WMA)
77 Holloway Rd.
London N7 8JZ, England
Irene Pilia, Info.Mgr.
PH: 71 7005771
FX: 71 7001105

Founded: 1985. **Members:** 3,000. **Staff:** 4. **Languages:** English. **National.** Promotes the interest of working parents and their children. Provides an informal support system to members by networking with local child care centers. Works to influence organizations, policy makers, and employers to improve child care facilities. **Awards:** Annual Employer of the Year. ● Annual Mother of the Year. ● Annual Carer of the Year.

Publications: *The Working Parents Handbook* (in English). ● *The Employer's Guide to Child Care* (in English). Book. ● *WMA Returners Pack* (in English). Book.

Conventions/Meetings: monthly executive committee meeting.

★1774★ WORLD'S WOMAN'S CHRISTIAN TEMPERANCE UNION
c/o Mrs. Gwen Stretton
27 Ankemoor Close
Shard End
Birmingham, W. Midlands B34 6TF,
England
Mrs. Gwen Stretton, President

Founded: 1883. **Languages:** English. **Multinational.** Women working to educate children and adults on the "evils of alcohol, tobacco, and narcotic drugs." Conducts drug abuse seminars and workshops for youth; sponsors professional training program for counselors. **Libraries:** Type: reference.

Publications: *White Ribbon* (in English), periodic. Bulletin. ● *Magazine*, periodic.

★1775★ YOUNG WOMEN'S CHRISTIAN ASSOCIATION - GREAT BRITAIN (YWCA - GB)
Clarendon House
52 Cornmarket St.
Oxford OX1 3EJ, England
F. Elizabeth Sharples, Exec.Dir.
PH: 865 726110
865 204805

Founded: 1855. **Members:** 20,000. **Staff:** 250. **Budget:** £8,000,000. **Languages:** English. **National.** Women and girls age 7 and older. Promotes fellowship and service among young women in Great Britain. Advocates peace, unity, and justice. Strives to enhance the social status of women in Great Britain. Offers encouragement and support to needy communities. Sponsors educational and career guidance programs. **Awards:** Periodic Women of the West.

Publications: *Update*, 3/year. Newsletter. ● *Common Concern*, periodic. Newsletter. ● *Annual Review*. Magazine. ● *Letters to Teenagers*. Booklet. Information for young single mothers.

Conventions/Meetings: periodic meeting.

★1776★ ZONTA INTERNATIONAL - ENGLAND
30 The Woodlands
Esher
Surrey KT10 8DB, England
Minika Wylde, Contact   PH: 81 3988852

Founded: 1917. Women professionals. Works to advance the status of women through maintaining contact with the United Nations and several of its agencies. Funds programs which enable women of developing countries to better their quality of life. Seeks to advance future leaders through mentoring and offering scholarship programs designed to encourage students, especially young women, to pursue nontraditional or enterprising careers. Addresses local issues regarding women's economic self-sufficiency, equal rights, aging, educational opportunities for women, and women's health and nutrition.

Publications: *Newsletter*, monthly. ● *Directory*, annual.

Finland

★1777★ ASSOCIATION OF FEMALE AGRONOMISTS
Runonlaulajantie 49 E
SF-00420 Helsinki, Finland
Pirjo Malkia, Secretary   PH: 0 5074346

Members: 300. **Languages:** Finnish, Swedish, English. **National.** Women who have studied agriculture or food sciences at the university level. Represents the economic, scientific, and technical interests of members. Fosters communication and exchange among women working in agriculture.

★1778★ CENTRAL ASSOCIATION OF WOMEN ENTREPRENEURS
   (CAWE)
(YK Yrittajanaisten Keskusliitoo)
Urhokekkosenkatu 8 C 36
SF-00100 Helsinki, Finland   PH: 0 6940045
Sinikka Lallukka, Exec. Dir.   FX: 0 6940250

Founded: 1947. **Members:** 7,000. **Local Groups:** 107. **Languages:** English, Finnish. **National.** Women entrepreneurs in Finland. Promotes the participation of women in Finland's economic structure. Assists women in small business development.

★1779★ FEDERATION FOR HOME ECONOMICS TEACHERS (FHET)
Snellmaninkatu 25 B 24
SF-00170 Helsinki, Finland
Marja-Liisa Lindroos, Exec. Dir.   PH: 0 1352033

Members: 2,400. **Languages:** Finnish, Swedish. **National.** Women home economics teachers in Finland. Promotes the development of home economics education in Finland. Works to establish and maintain high standards of qualification for teachers.

★1780★ FINNISH WHITE RIBBON ASSOCIATION
(SVL Suomen Valkonauhaliitto)
Liisankatu 27 A 3
SF-00170 Helsinki 17, Finland
Irja Eskelinen, Gen.Sec.   PH: 0 1351268

Founded: 1905. **Members:** 664. **Budget:** FM 900,000. **Local Groups:** 10. **Languages:** English, Finnish, Swedish. **National.** Women and women's organizations. Provides social and spiritual guidance to alcoholics and their families, drug addicts, youth, and women in prison. Maintains homes for girls. Provides counseling services; conducts courses and seminars.

Publications: *Valkonauha*, bimonthly.

Conventions/Meetings: periodic convention.

★1781★ MEDICAL WOMEN'S INTERNATIONAL ASSOCIATION -
   FINLAND (MWIA-F)
Granfeltintie 4
SF-00570 Helsinki, Finland
Eija Kiuru, Contact

Languages: Finnish. **National.** Finland branch of the Medical Women's International Association (see separate entry). Women physicians. Provides a forum for discussion of women's health care issues. Encourages women to enter the field of medicine. Works to overcome discrimination against female physicians. Sponsors research and educational programs.

★1782★ NATIONAL COUNCIL OF WOMEN OF FINLAND
Rauhankatu 7   PH: 0 1356626
SF-00170 Helsinki 17, Finland   FX: 0 1357318
Mrs. Elsie Hetemaki-Olander, President CBL: FINNWOMAN

National. Umbrella organization for women's groups in Finland. Promotes the interests of women. Coordinates activities. Disseminates information on women's issues.

★1783★ OPEN UNIVERSITY FOR WOMEN
Bulevardi 11 A1
SF-00120 Helsinki, Finland   PH: 0 649382
Aiska Hiltunen, Director   FX: 0 643193

Founded: 1980. **Staff:** 1. **Budget:** FM 500,000. **Languages:** Finnish, Swedish, German, French, Spanish, Russian, English. **National.** Independent women's educational organization. Annually plans and administers 70 courses for women in the areas of: women and politics; therapy; art and culture; and practical skill development. Researches feminist education and potential teaching strategies to achieve and maintain it. Instruction centers on growth rather than schooling. Believes in eliminating the wedge between teacher and learner, and views the two as learning partners. **Formerly:** Finnish Federation for Women's Liberation.

Conventions/Meetings: semiannual meeting. ● monthly meeting.

★1784★ SCANDINAVIAN ASSOCIATION OF OBSTETRICS AND
   GYNECOLOGY (SSOG)
(NFOG Nordisk Forening for Obstetrik och Gyneckologi)
Dept. of Obstetrics and Gynecology
Univ. of Helsinki
SF-00250 Helsinki, Finland   PH: 0 4711
Kari A. Teramo M.D., Exec. Officer   FX: 0 412192

Founded: 1933. **Members:** 2,780. **Budget:** FM 250,000. **National Groups:** 5. **Languages:** Swedish. **Multinational.** Gynecologists and obstetricians from Nordic countries. Conducts educational programs; sponsors competitions and bestows awards.

Publications: *Acta Obstetrica Gynecologicia Scandinavica*, periodic. Magazine. ● *Bulletin* (in Danish, English, Norwegian, and Swedish), semiannual.

Conventions/Meetings: biennial congress (exhibits) - 1994 June, Oulu, Finland.

★1785★ UNIONI-LEAGUE OF FINNISH FEMINISTS
(Unioni Naisasialiitto Suomessa)
Bulevardi 11 A 1
SF-00120 Helsinki, Finland   PH: 0 643158
Leena Ruusuvuori, Admin.   FX: 0 643193

Founded: 1892. **Members:** 1,200. **Staff:** 2. **Budget:** FM 1,500,000. **Languages:** English. **National.** College and university educated women and women's organizations. Promotes the development of Finnish women with a feminist perspective. Works to ensure women's influence in Finnish society. Seeks to abolish discrimination against women and raise the social and political consciousness of women. Conducts lectures and courses. Offers a crisis phone line and free legal services for women. Maintains feminist art gallery. **Libraries:** Type: open to the public. Holdings: 4,000; books, periodicals. Subjects: women's issues.

Publications: *Women's Voice*, annual. Magazine.

Conventions/Meetings: semiannual meeting. ● annual board meeting.

★1786★ WOMEN'S ORGANIZATION OF THE SWEDISH PEOPLE'S PARTY IN FINLAND
(Svenska Kvinnoforbundet)
Grasviksgatan 14
SF-00180 Helsinki, Finland   PH: 0 6932322
Yrsa Palin, Contact   FX: 0 6931968

Founded: 1907. **Members:** 3,000. **Staff:** 2. **Languages:** English, Swedish. **National.** Women promoting the moderate liberal Swedish People's Party in Finland. Represents interests of the Swedish-speaking and bilingual populations in Finland.

★1787★ YOUNG WOMEN'S CHRISTIAN ASSOCIATION - FINLAND
(YWCA)
P. Rautatiekatu 19 C 26
SF-00100 Helsinki, Finland   PH: 0 448066
Kaisa Rintala, Gen.Sec.   FX: 0 441087

National. Works to uphold Christian fellowship and service among young women in Finland. Promotes physical, mental, and spiritual growth of members.

France

★1788★ AMERICAN WOMEN'S GROUP IN PARIS (AWGP)
(AFAP Association des Femmes Americaines a Paris)
49, rue Pierre Charron
F-75008 Paris, France
Gayle George, Pres.   PH: 1 43591761

Founded: 1949. **Members:** 550. **Staff:** 1. **Languages:** English. **National.** Promotes Franco-American relations. Sponsors social and cultural activities. Grants scholarships to French women for graduate study in the United States.

Publications: *AWG Directory* (in English), annual. ● *Bulletin* (in English), monthly.

★1789★ ASSOCIATION OF AMERICAN WIVES OF EUROPEANS
(AAWE)
49, rue Pierre Charron
F-75008 Paris, France
Marissa Roufosse, Pres.   PH: 1 42560524

Founded: 1961. **Members:** 500. **Staff:** 1. **Languages:** English, French. **National.** American women married to Europeans and living permanently in or around Paris, France. Conducts social and educational activities for members and their children, enabling them to share common experiences and pass on American customs and traditions to their children. Sponsors Project for Dual National Students; studies causes and effects of bilingualism and bi-culturalism; produces and distributes information regarding college entrance exam procedures for students of dual citizenship and studies on bilingualism; compiles statistics on citizenship. Maintains biographical archives. **Computer Services:** Data base. **Committees:** Bilingualism; Children's Parties; Citizenship; Education; Seniors; Special Cultural Activities; Women's Outlook.

Publications: *Directory*, annual. ● *Newsletter*, monthly. ● *AAWAE Guide to Education*, annual. Lists bilingual schools in Paris and information pertaining to the French educational system. ● *Living in France*. Booklet. ● *Who Are We?*. Booklet.

Conventions/Meetings: monthly, guest speakers.

★1790★ ASSOCIATION POUR LA PREVENTION DE LA VIOLENCE EN PRIVE
6, Impasse des Orteaux
F-75020 Paris, France
Claude Mastre, Director   PH: 1 40240505

Members: 30. **Languages:** French, English. **National.** Works to improve conditions and increase awareness of domestic violence in France. Educates children and parents about preventing violence in the home in its early stages. Assists professionals working to eliminate domestic abuse. Maintains homes and shelters for victims of this type of abuse. Offers psychological advice and help to victims and individuals who commit domestic violence. Lobbies government to change laws and improve support programs involving domestic violence. Creates and conducts program to eradicate violence in the home. Maintains speakers' bureau.

Publications: *Newsletter* (in French), annual.

★1791★ ASSOCIATIONS DES CONJOINTS DE MEDECINS (ACOMED)
22, rue Garnier   PH: 46 403885
F-92200 Neuilly sur Seine, France   46 403240

Languages: French. **National.** Women in France married to medical doctors. Sponsors social activities for members. Fosters solidarity among members.

★1792★ COLLECTIF DES FEMMES MAGHREBINES
c/o Maison des Femmes
8, Cite Prost
F-75011 Paris, France

Languages: French. **National.** Protects and defends the rights of African women in France.

★1793★ CONGREGATION OF LA RETRAITE (LR)
(Congregation de la Retraite)
16, avenue du Belvedere
F-78100 Saint Germain-en-Laye, France
Sr. Darryll J. Candy RLR, Gen.Sec.   PH: 1 34519696

Founded: 1675. **Members:** 400. **Regional Groups:** 6. **Languages:** Dutch, English, French. **Multinational.** Religious women from 8 countries who publicly profess to live communally within the Catholic church and according to the teachings of the Gospel. Tends to the spiritual and human needs of others through teachings of the Gospel. Works to contribute to the building of a "human family" by offering educational programs, catechesm, human and spiritual guidance, and addressing instances of disbelief in the Gospel and injustices toward people. Offers retreats centered on the spiritual exercises of St. Ignatius.

Conventions/Meetings: general assembly - every 6 years.

★1794★ CONGREGATION DES SOEURS DE SAINTE MARIE-MADELEINE POSTEL (CSSMMP)
Abbaye Ste. Marie-Madeleine Postel
F-50390 St. Sauveur-le-Vicomte, France   PH: 416037

Founded: 1807. **Members:** 555. **Languages:** French. **Multinational.** Catholic women who have taken vows of chastity, poverty, and obedience; superiors general, councillors general, and provincial superiors in France, Indonesia, Italy, Northern Ireland, and the Netherlands. Members establish schools, hospitals, and serve the social needs of local communities. Provides children's services and sponsors charitable programs.

Conventions/Meetings: periodic convention.

★1795★ CONSEIL NATIONAL DES FEMMES FRANCAISES
11, rue de Viarmes
BP 115-01
F-75022 Paris Cedex 01, France   PH: 1 40399082
Paulette Laubie, President   FX: 1 47828028

Languages: French. **National.** Umbrella organization for women's groups in France. Promotes women's interests. Coordinates activities for women. Disseminates information on women's issues.

★1796★ DAUGHTERS OF CHARITY OF THE SACRED HEART OF JESUS (DCSHJ)
(FCSCJ Filles de la Charite du Sacre-Coeur de Jesus)
55, avenue de la Republique
F-91230 Montgeron, France
Sr. Colette Lussier, Superior Gen.   PH: 1 69427500

Founded: 1823. **Members:** 1,390. **Regional Groups:** 9. **Multinational.** Religious women. Promotes religious living. Activities include nursing and teaching.

Conventions/Meetings: biennial conference

★1797★ DAUGHTERS OF JESUS OF KERMARIA (DJ)
(FJ Filles de Jesus de Kermaria)
11, rue d'Arras
F-75005 Paris, France
Sr. Ellen Martin, Superior Gen.   PH: 1 46333290

Founded: 1834. **Members:** 1,960. **Languages:** English, French, Spanish. **Multinational.** Apostolic religious women in 13 countries. Works to honor Jesus through human development projects undertaken in conjunction with the Catholic church and in accordance to the teachings of the Gospel. Sponsors educational programs; ministers to the sick and neglected; works for the dignity of women. Provides in-service development programs.

Publications: *Directory*, periodic. ● *En Liaison*, periodic. ● *Kermaria*, periodic. Magazine.

★1798★ DIALOGUE DE FEMMES
12, rue Georges Berger
F-75017 Paris, France

Languages: French. **National.** Provides a forum for discussion relevant to women's issues, including work, family, and the effects of legislation and religion on the lives of women. Offers an opportunity for women researchers and intellectuals to be heard, explaining their work and sharing their knowledge. Maintains the motto: "we want our rights, nothing but our rights, but all our rights.".

Conventions/Meetings: meeting - 10/year.

★1799★ EUROPEAN ASSOCIATION AGAINST VIOLENCE AGAINST WOMEN AT WORK
(AVFT Association Europeene Contre les Violences Fatites aux Femmes au Travail)
71, rue St. Jacques
F-75005 Paris, France
Louis Marie-Victoire, Contact   PH: 1 45842424

Founded: 1985. **Members:** 100. **Staff:** 1. **Budget:** 600,000 Fr. **Languages:** French, German, Spanish, English. **National.** Works to defend women's rights in France. Sponsors programs to protect women from domestic violence and sexual harassment. Offers training programs to combat sexual harassment in the workplace. Conducts research on patterns of sexual harassment. Operates a resource center on women's issues for members' use.

Publications: *Projets Feministes*, periodic. Magazine.

Conventions/Meetings: periodic convention

★1800★ EUROPEAN ASSOCIATION FOR THE DEVELOPMENT OF INFORMATION AND TRAINING OF WOMEN - FRANCE (EUDIFF)
(Association Europeene pour le Developpement de l'Information et de la Formation des Femmes - France)
Institut de Cooperation Sociale
International ICOSI
4, ave. du Colonel Bonnet
F-75016 Paris, France
Monique Halpern, Contact

Languages: French. **National.** Circulates information on women and women's issues throughout France. Networks with organizations that also champion women's advancement. Demands that EC nations fully recognize women's rights. Supports women's development and equality; encourages women's participation in leadership roles. Facilitates exchange among members.

★1801★ FEDERATION DES ASSOCIATIONS DE VEUVES
28, place St. Georges
F-75000 Paris, France
Simone Loudot, President   PH: 1 42851830

Languages: French. **National.** Women working to offer support to widows in France. Offers financial, legal, and emotional counseling to recently widowed women and their children.

★1802★ FEDERATION FRANCAISE DU PRET A PORTER FEMININ (PROFEM)
5, rue Caumartin   PH: 1 42680840
F-75009 Paris, France   FX: 1 42680084
J. Belinski, Contact   TX: 680192

Members: 900. **Languages:** English, French. **National.** Promotes economic development programs for women in France. Provides financial support.

Conventions/Meetings: periodic conference.

★1803★ FEDERATION OF FRENCH-LANGUAGE GYNECOLOGISTS AND OBSTETRICIANS
(FGOLF Federation des Gynecologues et Obstetriciens de Langue Francaise)
Ainique Bandelscque
123, blvd. de Port-Royal
F-75674 Paris Cedex 14, France   PH: 1 42341138
Prof. E. Papiernik, Sec.Gen.   FX: 1 43269993

Founded: 1950. **Members:** 2,000. **Languages:** French. **Multinational.** French-speaking gynecologists and obstetricians. Promotes the provision of scientific study in the French language of all aspects of the biology of human reproduction. Conducts training sessions and travel and exchange programs; sponsors seminars. Maintains permanent committees to deal with special topics.

Publications: *Journal de Gynecologie Obstetrique et Biologie de la Reproduction*, bimonthly.

Conventions/Meetings: biennial congress (exhibits)

★1804★ GENERATION FEMMES D'ENTREPRISES (GFE)
47, rue du Marche
F-86006 Poitiers Cedex, France   PH: 49 609810
Claudine Andrault, Contact   FX: 49 416572

Founded: 1990. **Members:** 56. **Languages:** French. **National.** Women working in business and management. Promotes the rights of women working in management positions. Seeks to raise the status of working women. Works to eliminate sexism in the workplace. Acts as a forum for the exchange of information among women. Sponsors seminars and debates.

Publications: *Gazette* (in French), semiannual. Bulletin.

★1805★ GRAIN DE SEL
62, blvd. Garibaldi
F-75015 Paris, France   PH: 1 47835715
Denise Fuchs, Pres.   FX: 1 40560226

Founded: 1984. Members: 500. Languages: French, English. National. Works to improve the quality of life for women living in France. Supports democratic ideals and equality of the sexes. Encourages women to participate in the government. Promotes public awareness of political issues and how they relate to women. Acts as a forum for exchange of information among women in Europe. Encourages a positive portrayal of women in politics, business, and the media.

Publications: Grain de Sel (in French), periodic. Bulletin.

Conventions/Meetings: quarterly conference.

★1806★ HELPERS OF THE HOLY SOULS OF PURGATORY (HHS)
(AAP Axiliatrices des Ames du Purgatoire)
                                         PH: 1 45679090
16, rue St. Jean-Baptiste de la Salle   FX: 1 45669454
F-75006 Paris, France   TX: AUXIBAROUILLERE
Sr. France Delcourt, Superior Gen.   PARI

Founded: 1856. Members: 950. Languages: English, French, Spanish. Multinational. Women religious in 24 countires. Promotes religious living. Provides aid to the poor.

Publications: INTERCOM (in English, French, and Japanese), bimonthly. ● Membership List (in French), annual.

Conventions/Meetings: periodic meeting.

★1807★ INTERNATIONAL COUNCIL OF WOMEN (ICW)
(CIF Conseil International des Femmes)
13, rue Caumartin
F-75009 Paris, France   PH: 1 47421940
Jacqueline Barbet-Massin, Gen.Sec.   FX: 1 42662623

Founded: 1888. Members: 75. Staff: 3. Languages: French, German, Spanish. Multinational. National councils of women comprising national and local women's organizations. Serves as a medium for consultation among women on those actions necessary to promote the welfare of humankind, the family, children, and the individual. Advises women of their rights and their civic, social, and political responsibilities; works for the equal legal status of women and for the removal of all that restricts women from full participation in life. Supports international peace and arbitration. Areas of interest include advancement of women; education; human rights; literacy; role of women in economic and social development. Maintains consultative status with the Economic and Social Council of the United Nations, United Nations Educational, Scient ific and Cultural Organization, United Nations Children's Fund, World Health Organization, and the Council of Europe. Committees: Ageing; Arts and Letters/Music; Child and Family; Development; Economics; Education; Environment and Habitat; Health; Home Economics Consumer Affairs; International Relations and Peace; Laws and Status of Women; Mass Media; Migration and Refugees; Social Welfare; Women and Employment; Youth.

Publications: Triennial Report. ● Children's Stories from Many Lands. ● Side by Side.

Conventions/Meetings: triennial conference.

★1808★ INTERNATIONAL FEDERATION OF WIDOWS AND
     WIDOWERS ORGANIZATIONS
10, rue Cambaceres
F-75008 Paris, France
Aliette Bellavoine, President   PH: 1 42662329

Languages: French. Multinational. Promotes international cooperation among widows and widowers. Liaises with similar organizations worldwide.

Publications: Booklet.

★1809★ INTERNATIONAL SOCIETY AGAINST BREAST CANCER
     (ISABC)
(Societe Internationale pour la Lutte Contre le Cancer du Sein)
26, rue de la Faisanderie
F-75116 Paris, France
K.H. Hollmann M.D., Pres.   PH: 1 47047032

Founded: 1973. Members: 150. Languages: English, French. Multinational. Medical doctors, scientists, computer specialists, and industry representatives in 15 countries concerned about breast cancer. Provides diagnostic assistance; coordinates research programs; organizes workshops and seminars.

Publications: New Frontiers in Mammary Pathology (in English), periodic. Magazine.

Conventions/Meetings: biennial symposium (exhibits)

★1810★ INTERNATIONAL UNION OF WOMEN ARCHITECTS (IUWA)
(UIFA Union Internationale des Femmes Architectes)
14, rue Dumont d'Urville
F-75116 Paris, France   PH: 1 47208882
Solange d'Herbez de la Tour, Pres.   FX: 1 47233864

Founded: 1963. Languages: English, French, German, Spanish. Multinational. Women architects, landscapers, builders, and engineers representing 58 countries. Promotes the opinions and appreciation of female architects.

Publications: Congress Reports (in English and French), periodic. ● Exhibition Revues (in English and French), periodic.

Conventions/Meetings: triennial congress (exhibits)

★1811★ LITTLE SISTERS OF THE ASSUMPTION (LSA)
(PSA Petites Soeurs de l'Assomption)
57, rue Violet
F-75015 Paris, France   PH: 1 45790733
Sr. Celine Heon, Superior Gen.   FX: 1 45776803

Founded: 1865. Members: 1,653. Regional Groups: 16. Local Groups: 210. National Groups: 24. Languages: English, French, Italian, Portuguese, Spanish. Multinational. Roman Catholic women religious united to promote humane living conditions for the working class and the poor. Provides charitable services to the underprivileged.

★1812★ MEDICAL WOMEN'S INTERNATIONAL ASSOCIATION -
     FRANCE (MWIA-F)
10, ave. de Salonique
F-75017 Paris, France
Yvonne Perol, Contact

Languages: French. National. French national branch of the Medical Women's International Association (see separate entry). Women physicians. Provides a forum for discussion of women's health care issues. Encourages women to enter the field of medicine. Works to overcome discrimination against female physicians. Sponsors research and educational programs.

★1813★ MOUVEMENT FRANCAIS POUR LE PLANNING FAMILIAL
     (MFPF)
4, square St. Irenee
F-75011 Paris, France   PH: 1 48072910
Ms. Monique Bellanger, Contact   FX: 1 47007977

Languages: French. National. Works to enhance the quality of life for individuals living in France by promoting responsible parenthood and family planning. Advocates family planning as a basic human right. Attempts to stop the spread of AIDS and other sexually transmitted diseases. Sponsors programs in sex education, family planning, and health. Provides contraceptive and health care services. Acts as an advocate for family planning on a national level. Conducts research.

★1814★ NA'AMAT FEMMES PIONNIERES (NFP)
12, rue de l'Echiquier   PH: 1 45048549
F-75010 Paris, France   FX: 1 47702175

Languages: French. **Multinational.** Working and professional women. Works to advance the status of women by providing a variety of educational, community, and legal services. Believes that strong family relations are the foundation of a stable society. Members identify with the Zionist movement.

★1815★ RESEAU FEMMES ET DEVELOPPEMENT
c/o GRDR
8, rue Paul Bert   PH: 48 349594
F-93300 Aubervilliers, France   48 340167

Founded: 1983. **Members:** 570. **Staff:** 1. **Languages:** French, English. **National.** Promotes the role of women in all types of development projects. Encourages women to become involved in community development.

Publications: *Lettre d'Information*, bimonthly. Newsletter. ● *Bulletin*, annual.

★1816★ SALESIAN MISSIONARIES OF MARY IMMACULATE (SMMI)
(SSMMI Soeurs Salisiennes Missionaires de Marie Immaculate)
17, impasse Villa Remond
F-94250 Gentilly, France
Mother Luc Marie Ferron, Superior Gen.   PH: 1 46550930

Founded: 1872. **Members:** 1,056. **Regional Groups:** 5. **Languages:** English, French, Spanish. **Multinational.** Women religious dedicated to aiding impoverished people, especially women, in developing countries. Offers educational and medical services and is active in the social work and nursing professions. Has organized schools in Bangladesh, India, and Madagascar, including a training college for teachers.

Publications: *Newsletter* (in French), semiannual.

Conventions/Meetings: general assembly - every 6 years.

★1817★ SISTERS OF CHARITY (SCB)
(Soeurs de la Charite de Besancan)
131, Grande-Rue
Boite Postale 389
F-25018 Besancon, France
Sr. Catherine Belpois, Contact   PH: 81 820089

Founded: 1799. **Members:** 520. **Languages:** Arabic, English, French, Italian. **Multinational.** Religious women. Conducts charitable programs.

★1818★ SISTERS OF THE SACRED HEART OF JESUS (SSCJ)
(Soeurs du Sacre-Coeur de Jesus)
Villa des Otages 8
85, rue Haxo
F-75020 Paris, France
Sr. Isabelle Therrien SSCJ, Sec.Gen.   PH: 1 43640359

Founded: 1816. **Members:** 900. **Languages:** English, French, Spanish. **Multinational.** Roman Catholic women in 10 countries. Promotes personal development through educational, medical, social, and pastoral activities. Conducts religious training. **Libraries:** Type:. Holdings: 9,700. Subjects: religious life and culture.

Publications: *Together* (in English and French), bimonthly. ● *Yearbook* (in English, French, and Spanish), triennial.

Conventions/Meetings: general assembly - every 6 years.

★1819★ SISTERS OF STATION JOSEPH OF CLUNY (SJC)
(Soeurs de Station Joseph de Cluny)
21, rue Mechain
F-75014 Paris, France
Rev. Mother Marie Noel Lefrancois SJC,
     Superior Gen.   PH: 1 47079572

Founded: 1807. **Members:** 3,323. **Languages:** English, French. **Multinational.** Women involved in religion. Provides religious guidance, health care, educational, and community services.

Publications: *Cluny Mission* (in French), bimonthly.

Conventions/Meetings: general assembly - every 6 years.

★1820★ SISTERS OF STATION URSULA DE DOLE
(Religieuses de la Compagnie de Sainte Ursula de Dole)
9, rue Mont Roland
BP 338
F-39104 Dole Cedex, France
Sr. Cecile Machiels, Superior Gen.   PH: 84 722103

Founded: 1606. **Members:** 67. **Languages:** French. **National.** Women religious. Activities include education of the young and ministering to the sick and aged.

★1821★ SOEURS DU BON SAUVEUR (SBS)
93, rue Caponiere
F-14012 Caen Cedex, France
Sr. Genevieve Calmettes, Superior Gen.   PH: 31 305050

Founded: 1732. **Members:** 263. **Languages:** French. **Multinational.** Activities include the education of children (particularly deaf children) and care of the sick.

★1822★ WOMEN'S INTERNATIONAL CULTURAL FEDERATION (WICF)
(FICF Federation Internationale Culturelle Feminine)
62, rue de Rome
F-75008 Paris, France
Marie-Michell Perigot, Pres.

Founded: 1961. **National Groups:** 16. **Languages:** French. **Multinational.** Engravers, painters, sculptors, and other women artists working with plastic as a medium. Purpose is to unite women in the pursuit of cultural activities. Conducts study tours; organizes roundtables.

Publications: *Bulletin* (in English, French, German, and Italian), 3/year. ● *EXPRESSION* (in English, French, German, and Italian), semiannual.

Conventions/Meetings: semiannual, exposition

★1823★ WOMEN'S INTERNATIONAL LEAGUE FOR PEACE AND
     FREEDOM - FRENCH SECTION (WILPF/FS)
(LIFPL/SF Ligue Internationale de Femmes pour la Paix et la Liberte -
     Section Francaise)
24, quai Louis Bleriot
F-75016 Paris, France
Anne Picard, Pres.   PH: 1 42281502

Founded: 1915. **Members:** 200. **Languages:** English, French. **National.** Women in France working to obtain and preserve universal peace, freedom, and respect for human rights. Collaborates with similar agencies in other countries.

Publications: *Paix et Liberte*, quarterly.

Conventions/Meetings: periodic meeting.

★1824★ WOMEN'S RIGHTS LEAGUE
(Ligue du Droit des Femmes)
54, ave. de Choisy
F-75013 Paris, France
Anne Zelensky, President   PH: 1 45851137

Founded: 1974. **Members:** 3,000. **Staff:** 15. **Languages:** French. **National.** Association of feminists defending womens rights in the areas of: public image, politics, and legislation. Especially active in the defense of victims of domestic violence.

Conventions/Meetings: semiannual conference.

★1825★ WORLD UNION OF CATHOLIC WOMEN'S ORGANIZATIONS
(WUCWO)
20, Notre Dame des Champs
F-75006 Paris, France   PH: 1 45442765
Sr. Geraldine MacCarthy, Sec.Gen.   FX: 1 42840480

Founded: 1910. **Staff:** 3. **Regional Groups:** 5. **Languages:** English, French, German, Spanish. **Multinational.** Coordinates activities of organizations of Catholic women in 47 countries and represents them on an international level. **Committees:** AIDS; Environment; International; Procedures. **Commissions:** Development Cooperation; Ecumenism; Family; Human Rights; Women and the Church.

Publications: *WUCWO Newsletter*, quarterly.

★1826★ YOUNG WOMEN'S CHRISTIAN ASSOCIATION - FRANCE
(YWCA)
47, rue de Clichy
F-75009 Paris, France   PH: 1 48741508
Jacqueline Dom, Contact   FX: 1 42814001

National. Works to promote Christian fellowship and service among young women in France. Advocates peace and justice.

Germany

★1827★ AMNESTY FOR WOMEN
Steinorweg 2
20099 Hamburg, Germany   PH: 40 2802829

National. Strives to eliminate the exploitation, oppression, and maltreatment of women. Organizes programs and activities to raise public consciousness. Lobbies governmental agencies and organizations for recognition and protection of women's rights; supports development programs which improve the status of women.

★1828★ ASSOCIATION FOR INTERNATIONAL YOUTH-WORK -
CHRISTIAN WOMEN'S WORKING GROUP
(Verein fur Internationale Jungendarbeit - Arbeitsgemeinschaft
Christlischer Frauen)
Adenaurallee 37
W-5300 Bonn 1, Germany
Sabine Rudiger-Hahn, Contact   PH: 228 224433

Founded: 1882. **Members:** 2,400. **Regional Groups:** 23. **Languages:** English, German. **Multinational.** Provides opportunities for German, English, and French young women to: live and work abroad as providers of child care. Disseminates information about study programs, working conditions, and insurance matters. Conducts language courses and cultural programs.

Publications: *Mitteilungen* (in German), annual.

Conventions/Meetings: semiannual conference.

★1829★ BUNDESVERBAND UNTERNEHMERFRAUEN IM HANDWERK
Geschaftsstelle des UFH
Landesgewerbeamt Baden-Wurttemberg
Direktion Karlsruhe
Postfach 41 69
76026 Karlsruhe, Germany   PH: 721 1354010
Gerda Hambuch, President   FX: 721 1354020

Founded: 1988. **Members:** 6,000. **Languages:** Danish, German, English. **National.** Master craftswomen and women working in the craft sector. Promotes the improvement of social status and economic position of women in craft firms. Represents women's interests at a national level. Supports training; encourages further education of craftswomen. Works to establish an extensive network of work associations and organizations in Germany. Offers educational programs, meetings, and seminars. **Awards:** Annual Meisterfrau des Jahres (Master Craftswomen of the Year).

Publications: *Arbeitskreis Unternehmerfrauen im Handwerk Grundungsleitfaden*. Newsletter.

Conventions/Meetings: annual conference.

★1830★ CARITAS-GEMEINSCHAFT FUR PFLEGE- UND
SOZIALBERUFE
Maria-Theresia-Str. 10
79102 Freiburg, Germany   PH: 761 708610
Renate Heinzmann, President   FX: 761 7086116

Founded: 1937. **Members:** 3,000. **Staff:** 3. **Languages:** German. **National.** Society for men and women in nursing and social professions. Represents the political and corporate interests of nursing and health care professionals. Offers continuing education.

Publications: *Newspaper* (in German), bimonthly.

Conventions/Meetings: quarterly conference.

★1831★ DEUTSCHER FRAUENRING
Lessingstr. 9
61231 Bad Nauheim, Germany
Gertrud Wartenberg, President   PH: 6032 1714

Languages: German. **National.** Umbrella organization for women's groups in Germany. Supports and promotes women's interests. Coordinates activities for women. Disseminates information on women's topics.

★1832★ DEUTSCHER HAUSFRAUEN-BUND (DHB)
Coburger Str. 19   PH: 228 237718
53113 Bonn, Germany   228 237799
Siglinde Porsch, Contact   FX: 228 238858

Founded: 1915. **Members:** 100,000. **Staff:** 4. **State Groups:** 17. **Languages:** German. **National.** Housewives in Germany. Works to raise the legal and social status of housewives. Encourages recognition and appreciation of domestic work. Represents the interests of professional housekeepers. Active in consumer affairs on behalf of housewives. Offers educational workshops on home economics, the environment, consumer awareness, and nutrition. Cooperates with other home economics organizations. **Committees:** Family Issues.

Publications: *Moderne Hausfrau* (in German), monthly. Magazine. ● *Kongressdokumentationen* (in German), periodic. Monograph. Convention documentation.

Conventions/Meetings: quadrennial congress, International.

★1833★ DEUTSCHER HAUSFRAUENGEWERKSCHAFT (DHG)
c/o Ingrid Gripp
Querbrakenring 26
38442 Wolfsburg, Germany   PH: 5361 74255
Gerda Becker, President   TF: 5361 771958

Founded: 1979. **Members:** 40,000. **Budget:** DM 54,000. **Languages:** German. **National.** German housewives. Membership includes adult women and men from different professions. Seeks national recognition of the housewife/husband as a profession, requesting a state-subsidized income, child support, social security benefits. and retirement pensions. Offers prematrimony educational programs in schools.

Publications: *DHG Rundschau* (in German), quarterly. Newsletter.

Conventions/Meetings: biennial board meeting. ● annual general assembly (exhibits). ● biennial workshop.

★1834★ DEUTSCHER JURISTINNENBUND
Strasschensweg 28
53113 Bonn, Germany   PH: 228 238613
Dr. Hertha Englebrecht, Secretary   FX: 228 238749

Founded: 1948. **Members:** 1,700. **Budget:** DM 200,000. **Languages:** German, English. **National.** Women lawyers, judges, civil servants, economists, and law students. Seeks to enhance the status of women. Works to update legislation regarding: violence against women, women's pensions, cohabitation, abortion, and equal employment. Fosters communication among members; promotes international understanding. Conducts research and educational programs. **Committees:** Family Law; Criminal Law; Taxation Law; Old Age Pensions; Senior Citizens; Equality and Equal Chances.

Publications: *Aktuelle Informationen* (in German), quarterly. Newsletter. ● *Annual Report.* ● *Directory*, periodic.

Conventions/Meetings: annual general assembly.

★1835★ DEUTSCHER SEKRETARINNEN-VERBAND (DSV)
Geschaftsstelle
Lagewiessenstrasse 1A
67063 Ludwigshafen, Germany   PH: 621 695965
Marion Beuthling, Office Mgr.   FX: 621 632158

Founded: 1956. **Members:** 2,000. **Staff:** 2. **Local Groups:** 51. **Languages:** German, English. **National.** Women employed as secretaries, personal assistants, and educational institutions. Improves the status, and defends the professional interests, of secretaries. Offers secretarial vocational training. Provides counseling to individuals involved or interested in the secretarial profession. Offers educational programs and special events to the public. Affiliated with secretarial organizations nationally and internationally. **Libraries:** Type: not open to the public.

Publications: *Newsletter* (in German), periodic. ● *Assistenz*, periodic. Journal.

Conventions/Meetings: biennial general assembly - Germany. ● biennial congress - Germany.

★1836★ DEUTSCHER STAATSBERGERINNEN-VERBAND
Tempelhofer Damm 2
Platz der Luftbrucke
12101 Berlin, Germany
Helga Dirks-Norden, President   PH: 30 7858927

Languages: English. **National.** Works to ensure that German women experience the same rights as men.

★1837★ DEUTSCHER VERBAND BERUFSTATIGER FRAUEN (DVBF)
Schornstr. 8
81699 Munich, Germany   PH: 89 4485746
S. Kuschel, Contact   FX: 89 482901

Founded: 1931. **Members:** 1,000. **Languages:** German. **National.** Member of the International Federation of Business and Professional Women (IFBPW). Members have opportunity, through the IFBPW, to participate in congresses, develop worldwide contacts, and utilize the IFBPW international network while traveling. Goals include: professional education, training, and advancement to establish economic and social equalty for women; defense of the interests of working women; promotion and maintenance of local professional women's clubs; support of cooperation among women; and improvement of economic and social institutions serving working women. Encourages cooperation with other organizations and institutions nationally and internationally.

Publications: *DVBF Information* (in German), periodic. Newsletter.

Conventions/Meetings: semiannual conference. ● monthly regional meeting.

★1838★ DEUTSCHER VERBAND FRAU UND KULTUR
Briandstr. 2
42781 Haan, Germany
Margret Werner, Director   PH: 21294861

Founded: 1896. **Members:** 4,000. **Budget:** DM 10,000. **Languages:** German. **National.** Works to establish equal rights for women in all realms of society through the distribution of information. Encourages women's involvement in politics, the arts, environment, health, and social projects. Organizes lectures. Encourages continuing education. **Libraries:** Type: reference. archival material.

Publications: *Frau und Kultur* (in German), quarterly. Newsletter.

Conventions/Meetings: weekly meeting. ● monthly seminar. ● monthly conference.

★1839★ EUROPEAN ASSOCIATION FOR THE DEVELOPMENT OF
    INFORMATION AND TRAINING OF WOMEN - GERMANY (EUDIFF)
(Europaische Gesellschaft zur Forderung der Information und Ausbildung
    der Frauen)
Friedrich-Ebert-Stiftung
Godesberger Alee 149
53175 Bonn, Germany   PH: 228 883216
Monika Langkau-Herrmann, Contact   FX: 228 883538

Languages: German. **National.** Circulates information on women and women's issues throughout Germany. Networks with organizations that also champion women's advancement. Demands that EC nations fully recognize women's rights. Supports women's development and equality; encourages women's participation in leadership roles. Facilitates exchange among members.

★1840★ EUROPEAN DIABETES PREGNANCY STUDY GROUP
    (EDPSG)
c/o EASD
Auf'm Hennekamp 32
40225 Dusseldorf, Germany   PH: 211 316738

Founded: 1971. **Members:** 40. **Multinational.** A study group of the European Association for the Study of Diabetes. Members are diabetologists, obstetricians, pathologists, and pediatricians in 10 countries. Promotes better understanding and more effective investigation of the problems of pregnancy and diabetes.

Conventions/Meetings: annual symposium.

★1841★ EUROPEAN UNION OF WOMEN (EUW)
Nymphenburgerstr. 64
80335 Munich, Germany

Languages: German. **Multinational.** Women members of parliament, the Christian Democrats, and conservative political parties. Seeks to enhance women's influence in all aspects of public life. Works for the conservation of European heritage, human dignity, and freedom, while upholding Christian principles.

Publications: *Bulletin*, biennial.

Conventions/Meetings: biennial general assembly.

★1842★ FEDERATION DEMOCRATIQUE INTERNATIONALE DES
FEMMES
Unter den Linden 13
10117 Berlin, Germany

Languages: German, French. **Multinational.** Women united to uphold the principles of democracy. Works to combat sexual discrimination.

★1843★ FEMININ EUROPEANS OF MEDIUM AND SMALL
ENTERPRISES (FEM)
c/o Landesgewerbeamt Baden
Wurttemberg
Direktion Karlsruhe
Postfach 41 69
76026 Karlsruhe, Germany   PH: 721 1354010
Gerda J. Eertink, President   FX: 721 1354020

Founded: 1990. **Languages:** German, English. **Multinational.** Female entrepreneurs in Europe. Seeks to improve the status of female entrepreneurs in the European Community. Fosters international networking among members. Seeks to enable women to become independent through entrepreneurial activities. Supports members' continued training and education. Encourages increased public awareness of female entrepreneurship.

Conventions/Meetings: annual congress.

★1844★ FRAUEN IN LATEINAMERIKA
Eulen Baumstr. 287
44801 Bochum, Germany   PH: 234 70446

Languages: German. **Multinational.** Works to improve conditions for women in South America. Fosters multi-cultural understanding.

★1845★ FRAUEN-UNION DER CHRISTIAN DEMOKRATISCHEN UNION
DEUTSCHLANDS (FUCDU)
Konrad-Adenauer-Haus
Friedrich-Ebert-Alle 73-75
53113 Bonn, Germany   PH: 228 544315
Ingrid Sehrbrock, Secretary   FX: 228 544216

Founded: 1948. **Members:** 185,222. **Staff:** 5. **Local Groups:** 17. **Languages:** German, English. **National.** Represents the interests of women within the Christian Democratic Union. Ensures the recognition of women's rights within the platform and actions of the party. Works to mobilize women within the party. Recognizes the work and achievments of women in agriculture, industry, and business. Furthers awareness of women's issues among national and international political bodies and policy making.

Publications: *Frau und Politik* (in German), bimonthly. Magazine.

Conventions/Meetings: periodic meeting.

★1846★ FRAUENKOMMISSION DER EUROPAISCHEN BEWEGUNG
DEUTSCHLAND
Europa-Zentrum
Bachstr. 32   PH: 228 7290060
53115 Bonn, Germany   228 695734

Parties, alliances, and educational institutions. Observes the activities of the European Community in the area of the political involvement of women. Supports the execution of corresponding projects. **Awards:** Frauen fur Europa (recognition). **Alternate name:** Frauenkommission im Deutschen Rat der Europaischen Bewegung.

Conventions/Meetings: seminar - 3/year. ● conference - 3/year.

★1847★ FRIEDRICH EBERT FOUNDATION (FEF)
Godesberger Allee 149
53175 Bonn, Germany

Languages: English. **National.** Sponsors adult education programs for women. Provides a forum for women to meet and exchange information and experiences. Works for equal employment opportunities for women.

Publications: *Booklet*. Focuses on women's employment and equality.

Conventions/Meetings: periodic conference.

★1848★ GERMAN WOMEN'S COUNCIL
(Deutscher Frauenrat)
Simrockstr. 5   PH: 228 223008
53113 Bonn, Germany   228 223009
Birgit Rosenberg, Contact   FX: 228 218819

Founded: 1951. **Members:** 47. **Staff:** 11. **Languages:** German, English. **National.** Women's organizations in Germany united to enhance women's status. Lobbies governments, institutions, and other decision-making bodies to influence policies on women's issues. Works to: improve women's political and employment opportunities; achieve independent social security for women; and increase awareness of women's history. Fosters communication among members.

Publications: *Informationen fur die Frau* (in German), 10 times/year. Journal. ● *Handbuch der Deutschen Frauenorganisationen* (in German), periodic. Directory.

Conventions/Meetings: annual general assembly.

★1849★ GERMAN WOMEN'S ORGANIZATION FOR ALCOHOL FREE
CULTURE (GWOAFC)
(Deutscher Frauenbund fur Alkoholfreie Kultur)
K. Tuchosky Str. 7
63329 Egelsbach, Germany
Helga Rau, Pres.   PH: 6103 42731

Founded: 1900. **Members:** 290. **Budget:** DM 16,260. **Local Groups:** 6. **Languages:** English, German. **National.** Individuals in Germany. Disseminates information on the dangers of alcohol consumption; conducts seminars.

Publications: *Booklet*.

Conventions/Meetings: annual convention.

★1850★ INDEPENDENT WOMEN'S FEDERATION (UFV)
(Unabhangiger Frauenverband Bundesverband)
Friedrichstr. 175
13505 Berlin, Germany
Marinka Korzendorfer, Contact   PH: 30 2291685

Founded: 1989. **National.** Women's groups and interested individuals in Germany. Champions women's rights and the issues impacting them. Offers a forum for discussion; provides opportunities for involvement in the political process; disseminates information on objectives and activities. Calls for: the establishment of women's councils in factories and institutions, communities, municipal parliaments, and the People's Chamber; creation of a government post responsible for the monitoring of legislation affecting women; establishment of a women's support fund to promote women's projects and to finance the development of women's advice and cultural centers, babysitting, and other services. Conducts forums, hearings, panel discussions, and social events.

★1851★ INTERNATIONAL ASSOCIATION OF WOMEN
   PHILOSOPHERS (IAWP)
(Internationale Assoziation von Philosophinnen)
c/o Ulrike Ramming
Burknerstrasse 24
12047 Berlin, Germany   PH: 30 6938991
Ulrike Ramming, Exec. Officer   TX: 8044 ZURICH

Founded: 1974. **Members:** 200. **Languages:** English, French, German. **Multinational.** Women philosophers in 15 countries united to organize congresses and symposia. Maintains biographical archives.

Publications: *Rundbriefs* (in German), annual. Newsletter.

Conventions/Meetings: triennial symposium

★1852★ KOMMISSION GLEICHBERECHTIGUNG UND
   FAMILIENPOLITIK
c/o Freie Demokratische Partei
Baunscheidtstr. 15
53113 Bonn, Germany
Frau Tampe, Contact   PH: 228 547302

National. Political organization for women in Germany; section of the Free Democratic Party.

★1853★ KOORDINIERUNGS UND BERATUNGSZENTRUM FUR
   WEITERBILDUNG VON FRAUEN (KOBRA)
Knesebeckstr. 33/34   PH: 30 8825783
10623 Berlin, Germany   30 8825784
Margrit Zauner, Director   FX: 30 8836546

Founded: 1988. **Staff:** 11. **Languages:** German. **National.** Coordination and counseling center for the advancement of women. Offers practical advice and continuing education pertaining to the needs and concerns of women. Assists women, education representatives, and businesses. Provides counseling in career and continuing education planning, and assistance in administration and business. **Libraries:** Type: not open to the public.

Publications: *Frauen in Sozialen Berufen - Auswege aus die Sachgosse* (in German). Book. ● *Einstieg Ohne Abstieg* (in German). Book. ● *Booklet* (in German).

★1854★ KREIS KATHOLISCHER FRAUEN IM HELIAND-BUND
Lilienstr. 61
67112 Mutterstadt, Germany
Sigrid Doerry, Mgr. Dir.   PH: 6234 7544

Founded: 1926. **Members:** 2,500. **Budget:** DM 100,000. **Languages:** German. **National.** Catholic women professionals. Strives to effectively make an impact on society through: character building; Christian maturity; the church community; and personal example. Professes that the youth and Christian movements are bound together through a new style of living based on Christian teaching.

Conventions/Meetings: annual general assembly. ● semiannual conference. ● periodic regional meeting.

★1855★ MEDICAL WOMEN'S INTERNATIONAL ASSOCIATION (MWIA)
Herbert-Lewin-Str. 5   PH: 221 4004558
50931 Cologne, Germany   FX: 221 4004388
Dr. Carolyn Motzel, Sec.Gen.   TX: 08882161 BAEK

Founded: 1919. **Members:** 20,000. **Staff:** 1. **Regional Groups:** 8. **National Groups:** 44. **Languages:** English. **Multinational.** Women involved or interested in medicine in 67 countries. Provides women with an opportunity to exchange information about medical problems with worldwide implications; promotes friendship and understanding between women; secures members' cooperation in matters relating to international health. Seeks to encourage women to enter the field of medicine and allied sciences and to overcome discrimination against female physicians. Aids women in developing countries in obtaining fellowships and grants for research and travel; offers information and advice to members visiting other countries. **Committees:** Ethics and Resolution; Scientific and Research.

Publications: *Circular Letter*, quarterly. ● *Congress Report*, triennial. ● *Newsletter*, semiannual. ● *Women Physicians of the World*. Book.

Conventions/Meetings: triennial congress (exhibits) - 1995 May 7 - 12, The Hague, Netherlands; 1998, Nairobi, Kenya.

★1856★ NGO WOMEN'S FORUM
World University Service
Goebenstr. 35
65195 Wiesbaden, Germany
Ms. Petra Loch, Contact   PH: 6121 446648

Languages: German, English. **Multinational.** Non-governmental women's organizations in Africa, Asia, and Latin America. Promotes women's ideas and interests in development concepts. Works to raise awareness of gender issues. Seeks to improve women's working conditions and employment opportunities. Fosters cooperation and information exchange between women's groups and development programs.

Conventions/Meetings: meeting - 3/year.

★1857★ PRO FAMILIA: DEUTSCHE GESELLSCHAFT FUR
   SEXUALBERATUNG UND FAMILIEPLANUNG
Cronstettenstr. 30   PH: 69 550901
60322 Frankfurt am Main, Germany   FX: 69 552701
Ms. Elke Thoss, Exec. Dir.   TX: 882111 BFT BGMX

Languages: German. **National.** Promotes family planning as a basic human right. Works to reduce the number of unwanted pregnancies and abortions. Attempts to stop the spread of AIDS and other sexually transmitted diseases through education and contraceptive services. Sponsors programs in family planning, sex education, and health. Conducts research.

★1858★ SISTERS OF DIVINE PROVIDENCE (SDP)
(Schwestern von dir Gottlichen Vorschung)
Neubrueckenstrasse 22
48143 Munster, Germany
Sr. Petra Bade, Gen. Superior   PH: 251 511493

Founded: 1842. **Members:** 2,025. **Regional Groups:** 10. **National Groups:** 5. **Languages:** English, German, Portuguese. **Multinational.** Promotes religious living and teaching.

Conventions/Meetings: periodic general assembly.

★1859★ SOZIALDIENST KATHOLISCHER FRAUEN (SKF)
Agnes-Neuhaus-Str. 5   PH: 231 528126
44135 Dortmund, Germany   231 528127
Annelie Windheuser, Secretary   FX: 231 526751

Founded: 1899. **Members:** 9,500. **Staff:** 2,000. **Languages:** German. **National.** Catholic women. Serves the church, state, and society with a Christian attitude and according to Catholic teaching. Assists disadvantaged and endangered children, teenagers, women, and families, offering counseling and aid. Also serves as an adoption and foster care service, and provides 22 emergency shelters for women. Recognizes an obligation to serve society and those less fortunate. Proposes a solution to problems through feminine solidarity and Christian charity.

★1860★ TERRES DES FEMMES (TdF)
Kornhausstr. 12
PO Box 25 31
72015 Tubingen, Germany — PH: 7071 24289
Christa Stolle, Contact — FX: 7071 550352

Founded: 1981. **Members:** 250. **Staff:** 1. **Budget:** DM 150,000. **Regional Groups:** 9. **Languages:** German, French, Spanish, English. **National.** Works to eliminate human rights violations against women regardless of political opinion, race, or geographical origin. Provides assistance to women victims of maltreatment, persecution, and exploitation. Collaborates with other women's organizations to improve women's status. Disseminates information.

Publications: *Heir ist ewig Ausland Koreanische Frauen in der BRD* (in German). Book. ● *Tod als Ehrensache - Frauenschicksale* (in German). Book. ● *Unterdruckung - Flucht - Asyl Iran Fluchtlingsfrauen in der BRD* (in German). Book. ● *Rundbrief*, quarterly. Newsletter.

Conventions/Meetings: annual general assembly.

★1861★ UNION OF GERMAN CATHOLIC WOMEN
(Katholischer Deutscher Frauenbund)
Kaesenstr. 18
50677 Cologne, Germany — PH: 221 314930
Kriemhild Ramms, Contact — FX: 221 322954

Founded: 1903. **Members:** 220,000. **Staff:** 10. **Languages:** German, English. **National.** Fosters women's personal growth and development. Encourages women to assume leadership roles in the areas of: society, church, family, and business. Conducts ecumenical study programs. Conducts research on feminsit theology, women and the media, and social politics. **Libraries:** Type: reference. Holdings: 0; books. **Awards:** Best women's liturgical text..

Publications: *Die Christliche Frau* (in German), bimonthly. Magazine.

Conventions/Meetings: annual general assembly.

★1862★ VERBAND DER DEUTSCHEN LYCEUM CLUBS
Gustav-Adolf-Str. 19
73033 Goppingen, Germany
Dr. Renate Hees, Contact — PH: 7161 671410

Founded: 1905. **Members:** 850. **Languages:** German, French. **National.** Women with interests in the areas of: the arts, literature, sciences, and social sciences.

Conventions/Meetings: triennial congress.

★1863★ WOMEN'S ENTERPRISES
(Frauenbriebe)
Hamburger Allee 96
60486 Frankfurt am Main, Germany — PH: 69 700776
Susan Uschi, Director — 69 773066

Founded: 1984. **Members:** 7. **Staff:** 5. **Budget:** DM 6,000,000. **Languages:** German. Executes 'raison d'etre' seminars, vocational workshops, and consultation. Offers vocational training to unemployed women, namely: single mothers; older women (returning to the workforce); young female students who are deficient in work experience and are finding difficulty in securing a job. Established a vocational training center in 1987 financed through public funding.

Publications: *Frauen Starten in die Selbstandigkeit* (in German). Book. ●

Frauenporjekte - Planung, Finanzierung, Durchfuhrung (in German). Book. ● *Frauen Grunden Betriebe* (in German). Book.

Conventions/Meetings: semiannual general assembly - Frankfurt am Main Germany. ● annual seminar. ● annual workshop.

★1864★ WOMEN'S INTERNATIONAL DEMOCRATIC FEDERATION
(WIDF)
(FDIF Internationale Demokratische Frauenfoderation)
— PH: 30 2755028
— FX: 30 2793633 ATTN:
Dresdener Str. 43 — WID
Postfach 940 — TX: 114446 ATTN: WIDF
10132 Berlin, Germany — CBL: FEDEINTFEM
Brigitte Triems, Gen.Sec. — BERLIN

Founded: 1945. **Members:** 144. **Languages:** English, French, German, Spanish. **Multinational.** National organizations in 113 countries and territories. Seeks to unite women regardless of race, nationality, religion, or political opinion, so that they may work together to win, implement, and defend their rights as mothers, workers, and citizens. Defends the rights of children to life, well-being, and education; attempts to win and defend national independence and democratic freedoms, eliminate apartheid, racial discrimination, and fascism. Works for peace and universal disarmament. Organizes study trips; holds seminars.

Publications: *Newsletter*, periodic. ● *Women in Action*, periodic. Bulletin. ● *Women of the Whole World*, periodic.

Conventions/Meetings: triennial congress.

★1865★ WOMEN'S WORLD DAY OF PRAYER
(Weltgebetstag der Frauen)
Deutenbacherstr. 1
PO Box 1240
90544 Stein, Germany — PH: 911 680630
Eileen King, Exec. Dir. — FX: 911 680677

Founded: 1968. **Members:** 13. **Staff:** 4. **Budget:** US$2,321,000. **Languages:** German, Spanish, English. **Multinational.** Unites Christian women worldwide in a common day dedicated to prayer. Encourages an international awareness and mission of service among Christian women. Subjects of prayer of include: specified means of women's empowerment in specific developing countries; environmental protection and improvement techniques and programs; and the improved social welfare for disadvantaged women and children. Seeks to eliminate homelessness, poverty, and illiteracy among refugees, migrant workers, and agriculture laborers. Financially and prayerfully supports self-help/community groups.

Publications: *Order of Worship*. Booklet.

★1866★ YOUNG WOMEN'S CHRISTIAN ASSOCIATION - GERMANY
(Evangelische Frauenarbeit in Deutschland)
Emil-von-Behring-Str. 3
60439 Frankfurt, Germany
Susanne Lipka, Gen.Sec. — PH: 69 95890120

National. Works to promote Christian fellowship, service, and unity among young women in Germany. Upholds peace and justice.

Greece

★1867★ CONSEIL NATIONAL DES FEMMES HELLENES
38 Voulis St. — PH: 1 3227609
GR-105 57 Athens, Greece — 1 3232418
Effi Kalliga, President — FX: 1 7210384

National. Umbrella organization for women's groups in Greece. Promotes women's interests. Coordinates activities for women. Disseminates information on women's issues.

★1868★ ELLINIKO DIKTIO GYNEKON EVROPIS
22-24 Protarias Str.
GR-115 23 Athens, Greece
Tasso Gaitani, Contact
PH: 1 9613100

Founded: 1983. **Members:** 20. **Languages:** Greek, French, English. **Multinational.** Feminists from EEC countries. Pursues the exchange of information on the feminist movement among members of the EEC. Attempts to influence decision-making of the European Parliament on issues concerning the position of women in society. Areas of concern include: social security, professional training, maternity leave, and salary equality. Plans to implement employment assistance program for women.

Publications: *Bulletin* (in English and French), quarterly.

Conventions/Meetings: monthly convention.

★1869★ EUROPEAN ASSOCIATION FOR THE DEVELOPMENT OF INFORMATION AND TRAINING OF WOMEN - GREECE (EUDIFF)
(Europaiki Enossi gia tin Anaptixi tis Pairoforisis kai Epimorfosis ton Ginaikon)
16 Skoufa St.
Athens, Greece
PH: 1 3615098
Joanna Manganara, Contact
FX: 1 3069585

Languages: Greek. **National.** Circulates information on women and women's issues throughout Greece. Networks with organizations that also champion women's advancement. Demands that EC nations fully recognize women's rights. Supports women's development and equality; encourages women's participation in leadership roles. Facilitates exchange among members.

★1870★ FAMILY PLANNING ASSOCIATION OF GREECE (FPAG)
121 Solonos St.
GR-106 78 Athens, Greece
PH: 1 3606390
Ms. Liz Mestheneos, Contact
FX: 1 3606390

Languages: Greek. **National.** Works to enhance the quality of life for individuals living in Greece by promoting family planning and responsible parenthood. Works to stop the spread of AIDS and other sexually transmitted diseases through education and contraceptive services. Sponsors programs in family planning and health. Conducts research.

★1871★ FEDERATION OF GREEK WOMEN
120 Hippocratous Str.
GR-114 72 Athens, Greece
PH: 1 8027222

Founded: 1976. **Members:** 20,000. **Budget:** 800,000 Dr. **Languages:** Greek, French, German, English. **National.** Promotes equal opportunity for women in labor, family life, and social activities. Encourages women's participation in government to influence such policies as social security, legalized abortion, and women in the military. Participates in activities relating to world peace, environmental conservation, and drug use prevention. Conducts seminars on issues of interest. **Libraries:** Type: reference. Holdings: 0; books. Subjects: women's issues. **Committees:** Labor; Social Security; Press; Media; Public Relations; International Relations.

Conventions/Meetings: quadrennial convention (exhibits). • monthly meeting.

★1872★ GREEK FEMINIST NETWORK
(Telesilla)
109 Asklipiou
PH: 1 3628104
GR-114 72 Athens, Greece
FX: 1 3619287

Founded: 1989. **Members:** 470. **Budget:** US$8,000. **Languages:** Greek, English. **Multinational.** Promotes open communication channels among women in Greece and internationally. Collaborates with similar organizations to create models of action to fight oppression of women. Disseminates information.

Publications: *Telesilla* (in Greek), quarterly. Bulletin.

Conventions/Meetings: semiannual meeting.

★1873★ GREEK LEAGUE FOR WOMEN'S RIGHTS
41 Solonos St.
GR-106 72 Athens, Greece
Prof. Alice Yotopoulos-Marangopoulos,
PH: 1 3616236
President
FX: 1 3616236

Founded: 1920. **Members:** 2,000. **Budget:** US$1,850. **Languages:** Greek, French, English. **National.** Lawyers, sociologists, physicians, teachers, and workers. Aims to eradicate inequalities in the civil and political rights of men and women. Promotes women's involvement in government and other decision making positions. Works to ensure that family obligations do not impede women's career advancement; lobbies government for three months paid family leave, child care, and adjustment of children's school hours to parents' work hours. Conducts public awareness seminars to alter the traditional view of sex roles. Engages in research on sexual harrassment and the portrayal of women in media and advertising. Offers legal and emotional counselling to women. Disseminates information. **Libraries:** Type: reference. books. Subjects: women's issues. **Awards:** . **Committees:** Civil & Political Rights.

Publications: *Woman's Struggle* (in Greek and English), quarterly. Journal. • *Women, Work, and New Technologies* (in Greek). Book.

Conventions/Meetings: annual general assembly (exhibits) - Athens, Greece. • monthly board meeting (exhibits) - Athens, Greece. • periodic seminar (exhibits) - Athens, Greece.

★1874★ GREEK WOMEN'S ANTINUCLEAR MOVEMENT (EGAK)
NCRS Demeokritos
Aglina Ponoskeir
GR-153 10 Attiki, Greece
PH: 1 6513111
Dr. H. Gamari-Seale, Res. Scientist
FX: 1 6519430

Founded: 1985. **Members:** 2,000. **Staff:** 2. **Languages:** English, French, Greek. **National.** Individuals united to strengthen the peace movement in Greece and the world. Organizes lectures and marches. Conducts research and educational programs. Analyzes current events; conducts research on armament expenditures. Issues publications.

Conventions/Meetings: biennial conference.

★1875★ INTERNATIONAL ALLIANCE OF WOMEN (IAW)
(AIF Alliance Internationale des Femmes)
1 Lycavittou St.
GR-106 72 Athens, Greece
PH: 1 3626111
Alice Marangopoulos, Pres.
FX: 1 3622454

Founded: 1904. **Members:** 79. **Staff:** 2. **Languages:** English, French. **Multinational.** Women's organizations and individuals in 85 countries. Objectives are: to secure reforms necessary to establish a real equality of liberties, status, and opportunities between men and women; to urge women to use their rights and influence in public life to ensure that the status of every individual shall be based on the respect for human personality and not on sex, race, or creed; to work for understanding between nations. Promotes exchange of views and experiences. Holds seminars, conferences, and workshops, with special emphasis on developing countries. Arranges study tours. **Committees:** Legal Problems; Media, Environment, and Habitat. **Commissions:** Civil and Political; Economic; Education; Health; Social; United Nations Ad Hoc.

Publications: *Action Programme*, triennial. Booklet. • *Congress Reports*, triennial. Booklet. • *International Women's News Journal* (in English and French), quarterly.

Conventions/Meetings: triennial congress

★1876★ LEAGUE FOR WOMEN'S RIGHTS (LWR)
(Ligue Hellenique pour le Droit des Femmes)
41 Solonos St.
GR-106 72 Athens, Greece
Prof. A. Yotopoulos-Marangopoulos,   PH: 1 3616236
    President   FX: 1 3616236

Founded: 1920. Members: 3,000. Languages: English, French, Greek.
National. Promotes equality of the sexes in all areas of society. Works to
protect women's rights in politics, law, and education. Lobbies government
to pass laws to increase women's rights. Offers educational programs and
works to eradicate illiteracy among women. Supports affirmative action
measures. Sponsors legal and psychological counseling. Conducts research
on the role of women in society with special emphasis on sexual harassment.
Offers training and informational seminars. Libraries: Type: reference.
Holdings: books, periodicals. Subjects: women's issues. Awards: Annual
Best Journalist on Women's Issues. ● Annual Best Student Article on
Sexual Equality. Committees: Legal; Women's Employment and Working
Conditions; Education; Media; Women's Employment and Working Condi-
tions; Public Relations.

Publications: Woman's Struggle (in Greek and English), quarterly. Journal.

Conventions/Meetings: periodic meeting (exhibits) - Athens, Greece.

★1877★ LYCEUM CLUB OF GREEK WOMEN
(Likion ton Ellinidon)
14 Dimokritou St.   PH: 1 3611042
GR-106 73 Athens, Greece   1 3628978
Dr. Tota Valinakis, President   FX: 1 3607355

Founded: 1911. Members: 12,220. Staff: 9. Local Groups: 48. Languages:
Greek, French, English. National. Promotes the interests and concerns of
Greek women and also the preservation of Greek folk culture. Organized the
first Panhellenic Women's Congress. Contributes to women's education,
advancement, and the struggle against illiteracy. Works to protect women's
rights. Encourges the participation of women in politics and society in
general. Offers folk culture education, professional training programs, and
activities, such as trips to museums, exhibitions, and historical sites.
Conducts and supports research on Greek folk culture, costumes, music,
and dance. Provides services to handicapped children. Libraries: Type:
lending. Holdings: 0; books, periodicals, archival material. Awards: Scholarship. Recipient: handicapped children. ● Recognition. Recipient: overcom-
mers of illiteracy. Sections: Folk Dance; Greek Traditional Costume; Music;
Protection of Mother and Child; Art; Greek Communities Abroad; International Cultural Relations.

Publications: Bulletin, annual. Minutes of meetings.

Conventions/Meetings: annual general assembly (exhibits) - Athens,
Greece.

★1878★ MEDITERRANEAN WOMEN'S STUDIES INSTITUTE (KEGME)
(Institut d'Etudes des Femmes de la Mediterranee)
115 Harilaou Trikoupi
GR-114 73 Athens, Greece
Ketty Lazaris, President   PH: 1 3615660

Founded: 1982. Languages: Greek, French, English. Multinational. Participates in research and education on gender issues. Conducts vocational
training programs for young unemployed women and special projects for
women in Africa. Established as an advisory group to the Economic and
Social Council (United Nations) and the United Nations Educational, Scientific, and Cultural Organization and a board member of the European Network
for Women's Studies. Computer Services: Data base.

Publications: Newsletter, quarterly.

Conventions/Meetings: semiannual meeting.

★1879★ NON-ALIGNED WOMEN'S MOVEMENT
109 Asklipiou St.   PH: 1 3628104
GR-114 72 Athens, Greece   FX: 1 3619287

Founded: 1983. Members: 60. Budget: US$15,000. Languages: Greek,
English. National. Women of all ages. Supports the worldwide solidarity of
women and the struggle for women's liberation from social inequality.
Provides information about and conducts research in: prostitution and
pornography; birth control; health care; discrimination in the work place;
reproductive technology; reproductive rights; women and drugs; women and
policy; population control; women and work; and sexuality. Affiliated with
other organizations worldwide; participates in conventions abroad. Provides
an information center and library.

Publications: Newspaper, annual.

Conventions/Meetings: meeting - 3/year. ● annual, Bazaar.
always December. Athens, Greece.

★1880★ PANHELLENIC ASSOCIATION OF TELEPHONE OPERATORS
    OF OTE
(Panellinios Sylogos Tilefonitrion-Chiristrian OTE)
28-30 Derigny St.
GR-104 34 Athens, Greece
Filio Hadji, Secretary   PH: 1 8843911

Founded: 1964. Members: 180. Budget: 1,500,000 Dr. Languages: Greek,
English. National. Works to achieve women's equality in the telecommunications field. Represents and defends members' labor claims. Fosters solidarity
among members. Libraries: Type: reference. Holdings: books.

Publications: Anagenissi (in Greek), periodic. Newsletter.

Conventions/Meetings: annual general assembly - Athens, Greece.

★1881★ PROTOPORIAKI ORGANOSSI GYNAECON
Olympou str. 3
Aghia Paraskevi
GR-153 43 Athens, Greece
Eugenie Katsouridou-Dampassi, President   PH: 1 6398985

Founded: 1983. Members: 171. Budget: 170,000 Dr. Languages: French.
National. Promotes equal rights among the sexes in society and at the
workplace. Libraries: Type: reference.

Publications: Protopoziaki (in Greek), Three/year.

Conventions/Meetings: annual general assembly (exhibits) - always October. Athens, Greece.

★1882★ RESEARCH CENTRE OF WOMEN'S AFFAIRS
109 Asklipiou
GR-114 72 Athens, Greece   PH: 1 3628104
Matia Kaloudaki, Contact   FX: 1 3619287

Founded: 1987. Members: 40. Budget: 10,000 Dr. Languages: English.
National. Scientists and individuals from all classes and professions.
Promotes and presents the theoritical and practical matteres concerning
women. Collects and studies information on the women's movement.
Conducts research and educational programs on prostitution and women
and smoking. Libraries: Type: reference.   Subjects: women's
affairs.

Publications: Newspaper, annual.

Conventions/Meetings: semiannual meeting. ● periodic conference.

★1883★ WOMEN FOR MUTUAL SECURITY (WMS)
1 Romilias Str.   PH: 1 8843227
GR-146 71 Kastri, Greece   1 8843202
Margarita Papandreou, Coord.   FX: 1 8012850

Founded: 1985. National Groups: 20. Multinational. Women striving to demilitarize international relations. Challenges political decision makers to develop ways to resolve conflicts peacefully and to negotiate for the goal of disarmament. Works for the development and maintenance of solidarity among women of the world for the cause of world peace. Participates in decision making activities globally, such as: The Women's Defense Dialogue with NATO, The Warsaw Pact Women's Dialogue, Women Leaders and the NATO Defense Ministers Meeting, The Women's Summit, Women Leaders at the Moscow Summit, Women's International Gulf Peace Initiative, and the South Pacific International Policy Congress.

★1884★ WOMEN'S PANHELLENIC ORGANIZATION
(Panathinaiki)
26 Vas. Koustautinou St.   PH: 1 7234543
GR-116 35 Athens, Greece   1 8017380
Mika Ablianiti, Public Relations Coord.   FX: 1 7214459

Founded: 1983. **Members:** 4,000. **Languages:** Greek, English. **National.** Greek women over the age of 18. Promotes equal opportunities for women in Greek society, politics, and economics. Acts as liason with other women's associations and family institutions. Sponsors Greek cultural education programs for members.

Publications: *I Ellinida* (in Greek), quarterly. Magazine. **Also Cited As:** *The Greek Woman.*

Conventions/Meetings: annual convention. ● monthly meeting.

★1885★ WOMEN'S PANHELLENIC UNION
Parnassou str. 2
GR-105 61 Athens, Greece
Georgia Nicoloidou, Secretary   PH: 1 3245539

Founded: 1981. **Members:** 350. **Staff:** 1. **Languages:** Greek, French, English. **National.** Women in Greece united to strive for equal rights. Protests exploitation of women in the mass media and pornography. Promotes environmental conservation; conducts environmental seminars for young people. Conducts research on abortion. **Committees:** Anti-Abortion; Education and Formation.

Publications: *What You Must Know about Abortion* (in Greek). Booklet. ● *The Four Monsters of Today: Violence, Pollution, Drugs, AIDS* (in Greek). Booklet. ● *Ecological Declaration on the Chernobyl Disaster* (in Greek). Booklet.

★1886★ YOUNG WOMEN'S CHRISTIAN ASSOCIATION - GREECE
(YWCA)
Odos Amerikis 11
GR-106 72 Athens, Greece
Clio Fotinopoulou, Gen.Sec.   PH: 1 3624294

National. Works to promote Christian fellowship and service among young women in Greece. Advocates peace and justice.

Hungary

★1887★ ASSOCIATION OF HUNGARIAN WOMEN
Andrassy utca 124   PH: 1 1314734
H-1062 Budapest, Hungary   1 1125071
Ms. Judith Thorma Asbot, President   FX: 1 1317529

Founded: 1989. **Members:** 10,000. **Membership Dues:** 240 Ft annual. **Staff:** 2. **Budget:** US$50,000. **Languages:** English, Hungarian. **National.** Women's organizations and individuals seeking to achieve equal rights for women. Lobbies government on issues affecting women; encourages women to become involved in politics. Aims to enable women to balance family and career while fostering respect for motherhood. Supports programs in conservation, health care, and employment opportunities; operates

counseling center. Disseminates information on: women's unemployment; family planning; abortion; and legal advice. Participates in the International Day of Women (every March 8). Promotes AIDS awareness and prevention. **Libraries:** Type: reference. Holdings: 0; books. **Awards:** Annual (scholarship). Recipient: university graduates who have conducted research on women's issues. **Also Known As:** Hungarian Women's Association.

Conventions/Meetings: semiannual, Presentations on discrimination against women, and women in public life. (exhibits) - Budapest, Hungary.

★1888★ EUROPEAN BAPTIST WOMEN'S UNION (EBWU)
(EBF Europaische Baptistische Frauenunion)
Darno utca 5
H-1155 Budapest, Hungary
Julia Gero, Pres.

Founded: 1982. **Members:** 27. **Languages:** English, German. **Multinational.** A committee of the European Baptist Federation. Baptist women's unions seeking to unite Baptist women in a fellowship of prayer. Promotes friendships and international exchange of ideas and experiences. Works in cooperation with the Baptist World Alliance.

Publications: *News* (in English), periodic. Newsletter.

Conventions/Meetings: quinquennial conference

★1889★ NA'AMAT HUNGARY
Sigrid Reti
Ungvar utca 12
H-1068 Budapest, Hungary   FX: 1 2510577

Languages: Hungarian. **Multinational.** Working and professional women. Works to advance the status of women by providing a variety of educational, communtiy, and legal services. Believes that strong family relations are the foundation of a stable society. Members identify with the Zionist movement.

★1890★ PRO FAMILIA HUNGARIAN SCIENTIFIC SOCIETY (HSSFWW)
Keleti Karoly utca 5-7   PH: 1 1358530
H-1024 Budapest, Hungary   FX: 1 1159040
Dr. Arpad Meszaros, Secretary   TX: 224308 STATI H

Languages: Hungarian. **National.** Advocates family planning as a basic human right. Encourages public awareness of family planning and responsible parenthood. Works to reduce the number of unwanted pregnancies and abortions. Offers programs in sex education, family planning, and health care. Conducts research.

Iceland

★1891★ FAMILY PLANNING ADMINISTRATION - ICELAND
Frostaskjoli 32
I-107 Reykjavik, Iceland
Ms. Soley Bender, Contact   PH: 1 694980

Languages: Icelandic. **National.** Advocates family planning as a basic human right. Works to reduce the number of unwanted pregnancies and abortions. Encourages public awareness of family planning and responsible parenthood. Offers programs in sex education, family planning, and health. Conducts research.

★1892★ WOMAN'S ALLIANCE
(Kuennalistinn)
Lavgaveg 17
IS-101 Reykjavik, Iceland   PH: 1 13725
Ingibjorg Hafstad, Exec. Officer   FX: 1 27560

Founded: 1983. **Members:** 1,100. **Staff:** 3. **Local Groups:** 8. **Languages:**

English, Icelandic. **National**. Women in Iceland between the ages of 25 and 50 united to increase female representation in the Icelandic Parliament and national awareness of women's issues. Believes it is essential for women to be in policy-making positions in order to create national legislation that is founded in the experience and culture of women. Organizes fund-raising sales.

Conventions/Meetings: periodic meeting.

★1893★ WOMEN'S ASSOCIATION OF ICELAND
(Kvenretlindafelag Islands)
Hallbergarstooum
Tungotta 14
IS-101 Reykjavik, Iceland
Lara V. Julfusdottir, President

Languages: Icelandic. **National**. Promotes the interests of women in Iceland. Encourages cooperation and communication among women.

★1894★ YOUNG WOMEN'S CHRISTIAN ASSOCIATION - ICELAND
Aoalstoovar
KFUM og KFUK vio Holtaveg
IC-104 Reykjavik, Iceland
Dorarrin Bjornsson, Gen.Sec.   FX: 1 657414

National. Works to promote Chrsitain fellowhsip and service among young women in Iceland. Advocates unity, peace, and justice.

Ireland

★1895★ CAMOGIE ASSOCIATION
(Cumann Camogaiochta na n°Gael)
Pairc an Chrocaigh
Dublin 3, Ireland   PH: 1 726508
Sheila Wallace, Contact   FX: 1 366420

Founded: 1904. **Languages:** English, Gaelic. **National**. Provides girls and women of Ireland with the opportunity to participate in camogie, or hurling, a sport related to a version of field hockey. Promotes national culture and development of community spirit. Offers administrative, coaching, and refereeing programs. Sponsors competitions.

★1896★ CHERISH
2 Lower Pembroke St.
Dublin 2, Ireland   PH: 1 682744
Cora Pollard, Director   FX: 1 682184

Founded: 1972. **Staff:** 3. **Budget:** IR£55,000. **Languages:** English, French. **National**. Single mothers. Provides a support network to single mothers. Campaigns for legal reform to abolish the legal concept of illegitimacy and children's rights. Offers the following services: drop-in information center, weekly counselling meetings, courses in personal development, stress management guidance, health care programs, and seminars on how to disclose information to children about absentee parents. **Libraries:** Type: reference.

Publications: *Cherish News*, quarterly. Newsletter.

Conventions/Meetings: annual conference - Dublin, Ireland.

★1897★ COUNCIL FOR THE STATUS OF WOMEN
64 Lower Mount St.
Dublin 2, Ireland   PH: 1 607731

Languages: English. **National**. Works to enhance the political, economic, and social status of women in Ireland. Disseminates information.

★1898★ INTERNATIONAL FEDERATION OF FERTILITY SOCIETIES (IFFS)
c/o Prof. Robert F. Harrison
Rotunda Hospital, RCSI Dept. OB/GYN
Dublin 1, Ireland   PH: 1 727599
Prof. Robert F. Harrison, Sec.Gen.   FX: 431 5972149

Founded: 1953. **Languages:** English. **Multinational**. National fertility and sterility societies. Conducts congresses to study human reproduction and problems relating to fertility and sterility in humans and animals.

Publications: *International Journal of Fertility* (in English), quarterly.

Conventions/Meetings: triennial World Congress of Human Reproduction (exhibits)

★1899★ IRISH FAMILY PLANNING ASSOCIATION (IFPA)
Halfpenny Ct.
36-37 Lower Ormond Quay   PH: 1 730877
Dublin 1, Ireland   1 725394
Mr. Tony O'Brien, Exec. Dir.   FX: 1 726639

Languages: English. **National**. Works to improve the quality of life for individuals living in Ireland by promoting family planning and responsible parenthood. Advocates family planning as a basic human right. Offers programs in sex education, family planning, and health. Provides contraceptive and health care services. Conducts research.

★1900★ LADIES FOOTBALL ASSOCIATION IRELAND (ILFA)
32 Greencastle Park
Coolock   PH: 1 8479779
Dublin 17, Ireland   FX: 1 610931
Pauline O'Shaughnessy, Sec.   TX: 91397

Founded: 1970. **Members:** 4,000. **Budget:** IR£25,000. **Languages:** English. **National**. Soccer players and managers. Promotes ladies' soccer in Ireland. Encourages fellowship among players.

Conventions/Meetings: annual convention. ● quarterly meeting.

★1901★ MEDICAL WOMEN'S INTERNATIONAL ASSOCIATION - IRELAND (MWIA-I)
Knockoulart-Dublin Rd.
Shankill
Dublin, Ireland
Monica McWeeney, Contact

Languages: English. **National**. Irish national branch of the Medical Women's International Association (see separate entry). Women physicians. Provides a forum for discussion of women's health care issues. Encourages women to enter the field of medicine. Works to overcome discrimination against female physicians. Sponsors research and educational programs.

★1902★ MISSIONARY SISTERS OF OUR LADY OF THE HOLY ROSARY (MSHR)
c/o Sr. Therese Dillon
23 Cross Ave.
Blackrock, Dublin, Ireland
Sr. Therese Dillon, Superior Gen.   PH: 1 2881708

Founded: 1924. **Members:** 425. **Languages:** English. **Multinational**. Catholic sisters in Africa, Europe, and North and South America. Provides educational, medical, pastoral, and social services.

Publications: *Information Bulletin* (in English), bimonthly. ● *Vincula* (in English), bimonthly. Magazine. ● *The Second Burial of Bishop Shanahan* (in English). Book.

Conventions/Meetings: general assembly - every 6 years.

★1903★ NATIONAL ASSOCIATION OF WIDOWS - IRELAND
12 Upper Ormond Quay
Dublin 7, Ireland
Eileen Proctor, President

Languages: English. **National.** Represents the interests of widows. Makes available job training and placement, legal counseling, and discussion groups. Disseminates information.

★1904★ NATIONAL FEDERATION OF BUSINESS AND
PROFESSIONAL WOMEN'S CLUBS OF THE REPUBLIC IRELAND
29 Erne St.
Dublin 2, Ireland
Dr. Meda O'Callaghan Lehans, President   PH: 1 762966

Founded: 1960. **Languages:** English. **National.** Business and Professional women. Strives to improve the status of women in business and other professions. Encourages women to further their education. Seeks to help women to take part in public life.

Conventions/Meetings: monthly meeting. ● bimonthly conference.

★1905★ SISTERS OF STATION JOHN OF GOD (SSJG)
Spawell Rd.
Wexford, Ireland   PH: 53 42396
Sr. Columba Howard, Contact   FX: 53 41500

Founded: 1871. **Members:** 506. **Languages:** English, Gaelic. **Multinational.** Women religious in 6 countries. Provides educational, medical, pastoral, and social services.

★1906★ SISTERS OF STATION LOUIS (SSL)
(Soeurs de Saint Louis)
5 Grosvenor Rd.
Rathgar 6, Dublin, Ireland   PH: 1 977974
Sr. Anita Muldowney SSL, Gen.Sec. FX: 1 977774

Founded: 1842. **Members:** 558. **Languages:** English, French, Portuguese. **Multinational.** Women religious ministering in Belgium, Brazil, England, France, Ghana, Nigeria, Republic of Ireland, and the United States. Promotes the Christian values of justice, freedom, peace, and dignity. Serves the poor through education and medical assistance; provides counseling. Performs ecumenical work, especially for the good of the poor and the handicapped.

Publications: *Link* (in English), quarterly. Newsletter. ● *Newsletter* (in English), quarterly.

Conventions/Meetings: general assembly - every 6 years. ● annual regional meeting. ● annual meeting, interregional.

★1907★ WOMEN IN DEVELOPMENT EUROPE (WIDE)
c/o Irish Commission for Justice and
   Peace
169 Booterstown Ave.
Blackrock, Dublin, Ireland
Pauline Eccles, Acting Coord.

Founded: 1985. **Multinational.** All women working in NGOs in Europe and who support WIDE. Provides a forum for the exchange of information and bulid up more expertise on issues of importance to women's development needs in developing countries. Encourages and strengthens the national networks, development policies, priorities, especially in Southern Europe. Promotes purposeful contacts with women in partner countries so that their development priorities will become guiding principles of the organizations' activities. Lobbies European and international institutions.

Publications: *WIDE Bulletin*, quarterly. Current events.

Conventions/Meetings: annual meeting. ● quarterly executive committee meeting.

★1908★ WOMEN IN THE HOME (WITH)
12 Springfield Rd.
Templeogue
Dublin 6, Ireland
Norah T. Gilligan, Chairwoman   PH: 1 906778

Founded: 1981. **Members:** 300. **Budget:** IR£1,000. **Languages:** English. **National.** Women homemakers. Supports and encourages women who choose to stay at home to care for their families. Works to achieve equality for women working in the home. Establishes friendship groups for homemakers within their communities and functions as a forum for women to express opinions and influence society. Disseminates information. Conducts seminars and meetings.

Publications: *Report*. Newsletter.

Conventions/Meetings: annual general assembly.

★1909★ WOMEN'S AID
17A Sallymount Ave.
Ranelagh
Dublin 6, Ireland

National. Organizes programs and activities which further the advancement and development of women. Provides financial assistance, counseling, training, and advocacy services for women in need.

★1910★ WORLD FEDERATION OF METHODIST WOMEN (WFMW)
Inglenook
Royal Terrace Ln.
Dun Laoghaire, Dublin, Ireland   PH: 1 2803488
Edith W. Loane, Pres.   FX: (504)947-4018

Founded: 1939. **Members:** 6,000,000. **Budget:** US$30,000. **Regional Groups:** 9. **National Groups:** 64. **Languages:** English. **Multinational.** Methodist women in 64 countries. Promotes peace among nations, the establishment of human rights, and the elimination of discrimination against women in all countries. Conducts evangelistic activities, including healing ministries, and provides educational and social services. Exchanges information on religious, social, and economic concerns and issues related to women in the Third World. Organizes literacy and translation programs; develops counseling and educational programs on family issues such as training in food production, hygiene, causes of malnutrition, and family planning; enactment of legislation to prevent child abuse. Provides children's services. Conducts regional seminars.

Publications: *Handbook*, quinquennial. ● *Program Material*, annual. Booklet. ● *Tree of Life*, quarterly. Newsletter. ● *Methodist Women: A World Sisterhood*. Book.

Conventions/Meetings: quinquennial conference

★1911★ YOUNG WOMEN'S CHRISTIAN ASSOCIATION - IRELAND
49 St. John's Rd.
Sandymount 4, Dublin, Ireland
Daphne Murphy, Contact   PH: 1 2692205

National. Works to promote Christian fellowship and service among young women in Ireland. Advocates justice, peace, and unity.

Italy

★1912★ CARMELITE MISSIONARIES (CM)
(Carmelitans Missionarie)
Via del Casaletto 115
I-00151 Rome, Italy   PH: 6 535472
Sr. Maria Pilar Miguel Garcia, Sec.Gen. FX: 6 532279

Founded: 1860. **Members:** 1,830. **Regional Groups:** 235. **Languages:**

English, Spanish. **Multinational**. Roman Catholic women in 30 countries. Provides primary and secondary education; maintains health centers, hospitals, missions, mobile clinics, and welfare centers.

Publications: *Shelahani* (in English, French, and Spanish), annual.

Conventions/Meetings: convention - every 6 years. 1994, Rome, Italy.

★1913★ CONGREGATION OF OUR LADY OF THE RETREAT IN THE CENACLE (RC)
(Congregation de Notre Dame de la Retraite au Cenacle)
Piazza Madonna del Cenacolo 15
I-00136 Rome, Italy
Sr. Barbara Ehrler, Superior Gen.   PH: 6 3420054

Founded: 1826. **Members:** 838. **National Groups:** 12. **Languages:** English, French. **Multinational**. Congregation of Roman Catholic women. Members seek to awaken and deepen the faith of those they serve. Offers retreats for groups, individual spiritual direction, and religious education for people of all ages, especially adults.

★1914★ CONSIGLIO NAZIONALE DELLE DONNE ITALIANE
Via della Moscova 40/5
I-20121 Milan, Italy   PH: 2 29001235
Prof. Maria Pia Roggero, President   FX: 2 70632094

Languages: Italian. **National**. Umbrella organization for women's groups in Italy. Promotes the interests of women. Coordinates activities for women. Disseminates information on women's issues.

★1915★ DIP DONNA
P.za S. Salvatore in Lauro 15
I-00186 Rome, Italy   PH: 6 4451736
Gabriella Angelini, Chair   FX: 6 4998234

Founded: 1988. **Members:** 220. **Budget:** 110,000,000 Lr. **Languages:** English. **National**. Women professionals. Strives to elevate the status of women in society.

Publications: *Newsletter*, periodic.

Conventions/Meetings: annual congress.

★1916★ DISCALCED CARMELITE NUNS (DCN)
Corso d'Italia 38   PH: 6 8416578
I-00198 Rome, Italy   FX: 6 8440758

Founded: 1568. **Members:** 13,026. **Languages:** English, French, Italian, Spanish, Latin. **Multinational**. Catholic women in 77 countries. A branch of the Discalced Brothers of the Most Blessed Virgin Mary of Mount Carmel.

★1917★ EUROPEAN ASSOCIATION FOR THE DEVELOPMENT OF INFORMATION AND TRAINING OF WOMEN - ITALY (EUDIFF)
(Associazione Europea per lo Sviluppo dell'Informazione e della Formazione delle Donne - Italy)
Via Romagnosi 3
I-20121 Milan, Italy
Elvira Badaracco, Contact   PH: 2 874175

Languages: Italian. **National**. Circulates information on women and women's issues throughout Italy. Networks with organizations that also champion women's advancment. Demands that EC nations fully recognize women's rights. Supports women's development and equality; encourages women's participation in leadership roles. Facilitates exchange among members.

★1918★ FEDEREZIONE ITALIANA DONNE ARTI PROFESSIONI AFFARI (FIDAPA)
Via Roma 12
90133 I-Palermo, Italy
Eugenia Bono, President   PH: 91 6174653

Founded: 1930. **Members:** 9,000. **Languages:** Italian, English. **National**. Women professionals. Promotes mutual cooperation and understanding among professional women.

Publications: *Notiziario FIDAPA*, quarterly. Bulletin. ● *Widening Horizens*, semiannual. Newsletter. ● *FIDAPA Story*. Book.

Conventions/Meetings: annual general assembly.

★1919★ FRANCISCAN SISTERS OF PENANCE AND CHRISTIAN CHARITY (OSF)
(Franciscaines de la Peratence et de la Charite Chretienne)
Via Cassia 870
I-00189 Rome, Italy   PH: 6 3660335
Sr. Marietta Miller, Gen.Sec.   FX: 6 3652855

Founded: 1835. **Members:** 2,455. **Regional Groups:** 10. **Languages:** Dutch, English, German, Indonesian, Polish, Portuguese. **Multinational**. Women religious in 7 countries.

Conventions/Meetings: periodic convention.

★1920★ INTERNATIONAL FEDERATION OF WOMEN IN LEGAL AFFAIRS (FIFCY)
(Federation Internationale des Femmes des Carrieres Juridiques)
c/o Ms. Teresa Assension Brugiatelli
Via R. Giovagnoli 6
I-00152 Rome, Italy
Teresa Assensio Brugiatelli, President   PH: 6 5818107

Founded: 1928. **Members:** 195. **Budget:** 50,000 Lr. **Languages:** French, Spanish. **Multinational**. Women's groups and individual women. Concerned with human rights issues, especially that of women and children. Involved with legislation and legal matters.

Conventions/Meetings: annual congress.

★1921★ INTERNATIONAL RIGHT TO LIFE FEDERATION
44 Via Nicolo V.
I-00165 Rome, Italy
William Sherwin, Secretary   PH: 6 6380955

Languages: Italian. **National**. Individuals united to oppose abortion. Disseminates information on the potential health risks resulting from abortion.

★1922★ ISTITUTO INTERNAZIONALE SUORE DI SANTA MARCELLINA (ISM)
Piazza Cardinal Andrea Ferrari 5
I-20122 Milan, Italy   PH: 2 58306661
Sr. Maria Paola Albertario, Superior Gen.   FX: 2 55183049

Founded: 1838. **Members:** 902. **Staff:** 5. **Regional Groups:** 2. **Languages:** English, French, Italian, Portuguese, Spanish. **Multinational**. Professed sisters dedicated to religious education at all levels of instruction. Activities include apostolic work in hospitals, missionary programs, and charitable services. **Alternate name:** Istituto Marcelline.

★1923★ ISTITUTO DELLE SUORE MAESTRE DI SANTA DOROTEA (ISMSD)
Casa Generalizia
Via Raffaele Conforti 25
I-00166 Rome, Italy
Sr. Giovanna Lia Sardella, Sec.Gen.   PH: 6 6224041

Founded: 1838. **Members:** 876. **Multinational**. Roman Catholic religious women in Bolivia, Italy, and Zaire who prepare young people, particularly women, for leadership. Offers instruction in rural parochial and scholastic settings, providing spiritual and educational assistance, and striving to develop leaders who have been "risen" within the Christian community.

★1924★ ITALIAN ASSOCIATION FOR WOMEN IN DEVELOPMENT
(AIDOS)
Via dei Giubbonari 30
I-00186 Rome, Italy   PH: 6 6873214

Encourages women's participation in development projects. Works to improve women's economic status and access to education. Promotes preservation of the natural environment. Disseminates information on the dangers of female genital mutilation. Liaises with women's development organizations in third world countries. Maintains documentation center.

Publications: AIDoS News (in Italian), bimonthly. Newsletter. Circulation: 2,000. ● Newsletter (in English), annual.

Conventions/Meetings: periodic meeting.

★1925★ ITALY: WOMEN AND DEVELOPMENT NGO COORDINATION
(Coordinamento ONG Donne e Sviluppo)
Via Raffaele Cadorna 29
I-00187 Rome, Italy

Founded: 1984. Languages: Italian, English. National. Coordinates activities of nongovernmental organizations and local women's development groups. Facilitates solidarity and cooperation among women of the North and South to promote mutual understanding and problem solving. Unites women interested in international affairs. Maintains computerized documentation center. Conducts research; disseminates information.

★1926★ LITTLE SISTERS OF JESUS (LSJ)
(PSJ Petites Soeurs de Jesus)
Via Acque Salvie 2
Tre Fontane
I-00142 Rome, Italy
Sr. Mariyananda, Gen.Asst.   PH: 6 5925425

Founded: 1939. Members: 1,400. National Groups: 60. Languages: English, French. Multinational. Catholic women. Promotes contemplative religious life without monastic structure as inspired by Charles de Foucauld. Provides spiritual aid through residence and work to underprivileged populations throughout the world.

★1927★ MEDICAL WOMEN'S INTERNATIONAL ASSOCIATION - ITALY
L.B. Alberti 5
I-20149 Milan, Italy
Elvira Galluzi Camozzi, Contact

Languages: Italian. National. Italian national branch of the Medical Women's International Association (see separate entry). Women physicians. Provides a forum for discussion of women's health care issues. Encourages women to enter the field of medicine. Works to overcome discrimination against female physicians. Sponsors research and educational programs.

★1928★ MISSIONARY SISTERS OF THE CATHOLIC APOSTOLATE
(SAC)
(Suore Missionarie dell'Apostolato Cattolico)
Viale delle Mura Aurelie 7 B
I-00165 Rome, Italy   PH: 6 383635
Sr. Maria Knaus SAC, Superior Gen.   FX: 6 39379157

Founded: 1838. Members: 756. Languages: English, German, Italian. Multinational. Catholic sisters. Follows the teachings of St. Vincent Pallotti (1795-1850). Activities include nursing, teaching, and providing youth and social services.

Conventions/Meetings: general assembly - every 6 years.

★1929★ MISSIONARY SISTERS OF THE IMMACULATE HEART OF MARY (ICM)
(Soeurs Missionaires du Coeur Immacule de Marie)
Casa Generalizia
Via di Villa Troili 30
I-00163 Rome, Italy
Sr. Lieve Haentjens, Gen.Sec.   PH: 6 66417156

Founded: 1897. Members: 1,052. Local Groups: 11. Languages: English, French, Flemish. Multinational. Women religious in 20 countries. Conducts mission work.

Publications: Directory, annual. ● Focus, 5/year. Bulletin.

★1930★ MISSIONARY SISTERS OF THE PRECIOUS BLOOD (CPS)
(Missions°schwestern von Kostbaren Blut)
Via San Giovanni Eudes 93
I-00163 Rome, Italy
Sr. M. Manuela Randerath CPS,   PH: 6 66158559
  Superior Gen.   FX: 6 66158559

Founded: 1885. Members: 1,059. Regional Groups: 3. Languages: Dutch, English, French, German, Portuguese. Multinational. Roman Catholic nuns and novices in 17 countries who have taken vows to work as missionaries. Seeks to evangelize non-Christian societies.

★1931★ MISSIONARY SISTERS OF THE SOCIETY OF MARY (MSSM)
(SMSM Soeurs Missionaires de la Societe de Marie)
Via Cassia 1243
I-00189 Rome, Italy
Aileen Lanigan, Sec.Gen.   PH: 6 3767867

Founded: 1845. Members: 700. Languages: English, French. Multinational. Religious women in 26 countries. Activities include missionary work.

★1932★ MISSIONARY SISTERS OF STATION PETER CLAVER (SSPC)
(Suore Missionarie di San Pietro Claver)
Via dell'Olmata 16
I-00184 Rome, Italy
Mother M. Immacolata Nihoul, Superior   PH: 6 4880450
  Gen.   FX: 6 4871953

Founded: 1894. Members: 250. Languages: English, Italian, Spanish. Multinational. Religious women in 20 countries. Offers material and spiritual assistance to Catholic missions. Operates museum in Switzerland. Libraries: Type: reference. Holdings: 5,000.

Publications: Almanac (in English, French, German, Italian, Polish, Portuguese, and Spanish), periodic. Booklet. ● Echo from Africa and other Continents (in Dutch, English, French, German, Italian, Polish, Portuguese, and Spanish), periodic. Magazine.

★1933★ MOVIMENTO FEMMINILE REPUBBLICANO
c/o Partito Repubblicano Italiano
Piazza dei Caprettari 70
I-00186 Rome, Italy   PH: 6 6834037
Gabriella Poma, Sec.   FX: 6 6834039

Founded: 1945. Members: 10,000. Budget: 80,000,000 Lr. Regional Groups: 20. Languages: English, Italian. National. Political organization supporting women's rights in Italy; branch of the Italian Republican Party. Libraries: Type: reference. Holdings: 200. Subjects: women's studies. Computer Services: Data base.

Conventions/Meetings: annual conference.

★1934★ ORDER OF THE COMPANY OF MARY OUR LADY
(Ordine de la Campagnia di Maria Nostra Signora)
Via Nomentana 333
I-00162 Rome, Italy PH: 6 8417675
Maria Nieves Guerrero, Exec. Officer FX: 6 8412624

Founded: 1607. **Members:** 2,312. **Languages:** English, French, Spanish. **Multinational.** Catholic women in 19 countries. Activities include teaching and social work, especially among youth.

Conventions/Meetings: general assembly - every 6 years.

★1935★ PIOUS SOCIETY OF THE DAUGHTERS OF SAINT PAUL
(FSP)
(Figlia de San Paolo)
Via San Giovanni Eudes 25
I-00163 Rome, Italy PH: 6 66161000
Sr. Clorinda Carrara, Superior Gen. FX: 6 66157208

Founded: 1915. **Members:** 2,628. **Languages:** Chinese, English, French, Italian, Japanese, Korean, Portuguese, Spanish. **Multinational.** Professed sisters and religious congregations in 37 countries. Fosters evangelization.

Conventions/Meetings: meeting - every 6 years.

★1936★ SCHOOL SISTERS OF NOTRE DAME (SSND)
(Armen Schulschwestern von Unserer Lieben Frau)
PH: 6 66418065
Via della Stazione Aurelia 95 FX: 6 66411212
I-00165 Rome, Italy TX: MADONNA 00165
Sr. Patricia Flynn SSND, Gen. Superior ROMA

Founded: 1833. **Members:** 6,345. **Regional Groups:** 3. **National Groups:** 21. **Languages:** English, German. **Multinational.** Catholic women in 33 countries. Promotes religious life and teaching. Provides: staffing for women's colleges and residences; information to mothers in developing nations; courses on prayer and theology; basic elementary and secondary education; an alternative high school for girls; services to the elderly and education for the handicapped; ministry to the sick.

Publications: *Generalate News* (in English and German), periodic. Newsletter.

Conventions/Meetings: quinquennial meeting

★1937★ SISTERS OF CHARITY OF SAINTS BARTHOLOMEW
CAPITANIO AND VINCENT GEROSA (SCSBCVG)
(Suore di Carita delle Sante Bartholomea Capitanio e Vincenza Gerosa)
Via S. Sofia 13 PH: 2 58306230
I-20122 Milan, Italy FX: 2 58306174

Founded: 1932. **Members:** 6,450. **Languages:** English, Italian, Spanish. **Multinational.** Women religious. Activities include social and pastoral work in schools and hospitals. Provides educational programs and children's services.

Conventions/Meetings: general assembly - every 6 years.

★1938★ SISTERS OF CHARITY OF STATION JEANNE ANTIDE
THOURET (SCSJAT)
(Soeurs de la Charite de Sainte Jeanne Antide Thouret)
Via Santa Maria in Cosmedin 5 PH: 6 5746328
I-00153 Rome, Italy FX: 6 5757217

Founded: 1799. **Members:** 4,435. **Multinational.** Women religious in 21 countries. Offers charitable assistance to the spiritually and/or materially destitute.

★1939★ SISTERS OF CHRISTIAN CHARITY (SCC)
(Suore della Carita Cristiana)
Via di Boccea 761
I-00166 Rome, Italy PH: 6 6960829
Mother Gregoris Michels, Superior Gen. FX: 6 6962852

Founded: 1849. **Members:** 1,151. **Regional Groups:** 5. **National Groups:** 7. **Languages:** English, German, Italian, Spanish. **Multinational.** Religious women in the service of the Catholic church. Provides Catholic education on elementary, secondary, and college levels; sponsors retreats, catechesis, and pastoral ministry; serves the blind and handicapped. Areas of concern include health services, homemaking, and care for the poor, orphaned, and elderly. **Libraries:** Type: reference. Holdings: 3,500.

Publications: *Mother Pauline Leaflet*, 3/year. Bulletin. ● *Our Heritage*, semiannual. Magazine. ● *Paulinenbrief*, semiannual. Newsletter.

Conventions/Meetings: general assembly - every 6 years. ● periodic conference.

★1940★ SISTERS OF THE GOOD SHEPHERD (SGS)
(SBP Suore del Buon Pastore)
Via Raffaello Sardiello 20
I-00165 Rome, Italy PH: 6 66418545
Sr. Gabriela Botelho, Gen.Sec. FX: 6 66418864

Founded: 1835. **Members:** 6,218. **Languages:** English, French, German, Italian, Portuguese, Spanish. **Multinational.** Catholic women in 64 countries. Dedicated to promoting and addressing the social needs of women and children. Conducts charitable programs.

Publications: *Newsletter* (in Dutch, English, French, German, Italian, Japanese, Portuguese, Spanish, and Tamil), quarterly.

Conventions/Meetings: periodic convention.

★1941★ SISTERS OF NOTRE DAME DE NAMUR (SNDN)
(Suore di Nostra Signora di Namur)
c/o Sr. Ellen Gielty
Via Monte Altissimo 23
I-00141 Rome, Italy PH: 6 8922473
Sr. Ellen Gielty, Gen. Moderator FX: 6 891837

Founded: 1804. **Members:** 2,545. **Languages:** English, Flemish, French, Japanese, Portuguese, Spanish. **Multinational.** Catholic women in 14 countries. Provides religious, social, and educational services.

Publications: *Forum* (in English, Flemish, French, and Japanese), 3/year. Newsletter. ● *Quinilog* (in English, Flemish, French, Italian, Portuguese, and Spanish), 3/year. Newsletter. **Advertising:** not accepted. ● *International Directory Sisters of Notre Dame de Namur* (in English), annual.

★1942★ SISTERS OF STATION FRANCIS OF DILLINGEN (SSFD)
(SFD Suore Francescane di Dillingen)
Casa Generalizia
Via della Storta 783
I-00123 Rome, Italy
Sr. M. Irmtraud Eichelbronner, Superior PH: 6 3790080
Gen. FX: 6 3715697

Founded: 1241. **Members:** 1,323. **Regional Groups:** 1. **Languages:** English, German, Italian, Portuguese. **Multinational.** Catholic women in Brazil, Germany, India, Italy, Spain, Switzerland, and the United States. Members take vows of poverty, celibacy, and obedience, and are devoted to prayer and charitable works, especially for the good of the poor. Activities include: elementary, secondary, and vocational education; special education for the mentally and physically handicapped; care of the ill and aged; social services to families.

Conventions/Meetings: triennial general assembly

★1943★ SISTERS OF STATION JOHN THE BAPTIST (SSJB)
(CSSGB Congregazione Suore di San Giovanni Baptiste)
Circonvallazione Cornelia 65
I-00165 Rome, Italy
Rev. Mother Immacolata M. Vicidomini,
  Superior Gen.   PH: 6 6216445

Founded: 1878. **Members:** 420. **Regional Groups:** 6. **National Groups:** 9.
Languages: English, Italian, Portuguese, Spanish. **Multinational.** Women religious. Evangelizes and works for the development of young people, particularly those who are most needy. Engages in mission work in developing countries.

Publications: *ECHO* (in English, Italian, Portuguese, and Spanish), quarterly. Magazine. ● *Newsletter* (in English, Italian, Portuguese, and Spanish), monthly.

Conventions/Meetings: periodic general assembly

★1944★ SOCIETY OF STATION TERESA OF JESUS (STJ)
(Compania de Santa Teresa de Jesus)
Via Val Cannuta 134
I-00166 Rome, Italy   PH: 6 6637053
Sr. Mercedes Martin STJ, Sec.Gen.   FX: 6 6635750

Founded: 1876. **Members:** 1,936. **Languages:** English, French, Italian, Portuguese, Spanish. **Multinational.** Roman Catholic sisters in 20 countries. Conducts pastoral ministry. Provides primary, secondary, and junior college level education. Maintains missions and medical dispensary. Offers spiritual assistance. **Committees:** Educacion; Formacion; Missions; Vocaciones.

Publications: *Boletin STJ* (in Spanish and Portuguese), bimonthly. Bulletin. ● *Jesus Maestro* (in Spanish), monthly. Newsletter.

★1945★ UNIONE DONNE ITALIANE (UDI)
Via della Colonna Antonina   PH: 6 543492
I-00186 Rome, Italy   6 865884
Rosanna Marcodoppido, Contact   FX: 6 543492

Founded: 1944. **Members:** 50,000. **Budget:** 160,000,000 Lr. **Languages:** Italian, French. **National.** Fosters solidarity among Italian women in pursuit of the full recognition of women's rights in Italy.

Publications: *Noi Donne* (in Italian), monthly. Newsletter.

Conventions/Meetings: periodic meeting.

★1946★ UNIONE ITALIANA CENTRI EDUCAZIONE MATRIMONIALE E
  PREMATRIMONIALE (UICEMP)
Via Eugenio Chiesa 1
I-20122 Milan, Italy   PH: 2 783915
Ms. Antonietta Corradini, Secretary   FX: 2 5460758

Languages: Italian. **National.** Acts as an advocate for family planning and responsible parenthood. Promotes family planning as a basic human right and a means to improve the quality of life for individuals living in Italy. Works to stop the spread of AIDS and other sexually transmitted diseases. Offers programs in family planning, sex education, and health. Provides contraceptive services. Conducts research.

★1947★ WOMEN'S WORLD BANKING - ITALY (WWB)
Via S. Sofia 9/1
I-20122 Milan, Italy   PH: 2 58304820
Dr. Maria Grazia Randi, Contact   FX: 2 58304833

Founded: 1985. **Budget:** US$300,000. **Languages:** Italian, French, English. **National.** Financial institutions in Italy. Works to help securing financing for women in Italy with no credit and/or financial history. Lobbies government and financial institutions to change laws against women in private enterprise. Supports and encourages women entrepreneurs. Conducts training. **Committees:** Technical-Scientific; Formative Programs; Support New Entrepreneurships; International Programming.

Publications: *What Works: A Women's World Banking Newsletter*-New York. ● *Bulletin*, periodic.

★1948★ WORLD ASSOCIATION OF WOMEN ENTREPRENEURS
  (FCEM)
(Femmes Chefs d'Enterprises Mondiales)
Corso Europa 14   PH: 2 76021915
I-20122 Milan, Italy   FX: 2 780803
Maria Grazia Randi, Pres.   TX: 15223123 DEAMB I

Founded: 1946. **Members:** 28. **Languages:** English, French, German, Italian, Spanish. **Multinational.** National associations representing 33,000 women who own and manage their own businesses or who are managing directors of companies in which they have invested capital. Works to improve the professional status of women in industry; seeks professional recognition by national and official international entities. Facilitates access to the committees and boards of federations and other economic organizations; creates friendship and business links among members. Fosters exchange of experiences in different sectors of the economy. Sponsors seminars and workshops on financial and economic topics. Bestows awards.

Publications: *FCEM Directory*, periodic. ● *FCEM News*, 3/year. Newsletter.

Conventions/Meetings: annual congress (exhibits) - England.

★1949★ YOUNG WOMEN'S CHRISTIAN ASSOCIATION - ITALY
(Unione Cristiana Delle Giovani)
c/o Mirelle Bein
Corso Gramsci 3
I-10066 Torre Pellice, Italy
Mirelle Bein, Contact   PH: 12 191205

National. Works to promote Christian fellowship and service among young women in Italy. Advocates justice, peace, and unity.

Luxembourg

★1950★ ASSOCIATION DES FEMMES LIBERALES
5, rue Jean Webster
L-8273 Mamer, Luxembourg
Marcelle Sauber, Contact

Languages: French. **National.** Promotes the interests of women liberals in Luxembourg.

★1951★ CENTRE D'INFORMATION ET DE DOCUMENTATION DES
  FEMMES 'THERS BODE' (CID)
66, rue de Hollerich
L-1740 Luxembourg, Luxembourg
Danielle Roster, Contact   PH: 490583

Founded: 1992. **Members:** 350. **Staff:** 1. **Budget:** 400,000 LFr. **Languages:** French, German. **National.** Works to bring about public awareness of women's issues. Encourages research on the history and recent developments of the feminist movement. Supports women active in the arts, literature, and science, and provides opportunities for them to reveal their creations and findings to the public. Cooperates with other organizations and centers with similar objectives. **Libraries:** Type: reference. Holdings: books, periodicals, audio recordings, video recordings.

Publications: *Diese Stunden des Selbstvergessens* (in German). Book.

Conventions/Meetings: semiannual conference.

★1952★ CHRISTIAN SOCIAL WOMEN (CSW)
(CSF Femmes Chretiennes-Sociales)
4, rue de l'Eau   PH: 225731
L-1449 Luxembourg, Luxembourg   FX: 472716
Viviane Reding, President   TX: 60187 CSVGPLU

Founded: 1960. **Members:** 4,000. **Languages:** French, English. **National.** Women with political interests. Promotes women's issues in the political forum. Works to protect women's rights. Encourages Christian ideals. **Also Known As:** Christlich-Soziale Volkspartei, Europaische Volkspartei.

Conventions/Meetings: annual congress.

★1953★ CONSEIL NATIONAL DES FEMMES LUXEMBOURGEOISES
(CNFL)
BP 160
Luxembourg, Luxembourg   PH: 4772210
Mme. Ginette Schaak-Etienne, President   FX: 477202

Founded: 1975. **Members:** 10. **Languages:** French, English. **National.** Promotes the interests of women living in Luxembourg. Encourages protection of women's rights. Offers legal counsel to women.

Conventions/Meetings: monthly congress.

★1954★ EUROPEAN CENTRE OF THE INTERNATIONAL COUNCIL OF WOMEN (ECICW)
(CECIF Centre Europeen du Conseil International des Femmes)
     PH: 548256
28 Chemin Vert   548113
L-3878 Schifflange, Luxembourg   FX: 49921
Mme. Astrid Lulling, President   TX: 2985

Multinational. Umbrella organization for European women's groups. Promotes and supports women and women's groups. Coordinates activities among organizations. Disseminates information on women's issues. **Foreign language name:** Centro Europeo del Consejo Internacional de Mujeres.

★1955★ FEDERATION LUXEMBOURGEOISE DES FEMMES UNIVERSITAIRES
20, Cote d'Eich
L-1450 Luxembourg, Luxembourg
A. Schwall-Lacroix, Contact

National. Represents women who are students and graduates of universities. Encourages women's pursuit of higher education.

★1956★ FEDERATION NATIONALE DES FEMMES LUXEMBOURGEOISES
2, allee L. Goebel
L-1635 Luxembourg, Luxembourg
Ginette Schaack, Contact   PH: 444864

National. Promotes the interests of women in Luxembourg.

★1957★ FEMMES EN DETRESSE
BP 1024   PH: 490051
L-10 Luxembourg, Luxembourg   448181
Sylvie Vandivinit, President   FX: 406111

Founded: 1979. **Members:** 30. **Staff:** 25. **Budget:** 25,000 LFr. **Languages:** French. **National.** Provides financial and emotional support to women who are victims of domestic violence. Offers programs for single parents. Sponsors vocational training programs for women. Encourages public awareness of the problem of domestic violence. **Libraries:** Type: reference. Subjects: women's issues, especially domestic violence.

Publications: *Directory*, annual.

Conventions/Meetings: bimonthly conference.

★1958★ FEMMES AU PRESENT
1, rue E. Verhaeren
L-2660 Luxembourg, Luxembourg
Mady Molitor, Contact

National. Seeks to enhance women's status. Fosters communication among women throughout Luxembourg.

★1959★ FEMMES SOCIALISTES LUXEMBOURGEOISES (FS)
16, rue de Crecy
L-1364 Luxembourg, Luxembourg   PH: 455991
Lydie Err, Sec.Gen.   456575

Founded: 1972. **Members:** 1,500. **Languages:** German, French, English. **National.** Women of all backgrounds and social classes who support the ideals of the Socialist Party. Works to improve the quality of life for women living in Luxembourg. Promotes equal rights for men and women in society, at the workplace, and before the law. Supports policies that protect the worker.

Publications: *Femmes Contre le Harcelement Sexuel* (in French). Book.

Conventions/Meetings: quarterly convention (exhibits). ● annual congress (exhibits).

★1960★ MOUVEMENT LUXEMBOURGEOIS POUR LE PLANNING FAMILIAL ET L'EDUCATION SEXUELLE (MLPFES)
18-20, rue Glesener
L-1630 Luxembourg, Luxembourg
Ms. Gaby Delvaux, Contact   PH: 485976

Languages: French. **National.** Promotes family planning as a means to enhance the quality of life for individuals living in Luxembourg. Works to reduce the number of unwanted pregnancies and abortions. Attempts to stop the spread of AIDS and other sexually transmitted diseases. Offers programs in sex education, family planning, and health. Provides contraceptive and health care services. Conducts research.

★1961★ UNION DES DAMES ISRAELITES
34, rue Marechal-Foch
L-1527 Luxembourg, Luxembourg
Liliane David-Schlanger, Contact

National. Promotes unity among Israeli women living in Luxembourg.

★1962★ UNION DES FEMMES LUXEMBOURGEOISES (UFL)
113, route d'Arlon
L-8009 Strassen, Luxembourg
Christiane Meier, Secretary

Founded: 1945. **Members:** 700. **Languages:** Luxembourgish, German, French. **National.** A union organization comprised mainly of working-class women. Originally founded after WWII by female members of the resistence. Offers financial and moral support to women. Actively participates in legal projects that are in support of the needs of women. **Libraries:** Type: reference. Holdings: archival material.

Publications: *Newspaper*, periodic. ● *Fra & Mensch* (in Luxembourgish), periodic. Magazine.

Conventions/Meetings: bimonthly executive committee meeting.

★1963★ UNION LUXEMBOURGEOISE DU SOROPTIMIST INTERNATIONAL
17, rue des Chevaliers
L-5817 Fentange/Plateau, Luxembourg
Carmen Watgen-Mommer, Contact

National. Women engaged in business and professional occupations in Luxembourg. Seeks to elevate the status of women and to develop a spirit of friendship and unity among members. Promotes high ethical standards, human rights, goodwill, and peace.

Malta

★1964★ NATIONAL COUNCIL OF WOMEN - MALTA
23 St. Andrew St.
Valletta, Malta
Dolores Cristina, President   PH: 246982

National. Umbrella organization for women's groups in Malta. Supports and promotes women's interests. Coordinates activities for women. Disseminates information on women's issues.

Netherlands

★1965★ BOND VAN OUD-KATHOLIEKE VROUWEN IN NEDERLAND
Kon. Wilhelminalaan 3
NL-3818 HN Amersfoort, Netherlands
C.J.W Homan-Copper, Chair

Founded: 1927. **Members:** 400. **Budget:** 15,000 f. **Languages:** Dutch, English, German. **National**. Women from the 16 parishes of the Old Catholic church in the Netherlands. Seeks to enhance members' sense of personal responsibility to the church and community. Conducts educational and cultural activities. Fosters communication among members.

Publications: *ONS Contact* (in Dutch), monthly. Newsletter.

Conventions/Meetings: annual general assembly.

★1966★ DUTCH ORGANIZATION FOR SEXUAL REFORM
(Nederlandse Vereniging voor Sexuele Hervorming)
Postbus 64
NL-2501 CB The Hague, Netherlands
U. Teunis, Secretary   PH: 70 3469709

Founded: 1946. **Members:** 4,000. **Staff:** 2. **Budget:** 200,000 f. **Languages:** English. **National**. Individuals working for sexual reform in the Netherlands. Promotes and supports gender equality and sexual emancipation for women. Conducts political lobbying, discussion groups, and social meetings. Operates a telephone service for information on sexual issues.

Publications: *Sesctant* (in Danish), bimonthly.

Conventions/Meetings: monthly meeting (exhibits) - Netherlands.

★1967★ EUROPEAN NETWORK FOR POLICEWOMEN
Postbus 1102
NL-3800 BC Amersfoort, Netherlands   PH: 33 654019
Anita Hazenberg, Coord.   FX: 33 654083

Founded: 1989. **Staff:** 1. **Languages:** Dutch, French, Italian, Spanish, German, English. **Multinational**. Seeks to enhance the status of female police officers throughout Europe. Fosters mutual support and exchange of experiences among female police officers. Supports international research on topics of interest to policewomen. Encourages formation of national networks of policewomen.

Publications: *Facts, Figures and General Information about Policewomen in Europe* (in English). Book. ISBN:90-74260-02-0. ● *Newsletter*, quarterly. **ISSN:** 0924-7300. ● *Equal Treatment of Policewomen in the European Community*. Book. ISBN: 90-74260-01-2. ● *Everything You Always Wanted to Know about Policewomen but Were Afraid to Ask*. Videos.

Conventions/Meetings: biennial conference. ● annual meeting.

★1968★ FOUNDATION AGAINST TRAFFICKING OF WOMEN (FATW)
(STVH Stichting Tegen Vrouwen Handel)
Postbus 97799
NL-2509 GD The Hague, Netherlands
Marjan Wyers, Contact   PH: 70 324080

Founded: 1987. **Staff:** 3. **Budget:** US$150,000. **Local Groups:** 7. **Languages:** Dutch, English, Spanish. **National**. Individuals united to support victims of and bring an end to the trafficking of women. Coordinates the efforts of groups throughout the Netherlands working to end trafficking of women. According to the group, women are brought to the Netherlands under false pretenses and forced into indentured servitude as prostitutes. Their illegal alien status prevents appeals to the police, and threats against their family coerce good behavior. Seeks to: influence policy-making to eliminate the trafficking of women; furnish topical information to governments, organizations, and the public; foster research and create a network of concerned organizations and individuals. Maintains library of 800 volumes.

Publications: *Newsletter*, monthly. ● *Jaarverslag 1987-1988*. ● *Tussin Migrant en Handelswaar/Anne Vondeling Stichting*.

★1969★ FOUNDATION FOR WOMEN AND THE USE OF MEDICATION
(Stichting Vrouwen en Medicijngebruik)
Poeijersstraat 50
NL-5642 GD Eindhoven, Netherlands
Mrs. Ineke Thomeer, Contact   PH: 40 812292

Founded: 1980. **Staff:** 10. **Budget:** 50,000 f. **Languages:** Dutch, English. **National**. Provides counseling and support to women who have become, or are in danger of becoming, addicted to benzodiazepine (tranquilizers). Believes the prescription of tranquilizers over an extended period of time is "a form of superfluous medical interference." Aims to prevent dependence on tranquilizers through educational programs and information dissemination.

★1970★ FRAUEN IN DER EUREGIO MAAS-RHEIN
(Vrouen in de Euregio Mass-Rijn)
Recessenplein 47/A
NL-6218 Maastricht, Netherlands
A. Eulenberg, Secretary   PH: 43 472490

Founded: 1975. **Members:** 400. **Budget:** DM 10,000. **Languages:** German, Dutch, French. **Multinational**. Women from the Netherlands, Germany, and Belgium residing between the Maas and Rhein rivers. Works towards improving relations among women from the three countries. Holds discussions concerning: child rearing and care; school, health, and care for the elderly; and cultural awareness. Offers an educational program on women in menopause. **Also Known As:** Femmes de l'Euregio Meuse-Rhin.

Conventions/Meetings: semiannual meeting.

★1971★ GEREFORMEERDE VROUWENBOND
Steinlaan 8
NL-3743 CH Baarn, Netherlands   PH: 21 5413366

Founded: 1937. **Members:** 10,000. **Languages:** Dutch, English. **National**. Women interested in administering and attending bible lessons. Conducts church and community service activities. Fosters communication among members.

Publications: *Ingesprek* (in Dutch), monthly. Newsletter.

Conventions/Meetings: annual meeting.

★1972★ INTERNATIONAL ASSOCIATION OF LIBERAL RELIGIOUS WOMEN (IALRW)
Chezeeweg 18
Postbus 42
NL-4424 ZG Wemeldinge, Netherlands
Dr. Nelly de Rooy-Janse, Pres.   PH: 1192 2382

Founded: 1910. **Members:** 265,000. **Languages:** English. **Multinational**.

Women and liberal women's religious groups representing 18 countries. Objectives are to: forward liberal religious ideas and promote international peace and service; serve as a link between liberal religious women throughout the world and promote friendship and cooperation among them; open and maintain communications with women striving for a liberal religious life. Represents diverse religious movements including Unitarian Universalism, the Brahmo Samaj and liberal Buddhism, and liberal wings of conservative religious groups. Participates with other international groups in International Women's Year and Decade events. Sponsors Literacy Service Project for Women in 4 Brahmo Samaj village centers near Calcutta, India. Offers hospitality to members traveling in member countries.

Publications: *Newsletter*, annual.

Conventions/Meetings: triennial conference

★1973★ INTERNATIONAL INFORMATION CENTRE AND ARCHIVES
   FOR THE WOMEN'S MOVEMENT
(International Informatiecentrum en Archief voor de Vrouwenbeweging)
Keizersgracht 10
NL-106G NP Amsterdam, Netherlands   PH: 20 6277054
Nicolette van der Post, Contact   FX: 20 6233855

Founded: 1935. **Languages:** Dutch, English. Promotes the advancement of women worldwide. Fosters the exchange of information related to international women's movements. Conducts research programs. **Libraries:** Type: open to the public. Holdings: 0; books, periodicals, clippings, archival material. **Computer Services:** Data base, bibliographic; data base, inventory of current research; data base, address listing; data base, diary of events; data base, publications catalogs.

★1974★ MEDICAL WOMEN'S INTERNATIONAL ASSOCIATION -
   NETHERLANDS
Strandvlietlaan 17
NL-1191 C Ouderkerk, Netherlands
Carolin Roos, Contact

Languages: Dutch. **National.** Netherlands national branch of the Medical Women's International Association (see separate entry). Women physicians. Provides a forum for discussion of women's health care issues. Encourages women to enter the field of medicine. Works to overcome discrimination against female physicians. Sponsors research and educational programs.

★1975★ MEDUSA - LANDELIJK BUREAU ONTWIKKELING BELEID &
   HULPVERLENING SEKSUEEL GEWELD
Pausdam 1
NL-3512 HN Utrecht, Netherlands   PH: 30 368748
M.J.H. Smulders   FX: 30 367203

Founded: 1991. **Staff:** 9. **Languages:** Dutch, English. **National.** Serves nationally towards the prevention of sexual abuse. Provides referrals to victims in need of support services. Undertakes projects pertaining to sexual abuse. Offers information to authorties, officials, and professionals. Affiliated with: the National Network of Black Women Against (Sexual) Violence, composed of women of Moluccan or Caribbean descent who offer assistance to refugee and counseling organizations; LORO, a national network of regional projects related to sexual violence, welfare agencies, police officers, and medical professionals involved in the prevention of sexual abuse and the victimization it manifests. Maintains a documentation center.

Publications: *Vrouwen Tegen Verkrachting; Hulverlening in de Praktijk* (in Dutch). Book. ● *Lastig Gevallen, Aangerand, Verkracht? Informatie Over de Rechtsgang na Seksueel Geweld* (in Dutch). Book. ● *Eindverslagen Integratiegroepen Seksueel Geweldsbeleid* (in Dutch). Book. ● *Newsletter* (in Dutch), periodic. ● *Vrouw en Gezondheidszong* (in Dutch), semimonthly. Journal.

★1976★ NEDERLANDSE CHRISTEN VROUWENBOND (NCVB)
Postbus 662
NL-3800 AR Amersfoort, Netherlands
Stans Gehrels, Gen.Sec.   PH: 33 630165

Founded: 1919. **Members:** 52,000. **Staff:** 5. **Budget:** 1,315,000 f. **Languages:** Dutch, English. **National.** Christian women in the Netherlands. Conducts study programs with a Christian focus on issues of interest to women, including: health care, equal rights, division of labor, and salary equality. Organizes discussion groups on political, cultural, and environmental issues. Promotes women's development in developing countries. Offers training programs for members.

Publications: *Information* (in Dutch), monthly. Magazine.

Conventions/Meetings: monthly meeting.

★1977★ NEDERLANDSE VERENIGING VAN HUISVROUWEN (NVVH)
Jan van Nassaustraat 89
NL-2596 BR The Hague, Netherlands   PH: 70 3241347
Mrs. L. de Ryk, Contact   FX: 70 3244362

Founded: 1912. **Members:** 45,000. **Staff:** 6. **Budget:** 10,000,000 f. **Languages:** Dutch, English. **National.** Liaises with other women's groups in the Netherlands to enhance the status of women. Works to protect the environment and consumer interests. Conducts cultural and educational programs.

Publications: *Denken en Doen* (in Dutch), bimonthly. Magazine.

★1978★ NEDERLANDSE VERENIGING VOOR VROUWENBELANGEN
Noordeinde 2A
NL-2311 CD Leiden, Netherlands
Mies Kulken-Bos, President   PH: 71 120603

Languages: Dutch. **National.** Women in the Netherlands working to achieve equality with men.

★1979★ NETHERLANDS COUNCIL OF WOMEN (NCW)
(NVR Nederlandse Vrouwen Raad)
Groot Hertoginnelaan 41
NL-2517 The Hague, Netherlands   PH: 70 3469304

Founded: 1975. **Members:** 41. **Staff:** 18. **Languages:** Dutch. **National.** Women's organizations in the Netherlands. Seeks to make women aware of their position in society and the opportunities available for their advancement; encourages women to take full and equal responsibility in all areas of Dutch society. **Committees:** Equal Rights and Opportunities; International Work; Labour; Public Relations.

Publications: *Inforeeks* (in Dutch), quarterly. ● *Nieuwsbulletin* (in Dutch), bimonthly.

★1980★ RUTGERS STICHTING
Postbus 17430
Groot Heroginnelaan 201
NL-2502 CK Gravenhage, Netherlands   PH: 70 3631750
Ms. Doortje Braeken, Contact   FX: 70 3561049

Languages: Dutch. **National.** Advocates family planning as a basic human right and a means to enhance the quality of life for individuals living in the Netherlands. Works to stop the spread of AIDS and other sexually transmitted diseases. Offers programs in sex education, family planning, and health. Acts as an advocate for family planning on a national level. Conducts research.

★1981★ SISTERS OF CHARITY OF STATION CHARLES BORROMEO
(SCSCB)
(LCB Liefdezusters van de H. Carolus Borromeus)
Onder de Bogen
St. Servaasklooster 14
Postbus 206
NL-6200 AE Maastricht, Netherlands   PH: 43 219241
Sr. Louisie Satini, Superior Gen.   FX: 43 257262

Founded: 1837. Members: 1,260. Languages: Danish, Dutch, English, Indonesian, Norwegian, Swahili. Multinational. Pontifical religious congregation with members in 9 countries including Belgium, Denmark, Indonesia, the Netherlands, Norway, Philippines, Tanzania, and the United States. Activities include pastoral work, educational programs, nursing services, and aid to the elderly.

★1982★ SOCIETY OF JESUS, MARY AND JOSEPH (SJMJ)
(Societe de Jesus, Marie et Joseph)
Jagersboschlaan 17
NL-5262 LS Vught, Netherlands
Sr. Benedict Melchers SJMJ, Superior   PH: 73 561721
   Gen.   TX: 73510249

Founded: 1822. Members: 1,541. Languages: English, Indonesian, Dutch. Multinational. Religious women in 6 countries.

★1983★ UNIE VAN SOROPTIMISTENCLUBS IN NEDERLAND, SURINAME EN DE NEDERLANDSE ANTILLEN
Prins Bernhardplein 171
NL-1097 BL Amsterdam, Netherlands   PH: 20 6922921
Silvia van den Heuvel, Contact   FX: 20 6943531

Founded: 1928. Members: 2,000. Budget: 250,000 f. Languages: Dutch, English. Multinational. Professional women. Works to: maintain high ethical standards in society and business; obtain and preserve human rights; foster friendship and cooperation among Soroptimist organizations worldwide; hasten a spirit of universal understanding, service, and friendship. Involved in the areas of: economic and social development, education, environment, health, the status of women, and international goodwill and understanding.

Publications: De Nederlandse Soroptimist (in Dutch), 11/year.

Conventions/Meetings: quarterly meeting. ● monthly meeting, for individual clubs.

★1984★ UNIE VAN VROUWELIJKE ONDERNEMERS NEDERLAND
(UVON)
Ruitery 2A
NL-6221 EW Maastricht, Netherlands   PH: 43 255414
M.N.L. Van Halder, Secretary   FX: 43 255836

Founded: 1951. Members: 400. Languages: English. National. Women entrepreneurs. Promotes the interests of women professionals and entrepreneurs. Offers information regarding professional advancement, growth and networking opportunities. Provides information on technical and business developments in the business world locally and globally. Corresponds and cooperates with other professional associations.

Conventions/Meetings: semiannual meeting. ● semiannual meeting, national.

★1985★ UNIVERSITY WOMEN OF EUROPE (UWE)
(GEFOU Groupe Europeen des Femmes Diplomes des Universites)
Waalsdorperweg 71
NL-2597 HR The Hague, Netherlands
Dr. J. Gremmee, Contact   PH: 70 3246231

Founded: 1978. Members: 14. Budget: 3,500 f. Languages: English, French. Multinational. National federations and associations of female university graduates representing 15,000 individuals in 14 countries. Aims to monitor and influence political decisions affecting women worldwide and to address problems in higher education and universities. Encourages professional advancement of graduate women to decision-making positions. Maintains consultative status with the Council of Europe. Provides placement service. Maintains roster of women suitable for management or political positions. Compiles statistics reflecting the advancement of women toward equality. Committees: Reentry; University Teachers.

Publications: Conference Report, biennial.

Conventions/Meetings: annual conference.

★1986★ VERENIGING VAN VROUWEN MET ACADEMISCHE OPLEIDING (VVAO)
Postbus 13226
NL-3507 LE Utrecht, Netherlands   PH: 30 721588
Ms. H.I. Oudraad, Coord.Intl. Relations   FX: 30 722432

Founded: 1918. Members: 5,500. Staff: 1. Regional Groups: 33. Languages: Danish, English. National. Women graduates of accredited universities and institutions. Promotes the interests, primarily, of educated women. Works to develop professional and non-professional networks. Establishes contacts between university women on a national and international level. Encourages members to apply their education to the resolution of societal problems. Promotes the re-training of women re-entering the work force. Disseminates information on study and career opportunities. Conducts training and workshops to assist members with career development.

Publications: De Economische Zelfstandigheid van Vrouwen (in Danish). Bulletin. Seminar reports. ● Arbeidsparticipatie van Vrouwen: Springplank of Valkuil (in Danish). Booklet.

Conventions/Meetings: triennial convention.

★1987★ VROUWEN IN DE VOLKSPARTIJ VOOR VRIJHEID EN DEMOCRATIE
c/o Organisatie Vrouwenin de VVD
Postbus 30836   PH: 70 3613040
NL-2500 GV The Hague, Netherlands   FX: 70 608276

National. Branch of the Peoples' Party for Freedom and Democracy of the Netherlands (see separate entry). Political organization advocating the rights of women.

★1988★ WOMEN AGAINST SEXUAL VIOLENCE BY PUBLIC HEALTH WORKERS
(Seksueel Misbruik en Vernederingen van Vrouwen en Meiden door Hulpverleners)
p/a Hugo de Grootstr. 20
NL-6522 DE Nijmegen, Netherlands   PH: 80 232956

Founded: 1983. Members: 5. Budget: 8,000 f. Languages: Dutch, German, English. National. Provides information and advice for women and organizations; organizes workshops for training institutions on request; runs a documentation service at a regional and national level.

Conventions/Meetings: annual - Nijmegen, Netherlands.

★1989★ WOMEN AND ENVIRONMENT PROJECT
Damrak 28-30   PH: 20 6230823
NL-1012 LJ Amsterdam, Netherlands   FX: 20 6208049
Theo van Koolwijk, Contact   E-Mail: GEO2:BOTHENDS

Founded: 1986. Staff: 10. Languages: Dutch, Spanish, French, English. National. Women engaged in development programs to ensure environmental preservation. Conducts programs in agriculture and population control. Alternate name:: Both Ends.

Conventions/Meetings: meeting - 3 times/year.

★1990★ WOMEN AND PHARMACEUTICALS PROJECT (WPP)
(Vrouwen en Geneesmiddelen)
Postbus 4263
NL-1009 AG Amsterdam, Netherlands   PH: 20 6653115
Helmi Govers, Desk Mgr.   FX: 20 6684085

Multinational. Disseminates information to women on pharmaceutical "dumping" in the Third World. (Developed countries have been accused of "dumping" pharmaceuticals that have been banned in their country due to health and safety reasons in developing countries where there are no health or safety bans.).

★1991★ WOMEN'S EXCHANGE PROGRAMME INTERNATIONAL
   (WEP)
PO Box 25096
NL-3001 HB Rotterdam, Netherlands

Founded: 1988. **Languages:** Dutch. **Multinational**. Provides a forum for the international exchange of knowledge and experiences among women's organizations. Lobbies policymakers to account for women's opinions in international policy. Areas of concern include: reproductive rights, women's studies, and economic independence. Offers training programs. **Computer Services:** Data base, addresses of women's organizatons.

Publications: *WEP International Newsbulletin*, semiannual. Magazine.

★1992★ WOMEN'S GLOBAL NETWORK FOR REPRODUCTIVE
   RIGHTS (WGNRR)
N.Z. Voorburgwal 32
NL-1012 RZ Amsterdam, Netherlands   PH: 20 6209072
L. Vogels, Contact   FX: 20 6222450

Founded: 1978. **Members:** 1,530. **Staff:** 7. **Languages:** Dutch, English, French, German, Spanish. **Multinational**. International network of women's health groups, reproductive rights campaigns, clinics, health workers, and interested individuals. Supports women's right to decide if and when to have children; defends the right to safe, effective contraceptives, legal abortion, and freedom from sterilization abuse. Campaigns on issues including what the group considers the "dumping of dangerous contraceptives in the Third World," the lack of complete information that would provide women with the opportunity to make informed decisions on spacing and controlling births, and the lack of availability of safe contraceptive methods to women who want them. Seeks to raise public awareness of issues surrounding maternal mortality and illness. Serves as information clearinghouse for abortion, sterilization and research, testing, and distribution of contraceptives and other reproductive health and services issues. Maintains resource center.

Publications: *Newsletter* (in English and Spanish), quarterly.

Conventions/Meetings: triennial conference

★1993★ WOMEN'S INTERNATIONAL STUDIES EUROPE (WISE)
Heidelberglaan 2
NL-3584 CS Utrecht, Netherlands   PH: 30 531881
Dr. Margit Van der Steen, Contact   FX: 30 531619

Founded: 1990. **Members:** 350. **Languages:** Dutch, English. **Multinational**. Scholars, women's studies associations, and other interested individuals. Promotes teaching and research in the field of women's studies throughout the EC. Fosters exchange of ideas among members. **Divisions:** Women, Science and Technology; Women's Work, Resources, and State Policies; Contemporary Feminism and Its Strategies; Cultural Practice and Communication; Racism and Discrimination in Refugee and Immigration Policies in Europe.

Publications: *Wise Women's News*, quarterly. Newsletter. **Circulation:** 400. **Advertising:** accepted.

Conventions/Meetings: annual general assembly.

★1994★ WOMEN'S INTERNATIONAL ZIONIST ORGANIZATION -
   NETHERLANDS (WIZO)
Johann Siegerstraat 8
NL-1096 BH Amsterdam, Netherlands
L. Heijmans-Slager, Secretary   PH: 20 944269

Founded: 1920. **Members:** 2,400. **Regional Groups:** 15. **Languages:** English. **National**. National branch of WIZO in Holland. Raises funds to provide for women and children in Israel. Offers educational and cultural ativities. Works to promote the advancement of women in Israel.

Publications: *Newsletter*, periodic.

★1995★ WOUW VLECHTWERK
Postbus 33163
NL-3005 ED Rotterdam, Netherlands
M.E. Sonius-Southworth, Contact   PH: 10 4186573

Founded: 1981. **Members:** 1,000. **Membership Dues:** 10 f annual. **Budget:** 50,000 f. **Languages:** Dutch. **National**. Women in the Netherlands over 50 years of age. Encourages members to represent the interests of older women in politics and social development. Fosters communication among members. Offers educational programs.

Publications: *Newsletter* (in Dutch), quarterly.

Conventions/Meetings: annual convention - Rotterdam, Netherlands.

★1996★ YOUNG WOMEN'S CHRISTIAN ASSOCIATION -
   NETHERLANDS
   PH: 30 715525
F.C. Dondersstraat 23   FX: 30 715525
NL-3572 JB Utrecht, Netherlands   CBL: YWCA
Els te Siepe, Gen.Sec.   DONDERSSTRAAT

National. Works to promote Christian fellowship and service among young women in the Netherlands. Encourages peace, unity, and justice.

★1997★ ZONTA INTERNATIONAL - NETHERLANDS
Postbus 248
NL-6880 AE Velp, Netherlands
Mrs. Regina Smit, Contact

Founded: 1964. **Members:** 450. **Budget:** 11,300 f. **Languages:** Dutch, English. **National**. Business people and other professionals. Works to improve the legal, political, economic and professional status of women. Encourages high ethical standards in business. **Awards:** Annual Amelia Earhart (grant). Recipient: women graduate students of aerospace science. ● Young Women in Public Affairs.

Publications: *Zonta Newsbrief* (in Dutch), quarterly. Newsletter. ● *Directory*, annual. European members.

Northern Ireland

★1998★ ACTION CANCER
127 Marlborough Park S
Belfast, Antrim BT9 6HW, Northern
   Ireland   PH: 232 382455
Debbie Jones, Contact   232 661081

National. Works to heighten women's awareness of the importance of early cancer detection. Offers breast and cervical cancer screening services. Provides counseling service for cancer patients, families, and friends. Maintains research lab. Disseminates information.

★1999★ AIDS HELPLINE
310 Bryson House
28 Bedford St.
Belfast, Antrim BT2 7FE, Northern
   Ireland
Rosie Yeauen, Contact   PH: 232 249268

National. Makes available women counselors to offer advice to women concerned about AIDS. Offers home support. Conducts preventative education and a outreach programs. Promotes fundraising.

★2000★ AMALGAMATED TRANSPORT AND GENERAL WORKERS UNION WOMEN'S COMMITTEE
Transport House
102 High St.
Belfast, Antrim BT1 2BG, Northern
   Ireland
Avila Kilmurray, Contact   PH: 232 232381

National. Represents the interests of women members in the Amalgamated Transport and General Workers Union. Liaises with women's organizations to develop the active involvement of women in society.

★2001★ ASIAN WOMEN AND CHILDREN'S ASSOCIATION
275 Legahory Ct.
Craigavon, Armagh, Northern Ireland
Mrs. Ali, Contact

National. Promotes the interests of women in the Asian community in Northern Ireland. Organizes social, educational, and cultural activities for Asian women and children. Conducts classes for women, a play group for pre-school children, and an after school program for older children.

★2002★ BAHA'I WOMEN'S COMMITTEE OF NORTHERN IRELAND
69 Shore Rd.
Magheramorne, Larne BT40 3HW,
   Northern Ireland
Dr. Colette Ma'ani, Secretary   PH: 574 273796

Founded: 1989. **Members:** 93. **Budget:** £180. **Languages:** English. **National**. Baha'i women in Northern Ireland. Promotes Baha'i teachings and equality of the sexes. Encourages women to live by Baha'i principles. Seeks to create a more compassionate, understanding, and balanced society. Conducts presentations in women's groups, Baha'i communities and schools. Organizes activities; campaigns for peace in Northern Ireland.

Publications: *Community Life* (in English), monthly.

Conventions/Meetings: monthly meeting. ● periodic meeting.

★2003★ CENTRE FOR RESEARCH ON WOMEN (CROW)
University of Ulster
Coleraine, Derry BT52 1SA, Northern
   Ireland
Morag Stark, Contact   PH: 265 44141

National. Aims to contribute to the understanding of women's issues in Northern Ireland. Provides a forum for debate on issues of interest to women. Sponsors research on gender roles. Serves as a source of advice and expertise for researchers and teachers of women's studies.

★2004★ CHATTER BOX
c/o Cupar St. Clinic
Belfast, Antrim BT11, Northern Ireland   PH: 232 326574
Pat McConville, Contract   232 327613

National. Promotes improvement of women's general health and well-being. Offers counselling to depressed women. Disseminates information.

★2005★ EQUAL OPPORTUNITIES COMMISSION-NORTHEN IRELAND (EOC)
22 Great Victoria St.
Belfast, Antrim BT2 2BA, Northern
   Ireland
Mrs. I. Kingston, Contact   PH: 232 242752

National. Promotes equal opportunities between women and men. Strives to eliminate sex discrimination. Enforces sexual discrimination and equal pay legislation. Supports research on gender issues.

★2006★ FAINNE NA MBAN
c/o Glor Na Gael
145 Falls Rd.
Belfast, Antrim BT12, Northern Ireland
Geraldine Scullion, Contact   PH: 232 232608

National. Encourages women's involvement in the Irish language and culture. Sponsors events, classes, lectures, mini colleges, and discussions of interest to women.

★2007★ FAMILY PLANNING ASSOCIATION - NORTHERN IRELAND
14 Magazine St.
Derry, Northern Ireland
Evelyn Kerr, Contact   PH: 504 260016

National. Offers information and advice on issues of women's heath, sex education, and relationships. Supplies resources and offers consulting to professional counselors and educators. Operates pregnancy testing and counseling services.

★2008★ FEDERATION OF WOMEN'S INSTITUTES OF NORTHERN IRELAND
209/211 Upper Lisburn Rd.
Belfast, Antrim BT11, Northern Ireland
Mrs. Jean Mann, Chairman of the Board   PH: 232 301506

National. Umbrella organization of institutes studying women and women's issues. Promotes and supports the interests of women of Northern Ireland.

★2009★ GINGERBREAD-NORTHERN IRELAND
169 University St.
Belfast, Antrim BT7 1HR, Northern
   Ireland
Monica O'Prey, Contact   PH: 232 231417

National. Single parent groups in Northern Ireland. Promotes the interests and development of single parents and their families. Offers counseling; disseminates nformation.

★2010★ ICTU WOMEN'S COMMITTEE
c/o ICTU
3 Wellington Park
Belfast, Antrim BT9, Northern Ireland
Avila Kilmurray, Contact   PH: 232 681726

National. Umbrella organization for trade unions in Northern Ireland. Promotes women's enhanced status in the work place and community. Collaborates with community organizations on matters of common concern.

Conventions/Meetings: monthly meeting.

★2011★ IRISH ASSOCIATION FOR RESEARCH IN WOMEN'S
HISTORY
Dept. of Modern History, QUB
Belfast, Antrim BT7 1NN, Northern
Ireland
Dr. Mary O'Dowd, Contact   PH: 232 245133

Languages: English. **National.** Promotes research of women's history.
Disseminates information.

Publications: *Newsletter.* Information on publications and conferences on
women's history.

Conventions/Meetings: annual conference.

★2012★ IRISH WOMEN'S BOWLING ASSOCIATION
2 Downriver Ct.
102 Downview Park W
Belfast, Antrim BT15 5HZ, Northern
Ireland
Mrs. D. Sutton, Contact   PH: 232 771427

National. Encourages women to become involved in the sport of bowling in
Ireland. Organizes tournaments.

★2013★ LESBIAN LINE
Box 44
Belfast, Antrim, Northern Ireland
          PH: 232 238668

National. Offers advice, support, and information to lesbian women in
Northern Ireland. Provides a safe place for lesbian women to develop
friendships. Sponsors lesbian oriented social events.

★2014★ MASTECTOMY SUPPORT/ADVISORY SERVICE
Ulster Cancer Foundation
40 Eglantine Ave.
Belfast, Antrim BT9 6DX, Northern
Ireland
Betty M.E. McCrum, Contact   PH: 232 663281

Regional Groups: 10. **National.** Promotes awareness of breast care and
early detection of breast cancer. Supports the rehabilitation of women who
have breast cancer or breast surgery.

★2015★ METHODIST WOMEN'S ASSOCIATION - IRELAND
27 Magheralaye Park E
Lisburn, Antrim BT28 3BT, Northern
Ireland
Patricia E. Orr, Secretary   PH: 846 601529

Founded: 1972. **Members:** 4,000. **Languages:** English. **National.** Methodist
women in Ireland. Promotes application of the teachings of Jesus Christ to
life in the home, church, community, and world. Encourages fellowship
among Christian women to deepen their personal commitment to Jesus
Christ. Works to share in the mission of the World Church. Provides a link
with women of other churches nationally and internationally. Conducts rallies
and retreats.

Conventions/Meetings: annual conference.

★2016★ NISC WOMEN'S FOOTBALL TEAM
282 Shankill Rd.
Belfast, Antrim BT13, Northern Ireland
Mr. William Smith, Contact   PH: 232 333813

National. Women soccer players in Northern Ireland. Promotes participation
of females, ages 11 to 40, in the sport of soccer.

★2017★ NORTHERN IRELAND CHILDMINDING ASSOCIATION
17A Court St.
Newtownards, Down BT23 5NX,
Northern Ireland
Christine Best, Contact   PH: 811015

National. Promotes high standards of child care in Northern Ireland. Fosters
the development of child care facilities. Offers assistance and advice to child
care providers.

★2018★ NORTHERN IRELAND PRE-SCHOOL PLAYGROUPS
ASSOCIATION (NIPPA)
Enterprise House
Boucher Crescent
Boucher Rd.
Belfast, Antrim, Northern Ireland
Siobhan Fitzpatrick, Contact   PH: 232 662285

Founded: 1965. **Members:** 800. **Languages:** English. **National.** Promotes
the availability of child care facilities for women with children under 5 years of
age. Fosters children's educational and physical development.

★2019★ NORTHERN IRELAND RAPE CRISIS ASSOCIATION - RAPE
AND INCEST LINE (NIRCA-RAIL)
105 University St.
Belfast, Antrim BT7 1HD, Northern
Ireland   PH: 232 326803
Dominica McGouan, Director   FX: 232 237392

Founded: 1984. **Members:** 50. **Staff:** 4. **Budget:** £150. **Languages:** English.
National. Provides counseling and support groups for adult survivors of
sexual abuse and their families. Conducts research on sexual abuse. Offers
education to doctors, social workers, and teachers on the warning signs,
symptoms, and long and short-term effects on victims; provides awareness
training on characteristics of abusers. Operates rape crisis centers and
related bookshop in Northern Ireland. Disseminates information. **Libraries:**
Type: not open to the public.   **Computer Services:**
Information services.

Publications: *Journal* (in English), annual. ● *Bulletin* (in English), bimonthly.

★2020★ NORTHERN IRELAND WIDOWS ASSOCIATION
Primrose Hill
92 Derryloughan Rd.
Loughgall, Armagh, Northern Ireland
Mrs. Lily Abbott, Contact   PH: 762 891551

National. Promotes the interest of widows in Northern Ireland. Provides
meeting places where widows can overcome loneliness and discuss problems. Encourages widows to actively participate in society.

★2021★ NORTHERN IRELAND WOMEN'S EUROPEAN PLATFORM
(NIWEP)
c/o Northern Ireland Council for
Voluntary Action
127 Ormeau Rd.
Belfast, Antrim BT7 1SH, Northern
Ireland   PH: 232 321224
Liz Law, Contact   FX: 232 438350

National. Promotes the interests of women in Northern Ireland.

★2022★ PRESBYTERIAN WOMEN'S ASSOCIATION (PWA)
PWA Office
Church House
Belfast, Antrim BT1 6DW, Northern
Ireland   PH: 232 32284
D. Elizabeth McCaughan, Contact   FX: 232 236605

Founded: 1871. **Members:** 16,000. **Staff:** 4. **Budget:** £571,000. **Lan-**

guages: English. **National.** Encourages the union of women within the Church and the dedication of their lives to Christian service. Promotes Christianity nationally and abroad through thought, prayer, and financial support of missionaries. Provides a link with other Christian women in Ireland and worldwide facilitating fellowship and cooperation for a common purpose. Educates members through occasional workshops. **Committees:** Young Women's Group.

Publications: *Wider World* (in English), quarterly. Magazine.

Conventions/Meetings: annual conference, for committee members. - always in September. ● annual general assembly - always in May.

★2023★ SOROPTIMIST INTERNATIONAL OF NORTHERN IRELAND
191A Avenue Rd.
Lurgan, Armagh BT66 7BJ, Northern
    Ireland
Mrs. Anna M.C. Soye, Contact   PH: 762 322607

National. Promotes the interests of professional and business women in Northern Ireland. Supports the advancement of the status of women. Maintains high ethical standards. Works to defend human rights.

★2024★ ULSTER PREGNANCY ADVISORY ASSOCIATION
719A Lisburn Rd.
Belfast, Antrim BT9 7GU, Northern
    Ireland
Mrs. Joan Wilson, Director   PH: 232 381345

National. Offers counseling and support to women with unplanned pregnancies in Northern Ireland.

★2025★ UNITED KINGDOM FEDERATION OF BUSINESS AND
    PROFESSIONAL WOMEN-NORTHERN IRELAND
109 Shankbridge Rd.
Kells, Ballymena BT42 3NJ, Northern
    Ireland
Mrs. Mary E. Ardis, Contact   PH: 266 891533

Multinational. Business and professional women's groups. Aims to enable members to succeed in their careers. Encourages women to take an active part in public life and decision making at all levels. Strives to ensure that the same opportunities and facilities are available to both men and women. Undertakes studies of problems common to business and professional women world wide. Sponsors educational and training programs.

★2026★ WOMEN IN ALLIANCE
88 University St.
Belfast, Antrim BT7 1HE, Northern
    Ireland   PH: 232 324274
Eileen Bell, Contact   FX: 232 333147

National. Political organization for women in Northern Ireland; branch of the Alliance Party of Northern Ireland.

★2027★ WOMEN'S EXCHANGE AND INFORMATION GROUP
185 Donegall St.
Belfast, Antrim BT1 2FJ, Northern
    Ireland
C. Couvert, Contact   PH: 232 325426

National. Promotes the feminist movement in Northern Ireland. Organizes social and cultural events for women. Operates drop-in center; disseminates information. **Libraries:** Type: lending.   Subjects: feminist issues.

Publications: *Women's News.* Magazine.

★2028★ WOMEN'S FORUM - NORTHERN IRELAND
c/o Northern Ireland Council for
    Voluntary Action
127 Ormean Rd.
Belfast, Antrim BT7 1SH, Northern
    Ireland   PH: 232 321224
Miss Mary McGrane, Chair   232 321124

Founded: 1969. **Members:** 27. **Staff:** 1. **Languages:** English. **National.** Women's welfare organizations. Provides a forum for women's organizations to network and discuss problems of public welfare in Northern Ireland, focusing on the welfare of women and children. Monitors changes in health services and education. Disseminates information. Organizes speaking engagements. Conducts research and educational programs. **Formerly:** Women's Group on Public Welfare.

Publications: *Women Work*, periodic. Newsletter. ● *Pressures on the Young.* Booklet. ● *Caring in the Community.* Booklet. ● *Women into Europe.* Booklet.

Conventions/Meetings: meeting - 5/year. Belfast, AT, Northern Ireland. ● executive committee meeting - 5/year. Belfast, AT, Northern Ireland. ● semiannual seminar.

★2029★ WOMEN'S INFORMATION GROUP
c/o 37 Juniper Rise
Dunmurry
Belfast, Antrim BT17 0BG, Northern
    Ireland
Kathleen Feenan, Contact   PH: 232 628342

National. An umbrella organization for women's groups in Northern Ireland. Provides an opportunity for women's organizations to meet and exchange experiences. Disseminates information.

★2030★ WOMEN'S LAW AND RESEARCH GROUP
26 Mt. Merrion Ave.
Belfast, Antrim BT6 0FR, Northern
    Ireland
Eileen Evason, Contact   PH: 232 646949

Founded: 1975. **National.** Campaigns to reform laws to create equal opportunities for women and men. Supports research on women's issues.

★2031★ WOMEN'S STUDIES, WORKER'S EDU ASSOCIATION
1 Fitzwilliam St.
Belfast, Antrim BT9 6AW, Northern
    Ireland
Ann Hope, Contact   PH: 232 329718

National. Promotes women's education in Northern Ireland. Conducts day, evening, and weekend classes on women's issues. Provides tutor training.

★2032★ YOUTH ACTION YOUNG WOMEN'S GROUP
Youth Action
Hampton
Glenmachan Park
Belfast, Antrim BT4 2PJ, Northern
    Ireland
Kate Campbell, Contact   PH: 232 760067

Promotes the interests of young women in Northern Ireland. Communicates with other young women's groups. Disseminates information.

Conventions/Meetings: annual conference, Includes seminars.

Norway

★2033★ CENTRE FOR INTERNATIONAL WOMEN'S ISSUES (CEWI)
(Senter for Internasjonale Kvinne-Sporsmal)
Fr. Nansens Pl. 6
N-0160 Oslo, Norway   PH: 2 426245
Trine Lynggard, Exec. Dir.   2 423205

Founded: 1990. **Languages:** Norwegian, English. **National.** Originally founded as an information service following a television campaign describing developmental assistance for women internationally. Focuses on: arranging contact between national women's organizations and women's groups of developing countries; promoting solidarity among women; and educating women on environmental and developmental issues. Affiliated with 40 national women's organizations.

Publications: *Women Together* (in Norwegian), quarterly. Magazine.

Conventions/Meetings: semiannual conference.

★2034★ FEDERATION OF METHODIST WOMEN NORWAY (FMWN)
(MKN Metodist Kirkens Kuinneforbund Norge)
Metodistkirken i Norge
St. Olavsgate 28
Oslo 1, Norway
Anne Marie Nordby, Contact

Founded: 1968. **Members:** 2,000. **Budget:** 60,000 NKr. **Languages:** English, Norwegian. **National.** Christian women and women's organizations in Norway. Activities include missionary work outside of Norway.

Publications: *Metodistkirkens Kvinner* (in Norwegian), 5/year. Newsletter.

Conventions/Meetings: triennial convention.

★2035★ LEGAL ADVICE FOR WOMEN (JURK)
(Juridisk Raagivning for Kvinner)
Postboks 6756
St. Olavs Plass
N-0130 Oslo 1, Norway   PH: 2 112500427
Heidi Lversen, Administrator   2 112500428

Founded: 1974. **Members:** 19. **Staff:** 19. **Budget:** 13,000,000 NKr. **Languages:** English. **National.** Female students. Aim is to improve the legal position of women. Offers free legal advice on matters relating to family law, the law of inheritance, child law, social security law, labor law, housing law, and the law of damages. Subgroups assist battered women, female immigrants, and female prisoners; educate woman on legal matters; and act as liaison between women and the Government and organizations.

★2036★ NORSK FORENING FOR FAMILIEPLANLEGGING (NFF)
Roahellinga 15
N-0755 Oslo, Norway
Ms. Kari Rovang, Conact   PH: 2 209230

Languages: Norwegian. **National.** Advocates family planning and responsible parenthood as a means to improve the quality life. Attempts to reduce the number of unwanted pregnancies and abortions. Offers programs in sex education, family planning, and health. Provides contraceptive and health care services. Conducts research.

★2037★ NORSK KVINNESAKSFORENING
Fredrik Stangsgt 31 C
N-0264 Oslo 2, Norway
Irene Bauer, President

Languages: Norwegian. **National.** Promotes the interests of women in Norway. Fosters unity and friendly relations among women in Norway.

★2038★ NORWEGIAN HOUSEWIVES ASSOCIATION (NH)
(Norges Husmorforbund)
Oscarsgt. 43
Oslo 2, Norway   PH: 2 563097

Advocates: equal ownership of home assets between husbands and wives; equal tax and pension regulations between working women; equal resonsibility for the caring of children, state financial compesation for the loss of work due to illness of women; financial assistance for expenses of caring for handicapped or elderly family members; and financial compensation to family members nursing and caring for other family members. Supports the arts; encourages appreciation of the arts.

★2039★ WHITE RIBBON, NORWEGIAN WOMAN'S CHRISTIAN
TEMPERANCE UNION
(Huite Band, Norske Kvinners Kristne Avholdsforbund)
Mollergate 38
N-0179 Oslo 1, Norway
Silvia Molander, Sec.   PH: 2 205438

Founded: 1889. **Members:** 5,500. **Staff:** 2. **Local Groups:** 160. **Languages:** English, Norwegian. **National.** Women dedicated to reducing the consumption of alcohol in Norway. Coordinates public information campaigns in an attempt to influence authorities. Operates a treatment center for women alcoholics and their families. Organizes study groups.

Publications: *Det Hvite Band* (in Norwegian), 9/year. Newsletter.

Conventions/Meetings: biennial convention.

★2040★ WOMEN'S ORGANIZATION OF THE CONSERVATIVE PARTY
(Hoyrekvinners Landsforbund)
Postboks 1536
Vika
N-0117 Oslo, Norway   PH: 2 421241
Fiffi Sars, Gen.Sec.   FX: 2 422141

Founded: 1925. **Members:** 7,000. **Staff:** 1. **Budget:** 1,300,000 NKr. **Local Groups:** 100. **Languages:** Norwegian. **National.** Women in Norway; members of the National Organization of the Right. Goal is to increase the interest of and the participation by women in politics in Norway. Advocates equal rights for women and improved policy regarding families. Activities include fund-raising, children's services, and projects in Botswana.

Publications: *Convention Report* (in Norwegian), biennial. ● *Newsletter* (in Norwegian), monthly.

Conventions/Meetings: biennial convention (exhibits).

★2041★ YOUNG WOMEN'S CHRISTIAN ASSOCIATION - NORWAY
(Kristelige Foreninger av Unge Kvinner)
Postboks 6814
St. Olavs pl.
N-0130 Oslo 1, Norway   PH: 2 204475
Irene Wenaas Holte, Gen.Sec.   FX: 2 204759

National. Works to uphold Christian fellowship and service among young women in Norway. Promotes justice, peace, and unity.

Poland	Portugal

★2042★ MEDICAL WOMEN'S INTERNATIONAL ASSOCIATION - POLAND
Zarzad Glowny Ligi
Korbiet Polskich
Sekcja Lekarek
Electoralna Str. 13
PL-00-137 Warsaw, Poland
Ilona Szilagyi-Pagowska, Contact

Languages: Polish. **National.** Polish national branch of the Medical Women's International Association (see separate entry). Women physicians. Provides a forum for discussion of women's health care issues. Encourages women to enter the field of medicine. Works to overcome discrimination against female physicians. Sponsors research and educational programs.

★2043★ POLISH FEMINIST ASSOCIATION
Ulica Gorska 7M53
Warsaw, Poland

Languages: Polish. **National.** Works towards the furthering of the national feminist movement and the fostering of public awareness and recognition of women's rights.

★2044★ POLISH WOMEN'S LEAGUE
ulica Elektoralna 13
PL-00-137 Warsaw, Poland
Izabela Nowacka, Contact

Founded: 1913. **Members:** 120,000. **National.** Promotes the interests of women in Poland. Works to ensure equal rights for women in social, economic, political, and legal areas. Aims to improve women's standard of living in Poland. Offers professional training and educational programs. Encourages women to pursue satisfying employment and to become involved in public life. Seeks to raise the status of women working at home.

★2045★ TOWARZYSTWO ROZWOJU RODZINY (TRR)
Ul. Karowa 31
PL-00-324 Warsaw, Poland   PH: 22 268825
Mr. Jerzy Witczak, Secretary   FX: 22 268825

Languages: Polish. **National.** Promotes family planning as a basic human right and a means to improve the standard of living for individuals and families. Works to reduce the number of unwanted pregnancies and abortions. Attempts to stop the spread of AIDS and other sexually transmitted diseases. Offers programs in family planning, sex education, and health. Provides contraceptive and health care services.

★2046★ YOUNG WOMEN'S CHRISTIAN ASSOCIATION - POLAND
(Zwiazek Dziewczat I Kobiet Chrzescijanskich - Polska)
Spalska 3/4
PL-02-934 Warsaw, Poland
Kinga Stawikowska, Gen.Sec.   PH: 22 429221

National. Works to promote Christian fellowship and service among young women in Poland. Advocates justice, peace, and unity.

★2047★ ASSOCIACAO DE MULHERES AGRICULTORAS PORTUGESAS (AMAP)
Calcada Ribeiro dos Santos 19-r/c
P-1200 Lisbon, Portugal

Languages: Portuguese. **National.** Women working in the agricultural sector. Represents members interests.

★2048★ ASSOCIACAO DAS MULHERES DEMOCRATAS CRISTAS (AMDC)
Alameda Antonio Sergio 9-5 D
P-1700 Lisbon, Portugal

Languages: Portuguese. **National.** Women's political party in Portugal. Organizes social and political activities.

★2049★ ASSOCIACAO DAS MULHERES SOCIALISTAS (AMS)
R. Jose Ferrao Castelo Branco 42
P-2780 Paco d'Arcos, Portugal

Languages: Portuguese. **National.** Socialist women in Portugal. Promotes principles of the socialist party.

★2050★ ASSOCIACAO DAS MULHERES QUE TRABALHAM EM CASA (AMEC)
R. Qt das Palmeiras 39-7 Esq.
P-2780 Oerias, Portugal

Languages: Portuguese. **National.** Women who work at home. Works to raise the economic and social status of members.

★2051★ ASSOCIACAO PARA O PLANEAMENTO DA FAMILIA (APF)
38 Rua Artilharia um 2 Dto
P-1200 Lisbon, Portugal   PH: 1 3853993
Mr. Duarte Vilar, Exec. Dir.   FX: 1 3887379

Languages: Portuguese. **National.** Promotes family planning and responsible parenthood as a basic human right and as a means to improve the standard of living for individuals in Portugal. Works to stop the spread of AIDS and other sexually transmitted diseases through education and contraceptive services. Offers programs in family planning and health. Conducts research.

★2052★ ASSOCIACAO PORTUGUESA DE ESTUDOS SOBRE AS MULHERES (APEM)
Praca Manuel Cerveira Pereira, No. 3-5
     Esq.
P-1900 Lisbon, Portugal

Languages: Portuguese. **National.** Portuguese women and others seeking to advance the rights of women. Conducts research and disseminates information on the status of Portuguese women.

★2053★ ASSOCIACAO PORTUGUESA DAS MULHERES JURISTAS
Rua do Crucifixo 50-3
P-1100 Lisbon, Portugal

Languages: Portuguese. **National.** Women lawyers and law students in Portugal. Fosters the study of legal problems of special interest to women. Promotes the professional interests of members.

★2054★ COMISSAO PARA A IGUALDADE E PARA OS DIREITOS
DAS MULHERES
Avenida da Republica 32-1   PH: 1 7976081
P-1093 Lisbon Codex, Portugal   1 7976084
Madalena Barbosa, Coord.   FX: 1 7937691

Languages: Portuguese, English. **National**. Works to create awareness of
women's rights in Portugal. Provides a forum for collaboration among
women's organizations.

★2055★ COMISSAO DAS MULHERES DA UGT
    PH: 1 3976505
Rua de Buenos Aires 11   1 3976503
P-1200 Lisbon, Portugal   FX: 1 3974612

Languages: Portuguese. **National**. Women working to promote equality
between the sexes in Portugal. Disseminates information.

★2056★ COMISSAO NACIONAL DE MULHERES DA CGTP-IN
Rua de S. Pedro de Alcantara 63-2   PH: 1 3474964
P-1200 Lisbon, Portugal   FX: 1 3474140

Languages: Portuguese. **National**. Women in Portugal working to raise
awareness of women's issues. Fosters communication among members.

★2057★ CRUZ VERMELHA PORTUGUESA (CVP)
    PH: 1 605490
Jardim 9 de Abril, 1 a 5   1 605564
P-1293 Lisbon Codex, Portugal   FX: 1 3951045

Languages: Portuguese. **National**. Women members of the Portuguese Red
Cross. Provides health care and other relief services.

★2058★ DEPARTAMENTO DE MULHERES DO PARTIDO SOCIALISTA
(DMPS)
Largo do Rato   PH: 1 690376
P-1200 Lisbon, Portugal   FX: 1 693845

Languages: Portuguese. **National**. Socialist women in Portugal. Encourages
women's involvement in political life. Campaigns for the election of socialist
politicians.

★2059★ DEPARTAMENTO DE MULHERES DA UDP
Rua de Sao Bento 698-1
P-1200 Lisbon, Portugal   PH: 1 3385034

Languages: Portuguese. **National**. Works to improve the quality of life for
women in Portugal. Works for women's equality and development.

★2060★ EUROPEAN ASSOCIATION FOR THE DEVELOPMENT OF
INFORMATION AND TRAINING OF WOMEN - PORTUGAL (EUDIFF)
(Associacao Europeia para o Desenvolvimento da Informacao e des
Mulheres - Portugal)
Commissao de Mulheres da UGT
Rua Buenos Aires 11
P-1200 Lisbon, Portugal   PH: 1 676472
Elisa Damiao, Contact   FX: 1 67462

Languages: Portuguese. **National**. Circulates information on women and
women's issues throughout Portugal. Networks with organizations that also
champion women's advancement. Demands that EC nations fully recognize
women's rights. Supports women's development and equality; encourages
women's participation in leadership roles. Facilitates exchange among
members.

★2061★ INTERVENCAO FEMININA (IF)
Rua Luciano Cordeiro 24-6 A
P-1000 Lisbon, Portugal

Languages: Portuguese. **National**. Promotes the interests of women in
Portugal. Fosters solidarity among women.

★2062★ MOVIMENTO ESPERANCA E VIDA
Quinta da Fonteireira
Belas
P-2745 Queluz, Portugal
Margaret Kendall Villas Boas, Coord.

Languages: Portuguese. **National**. Catholic widows in Portugal. Counsels
women through the bereavment process.

Publications: *Newsletter*, bimonthly.

★2063★ MOVIMENTO DEMOCRATICO DAS MULHERES (MDM)
Avenida Duque de Loule 111-4   PH: 1 3528622
P-1000 Lisbon, Portugal   1 3527853

Languages: Portuguese. **National**. Women united to promote the principles
of democracy. Champions human rights, solidarity, freedom, and civic
involvement.

★2064★ MOVIMENTO PARA A EMANCIPACAO SOCIAL DAS
MULHERES PORTUGUESAS (UMAR)
Apartado 513
Torcatas
P-2800 Almada, Portugal

Languages: Portuguese. **National**. Defends and protects women's rights.
Works to raise the economic and social status of women to enable them to
participate in all sectors of society.

★2065★ MULHERES PORTUGUESAS SOCIAL-DOMOCRATAS (MSPD)
c/o Partido Social-Democrata
Rua Buenos Aires 39
P-1200 Lisbon, Portugal

National. Political organization advocating the rights of women in Portugal;
branch of the Social Democratic Party in Portugal.

★2066★ NATIONAL DEPARTMENT OF SOCIALIST WOMEN (NDSW)
Largo do Rato 2   PH: 1 690376
Lisbon, Portugal   FX: 1 693865
Maria Carmoramao, Coord.   TX: 62862

Members: 14,000. **Staff:** 1. **Languages:** French, Portuguese, Spanish.
National. Promotes equality among women and men. Investigates discriminatory practices against women; designs legislative programs to achieve
equality. Organizes activities and educational courses.

Conventions/Meetings: semiannual meeting.

★2067★ ORGANIZACAO DAS MULHERES COMUNISTAS (OMC)
Rua Soeiro Pereira Gomes
P-1699 Lisbon Codex, Portugal   PH: 1 7936272

Languages: Portuguese. **National**. Women promoting communist ideals and
policies in Portugal.

★2068★ SOROPTIMIST INTERNATIONAL - PORTUGAL
Rua Prof. Branco Rodrigues 265
P-1200 Lisbon, Portugal

Languages: Portuguese. **National**. Women engaged in social service
activities in Portugal. Works to improve educational programs, health
services, and environmental quality.

Romania

★2069★ MEDICAL WOMEN'S INTERNATIONAL ASSOCIATION - ROMANIA
Strada Danicieni nr. 8
71267 Bucharest, Romania
Maria Ciochirca, President

Languages: Romanian. **National.** Romanian national branch of the Medical Women's International Association (see separate entry). Women physicians. Provides a forum for discussion of women's health care issues. Encourages women to enter the field of medicine. Works to overcome discrimination against female physicians. Sponsors research and educational programs.

★2070★ SOCIETATEA DE EDUCATIE CONTRACEPTIVA SI SEXUALA (SECS)
Str. Iancu Cavaler de Flondor Nr. 2
Sect 2, Ofc. Post No. 20
73114 Bucharest, Romania   PH: 0 422686
Dr. Borbala Koo, Exec. Dir.   FX: 0 350866

Languages: Romanian. **National.** Works to improve the quality of life for individuals living in Romania by promoting responsible parenthood and family planning. Attempts to reduce the number of unwanted pregnancies and abortions. Offers programs in family planning, sex education, and health. Acts as an advocate for family planning on a national level.

★2071★ WOMEN'S ASSOCIATION OF ROMANIA
(Asociatia Femeilor din Romania)
Calea Victoriei 133-135, Sc. A, Et. 3
Cam 30-31
71102 Bucharest, Romania
Liliana Pagu, President

Founded: 1989. **National.** Purpose is to unite Romanian women in pursuit of equal rights. Fosters awareness among women of their social, cultural, and political responsiblities within society. Cooperates with other women's organizations to achieve equality, peace, and freedom.

Scotland

★2072★ CHURCH OF SCOTLAND WOMEN'S GUILD
121 George St.   PH: 31 2255722
Edinburgh EH2 4YN, Scotland   FX: 31 2203113
Lorna M. Paterson, Secretary   TX: 727935

Founded: 1887. **Members:** 66,000. **Staff:** 4. **Budget:** £106,000. **Languages:** English. **National.** Women who accept the beliefs of the Church of Scotland. Works towards uniting women of the church in the dedication of their lives to the beliefs and aims of Christianity through worship, fellowship, and service.

Publications: *Newsletter* (in English), quarterly.

Conventions/Meetings: annual meeting. ● annual conference.

★2073★ EDUCATIONAL INSTITUTE OF SCOTLAND
46 Moray Pl.
Edinburgh, Scotland   PH: 31 2256244

Founded: 1983. **Members:** 303,000. **Languages:** English. **National.** Works to enhance the status of women's education. Lobbies government on women's issues.

★2074★ ENGENDER, THE SCOTTISH WOMEN'S FOUNDATION
c/o Scotland on Sunday
20 N. Bridge
Edinburgh EH1 1YT, Scotland   PH: 31 2433657
Cathie Thomson   41 3570180

Founded: 1992. **Members:** 1,000. **Staff:** 2. **Budget:** £50,000. **Languages:** English. **National.** Campaigns and lobbies for the improved status and perception of women in Scotland. Engender, meaning "to sow," reflects the organizations purpose in helping to produce change for women in the areas of leadership roles, decision-making, and institutionalized discrimination. Conducts research in an effort to establish a factual base from which to legitimitaize the need for change. Provides a consulting service regarding the status of women in Scotland. Collects and disseminates information. Develops links among national women's organizations, and provides a forum in which women may meet to share knowledge. **Committees:** Research; Communication; Information Technology; Fund-Raising.

Publications: *Newsletter* (in English), periodic.

Conventions/Meetings: periodic conference.

★2075★ LADIES' GOLF UNION
The Scores
St. Andrews
Fife KY16 9AT, Scotland   PH: 33475811
Elaine Mackie, Contact   FX: 33472818

Members: 195,087. **National.** Amateur women golfers. Promotes and administers women's participation in amateur golf in the United Kingdom. Organizes matches.

Publications: *Booklet*, annual. Golfing clubs in Great Britain and abroad.

★2076★ NATIONAL COUNCIL OF WOMEN - SCOTTISH STANDING COMMITTEE
49 Kier St.
Bridge of Allan
Stirling FK9 4QJ, Scotland   PH: 786 832064

Languages: English. **National.** Promotes collaboration and exchange among women's groups. Conducts charitable and educational programs.

Publications: *Council* (in English), monthly. Newsletter.

★2077★ SCOTTISH ASSOCIATION OF FAMILY CONCILIATION SERVICES (SAFCOS)
127 Rose St.
South Ln.
Edinburgh EH2 5BB, Scotland   PH: 31 2201610
Susan Matheson, Director   FX: 31 2206895

Founded: 1987. **Languages:** English. **National.** Promotes the availability of family counseling and conciliation services in Scotland. Works to maintain high standards for the qualifications and accreditation of consiliators.

Publications: *Me and My Changing Family*. Booklet. ● *Children in Conciliation*. Booklet. ● *Divorce Counselling and Conciliation Services in Sweden and Scotland*. Booklet. ● *Annual Report*. ● *Bulletin*, semiannual.

★2078★ SCOTTISH CHILD AND FAMILY ALLIANCE (SCAPA)
55 Albany St.
Edinburgh EH1 3QY, Scotland
Anne Lancaster, Contact   PH: 31 5572780

Founded: 1983. **Members:** 200. **Languages:** English. **National.** Represents the interests of children and families in Scotland, fostering communication between professionals, parents, and government agencies and evaluating and reacting to policy proposals. Participates in conferences, seminars, and training services. List of publications available upon request.

★2079★ SCOTTISH CO-OPERATIVE WOMEN'S GUILD
95 Morrison St.
Glasgow G5 8LP, Scotland
Morag Frame, Secretary   PH: 41 4291457

Founded: 1892. **Members:** 1,600. **Languages:** English. **National**. Studies and implements the best means of strengthening and extending the women's co-operative movement locally, nationally, and internationally to promote women's economic development. Stimulates thought on all questions of social and political reform.

★2080★ SCOTTISH CONVENTION OF WOMEN (SCOW)
88 Main St.
Davidson's Mains
Edinburgh EH4 5AB, Scotland   PH: 31 3363630

Founded: 1977. **Languages:** English. **National**. National and regional women's organizations and individuals. Provides a forum for the discussion of women's issues and a framework for action.

★2081★ SCOTTISH COUNCIL FOR SINGLE PARENTS (SCSP)
13 Gayfield Sq.
Edinburgh EH1 3NX, Scotland   PH: 31 5563899

Founded: 1944. **Members:** 159. **Languages:** English. **National**. Organizations and individuals. Provides support, information, and counseling services to single parents. Organizes conferences and workshops. Offers training and assistance to agencies which help single parents. **Computer Services:** Data base.

★2082★ SCOTTISH TRADES UNION CONGRESS - WOMEN'S
COMMITTEE
16 Woodlands Terr.
Glasgow G3 6DF, Scotland
Ms. Ronnie McDonald, Contact   PH: 41 3324946

Founded: 1926. **Members:** 900,000. **Languages:** English. **National**. Seeks the improvement of the status of working women in Scotland. Offers educational programs for women in trade unions. Cooperates with other organizations pursuing equal treatment and opportunities for women.

Publications: *General Council Report*, periodic. ● *Annual Congress Report*. ● *Equal Voices*, periodic. Magazine. ● *Youth Agenda*, periodic. Bulletin. ● *Equal Opportunities in the Arts*. Booklet. ● *Scotland: A Land Fit for People*. Book.

★2083★ SCOTTISH WOMEN'S AID
13 N. Bank St.   PH: 31 2258011
Edinburgh EH1 2LP, Scotland   31 2253321

Founded: 1975. **Members:** 37. **Languages:** English. **National**. Women's aid groups. Offers information, counselling and support services, and shelters to battered women and their children. Monitors legisltation to ensure that battered women's rights and well-being are protected.

Publications: *Videos*.

★2084★ SCOTTISH WOMEN'S RURAL INSTITUTES
42 Heriot Row
Edinburgh EH3 6ES, Scotland
Mrs. Eileen Nicol, Gen.Sec.   PH: 31 2251724

Founded: 1917. **Members:** 38,500. **Languages:** English. **National**. Promotes the interests of women living in rural areas in Scotland. Offers educational and recreational activities to women residing in the country or interested in country living. Encourages home-grown food production, home industry, and craftsmanship. Addresses issues of family welfare and community matters. Works to preserve the traditions of rural Scotland. Promotes peaceful living and understanding.

Publications: *Scottish Home and Country*, monthly. Magazine.

★2085★ UNION OF CATHOLIC MOTHERS (SCOTTISH NATIONAL
COUNCIL)
34 Kirkwood Ave.
Clydebank G81 2SX, Scotland
Mrs. M. Lyden   PH: 41 9521570

Founded: 1942. **Members:** 2,786. **Languages:** English. **National**. Promotes the adherence to moral teachings of the Catholic church by women; encourages a respect for traditional Christian values within the family. Offers support services to struggling families.

Publications: *Newsletter*.

★2086★ WOMEN INTO COMPUTING
University of Glasgow
Dept. of Computer Science
Glasgow G12 8QQ, Scotland
Helen Watt, Contact   PH: 41 3398855

Founded: 1987. **Members:** 300. **National**. Supports the advancement of women in the computer industry. Encourages continued training and career development efforts.

Publications: *Women in Computing* (in English). Magazine. ● *Newsletter*, periodic.

★2087★ WOMEN OF THE YEAR ASSOCIATION
Tower Office
Jedburgh TD8 6NX, Scotland
Betty McLeish, Contact

Founded: 1981. **Members:** 350. **National**. Promotes women's role in society throughout the United Kingdom. Recognizes women who have distinguished themselves through charitable work.

Publications: *Newsletter*, annual.

★2088★ WOMEN'S AUXILIARY TO THE BAPTIST UNION OF
SCOTLAND
Failte
4 Argyle St.
Dundee DD4 7AL, Scotland
Mrs. G.C. Neilson, Secretary   PH: 382 43486

Founded: 1909. **Members:** 3,152. **Languages:** English. **National**. Women promoting the Baptist faith in Scotland. Organizes and overseas work of Baptist women. Offers assistance to the Baptist Union for the advancement of the demonimation.

Publications: *Annual Report*.

★2089★ WOMEN'S FORUM SCOTLAND
2/L 147 Kenmure St.
Pollokshields
Glasgow G41 2NU, Scotland
Karen Willey, Contact   PH: 41 4294106

Founded: 1990. **Members:** 21. **Languages:** English. **National**. Seeks equal opportunities for women and the full recognition of women's rights.

★2090★ WOMEN'S LEGAL DEFENSE FUND (WLDF)
12 Picardy Pl., Rm. 5
Edinburgh, Scotland
Ms. Shelley M. Mortimer, Office Mgr.   PH: 31 5571018

Founded: 1989. **Members:** 120. **Budget:** £3,200. **Languages:** English. **National**. Women lawyers and other professional women from ages 20 to 50. Seeks to enhance the social status of women in Scotland. Strives to eradicate sexual discrimination. Offers counseling and legal representation. Disseminates information.

Conventions/Meetings: quarterly board meeting - Edinburgh, Scotland.

★2091★ WOMEN'S SUPPORT PROJECT
871 Springfield Rd.
Glasgow G31 4HZ, Scotland   PH: 41 5545669
Jan Macleod, Dev. Worker   FX: 41 5540786

Founded: 1983. **Staff:** 2. **Budget:** £80,000. **Languages:** English. **National.** Offers emotional and material support to women and children who are victims of abuse. Administers training courses for organizations. Organizes discussion and support groups for women. Offers self-defense classes for women. Conducts research. **Libraries:** Type: lending; reference; open to the public. Holdings: books, video recordings, audio recordings. Subjects: male violence against women and children. **Telecommunication Services:** TDD, 41 5565205.

Publications: *Register and Services on Child Sexual Abuse in Scotland*, annual. Directory. ● *Resource List*, periodic. Directory. ● *Reports on Support Groups for Women Whose Children Have Been Sexually Abused*. Booklet. ● *Glasgow Women's Directory*. Information and contacts for women's organizations and services.

Spain

★2092★ AGORA FEMINISTA
Almagro 28
E-28010 Madrid, Spain   PH: 1 4102093

Languages: Spanish. **National.** Emphasizes importance of feminism in women's fight for equal treatment and status. Investigates women's social situation and disseminates findings.

★2093★ ASOCIACION ASISTENCIA A MUJERES VIOLADAS
O'Donnell 42, bajo
E-28009 Madrid, Spain   PH: 1 5740110

Languages: Spanish. **National.** Works with female rape victims. Seeks to eradicate all violence against women. Provides legal, medical, and psychological aid and advice.

★2094★ ASOCIACION ATENCION Y REINSERCION MUJER PROSTITUIDA (APRAMP)
Plaza del Angel 14, 1 izquierda
E-28012 Madrid, Spain   PH: 1 3693172

Languages: Spanish. **National.** Works with female prostitutes. Trains women in alternative job skills and offers educational assistance.

★2095★ ASOCIACION AYUDA A MADRES DE MINUSVALIDOS
Villa de Marin 47, 3 D
E-28029 Madrid, Spain   PH: 1 3147785

Languages: Spanish. **National.** Offers supportive services to pregnant women of low income. Provides information about prenatal care, child care, and maternal health.

★2096★ ASOCIACION CATOLICA MUJERES SEPARADAS Y DIVORCIADAS
Fuente del Berro 35, 2 derecha
E-28009 Madrid, Spain   PH: 1 4015433

Languages: Spanish. **National.** Separated and divorced, Catholic women. Offers counseling and help with various aspects of divorce and marital separation.

★2097★ ASOCIACION PARA LA DEFENSA DE LA IMAGEN PUBLICA DE LA MUJER
Cordoba 6, 202 bis
E-29001 Malaga, Spain   PH: 52 217044

Languages: Spanish. **National.** Works to replace cultural stereotypes of women with positive images. Investigates women's status and distributes the findings. Interacts with media.

★2098★ ASOCIACION ESPANOLA INVESTIGACION DE HISTORIA DE MUJERES (AEIHM)
Univ. Complutense
Facultad de G. e Historia
Historia Contemporanea, D-39
E-28040 Madrid, Spain   PH: 1 5499600

Languages: Spanish. **National.** Conducts research on the history of women. Strives to increase public awareness of women's place in history.

★2099★ ASOCIACION ESPANOLA MUJERES JURISTAS
Almagro 28, bajo
E-28010 Madrid, Spain   PH: 1 3081847

Languages: Spanish. **National.** Female judges, lawyers, and others working in the legal profession in Spain. Provides a forum for members to interact socially and professionally. Offers career development opportunities.

★2100★ ASOCIACION ESPANOLA MUJERES DE NEGOCIOS
Zurbano 26, 2 A
E-28010 Madrid, Spain   PH: 1 4102336

Languages: Spanish. **National.** Spanish, business women. Trains and informs women interested in business careers. Encourages female empowerment through productive employment.

★2101★ ASOCIACION ESPANOLA MUJERES PROFESIONALES Y TECNICAS
Bravo Murillo 357
E-28020 Madrid, Spain   PH: 1 4102336

Languages: Spanish. **National.** Spanish women working in professional and technical jobs. Investigates the work setting for women and seeks to abolish job-related discrimination. Provides career development opportunities for members.

★2102★ ASOCIACION ESPANOLA SEXOLOGIA CLINICA
Ayala 94
E-28001 Madrid, Spain   PH: 1 4133900

Languages: Spanish. **National.** Medical facilities specializing in sexual and reproductive issues. Works to provide access to medical and psychological assistance. Disseminates information.

★2103★ ASOCIACION INTERNACIONAL MUJERES EN LAS ARTES (AIMA)
Pedro de Valdivia 34
E-28006 Madrid, Spain
Prudencia Sanz, Contact   PH: 1 5612486

Founded: 1990. **Members:** 100. **Languages:** Spanish. **Multinational.** Women interested in promoting and defending all forms of art. Seeks to uphold values of quality, good taste, and ethics in art; and to increase awareness of the esthetic, intellectual, and ethical importance of human beings. Conducts educational programs. Organizes concerts, expositions, dramatic presentations, conferences, and dances. Publishes works by women. Awards prizes. Contributes to charity. Maintains a museum and a documentation center.

Conventions/Meetings: monthly meeting (exhibits).

★2104★ ASOCIACION LIBRERIAS DE MUJERES "UNA PALABRA
OTRA"
San Cristobal 17
E-28012 Madrid, Spain   PH: 1 5217043

Languages: Spanish. **National**. Women booksellers and women's bookstore owners. Functions as a forum for exchange of books and ideas. Encourages professional and social interaction among members.

★2105★ ASOCIACION MUJERES ARTISTAS
Boix y Moret 9, 1 A
E-28003 Madrid, Spain   PH: 1 2542554

Languages: Spanish. **National**. Female artists and patrons of women's art. Promotes display and creation of art by women. Supports the professional goals of women artists.

★2106★ ASOCIACION MUJERES DEMOCRATAS
Genova 13
E-28004 Madrid, Spain   PH: 1 4192027

Languages: Spanish. **National**. Women supporting democracy in Spain. Supports political agendas that reflect democratic goals. Works to increase public awareness of related issues.

★2107★ ASOCIACION MUJERES EN LA ENSENANZA
Plaza Tirso de Molina 5, 5 D
E-28012 Madrid, Spain   PH: 1 2692152

Languages: Spanish. **National**. Female teachers and women employed in the educational field. Seeks to improve quality of teaching and education. Works to maintain high standards for the teaching profession. Encourages professional development of members.

★2108★ ASOCIACION MUJERES INTERNACIONALISTAS
Barquillo 44, 2 izquierda
E-28004 Madrid, Spain   PH: 1 3193689

Languages: Spanish. **National**. Spanish women seeking an international community. Promotes cooperation and friendship among women worldwide.

★2109★ ASOCIACION MUJERES EN LA MUSICA
Almagro 28
E-28010 Madrid, Spain   PH: 1 7637649

Languages: Spanish. **National**. Female musicians and others. Works to help women establish themselves in musical careers.

★2110★ ASOCIACION MUJERES PARA EL OCIO Y TIEMPO LIBRE
Barquillo 44, 2 izquierda
E-28004 Madrid, Spain   PH: 1 3193689

Languages: Spanish. **National**. Women interested in shortening the work week and increasing opportunities for relaxation. Promotes career development programs.

★2111★ ASOCIACION MUJERES POR LA PAZ
Almagro 28
E-28010 Madrid, Spain   PH: 1 3081847

Languages: Spanish. **National**. Seeks to end violence, war, and crimes against women. Disseminates information about the effects of violence.

★2112★ ASOCIACION MUJERES PARA LA SALUD (AMS)
Sanchez Pacheco, 38
E-28003 Madrid, Spain
Soledad Muruaga Lopez de Guerenu,   PH: 1 4134383
    President & Dir.   FX: 1 4134383

Founded: 1983. **Members:** 5,000. **Staff:** 8. **Budget:** 45,000,000 Ptas.

Languages: English, Spanish. **National**. Promotes and supports women's health. Conducts educational and informational seminars on health and women's issues. Conducts research and disseminates information on contraception, in vitro fertilization, abortion, maternal and infant mortality, and health of migrant women. Maintains a health center providing medical attention and information; maintains an activities center for women offering workshops on women's issues, video forums, and general discussion groups. Organizes and coordinates activities with women's organizations. **Libraries:** Type: reference; lending. Holdings: books, archival material.

Publications: *La Boletina* (in Spanish), quarterly. Journal. Health, feminist, and organizational information. **Circulation:** 1,000. **Advertising:** not accepted.

★2113★ ASOCIACION NACIONAL MUJERES ESPANOLAS GITANAS
ROMI SERSENI
Meson de los Panos 1
E-28013 Madrid, Spain

Languages: Spanish. **National**. Works with Gypsy women in Spain. Offers supportive services and informational assistance.

★2114★ ASOCIACION SIMONE DE BEAUVOIR
Camarena 204, local 1
E-28047 Madrid, Spain   PH: 1 7194687

Languages: Spanish. **National**. Works to uphold the feminist ideals of Simone de Beauvoir. Encourages women to be politically active. Encourages fellowship among members.

★2115★ ASOCIACION SOLIDARIDAD CON MADRES SOLTERAS
(ASMS)
Almagro 28, bajo
E-28010 Madrid, Spain
Mercedes Montero Rumbao, President   PH: 1 3082150

Founded: 1984. **Staff:** 1. **Languages:** Spanish. **National**. Studies the social, economic, and legal conditions of single mothers. Works to increase public awareness of the needs of single mothers. Provides job finding assistance, child care services for working mothers, and educational programs. Conducts seminars and working groups.

Conventions/Meetings: annual general assembly.

★2116★ ASOCIACION UNIVERSITARIA DE ESTUDIOS DE LA MUJER
Apartado de Correos 523
E-25000 Lerida, Spain

Languages: Spanish. **National**. Studies women, women's issues, and society. Offers educational opportunities for women.

★2117★ ASSOCIATION OF FAMILIES AND WOMEN FROM THE
RURAL WORLD (AFWRW)
(Asociacion de Familias y Mujeres del Medio Rural)
                                         PH: 1 5704114
Rosario Pino 6, 9 A   1 5704229
E-28020 Madrid, Spain   FX: 1 5703208

Founded: 1982. **Members:** 5,800. **Budget:** 4,000,000 Ptas. **Languages:** Spanish, English. **National**. Women who live in rural areas. Works to improve the economic, social, and cultural conditions of women. Assists with, and manages projects for, rural women striving to create their own businesses. Promotes women's participation in the commercialization of agricultural products. Conducts educational courses and conferences.

Publications: *Hoja Informativa* (in Spanish), bimonthly. Bulletin. **Circulation:** 2,000.

Conventions/Meetings: annual Seminario Europeo de la Comision Europea

del COPA seminar   .. ● annual Jornada sobre la Salud de la Mujer
Rural - 1993 Nov..

★2118★ ATHENEA - INVESTIGACION E INTERVENCION (AREA MUJER)
Marques de Urquijo 24, 1 B
E-28008 Madrid, Spain   PH: 1 5593322

Languages: Spanish. **National.** Researches women and women's issues in Spain. Makes recommendations based on findings. Seeks to prevent discrimination and violence against women.

★2119★ AULA FORMACION FEMINISTA
Araucaria 9, bajo
E-28039 Madrid, Spain   PH: 1 3117097

Languages: Spanish. **National.** Offers education in feminist theory and women's issues. Seeks to increase awareness of women's concerns.

★2120★ CARITAS ESPANOLA
San Bernardo 99, bis 7
E-28015 Madrid, Spain   PH: 1 4455300

Languages: Spanish. **National.** Catholic organization of women in Spain involved in relief and social welfare programs. Programs include disaster assistance and financial support.

★2121★ CENTRE D'INVESTIGACIO HISTORICA DE LA DONA (CIHD)
Brusi 61
E-08023 Barcelona, Spain   PH: 3 2004567
Maria Milagro-Rivera, Director   FX: 3 4144454

Founded: 1982. **Members:** 80. **Languages:** Spanish, English. **National.** Studies women's role in history and provides educational courses. Seeks to increase public awareness of women's historical relevance and their role in society. Maintains speakers' bureau. **Libraries:** Type: not open to the public; reference. Holdings: 0. Subjects: women's studies. **Computer Services:** Data base, women's history.

Publications: *DUODA: Revista d'Estudiers Femininstes* (in Spanish and Catalan), semiannual. Journal.

★2122★ CENTRO PARA EL DESARROLLO DE LA MUJER IBEROAMERICANA
Nunez Morgado 4, oficina 92
E-28036 Madrid, Spain   PH: 1 3145192

Languages: Spanish. **National.** Seeks to aid Latin American women in the struggle for social, economic, and political equality. Supports and coordinates development projects.

★2123★ CENTRO DE ESTUDIOS DE LA MUJER
Plaza Tirso de Molina 5, 1 izquierda
E-28012 Madrid, Spain   PH: 1 4293070

Languages: Spanish. **National.** Conducts research on women's issues. Offers educational services for women. Disseminates information.

★2124★ CENTRO FEMINISTA DE ESTUDIOS Y DOCUMENTACION
Barquillo 44, 2 izquierda
E-28004 Madrid, Spain   PH: 1 3193689

Languages: Spanish. **National.** Studies women's issues and feminism. Researches social conditions of women. Maintains a documentation center specializing in women.

★2125★ CENTRO DE INVESTIGACION Y FORMACION FEMINISTA
Gaztambide 11, 2 izquierda
E-28015 Madrid, Spain   PH: 1 5440518

Languages: Spanish. **National.** Conducts research and trains women from a feminist perspective. Seeks to increase awareness of women's issues. Disseminates information.

★2126★ CENTRO PROMOCION Y DESARROLLO DE LA MUJER ESPANOLA-LATINOAMERICANA
Peal 16, 2
E-28018 Madrid, Spain   PH: 1 7857042

Languages: Spanish. **National.** Provides developmental opportunities and information for Spanish-Latin American women. Promotes eradication of legal, political, and social limitations.

★2127★ COLECTIVO DE APOYO SOCIOSANITARIO A LA MUJER PROSTITUTA
Ninas 17, apartado 412
E-28004 Madrid, Spain   PH: 1 5322748

Languages: Spanish. **National.** Works to improve the health of female prostitutes and to provide them with alternative employment. Seeks to eliminate the societal conditions that lead women to prostitution.

★2128★ COLECTIVO DE MUJERES LIBERTARIAS
Almagro 28
E-28010 Madrid, Spain   PH: 1 2419131

Languages: Spanish. **National.** Women fighting for freedom. Seeks to obtain equal rights and privileges for Spanish women.

★2129★ COMISION DE ASOCIACIONES DE MUJERES PARA EL SEGUIMIENTO DEL PIOM
Almagro 28
E-28010 Madrid, Spain   PH: 1 3080993

Languages: Spanish. **National.** Coordinates activities and supports the objectives of women's organizations.

★2130★ COMISION PARA LA INVESTIGACION DE MALOS TRATOS A LAS MUJERES
Almagro 28
E-28010 Madrid, Spain   PH: 1 3082704

Languages: Spanish. **National.** Researches violence against women. Offers help to victims of rape, incest, and domestic violence. Provides legal advice. Disseminates findings.

★2131★ COMITE REIVINDICATIVO CULTURAL DE LESBIANAS (CRECUL)
Barquillo 44, 2 izquierda
E-28004 Madrid, Spain
Elena Criado de Leon, President   PH: 1 3193689

Founded: 1991. **Languages:** Spanish. **National.** Works to increase awareness of problems lesbians face. Seeks to end sexual and gender discrimination in the workplace. Provides legal advice and encourages lesbians to work for their rights. Seeks to create a new social definition of lesbians that will allow them total equality. Conducts public educational and informational sexuality programs. Collects and disseminates summaries of films, books, and art works relevant to lesbians. Researches the history of lesbians and lesbianism.

Publications: *Mujeres y Punto* (in Spanish), quarterly. Magazine. **Advertising:** not accepted.

★2132★ COMMISSION FOR ABORTION RIGHTS (CAR)
(CDA Comision pro Derecho al Aborto)
Barquillo 44, 12 Q
E-28004 Madrid, Spain
Erika Laredo, Contact   PH: 1 3193689

Founded: 1981. Members: 16. Languages: Spanish. National. Doctors, students, teachers, and workers in Spain interested in guarding the reproductive rights of women including the right to a free abortion. Organizes educational programs on contraception; offers counseling and advice. Maintains speakers' bureau and biographical archives; compiles statistics.

Publications: *Hinojo y Perejil* (in Spanish), periodic. Bulletin. ● *Tribunal Against Aggressions Against Women for Abortion Rights*. Booklet.

★2133★ CONSEJO NACIONAL DE MUJERES DE ESPANA
Diputacion 306, principal
E-08009 Barcelona, Spain
Maria Luisa Olivada, President   PH: 3 2363289

Languages: Spanish. National. Works with women and investigates their needs. Strives for social, economic, and legal equality.

★2134★ CONTEMPORARY ARTIST WOMEN ASSOCIATION (CAWA)
Moratines 22, 1 A
E-28005 Madrid, Spain
Blanca Gutierret Ortiz, President

PH: 1 5170811
FX: 1 5175834

Founded: 1990. Members: 300. Languages: Spanish, French, German, Italian, Portuguese. Multinational. Female artists. Encourages, aids, directs, coordinates, and displays cultural or artistic projects produced by women and other marginalized groups. Maintains studios for artists. Offers advice on and produces portfolios for women's art. Interacts with other women's groups. Maintains a documentation center.

Publications: *MUAC* (in Spanish, German, Italian, Portuguese, and French), quarterly. Circulation: 2,000. Advertising: accepted.

★2135★ COORDINADORA DE COMISIONES PRO DERECHO AL
    ABORTO
Barquillo 44, 2 izquierda
E-28004 Madrid, Spain   PH: 1 3193689

Languages: Spanish. National. Coordinates activities and communication between reproductive rights organizations. Seeks to make safe, legal abortion accessible to all women.

★2136★ COORDINADORA ESTATAL DE MUJERES ABOGADAS
Arturo Soria 256
E-28003 Madrid, Spain   PH: 1 1029794

Languages: Spanish. National. Women lawyers. Supports the objectives of women working in the legal profession.

★2137★ COORDINADORA DE GRUPOS PARA LA LIBERACION
    SEXUAL
Barquillo 44, 2 izquierda
E-28004 Madrid, Spain   PH: 1 3193689

Languages: Spanish. National. Organizes activities of groups seeking to liberate women from employment, legal, social, and political discrimination.

★2138★ EUROPEAN ASSOCIATION FOR THE DEVELOPMENT OF
    INFORMATION AND TRAINING OF WOMEN - SPAIN (EUDIFF)
(Asociacion Europea para el Deslarrollo de la Informacion y Formation de las Mujeres - Spain)
Instituto de la Mujer
Almagro 36
E-28010 Madrid, Spain   PH: 1 3478000
Ana Balbas-Moreno, Contact   FX: 1 3199178

Languages: Spanish. National. Circulates information on women and women's issues throughout Spain. Networks with organizations that also champion women's advancement. Demands that EC nations fully recognize women's rights. Supports women's development and equality; encourages women's participation in leadership roles. Facilitates exchange among members.

★2139★ FEDERACION DE ASOCIACIONES DE MUJERES
    SEPARADAS-DIVORCIADAS
Santa Engracia 128, bajo B
E-28010 Madrid, Spain   PH: 1 4418560

Languages: Spanish. National. Works with groups comprised of separated and divorced women. Coordinates activities among such groups. Seeks equitable marriage laws. Provides information, support, and advice.

★2140★ FEDERACION DE ASOCIACIONES DE VIUDAS HISPANIA
Alfonso XI 4, 6a planta
E-28014 Madrid, Spain   PH: 1 25313577

Languages: Spanish. National. Works with groups that assist widows. Coordinates activities among such groups. Provides counseling, financial advice, and legal help.

★2141★ FEDERACION DE CLUBS VINDICACION FEMINISTA
Magdalena 29, 1 centro
E-28012 Madrid, Spain   PH: 1 3694488

Languages: Spanish. National. Feminist groups. Works to increase public awareness of women's issues and concerns. Promotes the development of women and women's organizations in Spain.

★2142★ FEDERACION ESPANOL DE MUJERES EMPRESARIAS, DE
    NEGOCIOS Y PROFESIONALES
Zurbano 26, 2 A
E-28010 Madrid, Spain   PH: 1 3180948

Languages: Spanish. National. Spanish women working in business and the professions. Promotes the development of career-oriented women. Supports the goals and objectives of members. Provides a forum for social and professional interaction.

★2143★ FEDERACION IBEROAMERICANA DE MUJERES DE
    EMPRESA (FIDE)
Manuel de Falla 3, 5 derecha
E-28036 Madrid, Spain   PH: 1 4586991

Languages: Spanish. Multinational. Latin American business women. Promotes the development of women employed in professional fields. Coordinates programs.

★2144★ FEDERACION INTERNACIONAL DE MUJERES DE
    CARRERAS JURIDICAS
Francisco Silvela 79, 2
E-28028 Madrid, Spain   PH: 1 2620011

Languages: Spanish. Multinational. Female judges and lawyers. Promotes the development of women employed in the legal profession. Provides a forum for members to interact socially and professionally.

★2145★ FEDERACION DE MUJERES PROGRESISTAS
Francisco Silvela 94, 1 derecha
E-28002 Madrid, Spain   PH: 1 5645181

Languages: Spanish. **National.** Women working to develop and incorporate progressive social policies. Works with other women's groups to achieve objectives.

★2146★ FEDERACION DE ORGANIZACIONES FEMINISTAS DEL ESTADO ESPANOL
Barquillo 44, 2 izquierda
E-28004 Madrid, Spain   PH: 1 3193689

Languages: Spanish. **National.** Works to unite Spanish feminist groups. Promotes ideals of feminism and supports objectives of member organizations. Disseminates information to groups and individuals. Coordinates activities.

★2147★ FEDERACION DE PLANIFICACION FAMILIAR DE ESPANA (FPFE)
Almagro 28   PH: 1 3199276
E-28010 Madrid, Spain   1 3082286
Ms. Isabel Fuster, President   FX: 1 3081589

Languages: Spanish. **National.** Works to improve the quality of life for individuals living in Spain by promoting responsible parenthood and family planning. Attempts to stop the spread of AIDS and other sexually transmitted diseases through education and contraceptive services. Offers programs in family planning and health care. Acts as an advocate for family planning on the national level.

★2148★ FORO DE ESTUDIOS SOBRE LA MUJER (FEM)
Ayala 53, 1 derecha
E-28001 Madrid, Spain   PH: 1 4026704

Languages: Spanish. **National.** Studies the status of women, women's history, and women's issues. Seeks to increase public awareness of women and their unique concerns. Disseminates information.

★2149★ FORUM DE POLITICA FEMINISTA
Barquillo 44, 2 izquierda
E-28004 Madrid, Spain   PH: 1 3193689

Languages: Spanish. **National.** Feminist women. Encourages women to be politically active and to fight for their rights. Provides opportunities for feminists to voice their opinions.

★2150★ GRUPO DE MUJERES FEMINISTAS INDEPENDIENTES
Barquillo 44, 2 izquierda
E-28004 Madrid, Spain   PH: 1 3193689

Languages: Spanish. **National.** Feminist women and women's groups. Works to empower women. Investigates women's issues from a feminist perspective. Conducts activities with other women's organizations.

★2151★ MEDICAL WOMEN'S INTERNATIONAL ASSOCIATION - SPAIN
Plaza Conde del Valle
Suchil 19-3D
E-28015 Madrid, Spain
Gloria Alouse Munarriz, Contact

Languages: Spanish. **National.** Spain national branch of the Medical Women's International Association (see separate entry). Women physicians. Provides a forum for discussion of women's health care issues. Encourages women to enter the field of medicine. Works to overcome discrimination against female physicians. Sponsors research and educational programs.

★2152★ MOVIMIENTO PARA LA LIBERACION E IGUALDAD DE LA MUJER (MLIM)
Campomanes 8, 2 C
E-28013 Madrid, Spain   PH: 1 5595234

Languages: Spanish. **National.** Works to achieve gender equality and to assist women in gaining access to all legal rights denied women. Organizes campaigns. Disseminates information.

★2153★ MUJERES POR COLOMBIA
Barquillo 44, 2 izquierda
E-28004 Madrid, Spain   PH: 1 3193689

Languages: Spanish. **National.** Spanish women working for peace in Colombia. Supports development activities.

★2154★ MUJERES PERUANAS ILLARY
Barquillo 44, 2 izquierda
E-28004 Madrid, Spain   PH: 1 3193689

Languages: Spanish. **Multinational.** Peruvian and Spanish women. Promotes fellowship between members. Coordinates activities.

★2155★ ORGANIZACION MUJERES DEMOCRATAS MANUELA MALASANA
Libertad 7, 3 derecha
E-28004 Madrid, Spain   PH: 1 5327666

Languages: Spanish. **National.** Women organized to fight for democracy and equality for all people. Coordinates activities. Disseminates information.

★2156★ ORGANIZACION DE MUJERES EMPRESARIAS Y GERENCIA ACTIVA (OMEGA)
Montesa 35, 3, oficina 312
E-28006 Madrid, Spain   PH: 1 4018926

Languages: Spanish. **National.** Women in business and management. Helps women seeking to create or expand businesses. Promotes and supports women in their professional endeavors. Provides a forum for social and career interaction among members.

★2157★ PLATAFORMA AUTONOMA FEMINISTA
Barquillo 44, 2 izquierda
E-28004 Madrid, Spain   PH: 1 3193689

Languages: Spanish. **National.** Feminist women. Promotes empowerment through self-reliance and independence. Investigates women's lives from a feminist perspective. Encourages fellowship among members.

★2158★ RED EUROPEA DE MUJERES
Barquillo 44, 2 izquierda
E-28004 Madrid, Spain   PH: 1 3193689

Languages: Spanish. **Multinational.** Works to gain independence and equality for European women. Organizes women and women's groups. Coordinates activities.

★2159★ SPANISH FEDERATION OF WOMEN IN MANAGEMENT AND ENTREPRENEURS
(Federacion Espanola de Mujeres Directivas y Empresarias)
Orense 6-8, B-7
E-28020 Madrid, Spain   PH: 1 5551855
Nieves Cervero, President   FX: 1 3207000

Founded: 1982. **Members:** 500. **Budget:** 1,000,000 Ptas. **Languages:** Spanish, English. **National.** Spanish business women. Works to improve conditions for women in business. Provides educational programs. Conducts competitions and awards prizes. Coordinates research on women's issues. Maintains a library and a documentation center.

Publications: *La Gaceta* (in Spanish), monthly. Newspaper. **Circulation:** 500. **Advertising:** accepted.

Conventions/Meetings: annual convention.

★2160★ UNION DE MUJERES POR EUROPA
Gran via 43, 2
E-28013 Madrid, Spain   PH: 1 2480869

Languages: Spanish. **Multinational.** European women. Supports fellowship among members of many nationalities. Promotes peaceful resolution of conflict. Works with other women's groups with similar goals.

★2161★ WOMEN'S INSTITUTE (WI)
(IM Instituto de la Mujer)
c/o Ministerio de Asuntos Sociales
Almagro 36   PH: 1 3478000
E-28010 Madrid, Spain   FX: 1 3199178
Matilde Vazquez, Contact   TX: 49156 IDL ME

Founded: 1983. **Members:** 160. **Budget:** 2,100,000 Ptas. **Languages:** English, Spanish. **National.** Promotes the equality and full participation of women in the cultural, economic, political, and social life of Spain. Works to effect change in social customs and individual behavior regarding women's rights. Advises and collaborates with government and public agencies in the coordination of research and creation and maintenance of women's social services. Cooperates with allied regional and international government and public institutions. Monitors media portrayal of women through participation in the Commission for Advice and Control of Advertising on Spanish Television. Receives and processes accusations of sex discrimination brought by women; offers advice, information, and referrals. Conducts research and public awareness campaigns; disseminates information. Organizes exhibitions and seminars on the situation of women in education, health, the law, the workplace, and other areas. Assists in operating Cultural Centers, Women's Advisory Centers, and women's homes and shelters. Maintains Annual Subsidy Plan for the funding of activities for women's advancement. Compiles statistics. **Libraries:** Type: reference. Holdings: books, archival material. Subjects: biographical and related materials. **Computer Services:** Data base, bibliographic, legislative, directory, and women's social indicators information. **Projects:** Annual Research Plan.

Publications: *Entre Nous*, semiannual. Newsletter. ● *Instituto de la Mujer "Catalogo de publicaciones"*, annual. ● *La Mujer Espana - Situacion Social*, periodic. ● *Mujer y Trabajo*, semiannual. Magazine. ● *Mujeres, Mulleres, Dones, Emakumear* (in Spanish), quarterly. Journal. Journal of general information on Spanish women. **ISSN:** 0213-7259. **Advertising:** not accepted. ● *Trabajo en Femenino*, semiannual. Newsletter. ● *La Mujer en Citras*. Newsletter. report with statistics. ● *Plan para la Igualdad de Oportunidades de las Mujeres (1988-1990)* (in English, French, and Spanish). Book. ● Videos.

★2162★ WOMEN'S WORLD BANKING IN SPAIN (WWB)
(Fundacion Laboral WWB en Espana)
Paseo del Marques de Zafra 7
E-28028 Madrid, Spain   PH: 1 3563004
Inger Berrgren Garnacho, President   FX: 1 3551066

Founded: 1988. **Members:** 370. **Staff:** 15. **Budget:** 60,000,000 Ptas. **Languages:** Spanish, English. **National.** Women in business, or those planning to start businesses. Works to create and expand female owned and operated enterprises. Promotes and supports women in their professional endeavors. Supplies information on financing. Provides assistance with formation and legality of written documents. Negotiates loans and credit agreements. Offers courses to women in management and general business subjects. Promotes and advertises women's businesses through fairs, expos, and business directories.

Conventions/Meetings: annual Feria de la Mujer convention (exhibits) - 1993 Nov. 25 - 27, Madrid, Spain.

★2163★ YOUNG WOMEN'S ASSOCIATION (YWA)
Almagro 28, bajo derecha
E-28010 Madrid, Spain   PH: 1 3196846
Purificacion Causapie Lopesino, President   FX: 1 3083294

Founded: 1987. **Members:** 5,500. **Staff:** 18. **Budget:** 100,000,000 Ptas. **Languages:** Spanish, English, Castilian. **National.** Young women, ages 18-30. Promotes social participation of women and works to improve their standard of living. Seeks to enhance women's opportunities for employment through the Centro de Empleo Mujeres Jovenes which provides aid in creating new businesses, management training, and professional orientation. Conducts educational programs to prevent unwanted pregnancies, sexually transmitted diseases, and AIDS. Maintains a documentation center specializing in young women and their relationship to the marketplace.

Publications: *Jovenas* (in Spanish), semiannual. Magazine. ● *Boletin Informativo* (in Spanish), monthly. Bulletin. ● *Boletina* (in Spanish), monthly. Bulletin.

Sweden

★2164★ EUROPEAN ASSOCIATION OF PERINATAL MEDICINE
(EAPM)
Unit of Pediatric Physiology
Univ. Hospital
S-751 85 Uppsala, Sweden
Dr. L.E. Bratteby, Sec.   PH: 18 167515

Founded: 1968. **Members:** 900. **Languages:** English. **Multinational.** Pediatricians, obstetricians, anesthesiologists, medical doctors, students, and nurses interested in perinatal medicine. Works to advance information and interest in perinatal medicine.

Publications: *Perinatal Medicine*, biennial.

Conventions/Meetings: biennial convention (exhibits)

★2165★ INTERNATIONAL ASSOCIATION OF WOMEN IN RADIO AND
TELEVISION (IAWRT)
c/o Christina Ruhnbro
Swedish Radio Co.
S-105 10 Stockholm, Sweden   PH: 8 7845000
Christina Ruhnbro, President   FX: 8 7842270

Founded: 1951. **Members:** 300. **Languages:** English, Swedish, Finnish. **National.** Women working professionally in radio and television broadcasting. Provides an international forum for women to share their professional interests and experiences. Works to raise the social and economic status of members. Promotes socially responsible radio and television broadcasting. Seeks to enhance exposure of women's issues in the media. **Formerly:** (1951) International Association of Radio Women.

Publications: *Newsletter*, quarterly. ● *Bulletin*, biennial. Includes register of professional media women.

Conventions/Meetings: biennial conference.

★2166★ JOINT ORGANIZATION OF NORDIC WOMEN'S RIGHTS
ASSOCIATIONS
Hornsgatan 52
S-118 21 Stockholm, Sweden   PH: 8 6443260
Fredrika Bremer, Exec. Officer   FX: 8 6433844

Members: 8. **Languages:** Swedish. **Multinational.** Representatives of women's rights organizations from Denmark (including the Faroe Islands), Finland, Norway, and Sweden. Purpose is to exchange information and organize conferences.

Conventions/Meetings: biennial.

★2167★ MEDICAL WOMEN'S INTERNATIONAL ASSOCIATION -
   SWEDEN
Alvagen 9
S-582 63 Linkoping, Sweden
Disa Lidman, Contact

Languages: Swedish, Finnish. **National.** Sweden national branch of the Medical Women's International Association (see separate entry). Women physicians. Provides a forum for discussion of women's health care issues. Encourages women to enter the field of medicine. Works to overcome discrimination against female physicians. Sponsors research and educational programs.

★2168★ MODERATE WOMEN'S ASSOCIATION
Box 1243
S-111 82 Stockholm, Sweden   PH: 8 6768105
Ulrika Johannesson, Contact   FX: 8 216123

Founded: 1920. **Members:** 35,000. **Staff:** 3. **Languages:** Swedish, English. **National.** Women supporting the Moderate Party of Sweden. Promotes women's perspectives on domestic and international politics. Disseminates information on current political issues. Fosters communication among members.

Conventions/Meetings: triennial convention (exhibits). ● periodic meeting (exhibits).

★2169★ NATIONAL ASSOCIATION OF THE INTERNATIONAL
   SOCIETY FOR IMMIGRANT WOMEN
(RIFFL Riksforbundet Internationelle Foreningan for Invandrarkvinnor)
Norrhullsgatan 45
S-113 45 Stockholm, Sweden   PH: 8 302189
T. Puurunan, Secretary   FX: 8 317011

Founded: 1974. **Members:** 2,500. **Languages:** Swedish, Finnish, English. **National.** Seeks to enhance the status of immigrant women. Works to motivate imigrant women to activism for their interests. Informs women of their rights and civic duties. Offers educational programs in languages, handicrafts, and women's issues.

Publications: *Invandrarkvinnan* (in Swedish), periodic. Magazine. ● *Invandrarkvinnor Berattar* (in Swedish). Book.

★2170★ RIKSFORBUNDET FOR SEXUELL UPPLYSNING (RFSU)
PO Box 17006
Rosenlundsgatan 13   PH: 8 6680940
S-104 62 Stockholm, Sweden   FX: 8 6685868
Ms. Katarina Lindahl, Exec. Dir.   TX: 14359 RFSUS

Languages: Swedish. **National.** Promotes family planning as a basic human right. Works to reduce the number of unwanted pregnancies and abortions. Attempts to stop the spread of AIDS and other sexually transmitted diseases. Offers programs in sex education, family planning, and health. Provides contraceptive and health care services. Conducts research.

★2171★ SWEDISH FEDERATION OF BUSINESS AND PROFESSIONAL
   WOMEN (SFBPW)
Drottninggatan 59, 3tr
S-111 21 Stockholm, Sweden   PH: 8 107414
Margareta Juhlin, Contact   FX: 8 107414

Founded: 1935. **Members:** 2,500. **Budget:** 300,000 SKr. **Languages:** English. **National.** Business and professional women. Promotes the advancement of women in education, business and employment. Champions equal rights; disseminates information; conducts programs, lectures, and seminars on women's issues.

Publications: *Women and Their Careers*. Booklet. ● *Power, Influence, Ownership*. Booklet. ● *YK-Forum*. Magazine. ● *Annual Report*, periodic.

Conventions/Meetings: biennial meeting (exhibits) - Sweden.

★2172★ SWEDISH ORGANIZATION OF EMERGENCY SHELTERS FOR
   BATTERED WOMEN
(Riksorganisationen fur Kvinnojourer i Sverige)
Hantverkargatan 7
Box 22114   PH: 8 6520720
S-104 22 Stockholm, Sweden   FX: 8 6549077
Ebon Kram, President   TX: 17041 ROKS

Founded: 1984. **Members:** 10,000. **Languages:** Swedish, English. **National.** An umbrella organization for women's shelters in Sweden. Works to prevent the physical, mental, and sexual abuse of women. Promotes women's independence and equality. Supports the creation of laws to improve the life and health of women. Disseminiates information. Conducts training courses and research projects. **Libraries:** Type: reference. Holdings: archival material. Subjects: women abuse issues.

Publications: *Kvinnotryck*, bimonthly. Magazine.

★2173★ WOMEN FOR PEACE (WP)
(KF Kvinner for Fred)
Tjarhovsgatan 9   PH: 8 6404181
S-116 21 Stockholm, Sweden   FX: 8 7021973

Founded: 1978. **Members:** 1,000. **National.** Works for peace and disarmament; social and economic justice; solidarity against poverty and oppression; and sustainable ecological development. Has organized peace marches in Paris, France, Minsk, Belarus, and Washington, DC, United States.

★2174★ WOMEN'S ASSOCIATION OF THE CENTRE PARTY (WACP)
(Centerns Kvinnoforbund)
Postfack 22039
S-104 22 Stockholm, Sweden
Ylva Schmidt, Gen.Sec.   PH: 8 6173800

Founded: 1933. **Members:** 60,000. **Staff:** 9. **Languages:** Swedish. **National.** Women interested in social and political issues in Sweden. Promotes women candidates in national and local elections. Areas of concern include environmental issues and equality between the sexes. Conducts seminars.

Publications: *Nya Budkavle* (in Swedish), bimonthly.

Conventions/Meetings: annual meeting - always June.

★2175★ WORLD WOMEN PARLIAMENTARIANS FOR PEACE
Parliament of Sweden
S-100 12 Stockholm, Sweden
Edna Madzongwe, Chair   PH: 8 700181

Languages: Swedish, Finnish. **Multinational.** Women members of national or supranational parliaments. Disseminates information on disarmament activities. Works to abolish military and political violence.

★2176★ YOUNG WOMEN'S CHRISTIAN ASSOCIATION - SWEDEN
          PH: 8 145330
          FX: 8 217522
Postfack 2054   TX: JUVENTUS 12442
S-103 12 Stockholm, Sweden   CBL: JUVENTUS
Jan Olov Soderberg, Gen.Sec.

National. Works to encourage Christian fellowship and service among young women in Sweden. Promotes justice, peace, and unity.

Switzerland

★2177★ ASSOCIATION SUISSE DES CONSEILLERES EN PLANNING FAMILIAL
c/o 3, ave. des Belles-Roches
CH-1004 Lausanne, Switzerland
Ms. Mary-Anna Barbey, Contact   PH: 21 384735

Languages: French, German, Italian. **National.** Promotes family planning and responsible parenthood as a means to improve the quality of life for individuals in Switzerland. Advocates family planning as a basic human right. Works to reduce the number of unwanted pregnancies and abortions. Offers programs in sex education, family planning, and health. Provides contraceptive and health care services. Conducts research.

★2178★ ASSOCIATION SUISSE POUR LES DROITS DE LA FEMME
Alemannengasse 42
CH-4058 Basel, Switzerland   PH: 61 6913051

Languages: French, German, Italian, English. **National.** Women in Switzerland united to promote and protect women's rights.

★2179★ BUREAU DE L'EGALITE
2, rue Henri-Fazy
CP 362
CH-1211 Geneva 3, Switzerland   PH: 22 3192065
Mrs. Marianne Frischknecht, Contact   FX: 22 3192942

Founded: 1987. **Languages:** French, English, German. **National.** State administrative officers. Strives to eliminate sexual discrimination. Promotes and protects the rights of women and men. Campaigns for matters involved with equal rights and all issues concerning women's lives. Conducts research on: family violence; women's needs in professional training; sexual harrasment in the work force; and custody cases dealing with sick children. **Libraries:** Type: open to the public. Holdings: books, clippings, video recordings. Subjects: legal information for women and men. **Awards:** Geneva's State. **Committees:** Professional Training; Professional Situation; Practical Life; Violence Towards Women.

Publications: *Actes du Colloque des 21-22, Sur la Violence a l'Egard des Femmes* (in French). ● *La Formation des Femmes* (in French). Booklet. ● *Femmes Pauvres dans Ville Riche*. Booklet.

Conventions/Meetings: bimonthly meeting.

★2180★ CAREER WOMEN'S FORUM (CWF)
Case Postale 39
CH-1211 Geneva 12, Switzerland
Denise Arbel, Pres.   PH: 22 7387196

Founded: 1982. **Members:** 150. **Staff:** 1. **Languages:** English, French. **Multinational.** Professional women active in the arts, business, and government in Geneva, Switzerland and surrounding areas. Provides a forum for business contacts.

Publications: *Bulletin* (in English and French), 3-4/year. ● *Directory* (in English and French), annual.

Conventions/Meetings: annual general assembly. ● monthly luncheon.

★2181★ EVANGELISCHER FRAUENBUND DER SCHWEIZ (EFS)
(FSFP Federation Suisse des Femmes Protestantes)
Winterthurerstr. 60
CH-8006 Zurich, Switzerland   PH: 1 3630608

Founded: 1947. **Members:** 180,000. **Staff:** 2. **Budget:** 3,000,000 SFr. **Languages:** German, French. **National.** Umbrella organization of Swiss protestant women's alliances. Addresses questions pertaining to faith, identity, gender roles, family and social life, and solidarity with the disadvantaged in Switzerland through the means of: education; seminars; and

dissemination of information. Maintains relations with a number of church and lay organizations, Swiss and foreign. Special commissions include: theology; "Journee Mondiale de Priere" (Worldly Day of Prayer); ecumenical feminine associations of French-speaking Swiss provinces; legal issues for women. Areas of involvement include: feminist theology; counseling; development; racism; bio-ethics; women and the church; and peace campaigns. Has taken an interest in, and collaborates with, Christian groups of South Africa.

Publications: *Schritte ins Offene* (in German), bimonthly. Magazine. ● *Approches* (in French), bimonthly. Magazine.

Conventions/Meetings: meeting - 3/year.

★2182★ FEDERATION SUISSE DES FAMILLES MONOPARENTALES (FSFM)
(SVAMV Schweizerischer Verband Alleinerziehender Mutter und Vater)
Kuttelgasse 8
Case Postale 4213
CH-8022 Zurich, Switzerland   PH: 1 2122511
Maja Feullmann Ph.D., Contact   FX: 1 2122445

Founded: 1984. **Staff:** 2. **Languages:** German, French. **National.** Self help groups for single parents in Switzerland. Seeks to improve the well-being of single parents and their children. Offers telephone counselling for legal, economic, pedagogical, and social problems. Represents rights of single parents in the workplace; encourages continuing education and career reentry. Organizes vacations and leisure activities. Fosters communication and solidarity among single parents. **Libraries:** Type: reference. Holdings: books.

Publications: *SVAMV-Aktuell* (in German), quarterly. Bulletin. ● *FSFM-Actuelle* (in French), quarterly. Bulletin.

Conventions/Meetings: semiannual - Zurich, Switzerland.

★2183★ GESELLSCHAFT SCHWEIZERISCHER BILDENDER KUNSTLERINNEN (GSBK)
(Societe Suisse des Femmes Peintres, Sculpteurs et Decorateurs)
Spalentorweg 10
CH-4051 Basel, Switzerland
Rita Kenel, Secretary   PH: 61 2612862

Founded: 1902. **Members:** 1,300. **Staff:** 2. **Budget:** 120,000 SFr. **Languages:** German, French. **National.** Female artists. Originally founded as response to the prohibition of admitting female artists into the Swiss Painters' and Sculptors' Association. Supports the professional and artistic objectives of, colleagues, and associates from the arts. Protects the artistic, legal, and financial interests of members. Organizes exhibits of members' artwork, and offers occupational programs. Defends interests of female artists through participation in all levels of Swiss government. Assists in provision of studios; supports the Swiss Insurance Fund for Creative Artists. Bestows financial grants to eligible members. **Awards:** Gertrud Schlatter-Fonds GSMBK (monetary). Recipient: piece of artwork in progress. **Formerly:** Gesellschaft Schweizerischer Malerinnen, Bilderinnen and Kunstgewerblerinnen.

Publications: *Schweizer Kunstlerinnen Heute* (in German). Catalogue of nature hiking exhibition 1984/85 and 1992/93. ● *Textilkunst Schweiz* (in German). Catalogue of nature hiking exhibition 1989/90. ● *Journal*, 3/year.

Conventions/Meetings: semiannual general assembly (exhibits).

★2184★ INTER-AFRICAN COMMITTEE ON TRADITIONAL PRACTICES
147, rue de Lausanne
CH-1202 Geneva, Switzerland   PH: 22 312420

Multinational. Works to eradicate traditional practices in Africa that are harmful to the emotional and physical health of women and children. Conducts research and compiles information.

Entries are listed geographically by country and alphabetically within each country

★2185★ INTERNATIONAL FEDERATION OF INFANTILE AND JUVENILE GYNECOLOGY (IFIJG)
(FIGIJ Federation Internationale de Gynecologie Infantile et Juvenile)
c/o Dr. I. Rey-Stocker
2, ave. Mercier Molin
CH-3960 Sierre, Switzerland
Dr. I. Rey-Stocker, Sec.

PH: 27 550392
FX: 27 554371

Founded: 1972. **Members:** 500. **Languages:** English, French, German. **Multinational.** Gynecologists and pediatricians in 43 countries. Promotes the diagnosis and treatment of gynecological problems during childhood and adolescence. Maintains the FIGO Joint Committee for the Study of Gynecological Problems in Childhood and Adolescence.

Publications: *Gynecologie* (in French), periodic. ● *Pediatric and Adolescent Gynecology* (in English), periodic.

Conventions/Meetings: annual European congress. ● triennial world congress - 1995.

★2186★ INTERNATIONAL FEDERATION OF UNIVERSITY WOMEN (IFUW)
(FIFDU Federation Internationale des Femmes Diplomes des Universites)
37, quai Wilson
CH-1201 Geneva, Switzerland
Dorothy Davies, Exec.Sec.

PH: 22 7312380
FX: 22 7380440

Founded: 1919. **Members:** 54. **Staff:** 10. **Languages:** English, French, Spanish. **Multinational.** National associations representing 200,000 women possessing degrees from institutions recognized by IFUW. Promotes understanding and friendship among university women of the world, irrespective of race, religion, or political opinions. Encourages international cooperation and the full application of members' knowledge and skills to national, regional, or worldwide problems. Works to further the development of education. Represents university women in international organizations. Administers fellowships and study grants; provides assistance for displaced university women. Undertakes studies and compiles reports dealing with the legal, social, political, economic and educational status of women. Conducts seminars. **Committees:** Fellowships; Relief; Status of Women and Cultural Relations.

Publications: *IFUW News* (in English and French), 5/year. ● *Triennial Report.*

Conventions/Meetings: triennial conference - 1995, Yokohama, Japan.

★2187★ ISIS - WOMEN'S INTERNATIONAL CROSS-CULTURAL EXCHANGE (ISIS-WICCE)
3, chemin des Campanules
Aire
CH-1219 Geneva, Switzerland
Valsa Verghese, Exec.Dir.

PH: 22 7964437
FX: 22 7960603

Founded: 1974. **Members:** 38. **Staff:** 6. **Budget:** US$450,000. **Languages:** English, French, Spanish. **Multinational.** International resource center organized to exchange information on women's issues. Seeks to improve the lives of women through information and communication networks. Promotes ideas and actions that help women combat sex discrimination and injustice. Sponsors a 3-month exchange program for women working on women's projects in various Third World cultures. Supports the International Feminist Network which coordinates campaigns on women's issues of justice, peace, sex discrimination, and violence. Provides information services on topics including food, health, violence against women, development, and communication. Responds to written and telephone requests; offers training and technical assistance in communication and information management; organizes internships for women activists working in fields involving women's issues. Operates documentation center; maintains feminist library.

Publications: *Monde des Femmes* (in French and English), biennial. ● *Women in Development: A Resource Guide for Organization and Action* (in English and French). Book.

Conventions/Meetings: annual workshop.

★2188★ MEDICAL WOMEN'S INTERNATIONAL ASSOCIATION - SWITZERLAND
Eleonorenstr. 9
CH-8001 Zurich, Switzerland
Ursula Jehle Bruhlmann, Contact

Languages: French, German, Italian, English. **National.** Switzerland national branch of the Medical Women's International Association (see separate entry). Women physicians. Provides a forum for discussion of women's health care issues. Encourages women to enter the field of medicine. Works to overcome discrimination against female physicians. Sponsors research and educational programs.

★2189★ MOTHER AND CHILD INTERNATIONAL (MCI)
(MEI Meres et Infants Internationale)
16, chemin Grande Gorge
CH-1255 Veyrier, Switzerland
Mrs. Gerda M. Santschi, Sec.

PH: 22 7840658
FX: 22 7840658

Founded: 1977. **Members:** 4,500. **Staff:** 2. **Budget:** US$300,000. **National Groups:** 34. **Languages:** English, French. **Multinational.** Medical professionals and individuals interested in improving maternal and neonatal care throughout the world, especially at the primary health care level. Objectives are to: promote and finance basic and applied research in the field of human reproduction, and publish and distribute the findings; improve the standards of medical and paramedical care in the field of obstetrics and gynecology; foster and finance research programs on social problems related to maternal and perinatal health; propose a curriculum for improving maternal and perinatal health to higher education institutions; disseminate scientific information concerning women, mothers, fetuses, newborns, and children. Supports projects to improve maternal and neonatal care in developing countries. **Councils:** Scientific.

Publications: *MCI Newsletter*, 3/year. ● *Proceedings of Congress*, triennial. ● *Proceedings of Workshop*, annual. ● *High Risk Mothers and Newborns - Detection, Management, and Prevention.* ● *Maternal and Child Care in Developing Countries - Assessment, Promotion.*

Conventions/Meetings: triennial International Congress for Maternal and Neonatal Health. ● annual convention, includes workshops..

★2190★ NATIONAL COUNCIL OF WOMEN OF SWITZERLAND (NCWC)
(Bund Schweizerischer Frauenorganizationen)
Altikofenstr. 182
Postfach 101
CH-3048 Worblaufen, Switzerland

PH: 31 9214848
FX: 31 9217115

National. Promotes cooperation among Swiss women for problem-solving activities nationally and internationally. Works towards the advancement of women and consolidation women to actively paticipate in matters of public interest. Defends the interests of women at federal, public, organizational levels; represents the interests of Swiss women at the international level. Organizes seminars, workshops, and conferences in an effort to support the exchange of opinions and information regarding women's issues. Conducts research and publishes discussion of the findings. **Committees:** Employment and Career; Legal and Insurance Issues; Social Issues; Economic Issues; Housing; Public Health; Mass Media; Education; National Service for Women; International Relations. **Foreign language name:** Alliance de Societe Feminines Suisses, Alleanza delle Societa Femminili Svizzere.

Conventions/Meetings: annual meeting.

★2191★ ORGANISATION GESTOSIS - SOCIETY FOR THE STUDY OF PATHOPHYSIOLOGY OF PREGNANCY (OG)
Geburtshilfe und Gynakologie FMH
Gerbergasse 14
CH-4051 Basel, Switzerland
Dr. Ernest T. Rippmann, Sec.Gen.
PH: 61 2615555
FX: 61 2615934

Founded: 1969. **Members:** 4,500. **Regional Groups:** 11. **Languages:** English, German. **Multinational.** Obstetricians, gynecologists, neonatologists, nephrologists, epidemiologists, pathologists, geneticists, immunologists, physiologists, and health officials in 75 countries in the field of EPH-Gestosis. (EPH-Gestosis is a term adopted by the society to describe a malady that may occur during pregnancy wherein a woman exhibits excessive accumulation of body water, protein in the urine, and/or abnormal elevation of blood pressure; EPH is derived from the terms for 3 conditions: edema, proteinuria, and hypertension; gestosis is derived from the word gestation and the suffix -osis which means disturbance. The condition is prevalent in socioeconomically depressed areas where poor hygiene and malnutrition aggravate the effects of inadequate prenatal care. The society reports that EPH-Gestosis occurs in 10% of births in the world's population, is responsible for as much as 50% of perinatal/fetal death, and is the cause of up to 33% of maternal mortality.) Objectives are to: disseminate information to medical and lay personnel and the public; foster research, preventive health care, and therapy; internationalize nomenclature, classification, and definitions in the field of EPH-Gestosis for diagnosis, therapy, and comparative techniques; standardize methods of investigation; serve as documentation center; foster exchange of scientists. Conducts discussion groups and study groups on topics such as edema, proteinuria, cytology, serumprotein, and hypertension. Suggests alterations of definitions of EPH-Gestosis as offered by International Classification of Diseases of the World Health Organization. Makes recommendations for the most modern and successful measures of prevention and treatment of EPH-Gestosis. Conducts postgraduate training at the Inter-University Center in Dubrovnik, Croatia. Sponsors symposia and workshops; conducts surveys. Operates Organisation Gestosis Press, a publishing house. Maintains small library. **Committees:** Consulting; Hypertension; Postgraduate Training. **Commissions:** Joint Commission Organisation Gestosis. **Divisions:** Editorial.

Publications: *Congress Volume*, annual. ● *Instruction Bulletin*, periodic. ● *International Journal of Feto-Maternal Medicine*, periodic.

Conventions/Meetings: annual congress - 1994, Dubrovnik, Croatia; 1995, Manila, Philippines; 1996, Tbilissi, Georgia.

★2192★ ORGANISATION FUR DIE SACHE DER FRAU (OFRA)
Bollwerk 39
CH-3011 Bern, Switzerland
PH: 31 223879

Languages: German. **National.** Works to raise awareness of the status of issues pertaining to women's rights and the women's movement. Encourages political action among women.

★2193★ SCHWEIZERISCHER BUND ABSTINENTER FRAUEN (SBAF)
Hohfurristr. 23
CH-8408 Winterthur, Switzerland
Annemarie Ruegg, President
PH: 52 256016

Founded: 1902. **Members:** 500. **Languages:** English, French, German. **National.** Women dedicated to a life of abstaining from alcohol consumption. Seeks to advance women's issues and public health. Encourages alcohol-free social activities. Enhances public awareness of abstinence through presentations at fairs and events. Disseminates information. **Formerly:** Ligue Suisee des Femmes Abstinentes.

Publications: *SBAF Mitteilungen* (in German), bimonthly. Newsletter. ● *En Geute* (in German). Book. ● *Bon Appetit* (in German). Book.

★2194★ SCHWEIZERISCHER LANDFRAUENVERBAND
Larstr. 10
CH-5200 Brugg, Switzerland
Rosmarie Kunz, President
PH: 56 411263

Founded: 1932. **Members:** 70,000. **Staff:** 1. **Budget:** 240,000 SFr. **Regional Groups:** 20. **Languages:** French, German. **National.** Active female farmers and naturalists. Encourages the professional development and improvement of the female farmer, steps towards the social betterment of the farming family, and the support and maintenance of nature. Represents the interests of the female farmer in federal agencies as well as ecological and other organizations. Addresses questions concerning argrarian policy. Divided into regional groups that carry out professional and cultural direction and events which are beneficial to the public at large.

Publications: *Die Bauerin* (in German), bimonthly. Newsletter.

Conventions/Meetings: annual executive committee meeting. ● quarterly board meeting. ● quarterly meeting.

★2195★ SCHWEIZERISCHER VERBAND DER AKADEMIKERINNEN (SVA)
(ASFU Association Suisse des Femmes Universitaires)
Klingentalstr. 67
CH-4057 Basel, Switzerland
Dr. F. DeSouza, Contact
PH: 61 6912142

Founded: 1924. **Members:** 1,345. **Budget:** 47,000 SFr. **Languages:** German, French, English. **National.** Women university graduates. Supports and protects the professional concerns of university-educated women through: assisting them in re-entering the workforce and beginning or continuing graduate studies; representing their interests vis a vis the federal govenrent; and participating with organizations pursuing similar objectives. Works towards the goals of: improving the position of educated women in the spheres of the economy and society; assisting members in developing professional contacts; and improving the interdisciplinary and international exchange of view points among university-educated women. **Committees:** Scholarship; Economic Status of Women; International Relations; European Relations.

Publications: *Heureka, die Zukunft der Forschung aus der Sicht von Frauen* (in German and French). Booklet. ● *Bulletin* (in German and French), semiannual. ● *Directory*, periodic.

Conventions/Meetings: bimonthly general assembly - Zurich, Switzerland; Basel, Switzerland.

★2196★ SOROPTIMIST INTERNATIONAL OF EUROPE (SIE)
(Soroptimist International d'Europe)
72, route de Florissant
CH-1206 Geneva, Switzerland
Marie-Irene Paleologue, Exec. Officer
PH: 22 3460880
FX: 22 7890443

Founded: 1924. **Members:** 22,310. **Regional Groups:** 34. **Languages:** English, French. **Multinational.** Women engaged in business and professional occupations, including that of homemaker. Participates in the struggle for peace, human rights, environmental protection, and the rights of women. Works to improve living conditions in developing countries through water sanitation projects; agricultural cooperatives and other income-generating projects; and leadership and management training for women. Is involved in drug abuse prevention, providing shelter to children, and aid to refugees; calls for legal assistance involving questions such as surrogate motherhood, in vitro fertilization, female circumcision, and early childhood marriage. Establishes standards of business ethics. Sponsors research; conducts seminars and symposia.

Publications: *Beinenu* (in English and Hebrew), annual. ● *Directory* (in English and French), annual. ● *The Link* (in English and French), quarterly. ● *Soroptima* (in Danish), 10/year. ● *Unions-Nachrichten* (in German), 10/year.

Conventions/Meetings: annual convention.

★2197★ UNION OF JEWISH WOMEN'S SOCIETIES IN SWITZERLAND
(BSIF)
(Bund Schweizerischer Israelischer Frauenvereine)
Schlossstr. 11
CH-8803 Rueschlikon, Switzerland   PH: 1 7242630
Beatrice Zucker, President   FX: 1 7240864

Founded: 1924. **Members:** 3,000. **Budget:** 8,000 SFr. **Languages:** German, French, English. **National.** Promotes networking among Jewish women's organizations in Switzerland. Represents the interests of Jewish women to authorities and organizations nationally and internationally; participates in governmental policy and decision making procedures, representing demands of Jewish women experiencing discrimination; studies and monitors legal protection measures of women against harassment and discrimination. Encourages education, development, and consciousness-raising of Jewish women. Sends delegates to national and international congresses and conferences. Implements strategies for bringing about public awareness of the status and struggles of women. Motivates members to actively take part in projects and activities working to improve the position of women. **Also Known As:** Union des Societes des Femmes Israelites Suisses.

Publications: *Newsletter* (in German and French).

Conventions/Meetings: annual convention. ● monthly meeting.

★2198★ UNITED METHODIST WOMEN IN SWITZERLAND AND IN FRANCE (UMWSF)
(Frauendienst der Evangelisch-Methodistischen Kirche in der Schweiz und in Frankreich)
Badenerstrasse 69
Postfach 469
CH-8026 Zurich, Switzerland
Hanni Handschin, Contact   PH: 1 2412342

Founded: 1971. **Members:** 6,000. **Budget:** 130,000 SFr. **Local Groups:** 100. **Languages:** English, French, German. **Multinational.** Women who are members of the United Methodist Church. Seeks to: share belief in Jesus Christ with women worldwide; establish a community of women within the Methodist Church; support the mission work of the church. Encourages solidarity among refugees and the economically disadvantaged. Provides services to the sick and aged; conducts religious services.

Publications: *Rundbrief* (in German), 5/year.

Conventions/Meetings: quadrennial meeting. ● annual meeting.

★2199★ VEREIN FRAU UND POLITIK
Manuelstr. 64
CH-3006 Bern, Switzerland
Erica Sardin-Toneatti, President   PH: 31 446923

Languages: German. **National.** Encourages political action among women. Provides information on the political process and on political issues of concern for women.

★2200★ WOMEN FOR PEACE (WP)
(FF Frauen fur den Frieden)
Postfach 380
CH-8025 Zurich, Switzerland

Founded: 1977. **Languages:** French, German, Italian. **National.** Works for the establishment of world peace; seeks to increase public awareness of social, economic, and military violence and to find solutions for their eradication. Coordinates national peace activities for women in Switzerland. Organizes demonstrations.

★2201★ WOMEN'S INFORMATION CENTER, THIRD WORLD (FIZ)
(FIZ Dritte Welt Frauens Informationszentrum)
Quellenstr. 25
CH-8005 Zurich, Switzerland
Brigitte Sporri, Exec. Officer   PH: 1 2718282

Founded: 1985. **Members:** 500. **Staff:** 5. **Budget:** 200,000 SFr. **Languages:** English, French, German, Portuguese, Spanish, Thai. **Multinational.** Development policy institutes; religious and social welfare organizations; women's associations; individuals. Seeks to increase awareness of the problems facing Third World women who emigrate to countries outside the Third World. Offers counseling and information programs to Third World women currently living in Switzerland or contemplating a move there. Disseminates information on Swiss working and living conditions and studies the extent and consequences of trafficking of Third World women in Switzerland. Serves as a liaison between women and institutions designed to aid them. **Computer Services:** Mailing lists, members.

Publications: *Annual Report.* ● *FIZ Newsletter* (in English, German, and Spanish), semiannual. ● *Rundbrief* (in English, French, German, and Spanish), semiannual. Newsletter.

Conventions/Meetings: annual conference, on subjects such as marriage agencies, trafficking of women, and forced prostitution.

★2202★ WOMEN'S INTERNATIONAL LEAGUE FOR PEACE AND FREEDOM - SWITZERLAND (WILPF)
(LIFPL Ligue Internationale de Femmes pour la Paix et la Liberte)
Case Postale 28
CH-1211 Geneva 20, Switzerland   PH: 22 7336175
Edith Ballantyne, Gen.Sec.   FX: 22 7401063

Founded: 1915. **National Groups:** 32. **Languages:** English, French, German, Spanish. **Multinational.** Women united to study, publicize, and help abolish the political, social, economic, and psychological causes of war, and to work toward building peace and respect for freedom. Seeks to achieve total and universal disarmament. Protests armaments, nuclear testing, military aggression, and violation of human rights through letters, petitions, visits, and demonstrations. Conducts seminars.

Publications: *Pax et Libertas* (in English and French), quarterly. Newsletter. **Advertising:** not accepted.

Conventions/Meetings: triennial congress

★2203★ WORLD FEDERATION OF UNITED NATIONS ASSOCIATIONS (WFUNA)
Palais des Nations
CH-1211 Geneva, Switzerland

Languages: French, English, German. **Multinational.** Disseminates information and educational materials on United Nations activities concerning women's issues. Lobbies authorities in different countries and educates the public on women's issues.

★2204★ WORLD YOUNG WOMEN'S CHRISTIAN ASSOCIATION (WORLD YWCA)
(Alliance Mondiale des Unions Chretiennes Feminines)
37, quai Wilson
CH-1201 Geneva, Switzerland   PH: 22 7323100
Elaine Hesse Steel, Sec.Gen.   FX: 22 7317938

Founded: 1894. **Languages:** English, French, Spanish. **Multinational.** Associations in 86 countries. Seeks to build a worldwide fellowship for young women to learn of and express the love of God. Works for the elimination of racism and racial discrimination, for economic and social justice, and for the building of a world community. Sponsors consultations on world issues and study programs for members. Attempts to make the public aware of world problems. Conducts human rights and rehabilitation projects and services for refugees and migrants. Current emphasis is on studying the problems of women in a changing world, peace, the environment, housing, health, and political and family life education. Conducts seminars.

Publications: *Annual Report.* ● *Common Concern*, quarterly. ● *Directory*, biennial.

Conventions/Meetings: quadrennial, world council - 1995.

★2205★ YOUNG WOMEN'S CHRISTIAN ASSOCIATION -
SWITZERLAND
(Alliance Nationale Suisse des Unions Chretiennes Feminines)
Teussenrain 13
CH-3454 Sumiswald, Switzerland
Inge Zinn, Treas.   PH: 34 711991

National. Works to promote Christian fellowship and service among young women in Switzerland. Encourages justice, peace, and unity. **Also Known As:** Schweizerischer Nationalverband Christlicher Vereine Junger Frauen.

Turkey

★2206★ ASSOCIATION OF DEMOCRACY FOR WOMEN
Sumer Sokak Ayas Apt. 25/7
Kizilay
Ankara, Turkey   PH: 4 2310066

National. Turkish women united to uphold the ideals of democracy. Supports women's rights.

★2207★ ASSOCIATION OF RESEARCH AND REVIEW OF WOMEN'S
SOCIAL LIFE
Akay Cad. 15/2
Kucukesat
TR-06660 Ankara, Turkey
Mufide Niron, President   PH: 4 4172604

National. Provides information on the social status and devlopment of women in Turkey. Conducts research.

★2208★ ASSOCIATION FOR SUPPORTING CONTEMPORARY LIVING
Hatay Sokak 8/17
Kizilay
Ankara, Turkey
Dr. Turkan Saylan, President   PH: 4 4257433

National. Promotes improved living conditions for women. Represents women's interests.

★2209★ ASSOCIATION OF TURKISH WOMEN PAINTERS
Bayindir Sokak 63/12
Kizilay
Ankara, Turkey
Naciye Izbul, President   PH: 4 4181403

National. Supports Turkish women painters. Provides a forum for the public to view women artist's works. Encourages artistic talents.

★2210★ ASSOCIATION OF WOMEN'S HEALTH PROTECTION
Mesrutiyet Caddesi 10/68
Kizilay
Ankara, Turkey

National. Works to provide quality health care to women and children throughout Turkey.

★2211★ ASSOCIATION OF WOMEN'S RIGHTS PROTECTION
(Kadin Haklarini Koruma Dernegi)
Yali Kosku
Vakif Hani 3 Kat
320 Yali Kosku Caddesi
Eminou
Istanbul, Turkey   PH: 1 5266094
Gonul Isler, Director   1 2457799

Founded: 1954. **Members:** 200. **Staff:** 7. **Budget:** US$1,000. **Languages:** English. **National.** Strives to protect women's rights under Turkish law. Seeks to improve awareness of women's rights and the status of women in society. Offers educational programs in writing, speaking, art, sewing, etc. Offers legal counseling. Conducts research on promotion of women's rights. **Libraries:** Type: reference.   **Awards:** Annual (recognition). Recipient: Individual who has contributed to the promotion of women's rights. **Committees:** Law; Travel; Education.

Publications: *Yenu Yasanti* (in Turkish), monthly. **Also Cited As:** *New Life*.

Conventions/Meetings: semiannual convention (exhibits). ● periodic meeting.

★2212★ BEDENSEL ENGELLILERI GUCLENDIRME VAKFI
Ilk Adim Mahallesi
Vezinli Sokak 7/6
Dikmen
Ankara, Turkey
Zeren Unal, Contact

Languages: Turkish. **National.** Women in Turkey working to improve opportunities for disabled individuals.

★2213★ CAMLICA KIZ LISELILER DERNEGI
Mesrutiyet Cad. Mesrutiyet Han 10/30
Ankara, Turkey
Evren Oktay, Contact

Languages: Turkish. **National.** Fosters the spiritual and intellectual growth of young girls and women.

★2214★ CANKAYA COCUK DOSTLARI DERNEGI
Buklum Sokak 76/2
Kavaklidere
Ankara, Turkey
Fecir Suar, Contact   PH: 4 4266683

Languages: Turkish. **National.** Women in Turkey working to enhance the welfare of children and improve child care. Promotes the advancement of maternal and infant healthcare.

★2215★ DEMET ISIK
Cagdas Yasami Destekleme Dernegi
Haytay Sokak 8/17
Kizilay
Ankara, Turkey

Works to raise awareness of women's issues in Turkey. Promotes equality between men and women.

★2216★ DIS ISLERI MENSUPLARI DAYANISMA DERNEGI
Dis Isleri Bakanligi
Tandogan
Ankara, Turkey

Wives of Turkish foreign affairs officers. Works to promote social activities among members.

★2217★ FAMILY PLANNING ASSOCIATION OF TURKEY
(Turkiye Aile Planlamasi Dernegi)
Atac Sokak 73/3
TR-06420 Ankara, Turkey
Dr. Kemal Demir, President   PH: 4 4311878

National. Promotes enhanced awareness of family planning services throughout Turkey. Advocates family planning as a basic human right. Disseminates information.

★2218★ FEDERATION OF WOMEN'S ASSOCIATIONS - TURKEY
Akay Caddesi 15/2
Kucukesat
TR-06660 Ankara, Turkey
Didar Eser, President   PH: 4 4172604

National. Represents women's interests in Turkey.

★2219★ FOUNDATION FOR THE ADVANCEMENT AND RECOGNITION
OF TURKISH WOMEN
Cinnah Caddesi 33/3
Cankaya
Ankara, Turkey   PH: 4 4409189
Semra Ozal, President   4 4406801

National. Promotes the development and enhanced status of Turkish women.

★2220★ FOUNDATION FOR THE SUPPORT OF WOMEN'S WORK
(FSWW)
Sipahioglu cad. 3/2
Yesilyurt   PH: 1 5758899
Istanbul, Turkey   1 5835025

Founded: 1986. **Languages:** English, Turkish. **National.** Professional women. Seeks to assist women's development in areas of education and training and economic independence through small business development. Offers assistance with childcare programs and counselling services.

★2221★ KADININ SOSYAL HAYATINI ARASTIRMA-INCELEME
DERNEGI
Akay Cad. 15/2
Bakanliklar
Ankara, Turkey   PH: 4 4172604
Mufide Niron, Contact   4 4389445

Languages: Turkish. **National.** Promotes the social and personal development of women in Turkey.

★2222★ KIZ IZCILER DERNEGI
Tunus Caddesi 81/13
Ankara, Turkey
Sevim Kocak, Contact   PH: 4 4262626

Languages: Turkish. **National.** Promotes the development of young women in Turkey. Encourages participation in community service activities.

★2223★ KORLERE ISIK DERNEGI
Cinnah Cad. 24/16
K. Dere
Ankara, Turkey
Perihan Ariburun, Contact   PH: 4 4271488

Languages: Turkish. **National.** Women in Turkey working to improve the welfare of visually impaired people.

★2224★ KOY OGRETMENLERI HABERLESME VE YARDIMLASMA
DERNEGI
Tumali Hilmi Cad. 61/20
K. Dere
Ankara, Turkey
Nimet Ardic, Contact   PH: 4 4185073

Languages: Turkish. **National.** Fosters public appreciation of theater and the arts. Conducts fundraisers to support community theatre programs.

★2225★ NATIONAL COUNCIL OF TURKISH WOMEN
15/2 Akay Caddesi
Kucukesat
TR-06660 Ankara, Turkey
Prof. Sveinc Karol, President   PH: 4 1172604

Languages: Turkish, English. **National.** Works to improve the status of and promote the interests of women in Turkey. Fosters friendly relations among members.

★2226★ OGRETILEBILIR COCKUKLARI KORUMA DERNEGI
Kuyuyazisi Caddesi
Kivrimli Sokak 27
Etlik
Ankara, Turkey   PH: 4 3210252
Zehra Atac, Contact   4 3237055

Languages: Turkish. **National.** Women in Turkey working to increase awareness of the challenges facing disabled children.

★2227★ PURPLE ROOF FOUNDATION FOR WOMEN'S SHELTER
c/o Canan Arin, Pres.
Cumhuriyet Cad. Fransiz Hastanesi Sok.
3/3 Ozbakir Ishani
Harbiye
Istanbul, Turkey   PH: 1 2486085
Susan Herner, Contact   FX: 1 2316872

Founded: 1990. **Staff:** 3. **Budget:** TL 275,000,000. **Languages:** Turkish, English. **National.** Works to eliminate violence against women. Seeks to raise public awareness of the prevalence of domestic violence. Fosters solidarity among victims of violence. Offers psychological and legal counselling, job placement services, educational classes, and assertiveness training programs. Plans to renovate and open a shelter for women. **Foreign language name:** Mor Cati Kadin Siginagi Vakfi.

Publications: *Bagir! Herkes Duysun* (in Turkish). Monograph. ● *Simdi Siginak Icin* (in Turkish). Monograph. ● Also publishes calendars.

Conventions/Meetings: weekly meeting.

★2228★ SOCIETY FOR PROMOTING TURKISH HANDICRAFTS
5/53 Karanfil Sokak
Kizilay
Ankara, Turkey
Mrs. Inci Erguvanli, Chair   PH: 4 4188537

Founded: 1953. **Members:** 52. **Staff:** 2. **Budget:** TL 250,000,000. **Languages:** Turkish, English. **National.** Women working to preserve and promote authentic Turkish handicrafts. Collects, exhibits, and markets antique and contemporary works of art. Conducts research on the origins of individual artifacts. Offers skill training in Turkish embroidery for women. Loans archives to various museums. **Libraries:** Type: reference.
books, archival material. Subjects: Turkish embroidery. **Committees:** Embroidery; Silver Jewelry; Copper Artifacts; Ceramic Artifacts; Kilim (flat weaving).

Conventions/Meetings: periodic meeting (exhibits).

★2229★ SOROPTIMIST INTERNATIONAL OF TURKEY
Abdi Ipekci cad. No 10
Gultepe
TR-80640 Istanbul, Turkey   PH: 1 214903
Mrs. Ayla Selcuk, President   FX: 1 843112

Founded: 1953. **Members:** 1,099. **Budget:** TL 115,000. **Regional Groups:** 34. **Languages:** English. **Multinational.** Women professionals and those working in management positions. Promotes high ethical standards in business, the professions, and other aspects of life. Advocates human rights for all people, and strives to advance the status of women. Seeks to develop a spirit of friendship and unity amony soroptimists of all countries. Administers an adult education center.

Publications: *Directory*, annual. ● *Soroptimist Dunyasi*, quarterly. **Also Cited As:** *Soroptimist World*.

Conventions/Meetings: annual general assembly (exhibits).

★2230★ TURK AMERIKAN KADINLARI DOSTLUK DERNEGI
Gunes Sokak 7/2
Ankara, Turkey
Gulten Das, Contact   PH: 4 4263033

Languages: Turkish. **National.** Women working to promote friendship, understanding, and cultural exchange between Turkish and American women.

★2231★ TURK ANNELER DERNEGI
40 Bahcelievler Sok. 12/B
Ankara, Turkey
Turkan Aksu, Contact   PH: 4 2132812

Languages: Turkish. **National.** Mothers in Turkey. Provides a forum for members to meet and develop friendly ties.

★2232★ TURK EL SANATLARINI TANITMA DERNEGI
Karanfil Sok. 5/53
Kizilay
Ankara, Turkey
Inci Erguvanli, Contact   PH: 4 4188537

Languages: Turkish. **National.** Women in Turkey working to promote and preserve traditional handicrafts and folk culture.

★2233★ TURK KADINLAR BIRLIGI
Gazi Mustafa Kemal Bulvari 94/3
Maltepe
Ankara, Turkey
Ayseli Goksoy, Contact   PH: 4 4274433

Languages: Turkish. **National.** Women in Turkey united to foster awareness of women's isssues.

★2234★ TURK KADINLARI KULTUR DERNEGI
Fevzi Cakmak Sok. 17/2
Demirtepe
Ankara, Turkey   PH: 4 4300836
Sahbat Gulay, Contact   4 4388024

Languages: Turkish. **National.** Women united to preserve traditional Turkish culture.

★2235★ TURK-PAKISTAN KADINLARI DOSTLUK DERNEGI
Mebusevleri 5, Caddesi 43
Tandogan
Ankara, Turkey
Kutsiye Kalafatoglu, Contact   PH: 4 2132807

Languages: Turkish. **National.** Women in Turkey and Pakistan engaged in cultural exchange. Fosters international understanding.

★2236★ TURKISH-AMERICAN WOMEN'S CULTURAL AND CHARITY ORGANIZATION
7/1 Gunes Sokak
Cankaya
Ankara, Turkey
Gulden Das, President   PH: 4 4278784

Founded: 1950. **Languages:** Turkish, English. **National.** English-speaking Turkish women united to promote educational and cultural activities. Fosters continuing education for women. Conducts literacy programs; operates a bookmobile. Works to improve public health through family planning, child care, and improved nutrition. Offers courses in handicrafts. **Libraries:** Type: lending. Holdings: 8,000; books. Subjects: children's books. **Awards:** Scholarship. Recipient: Female university students.

★2237★ TURKISH JURIST WOMEN'S ASSOCIATION
Bozdogan Kemeri Caddesi 1
Ogranci Kultur Sitasi Merkezi
Vezneciler
Istanbul, Turkey   PH: 1 5255856
Aysel Celikel, President   1 5281171

Women legal professionals. Promotes the interests of women lawyers and judges in Turkey.

★2238★ TURKISH MOTHERS ASSOCIATION
Menekse Sok, 8B, D. 22
Kizilay
Ankara, Turkey
Turkan Asku, President   PH: 4 4265818

Founded: 1959. **Members:** 10,000. **Staff:** 13. **Budget:** TL 175,000,000. **Regional Groups:** 40. **Languages:** Turkish, English. **National.** Provides psychological and emotional support for mothers. Believes that mothers have the collective duty to bring up a healthy nation and follow the commandments of Turkish statesman and soldier Kemal Ataturk (1881-1938). Advises women regarding contraception and family planning. Conducts educational programs for women and children; collects books to establish village libraries. Operates health clinics. Offers scholarships. **Awards:** Scholarship. **Projects:** Sewing and Handicrafts.

Conventions/Meetings: biennial conference.

★2239★ TURKISH RELIEF ASSOCIATION
Dr. Mediha Eldem Sokak
Kocatepe
Ankara, Turkey
Birsen Erden, President   PH: 4 4316220

National. Provides supports services to needy women and children throughout Turkey.

★2240★ TURKISH UNIVERSITY WOMEN'S ASSOCIATION
Basak Sokak 43/11
Kucukesat
TR-06442 Ankara, Turkey
Aymelek Tashan, President   PH: 4 4828509

National. Promotes the interests of women graduates of accredited universities and colleges in Turkey.

★2241★ TURKISH WOMEN CULTURAL ASSOCIATION
Fevzi Cakmak Sokak 17/2
Kizilay
Ankara, Turkey
Sebahat Gulay, President   PH: 4 2300836

National. Works to uphold the cultural heritage of women in Turkey. Coordinates social and cultural events.

★2242★ UNIVERSITELI KADINLAR DERNEGI
Illar Mah. 45, Sokak 13
Dikmen
Ankara, Turkey
Aymelek Tashan, Contact   PH: 4 4828509

Languages: Turkish. **National.** Women university graduates in Turkey. Works to enhance educational opportunities for women.

★2243★ UNIVERSITY OF ISTANBUL WOMEN'S RESEARCH AND
EDUCATION CENTER
Bozdgan Kemeri Caddesi 1
Ogrenci Kultur Sitesi Merkizi
Vezneciler
Istanbul, Turkey
Necla Arat, President   PH: 1 5119826

National. Sponsors research on issues of concern to Turkish women. Conducts educational programs.

★2244★ WOMEN SOLIDARITY FOUNDATION
Hisarparki Caddesi
Firuzaga Sokak 9/3
Ulus
Ankara, Turkey
Dr. Leziz Onaran, President   PH: 4 3090484

National. Fosters unity among women in Turkey.

★2245★ WOMEN'S LIBRARY AND INFORMATION CENTER
c/o Dr. Sirin Tekeli
Fener Mah. PTT Yani
Halic
Istanbul, Turkey   PH: 1 5349550
Dr. Sirin Tekeli, Contact   FX: 1 5237408

Founded: 1990. **Members:** 510. **Staff:** 1. **Languages:** English, French, German, Turkish. **National.** Seeks to raise awareness of women's issues. Promotes women's opportunities in politics, law, and education. Works to prevent sexism and improve women's health facilities. Publicizes women's artworks. **Libraries:** Type: open to the public. Holdings: 0; books, archival material, clippings, monographs, periodicals. **Committees:** Art; Literature; Archive Buildings.

Publications: *Haberler* (in Turkish), quarterly. Newsletter. Information on news, activities, and book reviews. ● Also publishes meeting proceedings and calendars.

Conventions/Meetings: annual.

★2246★ WOMEN'S RESEARCH AND EDUCATION CENTER (WREC)
Bozdogan Kemeri Caddesi No. 1
Vezneciler
Istanbul, Turkey   PH: 1 5119826
Prof. Necla Arat, Chair   FX: 1 5205473

Founded: 1990. **Staff:** 3. **Languages:** English. **National.** Promotes feminist research on Turkish women's status in social life, the legal system, politics, and labor markets. Conducts programs to further public awareness on women's issues and rights. Offers training courses to rural women not benefitted by traditional development programs. **Libraries:** Type: not open to the public.   Subjects: women's studies.

Publications: *Women's Rsearch and Education*, quarterly. Journal.

★2247★ YOUNG WOMEN'S CHRISTIAN ASSOCIATION - TURKEY
PH: 1 490415
24 Ozogul sokak   1 446747
Cihangir   CBL: EMISSARIUS
Istanbul, Turkey   ISTANBUL

National. Promotes the development of young women in Turkey. Upholds Christian beliefs and values in its programs. Works to instill self worth and self-esteem in young women.

Wales

★2248★ MERCHED Y WAWR
Penlan-Merwyn
Aberporth
Aberteifi, Dyfed, Wales
M. James, Contact   PH: 239 810999

Founded: 1967. **Members:** 9,500. **Languages:** English, Welsh. **National.** Welsh speaking women. Promotes the Welsh language, culture, and arts through educational programs and study trips.

Publications: *Y Wawr* (in Welsh), quarterly. Magazine.

Conventions/Meetings: periodic meeting.

★2249★ WALES ASSEMBLY OF WOMEN
Dyffryn
The Esplanade
Carmarthen, Wales
Helwen Humphreys MA   PH: 267 236188

Founded: 1984. **Members:** 300. **National.** Organizations and individuals. Seeks increased educational opportunity for women. Encourages women to ulitize their talents to full potential and to participate in local, national, and international issues.

★2250★ WELSH WOMEN'S AID
38-48 Crwys Rd.
Cardiff CF2 4NN, Wales   PH: 222 390874

Founded: 1978. **National.** Advocates for the welfare of battered women in Wales. Offers shelter to women and their children fleeing domestic violence. Encourages women to be self-reliant and confident in building their futures. Provides counselling services to women and children. Raises awareness of battered women and domestic violence among the public, media, police, courts, social services, etc. List of publications available upon request.

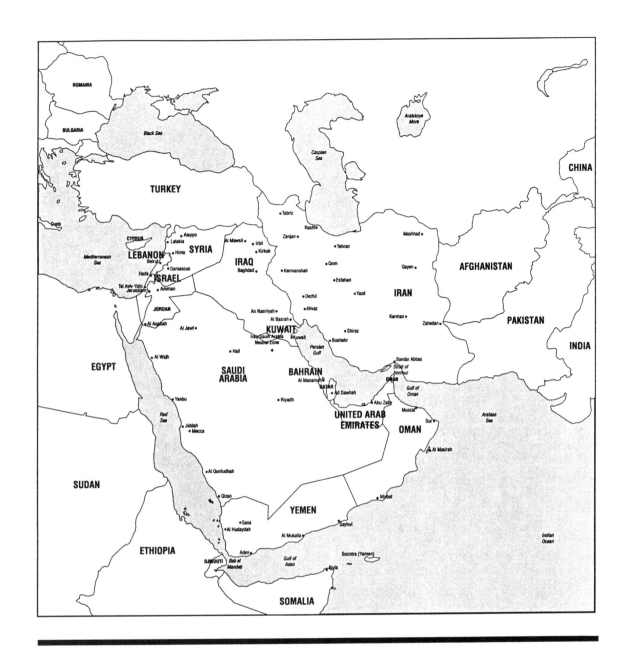

Middle East

Bahrain   Lebanon
Iran   Saudi Arabia
Iraq   Syrian Arab
Israel   Republic
Jordan   Yemen

Middle East

Bahrain

★2251★ BAHRAIN FAMILY PLANNING ASSOCIATION (BFPA)
PO Box 20326   PH: 232233
Manama, Bahrain   FX: 276408
Mr. Jaafar Al-Durazi, President   TX: 8200 BAFPA BN

Languages: Arabic, English. **National.** Encourages family planning and responsible parenthood as a means to enhance the quality of life for individuals living in Bahrain. Works to stop AIDS and other sexually transmitted diseases through education and contraceptive services. Provides programs in sex education, family planning, and health.

Iran

★2252★ CENTER FOR WOMEN'S STUDIES
PO Box 13145-654
Tehran, Iran

National. Promotes the study of women and women's issues in Iran. Strives to eliminate sex discrimination and achieve gender equality. Works to increase public awareness of women's working conditions, gender relations, and sex discrimination. Seeks to improve the standard of living of women, and to advance the role of women in positions of leadership.

★2253★ ISLAMIC WOMEN'S INSTITUTE
No. 1-275 Hedayat St.
N. Saddi
Tehran, Iran   PH: 21 3115656
Azam Alaie Taleghani, Director   FX: 21 3116201

Founded: 1980. **Staff:** 25. **Budget:** 5,500,000 Rl. **Languages:** Persian, English. Seeks to improve the status and standard of living of Iranian women through: implementing income-generating projects; providing legal counselling; conducting literacy and training programs; and assisting women in entrepreneurship endeavors. Conducts research related to women's employment, family legal and economic conflicts, and difficulties of the housewife. **Libraries:** Type: reference. Holdings: 0; books. **Divisions:** Cultural Activities; Economic; Training; Public Relations; Social Research.

Publications: *Payam Hajar* (in Persian and English), weekly. Magazine.

Conventions/Meetings: weekly meeting.

★2254★ MAHJUBAH
PO Box 14155-3987
Tehran, Iran

Languages: Arabic, Kurdish. **National.** Educates Muslim women on their role in society and responsibilities to family and home. Encourages women to avoid Western influence and follow Muslim principles.

★2255★ WOMEN'S ORGANISATION OF IRAN
Takte Jamshid Ave.
Tehran, Iran

Languages: Arabic, Kurdish. **National.** Umbrella organization of women's groups in Iran. Promotes the interests of women in Iran. Fosters positive relations among women and men.

Iraq

★2256★ GENERAL ARAB WOMEN FEDERATION (GAWF)
Hay al-Maghreb
Mahaela 304
Baghdad, Iraq   PH: 1 4227117
Mrs. Manal Y.A. Razzak, Sec.Gen.   TX: 213014

Founded: 1944. **Members:** 18. **Languages:** Arabic. **Multinational.** National women's federations in Arab countries. Seeks the liberation of occupied Arab territories, the liberation of Palestine, the establishment of Arab unity, the development of Arab society, and the defeat of colonialism. Particular concerns involve the status of Arab women. Works to: unify the Arab women's movement worldwide; reinforce solidarity among Arab women; publicize the important role of Arab women in the growth of their society. Combats ideas that deny the equality of men and women; promotes the partnership of men and women in child rearing. Seeks to make Arab women aware of their rights and how to assert them; aims to integrate women into Arab society and establish women as full participants in the Arab world. Provides Arab women with educational opportunities including courses and training for governmental responsibilities. Works to coordinate the efforts of Arab women in social and health services such as family planning and the care of children, the elderly, and the disabled. Sponsors research on such topics as the development of the women's movement in the Arab Gulf, demographics, the role of women in Arab society, and the effect of social and cultural change on the Arab family. Maintains biographical archives and hall of fame. Compiles statistics. Operates placement services; bestows awards. **Libraries:** Type: reference. Holdings: 16,000.

Publications: *Arab Women*, semiannual. Journal. ● *Nisa'al-Arab*, periodic. Newsletter. ● *Directory of Articles About Women Published in Arab Newspapers.* 7-volume set. ● *Directory of Women Periodicals in the Arab World.*

Conventions/Meetings: biennial conference

★2257★ GENERAL FEDERATION OF IRAQI WOMEN
Abi-Talib St.
Wazeeriyah
Baghdad, Iraq
Manal Razzaq, President

Languages: Arabic, English. **National.** Seeks to raise the economic and social status of women in Iraq. Fosters solidarity among women.

★2258★ IRAQI FAMILY PLANNING ASSOCIATION (IFPA)
Mansour City
Maari St.   PH: 1 4229202
PO Box 6028   FX: 1 4229859
Baghdad, Iraq   CBL: ALMANSOUR
Mr. Mizaal Al-Hatim, Exec. Dir.   BAGHDAD

Languages: Arabic. **National.** Works to improve the quality of life for individuals living in Iraq by promoting responsible parenthood and family planning. Advocates family planning as a basic human right. Offers programs in sex education, family planning, and health. Provides contraceptive and health services. Conducts research.

Israel

★2259★ COUNCIL OF WOMEN'S ORGANIZATIONS IN ISRAEL (CWOI)
26 Sh. Ben Maimon
92261 Jerusalem, Israel
Dr. Mina Westman, Pres.
PH: 2 631303
FX: 2 662811

Founded: 1952. **Members:** 9. **Staff:** 1. **Languages:** English. **National.** Voluntary women's movements representing 1,000,000 women. Seeks to enhance and strengthen the legal and social status of women in Israel. Publicizes the progress of the Israeli women's movement, including the passage of legislation, in order to support similar legal initiatives in developing countries. Provides assistance and support to Israeli experts traveling outside the country. **Awards:** Scholarship. Recipient: women studying Israeli regional development. **Committees:** Arts and Letters; Child and Family; Development; Economics; Education; Environment; Health; Home Economics and Consumer Affairs; International Relations and Peace; Mass Media; Migration and Refugees; Social Welfare; Women and Employment; Youth.

Publications: CWOI Newsletter, quarterly. Includes information on membership actvities.

★2260★ GOLDA MEIR MOUNT CARMEL INTERNATIONAL TRAINING CENTRE
PO Box 6111
31060 Haifa, Israel
PH: 4 375904
FX: 4 375913

Founded: 1961. **Members:** 24. **Languages:** Hebrew, English, Spanish, French. **National.** Professional workers, supervisors, and planners working to help women in developing countries. Offers training courses, study workshops, and seminars on: rural community development; organization of income-generating projects; early childhood education; and women's leadership. Provides work experience for women who wish to establish community-based help centers. Maintains relations with other organizations that work with women. Oversees projects and assesses results. **Libraries:** Type: reference. Holdings: 10,000; books.

Conventions/Meetings: quadrennial seminar - 1994.

★2261★ ISRAEL FAMILY PLANNING ASSOCIATION
9 Rambam St.
65601 Tel Aviv, Israel
Ms. Judith Abrahami-Einat, Exec. Dir.
PH: 3 5101511
     3 5101512
FX: 3 5102589

Languages: Arabic, Hebrew. **National.** Promotes responsible parenthood and family planning as a means to enhance the quality of life for individuals living in Israel. Works to stop the spread of AIDS and other sexually transmitted diseases through education and contraceptive services. Offers programs in sex education, family planning, and health. Acts as an advocate for family planning on the national level.

★2262★ ISRAEL WOMEN'S NETWORK
PO Box 3171
92193 Jerusalem, Israel
Linda Futterman, Director
PH: 2 439966
FX: 2 435976

Founded: 1984. **Members:** 600. **Membership Dues:** Sponsor, US$1,000 annual; Donor, US$500 annual; Friend, US$100 annual; Member, US$25 annual. **Staff:** 7. **Languages:** Hebrew, English. **National.** Raises public awareness of women's issues. Seeks to: advocate women's rights; achieve proportionate representation of women in national and local government; eliminate the income gap between men and women. Conducts leadership and assertiveness training programs. Initiates legislation for women's equali-

ty. Operates a discrimination hotline, providing free legal advice and referrals. **Libraries:** Type: reference. Holdings: books, periodicals, clippings. **Study Groups:** Civic Education. **Programs:** Health; Lobbying; Education.

Publications: Networking for Women (in English), quarterly. Newsletter. **Advertising:** not accepted. ● Directory of Women's Orgainzations in Israel (in Hebrew and Russian).

Conventions/Meetings: conference - 2-3/year.

★2263★ ISRAELI FEMINIST MOVEMENT (IFM)
82 Ben-Yehuda St.
63435 Tel Aviv, Israel
Holly Fernandez, Contact
PH: 3 5234917
FX: 3 5449191

Founded: 1972. **Languages:** English, Hebrew. **National.** Women in Israel. Advocates improved public awareness of feminist issues. Lobbies for specific legislation; encourages development of academic courses on the status of women in society. Maintains library; sponsors educational programs. Has coordinated demonstrations for equal rights and against violence towards women. Currently working to create a shelter for battered women in Tel Aviv.

Publications: IFM Newsletter (in Hebrew), 4-6/year. ● The Feminist Movement (in Hebrew), quarterly. Newsletter. Includes activities list and editorials.

Conventions/Meetings: annual.

★2264★ ISRAELI WOMEN'S PEACE NET - RESHET
PO Box 9668
91090 Jerusalem, Israel
Renee-Anne Gutter, Coord.
PH: 2 410002
FX: 2 419561

Founded: 1989. **Languages:** Hebrew, English. **National.** Israeli women working for peace between Israel and Palestine. Strives to increase women's participation in affecting peace. Organizes public and private meetings and conferences for discussion and exchange of ideas. Visits Palestinian women's organizations. Investigates human rights violations against women and children. Disseminates information and holds rallies intended to influence public opinion.

★2265★ MEDICAL WOMEN'S INTERNATIONAL ASSOCIATION - ISRAEL (MWIA-I)
24 Hubermanstr.
Tel Aviv, Israel
Gabriella Lichtenberg, Contact

Languages: Arabic, English. **National.** Israel national branch of the Medical Women's International Association (see separate entry). Women physicians. Provides a forum for discussion of women's health care issues. Encourages women to enter the field of medicine. Works to overcome discrimination against female physicians. Sponsors research and educational programs.

★2266★ NA'AMAT MOVEMENT OF WORKING WOMEN AND VOLUNTEERS
93 Arlozorov St.
62098 Tel Aviv, Israel
Masha Lubelsky, Sec.Gen.
PH: 3 431111
FX: 3 6954470

Founded: 1921. **Members:** 800,000. **Staff:** 1,000. **National Groups:** 14. **Languages:** English, French, German, Hebrew, Portuguese, Spanish. **Multinational.** Working and professional women in Argentina, Australia, Belgium, Brazil, Canada, Chile, England, France, Israel, Mexico, Peru, Spain, United States, and Uruguay. Works to advance the status of women by providing a variety of educational, community, and legal services. Sponsors: day-care centers for over 25,000 children; agricultural and vocational high schools for young people; adult education classes; legal aid; and counseling. Advances the cause of Zionism and champions the rights of Jewish women. **Departments:** Family and Community; Foreign Relations; Health; Ideological Education; Organization; Pre-School Education; Status of Women; Tourism,

Overseas, and Immigrant Absorption; Vocational Training; Working Woman. **Sections:** Arab Women; Single-Parent Families; Volunteer. **Alternate name::** NA'AMAT Israel. **Formerly:** Council of Working Women, Pioneer Women.

Publications: *NA'AMAT* (in Hebrew), monthly. Magazine. ● *NA'AMAT Newsletter* (in English and Spanish), quarterly. ● *NA'AMAT Woman* (in English), bimonthly. ● *Yediot* (in Arabic and Hebrew), monthly. ● Also publishes brochures.

Conventions/Meetings: quadrennial - next 1997.

★2267★ SOROPTIMIST INTERNATIONAL OF ISRAEL
4 Shneor St.
63326 Tel Aviv, Israel   PH: 3 299317
Margalit Normand, President   FX: 3 299317

Founded: 1954. **Members:** 400. **Languages:** Hebrew, English. **National.** Professional and business women. Promotes international goodwill and understanding. Cooperates with non-governmental organizations for the advancement of peace. Studies and conducts projects in economic and social development; education and culture; the environment; and human and women's rights. Encourages interaction among local and international clubs. Awards scholarships.

Publications: *Benenu* (in Hebrew), bimonthly.

Conventions/Meetings: annual convention.

★2268★ UNION OF PALESTINIAN WORKING WOMEN COMMITTEES
7 Ibn Abi Taleb St.
PO Box 25113
East Jerusalem, Israel

National. Professional women in business and management. Provides a forum for communication, discussion, and information exchange among professional Palestinian women. Promotes the advancement of women in the workplace.

★2269★ UNION OF WOMEN'S WORK COMMITTEES
PO Box 20576
Jerusalem, Israel

Provides a forum for communication, discussion, and information exhange among women professionals and workers. Promotes the advancement of women in the workplace.

★2270★ WOMAN TO WOMAN - HAIFA'S WOMEN'S CENTRE
(Isha L'Isha)
88 Arlosoroff
33276 Haifa, Israel   PH: 4 664949
Ms. Hannah Safran, Director   FX: 4 670780

Founded: 1982. **Members:** 150. **Budget:** 60,000 IS. **Languages:** Hebrew, Russian, Arabic, English. **National.** Promotes women's personal development programs in Israel. Campaigns for full civil rights and equal opportunities for women. Works to eliminate physical, sexual, and psychological violence against women; operates an anti-violence hotline. Campaigns against discriminatory government policies. Defends women's reproductive rights. Provides educational programs in auto mechanics, health and nutrition, and self-defense. Provides free initial legal consultation to women facing discrimination. Assists immigrant women in job placement and integration. **Libraries:** Type: reference. Holdings: books. Subjects: literature on women's issues in English and Hebrew. **Committees:** Education, Networking, and Resource Sharing; Women's Health Project; Multicultural Outreach; Jewish/Arab Coexistence.

Publications: *Isha L'Isha* (in Hebrew, Russian, Arabic, and English), bimonthly. Newsletter. Information on women's issues, upcoming events and programs. **Circulation:** 1,000.

Conventions/Meetings: monthly seminar.

★2271★ WOMEN IN BLACK (WIB)
PO Box 61128
91060 Jerusalem, Israel   PH: 2 430138

Founded: 1988. **Languages:** Hebrew, English. **Multinational.** Women who work for peace throughout the world. Strives to increase awareness of effects of war. Protests violence between Israelis and Palestinians.

Publications: *Women in Black* (in English and Hebrew), quarterly. Newsletter.

★2272★ WOMEN FOR FEMALE POLITICAL PRISONERS (WOFPP)
PO Box 31811
61318 Tel Aviv, Israel   PH: 3 5286050
Hava Keller, Contact   FX: 3 5286050

Founded: 1988. **Members:** 10. **Languages:** Hebrew, English. **National.** Promotes action programs to free female political prisoners within the Palestinian/Israeli struggle. Investigates and studies the condition of female political prisoners worldwide. Offers legal, material, and financial assistance to women prisoners.

Publications: *Newsletter* (in Hebrew, English, French, German, Spanish, Finnish, and Japanese), monthly.

★2273★ WOMEN FOR WOMEN - HAIFA SHELTER FOR BATTERED
      WOMEN
PO Box 4667
31046 Haifa, Israel   PH: 4 662114
Amy Holzer, Contact   4 643101

Founded: 1977. **Members:** 20. **Budget:** US$250,000. **Languages:** Hebrew, English. **National.** Promotes the rights and safety of women victims of domestic violence in Israel. Provides protection and support to abused women and their children. Raises public awareness of the plight of abused women through lectures and video presentations. Works to raise women's self-esteem. Offers legal consultation. Operates a children's educational activity center. Conducts child psychology projects.

★2274★ WOMEN'S INTERNATIONAL ZIONIST ORGANIZATION (WIZO)
(Organisation Internationale des Femmes Sionistes)
38 David Hamelech Blvd.   PH: 3 5421717
PO Box 64237   FX: 3 6958267
64237 Tel Aviv, Israel   CBL: ISRAWI ZO TEL-
Raya Jaglom, Contact   AVIV

Founded: 1920. **Members:** 250,000. **National Groups:** 50. **Languages:** English, French, German, Hebrew, Spanish. **Multinational.** Non-party, voluntary movement of Zionist women worldwide. Provides for the welfare of infants, children, youth, and the elderly; promotes the advancement of women in Israel. Works to strengthen the bond between world Jewry and Israel. Maintains 680 institutions and services in Israel including: shelters for battered wives and girls; rape crisis center; legal advice bureau; immigrant absorption; summer camps for needy mothers; care for war victims and one-parent families; book service and mobile library; employment clubs for the elderly. Offers supportive workshops and vocational training and advancement for women. **Telecommunication Services:** Phone referral system, battered wives hotline: 3 5461133; phone referral system, rape crisis hotline: 2 245554 (in Hebrew), 2 251430 (in Arabic).

Publications: *Bamat Haisha* (in Hebrew), bimonthly. ● *Report of the World WIZO Executive*, quadrennial. ● *Review* (in English), quarterly. ● *Review* (in German), 3/year. ● Also publishes leaflets and booklets.

Conventions/Meetings: annual. ● quadrennial World Conference - Israel.

★2275★ WOMEN'S ORGANIZATION FOR POLITICAL PRISONERS
(WOFPP)
PO Box 31811   PH: 3 5285060
Tel Aviv, Israel   FX: 3 528060

Founded: 1988. **Members:** 20. **Languages:** English, Hebrew. **National.** Women in Israel monitoring the status of women being held in prisons and detention centers. Provides legal services for women political prisoners. **Computer Services:** Mailing lists.

Publications: *Newsletter*, monthly. **Circulation:** 400. **Advertising:** not accepted.

Conventions/Meetings: weekly.

★2276★ WOMEN'S STUDIES CENTRE
PO Box 19591
East Jerusalem, Israel

Founded: 1990. **National.** Palestinian women working to construct a feminist agenda. Conducts research and training programs. Encourages women to participate politically for their benefit. Acts as an information clearinghouse. **Libraries:** Type: reference.

Publications: *Newsletter*, periodic.

★2277★ YOUNG WOMEN'S CHRISTIAN ASSOCIATION - ISRAEL
c/o Clothilde Khayat
20 Persian St.
35662 Haifa, Israel
Clothilde Khayat, Contact   PH: 4 514622

National. Promotes the development of young women in Israel. Upholds Christian beliefs and values in its programs. Works to instill self- worth and self-esteem in young women.

★2278★ YOUNG WOMEN'S CHRISTIAN ASSOCIATION - PALESTINE
YWCA of Jerusalem
PO Box 20044   PH: 2 284654
Jerusalem, Israel   2 282593
Doris Salah, Contact   FX: 2 284654

National. Promotes the development of young women in Palestine. Upholds Christian beliefs and values in its programs. Works to instill self worth and self-esteem in young women.

Jordan

★2279★ ARAB WOMEN'S ORGANIZATION
c/o Sahab Shaheen
PO Box 926775
Amman, Jordan
Sahab Shaheen, Contact

Languages: Arabic. **National.** Works to enhance the status of Arab women. Fosters friendly relations among women.

★2280★ BUSINESS AND PROFESSIONAL WOMEN CLUB
PO Box 91-415
Amman, Jordan

Founded: 1976. **Languages:** Arabic. **National.** Jordanian women who own businesses or are professionally employed. Works to improve women's status in economic, civil, and political life. Encourages women to further their education and training. Disseminates information and offers counselling to women on legal rights and obligations. Maintains documentation center.

★2281★ JORDANIAN ASSOCIATION FOR FAMILY PLANNING AND
PROTECTION (JAFPP)
Abdali-Amman Commercial Center Bldg.,
6th Fl.   PH: 6 678083
PO Box 8066   FX: 6 674534
Amman, Jordan   TX: 23046 IPPF JO
Mr. Basem Abu raad, Exec.Dir.   CBL: FAMPLAN

Founded: 1964. **Members:** 300. **Staff:** 69. **Budget:** 284,650 JD. **Local Groups:** 3. **Languages:** Arabic, English. **National.** Social workers and health care professionals in Jordan. Advocates responsible parenthood and family planning in Jordan. Operates family planning clinics and mobile units for rural areas. Offers advice to parents on issues such as child spacing, marital problems, and child rearing; encourages couples to plan children according to financial means. Provides medical assistance to couples with infertility problems and helps them to overcome the social stigma attached to infertility through counseling services. Conducts Annual family planning week; sponsors periodic lectures and workshops. Organizes family planning courses for social workers and volunteers.

Publications: *Selected Lectures in Family Planning.* ● Also publishes brochures, posters, and calendar.

Conventions/Meetings: 12-18 conferences/year.

★2282★ YOUNG WOMEN'S CHRISTIAN ASSOCIATION - JORDAN
PO Box 5014
Amman, Jordan
Leila Victor Diab, Gen.Sec.   PH: 6 655476
                                           6 641793

National. Promotes the development of young women in Jordan. Upholds Christian beliefs and values in its programs. Works to instill self- worth and self-esteem in young women.

★2283★ YOUNG WOMEN'S MOSLEM ASSOCIATION
Centre for Special Education   PH: 6 89482
PO Box 19124   6 712955
Amman, Jordan   FX: 6 722211
Mrs. Nojood Fawzi, Secretary   TX: 24599 SLHJO

Founded: 1972. **Members:** 55. **Languages:** English, Arabic. **National.** Seeks to improve the social and educational development of young women and girls in Jordan. Conducts educational and vocational programs for mentally disabled children. Operates a women's community college to provide young women with opportunites for advancement and participation in development programs. **Libraries:** Type: reference.

Lebanon

★2284★ CONSEIL DES FEMMES LIBANAISES
BP 165640
Beirut, Lebanon   PH: 1 382341
Laure Moghaizel, President   1 384470

National. Umbrella organization for women's groups in Lebanon. Supports and promotes women's interests. Coordinates activities. Disseminates information on women's issues.

★2285★ INSTITUTE FOR WOMEN'S STUDIES IN THE ARAB WORLD
(IWSAW)
Beirut Univ. College
PO Box 13-5053
Beirut, Lebanon   PH: 1 811968
Julinda Abu Nasr Ph.D., Dir.   TX: BUC 23389 LE

Founded: 1973. **Staff:** 7. **Languages:** Arabic, English, French. **Multinational.** Organized to encourage and evaluate research into the history, condition, and rights of women in the Arab world. Promotes a better understanding of the Arab woman. Provides education and assistance to Arab women. Offers in-service training program in social work, a basic living skills program for illiterate and semi-literate women, and a preschool training teachers course. Sponsors an income generating project for displaced women. Offers a course about women in the Arab world at Beirut University College. Has established a network of women's organizations, universities, and research centers for the exchange of information. Founded Lebanese chapter of th International Board on Books for Young Children. Maintains documentation center of materials published in Arabic, English, and French. Presents papers at regional and international conferences. **Computer Services:** Data base.

Publications: *Al-Raida* (in English), quarterly. ● Also publishes books and monographs.

Conventions/Meetings: annual conference.

★2286★ LEBANON FAMILY PLANNING ASSOCIATION (LFPA)
Corniche Mazraa, Al Maskan Bldg.
PO Box 118240   PH: 1 311978
Beriut, Lebanon   1 318575
Ms. Jumana El Kadi, Exec. Dir.   TX: 20426 LFPA

Languages: Arabic. **National.** Works to improve the quality of life for individuals living in Lebanon by promoting responsible parenthood and family planning. Advocates family planning as a basic human right. Offers programs in sex education, family planning, and health. Provides contraceptive and health care services. Conducts research.

★2287★ YOUNG WOMEN'S CHRISTIAN ASSOCIATION - LEBANON
PO Box 2041   PH: 1 369635
Beirut, Lebanon   TX: 23180 LE
Mona Khauli, Exec.Dir.   CBL: YWCA BEIRUT

National. Promotes the development of young women in Lebanon. Upholds Christian beliefs and values in its programs. Works to instill self-worth and self-esteem in young women.

Saudi Arabia

★2288★ MUSLIM WORLD LEAGUE (MWL)
Al-Moa'bdah
PO Box 538
Makkah Al-Mukarramah, Saudi Arabia

Languages: Arabic, English. **National.** Conducts women's development and children's welfare programs in Saudi Arabia. Promotes Muslim values, world peace, and human rights; opposes all wars and discrimination. **Awards:** Scholarship. Recipient: female students.

Publications: *Women's Rights in Islam.* Book. ● *Women During the Pre-Islamic Era and Islam.* Book. ● *Muslim Woman Between Two Perspectives.* Book.

★2289★ SAUDI ARABIA WOMEN'S ASSOCIATION
BP 6
Riyadh, Saudi Arabia
Mrs. Semiar Khashoggi Yassin, President

National. Umbrella organization for women's groups in Saudi Arabia. Promotes and supports women's interests. Coordinates activities; disseminates information on women's issues.

Syrian Arab Republic

★2290★ SYRIAN FAMILY PLANNING ASSOCIATION (SFPA)
PO Box 2282   PH: 11 330714
Al-Jala St., Saegh Bldg. 25   TX: 412823 SFPASY SY
Damascus, Syrian Arab Republic   CBL: FAMPLAN
Ms. Zinab Khanadan Sabri, Exec. Dir.   DAMASCUS

Languages: Arabic. **National.** Promotes family planning and responsible parenthood as a means to improve the quality of life for individuals living in Syria. Advocates family planning as a basic human right. Offers programs in sex education, family planning, and health. Provides contraceptive services. Conducts research.

★2291★ UNION GENERALE DES FEMMES ARABES SYRIENNES
Rue Mahdi Ben Barakeh
Abou Roumane
Damascus, Syrian Arab Republic   PH: 11 332077
Mme. B. Tawaklna, President   11 336769

National. Umbrella organization for women's groups in Syria. Supports the interests of women. Coordinates activities for women. Disseminates information.

Yemen

★2292★ YEMEN FAMILY CARE ASSOCIATION (YFCA)
PO Box 795
Al-Tahreer Sq.   PH: 1 78044
Near Arab Bank   FX: 1 270948
Sana'a, Yemen   TX: 2965 YFCA YE
Dr. Yahia Al-Babily, Exec. Dir. CBL: FAMPLAN SANA'A

Languages: Arabic. **National.** Promotes family planning and responsible parenthood. Works to reduce the number of unwanted pregnancies and abortions and stop the spread of sexually transmitted diseases such as AIDS. Offers programs in sex education, family planning, and health. Provides contraceptive and health care services. Conducts research.

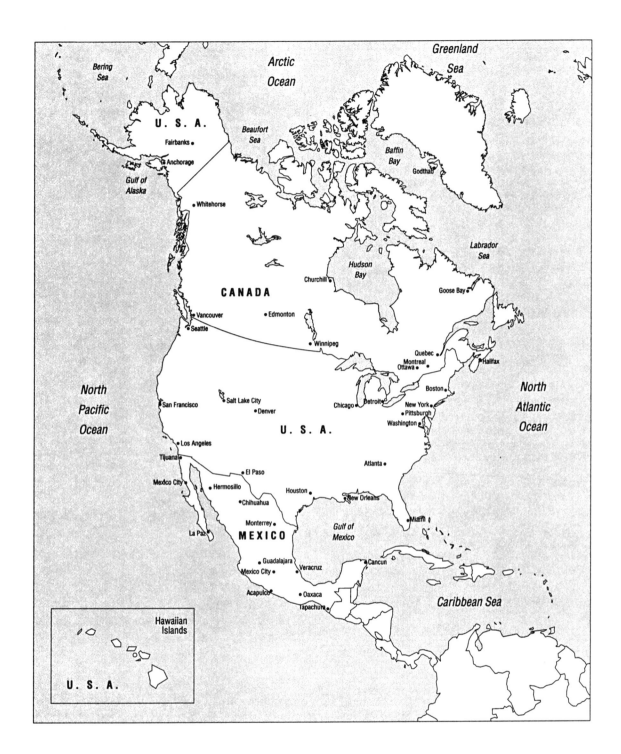

North America

Canada   Mexico   United States

North America

Canada

★2293★ 2 SPIRITED PEOPLE OF THE 1ST NATIONS
476 Parliament St., Ste. 202
Toronto, ON, Canada M4X 1P2   PH: (416)961-4725

National. Works to represent lesbian and gay Native Americans throughout Canada. Provides support to those infected with the HIV-virus.

Publications: *Sacred Fire*, periodic. Newsletter.

★2294★ ACTION EDUCATION DES FEMMES
50, rue Vaughan
Ottawa, ON, Canada K1M 1X1
Marie Lynne Tremblay, Exec. Officer   PH: (613)741-9978

Members: 525. **Languages:** French, English. **National**. Promotes the educational interests and concerns of French speaking women throughout Canada.

Publications: *Bulletin*, 3/year. ● *Newsletter*, 3/year.

Conventions/Meetings: annual - Ottawa, ON, Canada.

★2295★ ADVOCATES FOR COMMUNITY BASED TRAINING AND EDUCATION FOR WOMEN (ACTEW)
No. 301, 801 Eglinton Ave. W   PH: (416)783-3590
Toronto, ON, Canada M5N 1E3   FX: (416)787-1500

Members: 55. **Languages:** English. **National**. Umbrella organization of agencies, networks, and groups working on the local level to support existing education and training opportunities for women (particularly lower income, refugee, and older women). Encourages the creation of new programs. Active in areas such as research, lobbying, and advocacy.

Conventions/Meetings: monthly meeting.

★2296★ ALLIANCE FOR LIFE
(Alliance pour la Vie)
B 1-90 Garry St.   PH: (204)942-4772
Winnipeg, MB, Canada R3C 4H1   TF: (800)665-0570
Anna M. Desilets, Exec. Dir.   FX: (204)943-9283

Founded: 1968. **Staff:** 8. **Local Groups:** 255. **Languages:** English, French. **National**. Promotes recognition of the right to life of all human beings from conception to natural death. Offers educational programs. Researches such issues as abortion, euthanasia, and infanticide; disseminates information. Operates speaker's bureau. **Libraries:** Type: reference.

Publications: *Actualite Vie* (in French), quarterly. ● *Prolife News* (in English), monthly. ● Also publishes pamphlets and booklets.

Conventions/Meetings: annual conference.

★2297★ AQUELARRE LATIN AMERICAN WOMEN'S CULTURAL SOCIETY
PO Box 65535, Sta. F   PH: (604)251-6678
Vancouver, BC, Canada V5N 5K6   FX: (604)731-5279

Languages: English. **National**. Women's social and cultural organization in Canada. Works to foster appreciation for Latin American art, music, and crafts.

★2298★ BALTIC WOMEN'S COUNCIL - CANADA
53 Waterford Dr., Ste. 306
Weston, ON, Canada M9R 2N7
Eddite Lynch, Contact   PH: (416)244-4024

Members: 60. **National**. Political women's organization. Supports complete autonomy among the Baltic countries. Works to strenthen relations among women of Baltic origin.

Conventions/Meetings: annual convention - always spring.

★2299★ CAMPAIGN LIFE COALITION
1355 Wellington St., Ste. 100
Ottawa, ON, Canada K1Y 3C2   PH: (613)729-0379
Sue Hierlihy, Contact   FX: (613)729-7611

National. Individuals in Canada who opposes abortion. Advocates fetal rights. Promotes recogintion of the right to life for all human beings from conception to natural death.

★2300★ CANADIAN ABORTION RIGHTS ACTION LEAGUE (CARAL)
(Association Canadienne pour le Droit a l'Avortement)
344 Bloor St. W, Ste. 306   PH: (416)961-1507
Toronto, ON, Canada M5S 3A7   (416)961-5571
Jane Holmes, Exec.Coord.   FX: (416)961-5771

Founded: 1974. **Members:** 15,000. **Membership Dues:** Limited income., C$3; Individual., C$10; Family., C$15; Member groups., C$25; Friends of membership., C$250. **Staff:** 2. **Regional Groups:** 34. **Languages:** English, French. **National**. Individuals in Canada promoting women's reproductive freedoms. Defends the right to safe, effective contraceptives and legal abortion. Offers support to physicians who provide abortion services. Engages in political lobbying and advocacy. Disseminates information; offers educational programs. Maintains verticle files on abortion and related issues. Provides speakers bureau. **Awards:** Norma Scarborough Award. **Committees:** RU-486 (Abortion Pill). **Formerly:** Canadian Association for Repeal of the Abortion Law.

Publications: *Pro-Choice News*, 3/year. **ISSN:** 0836-7221. **Circulation:** 16,000. **Advertising:** not accepted. ● *Abortion: Medical Facts*. ● *Abortion in Law and History*. ● *Freedom of Choice* (in English and French). ● *RU 486: The Abortion Pill* (in English and French).

Conventions/Meetings: annual general assembly - always Spring. Toronto, ON, Canada. ● semiweekly board meeting.

★2301★ CANADIAN ADVISORY COUNCIL ON THE STATUS OF WOMEN
(Conseil Consultatif Canadien sur la Situation de la Femme)
110 O'Connor St. W, 9th Fl.
Ottawa, ON, Canada K1P 5M9   PH: (613)992-4975
Glenda P. Simms, President   FX: (613)992-1715

Founded: 1973. **Members:** 40. **Staff:** 3. **Languages:** English, French. **National**. Counsels the government of Canada, and keeps the public apprised on issues of concern to women. Works to promote equal status for women. Seeks to improve women's lives by affecting change in federal laws and policies.

Publications: *Women Speak out in Agriculture*, annual.

Conventions/Meetings: periodic meeting.

★2302★ CANADIAN ALLIANCE OF WOMEN
45 Northridge Rd.
Ile Bizard, PQ, Canada H9E 1A8
Hon. Judge Claire Kirkland-Casgrain,
President

Languages: English. **National.** Seeks to raise public awareness of women's issues. Promotes women's rights.

★2303★ CANADIAN ASSOCIATION FOR THE ADVANCEMENT OF
WOMEN AND SPORT AND PHYSICAL ACTIVITY (CAAWS)
(Association Canadienne pour l'Advancement des Femmes du Sport et de l'Activite)
1600 James Naismith Dr.
Gloucester, ON, Canada K1B 5N4
Marge McGregor, Exec. Officer   PH: (613)748-5793

Founded: 1981. **Members:** 300. **Staff:** 1. **Languages:** English. **National.** Promotes and supports the involvement of women and girls in sports and physical activity. Seeks to ensure that women have equal access to a broad range of opportunities as both leaders and participants in sport-related activities. **Commissions:** Research; Community Initiatives; Coaching.

Publications: *Action Bulletin* (in French and English), periodic. ● *Newsletter* (in French and English), periodic.

★2304★ CANADIAN ASSOCIATION AGAINST SEXUAL HARASSMENT
IN HIGHER EDUCATION (CAASHHE)
(Association Canadienne Contre le Harcelement Sexuel en Milieu d'Enseignment Superieur)
University of Victoria
School of Social Work
Box 1700
Victoria, BC, Canada V8W 2Y2
Prof. Barbara Whittington, President

Languages: English, French. **National.** Works to prevent sexual harrassment in Canadian universities and colleges. Protects the rights of students and professional women.

★2305★ CANADIAN ASSOCIATION OF SEXUAL ASSAULT CENTRES
77 E. 20th Ave.
Vancouver, BC, Canada V5V 1L7   PH: (604)872-8212
Lee Lakeman, Contact   FX: (604)876-8450

Members: 50. **Languages:** English, French. **National.** Organization of grassroots groups concerned with issues of sexual assault. Lobbies for more stringent laws to punish offenders. Disseminates information and educational materials.

Conventions/Meetings: annual convention.

★2306★ CANADIAN ASSOCIATION OF WOMEN BUSINESS OWNERS
(CAWBO)
2007 The Chase
Mississauga, ON, Canada L5M 2W2
Marcie Weinman, President   PH: (416)820-9206

Founded: 1980. **Languages:** English. **National.** Supports and promotes the activities of women in business. Seeks to increase women's visibility in the business community. Offers financial and marketing advice. Promotes leadership, efficiency, and competition. Encourages the development of cottage industries.

★2307★ CANADIAN ASSOCIATION OF WOMEN EXECUTIVES AND
ENTREPRENEURS
(Association Canadienne des Femmes Cadres et Entrepreneurs)
456 Danforth Ave.
Toronto, ON, Canada M4K 1P4   PH: (416)596-7923
Carol Bulmer, President   FX: (416)778-4295

Founded: 1976. **Members:** 250. **Staff:** 3. **Languages:** English, French. **National.** Women working in middle and upper level management positions. Seeks to foster a growth environment for women executives and business owners. Strives to increase the visibility of professional women in Canada. Works to influence the media and government on issues of concern to the business community. Provides a forum for women to establish professional contacts. Participates in trade shows. **Committees:** Program; Business Owners; Member Communications; Public Relations.

Publications: *Canadian Association of Women Executives and Entrepreneurs Newsletter* (in English), quarterly.

Conventions/Meetings: annual meeting. ● periodic dinner.

★2308★ CANADIAN CONGRESS FOR LEARNING OPPORTUNITIES
FOR WOMEN
47 Main St.
Toronto, ON, Canada M4E 2V6
Aisla Thomson, Exec. Dir.   PH: (416)699-1909

Founded: 1979. **Members:** 600. **Staff:** 2. **Regional Groups:** 12. **Languages:** English, French. **National.** Works to achieve greater social, political, and economic equity for women through educational opportunities. Encourages women to participate in formal, informal, and experiential learning. Fosters the availability of equal education for females and males. Conducts research on women, literacy, and learning. **Libraries:** Type: open to the public.

Publications: *Women's Education des Femmes* (in English and French), quarterly. Magazine. **ISSN:** 0714-9788.

Conventions/Meetings: semiannual Board of Directors.

★2309★ CANADIAN CONSTRUCTION WOMEN
3636 E. 4th St.
Vancouver, BC, Canada V5M 1M3
Patti Dewhurst, Exec. Officer   PH: (604)736-6311

Languages: English. **National.** Women working in the construction field. Functions as a support group for members. Offers an opportunity for women to network with one another and share concerns.

Conventions/Meetings: monthly dinner. ● monthly executive committee meeting.

★2310★ CANADIAN COUNCIL OF MUSLIM WOMEN
(Conseil Canadien des Femmes Musulmanes)
PO Box 128
Seba Beach, AB, Canada T0E 2B0
Dr. Lila Fahlman, President   PH: (403)797-3855

Founded: 1982. **Members:** 1,000. **Languages:** English, French. **National.** Works to foster greater understanding between Muslim women and those of other faiths in Canada. Encourages members to study the Koran, gain knowledge of their faith, and communicate with Muslim women worldwide. Coordinates the activities of Muslim women's organizations throughout Canada. Maintains speakers' bureau.

Publications: *The Muslim Woman* (in English and French), quarterly. Newsletter.

Conventions/Meetings: annual meeting.

★2311★ CANADIAN DAUGHTERS' LEAGUE
3721 Frances St.
Burnaby, BC, Canada V5C 2N9
Emma Romak, Contact   PH: (604)299-2136

Founded: 1923. **Members:** 800. **National.** Canadian-born women. Fosters Canadian national spirit, and promotes interests which pertain to Canada. **Awards:** Periodic (scholarship). Recipient: women excelling in literature, art, or music.

Conventions/Meetings: biennial conference. ● annual convention.

★2312★ CANADIAN FEDERATION OF BUSINESS AND
   PROFESSIONAL WOMEN'S CLUBS
56 Sparks St., No. 308
Ottawa, ON, Canada K1P 5A9
Shirley Cote, Secretary   PH: (613)234-7619

Founded: 1930. **Members:** 3,000. **Membership Dues:** C$25 annual. **Staff:** 1. **Languages:** English, French. **National.** Canadian women engaged in business, the professions, or industry. Works to enhance the economic, social, and employment status of women. Encourages women to become active in government at every level. Strives to improve business service standards. Networks with related organizations to promote common concerns.

Publications: *Business and Professional Women* (in English and French), quarterly. Magazine.

Conventions/Meetings: biennial convention - even-numbered years.

★2313★ CANADIAN FEDERATION OF UNIVERSITY WOMEN (CFUW)
(FCFDU Federation Canadienne des Femmes Diplomees des
   Universites)
55 Parkdale Ave.
Ottawa, ON, Canada K1Y 1E5   PH: (613)722-8732
Elizabeth Cureton, President   FX: (613)722-8732

Founded: 1919. **Members:** 11,500. **Languages:** English, French. **National.** Women graduates of Canadian universities. Promotes continuing education for women. Fosters communication and fellowship among members. **Committees:** Education; Fellowships; International Relations; Legislation, Libraries, and Creative Arts; Status of Women and Human Rights.

Publications: *CFUW-FCFDU Journal* (in English and French), 3/year.

Conventions/Meetings: annual meeting.

★2314★ CANADIAN LADIES GOLF ASSOCIATION (CLGA)
(Association Canadienne des Golfeuses)
1600 James Naismith Dr., No. 214
Gloucester, ON, Canada K1B 5N4   PH: (613)748-5642
Esther Cox, President   FX: (613)748-5720

Founded: 1913. **Members:** 92,000. **Staff:** 3. **Regional Groups:** 9. **Languages:** English, French. **National.** Women interested in the sport of golf in Canada. Promotes the game of golf for women. Works to ensure understanding and maintainance of rules, regulations, handicapping, and course ratings. Maintains speakers' bureau. **Committees:** Rules and Handicap; Championship.

Publications: *CLGA Yearbook* (in English), annual. Magazine.

Conventions/Meetings: semiannual board meeting. ● annual meeting - always March. ● periodic competition.

★2315★ CANADIAN PELVIC INFLAMMATORY DISEASE SOCIETY
PO Box 33804, Sta. D
Vancouver, BC, Canada V6J 4L6
Jill Weiss, Coord.   PH: (604)684-5704

Founded: 1985. **Members:** 300. **Membership Dues:** unemployed, C$2 annual; individual, C$5 annual; organization, C$10 annual. **Staff:** 1. **Budget:** C$100,000. **Languages:** English, French. Women with Pelvic Inflammatory Disease (PID), medical professionals, health care organizations, and interested individuals. (PID is a bacterial infection or inflammation of a women's pelvic organs which can result in scarring and adhesion of the pelvic organs, infertility, recurring or chronic infecion, ectopic pregnancy, chronic abdominal pain, disability, and death.) Provides information and support to women with PID and their families. Promotes public education and the prevention of PID; produces and distributes educational materials; supports research on prevention of PID. Maintains speakers' bureau. **Libraries:** Type:. Holdings: 2,000; books, clippings. Subjects: medical research on PID. **Computer Services:** Data base, medical information on PID. **Telecommunication Services:** Phone referral system, free information on PID.

Publications: *Booklet* (in English). ● *News Coverage of PID*. Videos. ● *Chlamydia and PID*. Videos.

Conventions/Meetings: annual.

★2316★ CANADIAN RESEARCH INSTITUTE FOR THE
   ADVANCEMENT OF WOMEN (CRIAW)
(ICREF Institute Canadien de Recherches sur les Femmes)
151 Slater St., Ste. 408
Ottawa, ON, Canada K1P 5H3   PH: (613)563-0681
Linda Clippingdale, Exec. Dir.   FX: (613)563-7739

Founded: 1976. **Members:** 1,100. **Membership Dues:** Student and low-income individuals., C$15; Regular., C$25; Supporting., C$50; Sustaining., C$150; Institutional., C$100. **Staff:** 3. **Languages:** English, French. **National.** Individuals and institutions interested or engaged in the study of women and women's issues. Promotes and encourages research by and for women on all aspects of the female experience. Advocates the active participation of women in the research process. Disseminates information. Maintains speakers' bureau. **Libraries:** Type: open to the public. Holdings: books, audio recordings, video recordings.

Publications: *CRIAW Newsletter* (in English and French), quarterly. ● *Funding Directory* (in English and French), biennial. ● *The CRIAW Papers* (in English and French). Book. ● *Feminist Perspectives* (in English and French). Book. ● *Resources for Research and Action* (in English and French). Book.

Conventions/Meetings: annual conference - always November.

★2317★ CANADIAN VOICE OF WOMEN FOR PEACE (VOW)
(VFCP Voix des Femmes Canadiennes pour la Paix)
736 Bathurst St., Ste. 215
Toronto, ON, Canada M5S 2R4   PH: (416)537-9343
Grace Hartman, Chwm.   FX: (416)531-6214

Founded: 1960. **Members:** 1,000. **Local Groups:** 10. **Languages:** English, French. **National.** Women promoting peace. Acts as a resource center for information on peace and women's issues. Conducts educational programs; maintains speaker's bureau and biographical archive. **Committees:** Chemical/Biological Weapons Watch; Women's Commonwealth Conference.

Publications: *Atlantic Peace Letter* (in English), quarterly. ● *BC Voice* (in English), quarterly. ● *Ontario Newsletter* (in English), quarterly. ● *Voices* (in English), quarterly. ● Also publishes educational brochures.

Conventions/Meetings: biennial meeting - always fall, Canada.

★2318★ CANADIAN WOMEN'S FOUNDATION
(Fondation des Femmes Canadiennes)
214 Merton St., Ste. 208
Toronto, ON, Canada M4S 1A6   PH: (416)484-8268
                                       FX: (416)486-8604

Languages: English, French. **National.** Seeks to effect long-term social changes in Canada that will contribute to the equal treatment of females. Offers funding for projects and programs designed to assist women and girls in the achievement of economic independence and self-reliance. Engages in partnerships with women's community and grassroots groups. **Awards:** Periodic (grant).

Publications: *Initiative* (in English and French), semiannual. Newsletter.

Conventions/Meetings: board meeting - 3/year.

★2319★ CATHOLIC WOMEN'S LEAGUE OF CANADA
No. 1, 160 Murray Pk. Rd.
Winnipeg, MB, Canada R3J 3X5
M. Fall, Exec. Dir.   PH: (204)885-4856

Members: 118,000. **Languages:** English. **National.** Religious-based women's organization. Promotes principles of the Catholic faith. Assists and provides services to charitable organizations.

Publications: *The Canadian League* (in English). Newsletter.

Conventions/Meetings: annual meeting.

★2320★ CHILDBIRTH BY CHOICE TRUST
344 Bloor St. W, Ste. 306
Toronto, ON, Canada M5S 1W9   PH: (416)961-1507
Robin Rowe, Admin.   FX: (416)961-5771

Founded: 1982. **Staff:** 1. **Languages:** English. **National.** Advocates educational programs and disseminates information on abortion, reproductive choice, and contraception issues to the public, schools, and libraries. Maintains resources for researchers.

Publications: *Abortion in Law and History: The Pro-Choice Perspective.* ● *Childbirth by Choice.* ● *Abortion: Medical Facts.*

★2321★ COALITION OF CANADIAN WOMEN'S GROUPS
    INTERNATIONAL PEACE CONFERENCE
Seton Anne, Rm. 9-10
166 Bedford Hwy.
Halifax, NS, Canada B3M 2J6

Languages: English. **National.** Women working for peace and disarmament. Fosters international understanding.

★2322★ COALITION FOR REPRODUCTIVE CHOICE
PO Box 51, Sta. L
Winnipeg, MB, Canada R3H 0Z4
Susan Riley, Chair   PH: (204)453-7774

Founded: 1982. **Members:** 3,500. **Membership Dues:** C$10 annual. **Staff:** 1. **Languages:** English. **National.** Works to guarantee the reproductive rights of women. Supports the decriminalization of abortion, and promotes safe, legal access to same. Assists in the establishment of clinics while striving to enhance the quality and availability of healthcare, pregnancy counselling, and contraception for women. Disseminates educational materials to the public and engages in political lobbying. Maintains speakers' bureau. **Libraries:** Type: open to the public. **Computer Services:** Mailing lists. **Committees:** Lobbying.

Publications: *Manitoba Pro-Choice News* (in English), periodic. Newsletter. ● *Profile* (in English), periodic. Provides current information on abortion access, legal issues, healthcare, and related political developments.

Conventions/Meetings: monthly board meeting.

★2323★ DES ACTION CANADA
PO Box Snowdon 233
Montreal, PQ, Canada H3X 3T4   PH: (514)482-3204
Lisa Laporte, Exec. Dir.   FX: (514)482-1445

Founded: 1982. **Members:** 1,000. **Staff:** 2. **Regional Groups:** 9. **Languages:** French, English. **National.** DES (diethylstilbestrol) exposed women, doctors, and concerned individuals. (DES was prescribed for pregnant women between 1941 and 1971 in the belief that it would prevent miscarriages. It has since been found to cause medical problems in mothers and their children.) Seeks to detect, instruct, support, and defend the rights of individuals exposed to DES. Promotes the prevention of similar health concerns, especially in the field of reproductive health care. Disseminates written materials as well as audio-visual aids on medical concerns related to DES exposure. Offers physician referrals and peer counseling. Sponsors educational programs.

Publications: *Newsletter* (in English), quarterly. ● *Bulletin D.E.S.* (in French), quarterly. ● *Fertility and Pregnancy Guide for DES Daughters and Sons.* ● *Breast Cancer: Risk, Protection, Detection, and Treatment.* ● *Nursing Curriculum.*

Conventions/Meetings: annual meeting. ● annual board meeting.

★2324★ DISABLED WOMEN'S NETWORK CANADA (DAWN Canada)
658 Danforth Ave., Ste. 203
Toronto, ON, Canada M4J 1L1   PH: (416)406-1080
Pat Israel, Chair   FX: (416)406-1082

Founded: 1985. **Members:** 300. **Staff:** 2. **Languages:** English, French. **National.** Women with disabilities, organizations concerned with disability issues, and non-disabled supporters. A feminist organization that recognizes and addresses issues of concern to women with disabilities such as: poverty; employment equity; violence against women; parenting; health; access to services; and education. Provides information regarding issues of concern to disabled women, women's organizations, and the government. Allows women with disabilities the opportunity to participate in the women's movement. Cooperates with other groups involved in the quest for social justice nationally and internationally. Offers role models to girls with disabilites. Participates in research. **Telecommunication Services:** TDD, (416)406-1081.

Publications: *Beating the Odds: Violence and Women with Disabilities* (in English). Book. ● *New Reproductive Technologies* (in English). Book. ● *Meeting Our Needs: An Access Manual for Transition Houses* (in English). Book. ● *Who Do We Think We Are?: Self-Image and Women with Disabilities.* Book. ● *Different Therefore Unequal: Employment and Women with Disabilities* (in English). Book. ● *The Only Parent in the Neighbourhood: Mothering and Women with Disabilities* (in English). Book. ● *Thriving* (in English and French), quarterly. Newsletter.

★2325★ EDUCATION WIFE ASSAULT
427 Bloor St. W
Toronto, ON, Canada M5S 1X7
Marsha Sfeir, Coord.   PH: (416)968-3422

Founded: 1978. **Languages:** English. **National.** Works to prevent violence against women in all its forms, particularly spouse abuse. Strives to increase public awareness through education, training, and dissemination of information. Provides supportive services to: professionals in the legal and health care fields; students; community groups and agencies; social service workers; counselors; women who have suffered assault, along with their family members and friends; men dealing with their own violent behaviors. Maintains a public resource center and crisis service.

Publications: *Education Wife Assault Newsletter*, periodic. ● *Annotated Bibliography on Violence Against Women* (in English). Book. Summarizes relevant research. ● *Pornography: A Feminist Survey*, Annotated bibliography of feminist works. Book. ● *Understanding Wife Assault* (in English and French). Book. Training manual for counselors and advocates. ● *Wife Abuse.* Book. Program manual. ● *Wife Abuse - Understanding the Issues.* Book. Workshop manual for community groups.

★2326★ EMUNAH WOMEN OF CANADA
5253 Decarie Blvd., Ste. 110   PH: (514)485-2397
Montreal, PQ, Canada H3W 3C3   (514)485-2539
Roslyn Schneidman, Exec. VP   FX: (514)483-3624

Founded: 1942. **Members:** 1,500. **Languages:** English. **National.** Religious women. Promotes religious consciousness among women in Canada. Provides social programs for children and youth. Offers religious and secular education programs, and vocational training. Conducts leadership seminars; bestows awards.

Publications: *Newsletter* (in English), semiannual.

Conventions/Meetings: board meeting - 3/year. Canada. ● triennial (exhibits) - Canada. ● monthly Council - Canada.

★2327★ FEDERATED WOMEN'S INSTITUTES OF CANADA (FWIC)
251 Bank St., Ste. 606
Ottawa, ON, Canada K2P 1X3   PH: (613)234-1090
Arlene Strugnell, Exec. Dir.   FX: (613)234-1090

Founded: 1919. **Members:** 31,000. **Staff:** 1. **Regional Groups:** 10. **Languages:** English. **National.** Provincial women's institutes in Canada. Promotes the study of women and women's issues in Canada. Acts as a forum for women's institutes to discuss common interests. Fosters women's leadership in the promotion of Canadian agriculture and other aspects of community living. Works to involve women in the activities of national and international events. **Awards:** Annual Hazel Stiles (scholarship). ● Annual Muriel Bronson (scholarship). **Committees:** Agriculture; Canadian Industries; Citizenship and Legislation; Educational and Cultural Activities; Environment; Home Economics and Health; International Affairs.

Publications: *Federated News* (in English), 3/year.

Conventions/Meetings: triennial - next 1994. Canada. ● annual board meeting - always spring. Canada. ● annual executive committee meeting - always fall. Canada.

★2328★ FEDERATION NATIONALE DES FEMMES CANADIENNES-FRANCAISES (FNFCF)
325, rue Dalhousie, Ste. 525
Ottawa, ON, Canada K1N 7G2   PH: (613)232-5791
Diane Vachon, Director   FX: (613)232-6679

Founded: 1914. **Staff:** 4. **Budget:** C$6,000,000. **Regional Groups:** 50. **Languages:** French. **National.** Works to improve women's economic and political status and living conditions. Fosters cooperation among women's groups with similar concerns. **Awards:** Periodic (scholarship).

Publications: *Femmes d'Action*, 5/year. Magazine. ● *Femmes de la Diaspora Canadiene-Francaise* (in French). Book. ● *Une Affaire d'Argent* (in French). Book. ● *Legalite pour l'Egalite* (in French). Book. ● *Ou en Sommes-Nous?* (in French). Booklet.

Conventions/Meetings: bimonthly meeting - Canada.

★2329★ FRIENDS OF BREASTFEEDING SOCIETY
RR No. 2
Chesley, ON, Canada N0G 1L0
Catherine Young, Contact   PH: (519)363-3778

Founded: 1986. **National.** Encourages mothers to breastfeed through dissemination of information and display of posters in clinics and hospitals.

Conventions/Meetings: periodic meeting.

★2330★ GENERATIONS
CP 186
Succ. Place d'Armes
Montreal, PQ, Canada J2Y 3G7
Jocalyn Paiment, Contact   PH: (514)288-1444

Members: 900. Promotes healthy relations among parents and their children. Offers support groups and family counselling.

Publications: *Generations*, quarterly.

★2331★ GIRL GUIDES OF CANADA
50 Merton St.
Toronto, ON, Canada M4S 1A3   PH: (416)487-5281
Barbara Meisner, Acting Exec.Dir.   FX: (416)487-5570

Founded: 1910. **Members:** 270,000. **Staff:** 45. **Budget:** C$4,000,000. **Languages:** English. **National.** Girls and adult women sponsors. Works to assist girls and young women in becoming responsible citizens. Promotes the personal and social development of members. Encourages members to offer leadership and service to the local, national, and/or global communities. Offers programs that foster self-esteem and self-confidence. **Awards:** Scholarship.

Publications: *Canadian Guider* (in English), 5/year.

Conventions/Meetings: annual - always May/June.

★2332★ HADASSAH - WIZO ORGANIZATION OF CANADA
1310 Greene Ave.
Montreal, PQ, Canada H3Z 2B8   PH: (514)937-9431
Esther Matlow, Contact   FX: (514)933-6483

Founded: 1917. **Members:** 18,500. **Membership Dues:** C$10 annual. **Staff:** 10. **National.** Women in Canada working to promote Jewish cultural awareness. Organizes fundraising activities for non-political projects in Israel. Offers support to needy individuals in Israel. Affirms democratic principles and aims.

Publications: *Orah* (in English), periodic. Magazine.

Conventions/Meetings: triennial convention.

★2333★ IMMIGRANT AND VISIBLE MINORITY WOMEN AGAINST ABUSE
PO Box 3188, Sta. C
Ottawa, ON, Canada K1Y 4J4   PH: (613)839-5401
Gina Witteveen Salinas, Contact   FX: (613)839-2717

Works to eradicate domestic violence among immigrant and minority populations through awareness programs, legislation development, advocacy, counseling, and information dissemination. Offers support services to victims.

★2334★ INFANT - MATERNAL NUTRITION EDUCATION
10 Trinity Sq.
Toronto, ON, Canada M5G 1B1   PH: (416)595-9819
Elisabeth Sterken, Exec. Dir.   (416)488-3368

Members: 3,000. **Membership Dues:** Individual, C$30; Outside of Canada, C$35; Group, C$45; Institutional, C$250. **National.** Promotes breastfeeding as a means towards better maternal and infant health. Seeks to ensure that women receive accurate information about infant feeding. Monitors marketing of baby formula, including public advertising, distribution of free samples to new mothers, promotion to health are facilities, and gifts to health care workers. Conducts research and disseminates information about infant feeding and maternal health. Lobbies for complete adoption and enforcement of the WHO/UNICEF International Code.

Publications: *INFACT Newsletter*, quarterly. ● *INFACT*. Booklet. ● *Protecting, Promoting, and Supporting Breastfeeding: The Special Role of Maternity Service*. Booklet. ● *The Politics of Breastfeeding*. Book.

Conventions/Meetings: annual meeting.

★2335★ INFERTILITY AWARENESS ASSOCIATION OF CANADA (IAAC)
(Association Canadienne de Sensibilisation a l'Infertilite)
1785 Alta Vista Dr., Ste. 104   PH: (613)738-8968
Ottawa, ON, Canada K1G 3Y6   TF: (800)263-2929
Trish Maynard, National Coord.   FX: (613)738-0159

Founded: 1990. **Members:** 600. **Membership Dues:** Individuals., C$30;

Institutions., C$50. **Staff:** 2. **Budget:** C$150,000. **Regional Groups:** 5. **Languages:** English, French. **National.** Individuals and organizations working to increase the awareness and understanding of the causes, treatments, and the emotional impact of infertility. Represents the interests of those with infertility concerns. Collaborates with infertility support groups to advance the organization's agenda. Disseminates information through media interviews, seminars, and educational materials. Maintains resource center and speakers' bureau. **Committees:** Fundraising; Chapter Development; Publications and Education; Membership Development.

Publications: *Infertility Awareness* (in English and French), bimonthly. Newsletter.

Conventions/Meetings: biennial conference (exhibits) - Canada.

★2336★ INTERNATIONAL COUNCIL OF JEWISH WOMEN (ICJW)
c/o Helen Marr
1110 Finch Ave. W, Ste. 518
Downsview, ON, Canada M3J 2T2   PH: (416)665-8251
Helen Marr, Pres.   FX: (416)665-8702

Founded: 1912. **Members:** 1,500,000. **Languages:** English, French, Spanish. **Multinational.** National organizations linking nearly 1,500,000 Jewish women. Objectives are to: promote friendly relations, understanding, and mutual support among Jewish women; uphold and strengthen the bonds of Judaism; show solidarity with Israel and support the efforts of Israel to secure a just and lasting peace; promote economic security and social, educational, and cultural development in Israel; further the highest interests of humanity; cooperate with national and international organizations working for goodwill among all peoples and for equal rights for humanity. Supports the Universal Declaration of Human Rights of the United Nations, and encourages work for the improvement of the social, economic, and legal status of all women under Jewish and civil law. Holds seminars and workshops; sponsors field trips. Provides children's services. Conducts research and educational programs. Maintains speakers' bureau and information and service center. **Committees:** Anti-Semitism and Racism; Community Services; Environment; European Regional; Extension and Field Services; Habitat; Herczeg Seminar; Inter-Affiliate Travel; Interfaith; Jewish Education; Latin American Regional; North American Regional; Public Relations; Resolutions; South East Asian Pacific Regional; Status of Women.

Publications: *Directory of ICJW Affiliates*, triennial. ● *ICJW Newsletter* (in English and Spanish), semiannual. ● *Links Around the World* (in English and Spanish), 3/year. **Circulation:** 500. **Advertising:** accepted. ● *International Kosher Cookbook*.

Conventions/Meetings: triennial meeting. ● periodic regional conferences.

★2337★ INTERNATIONAL INDIGENOUS WOMEN'S COUNCIL
c/o Native Women's Association of
  Canada
9 Melrose Ave.
Ottawa, ON, Canada K1Y 1T8   PH: (613)722-3033

Members: 120. **Multinational.** Umbrella organization of Native American women's groups throughout the world. Promotes the interests of native women throughout the world.

★2338★ JEWISH WOMEN'S FEDERATION
4600 Bathurst St.   PH: (416)635-2883
Willowdale, ON, Canada M2R 3V2   FX: (416)635-1408

Members: 20,000. **National.** Umbrella organization for Jewish women's groups. Promotes the spirit of Judaism.

Publications: *Newsletter.*

Conventions/Meetings: Jewish Women's Festival.

★2339★ KIDS' FIRST PARENT ASSOCIATION OF CANADA
Lakeview Postal Outlet
6449 Crowchild Trail SW
PO Box 36032
Calgary, AB, Canada T3E 7C6   PH: (403)289-1440
Dianne Klein, Contact   (403)281-5713

Members: 5,000. **Membership Dues:** C$15. **Languages:** English. **National.** Promotes the well-being of children; protects parents' rights to choose how and in what environment to raise their children.

Publications: *Kids' First Newsletter* (in English), quarterly.

Conventions/Meetings: quarterly meeting.

★2340★ LA LECHE LEAGUE CANADA
18C Industrial Dr.
Box 29
Chesterville, ON, Canada K0C 1H0   PH: (613)448-1842
Carol Luck, Exec. Dir.   FX: (613)448-1845

Founded: 1961. **Members:** 3,060. **Staff:** 5. **Budget:** C$330,000. **Languages:** English. **National.** Women who breast-feed and health professionals. Promotes breastfeeding for the benefit of mothers and infants. Offers information and assistance to women who decide to breast-feed their infants. Provides mother-to-mother support through monthly meetings and telephone help-line services. Presents public education programs; administers professional education for health practitioners. Works with other breastfeeding groups to discuss health-related topics. Sponsors seminars. **Libraries:** Type: lending.

Publications: *The Womanly Art of Breastfeeding.* ● *The Breastfeeding Answer Book.* ● Publishes leaflets on topics such as breast-feeding twins, breast-feeding and working, increasing your milk, and other related topics.

Conventions/Meetings: annual conference.

★2341★ LITTLE SISTERS OF THE HOLY FAMILY (PSSF)
(Petites Soeurs de la Sainte-Famille)
1820 W. Galt St.
Sherbrooke, PQ, Canada J1K 1H9
Sr. Jeannine Vachon, Sec.   PH: (819)823-0345

Founded: 1880. **Members:** 600. **Languages:** English, French, Spanish. **Multinational.** Catholic nuns in 5 countries dedicated to aiding the priesthood. Provides: domestic services in seminaries, priests' residences, and bishops' houses; nursing and health services in community infirmaries; secretarial services.

★2342★ LYCEUM CLUB AND WOMEN'S ART ASSOCIATION OF CANADA (WAA)
23 Prince Arthur Ave.
Toronto, ON, Canada M5R 1B2
A. Lynn Cumine, President   PH: (416)922-2060

Founded: 1887. **Members:** 80. **Languages:** English. **National.** Women interested and involved in the arts in Canada. Supports the work of young artists throughout Canada. Provides studio space for artists' work. Hosts luncheons, seminars, and workshops. **Libraries:** Type: reference; lending.
   Awards: National Ballet of Canada (scholarship). Recipient: Young Canadian artists. ● Ontario College of Art (scholarship). Recipient: Young Canadian artists. ● University of Toronto Faculty of Music (scholarship). Recipient: Young Canadian artists. ● Royal Conservatory of Music (scholarship). Recipient: Young Canadian artists. ● Annual Derazy Violin. Recipient: Violin student selected by the Royal Conservatory of Music.

Conventions/Meetings: semimonthly. ● monthly executive committee meeting.

★2343★ MATCH INTERNATIONAL CENTRE (MIC)
1102-200 Elgin St.   PH: (613)238-1312
Ottawa, ON, Canada K2P 1L5   FX: (613)238-6867

Languages: English. **Multinational.** Women in Canada united to improve standards of living for women internationally. Enables women to contribute socially, politically, and economically to the development of their community. Seeks to erradicate conditions of violence, poverty, and landlessness. Fosters communication among women worldwide. Receives financial support from some provincial governments and the Canadian International Development Agency. **Libraries:** Type: open to the public. Subjects: women's development issues in French, Spanish, and English.

Publications: *Match News* (in English and French), quarterly. Newsletter.

★2344★ MEDIAWATCH
(Evaluation - Medias)
1820 Fir St., No. 250
Vancouver, BC, Canada V6J 3B1
Suzanne Strutt, Exec. Dir.   PH: (604)731-0457

Members: 350. Works to improve the media's representation of women.

Publications: *The Bulletin.*

★2345★ MEDICAL WOMEN'S INTERNATIONAL ASSOCIATION -
CANADA (MWIA-C)
212, 222 16th Ave. NE
Calgary, AB, Canada T2E 1J8
Janette Hurley, Contact

Languages: English. **National.** Canada branch of the Medical Women's Association International (see separate entry). Women physicians. Provides a forum for discussion of women's health care issues. Encourages women to enter the field of medicine. Works to overcome discrimination against female physicians. Sponsors research and educational programs.

★2346★ MISSIONARY SISTERS OF OUR LADY OF THE ANGELS
(MNDA)
c/o Gilberte Giroux
323, rue Queen
Lennoxville, PQ, Canada J1M 1K8   PH: (819)346-8011
Gilberte Giroux, Exec. Officer   FX: (819)346-8011

National. Women religious in Canada. Conducts charitable programs.

★2347★ NA'AMAT CANADA (NC)
7005 Kildare Rd.   PH: (514)488-0792
Montreal, PQ, Canada H4W 1C1   FX: (514)487-6727

Multinational. Working and professional women. Works to advance the status of women by providing a variety of educational, community, and legal services. Believes that strong family relations are the foundation of a stable society. Members identify with the Zionist movement.

★2348★ NATIONAL ACTION COMMITTEE ON THE STATUS OF
WOMEN (NACSW)
(Comite Canadien d'Action sur le Statut de la Femme)
57 Mobile Dr.
Toronto, ON, Canada M4A 1H5   PH: (416)759-5252
Beverly Bain, Contact   FX: (416)759-5370

Founded: 1971. **Members:** 500. **Staff:** 5. **Regional Groups:** 13. **Languages:** English, French. **National.** Women's organizations, centers, services, church committees, unions, and political parties. Works to improve the status of women in Canada within the public and governmental arenas. Encourages women's full social, legal, and political participation. Promotes and safeguards anti-sexist, anti-racist, and anti-heterosexist principles. Programs include: state-subsudized training programs for women, language training for immigrant women; recognition of older women as positive participants within

the work force; and investigation into the violation of human rights of minorities by police officers. Lobbies government to establish firmer legislative actions against agressors in violent crimes, national child care programs, and reversal of taxations on child support payments. **Libraries:** Type: open to the public. Holdings: clippings, periodicals.

Publications: *Feminist Action Feministe* (in English and French), periodic. Newsletter. ● *Action Now*, 9/year. Bulletin. ● *Profile: Issues of importance to the Canadian feminist movement.* Booklet.

★2349★ NATIONAL ASSOCIATION OF WOMEN IN CONSTRUCTION -
CANADA (NAWIC)
11508 119 St.
Edmonton, AB, Canada T5G 2X7   PH: (403)454-6585
Iris Potter, Contact   FX: (403)452-1959

Founded: 1955. **National.** Women owners and employees of construction businesses united to attain equal rights. Promotes high standards in the construction industry. Represents member's interests.

Publications: *Newsletter*, quarterly.

★2350★ NATIONAL ASSOCIATION OF WOMEN AND THE LAW
(NAWL)
(Association Nationale de la Femme et du Droit)
1 Nicholas St., Ste. 604
Ottawa, ON, Canada K1N 7B7
Cheryl Boom, Contact   PH: (613)238-1544

Members: 1,000. **National.** Lawyers, students, and professionals in Canada. Seeks to secure equal rights under the law for women, ethnic minorities, and the disabled.

Publications: *Jurisfemme*, quarterly. Newsletter.

Conventions/Meetings: biennial conference. ● semiannual executive committee meeting.

★2351★ NATIONAL CLEARINGHOUSE ON FAMILY VIOLENCE
Family Violence Prevention Division
Brooke Claxton Bldg.
Ottawa, ON, Canada K1A 1B5

National. Seeks to eradicate domestic violence. Compiles, publishes, and disseminates information on domestic violence and child abuse.

★2352★ NATIONAL COUNCIL OF WOMEN OF CANADA
270 MacLaren St., No. 20   PH: (613)233-4953
Ottawa, ON, Canada K2P 0M3   (613)230-6834
Katherine Tait, Contact   FX: (613)232-8419

State Groups: 4. **National Groups:** 24. **National.** Umbrella organization for women's groups in Canada. Strives for the improvement of the quality of life and status of women in public and private life.

Publications: *Newsletter*, quarterly. ● *Yearbook*, annual.

Conventions/Meetings: annual meeting - 1994 May, Vancouver, BC, Canada.

★2353★ NATIONAL EATING DISORDER INFORMATION CENTRE
College Wing, 1-304
200 Elizabeth St.
Toronto, ON, Canada M5G 2C4   PH: (416)340-4156
Merryl Bear, Coord.   (416)340-4188

Founded: 1985. **Staff:** 2. **Budget:** C$100,000. **Languages:** English. **National.** Individuals interested in problems associated with women who suffer from eating disorders. Provides information and resources on causes, symptoms of, and therapeutic and health care treatments for eating disorders and the preoccupation with food and weight. Aims to raise awareness on eating disorders through conducting lectures and workshops. **Libraries:** Type: reference. Holdings: books, video recordings.

Publications: *Bulletin* (in English), 5/year.

Conventions/Meetings: annual Eating Disorders Awareness Week.

★2354★ NATIONAL ORGANIZATION OF IMMIGRANTS AND VISIBLE MINORITY WOMEN OF CANADA
(Organisation Nationale des Femmes Appartenant a une Minorite Visible du Canada)
251 Bank St.
Ottawa, ON, Canada K2P 1X3
Shelley Das, Contact   PH: (613)232-0689
Founded: 1988. **Languages:** English, French. **National.** Defends minority and immigrant women against sexism, racism, and violence; safeguards human rights. Assists minority and immigrant women in integrating into society. **Committees:** Advocacy; Constitution and Policy.

Publications: *NOIVMWC News,* quarterly. Newsletter.

★2355★ NATIVE WOMEN'S ASSOCIATION OF CANADA
9 Melrose Ave.
Ottawa, ON, Canada K1Y 1T8   PH: (613)722-3033
Virginia Meness, Exec. Dir.   FX: (613)722-7687
Founded: 1974. **Members:** 120,000. **Staff:** 4. **Regional Groups:** 4. **State Groups:** 12. **Languages:** English. **National.** Aboriginal women. Holds the beliefs that individuals in minority groups need protection from the political majority and that rights must be enforced, not merely endorsed. Supports the interpretation of human rights and freedoms as outlined by the United Nations. Endeavors to defend aboriginal peoples in the areas of: fundamental freedoms; democratic, mobility, legal, and equal rights; official language; and minority language educational rights. Strives to develop effective legislation. **Awards:** Annual (scholarship). Recipient: students who demonstrate a commitment to improving the situation of aboriginal women.

Publications: *An Aboriginal Charter of Rights and Freedoms* (in English and French). Booklet.

Conventions/Meetings: annual general assembly - always October.

★2356★ NUESTRA VOZ, A VOICE FOR GUATEMALAN WOMEN
1395 Lawrence Ave. W
PO Box 20092
Toronto, ON, Canada M6L 1A7   FX: (416)766-2659
Languages: Spanish, English. **Multinational.** Promotes public awareness of Guatemalan women's struggle for equality, justice, and peace. Provides a forum for cooperation and information exchange between Canada and Guatemala. Offers assistance to women in refugee camps. Disseminates information.

Publications: *We Are No Longer Afraid.* Book. ● *Newsletter,* semiannual.

Conventions/Meetings: periodic workshop.

★2357★ OLDER WOMEN'S NETWORK (OWN)
St. Paul's Centre
B4 427 Bloor St. W
Toronto, ON, Canada M5S 1X7   PH: (416)924-4188
Membership Dues: organization, C$25; individual, C$15. Women over 55. Represents interests of older women. Works to secure housing, health, and financial benefits for older women through legal support. Promotes a positive image of older women among the media and public. Works to achieve equal rights and freedom of reproductive choice for women.

Publications: *Contact,* quarterly. Newsletter.

★2358★ ORIGINAL WOMEN'S NETWORK - RESOURCE CENTRE FOR ABORIGINAL WOMEN (OWN)
294 Ellen St.
Winnepeg, MB, Canada R3A 1A9   PH: (204)942-2711
Kathy Mallett, Exec. Dir.   FX: (204)942-3445
Founded: 1985. **Members:** 150. **Membership Dues:** Individual and youth (13-17)., C$1 annual. **Staff:** 6. **Budget:** C$100,000. **Languages:** English. **National.** Aboriginal women. Provides communication, information, and support services. Raises awareness of aboriginal women's issues and the contributions they make to society. Promotes individual and organizational development of aboriginal women. Offers a women's business education, skills-training program entitled, "Ikwewak Anokiiwaad" (Women Working). Maintains an aboriginal women's radio broadcasting program entitled "Not Vanishing." Also undertakes public speaking and personal development radio/audio workshops. Provides Aboriginal Women's Speakers Bureau.

Publications: *Working Together Community Calendar.* ● *Aboriginal Women's Community Bulletin* (in English). ● *Aboriginal Women's Resource Directory* (in English).

Conventions/Meetings: monthly board meeting. ● bimonthly meeting. ● annual meeting - always June.

★2359★ OSTEOPOROSIS SOCIETY OF CANADA
(Societe de l'Osteoporose du Canada)
PO Box 280, Sta. Q
Toronto, ON, Canada M4T 2M1   PH: (416)696-2663
Kathryn D. Robins, Exec. Dir.   FX: (416)696-2673
Founded: 1982. **Members:** 14,000. **Staff:** 3. **Budget:** C$300,000. **Languages:** English, French. **National.** Individuals and organizations interested in the prevention, diagnosis, and treatment of osteoporosis. Supports research programs that seek to improve the quality of life for women with osteoporosis. Promotes education about osteoporosis among professional health practitioners. Disseminates informational materials to women with osteoporosis, physicians, and the public. Offers audio visual programs; participates in public forums. **Libraries:** Type: reference. **Awards:** Grant. Recipient: Canadian researchers focusing on osteoporosis and related areas. **Committees:** Public Information and Education; Professional Education; Communications and Industry Relations; Rehabilitation and Support Groups; Fundraising and Donor Development; Member and Community Services; Public Policy; Research.

Conventions/Meetings: annual - usually June. Toronto, ON, Canada.

★2360★ PAKISTANI WOMEN'S ASSOCIATION
190 Coltrin Rd.
Rockcliffe, ON, Canada K1M 0C5   PH: (613)749-5281
Khalida Hakim, Contact   (613)236-6646
Fosters unity, friendship, and cultural exchange among Pakistani and Canadian women.

★2361★ PLANNED PARENTHOOD FEDERATION OF CANADA (PPFC)
(FPNC Federation pour le Planning des Naissances Canada)
1 Nicholas St., Ste. 430
Ottawa, ON, Canada K1N 7B7   PH: (613)238-4474
Ms. Winnifred Kalagian, President   FX: (613)238-1162
Languages: English. **National.** Promotes family planning and responsible parenthood. Encourages public awareness of contraceptive methods and the need for family planning. Works to reduce the number of unwanted pregnancies and abortions. Sponsors programs in family planning, sex education, and sexually transmitted diseases, especially AIDS. Provides contraceptive services. Acts as an advocate for family planning issues on a national level. Conducts research.

★2362★ RESEAU D'ACTION ET D'INFORMATION POUR LES
    FEMMES (RAIF)
PO Box 360
88, place Ste. Foi
Ste. Foi, PQ, Canada G1Z 1C0
Marcelle Dolment, Contact   PH: (418)658-1973

Founded: 1973. Members: 100. Languages: French, English. Conducts research and disseminates information on women's issues. Lobbies government on women's rights.

Publications: *RAIF: Magazine on Information for Women.*

★2363★ SEXUALITY INFORMATION AND RESOURCES CLEARING
    HOUSE (SIRCH)
1 Nicholas St., Ste. 430
Ottawa, ON, Canada K1N 7B7   PH: (613)238-4474
Gillian Phillips, Director   FX: (613)238-1162

Founded: 1990. Staff: 6. Budget: C$600,000. Languages: English. National. Provides information services on sexuality issues. Compiles statistics. Offers educational programs.

Publications: *Bulletin*, periodic. ● *Directory*, annual. ● *Newsletter*, quarterly.

Conventions/Meetings: semiannual meeting.

★2364★ SISTERS OF CHARITY OF STATION VINCENT DE PAUL
150 Bedford Hwy.
Halifax, NS, Canada B3M 3J5
Sr. Theresa Corcoran, Gen.Sec.   PH: (902)453-3400

Founded: 1849. Members: 970. Staff: 198. Languages: English. Multinational. Catholic sisters in 6 countries involved in education, health care, social services, and pastoral ministry.

Publications: *The Sisters of Charity.*

★2365★ SISTERS OF STATION ANNE (SSA)
1950, rue Provost
Lachine, PQ, Canada H8S 1P7   PH: (514)637-1254
Sr. Yvette Bellerose SSA, Gen. Superior   FX: (514)637-5400

Founded: 1850. Members: 1,144. Languages: Creole, English, French, Spanish. Multinational. Roman Catholic women in 5 countries.

★2366★ SOCIETY FOR CANADIAN WOMEN IN SCIENCE AND
    TECHNOLOGY (SCWIST)
(SCST Societe des Canadiennes dans la Science et la Technologies)
                                     PH: (604)291-5163
515 W. Hastings St., No. 2423   FX: (604)291-5112
Vancouver, BC, Canada V6B 5K3   E-Mail: Internet:
Jacqueline Gill, President   SCWIST@SFU.CA

Founded: 1981. Members: 170. Membership Dues: Individuals., C$25; Students or unemployed individuals., C$10. Staff: 1. Languages: English. National. Individuals who seek to encourage equal opportunities for women in scientific, technological, and engineering careers. Promotes the development of women's careers in these areas. Informs the public about women's careers in science and technology to change social attitudes on the stereotyping of careers in these areas. Assists educators through the presentation of current information on careers, career training, science, and scientific policies. Offers summer work placement for 17-18 year old women in science and math fields. Sponsors science workshops for elementary school teachers and career exploration conferences. Conducts field trips.

Awards: Annual Dr. Margaret Lowe Benston Memorial Scholarship (scholarship). Recipient: female student at British Columbia Institute of Technology. Computer Services: Data base, registry of Women in Science, Engineering and Technology. Committees: Ms. Infinity; Journal; Female Friendly Science; Parent Education.

Publications: *Imagine the Possibilities* (in English). Book. ● *SCWIST News* (in English), bimonthly. Newsletter. ● What Do Scientists Do?, a 4-part video series on science careers.

★2367★ SOROPTIMIST FOUNDATION OF CANADA
185 Woodbridge Dr. SW, No. 22
Calgary, AB, Canada T2W 3X7
Marguerite Duguid, Secty. & Treasurer   PH: (403)249-9191

Founded: 1963. Members: 600. National. Works to: advance women in society; secure human rights; preserve high ethical standards in the work place. Encourages fellowship and cooperation among Soroptimists globally; fosters international understanding. Awards: Periodic (grant).

★2368★ SOUTH ASIAN WOMEN'S GROUP
PO Box 1022
1/2 Bloor St. W
Toronto, ON, Canada M6H 1M2   PH: (416)537-2276
Nirmala Nathan, Contact   FX: (416)537-9472

Members: 150. Provides support to women from South Asia. Offers cultural exchange programs and recreational activities to assist Asian women's integration into society and development of new friendships. Responds to social, educational, cultural, health, and legal needs of women immigrants.

Publications: *South Asian Women's Update.* Newsletter.

★2369★ TRAVELSHARE
1315, 44 Victoria St.
Toronto, ON, Canada M5C 1Y2
Genie Field, Contact   PH: (416)363-6491

Members: 1,000. National. Accomodates women who wish to find female travelling partners for safety and companionship.

Publications: *Travelshare*, monthly. Newsletter.

Conventions/Meetings: monthly meeting.

★2370★ UNITED CHURCH WOMEN (UCW)
85 St. Clair Ave. E
Toronto, ON, Canada M4T 1M8   PH: (416)925-5931
Ann Clark, Contact   FX: (416)925-3394

Founded: 1962. Members: 100,000. Staff: 1. Budget: C$30,000. Languages: English. National. Lay women of the United Church of Canada. Promotes unity among members to uphold the beliefs and missions of the church. Advocates members' growth in Christian understanding, faith, and experience. Fosters leadership in the activities of the church among members. Encourages acceptance and understanding of other ecumenical beliefs throughout Canada. Promotes support and fellowship among members. Maintains relationships with other national and international women's organizations.

Conventions/Meetings: annual, Presidents and Vice Presidents meeting. - Toronto, ON, Canada. ● annual executive committee meeting - Toronto, ON, Canada.

★2371★ WESTERN BUSINESS WOMEN'S ASSOCIATION
1250 Homer St.
Vancouver, BC, Canada V6B 2Y5   PH: (604)688-0951
Elizabeth Reymond, President   (604)681-4545

Members: 120. Provides a network and support to women in business. Offers mentorship program.

Publications: *WBA Newsletter*, annual.

Conventions/Meetings: monthly meeting.

★2372★ WIDOW TO WIDOW PROGRAM
Y.M.-Y.W.H.A. and N.H.S. of Montreal
5500 Westbury Ave.
Montreal, PQ, Canada H3W 2W8

National. Offers services to widows, including housing assistance, legal counseling, health improvement, and job placement. Educates the public and professional counsellors on the stresses of bereavement.

★2373★ WIDOWS HELPING OTHERS
Family Service Bldg.
5339 207th St.
Langley, BC, Canada V3A 2E6
Catherine Farrar, Secretary   PH: (604)534-7921

Languages: English. **National.** Sponsors social programs for widowed women. Operates telephone referral service.

Conventions/Meetings: annual conference.

**★2374★ WOMEN AND ENVIRONMENTS EDUCATION AND
  DEVELOPMENT FOUNDATION (WEED)**
736 Bathurst St.
Toronto, ON, Canada M5S 2R4   PH: (416)516-2379

Founded: 1987. **Members:** 1,000. **Languages:** English. **National.** Women experts in environmental studies and issues. Works to implement community development projects to improve the environment. Provides a forum for discussion, information exchange, and the conducting of research related to women in the fields of planning, health, workplace, design, economy, urban and rural sociology, and community development. Initiates and organizes community projects. Advocates environmental protection, anti-discriminatory zoning practices, and the development of affordable housing.

Publications: *Women and Environments* (in English), quarterly. Magazine. **Advertising:** accepted. ● *Whitewash.* Book. Information on removing chlorine bleach from feminine sanitary products and baby diapers.

★2375★ WOMEN INVENTORS PROJECT
1 Greensboro Dr., Ste. 302   PH: (416)243-0668
Etobicoke, ON, Canada M9W 1C8   FX: (416)243-0688

Founded: 1986. **Languages:** English, French. **National.** Encourages innovative women and girls in professional and academic pursuits in science and technology. Works to further the issuing of patents to women and women's access to funding for research and inventions and to increase the number of women inventor/entrepreneur role models. Maintains that education and encouragement aimed towards women's contributions to innovation, science, and industry are vital to preserving Canada's competitiveness in the global economy. Develops and supplies resource materials for women inventors, entrepreneurs, professionals, and scholars.

Publications: *The Book for Women Who Invent or Want To* (in English and French). ● *Inventors Want To Know: A Reference Guide on Entrepreneurship and Innovation for Information Providers* (in English). ● *Daughters of Invention: An Invention Workshop for Girls* (in English). Includes over 20 biographies of women inventors. ● *Focus* (in English), quarterly. Newsletter. ● *What If?* (in English). Video. ● *Women Inventors* (in English). Video. ● *Workshop on Women, Entrepreneurship and Innovation: Facilitator's Guide* (in English). ● *Course Materials on Invention and Innovation for Schools* (in English). ● *Inventing Women* (in English). Video. ● *Workshop Kit for Advisors to Entrepreneurship and Inventors* (in English).

Conventions/Meetings: Workshop on Women, Entrepreneurship and Innovation.

★2376★ WOMEN IN SCIENCE AND ENGINEERING (WISE)
(Corp. des Femmes en Sciences et en Genie)
6519B Mississauga Rd.
Mississauga, ON, Canada L5N 1A6   PH: (416)567-7190
Mildred Minty, President   FX: (416)567-7191

Founded: 1977. **Members:** 300. **Regional Groups:** 7. **Languages:** English. **National.** Women scientists and engineers, educators in the sciences, and interested individuals. Encourages young women to strive for higher education and achievement. Promotes the involvement of women in Canada's scientific and engineering industries. Supports women entering scientific and engineering professions. Operates as an information center for Canadian women seeking information on scientific and engineering education and professions. Provides the Canadian government with information on the experiences of women scientists and engineers in the workplace and in academia. Fosters networking and support among members. Sponsors career information presentations at the junior and senior high school levels. Disseminates posters and videos encouraging young women in schools to remain active in scientific-focused curriculums. Works with other Canadian women's organizations to organize conferences.

Publications: *Newsletter* (in English), quarterly. Highlights of chapter activities and national issues.

Conventions/Meetings: annual.

★2377★ WOMEN ON STAMPS STUDY UNIT (WOSSU)
c/o Betty M. Killingbeck
905 Birch Ave.
Peterborough, ON, Canada K9H 6G7
Betty M. Killingbeck, Pres.   PH: (705)742-1714

Founded: 1979. **Members:** 123. **Multinational.** A study unit of the American Topical Association. Individuals interested in collecting postal items relating to women. Purposes are to aid members in formulating collections and to disseminate information on the subject. Maintains biographical archives. Offers award for topical exhibiting at the ATA Annual Topex. Members engage in continuing research.

Publications: *The Topical Women*, bimonthly. Newsletter. Includes member profiles and calendar of events. **Circulation:** 100. **Advertising:** accepted. ● *Women Artists Lists.* Book. ● *List of Women Stamp Designers.* Book. ● *List of Women's Art on Stamps.* Book. ● *List of Women Athletes on Stamps.* Book. ● *List of Family of Queen Elizabeth II.* Book.

★2378★ WOMEN OF UNIFARM
14815 - 119 Ave.
Edmonton, AB, Canada T5L 4W2
Verna Kette, Contact   PH: (403)451-5912

Founded: 1970. **Members:** 150. Women farmers and ranchers. Works to improve education, health, and welfare for rural women. Monitors legal developments affecting rural life. Cooperates with Unifarm and similar organizations to achieve goals.

Publications: *Newsletter.*

Conventions/Meetings: annual convention - always January. ● periodic board meeting.

★2379★ WOMEN WHO EXCEL
PO Box 3533, Sta. C
Hamilton, ON, Canada L8H 7M9
Christine Whitlock, Contact   PH: (416)547-7135

Members: 120. Advances interests of women in the business world.

Publications: *Networks.* Newsletter. 3/year. ● *Directory*, periodic.

Conventions/Meetings: annual meeting. ● monthly dinner.

★2380★ WOMEN WHO LOVE TOO MUCH
c/o Catholic Family Services
No. 1013 Wilson Ave., Ste. 201
Downsview, ON, Canada M3K 1G1   PH: (416)636-9963

Support group for women striving to take control of their lives. Group based on the publication, *Women Who Love Too Much*, by Robin Norwood.

★2381★ WOMEN'S ECONOMIC FORUM
PO Box 7473
Sandwich Postal Sta.
Windsor, ON, Canada N9C 4G1
Katherine Ruth, President   PH: (519)255-7447

Members: 100. **National.** Promotes the networking and professional development of business women. Maintains speakers' bureau.

Publications: *Directory*, periodic.

Conventions/Meetings: annual seminar.

★2382★ WOMEN'S EMPLOYMENT OUTREACH (WEO)
91 Douglas Ave.
Fredericton, NB, Canada E3A 2N6   PH: (506)450-0128
Susan Adams, Contact   FX: (506)450-0126

Languages: English. **National.** Assists women in finding employment. Offers guidance in resume writing, interviewing techniques, and goal setting. Conducts programs to help women improve their self confidence and communication skills.

★2383★ WOMEN'S HEALTHSHARING COLLECTIVE
14 Skey Ln.
Alley Behind 72 Fexley St.   PH: (416)532-0812
Toronto, ON, Canada M6S 3S5   FX: (416)588-6038

Members: 12. **National.** Promotes women's mental and physical health awareness. Collects and disseminates information regarding women's health concerns.

Publications: *Healthsharing: Canadian Women's Health Quarterly.* Magazine.

★2384★ WOMEN'S INITIATIVES FOR SUCCESSFUL
       ENTREPRENEURSHIP
784 Richmond St.
London, ON, Canada M6A 3H5
Ann Hubbell, Contact   PH: (519)433-2180

Staff: 7. Sponsors mentoring program for women in the scientific and technological fields. Encourages female high school students to pursue careers in the sciences. **Awards:** Annual (scholarship). Recipient: female science student.

★2385★ WOMEN'S INTER-CHURCH COUNCIL OF CANADA
77 Charles St. W
Toronto, ON, Canada M5S 1K5
Donna Hunter, Exec. Dir.

Languages: English. **National.** Female members of Christian and Catholic churches. Conducts community service activities.

★2386★ WOMEN'S INTERNATIONAL LEAGUE FOR PEACE AND
       FREEDOM - CANADA SECTION (WILPF)
PO Box 4781, Sta. E
Ottawa, ON, Canada K1S 5H9
Marcy Rnic, President   PH: (613)253-6395

Languages: English. **National.** Women in Canada working to obtain and preserve world peace. Organizes campaigns against disarmament, apartheid, and human rights. Cooperates with local disarmament coalitions and other groups promoting social, economic, and political justice in Canada and abroad.

Publications: *WILPF News* (in English), periodic. ● Also publishes pamphlet.

★2387★ WOMEN'S LEGAL EDUCATION AND ACTION FUND (LEAF)
489 College St., Ste. 403
Toronto, ON, Canada M6G 1A5   PH: (416)963-9654
Joanne St. Lewis, Exec. Dir.   FX: (416)963-8455

Founded: 1985. **Members:** 2,500. **Staff:** 15. **Languages:** English. **National.** Promotes women's equality through test case litigation and public education, based on the equality provisions in the Canadian Charter of Rights and Freedoms. Provides resources on gender equality and legal issues.

Publications: *LEAF Lines* (in English), quarterly. Newsletter.

★2388★ WORLD ASSOCIATION OF WOMEN JOURNALISTS AND
       WRITERS-CANADA
3945 St. Martin Blvd. W
Laval, PQ, Canada H7T 1B7   PH: (514)688-6380
Pierrette Pare-Walsh, President   FX: (514)681-1682

Founded: 1969. **Members:** 400. **Regional Groups:** 1. **Languages:** English, French, Spanish. **National.** Canadian branch of the World Association of Women Journalists and Writers. Women journalists, writers, and communicators. Promotes the interests of women in these fields. Encourages members to take advantage of opportunities in their professional fields. Supports the exchange of knowledge, ideas, experiences, and cultural values among members. Works to enhance the professional status of women through seminars and conferences.

Publications: *Newsletter* (in English, French, and Spanish), semiannual.

Conventions/Meetings: biennial congress

★2389★ YOUNG WOMEN'S CHRISTIAN ASSOCIATION OF CANADA
       (YWCA of Canada)
80 Gerrard St. E
Toronto, ON, Canada M5B 1G6   PH: (416)593-9886
Adrienne Clements, Director   FX: (416)971-8084

Founded: 1893. **Members:** 2,500,000. **Budget:** C$3,000,000. **Local Groups:** 45. **Languages:** English, French. **National.** Member associations. Acts in accordance with the constitutional funtions of the World YWCA: providing a network for the apportionment of resources and exchange of experience among national associations; promoting international understanding, improved social and economic conditions, and human rights. Accepts a responsibilty to work towards development fronted by women, influenced by Christianity, and guided by an attitude that development is a fundamental human right. Contributes to development through: emphasizing the necessity for building and strengthening world-wide development education programs advancing social awareness that leads to a respect for the completeness and equality of all people; recognizing and addressing serious economic, social, cultural, and spiritual needs of women; working towards transforming society from an hierarchical model to one of equality and democracy; achieving equity through the sharing of knowledge and techology; securing the participation of women in all areas of development; and adopting technologies for projects that will protect the environment. Strives to secure the dignity of every human being and a just society. Encourages self-determination and personal development of women and girls. Functions as a voice for women, a source of consultion on women's issues, and a supporter and defender of social change. Community services include: shelters for abused women; child care; advocacy on issues affecting women; leadership programs; fitness programs; micro-entrepreneurship programs.

Publications: *Annual Report.* ● *Journal*, quarterly. ● *Fresh Start.* ● *Directory.*

Conventions/Meetings: annual meeting.

Mexico

★2390★ ASOCIACION MEXICANA DE MUJERES EN LA CIENCIA
Apartado Postal 74
09081 Mexico City, DF, Mexico

PH: 5 6706897
FX: 5 6706897

Languages: Spanish. **National.** Women students and professionals in the fields of natural and physical science. Works to enhance the status of women scientists in Mexico.

★2391★ CENTER OF RESEARCH AND STRUGGLE AGAINST DOMESTIC VIOLENCE (CECOVID AC)
(CECOVID AC Centro de Investigacion y Lucha Contra la Violencia Domestica)
Apartado Postal 211
06000 Mexico City, DF, Mexico
Ana Maria Martinez, Gen.Coord.

PH: 5 5798051
FX: 5 6961256

Founded: 1987. **Members:** 10. **Staff:** 5. **Budget:** US$50,000. **Languages:** English, Spanish. **National.** Mexican women. Seeks to end violence against women through public education and women's empowerment. Maintains a shelter; provides psychological counseling for battered women and children. Conducts workshops and self-help groups on self-esteem and overcoming violence. Investigates domestic violence; disseminates information.

Publications: *Aproximaciones a las Caracteristicas de la Violencia Domestica* (in Spanish). Book.

★2392★ CENTRO DE APOYO PARA MUJERES VIOLADAS (CAMVAC)
Apartado Postal 12-890
03020 Mexico City, DF, Mexico
Ma. del Carmen Sanchez Ruiz,
Secretary

PH: 5 5192553

Founded: 1979. **Languages:** Spanish. **Multinational.** Provides support for the psychological, medical, and legal needs of victims of sexual violence. Conducts research on sexual assault issues. Offers seminars and courses; provides children's services. Maintains biographical archives. **Computer Services:** Data base.

Conventions/Meetings: annual assembly - always Mexico City.

★2393★ CENTRO DE INVESTIGACION Y CAPACITACION DE LA MUJER
Santa Maria La Ribera 107, Int. 3
Colonia Santa Maria La Ribera
Mexico City, DF, Mexico

PH: 5 416799

Languages: Spanish. **National.** Promotes the study of women and women's issues in Mexico. Works to enhance the political and economic status of women. Defends women's rights. Conducts research.

★2394★ CENTRO PARA MUJERES ''CIDHAL''
Calle de las Flores 12
Col Acapantzingo 1-579
Cuernavaca, Morelos, Mexico

PH: 182058
FX: 182058

Languages: Spanish. **National.** Protects and defends women's rights in Mexico. Fosters friendly relations among women.

★2395★ COLECTIVO FEMINISTA COATLICUE
Apartado Postal 2-16809
2800 Colima, Mexico

PH: 332 29599

Languages: Spanish. **National.** Provides a forum for discussion and implementation of action on feminist issues. Fosters feminist solidarity and mobilization.

★2396★ COLECTIVO DE LUCHA EN CONTRA DE LA VIOLENCIA HACIA LAS MUJERES
Baja California
No. 261, 6 piso
Col. Hipodromo Condenzo, Mexico

Languages: Spanish. Works towards the support and development of legislation which povides firmer action against aggressors of violence against women and protection and support of victims. Provides information designed to raise pubic awareness of the prevalence of violence against women.

★2397★ CONSEJO NACIONAL DE MUJERES DE MEXICO
Cuvier 45
5 Mexico City, DF, Mexico
Sra. M. Lavalle Urbina, President

PH: 5 5459141

Languages: Spanish. **National.** Umbrella organization for women's groups in Mexico. Supports the interests of women. Coordinates activities. Disseminates information on women's issues.

★2398★ DIFUSION CULTURAL FEMINISTE
Av. Universidad 1855, piso 4
Col. Oxtopulco Universida
04310 Mexico City, DF, Mexico

PH: 5 5507306

Languages: Spanish. **National.** Works to further the feminist movement through information dissemination, lectures, and education. Strives to unite and mobilize women in action on feminist issues.

★2399★ FEDERACION NACIONAL DE MUJERES INSURGENTES
Cerrada Monte Camerum 62-10
Loma de Chapultepec
06170 Mexico City, DF, Mexico

Languages: Spanish. **National.** Politically active women working for equality between the sexes in Mexico. Disseminates information.

★2400★ FUNDACION MEXICANA PARA LA PLANEACION FAMILIAR (MEXFAM)

PH: 5 5737348
5 5737268
Calle Juarez 208
Tlalpan
FX: 5 5732318
14000 Mexico City, DF, Mexico
TX: 3831764338 XFAMME
Emilio Carrillo, President
CBL: MEXFAM

Languages: Spanish. **National.** Promotes responsible parenthood and family planning. Advocates family planning as a basic human right. Works to reduce the number of unwanted pregnancies and abortions. Encourages public awareness of family planning, contraception, and sexually transmitted diseases. Offers educational programs for teens and adults. Acts as an advocate for family planning on a national level. Conducts research.

★2401★ INTERDISCIPLINARY PROGRAM ON WOMEN'S STUDIES
(PIEM Programa Interdisciplinario de Estudios de la Mujer)
Camino al Ajusco 20
Colonia Pedregal de Sta. Teresa
01000 Mexico City, DF, Mexico
Elena Urrutia, Coord.

PH: 5 6455955
FX: 5 6450464

Founded: 1983. **Staff:** 20. **Budget:** 200,000 MP. **Languages:** Spanish, English. **National.** Seeks to enhance the status of women in Mexico. Sponsors educational and research programs on women's issues.

★2402★ MEXICAN SOCIETY FOR WOMEN'S RIGHTS (MSWR)
(SWPDM Sociedad Mexicana Pro-Derechos de la Mujer)
Alpina 37
Tizapan, San Angel
01090 Mexico City, DF, Mexico   PH: 5 55076711
Lucero Gonzalez, Vice President   FX: 5 5507671

Founded: 1990. **Members:** 11. **Staff:** 3. **Languages:** English, Spanish. **National.** Seeks to establish a new philanthropic trend among women for women. Assists women's groups financially and organizationally. Supports and promotes women and women's groups working to improve their society and their standard of living. Seeks to improve legal and social conditions such as self-worth and dignity to eliminate discrimination and inequality of opportunity.

★2403★ NA'AMAT PIONERAS (NP)
Vicente Suarez 67   PH: 5 2865589
06140 Collondesa 11, DF, Mexico   FX: 5 5692016

Languages: Spanish. **Multinational.** Working and professional women. Works to advance the status of women by providing a variety of educational, community, and legal services. Believes that strong family relations are the foundation of a stable society. Members identify with the Zionist movement.

★2404★ RED DE GRUPOS POR LA SALUD DE LA MUJER Y DEL
     NINO (REGSAMUNI)
Revolucion 1133-3, Col. Mixcoac
Apartado Postal 22-443
03910 Mexico City, DF, Mexico   PH: 5 5935336
Dra. Leticia Quesnel Galvan   FX: 5 5935336

Founded: 1987. **Members:** 6. **Staff:** 4. **Languages:** English, Spanish. **National.** Women working to improve the health of women and children in Mexico. Seeks to empower women and improve their standard of living. Conducts educational and informational courses for women and women's organizations on nutrition, sexuality, lactation and breastfeeding, and other women's health issues. Trains health workers; conducts research.

Publications: *Dialogos de Salud Popular* (in Spanish), quarterly. Bulletin. **Circulation:** 500. **Advertising:** accepted.

Conventions/Meetings: biennial workshop.

★2405★ RED CONTRA LA VIOLENCIA HACIA LAS MUJERES
Xola 1454, Colonia Narvante
Colonia Narvante
03020 Mexico City, DF, Mexico

Languages: Spanish. **National.** Supports and develops legislation and policies to eliminate violence against women; aims towards firmer action against aggressors against women and increased support and protection of victims.

★2406★ WOMAN TO WOMAN, MEXICO
(Mujer a Mujer)
Apartado Postal 24-553
Col. Roma   PH: 5 2070834
06701 Mexico City, DF, Mexico   FX: 5 5841068
Mercedes Lopez, Contact   E-Mail: PeaceNet: igc:mam

Languages: English, Spanish. **National.** Provides a network for grassroots and feminist organizations. Promotes cooperation and communication among women's groups; organizes exchanges, workshops, tours, and retreats. Encourages the sharing of views and strategies relevant to the women's movement and the age of internationalism. Promotes increased participation of women in North American economics. Areas of interest include: labor organization, community development and mobilization, lesbian issues, health, education, and violence against women.

Publications: *Correspondencia* (in English and Spanish), quarterly. Journal.

★2407★ YOUNG WOMEN'S CHRISTIAN ASSOCIATION - MEXICO
(Asociacion Cristiana Femenina National - Mexico)
c/o Sra. Emilia Hernandez Ibarra
YWCA of Guadalajara
J. Gpe. Montenegro 1614
44100 Guadalajara, Jalisco, Mexico
Sra. Emilia Hernandez Ibarra, Contact

National. Promotes the development of young women in Mexico. Upholds Christian beliefs and values. Works to instill self-worth and self-esteem in young women.

United States

★2408★ 9 TO 5, NATIONAL ASSOCIATION OF WORKING WOMEN
614 Superior Ave. NW, Rm. 852
Cleveland, OH 44113   PH: (216)566-9308
Karen Nussbaum, Exec.Dir.   FX: (216)566-0192

Founded: 1973. **Members:** 13,000. **Staff:** 14. **Budget:** US$600,000. **Local Groups:** 25. **Languages:** English. **National.** Women office workers. Seeks to build a national network of local office worker chapters that strives to gain better pay, proper use of office automation, opportunities for advancement, elimination of sex and race discrimination, and improved working conditions for women office workers. Works to introduce legislation or regulations at state level to protect video display terminal operators. Produces studies and research in areas such as reproductive hazards of Video Display Terminals (VDTs), automation's effect on clerical employment, family and medical leaves, and stress. Conducts Annual summer school for working women. Maintains speakers' bureau.

Publications: *9 to 5*, 5/year. Newsletter. **Circulation:** 12,000. **Advertising:** accepted. ● *9 to 5: Working Woman's Guide to Office Survival.* Booklet. ● *Guide to Combatting Sexual Harassment.* Booklet.

Conventions/Meetings: annual conference.

★2409★ 9 TO 5 WORKING WOMEN EDUCATION FUND (WWEF)
614 Superior Ave. NW
Cleveland, OH 44113   PH: (216)566-1699
Tami O'Dell, Exec.Dir.   FX: (216)566-0192

Founded: 1973. **Languages:** English. **National.** Conducts research on the concerns of women office workers. Topics include: the future of office work; automation; health and safety issues; affirmative action; family and medical leave; pay equity; flex-time; job-sharing. Conducts public presentations and seminars upon request; provides speakers. Compiles statistics; has conducted a national survey on women and stress. Maintains biographical archives, and library on the history of working women.

Conventions/Meetings: annual conference.

★2410★ ABORTION RIGHTS MOBILIZATION (ARM)
175 5th Ave., Ste. 814
New York, NY 10010
Lawrence Lader, Pres.   PH: (212)673-2040

Languages: English. **National.** Works to guarantee a woman's legal right to abortion as decreed by the U.S. Supreme Court.

★2411★ AD HOC COMMITTEE IN DEFENSE OF LIFE
1187 Natl. Press Bldg.
Washington, DC 20045
Robert McFadden, Bureau Chief   PH: (202)347-8686

Founded: 1974. **Staff:** 3. **Languages:** English. **National.** Seeks to have the Roe vs. Wade decision repealed. (The Roe vs. Wade decision, handed down by the Supreme Court in 1973, interpreted the concept of personal liberty guaranteed by the Constitution to include a woman's right to decide whether or not to terminate her pregnancy.) Disseminates information opposing abortion and euthanasia; lobbies for legislation against abortion and euthanasia. Maintains library of documents, clippings, and reports on pro-life issues.

Publications: *Lifeletter*, 12-18/year. Newsletter. Includes information on lobbying efforts.

★2412★ ADVERTISING WOMEN OF NEW YORK (AWNY)
153 E. 57th St.
New York, NY 10022
Nancy Meagan, Exec.Dir.
PH: (212)593-1950
FX: (212)759-2865

Founded: 1912. **Members:** 850. **Staff:** 4. **Languages:** English. **National.** Women engaged in an executive or administrative capacity in advertising, publicity, marketing, research, or promotion. Conducts professional development seminars and a career clinic to provide personal job counseling. The affiliated Advertising Women of New York Foundation funds scholarship programs and conducts an Annual career conference for college seniors and graduate students and other educational and charitable programs. Membership concentrated in the New York City area. Maintains speakers' bureau. **Committees:** AAF College Competition; Addy's Competition; Awards and Citations; Cannes Film Festival; Career Council; College Career Conference; College Internship; Industry Programs; Membership Development; Public Relations; Reception and Hospitality; Scholarship; Special Events

Publications: *Advertising Women of New York—Annual Roster*. Membership directory. **Circulation:** 800. ● *AWNY Matters: A Monthly Report from the Advertising Women of New York*. Newsletter informing members of social events and trends impacting the advertising industry. **Advertising:** accepted. ● *AWNY News*, 3/year. Membership activities newsletter. **Circulation:** 800.

Conventions/Meetings: monthly luncheon.

★2413★ ADVOCACY INSTITUTE - WOMEN VS. SMOKING NETWORK
1739 Rhode Island Ave. NW, Ste. 600
Washington, DC 20036
Michele Block M.D., Director
PH: (202)659-8475

Languages: English. **National.** Educates women about the negative effects of tobacco use. Disseminates information.

★2414★ ADVOCACY AND RESEARCH INSTITUTE ON LATINO WOMEN
The Women's Bldg.
79 Central Ave.
Albany, NY 12206
Sonia Ivette Dueno, Exec.Dir.
PH: (518)432-6498

National. Promotes the interests of Hispanic American women. Advocates research and programs that focus on issues of interest to Hispanic American women.

★2415★ ADVOCATES FOR AFRICAN FOOD SECURITY: LESSENING THE BURDEN FOR WOMEN
866 United Nations Plaza, Ste. 120
New York, NY 10017

Languages: English. **National.** Works to eradicate hunger throughout Africa by assisting African women to obtain means of nourishment for their families. Conducts women's and children's programs.

★2416★ AFL-CIO - COMMITTEE ON SALARIED AND PROFESSIONAL WOMEN
Department for Professional Employees
815 16th St. NW, No. 707
Washington, DC 20006
Gloria Johnson, Chair
PH: (202)638-0320

Founded: 1974. **National.** Explores the problems facing women in professional and technical occupations. Encourages organizing and union participation among white collar women workers.

★2417★ AFL-CIO - WOMEN'S ACTIVITIES
815 16th St. NW
Washington, DC 20006
Cynthia McCaughan, Coordinator
PH: (202)637-5272

Founded: 1955. **National.** Works to ensure women's equal rights in AFL-CIO policies and activities. Encourages women's organization in labor.

★2418★ AFRICA STUDIES ASSOCIATION - WOMEN'S CAUCUS
Emory University
Atlanta, GA 30322
Edna Bay, Contact
PH: (404)329-6410

National. Promotes the interests of African and African American women. Works to bring attention to the issues facing African women. Fosters exchange of information about research and studies of women in Africa.

Publications: *Newsletter*.

★2419★ AFRICAN AMERICAN WOMEN IN DEFENSE OF OURSELVES (AAWDO)
317 S. Division, Ste. 199
Ann Arbor, MI 48104
PH: (313)918-2702

National. Originally formed to oppose the nomination and confirmation of Supreme Court Justice Clarence Thomas. Opposed the "racist and sexist treatment of Anita Hill." Facilitates information sharing among members to organize members as a strongforce against sexual harassment.

★2420★ AFRICAN AMERICAN WOMEN'S ASSOCIATION
PO Box 55122
Brightwood Sta.
Washington, DC 20011
Mary P. Doughterty, President
PH: (202)966-6645

National. Works to establish closer relationships and understanding between the women of Africa and the Americas through cultural, educational, charitable, and social activities.

Publications: *Newsletter*.

★2421★ AFRICAN-AMERICAN WOMEN'S CLERGY ASSOCIATION (AWCA)
PO Box 1493
Washington, DC 20013
Rev. Imagene B. Stewart, Chairperson
PH: (202)797-7460

Founded: 1969. **Members:** 167. **Local Groups:** 20. **Languages:** English. **National.** Lay and ordained women clergy. Seeks to promote and encourage the clergy as a profession for women. Operates shelter for homeless and battered women in Washington, DC. Provides scholarships for women interested in the clergy; bestows Social Activist of the Year Award.

Conventions/Meetings: annual meeting.

★2422★ AFRICAN METHODIST EPISCOPAL CHURCH - WOMEN'S
MISSIONARY SOCIETY
1134 11th St. NW
Washington, DC 20001
Delores L. Kennedy Wiliams, President   PH: (202)371-8886

Multinational. Promotes the training, education, and welfare of disadvantaged women, youths, and children throughout the Bahamas, Bermuda, Canada, Central African Republic, Dominican Republic, England, Guyana, Haiti, Jamaica, Namibia, South Africa, Suriname, Trinidad and Tobago, and the United States. Works for the empowerment of women struggling to break the cycle of poverty and second class citizenship. Monitors legislation; lobbies governments.

Publications: *Magazine.*

★2423★ AGENCY FOR INTERNATIONAL DEVELOPMENT - WOMEN
IN DEVELOPMENT
320 21st St. NW, Rm. 3725A
Department of State
Washington, DC 20523
Kay Davies, Director   PH: (202)647-3992

Founded: 1974. **Members:** 13,500. **Local Groups:** 50. **Languages:** English. **Multinational.** Family therapists, psychologists, psychiatrists, social workers, and interested individuals. Works to include women in the development of their countries. Conducts research; organizes conferences and community projects; and training in development skills. Maintains a public resource center on women's issues. **Libraries:** Type: reference; open to the public. Holdings: 6,000. Subjects: documents on women in developing countries.

★2424★ ALAN GUTTMACHER INSTITUTE (AGI)
111 5th Ave.
New York, NY 10003   PH: (212)254-5656
Jeannie I. Rosoff, Pres.   FX: (212)254-9891

Founded: 1968. **Budget:** US$4,000,000. **Languages:** English. **National.** Fosters sound public policies on voluntary fertility control and population issues and encourages responsive reproductive health programs through policy analysis, public education, and research. Compiles statistics on the provision of services relating to reproductive health care. Offers technical assistance. Until 1977, served as the Research and Development Division of Planned Parenthood Federation of America. **Divisions:** Communications and Development; Public Policy; Research.

Publications: *Annual Report.* ● *Family Planning Perspectives*, bimonthly. Professional journal focusing on reproductive health issues. **ISSN:** 0014-7354. **Circulation:** 15,000. **Advertising:** accepted. ● *International Family Planning Perspectives* (in English, French, and Spanish), quarterly. Journal. Highlighting population and reproductive health research and program achievements in developing countries. **ISSN:** 0162-2749. **Circulation:** 30,000. **Advertising:** accepted. ● *Washington Memo*, 20/year. Newsletter. **ISSN:** 0739-4179. **Circulation:** 5,000. **Advertising:** not accepted **Also Cited As:** *Planned Parenthood-World Population Washington Memo.* ● *Preventing Pregnancy, Protecting Health: A New Look at Birth Control in the U.S..* Booklet. ● *Abortion Factbook.* Booklet.

Conventions/Meetings: board meeting - 3/year.

★2425★ ALL NATIONS WOMEN'S LEAGUE (ANWL)
c/o Madeleine Thibault
Jackson Heights, Queens
PO Box 428
New York, NY 11372
Madeleine Thibault, Pres.   PH: (718)672-1243

Founded: 1970. **Members:** 50. **Membership Dues:** US$20 annual. **Budget:** US$100,000. **State Groups:** 2. **Local Groups:** 2. **Languages:** English. **National.** Women over the age of 18 from all parts of the world. Purpose is to promote a mutual understanding of women's problems and the need for

community integration. Seeks to improve the cultural, educational, and professional status of women throughout the world. Works to broaden public awareness of the goals, concerns, ideas, and problems of women. Sponsors cultural events, educational and health programs, and lectures. Educational activities for children include classes in music, painting, and crafts. Offers vocational rehabilitation programs for unemployed women; operates counseling office. Bestows awards; operates charitable program; maintains speakers' bureau.

Publications: *Bulletin*, periodic. ● *Magazine*, periodic. ● *Newsletter*, periodic.

Conventions/Meetings: monthly conference - New York, NY, United States. ● annual meeting (exhibits) - always March.

★2426★ ALLIANCE OF MINORITY WOMEN FOR BUSINESS AND
POLITICAL DEVELOPMENT
c/o Brenda Alford
PO Box 13933
Silver Spring, MD 20911-3933
Brenda Alford, Pres.   PH: (301)565-0258

Founded: 1982. **Budget:** US$50,000. **Languages:** English. **National.** Organizations in support of minority women in business and politics. Seeks to increase number of minority women business owners as elected officials.

★2427★ ALLIANCE OF WOMEN BIKERS (AWB)
PO Box 484
Eau Claire, WI 54702
Debby Berry, Contact

Founded: 1977. **Members:** 300. **Languages:** English. **National.** International organization of women ages 18 to 65. Supports women motorcyclists; disdains a tough, macho, stay-out-of-my-way image; educates sexist motorcycle magazines; lobbies against laws that the alliance believes violate their rights as bikers and citizens. Has held motorcycle shows for inmates of women's prisons; seeks to provide social contact to incarcerated women. Motto is: "Sisters Helping Sisters.".

Conventions/Meetings: semiannual meeting.

★2428★ ALLIANCE OF WOMEN ROAD RIDERS AND ASSOCIATES
(AWRRA)
PO Box 3116
Falls Church, VA 22043
Courtney Caldwell, Bd.Chm.   PH: (703)237-2824

Founded: 1985. **Members:** 300. **Membership Dues:** US$25. **State Groups:** 5. **Languages:** English. **National.** Women motorcycle enthusiasts. Promotes a positive image of motorcyclists. **Formerly:** American Women Road Riders' Alliance.

★2429★ ALPHA CHI OMEGA
5939 Castle Creek Parkway Dr.
Indianapolis, IN 46250-4343
Nancy Leonard, Dir.   PH: (317)579-5050

Founded: 1885. **Members:** 120,000. **Languages:** English. **National.** Social sorority. Presents Award of Achievement biennially. Sponsors Alpha Chi Omega Foundation.

Publications: *Lyre*, quarterly.

Conventions/Meetings: biennial meeting - always June.

★2430★ ALPHA DELTA KAPPA
1615 W. 92nd St.
Kansas City, MO 64114
Opal L. Lunsford, Exec. Administrator   PH: (816)363-5525

National. Seeks to recognize outstanding women educators actively engaged in teaching, administration, or a specialized field of the teaching profession. Works to build a fraternal fellowship among women educators. Promotes high standard in education and assists in strengthening the status and advancement of women in the teaching profession.

Publications: *The Kappan.* Magazine.

★2431★ ALPHA EPSILON PHI
6100 Channingway Blvd., Ste. 302
Columbus, OH 43232   PH: (614)866-6814
Bonnie Rubenstein, Exec.Dir.   FX: (614)866-6819

Founded: 1909. **Members:** 50,000. **Languages:** English. **National.** Social sorority.

Publications: *Columns of Alpha Epsilon Phi*, quarterly.

Conventions/Meetings: biennial meeting.

★2432★ ALPHA GAMMA DELTA
8701 Founders Rd.   PH: (317)872-2655
Indianapolis, IN 46268   FX: (317)875-5824

Founded: 1904. **Members:** 102,000. **Languages:** English. **National.** Social sorority.

Conventions/Meetings: biennial meeting.

★2433★ ALPHA IOTA
PO Box 178
Ramona, CA 92065
Ruth O'Hara, Exec. Officer   PH: (619)789-0781

Founded: 1925. **Members:** 65,000. **Regional Groups:** 12. **Languages:** English. **National.** Honorary sorority - business.

Publications: *Alpha Iota Note Book*, quarterly.

Conventions/Meetings: biennial meeting. ● annual regional meeting.

★2434★ ALPHA KAPPA ALPHA
5656 S. Stony Island Ave.
Chicago, IL 60637
Allison Harris, Exec.Dir.   PH: (312)684-1282

Members: 100,000. **Multinational.** Greek organization for black women throughout Africa, the Bahamas, Germany, the United States, and the Virgin Islands. Works to improve the quality of life for black women worldwide. Addresses issues such as job discrimination, affirmative action, education, access to nontraditional jobs, pay equity, poverty, economic development, teenage pregnancy, child care, housing, domestic violence, families, and health.

★2435★ ALPHA OMICRON PI
9025 Overlook Blvd.
Brentwood, TN 37027   PH: (615)370-0920
Melanie Doyle, Exec.Dir.   FX: (615)371-9736

Founded: 1897. **Members:** 90,000. **Staff:** 30. **Regional Groups:** 10. **Languages:** English. **National.** Social sorority. Conducts charitable, research, and educational programs. **Libraries:** Type: reference. **Computer Services:** Data base, membership information.

Publications: *Directory*, annual. ● *The Piper*, monthly. **Circulation:** 90,000. **Advertising:** accepted. ● *To Dragma*, quarterly. **Circulation:** 90,000. **Advertising:** not accepted.

Conventions/Meetings: biennial meeting (exhibits)

★2436★ ALPHA PHI INTERNATIONAL FRATERNITY
1930 Sherman Ave.
Evanston, IL 60201
Mrs. Joyce Shumway, Contact   PH: (312)475-0663

Founded: 1872. **Multinational.** Promotes the interests of women at universities and colleges worldwide. Fosters information exchange and fellowship between members.

Publications: *Alpha Phi Quarterly.* Magazine.

★2437★ ALPHA PI CHI
PO Box 255
Kensington, MD 20895
Magoline Carney, Pres.   PH: (301)559-4330

Founded: 1963. **Members:** 1,300. **Languages:** English. **National.** Service sorority - business and professional women. Conducts fundraising activities for civil rights organizations and black charities. Sponsors Talent a Rama, a charity showcase of young amateurs. Local chapters "adopt" senior citizens' homes. **Awards:** Periodic (scholarship).

Publications: *The President Speaks*, quarterly. Newsletter.

Conventions/Meetings: triennial meeting.

★2438★ ALPHA SIGMA ALPHA SORORITY
1201 E. Walnut St.
Springfield, MO 65802
Rose Marie Fellin, Contact   PH: (417)869-0980

Founded: 1901. **National.** Social sorority. Fosters fellowship among members.

★2439★ ALPHA SIGMA TAU
PO Box 59252
Birmingham, AL 35259
Lenore Seibel King, Dir.   PH: (205)945-0318

Founded: 1899. **Members:** 28,612. **Languages:** English. **National.** Social sorority. **Awards:** Annual (scholarship).

Publications: *The Anchor*, semiannual. ● *Crest*, semiannual. Newsletter.

Conventions/Meetings: biennial conference - 1994 June 19 - 25, Syracuse, NY, United States; 1996 June 23 - 29; 1998 June 21 - 1996 June 28, Innisbrook, FL, United States.

★2440★ ALPHA XI DELTA
8702 Founders Rd.
Indianapolis, IN 46268
Diane C. Gregory, Exec.Dir.   PH: (317)872-3500

Founded: 1893. **Members:** 97,000. **Languages:** English. **National.** Social sorority.

Publications: *The Quill of Alpha Xi Delta*, quarterly.

Conventions/Meetings: biennial meeting.

★2441★ ALWAYS CAUSING LEGAL UNREST (ACLU)
PO Box 2085
Rancho Cordova, CA 95741-2085
Steven Paskey, Contact   PH: (408)427-2858

Founded: 1990. **Members:** 200. **Local Groups:** 5. **Languages:** English. **National.** Feminists; anti-pornography activists; individuals interested in an "alternative to First Amendment fundamentalism." Urges corporations to place public safety and welfare and women's rights over profit and discourages the "conservative values" including trademark laws, private property rights, individual privacy, and monetary profit. Encourages women to learn self defense and weaponry. Sponsors Pushing Buttons Campaign, in which buttons bearing slogans against media violence and for women's self-defense are worn in an effort to gain widespread public and legislative awareness and support. Advocates "recourse against male supremacists and their various political organs." Promotes the use of humor in generating public awareness of what the group sees as an overemphasis on conservative values. Disseminates information.

Publications: *Nemesis: Justice Is A Woman With A Sword.* Booklet.

★2442★ AMERICAN ACADEMY OF HUSBAND-COACHED CHILDBIRTH
(AAHCC)
PO Box 5224
Sherman Oaks, CA 91413
Marjie Hathaway, Exec. Dir.   PH: (818)788-6662

Founded: 1970. **Members:** 1,200. **Languages:** English. **National.** Trains instructors in the Bradley method of natural childbirth.

Publications: *Directory of Instructors*, 2-3/year. ● *Fetal Advocate*, periodic.

★2443★ AMERICAN ACADEMY OF MEDICAL ETHICS
4205 McAuley Blvd., Ste. 420
Oklahoma City, OK 73120
Curtis E. Harris, Pres.

Members: 8. **Languages:** English. **National.** Umbrella organization of medical groups representing 25,000 pro-life doctors. Opposes abortion; lobbies and testifies in Congress.

Publications: *Issues in Law and Medicine*, periodic.

Conventions/Meetings: periodic seminar.

★2444★ AMERICAN ACADEMY OF NATURAL FAMILY PLANNING
(AANFP)
615 S. New Ballas Rd.
St. Louis, MO 63141
Charmaine Champanine, Pres.   PH: (314)569-6495

Founded: 1982. **Members:** 300. **Budget:** US$75,000. **Languages:** English. **National.** Individuals who participate in natural family planning instruction. (Natural family planning refers to methods that do not employ contraceptive devices of any kind, using instead the natural phases of fertility.) Seeks to improve the quality of natural family planning services by establishing specific certification and accreditation requirements for teachers and educational programs. Conducts training programs throughout the U.S. and England. Promotes public recognition and acceptance of natural family planning; disseminates information; bestows awards. **Computer Services:** Mailing lists. **Committees:** Ad Hoc Committee for the Study of Commissions; Continuing Education; Ethics; Legislative; Public Relations; Science and Research. **Commissions:** Interim Commission for Certification. **Subcommittees:** Awards; Credentials. **Committees:** Science and Research. **Commissions:** Interim Commission for Certification.

Publications: *Academy Activity*, quarterly. Newsletter. ● *Client Connection*, quarterly. ● *Membership Directory*, annual.

Conventions/Meetings: annual congress (exhibits).

★2445★ AMERICAN ACADEMY OF RELIGION - WOMEN'S CAUCUS
Washington University
Women's Studies
Box 1078
St. Louis, MO 63130-4899
Jacqueline Pastif, Contact   PH: (314)889-5000

National. Promotes the role of women in religion and theological studies in the United States.

★2446★ AMERICAN AGRI-WOMEN (AAW)
c/o Sandy Greiner
Rte. 2, Box 193
Keota, IA 52248   PH: (515)363-2293
Sandy Greiner, Pres.   FX: (515)636-2293

Founded: 1974. **Members:** 42. **Budget:** US$60,000. **State Groups:** 20. **Languages:** English. **National.** Farm and ranch women's organizations representing 35,000 interested persons. Promotes agriculture; seeks to present the real identity of American farmers to the rest of the population and to develop an appreciation of "the interdependence of the components of the agricultural system." Supports a marketing system which makes quality food and fiber available to all on a reasonable cost basis and at a fair profit to the farmer. Believes that the family farm system is the bulwark of the private enterprise system, and as such must be preserved. Works in areas of legislation, regulations, consumer relations, and education. Maintains resource center and speakers' bureau. Is establishing an oral history project of America's farm and ranch women entitled From Mules to Microwaves; conducts research programs. **Awards:** Periodic Leaven Award for Outstanding Achievement. **Committees:** Agriculture Chemical; Agriculture Labor/Management; Animal Welfare; Dairy; Energy; Food Safety; Fruit and Vegetables; Grain; Land Use; Legislation; Livestock; Religion; Rural Economic Development; Trade and Marketing; Water Resources.

Publications: *American Agri-Women*, annual. Directory. Contains listing of officers of affiliate organizations of farm and ranch women. ● *Voice of the American Agri-Woman*, bimonthly. Newsletter. **Circulation:** 5,000.

Conventions/Meetings: annual meeting (exhibits) - always November.

★2447★ AMERICAN AGRI-WOMEN RESOURCE CENTER (AAWRC)
c/o Marjorie Wendzel
785 N. Bainbridge Center
Watervliet, MI 49098
Marjorie Wendzel, Treas.   PH: (616)468-3649

Founded: 1974. **Members:** 35,000. **Regional Groups:** 40. **Languages:** English. **National.** Farm women concerned with the advancement of agricultural production within the free enterprise system. Objectives are: to formulate and disseminate educational materials which accurately represent agripolitan America for use by teachers and the public; to initiate and promote an educational program to advance the interests and welfare of agriculture. Provides training for women in leadership, public relations, and self-esteem. Conducts the Agricultural Commodity Lessons which illustrates, explains, and informs in various subject areas from kindergarten to 8th grade levels.

Publications: *American Agri-Women Resource Guide*, periodic.

Conventions/Meetings: annual meeting, workshops and exhibits (exhibits).

★2448★ AMERICAN ANTHROPOLOGICAL ASSOCIATION -
ASSOCIATION FOR FEMINIST ANTHROPOLOGY
1703 New Hampshire Ave.
Washington, DC 20009
Jane Collins, Chair   PH: (202)232-8800

National. Anthropologists interested in a feminist approach within the discipline. Concerns include: women and human rights; women's body control; gender and the anthropology curriculum

★2449★ AMERICAN ASSOCIATION FOR ADULT AND CONTINUING
EDUCATION - WOMEN'S ISSUES, STATUS, AND EDUCATION UNIT
1112 16th St. NW, Ste. 420
Washington, DC 20036
Ellen Ironside, Director   PH: (202)463-6333

National. Promotes the interests of women in the field of adult and continuing education. Calls attention to women's issues as part of the national agenda for the AAACE.

★2450★ AMERICAN ASSOCIATION FOR THE ADVANCEMENT OF
SCIENCE - NATIONAL NETWORK OF WOMEN IN SCIENCE
Office of Opportunities in Science
1333 H St. NW
Washington, DC 20005
Dr. Shirley Malcolm, Head   PH: (202)326-6670

Founded: 1978. National. Promotes the interests of women in science.
Seeks to provide access to scientific career information to female students.
Fosters the professional advancement of American Indian, African American,
Hispanic American, and Puerto Rican women in science and engineering.

Publications: Newsletter.

★2451★ AMERICAN ASSOCIATION FOR COUNSELING AND
DEVELOPMENT - COMMITTEE ON WOMEN
5999 Stevenson Ave.
Alexandria, VA 22304
Linda K. Kemp, Chair   PH: (703)823-9800

National. Works to enhance the identification, awareness, and response to
women's issues within the counseling profession. Promotes the development
of training and orientation programs on gender-fair professional practices and
issues.

★2452★ AMERICAN ASSOCIATION OF GYNECOLOGICAL
LAPAROSCOPISTS (AAGL)
13021 E. Florence Ave.
Santa Fe Springs, CA 90670
Jordan M. Phillips M.D., Bd.Chm.   PH: (310)946-8774

Founded: 1972. Members: 5,200. Staff: 12. Languages: English. National.
Physicians who specialize in obstetrics and gynecology and who are
interested in gynecological endoscopic procedures. Purposes are to: teach;
demonstrate; exchange ideas; distribute literature; stimulate interest in
gynecological laparoscopy; maintain and improve medical standards in
medical schools and hospitals regarding gynecological laparoscopy; maintain
and improve the ethics, practice, and efficiency of the medical practice
pertaining to obstetrics and laparoscopy. Telecommunication Services:
Electronic bulletin board.

Publications: News Scope—American Association of Gynecology, 3/year.
Newsletter. Contains research updates. Circulation: 5,200. ● Gynecological
Laparoscopy: Principles and Techniques. Book. ● Endoscopy in Gynecology.
Book. ● Microsurgery in Gynecology. Book. ● Female Endoscopic Steriliza-
tion. Book.

Conventions/Meetings: annual meeting. ● periodic conference.

★2453★ AMERICAN ASSOCIATION FOR HIGHER EDUCATION -
WOMEN'S CAUCUS
1 Dupont Circle, Ste. 600
Washington, DC 20036
Judy Corcillo, Chair   PH: (202)293-6440

National. Promotes the interests of women involved in higher education
professions. Works to assist women in the development of their professional
education careers.

★2454★ AMERICAN ASSOCIATION OF IMMUNOLOGISTS -
COMMITTEE ON THE STATUS OF WOMEN
9650 Rockville Pike
Bethesda, MD 20814
          PH: (301)530-7178

Promotes the interests of women immunologists.

★2455★ AMERICAN ASSOCIATION OF LAW SCHOOLS -
COMMITTEE ON WOMEN
University of Southern California Law
School
Los Angeles, CA 90089-0071   PH: (213)743-7302

Promotes the interests of women law school educators and women enrolled
in law schools throughout the United States. Addresses issues of interests to
women involved in the law profession.

★2456★ AMERICAN ASSOCIATION OF PRO-LIFE OBSTETRICIANS
AND GYNECOLOGISTS (AAPLOG)
850 Elm Grove Rd.
Elm Grove, WI 53122   PH: (414)789-7984
David V. Foley M.D., Pres.   FX: (414)782-8788

Founded: 1973. Members: 800. Membership Dues: Resident, US$5;
Retired, US$10; Active, US$75. Staff: 2. Regional Groups: 9. Languages:
English. National. Obstetricians and gynecologists who oppose abortions,
perform no abortions, and take no part in arranging abortions. Seeks "to
draw attention to the value of all human life from the moment of conception."
Supports programs that assist unwed mothers who choose to have their
babies. Conducts research on complications experienced by women who
have had legal abortions and compiles statistics on illnesses and deaths;
studies the long-range effects of abortion on fertility and reproductive
capability. Presents awards to congresspersons and physicians who have
demonstrated strong support for the protection of human life beginning with
conception. Offers postgraduate course on the subject of care and concern
for women experiencing mental and physical trauma after abortions.

Publications: Directory, triennial. ● Newsletter, quarterly.

Conventions/Meetings: annual conference.

★2457★ AMERICAN ASSOCIATION OF PRO-LIFE PEDIATRICIANS
(AAPLP)
11055 S. St. Louis Ave.
Chicago, IL 60655
E. F. Diamond M.D., Sec.   PH: (708)448-9290

Founded: 1978. Members: 510. State Groups: 50. Languages: English.
National. Members of the American Academy of Pediatrics (see separate
entry) interested in issues such as abortion, infanticide, and definition of
death. Coordinates member activities; publicizes political trends; educates
members.

Publications: Newsletter, quarterly. ● This Curette for Hire. Book.

Conventions/Meetings: annual conference. ● semiannual meeting.

★2458★ AMERICAN ASSOCIATION OF RETIRED PERSON -
WOMEN'S INITIATIVE NETWORK
1909 K St. NW
Washington, DC 20049
Margaret Arnold, Sr. Program Specialist   PH: (202)434-2642

National. Advocates and supports policies, programs, and legislation that
improve the status of mid-life and older women. Works to correct inequities in
employment opportunities, practices, and policies affecting older women.
Promotes greater recognition of the significant contributions of women to
families, communities, the nation, and the world.

★2459★ AMERICAN ASSOCIATION OF UNIVERSITY PROFESSORS -
COMMITTEE ON THE STATUS OF WOMEN IN THE ACADEMIC
PROFESSION
1012 14th St. NW, Ste. 500
Washington, DC 20005
Leslie Lee Francis, Secretary   PH: (202)737-5900

National. Women faculty members of U.S. colleges and universities working
to obtain equitable treatment in personnel decisions. Promotes the status of

women professors; represents members' interests. Lobbies government on legislation affecting the equal rights of women.

★2460★ AMERICAN ASSOCIATION OF UNIVERSITY WOMEN EDUCATIONAL FOUNDATION (AAUWEF)
1111 16th St. NW
Washington, DC 20036   PH: (202)785-7700
Anne L. Bryant, Exec.Dir   FX: (202)872-1425

Founded: 1958. Languages: English. National. An arm of the American Association of University Women Established to: expand AAUW's primary emphasis on educational work; facilitate the building of endowments for fellowships, research, and public service projects; supplement and further specified areas of AAUWEF concern; assume administrative and managerial responsibilities Encourages development of the Educational Center in Washington, DC, as a center for women scholars throughout the world; seeks support from other foundations for research and educational projects; also receives contributions from AAUW members. Is especially concerned with women's participation in the community and in higher education. Libraries: Type: reference. Holdings: 500. Awards: Periodic American International Fellowship (monetary). ● Periodic Research and Project Endowment (monetary). ● Periodic Eleanor Roosevelt Fund for Women and Girls (grant).

Conventions/Meetings: biennial meeting.

★2461★ AMERICAN ASSOCIATION OF WOMEN (AAW)
2210 Wilshire Blvd., Ste. 174
Santa Monica, CA 90403   PH: (310)395-0244
Leslie C. Dutton, Pres. & Editor   FX: (310)394-6470

Founded: 1984. Membership Dues: Individual, US$10; Business, US$100; Founding, US$500. Staff: 4. Languages: English. National. Participants include retired career women, working mothers, and formerly elected officials. Seeks to disseminate contrasting viewpoints on issues. Encourages women to take part in the debate on public policy. Bestows awards; operates speakers' bureau. Libraries: Type: reference. Holdings: 0; periodicals, clippings. Committees: Crime Prevention and Reporting; Family Health Issues; Health Care Costs and Quality; Illegal Immigration and Social Security; Insurance Rates for Women; Pension Fund Investment Practices; Public Health Crisis: The AIDS Epidemic; Safer Blood Products; Public Health and Safety Issues.

Publications: AAW Issue Papers, periodic. ● American Association of Women, 2-4/year. Newsletter. Circulation: 27,000.

Conventions/Meetings: annual conference.

★2462★ AMERICAN ASSOCIATION OF WOMEN IN COMMUNITY AND JUNIOR COLLEGES (AAWCJC)
Middlesex Community College
100 Training Hill Rd.
Middletown, CT 06457   PH: (203)344-3001
Leila Gonzalez Sullivan, Pres.   FX: (203)344-7488

Founded: 1973. Members: 2,300. Budget: US$120,000. Regional Groups: 10. State Groups: 51. Languages: English. National. Women faculty members, administrators, staff members, students, and trustees of community colleges. Objectives are to: develop communication and disseminate information among women in community, junior, and technical colleges; encourage educational program development; obtain grants for educational projects for community college women. Disseminates information on women's issues and programs. Conducts regional and state professional development workshops and forums. Maintains placement services. Awards: Annual Mildred Bulpitt Woman of the Year (recognition).

Publications: AAWCJC Journal, annual. Research on women's issues. Circulation: 2,300. ● AAWCJC Quarterly. Newsletter. Includes book reviews; calendar of events; educational opportunities.

Conventions/Meetings: annual meeting (exhibits).

★2463★ AMERICAN ASSOCIATION OF WOMEN DENTISTS (AAWD)
401 N. Michigan Ave.
Chicago, IL 60611-4267   PH: (312)644-6610
Christine Norris, Exec.Dir.   FX: (312)245-1084

Founded: 1921. Members: 2,000. Budget: US$100,000. Regional Groups: 17. Languages: English. National. Female dentists and dental students. Encourages young women to pursue an academic degree in dentistry and to advance the status of women already in the dental profession. Awards: Periodic Colgate-Palmolive.

Publications: American Association of Women Dentists Chronicle, bimonthly. Newsletter. Includes book reviews, listings of employment opportunities, obituaries, research updates, and statistics. Circulation: 2,000. ● Directory, annual.

Conventions/Meetings: annual meeting. ● in conjunction with the American Dental Association.

★2464★ AMERICAN ASSOCIATION FOR WOMEN PODIATRISTS
1300 State Hwy.
Ocean Township, NJ 07712
Margaret Zakanycz, Contact   PH: (201)531-0490

National. Women podiatrists. Promotes the interests of members. Offers guidance and financial assistance to female students studying podiatry. Assists graduates of podiatry in establishing practices.

Publications: Newsletter.

★2465★ AMERICAN ASTRONOMICAL SOCIETY - COMMITTEE ON THE STATUS OF WOMEN IN ASTRONOMY
2000 Florida Ave. NW, Ate. 300
Washington, DC 20009
Roger Bell, Secretary   PH: (202)328-2010

National. Works to monitor and study the status of women involved in fields focusing around the science of astronomy. Promotes women's development in astronomy.

★2466★ AMERICAN ATHEIST WOMEN (AAW)
PO Box 140195
Austin, TX 78714-0195
Dr. Madalyn Murray O'Hair, Exec.Dir. PH: (512)458-1244

Founded: 1960. Members: 35,000. Languages: English. National. Female atheists united for the enrichment and beautification of life and to emphasize the need for quality living. Conducts leadership education/training program. Sponsors programs for children; maintains speakers' bureau and biographical archives; compiles statistics.

Conventions/Meetings: annual meeting.

★2467★ AMERICAN BAPTIST WOMEN'S MINISTRIES (ABW)
PO Box 851
Valley Forge, PA 19482-0851
Donna Anderson, Contact   PH: (215)768-2288

Founded: 1951. Members: 750,000. Staff: 3. Regional Groups: 31. Local Groups: 5,000. Languages: English. National. Women who belong to an American Baptist church. Seeks to undergird the total program of the American Baptist Churches of the U.S.A., through support of missions and church service projects. Conducts studies and acts in matters involving Christian social concern, including local, national, and international affairs; sponsors programs to meet the specific needs of women as well as to integrate them into the life of the church. Trains women in leadership skills. Formerly: (1965) National Council of American Baptist Women, American Baptist Women.

Publications: *The American Baptist Woman*, 3/year. ● *Directory*, annual.

Conventions/Meetings: biennial meeting - always June. ● annual conference - always July, Green Lake.

★2468★ AMERICAN BAR ASSOCIATION - COMMISSION ON WOMEN IN THE PROFESSION
750 N. Lakeshore Dr.
Chicago, IL 60611
Elaine Weiss, Director   PH: (312)988-5676

National. Assesses the status of women in the legal profession by identifying barriers to advancement and key issues of concern to women lawyers. Develops educational materials, programs, and research to address the discrimination women lawyers encounter. Makes recommendations to the ABA for action to address identified problems and barriers. Provides assistance to individuals and organizations interested in studying issues of concern to women lawyers.

Publications: *Lawyers and Balanced Lives: A Guide to Drafting and Implementing Workplace Policies for Lawyers.*

★2469★ AMERICAN BAR ASSOCIATION - COMMITTEE ON THE RIGHTS OF WOMEN
1800 M St. NW
Washington, DC 20036
Leslie Harris, Co-Chair   PH: (202)822-6644

Founded: 1970. **National.** Works to educate the profession on issues affecting women. Promotes the improvement of the status of women within the law profession.

★2470★ AMERICAN BOARD OF OBSTETRICS AND GYNECOLOGY (ABOG)
936 N. 34th St., Ste. 200
Seattle, WA 98103
James A. Merrill M.D., Exec.Dir.   PH: (206)547-4884

Founded: 1927. **Members:** 15. **Languages:** English. **National.** Certification board to establish qualifications, conduct examinations, and certify as diplomates those doctors whom the board finds qualified to specialize in obstetrics and gynecology. **Committees:** Residency Review. **Divisions:** Gynecologic Oncology; Maternal Fetal Medicine; Reproductive Endocrinology.

Publications: *Bulletin*, annual.

Conventions/Meetings: annual executive committee meeting.

★2471★ AMERICAN BUSINESS WOMEN'S ASSOCIATION (ABWA)
9100 Ward Pky.
PO Box 8728
Kansas City, MO 64114   PH: (816)361-6621
Carolyn B. Elman, Exec.Dir.   FX: (816)361-4991

Founded: 1949. **Members:** 90,000. **Local Groups:** 1,800. **Languages:** English. **National.** Women in business, including women owning or operating their own businesses, women in professions, and women employed in any level of government, education, or retailing, manufacturing, and service companies. Provides opportunities for businesswomen to help themselves and others grow personally and professionally through leadership, education, networking support, and national recognition. Offers leadership training and discounted CareerTrack programs, a resume service, credit card and member loan programs, and various travel and insurance benefits. Annually Awards more than $2.5 million to women students through chapter scholarship programs; also awards scholarships nationally through the Stephen Bufton Memorial Educational Fund. Sponsors American Business Women's Day and American Business Women's Strut annually on Sept. 22. **Awards:** Periodic National Top Ten Business Women of ABWA (recognition). ● Annual Local Woman of the Year (recognition).

Publications: *CONNECT*, bimonthly. Newsletter. ● *Women in Business*, bimonthly. Magazine. **ISSN:** 0043-7441. **Circulation:** 104,000. **Advertising:** accepted.

Conventions/Meetings: annual meeting (exhibits) - 1993 Sept. 29 - Oct. 3, Indianapolis, IN, United States; 1994 Oct. 5 - 9, Denver, CO, United States. ● periodic regional meeting.

★2472★ AMERICAN CHEMICAL SOCIETY - WOMEN CHEMISTS COMMITTEE
1155 16th St. NW
Washington, DC 20036
Eileen Reilley, Contact   PH: (202)872-4456

National. Represents the interests of more than 23,000 women chemists in the United States. Works to develop programs to insure full participation of women chemists in their profession. Monitors legislation affecting women chemists.

Publications: *Newsletter*, semiannual.

★2473★ AMERICAN CITIZENS CONCERNED FOR LIFE EDUCATION FUND - ACCL COMMUNICATIONS CENTER (ACCL)
PO Box 179
Excelsior, MN 55331
Gloria Ford, Pres.   PH: (612)474-0885

Founded: 1973. **Languages:** English. **National.** Individuals engaged in educational, legislative, research, and service activities directed toward increasing respect, protection, and support for human life. Believes that society should encourage recognition of the humanity of the unborn. Purposes are: to encourage among the public an understanding of the dignity and worth of each human life whatever his or her circumstances; to foster respect for human life before and after birth, particularly for the defenseless, the incompetent, and the impaired and incapacitated; to promote, encourage, and sponsor legislative measures that will support these goals. Activities are focused in the area of education of the public on issues such as abortion, alternatives to abortion, euthanasia, ethics and morality, the disabled, and the elderly. Maintains resource center and speakers' bureau. **Formerly:** (1974) American Citizens for Life.

Publications: *ACCL Communications Center Resource Catalog*, annual. Directory. ● *Communications Center Update*, 3/year. Newsletter. Includes book reviews and editorials. ● *Counseling the Individual Experiencing a Troubled Pregnancy*. Book.

★2474★ AMERICAN COALITION FOR LIFE (ACL)
PO Box 44415
Ft. Washington, MD 20749
Ray Allen, Exec. Officer   FX: (301)292-0609

Founded: 1981. **Languages:** English. **National.** Individuals and businesses dedicated to extending "compassion to the preborn." Concerned with human life issues, in particular abortion, infanticide, and euthanasia. Lobbies Congress.

Publications: *Adopt A Congressman*. Booklet. ● *Congressional Life Index*. Book.

★2475★ AMERICAN COLLEGE OF HOME OBSTETRICS (ACHO)
PO Box 508
Oak Park, IL 60303
Gregory White M.D., Pres.   PH: (708)383-1461

Founded: 1978. **Members:** 40. **Languages:** English. **National.** Physicians interested in cooperating with families who wish to give birth in the home. Objective is to accumulate and exchange data on home birth. Maintains speakers' bureau; compiles statistics. Plans to conduct research. **Computer Services:** Information services, obstetrical log.

Publications: *Newsletter*, periodic.

Conventions/Meetings: annual seminar.

★2476★ AMERICAN COLLEGE OF OBSTETRICIANS AND
     GYNECOLOGISTS
409 12th St. SW
Washington, DC 20024
Warren H. Pearse M.D., Exec.Dir.   PH: (202)638-5577

Founded: 1951. **National.** Obstetricians and gynecologists in the United States. Promotes the OB/GYN profession. Sponsors continuing professional development programs. **Libraries:** Type: reference. Holdings: 8,000. **Formerly:** American Academy of Obstetrics and Gynecology.

Publications: *Bulletin*, periodic. ● *Directory of Fellows*, biennial. ● *Newsletter*, monthly. ● *Obstetrics and Gynecology*, monthly. ● Also publishes manuals and booklets.

★2477★ AMERICAN COLLEGE OF OBSTETRICIANS AND
     GYNECOLOGISTS - NURSES ASSOCIATION
409 12th St. SW
Washington, DC 20024-2188
Judity Serevino, Deputy Dir.   PH: (202)638-0026

National. Promotes the interests of OB/GYN nurses. Establishes and promotes high standards of prenatal women's health nursing practice, education and research. Maintains a fetal heart rate monitoring national education program. Produces videos on teen pregnancy, childbirth, substance abuse, and parenting.

Publications: *Newsletter.* ● *Journal of Obstetrics, Gynecologic, and Neonatal Nursing.* ● *Clinical Issues in Prenatal and Women's Health Nursing.* ● *NAACOG's Women's Health Nursing Scan.*

★2478★ AMERICAN COLLEGE OF OSTEOPATHIC OBSTETRICIANS
     AND GYNECOLOGISTS (ACOOG)
900 Auburn Rd.
Pontiac, MI 48342-3365   PH: (313)332-6360
J. Polsinelli D.O., Exec.Dir.   FX: (313)332-4607

Founded: 1934. **Members:** 565. **Staff:** 3. **Budget:** US$312,000. **Languages:** English. **National.** Osteopathic physicians and surgeons specializing in obstetrics and gynecology. Conducts educational programs, and reviews osteopathic obstetric and gynecologic residency training programs. Holds an Annual postgraduate course. Bestows awards; offers research grants. **Computer Services:** Mailing lists. **Committees:** Continuing Post Graduate Education; Editorial and Research; Malpractice; Policy Guidelines; Residency Evaluation; Special Committee for Examination of Residents.

Publications: *ACOOG Newsletter*, quarterly. Includes legislative news, calendar of events, employment listings, and lists of residents completing training and newly certified physicians. **Circulation:** 600. ● *American College of Osteopathic Obstetricians and Gynecologists Membership Directory*, annual. **Circulation:** 700. **Advertising:** not accepted.

Conventions/Meetings: annual meeting (exhibits) - usually March. 1994 Mar. 14 - 18, Scottsdale, AZ, United States; 1995, Orlando, FL, United States. ● annual Ortho-ACOOG Resident Thesis Competition competition.

★2479★ AMERICAN COLLEGIANS FOR LIFE (ACL)
PO Box 1112
Washington, DC 20013
Elizabeth Dever, Contact

Founded: 1982. **Members:** 5,000. **Staff:** 10. **Budget:** US$40,000. **State Groups:** 15. **Local Groups:** 350. **Languages:** English. **National.** Pro-life university students working to restore "respect for human life." Organizes student protests. Sponsors educational programs; bestows award.

Publications: *VITA*, monthly. Newsletter. **Circulation:** 5,000. **Advertising:** accepted.

Conventions/Meetings: annual conference (exhibits).

★2480★ AMERICAN COUNCIL FOR CAREER WOMEN (ACCW)
c/o Joan Savoy
PO Box 50825
New Orleans, LA 70150
Joan Savoy, Pres.   PH: (504)525-0375

Founded: 1979. **Members:** 5,175. **Budget:** US$30,000. **Languages:** English. **National.** Corporations, organizations, and individuals concerned about the interests of career women. Purpose is to promote leadership and professional development among women. Seeks to enhance opportunities for career women in all educational and employment endeavors. Provides a forum for the discussion of issues, opportunities, and problems concerning women in business. Encourages higher business standards and improved business methods among men and women; works to maintain the integrity of and improve the business conditions for working women. Promotes heightened public awareness of and the demand for opportunities, products, and services for women; seeks to educate the public to the opportunities available to women. **Awards:** Periodic Achievers Award. Recipient: Businesswomen. **Computer Services:** Information services; mailing lists. **Committees:** Market Research; Media Access.

Publications: *American Council for Career Women Membership Roster*, annual. ● *News/Views*, quarterly. Newsletter.

Conventions/Meetings: annual conference (exhibits) - always August. New Orleans, LA, United States. ● annual seminar.

★2481★ AMERICAN COUNCIL ON EDUCATION - OFFICE OF WOMEN
     IN HIGHER EDUCATION
1 Dupont Circle
Washington, DC 20036-1193
Donna Shavlik, Director   PH: (202)939-9390

National. Seeks to advance the status of women in academic administration professions.

★2482★ AMERICAN EDUCATIONAL RESEARCH ASSOCIATION -
     RESEARCH ON WOMEN AND EDUCATION GROUP
San Jose State University
Department of Mathematics and
     Computer Science
San Jose, CA 95192-0103
Joanne Rossi Becker, Chair   PH: (408)924-5112

Founded: 1973. **National.** Promotes the study and research of issues concerning women and girls in education. Provides a forum for communication among researchers and practitioners who are concerned about women in education. Supports pay equity within education professions.

Publications: *Newsletter.*

★2483★ AMERICAN FARM BUREAU FEDERATION - WOMEN'S
     COMMITTEE
225 Touhy Ave.
Park Ridge, IL 60068
Marsha Purcell, Director   PH: (312)399-5764

Founded: 1919. **National.** Women involved in farming and ranching. Promotes the agriculture industry in the United States. Works to address the special problems facing farm and ranch families.

★2484★ AMERICAN FEDERATION OF STATE, COUNTY AND
     MUNICIPAL EMPLOYEES - WOMEN'S RIGHTS DEPARTMENT
1625 L St. NW
Washington, DC 20036
Cathy Collette, Director   PH: (202)429-5090

National. Works to advance the interests of women working for state, county, and municipal governments. Supports women's rights in regards to issues such as pay equity, sexual harassment, and child abuse.

Publications: *Public Employee*, bimonthly. ● *Leader*, weekly. ● *Women's Letter*, quarterly.

★2485★ AMERICAN FEDERATION OF TEACHERS - WOMEN'S RIGHTS COMMITTEE
555 New Jersey Ave. NW
Washington, DC 20001
Barbara Van Blake, Director   PH: (202)879-4400

National. Promotes the interests of women teachers. Concerned with issues such as: integrating women's history into the curriculum; sexual harassment, child care options, and pay equity. Lobbies the AFT on issues affecting women in the teaching profession. Conducts research and education programs. Maintains speakers' bureau; compiles statistics.

★2486★ AMERICAN FEDERATION OF TELEVISION AND RADIO ARTISTS - NATIONAL WOMEN'S DIVISION
260 Madison Ave.
New York, NY 10016
Virginia Williams, President   PH: (212)532-0800

Founded: 1973. **National**. Promotes the interests of women in radio and television broadcasting. Focuses on issues and concerns to women, including employment and improving the image of women in the media.

★2487★ AMERICAN FERTILITY SOCIETY (AFS)
2140 11th Ave. S, Ste. 200
Birmingham, AL 35205-2800   PH: (205)933-8494
Nancy C. Hayley, Adm.Dir.   FX: (205)930-9904

Founded: 1944. **Members:** 10,000. **Staff:** 16. **Languages:** English. **National**. Gynecologists, obstetricians, urologists, reproductive endocrinologists, veterinarians, research workers, and others interested in reproductive health in man and animals. Seeks to extend knowledge of all aspects of fertility and problems of infertility and mammalian reproduction; provides a rostrum for the presentation of scientific studies dealing with these subjects. Offers patient resource information and placement service. Maintains film library. Conducts six to eight workshops and six regional postgraduate courses per year.

Publications: *American Fertility Society*, biennial. Directory. Arranged alphabetically and geographically. **Advertising:** accepted. ● *Fertility News*, quarterly. Newsletter. Includes new member and regional postgraduate course listings. ● *Fertility and Sterility*, monthly. Journal. Includes book reviews and announcements of meetings, courses, services, and employment opportunities. **ISSN:** 0015-0282. **Circulation:** 14,000. **Advertising:** accepted. **Alternate Formats:** microform.

Conventions/Meetings: annual meeting (exhibits) - 1993 Oct. 9 - 14, Montreal, PQ, Canada; 1994 Oct. 5 - 10, San Antonio, TX, United States; 1995 Oct. 7 - 12, Seattle, WA, United States.

★2488★ AMERICAN FILM INSTITUTE - DIRECTING WORKSHOP FOR WOMEN
2021 N. Western Ave.
PO Box 27999
Los Angeles, CA 90027
Tess Martin, Contact   PH: (213)856-7722

National. Promotes the involvement of women in film direction. Provides a forum for experience sharing and hands-on production work among members.

★2489★ AMERICAN FOLKLORE SOCIETY - WOMEN'S SECTION
George Mason University
Department of English
Fairfax, VA 22030
Peggy Yocum, Chair   PH: (703)323-2220

National. Works to advance the interests of women folklorists. Fosters exchange and communication between members.

★2490★ AMERICAN FOUNDATION FOR MATERNAL AND CHILD HEALTH (AFMCH)
439 E. 51st St., 4th Fl.
New York, NY 10022
Doris Haire, Pres.   PH: (212)759-5510

Founded: 1972. **Staff:** 1. **Languages:** English. **National**. Serves as a clearinghouse for interdisciplinary research on maternal and child health; focuses on the perinatal or birth period and its effect on infant development. Sponsors medical research designed to improve application of technology in maternal and child health; conducts educational programs; compiles statistics. **Libraries:** Type: reference.

★2491★ AMERICAN FRIENDS SERVICE COMMITTEE - NATIONWIDE WOMEN'S PROGRAM
1501 Cherry St.
Philadelphia, PA 19102
Joyce Miller, Co-Chair   PH: (215)241-7181

Founded: 1975. **National**. Works to address women's issues and interests in the activities of the AFSC. Encourages programs that involve women in social services activities.

★2492★ AMERICAN GI FORUM WOMEN
c/o Marianne Martinez
9948 S. Plaza, Apt. 1-D
Omaha, NE 68127
Marianne Martinez, Chair   PH: (402)593-1248

Founded: 1948. **Members:** 6,000. **Languages:** English. **National**. Women ages 14 and over who are American citizens and are either married or related to members of the American GI Forum of United States. Seeks to "secure the blessing of American democracy at every level of life" for all citizens and support the interests of persons of Hispanic ancestry through upholding and defending the U.S. Constitution and fostering religious and political freedom. **Awards:** Periodic (scholarship). **Committees:** Education; Queen Scholarship.

Publications: *The Forumeer*, monthly. Newsletter. Membership activities. **Circulation:** 6,000.

Conventions/Meetings: annual conference (exhibits). ● periodic competition.

★2493★ AMERICAN GOLD STAR MOTHERS (AGSM)
2128 Leroy Pl. NW
Washington, DC 20008
Winona L. Tucker, Pres.   PH: (202)265-0991

Founded: 1928. **Members:** 4,000. **Staff:** 13. **State Groups:** 34. **Local Groups:** 385. **Languages:** English. **National**. Natural mothers whose sons or daughters died in the line of duty in the armed forces during World Wars I and II, the Korean Conflict, the Vietnam hostilities, or in other strategic areas. Seeks to: inspire patriotism and a sense of individual obligation to the community, state, and nation; assist veterans and their dependents with claims made to the Veterans Administration; perpetuate the memory of individuals who died in our wars; promote peace and good will for the U.S. and all other nations. Mothers work as volunteers in VA Medical Centers and at Vietnam Veterans Memorial Fund. **Committees:** Veterans Administration Voluntary Service.

Publications: *Gold Star Mother*, bimonthly. Newsletter. **Advertising:** not accepted.

Conventions/Meetings: annual meeting - always June/July.

★2494★ AMERICAN GYNECOLOGICAL AND OBSTETRICAL SOCIETY
(AGOS)
c/o James R. Scott, M.D.
University of Utah
50 N. Medical Dr.
Salt Lake City, UT 84132
James R. Scott M.D., Sec.   PH: (801)581-5501

Founded: 1981. Members: 300. Languages: English. National. To cultivate
and promote knowledge concerning obstetrics and gynecology. Fosters the
gathering, promotion, and dissemination of theoretical and practical knowledge on subjects relating to obstetrics and gynecology. Holds learning
workshops. Awards: Periodic Association Foundation Prize.

Publications: Transactions, annual. Bulletin.

Conventions/Meetings: annual meeting - 1993 Sept. 9 - 11, Carlsbad, CA,
United States; 1994 Sept. 8 - 10, Hot Springs, VA, United States.

★2495★ AMERICAN HISTORY ASSOCIATION - WOMEN AND
MINORITIES
400 A St. SE
Washington, DC 20003
Noralee Frankle, Asst.Dir.   PH: (202)544-2422

National. Promotes the status of women historians. Advances the study and
scholarship of the history of women and minorities.

Publications: Directory of Women Historians.

★2496★ AMERICAN HUMANIST ASSOCIATION - FEMINIST CAUCUS
Box 21506
San Jose, CA 95151
Meg Bowman, Chair   PH: (408)924-5325

National. Women promoting secular humanism. Works to advance the
interests of women in the humanistic ideology.

★2497★ AMERICAN INSTITUTE OF ARCHITECTS - WOMEN IN
ARCHITECTURE COMMITTEE
1735 New York Ave. NW
Washington, DC 20006
Jean Barber, Director   PH: (202)626-7305

National. Reviews, monitors, and develops policies and programs that
ensure equal opportunities for women in the architecture profession. Seeks
full integration of women in the profession. Sponsors a women in architecture
speakers' bureau. Conducts educational outreach programs.

★2498★ AMERICAN INSTITUTE OF CERTIFIED PLANNERS -
WOMEN'S RIGHTS COMMITTEE
1776 Massachusetts Ave. NW
Washington, DC 20036   PH: (202)872-0611

National. Promotes the interests of women certified planners. Advances
issues and concerns of special interest to women.

★2499★ AMERICAN JEWISH COMMITTEE - WOMEN'S DIVISION
165 E. 56th St.
New York, NY 10022
Joanne Hoffman, Contact   PH: (212)751-4000

Languages: English. National. Works to improve the status of women in the
Jewish community. Maintains the Center on Sexual Equality. Conducts
educational programs on social, economic, and legal issues affecting women.
Lobbies governmental and private organizations.

★2500★ AMERICAN JEWISH CONGRESS - COMMITTEE FOR
WOMEN'S EQUALITY
15 E. 84th St.
New York, NY 10028
Harriet Kurlander, Director   PH: (212)360-1560

Founded: 1985. National. Provides a forum for inquiry and discussion of
issues important to Jewish women. Works for the equality of women in
political, social, legal, and economic areas. Strives to educate members on
topics such as reproductive rights, economic equity, child care, equality in
religious life, and the equality of women in Jewish communal life.

★2501★ AMERICAN LEGION AUXILIARY (ALA)
777 N. Meridian St.
Indianapolis, IN 46204   PH: (317)635-6291
Miriam Junge, Sec.   FX: (317)636-5590

Founded: 1919. Members: 1,000,000. Staff: 25. State Groups: 54. Local
Groups: 12,000. Languages: English. National. Mothers, wives, sisters,
daughters, granddaughters, and great granddaughters of members of the
American Legion or of all men and women who were in the U.S. Armed
Forces during World War I or II, the Korean War, the Vietnam War, Grenada/
Lebanon, Panama, or Persian Gulf; women whose close male relatives lost
their lives in war service or died after honorable discharge; women who
served in the armed forces during peacetime. Maintains museum and
sponsors competitions. Committees: Americanism; Education; Girls State;
Junior Activities; Leadership; Legislative; National Security; Poppy; Public
Relations; Veterans Affairs and Rehabilitation; National Security; Poppy;
Public Relations.

Publications: National News, bimonthly. Newsletter.

Conventions/Meetings: annual meeting.

★2502★ AMERICAN LIBRARY ASSOCIATION - COMMITTEE ON PAY
EQUITY
50 E. Huron St.
Chicago, IL 60611   PH: (312)944-6780

Works for equal rights and pay equity for women librarians. Advances the
interests of women librarians in the ALA's national agenda.

★2503★ AMERICAN LIBRARY ASSOCIATION - COMMITTEE ON THE
STATUS OF WOMEN IN LIBRARIANSHIP
50 E. Huron St.
Chicago, IL 60611
Margaret Myers, Contact   PH: (312)944-6780

National. Works to advance the interests of women librarians in the ALA.
Coordinates the collection and dissemination of information on the status of
women in librarianship. Produces programs and publications desinged to
enhance the opportunities and image of women in the library profession. Is
currently working on an oral history project of minority women in librarianship.

★2504★ AMERICAN LIBRARY ASSOCIATION - FEMINIST TASK
FORCE
50 E. Huron St.
Chicago, IL 60611
Eunice Raigrodski, Contact   PH: (312)944-6780

Founded: 1970. National. Addresses sexism in libraries and library administration. Focuses on issues affecting women libraries.

★2505★ AMERICAN LIBRARY ASSOCIATION - SOCIAL
RESPONSIBILITIES ROUND TABLE - GAY AND LESBIAN TASK
FORCE (ALA/SRRT/GLTF)
Office of Library Outreach Services
50 E. Huron
Chicago, IL 60611
Roland C. Hansen, Co-Chair
PH: (312)280-4294
TF: (800)545-2433
FX: (312)440-9374

Founded: 1970. **Languages:** English. **National.** Division of the Social
Responsibilities Round Table of the American Library Association. Purposes
are to help get more and better materials concerning gays into libraries and
out to patrons and to deal with discrimination against gay people in libraries.
Maintains information clearinghouse. **Awards:** Annual Gay/Lesbian Book
Award (recognition).

Publications: *GLTF Newsletter*, quarterly. **ISSN:** 1045-2893. **Circulation:**
250. **Advertising:** not accepted.

Conventions/Meetings: annual meeting (exhibits) - 1994 June 23 - 30,
Miami, FL, United States.

★2506★ AMERICAN LIBRARY ASSOCIATION - WOMEN'S STUDIES
SECTION
50 E. Huron St.
Chicago, IL 60611
Margarete S. Klein, Contact
PH: (312)944-6780

National. Promotes the study of women and issues affecting the lives of
women. Works within the ALA to advance the interests of women on the
national agenda.

★2507★ AMERICAN LIFE LEAGUE (ALL)
PO Box 1350
Stafford, VA 22554
Judie Brown, Pres.
PH: (703)659-4171
FX: (703)659-2586

Founded: 1979. **Members:** 250,000. **Staff:** 50. **Budget:** US$8,200,000.
Languages: English. **Multinational.** Serves as a pro-life service organization
providing educational materials, books, flyers, and programs for local, state,
and national pro-life, pro-family organizations. Sponsors international pro-life
meetings, training sessions, and seminars. Special fields of interest: abortion;
euthanasia; organ transplantation; population; world hunger. Sponsored
Coalition for Unborn Children project. **Divisions:** Advocates; Anastasia Book
Publishers; Athletes for Life; Castello Institute of Stafford; Dentists for Life;
Executives for Life; Teen American Life League.

Publications: *All About Issues*, monthly. Magazine. ● *Communique*, periodic.
Newsletter. ● *Voice*, periodic. Magazine. ● *Choice in Matters of Life and
Death*. Book. ● *The Living Will*. Book.

★2508★ AMERICAN MATHEMATICAL SOCIETY - JOINT COMMITTEE
ON WOMEN IN THE MATHEMATICS SCIENCES
Texas A & M University
Department of Mathematics
College Station, TX 77843
Susan Geller, Chair
PH: (409)845-7531

National. Promotes the interests of women mathematicians. Works to
abolish disadvantages and discriminations that women face in the mathematics sciences. Disseminates information on activities that enhance the status
of women in the mathematics sciences.

★2509★ AMERICAN MEDICAL WOMEN'S ASSOCIATION (AMWA)
801 N. Fairfax St., Ste. 400
Alexandria, VA 22314
Eileen McGrath, Exec. Dir.
PH: (703)838-0500
FX: (703)549-3864

Founded: 1915. **Members:** 11,000. **Staff:** 15. **Budget:** US$1,500,000. **Local
Groups:** 160. **Languages:** English. **National.** Women holding a M.D. or D.O.
degree from approved medical colleges; women interns, residents, and
medical students. Seeks to find solutions to problems common to women

studying or practicing medicine, such as career advancement and the
integration of professional and family responsibilities. Provides student
members with educational loans and personal counseling. Accredited to
sponsor continuing medical education programs. Maintains Friends of
American Medical Women's Association, an auxiliary organization for hus-
bands, relatives, and supporters of AMWA. **Awards:** Periodic Elizabeth
Blackwell Medal (recognition). ● Periodic Janet M. Glasgow Achievement
Award (recognition). Recipient: women medical students. ● Periodic Caroll L.
Birch Manuscript Award (recognition). Recipient: women medical students.
Committees: Archives; Credentials; Legislative; Medical Education and
Research; Medical Opportunities and Practice; Publicity and Public Relations;
Student Loans, Fellowships, and Grants; Women's Health.

Publications: *Journal*, bimonthly. ● *Newsletter*, quarterly. ● *What's Happen-
ing in AMWA*, semiannual. Newsletter. **Circulation:** 13,000.

Conventions/Meetings: annual meeting - 1993 Nov. 3 - 7, New York, NY,
United States; 1994 Nov. 2 - 6, Orlando, FL, United States; 1995 Nov. 1 - 5,
Seattle, WA, United States; 1996 Nov. 6 - 10, Boston, MA, United States.

★2510★ AMERICAN METEOROLOGICAL SOCIETY - BOARD ON
WOMEN AND MINORITIES
45 Beacon St.
Boston, MA 02108
Susan F. Zevin, Chair
PH: (617)227-2425

National. Promotes the interests of women and other minorities in the
meteorological sciences. Maintains a clearinghouse of resource information
on women in meteorology.

★2511★ AMERICAN MUSICOLOGICAL SOCIETY - COMMITTEE ON
THE STATUS OF WOMEN
Middlebury College
Department of Music
Middlebury, VT 05753
Susan Cook, Chair
PH: (802)388-3711

National. Promotes the interests of women musicologists in the United
States. Provides a forum for the discussion of issues affecting women
musicologists.

★2512★ AMERICAN NATIONAL CATTLE WOMEN (ANCW)
5420 S. Quebec
PO Box 3881
Englewood, CO 80155
Karrie Patterson, Exec.V.Pres.
PH: (303)694-0313
FX: (303)694-0313

Founded: 1952. **Members:** 10,000. **Staff:** 4. **Regional Groups:** 7. **State
Groups:** 40. **Languages:** English. **National.** Women who are actively
employed or interested in the cattle industry. Purposes are to assist the
National Cattlemen's Association, the National Live Stock and Meat Board,
and other beef-related organizations in carrying out all activities necessary for
the betterment of the cattle industry in the U.S. and to serve as a public
clearinghouse for information concerning that industry. Conducts National
Beef Cook-Off each September. Sponsors Beef Cattle Drive for Hunger to
raise funds for distribution of beef gift certificates to the needy. **Committees:**
Agriculture Day; Beef for Father's Day; Cookbook; Legislation; Publicity
Promotion and Consumer Relations.

Publications: *ANCW Directory*, annual. ● *ANCW Newsletter*, bimonthly.

Conventions/Meetings: semiannual meeting (exhibits). ● periodic meeting.

★2513★ AMERICAN NEWS WOMEN'S CLUB (ANWC)
1607 22nd St. NW
Washington, DC 20008
Margot Phillips, Pres.
PH: (202)332-6770

Founded: 1932. **Members:** 300. **Staff:** 1. **Languages:** English. **National.**
Women who write news for all media, government agencies, nonprofit

organizations, or free-lance; women in the news who hold high ranking in government or as professional women in the arts, sciences, education, civic affairs, government, or social service are associates and affiliates. Encourages friendly understanding between members and those whom they must contact in their profession. Sponsors social events; maintains club house. **Committees:** Education; Development; Professional Activities; Special Events.

Publications: *American News Women's Club*, annual. Directory. ● *Shop Talk*, monthly. Magazine.

Conventions/Meetings: periodic seminar.

★2514★ AMERICAN PHARMACEUTICAL ASSOCIATION - COMMITTEE ON WOMEN'S AFFAIRS
2215 Constitution Ave. NW
Washington, DC 20037
Maude Babington, Director   PH: (202)429-7537

National. Promotes the interests of women pharmacists and pharmacologists in the United States. Provides a forum for the discussion of issues affecting women in pharmaceutical professions.

★2515★ AMERICAN PHILOLOGICAL ASSOCIATION - COMMITTEE ON THE STATUS OF WOMEN AND MINORITIES
University of Colorado, Boulder
Department of Classics
Campus Box 248
Boulder, CO 80309
Joy K. King, Chair   PH: (303)492-6257

National. Promotes the interests of women and minorities working in the study of philology.

★2516★ AMERICAN PHILOLOGICAL ASSOCIATION - WOMEN'S CLASSICAL CAUCUS
College of New Rochelle
Department of Classics
New Rochelle, NY 10801
Barbara McManus, Treas.   PH: (914)654-5399

National. Promotes feminist works on classical antiquity. Works to eliminate sexist, ageist, and homophobic practices and attitudes throughout the field of philology.

★2517★ AMERICAN PHYSICAL SOCIETY - COMMITTEE ON THE STATUS OF WOMEN IN PHYSICS
335 E. 45th St.
New York, NY 10017
Miriam A. Forman, Director   PH: (212)682-7341

National. Addresses the career development of women physicists. Gathers and maintains data on women in physics.

★2518★ AMERICAN PLANNING ASSOCIATION - PLANNING AND WOMEN DIVISION
1776 Massachusetts Ave. NW
Washington, DC 20036
Carol Barrett, Director   PH: (202)872-0611

National. Women planners in the United States. Represents the interests of women involved in the planning industry.

★2519★ AMERICAN POLITICAL SCIENCE ASSOCIATION - COMMITTEE ON THE STATUS OF WOMEN IN POLITICAL SCIENCE
1527 New Hampshire Ave. NW
Washington, DC 20036
Sheila Mann, Asst.Dir.   PH: (202)483-2512

National. Works to advance the interests of women in the field of political science. Strives to improve the representation of women authors in scholarly journals.

★2520★ AMERICAN POSTAL WORKERS UNION (AFL-CIO) - POST OFFICE WOMEN FOR EQUAL RIGHTS
460 W. 34th St., 9th Fl.
New York, NY 10001
Josie McMillian, President   PH: (212)563-7553

National. Represents the interests of women postal workers. Works to improve the status of women in the postal union. Seeks an end to discriminatory practices affecting women in the United States postal service.

★2521★ AMERICAN PRO-LIFE COUNCIL (APLC)
1612 S. Prospect Ave.
Park Ridge, IL 60068
John de Paul Hansen, Pres.   PH: (708)692-2183

Founded: 1980. **Members:** 50,000. **Languages:** English. **National.** Provides right-to-life activists with insurance, credit union, and other programs containing pro-life provisions. Has established American Pro=life Assurance Society and a general insurance agency, and uses profits to fund pro-life causes.

★2522★ AMERICAN PSYCHIATRIC ASSOCIATION - ASSOCIATION OF WOMEN PSYCHIATRISTS
9802 Farnham Rd.
Louisville, KY 40223
Kathy Garvin, Exec.Asst.   PH: (502)588-6185

National. Women psychiatrists. Works to promote the status of women psychiatrists in the profession. Provides a forum for communication and exchange among members. Collects and disseminates information on women's mental health issues.

★2523★ AMERICAN PSYCHIATRIC ASSOCIATION - COMMITTEE ON WOMEN AND WOMEN'S CAUCUS
1400 K St. NW
Washington, DC 20005
Jean Spurlock, Deputy Medical Dir.   PH: (202)682-2000

National. Defines and recommends action to meet the mental health needs of women in the United States. Promotes the involvement of women psychiatrists in academic, research, administration, and professional organizations.

★2524★ AMERICAN PSYCHOLOGICAL ASSOCIATION - COMMITTEE ON WOMEN IN PSYCHOLOGY
Department of Medical Psychology
4301 Jones Bridge Rd.
Bethesda, MD 20804
Sheryl Gallant, Chair   PH: (301)295-3270

National. Promotes the interests of women psychologists in the United States. Studies the role of women psychologists in the profession.

★2525★ AMERICAN PSYCHOLOGICAL ASSOCIATION - DIVISION OF THE PSYCHOLOGY OF WOMEN
750 1st St. NE
Washington, DC 20002-4242
Gwendolyn Puryear Keita, Director   PH: (202)336-6044

National. Promotes research into, and practice of, feminist psychology. Works for the equitable treatment of women throughout society and within the discipline of psychology.

★2526★ AMERICAN PSYCHOLOGICAL ASSOCIATION - WOMEN'S CAUCUS
1200 17th St. NW
Washington, DC 20036
Judith Alpert, Chair   PH: (202)691-6587

National. Works for the improved research, education, training, and practice involving women and gender issues. Promotes the career status of women in psychology.

★2527★ AMERICAN PSYCHOLOGICAL ASSOCIATION - WOMEN'S PROGRAM
750 1st St. NE
Washington, DC 20009   PH: (202)336-6044

Languages: English. **National.** Women members of American Psychological Association. Encourages women to pursue mental health careers. Offers advice and financial assistance to female students in psychology. Disseminates information.

★2528★ AMERICAN PUBLIC HEALTH ASSOCIATION - WOMEN'S CAUCUS
1015 15th St. NW
Washington, DC 20005
Shauna Heckert, Chair   PH: (202)789-5600

National. Provides a forum for the discussion of women's health issues. Addresses concerns of discrimination in women's health care in the United States.

★2529★ AMERICAN RAPE PREVENTION ASSOCIATION
50 Muth Dr.
Orinda, CA 94563
Margot C. Spott, Co-Pres.   PH: (415)254-0963

Founded: 1943. **Members:** 68,000. **Regional Groups:** 3. **Languages:** English. **National.** Professionals in life sciences. Investigates relationship between incest and rape; domestic violence and rape; sexual harassment and rape; and murder and rape; researches how to prevent such violence against women. Works to prevent violence against women through increasing public awareness of its causes and effects.

Publications: *JARPA* (in English).

★2530★ AMERICAN RIGHTS COALITION (ARC)
PO Box 487
Chattanooga, TN 37401   PH: (615)698-7960
Charlie Wysong, Founder   TF: (800)634-2224

Languages: English. **National.** Christian, pro-life organization. Ministers to women who have had negative experiences with abortion. Assists women in pursuit of legal recourse in cases where fraud, malpractice, or misrepresentation are indicated. People who contact ARC are referred to local volunteer "support teams" who channel them to the appropriate resources. Encourages women to join Christian post-abortion "healing groups" and to attend church. Works to fight abortion through legislative means.

Publications: *The Abortion Injury Report* (in English), bimonthly. Bulletin. Features reprints of news stories on abortion/right-to-life related issues. ● Books, manuals, and videos.

★2531★ AMERICAN SOCIETY OF ALLIED HEALTH PROFESSIONS - WOMEN'S ISSUES SECTION
1101 Connecticut Ave. NW, Ste. 700
Washington, DC 20036
Carolyn M. Del Polito, Exec.Dir.   PH: (202)857-1150

Founded: 1967. **National.** Professional organization of women involved in allied health professions. Promotes the interests of members.

★2532★ AMERICAN SOCIETY OF BIO-CHEMISTRY AND MOLECULAR BIOLOGY - COMMITTEE ON EQUAL OPPORTUNITIES FOR WOMEN
9650 Rockville Pike
Bethesda, MD 20814
Charles Hancock, Contact   PH: (301)530-7145

National. Promotes the interests of women involved in the fields of bio-chemistry and molecular biology. Works to involve women more actively in these scientific areas.

★2533★ AMERICAN SOCIETY OF CHILDBIRTH EDUCATORS (ASCE)
PO Box 1630
Sedona, AZ 86336
Dr. James C. Sasmor, Corporate Sec.   PH: (602)284-9897

Founded: 1972. **Languages:** English. **National.** Seeks to provide a medium for the exchange and dissemination of information relating to prepared childbirth as a shared family experience and disseminate information to qualified professionals regarding standards, techniques, and skills relevant to the concept of prepared birth.

★2534★ AMERICAN SOCIETY OF CHURCH HISTORY - WOMEN IN THEOLOGY AND CHURCH HISTORY
Lutheran Theological Seminary
7301 Germantown Ave.
Philadelphia, PA 19119
Faith Burgess, Chair   PH: (215)248-4616

National. Promotes the involvement of women in the study of theology. Seeks to advance the importance of women in the development of the church.

★2535★ AMERICAN SOCIETY FOR COLPOSCOPY AND CERVICAL PATHOLOGY (ASCCP)
c/o American College of Obstetricians
 and Gynecologists
409 12th St. SW
Washington, DC 20024   TF: (800)787-7227
Kathleen Poole, Admin.Dir.   FX: (202)484-5107

Founded: 1964. **Members:** 2,000. **Staff:** 2. **Languages:** English. **National.** Obstetricians, gynecologists, nurses, and other individuals interested in promoting the accurate and ethical application of colposcopy (the examination of the lower genital tract by means of a colposcope). Organizes and approves training programs in colposcopy. Conducts research and postgraduate courses. **Awards:** Annual Coloscopy Recognition Award. **Computer Services:** Data base, membership information. **Committees:** Education; Pathology; Practice. **Task Forces:** Audio-Visual Development; Non-Ob/Gyn Colposcopist. **Committees:** Pathology; Practice. **Task Forces:** Audio-Visual Development.

Publications: *Colposcopist*, quarterly. Magazine. ● *Membership Directory*, biennial.

Conventions/Meetings: biennial meeting (exhibits) - 1993 Nov. 18 - 23, Maui, HI, United States; 1994 Mar., Orlando, FL, United States.

★2536★ AMERICAN SOCIETY FOR EIGHTEENTH CENTURY STUDIES - WOMEN'S CAUCUS
Mail Location 368
University of Cincinnati
Cincinnati, OH 45221
Felicia Sturzer, Chair   PH: (513)556-3820

National. Promotes the study of women writers and characters of eighteenth century literature. Works to address issues that affect women in the study of eighteenth century literature. Fosters information exchange among members.

★2537★ AMERICAN SOCIETY FOR PSYCHOPROPHYLAXIS IN OBSTETRICS (ASPO/LAMAZE)
1101 Connecticut Ave. NW, Ste. 700   PH: (202)857-1128
Washington, DC 20036   TF: (800)368-4404
Linda Harmon, Exec.Dir.   FX: (202)223-4579

Founded: 1960. **Members:** 5,000. **Budget:** US$2,500,000. **Local Groups:** 25. **Languages:** English. **National.** Physicians, nurses, nurse-midwives, certified teachers of psychoprophylatic (Lamaze) method of childbirth, other professionals, parents, and others interested in Lamaze childbirth preparation and family-centered maternity care. Disseminates information about the theory and practical application of psychoprophylaxis in obstetrics; administers teacher training courses and certifies qualified Lamaze teachers; provides educational lectures, public forums, films, and written materials; maintains national and local teacher and physician referral service. Also presents materials to prospective parents concerning the demands of childrearing. National office serves as information clearinghouse. **Libraries:** Type: reference. Holdings: 0. **Awards:** Semiannual Elizabeth Bing (scholarship). **Computer Services:** Mailing lists, educational programs. **Committees:** Appeals and Mediation; Certification; Chapter Formation and Development; Education and Public Information. **Task Forces:** Outreach.

Publications: *Genesis*, bimonthly. Newsletter. Contains book and film reviews and calendar of events.. **Circulation:** 5,000. ● *Perinatal Education*, quarterly. Journal. **Circulation:** 5,000. **Advertising:** not accepted.

Conventions/Meetings: annual meeting (exhibits) - 1994, Chicago, IL, United States; 1995, Washington, DC, United States.

★2538★ AMERICAN SOCIETY FOR PUBLIC ADMINISTRATION - SECTION FOR WOMEN IN PUBLIC ADMINISTRATION
Evergreen State College
3306 Windolp Loop NW
Olympia, WA 98502
Camilla Stivera, Chair   PH: (206)866-6000

National. Promotes the interests of women in public administration professions. Provides a forum for information exchange between members.

★2539★ AMERICAN SOCIETY OF WOMEN ACCOUNTANTS (ASWA)
1755 Lynnfield Rd., Ste. 222
Memphis, TN 38119-7235   PH: (901)680-0470
Allison Conte, Exec.Dir.   FX: (901)680-0505

Founded: 1938. **Members:** 8,000. **Staff:** 4. **Budget:** US$500,000. **Local Groups:** 140. **Languages:** English. **National.** Professional society of women accountants, educators, and others in the field of accounting. Assists women accountants in their careers and promotes development in the profession. Conducts educational and research programs; training seminars; bestows awards.

Publications: *Coordinator*, monthly. Newsletter. Includes calendar of events, listings of new officers and directors, and recognizes distinguished members. **ISSN:** 0744-8937. **Circulation:** 8,000. ● *Membership Directory*, annual.

Conventions/Meetings: annual conference (exhibits) - 1993 Oct. 28 - 30, Minneapolis, MN, United States.

★2540★ AMERICAN STUDIES ASSOCIATION - WOMEN'S COMMITTEE
University of Maryland
Taliafero Hall
College Park, MD 20742
Lee Chambers-Schiller, Chair   PH: (301)454-2533

National. Promotes the study of women's issues within the American studies discipline. Seeks to bring awareness to the importance of women's involvement in the course of American history.

★2541★ AMERICAN VICTIMS OF ABORTION (AVA)
419 7th St. NW, Ste. 500   PH: (202)626-8800
Washington, DC 20004   FX: (202)737-9189

Founded: 1985. **State Groups:** 50. **Languages:** English. **National.** Individuals who have been affected by abortion including mothers, fathers, grandparents, and other relatives, doctors, nurses, and counselors. Works to expose "the truth of abortion's tragedy" and increase public awareness of "Post-Abortion Syndrome," which the association says is the physical, psychological, and emotional trauma suffered by the "secondary victims" of abortions. Conducts public awareness campaigns, legislative initiatives, and judicial activities. Maintains counseling referral service and speakers' bureau; encourages further research of "Post-Abortion Syndrome.".

Publications: *AVA Newsletter*, quarterly.

★2542★ AMERICAN WAR MOTHERS (AWM)
2615 Woodley Pl. NW
Washington, DC 20008
LaVita G. Orand, Contact   PH: (202)462-2791

Founded: 1917. **Members:** 3,500. **Staff:** 2. **Budget:** US$52,000. **State Groups:** 28. **Local Groups:** 195. **Languages:** English. **National.** Natural mothers of veterans, servicemen, and servicewomen. Holds Veterans' Day services at the U.S. Capitol and Mothers' Day services at Arlington Cemetery. Conducts volunteer services in VA hospitals. **Awards:** Biennial (recognition). **Committees:** Americanism; Hospitalization; Legislative; Memorials.

Publications: *American War Mothers Newsletter*, quarterly.

Conventions/Meetings: biennial meeting - always odd-numbered years.

★2543★ AMERICAN WOMAN'S ECONOMIC DEVELOPMENT (AWED)
641 Lexington Ave.
New York, NY 10022   PH: (212)688-1900
Rosalind Paaswell, CEO   FX: (212)688-2718

Founded: 1975. **Members:** 6,000. **Staff:** 20. **Languages:** English. **National.** Women owning or planning to form small businesses. Sponsors 18-month training and technical assistance program. Provides management training, on-site analysis of businesses, volunteer advisers who work in specific problem areas, assistance in preparing a business plan, and continued support after the program is completed. Nine-week mini-programs are also available. Staff is composed of experienced business people and specialists from university business schools and major corporations. Operates telephone counseling hot-line.

Publications: *AWED's in Business*, bimonthly. Newsletter. **Advertising:** accepted.

Conventions/Meetings: annual conference. ● periodic seminar.

★2544★ AMERICAN WOMAN'S SOCIETY OF CERTIFIED PUBLIC ACCOUNTANTS (AWSCPA)
401 N. Michigan Ave.
Chicago, IL 60611   PH: (312)644-6610
Bonnie Engle, Exec.Dir.   FX: (312)321-6869

Founded: 1933. **Members:** 4,000. **Staff:** 8. **Local Groups:** 45. **Languages:** English. **National.** Citizens of the U.S. who hold certified public accountant certificates; those who have passed the CPA examination but do not have certificates are associates; women holding degrees comparable to CPA certificates but who are not U.S. citizens are international associates. Works to improve the status of professional women and to make the business community aware of the professional capabilities of the woman CPA. Conducts statistical survey of members; offers specialized education and research programs.

Publications: *AWSCPA Newsletter*, quarterly. ● *Issues Paper*, annual. ● *Membership Roster*, annual. Directory.

Conventions/Meetings: annual meeting.

★2545★ AMERICAN WOMEN COMPOSERS (AWC)
1690 36th St. NW, Ste. 409
Washington, DC 20007
Judith Shatin, Pres.   PH: (202)342-8179

Founded: 1976. **Members:** 350. **Membership Dues:** senior composers. students, US$15; individual, US$30; institution, US$40. **Staff:** 2. **Regional Groups:** 3. **Languages:** English. **National.** Composers, performers, musicologists, and associate members. Seeks to help women attain recognition as composers by promoting and supporting the works of women composers and performers in the U.S. and by working to increase public awareness of women's contributions to American musical culture. Produces recordings of women's music. Sponsors live programs and music festivals. **Libraries:** Type: reference. Holdings: 3,000; audio recordings, archival material. **Computer Services:** Mailing lists.

Publications: *AWC News/Forum*, annual. Journal. Articles about women in music, and lists of competitions. contests, fellowships, and prizes. **ISSN:** 0193-8050. **Circulation:** 700. **Advertising:** accepted. ● *AWC News-Update*, semiannual. Newsletter.

Conventions/Meetings: periodic seminar. ● annual competition.

★2546★ AMERICAN WOMEN IN RADIO AND TELECOMMUNICATION (AWRT)
1101 Connecticut Ave. NW, Ste. 700
Washington, DC 20036   PH: (202)429-5102
Donna Cantor, Exec.Dir.   FX: (202)223-4578

Founded: 1951. **Members:** 1,800. **Staff:** 4. **Regional Groups:** 5. **Local Groups:** 47. **Languages:** English. **National.** Professional women in administrative, creative, or executive positions in the broadcasting industry (radio, television stations, cable, and networks) as well as advertising, government, and charitable agencies, corporations, and service organizations, whose work is substantially devoted to radio and television. Maintains AWRT Educational Foundation, chartered 1960. Maintains speakers' bureau and charitable program; sponsors competitions. **Awards:** Periodic Silver Satellite for Outstanding Accomplishment. **Computer Services:** Mailing lists. **Committees:** Affirmative Action; Professional Development Speakers' Bureau. **Projects:** Soaring Spirits: Programming for Hospitalized Children; Symposium on Careers. **Formerly:** Association of Women Broadcasters.

Publications: *American Women in Radio & TV*, annual. Directory. ● *News and Views*, bimonthly. Newsletter. ● *Women on the Job - Careers in the Electronic Media*. Book.

Conventions/Meetings: annual meeting (exhibits) - 1994 May, Minneapolis, MN, United States.

★2547★ AMERICAN WOMEN'S ASSOCIATION FOR RENEWABLE ENERGY (AWARE)
Box U   PH: (201)728-2593
Hewitt, NJ 07421   FX: (201)728-2597

Founded: 1992. **Members:** 15. **Staff:** 2. **Languages:** English. **National.** Women promoting the implementation of renewable energy sources. Sponsors research to develop new sources of renewable energy. Disseminates information.

★2548★ AMERICAN WOMEN'S HOSPITALS SERVICE COMMITTEE OF AMWA (AWHS/AMWA)
801 N. Fairfax St., Ste. 400
Alexandria, VA 22314   PH: (703)838-0500
Dr. Anne Barlow, Chair   FX: (703)549-3864

Founded: 1917. **Languages:** English. **National.** Committee of American Medical Women's Association. International philanthropic medical relief service that supports medical and hospital services conducted by women doctors and nurses for the care of the indigent sick and prevention of disease. Current activities, carried on in Bolivia, Haiti, and the U.S., include family planning and fostering health education through demonstrations, home visits, and giving financial aid to hospitals and clinics.

Conventions/Meetings: semiannual meeting.

★2549★ AMERICAN WOMEN'S SELF-DEFENSE ASSOCIATION (AWSDA)
713 N. Wellwood Ave.   PH: (516)226-8383
Lindenhurst, NY 11757   (516)226-5454
Elizabeth Kennedy, Exec. Dir.   E-Mail: eileen@camb.com.

Languages: English. **National.** Promotes rape prevention awareness and self-defense for women. Operates national advertising campaign. Provides free rape prevention classes. Trains teachers in self-defense and rape prevention. Unites individuals interested in women's self-defense and encourages cooperation and information exchange among them. Motto is: "You have an absolute right to defend yourself." Maintains that an individual has a legal and moral right to protect him/herself. **Computer Services:** Data base, services available for survivors of violent crimes.

Publications: *Newsletter*, quarterly.

Conventions/Meetings: annual seminar.

★2550★ AMERICANS UNITED FOR LIFE (AUL)
343 S. Dearborn, Ste. 1804
Chicago, IL 60604
Guy M. Condon, Pres.   PH: (312)786-9494

Founded: 1971. **Staff:** 30. **Languages:** English. **National.** Pro-life legal and educational organization concerned with protecting human life at all stages of development. Conducts legal and legislative activites including provision of testimony, model abortion statutes, and legal briefs in cases involving abortion and euthanasia. Offers summer internship to qualified law students. Operates Americans United for Life Legal Defense Fund to promote the reversal of the 1973 U.S. Supreme Court Roe vs. Wade ruling which affirmed the legal rights of women to choose to have an abortion; provides legal assistance to individuals challenging the Roe vs. Wade decision. **Libraries:** Type: reference. Holdings: books, periodicals, clippings.

Publications: *AUL Briefing Memo*, periodic. Newsletter. Provides analysis of pro-life legal topics. ● *AUL Forum*, monthly. Newsletter. ● *AUL Insights*, periodic. Newsletter. ● *Lex Vitae*, quarterly. Bulletin. ● *Life Docket*, monthly. Newsletter.

Conventions/Meetings: annual Legislator's Educational Conference.

★2551★ AMIT WOMEN (AW)
817 Broadway   PH: (212)477-4720
New York, NY 10003   TF: (800)221-3117
Norma Holzer, Pres.   FX: (212)353-2312

Founded: 1925. **Members:** 89,000. **Staff:** 50. **Regional Groups:** 9. **Local Groups:** 425. **Languages:** English. **National.** Religious-Zionist organization of Jewish women. Provides child care, social welfare education, and vocational training programs for youth and newcomers to Israel in an atmosphere of Jewish tradition. Serves as Israel Ministry of Education's Official Reshet (network) for religious secondary technological and vocational education. Sponsors and maintains children's villages, vocational high schools, settlement houses, community centers, and other institutions in

Israel. Distributes Passover supplies to the needy; conducts musicals and lectures for adults; provides aid to graduates. Participates in reforestation and land reclamation activities through Jewish National Fund. Conducts educational programs on life in Israel and the Jewish cultural and religious heritage; produces films and other materials. Maintains speakers' bureau. **Awards:** Annual America-Israel Friendship Award. **Departments:** Social Services; Vocational Education; Youth Aliyah and Child Restoration.

Publications: *Amit Woman*, 5/year. ● *Not for Presidents Only*, 10/year. Newsletter. ● *Program Guide*, bimonthly. ● *Biography of Bessie Gotsfeld*. Book.

Conventions/Meetings: biennial conference.

★2552★ AMVETS AUXILIARY (AA)
4647 Forbes Blvd.
Lanham, MD 20706   PH: (301)459-6255

Founded: 1946. **Members:** 30,000. **Staff:** 2. **State Groups:** 38. **Local Groups:** 581. **Languages:** English. **National**. Wives, mothers, sisters, daughters, and granddaughters of members of AMVETS - American Veterans of World War II, Korea and Vietnam; women relatives of deceased veterans who would have been eligible for membership; female veterans who served honorably in the Armed Forces of the United States or in the Armed Forces of allied countries from Sept. 16, 1940 to present. Carries out nationwide hospital program for veterans, civil defense and Americanism activities, and child welfare projects. **Awards:** Annual (scholarship).

Publications: *Newsletter*, quarterly.

Conventions/Meetings: annual meeting - always August. ● annual executive committee meeting - always April.

★2553★ ANANDA MARGA UNIVERSAL RELIEF TEAM, AMURT & AMURTEL (WOMEN'S BRANCH)
302 W. Mulberry
PO Box 15963
San Antonio, TX 78212
Sid Jordan, President

Languages: English. **National**. Provides community development and relief services to women in need. Conducts educational programs.

★2554★ ARAB WOMEN'S COUNCIL (AWC)
PO Box 5653
Washington, DC 20016
Najat Khelil, Pres.

Founded: 1982. **Members:** 200. **State Groups:** 2. **Languages:** English. **National**. Arab, American, and Arab-American women. Seeks to inform the public on Arab women and their culture. Sponsors annual essay contest for high school juniors and seniors. Initiated a hunger strike to protest Israel's blockage of food and water to west Beirut, Lebanon in July, 1982. Conducts seminars for Arab-American women; provides lecture series and cultural events such as dance performances, fashion shows, art exhibitions, poetry readings, and other events related to the Arab community. Maintains Arab Women's Council Research and Education Fund. Maintains speakers' bureau and charitable program. **Libraries:** Type: reference. Holdings: 0; books, periodicals. Subjects: issues relevant to the Middle East. **Committees:** Education; Information; Youth.

Conventions/Meetings: annual meeting.

★2555★ ARCHCONFRATERNITY OF CHRISTIAN MOTHERS (ACM)
220 37th St.
Pittsburgh, PA 15201
Rev. Bertin Roll, Dir.   PH: (412)683-2400

Founded: 1881. **Members:** 3,400. **Languages:** English. **National**. Parish confraternities interested in the home-education, character formation, and personality development of children guided primarily by mothers.

Publications: *The Christian Mother*, quarterly. Bulletin.

★2556★ ARMENIAN INTERNATIONAL WOMEN'S ASSOCIATION (AIWA)
PO Box 654
Belmont, MA 02178   PH: (617)237-6858
Dr. Barbara Merguerian, President   FX: (617)237-1842

Founded: 1990. **Members:** 200. **Budget:** US$7,000. **Languages:** English. **Multinational**. Women of Armenian heritage or interested in Armenian culture. Aims to unite Armenian women worldwide to address critical issues. Works to establish contacts with other women's organizations, Armenian and non-Armenian. Provides a forum for dialogue and negotiation of issues of concern to Armenian women. Compiles information related to the changing role of women in society. Plans to establish an Armenian women archives. Promotes the recognition of Armenian women and their role and equal rights in society. Offers information to the media and public on Armenia and Armenian activities. Sponsors programs, issues publications, and organizes discussion groups and workshops concerning Armenian culture and issues. **Committees:** Program; Directory; Communications; Membership; Human Rights; Archives.

Publications: *Newsletter* (in English), semiannual. ● *Directory* (in English), periodic.

Conventions/Meetings: annual meeting.

★2557★ ARMENIAN WOMEN'S WELFARE ASSOCIATION (AWWA)
431 Pond St.
Jamaica Plain, MA 02130   PH: (617)522-2600
Anita Hedison, Pres.   FX: (617)524-7024

Founded: 1921. **Members:** 500. **Languages:** English. **National**. Women interested in helping with charitable work. Maintains nursing home to care for the aged.

Conventions/Meetings: annual meeting - always May. Boston, MA, United States.

★2558★ ARTTABLE
301 E. 57th St.
New York, NY 10022   PH: (212)593-6310
Caroline Goldsmith, Exec.Dir.   FX: (212)715-1507

Founded: 1981. **Members:** 500. **Staff:** 3. **Regional Groups:** 2. **Languages:** English. **National**. Invitational organization for women leaders in the visual arts profession. Seeks to create understanding of the field and enrich the cultural life of society. Creates forum for idea exchange. Sponsors educational programs; bestows awards.

Publications: *ArtWire*, semiannual. Newsletter. **Circulation:** 500. **Advertising:** not accepted.

Conventions/Meetings: bimonthly meeting.

★2559★ ASIAN-INDIAN WOMEN IN AMERICA (AIWA)
RD 1, Box 98
Palisades, NY 10964   PH: (914)365-1066
Ms. Uma Shah, Pres.   FX: (914)425-5804

Founded: 1980. **Members:** 175. **Languages:** English. **National**. Asian-Indian women, primarily professionals, who live in the U.S. Provides social, financial, and cultural services to Asian-Indian women in the U.S. Addresses issues affecting women in the U.S., including spouse abuse, single-parent families, and career development. Offers counseling for families and battered women; provides financial consultation services. Works with other groups on issues of concern to Asian-Indian women; sponsors social gatherings to aid the acculturation of members; conducts workshops. Monitors political developments in India. Maintains speakers' bureau. Plans to conduct support group.

Publications: *AIWA Newsletter*, 3-4/year. **Advertising:** accepted. ● *Commu-*

nity News Bulletin, monthly. Lists events of interest, job opportunities, and support information. **Advertising:** not accepted. ● *Membership Directory*, annual. ● *Newsletter*, 3-4/year. ● *Asian-Indian Women's Directory*.

Conventions/Meetings: bimonthly meeting. ● biennial meeting.

★2560★ ASIAN INDIAN WOMEN'S NETWORK (AINN)
8391 Satinwood Circle
Westminster, CA 92683   PH: (714)894-2608
Angela Anand, President   FX: (714)898-0894

Founded: 1987. **Members:** 200. **Languages:** English. Provides a forum for the discussion of issues concerning the professional and personal development of Asian women. Offers support services and maintains a network designed to assist the career and business growth of and opportunities for women. Recognizes the contributions Asian women have made to society. Helps newly arrived Asian immigrants through the acculturation process. Organizes mentorship programs.

Publications: *Newsletter*, quarterly. ● *Directory*. of membership.

Conventions/Meetings: quarterly meeting.

★2561★ ASSOCIATION OF AFRICAN-AMERICAN WOMEN BUSINESS
   OWNERS (BWE)
c/o Brenda Alford
Brasman Research
PO Box 13933
Silver Spring, MD 20911-3933
Tracy Mason, Pres.   PH: (301)565-0258

Founded: 1982. **Members:** 850. **Staff:** 3. **Local Groups:** 10. **Languages:** English. **National.** Small business owners in all industries, particularly business services. Seeks to assist in developing a greater number of successful self-employed black women through business and personal development programs, networking, and legislative action. Is conducting a 2-year project identifying black women business owners as role models and historical figures; plans to establish an archive.

Publications: *Chronicle of Minority Business*, quarterly. Journal.

Conventions/Meetings: biennial workshop, training program - always odd-numbered years. ● periodic regional meeting - always even-numbered year.

★2562★ ASSOCIATION OF BLACK CATHOLICS AGAINST ABORTION
   (ABC)
1011 1st Ave.
New York, NY 10022   PH: (212)371-1000
Dr. Delores Bernadette Grier, Pres.   FX: (212)319-8265

Languages: English. **National.** African-American Catholics who oppose abortion. Conducts educational programs, workshops, and conferences.

★2563★ ASSOCIATION OF BLACK WOMEN IN HIGHER EDUCATION
   (ABWHE)
c/o Lenore R. Gall
234 Hudson Ave.
Albany, NY 12210   PH: (518)472-1791
Lenore R. Gall, Pres.   (212)988-5677

Founded: 1979. **Members:** 350. **Languages:** English. **National.** Faculty members, education administrators, students, retirees, consultants, managers, and affirmative action officers. Objectives are to nurture the role of black women in higher education, and to provide support for the professional development goals of black women. **Computer Services:** Mailing lists.

Publications: *ABWHE Newsletter*, quarterly.

Conventions/Meetings: biennial conference (exhibits) - always odd-numbered years. ● periodic seminar. ● periodic workshop.

★2564★ ASSOCIATION OF BLACK WOMEN HISTORIANS
PO Box 19753
Durham, NC 27707
Sylvia M. Jacobs, Director   PH: (919)493-1024

National. Promotes the interests of African American women historians. Provides a forum for information exchange between members.

★2565★ ASSOCIATION FOR COUPLES IN MARRIAGE ENRICHMENT
   (ACME)
PO Box 10596
Winston-Salem, NC 27108   PH: (919)724-1526
Chi-Chi Messick, Contact   TF: (800)634-8325

Founded: 1973. **Members:** 2,500. **Staff:** 4. **Budget:** US$200,000. **State Groups:** 40. **Local Groups:** 100. **Languages:** English. **National.** Married couples united to: promote and support effective community services to foster successful marriages; improve public acceptance and understanding of marriage as a relationship capable of fostering personal growth and mutual fulfillment; educate and assist married couples in seeking growth and enrichment in their marriages. Conducts marriage enrichment retreats and growth groups, marital communication training courses, enrichment programs, and basic and advanced training workshops. Grants certification to leader couples; conducts state, regional, international, and national conferences. Bestows awards annually. **Committees:** Selection; Training and Certification.

Publications: *Marriage Enrichment*, monthly. Newsletter.

Conventions/Meetings: periodic conference.

★2566★ ASSOCIATION FOR GAY, LESBIAN, AND BISEXUAL ISSUES
   IN COUNSELING (AGLBIC)
Box 216
Jenkintown, PA 19046
Robert Rohde, Sec.-Treas.

Founded: 1974. **Members:** 210. **Languages:** English. **National.** Counselors and personnel and guidance workers concerned with lesbian and gay issues. Seeks to eliminate discrimination against and stereotyping of gay and lesbian individuals, particularly gay counselors. Works to educate heterosexual counselors on how to overcome homophobia and to best help homosexual clients. Provides a referral network and support for gay counselors and administrators; encourages objective research on gay issues. Maintains speakers' bureau.

Publications: *AGLBIC News*, 4/year. Newsletter.

Conventions/Meetings: annual meeting (exhibits) - 1994 Apr. 24 - 27, Minneapolis, MN, United States; 1995 Apr. 27 - 30, Denver, CO, United States.

★2567★ ASSOCIATION OF GAY AND LESBIAN PSYCHIATRISTS
   (AGLP)
24 Olmstead St.
Jamaica Plain, MA 02130
Marshall Forstein M.D., Pres.   PH: (617)522-1267

Founded: 1975. **Members:** 500. **Languages:** English. **National.** Gay, lesbian, and bisexual members of the American Psychiatric Association and other psychiatrists throughout North America. Objectives are to: provide support and encouragement for gay and lesbian psychiatrists; serve as a vehicle for the promotion of social and legal equality for all gay people; further the understanding of members, colleagues, and the public in matters relating to homosexuality; promote improved mental health services for gays and lesbians; encourage research in areas related to homosexuality. Provides, by mail, referrals to private gay-sympathetic therapists. Maintains speakers' bureau; bestows awards; presents papers and panels. **Committees:** Education; Issues.

Publications: *Newsletter of the Association of Gay and Lesbian Psychia-*

trists, quarterly. Includes book reviews, calendar of events, and obituaries. **Circulation:** 325. **Advertising:** accepted.

Conventions/Meetings: annual meeting. ● periodic seminar (exhibits). ● annual meeting - always fall. Washington, DC, United States.

★2568★ ASSOCIATION FOR INTERDISCIPLINARY RESEARCH IN VALUES AND SOCIAL CHANGE
419-7th NW, Ste. 500
Washington, DC 20004
Marie Hagan, Contact   PH: (202)626-8800

Languages: English. **National.** Professionals who oppose abortion. Serves as a forum for exchange of ideas and research on abortion. Acts as a clearinghouse for information on abortion and abortion's effects on society. Promotes the idea that abortion is detrimental to the American family network.

Conventions/Meetings: annual meeting - always June.

★2569★ ASSOCIATION FOR PROFESSIONAL INSURANCE WOMEN
1 Liberty Plaza
New York, NY 10006
Marsha A. Cohen, President   PH: (212)225-7500

National. Promotes the interests of women involved in the insurance industry. Provides a forum for the exchange of information between members.

★2570★ ASSOCIATION FOR RECOGNIZING THE LIFE OF STILLBORNS (ARLS)
11128 W. Frost Ave.
Littleton, CO 80127
Frank J. Pavlak, Exec. Officer   PH: (303)978-9517

Founded: 1983. **Languages:** English. **National.** Offers Certificates of Life (for a fee) to parents who have experienced a miscarriage, stillbirth, or early infant death to serve as tangible evidence that their babies were once alive.

★2571★ ASSOCIATION OF REPRODUCTIVE HEALTH PROFESSIONALS (ARHP)
2401 Penn Ave. NW, Ste. 350
Washington, DC 20037-1718   PH: (202)466-3825
Dennis J. Barbour J.D., Exec.Dir.   FX: (202)466-3826

Founded: 1963. **Members:** 600. **Staff:** 2. **Languages:** English. **National.** Physicians, scientists, educators, and reproductive health professionals. Educates the public and health care professionals on matters pertaining to reproductive health, including sexuality, contraception, prevention of sexually transmitted disease, family planning, and abortion. Promotes consumer knowledge and the attainment of professional skills relevent to reproductive health. Supports the right of women to decide to sustain or terminate their pregnancies. Advocates public policies supportive of reproductive health. Collaborates with other professional organizations, government agencies, nonprofit organizations, and corporations on mutual reproductive health concerns. Sponsors scientific meetings, educational programs, and other forums for the Exchange of information among reproductive health care providers.

Publications: *American Journal of Gynecologic Health*, bimonthly. ● *Newsletter*, quarterly.

Conventions/Meetings: annual meeting (exhibits).

★2572★ ASSOCIATION FOR THE SEXUALLY HARASSED (ASH)
PO Box 27235
Philadelphia, PA 19118
Cheryl Gomez-Preston, Exec.Dir.   PH: (215)482-3528

Founded: 1988. **Languages:** English. **National.** Employers, talk shows, attorneys, organizations, schools, victims of sexual harassment, and other interested individuals. Seeks to create a national awareness of sexual harassment. Offers: experts for talk shows; mediation trouble shooter services to resolve sexual harassment problems between the employee and employer to prevent litigation; telephone counseling; consultation services for the litigator and client; assistance to businesses to help in the development of sexual harassment guidelines. Sponsors educational programs for school children. Conducts pro-active, preventative sexual harassment training workshops; compiles statistics. Maintains speakers' bureau. **Libraries:** Type: reference.

Publications: *ASH Handbook on Sexual Harassment.* ● *When No Means No.* Book.

★2573★ ASSOCIATION FOR UNION DEMOCRACY - WOMEN'S PROJECT FOR UNION DEMOCRACY
YWCA Bldg.
30 3rd Ave.
Brooklyn, NY 11217
Susan Jennik, Exec.Dir.   PH: (718)855-6650

National. Assists women fighting for job equality within labor unions. Works to increase women's involvement and influence within unions.

★2574★ ASSOCIATION FOR VOLUNTARY SURGICAL CONTRACEPTION - UNITED STATES (AVSC)
79 Madison Ave.
New York, NY 10016   PH: (212)561-8000
Hugo Hoogenboom, Exec.Dir.   FX: (212)779-9439

Founded: 1943. **Staff:** 150. **Languages:** English. **National.** Aim is to give men and women access to safe and effective voluntary surgical contraception. Is concerned with the quality of life on earth and the quality and availability of voluntary surgical contraception services. Supports programs in the U.S. and service delivery and training programs in developing countries. Disseminates information on voluntary surgical contraception. Sponsors research studies on medical, public health, legal, psychological, ethical, and socioeconomic aspects of voluntary sterilization. Promotes safer, simpler techniques in surgical contraception. Fosters, stimulates, and supports voluntary surgical contraception activities in various types of health programs all over the world by providing local medical groups with training equipment and technical assistance. **Libraries:** Type: reference. Holdings: 3,000. Subjects: sterilization and birth control. **Committees:** Medical; Research and Evaluation.

Publications: *AVSC News*, quarterly. Newsletter. Provides information on research, legal issues, and new medical technologies. **ISSN:** 0001-2904. **Circulation:** 3,000.

Conventions/Meetings: annual meeting.

★2575★ ASSOCIATION OF WA-TAN-YE CLUBS
808 N. Kentucky
Mason City, IA 50401
Arlene J. VanHorn, Sec.

Founded: 1921. **Members:** 27. **Languages:** English. **National.** Business and professional women's clubs. Works to increase members' sense of civic responsibility through community service. Provides a forum for exchange between members. "Wa-tan-ye" is a Native American word meaning "foremost." Membership is by invitation only.

Publications: *The Wa-Tan-Yan*, 9/year. Includes information on new community projects.

Conventions/Meetings: annual meeting - always fall.

★2576★ ASSOCIATION FOR WOMEN IN COMPUTING (AWC)
41 Sutter St., Ste. 1006
San Francisco, CA 94104
Cheryl Deichter, Pres.   PH: (415)905-4663

Founded: 1978. **Members:** 650. **Local Groups:** 37. **Languages:** English. **National.** Individuals interested in promoting the education, professional development, and advancement of women in computing. Sponsors seminars at local and national levels. Maintains speakers' bureau; bestows awards; compiles statistics. **Committees:** Technical Review.

Publications: *Directory*, annual. ·

Conventions/Meetings: annual conference, with workshop.

★2577★ ASSOCIATION FOR WOMEN IN DEVELOPMENT (AWID)
Virginia Tech
10 Sandy Hall
Blacksburg, VA 24061-0338   PH: (703)231-3765
Norge W. Jerome, Pres.   FX: (703)231-6741

Founded: 1982. **Members:** 1,067. **Languages:** English. **National.** Individuals and institutions, including government and United Nations agencies, private research and consulting firms, private voluntary agencies, and universities with a focus on international development, particularly as it affects women. Purpose is to ensure the participation of women as full and active partners in a more equitable process of development, and to guarantee them a share of its benefits. Seeks to: heighten public awareness of the interdependence among individuals, institutions, and nations in development; increase research and action by encouraging interaction among scholars, practitioners, and policymakers in women in development; improve communication and education on problems and solutions relating to women in development.

Publications: *AWID Newsletter*, bimonthly. ● *Special Papers Series*. Monograph.

Conventions/Meetings: biennial conference.

★2578★ ASSOCIATION FOR WOMEN GEOSCIENTISTS (AWG)
Macalester Coll. Geology Dept.
1600 Grand Ave.   PH: (612)696-6448
St. Paul, MN 55015-1899   FX: (612)696-6122
Janet L. Wright, Pres.   E-Mail: Internet

Founded: 1977. **Members:** 900. **Membership Dues:** Low income and student, US$20; Professional, US$40; Sustaining, US$55; Institutional, US$100; Corporate, US$500. **Budget:** US$40,000. **Regional Groups:** 18. **Languages:** English. **National.** Women and men geologists, geophysicists, petroleum engineers, geological engineers, hydrogeologists, paleontologists, geochemists, and other geoscientists. Aims to: encourage the participation of women in the geosciences; exchange educational, technical, and professional information; enhance the professional growth and advancement of women in the geosciences. Provides information on opportunities and careers available to women in the geosciences. Conducts workshops and seminars on job hunting techniques, management skills, and career and professional development. Sponsors educational booths and programs at geological society conventions. Operates charitable program; sponsors competitions. Maintains career profiles of women geoscientists, speakers' bureau, and Association for Women Geoscientists Foundation (educational arm). **Computer Services:** Data base; mailing lists. **Committees:** Career Development; Education; Field Trips; Public Affairs.

Publications: *Gaea*, bimonthly. Newsletter. ● *Membership Directory*, annual. ● *Careers in the Geosciences*. Book.

Conventions/Meetings: annual meeting (exhibits).

★2579★ ASSOCIATION FOR WOMEN IN MATHEMATICS (AWM)
4114 Computer and Space Science
  Bldg.
University of Maryland
College Park, MD 20742-2461
Ginny Reinhart, Exec.Dir.   PH: (301)405-7892

Founded: 1971. **Members:** 4,000. **Budget:** US$40,000. **Languages:** English. **National.** Mathematicians employed by universities, government, and private industry; students. Seeks to improve the status of women in the mathematical profession, and to make students aware of opportunities for women in the field. Membership is open to all interested individuals, regardless of sex. Operates resource center at Wellesley College. **Awards:** Annual Louise Hay Award for Contributions to Mathematics Education. ● Periodic Anne T. Schafer Mathematics Prize. ● Periodic Travel Grants. **Committees:** Journals and Speakers; Maternity Leave Policies; Math Education.

Publications: *Association for Women in Mathematics*, bimonthly. Newsletter. Contains articles by and about women in mathematics. **Circulation:** 4,000. **Advertising:** accepted. ● *Directory of Women in the Mathematical Sciences*, periodic. ● *Careers for Women in Mathematics*. Book. ● *Profiles of Women in Mathematics: The Emmy Noether Lectures*. Book.

Conventions/Meetings: semiannual meeting.

★2580★ ASSOCIATION FOR WOMEN PSYCHIATRISTS
PO Box 191079-350
Dallas, TX 75219-0179
Ruth Barnhouse, Contact   PH: (214)855-5104

National. Promotes the interests of women psychiatrists in the United States. Works to improve the status of women within the profession. Provides a forum for information exchange and experience sharing between members.

★2581★ ASSOCIATION FOR WOMEN IN PSYCHOLOGY (AWP)
c/o Angela Rose Gillem
526 W. Sedgwick St.
Philadelphia, PA 19119
Angela Rose Gillem Ph.D., Recorder

Founded: 1969. **Members:** 1,500. **Budget:** US$35,000. **Languages:** English. **National.** Seeks to: end the role that the association feels psychology has had in perpetuating unscientific and unquestioned assumptions about the "natures" of women and men; encourage unbiased psychological research on sex and gender in order to establish facts and expose myths; encourage research and theory directed toward alternative sex-role socialization, child rearing practices, life-styles, and language use; educate and sensitize the science and psychology professions as well as the public to the psychological, social, political, and economic rights of women; combat the oppression of women of color; encourage research on issues of concern to women of color; achieve equality of opportunity for women and men within the profession and science of psychology. Conducts business and professional sessions at meetings of regional psychology associations. Maintains hall of fame, archives, and speakers' bureau. Monitors sexism in APA. **Awards:** Annual Distinguished Publication. ● Annual Women of Color Psychologies Unpublished Manuscript. ● Annual Lesbian Psychologies Unpublished Manuscript. ● Periodic Prize for Student Research on Women and Gender.

Publications: *AWP Membership Directory*, annual. ● *Newsletter*, quarterly. ● *Feminist Mental Health Agenda for the Year 2000*. Book.

Conventions/Meetings: annual conference (exhibits) - always March. ● periodic regional meeting.

★2582★ ASSOCIATION FOR WOMEN IN SCIENCE (AWIS)
1522 K St. NW, Ste. 820
Washington, DC 20005
Catherine Didion, Exec.Dir.
PH: (202)408-0742
TF: (800)886-2947
FX: (202)408-8321

Founded: 1971. **Members:** 3,700. **Local Groups:** 46. **Languages:** English. **National**. Professional women and students in life, physical, and social sciences and engineering. Promotes equal opportunities for women to enter the scientific workforce and to achieve their career goals; provides educational information to women planning careers in science; networks with other women's groups; monitors scientific legislation and the status of women in science. Provides advice and support to women involved in equal opportunity legislation; assists local chapters with programming and support services. Operates AWIS Educational Foundation; promotes appreciation of past accomplishments of women scientists. **Awards:** Annual (scholarship). Recipient: Predoctoral students. **Committees:** Affirmative Action; Education; Legislative.

Publications: *Association for Women in Science*, periodic. Directory. ● *AWIS*, bimonthly. Magazine. Features analytical articles on the status of women in science; includes book reviews; lists employment, grant, and educational opportunities. **ISSN:** 0160-256X. **Circulation:** 4,000. **Advertising:** accepted. ● *Resources for Women in Science Series*, periodic. Book. ● *Gender and Science*. Book. ● *Bibliography of Science Education Resources*. Book. ● *Grants-at-a-Glance*. Book. ● *Careers in Science*. Book.

Conventions/Meetings: periodic meeting.

★2583★ ASSOCIATION FOR WOMEN IN SOCIAL WORK
University of Pennsylvania
Women's Center
119 Houston Hall
3417 Spruce St.
Philadelphia, PA 19104-6303
Elena M. DiLapi, Director
PH: (215)898-8611

National. Promotes the interests of women involved in social work and social services. Works to advance the status of women in the profession. Addresses issues affecting women in social work.

★2584★ ASSOCIATION OF WOMEN SOIL SCIENTISTS (AWSS)
c/o Margie Faber
8 Windham Rd.
Enfield, CT 06082
Margie Faber, Sec.-Treas.
PH: (203)688-7725

Founded: 1981. **Members:** 200. **Languages:** English. **National**. Women who are soil scientists, soil conservationists, soil agriculturists, research scientists, professors, and students. Identifies women in the field and provides them with communication opportunities, technical and career information, assistance, and encouragement.

Publications: *Membership Directory*, periodic. ● *Newsletter*, 3/year.

Conventions/Meetings: periodic meeting.

★2585★ ASSOCIATION FOR WOMEN IN SPORTS MEDIA (AWSM)
PO Box 4205
Mililani, HI 96789
Cathy Henkel, Pres.
PH: (800)343-6319

Founded: 1986. **Members:** 500. **Languages:** English. **National**. Women sportswriters, copy editors, broadcasters and sports information directors. Supports and fosters advancement of women involved in sports media. Sponsors educational programs; awards college journalists summer internships.

Publications: *AWSM Newsletter*, quarterly. **Circulation:** 500. **Advertising:** not accepted.

Conventions/Meetings: annual meeting.

★2586★ ASSOCIATION FOR WOMEN VETERINARIANS (AWV)
32205 Allison Dr.
Union City, CA 94587
Chris Stone Payne D.V.M., Sec.
PH: (510)471-8379

Founded: 1947. **Members:** 625. **Languages:** English. **National**. Women veterinarians; students of veterinary medicine. Seeks to advance the status of women in veterinary medicine. **Awards:** Annual AWV Service Award. ● Annual Outstanding Woman Veterinarian. ● Periodic (scholarship). **Computer Services:** Data base, members. **Committees:** Archives; Historical; Outstanding Woman Veterinarian; Publicity; Survey.

Publications: *AWV Bulletin*, quarterly. **Advertising:** accepted. ● *Roster of Women Veterinarians*, periodic. Directory.

Conventions/Meetings: annual meeting.

★2587★ ASSOCIATION OF WOMEN'S MUSIC AND CULTURE
2124 Kittredge St., No. 104
Berkeley, CA 94704
Jim Cruise, Contact
PH: (415)655-4334

National. Feminist professional organization engaged in the enhancement of women's music and culture. Offers support, recognition, educational opportunity, networking, and resources for women as individuals, businesses, and organizations.

★2588★ ASTRAEA NATIONAL LESBIAN ACTION FOUNDATION
666 Broadway, Ste. 520
New York, NY 10012
Katherine T. Acey, Exec.Dir.
PH: (212)529-8021

Founded: 1977. **National**. Multi-cultural organization that seeks to empower lesbian women and girls through financial and organizational support. Supports projects that actively work to eliminate all forms of oppression that affect lesbians in the United States. Sponsors programs that encourages the work of lesbian writers.

★2589★ AUXILIARIES OF OUR LADY OF THE CENACLE (AOLC)
3820 W. Pine Blvd.
St. Louis, MO 63108-3308
Sr. Agnes Sauer, Regional Dir.
PH: (314)535-2461

Founded: 1878. **Members:** 140. **Regional Groups:** 2. **Languages:** English. **National**. Catholic women of all ages and professions interested in a religious, but fully secular life. Vows are received through the Congregation of Our Lady of the Retreat in the Cenacle, and are renewed annually. Members serve God through their own professions, talents, lifestyles, or other apostolic works. Promotes apostolic and personal spiritual growth and development. Activities are usually church-related.

Publications: *AC Highlights*, quarterly. Newsletter. ● *Directory*, semiannual. ● *Feuilles de Liaison des Auxiliares de Notre Dame Du Cenacle*, bimonthly. Newsletter.

Conventions/Meetings: semiannual meeting.

★2590★ BAHA'I INTERNATIONAL COMMUNITY
866 United Nations Plaza, Ste. 120
New York, NY 10017

Languages: English. **Multinational**. Works to achieve equality between men and women. Encourages women's participation in political and social life. Believes equality between both sexes is a prerequisite to world peace. Offers health and educational programs; conducts training in literacy, crafts, and agriculture.

Publications: *One Country* (in English), quarterly. Newsletter. ● *Journal of Baha'i Studies* (in English), quarterly.

Conventions/Meetings: periodic seminar.

★2591★ BALTIC WOMEN'S COUNCIL - UNITED STATES (BWC)
c/o Helga Ozolins
414 Abington Pl.
East Meadow, NY 11554
Helga Ozolins, Pres.   PH: (718)672-5558

Founded: 1947. **Languages:** English. **Multinational.** Estonian, Latvian, and Lithuanian women's clubs in the U.S. and overseas. To unite the women of Estonian, Latvian, and Lithuanian origin; to preserve native culture; to assist with the development of their countries of birth; to promote the spirit of Baltic solidarity and friendship among the young generations. Sponsors literary, arts, and musical events. Works for reunification of Baltic refugee families. **Divisions:** Estonian; Latvian; Lithuanian.

Conventions/Meetings: annual - always March. New York, NY, United States.

★2592★ BAPTIST WORLD ALLIANCE - WOMEN'S DEPARTMENT
6733 Curran St.
McLean, VA 22101   PH: (703)790-8980
Beth H. MacClaren, Director   FX: (703)903-9544

Founded: 1951. **Languages:** English. **Multinational.** Women members of churches affiliated with the Baptist World Alliance. Works towards linking Baptist women together worldwide. Aims to evangelize and minister to women. Committed to prayer and practical ministry which will meet basic human needs. Promotes the worldwide Baptist Women's Day of Prayer on the first Monday of each November as a means of encouraging global sympathy and understanding among women. Disseminates information on the educational, economic, and health status of women worldwide. Conduct leadership training for women.

Publications: *Together* (in English and Spanish), semiannual. Newsletter. **Circulation:** 82,000. ● *Together in Leadership*, periodic.

Conventions/Meetings: quinquennial conference - 1995 July, Buenos Aires, Argentina. ● congress - 3/year.

★2593★ BASS'N GAL
PO Box 13925
2007 Roosevelt
Arlington, TX 76013   PH: (817)265-6214
Sugar Ferris, Pres.   FX: (817)265-6290

Founded: 1976. **Members:** 26,376. **Staff:** 6. **Budget:** US$150,000. **State Groups:** 88. **Languages:** English. **National.** Women's organizations interested in the sport of bass fishing. Objectives include: to bring together women anglers of the U.S; to help improve members' skills as anglers through the exchange of techniques and ideas; to stimulate public awareness of bass fishing as a major sport and a relaxing pastime. Hopes to educate and introduce youth to the pleasures of fishing; encourages concern for the preservation of U.S. natural resources, and provides organized moral and political support and encouragement to state Fish and Game Departments. Strives to bring an end to discrimination against women in participation of certain outdoor activities, dispelling old beliefs that women do not have the skill or experience to compete with their male counterparts on the same level. Conducts youth fishing projects through affiliated club programs and local level seminars by affiliated clubs.

Publications: *Bass'n Gal*, 6/year. Magazine.

Conventions/Meetings: bimonthly competition.

★2594★ BAY AREA PHYSICIANS FOR HUMAN RIGHTS (BAPHR)
4111 18th St., No. 6
San Francisco, CA 94114   PH: (415)558-9353
Leonard Simpson M.D., Pres.   FX: (415)558-0466

Founded: 1977. **Members:** 350. **Budget:** US$50,000. **Languages:** English. **National.** Graduates of and students in approved schools of medicine and osteopathy; dentist and podiatrists. Objectives are: to improve the quality of medical care for gay and lesbian patients; to educate physicians, both gay and nongay, in the special problems of gay and lesbian patients; to educate the public about health care needs of the homosexual; to maintain liaison with public officials about gay and lesbian health concerns; to offer the gay and lesbian physician support through social functions and consciousness-raising groups. Sponsors research into medical problems and issues which are of special interest to homosexual patients. Provides medical and physician referral service and monthly educational programs; operates speakers' bureau; compiles statistics; bestows awards. Membership is concentrated in the San Francisco, CA Bay Area. **Committees:** Education; Journal Club; Public Relations; Scientific Affairs; Social Concerns; Support.

Publications: *BAPHRON*, bimonthly. Newsletter. Concerned with medical-related human rights issues, especially gay and lesbian rights and public policy on AIDS. **Circulation:** 1,000. **Advertising:** accepted. ● *Medical Evaluation of Persons at Risk of HIV Infection.* Monograph.

Conventions/Meetings: annual conference (exhibits).

★2595★ BEREAVED PARENTS (BP)
PO Box 3147
Scottsdale, AZ 85271   PH: (602)945-0342
Lewis Bove, Pres.   FX: (602)423-0198

Founded: 1987. **Members:** 110. **State Groups:** 6. **Local Groups:** 1. **Languages:** English. **National.** Parents of children who have died during autoerotic asphyxiation (AEA); medical professors; clergy. (AEA involves voluntary deprivation of oxygen, at the time of sexual climax; since AEA is usually performed alone, it often results in accidental death.) Conducts research and provides information on AEA and to provide counseling to families affected by AEA. Offers educational programs; operates charitable program. **Alternate name::** The Bereaved.

Conventions/Meetings: annual meeting.

★2596★ BETA SIGMA PHI
1800 W. 91st Pl.
Box 8500
Kansas City, MO 64114   PH: (816)444-6800
John J. Ross, Pres.   TF: (800)821-3989
          FX: (816)333-6206

Founded: 1931. **Members:** 250,000. **Staff:** 63. **Languages:** English. **National.** Social, service, and cultural society - business and professional women and housewives, over age 18. Sponsors writing competitions. Operates charitable program. **Awards:** Annual Walter W. Ross Scholarship. **Telecommunication Services:** Electronic bulletin board.

Publications: *Chapter Listing*, annual. Directory. ● *The Torch of Beta Sigma Phi*, 10/year. Newsletter.

Conventions/Meetings: annual regional meeting.

★2597★ BIOPHYSICAL SOCIETY - COMMITTEE ON PROFESSIONAL OPPORTUNITIES FOR WOMEN (CPOW)
9650 Rockville Pike
Bethesda, MD 20614
Joyce Jentof, Chair

Members: 200. **Languages:** English. **National.** Professionals in biophysics and related fields working to improve the status of women in the profession. Investigates women's needs; identifies employment, educational, and financial aid opportunities; and provides opportunities for women to exchange ideas. Lobbies the parent organization on women's issues.

Publications: *Spectrum* (in English).

★2598★ BIRTHRIGHT, UNITED STATES OF AMERICA
686 N. Broad St.   PH: (609)848-1819
Woodbury, NJ 08096   TF: (800)848-5683
Denise F. Cocciolone, Exec.Dir.   FX: (609)848-2380

Founded: 1968. **Regional Groups:** 38. **Local Groups:** 617. **Languages:** English. **National.** Groups operating independently in the U.S. to help pregnant women find alternatives to abortion. All chapters are private and interdenominational, supported by contributions, and operated by volunteers. Operates childbirth education classes, telephone counseling, and parenting programs. Maintains speakers' bureau.

Publications: *The National Pulse*, bimonthly. Newsletter.

Conventions/Meetings: annual meeting - always June.

★2599★ BLACK AMERICANS FOR LIFE
419 7th St. NW, Ste. 500
Washington, DC 20004   PH: (202)626-8833

Languages: English. **National.** Individuals working to educate the black community on pro-life and pro-family issues. Promotes alternatives to abortion for women with crisis pregnancies; strives to be a visible presence defending the rights of the unborn in the black community. Asserts that black women are twice as likely as white women to have abortions; believes that abortions are counterproductive to advances made through civil rights efforts. Provides information on resources and available speakers.

★2600★ BLACK, INDIAN, HISPANIC, AND ASIAN WOMEN IN ACTION
  (BIHA)
122 W. Franklin Ave., Ste. 306
Minneapolis, MN 55404
Alice O. Lynch, Contact   PH: (612)870-1193

Founded: 1983. **Members:** 200. **Staff:** 3. **Budget:** US$200,000. **Languages:** English. **National.** Strives to empower Black, Indian, Hispanic, and Asian communities through implementation of educational projects. Acts as an advocate for communities of color in the areas of family violence, chemical dependence, education, and physical and mental health. Works for social change, the health of the family and advancement of socioeconomic status.

Publications: *Unison*, quarterly. Newsletter. **Circulation:** 1,000. **Advertising:** not accepted.

Conventions/Meetings: annual meeting.

★2601★ BLACK PROFESSIONAL WOMEN'S NETWORK
123 E. 44th St., Ste. 2E
New York, NY 10036
Paulette M. Owens, President   PH: (212)302-2924

National. Promotes the interests of and defends the rights of professional African American women in the United States. Provides a forum for information exchange and experience sharing between members.

★2602★ BLACK WOMEN IN CHURCH AND SOCIETY (BWCS)
c/o Interdenominational Theological
  Center
671 Beckwith St. SW
Atlanta, GA 30314   PH: (404)527-7740
Jacquelyn Grant Ph.D., Dir.   FX: (404)527-0901

Founded: 1982. **Staff:** 2. **Languages:** English. **National.** Women in ministry, both ordained and laity. Seeks to provide: structured activities and support systems for black women whose goals include participating in leadership roles in church and society; a platform for communication between laywomen and clergywomen. Conducts research into questions and issues pivotal to black women in church and society. Sponsors charitable programs; compiles statistics. Maintains a research/resource center. **Libraries:** Type: reference. Subjects: black theology, liberation, and feminism. **Computer Services:** Mailing lists. **Programs:** Black Women in Ministry Internship.

Publications: *Black Women in Ministry*, quadrennial. Directory.

Conventions/Meetings: annual meeting. ● semiannual seminar.

★2603★ BLACK WOMEN ORGANIZED FOR EDUCATIONAL
  DEVELOPMENT (BWOED)
518 17th St., Ste. 202
Oakland, CA 94612   PH: (510)763-9501
Dezie Woods-Jones, Exec.Dir.   FX: (510)763-4327

Founded: 1984. **Languages:** English. **National.** Fosters self-sufficiency in and encourages empowerment of low-income and socially disadvantaged women by establishing and maintaining programs that improve their social and economic well-being. Sponsors mentor program for junior high-age young women in low-income urban areas; offers support groups, workshops, and seminars. Maintains Black Women's Resource Center, an information and referral service for African American women and youth.

Publications: *BWOED Newsletter*, quarterly.

Conventions/Meetings: periodic seminar.

★2604★ BLACK WOMEN IN PUBLISHING (BWIP)
PO Box 6275, F.D.R. Sta.
New York, NY 10150
Dolores Gordon, Pres.   PH: (212)772-5951

Founded: 1979. **Languages:** English. **National.** Women designers, editors, financial analysts, freelancers, personnel directors, photographers, production managers, authors, entrepreneurs, and publicists within the print industry. A networking and support group whose purpose is to encourage minorities interested in all sectors of the print industry, including book, newspaper, and magazine publishing. Promotes the image of minorities working in all phases of the book, newspaper, and magazine industries; recognizes achievements of minorities in the media. Works for a free and responsible press. Facilitates the exchange of ideas and information among members, especially regarding career planning and job security. Keeps members informed about the publishing industry and their impact on it. Encourages and works to maintain high professional standards in publishing. Collaborates with other organizations in striving to improve the status of women and minorities. Sponsors lectures, panel discussions, seminars, workshops, radio talk shows, and other programs on topics such as computers in publishing, magazine publishing, trends in multicultural literature for children, career paths publishing, getting work published, starting a publishing firm, author readings, awards presentations, and women and stress. Organizes social events. Maintains biographical archives, placement service, and a resume bank in collaboration with major corporations. **Committees:** Career and Educational Services; Public Relations; Speakers.

Publications: *Interface*, bimonthly. Newsletter. **Advertising:** not accepted.

Conventions/Meetings: annual. ● monthly meeting.

★2605★ BLACK WOMEN IN SISTERHOOD FOR ACTION
PO Box 1592
Washington, DC 20013
Verna S. Cook, President

Founded: 1980. **National.** Works to develop and promote alternative strategies for educational and career development for African American women in the United States. Provides a forum for information exchange and experience sharing among members.

★2606★ BLACK WOMEN UNITED
6551 Loisdale Ct., Ste. 714
Springfield, VA 22150
Virginia Williams, President   PH: (703)922-5757

Founded: 1985. **Members:** 100. **Languages:** English. **National.** African American women working for equality. Lobbies government for black women's needs.

★2607★ BLACK WOMEN FOR WAGES FOR HOUSEWORK - UNITED STATES
PO Box 86681
Los Angeles, CA 90086-1698
Margaret Prescod, Co-Founder   PH: (213)221-1698

National. Network of black women working to dismantle the "hierarchy of work and wealth by refusing forced labor and claiming reparations for slavery, imperialism, and unwaged work." Campaign issues include racism, immigration controls, welfare, low wages, rape, prostitution, police accountability, civil and human rights, gays/lesbians, peace, and ecology.

★2608★ BLACK WOMEN'S AGENDA
208 Auburn Ave. NE
Atlanta, GA 30303
Dolly D. Adams, President   PH: (404)524-8279

Founded: 1977. **National.** Promotes equal opportunites for African American women in all areas of society. Educates the public about economic, social, and civil liberties issues relevant to the lives of African American women. Recommends policy changes to government to secure equal rights for African American women and their families.

★2609★ BLACK WOMEN'S EDUCATIONAL ALLIANCE (BWEA)
6625 Greene St.
Philadelphia, PA 19119
Deidre Farmbey, Pres.

Founded: 1976. **Members:** 300. **Local Groups:** 2. **Languages:** English. **National.** Active and retired women in the field of education. Seeks a strong union among members in order to foster their intellectual and professional growth. Conducts public awareness programs to improve educational standards and delivery of educational services; works for equal opportunities for women. Maintains speakers' bureau; conducts instructional seminars and workshops. **Awards:** Periodic (scholarship). **Committees:** Career Mobility; Political Education; Scholarship.

Publications: *BWEA Bulletin*, periodic. ● *BWEA Newsletter*, semiannual.

Conventions/Meetings: biennial meeting.

★2610★ BLACK WOMEN'S NETWORK (BWN)
PO Box 12072
Milwaukee, WI 53212
Joan Prince, Pres.   PH: (414)562-4500

Founded: 1979. **Members:** 56. **Languages:** English. **National.** Black professional women organized to improve the political, economic, and educational conditions of minority women. Offers support services and networking opportunities to address issues affecting African-American women.

Publications: *Cross Roads*, quarterly. Newsletter.

Conventions/Meetings: annual meeting.

★2611★ BLUE STAR MOTHERS OF AMERICA (BSM)
c/o Margaret Wood
119 W. 2nd St., No. 706
Xenia, OH 45385
Margaret Wood, Pres.   PH: (513)372-9577

Founded: 1942. **Members:** 2,200. **State Groups:** 6. **Local Groups:** 166. **Languages:** English. **National.**

Publications: *Blue Star Mother Yearbook*.

Conventions/Meetings: annual conference - always October.

★2612★ B'NAI B'RITH WOMEN (BBW)
1828 L St. NW, Ste. 250
Washington, DC 20036   PH: (202)857-1300
Elaine K. Binder, Exec.Dir.   FX: (202)857-1380

Founded: 1897. **Members:** 100,000. **Regional Groups:** 12. **Local Groups:** 600. **Languages:** English. **Multinational.** Jewish women's organizations. Engages in activities that support women and their families through public affairs advocacy and national and local education projects. Community activities include human relations, caregiving for older adults, philanthropy, and youth projects. Founded and maintains a home for emotionally disturbed boys in Jerusalem, Israel. **Awards:** Biennial B'nai B'rith Women Perlman. **Formerly:** (1957) Women's Supreme Council.

Publications: *Women's World*, 4/year. Newsletter. Includes book reviews. **ISSN:** 0043-759X. **Circulation:** 100,000. **Advertising:** not accepted.

Conventions/Meetings: biennial convention - 1994, Orlando, FL, United States.

★2613★ BREAST CANCER ADVISORY CENTER (BCAC)
PO Box 224
Kensington, MD 20895
Rose Kushner, Exec.Dir.   FX: (301)949-1132

Founded: 1975. **Staff:** 2. **Languages:** English. **National.** Medical service group for people, mostly women, with breast cancer patients. Makes referrals; disseminates information; gives lectures. **Libraries:** Type: reference. Subjects: breast cancer.

Publications: *Alternatives: New Developments in Breast Cancer*. Book.

★2614★ BUDDHIST CHURCHES OF AMERICA FEDERATION OF BUDDHIST WOMEN'S ASSOCIATIONS (BCAFBWA)
c/o Buddhist Churches of America
1710 Octavia St.
San Francisco, CA 94109   PH: (415)776-5600
Rev. Seikan Fukuma, Exec.Dir.   FX: (415)771-6293

Founded: 1952. **Members:** 15,000. **Languages:** English. **National.** Women members of Buddhist churches of Jodo Shinshu faith. Promotes American Buddhism through publications, community service, fundraising, and recreational and educational programs. Makes Annual contributions to welfare organizations.

Conventions/Meetings: annual meeting.

★2615★ BUSINESS AND PROFESSIONAL WOMEN'S FOUNDATION (BPWF)
2012 Massachusetts Ave. NW   PH: (202)293-1200
Washington, DC 20036   FX: (202)861-0298

Founded: 1956. **Languages:** English. **National.** Dedicated to improving the economic status of working women through their integration into all occupations. Conducts and supports research on women and work, with special emphasis on economic issues. Sponsors BPW Foundation Loan Fund for Women in Engineering and BPW/Sears-Roebuck Loan Fund for Women in Graduate Business Studies. Maintains Marguerite Rawalt Resource Center of 20,000 items on economic issues involving women and work and provides public reference and referral service. Established by BPW/USA, the National Federation of Business and Professional Women's Clubs. **Awards:** Periodic LenaLake Forrest Fellowship. ● Periodic Sally Batter Memorial Fund for Latina Research. ● Periodic (scholarship). Recipient: women in health professions.

Publications: *Annual Report*.

Conventions/Meetings: annual meeting - always July.

★2616★ BYELORUSSIAN-AMERICAN WOMEN ASSOCIATION (BAWA)
146 Sussex Dr.
Manhasset, NY 11030
Vera Bartul, Pres.   PH: (516)627-9195

Founded: 1956. **Members:** 300. **State Groups:** 4. **Languages:** English. **Multinational.** Women of Byelorussian birth or descent and those related by marriage to Byelorussian-Americans. Aims to preserve national identity, cultural heritage, and traditions. Extends relief to needy Byelorussians at home and abroad in the form of packages and financial contributions. Organizes and supports school programs of Byelorussian supplementary schools. Also organizes shows and exhibitions of fine arts and ethnic crafts. Offers Byelorussian language classes.

Publications: *Woman's Page in Belarus*, periodic. Newsletter.

Conventions/Meetings: biennial conference, with symposium.

★2617★ CAMPING WOMEN (CW)
7623 Southbreeze Dr.
Sacramento, CA 95828
Gail Sanabria, Pres.   PH: (916)689-9326

Founded: 1976. **Members:** 200. **Local Groups:** 6. **Languages:** English. **National.** Individuals seeking to enhance women's camping skills; women interested in camping, backpacking, hiking, canoeing, white water rafting, biking, skiing, birdwatching, and other outdoor activities. Objectives are to: provide opportunities for women to experience an outdoor program in a supportive atmosphere; help women develop a sense of "at-homeness" in the outdoors; develop women's camping abilities and leadership skills. Provides skills training in campcraft, watercraft, snow camping, and leadership. Bestows awards and certificates.

Publications: *Camping Women Trails*, 10/year. Newsletter. **Advertising:** accepted. ● *Membership Directory*, annual.

Conventions/Meetings: annual invitational camp - always August.

★2618★ CAMPUS MINISTRY WOMEN (CMW)
802 Monroe
Ann Arbor, MI 48104
Ann Marie Coleman, Treas.   PH: (313)662-5189

Founded: 1970. **Members:** 250. **Languages:** English. **National.** Protestant, Catholic, and Jewish women; interested men are associate members. To serve as a network to empower women to be effective ministers in college and university settings. Provides professional and educational resources to women as they locate and acquire campus ministry positions and develop their skills and careers. Promotes interfaith cooperation; enables women to participate in the development and teaching of a feminist theology reflecting interfaith awareness. Serves as a forum for sharing campus ministry programs and resources. Supports women who are victims of racism, religious bigotry, or discrimination because of their sexual preference; allots money for projects for such women. Advocates hiring and promoting women in religious and campus structures; provides grievance and crisis intervention. Assists in funding local projects by and for women. **Awards:** Periodic (scholarship).

Publications: *Directory*, periodic. ● *Newsletter*, 5-6/year.

Conventions/Meetings: annual conference. ● periodic meeting.

★2619★ CAPITOL HILL WOMEN'S POLITICAL CAUCUS (CHWPC)
Longworth House Office Bldg.
PO Box 599
Washington, DC 20515
Liz Ryan, Co-Chwm.   PH: (202)986-0994

Founded: 1971. **Members:** 300. **Languages:** English. **National.** A chapter of the National Women's Political Caucus. Individuals dedicated to equal rights and equal opportunities for all people. Purpose is to promote and increase the election, appointment, and participation of women in local, state, and national political and governing processes. Works to increase the political power of women and to combat the inequities of employment and salaries for women on Capitol Hill. Believes equal political and governmental participation will enhance the quality of life for all Americans. Monitors and encourages the enactment of legislation beneficial to women, including the Equal Rights Amendment; acts as clearinghouse of legislative information. Sponsors job seminars and programs in personal and professional development. Promotes national organization's goals and works closely with NWPC in its efforts. Compiles statistics; operates speakers' bureau. **Task Forces:** Candidate Support; Democratic; Fundraising; Sexual Harassment; Job Service; Legislation; Networking; Press; Republican; Legislation; Networking; Press.

Publications: *Directory*, annual. ● *Equal Times Newsletter*, bimonthly. ● *The Last Plantation: How Women Fare on Capitol Hill.* Book.

Conventions/Meetings: monthly meeting.

★2620★ CASA PENSAMIENTO DE MUJER
Degetau No. 55
Aibonito, PR 00609   PH: (809)735-3200
Aida Iris Cruz Alicea, Coord.   FX: (809)735-3200

Founded: 1990. **Members:** 17. **Staff:** 2. **Budget:** US$44,800. **Languages:** English, Spanish. **National.** Works to raise public awareness of domestic violence, rape, and other crimes against women. Offers emotional and legal counselling to abused women. Conducts community education programs; disseminates information. **Libraries:** Type: reference.

Publications: *Pensamiento de Mujer* (in Spanish), quarterly. Bulletin. ● *SIDA un Mal de Nuestros Tiempos* (in Spanish). Monograph. ● *Que es el Norplant?* (in Spanish). Monograph.

★2621★ CATALYST
250 Park Ave. S
New York, NY 10003
Felice N. Schwartz, Pres.   PH: (212)777-8900

Founded: 1962. **Staff:** 43. **Budget:** US$2,300,000. **Languages:** English. **National.** A national research and advisory organization that helps corporations foster career and leadership development of women. Works to: identify and analyze human resource issues such as impediments to women's progress in the corporation, balancing work and family, and managing a diverse work force. Develops cost-effective and transferable models that help employers manage the two-gender work force. Services include: Corporate Board Resource to assist employers in locating qualified women for board directorships; speakers' bureau; Information Center, which holds current statistics, print media, and research materials on women in business. Organization is unrelated to another group of the same name (see separate entry).

Publications: *Perspective on Current Corporate Issues*, monthly. Newsletter.

Conventions/Meetings: annual dinner.

★2622★ CATHOLIC DAUGHTERS OF THE AMERICAS (CDA)
10 W. 71st St.
New York, NY 10023
Lorraine McMahon, Exec.Sec.   PH: (212)877-3041

Founded: 1903. **Members:** 145,000. **Staff:** 10. **State Groups:** 35. **Local Groups:** 1,531. **Languages:** English. **National.** Society of Catholic women. Supports religious and charitable projects; conducts study and discussion groups and poetry, essay, art, and poster contests. **Awards:** Periodic (scholarship). Recipient: teachers. **Committees:** Apostolate; Community; Renewal; Youth.

Publications: *Share*, quarterly. Magazine.

Conventions/Meetings: biennial meeting - always July. 1994, Des Moines, IA, United States.

★2623★ CATHOLICS FOR A FREE CHOICE (CFFC)
1436 U St. NW, No. 301
Washington, DC 20009   PH: (202)986-6093
Frances Kissling, Pres.   FX: (202)332-7995

Founded: 1972. **Budget:** US$1,200,000. **Languages:** English. **National.** Catholics within the Roman Catholic church who support the right to legal reproductive health care, especially to family planning and abortion. Goal is to preserve the right of women's choices in childbearing and child rearing. Advocates social and economic programs for women, families, and children. Engages in public education on being Catholic and pro-choice. **Libraries:** Type: reference.

Publications: *Conscience: A Newsjournal of Prochoice Catholic Opinion*, quarterly. Magazine. Serves as a forum for dialogue on ethical questions related to human reproduction; contains book reviews. **ISSN:** 0740-6835. **Circulation:** 8,000. **Advertising:** accepted.

Conventions/Meetings: periodic meeting (exhibits).

★2624★ CATHOLICS UNITED FOR LIFE (CUL)
c/o Dennis Musk
3050 Gap Knob Rd.
New Hope, KY 40052   PH: (502)325-3061
Dennis Musk, Treas.   FX: (502)325-3091

Founded: 1975. **Languages:** English. **National.** Disseminates information on Catholic moral and social teachings regarding family life, marriage, and the value of human life. Provides speakers to family life, pro-life, or natural family planning conventions; suggests alternatives to abortion; teaches techniques of Sidewalk Counseling, through which individuals conduct legal vigils outside of abortion centers. Maintains chapel and holds daily services. **Libraries:** Type: reference. Holdings: 10,000. Subjects: theology, history, papal teachings, and hagiology (literature dealing with venerated persons or writings).

Publications: *Newsletter*, every 6 weeks. **Circulation:** 100,000.

Conventions/Meetings: periodic regional meeting.

★2625★ CENTER FOR ADVANCEMENT OF SOMALI WOMEN AND
          CHILDREN (CASWC)
1025 Vermont Ave. NW, Ste. 920   PH: (202)347-3507
Washington, DC 20005   FX: (202)347-3418

Founded: 1992. **Budget:** US$100,300. **Languages:** English. **National.** Women working to rehabilitate Somalia's infrastructure after its destruction by civil war. Aims to: restore sense of well being to Somali women and children; improve health care through education and preventative measures; enhance financial status through loans and employment opportunities; and provide counselling. Plans to rebuild the Women's Center in Hargeisa.

★2626★ CENTER FOR THE AMERICAN WOMAN AND POLITICS
          (CAWP)
Eagleton Inst. of Politics
Rutgers University
90 Clifton Ave.
New Brunswick, NJ 08901   PH: (908)828-2210
Ruth B. Mandel, Dir.   FX: (908)932-6778

Founded: 1971. **Staff:** 8. **Languages:** English. **National.** Research, education, and public service center that aims to develop and disseminate information about U.S. women's political participation and to encourage women's involvement in public life. Sponsors workshops and courses. **Libraries:** Type: reference. Holdings: books, periodicals. Subjects: women in politics. **Computer Services:** Information services, women in public office.

Publications: *CAWP News & Notes*, 3/year. Newsletter. Reports on events, organizations, and news related to women in politics and public leadership. **Advertising:** not accepted. ● *Subscriber Information Services*, 3/year.

Magazine. Contains fact sheets, reports, and timely information on the political status of women.

Conventions/Meetings: periodic conference.

★2627★ CENTER FOR GLOBAL ISSUES AND WOMEN'S
          LEADERSHIP
Douglass College
27 Clifton Ave.
New Brunswick, NJ 08903   PH: (908)932-8782
Charlotte Bunch, Director   FX: (908)932-1180

Founded: 1989. **Members:** 7. **Staff:** 2. **Budget:** US$200,000. **Languages:** English, Spanish. **National.** Seeks to create visibility of women's opinions and perspectives. Works to increase women's participation and influence in decision-making activities nationally and internationally. Fosters collaboration among women leaders worldwide. Conducts activities to raise awareness that "violence against women violates human rights.". **Libraries:** Type: reference. Holdings: periodicals, books. Subjects: violence against women.

Publications: *Women, Violence, and Human Rights* (in English). Booklet. ● *Gender and Violence: A Human Rigths and Development Issue* (in English). Book. ● *International Feminism: Networking Against Female Sexual Slavery* (in English). Book.

Conventions/Meetings: annual meeting - New Brunswick, NJ, United States.

★2628★ CENTER FOR HUMANE OPTIONS IN CHILDBIRTH
          EXPERIENCES (CHOICE)
5426 Madison St.
Hilliard, OH 43026-2418
Abby Kinne, Dir.   PH: (614)263-2229

Founded: 1977. **Members:** 1,200. **Local Groups:** 1. **Languages:** English. **National.** Medical professionals, paraprofessionals, and interested individuals. Purpose is to teach and encourage parents, parents-to-be, groups, and interested individuals working in family-oriented childbirth in hospital birth centers and out-of-hospital situations. Trains and certifies attendants to attend or coach births. Acts as consumer advocate for hospital births. Services include: medical referrals; childbirth education classes; supplementary prenatal care. Sponsors community educational programs; operates speakers' bureau; compiles statistics. **Libraries:** Type: lending.

★2629★ CENTER FOR LESBIAN AND GAY STUDIES (CLAGS)
CUNY Graduate Center
33 W. 42 St.
New York, NY 10036
Martin Duberman, Exec. Offcr.   PH: (212)642-1600

Founded: 1986. **Members:** 1,300. **Languages:** English. **National.** Promotes lesbian/gay studies at the University level. Encourages the development of courses and degree programs in lesbian/gay studies and history; works to recognize the contributions of homosexuals in the arts and sciences. Maintains speakers' bureau and lesbian/gay collection at The Mina Rees Library of The Graduate School, City University of New York. Plans to produce publications; conduct surveys; provide courses, research grants, and bestows awards in the field of Lesbian/Gay studies.

Publications: *Directory*, periodic.

Conventions/Meetings: periodic conference.

★2630★ CENTER FOR THE PACIFIC-ASIAN FAMILY
543 N. Fairfax, Rm. 108
Los Angeles, CA 90036   PH: (213)653-4045

National. Works to improve the welfare of Asian families living in the United States. Coordinates social activities.

★2631★ CENTER FOR POPULATION OPTIONS (CPO)
1025 Vermont Ave. NW, Ste. 210
Washington, DC 20005   PH: (202)347-5700
Judith Senderowitz, Exec.Dir. & Pres.   FX: (202)347-2263

Founded: 1980. **Staff:** 30. **Budget:** US$2,000,000. **Languages:** English. **National.** Objectives are to: reduce the incidence of unintended teenage pregnancy and childbearing and promote adolescent health through education; to prevent the proliferation of the human immunodeficiency virus (HIV) among adolescents; motivate teens to think and act responsibly about birth control and parenting; conduct programs and advocacy campaigns to assure minors' access to family planning information and services. Provides technical assistance on program planning, implementation, and evaluation of sexuality education in the U.S. and, through International Clearinghouse on Adolescent Fertility, to health, education, and social service workers worldwide. Operates Support Center for School-Based Clinics and media project. Monitors legislative activities for various organizations concerned with youth issues. Conducts research to evaluate promising prevention strategies. **Libraries:** Type: reference. Holdings: 2,500. Subjects: sexual education, family planning, and other adolescent fertility-related issues. **Awards:** .

Publications: *Clinic News*, quarterly. Newsletter. ● *Options*, quarterly. Newsletter. ● *Passages* (in English, French, and Spanish), quarterly. Magazine.

Conventions/Meetings: semiannual meeting - always fall.

★2632★ CENTER FOR POPULATION OPTIONS' MEDIA PROJECT
(CPOMP)
3733 Motor Ave., Ste. 204
Los Angeles, CA 90034   PH: (310)559-5700
Jennifer Daves, Dir.   FX: (310)599-5784

Founded: 1983. **Staff:** 3. **Budget:** US$300,000. **Languages:** English. **National.** Serves as an advisory and information resource for the entertainment industry to encourage positive and relevant messages about family planning, sexuality, and reproductive health, especially in programming directed toward adolescents. Conducts research and charitable programs. Operates speakers' bureau. A project of the Center for Population Options. **Awards:** Annual Media Awards.

★2633★ CENTER FOR REPRODUCTIVE LAW AND POLICY (CRLP)
120 Wall St.
New York, NY 10005   PH: (212)514-5534
Janet Benshoof, Pres.   FX: (212)514-5538

Founded: 1992. **Staff:** 20. **Languages:** English. **National.** Reproductive rights attorneys and activists united to secure women's reproductive freedoms in the U.S. and around the world. Is currently working as lead counsel in challenging restrictive abortion laws in Guam, Louisiana, Mississippi, North Dakota, Pennsylvania, Tennessee, and Utah. Also focuses on other aspects of health law, including the rights of pregnant women. Disseminates information on maintaining women's reproductive rights to policy makers, governmental agencies, private institutions, medical and health organizations, and the public. Maintains speakers' bureau. **Libraries:** Type: reference.

Publications: *Reproductive Freedom News*, biweekly. Newsletter. **Circulation:** 7,000. **Advertising:** not accepted.

★2634★ CENTER FOR THE STUDY, EDUCATION, AND
ADVANCEMENT OF WOMEN
University of California, Berkeley
Bldg. T-9, Rm. 112
Berkeley, CA 94720   PH: (415)642-4786

Founded: 1972. **National.** Promotes the educational and career interests of women in the United States. Conducts programs that address issues affecting women in education and career development.

★2635★ CENTER FOR THE STUDY OF PARENT INVOLVEMENT
(CSPI)
JFK University
370 Camino Pablo
Orinda, CA 94563   PH: (510)254-0110
Daniel Safran Ph.D., Dir.   FX: (510)254-4870

Founded: 1973. **Budget:** US$150,000. **Languages:** English. **National.** Collects and disseminates information on parent involvement; brings parent leaders, educators, and parent/community workers together; provides consultation in planning, training, and evaluating parent involvement. Offers workshops for teachers to prepare them to work with parents in their roles as volunteers, decision-makers, and advocates for their children; also sponsors workshops for parents, teachers, administrators, counselors, and other human service workers on parenting and family development issues. Works with federal, state, and local education agencies on issues such as teacher preparation, family involvement in education, and family and community outreach. **Libraries:** Type: reference.

Conventions/Meetings: annual conference.

★2636★ CENTER FOR WOMEN POLICY STUDIES (CWPS)
2000 P St. NW, Ste. 508
Washington, DC 20036   PH: (202)872-1770
Leslie R. Wolfe, Exec.Dir.   FX: (202)296-8962

Founded: 1972. **Membership Dues:** Associate, US$50. **Staff:** 8. **Languages:** English. **National.** Purpose is to educate the public and policymakers regarding issues of women's equity. Conducts studies of such issues as rape and domestic violence, occupational segregation and its roots in education, Social Security equity for women, and sexual harassment in the workplace. Conducts programs such as Educational Equity Policy Studies on math, science, and technology education for girls and women of color. Operates National Resource Center on Women and AIDS and the Law and Pregnancy Program. Has testified before congressional and governmental committees and commissions. Sponsors policy seminars; operates speakers' bureau.
Awards: Annual Wise Woman.

Publications: *Earnings Sharing in Social Security: A Model for Reform*. Book. ● *The SAT Gender Gap*. Book. ● *Violence Against Women as Bias-Motivated Hate Crime*. Book. ● *Guide to Resources on Women and AIDS*. Book.

Conventions/Meetings: periodic meeting.

★2637★ CENTER FOR WOMEN'S STUDIES AND SERVICES (CWSS)
2467 E St.
San Diego, CA 92102
Carol Council, Dir.   PH: (619)233-8984

Founded: 1969. **Members:** 977. **Staff:** 16. **Budget:** US$450,000. **Local Groups:** 2. **Languages:** English. **National.** A feminist organization founded to meet the unmet needs of women via feminist services and programs and to advance the cause of women's rights. Offers: feminist-oriented counseling on a one-to-one basis or in groups; crisis hot-line for victims of sexual assault and family violence; shelter for battered women; family and relationship counseling; legal counseling and assistance for battered women; information on and referral to other women's programs and organizations and to human service agencies. Conducts classes in the community and special workshops (Sexual Assault Prevention, Family Violence, and Assertiveness Training). Projects include: Dissolution Clinic - Uncontested Divorces, Rape Crisis Center, Shelter for Battered Women, and Temporary Restraining Order Legal Clinic. Maintains speakers' bureau. **Formerly:** (1971) Center for Women's Studies.

Publications: *CWSS Newsletter*, quarterly. Analyzes current events with an emphasis on the women's and gay movements for equality. **Circulation:** 1,500. ● *Bylines by Women*. Book. ● *The Year of the Fires*. Book. ● *Double Jeopardy: Young and Female in America*. Book. ● *Rainbow Snake*. Book.

★2638★ CHI ETA PHI SORORITY
3029 13th St. NW
Washington, DC 20009
Mary H. Morris R.N., Contact

PH: (202)232-3858
FX: (202)232-3858

Founded: 1932. **Members:** 5,000. **Staff:** 1. **Languages:** English. **National.** Professional sorority - registered and student nurses. Objectives are to: encourage continuing education; stimulate friendship among members; develop working relationships with other professional groups for the improvement and delivery of health care services. Sponsors leadership training seminars every two years and holds additional seminars at the local, regional, and national levels. Offers educational programs for entrance into nursing and allied health fields. Maintains health screening and consumer health education programs; volunteers assistance to senior citizens; sponsors recruitment and retention programs for minority students in nursing. Operates speakers ' bureau on health education and biographical archives on African-American nurses. **Awards:** Periodic (scholarship). **Computer Services:** Data base; mailing lists.

Publications: *Chi Line*, semiannual. Newsletter. Includes membership activities. **Circulation:** 4,000. **Advertising:** accepted. ● *The Directory*, biennial. ● *Glowing Lamp - Journal of Chi Eta Phi Sorority*, annual. **Circulation:** 4,000. **Advertising:** accepted. ● *History of Chi Eta Phi Sorority*. Book. ● *Mary Eliza Mahoney, America's First Black Professional Nurse*. Book.

Conventions/Meetings: annual conference (exhibits) - always July. 1994 July 11 - 15, Richmond, VA, United States; 1995 July 10 - 15, New Orleans, LA, United States.

★2639★ CHILDBIRTH EDUCATION FOUNDATION (CEF)
PO Box 5
Richboro, PA 18954
James E. Peron, Founder & Exec.Dir.

PH: (215)357-2792

Founded: 1972. **Members:** 18,000. **Languages:** English. **National.** Physicians, nurses, childbirth educators, childbirth reform activists, concerned parents, and individuals dedicated to providing alternatives for a more meaningful childbirth experience, and to promoting reform in childbirth issues and in the treatment of the newborn. Promotes home births, birthing centers, certified nurse-midwife pregnancy management and delivery, family togetherness and infant bonding, "nonviolent birth" for mother and child, and breast-feeding. Distributes literature to libraries, parents, maternal care providers, and educators regarding childbirth, trends in childbirth, safe alternatives, the avoidance of "violence in birth," and the treatment of newborns and infants. Compiles statistics and conducts extensive research related to childbirth, newborn, and infant care; provides seminars and educational workshops for childbirth educators, Lamaze instructors, the La Leche League International, and right-to-life and birthright organizations. Provides referrals and film and videotape services to childbirth educators and maternal and child-care organizations. Maintains speakers' bureau. Sponsors charitable programs. **Libraries:** Type: reference. **Computer Services:** Mailing lists. **Committees:** Childbirth Education; Medical Advisory; Medical/Legal Advisory; Medical Referral; National Public Relations.

Publications: *CEF Newsletter*, semiannual. ● *Membership Directory*, periodic. ● *Bulletin*, periodic.

Conventions/Meetings: annual conference, with symposium.

★2640★ CHILDBIRTH WITHOUT PAIN EDUCATION ASSOCIATION (CWPEA)
20134 Snowden
Detroit, MI 48235-1170
Flora Hommel, Exec.Dir.

PH: (313)341-3816

Founded: 1958. **Members:** 3,000. **Staff:** 11. **Budget:** US$50,000. **Languages:** English. **National.** Former and current students of the Lamaze-Pavlov (psychoprophylactic) method of painless childbirth; physicians, nurses, and interested individuals. Sponsors lectures, classes, and films for women with or without partners, nurses, and medical and lay groups about the method, which is based on conditioning reflexes to help prevent pain, thus allowing for natural, usually drug-free childbirth. Works to provide a method-trained registered nurse (monitrice) in attendance at the birth where possible. Collects data for further development of the method; surveys maternity services; presents awards. Sponsors childbirth teacher and monitrice training and certification. Provides teen pregnancy programs. Offers referral service. **Libraries:** Type: reference. Holdings: 100; books. Subjects: pregnancy and childbirth. **Committees:** Film; Speakers' Bureau. **Divisions:** Education; Nursing; Research.

Publications: *Childbirth Without Pain Education Association Memo*, bimonthly. Newsletter. Includes association news and book reviews. **Circulation:** 1,500. **Advertising:** accepted.

Conventions/Meetings: annual - always June. Detroit, MI, United States.

★2641★ CHINESE WOMEN'S BENEVOLENT ASSOCIATION (CWBA)
22 Pell St., No. 3
New York, NY 10013
Mrs. Woongan Mei Lee, Pres.

PH: (212)267-4764

Founded: 1942. **Members:** 100. **Languages:** English. **National.** Chinese women who volunteer in fundraising drives, aid students, and conduct other philanthropic activities. Provides interpreting and translating services when needed.

★2642★ CHRISTIAN AMERICANS FOR LIFE (CAFL)
PO Box 977
Tulsa, OK 74102
Dr. Billy James Hargis, CEO

PH: (918)665-2345

Founded: 1972. **Members:** 10,000. **Staff:** 3. **Languages:** English. **National.** Campaigns against abortion. Maintains program to support adoption instead of abortion. Compiles statistics, mails letters, and conducts research programs.

Publications: *Hotline*, monthly. Newsletter. ● *Thou Shalt Not Kill.My Babies*. Book.

★2643★ CHURCH WOMEN UNITED (CWU)
475 Riverside Dr., Rm. 812
New York, NY 10115-0832
Patricia Rumer, Gen.Dir.

PH: (212)870-2347

Founded: 1941. **Staff:** 24. **Budget:** US$1,579,000. **State Groups:** 52. **Local Groups:** 1,750. **Languages:** English. **National.** Ecumenical movement uniting Protestant, Roman Catholic, Orthodox, and other Christian church women into one Christian community. Supports peace, human rights, justice, and the empowerment of women. Works to strengthen the presence of ecumenical women in both the national and global arenas through offices in Washington, DC and the United Nations. Activities include Intercontinental Grants for Mission, Citizen Action, Assignment: Poverty of Women, and ecumenical and international relations. Sponsors World Day of Prayer (first Friday in March), May Fellowship Day (first Friday in May), and World Community Day (first Friday in November). **Programs:** T.V. Tune=-In U.S.A..

Publications: *Church Woman*, quarterly. Magazine. ● *Lead Time*, bimonthly. Newsletter.

Conventions/Meetings: periodic conference.

★2644★ CIRCLES OF EXCHANGE (COE)
9594 1st Ave. NE, No. 333
Seattle, WA 98115
Nan Hawthorne, Exec. Officer

PH: (206)298-1943

Founded: 1984. **Members:** 205. **Staff:** 3. **Languages:** English. **National.** Primarily women involved in round-robin correspondence and literary exchange focusing on spirituality. Sponsors competitions.

Publications: *Correspondence Directory*, biennial. ● *Mooncircles*, 8/year. Bulletin. **Circulation:** 205. **Advertising:** accepted. ● *Yearbook*. Includes members' writing and artwork contributions and epistolary excerpts from previous year.

★2645★ CLEARINGHOUSE ON FEMICIDE
PO Box 12342
Berkeley, CA 94701-3342
Chris Domingo, Founder   PH: (510)845-7005

Founded: 1989. **Members:** 100. **Staff:** 1. **Languages:** English. **National**. Women activists, teachers, students, organizers, writers, lawyers, and other interested individuals. Provides research findings and information regarding misogyny and femicide. Organizes lectures and workshops. Seeks to: raise awareness of activists; gather information about femicide; organize and mobilize women to fight against it. Maintains that femicide and violence against women are often an overt expression by men of their feelings of powerlessness against the feminist movement. **Libraries:** Type: open to the public. Holdings: archival material, clippings, audio recordings, video recordings, books. **Awards:** Periodic Berkeley Commission on the Status of Women Certificate (recognition). **Computer Services:** Data base, articles pertaining to femicide. **Telecommunication Services:** Teletype.

Publications: *Memory and Rage* (in English), periodic. ● *Local Updates* (in English), periodic. Bulletin. ● *Femicide: The Politics of Woman Killing* (in English).

★2646★ CLEARINGHOUSE ON WOMEN'S ISSUES (CWI)
PO Box 70603
Friendship Heights, MD 20813
Elaine L. Newman, Pres.

Founded: 1972. **Members:** 400. **Languages:** English. **National**. Nonpartisan clearinghouse for national, regional, state, and local women's and civil rights organizations. Purpose is to exchange and disseminate educational information and materials on issues related to discrimination on the basis of sex and marital status, with particular emphasis on public policies affecting the economic and educational status of women.

Publications: *Newsletter*, 9/year. **Circulation:** 400.

Conventions/Meetings: meeting - 9/year.

★2647★ CO-ETTE CLUB
2020 W. Chicago Blvd.
Detroit, MI 48206
Mary-Agnes Miller Davis, Founder &
   Chm.   PH: (313)867-0880

Founded: 1941. **Local Groups:** 35. **Languages:** English. **National**. Teenage high school girls "outstanding in one or all of the following categories - Academic Scholarship, School and Community, Extra-Curriculars, Community Volunteer Service, and Leadership"; membership consists primarily of black girls, but is open to any girl; number of members limited to 35 per chapter. Helps members channel interests and become leaders in educational, cultural, and artistic activities on local and national levels; maintains speakers' bureau and museum. Offers placement services. Raises funds for United Negro College Fund and contributes to local charity and social service groups in each community. Founder of the Metropolitan Detroit Teen Conference Coalition. **Awards:** Annual John Fitzgerald Kennedy Memorial. Recipient: Teenage high school girl for distinguished humanitarian service or professional excellence. **Committees:** Charity Ball; Community and Cultural Affairs; Graduation Celebration; High School Graduation Celebration; Personal Service; Speakers' Bureau; Volunteer.

Publications: *Co-Ette Manual*, annual. Booklet. ● *Co-Ette Souvenir*, annual. Magazine. ● *Membership Directory*, periodic. ● *Newsletter*, periodic.

Conventions/Meetings: semiannual meeting.

★2648★ COAL EMPLOYMENT PROJECT (CEP)
17 Emory Pl.
Knoxville, TN 37917   PH: (615)637-7905
Carol J. Davis, Exec.Off.   FX: (615)637-3945

Founded: 1977. **Staff:** 3. **Budget:** US$160,000. **Local Groups:** 12. **Languages:** English. **National**. Female coal miners, their supporters, union members, and others who work in the coal industry. To help women obtain and retain coal mining jobs and to end discrimination against women in the coal industry. Works on issues vital to women coal miners such as legal rights, health and safety in the coal mines, sexual harassment, training for women miners, union support, child care, family leave, and pregnancy while employed as a miner. Pursues legal remedies for alleged injustices. Works closely with the Coal Mining Women's Support Teams, founded by the CEP. Organizes local support groups and education in the fields of legal and occupational rights. Conducts ongoing research and surveys on issues of importance to women miners and other nontraditional careers for women. **Libraries:** Type: reference.

Publications: *Coal Mining Women's Support Team News*, bimonthly. Newsletter.

Conventions/Meetings: annual conference.

★2649★ COALITION AGAINST TRAFFICKING IN WOMEN
323 E. Park Ave.
State College, PA 16803
Kathleen Barry, Exec. Dir.   PH: (814)867-7575

Languages: English. **National**. Works to prevent exploitation of women. Conducts research; disseminates information.

★2650★ COALITION OF ASIAN SISTERS AGAINST SEXUAL
   EXPLOITATION (CASSE)
c/o Third World Women's Archives
PO Box 2651
New York, NY 10009

Languages: English. **National**. Protects and defends Asian women from sexual exploitation. Offers psychological, medical, and legal assistance to sexually exploited women.

★2651★ COALITION OF LABOR UNION WOMEN (CLUW)
15 Union Sq. W
New York, NY 10003   PH: (212)242-0700
Chrystl Lindo-Bridgeforth, Exec.Officer   FX: (212)255-7230

Founded: 1974. **Members:** 18,000. **Local Groups:** 72. **Languages:** English. **National**. Aims to: unify all union women in order to determine common problems within unions and deal effectively with objectives; promote unionism and encourage unions to be more aggressive in their efforts to bring unorganized women under collective bargaining agreements; inform members about what can be done within the labor movement to achieve equal opportunity and correct discriminatory job situations; educate and inspire union brothers to help achieve affirmative action in the workplace. Seeks to encourage members, through action programs of the coalition, to become more active participants in the political and legislative processes of their unions, to seek election to public office or selection for governmental appointive office at local, county, state, and national levels, and to increase their participation in union policymaking. Bestows awards; operates speakers' bureau. Conducts training programs and project on empowerment of union women. Maintains Coalition of Labor Union Women Center for Education and Research. **Committees:** Education; Minority; Organizing the Unorganized; Political Action.

Publications: *Newsletter*, bimonthly. ● *Bargaining for Family Issues*. Book. ● *Is Your Job Making You Sick?*. Book.

Conventions/Meetings: biennial meeting.

★2652★ COALITION OF LABOR UNION WOMEN CENTER FOR EDUCATION AND RESEARCH (CLUWCER)
15 Union Sq. W
New York, NY 10003
Crystl L. Bridgefurth, Exec.Dir.   PH: (212)242-0700

Founded: 1978. **Budget:** US$50,000. **Languages:** English. **National**. Education arm of the Coalition of Labor Union Women. Promotes the full participation of women in their unions. Provides direction and assistance in the development of union policies and programs that reflect the concerns of women in the workplace. Serves as information and referral clearinghouse. Develops and conducts education and training programs for working women; emphasizes leadership training so that women may become more involved and may advance in the union. Conducts research on issues concerning working women, particularly labor union women. Sponsors Reproductive Rights Project. Maintains speakers' bureau; compiles statistics.

Conventions/Meetings: periodic meeting.

★2653★ COALITION OF LEADING WOMEN'S ORGANIZATIONS
825 8th Ave.
New York, NY 10019
Marcella Rosen, Chair   PH: (212)474-5000

National. Umbrella organization of women's organizations in the United States. Promotes the interests of women in all areas of society, including legal, economic, social, and political.

★2654★ COALITION FOR WOMEN'S APPOINTMENTS (CWA)
c/o Natl. Women's Political Caucus
1275 K St. NW, Ste. 750
Washington, DC 20005-4051   PH: (202)898-1100
Harriett Woods, Pres.   FX: (202)898-0458

Founded: 1976. **Members:** 84. **Staff:** 2. **Languages:** English. **National**. Organization coordinated by the National Women's Political Caucus. Seeks to promote the appointment and promotion of women to high level government positions and to assist women seeking appointment or election to the state or federal bench. The coalition evaluates and monitors appointments to determine their impact on issues affecting women. Compiles statistics and maintains biographical archives.

★2655★ COALITION OF WOMEN'S ART ORGANIZATIONS (CWAO)
123 E. Beutel Rd.
Port Washington, WI 53074
Dorothy Provis, Pres.   PH: (414)284-4458

Founded: 1977. **Languages:** English. **National**. Women art organizations and professionals. Works to protect and improve the rights of all artists. In 1984, reorganized as an advocacy organization dedicated to alerting its national network to issues in the arts. Advocates for the passage of consignment legislation on the state level; supports the National Heritage Resource Act.

Publications: *CWAO News*, monthly. Newsletter.

Conventions/Meetings: annual conference - always February.

★2656★ COLONIAL DAMES OF AMERICA (CDA)
421 E. 61st St.
New York, NY 10021
Mrs. Hill Dawson Penniman, Pres.Gen.   PH: (212)838-5489

Founded: 1890. **Members:** 2,000. **Staff:** 8. **Local Groups:** 26. **Languages:** English. **National**. Women whose ancestors served an armed forces commission for or held public office in one of the 13 North American colonies. Collects and preserves educational resources, including manuscripts, relics, and mementos of the colonial period in American history; commemorates the important colonial events of the U.S. and of the 13 colonies. Seeks to disseminate information about and create popular interest in colonial history.

Maintains Abigail Adams Smith Museum in New York City. Provides educational programs.

Conventions/Meetings: annual meeting - New York, NY, United States.

★2657★ COMISION FEMENIL MEXICANA NACIONAL (CFMN)
379 S. Loma Dr.
Los Angeles, CA 90017
Maggie Cervantes, Pres.   PH: (213)484-1515

Founded: 1970. **Members:** 5,000. **Regional Groups:** 23. **State Groups:** 20. **Local Groups:** 10. **Languages:** English. **National**. Advocates Latin women's rights; works to advance Hispanic women politically, socially, economically, and educationally. Maintains: Chicana Service Action Center, which provides jobs skills training; Centro de Ninos, bilingual child development programs; Casa Victoria group home for teens. Bestows awards; maintains speakers' bureau; compiles statistics. Conducts research. **Computer Services:** Data base, information on women's and Hispanic organizations and national Latino leaders. **Committees:** Development; Education; Health/Welfare; Legislative; Reproductive Rights; Teen Pregnancy.

Publications: *Annual Report*. ● *La Mujer*, semiannual. Journal. Includes statistics. **Circulation:** 3,000. **Advertising:** not accepted. ● *Newsletter*, periodic.

Conventions/Meetings: annual meeting.

★2658★ COMMAND TRUST NETWORK (CTN)
PO Box 17082
Covington, KY 41017   PH: (606)331-0055
Kathleen Anneken, Exec. Officer   FX: (606)331-0055

Founded: 1988. **Languages:** English. **National**. Individuals concerned with the effects of silicone breast implants. Seeks to inform the public and motivate women with implants to consider all possible options. Disseminates information on medical studies, legal referrals, research, choosing a doctor, implant removel procedures, and other related topics.

Publications: *Newsletter*, quarterly. ● *Elective Surgery*. Booklet.

Conventions/Meetings: annual conference.

★2659★ COMMISSION OF THE STATUS AND ROLE OF WOMEN (CSRW)
1200 Davis St.
Evanston, IL 60201   PH: (312)869-7330
Joetta Rinehart, Pres.   FX: (708)475-5061

Founded: 1970. **Members:** 48. **Staff:** 4. **Regional Groups:** 72. **Languages:** English. **National**. A commission of the United Methodist Church. Laypersons and clergy interested in the status of women in the UMC. Works to protect the rights of women, both lay and clergy, in the UMC. Assists individuals with recognizing and bringing complaints of sexual harassment or discrimination to the appropriate church disciplinary body or civil authorities. Maintains speakers' bureau. Conducts educational and research programs.

Publications: *The Flyer*, quarterly. Newsletter.

Conventions/Meetings: semiannual conference.

★2660★ COMMISSION FOR WOMEN'S EQUALITY (CWE)
c/o American Jewish Congress
15 E. 84th St.
New York, NY 10028   PH: (212)879-4500
Hanita Blumfield, Dir.   FX: (212)249-3672

Founded: 1984. **Members:** 200. **Staff:** 2. **Regional Groups:** 15. **Languages:** English. **National**. Feminists, elected officials, professionals, academics, and Jewish communal leaders working to define feminism within a context compatible with Judaism. Areas of concern include: reproductive freedom, economic equity, child care, equality in religious life, and the empowerment of women in politics and in Jewish communal life. A commission of the

American Jewish Congress. **Formerly:** (1991) National Commission for Women's Equality.

Publications: *International Jewish Feminist Directory*, periodic.

Conventions/Meetings: quarterly meeting. ● periodic conference.

★2661★ COMMITTEE OF 200 (C200)
625 N. Michigan Ave., Ste. 500
Chicago, IL 60611-3108
Lydia Lewis, Exec.Dir.   PH: (312)751-3477

Founded: 1982. **Members:** 320. **Staff:** 3. **Languages:** English. **National.** Women executives who are recognized as leaders in their industries. (Though originally intended to have a membership of 200 top-ranking businesswomen, the committee is no longer limited to 200). Encourages successful entrepreneurship by women and the active participation of women business owners and senior corporate executives in business, economic, social, and educational concerns. Seeks to strengthen the influence of women business leaders. Provides forum for exchange of ideas and enhancement of business opportunities for women.

Publications: *Network*, monthly. Bulletin. ● *Update*, semiannual. Newsletter.

Conventions/Meetings: semiannual conference.

★2662★ COMMITTEE TO DEFEND REPRODUCTIVE RIGHTS (CDRR)
25 Taylor St., Ste. 704
San Francisco, CA 94102
Laura Weide, Coordinator   PH: (415)441-4434

Founded: 1977. **Members:** 1,200. **Membership Dues:** US$25. **Staff:** 1. **Languages:** English. **National.** Individuals interested in reproductive rights; health organizations. Conducts community education and activism concerning reproductive rights including abortion, sterilization, and prenatal care. Provides speakers for high schools, community colleges, and universities. Maintains speakers' bureau. **Libraries:** Type: reference. **Committees:** Consumer Alert; Just Us for Justice.

Publications: *CDRR News*, quarterly. Newsletter. **Circulation:** 1,200. **Advertising:** not accepted.

Conventions/Meetings: semiannual meeting.

★2663★ COMMITTEE TO EXPOSE, OPPOSE, AND DEPOSE PATRIARCHY (CEODP)
8319 Fulham Ct.
Richmond, VA 23227 1712
Donna Gorman, Exec. Officer   PH: (804)266-7400

Founded: 1984. **Staff:** 1. **Languages:** English. **National.** Individuals who oppose institutions deemed to be "patriarchal" (administered exclusively for the benefit of males) and that "characteristically lie, practice double-think," "control and dominate" minorities, and are animated by a "love for death" (as in supporting militarism, war, and capital punishment).

★2664★ COMMITTEE TO RESIST ABORTION (CRA)
1626 2nd Ave.
New York, NY 10028
Hugo Carl Koch, Chm.

Founded: 1983. **Languages:** English. **National.** Individuals who, after prolonged opposition to legalized abortion, created the committee as a means to intensify their protest. Seeks to: oppose abortion by mobilizing a nationwide anti-abortion income tax strike, during which participants would refuse to pay all or part of their federal income tax; prepare and present a petition to the U.N. General Assembly alleging that legalized abortion in the U.S. is an act of racial and class oppression constituting genocide under the terms of the U.N. charter. Maintains communication with antiabortion groups and interested individuals; collects supporting sociological and economic data.

Publications: *Newsletter*, periodic.

★2665★ COMMITTEE ON THE ROLE AND STATUS OF WOMEN IN EDUCATIONAL RESEARCH AND DEVELOPMENT
c/o Emily Lowe Brizendine
California State University
Department of Educational Leadership   PH: (510)658-7013
Hayward, CA 94542   (510)881-3106
Emily Lowe Brizendine, Chairperson   FX: (510)727-2283

Founded: 1972. **Members:** 7. **Languages:** English. **National.** A standing committee of the American Educational Research Association. Persons affiliated with elementary and secondary schools and universities. To assess and enhance the status of women in educational research at universities, research and development centers, and on an international level. Projects include preparation of a roster of women in educational research and development of career materials for educational research. Compiles statistics.

Publications: *Directory*, periodic.

Conventions/Meetings: annual meeting - always spring.

★2666★ COMMITTEE ON SOUTH ASIAN WOMEN (COSAW)
Texas A & M University
Psychology Dept.
College Station, TX 77843   PH: (409)845-2576
Dr. Jyotsna Vaid, Contact   FX: (409)845-4727

Founded: 1982. **Languages:** English. **National.** Organizations and individuals promoting the interests and exploring the needs of women of South Asian origin or interests. Publishes literary works of South Asian women regarding the women's struggle in South Asia (India, Pakistan, Bangladesh, Afghanistan, Nepal, Bhutan, and Sri Lanka) and the experiences of women South Asian immigrants. Conducts educational programs. Maintains speakers' bureau. **Libraries:** Type: reference.

Publications: *Bulletin*, semiannual. **ISSN:** 0885-4319. **Circulation:** 400. **Advertising:** accepted.

Conventions/Meetings: annual meeting.

★2667★ COMMITTEE ON THE STATUS OF WOMEN IN ANTHROPOLOGY
Arizona State University
Department of Anthropology
Tempe, AZ 85287
Louisa R. Stark, Chair   PH: (602)965-6213

Members: 8. **Languages:** English. **National.** Promotes the interests of women working and studying in anthropology.

★2668★ COMMITTEE ON THE STATUS OF WOMEN IN THE ECONOMICS PROFESSION (CSWEP)
c/o Dr. Elizabeth Hoffman
KEGSM
Univ. of Arizona
Tucson, AZ 85721   PH: (602)621-6227
Dr. Elizabeth Hoffman, Chair   FX: (602)621-2606

Founded: 1972. **Languages:** English. **National.** A standing committee of American Economic Association. Women economists in the U.S. Purpose is to support and facilitate equality of opportunity for women economists. Disseminates information about job opportunities, research funding, and research related to the status of women in economics. Sponsors technical sessions. **Computer Services:** Mailing lists; data base, employment information.

Publications: *Newsletter*, 3/year. ● *Women in Economics, The CSWEP Roster*, biennial. Directory.

Conventions/Meetings: annual convention (exhibits).

★2669★ COMMITTEE ON THE STATUS OF WOMEN IN GEOGRAPHY
(CSWG)
Geography Department
Florida State University
Boca Raton, FL 33431
David Lee, Chair   PH: (305)393-3252

Members: 7. **Languages:** English. **National.** Investigates the status of women geographers. Supports and promotes women in the profession. Works to eliminate financial and discriminatory obstacles to women's success.

Publications: *Association of American Geographers Newsletter* (in English).

★2670★ COMMITTEE ON THE STATUS OF WOMEN IN LINGUISTICS
(CSWL)
1325 18th St. NW, Ste. 211
Washington, DC 20036
Penelope Eckert, Chair   PH: (202)835-1714

Founded: 1973. **Members:** 6. **Languages:** English. **National.** A committee of the Linguistic Society of America. Purpose is to guarantee equality of opportunity in training and employment to all members. Studies and publicizes the official policies of institutions and organizations employing and representing linguists; investigates and makes reports on patterns of discrimination against women; makes available information about grievance and appeal agencies; communicates information about federal and state regulations regarding the status of women in academic institutions to colleges and universities employing linguists. Maintains up-to-date statistical data; presents recommendations for affirmative action at LSA meetings.

Conventions/Meetings: annual meeting.

★2671★ COMMITTEE ON THE STATUS OF WOMEN IN
MICROBIOLOGY (CSWM)
c/o Dr. Anne Morris Hooke
Miami University
Dept. of Microbiology   PH: (513)529-2028
Oxford, OH 45056   FX: (513)529-2431
Dr. Anne Morris Hooke, Chairperson   E-Mail: AMHOOK@ MIMIU

Founded: 1972. **Members:** 6. **Languages:** English. **National.** A committee of the American Society for Microbiology. Microbiologists investigating the status of women in microbiology in relation to their male counterparts in the work place and within their professional society. Reports findings and conducts seminars at the Annual meeting of the ASM. Works toward full and equal opportunity for educational, career, and personal development for male and female microbiologists. **Awards:** Annual Alice Evans Award.

Publications: *The Communicator,* quarterly. Newsletter.

★2672★ COMMITTEE ON THE STATUS OF WOMEN IN PHILOSOPHY
(CSWP)
c/o Helen Langine
Philosohy
Rice Univ.
Houston, TX 77251
Alison Jaggar, Chairperson   PH: (713)527-4994

Founded: 1970. **Members:** 8. **Languages:** English. **National.** A committee of the American Philosophical Association. Individuals appointed by APA to report on and further the professional status of women in philosophy. Collects and disseminates information on the status of women in philosophy; works to facilitate an understanding of issues of gender and of the range of positions respresented in feminist theories.

Publications: *Feminism and Philosophy Newsletter,* periodic.

Conventions/Meetings: periodic meeting.

★2673★ COMMITTEE ON THE STATUS OF WOMEN IN SOCIOLOGY
(CSWS)
c/o American Sociological Association
1722 N St. NW
Washington, DC 20036   PH: (202)833-3410
Carla B. Howery, Contact   FX: (202)785-0146

Founded: 1970. **Members:** 6. **Staff:** 1. **Languages:** English. **National.** A standing committee of the American Sociological Association. Primary task is to monitor and further the status of women in the sociological profession.

Conventions/Meetings: annual conference (exhibits) - 1994 Aug. 5 - 9, Los Angeles, CA, United States.

★2674★ COMMITTEE ON WOMEN IN ASIAN STUDIES (CWAS)
c/o Jyotsna Vaid
Texas A & M Univ.
Dept. of Psychology
Collegen Station, TX 77843   PH: (409)845-2576
Sucheta Mazumdar, Chair   FX: (409)845-4727

Founded: 1972. **Budget:** US$5,000. **Languages:** English. **National.** Scholars, students, writers, and professionals in any field that deals with gender issues in Asia. Studies the social, economic, and political position of Asian women, including issues such as women and poverty in the Third World, sexual division of labor in south India, and women's education in the Third World. Seeks to further gender-disaggregated research, teaching, and publication concerning the lives of males and females in Asian populations; promotes the role of women in the Asian studies profession. Disseminates research results and information; sponsors workshops.

Publications: *CWAS Newsletter,* 3/year. Includes book reviews, conference news and announcements, film and publications announcements, profiles of people in the field, and research reports. **ISSN:** 0738-3207. **Circulation:** 200.

Conventions/Meetings: annual meeting. ● periodic conference.

★2675★ COMMITTEE ON WOMEN IN PHYSIOLOGY
9650 Rockville Pike
Bethesda, MD 20814
Dr. Helen Cooke, Contact   PH: (301)530-7164

Languages: English. **National.** Works to improve the status of women in the fields of physiology and neurophysiology. Organizes informational and educational programs. Conducts research. Disseminates information.

Publications: *The Physiologist* (in English). ● *American Journal of Physiology* (in English). ● *Journal of Applied Physiology* (in English). ● *Physiological Review* (in English). ● *Journal of Neurophysiology.*

★2676★ COMMITTEE OF WOMEN IN STATISTICS
1429 Duke St.
Alexandria, VA 22314
Caroline Morgan, President

Languages: English. **National.** Professionals in statistics. Works to increase awareness among professionals in the field of the needs and problems of women. Promotes and supports women working in statistics. Encourages women to pursue careers in statistics and to network with other professionals.

★2677★ COMMUNICATIONS WORKERS OF AMERICA - WOMEN'S
COMMITTEE (AFL/CIO)
1925 K St. NW
Washington, DC 20006   PH: (202)728-2300

Members: 12. **Languages:** English. **National.** Promotes the interests of women working in the communications industries. Works to improve job security, child care benefits, and professional conduct. Investigates political concerns of women; alcohol and drug abuse; domestic violence; handicapped and minority women's needs; and financial issues concerning women. Seeks to increase members' awareness of women's issues.

Publications: *CWA News* (in English).

★2678★ THE COMPASSIONATE FRIENDS (TCF)
PO Box 3696
Oak Brook, IL 60522-3696   PH: (708)990-0010
Therese Goodrich, Exec.Dir.   FX: (708)990-0246

Founded: 1972. **Staff:** 8. **Local Groups:** 655. **Languages:** English. **National.** Nondenominational, informal, selfhelp organization open to parents who have experienced the death of a child. Purposes are: to promote and aid parents in the positive resolution of grief; to foster the physical and emotional health of bereaved parents and siblings. Chapters offer support and understanding by providing "telephone friends" who may be called, identifying sharing groups that meet monthly, and disseminating information concerning the grieving process. Maintains speakers' bureau; bestows awards. **Libraries:** Type: reference.

Publications: *Annual Report.* ● *Sibling Newsletter*, quarterly. ● *Videos.* on parental grief.

Conventions/Meetings: annual conference - always July. ● semiannual regional meeting.

★2679★ CONCERN FOR HEALTH OPTIONS - INFORMATION, CARE
  AND EDUCATION
(CHOICE)
1233 Locust St., Fl. 3
Philadelphia, PA 19107   PH: (215)985-3355
Lisa Shulock, Exec.Dir.   FX: (215)985-3369

Founded: 1971. **Members:** 1,500. **Staff:** 30. **Budget:** US$1,000,000. **Languages:** English. **National.** Concerned with reproductive health care, child care, and HIV/AIDS. Goal of CHOICE, which began as an outgrowth of the Clergy Consultation Service, is to make available, with dignity and concern, high-quality medical and social services to all people at every economic level. Operates resource information hotlines; provides training and consulting services. Conducts training programs, seminars, and workshops. **Libraries:** Type: reference.

Publications: *The Choice is Yours*, periodic. Directory. HIV testing services. ● *Where to Find*, periodic. Directory of family planning services. **Circulation:** 8,800. **Advertising:** not accepted.

★2680★ CONCERNED WOMEN FOR AMERICA (CWA)
370 L'Enfant Promenade SW, Ste. 800
Washington, DC 20024   PH: (202)488-7000
Beverly LaHaye, Pres.   FX: (202)488-0806

Founded: 1979. **Members:** 600,000. **Staff:** 30. **Budget:** US$8,000,000. **Regional Groups:** 2,500. **Languages:** English. **National.** Educational and legal defense foundation that seeks to protect the rights of the family and preserve traditional American values.

Publications: *Newsletter*, 11/year.

Conventions/Meetings: annual conference.

★2681★ CONGREGATION OF SISTERS OF STATION AGNES
475 Gillett St.
Fond du Lac, WI 54935
Sr. Jean Steffes CSA, Gen. Superior   PH: (414)923-2121

Founded: 1858. **Members:** 487. **Local Groups:** 62. **Languages:** English. **Multinational.** Religious women serving rural and urban communities throughout the U.S. and Latin America. Promotes justice for the economically poor; works to further the role of women in the Catholic church and society; collaborates with the laity and clergy of other faiths in service programs.

Provides staffing at 4 hospitals, a home for the aged, and a coeducational college. Places and supports missionaries in Nicaragua.

★2682★ CONGRESSIONAL CAUCUS FOR WOMEN'S ISSUES (CCWI)
2471 Rayburn House Office Bldg.
Washington, DC 20515
Lesley Primmer, Exec.Dir.   PH: (202)225-6740

Founded: 1977. **Members:** 170. **Staff:** 4. **Languages:** English. **National.** Bipartisan legislative service organization of the U.S. House of Representatives with the goal of improving the status of American women and eliminating discrimination "built into many federal programs and policies." Supports legislation to improve women's status. Focuses on equal treatment of women with regard to Social Security, federal and private pensions, insurance, and child support enforcement. Seeks to improve health care for American women through increased funding for research on women's health issues and improved access to health care services.

★2683★ CONGRESSIONAL CLUB (CC)
2001 New Hampshire Ave. NW
Washington, DC 20009
Doris Matsui, Pres.   PH: (202)332-1155

Founded: 1908. **Members:** 650. **Languages:** English. **National.** Wives of present and former U.S. Representatives, Senators, Cabinet members, and Supreme Court Justices. The wives of the President and Vice President of the U.S. and the wife of the Speaker of the House are honorary members. Fosters communication among members. **Committees:** Archives; Community Service; Cookbook; Decorating; Diplomatic; Founders Day; Museum and Foundation; Press; Year Book.

Publications: *Directory*, biennial.

Conventions/Meetings: weekly luncheon.

★2684★ COORDINATING COMMITTEE ON WOMEN IN THE
  HISTORICAL PROFESSION - CONFERENCE GROUP ON WOMEN'S
  HISTORY (CCWHP/CGWH)
124 Park Pl.
Brooklyn, NY 11217   PH: (718)638-3227
Barbara Winslow, Exec.Dir.   FX: (718)499-7595

Founded: 1969. **Members:** 800. **Regional Groups:** 14. **Languages:** English. **National.** Women historians and others interested in women's history. Works to encourage and help develop research and instruction in the field of women's history, advance the status of women at all levels and increase their numbers, and to oppose discrimination against women in the profession. Assists members in establishing panels in different conferences; promotes networking.

Publications: *CCWHP/CGWH Newsletter*, 5/year. **Circulation:** 800. **Advertising:** accepted.

Conventions/Meetings: annual meeting.

★2685★ COSMETIC EXECUTIVE WOMEN (CEW)
217 E. 85th St., Ste. 214
New York, NY 10028
Lee MacCallum, Pres.   PH: (212)759-3283

Founded: 1954. **Members:** 600. **Regional Groups:** 1. **Languages:** English. **National.** Women who have served for more than three years in executive positions in the cosmetic and allied industries. Unites women executives in the cosmetic field for industry awareness and business advancement. **Awards:** Annual Cosmetic Executive Women Achiever.

Publications: *CEW Wavelength*, periodic. Newsletter. ● *Membership Roster*, periodic. Directory.

Conventions/Meetings: periodic seminar. ● periodic luncheon.

★2686★ COSMOPOLITAN ASSOCIATES (CA)
PO Box 1491
West Caldwell, NJ 07007
Gisela Lange, Pres.   PH: (201)992-2232

Founded: 1947. **Members:** 604. **Local Groups:** 13. **Languages:** English. **National.** Foreign-born women living in the U.S. Purposes are to: retain affiliations with the homelands of members; provide for socialization and companionship; encourage formation of local chapters. Conducts charitable program.

Publications: *Newsletter*, monthly.

Conventions/Meetings: annual meeting.

★2687★ COUNCIL OF ASIAN AMERICAN WOMEN
232 E. Capitol St. NE
Washington, DC 20003
Virginia Kee, President   PH: (202)544-3181

Founded: 1977. **National.** Promotes the interests of Asian American women. Increases the awareness of Asian American women in the areas of politics, business, and public policy.

★2688★ COUNCIL ON BATTERED WOMEN
PO Box 54737
Atlanta, GA 30308
Constance Rushing, President   PH: (404)873-1766

Founded: 1977. **Members:** 350. **Languages:** English. **National.** Offers help to female victims of domestic violence. Provides temporary shelter for women and children; a crisis telephone service; and personal, in-person counseling. Conducts community educational and advocacy programs to increase public awareness of the causes and effects of domestic violence and spouse abuse.

Publications: *Volunteer Newsletter* (in English). ● *Volunteer Voice* (in English).

★2689★ COUNCIL ON RESIDENT EDUCATION IN OBSTETRICS AND GYNECOLOGY (CREOG)
409 12th St. SW
Washington, DC 20024
DeAnne Nehra, Exec.Dir.   PH: (202)863-2554
                               FX: (202)484-5107

Founded: 1967. **Members:** 450. **Staff:** 3. **Languages:** English. **National.** A semiautonomous nonregulatory organization founded by the American College of Obstetricians and Gynecologists and comprised of national specialty organizations. Works to promote and maintain high standards of resident training in obstetrics and gynecology. Services include: consultative site visits to residency programs; clearinghouse for residency positions; conferences; a resident data bank; national in-training examination. **Committees:** Education; In-Training Examination; Program Directors Services.

Publications: *Basic Science Monographs in Obstetrics and Gynecology*, periodic. Series on metabolism, genetics, maternal physiology, pharmacology, microbiology, and other aspects of reproductive health. Contains bibliography. ● *Council on Resident Education in Obstetrics and Gynecology—Council News*, 3/year. Newsletter. Membership activities and *CREOG Directory of Obstetric and Gynecologic Residency Programs* update. ● *CREOG Directory of Obstetric and Gynecologic Residency Programs and Directors*, annual. Lists accredited residency programs in the U.S. and Canada.

Conventions/Meetings: annual conference. ● annual meeting.

★2690★ COUNTRY WOMEN'S COUNCIL UNITED STATES OF AMERICA (CWC)
c/o Mrs. Henry Buff
3500 Henbet Dr.
West Columbia, SC 29169
Mrs. Henry Buff, Chm.   PH: (803)794-7548

Founded: 1939. **Members:** 67. **Languages:** English. **Multinational.** Rural women's organizations. Aims are to: help in the economic, social, and cultural development of rural women; stimulate interest in the international aspects of rural and home life; further friendship and understanding among country women and homemakers of all nations.

Publications: *News Sheet*, semiannual. Newsletter. ● *United States of America - Our Way of Life*. Book. ● *United States of America - People and Places*. Book.

Conventions/Meetings: annual conference - usually fall.

★2691★ COUPLE TO COUPLE LEAGUE (CCL)
PO Box 111184
Cincinnati, OH 45211
John F. Kippley, Pres.   PH: (513)661-7612

Founded: 1971. **Staff:** 20. **Local Groups:** 450. **Languages:** English. **National.** Married and engaged couples interested in natural family planning (a method of spacing pregnancies through reliance on the woman's natural fertility cycle). Believes natural birth control strengthens family bonds and is healthier and more morally acceptable than artificial birth control devices. Sponsors local teaching groups where couples are taught basic natural family planning techniques. Provides special training program for those who wish to become CCL teaching couples. Promotes premarital chastity through speakers and materials.

Publications: *CCL Family Foundations*, bimonthly. Newsletter. ● *The Art of Natural Family Planning*. Book. ● *Breastfeeding and Natural Child Spacing*. Book. ● *Fertility, Cycles and Nutrition*. Book.

Conventions/Meetings: biennial meeting.

★2692★ CUBAN WOMEN'S CLUB (CWC)
970 SW 1st St., No. 406
Miami, FL 33130
Dr. Dolores Rovirosa, Treas.   PH: (305)324-5201

Founded: 1968. **Members:** 500. **Membership Dues:** US$24 annual. **Languages:** English. **National.** Women of Cuban descent. Promotes the general social welfare of women; sponsors cultural activities and other social functions. Works in cooperation with other organizations. Conducts charitable and educational programs.

Awards: Annual Floridana.
● Periodic (scholarship). ● Periodic (monetary).

Publications: *Directory*, periodic. **Advertising:** not accepted.

Conventions/Meetings: annual meeting. ● periodic competition.

★2693★ CUSTODY ACTION FOR LESBIAN MOTHERS (CALM)
PO Box 281
Narberth, PA 19072
Rosalie G. Davies, Coordinator   PH: (215)667-7508

Founded: 1974. **Staff:** 1. **Languages:** English. **National.** Provides free legal and counseling services for lesbian mothers seeking child custody. Primary commitment is to aid the mother in keeping her children; broader goal is to bring cases to court so the attitudes of judges and the courts may be challenged. Volunteers (usually lesbian mothers) advise mothers of their options, provide them with support and understanding, and accompany them through all phases of the legal process. Supports litigation addressing constitutional rights on the basis of sexual preference. Maintains nationwide contact with lesbian mother groups and attorneys who are either providing a similar counseling service or doing research in this area.

Conventions/Meetings: bimonthly board meeting.

★2694★ THE CYBELE SOCIETY (TCS)
W. 1603 9th Ave.
Spokane, WA 99204
Loel Fenwick M.D., Exec.Dir.   PH: (509)838-2332

Founded: 1978. **Languages:** English. **National.** Maternity care providers, physicians, nurses, nurse-midwives, and administrators. To promote maternity care that recognizes and adapts to the family's physical and emotional needs; to assist providers in keeping informed on changes in maternal/ newborn care. Sponsors continuing medical education programs for physicians and nurses. Conducts regional multidisciplinary conference. Maintains resource center of books and articles on family-centered maternity care. Acts as national clearinghouse for information on family-centered maternity care. Compiles statistics; maintains biographical archives. The society is named for Cybele, the Greek goddess of growth of natural things.

Publications: *The Cybele Report*, quarterly. Magazine.

Conventions/Meetings: annual meeting.

★2695★ DAKOTA WOMEN OF ALL RED NATIONS (DWARN)
PO Box 423
Rosebud, SD 57570
Lorelei DeCora, Chair

Founded: 1978. **Languages:** English. **National.** Grass roots organization of American Indian women seeking to advance the Native American movement. Is establishing local chapters to work on issues of concern such as sterilization abuse and women's health, adoption and foster-care abuse, community education, political imprisonment, legal and juvenile justice problems, and problems caused by energy resource development by multinational corporations on Indian land. Supports leadership roles for American Indian women.

Conventions/Meetings: annual conference.

★2696★ DAMES OF THE LOYAL LEGION OF THE UNITED STATES
   OF AMERICA (DLL)
138 Montrose Ave., No. 43
Rosemont, PA 19010
Mrs. Russell Bement, Pres.

Founded: 1899. **Members:** 225. **State Groups:** 5. **Languages:** English. **National.** Lineal and collateral female descendants of commissioned officers of the regular and volunteer forces of the United States during the Civil War; mothers, wives, and widows of companions of the Military Order of the Loyal Legion of the U.S. **Committees:** Memorial; Patriotic Education.

Conventions/Meetings: annual general assembly - always October.

★2697★ DAUGHTERS OF THE CINCINNATI (DC)
122 E. 58th St.
New York, NY 10022
Caroline Slee, Contact   PH: (212)319-6915

Founded: 1894. **Members:** 550. **Languages:** English. **National.** Women descendants of the officers of George Washington's Continental Army or Navy. Works to preserve patriotic ideals. **Awards:** Periodic (scholarship). Recipient: high school seniors who are daughters of commissioned officers of the armed services.

Publications: *Year Book*, annual.

Conventions/Meetings: annual meeting - always January. New York, NY, United States.

★2698★ DAUGHTERS OF EVRYTANIA (DE)
121 Greenwich Rd.
Charlotte, NC 28211
Theodora Retsios, Pres.   PH: (704)366-6571

Founded: 1948. **Members:** 600. **Languages:** English. **Multinational.** Women with an interest in the province of Evrytania, Greece; especially in helping the schools and hospitals in that area.

Conventions/Meetings: annual meeting.

★2699★ DAUGHTERS OF HIRSUTISM ASSOCIATION OF AMERICA
   (DOHA)
203 N. LaSalle St., Ste. 2100
Chicago, IL 60601
Jennifer M. Smith, Contact   PH: (312)558-1365

Founded: 1981. **Members:** 2,100. **Staff:** 4. **Budget:** US$25,000. **State Groups:** 2. **Languages:** English. **National.** Individuals with Hirsutism and their families and specialists in the treatment of Hirsutism. (Hirsutism is a hormonal imbalance causing excessive growth of facial and body hair in women.) Promotes understanding, support, and acceptance of Hirsute women. Provides seminars, workshops, and referral services for counseling, electrologists, endocrinology, dermatologists, and networking. Conducts research programs; maintains speakers' bureau; compiles statistics. **Computer Services:** Data base; mailing lists.

Publications: *Newsletter*, quarterly.

Conventions/Meetings: monthly conference.

★2700★ DAUGHTERS OF ISABELLA, INTERNATIONAL CIRCLE (DIIC)
375 Whitney Ave.
New Haven, CT 06511
Janet Hagen, Office Mgr.   PH: (203)865-2570

Founded: 1897. **Members:** 100,000. **Local Groups:** 800. **Languages:** English. **National.** Catholic women who seek to emulate the accomplishments and virtues of Queen Isabella (1451-1504), ruler of Aragon and Castile. Promotes friendship and seeks to unite the energies and resources of members "for the advancement of all that is best and truest in life." Sponsors Queen Isabella Foundation. Has established a family center at Catholic University of America. **Awards:** Periodic (scholarship).

Conventions/Meetings: biennial congress.

★2701★ DAUGHTERS OF THE NILE, SUPREME TEMPLE (DNST)
c/o Geraldine Neely
9832 Watts Branch Dr.
Rockville, MD 20850
Geraldine Neely, Sec.   PH: (301)279-7470

Founded: 1913. **Members:** 81,000. **Staff:** 6. **Local Groups:** 147. **Languages:** English. **National.** Mothers, wives, sisters, daughters, and widows of Shriners. Assists with philanthropic work of the Shriners' hospitals for crippled children.

Conventions/Meetings: annual meeting - always June.

★2702★ DAUGHTERS OF PENELOPE (DP)
1909 O St. NW, No. 500
Washington, DC 20009
Helen G. Pappas, Exec.Dir.   PH: (202)234-9741

Founded: 1929. **Members:** 12,000. **Local Groups:** 364. **Languages:** English. **National.** Women's fraternal organization. Awards scholarships to girls of Greek descent and participates in other philanthropic activities. Sponsors Daughters of Penelope Foundation. **Committees:** Cooley's Anemia; Pap Cancer Institute; Penelope House for Abused Women; Special Olympics; Youth Activities.

Conventions/Meetings: annual Supreme Council. ● biennial banquet.

★2703★ DAUGHTERS OF SCOTIA (DOS)
104 Buckingham Ave.
Syracuse, NY 13210
Marget Montgomery, Grand Rec.Sec.　　PH: (315)472-4050

Founded: 1895. **Members:** 5,000. **Local Groups:** 67. **Languages:** English. **National.** Women of Scottish descent or birth. Contributes to arthritis, Alzheimers, cancer, diabetes, and heart research programs.

Conventions/Meetings: annual meeting - always September. 1994, Worcester, MA, United States.

★2704★ DAUGHTERS OF UNION VETERANS OF THE CIVIL WAR, 1861-1865 (DUV)
503 S. Walnut St.
Springfield, IL 62704
Ms. Anna Kemison, Treas.　　PH: (217)544-0616

Founded: 1885. **Members:** 6,000. **Staff:** 1. **Regional Groups:** 21. **Local Groups:** 194. **Languages:** English. **National.** Lineal descendants of Union veterans of the U.S. Civil War. Objectives are to perpetuate the memories of veterans of the U.S. Civil War, their loyalty to the Union, and their sacrifices for its preservation. Seeks to: keep alive the history of those who participated in the struggle for the maintenance of our free government; aid the descendants of Union veterans of the Civil War; assist those who are worthy and needy; cooperate in movements relating to veterans, civic, and welfare projects; inculcate a love of country and patriotism; promote equal rights and universal liberty; honor Union veterans of the Civil War by placing flowers on graves on Memorial Day. Conducts genealogical projects. Supports and maintains public museum in Springfield, IL. Conducts charitable work in veterans' hospitals. Supports local historical societies. Takes part in patriotic ceremonial programs and holiday observances. Conducts specialized education programs and sponsors competitions. **Libraries:** Type: reference. Subjects: genealogy. **Awards:** Periodic (scholarship). **Committees:** Heritage; Legislative; Youth.

Publications: *General Orders*, quarterly. Newsletter. ● *Roster of National Members*, annual. Directory.

Conventions/Meetings: annual meeting - always August.

★2705★ DELEGATION FOR FRIENDSHIP AMONG WOMEN (DFW)
2219 Caroline Ln.
South St. Paul, MN 55075　　PH: (612)455-5620
Mary Pomeroy, Sec.　　FX: (612)445-5620

Founded: 1962. **Members:** 144. **Budget:** US$72,000. **Languages:** English. **Multinational.** Women who have displayed leadership qualities in the fields of academia, architecture, business, journalism, law, and science. Promotes better understanding and cultural exchange between women and women's organizations in developing nations and American women. Sponsors networks for the health, education, and welfare of women and children. Arranges programs for women visiting the U.S. from developing countries; provides speakers for women's activities. Maintains biographical archives. **Libraries:** Type: reference. Holdings: 600.

Publications: *Bulletin*, periodic. ● *Newsletter*, periodic.

Conventions/Meetings: annual meeting.

★2706★ DELTA DELTA DELTA
2313 Brookhollow Plaza Dr.
PO Box 5987
Arlington, TX 76005　　PH: (817)640-8001
Cari Cook, Exec. Dir.　　FX: (817)652-0212

Founded: 1888. **Members:** 152,000. **Languages:** English. **National.** Social sorority.

Publications: *The Trident*, quarterly. Magazine.

Conventions/Meetings: biennial meeting - even-numbered years.

★2707★ DELTA GAMMA
3250 Riverside Dr.
PO Box 21397
Columbus, OH 43221-0397　　PH: (614)481-8169
Margaret Hess Watkins, Exec.Dir.　　FX: (614)481-0133

Founded: 1873. **Members:** 143,000. **Staff:** 33. **Budget:** US$2,400,000. **Languages:** English. **National.** Social sorority. Delta Gamma Foundation serves as channel for philanthropic activities. Sponsors annual seminar for alumnae advisers to collegiate chapters and rush seminar for collegiate officers. Maintains biographical archives, hall of fame, and museum. Bestows awards; compiles statistics.

Publications: *Anchora*, quarterly. Magazine. Contains alumni and collegiate news. **Circulation:** 90,000. **Advertising:** not accepted. ● *History of Delta Gamma Series*, decennial. Monograph. ● *Shield*, triennial. Booklet.

Conventions/Meetings: biennial meeting - always June. ● biennial seminar - always June. 1994 June, New Orleans, LA, United States.

★2708★ DELTA KAPPA GAMMA SOCIETY INTERNATIONAL
PO Box 1589
Austin, TX 78767
Dr. Theresa Fechek, Exec. Coordinator　　PH: (512)478-5748

Founded: 1929. **Members:** 168,000. **Staff:** 20. **Languages:** English. **Multinational.** Honorary society for women in education. **Awards:** Periodic Educator's Award for Women Authors. ● Periodic (scholarship).

Publications: *Delta Kappa Gamma Bulletin*, quarterly. ● *Delta Kappa Gamma News*, 8/year. Newsletter. ● *International Directory*, annual.

Conventions/Meetings: biennial meeting.

★2709★ DELTA PHI EPSILON
1425 Bedford St., Ste. 1-G
Stamford, CT 06905
Dolores Engbar, Exec. Officer　　PH: (203)353-0011

Founded: 1917. **Members:** 28,604. **Staff:** 5. **Regional Groups:** 40. **State Groups:** 29. **Languages:** English. **National.** Social sorority.

Publications: *Triad*, semiannual. Magazine.

Conventions/Meetings: biennial leadership school - next 1994.

★2710★ DELTA SIGMA THETA SORORITY
1707 New Hampshire Ave. NW
Washington, DC 20009
Rosalind McKinney, Exec.Dir.　　PH: (202)483-5460

Founded: 1913. **National.** Promotes educational and economic development, physical and mental health, political awareness and involvement, and international awareness and involvement among women.

★2711★ DELTA ZETA
202 E. Church St.
Oxford, OH 45056
Cynthia W. Menges, Exec.Dir.　　PH: (513)523-7597

Founded: 1902. **Members:** 138,000. **Languages:** English. **National.** Social sorority.

Publications: *LAMP of Delta Zeta*, quarterly. Magazine.

Conventions/Meetings: biennial meeting.

★2712★ DEMOCRATIC NATIONAL COMMITTEE - WOMEN'S DIVISION
430 S. Capitol St. SE
Washington, DC 20003
Lynn Cutler, Co-chair　　PH: (202)836-8017

Languages: English. **National.** Supports and promotes women's needs within the Democratic Party.

★2713★ DEPARTMENT OF CIVIL RIGHTS, AFL-CIO
815 16th St. NW
Washington, DC 20006
Richard Womack, Dir.   PH: (202)637-5270

Founded: 1955. **Languages:** English. **National**. Staff arm AFL-CIO Civil Rights Committee. Serves as official liaison with women's and civil rights organizations and government agencies working in the field of equal opportunity; helps to implement state and federal laws and AFL-CIO civil rights policies; aids affiliates in the development of affirmative programs to expand opportunities for minorities and women; prepares and disseminates special materials on civil rights; speaks at union and civil rights institutes, conferences, and conventions; helps affiliates resolve complaints involving unions under Title VII of the 1964 Civil Rights Act and Executive Order 11246.

Publications: *AFL-CIO and Civil Rights*, biennial. Newsletter.

Conventions/Meetings: biennial meeting.

★2714★ DEPRESSION AFTER DELIVERY (DAD)
PO Box 1282
Morrisville, PA 19067   PH: (215)295-3994
Nancy Berchtold, Exec.Dir.   TF: (800)944-4773

Founded: 1986. **Members:** 10,000. **State Groups:** 70. **Languages:** English. **National**. Women who have experienced postpartum adjustment problems, depression, or psychosis; professionals in the health care industry. Provides support to members and their families. Acts as a clearinghouse for information on postpartum depression and psychosis. Maintains referral service; operates hot-line.

Publications: *Newsletter*, quarterly.

Conventions/Meetings: annual meeting. ● annual conference.

★2715★ DISABLED WOMYN'S EDUCATIONAL PROJECT
PO Box 8773
Madison, WI 53708-8773
Catherine Odette, Exec.Officer   PH: (608)256-8883

Founded: 1988. **Staff:** 6. **Languages:** English. **National**. Lesbians with disabilities. Promotes members' interests. Supports legislation affecting members' needs. Maintains a speakers' bureau. **Libraries:** Type: reference. Holdings: books, clippings, periodicals, artwork. **Committees:** Political Action.

Publications: *Dykes, Disability, and Stuff*, quarterly. Newsletter. **Circulation:** 750. **Advertising:** accepted. ● *The Time for Access is Now*. Book. ● *Building Community Through Access*. Book.

★2716★ DISPLACED HOMEMAKERS NETWORK
1411 K St. NW
Washington, DC 20005
Jill Miller, Exec.Dir.   PH: (202)628-6767

National. Works to empower displaced homemakers of all racial and ethnic backgrounds. Assists them in achieving economic independency. Cooperates with lawmakers and business leaders to create and strengthen programs that support these efforts. Sponsors public education projects on the needs of displaced homemakers.

★2717★ DOMESTIC VIOLENCE PROJECT
PO Box 7052
Ann Arbor, MI 48107
Susan McGee, Director   PH: (313)973-0242

Founded: 1976. **Languages:** English. **National**. Provides medical, psychological, and legal counseling services for female victims of domestic violence. Offers temporary shelter. Investigates domestic violence against women and other women's issues. Maintains a crisis line for women in need.

★2718★ EAGLE FORUM (EF)
Box 618
Alton, IL 62002   PH: (618)462-5415
Phyllis Schlafly, Pres.   FX: (618)462-8909

Founded: 1975. **Members:** 80,000. **Languages:** English. **National**. Men and women advocating issues involving family, education, and national defense through local, state, and federal government. Supports pro-family and conservative philosophy. Promotes traditional morality, private enterprise, and national defense. Opposes ratification of the Equal Rights Amendment because the forum claims it is inconsistent with the rights of women, families, and individuals. Plans are: to increase tax exemptions for children and end what the forum calls unfair tax discrimination against the traditional family that now exists in the income tax code; to rebuild a strong national defense. Strives to strengthen parents' and pupils' rights in education. Bestows Fulltime Homemaker Award. Maintains a relationship with Eagle Forum Education and Legal Defense Fund and Eagle Forum PAC. **Committees:** Education; Family; National Defense.

Publications: *Phyllis Schlafly Report*, monthly. Newsletter. Provides commentaries on education, national defense, politics, economics, and social, public, and foreign policy. **ISSN:** 0556-0152. **Circulation:** 40,000. **Advertising:** not accepted.

Conventions/Meetings: annual meeting.

★2719★ ECUMENICAL CELEBRATIONS (EC)
475 Riverside Dr., Rm. 812
New York, NY 10115   PH: (212)870-2348
Rev. Mary Cline Detrick, Dir.   FX: (212)870-2338

Founded: 1941. **Regional Groups:** 8. **State Groups:** 52. **Local Groups:** 1,750. **Languages:** English. **National**. Project of Church Women United. Participants include Protestant, Roman Catholic, Orthodox, and other Christian women. Plans, produces, and promotes World Day of Prayer (first Friday of March), May Fellowship Day (first Friday of May), and World Community Day (first Friday of November). Celebrations include worship, prayer, study, and action. Utilizes resources such as worship services, posters, feature stories, and radio and television advertisements.

Publications: *The Churchwoman*, quarterly. Newsletter. ● *Wellsprings*. Booklet. Bible study guide.

★2720★ ELECTRICAL WOMEN'S ROUND TABLE (EWRT)
PO Box 292793
Nashville, TN 37229-2793
Ann Cox, Exec.Dir.   PH: (615)890-1272

Founded: 1927. **Members:** 450. **Budget:** US$60,000. **Local Groups:** 15. **Languages:** English. **National**. Women and men holding positions connected with the electrical industry or allied fields in roles such as communicator, educator, information specialist, and researcher. Objectives are to: promote knowledge and expertise among members in the fields of electrical energy, energy resources, and energy conservation; increase recognition and encourage upward mobility of women in the electrical industry; advance consumer education. Acts as a forum, promotes research, conducts workshops, and reviews new audiovisual and printed materials. **Awards:** Annual Julia Keine and Lyle Mamer Fellowship.

Publications: *Electrical Women's Round Table—Membership Directory*, annual. **Circulation:** 500. ● *Electrical Women's Round Table—National Newsletter*, quarterly. Articles on efficient use of electrical energy from an administrative standpoint.

Conventions/Meetings: annual conference - 1993 Oct. 13 - 15, Indianapolis, IN, United States.

★2721★ EMUNAH WOMEN OF AMERICA (EWA)
7 Penn Plaza
New York, NY 10001   PH: (212)564-9045
Shirley Singer, Exec.Dir.   TF: (800)225-5528

Founded: 1948. **Members:** 38,000. **Staff:** 15. **Local Groups:** 40. **Languages:** English. **National**. A network of chapters throughout North America, with affiliated branches in 30 countries throughout the world. Women working to support and maintain 225 institutions in Israel where over 20,000 needy children are cared for in kindergartens, day care centers, nurseries, girls' homes, vocational training schools, and community colleges. Sponsors tours to Israel.

Publications: *Dinner Journal*, annual. ● *The Emunah Connection*, quarterly. Newsletter. ● *The Emunah Woman*, quarterly. Newsletter. ● *Lest We Forget*, quarterly. Newsletter.

Conventions/Meetings: annual meeting - usually May.

★2722★ ENDOMETRIOSIS ASSOCIATION (EA)
8585 N. 76th Pl.
Milwaukee, WI 53223
Mary Lou Ballweg, Exec.Dir.   PH: (414)355-2200

Founded: 1980. **Staff:** 8. **Languages:** English. **National**. Women who have endometriosis and others interested in the condition. (Endometriosis is a disorder in which endometrial tissue, which lines the uterus, is also found in other locations in the body, usually the abdomen. Symptoms can include extremely painful menstruation, infertility, painful sexual intercourse, and heavy or irregular bleeding.) Disseminates information on the treatment, research, and attitudes concerning endometriosis. Offers selfhelp support, telephone counseling, and informational meetings for women with endometriosis and others. Conducts public education programs; maintains speakers' bureau; gathers data on individual experiences with endometriosis. **Libraries:** Type: reference.   **Committees:** Community Education; Correspondence; Crisis Call; Data Bank; Scientific.

Publications: *Endometriosis Association Newsletter*, bimonthly. Includes news, tips, reviews, and research reports; also covers association and chapter news and activities. **Circulation:** 10,000. **Advertising:** not accepted. ● *Overcoming Endometriosis*. Book. ● *You're Not Alone.Understanding Endometriosis*. Videos. ● *The Choice is Ours: New Surgeries for Endometriosis*. Videos.

Conventions/Meetings: periodic meeting.

★2723★ EPISCOPAL WOMEN'S CAUCUS (EWC)
PO Box 5172
Laurel, MD 20726

Founded: 1971. **Members:** 800. **Languages:** English. **National**. Lay and ordained men and women concerned with the full ministry of all women and minorities in the church. Provides network of people involved in similar issues.

Publications: *RUACH*, quarterly. Newsletter. **Circulation:** 1,000. **Advertising:** not accepted. ● *Collection of Statements, Papers, and Resources on Inclusive Language*. Book.

Conventions/Meetings: annual conference.

★2724★ EPSILON SIGMA ALPHA
363 W. Drake Rd.
Ft. Collins, CO 80526
B. J. Clark, Exec.Dir.   PH: (303)223-2824

Founded: 1929. **Members:** 25,000. **Staff:** 15. **Budget:** US$700,000. **Languages:** English. **National**. Leadership service sorority. **Awards:** Annual International Diana Award.

Publications: *Jonquil*, semiannual. Newsletter.

Conventions/Meetings: annual meeting - always July.

★2725★ EQUALITY NOW
PO Box 20646
Columbus Circle Sta.
New York, NY 10023
Jessica Neuwirth, Contact

Multinational. Protects and defends the civil, political, economic, and social rights of women and girls worldwide. Promotes awareness of reproductive rights. Conducts letter writing, fax, and video campaigns against: rape, domestic violence, female infanticide, genital mutilation, sexual harassment, pornography, and discrimination.

★2726★ EQUITY INSTITUTE
PO Box 30245
Bethesda, MD 20814
Mary Ellen Verheyden-Hillard, President   PH: (301)654-2904

Founded: 1980. **National**. Promotes equal rights for women and girls throughout the United States. Disseminates information on equity for women and girls.

★2727★ EQUITY POLICY CENTER (EPOC)
2000 P St. NW, No. 508
Washington, DC 20036   PH: (202)872-1770
Elisabeth Prugl, Dir.   TX: 6503488207

Founded: 1978. **Members:** 230. **Staff:** 2. **Budget:** US$100,000. **Languages:** English. **National**. Research, communications, and educational organizations concerned with global women's issues and developments. Identifies and studies critical areas in national and international development programs where women's interests have been neglected, and suggests policy and programmatic improvements. Provides assistance to planners and programmers in the review and analysis of ongoing projects and their impact on women. Offers internship program and represents women in development in U.S. and United Nations preparations for world conferences and meetings. Arranges seminars and provides speakers for universities and government agencies and foundations. **Libraries:** Type: reference.   Subjects: unpublished materials on development issues. **Committees:** Policy Research on Home-based work.

★2728★ ETA PHI BETA
1724 Mohawk Blvd.
Tulsa, OK 74110
Elizabeth Anderson, Pres.   PH: (918)425-8612

Founded: 1942. **Members:** 8,000. **Regional Groups:** 6. **Languages:** English. **National**. Professional sorority - business. Conducts national projects concerning retarded citizens and retarded children. Conducts leadership and career programs and seminars; sponsors competitions. Operates speakers' bureau; provides children's services; maintains charitable program. **Awards:** Periodic Queen Bee (scholarship). ● Periodic (grant). **Committees:** Archives; Talent; Teenage Pregnancy and Parenting; Youth Career.

Publications: *Beeline*, semiannual. Newsletter. ● *Membership Directory*, biennial. ● *News*, quarterly. Newsletter.

Conventions/Meetings: biennial meeting (exhibits). ● biennial regional meeting - always odd-numbered years.

★2729★ ETERNAL LIFE
PO Box 787
Bardstown, KY 40004   PH: (502)348-3963

Languages: English. **National**. Orthodox, lay Catholics. Seeks to oraganize a Catholic response to "exploitive and sinful sexual behaviors and attitudes" such as abortion, fetal experimentation, euthanasia, sterilization, premarital sex, homosexuality, divorce, pornography, artificial insemination, and contraception. Promotes family-centered sexuality and spirituality by bringing the perspective of Catholic teachings into the prolife movement.

Publications: *Eternal Life*, monthly. Newsletter.

★2730★ EVANGELICAL AND ECUMENICAL WOMEN'S CAUCUS
(EEWC)
PO Box 209
Hadley, NY 12835
Florence Brown, Exec.Dir.   PH: (518)696-2406

Founded: 1974. **Members:** 300. **Staff:** 2. **Regional Groups:** 9. **Local Groups:** 12. **Languages:** English. **National.** Christian feminists, churches, seminaries, and colleges. Aims to: encourage evangelical women to work for change in their churches and in society; present God's teaching on female-male equality to the whole body of Christ's church; call men and women to "mutual submission and active discipleship." Believes that the Bible, when properly understood, supports the basic equality of the sexes. Holds special events and retreats. Maintains archives of EWCI activities.

Publications: *Update*, quarterly. Newsletter.

Conventions/Meetings: biennial conference - next 1994.

★2731★ EX-PARTNERS OF SERVICEMEN (WOMEN) FOR EQUALITY
(EXPOSE)
PO Box 11191
Alexandria, VA 22312   PH: (703)941-5844
Mary Wurzel, Pres.   (703)255-2917

Founded: 1980. **Members:** 5,000. **Languages:** English. **National.** Ex-military spouses whose purpose is to alert members of Congress to the need for change in laws concerning military benefits after divorce. Aims to educate past, present, and future military spouses as to the state of their benefits after divorce. Seeks legislation that treats marriage as an economic partnership. Feels that in the event of divorce, retirement pay should be divided (prorated). Operates telephone hot-line. Has achieved legislation for the direct payment of court-awarded monies from ex-spouses' retirement pay for alimony, child support, property settlement, medical care for most of those already divorced and those contemplating divorce, and courts' ability to award survivor benefits.

Publications: *Ex-Partners of Servicemen for Equality—Newsletter*, bimonthly. ● *Guide for Military Separation or Divorce*. Booklet.

Conventions/Meetings: annual meeting.

★2732★ EXECUTIVE WOMEN INTERNATIONAL (EWI)
515 S. 700 E, Ste. 2E
Salt Lake City, UT 84102   PH: (801)263-3296
Lois Trayner-Allinder, Pres.   FX: (801)268-6127

Founded: 1938. **Members:** 5,000. **Staff:** 4. **Budget:** US$500,000. **Local Groups:** 87. **Languages:** English. **Multinational.** Women holding key positions in business professions. **Awards:** Periodic (scholarship).

Publications: *Executive Women International*, annual. Directory. **Circulation:** 5,000. **Advertising:** not accepted. ● *Pulse*, quarterly. Newsletter. **Circulation:** 5,500. **Advertising:** not accepted.

Conventions/Meetings: annual meeting (exhibits) - always fall. 1994, Honolulu, HI, United States; 1995 Sept. 6 - 10, Washington, DC, United States; 1996 Sept. 25 - 29, Dallas, TX, United States.

★2733★ FAMILY OF THE AMERICAS FOUNDATION (FAF)
PO Box 1170   PH: (301)627-3346
Dunkirk, MD 20754-1170   TF: (800)443-3395
Mercedes Wilson, Exec.Dir.   FX: (301)627-0847

Founded: 1977. **Members:** 270. **Staff:** 10. **Languages:** English. **National.** Promotes teaching of the Ovulation Method of birth regulation in which a woman is taught to recognize the fertile phase of her menstrual cycle by analyzing the appearance of mucus secreted from the cervix. Maintains permanent teacher training centers; certifies instructors of the method.

Conducts regional, national, and international workshops to present new scientific information concerning the method and to train new and existing teachers; assists in the planning and implementation of local workshops. Sponsors teacher training and preparation of instructional materials for developing countries. Holds conferences to educate the public about the use of natural family planning in developed and developing countries. Participates in conferences with medical, religious, government, and educational personnel. Assists parents in providing effective sex education for their children; teaches adolescents about fertility and the importance of accepting responsibility for their sexual behavior. Provides referral services and technical assistance. Offers standard teacher certification programs for Master Teachers and Master Trainers. **Libraries:** Type: reference. Subjects: family planning.

Publications: *Love and Fertility* (in French and Spanish). Book.

Conventions/Meetings: annual congress.

★2734★ FAMILY CARE INTERNATIONAL
588 Broadway, Ste. 510   PH: (212)941-5300
New York, NY 10012   FX: (212)941-5563
Jill W. Sheffield, President   TX: 210474 FAMCARUR

Founded: 1985. **Staff:** 12. **Budget:** US$1,900,000. **Languages:** English, Spanish, French. **Multinational.** Promotes women's health and well-being worldwide, focusing specifically on maternal mortality. Seeks to reduce maternal mortality by at least 50 percent by the year 2000. Supports initiatives to raise the socio-economic and educational status of women as a condition for improved health for women. Furthers the availability of family planning and maternal health information services. Fosters the exchange of information and global networking. Develops community education and training programs. Serves as an information clearinghouse.

Publications: *Meeting of Partners for Safe Motherhood*. Booklet. ● *Safe Motherhood: Action Kit* (in English, Spanish, and French). ● *Safe Motherhood Initiative* (in English, Spanish, French, and Arabic). Booklet.

Conventions/Meetings: periodic conference.

★2735★ FAMILY HEALTH INTERNATIONAL (FHI)
PO Box 13950
Durham, NC 27709   PH: (919)544-7040
Dr. Malcolm Potts, Pres.   FX: (919)544-7261

Founded: 1971. **Staff:** 230. **Languages:** English. **National.** Biomedical researchers and technical assistants. Promotes increased availability, safety, effectiveness, acceptability, and ease of using family planning methods. Works to improve the delivery of voluntary fertility planning and primary health care services, and reduce the spread of sexually transmitted diseases, especially HIV infection. Conducts, analyzes, and disseminates research on contraception and distribution of family planning services. Supports a program of contraceptive safety and health records.
        Divisions: AIDSTECH; Biostatistics and Quality Assurance; Clinical Trials; Field Development and Training; Materials Technology; Program Evaluation, Regulatory Affairs; Reproductive Epidemiology and Sexually Transmitted Diseases.

Publications: *Report*, biennial. Journal. ● *Family Health International—Network* (in English, French, and Spanish), quarterly. Newsletter. Reproductive health and family planning for health care personnel and policymakers in developing countries. **ISSN:** 0270-3637. **Circulation:** 11,800. **Advertising:** not accepted. ● *Publications Catalog*, annual.

★2736★ FAT LIP READERS THEATER (FLRT)
PO Box 29963
Oakland, CA 94604
Laura Bock, Contact   PH: (415)664-6842

Founded: 1981. **Members:** 12. **Languages:** English. **National.** Women who do not look upon being fat as an illness and are not intent on finding its cure.

Original scripts dramatizing the experience of growing up fat and female in America are performed. Members are determined to fight misinformation and stereotypes about being fat within a theatrical and entertaining medium. Conducts workshops and classes for universities, professional associations, medical and health workers, and the public.

Publications: *Nothing to Lose.* Videos.

★2737★ FEDERALLY EMPLOYED WOMEN (FEW)
1400 I St. NW, Ste. 425
Washington, DC 20005   PH: (202)898-0994
Karen R. Scott, Exec.Dir.   FX: (202)898-0998

Founded: 1968. **Local Groups:** 200. **Languages:** English. **National**. Men and women employed by the federal government; associate members are persons who support the goals and objectives of FEW. Seeks to end sex discrimination in government service; to increase job opportunities for women in government service and to further the potential of all women in the government; to improve the merit system in government employment; to assist present and potential government employees who are discriminated against because of sex; to work with other organizations and individuals concerned with equal employment opportunity in the government. Provides speakers and sponsors seminars to publicize the Federal Women's Program; furnishes members with information on pending legislation designed to end discrimination against working women; informs members of opportunities for training to improve their job potential; issues fact sheets interpreting civil service rules and regulations. **Awards:** Annual Distinguished Service Award. ● Periodic (recognition). **Committees:** Compliance; Cultural Awareness; Legal; Legislative; Public Relations; Training.

Publications: *News and Views*, bimonthly. Newsletter.

Conventions/Meetings: annual conference (exhibits) - always July. 1994 July, Washington, DC, United States.

★2738★ FEDERATED WOMEN IN TIMBER (FWIT)
2543 Mt. Baker Hwy.
Bellingham, WA 98226
Judy Marr, Chm.   PH: (206)592-5330

Founded: 1979. **State Groups:** 11. **Languages:** English. **National**. Women from Alaska, California, Idaho, Montana, Colorado, Wyoming, Wisconsin, Oregon, Washington, Minnesota, and Michigan associated with the timber industry. Informs members of government, the communications media, and the public about the effect government-imposed restrictions on forest land have on timber communities. Lobbies against additional lands being designated as federal reserve or wilderness areas. Sponsors speakers' bureau; conducts research projects.

Publications: *Newsletter*, periodic.

Conventions/Meetings: annual meeting - always fall.

★2739★ FEDERATION OF EASTERN STARS (FES)
PO Box 02098
Detroit, MI 48202
Lucille F. McCants, Pres.   PH: (313)894-0790

Founded: 1962. **Members:** 105,000. **Languages:** English. **National**. Women's division of the Federation of Masons of the World. Seeks the unification of Easternism. Conducts charitable and community work.

Conventions/Meetings: biennial meeting.

★2740★ FEDERATION OF EASTERN STARS OF THE WORLD (FESW)
PO Box 1296
Austin, TX 78767
Ada C. Anderson, Exec.Sec.   PH: (512)477-5380

Founded: 1947. **Members:** 57,000. **Staff:** 2. **Languages:** English. **Multina-**tional. Organization with 87 Grand Chapters. Seeks to unify all Eastern Stars

Conventions/Meetings: biennial meeting.

★2741★ FEDERATION OF FEMINIST WOMEN'S HEALTH CENTERS (FFWHC)
1680 Vine St., Ste. 1105
Los Angeles, CA 90028-8837   PH: (213)957-4062
Carol Downer, Exec.Dir.   FX: (213)957-4064

Founded: 1975. **Members:** 163. **Staff:** 2. **Languages:** English. **National**. Women's health clinics and interested individuals. Works to secure reproductive rights for women and men, educate women about the normal functions of their bodies, and improve the quality of women's health care. Coordinates activities of women's health centers.

Publications: *A New View of a Woman's Body.* Book. ● *Woman-Centered Pregnancy.* Book. ● *How to Stay Out of the Gynecologist's Office.* Book.

Conventions/Meetings: annual meeting.

★2742★ FEDERATION OF FRENCH AMERICAN WOMEN (FFFA)
240 Highland Ave.
Fall River, MA 02720
Marthe W. Whalon, Pres.   PH: (508)678-1800

Founded: 1951. **Members:** 10,000. **Local Groups:** 49. **Languages:** English. **Multinational**. Members of French fraternal organizations. Promotes French culture. Conducts oral history program, French speaking contests, youth festivals, ethnic vacations, and reunions. Maintains biographical archives and hall of fame. Bestows awards; compiles statistics.

Publications: *Le Bulletin*, semiannual. Reports on membership activities.

Conventions/Meetings: biennial congress. ● semiannual conference.

★2743★ FEDERATION OF JEWISH WOMEN'S ORGANIZATIONS (FJWO)
1265 Broadway, Rm. 608
New York, NY 10001
Sylvia N. Rachlin, Pres.   PH: (212)684-2888

Founded: 1896. **Members:** 300. **Staff:** 1. **Languages:** English. **National**. Umbrella organization of Jewish women's groups representing 120,000 women. Serves as clearinghouse of information; maintains liaison between member groups and municipal and recognized private agencies; encourages interest in education, health, religion, social service, civic improvements, and city, state, and national welfare legislation; promotes efficiency by providing guidance and preventing duplication of efforts. Holds forums and lectures; equips synagogues in municipal institutions; conducts activities for armed forces and veterans.

Publications: *Horizons*, monthly. Newsletter.

Conventions/Meetings: annual meeting (exhibits).

★2744★ FEDERATION OF ORGANIZATIONS FOR PROFESSIONAL WOMEN (FOPW)
2001 S St. NW, Ste. 500
Washington, DC 20009   PH: (202)328-1415
Dr. Viola Young-Horvath, Dir.   FX: (202)462-5241

Founded: 1972. **Members:** 230. **Staff:** 3. **Budget:** US$25,000. **Languages:** English. **National**. Women's groups concerned with economic, educational, and social equality for women; interested individuals. Works to enhance the educational and employment status of women. Acts as a forum for the exchange of ideas and to provide mutual support. Provides information on selected public policy issues to affiliate groups. Offers research and policy analyses. Accepts internships. Conducts seminars and training programs; compiles statistics. Maintains referral service. Sponsors networking events. Affiliated with 30 women's groups and organizations. **Computer Services:**

Mailing lists, for members only. **Committees:** Career Development; Metaskills; Professional Women' Legal Fund and related support group; Public Policy/Legislation.

Publications: *A Woman's Yellow Book*, periodic. Directory. ● *ALERT*, bimonthly. Newsletter.

Conventions/Meetings: annual conference (exhibits) - always winter. ● annual meeting.

★2745★ FEDERATION OF WOMAN'S EXCHANGES (FWE)
62 Grove Park Circle
Memphis, TN 38117
Ann Uhlhorn, Pres.   PH: (901)761-3913

Founded: 1934. **Members:** 39. **State Groups:** 16. **Languages:** English. **National.** Groups known as Woman's Exchanges which operate voluntary nonprofit consignment shops. (Consignment shops provide a sales outlet for high-quality handcrafts and home-cooked foods; the profits from such shops are disbursed among other local voluntary nonprofit groups according to local needs.) Purposes are to: provide a market for handcrafted products; share information on effective shop management techniques; provide consultation to potential Woman's Exchanges; insure that the shops of prospective members are nonprofit and staffed by volunteers.

Publications: *Directory of Exchanges*, annual.

Conventions/Meetings: annual conference.

★2746★ FEMINIST ARAB-AMERICAN NETWORK
c/o NAJDA
PO Box 7152
Berkeley, CA 94707

Languages: English. **National.** Arab-American women united to promote the principles of feminism. Works to eliminate sexual and ethnic discrimination.

★2747★ FEMINIST CENTER FOR HUMAN GROWTH AND
DEVELOPMENT (FCHGD)
300 E. 75th St., Ste. 26-D
New York, NY 10021
Charlotte Schwab Ph.D., Exec.Dir.   PH: (212)686-0869

Founded: 1976. **Languages:** English. **National.** An educational organization that provides resources, information, and a referral support system for people who need personal or career counseling. Goal is to formulate a "new theory of personality development that will help to free women and men from the social, political and cultural limitations that now form the basis of existing psychological theories." Conducts nonsexist and feminist lectures, panels, and counseling. Sponsors participatory and experiential workshops and groups on such topics as relationships, self-identity, self-esteem, goal setting, risk taking, networking, assertiveness, and positive communication. Offers a nonsexist therapy training program for human resources personnel and others interested in counseling women and men.

Publications: *A Model for Positive Self Identity and Self Defined Success.* Book. ● *Model for Effective Positive Communication.* Book.

★2748★ FEMINIST INSTITUTE
PO Box 30563
Bethesda, MD 20824
Carolyn H. Sparks, President   PH: (301)951-9040

National. Promoting feminist social change through social action, education, and research projects that "illuminate and celebrate women's freedom and autonomy." Serves as a clearinghouse; maintains speakers' bureau.

★2749★ FEMINIST INTERNATIONAL NETWORKING ON THE NEW
REPRODUCTIVE TECHNOLOGIES (FINNRET)
c/o Women's Studies
University of Massachusetts
Amherst, MA 01003

Languages: English. **National.** Conducts research and disseminates information on reproductive and contraceptive technologies.

★2750★ FEMINIST MAJORITY FOUNDATION
675 Massachusetts Ave.
Cambridge, MA 02139
Eleanor Smeal, President

Languages: English. **National.** Campaigns to legalize RU 486 (the French abortion pill) in the United States. Disseminates information.

Publications: *RU 486 Report.* Booklet.

★2751★ FEMINIST TEACHER EDITORIAL COLLECTIVE (FTEC)
Indiana University
Ballantine Hall 442
Bloomington, IN 47405
Elisabeth Daumer, Treas.   PH: (812)855-5597

Founded: 1984. **Languages:** English. **National.** Teachers and students; schools, libraries, archives, and women's organizations. Opposes sexism, racism, and other forms of oppression in the classroom. Encourages innovative teaching practices that challenge traditional educational, disciplinary, and research methodologies.

Publications: *Feminist Teacher*, 3/year. Journal. Provides a forum for new ideas in the classroom. Includes feminist teacher network news, information on teaching resources, and book reviews. **Price:** US$12/year for individuals (in U.S.); US$17/year for individuals (outside U.S.); US$20/year for institutions (in U.S.); US$25/year for institutions (outside U.S.).. **ISSN:** 0882-4843. **Circulation:** 900.

★2752★ FEMINISTS FOR ANIMAL RIGHTS (FAR)
Box 694, Cathedral Sta.
New York, NY 10025
Barya Bauman, Exec. Officer   PH: (212)866-6422

Founded: 1982. **Members:** 250. **Regional Groups:** 3. **Languages:** English. **National.** Feminist vegetarians dedicated to ending all forms of animal abuse. Believes that violence against animals is directly related to violence against women. Seeks an end to: violence against animals in the forms of trapping animals for fur, animal experimentation, animals used for entertainment, killing animals for their flesh; the exploitation of women in the forms of pornography and prostitution. Works to eliminate all products derived from or tested on animals including food, clothing, and household products. Provides educational materials.

Publications: *Feminists for Animal Rights Newsletter*, semiannual. **Advertising:** accepted.

★2753★ FEMINISTS FIGHTING PORNOGRAPHY (FFP)
PO Box 6731, Yorkville Sta.
New York, NY 10128
Page Mellish, Exec. Officer

Founded: 1984. **Staff:** 1. **Languages:** English. **National.** Combats pornography by lobbying the federal government. Maintains speakers' bureau; conducts slide shows.

Publications: *Backlash Times*, annual. Magazine.

★2754★ FEMINISTS FOR LIFE (FFL)
811 E. 47th St.
Kansas City, MO 64110   PH: (816)753-2130

Feminists who advocate pro-life principles. A secular, national organization which supports equal opportunity and equal rights legal protection, as well as the protection of human life, maintaining a clear anti-abortion, anti-capital punishment, and anti-euthenasia position. Statement of purpose: ''As seekers of peace and equality and protectors of life, we pursue constructive, non-violent solutions to human problems. Since feminism rests upon the principles of justice, non-violence, and non-discrimination, abortion and other forms of institutionalized killing are inconsistent with these founding principles. We seek to identify and correct those practices which exploit women and children and deny them their true equality. As feminist women and men, we must be consistent in our demand for human rights.''

★2755★ FEMINISTS FOR LIFE OF AMERICA (FFL)
811 E. 47th St.
Kansas City, MO 64110   PH: (816)753-2130
Rosemary Bottcher, Exec.V.Pres.   FX: (816)753-7741

Founded: 1972. **Members:** 4,000. **Budget:** US$25,000. **State Groups:** 47. **Languages:** English. **National.** Individuals united to secure the right to life, from conception to natural death, of all human beings. Seeks legal and social equality of all persons regardless of sex. Supports a Human Life Amendment, Equal Rights Amendment, and other methods of achieving respect for life and equality of the sexes as necessarily compatible goals. Activities include workshops, speakers' bureau, debates, and research of current literature on abortion and feminism.

Publications: *Sisterlife*, quarterly. Newsletter. **Circulation:** 5,000. **Advertising:** accepted. ● *Profile Feminism: Different Voices*. Book.

Conventions/Meetings: semiannual conference.

★2756★ FINANCIAL WOMEN INTERNATIONAL (FWI)
7910 Woodmont Ave.
Bethesda, MD 20814   PH: (301)657-8288
Sylvia Straub, Exec.VP   FX: (301)913-0001

Founded: 1921. **Members:** 11,000. **Staff:** 4. **Budget:** US$1,500,000. **State Groups:** 51. **Local Groups:** 350. **Languages:** English. **Multinational.** Women officers and managers in the financial industry. Maintains FWI Educational Foundation.

Publications: *Financial Women Today*, monthly. Newsletter. **Circulation:** 11,000. ● *FWI Management*, quarterly. Journal.

Conventions/Meetings: annual conference.

★2757★ FOR LIFE
1111 N. Trade St.
Tryon, NC 28782
Rev. Ralph D. Kuether, Exec.Dir.   PH: (704)859-5392

Founded: 1973. **Staff:** 2. **Languages:** English. **National.** Purpose is to make available as wide a variety of pro-life materials as possible. Distributes material including films, videotapes, slide and filmstrip presentations, plays, puppet shows, stories, books, monographs, pamphlets, fundraising items, reprints, and transcripts; produces new material and assists others in printing and marketing material.

★2758★ FOUNDATION FOR WOMEN'S RESOURCES
700 N. Fairfax St., Ste. 302
Alexandria, VA 22314
Martha P. Farmer, Exec.Dir.   PH: (703)549-1102

Founded: 1974. **National.** Promotes the achievements and advancements of women. Supports reforms in education to improve the levels of education provided to women and girls. Studies issues affecting women's lives.

★2759★ GAMMA PHI BETA
12737 E. Euclid Dr.
Englewood, CO 80111-6445   PH: (303)799-1874
Marjory M. Shupert, Exec.Dir.   FX: (303)799-1876

Founded: 1874. **Members:** 101,000. **Staff:** 15. **Languages:** English. **National.** Social sorority. Awards scholarships, fellowships, and grants-in-aid to women students. Operates job networking service for members who are traveling or moving. Maintains camp for ''special'' girls.

Publications: *Alumnae Directory*, quinquennial. ● *THE CRESCENT*, quarterly. Newsletter.

Conventions/Meetings: biennial meeting - next 1994.

★2760★ GAMMA PHI DELTA SORORITY
2657 W. Grand Blvd.
Detroit, MI 48208
Willie B. Kennedy, Contact   PH: (313)872-8597

Founded: 1943. **National.** Supports the activities of business and professional African American women. Enhances the social and economic welfare of the community by promoting high educational standards, encouraging business and job development, and strengthening support services to families.

★2761★ GAMMA SIGMA SIGMA
112A Jefferson Heights
Catskill, NY 12414
Sharon Tompkins, Pres.   PH: (518)943-3229

Founded: 1952. **Members:** 3,500. **Staff:** 1. **Budget:** US$124,000. **Regional Groups:** 4. **Languages:** English. **National.** Service sorority. Works with charitable organizations. **Awards:** Periodic Volunteers of Distinction. ● Periodic Distinguished Service. ● Periodic Woman of the Year.

Publications: *Perspectives*, 3/year. Newsletter.

Conventions/Meetings: biennial meeting. ● periodic convention.

★2762★ GAY COMMUNITY NEWS PRISONER PROJECT (GCNPP)
62 Berkeley St.
Boston, MA 02116
Rebecca Lavine, Dir.

Founded: 1980. **Staff:** 1. **Languages:** English. **National.** Lesbian and gay prisoners. Supports prisoners by providing them with information on acquired immune deficiency syndrome (AIDS), pen pals, and book donations. Seeks to educate the gay community about what the group considers inequities in the justice system including bias against prisoners who are incarcerated because they cannot afford adequate legal assistance, racism in the prison system, and anti-gay bias in prisons.

Publications: *Newspaper*, weekly. Newsletter.

★2763★ GAY AND LESBIAN ALLIANCE AGAINST DEFAMATION
(GLAAD/NY)
150 W. 26th St., Ste. 503
New York, NY 10001   PH: (212)807-1700
Ellen Carton, Exec.Dir.   FX: (212)807-1806

Founded: 1985. **Members:** 10,000. **Staff:** 5. **Regional Groups:** 13. **Languages:** English. **National.** Seeks to: oppose media and public defamation of gay and lesbian individuals through education; replace ''bigoted and misinformed representations'' of lesbians and gays with positive images of the gay community; organize the gay community to respond to defamation and assert its right to be treated with dignity. Works to: identify and respond to public expressions of homophobia and bring instances of gay defamation to the attention of the gay community; counter attacks on the legal rights and physical well-being of gays and lesbians, particularly in the media. Promotes positive images of gays and lesbians by convincing those in the broadcasting and publishing fields to devote time and space to gay-related issues, events, and groups; monitors and reports occurrences of defamation in the media; offers suggestions and editorial style guidelines for news stories. Encourages members of the gay community to voice their protest against those responsible for gay defamation. Works to attain national media attention for civil rights battles fought by gays. Operates PhoneTree, through which members telephone television and radio stations to protest media defamation and bigotry. Operates MediaGrams campaign. Sponsors fundraising events. Produces Naming Names, a radio and television commentary on the portrayal of the gay community in the press. Provides services and information nationwide. **Awards:** Annual GLADD Media. **Committees:** Public Relations; Visibility Action.

Publications: *GLAAD Bulletin*, bimonthly. ● *GLAAD Tidings*, weekly. Newsletter. ● *Media Guide to the Lesbian and Gay Communities*. Book.

Conventions/Meetings: bimonthly meeting.

★2764★ GAY AND LESBIAN PARENTS COALITION INTERNATIONAL
(GLPCI)
Box 50360
Washington, DC 20091
Wayne E. Schwandt, Dir. of   PH: (202)583-8029
Development   (202)583-2158

Founded: 1979. **Members:** 1,000. **Local Groups:** 35. **Languages:** English. **National.** Gay and lesbian parents organizations. Acts as clearinghouse for information concerning gay and lesbian parenting. Strives to prove that parenting and homosexuality are compatible. Supports passage of legislation created to eliminate discrimination due to sexual orientation. Coordinates the establishment of support groups for parents and children; conducts educational outreach programs to educate professionals and the public on problems and special concerns related to gay parenthood. Maintains speakers' bureau and bibliographic archives.

Publications: *Annual Report*. **Advertising:** not accepted. ● *Bibliography of Gay and Lesbians and Their Families*, annual. Journal. **Advertising:** accepted. ● *Conference Proceedings*, annual. ● *Gay and Lesbian Parents Coalition International—Network*, quarterly. Newsletter. News of interest to gay and lesbian parents. Also inclu des association news and book and movie reviews. **Advertising:** accepted.

Conventions/Meetings: annual conference (exhibits).

★2765★ GAY MEDIA TASK FORCE (GMTF)
71-426 Estellita Dr.
Rancho Mirage, CA 92270   PH: (619)568-6711
Newton E. Deiter Ph.D., Exec.Dir. FX: (619)568-3241

Founded: 1972. **Staff:** 2. **Budget:** US$12,000. **Regional Groups:** 3. **Languages:** English. **National.** Purpose is to provide resources and consultative services to the media relative to the gay and lesbian community. Monitors the media actively; works with authors to promote accuracy in nonfiction works concerning gays. Represents gays before Congress, the Federal Communications Commission, and other decision-making bodies on issues brought to the attention of the task force by members of the gay community throughout the U.S. **Libraries:** Type: reference.

★2766★ GAY NURSES' ALLIANCE (GNA)
800 N. West St.
Wilmington, DE 19801-1886
Jim Welch R.N., Contact

Founded: 1974. **Members:** 300. **Languages:** English. **National.** Women and gay nurses and nursing students. Works to: provide a forum for discussion among gay nurses; foster an awareness that gay people are both patients and members of the nursing profession; eliminate stereotypes about gay people; aid gay nurses experiencing job discrimination; improve the quality of care rendered to gay patients; diagnose and treat homophobia (fear of gays and lesbians). Conducts seminars and workshops; maintains archives.

Publications: *Signal*, 4-5/year. Newsletter.

Conventions/Meetings: annual meeting.

★2767★ GAY OFFICERS' ACTION LEAGUE (GOAL)
510 E. 20th St., Apt 11C
New York, NY 10009
Peter Guardino, Contact   PH: (212)674-7849

Founded: 1982. **Languages:** English. **National.** Professional and fraternal organization of gay or lesbian active and former employees of the police department and criminal justice system in New York City. Bestows awards; maintains speakers' bureau.

Publications: *GOAL Gazette*, 10/year. **Advertising:** accepted.

Conventions/Meetings: monthly meeting.

★2768★ GAY VETERANS ASSOCIATION (GVA)
346 Broadway, Ste. 814
New York, NY 10013
Boyd Masten, Pres.   PH: (212)787-0329

Founded: 1984. **Members:** 100. **Languages:** English. **National.** Gays and lesbians who have served in the U.S. Armed Forces. Advocates and works to secure equal rights and privileges for all veterans regardless of sexual orientation; aims to ensure that all veterans may participate in any and all veterans' activities. Serves as a forum to aid, support, and bring together gay veterans; seeks cooperation with other gay and veteran organizations in an effort to broaden their constituency. Offers services to gay veterans, including counseling and psychotherapy, programs aiding homeless veterans, and monitoring AIDS patients in Veterans Administration hospitals. Monitors and attempts to influence legislation affecting gay and lesbian veterans and active military personnel. **Computer Services:** Mailing lists. **Committees:** Health, Education, and Welfare; Public Relations; Social.

Publications: *On Alert*, monthly. Newsletter. Includes calendar of events. **Circulation:** 120. **Advertising:** accepted. **Also Cited As:** *GVA Newsletter*.

Conventions/Meetings: monthly meeting.

★2769★ GENERAL COMMISSION ON THE STATUS AND ROLE OF
WOMEN (GCSRW - UMC)
1200 Davis St.
Evanston, IL 60201
Kiyoko Kasai Fujiu, Gen. Secretariat   PH: (708)869-7330

Founded: 1972. **Members:** 48. **Budget:** US$375,000. **Languages:** English. **National.** Representatives of both sexes and each ethnic group within the United Methodist church. Purpose is to challenge the church to make a continuing commitment to the full and equal responsibility and participation of women in the total life and mission of the church, sharing fully in the power and policymaking at all levels of the church. Feels that the church cannot be an effective witness to society until it has examined its own faithfulness to the full inclusiveness of all persons. Believes that many individuals feel excluded from a relationship with God when God is referred to only in masculine terms, but recognizes that some persons feel it necessary to use masculine gender in order to "be true to the sacred images of God." Works to foster an awareness of issues, problems, and concerns related to the status and role of women within the denomination; develops strategies to rectify adverse situations; recommends plans and curricula for new understanding of theological and biblical history. Acts as catalyst to achieve full utilization of women in total employment both in and out of the church. **Programs:** Education and Advocacy; Issue Development; Monitoring and Research.

Publications: *The Flyer*, 5/year. Newsletter. Provides a link between the national and the local commissions on the status and role of women in the United Methodist Church. **Circulation:** 13,000.

Conventions/Meetings: semiannual. ● annual conference.

★2770★ GENERAL FEDERATION OF WOMEN'S CLUBS (GFWC)
1734 N St. NW
Washington, DC 20036-2990
Ann Holland, Pres.
PH: (202)347-3168
TF: (800)443-GFWC
FX: (202)835-0246

Founded: 1890. **Members:** 350,000. **Staff:** 21. **Budget:** US$1,300,000. **Regional Groups:** 8. **State Groups:** 52. **Languages:** English. **National.** International women's volunteer service organization with members from 8500 U.S. clubs. Provides volunteer leadership training and development. Serves state and local clubs in community service programs in the following areas: the arts; conservation; education; home life; public affairs; international affairs. Has established Women's History and Resource Center to promote and document volunteer achievement.

Publications: *GFWC Clubwoman*, quarterly. Magazine. **ISSN:** 0745-2209. **Advertising:** accepted.

Conventions/Meetings: annual meeting (exhibits) - always June.

★2771★ GIRL FRIENDS (GF)
c/o Rachel Norcom Smith
2228 Lansing Ave.
Portsmouth, VA 23704
Rachel Norcom Smith, Exec. Officer
PH: (804)397-1339

Founded: 1927. **Members:** 1,200. **Budget:** US$120,000. **Local Groups:** 40. **Languages:** English. **National.** Black women "who have been friends over the years." Primary aim is to "keep the fires of friendship burning." Conducts charitable projects and contributes annually to a selected charity. Bestows awards. **Committees:** Courtesy; National Project; Publicity/Public Relations.

Publications: *The Chatterbox*, annual. Magazine. ● *Chatterletter*, biennial. Newsletter. ● *Directory*, quinquennial. ● *President's News and Friendship Letter*, annual. Newsletter.

Conventions/Meetings: annual meeting - usually May. 1994, Columbia, SC, United States.

★2772★ GIRLS CLUBS OF AMERICA
30 E. 33rd St.
New York, NY 10016
Ellen Claire Wahl, Contact
PH: (212)689-3700

Founded: 1945. **National.** Promotes the development of young girls through development programs in self-sufficiency and responsibility.

★2773★ GLOBAL COM OF PARLIAMENTARIANS ON POPULATION AND DEVELOPMENT
304 E. 45th St., 12th Fl.
New York, NY 10017

Languages: English. **Multinational.** Advises parliament on issues concerning: women's development, population control, and children's welfare. Works to abolish discriminatory marital practices. Provides a forum for women members of parliament to discuss strategies to enhance the status of women, improve education, achieve peaceful international relations, and preserve the environment. **Committees:** Women and Population.

Publications: *Newsletter*, quarterly. ● *Bulletin*, periodic.

★2774★ GLOBAL FUND FOR WOMEN
2400 Sand Hill Rd., Ste. 100
Menlo Park, CA 94025
Anne Firth Murray, Contact
PH: (415)854-0420
FX: (415)854-8050

Founded: 1987. **Budget:** US$1,500,000. **Languages:** English, Spanish, French. **Multinational.** Provides timely funding and support to groups that are committed to the well-being and advancement of women and involved in resolving controversial and difficult issues. Promotes increased awareness of the importance of the full participation of women internationally. **Awards:** Grant.

★2775★ GLOBAL WOMEN OF AFRICAN HERITAGE (GWAH)
PO Box 1033, Cooper Sta.
New York, NY 10003
Thelma Dailey-Stout, Founder & Pres.
PH: (212)547-5696

Founded: 1982. **Languages:** English. **National.** Women of African heritage worldwide. Purpose is to bring together women of African heritage to share common experiences and knowledge. Also seeks to share this knowledge with women who are not of African heritage.

★2776★ GOLD STAR WIVES OF AMERICA (GSW)
c/o Rose E. Lee
540 N. Lombardy St.
Arlington, VA 22203
Rose E. Lee, Pres.
PH: (703)527-7706

Founded: 1945. **Members:** 13,000. **Budget:** US$62,000. **Regional Groups:** 8. **Local Groups:** 53. **Languages:** English. **National.** Widows of servicemen who died while on active duty or from service-connected disabilities. Promotes patriotism. Conducts volunteer work in veteran and civilian hospitals. Testifies before congressional committees on behalf of service widows. Notifies widows and their children of changes in VA benefits. **Computer Services:** Mailing lists. **Committees:** Community Service; Education; Fundraising; Hospital Service; Legislation.

Publications: *Gold Star Wives Newsletter*, quarterly. Covers the volunteer activities of the association. Includes legislation report. **Advertising:** not accepted.

Conventions/Meetings: annual meeting.

★2777★ G.O.P. WOMEN'S POLITICAL ACTION LEAGUE (GOPAL)
2000 L St. NW, Ste. 200
Washington, DC 20036
Maureen E. Reagan, Chair
PH: (202)785-8242

Founded: 1985. **Languages:** English. **National.** Individual contributors to Republican female candidates' campaigns for public office. Promotes the election of Republican women to state and federal office primarily through contributions to their campaign committees. Sponsors fundraising activities and solicits direct contributions.

★2778★ GRACE OF GOD MOVEMENT FOR THE WOMEN OF THE WORLD (GGMWW)
c/o 3HO Found.
1620 Preuss Rd.
Los Angeles, CA 90035
Guru Amrit, Exec.Sec.
PH: (310)552-3416

Founded: 1970. **Local Groups:** 110. **Languages:** English. **National.** Purpose is "to provide women with the techniques and knowledge to fulfill their divine potential to live healthy, happy and holy lives as the Grace of God." Provides specialized Kundalini Yoga exercises; recipes for diet; information on feminine health; training courses in vegetarian cooking; and literature for women regarding child training and male/female interpersonal relationships. Conducts annual training camp in New Mexico at which women learn music, cooking, martial arts, outdoor living, and psychological and sociological understanding of the self.

Publications: *Women in Training*. Book.

★2779★ GRAIL MOVEMENT (GM)
c/o Grailville
932 O'Bannonville Rd.
Loveland, OH 45140
Martha Heidkamp, Trustee
PH: (513)683-2340

Founded: 1940. **Languages:** English. **National.** U.S. branch of the International Grail Movement. Christian women's movement working for human liberation through efforts in personal renewal, community development, religious search, education, medical-social agencies, and the arts. Works to develop creative alternatives to present lifestyles and institutions. Activities are primarily educational. Conducts programs on topics such as ecology, women's issues, social justice, and spirituality.

Conventions/Meetings: annual conference.

★2780★ GRASSROOTS ORGANIZATION OPERATING TOGETHER IN SISTERHOOD (GROOTS)
1 Sherman Sq., No. 27L
New York, NY 10023

Founded: 1985. **Multinational.** International women's leadership development network. Promotes and supports the development of women throughout the world. Collaborates with other grassroots organizations on housing, health, education, income operation, and child care for women.

Publications: *GROOTS Network News*, periodic. Newsletter.

★2781★ GREY NUNS - PARTNERS IN MINISTRY
10 Pelham Rd.
Lexington, MA 02173-5799
Sr. Marie Mansfield, Exec. Officer   PH: (617)862-4700

Members: 3. **Staff:** 2. **Languages:** English. **National.** Public ministry arm of the Sisters of Charity of Montreal. Advocates on behalf of the poor; works for social justice; promotes respect for human rights and the environment. Conducts health care programs; makes available services assisting the elderly and homeless.

★2782★ GROUP B STREP ASSOCIATION
PO Box 16515
Chapel Hill, NC 27516
Gina Burns, Pres.   PH: (919)932-5344

Founded: 1990. **Members:** 3,000. **Membership Dues:** US$15. **State Groups:** 50. **Languages:** English. **National.** Seeks to educate the public about Group B Strep (GBS) infections during pregnancy. Promotes screening of mothers and the development of a vaccine. Seeks to control the disease which is a leading cause of life-threatening infections in newborns. Acts as a support group; provides educational programs.

Publications: *Update*, semiannual. Newsletter.

Conventions/Meetings: annual meeting.

★2783★ HADASSAH, THE WOMEN'S ZIONIST ORGANIZATION OF AMERICA (HWZOA)
50 W. 58th St.
New York, NY 10019
Beth Wohlgelernter, Exec.Dir.   PH: (212)355-7900
                                        FX: (212)303-8282

Founded: 1912. **Members:** 385,000. **Staff:** 150. **Regional Groups:** 36. **State Groups:** 1,500. **Languages:** English. **Multinational.** Conducts many community services in the U.S. and Israel. Provides "basic Jewish education as a background for intelligent and creative Jewish living in America." Organizes programs in Jewish education, Zionist and American affairs, leadership development, singles, young leaders, health care professionals, seniors, and Young Judaea clubs and camps. Built and maintains Hadassah Medical Organization encompassing the Hadassah University Hospital on Mt. Scopus, Israel and the Hadassah Hebrew University Medical Center at Ein Karem, Israel. Maintains Hadassah College of Technology in Jerusalem, Israel, providing courses in computer science, medical and dental technology, electro-optics, printing, hotel managment and graphics; operates Hadassah Career Counseling Institute for high school students, young adults, and new immigrants. Is the principal agency in the U.S. for support of Youth Aliyah villages and day-centers for immigrant and deprived youth. Participates in land purchase and reclamation programs of the Jewish National Fund. Maintains Hadassah International, which works worldwide to raise funds and support for medical activities and to encourage cooperation in public health

and community medicine. Sponsors Young Judaea for American Jewish young people, ages 9 through 30. Conducts three month live-in program for adults wishing to volunteer their services in Israel. Operates speakers' bureau. **Libraries:** Type: reference. Holdings: 5,000. Subjects: Judaism and Zionism. **Awards:** Periodic Henrietta Szold. **Committees:** Aliyah; American Affairs; Audio-Visual; Communications; Hadassah-Israel Education Services; Jewish Education; Jewish National Fund; Outreach Program; Public Affairs; Soviet Jewry; Travel; Visual Aids; Young Leaders; Youth Aliyah; Zionist Affairs. **Divisions:** Hadassah Associates; Vanguard.

Publications: *The American Scene*, 3/year. Magazine. ● *Hadassah Associates Medbriefs*, quarterly. Newsletter. ● *Hadassah Headlines*, quarterly. Newsletter. Contains medical news. **Advertising:** not accepted. ● *Hadassah Magazine*, monthly. Contains articles on art, medicine, parenting, Hadassah projects, and Hebrew education. **ISSN:** 0017-6516. **Advertising:** accepted. **Alternate Formats:** microform. ● *Textures: Hadassah National Jewish Studies Bulletin*, 3/year. Contains articles on Jewish art, culture, and thought. Examines daily life in Israel; discusses Hebrew texts, literature, and poetry. **Advertising:** not accepted. ● *Zionist Affairs Update*, 20/year. Newsletter.

Conventions/Meetings: annual meeting. ● periodic seminar. ● periodic workshop.

★2784★ HEALTHY MOTHERS, HEALTHY BABIES (HMHB)
409 12th St. SW, Rm. 309   PH: (202)863-2458
Washington, DC 20024   TF: (800)673-8444
Lori Cooper, Exec.Dir.   FX: (202)484-5107

Founded: 1980. **Members:** 104. **Staff:** 2. **Languages:** English. **National.** Coalition of national and state organizations concerned with maternal and child health. Serves as a network through which members share ideas and information regarding issues such as prenatal care, nutrition for pregnant women, and infant mortality. **Committees:** Adolescent Pregnancy; Breastfeeding; Genetics; Injury Prevention; Low-Income; Oral Health; Substance Use in Pregnancy; Immunization Education and Action.

Publications: *Healthy Mothers, Healthy Babies*, quarterly. Newsletter. ● *Compendium of Program Ideas for Serving Low-Income Women*. Book.

Conventions/Meetings: biennial - always fall. Washington, DC, United States.

★2785★ HELEN DINER MEMORIAL WOMEN'S CENTER, AMBITIOUS AMAZONS
PO Box 811
East Lansing, MI 48826   PH: (517)371-5257

Languages: English. **National.** Promotes the rights of lesbians throughout the United States. Opposes discrimination against homosexuals. Communicates with other organizations with similar interests.

Publications: *Lesbian Connection - For, By, and About Lesbians*, periodic. Newsletter.

★2786★ HELPING OTHER PARENTS IN NORMAL GRIEVING (HOPING)
Sparrow Hospital
1215 E. Michigan Ave.
PO Box 30480
Lansing, MI 48909
Carolyn R. Wickham, Hospital
Coordinator   PH: (517)483-3873

Founded: 1981. **Members:** 1,500. **Staff:** 1. **Regional Groups:** 25. **State Groups:** 50. **Local Groups:** 1. **Languages:** English. **National.** Medical professionals, social service workers, and clergy; parents who have experienced a miscarriage, stillbirth, or the death of an infant. Provides support to newly bereaved parents through trained parents who have suffered a similar loss and resolved their grief. Promotes community education regarding the effect that a miscarriage, stillbirth, or neonatal death has on parents.

Conducts in-service programs for nurses and residents. Maintains speakers' bureau; offers educational programs. **Libraries:** Type: reference.

Publications: *Hoping Newsletter*, quarterly. **Advertising:** not accepted. ● *Oh My Children*. Book. ● *Parent to Parent Support Manual*. Book.

Conventions/Meetings: monthly meeting.

★2787★ HISPANIC WOMEN'S COUNCIL
5803 E. Beverly Blvd.
Los Angeles, CA 90022
Lourdes Saab, Exec.Dir.   PH: (213)725-1657

National. Dedicated to the empowerment of Hispanic American women through education and career leadership development programs. Seeks to provide young Hispanic American women with career role models and instill self-esteem.

★2788★ HISTORY OF SCIENCE SOCIETY - WOMEN'S COMMITTEE
215 S. 34th St.
Philadelphia, PA 19104-6310
Elizabeth Keeney, President   PH: (215)898-8575

Founded: 1972. **Members:** 7. **Languages:** English. **Multinational.** Women who study the history of science or who are interested in the history of women in science. Conducts research and disseminates information to members.

★2789★ HISTORY OF WOMEN RELIGIOUS
c/o Karen Kennelly
12001 Chalon Rd.
Los Angeles, CA 90049
Karen Kennelly, Contact

National. Promotes the study of women in religion and theology. Provides a forum for the exchange of study results and information.

★2790★ HOLLYWOOD WOMEN'S POLITICAL COMMITTEE (HWPC)
10536 Culver Blvd.
Culver City, CA 90232   PH: (310)559-9334
Margery Tabankin, Exec.Dir.   FX: (310)838-2367

Founded: 1984. **Members:** 200. **Staff:** 7. **Languages:** English. **National.** Women working in the entertainment industry and related fields. Raises funds for federal political candidates, grass roots organizations, and state-wide initiatives that pledge to represent the group's beliefs on nuclear disarmament, increased environmental protection, improved public education, and expanded civil rights for women. Seeks to heighten community involvement in national politics.

★2791★ HOMOSEXUAL INFORMATION CENTER (HIC)
115 Monroe
Bossier City, LA 71111-4539
W. E. Glover, Sec.   PH: (318)742-4709

Founded: 1968. **Languages:** English. **National.** Consultants in the field of homosexuality. Provides speakers for college classes and civic and church groups. Broadcasts radio interviews and discussions with gays and lesbians and informed persons; counsels veterans on their rights in upgrading less-than-honorable discharges; helps with legal cases in instances where decisions may change present antisex laws; refers individuals with legal, medical, and other personal problems to sympathetic, qualified counselors, and agencies for help. **Libraries:** Type: reference. Holdings: 5,500; books, periodicals, audio recordings. Subjects: the gay movement.

Publications: *A Selected Bibliography of Homosexuality*, periodic. Book. ● *Directory of Homosexual Organizations and Publications: A Field Guide to the Homosexual Movement in the United States and Canada with Topical Index*, periodic. Includes listing of research centers. ● *Homosexual Information Center—Newsletter*, periodic. Contains articles on sexual freedom,

freedom of the press, and civil rights. Includes book reviews. ● *Prostitution is Legal*. Book. ● *Seeds of the American Sexual Revolution*. Book.

Conventions/Meetings: annual meeting - always July. Los Angeles, CA, United States.

★2792★ HOMOSEXUALS ANONYMOUS FELLOWSHIP SERVICES (HAFS)
PO Box 7881
Reading, PA 19603-7881
John J., Service Coordinator   PH: (215)376-1146
                                        TF: (800)253-3000

Founded: 1980. **Members:** 400. **Staff:** 2. **Budget:** US$75,000. **Regional Groups:** 55. **Languages:** English. **National.** Serves as a selfhelp group based on Christian fellowship for individuals seeking "freedom from homosexuality." Seeks to help each other realize their true identity as part of "God's heterosexual creation." Sponsors training seminars utilizing a 14-step program and Christian ministry to assist homosexuals towards recovery. Offers support and guidance through meetings; holds training sessions.

Publications: *HA Newsletter*, bimonthly. Includes directory. ● Also publishes brochures and monographs.

Conventions/Meetings: annual conference.

★2793★ HOUSE OF RUTH (HOR)
501 H St. NE
Washington, DC 20002
Ellen M. Rocks, Exec.Dir.   PH: (202)547-6173

Founded: 1976. **Staff:** 65. **Languages:** English. **National.** Supported by individuals, churches, synagogues, service organizations, local businesses, private foundations, and local government service contracts. Provides shelter, on an emergency and temporary basis, for pregnant and battered women and homeless and destitute families; offers support services and individual and group counseling. Maintains second stage or transitional housing for former shelter residents. Sponsors speakers' bureau; holds volunteer training workshops.

Publications: *Friends*, quarterly. Newsletter. Includes calendar of events and "needs" lists. **Advertising:** not accepted.

★2794★ HUMAN LIFE CENTER (HLC)
University of Steubenville
Steubenville, OH 43952   PH: (614)282-9953
Mike Marker, Dir.   FX: (614)282-0769

Founded: 1972. **Staff:** 14. **Languages:** English. **National.** Seeks to: promote the sanctity of human life from conception to natural death; help married couples, families, and individuals to lead value-oriented lives; offer an integrated approach to sexuality corresponding to Judeo-Christian moral values. Holds seminars, educational programs, and workshops. Maintains speakers' bureau. HLC is the only university-based program of its kind in the U.S. **Libraries:** Type: reference. Holdings: 4,000.

Publications: *Human Life Issues*, quarterly. Journal. ● *International Review*, quarterly. Journal.

★2795★ HUMAN LIFE FOUNDATION (HLF)
150 E. 35th St., Rm. 840
New York, NY 10016
J.P. McFadden, Pres.   PH: (212)685-5210

Founded: 1977. **Languages:** English. **National.** Serves as a charitable and educational foundation. Produces publications addressing issues such as abortion, euthanasia, infanticide, and family concerns. Offers financial support to organizations that provide women with alternatives to abortion.

Publications: *Human Life Review*, quarterly. Journal.

★2796★ HUMAN LIFE INTERNATIONAL (HLI)
7845 Airpark Rd., Ste. E
Gaithersburg, MD 20879   PH: (301)670-7884
Paul Marx, Pres.   FX: (301)869-7363

Founded: 1981. **Members:** 500,000. **Budget:** US$2,500,000. **Regional Groups:** 32. **State Groups:** 8. **Languages:** English. **National.** Serves as a research, educational, and service program offering positive alternatives to what the group calls the antilife/antifamily movement. Explores and comments on various dimensions of human life issues. Provides research on topics such as: Christian sexuality, natural family planning, and all forms of mechanical and medical fertility control programs including abortion, infanticide, and euthanasia. Compiles statistics. Bestows awards; operates charitable program and speakers' bureau. **Libraries:** Type: reference. Holdings: 500. **Departments:** Populations Research Institute.

Publications: *Escoge la Vida* (in Spanish), quarterly. Magazine. ● *HLI Reports*, monthly. Newsletter. Includes information on population and developmental issues worldwide. **Circulation:** 29,000. **Advertising:** not accepted. ● *Sorrow's Reward*, quarterly. Newsletter. Reports on international developments in the study and treatment of what the group calls Post-Abortion Syndrome. Includes book reviews. **Advertising:** not accepted. ● *The Best of Natural Family Planning*. Book. ● *Death Without Dignity*. Book. ● *Deceiving Birth Controllers*. Book. ● *Confessions of a Prolife Missionary*. Book.

Conventions/Meetings: annual conference (exhibits). ● annual meeting.

★2797★ HUMAN RIGHTS CAMPAIGN FUND (HRCF)
1012 14th St. NW, Ste. 600
Washington, DC 20005
Tim McFeeley, Exec.Dir.   PH: (202)628-4160

Founded: 1980. **Members:** 62,000. **Staff:** 37. **Budget:** US$4,500,000. **Languages:** English. **National.** To advance the cause of lesbian and gay civil rights by lobbying Congress and political candidates who support gay and lesbian civil rights and increased funding for women's health concerns and AIDS research and treatment. Promotes responsible AIDS policy, including increased federal funding for AIDS research, education, and treatment programs. Encourages: legislative protection for lesbian and gay men in employment, housing, public accomodations, military service, and immigration matters; recognition of the legitimacy of gay and lesbian families and the repeal of laws criminalizing gay and lesbian Americans. Works for the elimination of anti-gay violence and the collection of data detailing crimes committed against gay men and lesbians. Provides financial contributions to supportive congressional candidates. Conducts fundraising events; maintains speakers' bureau. **Awards:** for the advancement of lesbian and gay civil rights.. **Computer Services:** Data base, voting records of members of Congress. **Projects:** Fairness Fund.

Publications: *Annual Report*. ● *Capitol Hill Update*, bimonthly. Bulletin. ● *Momentum*, quarterly. Newsletter. Details of legislative issues pertaining to lesbian and gay rights.

★2798★ INDIGENOUS WOMEN'S NETWORK (IWN)
PO Box 174
Lake Elmo, MN 55042
Ingrid Washinawatok, Co-Chair PH: (612)770-3861

Founded: 1989. **Members:** 300. **Languages:** English. **National.** Individuals seeking to increase visibility of the indigenous women of the Western Hemisphere. Encourages the resolution of contemporary problems through traditional values. Opearates speakers' bureau; sponsors educational programs; conducts research.

Publications: *Indigenous Woman*, semiannual. Magazine. **Circulation:** 4,000. **Advertising:** accepted. ● *Indigenous Environmental Perspectives - A North American Primer*. Booklet.

Conventions/Meetings: biennial meeting.

★2799★ INFORMED HOMEBIRTH - INFORMED BIRTH AND
    PARENTING (IH/IBP)
PO Box 3675
Ann Arbor, MI 48106
Rahima Baldwin, Pres.   PH: (313)662-6857

Founded: 1977. **Members:** 1,000. **Staff:** 4. **Languages:** English. **National.** Expectant and new parents, childbirth educators, midwives, nurses, pre-school and elementary school teachers, and others interested in safe childbirth alternatives. Seeks to provide information on alternatives in childbirth methods, parenting, and education. Sponsors Childbirth Educator Training Program leading to certification as Childbirth Educator; Childbirth Assistant Training emphasizing practical skills to help the birthing woman and the primary caregiver. Maintains mail order book service on alternative education. Offers cassette tape course for interested couples and childbirth educators who live in areas where classes are not available; conducts correspondence course to train shildbirth educators. **Divisions:** Educational.

Publications: *Openings*, quarterly. Newsletter. Includes association news, calendar of events, newly certified teacher listings, new resources, and schedule of upcoming workshops. **Circulation:** 600. **Advertising:** not accepted. ● *Special Delivery*, quarterly. Newsletter. Contains articles on midwifery and birth, book reviews, calendar of events, and schedule of upcoming workshops. **Circulation:** 1,500. **Advertising:** accepted.

Conventions/Meetings: annual conference.

★2800★ INSTITUTE OF ELECTRICAL AND ELECTRONICS
    ENGINEERS - TASK FORCE ON WOMEN AND MINORITIES
1828 L St. NW
Washington, DC 20036-5104   PH: (202)785-0017

Languages: English. **National.** Supports and promotes the needs of women and minority electrical and electronics engineers. Investigates women's issues.

Publications: *IEEE Spectrum* (in English). ● Also publishes technical works.

★2801★ INSTITUTE FOR FEMINIST STUDIES
1005 Market St., Ste. 305
San Francisco, CA 94103   PH: (415)621-4220

National. Promotes the study of women's issues, including the suffrage movements in the United States and Great Britain and violence against women. Maintains an archive of feminist materials.

★2802★ INSTITUTE FOR REPRODUCTIVE HEALTH (IRH)
433 S. Beverly Dr.   PH: (310)553-5821
Beverly Hills, CA 90212   TF: (800)562-4426
Vicki Hufnagel M.D., Med.Dir. FX: (213)854-4549

Staff: 10. **Languages:** English. **National.** Persons supporting informed, responsible health care for women and working toward the passage of regulatory legislation for informed consent. Conducts research and disseminates information on women's health issues including: technological advances, education, social and behavioral sciences, and belief systems; uterine endocrinology, female reconstructive surgery, sexually-transmitted diseases and their effect on female fertility; substance abuse and obstetrical problems; analysis of risks and losses due to hysterectomy and surgical abuses against women.

Publications: *Women's Health Quarterly*. Magazine.

Conventions/Meetings: periodic meeting.

★2803★ INSTITUTE FOR RESEARCH ON WOMEN'S HEALTH
1616 18th St. NW, Ste. 109
Washinton, DC 20009
Dr. Margaret Jensvold, Director PH: (202)483-8643

Languages: English. **National.** Promotes the study of women's health concerns. Conducts research and educational programs on the physical and mental health of women. Administers policy studies on gender issues, sexual harrassment, and discrimination.

Publications: *Booklet.*

★2804★ INSTITUTE OF WOMEN TODAY (IWT)
7315 S. Yale
Chicago, IL 60621
Sr. Margaret Ellen Traxler, Dir.   PH: (312)651-8372

Founded: 1974. **Members:** 889. **Staff:** 14. **Languages:** English. **National.** Sponsored by church-related Protestant, Catholic, and Jewish women's organizations to examine religious and historical origins of women's liberation. Endeavors to bring church-related women into the women's movement so that the principles of faith will be reflected in the women's struggle for equality. Conducts workshops and research. Provides legal services to women in prisons. Maintains archives.

Conventions/Meetings: annual meeting.

★2805★ INSTITUTE FOR WOMEN'S POLICY RESEARCH (IWPR)
1400 20th St. NW, Ste. 104
Washington, DC 20036

Founded: 1987. **Members:** 1,000. **Staff:** 6. **Budget:** US$500,000. **Languages:** English. **National.** Mostly researchers. Conducts independent, scientific research on women's issues, particularly in the United States; reveals findings to the public for debate and policymaking purposes. Areas of concern include: work and family, employment and wages, poverty and welfare, and health care accessibility and cost. Analyzes the ethnic, racial, and socio-economic diversity of women.

Publications: *Research News Reporter* (in English), bimonthly. Newsletter. ● *Products Mailing* (in English), quarterly. Bulletin. ● *Journal* (in English), quarterly.

Conventions/Meetings: biennial conference - 1995, Washington, DC, United States.

★2806★ INSTITUTE FOR WOMEN'S STUDIES IN THE ARAB WORLD
Beirut University College
475 Riverside Dr., Rm. 1846
New York, NY 10115
Dr. Julinda Abu Nasr, Dir.   PH: (212)870-2592

National. Promotes the study of Arab women and issues affecting their development. Conducts research and sponsors action programs to improve the living conditions of women and chidren in the Arab world.

★2807★ INTENSIVE CARING UNLIMITED (ICU)
910 Bent Ln.
Philadelphia, PA 19118   PH: (215)233-6994
Lenette S. Moses, Co-Founder   FX: (215)233-5795

Founded: 1983. **Languages:** English. **National.** Support organization for parents children born prematurely or with special problems; parents experiencing a high-risk pregnancy, miscarriage, or infant death; health care professionals. Offers emotional and educational support and information on care of babies and young children with special medical or developmental problems. Conducts training courses on peer support, counseling, and in-house hospital informational programs. Provides referral services and speakers' bureau. **Libraries:** Type: reference. Holdings: 2,000.

Publications: *Intensive Caring Unlimited* (in English and Spanish), quarterly. Newsletter. Includes medical reports. **Circulation:** 3,000.

Conventions/Meetings: annual meeting - always June.

★2808★ INTER-AMERICAN COMMISSION OF WOMEN (CIM)
c/o Organization of American States
1889 F St. NW, Rm. 880
Washington, DC 20006
Linda J. Poole, Exec.Sec.   PH: (202)458-6084

Founded: 1928. **Members:** 32. **Staff:** 5. **Budget:** US$600,000. **Languages:** English. **Multinational.** Specialized agency of the Organization of American States (see separate entry) dealing with issues concerning women. Commission is composed of one delegate for each member country of OAS. Mobilizes, trains, and organizes women "so that they may fully participate in all fields of human endeavor, on a par with men, as two beings of equal value, coresponsible for the destiny of humanity." Informs the OAS general assembly and member governments on: civil, political, social, economic, and cultural status of women in the Americas; progress achieved in the field as well as problems to be considered; development of a plan of action following the Decade of Women (1976-85) of strategies for full and equal participation by women by the year 2000. Serves as liaison for women's groups throughout the hemisphere, and conducts research on laws affecting women. Maintains library; operates a regional information center in Santiago, Chile; finances development projects in Latin America and the Caribbean.

Publications: *Final Report-Assembly of Delegates*, biennial. ● *Mujeres* (in English and Spanish), 2-3/year. ● Series: *Studies*, periodic.

★2809★ INTER-AMERICAN DEVELOPMENT BANK'S WIVES ASSOCIATION (IADBWA)
7945 MacArthur Blvd., Rm. 200
Cabin John, MD 20818
Libis Buguna, Pres.   PH: (301)493-6591

Founded: 1965. **Members:** 800. **Staff:** 2. **Languages:** English. **National.** Wives of bank employees; wives of bank officers and of former bank employees are nonvoting members. Purpose is to promote friendship, cooperation, cultural exchange, and understanding among members and their families. Seeks to heighten members' awareness of the opportunities for personal growth in the Washington, DC area. Facilitates contact and collaboration among all institutions organized with similar aims and interests; cooperates with area institutions in aiding the Washington, DC Spanish-speaking community. Offers language classes, information seminars, and other educational programs. **Libraries:** Type: reference. **Committees:** Communications; Madrinas; Neighborhood.

Publications: *Newsletter*, monthly.

Conventions/Meetings: annual meeting.

★2810★ INTERAGENCY COMMITTEE ON WOMEN'S BUSINESS ENTERPRISE
1441 L St. NW, Rm. 414
Washington, DC 20416
Lindsey Johnson, Director   PH: (202)653-8000

Founded: 1979. **Languages:** English. **National.** Supports and promotes women in small business. Works to increase governmental responsiveness to the needs of women business owners. Investigates and disseminates information on women's business issues. Researches federal, State, and local governments and their policies relevant to women in business.

Publications: *Women Along Business Lines* (in English).

★2811★ INTERCAMBOS
PO Box 390543
Mountain View, CA 94039
Sylvia Castillo, Contact   PH: (415)962-8324

Founded: 1980. Hispanic women and other individuals interested in issues related to Hispanic culture. Acts as a clearinghouse of information on Hispanic women, including issues of education, career, and civic leadership.

Publications: *Journal*, quarterly.

★2812★ INTERNATIONAL ADVISORY COUNCIL FOR HOMOSEXUAL MEN AND WOMEN IN ALCOHOLICS ANONYMOUS (IAC)
PO Box 90
Washington, DC 20044-0090

Founded: 1980. **Members:** 1,000. **Languages:** English. **Multinational.** Regular groups of Alcoholics Anonymous World Services specifically composed of lesbians and gays. Purpose is to serve the lesbian and gay members of AA and to provide advice and support to other members of AA. Works for unity and service with AA for the betterment of the lesbian and gay members and AA; advocates freedom in communication as an important aid to recovery. Provides alcoholism professionals with information about lesbian and gay AA groups for use in counseling lesbian and gay alcoholics. Assists in the exchange of recorded tapes of lesbian and gay AA speakers. **Committees:** Group Needs; Lesbian Outreach; Literature; Loners; Public Information.

Publications: *Newsletter*, periodic. ● *World Directory of Gay/Lesbian Groups of Alcoholics Anonymous*, annual.

Conventions/Meetings: semiannual meeting.

★2813★ THE INTERNATIONAL ALLIANCE, AN ASSOCIATION OF EXECUTIVE AND PROFESSIONAL WOMEN (TIA)
8600 LaSalle Rd., Ste. 308
Baltimore, MD 21286   PH: (410)321-6699
Marian E. Goetze, Exec.V.Pres.   FX: (410)823-2410

Founded: 1980. **Members:** 147. **Staff:** 2. **Budget:** US$60,000. **Languages:** English. **Multinational.** Local networks of professional and executive women; individual businesswomen without a network affiliation are alliance associates. Seeks to: promote recognition of the achievements of women in business; encourage placement of women in senior executive positions; maintain high standards of professional competence among members. Facilitates communication on an international scale among professional women's networks and their members. Represents members' interests before policymakers in business and government. Sponsors programs that support equal opportunity and enhance members' business and professional skills. Operates appointments and directors service. Conducts seminars, symposia, and workshops; maintains speakers' bureau. **Awards:** Periodic 21st Century Award (recognition). **Committees:** Corporate Development; Directors Resource Bank; Government Relations; Marketing; Public Relations. **Councils:** Network of Representatives.

Publications: *Membership Directory*, annual. ● *The Alliance*, bimonthly. Newsletter. Includes calendar of events and research updates. **Circulation:** 5,000. **Advertising:** accepted.

Conventions/Meetings: annual conference (exhibits).

★2814★ INTERNATIONAL ASSOCIATION OF MINISTERS WIVES AND MINISTERS WIDOWS (IAMWMW)
305 Dexter St. E
Chesapeake, VA 23324
Dr. Shirley Alexander Hart, Exec. Officer   PH: (804)543-0427

Founded: 1941. **Members:** 35,000. **Staff:** 20. **Budget:** US$200,000. **Regional Groups:** 7. **National Groups:** 11. **Languages:** English. **Multinational.** Wives and widows of ministers of 85 religious denominations. Seeks to erase barriers existing between religious communions. Sponsors competitions; conducts research; compiles statistics. Maintains museum, archives, hall of fame, and speakers' bureau. **Libraries:** Type: reference. Holdings: 10,000. **Awards:** Annual Christian Service (scholarship). **Committees:** Archives; Endowment; Human Relations; Public Relations; Social Concerns. **Departments:** Education; Student Affairs.

Publications: *The Ministers' Wives Herald*, quarterly. Journal. **Circulation:** 2,200. **Advertising:** accepted. ● *Prayers for All Seasons*, annual. Booklet.

Conventions/Meetings: annual conference - always June.

★2815★ INTERNATIONAL ASSOCIATION OF PARENTS AND PROFESSIONALS FOR SAFE ALTERNATIVES IN CHILDBIRTH (NAPSAC)
Rt. 1, Box 646
Marble Hill, MO 63764-9725
Lee Stewart, Pres.   PH: (314)238-2010

Founded: 1975. **Members:** 2,000. **Membership Dues:** US$20 annual. **Staff:** 2. **Budget:** US$50,000. **National Groups:** 6. **Languages:** English. **Multinational.** Parents, midwives, physicians, nurses, health officials, social workers, and childbirth educators in 10 countries who are "dedicated to exploring, examining, implementing, and establishing family-centered childbirth programs which meet the needs of families as well as provide the safe aspects of medical science." Promotes education concerning the principles of natural childbirth; facilitates communication and cooperation among parents, medical professionals, and childbirth educators; assists in the establishment of maternity and childbearing centers. Provides educational opportunities to parents and parents-to-be, enabling them to assume more personal responsibility for pregnancy, childbirth, infant care, and child rearing. **Computer Services:** Data base; mailing lists.

Publications: *NAPSAC Directory of Alternative Birth Services and Consumer Guide*, periodic. Lists midwives, birth centers, noninterventive physicians, and educators for safe alternatives in childbirth. **Circulation:** 500. **Advertising:** accepted. ● *NAPSAC News*, quarterly. Newsletter. Includes association news, book reviews, and calendar of events. **ISSN:** 0192-1223. **Circulation:** 2,000. **Advertising:** accepted. ● *Safe Alternatives in Childbirth*. Book. ● *Five Standards for Safe Childbearing*. Book. ● *21st Century Obstetrics Now*. Book. ● *Transitions*. Book. ● *Childbirth Activists Handbook*.

Conventions/Meetings: quadrennial conference (exhibits) - next 1994.

★2816★ INTERNATIONAL ASSOCIATION FOR PERSONNEL WOMEN (IAPW)
PO Box 969
Andover, MA 01810-0017   PH: (508)474-0750
Brenda Jackson, Pres.   FX: (508)474-0750

Founded: 1950. **Members:** 1,500. **Local Groups:** 18. **Languages:** English. **Multinational.** Professional association of personnel executives in business, industry, education, and government. Established to expand and improve the professionalism of women in personnel management. **Committees:** Communications; Professional Development; Professional Issues.

Publications: *Connections*, bimonthly. Newsletter. **Circulation:** 1,600. **Advertising:** accepted. ● *Membership Roster*, annual. Directory.

Conventions/Meetings: annual conference (exhibits).

★2817★ INTERNATIONAL ASSOCIATION OF PHYSICAL EDUCATION AND SPORT FOR GIRLS AND WOMEN (IAPESGW)
c/o Ruth M. Schellberg
50 Skyline Dr.
Mankato, MN 56001
Ruth M. Schellberg, Exec.Officer   PH: (507)345-3665

Founded: 1949. **Members:** 400. **Multinational.** Organizations in 54 countries with an interest in physical education for girls and women. Seeks to: bring together women working in physical education or sports; cooperate with organizations that encourage women's services; promote the exchange of persons and ideas between member organizations. Conducts research into problems affecting physical education and sport for women.

Publications: *Report Following Congresses*, quadrennial.

Conventions/Meetings: quadrennial congress.

★2818★ INTERNATIONAL ASSOCIATION OF WOMEN MINISTERS
(IAWM)
c/o Rev. Carol S. Brown
579 Main St.
Stroudsburg, PA 18360
Rev. Carol S. Brown, Treas.   PH: (717)421-7751

Founded: 1919. **Members:** 400. **Languages:** English. **Multinational.** Women in 20 countries who are licensed, ordained, or otherwise authorized by any evangelical denomination to preach or who are preparing for the ministry. Promotes equal ecclesiastical rights for women and encourages young women to take up ministerial work. Conducts research on the ecclesiastical status of women.

Publications: *Woman's Pulpit*, quarterly. Newsletter. Covering developments affecting the role of women in organized religion. **ISSN:** 0043-7397. **Circulation:** 450. **Advertising:** not accepted.

Conventions/Meetings: annual assembly.

★2819★ INTERNATIONAL BLACK WOMEN'S CONGRESS (IBWC)
1081 Bergen St.
Newark, NJ 07112
Dr. La Francis Rodgers-Rose, Pres.
PH: (201)926-0570
FX: (201)926-0818

Founded: 1983. **Members:** 5,800. **Membership Dues:** Lifetime, US$750; Organization, US$100 annual; Regular, US$35 annual; Student/senior, US$10 annual. **Budget:** US$125,000. **State Groups:** 9. **Languages:** English. **Multinational.** Women of African descent; interested individuals. Objective is to unite members for mutual support and socioeconomic development through: annual networking tours to Africa; establishing support groups; assisting women in starting their own businesses; assisting members in developing resumes and other educational needs; offering to answer or discuss individual questions and concerns. Conducts workshops and charitable program; compiles statistics. Operates speakers' bureau. **Libraries:** Type: reference. Holdings: 100. **Awards:** Annual Oni Award. **Committees:** Business Development; Support Group Network; Undergraduate; Youth.

Publications: *International Black Women's Directory*, periodic. ● *Oni Newsletter*, quarterly.

Conventions/Meetings: annual meeting (exhibits) - 1993 Sept. 24 - 26, Newark, NJ, United States; 1994 Sept. 23 - 25, Newark, NJ, United States.

★2820★ INTERNATIONAL CENTER FOR RESEARCH ON WOMEN
(ICRW)
1717 Massachusetts Ave. NW, Ste. 302
Washington, DC 20036
Mayra Buvinic, Pres.
PH: (202)797-0007
FX: (202)797-0007

Founded: 1976. **Staff:** 22. **Budget:** US$1,900,000. **Languages:** English. **Multinational.** Purpose is to improve the productivity and incomes of women in developing countries worldwide. Provides technical services for the design, implementation, and evaluation of development projects that integrate women into mainstream economic roles. Disseminates research findings to policymakers and others throughout the world who are concerned with economic and socioeconomic issues of the Third World. Conducts policy roundtables. Compiles statistics on women in developing countries; conducts research and educational programs. **Libraries:** Type:. Holdings: 15,000. Subjects: changing roles of women, income generation for women in developing nations.

Publications: *International Center for Research on Women—Papers*, periodic. Monograph. Series of papers covering women's socioeconomic status, health, and nutrition in developing countries and women's participation in development.

Conventions/Meetings: periodic meeting.

★2821★ INTERNATIONAL CESAREAN AWARENESS NETWORK (ICAN)
PO Box 152
Syracuse, NY 13210
Esther Booth Zorn, Pres.   PH: (315)424-1942

Founded: 1982. **Members:** 2,000. **Regional Groups:** 80. **Languages:** English. **Multinational.** Women and men concerned with the increasing rate of cesarean births. Objectives are: to promote vaginal births; to offer encouragement, information, and support for women wanting vaginal births after cesarean (VBAC); to assist in organizing and informing new parents and cesarean parents on preventing future cesareans by opposing unnecessary medical intervention during the birth process and by working to make hospital routines more responsive to women in labor. Offers teacher training and course materials. Sponsors childbirth education certification program, Birth Works, a birth education program that emphasizes a holistic approach. Provides support network to link women anticipating a VBAC and VBAC mothers, supportive physicians, midwives, and child birth educators. Compiles statistics. **Libraries:** Type: reference. Holdings: 300; periodicals, clippings. **Computer Services:** Mailing lists. **Committees:** Education. **Formerly:** (1992) Cesarean Prevention Movement.

Publications: *The Clarion*, quarterly. Includes research and informational articles, book reviews and chapter news. **Circulation:** 10,000. **Advertising:** accepted. ● *Cesarean Facts*. Booklet.

Conventions/Meetings: biennial conference.

★2822★ INTERNATIONAL CHILDBIRTH EDUCATION ASSOCIATION
(ICEA)
PO Box 20048
Minneapolis, MN 55420
Doris Olson, Mgr.   PH: (612)854-8660

Founded: 1960. **Members:** 12,000. **Membership Dues:** Individual, US$20. **Staff:** 8. **Budget:** US$500,000. **Local Groups:** 275. **Languages:** English. **Multinational.** Purposes are: to further the educational, physical, and emotional preparation of expectant parents for childbearing and breastfeeding; to increase public awareness on current issues related to childbearing; to cooperate with physicians, nurses, physical therapists, hospitals, health, education, and welfare agencies, and other individuals and groups interested in furthering parental participation and minimal obstetric intervention in uncomplicated labors; to promote development of safe, low-cost alternatives in childbirth that recognize the rights and responsibilities of those involved. Develops, publishes, and distributes literature pertaining to family-centered maternity care. Offers a teacher certification progran for childbirth educators. Conducts workshops. Operates mail order book store in Minneapolis, MN which makes available literature on all aspects of childbirth education and family-centered maternity care. **Awards:** Periodic ICEA Virginia Larso Research Award. **Committees:** Breastfeeding; Cesarean Options; Community Outreach.

Publications: *ICEA Bookmarks*, quarterly. Bulletin. ● *International Journal of Childbirth Education*, 4/year. ● *Membership Directory*, annual.

Conventions/Meetings: annual meeting (exhibits).

★2823★ INTERNATIONAL CHRISTIAN WOMEN'S FELLOWSHIP (ICWF)
PO Box 1986
Indianapolis, IN 46206
Janice R. Newborn, Pres.   PH: (317)353-1491

Founded: 1949. **Members:** 136,870. **Staff:** 4. **Budget:** US$200,000. **Languages:** English. **Multinational.** Women who are members of the Christian Church (Disciples of Christ) and others who accept the purpose of the CWF. Administered by Department of Church Women, Division of Homeland Ministries, and Christian Church. Objective is "to provide opportunities for spiritual growth, enrichment, education, and creative ministries to enable women to develop a sense of personal responsibility for the whole mission of the Church of Jesus Christ," through a program of study, worship, and service and through preparation of women for fuller participation in the total church life. Provides materials to local groups for programs on topics such as stewardship of life, Christian social relations, local church concerns, and the world mission of the church. **Programs:** Developing; International CWF Cabinet and Executive; Leader Development; Organizational Resources; Social Action Involvement; Status of Women.

Publications: *Guideposts for Christian Women's Fellowship*, annual. Journal. ● *World CWF Newsletter*, annual. ● *Yearbook*.

Conventions/Meetings: biennial meeting. ● quadrennial general assembly - 1994 June, West Lafayette, IN, United States.

★2824★ INTERNATIONAL COMMITTEE FOR WORLD DAY OF
    PRAYER (ICWDP)
475 Riverside Dr., Rm. 812
New York, NY 10115   PH: (212)870-3049
Eileen King, Exec.Dir.   FX: (212)870-2338

Founded: 1967. **Regional Groups:** 100. **Languages:** English. **Multinational.** Christian women united to observe a common day of prayer established on the first Friday in March. Through World Day of Prayer, which began in 1887, women "affirm their faith in Jesus Christ; share their hopes and fears, their joys and sorrows, their opportunities and needs." Encourages women to "become aware of the whole world and no longer live in isolation; to share the faith experience of Christians in other countries and cultures; to take up the burdens of other people and pray with and for them; to become aware of their talents and use them in the service of society." Affirms "that prayer and action are inseparable and that both have an imponderable influence in the world.".

Publications: *World Day of Prayer Journal*, annual. Reports on World Day of Prayer services. **Advertising:** not accepted.

Conventions/Meetings: quadrennial.

★2825★ INTERNATIONAL CONFEDERATION OF CHRISTIAN FAMILY
    MOVEMENTS (ICCFM)
505 E. Huron St., Ste. 607
Ann Arbor, MI 48104   PH: (313)747-8822
Susan Hamilton, Contact   FX: (313)428-9481

Founded: 1967. **Members:** 120,000. **Budget:** US$20,000. **Languages:** English, Spanish. **Multinational.** Seeks to facilitate communication, service, and ecumenism among Christian families worldwide. Concerned with issues affecting the family, children, and women.

Publications: *LINK/LAZO* (in English and Spanish), 3/year.

Conventions/Meetings: triennial World Assembly of Families.

★2826★ INTERNATIONAL CONGRESS ON WOMEN IN MUSIC (ICWM)
PO Box 12164
La Crescenta, CA 91224-0864
Jeannie G. Pool, Coordinator   PH: (818)248-1249

Founded: 1977. **Members:** 290. **National Groups:** 4. **Languages:** English. **Multinational.** Musicologists, scholars in women's studies, performers, composers, and feminist activists in 31 countries. Objectives are to: encourage performance, recording, and publication of classical concert music by women; establish courses on women at music on the college level; develop classroom materials at the primary and secondary school levels that include information on women's active and creative participation in music. Makes available information relating to the activities and accomplishments of women in music. Provides a forum for the discussion of issues and prospects for women in the music professions. Conducts performances, panels, and workshops.

Publications: *Annual Membership Directory*. ● *Newsletter*, quarterly. ● *Working Papers on Women in Music*, quarterly. Journal.

Conventions/Meetings: annual , with exhibits and music festival conference (exhibits).

★2827★ INTERNATIONAL CORRESPONDENCE SOCIETY OF
    OBSTETRICIANS AND GYNECOLOGISTS (ICSOG)
63 Great Rd.
Maynard, MA 01754   PH: (508)897-5552
Dean M. Laux, Publisher   FX: (508)897-6824

Founded: 1960. **Members:** 4,200. **Languages:** English. **Multinational.** Physicians concerned with obstetrics and gynecology and related surgery; medical schools and libraries; civilian and military hospitals; others with research interests. **Committees:** Editorial Advisory Board.

Publications: *The Collected Letters*, monthly. Newsletter.

★2828★ INTERNATIONAL COUNCIL OF AFRICAN WOMEN (ICAW)
PO Box 91812
Washington, DC 20090-1812
Nkenge Toure, Co-Coord.   PH: (202)546-8459

Founded: 1982. **Languages:** English. **Multinational.** Promotes the worldwide networking and development of African women. Concerns isnclude: violence against women, reproductive rights, and self-help programs. Disseminates information.

★2829★ INTERNATIONAL COUNCIL OF SEX EDUCATION AND
    PARENTHOOD (ICSEP)
c/o Dr. Patricia Schiller
5010 Wisconsin Ave. NW
Washington, DC 20016
Dr. Patricia Schiller, Dir.   PH: (202)686-2523

Founded: 1980. **Members:** 1,008. **Staff:** 2. **National Groups:** 44. **Languages:** English. **Multinational.** Individuals in 44 countries working in medicine, psychology, social work, nursing, and family planning. Fosters training, research, and program development in family health and relations. Conducts surveys and research on family life and sex education and counseling; develops curricula and technical materials; provides material for educational and clinical use. Sponsors summer institutes in conjunction with government, educational, and health-related organizations. Maintains library on sex education and counseling materials; operates speakers' bureau.

Publications: *International Register of Family Health Fellows*, periodic. ● *News and Views*, quarterly. Newsletter.

Conventions/Meetings: annual conference.

★2830★ INTERNATIONAL DALKON SHIELD VICTIMS EDUCATION
    ASSOCIATION (IDEA)
212 Pioneer Bldg.
Seattle, WA 98104   PH: (206)329-1371
Constance Miller, Treas.   FX: (206)623-4251

Founded: 1986. **Members:** 2,000. **Staff:** 1. **State Groups:** 2. **Languages:** English. **Multinational.** Women who have contracted illnesses and/or been disabled through use of the Dalkon Shield intrauterine contraceptive device; their supporters. Promotes public education about the dangers of using the Dalkon Shield. Disseminates information regarding Dalkon Shield injuries, claim resolution, and related topics. Offers seminars. Maintains speakers' bureau. **Libraries:** Type: reference.

Conventions/Meetings: annual meeting - always June. Seattle, WA, United States.

★2831★ INTERNATIONAL DIVISION OF THE NATIONAL COUNCIL OF
    NEGRO WOMEN (NCNW/ID)
1211 Connecticut Ave., Ste. 202
Washington, DC 20036
Galya Cook, Exec. VP   PH: (202)659-0006

Founded: 1975. **Languages:** English. **Multinational.** Seeks to improve the social and economic status of women. Collaborates with women's, governmental and nongovernmental organizations to conduct development programs. Works to: alleviate hunger and malnutrition; conserve natural resources; increase agricultural productivity; improve health. Provides skill training programs.

★2832★ INTERNATIONAL FEDERATION ON AGEING - GLOBAL LINK ON MIDLIFE AND OLDER WOMEN
1009 K St. NW
Washington, DC 20049

Members: 100. **Languages:** English. **Multinational.** Umbrella organization for groups working on behalf of elderly persons. Works to empower older women. Seeks to: achieve income security and income generation for older women; improve access health care; and eliminate age and sex discrimination.

Publications: *Midlife and Older Women in Latin America and the Caribbean* (in Spanish and English). Booklet. • *Ageing International*, periodic. Newsletter.

★2833★ INTERNATIONAL FEDERATION FOR FAMILY LIFE PROMOTION (IFFLP)
1511 K St. NW, Ste. 326   PH: (202)783-0137
Washington, DC 20005   FX: (202)783-7351
Claude A. Lanctot M.D., Exec.Dir.   TX: 4972704 FIDAF

Founded: 1974. **Members:** 130. **Staff:** 4. **Budget:** US$800,000. **Languages:** English. **Multinational.** Organizations and individuals interested in natural family planning and family life education. Objectives are to: provide leadership, guidance, and education in fields of family life education; conduct research in natural family planning; stimulate and assist in the formation of natural family planning and family life education organizations. Offers educational programs in primary health care and breast-feeding promotion. Conducts training workshops for program coordinators. **Libraries:** Type: reference. **Committees:** Training Research.

Publications: *IFFLP Bulletin* (in English, French, and Spanish), semiannual. Features articles on family planning, zonal development programs, and primary health care. **Circulation:** 1,500. • *Message to Members* (in English, French, and Spanish), annual. Magazine. • *Presentation Summaries*, triennial. Newsletter. • *NFP: Development of National Programs*. Monograph. • *NFP: Program Evaluation Instrument and Guide*. Book.

Conventions/Meetings: triennial congress. • annual meeting.

★2834★ INTERNATIONAL FEDERATION OF WOMEN LAWYERS (IFWL)
186 5th Ave.
New York, NY 10010
Dora Aberlin, Hon. Life Pres.   PH: (212)206-1666

Founded: 1944. **Languages:** English. **Multinational.** Women lawyers in 70 countries. Seeks to: advance the science of jurisprudence and protect women and children; advance the diffusion of knowledge of the laws of various countries; create better international relations. Holds consultative status with the United Nations (see separate entry); maintains liaison representatives at the United Nations, the International Labour Organization, and the United Nations Educational, Scientific and Cultural Organization (see seperate entries). **Committees:** Comparative Laws; Scholarship Facilitation; United Nations.

Publications: *La Abogada Internacional*, biennial. • *La Abogada Newsletter*, quarterly.

Conventions/Meetings: biennial - next 1994.

★2835★ INTERNATIONAL FEDERATION OF WOMEN'S TRAVEL ORGANIZATIONS (IFWTO)
4545 N. 36th St., Ste. 126
Phoenix, AZ 85018   PH: (602)956-7175
Paula Chavez, Exec.Dir.   FX: (602)957-0545

Founded: 1969. **Members:** 64. **Regional Groups:** 3. **National Groups:** 38. **Languages:** English. **Multinational.** Travel clubs in 14 countries representing 5000 women engaged in the sale and promotion of travel. Seeks to: improve and make more effective the status of women within the travel industry; assist in the development of women's travel organizations in areas where none exist; be involved in the planning and development of industrial affairs; promote further international goodwill and understanding. Presents Benger-Sullivan Award and SPIRIT award; maintains speakers' bureau. **Committees:** Education; Publicity; Research.

Publications: *Directory*, annual. Membership activities newsletter; includes regional news. • *Federation Footnotes*, periodic.

Conventions/Meetings: annual, educational seminars, workshops, lectures, and exhibits (exhibits) - always spring.

★2836★ INTERNATIONAL GAY AND LESBIAN HUMAN RIGHTS COMMISSION (IGLHRC)
520 Castro St.
San Francisco, CA 94114   PH: (415)255-8680
Julie Dorf, Exec.Dir.   FX: (415)255-8662

Founded: 1990. **Staff:** 2. **Budget:** US$80,000. **Languages:** English. **Multinational.** Lesbian and gay activists worldwide. Monitors, documents, exposes, and mobilizes response to human rights violations against lesbians, gays, bisexuals, and people with HIV and AIDS worldwide. Promotes the repeal of sodomy laws and AIDS education and prevention. Acts as a clearinghouse for information on lesbian and gay human rights violations. Conducts volunteer training workshops. Offers educational presentations. **Libraries:** Type: reference. **Telecommunication Services:** Electronic bulletin board. **Committees:** Research. **Sections:** Eastern Europe Support Group; Emergency Response Network; Latin American Support.

Publications: *TEMA International*, quarterly. **Circulation:** 1,000. **Advertising:** not accepted.

Conventions/Meetings: periodic conference.

★2837★ INTERNATIONAL LADIES' GARMENT WORKERS' UNION (ILGWU)
1710 Broadway
New York, NY 10019
Jay Mazur, Pres.   PH: (212)265-7000

Founded: 1900. **Members:** 173,000. **Languages:** English. **Multinational.** AFL-CIO.

Publications: *Justice*, 11/year. Newsletter. Informs members of union news, membership activities, and social and political issues. **ISSN:** 0022-7013. **Circulation:** 300,000.

Conventions/Meetings: triennial meeting.

★2838★ INTERNATIONAL LEAGUE OF WOMEN COMPOSERS (ILWC)
Southshore Rd., Box 670
Pt. Peninsula
Three Mile Bay, NY 13693
Elizabeth Hayden Pizer, Chairperson   PH: (315)649-5086

Founded: 1975. **Members:** 400. **Languages:** English. **Multinational.** Established professional women composers representing 25 countries. Works to: obtain more commissions, recordings, and performances for women composers; develop areas which are insufficiently accessible to women composers. Holds concerts; sponsors radio series; conducts Search for New Music competition.

Publications: *ILWC Journal*, 3/year. Covers the activities of women composers. Includes awards and competitions, book reviews, new recordings, and opportunities for members. **ISSN:** 0748-5735. **Circulation:** 400. **Advertising:** accepted. ● *ILWC Membership Directory*, annual. **Circulation:** 400.

★2839★ INTERNATIONAL LIFE SERVICES, INC. (ILSI)
2606 1/2 W. 8th St.
Los Angeles, CA 90057   PH: (213)382-2156
Sr. Paula Vandegaer SSS, Exec.Dir.   FX: (213)382-4203

Founded: 1985. **Staff:** 5. **Languages:** English. **Multinational.** A Judeo-Christian oriented research and educational association. Works to promote the pro-life movement; fosters respect for human life from the moment of conception until natural death. Recognizes God as the legitimate power over life and death. Promotes alternatives to abortion and euthanasia including premarital chastity and natural family planning; recognizes the family as the cornerstone of Judeo-Christian society. Opposes school-based health clinics that make available to teenagers contraceptives and abortion information. Operates speakers' bureau; compiles statistics. Conducts seminars and workshops on leadership, crisis pregnancy and post- abortion counseling, and bio-ethical and euthanasia issues. **Divisions:** Counseling; Education.

Publications: *ILSI Newsletter*, periodic. ● *Living World*, quarterly. Magazine. ● *Pro-Life Resource Manual*, biennial. Directory.

Conventions/Meetings: annual conference. ● annual Learning Center conference - always spring. Los Angeles, CA, United States.

★2840★ INTERNATIONAL LUTHERAN WOMEN'S MISSIONARY
    LEAGUE (ILWML)
3558 S. Jefferson Ave.   PH: (314)268-1531
St. Louis, MO 63118-3810   TF: (800)252-LWML
Shirley Meckfessel, Office Mgr.   FX: (314)268-1532

Founded: 1942. **Members:** 200,000. **State Groups:** 44. **Local Groups:** 6,000. **Languages:** English. **Multinational.** Women's groups within the congregations of the Lutheran Church-Missouri Synod in the U.S. and Canada. Works to develop a program of mission education, inspiration, and service for the women of the Lutheran Church-Missouri Synod, and to gather voluntary funds for mission projects. **Committees:** Christian Growth; Member Development; Mission Projects; Mission Service; Program Resources.

Publications: *Convention Manual*, biennial. Booklet. ● *Lutheran Woman's Quarterly*. Newsletter.

Conventions/Meetings: biennial meeting - 1995 June 22 - 25, Kansas City, MO, United States; 1997 June 26 - 29, Charlotte, NC, United States.

★2841★ INTERNATIONAL NETWORK ON FEMINIST APPROACHES
    TO BIOETHICS
Dept. of Philosophy
Indiana University
425 University Blvd.
Indianapolis, IN 46202   PH: (317)274-8926
Prof. Anne Donchin, Contact   FX: (317)274-2347

Founded: 1992. **Members:** 75. **Languages:** English. **Multinational.** Works to: develop a more inclusive theory of bioethics, encompassing the views and experiences of women and other minorities; reexamine the principles of the prevailing discourse; create new methodologies and strategies of change. Organizes presentations at professional meetings; conducts research. **Committees:** Steering.

Publications: *Newsletter of the International Network on Feminist Approaches to Bioethics*. ● *Directory*, periodic.

Conventions/Meetings: triennial meeting.

★2842★ INTERNATIONAL NETWORK FOR WOMEN IN ENTERPRISE
    AND TRADE
PO Box 6178
McLean, VA 22106
Christina Lane, President   PH: (703)893-8541

Multinational. Assists and supports women throughout the world to develop and implement effective business strategies and enterprise development initiatives.

★2843★ INTERNATIONAL NETWORK OF WOMEN IN TECHNOLOGY
    (WITI)
4641 Burnet Ave.   PH: (818)990-1987
Sherman Oaks, CA 91403   E-Mail:
Carolyn Leighton, Exec. Dir.   WITI@cup.portal.com

Women in technology. Works towards developing links with industry, government, and academia in an effort to improve the status and advance the management roles of women in technology. Provides women with information and expertise necessary to allot them professional insight that will assist them in advancing in the technogical industries. Strives to have the intelligence and creativity of women recognized within the technological industries. Works with other organizations which are also dedicated to improving the position and increase the participation of women in technical leadership.

★2844★ INTERNATIONAL PLANNED PARENTHOOD FEDERATION -
    WESTERN HEMISPHERE REGIONAL (IPPF/WHR)
                                        PH: (212)995-8800
902 Broadway, 10th Fl.   FX: (212)995-8853
New York, NY 10010   TX: 620661
Hernan Sanhueza, Regional Dir.   CBL: WHIPPFE

Founded: 1952. **Budget:** US$13,500,000. **Languages:** English. **Multinational.** Division of International Planned Parenthood Federation. National family planning organizations in Canada, Latin America, Caribbean Islands, and the United States. Views family planning as "the expression of the human right of couples to have only the children they want and to have them when they want them." Works to extend the practice of voluntary family planning by providing information, education, and services to couples. Seeks to persuade governments to establish national family planning programs. Conducts research programs; maintains speakers' bureau; sponsors specialized education programs. **Libraries:** Type: reference. Holdings: 10,000. **Sections:** Program Support; Resource Development.

Publications: *Annual Report*. Bulletin. ● *Forum* (in English and Spanish), quarterly. Magazine. Includes calendar of events. Distributed primarily to affiliated family planning programs.

Conventions/Meetings: annual regional meeting - always Fall.

★2845★ INTERNATIONAL SOCIETY FOR THE ADVANCEMENT OF
    HUMANISTIC STUDIES IN GYNECOLOGY (ISFAHSIG)
1750 S. Newport Way
Denver, CO 80224-2212   PH: (303)756-6140
Jack Drose, Exec.Sec.   FX: (303)757-3983

Founded: 1969. **Members:** 250. **Staff:** 1. **Budget:** US$90,000. **Languages:** English. **Multinational.** Obstetricians, gynecologists, urologists, surgeons, radiologists, and opthalmologists; professionals who support humanistic studies in obstetrics and gynecology. Works to: promote and further education on the humanistic aspects of medicine; improve the quality of medical care. Contributes to the continuing education of health practitioners working for the betterment of human reproduction and the resolution of social, political, and economic problems in the field. Facilitates exchange of professional, philosophical, and scientific information among health professionals and experts on the nontechnical aspects of human relationships related to reproduction.

Conventions/Meetings: annual conference - 1994 Feb. 26 - Mar. 5, Tammaron, CO, United States; 1995, Snowmass, CO, United States.

★2846★ INTERNATIONAL SOCIETY FOR IMMUNOLOGY OF REPRODUCTION (ISIR)
c/o Contraceptive Development Branch,
    NICHD
National Institutes of Health
Executive Plaza S, Ste. 450
6120 Executive Blvd.
Bethesda, MD 20892   PH: (301)496-7339
Nancy J. Alexander Ph.D., Sec.Gen.   FX: (301)496-8678

Founded: 1976. **Members:** 350. **Regional Groups:** 6. **Languages:** English. **Multinational.** Scientists and physicians interested in the immunological and genetic processes involved in reproduction. Seeks to encourage and develop research on immunological processes through scientific publications, workshops, and colloquia. **Committees:** Ethics; Standardization.

Publications: *ISIR Newsletter*, semiannual. Provides minutes of meetings, notices of upcoming meetings, and general news updates. **Advertising:** not accepted. ● *Journal of Reproductive Immunology*.

Conventions/Meetings: triennial congress

★2847★ INTERNATIONAL SOCIETY FOR PREVENTION OF INFERTILITY (ISPI)
1430 2nd Ave., Ste. 103
New York, NY 10021   PH: (212)774-5500
Masood A. Khatamee, Exec.Dir.   FX: (212)744-6536

Founded: 1990. **Languages:** English. **Multinational.** Physicians specializing in obstetrics and gynecology; scientists representing public and private teaching hospitals, medical school faculties, and university research departments; practitioners who work with infertile men and women. Objectives are to: study sexually transmitted infectious diseases (STDs) and their effects on human fertility; reduce the incidence of infection and the possibility of resulting infertility. Coordinates and encourages research that can lead to successful forms of treatment and control of STDs, thus enhancing the opportunities for childless couples to achieve intrauterine pregnancies and bear healthy children. Encourages the exchange of information among those involved in research on and treatment of STDs. Designs educational and informational strategies intended for the prevention of infertility. Organizes lectures, seminars, and symposia.

Conventions/Meetings: annual world conference (exhibits).

★2848★ INTERNATIONAL SOCIETY OF REPRODUCTIVE MEDICINE (ISRM)
c/o Donald C. McEwen
11 Furman Ct.
Rancho Mirage, CA 92270   PH: (619)340-5080
Donald C. McEwen M.D., Sec.   FX: (619)340-6920

Founded: 1968. **Members:** 300. **Staff:** 4. **Languages:** English. **Multinational.** Research specialists in reproductive medicine, obstetrics/gynecology, and endocrinology; associate members are laypersons interested in world population problems. Encourages basic and clinical research on the physiology of reproduction with special emphasis on the normal reproductive process, methods for enhancement of fertility, conception control, the pharmacology of steroids and polypeptides, and the immunology of reproduction. Fosters discussion and evaluation of new concepts, controversies in management of patients with reproductive disorders, and clinical relevance of advances in reproductive biology. Disseminates information and promotes continuing education for physicians and scientists. Bestows awards.

Publications: *Annual Proceedings*. Published in The International Journal of Fertility.

Conventions/Meetings: annual conference. ● periodic scientific meeting.

★2849★ INTERNATIONAL SOCIETY OF WOMEN AIRLINE PILOTS (ISA)
PO Box 66268
Chicago, IL 60666-0268
Sue Nielsen, Sec.

Founded: 1978. **Members:** 350. **Languages:** English. **Multinational.** Women airline pilots employed as flight crew members or holding seniority numbers with a major air carrier that operates at least 1 aircraft with a gross weight of 90,000 pounds or more. Fosters international cooperation and exchange among women in the profession. Operates information bank for women interested in entering the field. Maintains speakers' bureau and biographical archives. Recognizes members attaining the rank of captain. Operates Husbands of Airline Pilots auxiliary.

Publications: *International Society of Women Airline Pilots Membership Roster*, annual. **Circulation:** 350. ● *International Society of Women Airline Pilots Newsletter*, quarterly. **Circulation:** 350.

Conventions/Meetings: annual - always 2nd week in May.

★2850★ INTERNATIONAL WOMEN'S ANTHROPOLOGY CONFERENCE (IWAC)
Anthropology Department
25 Waverly Pl.
New York University
New York, NY 10003
Dr. Linda Basch, Sec.-Treas.   PH: (212)998-8550

Founded: 1978. **Languages:** English. **Multinational.** Women anthropologists and sociologists who are researching and teaching topics such as women's role in development, feminism, and the international women's movement. Encourages the exchange of information on research, projects, and funding; addresses policies concerning women from an anthropological perspective. Conducts periodic educational meetings with panel discussions.

Publications: *Bulletin*, periodic. ● *IWAC Newsletter*, semiannual.

Conventions/Meetings: semiannual conference.

★2851★ INTERNATIONAL WOMEN'S FISHING ASSOCIATION (IWFA)
PO Drawer 3125
Palm Beach, FL 33480

Founded: 1955. **Members:** 260. **Languages:** English. **Multinational.** Sportfisherwomen. Promotes angling competition among women anglers; encourages conservation; fosters fishing tournaments of all kinds. **Awards:** Periodic (scholarship). Recipient: Graduate students in marine sciences.

Publications: *Hooks and Lines*, bimonthly. Newsletter. **Advertising:** not accepted. ● *Yearbook*.

Conventions/Meetings: annual meeting - always April.

★2852★ INTERNATIONAL WOMEN'S FORUM (NWF)
1146 19th St. NW, Ste. 600
Washington, DC 20036
Cindy M. Ryan, Pres.   PH: (202)775-8917

Founded: 1980. **Members:** 29. **Languages:** English. **Multinational.** Domestic and international women's networks that seek to bring together women of influence and achievement and allow them to share ideas, experiences, and resources, and to solidify relationships that can enhance their effectiveness. Each state or local network is autonomous and may have different goals.

Publications: *Connection*, periodic. Newsletter. **Advertising:** not accepted.

Conventions/Meetings: annual meeting.

★2853★ INTERNATIONAL WOMEN'S HEALTH COALITION (IWHC)
24 E. 21st St., 5th Fl.
New York, NY 10010
Joan B. Dunlop, Pres.
PH: (212)979-8500
FX: (212)979-9009

Founded: 1980. **Staff:** 18. **Budget:** US$2,100,000. **Languages:** English.
Multinational. Seeks to promote and provide high quality reproductive health care for women in developing countries. Provides technical assistance, supports innovative health care projects and policy-oriented field research in Africa, Asia and Latin America. Sponsors international symposia; produces public education materials.

★2854★ INTERNATIONAL WOMEN'S RIGHTS ACTION WATCH
(IWRAW)
Hubert Humphrey Institute of Public
Affairs
Women, Public Policy and Development
Project
University of Minnesota
301 19th Ave. S
Minneapolis, MN 55455
Arvonne S. Fraser, Director
PH: (612)625-2505

Founded: 1985. **Languages:** English. **Multinational.** International network of women's rights activists and scholars. Monitors laws and policies worldwide in accordance with the principles established in the Convention on the Elimination of All Forms of Discrimination, an international treaty recognizing the securing of women's rights as a foundation for development. Offers legal services to women. Compiles information on the status of women; calls attention to violations of women's rights.

Publications: *Women's Watch* (in English and Spanish), quarterly. Newsletter. ● *Convention on the Elimination of All Forms of Discrimination Against Women* (in English, Spanish, and French). Booklet. The International bill of rights for women. ● *Reproductive Rights: How Signatures to the UN Convention on the Elimination of All Forms of Discrimination Against Women are Measuring Up* (in English, Spanish, and French). Book. ● *Assessing the Status of Women* (in English, Spanish, French, and Arabic). Book. ● *Women, Law and Land at the Local Level: Claiming Women's Human Rights in Domestic Legal Systems.* Book. ● *Women's Human Rights and Reproductive Rights: Status, Capacity and Choice* (in English, Spanish, and Portuguese). Booklet. ● *Measuring Equality: A Comparative Perspective on Women's Legal Capacity and Constitutional Rights in Five Commonwealth Countries.* Book.

★2855★ INTERNATIONAL WOMEN'S TRIBUNE CENTRE (IWTC)
PH: (212)687-8633
777 United Nations Plaza, 3rd Fl.
New York, NY 10017
Dr. Anne S. Walker Ph.D., Dir.
FX: (212)661-2704
CBL: TRIBCEN NY
E-Mail: IWTC@IGC.ORG

Founded: 1976. **Staff:** 8. **Budget:** US$600,000. **Languages:** English.
Multinational. Women's development communications service responding to requests for information and technical assistance from individuals around the world who are involved in women's projects in the Third World. Seeks to develop communication methods and educational materials in collaboration with regional women's groups. Acts as a clearinghouse for and about women in development activities; provides advisory services in low-cost media, women's resource centers, communications techniques, and organizational developments; compiles resource books. **Libraries:** Type: reference. Holdings: 5,550; books, periodicals, clippings, archival material.

Publications: *The Tribune* (in English, French, and Spanish), quarterly. Newsletter. Covers women's projects throughout the developing world. Includes bibliographies and calendar of events. **ISSN:** 0738-9779. **Circulation:** 17,000. **Advertising:** not accepted. ● *The Women $hare Funding Newsnote* (in English, French, and Spanish), periodic. Bulletin. Includes information on new grant programs and policy initiatives.

Conventions/Meetings: periodic workshop.

★2856★ INTERNATIONAL WOMEN'S WRITING GUILD (IWWG)
Box 810, Gracie Sta.
New York, NY 10028-0082
Hannelore Hahn, Exec.Dir.
PH: (212)737-7536

Founded: 1976. **Members:** 6,000. **Staff:** 4. **Languages:** English. **Multinational.** Women writers in 24 countries interested in expressing themselves through the written word professionally and for personal growth. Facilitates manuscript submissions to literary agents. Conducts writing workshops and educational conferences. Participates in international network. Maintains health insurance program at group rates; bestows Artist of Life Award.

Publications: *International Women's Writing Guild—Network*, bimonthly. Magazine. Offers information to assist women writers publish their work. Also includes calendar of events, awards listings, and employment opportunities. **Advertising:** accepted.

Conventions/Meetings: annual conference - always July/August.

★2857★ IOTA PHI LAMBDA
503 Patterson St.
Tuskegee, AL 36088
Mrs. Billie O. Glover, Exec.Dir.
PH: (205)727-5210

Founded: 1929. **Members:** 5,000. **Staff:** 1. **Regional Groups:** 5. **Languages:** English. **National.** Business and professional civic sorority. Seeks to: develop leadership expertise among business and professional women; promote increased interest in business education among high school and college girls through planned programs and scholarships; encourage the development of personalities for all areas of leadership through provision of educational opportunities; establish and promote civic and social service activities for youth and adults. Conducts children's services and tutoring sessions. Provides educational, tutorial, senior citizen, and health programs. **Libraries:** Type: reference. Holdings: 0. **Awards:** Periodic Lola M. Parker Achievement. ● Periodic Mahala S. Evans. ● Periodic Alice Pallen (scholarship).

Publications: *Convention Proceedings*, biennial. Booklet. ● *Journal*, annual. ● *Let's Chat*, semiannual. Magazine. ● *Membership Directory*, biennial.

Conventions/Meetings: biennial convention - always July. ● biennial conference.

★2858★ IOTA SIGMA PI
c/o Dr. Martha Thompson
Oregon Health Sciences University
School of Dentistry
611 SW Campus Dr.
Portland, OR 97201-3097
Dr. Martha Thompson, Senior Natl.Dir.
PH: (503)494-8966
FX: (503)494-4666

Founded: 1902. **Members:** 10,000. **Languages:** English. **National.** Professional honor sorority - chemistry. **Awards:** Triennial Agnes Fay Morgan Research. Recipient: woman chemist under age 40. ● Annual Anna Louise Hoffman. Recipient: female chemistry graduate students. ● Annual Gladys Emerson (scholarship).

Publications: *Directory*, triennial. ● *The Iotan*, 3/year. Newsletter.

Conventions/Meetings: triennial meeting.

★2859★ IOTA TAU TAU
1505 Stovall Circle
Hartwell, GA 30643
Selma C. Parris, Supreme Dean
PH: (706)376-9373

Founded: 1925. **Members:** 500. **Staff:** 1. **Languages:** English. **National.** Law students and attorneys working "for the advancement of women in the legal profession." Sponsors placement service. **Awards:** . **Committees:** Scholarship.

Publications: *The Double Tau*, biennial.

Conventions/Meetings: biennial conference - always fall.

★2860★ IPAS: ISSUES IN ABORTION CARE
303 E. Main St.
PO Box 100
Carrboro, NC 27510   PH: (919)967-7052

Multinational. Promotes safe, respectful abortion care to women throughout the world. Works to establish appropriate and timely treatment for abortion complications. Fosters options for safe, voluntary abortions. Provides comprehensive family planning counseling and services to reduce the need for abortion.

Publications: *Advances in Abortion Care*, periodic. Journal. Practical issues relevant to the delivery of abortion care, including appropriate technologies, clinical updates, and research results. ● *Issues in Abortion Care*. Booklet. ● *A Quality of Care Framework for Abortion Care*. Booklet. Elements of service delivery that are essential to making abortion care safe, effective, and acceptable.

★2861★ IRIS FILMS - IRIS FEMINIST COLLECTIVE
Box 5353
Berkeley, CA 94705   PH: (510)658-5763
Frances Reid, Pres.   FX: (510)658-4783

Founded: 1975. **Members:** 3. **Staff:** 3. **Languages:** English. **National.** Produces realistic, entertaining films with strong positive images of women; seeks to share skills and to open the film field to more women. Produces films for women's groups, organizations, and companies. Conducts seminars, workshops, and classes in film and feminist film theory. **Divisions:** Production. **Formerly:** (1978) Iris Films.

★2862★ JANE ADDAMS CONFERENCE
6 N. Michigan Ave., No. 1313
Chicago, IL 60602   PH: (312)346-3111
Anne Markowitch, President   FX: (312)782-0748

Founded: 1984. **Members:** 300. **Budget:** US$120,000. **Languages:** English. **Multinational.** Multi-ethnic, multi-racial, mostly professional women. Promotes and develops women's leadership in the international arena. Works to awaken international and intercultural understanding through the support of women who have influence reaching international level, educate women on how to have an influence on critical issues, encourage women to pursue leadership positions to become participants in the decision-making process, and provide a forum for the sharing of information and negotiation among national and international organizations. Sponsors lectures, workshops, and writers' series. **Awards:** Biennial Jane Addams International Women's Leadership Award.

Publications: *Briefings*, quarterly. Newsletter. ● Also publishes occasional papers.

Conventions/Meetings: annual dinner.

★2863★ JEWISH ANTI-ABORTION LEAGUE
PO Box 262, Gravesend Sta.
Brooklyn, NY 11223
Arthur Tomases M.D., Pres.   PH: (718)336-0053

Founded: 1979. **Members:** 800. **Staff:** 2. **Languages:** English. **National.** Religious Jews and other individuals who oppose abortion. Provides counseling, education, and adoption assistance programs. Conducts lobbying activities. Maintains speakers' bureau.

Conventions/Meetings: periodic conference.

★2864★ JEWISH LESBIAN DAUGHTERS OF HOLOCAUST SURVIVORS (JLDHS)
PO Box 8773
Madison, WI 53708-8773
Catherine Odette, Exec. Officer

Founded: 1985. **Members:** 150. **Languages:** English. **Multinational.** Provides networking, support, and educational services for lesbians who share the experience of being children of survivors of the Nazi efforts to exterminate the Jews of Europe and North Africa between 1933 and 1945. Offers internal educational programs. Maintains speakers' bureau. **Libraries:** Type: not open to the public.

Publications: *Directory*, semiannual.

Conventions/Meetings: semiannual conference.

★2865★ JEWISH WAR VETERANS OF THE U.S.A. - NATIONAL LADIES AUXILIARY (JWVA)
1811 R St. NW
Washington, DC 20009
Charlotte Steinburg, Admin.   PH: (202)667-9061

Founded: 1928. **Members:** 11,484. **Staff:** 4. **Budget:** US$100,000. **Regional Groups:** 300. **Languages:** English. **National.** Sisters, wives, mothers, daughters, widows, and lineal descendants of Jewish veterans of wars of the United States. Sends gifts to servicemen overseas; conducts youth programs; provides service to hospitalized veterans. Has furnished a surgical wing at Chaim Sheba Medical Center in Israel and has contributed equipment to an amniotic laboratory there. Provides children's services; conducts charitable program. **Awards:** Periodic (scholarship). ● Annual for Humanity. Recipient: military academies. **Committees:** Action and Jewish Affairs; Aid to Israel; Americanism; Child Welfare; Community Relations; Consumer Affairs; Hospital; Leadership; Legislation; MIA/POW Red Ribbon Campaign; Scholarship; Servicemen's Service; United Nations; Veterans Administration Volunteer Service; Veterans Service.

Publications: *Bulletin*, quarterly.

Conventions/Meetings: semiannual meeting.

★2866★ JEWISH WOMEN'S RESOURCE CENTER (JWRC)
National Council of Jewish Women, New
   York Section
9 E. 69th St.
New York, NY 10021
Emily Milner, Coord.   PH: (212)535-5900

Founded: 1978. **Staff:** 1. **Languages:** English. **National.** A division of the National Council of Jewish Women. Information collective on Jewish women. Maintains a directory (in file form) of Jewish women in the arts and Rosh Chodesh groups. Sponsors Jewish Women's Poetry Project, women's selfhelp groups, film festival and lectures. **Libraries:** Type: reference. Holdings: 5,000. Subjects: birth ceremonies, egalitarian marriage contracts, and Passover Haggadot. **Committees:** Library; Poetry; Programming.

Publications: *JWRC Newsletter*, 3/year.

Conventions/Meetings: annual conference.

★2867★ JUDEAN SOCIETY (JS)
1075 Space Pkwy., No. 336
Mountain View, CA 94043
Mrs. Frances A. Miller, Founder   PH: (415)964-8936

Founded: 1952. **Languages:** English. **National.** Divorced Catholic women who meet to offer personal comfort and inspiration to one another; other women of various religions concerned with divorce, separation, and their accompanying problems. Provides educational material regarding Catholic doctrine in terms of the Catholic divorced lifestyle. Encourages all divorced Catholics to remain in harmony with the church. Provides special counseling for marriage investigations and for the return to the sacraments for invalidly married Catholics. Sponsors retreats, workshops, Days of Recollection, and home masses to inspire and strengthen members' efforts to continue to do the will of God; also sponsors social activities. Maintains speakers' bureau. Conducts educational classes on Catholic doctrine regarding marriage and divorce, life after civil divorce, self-discovery, and personal growth.

Publications: *Steps to Effective Living.* Book. ● *Life After Divorce.* Book.

★2868★ JULIA DE BURGOS SHELTER FOR BATTERED WOMEN
GPO Box 2433
San Juan, PR 00936-2433   PH: (809)781-3500
Evangelista Colon   (809)781-2570

Founded: 1979. **Members:** 70. **Staff:** 12. **Budget:** US$251,000. **Languages:** Spanish, English. **National.** Works to raise public awareness of the nature and prevalence of domestic violence. Provides shelter, counselling, and referrals to abused women and their children. Conducts educational workshops, tutoring, sports, and art activities for children. Participates in educational radio and television programming. Engages in research. **Foreign language name:** Casa Protegida Julia de Burgos.

★2869★ JUSTICE FOR WOMEN (JFW)
100 Witherspoon St., Rm. 4608A
Louisville, KY 40202   PH: (502)569-5385
Rev. Mary J. Kuhns, Assoc.   FX: (502)569-5018

Founded: 1988. **Members:** 21. **Languages:** English. **National.** Division of United Presbyterian Church in the U.S.A. Women's Ministry Unit. Purpose is "to serve as the focal point for the identification of issues and churchwide policy relating to the status of women and their position within the church and society." Addresses issues of feminist theologies, inclusive language, and reproductive rights. Among its responsibilities are: evaluating programs of the church's agencies and governing units in terms of their compliance with denominational policies concerning the status of women; providing resources to task forces and committees on women in denomination's area structures. Conducts research on the status of women; sponsors training workshops. **Committees:** Internal Concerns; Reflection and Direction; Sexuality; Women and Economic and Environmental Justice.

Publications: *Newsletter,* quarterly.

Conventions/Meetings: meeting - 3/year.

★2870★ KAPPA ALPHA THETA
8740 Founders Rd.
Indianapolis, IN 46268
Marcia H. Bond, Exec.Dir.   PH: (317)876-1870

Founded: 1870. **Members:** 150,000. **Staff:** 30. **Languages:** English. **National.** Social sorority. Conducts educational programs. **Awards:** .

Publications: *Kappa Alpha Theta Magazine,* quarterly.

Conventions/Meetings: annual meeting. ● biennial conference.

★2871★ KAPPA DELTA
2211 S. Josephine St.
Denver, CO 80210   PH: (303)777-4900
Pat B. Nieman, Pres.   TF: (800)228-5326

Founded: 1897. **Members:** 126,000. **Languages:** English. **National.** Social sorority.

Publications: *The Angelos,* quarterly. Newsletter.

Conventions/Meetings: biennial meeting.

★2872★ KAPPA DELTA PHI
12201 E. Sunland Rd.
Columbus, IN 47203
Loretta Katterhenry, Chair   PH: (812)546-5350

Founded: 1925. **Members:** 2,000. **Languages:** English. **National.** Social civic sorority. Raises funds for civic projects of the American Occupational Therapy Association.

Publications: *Kadelphian,* periodic. Directory. ● *Kadelphian,* bimonthly. Magazine. ● *National Bulletin,* monthly.

Conventions/Meetings: annual meeting.

★2873★ KAPPA KAPPA GAMMA
530 E. Town St.
Box 2079
Columbus, OH 43216
J. Dale Brubeck, Exec.Dir.   PH: (614)228-6515

Founded: 1870. **Members:** 150,000. **Budget:** US$2,000,000. **Languages:** English. **National.** Social sorority. Serves as a network for career information; offers placement service. Maintains biographical archives and Heritage Museum with exhibits pertaining to the history of women and sorority memorabilia. Sponsors charitable activities and philanthropy program. **Awards:** Periodic (grant). ● Periodic (scholarship). ● Periodic Alumnae Achievement. **Computer Services:** Mailing lists. **Committees:** Extension; History; Housing; Panhellenic Affairs; Ritual. **Councils:** Associate; Fraternity.

Publications: *The Key,* quarterly. Newsletter. ● *Proceedings,* biennial. Bulletin.

Conventions/Meetings: biennial conference.

★2874★ KAPPA KAPPA IOTA
1875 E. 15th St.
Tulsa, OK 74104
Jean Terrell, Exec.Sec.   PH: (918)744-0389

Founded: 1921. **Members:** 11,500. **Staff:** 2. **State Groups:** 26. **Languages:** English. **National.** Professional sorority - education. Supports foundations for battered adults and children. **Awards:** Periodic (scholarship). Recipient: future teachers. **Formerly:** (1931) Blue Blue Violet.

Publications: *Bulletin,* semiannual. ● *Newsletter,* periodic.

Conventions/Meetings: annual meeting - 1994 June 29 - July 2, Birmingham, AL, United States.

★2875★ KOVALEVSKAIA FUND
6547 17th Ave. NE
Seattle, WA 98115
Dr. Ann Hibner Koblitz, Director

Multinational. Aims to encourage women to participate in the fields of science and technology in developing countries through appropriate forms of support. Seeks to increase the contact and cooperation between women scientists in diferent countries. Studies connections between the status of women and scientific-technological development.

Publications: *Kovalevskaia Fund,* periodic. Newsletter.

★2876★ LADIES AGAINST WOMEN (LAW)
48 Shattuck Sq., Ste. 70
Berkeley, CA 94704
Mrs. T. "Bill" Banks, Lady Chair-Man   PH: (510)841-6500

Founded: 1980. **Members:** 12,000. **Budget:** US$80,000. **Local Groups:** 26. **Languages:** English. **National.** "Decent ladies with a moral imperative to return to the Good Old Days"; male authority figures; supporting groups such as Moral Sorority and Another Mother for World Domination. Conducts seminars for "uppity women" designed to promote stress reduction through apathy; sponsors consciousness-lowering sessions. Supports right-thinking with fundraiser, including an endangered accessories fashion show (Save the Stoles), bakesales for the Pentagon, guest disruptions of women's events, and picket-reception-lines for "real ladies." Advocates banning books, not bombs. Operates speakers' bureau on issues such as "repealing the women's vote, and the need for a national dress code.".

Publications: *National Embroiderer*, periodic. Newsletter.

Conventions/Meetings: periodic conference.

★2877★ LADIES AUXILIARY, MILITARY ORDER OF THE PURPLE
    HEART, UNITED STATES OF AMERICA (LAMOPH)
419 Franklin St.
Reading, MA 01867
Nancy C. Klare, Sec.   PH: (617)944-1844

Founded: 1932. **Members:** 4,500. **Staff:** 4. **Budget:** US$150,000. **Regional Groups:** 5. **State Groups:** 16. **Local Groups:** 210. **Languages:** English. **National.** Female lineal descendants and adopted females descendants of veterans who have been wounded in combat and awarded the Purple Heart. Activities include: hospital work; child welfare; Americanism and community service; rehabilitation projects. **Computer Services:** Mailing lists. **Committees:** Americanism; Civil Defense; Freedom's Foundation.

Publications: *Directory of Departments and Units*, annual. ● *Newsletter*, 10/year. ● *The Purple Heart*, bimonthly. Magazine. ● *Directory of Unit and Departments*, periodic.

Conventions/Meetings: annual conference - usually August.

★2878★ LADIES AUXILIARY TO THE VETERANS OF FOREIGN WARS
    OF THE UNITED STATES (LAVFWUS)
406 W. 34th St.
Kansas City, MO 64111
Rosemary Mazer, Sec.-Treas.   PH: (816)561-8655

Founded: 1914. **Members:** 767,000. **Staff:** 29. **State Groups:** 51. **Local Groups:** 7,091. **Languages:** English. **National.** Wives, widows, mothers, stepmothers, grandmothers, daughters, foster daughters, stepdaughters, granddaughters, sisters, half sisters, stepsisters, and foster sisters of overseas campaign medal service veterans; women eligible for VFW. Conducts voluntary hospital and rehabilitation work and sponsors various patriotic, Americanism, and youth activities. Supports VFW National Home, Eaton Rapids, MI. Sponsors patriotic art competition. **Awards:** Annual Better World. ● Periodic Unsung Heroine. ● Periodic (scholarship). Recipient: for cancer research. ● Periodic (grant). ● Periodic (monetary). **Programs:** Americanism; Buddy Poppy Sale; Cancer Aid and Research Fund; Community Activities; Junior Girls Units; Legislative; Loyalty Day (May 1); National Home Fund; Rehabilitation; Safety; VA Voluntary Service and Hospital Work; Youth Activities.

Publications: *Directory*, annual. ● *National Auxiliary*, 8/year. Magazine. ● *Program Book*, annual.

Conventions/Meetings: annual meeting - always August. ● conference - usually March.

★2879★ LADIES OF THE GRAND ARMY OF THE REPUBLIC (LGAR)
204 E. Sellers Ave.
Ridley Park, PA 19078
Elizabeth B. Koch, Exec. Officer   PH: (215)521-1328

Founded: 1885. **Members:** 2,000. **Staff:** 11. **State Groups:** 26. **Local Groups:** 25. **Languages:** English. **National.** Female lineal descendants of soldiers, sailors, and marines honorably discharged as Union Civil War veterans. Programs include assistance to veterans and presentation of flags to youth and civic groups. Maintains museum; compiles statistics. **Awards:** . **Committees:** Child Welfare; Community Service; Grand Army of the Republic; Memorial; Veterans and Hospital Service.

Publications: *Bugle Call*, quarterly. Newsletter. ● *Journal*, annual. ● *Roster*, annual. Directory. ● *Roster of Officers - Past Officers*, annual. Directory.

Conventions/Meetings: annual congress - always August.

★2880★ LADIES - LIFE AFTER DIVORCE IS EVENTUALLY SANE
PO Box 2974
Beverly Hills, CA 90213

Founded: 1983. **Members:** 15. **Languages:** English. **National.** Ex-wives of famous men. Support group for divorced wives of celebrities that originated during a USA Cable show titled Are You Anybody? Seeks to form a network of support among other ex-wives in similar situations, and to assist in creating informal groups called LADIES Too whose members are ex-wives of non-famous men. Plans to offer discussion panels for other women's groups.

Conventions/Meetings: monthly meeting.

★2881★ LADIES ORIENTAL SHRINE OF NORTH AMERICA (LOS of
    NA)
1111 E. 54th St., Ste. 111
Indianapolis, IN 46220   PH: (317)259-1996
Betty J. Rathbun, Grand Recorder   FX: (317)253-4501

Founded: 1914. **Members:** 32,000. **Languages:** English. **National.** Wives, mothers, sisters, and daughters of members of the Imperial Council of the Ancient Arabic Order Nobles of the Mystic Shrine for North America. Conducts projects to raise funds for the Shriners' Hospitals for Crippled and Burned Children. **Committees:** Hospital.

Publications: *Proceedings*, annual. Magazine.

Conventions/Meetings: annual grand council session meeting - always May. Louisville, KY, United States; Denver, CO, United States.

★2882★ LADIES PROFESSIONAL BOWLERS TOUR (LPBT)
7171 Cherryvale Blvd.
Rockford, IL 61112   PH: (815)332-5756
John F. Falzone, Pres.   FX: (815)332-9636

Founded: 1981. **Members:** 280. **Staff:** 4. **Budget:** US$1,500,000. **Languages:** English. **National.** Professional women bowlers. Conducts women's world-class championship professional bowling tournaments; presents special competition player awards for outstanding performances. Compiles annual and career competition statistics. Supplies photographic and other promotional services to the bowling industry.

Publications: *Ladies Professional Bowlers Tour*, bimonthly. Newsletter. **Advertising:** not accepted. ● *Ladies Professional Bowlers Tour—Official Rules and Regulations*, annual. Booklet. Includes membership listing, policies, and procedures for all Ladies Pro Bowlers Tour tournaments, and tournaments conducted for others by the LPBT. **Circulation:** 1,000. **Advertising:** not accepted. ● *LPBT Booster Club News*, quarterly. Newsletter. Contains news and highlights for bowling fans. **Circulation:** 500. **Advertising:** not accepted. ● *LPBT Tour Guide*, annual. Directory. Program covering previous year's professional tournaments, records, statistics, and profiles of top women bowlers. Includes biographies. **Circulation:** 40,000. **Advertising:** accepted.

★2883★ LADIES PROFESSIONAL GOLF ASSOCIATION (LPGA)
2570 Volusia Ave., Ste. B
Daytona, FL 32114
Charles S. Mechem, Commissioner   PH: (904)254-8800

Founded: 1950. **Members:** 678. **Staff:** 22. **Budget:** US$12,000,000. **Languages:** English. **National.** Professional women golfers and educators. Compiles statistics on tournaments, money winnings, and scoring. Assists members in finding golfing positions. Provides major retirement program for members; maintains hall of fame; bestows awards. **Divisions:** Teaching; Tournament.

Publications: *Fairway*, annual. Magazine. Includes player profiles, golf fashion section, statistics, tournament reports, and tournament schedule. **Advertising:** accepted. ● *Ladies Professional Golf Association—Schedule Directory*, annual. Lists tournament date, venue, purse, defending champion, and contact telephone number. **Advertising:** not accepted. ● *Player Guide*, annual. Book. Media guide including player biographies, tournament histories and information, LPGA records and statistics, and information on LPGA awards. **Advertising:** not accepted.

Conventions/Meetings: annual conference (exhibits).

★2884★ LADYSLIPPER
PO Box 3124   PH: (919)683-1570
Durham, NC 27715   TF: (800)834-6044
Laurie Fuchs, Dir.   FX: (919)682-5601

Founded: 1976. **Staff:** 8. **Languages:** English. **National.** Seeks to increase public awareness of the achievements of women artists and musicians and expand the scope and availability of musical and literary recordings by women. Makes available information on recordings by female musicians, writers, and composers.

Publications: *Ladyslipper Catalog: Resource Guide to Records, Tapes, Compact Discs, and Videos by Women*, annual. Directory. Arranged by artist; includes music reviews. **Advertising:** accepted.

★2885★ LAMBDA LEGAL DEFENSE AND EDUCATION FUND (LLDEF)
666 Broadway, 12th Fl.
New York, NY 10012   PH: (212)995-8585
Kevin M. Cathcart, Contact   FX: (212)995-2306

Founded: 1973. **Members:** 22,000. **Membership Dues:** student and limited income, US$25; full, US$40. **Staff:** 23. **Budget:** US$1,800,000. **Languages:** English. **National.** Purpose is to defend the civil rights of gay persons and people with AIDS in areas such as employment, housing, education, child custody, and the delivery of medical and social services. Engages in test case litigation as counsel or cocounsel; files briefs as "a friend of the court" to present statistical and educational information and to help inform the court of the needs of lesbians, gay men, and people with AIDS. Provides resources and assistance to attorneys working on behalf of gay clients. Maintains a national network of cooperating attorneys. Helps inform the gay community about its rights and recent legal developments. Educates the public and the legal community about issues and concerns of gay persons and people with AIDS. Operates speakers' bureau; sponsors seminars; compiles statistics. Maintains files containing court decisions and copies of briefs and pleadings. **Awards:** Periodic Jay C. Lipner Liberty Award for service combatting AIDS. ● Periodic Lambda Liberty Award for service in the gay/lesbian community. **Committees:** Development; Education; Legal.

Publications: *AIDS Update*, 6/year. Newsletter. Covers nationwide litigation, legislation, and advocacy relating to AIDS. Focuses on AIDS-related job, housing, and insurance discrimination. **Circulation:** 2,000. **Advertising:** not accepted. ● *Lambda Update*, periodic. Newsletter. Reports on the court cases in which LLDEF is involved and issues of concern to the organization and its members. **Circulation:** 20,000. **Advertising:** not accepted. ● *AIDS Bibliography*. Book. ● *Domestic Partnership: Issues and Legislation*. Book. ● *Lambda Archives*. Book. ● *Pride at Work*. Book.

Conventions/Meetings: annual meeting.

★2886★ LARGESSE
74 Woolsey St.
New Haven, CT 06513-3719
Karen Stimson, Dir.   PH: (203)787-1624

Founded: 1983. **Staff:** 2. **Local Groups:** 2. **Languages:** English. **Multinational.** Organizations, advocates, and people of size concerned about what the group views as "fat oppression". Acts as a support and information resource for people and groups who promote "size acceptance" and oppose bias against those who are overweight. Largesse believes that "no woman in our society is too thin to feel fat," and that this preoccupation with body shape is an important facet of society's oppression of women. Seeks "the empowerment of all women, regardless of size or shape"; works to educate the women's movement and the public about fat women's issues. Operates speakers' bureau. **Libraries:** Type: reference. Holdings: archival material, clippings, video recordings, audio recordings. Subjects: fat activism. **Task Forces:** Fat Action Today; Amazon Liaison.

Publications: *Affirmations for Size Esteem*, periodic. Newsletter.

★2887★ LATIN AMERICAN PROFESSIONAL WOMEN'S ASSOCIATION
3516 N. Broadway
Los Angeles, CA 90031
Alicia Fuentes Unger, Treas.   PH: (213)227-9060

Founded: 1975. **National.** Promotes the business and professional development of Latin American women. Sponsors programs that address issues affecting the development of Latin American women.

★2888★ LATINAS FOR REPRODUCTIVE CHOICE
1900 Fruitvale Ave.
PO Box 7567
Oakland, CA 94601
Dr. Luz Alvarez Martinez, Director   PH: (510)534-1362

Founded: 1990. **Languages:** English. **National.** A project of the National Latina Health Organization. Works to increase awareness and discussion of reproductive rights within the Latino community. Strives to ensure that the interests of Latinas on abortion and on reproductive health issues are sufficiently represented by the presence of Latina individuals on boards of mainstream reproductive rights groups. Promotes self-help and self-responsibility for one's personal health and lifestyle. Encourages the Latino community to become involved in the struggle for full reproductive freedom, including: access to bilingual, quality, health care and prenatal care; freedom from sterilization abuses; education and information on sexuality and contraception; access to alternative forms of birth control. Monitors and seeks to influence elected officials with respect to reproductive rights legislation. Sponsors outreach programs. Conducts periodic workshops, conferences, and forums.

Publications: *Newsletter*, quarterly.

★2889★ LEADERSHIP CONFERENCE OF WOMEN RELIGIOUS OF THE U.S.A. (LCWR)
8808 Cameron St.
Silver Spring, MD 20910   PH: (301)588-4955
Sr. Margaret Cafferty PBVM, Exec.Dir.   FX: (301)587-4575

Founded: 1956. **Members:** 896. **Staff:** 7. **Regional Groups:** 15. **Languages:** English. **National.** Chief administrative officers of Roman Catholic communities of women religious in the U.S. Offers opportunity for discussion and exchange of ideas and information relative to women religious and to administration/leadership in religious orders. Organizes and promotes studies of matters of common interest. Provides information on matters affecting religious orders. Maintains national file of source references.

Publications: *Directory*, annual. ● *Newsletter*, monthly.

Conventions/Meetings: annual general assembly.

★2890★ LEAGUE OF BLACK WOMEN
405 N. Wabash Ave.
Chicago, IL 60611
Bobbie Smith, President

Founded: 1970. **Members:** 500. **Languages:** English. **National.** African American women working to help one another with career problems such as development and promotion. Encourages women to become financially self-reliant and fosters confidence in women. Conducts programs on raising self-awareness, self-motivation, self-direction, and self-assertiveness.

★2891★ LEAGUE OF WOMEN VOTERS EDUCATION FUND (LWVEF)
1730 M St. NW
Washington, DC 20036
Gracia Hillman, Exec.Dir.   PH: (202)429-1965

Founded: 1957. **Staff:** 13. **Budget:** US$2,675,000. **Languages:** English. **National.** Educational arm of the League of Women Voters of the United States (see separate entry). Conducts research on a variety of public policy issues including economic policy, nuclear and solid waste, social welfare, child care, and health care. Encourages more effective citizen participation in government. Organizes seminars. **Departments:** Election Services and Litigation; Research and Citizen Education.

Publications: *Annual Report.* ● *Safety on Tap: A Citizen's Drinking Water Guide.* Book. ● *Residential Debates: 1988 and Beyond.* Book. ● *Nuclear Waste Primer.* Book. ● *Understanding Economic Policy.*

★2892★ LEAGUE OF WOMEN VOTERS OF THE UNITED STATES
  (LWVUS)
1730 M St. NW
Washington, DC 20036   PH: (202)429-1965
Gracia Hillman, Exec.Dir.   FX: (202)429-0854

Founded: 1920. **Members:** 110,000. **Staff:** 50. **Budget:** US$3,550,000. **Regional Groups:** 32. **State Groups:** 50. **Local Groups:** 1,250. **Languages:** English. **National.** Voluntary organization of citizens (men and women) 18 years old or over. Promotes political responsibility through informed and active participation of citizens in government and acts on selected governmental issues. Members select and study public policy issues at local, state, and national levels and take political action on these issues. Leagues at all levels distribute information on candidates and issues and campaign to encourage registration and voting. Does not support or oppose candidates or political parties. National concerns include government, international relations, natural resources, and social policy. Evolved from the National American Woman Suffrage Association.

Publications: *Annual Report.* ● *National Voter*, bimonthly. Newsletter. ● *Report From the Hill*, bimonthly. Bulletin.

Conventions/Meetings: biennial meeting (exhibits). ● biennial meeting.

★2893★ LEGAL ADVOCATES FOR WOMEN (LAW)
320 Clement
San Francisco, CA 94118
Ginny Foat, Exec.Dir.

Founded: 1984. **Languages:** English. **National.** Aims to educate women about their rights and responsibilities within the legal system and to improve the legal status and social condition of women. Works with and monitors legal cases such as those involving sexual harassment, discrimination, and physical abuse of wives by their husbands. Is currently developing a women's prison network to improve prison conditions and aid women following their release. Provides educational materials, expertise, and referrals; conducts research; maintains speakers' bureau.

Publications: *Legal Case Studies*, periodic. Monograph.

Conventions/Meetings: annual board meeting.

★2894★ LEGION OF YOUNG POLISH WOMEN (LYPW)
c/o Copernicus Center
5216 W. Lawrence
Chicago, IL 60630
Lucie Bucki, Pres.

Founded: 1939. **Members:** 200. **Languages:** English. **National.** Women of Polish descent interested in promoting the cultural and social goals of the Polish American community and assisting Poles throughout the world. Provides financial assistance to Polish and American institutions and foundations. Sends medical supplies to Poland and participates in funding

scholarships, exhibits, competitions, and publications. Since 1945, has sponsored the presentation of debutantes at the Annual White and Red Ball.

Conventions/Meetings: monthly meeting.

★2895★ LESBIAN FEMINIST LIBERATION (LFL)
Gay Community Center
208 W. 13th St.
New York, NY 10011   PH: (212)924-2657
Eleanor Cooper, Spokeswoman   (212)627-1398

Founded: 1973. **Members:** 20. **Languages:** English. **National.** Women united to promote lesbian and women's rights. Works to change the attitudes and institutions that limit or deny women the control of their own lives and bodies. Activities include: coalitions with feminist and gay groups; lobbying; direct confrontation tactics (such as nonviolent demonstrations and sit-ins); educational programs. Conducts dances, concerts, sports events, and conferences.

★2896★ LESBIAN, GAY AND BISEXUAL PEOPLE IN MEDICINE
  (LGBPM)
c/o American Med. Student Association
1890 Preston White Dr.   PH: (703)620-6600
Reston, VA 22091   FX: (703)620-5873

Founded: 1976. **Members:** 350. **Local Groups:** 35. **Languages:** English. **National.** Standing committee of the American Medical Student Association. Practicing physicians and physicians in training; others interested in gay/lesbian issues. Purposes are to improve the quality of health care for gay patients; to improve working conditions and professional status of gay health professionals and students. Administers educational workshops for health professionals; designs training materials; conducts research on the health problems of gay people and surveys on admissions, hiring, and promotion policies of medical schools and hospitals; provides referrals; sponsors support groups for gay professionals to meet, socialize, and organize; presses for legislative and political action to end discrimination against gay people. Maintains speakers' bureau.

Publications: *LGBPM Newsletter*, semiannual.

Conventions/Meetings: annual conference (exhibits). ● semiannual workshop.

★2897★ LESBIAN AND GAY CAUCUS OF PUBLIC HEALTH
  WORKERS (LGCPHW)
Mailbox No. 113
1601 17th St. NW
Washington, DC 20009
Joshua Lipsman, Chair

Founded: 1975. **Members:** 150. **Languages:** English. **National.** A caucus of the American Public Health Association. Public health workers in the fields of administration, government, nursing, direct care, and teaching. Promotes dissemination of information on the health needs of lesbians and gay men. Serves as a support network for gay public health workers. The caucus believes homophobia interferes with the proper delivery of health care to gays and lesbians, restricts or eliminates their contributions as health workers, and causes physical and mental health problems. Holds scientific sessions on gay and lesbian health issues at Annual meeting.

Conventions/Meetings: annual meeting.

★2898★ LESBIAN HERSTORY EDUCATIONAL FOUNDATION (LHEF)
PO Box 1258
New York, NY 10116
Joan Nestle, Sec.   PH: (212)874-7232

Founded: 1974. **Budget:** US$50,000. **Languages:** English. **Multinational.** Works to gather, preserve, and share information on the lives and activities of lesbians worldwide. Maintains Lesbian Herstory Archives resource room including periodicals, diaries, tapes, photographs, poetry, prose, research papers, graphics, and other memorabilia on all aspects of the lesbian culture. Makes available guest speakers and offers slide shows for schools and community groups.

Publications: *Lesbian Herstory Archives Newsletter*, periodic. Lists bibliographies and reviews lesbian cultural material; includes research updates. **Circulation:** 8,000.

★2899★ LESBIAN MOTHERS NATIONAL DEFENSE FUND (LMNDF)
PO Box 21567
Seattle, WA 98111
Jenny Sayward, Contact   PH: (206)325-2643

Founded: 1974. **Members:** 450. **Languages:** English. **National**. Provides legal, emotional, and financial support for lesbian mothers involved with custody problems. Monitors and reports on judicial and legislative activities and decisions affecting gay and lesbian parents. Conducts specialized education. Provides alternative conception and adoption information, information bank, and lawyer referral service. Maintains speakers' bureau. **Libraries:** Type: reference.

Publications: *Mom's Apple Pie*, quarterly. Newsletter. Reports on lesbian custody cases, current legislation, and other issues surrounding lesbian parenting. Includes book reviews. **Circulation:** 450.

★2900★ LESBIAN RESOURCE CENTER (LRC)
1208 E. Pine St.
Seattle, WA 98122
Cherie Larson, Dir.   PH: (206)322-3953

Founded: 1971. **Staff:** 3. **Budget:** US$80,000. **Languages:** English. **National**. Provides classes, support groups, workshops, social activities, and information on housing, employment, and lesbian community groups. Represents the lesbian community in areas of political and social concern. Operates telephone referral service; maintains speakers' bureau. **Libraries:** Type: lending.   **Alternate name:** Pacific Women's Resources. **Formerly:** (1973) Gay Women's Alliance.

Publications: *Lesbian Resource Center Community News*, monthly. Newsletter. Covers community and center events; includes calendar, editorials, and news stories. **Circulation:** 5,500. **Advertising:** accepted.

★2901★ LIBERTARIANS FOR GAY AND LESBIAN CONCERNS (LGLC)
PO Box 447
Chelsea, MI 48118
James Hudler, Coordinator

Founded: 1981. **Members:** 100. **Budget:** US$30,000. **Regional Groups:** 3. **State Groups:** 6. **Local Groups:** 4. **Languages:** English. **National**. Gay and nongay libertarians and other interested individuals. Seeks to heighten awareness among libertarians regarding gay concerns. Promotes libertarianism as practical, moral alternative to traditional "left-right" party politics. Provides gay outreach program through local chapters in San Francisco, CA and New York City, Ann Arbor, MI, and through an informal network in 13 states and Canada. Maintains biographical archive. Conducts charitable programs. **Libraries:** Type: reference.   **Computer Services:** Database.

Publications: *LGLC Newsletter*, bimonthly.

Conventions/Meetings: annual conference.

★2902★ LIBERTY GODPARENT HOME (LGH)
1000 Villa Rd.   PH: (804)384-3043
Lynchburg, VA 24503   TF: (800)542-4453
Dr. Gregg Albers, Exec.V.Pres.   FX: (804)384-3730

Founded: 1982. **Languages:** English. **National**. Offers an alternative to abortion by meeting the immediate and long-term needs of teens in crisis pregnancy situations. Goal is "to change one life and save another through

sharing the gospel of Jesus Christ" via the ministry's educational and outreach program. The program consists of three divisions: the Pregnancy Crisis Center offers a hot line, free pregnancy testing, educational materials and counseling about alternatives to abortion; the Maternity Home, a residential care facility for women aged 12-21, offers life skills training, health services, counseling, and Christian education which centers on sharing the principles of the Bible and the claims of Jesus Christ and encouraging each woman to attend church regularly; the Adoption Agency places children in "dedicated, Bible-believing Christian families" which have been screened and spiritually prepared for the adoption by the ministry. Offers guidance in the establishment of local pregnancy crisis centers. Operates speakers' bureau. **Formerly:** (1986) Save-A-Baby.

Publications: *What About Me*. Booklet.

★2903★ THE LINKS
1200 Massachusetts Ave. NW
Washington, DC 20005
Mary P. Douglas, Contact   PH: (202)842-8686

Founded: 1946. **National**. African American women committed to the development of the community through educational, cultural, and civic activities. Sponsors charitable programs.

★2904★ LITHUANIAN AMERICAN ROMAN CATHOLIC WOMEN'S
          ALLIANCE (LCW)
3005 N. 124th St.
Brookfield, WI 53005
Dale Murray, Pres.   PH: (414)786-7359

Founded: 1914. **Members:** 1,000. **Staff:** 3. **State Groups:** 6. **Local Groups:** 22. **Languages:** English. **National**. Catholic-Lithuanian women or women married to Lithuanians who are interested in their heritage, and in the politics of Lithuania and America. Conducts regional seminars and charitable programs. Maintains archives at Kent State University in Ohio. Operates speakers' bureau. **Awards:** Periodic (scholarship).

Publications: *Newsletter*, quarterly.

Conventions/Meetings: biennial meeting.

★2905★ LUBAVITCH WOMEN'S ORGANIZATION (LWO)
398 Kingston Ave.
Brooklyn, NY 11225   PH: (718)493-1773
Shterna Spritzer, Pres.   FX: (718)604-0594

Founded: 1955. **Members:** 12,000. **Budget:** US$100,000. **Regional Groups:** 136. **Languages:** English. **National**. Jewish women and girls. Sponsored by the Lubavitch Movement. Purposes are: to bring Jewish heritage and culture to Jewish women and girls; to enhance their knowledge and practice of Jewish traditions and customs, including religious candle lighting rituals, establishment and maintenance of Kosher homes, family and marriage laws, and holidays; to increase public awareness of Jewish culture, heritage, and tradition. Conducts adult education classes on Jewish laws and customs. Sponsors charitable programs; offers children's services; operates speakers' bureau. **Committees:** Education; Family Life; Jewish Dietary Laws; Sabbath. **Alternate name:** Agudas Nshei Ub nos Chabad.

Publications: *Convention Journal*, annual. ● *International N'shei Chabad Newsletter*, semiannual. ● *N'shei Chabad Newsletter*, bimonthly. ● *Yiddish Heim*, quarterly. Journal. ● *Shlichus - Meeting the Outreach Challenge*. Book. ● *All the Days of Her Life*. Book. ● *The Modern Jewish Woman: A Unique Perspective*. Book.

Conventions/Meetings: annual meeting (exhibits) - New York, NY, United States. ● annual conference. ● annual Week of the Jewish Woman workshop.

★2906★ LUTHERANS FOR LIFE (LFL)
PO Box 819
Benton, AR 72015
Rev. Edward Fehskens, Exec.Dir.
PH: (501)794-2212
FX: (501)794-1437

Founded: 1978. **Members:** 8,000. **Staff:** 6. **State Groups:** 14. **Local Groups:** 270. **Languages:** English. **National.** Pro-life, pan-Lutheran educational and outreach organization seeking to promote respect for life at all stages from conception to natural death. Assists Lutheran colleges, congregations, and seminaries in establishing programs that educate the public about euthanasia, abortion, infanticide, and related life issues; helps church bodies reexamine their stances on these issues; provides resources on life issues. Encourages participation in public policy-making processes. Offers referral services to individuals experiencing crises and need; supports creation of crisis pregnancy and post-abortion counseling services. Operates speakers' bureau. **Libraries:** Type: reference. Holdings: books, periodicals. Subjects: abortion and related issues. **Committees:** Health Professional; Legal; Medical; Theological.

Publications: *Life Date*, quarterly. Newsletter. Reports on the care of children, unwed mothers, disabled persons, and the poor. Covers issues such as abortion, adoption, and euthanasia. **Circulation:** 8,000. • *Living*, quarterly. Magazine. Pro-life issues. • *Videos*.

Conventions/Meetings: annual meeting. • periodic regional meeting.

★2907★ LYDIA - A WOMEN'S COOPERATIVE INTERCHANGE
1257 E. Siena Heights Dr.
Adrian, MI 49221
Corinne Florek, Contact
PH: (517)265-5135

Languages: English. **National.** Participants are worker-owners, primarily women, involved in the cooperative form of business organization. Promotes the cooperative workplace as an employment alternative. Disseminates information on the ownership, control, and financing of a cooperative business. Offers educational programs.

Publications: *Cooperative Workplace: the Principles of Participation*. Book. • *Cooperative Workplace: A Working Alternative*. Book.

★2908★ MADRE
121 W. 27th St., Rm. 301
New York, NY 10001
Vivian Stromberg, Exec. Dir.

Members: 22,000. **Multinational.** Promotes friendship, international understanding, and cultural exchange between women and children in the United States, Central America, and the Caribbean. Provides a network of support and health care assistance to communities stricken by war, poverty, and violence. Organizes training and literacy projects for rural communities.

Publications: *Newsletter*, periodic.

★2909★ MANAVI - ASSOCIATION INDIAN WOMEN IN AMERICA (AIWA)
PO Box 614
Bloomfield, NJ 07003
Shamita Das Dasgupta, Contact
PH: (908)687-2662

Founded: 1985. **Members:** 130. **Budget:** US$10,000. **Languages:** English. **National.** Works to eradicate violence and discrimination against South Asian women residing in the United States, including customs that support the oppression and exploitation of women. Supports women's movements in South Asian countries through fund-raising efforts for specific projects. Conducts educational workshops at colleges, universities, and mainstream institutions; strives to sensitize the public to issues pertaining to South Asian women, their cultures, and their struggles. Offers counseling, financial assistance, and legal advocacy and referrals to women. Disseminates information. **Libraries:** Type: reference. Holdings: video recordings, books. **Committees:** Outreach.

Publications: *Manavi Newsletter* (in English), 3/year. • *Services Directory*.

Conventions/Meetings: semiannual meeting.

★2910★ MARCH FOR LIFE FUND (ML)
Box 90300
Washington, DC 20090
Nellie J. Gray, Pres.
PH: (202)543-3377
FX: (202)543-8202

Founded: 1974. **Languages:** English. **National.** Promotes the right to life of all individuals, born and pre-born. Advocates a mandatory Human Life Amendment to the U.S. Constitution. Sponsors Annual March for Life whereby pro-lifers come from across the nation to march in Washington, D.C. in protest to the 1973 U.S. Supreme Court decision legalizing abortion. Each year on Jan. 22 (date of march), ML sends the President, each member of Congress, and the U.S. Supreme Court a typed message and red roses on behalf of the unborn. Conducts lobbying activities and presents testimony from the pro-life viewpoint. Provides seminars; operates speakers' bureau. **Formerly:** (1992) March for Life.

Publications: *Action Memo*, periodic. Bulletin. • *Annual Report*. • *Student Contests*, annual. Bulletin.

★2911★ MARY'S PENCE
PO Box 29078
Chicago, IL 60629-9078
Maureen Gallagher, Contact
PH: (312)783-3177

National. Catholic women's organization that promotes alternative ministries, such as women's shelters, legal services, housing advocacy, economic development, education and literacy programs, and centers for creative theology.

★2912★ MATERNITY CENTER ASSOCIATION (MCA)
48 E. 92nd St.
New York, NY 10128
Ruth W. Lubic, Gen.Dir.
PH: (212)369-7300
FX: (212)369-8747

Founded: 1918. **Members:** 600. **Staff:** 22. **Languages:** English. **National.** Laypersons, physicians, nurses, nurse-midwives, and public health workers interested in improvement of maternity care, maternal and infant health, and family life. Maintains Childbearing Center for low-risk families. Conducts classes for expectant parents. Sponsors research; administers nurse-midwifery student assistance fund. Co-sponsors community-based Nurse-Midwifery Education Program. **Libraries:** Type: reference. **Committees:** Medical Board; Research Advisory.

Publications: *Special Delivery*. Newsletter. Contains information on the activities of the organization. **Circulation:** 1,000. • *The Birth Atlas*. Book. • *Preparation for Childbearing*. Book.

Conventions/Meetings: annual meeting - New York, NY, United States.

★2913★ MATH/SCIENCE NETWORK
Preservation Park
678 13th St., Ste. 100
Oakland, CA 94612
Rebecca Failor, Contact
PH: (510)893-6284

Founded: 1974. **National.** Works to promote the participation of women and girls in science and mathematics. Collects and disseminates information relating to the issues of the underrepresentation of women in math and science.

★2914★ MEDIA FUND FOR HUMAN RIGHTS (MFHR)
PO Box 8185
Universal City, CA 91608
R.J. Curry, Exec.Dir.
PH: (818)902-1476

Founded: 1983. **Staff:** 1. **Languages:** English. **National.** An educational foundation of the Gay and Lesbian Press Association. Seeks to: reeducate the media and the American public about lesbians and gays; utilize the media to change attitudes that deny gays full benefits of citizenship; enable gays to report their news; promote the accessibility of gay history nationwide.

★2915★ MEDIA WATCH (MW)
PO Box 618
Santa Cruz, CA 95061-0618   PH: (408)423-6355
Ann Simonton, Dir.   FX: (408)423-9119

Founded: 1984. Members: 800. Local Groups: 3. Languages: English. National. Individuals dedicated to improving the image of women in the media. Believes women and girls worldwide suffer from a lack of self-esteem which is instilled and maintained by the profusion of sexist, racist, and violent images of women in the media. Works to educate the public concerning the consequences of sexually objectifying women and children in the media with the goal of helping people become critical consumers of all forms of mass media. Stages public protests, boycotts, letter writing campaigns, and fundraising events. Maintains speakers' bureau; conducts children's programs and educational workshops and seminars. Compiles statistics. Libraries: Type: reference.

Publications: Media Watch News, quarterly. Includes items illustrating the dehumanization of women by the media and announcements of current boycott campaigns.

★2916★ MEDICAL WOMEN'S INTERNATIONAL ASSOCIATION -
     UNITED STATES
1310 Wyngate Rd.
Wynnewood, PA 19096
Estherina Shems, Contact

Languages: English. National. U.S. branch of the Medical Women's International Association (see separate entry). Women physicians. Provides a forum for discussion of women's health care issues. Encourages women to enter the field of medicine. Works to overcome discrimination against female physicians. Sponsors research and educational programs.

★2917★ MELPOMENE INSTITUTE FOR WOMEN'S HEALTH
     RESEARCH (MIWHR)
1010 University Ave.
St. Paul, MN 55104
Judy Mahle Lutter, Pres.   PH: (612)642-1951

Founded: 1981. Members: 1,400. Staff: 4. Budget: US$180,000. Languages: English. National. Individuals professionally trained in healthcare, physical activity, and sports for girls and women. Researches and disseminates information on issues such as body image, osteoporosis, athletic amenorrhea, exercise and pregnancy, and ageing. Offers undergraduate and graduate internships, and volunteer programs. Provides consulting services for program evaluations. Sponsors competitions and physical activities. Operates speakers' bureau. Libraries: Type: reference. Awards: . Computer Services: Data base, health related articles arranged by category and keyword.

Publications: Melpomene Journal, 3/year. Examines the relationship between physical activity and lifestyles. Features research reports, scientific bibliographies, and personal profiles. Circulation: 2,500. Advertising: not accepted. Also Cited As: Melpomene Report. ● Newsletter, quarterly. ● The Bodywise Woman. Book.

Conventions/Meetings: periodic conference.

★2918★ MEXICAN AMERICAN WOMEN'S NATIONAL ASSOCIATION
     (MANA)
1030 15th St. NW, Ste. 468
Washington, DC 20005   PH: (202)898-2036

Founded: 1974. Members: 2,000. Local Groups: 12. Languages: English. National. Promotes leadership and economic and educational development

for Mexican-American and other Hispanic women. Areas of concern include pay equity, adolescent pregnancy, and children in poverty. Offers leadership development course, which includes training at the national and local levels; operates Hermanitas Project, an Annual conference on self-image building and career counseling for high school Hispanic girls. Awards: Annual (scholarship).

Publications: Newsletter, quarterly. ● Issue Updates, periodic. Bulletin.

Conventions/Meetings: biennial conference.

★2919★ MIDDLE EAST STUDIES ASSOCIATION - ASSOCIATION OF
     MIDDLE EAST WOMEN'S STUDIES
University of Arizona
1232 N. Cherry Ave.
Tucson, AZ 85721
Nancy Dishaw, Sec.   PH: (602)621-5850

National. Promotes the study of issues affecting Arab American women.

★2920★ MIDWEST PARENTCRAFT CENTER (MPC)
3921 N. Lincoln
Chicago, IL 60613
Margaret Gamper R.N., Exec.Dir.   PH: (312)725-7767

Founded: 1950. Staff: 2. Languages: English. National. Prenatal instructors, parents, and professionals involved in parenting and pregnancy. To instruct and educate expectant mothers and others in the Gamper Method of childbirth. (The Gamper Method, based on the teachings of several 19th century physicians and developed by Margaret Gamper in 1946, is designed to prepare the prospective mother for childbirth by instilling self-determination and confidence in her ability to work with the physiological changes of her body during pregnancy, labor, and delivery.) Conducts prenatal and grandparenting classes and workshops; operates in-service programs for hospitals and clinics; sponsors programs on topics such as grieving and history of birth procedures. Disseminates teaching aids including slides, films, records, and tapes. Grants childbirth educator certificates to qualified applicants who have taught Gamper Method classes under the supervision of an instructor. Operates charitable program and speakers' bureau. The center's activities are currently concentrated in Ohio, Illinois, Indiana, Wisconsin, and Michigan. Libraries: Type: reference. Holdings: 6,000; books, periodicals. Subjects: childbirth, midwifery, marriage, sexuality, and childcare.

Publications: Heir Raising News, quarterly. Newsletter. ● Preparation for the Heir Minded. Book.

Conventions/Meetings: annual conference.

★2921★ MIDWIFERY TODAY AND CHILDBIRTH EDUCATION
PO Box 2672
Eugene, OR 97402
Jan Tritten, Editor   PH: (503)344-7438

National. Midwives, nurses, childbirth educators, and other professionals. Works to increase awareness of childbirth education to women throughout the United States. Provides information on childbirth methods in order to keep birth options open to women. Encourages networking among members and other organizations with similar interests.

Publications: Magazine, quarterly.

Conventions/Meetings: annual conference.

★2922★ MIDWIVES ALLIANCE OF NORTH AMERICA (MANA)
PO Box 1121
Bristol, VA 24203
Karen Moran, Exec.Dir.

Founded: 1982. Members: 900. Budget: US$55,000. Regional Groups: 8. Languages: English. Multinational. Midwives, student/apprentice midwives, and persons supportive of midwifery. Seeks to expand communication and support among midwives. Works to promote basic competency in midwives; develops and encourages guidelines for their education. Offers legal, legislative, and political advice and resource referrals; conducts networking on local, state, and regional bases; provides advice regarding insurance issues. Operates speakers' bureau; compiles statistics. **Committees:** Affirmative Action; AIDS; Communications; Credentialing; Education; Ethics; Finance; Fund-Raising; Public Relations; Standards and Practice; Statistics; Students. **Sections:** International.

Publications: *MANA News*, quarterly. Newsletter.

Conventions/Meetings: annual conference (exhibits).

★2923★ MINORITY BUSINESS WOMEN'S EXCHANGE
1500 Massachusetts Ave., Ste. 831-A
Washington, DC 20005
Willett Thomas, Contact

Languages: English. **National.** Seeks to enhance the personal and professional growth of minority women in business. Represents members' interests.

★2924★ MISSIONARY WOMEN INTERNATIONAL (MWI)
60180 CR 113 S
Elkhart, IN 46517
Opal Speicher, Pres.   PH: (219)875-3146

Founded: 1944. **Members:** 6,000. **Languages:** English. **Multinational.** Promotes fellowship among church women. Raises funds for missions. Sponsors retreats and leadership training. Operates under the auspices of the Missionary Church.

Publications: *Corner to Corner Newsletter*, monthly. ● *Prayer Projects*, annual. Magazine.

Conventions/Meetings: annual meeting - always October. Ft. Wayne, IN, United States. ● periodic conference.

★2925★ MISTRESSES ANONYMOUS (MA)
1320 Spur Dr. S
Islip, NY 11751
Melissa Sands, Pres.

Languages: English. **National.** Selfhelp organization for women involved with married men. Conducts specialized education program; compiles statistics. Maintains Foundation of Mistress Research.

Publications: *Triangle Tabloid*, periodic. Newsletter. ● *The Making of the American Mistress*. Book. ● *The Seocnd Wife's Survival Manual*. Book.

★2926★ MOMS IN TOUCH INTERNATIONAL (MITI)
PO Box 1120
Poway, CA 92074-1120   PH: (619)679-7953
Fern Nichols, Pres.   FX: (619)679-7953

Founded: 1984. **Staff:** 3. **Regional Groups:** 20,000. **Languages:** English. **Multinational.** Mothers, grandmothers, and other interested individuals united to provide support and prayer for children and educational systems.

Publications: *Heart to Heart from Moms in Touch*, quarterly. Newsletter. **Circulation:** 20,000.

Conventions/Meetings: annual meeting. ● periodic conference.

★2927★ MOTHERS AT HOME
8310-A Old Courthouse Rd.
Vienna, VA 22182
Cathy Myers, Pres.   PH: (703)827-5903

Founded: 1983. **Languages:** English. **National.** Dedicated to the support of mothers who choose to stay at home to raise their families. Serves as a forum for the exchange of information among members. Provides information

at congressional hearings. Conducts research and seminars; compiles statistics; maintains speakers' bureau. **Committees:** Congressional Liaison; Development; Editorial; Marketing; Mothering Education; Public Relations; Research.

Publications: *Welcome Home*, monthly. Magazine. Aimed at boosting the morale and image of mothers at home. ● *What's a Smart Woman Like You Doing at Home?*. Book. ● *Discovering Motherhood*. Book.

★2928★ MOTHERS WITHOUT CUSTODY (MWOC)
PO Box 27418
Houston, TX 77227-7418
Jennifer Isham, Pres.   PH: (713)840-1622

Founded: 1981. **Members:** 500. **Local Groups:** 20. **Languages:** English. **National.** Women living apart from one or more of their minor children for any reason, including court decisions, exchange of custody with an ex-spouse, intervention by a state agency, or childnapping by an ex-spouse. Provides support to women currently exploring their child custody options during and after divorce. Helps establish local selfhelp groups that meet monthly and organize social events for mothers alone and mothers visiting their children. Has estimated that there are 1.5 million mothers living apart from minor children. Provides member exchange.

Publications: *Mother-to-Mother*, bimonthly. Newsletter.

Conventions/Meetings: annual conference.

★2929★ MS. FOUNDATION FOR WOMEN (MFW)
141 5th Ave., Ste. 6-S
New York, NY 10010
Marie C. Wilson, Exec.Dir.   PH: (212)353-8580

Founded: 1972. **Budget:** US$1,500,000. **Languages:** English. **National.** Goals are to eliminate sex discrimination and to improve the status of women and girls in society. Provides funds and technical assistance to activist, community-based self-help feminist projects working on issues of economic development, nonsexist multicultural education, reproductive rights, health and AIDS, and prevention of violence to women and children. Evaluates community-based women's groups and helps them to strengthen their programs. **Computer Services:** Data base, organization's supporters.

Publications: *Newsletter*, quarterly. ● *Report*, annual. ● *Directory*, periodic. Grant listings.

Conventions/Meetings: annual Regional and National Economic Development Institute meeting.

★2930★ NAJDA: WOMEN CONCERNED ABOUT THE MIDDLE EAST
PO Box 7152
Berkeley, CA 94707
Alice Kawash, Pres.   PH: (510)549-3512

Founded: 1960. **Members:** 500. **Languages:** English. **National.** Arab-American women, Americans women married to Arabs, and others interested in the Arab world. Promotes understanding between Americans and Arabs by offering educational programs and audiovisual presentations on Middle Eastern history, art, culture, and current events. Raises funds for educational institutions in the Occupied Territories; provides humanitarian relief to Palestinian women and children. Sponsors poetry readings and other cultural performances. (Najda is an Arabic word meaning "assistance in time of need"). **Awards:** Periodic (scholarship). Recipient: women in the Gaza Strip and West Bank.

Publications: *Middle East Resources*, quarterly. Journal. Designed for teachers. ● *Najda Newsletter*, bimonthly. ● *The Arabic Cookbook*. ● *The Arab World Notebook for the Secondary School Level*.

Conventions/Meetings: periodic workshop.

★2931★ NATIONAL ABORTION FEDERATION (NAF)
1436 U St. NW, Ste. 103
Washington, DC 20009
Barbara Radford, Exec.Dir.
PH: (202)667-5881
TF: (800)772-9100
FX: (202)667-5890

Founded: 1977. **Members:** 300. **Staff:** 10. **Budget:** US$900,000. **Languages:** English. **National.** National professional forum for abortion service providers (physician offices, clinics, feminist health centers, planned parenthood affiliates) and others committed to making safe, legal abortions accessible to all women. Unites abortion service providers into a professional community dedicated to health care; upgrades abortion services by providing standards and guidelines; serves as clearinghouse of information on variety and quality of services offered; keeps abreast of educational, legislative, and public policy developments in reproductive health care. Provides consultations, training workshops, and seminars. Operates telephone hot-line. **Libraries:** Type: reference. Holdings: 225. Subjects: abortion, contraception, sexuality, sociology, health, and medicine.

Publications: *Annual Meeting Workbook.* Booklet. • *Government Relations Report*, periodic. Booklet. • *Meeting Notes*, periodic. Bulletin. • *Membership Directory*, annual. • *Membership News*, periodic. Newsletter. • *National Abortion Federation*, semiannual. Newsletter. Contains information pertinent to keeping abortion safe, legal, and accessible. Includes book reviews, calendar of events, and research updates. **Circulation:** 500. • *Risk Management Workbook*, semiannual. Booklet. • *Consumer's Guide to Abortion Services* (in English and Spanish). Book. • *Unsure About Your Pregnancy? A Guide to Making the Right Decision.* Book.

Conventions/Meetings: annual meeting (exhibits).

★2932★ NATIONAL ABORTION RIGHTS ACTION LEAGUE (NARAL)
1156 15th St. NW, Ste. 700
Washington, DC 20005
Kate Michelman, Exec.Dir.
PH: (202)973-3000
FX: (202)408-4698

Founded: 1969. **Members:** 400,000. **Staff:** 40. **Budget:** US$4,000,000. **State Groups:** 41. **Languages:** English. **National.** To develop and sustain a pro-choice political constituency in order to maintain the right to legal abortion for all women. Initiates and coordinates political action of individuals and groups concerned with maintaining the 1973 Supreme Court abortion decision affirming the choice of abortion as a constitutional right. Maintains lobbyist; briefs members of Congress; testifies at hearings on abortion and related issues; organizes affiliates in states to build political awareness; trains field representatives. Supports pro-choice candidates for elected office. Maintains speakers' bureau; compiles statistics. **Committees:** NARAL-PAC. **Divisions:** Affiliate Development; Communication; Development; Legal/Research; Legislative.

Publications: *NARAL Newsletter*, quarterly. Provides updates on legislation regarding abortion. **Circulation:** 270,000.

Conventions/Meetings: biennial conference.

★2933★ NATIONAL ACTION FOR FORMER MILITARY WIVES
(NAFMW)
1700 Legion Dr.
Winter Park, FL 32789
Lois N. Jones, Pres.
PH: (407)628-2801

Founded: 1979. **Members:** 5,000. **Languages:** English. **National.** Seeks federal legislation that: provides for retroactive, pro-rata sharing of military retirement pay; requires mandatory assignment of the Survivors Benefit Plan to current and former spouses of service members; restores all medical, commissary, and exchange privileges to former spouses; prevents instances of double taxation on benefits shared by ex-spouses. Advises former military wives in the process of divorce. Offers children's services; compiles statistics.

Publications: *Newsletter*, 2-4/year.

Conventions/Meetings: monthly meeting.

★2934★ NATIONAL ACTION FORUM FOR MIDLIFE AND OLDER
WOMEN
Health Sciences Center
State University of New York
Stony Brook, NY 11794
Jane Porcino, Contact

Languages: English. **National.** Promotes interests of older women. Conducts research on the medical, sociological, and psychological aspects of ageing.

Publications: *Hot Flash* (in English), periodic. Newsletter.

★2935★ NATIONAL ALLIANCE OF BREAST CANCER
ORGANIZATIONS (NABCO)
1180 Ave. of the Americas, 2nd Fl.
New York, NY 10036
Amy Langer, Exec.Dir.
PH: (212)719-0154
FX: (212)768-8828

Founded: 1986. **Members:** 300. **Languages:** English. **National.** Breast centers; hospitals; government health offices; and support and research organizations providing information about breast cancer and breast diseases from early detection through continuing care. Serves as a resource for: organizations requiring information about breast cancer programs and organizations and medical advances; individuals seeking information about research, developments, and treatment options for breast cancer. Seeks to influence public and private health policy on issues pertaining to breast cancer, such as insurance reimbursement, health care legislation, and research funding priorities. Offers advice on how to propose and lobby for or against legislation regarding discrimination, informed consent, and third-party reimbursement . Disseminates educational materials and information on support groups, breast care centers, and hospital programs. **Committees:** Medical Advisory.

Publications: *NABCO News*, quarterly. Newsletter. Monitors developments relating to breast cancer. • *NABCO's Resource List*, annual. Directory. Contains information on materials and organizations that provide information about breast cancer.

★2936★ NATIONAL ASSEMBLY OF RELIGIOUS WOMEN (NARW)
529 S. Wabash, Rm. 404
Chicago, IL 60605
Sr. Judy Vaughan CSJ, Coordinator
PH: (312)663-1980
FX: (312)663-9161

Founded: 1970. **Members:** 3,000. **Staff:** 3. **Languages:** English. **National.** Women of faith; associate members are men. Organized to provide a forum for Catholic feminist women to network, speak out, and act on issues of social justice and ministry. Conducts leadership training programs for a Ministry for Justice. Offers resources and program materials on women's issues, concerns, and strategies for change.

Publications: *Probe*, bimonthly. Newsletter. Covers various justice issues having an impact on women in the church and society.

Conventions/Meetings: annual conference. • periodic workshop.

★2937★ NATIONAL ASSOCIATION OF BLACK WOMEN ATTORNEYS
(NABWA)
3711 Macomb St. NW, 2nd Fl.
Washington, DC 20016
Mabel D. Haden, Pres.
PH: (202)966-9693
(202)966-9692
FX: (202)244-6648

Founded: 1972. **Members:** 500. **Staff:** 4. **Budget:** US$30,000. **Regional Groups:** 8. **State Groups:** 10. **Local Groups:** 2. **Languages:** English. **National.** Black women who are members of the bar of any U.S. state or territory; associate members include law school graduates, paralegals, and law students. Seeks to: advance jurisprudence and the administration of justice by increasing the opportunities of black and non-black women at all levels; aid in protecting the civil and human rights of all citizens and residents of the U.S; expand opportunities for women lawyers through education; promote fellowship among women lawyers. Provides pre-law and student counseling; serves as job placement resource for firms, companies, and others interested in the field. Sponsors brief-writing contest. Operates telephone referral service. Maintains hall of fame; offers charitable program. **Awards:** Periodic (scholarship). **Computer Services:** Data base; mailing lists.

Publications: *Convention Bulletin*, annual. ● *NABWA News*, quarterly. Newsletter.

Conventions/Meetings: annual conference (exhibits). ● periodic regional meeting.

★2938★ NATIONAL ASSOCIATION OF BLACK WOMEN
    ENTREPRENEURS (NABWE)
PO Box 1375
Detroit, MI 48231   PH: (313)341-7400
Marilyn French-Hubbard, Founder   FX: (313)342-3433

Founded: 1979. **Members:** 3,000. **Staff:** 5. **Budget:** US$230,000. **Regional Groups:** 4. **State Groups:** 28. **Languages:** English. **National.** Black women who own and operate their own businesses; black women interested in starting businesses; organizations and companies desiring mailing lists. Acts as a national support system for black businesswomen in the U.S. and focuses on the unique problems they face. Objective is to enhance business, professional, and technical development of both present and future black businesswomen. Maintains speakers' bureau and national networking program. Offers symposia, workshops, and forums aimed at increasing the business awareness of black women. Shares resources, lobbies, and provides placement service. **Awards:** Annual Black Woman Entrepreneur of the Year.

Publications: *Making Success Happen Newsletter*, bimonthly. ● *Membership Directory*, annual.

Conventions/Meetings: annual conference (exhibits).

★2939★ NATIONAL ASSOCIATION OF BUSINESS AND INDUSTRIAL
    SALESWOMEN (NABIS)
90 Corona, Ste. 1407
Denver, CO 80218
A. K. Lovejoy, Acting Exec.Dir.   PH: (303)777-7257

Founded: 1980. **Staff:** 2. **Languages:** English. **National.** Women who sell business and industrial products or services. Facilitates the exchange of ideas and experiences in an effort to further professional and personal development for women in business and industrial sales. Encourages women to enter the sales field; seeks recognition of saleswomen's needs through trade publications and other media. Provides resource services to corporations and individuals. Maintains career counseling and search services.

Publications: *Interchange*, periodic. Newsletter.

★2940★ NATIONAL ASSOCIATION OF CHILDBEARING CENTERS
    (NACC)
3123 Gottschall Rd.
Perkiomenville, PA 18074   PH: (215)234-8068
Eunice K. M. Ernst, Admin.   FX: (215)234-0994

Founded: 1983. **Members:** 400. **Staff:** 4. **Budget:** US$200,000. **Regional Groups:** 6. **State Groups:** 1. **Languages:** English. **National.** Birth centers; interested individuals and businesses that support the group's work. Acts as national information service on freestanding birth centers for state health departments, insurance companies, government agencies, consultants, hospitals, physicians, certified nurse-midwives, nurses, and families; promotes quality care in freestanding birth centers through state licensure and national standard-setting mechanisms, educational workshops, and support of professional education for midwives. Provides standards for certification of birth centers. Conducts regional workshops on financing, managing, operating, and marketing freestanding birth centers. Compiles statistics; offers telephone referral services. **Libraries:** Type: reference. **Computer Services:** Data base.

Publications: *Membership Directory*, periodic. ● *NACC News*, annual. Magazine.

Conventions/Meetings: annual meeting (exhibits).

★2941★ NATIONAL ASSOCIATION OF COLLEGIATE WOMEN
    ATHLETIC ADMINISTRATORS (NACWAA)
University of Minnesota
Athletic Department
Minneapolis, MN 55455
Chriz Voelz, Pres.   PH: (612)624-8000

Founded: 1979. **Members:** 350. **Languages:** English. **National.** Women working in athletic administration at U.S. colleges and universities. Seeks to increase members' professional skills. Serves as a forum for the exchange of information among members and as an advocate for opportunities for women in sport.

Publications: *CCWA Newsletter*, quarterly.

Conventions/Meetings: annual meeting, with workshops and seminars. - always fall.

★2942★ NATIONAL ASSOCIATION OF COLORED WOMEN'S CLUBS
    (NACWC)
5808 16th St. NW
Washington, DC 20011
Carole A. Early, Hdqtrs.Sec.   PH: (202)726-2044

Founded: 1896. **Members:** 45,000. **Staff:** 4. **State Groups:** 38. **Local Groups:** 1,000. **Languages:** English. **National.** Federation of black women's clubs. Carries on program of civic service, education, social service, and philanthropy. Sponsors National Association of Girls Clubs. **Committees:** Home and Child; Legislation; Mother; Women in Industry; Young Adults.

Publications: *National Notes*, quarterly. Newsletter.

Conventions/Meetings: biennial meeting (exhibits) - next 1994.

★2943★ NATIONAL ASSOCIATION OF COMMISSIONS FOR WOMEN
    (NACW)
c/o D.C. Commission for Women
Rm. N-354, Reeves Center
2000 14th St. NW
Washington, DC 20009   PH: (202)628-5030
Claire Bigelow, Dir.   FX: (202)939-8763

Founded: 1970. **Members:** 128. **Staff:** 1. **Budget:** US$50,000. **Regional Groups:** 33. **State Groups:** 40. **Local Groups:** 200. **Languages:** English. **National.** State, city, and county commissions that focus on the status of women. Aim is to strengthen and coordinate the vital work of the state and local commissions, in seeking to further the legal, social, political, economic, and educational equality of American women, that they may make their fullest contribution to society. Works to: eliminate discrimination based on sex, race, age, religion, national origin, or marital status in all phases of American society; foster the dissemination of information and provide counsel on opportunities for the effective participation of women in the private and public sector; create greater public awareness of the role and function of commissions on the status of women and provide a national focus on issues affecting women; strenghten commissions, coordinate their efforts nationwide, and provide a unified voice; act as a central clearinghouse and networking resource for information and activities of commissions across the country; foster a closer relationship and fuller exchange of ideas among members. Offers guidance in the designing of new strategies and programs on critical contemporary issues of concern to women; assists efforts to broaden the base of involvement of women of color and those of different backgrounds; works with other national women's groups on issues requiring collective action. Presents testimony at public hearings; monitors legislation of special interest to women. Maintains speakers' bureau; compiles statistics. Conducts research, workshops, and leadership training programs. **Libraries:** Type: reference. **Committees:** Friends of NACW.

Publications: *Breakthrough*, quarterly. Newsletter. Reports on news and activities of regional, state, and local commissions; includes legislative updates. **Circulation:** 3,000. **Advertising:** accepted. ● *Directory of National, Regionalal, State and Local Commissions*, periodic.

Conventions/Meetings: annual conference (exhibits).

★2944★ NATIONAL ASSOCIATION OF CUBAN-AMERICAN WOMEN OF THE U.S.A. (NACAW-USA)
(Asociacion Nacional de Mujeres Cubanoamericanas, de los Estados Unidos de America)
2119 S. Webster
Ft. Wayne, IN 46802   PH: (219)745-5421
Dr. G. F. del Cueto Beecher, Pres.   FX: (219)744-1363

Founded: 1972. **Members:** 5,700. **State Groups:** 35. **Languages:** English. **National.** To address current issues, concerns, and problems affecting Hispanic and minority women, and to achieve goals such as equal education and training, fair immigration policy, and meaningful work with adequate compensation. Coordinates activities with national Hispanic and other minority organizations; responds to female concerns from minority and majority populations; encourages participation in related task forces, legislative activities, and professional endeavors; acts as clearinghouse and referral center. Supports bilingual and bicultural education at the local, state, and national levels. Disseminates information on postsecondary educational opportunities and sources of financial aid in particular cities. Produces biweekly bilingual radio program. Conducts placement service; compiles statistics. **Libraries:** Type: reference. Holdings: 2,000. Subjects: Cuban history and human rights violations in Cuba.

Publications: *Newsletter*, periodic.

Conventions/Meetings: periodic meeting.

★2945★ NATIONAL ASSOCIATION FOR GIRLS AND WOMEN IN SPORT (NAGWS)
1900 Association Dr.
Reston, VA 22091
Peggy Kellers, Exec.Dir.   PH: (703)476-3450

Founded: 1899. **Members:** 9,000. **Membership Dues:** US$85 annual. **Staff:** 3. **Regional Groups:** 6. **State Groups:** 50. **Languages:** English. **National.** An association of the American Alliance for Health, Physical Education, Recreation and Dance. Teachers, coaches, athletic trainers, officials, athletic administrators, and students. Supports and fosters the development of quality sports programs that will enrich the lives of all participants. Sponsors coaches clinics; holds seminars and training sessions for leadership development. Maintains speakers' bureau and National Coaches Council which assists in organization and development of teams, offers grants , and emphasizes quality coaching. Conducts search programs. **Committees:** Coaching Certification; Latin American/Caribbean Project; Advocacy and Liaison; Coaching Enhancement; Minority Representation; Professional Development and Leadership; Student Representation.

Publications: *Newsletter*, 3/year. ● *Coaching the Female Athlete/Sport Leadership Conference Handbook*.

Conventions/Meetings: annual meeting (exhibits).

★2946★ NATIONAL ASSOCIATION OF INSURANCE WOMEN - INTERNATIONAL (NAIW)
1847 E. 15th
PO Box 4410   PH: (918)744-5195
Tulsa, OK 74159   TF: (800)766-6249
Jane R. Seago, Exec.V.Pres.   FX: (918)743-1968

Founded: 1940. **Members:** 20,000. **Staff:** 8. **Regional Groups:** 9. **Local Groups:** 422. **Languages:** English. **National.** Women in the insurance business. Sponsors insurance educational programs. Awards Certified Professional Insurance Woman (Man) certificate to qualified members who have passed one of several sets of national examinations.

Programs: Communicate with Confidence Speak-Off; Drinking and Driving Awareness; Grass Roots Political Participation; Officer Training.

Publications: *Today's Insurance Woman*, bimonthly. Magazine. Provides members with information on decision-making, risk management,personal planning, and education. **Circulation:** 21,500. **Advertising:** accepted.

Conventions/Meetings: annual meeting (exhibits) - 1994 June 22 - 25, New Orleans, LA, United States; 1995 June, Baltimore, MD, United States.

★2947★ NATIONAL ASSOCIATION OF MBA WOMEN
7701 Georgia Ave. NW
Washington, DC 20012
Sharon Griffith, President   PH: (202)723-1267

National. Works to improve career opportunities for women with M.B.A. degress as well as providing networking and scholarship opportunities.

★2948★ NATIONAL ASSOCIATION OF MEDIA WOMEN (NAMW)
1185 Niskey Lake Rd. SW
Atlanta, GA 30331
Mrs. Xernona Brady, Pres.   PH: (404)344-5862

Founded: 1965. **Members:** 300. **Local Groups:** 14. **Languages:** English. **National.** Women professionally engaged in mass communications. Purposes are: to enrich the lives of members through an exchange of ideas and experiences; to sponsor studies, research, and seminars to find solutions to mutual problems; to create opportunities for women in communications. **Awards:** Annual (scholarship). Recipient: woman student in mass communications. ● Annual Media Woman of the Year.

Publications: *Media Woman*, annual. Journal.

Conventions/Meetings: annual conference.

★2949★ NATIONAL ASSOCIATION OF MILITARY SPOUSES (NAMS)
13956 Cedar Rd., Ste 132
Box 188009   PH: (216)991-7228
University Heights, OH 44118   TF: (800)472-5620
Toni K. Chandler, Exec.Dir.   FX: (216)371-9767

Founded: 1991. **Membership Dues:** US$12 annual. **Languages:** English. **National.** Support and service organization for spouses of military personnel. Offers information on rights and benefits, investment programs, legal and employment referrals, and merchandise discounts. Is developing Outreach program.

Publications: *Spouse Talk*, quarterly. Newsletter.

Conventions/Meetings: biweekly support group.

★2950★ NATIONAL ASSOCIATION OF MILITARY WIDOWS (NAMW)
4023 25th Rd. N
Arlington, VA 22207
Jean Arthurs, Pres.   PH: (703)527-4565

Founded: 1978. **Members:** 7,000. **Languages:** English. **National.** Widows of careermen and reservists in all branches of the uniformed services whose husbands died either during active service or following disability or nondisability retirement. Seeks equitable legislation and survivor benefit programs, and monitors all legislation and programs affecting military widows in Congress, the Department of Defense, and Veterans Administration.

Publications: *National Association of Military Widows—Newsletter*, quarterly. Reports on issues affecting military widows. **Circulation:** 7,000. **Advertising:** not accepted.

★2951★ NATIONAL ASSOCIATION OF MINORITY POLITICAL WOMEN
(NAMPW)
6120 Oregon Ave. NW
Washington, DC 20015
Mary E. Ivey, Pres.   PH: (202)686-1216

Founded: 1983. **Members:** 500. **Languages:** English. **National**. Professional women of all ages interested in the U.S. political process. Conducts research and educational programs. **Awards:** Annual Diamond Award. ● Periodic (scholarship).

Conventions/Meetings: annual meeting.

★2952★ NATIONAL ASSOCIATION OF MINORITY WOMEN IN
BUSINESS (NAMWIB)
906 Grand Ave., Ste. 200
Kansas City, MO 64106
Inez Kaiser, Pres.   PH: (816)421-3335
                                       FX: (816)421-3336

Founded: 1972. **Members:** 5,000. **Languages:** English. **National**. Minority women in business ownership and management positions; college students. Serves as a network for the exchange of ideas and information on business opportunities for minority women in the public and private sectors. Conducts research. Maintains speakers' bureau, hall of fame, and placement service; compiles statistics; bestows awards to women who have made significant contributions to the field.

Publications: *Today*, bimonthly. Newsletter. **Advertising:** accepted.

Conventions/Meetings: annual conference (exhibits). ● semiannual conference. ● periodic workshop. ● periodic seminar. ● periodic luncheon.

★2953★ NATIONAL ASSOCIATION OF NEGRO BUSINESS AND
PROFESSIONAL WOMEN'S CLUBS (NANBPWC)
1806 New Hampshire Ave. NW
Washington, DC 20009
Ellen A. Graves, Exec. Officer   PH: (202)483-4206
                                       FX: (202)462-7253

Founded: 1935. **Members:** 10,000. **Budget:** US$500,000. **Regional Groups:** 6. **Local Groups:** 350. **Languages:** English. **National**. Business and professional women committed to rendering service through club programs and activities. Seeks to direct the interest of business and professional women toward united action for improved social and civic conditions, and to provide enriching and ennobling experiences that will encourage freedom, dignity, self-respect, and self-reliance. Offers information and help regarding education, employment, health, housing, legislation, and problems of the aged and the disabled. Sponsors educational assistance program, which includes local and national scholarships. Conducts consumer education and prison reform programs. Maintains youth department clubs. Provides placement services; operates speakers' bureau; compiles statistics. **Awards:** Periodic for National and Community Service. **Committees:** Economic Development; Educational Assistance; International Affairs; Political and Legislative Action; Social Welfare and Health. **Councils:** Business Women's.

Publications: *Convention Proceedings*, annual. Booklet. ● *Directory*, annual. ● *President's Newsletter*, monthly. ● *Program Idea Exchange*, bimonthly. Newsletter. ● *Responsibility*, quarterly. Magazine.

Conventions/Meetings: annual meeting (exhibits).

★2954★ NATIONAL ASSOCIATION FOR PROFESSIONAL
SALESWOMEN (NAPS)
1730 N. Lynn St., Ste. 502
Arlington, VA 22209
Sally Drew, Pres.   PH: (703)812-8642
                                       FX: (703)276-8196

Founded: 1980. **Members:** 2,000. **Staff:** 1. **Budget:** US$100,000. **Local Groups:** 30. **Languages:** English. **National**. Women actively involved or interested in professional sales and marketing careers. Conducts seminars, surveys, and research projects. Participates in television and radio programs. Operates speakers' bureau. Compiles statistics; sponsors competitions.

Libraries: Type: reference. Holdings: 450. Subjects: business and sales. **Awards:** .

Publications: *Successful Saleswoman*, monthly. Newsletter. Includes membership activities news and book reviews. **ISSN:** 0886-1498. **Circulation:** 4,000. ● *On the Right Track: A Guide to a Successful Sales Career*. Book.

Conventions/Meetings: annual conference, with training seminars and exhibits. (exhibits) - 1993 Oct. 6 - 10, San Diego, CA, United States.

★2955★ NATIONAL ASSOCIATION OF RAILWAY BUSINESS WOMEN
(NARBW)
c/o Carmen Taliaferro
2720 Mayfield Rd.
Cleveland Heights, OH 44106   PH: (216)321-0971
Carmen Taliaferro, Pres.   TF: (800)348-6272

Founded: 1921. **Members:** 2,500. **Staff:** 20. **Regional Groups:** 6. **State Groups:** 46. **Languages:** English. **National**. Women who work for railroads. Purposes are to: stimulate interest in the railroad industry; foster cooperation and understanding among members and people in related fields; promote good public relations for the railroad industry; further the educational, social, and professional interests of members. Conducts charitable, benevolent, and social welfare projects. Maintains a residence for retired members at Green Valley, AZ. **Awards:** Periodic Railroad Woman. ● Periodic (scholarship).

Publications: *Capsule*, monthly. Newsletter.

Conventions/Meetings: annual meeting - always May. ● annual regional meeting. ● periodic banquet.

★2956★ NATIONAL ASSOCIATION OF UNIVERSITY WOMEN (NAUW)
1553 Pine Forest Dr.
Tallahassee, FL 32301
Ruth R. Corbin, Pres.   PH: (904)878-4660

Founded: 1923. **Members:** 4,000. **Regional Groups:** 5. **Local Groups:** 92. **Languages:** English. **National**. Women college or university graduates. Works to promote constructive work in education, civic activities, and human relations; studies educational conditions with emphasis on problems affecting women; encourages high educational standards and stimulates intellectual attainment among women generally. Theme is "Women of Action: Reaching, Risking, Responding." Offers tutoring and sponsors After High School-What? youth development program. Maintains placement service. **Awards:** Periodic (scholarship). ● Annual Fellowship. **Committees:** Literacy Program Development; National and International Affairs; Necrology; Political Awareness; Youth Programs.

Publications: *Bulletin*, biennial. ● *Directory of Branch Presidents and Members*, annual. ● *Journal of the National Association of University Women*, biennial.

Conventions/Meetings: biennial - usually Summer.

★2957★ NATIONAL ASSOCIATION OF WOMEN BUSINESS OWNERS
(NAWBO)
600 S. Federal St., Ste. 400
Chicago, IL 60605
Virginia Littlejohn, Exec.Dir.   PH: (312)922-6222

Founded: 1974. **Members:** 3,000. **Staff:** 3. **Budget:** US$450,000. **Local Groups:** 44. **Languages:** English. **National**. Women who own and operate their own businesses. Purposes are to: identify and bring together women business owners in mutual support; to communicate and share experience and talents with others; to use collective influence to broaden opportunities for women in business. Services offered include: workshops and seminars; information clearinghouse, referral service, and reader service; representation before governmental bodies; liaison with groups of similar orientation.
Computer Services: Data base, women-owned businesses.
Committees: Corporate Relations; Leadership Development; Public Affairs; Public Relations.

Publications: *Annual Membership Roster*. Directory. ● *Statement*, bimonthly. Newsletter. Includes calendar of events. **Also Cited As:** *NAWBO Statement*.

Conventions/Meetings: annual meeting (exhibits) - always June.

★2958★ NATIONAL ASSOCIATION FOR WOMEN IN CAREERS (NAFWIC)
PO Box 81525
Chicago, IL 60681-0525   PH: (312)938-7662
Pat Surbella, CEO & Pres.   FX: (312)819-1220

Founded: 1981. **Members:** 1,500. **Staff:** 6. **State Groups:** 8. **Languages:** English. **National.** Service organization for women representing various economic sectors including corporations, personally-owned businesses, nonprofit and sales organizations, retail outlets, financial institutions including government and health agencies, educational institutions, and associations. Provides support, networking, and skill-development services for all women to enhance their potential for greater success and enable them to meet future challenges for personal and career growth. Attempts to help women integrate who they are with what they do and to balance the demands of career growth and private life. Conducts seminars and charitable programs; provides job referral, career planning, and professional speakers. **Awards:** Periodic (scholarship). **Committees:** Communications; Educational and Career Development; Employment Opportunities; Networking; Public Relations.

Publications: *Directory*, periodic.

Conventions/Meetings: annual meeting.

★2959★ NATIONAL ASSOCIATION OF WOMEN IN CHAMBERS OF COMMERCE (NAWCC)
PO Box 4552
Grand Junction, CO 81502-4552
Marie Davis Shope, Corp.Sec.-Treas.   PH: (303)242-0075

Founded: 1985. **Members:** 100. **Languages:** English. **National.** Professional women affiliated with a chamber of commerce. Fosters members' growth and prosperity by providing education and management direction, information for business improvement, and opportunities for networking. Encourages women to work to realize their potential. Promotes and supports local chambers of commerce. **Computer Services:** Data base, membership information.

Publications: *NAWCC Membership Directory*, annual. ● *NAWCC Update*, quarterly. Newsletter.

Conventions/Meetings: annual conference, with seminars..

★2960★ NATIONAL ASSOCIATION OF WOMEN IN CONSTRUCTION (NAWIC)
327 S. Adams St.   PH: (817)877-5551
Ft. Worth, TX 76104   TF: (800)552-3506
Paula Clements-Zang, Exec.Dir.   FX: (817)877-0324

Founded: 1954. **Members:** 8,800. **Budget:** US$1,000,000. **Regional Groups:** 14. **Local Groups:** 238. **Languages:** English. **National.** Professional women in the construction industry. Educates members in new construction techniques. Local chapters maintain employment services and sponsor Block-Kid Building Contests for elementary students, career days, workshops, study courses, and educational programs. **Awards:** Periodic (scholarship). Recipient: students of engineering construction or architecture. **Committees:** Education Foundation; Industry Support/Association Liaison; Legislative Awareness; NAWIC Business Roundtable; NAWIC Education; NAWIC/Workforce 2000; Occupation Research and Referral; Organization and Extension; Professional Educati on; Public Relations/Marketing; Tradeswomen; Women's Business Enterprise/Women Business Owners.

Publications: *NAWIC Image*, monthly. Magazine. **Circulation:** 10,000. **Advertising:** not accepted.

Conventions/Meetings: annual conference - 1993 Sept. 1 - 4, Dallas, TX,

United States; 1994, Chicago, IL, United States; 1995, Denver, CO, United States; 1996, Washington, DC, United States.

★2961★ NATIONAL ASSOCIATION FOR WOMEN IN EDUCATION (NAWE)
1325 18th St. NW, Ste. 210
Washington, DC 20036-6511   PH: (202)659-9330
Dr. Patricia A. Rueckel, Exec.Dir.   FX: (202)457-0946

Founded: 1916. **Members:** 1,900. **Staff:** 4. **Budget:** US$350,000. **State Groups:** 19. **Languages:** English. **National.** Women holding positions in academic administration, student affairs, and counseling including student and academic deans, college presidents, professors of education, and directors of residence halls. Promotes study of trends in women's education. **Awards:** Periodic Ruth Strang Research. **Committees:** Intercultural Education; Minority Concerns; Professional Employment Practices. **Divisions:** Activities and Services; Administration; Continuing Education; Counseling; Special Programs; Special Services.

Publications: *About Women on Campus*, quarterly. Newsletter. ● *Directory*, annual. ● *Journal*, quarterly. ● *Newsletter*, quarterly.

Conventions/Meetings: annual conference - 1994, Washington, DC, United States; 1995, Orlando, FL, United States; 1996, San Francisco, CA, United States.

★2962★ NATIONAL ASSOCIATION OF WOMEN HIGHWAY SAFETY LEADERS (NAWHSL)
721 Dragoon Dr.
Mt. Pleasant, SC 29464-3020
Mrs. Larry T. Riggs, Pres.   PH: (803)884-7724

Founded: 1967. **Members:** 3,000,000. **Budget:** US$75,000. **Regional Groups:** 10. **State Groups:** 50. **Languages:** English. **National.** Women and representatives of women's organizations with interests in traffic safety. Objectives are to reduce traffic crashes, injuries, and deaths by: supporting and implementing the National Highway Safety Standards in communities and states, and nationwide; encouraging each political subdivision to assume its responsibility for highway safety; aiming at more uniformity in traffic safety programs and regulations within the 50 states, the District of Columbia, and Puerto Rico. Conducts educational programs including seminars and workshops; maintains speakers' bureau. **Committees:** Alcohol/Drugs; Child Passenger Safety Seat Usage; Highway Environment; Mature Driver; Safety Belt; School Bus Safety.

Publications: *NAWHSL Directory*, annual. ● *President's Newsletter*, monthly. ● *Regionalal Director's Newsletter*, monthly. ● *State Representatives Newsletter*, periodic. ● *Buckle Up*. Booklet. ● *Look, Listen and Live*. Booklet. ● *Road Environment*. Booklet.

Conventions/Meetings: annual conference.

★2963★ NATIONAL ASSOCIATION OF WOMEN JUDGES (NAWJ)
c/o Natl. Center for State Courts
300 Newport Ave.
Williamsburg, VA 23187-8798   PH: (804)253-2000
Karen S. Heroy, Staff Dir.   FX: (804)220-0449

Founded: 1979. **Members:** 1,100. **Budget:** US$137,600. **Regional Groups:** 14. **Languages:** English. **National.** Individuals holding judicial or quasi-judicial positions. Objectives are to: promote the administration of justice; discuss and formulate solutions to legal, educational, social, and ethical problems encountered by women judges; increase the number of women judges so that the judiciary more appropriately reflects the role of women in a democratic society; address other issues particularly affecting women judges. Conducts research and educational programs and referral services; compiles statistics. **Awards:** Annual Honoree of the Year.

Publications: *NAWJ Annual Directory*, periodic. ● *NAWJ Newsletter*, 3/year.

Conventions/Meetings: annual conference - 1993 Oct. 7 - 11, Philadelphia, PA, United States; 1994 Sept. 29 - Oct. 2, Scottsdale, AZ, United States.

★2964★ NATIONAL ASSOCIATION OF WOMEN LAWYERS (NAWL)
750 N. Lake Shore Dr.
Chicago, IL 60611
Patricia O'Mahoney, Exec.Dir.
PH: (312)988-6186
FX: (312)988-6281

Founded: 1911. **Members:** 1,200. **Staff:** 1. **Languages:** English. **National.** Women lawyers who have been admitted to practice in any state or territory of the U.S. Maintains 17 committees. **Awards:** Annual Toch Membership Trophy.

Publications: *Membership Directory*, biennial. ● *Presidents Newsletter*, quarterly. ● *Women Lawyers Journal*, quarterly.

Conventions/Meetings: annual conference - always August. Kansas City, KS, United States; Miami, FL, United States.

★2965★ NATIONAL BAR ASSOCIATION - ASSOCIATION OF BLACK WOMEN ATTORNEYS
134 W. 32nd St., Ste. 602
New York, NY 10001
Leslie R. Jones, President
PH: (212)244-4270

National. Encourages African American women in the development of their professional careers. Assists in the development of legal assistance programs in the African American community.

★2966★ NATIONAL BAR ASSOCIATION - WOMEN LAWYERS DIVISION
1211 Connecticut Ave. NW, Ste. 702
Washington, DC 20036
Brenda Girton, Pres.
PH: (202)291-1979
FX: (202)347-7127

Founded: 1972. **Members:** 300. **Languages:** English. **National.** Women lawyers, law students, and other individuals. Purposes are to: provide a forum to discuss and address issues unique to women in the legal profession; promote professional growth and honor achievements of minority attorneys; promote admission to practice at all levels of the judicial system; foster interactions between minority and other bar associations; encourage participation in community service. **Awards:** Periodic (scholarship).

Publications: *Newsletter*, periodic.

Conventions/Meetings: annual breakfast. ● periodic seminar. ● annual meeting.

★2967★ NATIONAL BATTERED WOMEN'S LAW PROJECT
799 Broadway, Rm. 402
New York, NY 10003
Joan Zorza, Sr. Attorney
PH: (212)674-8200
FX: (212)535-5104

Founded: 1990. **Staff:** 2. **Budget:** US$131,000. **Languages:** English. **National.** Offers consulting services on legal action for victims of domestic violence and on securing child custody rights. Analyzes and works to improve federal and state legislature regarding family law. Serves as an information clearinghouse. Disseminates public education materials. Provides training programs for lawyers, judges, and defenders of battered women.

Publications: *The Women's Advocate* (in English), bimonthly. Magazine.

★2968★ NATIONAL BLACK SISTERS' CONFERENCE (NBSC)
1001 Lawrence St. NE, Ste. 102
Washington, DC 20017
Sr. Gwynette Proctor, Exec.Dir.
PH: (202)529-9250

Founded: 1968. **Members:** 150. **Budget:** US$40,000. **Languages:** English. **National.** Black religious women. Seeks to develop the personal resources of black women; challenges society, especially the church, to address issues of racism in the U.S. Activities include: retreats; consulting, leadership, and

cultural understanding; formation workshops for personnel. Maintains educational programs for facilitating change and community involvement in inner-city parochial schools and parishes. Operates Sojourner House to provide spiritual affirmation for black religious and laywomen. Maintains speakers' bureau. **Committees:** Education.

Publications: *Signs of Soul*, 4/year. Newsletter. Reports on black members of the Catholic church. Includes employment opportunities and obituaries of members. **Advertising:** not accepted. ● *Joint Black Clergy and Black Sisters*. Book.

Conventions/Meetings: annual conference (exhibits).

★2969★ NATIONAL BLACK WOMEN'S CONSCIOUSNESS RAISING ASSOCIATION (BWCR)
1906 N. Charles St.
Baltimore, MD 21218
Dr. Elaine Simon, Exec.Dir.
PH: (410)727-8900

Founded: 1975. **Members:** 750. **Languages:** English. **National.** Black women interested in women's rights and women's issues. Acts as a support group for women. Provides educational and informational workshops and seminars on subjects of concern to black women and women in general. **Awards:** Periodic Academic Achievement.

Publications: *BWCR*, semiannual. Newsletter.

Conventions/Meetings: annual (exhibits) - Baltimore, MD, United States.

★2970★ NATIONAL BLACK WOMEN'S HEALTH PROJECT (NBWHP)
1237 Ralph David Albernathy Blvd. SW
Atlanta, GA 30310
Cynthia Newbille-Marsh, Dir.
PH: (404)758-9590
TF: (800)ASK-BWHP
FX: (404)752-6756

Founded: 1981. **Members:** 2,000. **Staff:** 19. **Budget:** US$1,600,000. **Regional Groups:** 5. **State Groups:** 26. **Local Groups:** 150. **Languages:** English. **National.** Encourages mutual and selfhelp advocacy among women to bring about a reduction in health care problems prevalent among black women. Urges women to communicate with health care providers, seek out available health care resources, become aware of selfhelp approaches, and communicate with other black women to minimize feelings of powerlessness and isolation, and thus realize they have some control over their physical and mental health. Points out the higher incidence of high blood pressure, obesity, breast and cervical cancers, diabetes, kidney disease, arteriosclerosis, and teenage pregnancy among black women than among other racial or socioeconomic groups. Also notes that black infant mortality is twice that of whit es and that black women are often victims of family violence. Offers seminars outlining demographic information, chronic conditions, the need for health information and access to services, and possible methods of improving the health status of black women. Sponsors Center for Black Women's Wellness. Maintains speakers' bureau. Conducts gender and race specific health research programs. Plans to: establish black women's wellness centers; develop Empowerment Though Wellness curriculum. **Libraries:** Type: reference. **Computer Services:** Data base.

Publications: *Annual Report*. ● *Vital Signs*, quarterly. Newsletter. **Circulation:** 5,000. **Advertising:** not accepted. ● *On Becoming a Woman: Mothers and Daughters Talking Together*. Videos.

Conventions/Meetings: semiannual - Atlanta, GA, United States.

★2971★ NATIONAL BLACK WOMEN'S POLITICAL LEADERSHIP CAUCUS
3005 Bladensburg Rd. NE, No. 217
Washington, DC 20018
Juanita Kennedy Morgan, Dir.
PH: (202)529-2806

Founded: 1971. **Regional Groups:** 3. **State Groups:** 33. **Languages:** English. **National.** Women interested in understanding their political role and the need for females to work toward equality; auxiliary membership includes men, senior citizens, and youths. Works to educate and incorporate all black women and youth in the political and economic process through participation. Encourages women to familiarize themselves with the role of city, state, and federal governments. Presents awards for humanitarianism; trains speakers and conducts research on the black family and on topics concerning politics and economics; compiles statistics. Holds legislative, federal, state and local workshops. Provides placement service; offers children's services; operates charitable program. **Committees:** Cultural Affairs; Educational; Energy Conservation; Legislative; Older Americans; Registration and Voting; Youth Directive Workshop. **Departments:** Local, State and Federal; Men's Auxiliary; Older Americans and Youth Auxiliary.

Publications: *Newsletter*, semiannual.

Conventions/Meetings: annual conference.

★2972★ NATIONAL CATHOLIC WOMEN'S UNION (NCWU)
3835 Westminster Pl.
St. Louis, MO 63108-3492
Rev. John H. Miller CSC, Dir.   PH: (314)371-1653

Founded: 1916. **Members:** 10,900. **State Groups:** 7. **Local Groups:** 170. **Languages:** English. **National.** Individual Catholic women and affiliated societies interested in Catholic social action. Sponsors religious activities, works of charity, mission activities, and maternity guilds. Promotes vocations to the priesthood and the religious life. Headquarters, publications office, and various programs are maintained by Central Bureau, Catholic Central Union of America. **Libraries:** Type: reference. **Sections:** Church Vestments and Altar Linens; Medical Mission Units; Mission and Sewing Circles; Study Clubs.

Conventions/Meetings: annual conference.

★2973★ NATIONAL CENTER FOR EDUCATION IN MATERNAL AND
    CHILD HEALTH (NCEMCH)
2000 15th St. N, Ste. 701
Arlington, VA 22201-2617   PH: (703)524-7802
Dr. Rochelle Mayer, Dir.   FX: (703)524-9335

Founded: 1981. **Staff:** 28. **Languages:** English. **National.** Provides information services to professionals and the public on maternal and child health. Collects and disseminates information on available materials, programs, and research. Offers summer internships for graduate students in public health schools. **Libraries:** Type: reference. Holdings: 8,000; books, periodicals, clippings, audio recordings, video recordings. **Formerly:** (1982) National Clearinghouse for Human Genetic Diseases.

Publications: *Abstracts of Active Projects*, annual. Directory. Lists current grants of the Maternal and Child Health Bureau, U.S. Deptartment of Health and Human Services. **Advertising:** not accepted. ● *MCH Bureau Active Projects: An Annotated Listing*, annual. Directory. ● *MCH Program Interchange*, monthly. Directory. Lists new publications in maternal and child health. **Advertising:** not accepted. ● *Reaching Out: A Directory of National Organizations Related to Maternal and Child Health*, periodic. ● *Starting Early: A Guide to Federal Resources in Maternal and Child Health*, periodic. Directory.

★2974★ NATIONAL CENTER FOR LESBIAN RIGHTS (NCLR)
1663 Mission St., 5th Fl.
San Francisco, CA 94103   PH: (415)621-0674
Liz Hendrickson, Exec.Dir.   FX: (415)621-6744

Founded: 1977. **Membership Dues:** Student and low income, US$20 annual; Individual, US$35 annual; Institution, US$50 annual; Family, US$60 annual; Sustaining, US$100 annual. **Staff:** 5. **Budget:** US$305,000. **Languages:** English. **National.** A public interest law firm specializing in sexual orientation discrimination cases, particularly those involving lesbians. Activities include: legal counseling and representation, community education, and technical assistance. Provides legal services to lesbians and gay men on issues of custody and foster parenting, employment, housing, the military, and insurance.

Publications: *NCLR Newsletter* (in English and Spanish), 3/year. **Circulation:** 5,000. **Advertising:** not accepted. ● *Lesbian Mother Litigation Manual*. Book. ● *Recognizing Lesbianism and Gay Families: Strategies for Extending Employment Benefits*. Book. ● *Lesbians Choosing Motherhood: Legal Issues in Donor Insemination*. Book.

★2975★ NATIONAL CENTER ON WOMEN AND FAMILY LAW
    (NCOWFL)
799 Broadway, Rm. 402
New York, NY 10003   PH: (212)674-8200
Laurie Woods, Exec.Dir.   FX: (212)533-5104

Founded: 1979. **Staff:** 5. **Languages:** English. **National.** Litigates and provides technical assistance to legal services staff and other advocates on women's issues in family law. Provides consultations and participates in impact litigation as co-counsel or amicus. Maintains files on custody, support, divorce, division of property, battery, and rape. Compiles statistics. **Libraries:** Type: reference.   Subjects: women's issues in family law.

Publications: *Newsletter*, bimonthly.

★2976★ NATIONAL CHAMBER OF COMMERCE FOR WOMEN
    (NCCW)
10 Waterside Plaza, Ste. 6H
New York, NY 10010
Maggie Rinaldi, Exec.Dir.   PH: (212)685-3454

Founded: 1977. **Members:** 4,700. **Budget:** US$130,000. **Languages:** English. **National.** Coalition of corporations, state agencies, and concerned individuals. Works with local, regional, and state redevelopment agencies to expand business opportunities for women. Conducts research and pay comparison surveys. Compiles statistics. Maintains placement service and speakers' bureau. **Computer Services:** Data base, women's businesses. **Committees:** Chamber's Speakers' Bureau; National Job Bank Census; Women in Home-Based Small Business; Working Women and Consumers in Health Care Industries.

Publications: *Enrich!*, bimonthly. Newsletter. Analyzes opportunities, trends, and techniques for women who manage small businesses in commercial space or their homes. **Circulation:** 4,700. **Advertising:** accepted.

Conventions/Meetings: annual conference - New York, NY, United States.

★2977★ NATIONAL CHASTITY ASSOCIATION (NCA)
PO Box 402
Oak Forest, IL 60452
Mary Meyer, Pres. & Founder

Founded: 1988. **Members:** 600. **Languages:** English. **National.** Persons who believe in abstaining from premarital sex and who agree with or most of the group's "nineteen desires," which include the desire to marry someone who is one's best friend, the desire to marry someone who will be totally faithful and honest, and the desire to be in love with one's spouse throughout life. Facilitates contact among members. Presents the NCA's alternative value system as "a model of logic which will help many people clarify their own goals and methods, whatever they are, regarding relationships." Maintains speakers' bureau. The NCA is not affiliated with any religious organization.

Publications: *National Membership List*, monthly. Directory.

★2978★ NATIONAL CLEARINGHOUSE FOR THE DEFENSE OF
    BATTERED WOMEN (NCDBW)
125 S. 9th St., Ste. 902
Philadelphia, PA 19107   PH: (215)351-0010
Sue Osthoff, Director   FX: (215)351-0779

Founded: 1987. **Languages:** English. **National.** Provides legal services to battered women who have killed or assaulted their abusers while attempting to protect themselves or their children from brutal and life threatening violence. Compiles statistics.

Publications: *Directory*, annual. Bibliography. ● *Double Time*, periodic. Newsletter.

★2979★ NATIONAL CLEARINGHOUSE ON MARITAL AND DATE RAPE (NCOMDR)
2325 Oak St.
Berkeley, CA 94708
Laura X, Contact   PH: (510)524-1582

Founded: 1980. **Members:** 500. **Staff:** 2. **Budget:** US$35,000. **Languages:** English. **National.** Students, attorneys, legislators, faculty members, rape crisis centers, shelters, and other social service groups. Operates as speaking/consulting firm. Is presently launching a nation-wide call for members to help marital, cohabitant, and date rape victims and to stop the rape of potential victims by vigorously educating the public and by providing resources to battered women's shelters, crisis centers, district attorneys and legislators through media appearances and lectures at college campuses and conferences. Ultimate goal is to "make intimate relationships truly egalitarian". Holds training sessions and workshops. Provides phone consultation for the media, prosecutors, expert witnesses, victim/witness advocates, legislators, police, rape crisis workers, and others. Offers sociological and legal research on court cases and legislation. Compiles statistics. Maintains speakers' bureau. **Libraries:** Type: reference.   **Formerly:** (1969) Women's History Research Center.

Publications: *State Law Chart on Marital Rape*. Booklet. ● *Prosecution Statistics on Marital Rape*. Booklet. ● *Date Rape*. Booklet.

★2980★ NATIONAL CLEARINGHOUSE ON WOMEN AND GIRLS WITH DISABILITIES
Educational Equity Concepts
114 E. 32nd St., Ste. 306
New York, NY 10016   PH: (212)725-1803

National. Promotes the special interests of women and girls with disabilities. Provides information on programs and projects focusing on issues related to women and disabilities.

★2981★ NATIONAL COALITION OF 100 BLACK WOMEN (NCBW)
300 Park Ave., 2nd Fl.
New York, NY 10022   PH: (212)974-6140
Jewell Jackson-McCabe, Chm.   FX: (212)838-0542

Founded: 1981. **Members:** 6,000. **Languages:** English. **National.** African-American women actively involved with issues such as economic development, health, employment, education, voting, housing, criminal justice, the status of black families, and the arts. Seeks to provide networking and career opportunities for African-American women in the process of establishing links between the organization and the corporate and political arenas. Encourages leadership development; sponsors role-model and mentor programs to provide guidance to teenage mothers and young women in high school or who have graduated from college and are striving for career advancement. Bestows Candace Awards honoring outstanding African-American women and men. **Committees:** Arts and Culture; Community Action; Economic Development; Education; Employment; Health; Political Action.

Publications: *National Coalition of 100 Black Women—Statement*, semiannual. Newsletter. Reports on the activities and achievements of black women. **Circulation:** 6,000.

Conventions/Meetings: biennial meeting - next 1994.

★2982★ NATIONAL COALITION AGAINST DOMESTIC VIOLENCE (NCADV)
PO Box 34103
Washington, DC 20043-4103
Deborah White, Coordinator   PH: (202)638-6388

Founded: 1978. **Members:** 1,200. **State Groups:** 50. **Local Groups:** 1,250. **Languages:** English. **National.** Grass roots coalition of battered women's service organizations and shelters. Supplies technical assistance and makes referrals on issues of domestic violence. Provides training personnel; offers child advocacy training. Maintains speakers' bureau. Compiles statistics. **Libraries:** Type: lending. Holdings: video recordings. **Task Forces:** Child Advocacy; Formerly Battered Women; Jewish Woman; Lesbian; Rural; Women of Color.

Publications: *National Coalition Against Domestic Violence—Voice*, quarterly. Newsletter. **Advertising:** accepted. ● *Step Toward Independence: Economic Self-Sufficiency*. Book. ● *Naming the Violence: Speaking Out About Lesbian Battering*. Book. ● *Guidelines for Mental Health Practitioners in Domestic Violence Cases*. Book.

Conventions/Meetings: biennial conference (exhibits).

★2983★ NATIONAL COALITION AGAINST SEXUAL ASSAULT (NCASA)
PO Box 21378
Washington, DC 20009
Marybeth Carter, Pres.   PH: (202)483-7165

Founded: 1978. **Members:** 500. **Staff:** 3. **Regional Groups:** 6. **Languages:** English. **National.** Works to build a network through which individuals and organizations working against sexual assault can share expertise, experience, and information. Acts as an advocate for and on behalf of rape victims. Disseminates information on sexual assault. Sponsors Sexual Assault Awareness Month in April. Compiles statistics.   **Committees:** Fundraising; International Issues and Education; Legislation; Victim/Survivor; White Women Against Racism; Women of Color.

Publications: *Newsletter*, quarterly.

Conventions/Meetings: annual conference - always July or August.

★2984★ NATIONAL COALITION FOR SEX EQUITY IN EDUCATION (NCSEE)
1 Redwood Dr.
Clinton, NJ 08809   PH: (908)735-5045
Theodora Martin, Mgr.   FX: (908)735-9674

Founded: 1979. **Members:** 300. **Languages:** English. **National.** Educators, administrators, consultants, authors, and filmmakers, and any individuals working for the advancement of equity in education. Provides leadership and advocacy to restructure education; conducts research and development activities; encourages professional development of members; collaborates with and seeks to influence other organizations. Encourages members' pursuit of gender equality projects. Maintains archives. **Awards:** Annual (grant). **Computer Services:** Mailing lists. **Committees:** Communications; Legislative; Planning and Development. **Task Forces:** Computer/Technology; Curriculum Content; Early Childhood; Health; Male Issues; Multicultural; Religion and Spirituality; School Restructuring; Sexual Harrassment; Teacher Preparation/Staff Development; Vocational Issues.

Publications: *NCSEE News*, quarterly. Newsletter. **Advertising:** not accepted. ● *Directory*, annual.

Conventions/Meetings: annual meeting (exhibits).

★2985★ NATIONAL COALITION FOR WOMEN AND GIRLS IN
EDUCATION (NCWGE)
c/o Displaced Homemakers Network
1625 K St. NW, Ste. 300
Washington, DC 20006
Jill Miller, Exec.Dir. PH: (202)467-6346

Founded: 1975. **Members:** 60. **Languages:** English. **National.** National
organizations opposing sex discrimination in education. Purpose is to
promote national policies that assure educational equity for females.
Monitors actions of agencies responsible for enforcing civil rights laws;
advocates legislation guaranteeing women and girls equal opportunities in
education. **Task Forces:** Enforcement; Higher Education; Legislation; Literacy; Math/Science Education; Vocational Education.

Conventions/Meetings: biweekly meeting - always Monday.

★2986★ NATIONAL COMMISSION ON WORKING WOMEN (NCWW)
1325 G St. NW, Lower Level
Washington, DC 20005
Cynthia Marano, Dir. PH: (202)737-5764

Founded: 1977. **Members:** 30. **Languages:** English. **National.** A commission of Wider Opportunities for Women which oversees advisory and trend
analysis functions. Advocates for the needs and concerns of low-wage
women workers. Conducts public education on issues such as pay equity,
child care, literacy, and the image of women on television. Works to mobilize
corporate, public policy, labor, advocacy, media, and educational and training
representatives to effectively respond to the needs of working women.
Conducts research. **Awards:** Periodic Women at Work.

★2987★ NATIONAL COMMISSION ON WORKING WOMEN OF WIDER
OPPORTUNITIES FOR WOMEN
1325 G St. NW
Washington, DC 20005 PH: (202)737-5764

Languages: English. **National.** Works to advance the status of women
laborers throughout the United States. Disseminates statistical information
on working mothers and their children.

★2988★ NATIONAL COMMITTEE FOR A HUMAN LIFE AMENDMENT
(NCHLA)
1511 K St. NW, Ste. 335
Washington, DC 20005 PH: (202)393-0703
Michael A. Taylor, Exec.Dir. FX: (202)347-1383

Founded: 1974. **Staff:** 10. **Languages:** English. **National.** Seeks to overturn
the U.S. Supreme Court decision on abortion by means of a Human Life
Amendment. Is also involved in other pro-life legislation and education on the
national level. Provides grass roots assistance on the effective organization
of congressional districts.

★2989★ NATIONAL COMMITTEE ON PAY EQUITY (NCPE)
1126 16th St. NW, Rm. 411
Washington, DC 20036 PH: (202)331-7343
Susan Bianchi-Sand, Exec.Dir. FX: (202)331-7406

Founded: 1979. **Members:** 381. **Staff:** 4. **Languages:** English. **National.**
Individuals and women's groups, labor unions, professional associations,
minority and civil rights groups, and governmental and educational groups.
Educates the public about the historical, legal, and economic basis for pay
inequities between men and women and white people and people of color.
Sponsors speakers' bureau; acts as an information clearinghouse on pay
equity activities. Promotes grassroots activism. **Task Forces:** Labor/Collec-
tive Bargaining; Legislation; Litigation; Private Sector; Research and EEO
Agency Enforcement.

Publications: *Newsnotes*, 2-4/year. Newsletter. Includes international news,
federal legislation updates, and litigation reports. **Circulation:** 4,500. **Advertising:** not accepted. ● *Pay Equity: An Issue of Race, Ethnicity, and Sex.*

Book. ● *Bargains for Pay Equity: A Strategy Manual.* Book. ● *Pay Equity
Bibliography and Resource Listing.* Book.

Conventions/Meetings: annual meeting. ● periodic conference.

★2990★ NATIONAL CONFERENCE OF PUERTO RICAN WOMEN
(NACOPRW)
5 Thomas Circle NW
Washington, DC 20005
Ana M. Lopez Fontana, Exec.Dir. PH: (202)387-4716

Founded: 1972. **Members:** 3,000. **Budget:** US$25,000. **State Groups:** 17.
Languages: English. **National.** Promotes full participation of Puerto Rican
and other Hispanic women in the economic, social, and political life of the
U.S. and Puerto Rico. Collaborates with other national organizations
committed to equal rights for all. Encourages the formation of local chapters
in all Puerto Rican communities and fosters closer ties among them.
Sponsors competitions.

Publications: *Ecos Nacionales*, 3/year. Newsletter. Covers issues affecting
Puerto Rican and other Hispanic women; includes association news, book
reviews, chapter news, and employment opportunities. ● *Fact Sheets*,
periodic. Bulletin. ● *Membership Directory*, annual.

Conventions/Meetings: annual conference (exhibits).

★2991★ NATIONAL CONFERENCE OF WOMEN'S BAR
ASSOCIATIONS (NCWBA)
PO Box 77
Edenton, NC 27932-0077 PH: (919)482-8202
Mary Ann Coffey, Exec.Dir. FX: (919)482-8202

Founded: 1981. **Members:** 110. **Membership Dues:** US$25 annual. **Staff:** 1.
Languages: English. **National.** State and local women's bar associations.
Promotes the interests of women lawyers. Serves as a forum for information
exchange among women's bar associations. Maintains National Foundation
for Women's Bar Associations. Conducts educational programs; maintains
speakers' bureau; compiles statistics. **Awards:** Annual NCWBA Public
Service.

Publications: *NCWBA Newsletter*, quarterly.

Conventions/Meetings: semiannual meeting - 1994 Feb., Kansas City, MO,
United States; 1994 Aug., New Orleans, LA, United States.

★2992★ NATIONAL CONGRESS OF NEIGHBORHOOD WOMEN
(NCNW)
249 Manhattan Ave.
Brooklyn, NY 11211
Dr. Sandy Shieln, Exec. Officer PH: (718)388-6666

Founded: 1975. **Budget:** US$550,000. **Regional Groups:** 26. **Local Groups:**
26. **Languages:** English. **National.** Low-and moderate-income women from
diverse ethnic and racial backgrounds united to: bring about neighborhood
stabilization and revitalization; raise awareness of women's roles in neighborhood activities and organizations as well as on issues affecting low-income
women; provide a voice for a new women's movement that reflects family
and neighborhood values while promoting women's empowerment. Current
projects include: Neighborhood Women College Program, which offers
associate arts degree programs; Project Prepare, which seeks to prepare
individuals to get a job through adult education classes, work experience,
resume writing, child care, and counseling support. Maintains local advisory
board and support groups. Offers speakers' bureau and placement service.
Compiles statistics on women, poverty, and neighborhood development.
Libraries: Type: reference. Holdings: 0; clippings, periodicals, audio recordings, video recordings. **Computer Services:** Mailing lists.

Publications: *Neighborhood Women Network News*, bimonthly. Newsletter.
● *Leadership Training Manual.* Book. ● *Neighborhood Women: Putting It
Together.* Book.

Conventions/Meetings: periodic meeting.

★2993★ NATIONAL COUNCIL OF ADMINISTRATIVE WOMEN IN EDUCATION (NCAWE)
476 12th St., No. 11
Brooklyn, NY 11215
Dr. Jill Berman, Pres.   PH: (718)499-1593

Founded: 1915. **Members:** 1,300. **Local Groups:** 7. **Languages:** English. **National.** Women educators in administrative or supervisory positions in a public or private school system, college or university, foundation, agency, government or nongovernment education programs; also offers auxiliary and associate memberships. Encourages women to prepare for careers in educational administration and to urge educational institutions, systems, and agencies to employ and advance women in this field. Monitors national and local legislation pertaining to women's education. Works to eliminate discrimination against women in educational administration. Circulates information on job openings. Maintains speakers' bureau; conducts research. Sponsors competitions. **Committees:** Leadership Research Grant Award; Legislation; Liaison to Women's Organizations; Women's Issues.

Publications: *Administration Study on Status of Women Administration in Education*, periodic. Monograph. ● *Leadership in Education Journal*, semiannual. ● *National Council of Administration in Education Directory*, annual. ● *NCAWE News*, semiannual. Newsletter.

Conventions/Meetings: annual conference (exhibits).

★2994★ NATIONAL COUNCIL OF CAREER WOMEN (NCCW)
4200 Wisconsin Ave. NW, Ste. 106-210
Washington, DC 20016
Patricia Whittaker, Pres.   PH: (202)310-4200

Founded: 1975. **Members:** 355. **Budget:** US$25,000. **Languages:** English. **National.** Women interested in achieving maximum potential in the business world and individual careers; corporate sponsors. Seeks to enhance the image and role of women in the business and professional world, through professional skill development, education, mentoring, and networking. **Committees:** Communications; Public Relations; Special Projects; Support Groups.

Publications: *Membership Directory*, annual. **Advertising:** accepted. ● *NCCW News*, bimonthly. **Advertising:** accepted.

Conventions/Meetings: annual conference - always spring. Washington, DC, United States. ● bimonthly meeting.

★2995★ NATIONAL COUNCIL OF CATHOLIC WOMEN (NCCW)
1275 K St. NW, Ste. 975
Washington, DC 20005   PH: (202)682-0334
Annette Kane, Exec.Dir.   FX: (202)682-0338

Founded: 1920. **Staff:** 10. **Budget:** US$600,000. **Languages:** English. **National.** Federation of 7000 national, state, diocesan, interparochial, and parochial organizations of Catholic women. Serves as a forum for Catholic women to share resources, speak on current issues in the church and society, and develop leadership and management skills. Is engaged in initiating and developing programs in religious, educational, social, and service areas. Members serve on private and public policymaking bodies monitoring a variety of social justice issues. Works to raise funds for foreign relief in conjunction with Catholic Relief Services, Works of Peace, Help-a-Child, and Madonna Plan (see separate entry). **Commissions:** Community Affairs; Church Communities; Family Affairs; International Affairs.

Publications: *Catholic Woman*, bimonthly. Newsletter. **Circulation:** 10,500.

Conventions/Meetings: annual meeting - 1993 Sept. 16 - 20, Chicago, IL, United States.

★2996★ NATIONAL COUNCIL ON CHILD ABUSE AND FAMILY VIOLENCE (NCCAFV)
1155 Connecticut Ave. NW, Ste. 300
Washington, DC 20036   PH: (202)429-6695
Alan Davis, Pres.   TF: (800)222-2000

Founded: 1984. **Staff:** 6. **Languages:** English. **National.** To support community-based prevention and treatment programs that provide assistance to children, women, the elderly, and families who are victims of abuse and violence. Is concerned with the cyclical and intergenerational nature of family violence and abuse. Seeks to increase public awareness of family violence and promote private sector financial support for prevention and treatment programs. Collaborates with similar organizations to form an informal network; organized National Alliance on Family Violence. Provides technical assistance program to aid community-based organizations in obtaining nonfederal funding. Collects and disseminates information regarding child abuse, domestic violence, and elder abuse. **Programs:** Information Services; Professional Planning and Placement; Technical Assistance; Volunteer Recruitment and Training.

Publications: *INFORUM*, periodic. Newsletter.

★2997★ NATIONAL COUNCIL OF CHURCHES - WOMEN IN MINISTRY GROUP
475 Riverside Dr., Rm. 861
New York, NY 10115   PH: (212)870-2146

Founded: 1973. **Members:** 12. **Staff:** 1. **Budget:** US$26,000. **Languages:** English. **National.** National denominational staff who represent the interests of women in leadership positions within a church. Works to eliminate discrimination, sexual harassment, and other employment-related offenses against women working in the church. Acts as a forum for discussion among staffs with female clergy. Promotes programs for women on an ecumenical rather than a denominational basis. Conducts research programs. Compiles statistics.

Conventions/Meetings: semiannual meeting.

★2998★ NATIONAL COUNCIL, DAUGHTERS OF AMERICA (DA)
PO Box 154
Harrisburg, OH 43126
Ruth Shannon, Sec.   PH: (614)877-9462

Founded: 1891. **Members:** 9,000. **Staff:** 5. **State Groups:** 23. **Languages:** English. **National.** Fraternal society for women and men. Maintains Helping Hand System for deceased members' children. **Awards:** Periodic (scholarship).

Publications: *Newsletter*, periodic.

Conventions/Meetings: biennial meeting - always October. 1994 Oct., Pittsburgh, PA, United States; 1995 Oct., Ashville, NC, United States.

★2999★ NATIONAL COUNCIL OF HISPANIC WOMEN (NCHW)
L'Enfant Plaza Sta.
PO Box 23266
Washington, DC 20026   PH: (202)401-3670
Carmen C. Cardona, Pres.   FX: (202)401-1971

Members: 2,000. **Languages:** English. **National.** Hispanic women, universities, corporations, and government representatives interested in strengthening the role of Hispanic women in society. Seeks to: express the concerns and interests of Hispanic women by participating in the decision-making process; promote ideals that will keep the U.S. safe and strong; improve the social and economic conditions of the Hispanic community; assist Hispanics in establishing themselves in the mainstream of society; foster the exchange of ideas with other groups. Participates in public policy debates, conferences, and television interviews.

Publications: *NCHW Newsletter*, quarterly.

Conventions/Meetings: annual conference.

★3000★ NATIONAL COUNCIL OF JEWISH WOMEN (NCJW)
53 W. 23rd St.
New York, NY 10010
Iris Gross CAE, Exec.Dir.
PH: (212)645-4048
FX: (212)645-7466

Founded: 1893. **Members:** 100,000. **State Groups:** 39. **Local Groups:** 200. **Languages:** English. **National.** Sponsors programs of education, social action, and community service for youth, the elderly, and women. Aims to improve the quality of life for individuals of all ages, races, religions, and socioeconomic levels. Advocates measures affecting social welfare, constitutional rights, civil liberties, and equality for women. Maintains the Research Institute for Innovation in Education at Hebrew University, Jerusalem, Israel. Established Center for the Child in New York to conduct research on issues and actions necessary to shape policies affecting children. Develops community service projects and training materials. **Committees:** Israel Affairs; National Affairs/Community Services.

Publications: *NCJW Journal*, quarterly. Covers constitutional rights, aging, family and child welfare, and Israeli and Jewish life. **ISSN:** 0161-2115. **Circulation:** 100,000. **Advertising:** accepted. ● *NCJW Washington Newsletter*, quarterly. Reports on legislative issues. **Circulation:** 5,000.

Conventions/Meetings: triennial meeting (exhibits) - next 1995.

★3001★ NATIONAL COUNCIL OF NEGRO WOMEN (NCNW)
1167 K St. NW
Washington, DC 20006
Dorothy I. Height, Pres.
PH: (202)659-0006

Founded: 1935. **Members:** 40,000. **Staff:** 53. **Budget:** US$1,500,000. **Local Groups:** 240. **Languages:** English. **National.** Promotes the interests of African American women.

Publications: *Black Woman's Voice*, periodic. Newsletter. ● *Sisters Magazine*, quarterly.

Conventions/Meetings: biennial meeting (exhibits) - usually November.

★3002★ NATIONAL COUNCIL FOR RESEARCH ON WOMEN (NCRW)
Sara Delano Roosevelt Memorial House
47-49 E. 65th St.
New York, NY 10021
Mary Ellen Capek, Exec.Dir.
PH: (212)570-5001
FX: (212)570-5380

Founded: 1982. **Members:** 75. **Staff:** 7. **Budget:** US$400,000. **Languages:** English. **National.** National network of organizations representing the academic community, policymakers, and others interested in women's issues. Purpose is to bring institutional resources to bear on feminist research, policy analysis, and educational programs addressing legal, economic, and social inequities. Promotes collaborative research on issues affecting women; acts as clearinghouse. Houses the National Network of Women's Caucuses and Committees in the Disciplinary and Professional Associations. **Computer Services:** Data base, works of women's research.

Publications: *Annual Report.* ● *Directory of Members*, periodic. ● *Directory of National Women's Organizations*, periodic. ● *Directory of Women's Media*, periodic. ● *Directory of Work-In-Progress and Recent Publications*, periodic. Online database in print. ● *Women's Mailing List Directory*, periodic. ● *Women's Research Network News*, 3-4/year. Newsletter. Reports on member centers' activities, women's caucuses, and research; includes information on new books, fellowships, study and job opportunities. ● *Mainstreaming Minority Women's Studies.* Book. ● *Risk, Resiliency, and Resistance: Current Reseach on Adolescent Girls.* Book. ● *Women in Academe: Progress and Prospects, A Task Force Report.* Book.

Conventions/Meetings: annual conference.

★3003★ NATIONAL COUNCIL OF WOMEN OF FREE CZECHOSLOVAKIA (NCWFC)
77 Sprain Valley Rd.
Scarsdale, NY 10583
Betka Papanek, Pres.
PH: (914)723-9314

Founded: 1951. **Members:** 125. **Staff:** 1. **Local Groups:** 4. **Languages:** English. **National.** Women of Czechoslovak origin or background. "Carries on the democratic program of the National Council of Women of Czechoslovakia disbanded by the communists." Supports aged, ill, and disabled Czechoslovak refugees. Conducts cultural, educational, and welfare activities; sponsors exhibits of art and handcrafts. **Committees:** Cultural; International Relations; Social Welfare.

Publications: *Bulletin*, 3/year.

Conventions/Meetings: annual - New York, NY, United States.

★3004★ NATIONAL COUNCIL ON WOMEN IN MEDICINE
1300 York Ave., Rm. D-115
New York, NY 10021
Laura Scharf, Exec.Dir.
PH: (212)535-0031

National. Women working in the field of medicine. Seeks the improvement of health services for women in the United States.

★3005★ NATIONAL COUNCIL OF WOMEN OF THE UNITED STATES (NCW)
777 United Nations Plaza
New York, NY 10017
Alicia Paolozzi, Pres.
PH: (212)697-1278
FX: (212)972-0164

Founded: 1888. **Members:** 500. **Languages:** English. **National.** Works for the education, participation, and advancement of women in all areas of society. Serves as information center and clearinghouse for affiliated women's organizations. Conducts projects and sponsors conferences on national and international problems and matters of concern to women and shares the results with affiliated groups. Has observer status at the United Nations. **Awards:** Annual Woman of Conscience. **Committees:** Arts and Letters; Child and Family; Economics; Education; Environment and Habitat; Health; Home Economics; Human Rights; International Hospitality; International Relations; Laws and Status of Women; Laws and Suffrage; Mass Media; Migration; Public Policy; Social Welfare; Women and Employment. **Projects:** Racial and Ethnic Harmony.

Publications: *National Council of Women of the U.S.*, quarterly. Bulletin. Reports on council programs and activities of member organizations. Includes awards announcements, book reviews, and calendar of events. **Circulation:** 1,200.

★3006★ NATIONAL DEAF WOMEN'S BOWLING ASSOCIATION (NDWBA)
33 August Rd.
Simsbury, CT 06070
Kathy M. Darby, Sec.-Treas.
PH: (203)651-8234

Founded: 1974. **Members:** 160. **Languages:** English. **National.** Hearing impaired bowlers. Promotes fellowship and fair play among participants.

Publications: *NDWBA Constitution and By Laws.* Booklet.

Conventions/Meetings: annual competition, singles, doubles, team, queen's, and world championship. - always July. 1994 July, Baltimore, MD, United States; 1995 July, Atlantic City, NJ, United States; 1996 July, St. Louis, MO, United States.

★3007★ NATIONAL DEFENSE COMMITTEE OF THE DAUGHTERS OF THE AMERICAN REVOLUTION (NDCDAR)
1776 D St. NW
Washington, DC 20006-5392
Phyllis Schlafly, Chm.   PH: (202)879-3261

Founded: 1926. **Staff:** 2. **Local Groups:** 3,000. **Languages:** English. **National.** Objective is to assist members of the National Society, Daughters of the American Revolution in carrying out their patriotic, educational, and historical purposes. Advocates a strong military defense as being essential for national sovereignty and independence. Provides information to alert its members of potential external and internal threats to national independence.

Publications: *DAR National Defender*, 9/year. Newsletter.

Conventions/Meetings: annual meeting - Washington, DC, United States.

★3008★ NATIONAL FAMILY PLANNING AND REPRODUCTIVE HEALTH ASSOCIATION (NFPRHA)
122 C St. NW, Ste. 380
Washington, DC 20001   PH: (202)628-3535
Judith M. DeSarno, Exec.Dir.   FX: (202)737-2690

Founded: 1971. **Members:** 1,000. **Budget:** US$1,000,000. **Languages:** English. **National.** Hospitals, state and city departments of health, health care providers, private nonprofit clinics, and consumers concerned with the maintenance and improvement of family planning and reproductive health services. Serves as a national communications network and advocacy organization. Maintains contact with Congress and government agencies in order to monitor government policy and regulations. **Awards:** Periodic Public service. **Committees:** Consumer Affairs Council; Development; International and Domestic Public Affairs; Minority Development.

Publications: *NFPRHA Alert*, periodic. Bulletin. ● *NFPRHA News*, bimonthly. Newsletter. ● *NFPRHA Report*, bimonthly. Newsletter.

Conventions/Meetings: annual meeting (exhibits) - Washington, DC, United States.

★3009★ NATIONAL FEDERATION OF BUSINESS AND PROFESSIONAL WOMEN'S CLUBS (BPW/USA)
2012 Massachusetts Ave. NW
Washington, DC 20036
Barbara Sido, Deputy Exec.Dir.   PH: (202)293-1100

Founded: 1919. **Members:** 125,000. **Staff:** 40. **Budget:** US$3,070,000. **Regional Groups:** 53. **Local Groups:** 3,500. **Languages:** English. **National.** Business and professional women and men representing 300 occupations. To promote full participation, equal opportunities, and economic self-sufficiency for working women. Has created Congressional Lobby Corps to influence elected officials on issues concerning women. Sponsors National Business Women Week, held the third week in October, and Business and Professional Women's Foundation as research and education arm of the federation. Organizes the National Council on the Future of Women in the Workplace, which encourages corporate/private sector cooperation on issues such as dependent care and employer responsiveness to the needs of working women. Provides nationwide career and personal training seminars. **Libraries:** Type: reference. Holdings: 20,000. **Committees:** BPW/USA PAC; Issues Management; Legislation; Young Career Women.

Publications: *National Business Woman*, bimonthly. Newsletter. Covers women's socioeconomic issues such as pay equity and child care; includes association news. **ISSN:** 0027-8831. **Circulation:** 125,000. **Advertising:** accepted.

Conventions/Meetings: annual workshop (exhibits).

★3010★ NATIONAL FEDERATION OF CUBAN AMERICAN REPUBLICAN WOMEN (NFCARW)
2119 S. Webster St.
Ft. Wayne, IN 46804   PH: (219)745-5421
Dr. Graciela Beecher, Exec.Dir.   FX: (219)744-1363

Founded: 1982. **Members:** 350. **Membership Dues:** US$10 annual. **Staff:** 1. **Regional Groups:** 4. **State Groups:** 15. **Local Groups:** 31. **Languages:** English. **National.** Encourages women of Cuban orgin to participate in the Republican party. Represents the interests of Cuban-American women in the Republican party and at the Republican National Convention. Supports the principles, policies, and candidates of the party. Coordinate the activities of other recognized Cuban-American organizations on the local and state levels. Acts as a voice to the Republican party for individuals "suffering under the communist rule of Castro.".

Conventions/Meetings: periodic meeting.

★3011★ NATIONAL FEDERATION OF DEMOCRATIC WOMEN (NFDW)
2215 45th Ave.
Spokane, WA 99223
Charlotte Coker, Exec. Officer   PH: (509)448-0611

Founded: 1972. **Members:** 300,000. **Budget:** US$50,000. **Regional Groups:** 4. **State Groups:** 42. **Languages:** English. **National.** Democratic women's organizations; state, local, and regional clubs; individuals. Organized to develop leadership among women locally and nationally, both as party workers and elected public officials. Goal is to unite the women of the party and to encourage full participation of women on every level of the party structure by promoting the exchange of ideas and communication. Maintains biographical archives and special study groups; conducts specialized education programs; offers an internship. **Committees:** Legislative; Status of Women.

Publications: *The Communicator*, quarterly. Newsletter. Includes president's message and regional reports. **Circulation:** 500. **Advertising:** accepted. ● *Directory*, semiannual.

Conventions/Meetings: annual (exhibits). ● meeting.

★3012★ NATIONAL FEDERATION OF GRANDMOTHER CLUBS OF AMERICA (NFGCA)
203 N. Wabash Ave., Ste. 702
Chicago, IL 60601
Margaret Day, Office Mgr.   PH: (312)372-5437

Founded: 1938. **Members:** 8,000. **Staff:** 2. **Local Groups:** 300. **Languages:** English. **National.** Women who have grandchildren or have acquired them through marriage or adoption. Sponsors National Grandmother's Day (second Sunday in October). Raises funds to support research on children's diseases, especially leukemia.

Publications: *Autumn Leaves*, quarterly. Includes memorial list and club highlights. **Circulation:** 4,000. **Advertising:** not accepted.

Conventions/Meetings: annual meeting.

★3013★ NATIONAL FEDERATION OF PARENTS AND FRIENDS OF GAYS (NF/PFOG)
8020 Eastern Ave. NW
Washington, DC 20012
Eugene M. Baker, Exec.Sec.   PH: (202)726-3223

Founded: 1980. **Members:** 525. **Languages:** English. **National.** Individual counselors and peer-counseling support groups whose primary purpose is to serve and advise others who are concerned with or are attempting to understand and cope with homosexuality and related issues. Provides counseling for children, parents, and spouses of gays. Seeks for homosexuals the same basic human and civil rights, liberties, and opportunities that are afforded to heterosexuals. Develops and promotes educational programs and activities that eliminate ignorance, fear, and misinformation pertaining to human sexuality. Provides speakers, panelists, and participants in group discussions. Sponsors educational and conscience-raising workshops and seminars. **Libraries:** Type: reference.

Publications: *International Directory*, semiannual.

★3014★ NATIONAL FEDERATION OF PRESS WOMEN (NFPW)
Box 99
Blue Springs, MO 64013
Marj Carpenter, Pres.
PH: (816)229-1666
FX: (816)229-1676

Founded: 1937. **Members:** 4,000. **Budget:** US$180,000. **State Groups:** 51. **Languages:** English. **National.** Federation of state associations of professional women and men in all phases of communications on a full-time or free-lance basis. Purposes are to: encourage the highest standards of professionalism in journalism; provide for exchange of ideas, knowledge, and experience. Conducts Annual communications contest. Offers specialized education programs. **Awards:** Periodic (grant). ● Periodic (scholarship). **Committees:** Youth Project; Communicator of Achievement; Education Fund; Legal Education.

Publications: *Agenda*, bimonthly. Newsletter. ● *Directory*, annual. ● *Press Woman*, bimonthly. Magazine. **ISSN:** 0032-7824. **Circulation:** 5,000. **Advertising:** not accepted.

Conventions/Meetings: annual conference (exhibits) - always June.

★3015★ NATIONAL FEDERATION OF REPUBLICAN WOMEN (NFRW)
310 1st St. SE
Washington, DC 20003
Huda Jones, Pres.
PH: (202)547-9341
FX: (202)547-8485

Founded: 1938. **Members:** 160,000. **Staff:** 10. **State Groups:** 52. **Local Groups:** 2,600. **Languages:** English. **National.** Purposes are: to provide an organization through which women who share the principles of the Republican Party can join in Republican activities; to distribute political educational materials; to recruit and support qualified and electable Republican candidates; to encourage more women to seek public office and to provide them with campaign expertise through NFRW-sponsored Campaign Management Schools across the country; to provide research material and legislative information to federation members. Operates hot line. **Committees:** Americanism; Campaign; Candidate Recruitment; Community Relations; Heritage; Legislation and Research; Minority Outreach; New Founders; Public Relations; Senior Americans.

Publications: *The Republican Woman*, bimonthly. Magazine. Contains articles on the Federation and the Republican Party, administrative policies, and legislative activities in Congress. **Circulation:** 140,000. **Advertising:** not accepted. ● *Consider Yourself for Public Office*. Book. ● *Crime: You Don't Have To Live With It*. Book. ● *Lobby, Who Can? You Can!*. Book.

Conventions/Meetings: biennial meeting.

★3016★ NATIONAL FORT DAUGHTERS OF '98, AUXILIARY UNITED SPANISH WAR VETERANS
6210 Lavarne Ave.
Parna, OH 44128
Martha Kolley, Ft.Capt.
PH: (216)661-3573

Founded: 1934. **Members:** 700. **Staff:** 18. **State Groups:** 8. **Local Groups:** 40. **Languages:** English. **National.** Daughters, daughters-in-law, and other female descendants and legal relatives of veterans of the Spanish American War. Objective is to unite the descendants of Spanish American War veterans and perpetuate the memory of these veterans. Donates clothing and funds to homes for needy children. **Awards:** Periodic Clara Barten (scholarship). **Programs:** Americanism; Child Welfare.

Publications: *Bulletin*, periodic. Includes directory. ● *Proceedings*, annual.

Conventions/Meetings: annual meeting.

★3017★ NATIONAL FOSTER PARENT ASSOCIATION (NFPA)
Information and Services Office
226 Kilts Dr.
Houston, TX 77024
Gordon Evans, Dir.
PH: (713)467-1850
FX: (713)827-0919

Founded: 1972. **Members:** 3,300. **Budget:** US$100,000. **Regional Groups:** 10. **State Groups:** 43. **Local Groups:** 71. **Languages:** English. **National.** Foster parents, child social service line workers and administrators, and citizen child-advocates; interested associations. Seeks to identify and advocate the needs of children in foster care and those who care for them. Offers technical assistance and organizational skills training to state and local foster parent associations. Works to improve the foster parenting image nationwide and educate the courts, legislators, and the public to the needs of children in the foster care system. Has established a communication network among child advocacy organizations and developed a model recruitment plan to promote organized recruitment, development, and retention of foster family homes. Informs foster parents of their legal rights; encourages mandatory parenting skills training and a minimum requirement of preservice training for all foster parents. Operates Information and Services office to provide information on foster care issues. Maintains speakers' bureau; compiles statistics. Plans to conduct data accumulation project on foster care. **Libraries:** Type: reference. Subjects: Foster Care. **Awards:** Annual (scholarship). ● Periodic (recognition). **Committees:** Public Education Project; Public Relations.

Publications: *National Foster Parent Association—National Advocate*, bimonthly. Covers foster care issues nationwide; includes legislative news, innovative programs, and personal articles by foster parents. **Circulation:** 3,500. **Advertising:** accepted.

Conventions/Meetings: annual conference (exhibits) - 1994, Grand Rapids, MI, United States.

★3018★ NATIONAL FOUNDATION FOR WOMEN BUSINESS OWNERS
1825 I St. NW, Ste. 800
Washington, DC 20006
Sharon Hardary, Exec.Dir.
PH: (202)833-1854

National. Concerned with the leadership and career training of women entrepreneurs and women in management in the United States. Performs data collection and disseminates facts and statistics on women business owners.

★3019★ NATIONAL GAY ALLIANCE FOR YOUNG ADULTS (NGAYA)
PO Box 190712
Dallas, TX 75219
Scott Barea, Contact
PH: (817)381-0343
TF: (800)929-0867

Founded: 1985. **Languages:** English. **National.** Gay youth and individuals, businesses, and organizations supportive of gay youth. Seeks to: develop and promote the lifestyles of young gay men and women through education and socialization; educate both the general and gay communities about the special needs and issues of gay youth; initiate and conduct new projects; cooperate with existing projects having similar goals. Sponsors A New Tomorrow and the Texas Gay Youth Fund (fund-raising programs), Pen-Friend, National Gay Youth Awareness Week, and counselor seminars. Compiles statistics. **Computer Services:** Data base, information for gay youth.

Publications: *Annual Report*. ● *NGAYA News*, monthly. Newsletter.

Conventions/Meetings: periodic conference, with seminars.

★3020★ NATIONAL GAY AND LESBIAN TASK FORCE (NGLTF)
1734 14th St. NW
Washington, DC 20009-4309
Ms. Urvashi Vaid, Exec. Officer
PH: (202)332-6483
FX: (202)332-0207

Founded: 1973. **Members:** 18,000. **Staff:** 16. **Budget:** US$1,039,350. **Languages:** English. **National.** Dedicated to the elimination of prejudice against persons based on their sexual orientation. Lobbies U.S. Congress; organizes on the "grass roots" level; demonstrates and engages in direct action for gay freedom and full civil rights. Works with the media to cover gay issues and the lives of gay people; assists other associations and foundations in working effectively with the homosexual community. Represents national gay/lesbian community on AIDS policy issues and works for a responsible, nondiscriminatory national AIDS policy. Engages in sodomy law reform and repeal of military policy on homosexuals. Offers technical assistance, leadership training, education, and resource support. Maintains speakers' bureau. **Projects:** Anti-Violence; Campus; Civil Rights; Lesbian/ Gay Families; Media; Privacy; Legislative.

Publications: *Campus Organizing Newsletter*, semiannual. ● *National Gay and Lesbian Task Force—Task Force Report*, quarterly. Newsletter. Reports on activities of the task force, and on governmental a ctions affecting gays and lesbians. **Advertising:** not accepted. ● *Dealing With Violence: A Guide for Gay and Lesbian People*. Book. ● *Gay and Lesbian Rights Protection in the U.S.*. Book.

Conventions/Meetings: annual Creating Change conference - always November. ● annual conference.

★3021★ NATIONAL HOOK-UP OF BLACK WOMEN (NHBW)
c/o Wynetta Frazier
5117 S. University Ave.
Chicago, IL 60615
Wynetta Frazier, Pres.   PH: (312)643-5866

Founded: 1975. **Members:** 500. **Regional Groups:** 8. **Local Groups:** 9. **Languages:** English. **National.** Black women from business, professional, and community-oriented disciplines representing all economic, educational, and social levels. Purpose is to provide a communications network in support of black women who serve in organizational leadership positions, especially those elected or appointed to office and those wishing to elevate their status through educational and career ventures. Works to form and implement a Black Women's Agenda that would provide representation for women, families, and communities and that would help surmount economic, educational, and social barriers. Supports efforts of the Congressional Black Caucus in utilizing the legislative process to work toward total equality of opportunity in society. Seeks to highlight the achievements and contributions of black women. Sponsors workshops. Operates speakers' bureau. **Awards:** Periodic Distinguished Community Service. ● Periodic Distinguished Family Service. ● Periodic Outstanding Leadership. ● Annual (scholarship). **Committees:** Education; Health; Women's; Youth Mentoring.

Publications: *Hook-Up News and Views*, quarterly. Newsletter.

Conventions/Meetings: semiannual meeting - 1993 Sept., Washington, DC, United States; 1994 Apr., Brazil.

★3022★ NATIONAL INFERTILITY NETWORK EXCHANGE (NINE)
c/o Ilene Stargot
PO Box 204
East Meadow, NY 11554
Ilene Stargot, Pres.   PH: (516)794-5772

Founded: 1988. **Languages:** English. **National.** Peer support group for individuals and couples suffering from infertility. Offers education programs and referral service; advocates on behalf of participants. Maintains speakers' bureau.

Publications: *News from NINE*, 6/year.

Conventions/Meetings: monthly meeting.

★3023★ NATIONAL INSTITUTE FOR WOMEN OF COLOR (NIWC)
1301 20th St. NW, Ste. 702
Washington, DC 20036
Sharon Parker, Bd.Chm.   PH: (202)298-1118

Founded: 1981. **Staff:** 2. **Budget:** US$100,000. **Languages:** English.

National. Aims to: enhance the strengths of diversity; promote educational and economic equity for black, Hispanic, Asian-American, Pacific-Islander, American Indian, and Alaskan Native women. Focuses on mutual concerns and needs, bringing together women who have traditionally been isolated. (NIWC uses the phrase "women of color" to convey unity, self-esteem, and political status and to avoid using the term "minority," which the institute feels has a negative psychological and social impact.) Serves as a networking vehicle to: link women of color on various issues or programs; promote women of color for positions on boards and commissions; ensure that women of color are visible as speakers or presenters at major women's conferences, as well as planners or program developers; support and initiate programs; educate women and the public about the status and culture of the various racial/ethnic groups they represent; promote cooperative efforts between general women's organizations and women of color, while raising awareness about issues and principles of feminism. Provides technical assistance; conducts internship and leadership development programs; compiles statistics.

Publications: *Network News*, periodic. Newsletter. ● *Bulletin*, periodic.

Conventions/Meetings: periodic conference.

★3024★ NATIONAL INTERCOLLEGIATE WOMEN'S FENCING
ASSOCIATION (NIWFA)
3 Derby Ln.
Dumont, NJ 07628
Sharon Everson, Pres.   PH: (201)384-1722

Founded: 1929. **Members:** 18. **Languages:** English. **National.** Degree-granting colleges and universities with varsity women's fencing teams. Promotes fencing for women in colleges and universities. Conducts fencing matches, workshops, and clinics. Sponsors and determines members of All-American Women's Fencing Team (chosen annually). Maintains archives. **Committees:** All-American Selection; Bout; Olympians.

Publications: *Directory*, annual. ● *National Intercollegiate Women's Fencing Association—Newsletter*, periodic.

Conventions/Meetings: annual meeting.

★3025★ NATIONAL JUDICIAL EDUCATION PROGRAM TO PROMOTE
EQUALITY FOR WOMEN AND MEN IN THE COURTS
99 Hudson St., 12th Fl.
New York, NY 10013   PH: (212)925-6635
Lynn Hecht Schafran, Dir.   FX: (212)226-1066

Founded: 1980. **Languages:** English. **National.** A project of the NOW Legal Defense and Education Fund in cooperation with the National Association of Women Judges. Works to eliminate gender bias in the courts by making judges aware of stereotypes, myths, and biases pertaining to the roles of men and women, and how those biases can affect judicial decision-making and the courtroom environment. Serves as a clearinghouse for data on gender bias in the courts. Conducts courses, seminars, and other educational programs for judges, lawyers, and the public. Collaborates with state and national judicial colleges and state task forces; participates in legal conferences, law school programs, and continuing education projects.

★3026★ NATIONAL LADIES AUXILIARY TO VETERANS OF WORLD
WAR I OF THE U.S.A.
PO Box 2907
Bay St. Louis, MS 39521-2907
Pauline Charping, Sec.-Treas.   PH: (601)467-9799

Founded: 1953. **Members:** 20,000. **Staff:** 1. **Regional Groups:** 10. **State Groups:** 48. **Local Groups:** 1,000. **Languages:** English. **National.** Female relatives of Veterans of World War I of U.S.A. Conducts patriotic, historical, and educational programs. **Committees:** Americanism; Hospital-Community Services; Veterans Administration Voluntary Services.

Publications: *Torch*, monthly. Newsletter.

Conventions/Meetings: annual meeting.

★3027★ NATIONAL LEAGUE OF AMERICAN PEN WOMEN (NLAPW)
1300 17th St. NW
Washington, DC 20036
Muriel C. Freeman, Pres.   PH: (202)785-1997

Founded: 1897. Members: 5,000. Staff: 3. Budget: US$129,000. Regional Groups: 200. State Groups: 42. Local Groups: 5. Languages: English. National. Writers, composers, artists, and professional women in the creative arts. Promotes the professional development of members. Conducts and encourages literary, educational, and charitable activites in the fields of art, letters, and music. Fosters the exchange of ideas and techniques through workshops, discussion groups, and professional lecturers; sponsors art exhibit and contests. Maintains biographical archives, hall of fame, research all of fame, and research programs. Libraries: Type: reference. Holdings: 3,000. Awards: Periodic certificate of proficiency. ● Periodic (scholarship). Computer Services: Mailing lists; data base. Divisions: Art; Letter; Music.

Publications: National League of American Pen Women—Roster, biennial. Membership directory. Circulation: 5,000. Advertising: not accepted. Alternate Formats: online. ● The Pen Woman, 5/year. Membership activities magazine. Includes book listings and obituaries. Circulation: 5,000. Advertising: accepted. Alternate Formats: online.

Conventions/Meetings: biennial conference - 1994 Apr., New York, NY, United States.

★3028★ NATIONAL MARRIAGE ENCOUNTER (NME)
4704 Jamerson Pl.   PH: (407)282-8120
Orlando, FL 32807   TF: (800)828-3351
Chuck and Sandy Ogg, Bus.Admins.   FX: (407)282-8120

Founded: 1970. Regional Groups: 8. Languages: English. National. Offers weekend retreat programs organized by married couples and a member of the clergy. Retreats are aimed at encouraging communication between married partners and emphasizing personal and religious growth.

Publications: National Marriage Encounter Newsletter, quarterly.

Conventions/Meetings: annual Conference of Encountered Couples.

★3029★ NATIONAL MASTER FARM HOMEMAKERS' GUILD (NMFHG)
c/o Eleanor Strait
RR 1, Box 72
Keosauqua, IA 52565
Eleanor Strait, Pres.   PH: (319)293-3266

Founded: 1929. Members: 535. State Groups: 6. Languages: English. National. Outstanding farm women selected as leaders in local, state, or national affairs by groups working with land grant colleges. Works to: create a desire to give service to home, community, state, and nation; promote high standards of living in farm homes; provide hospitality to international visitors. Conducts charitable programs.

Conventions/Meetings: annual meeting - 1993 Sept. 30 - Oct. 2, Topeka, KS, United States.

★3030★ NATIONAL NETWORK OF HISPANIC WOMEN
12021 Wilshire Blvd., Ste. 353
Los Angeles, CA 90025
Celia Torres, Chair   PH: (213)225-9895

Founded: 1980. National. Promotes the development of Hispanic American women in business and management.

★3031★ NATIONAL NETWORK OF MINORITY WOMEN IN SCIENCE (MWIS)
c/o American Association for the
  Advancement of Science
Directorate for Educ. and Human
  Resources Programs
1333 H St. NW
Washington, DC 20005
Audrey B. Daniel, Coordinator   PH: (202)326-6670

Founded: 1978. Members: 400. Regional Groups: 1. State Groups: 2. Local Groups: 3. Languages: English. National. Asian, Black, Mexican American, Native American, and Puerto Rican women involved in science related professions; other interested persons. Promotes the advancement of minority women in science fields and the improvement of the science and mathematics education and career awareness of minorities. Supports public policies and programs in science and technology that benefit minorities. Compiles statistics; serves as clearinghouse for identifying minority women scientists. Offers writing and conference presentations, seminars, and workshops on minority women in science and local career conferences for students. Local chapters maintain speakers' bureaus and placement services, offer children's services, sponsor competitions.

Publications: MWIS, annual. Annual report.

Conventions/Meetings: annual (exhibits).

★3032★ NATIONAL NETWORK OF WOMEN'S FUNDS (NNWF)
1821 University Ave. W, Ste. 409N
St. Paul, MN 55104   PH: (612)641-0742
Carol Mollner, Exec. Officer   FX: (612)647-1401

Founded: 1985. Budget: US$270,000. Languages: English. National. Women's foundations and federations dedicated to generating increased resources for programs that benefit women and girls. Works to publicize what the Network views as the low percentage of funds offered by foundations and corporations to programs serving women and girls. Works to increase funding for programs for women and girls, primarily by supporting the development and growth of women's foundations and federations. Maintains clearinghouse of information about women's funds.

Conventions/Meetings: annual conference. ● annual regional meeting.

★3033★ NATIONAL ORGANIZATION OF ADOLESCENT PREGNANCY AND PARENTING (NOAPP)
4421A East-West Hwy.
Bethesda, MD 20814   PH: (301)913-0378
Kathleen Sheeran, Exec.Dir.   FX: (301)913-0380

Founded: 1979. Members: 2,000. Languages: English. National. Professionals, policymakers, community and state leaders, and other concerned individuals and organizations. Promotes comprehensive and coordinated services designed for the prevention and resolution of problems associated with adolescent pregnancy and parenthood. Supports families in expanding their capability of nurturing children and setting standards that encourage their healthy development through loving, stable relationships. Programs include: providing advocacy services at local, state, and national levels for pregnant adolescents and school-age parents (and their children); sharing information and promoting public awareness; coalition building assistan ce.

Publications: Directory of Adolescent Pregnancy and Parenting Program, periodic. ● NOAPP Network Newsletter, quarterly. Contains resource reviews, state highlights, legislative focus, and successful program models.

Conventions/Meetings: annual conference (exhibits). ● periodic conference. ● periodic workshop.

★3034★ NATIONAL ORGANIZATION OF EPISCOPALIANS FOR LIFE
(NOEL)
10523 Main St.
Fairfax, VA 22030
Mary Ann Dacey, Exec.Dir.   PH: (703)591-6635

Founded: 1966. **Members:** 16,000. **Staff:** 2. **Languages:** English. **National.** Episcopalians organized to reaffirm their faith and reestablish moral responsibility in the Christian response to human life issues. Focuses on issues concerning the protection and enhancement of human existence in accordance with God's laws. Objectives are: to offer education within the Protestant Episcopal Church on the value, dignity, and sanctity of human life; to provide support for the church in teaching life issues; to offer viable alternatives to abortion; to disseminate information through educational programs of a religious, ethical, and scientific nature. Supports National Organization of Episcopalians for Life: Research and Education Foundation. Offers workshops, seminars, and a pro-life ministry. Maintains tape ministry and speakers' bureau. **Alternate name:** NOEL.

Publications: *The Noel News*, quarterly. Newsletter. Newsletter; includes calendar of events and member news.

Conventions/Meetings: annual meeting.

★3035★ NATIONAL ORGANIZATION OF ITALIAN-AMERICAN WOMEN
(NOIAW)
445 W. 59th St., Rm. 1248
New York, NY 10019   PH: (212)237-8574
Barbara Gerard, Pres.   FX: (212)489-6130

Founded: 1980. **Members:** 800. **Staff:** 1. **Regional Groups:** 4. **State Groups:** 21. **Languages:** English. **National.** Women who have at least one parent of Italian heritage. Objectives are to: foster interests and address problems and concerns of Italian-American women; provide network of resources and support for professional, political, and social advancement; increase cultural, educational, and financial opportunities of young people of Italian-American origin; promote awareness and perpetuation of Italian culture and ethnic identity; foster ethnic pride and develop role models for younger Italian-Americans; modify traditional images of women of Italian descent and expand their career choices; help serve the interests of Italian-American communities; provide liaison and promote greater unity with other Italian-American groups and women's ethnic groups. Encourages Italian - American women to monitor and participate in the political process and to serve health and welfare interests of the Italian-American community. Conducts film presentations; sponsors forums, workshops, seminars, cultural events, and networking meetings; conducts selfhelp programs. Sponsors Mentor Program for female college students whereby each student is "adopted" by a member who has a career in the student's chosen field. **Awards:** Periodic (scholarship).

Publications: *NOIAW Newsletter*, quarterly. Memberhisp activities newsletter; contains regional updates and book reviews. **Advertising:** not accepted.

Conventions/Meetings: annual luncheon. ● periodic conference.

★3036★ NATIONAL ORGANIZATION OF MOTHERS OF TWINS
CLUBS (NOMOTC)
PO Box 23188
Albuquerque, NM 87192-1188
Lois Gallmeyer, Exec.Sec.   PH: (505)275-0955

Founded: 1960. **Members:** 15,500. **Budget:** US$85,000. **Local Groups:** 410. **Languages:** English. **National.** Twin clubs seeking to broaden the understanding of those aspects of child development and rearing which relate especially to twins through the interchange of information among parents, educators, doctors, and others. Goals are: to make information about twins available to the public; to increase awareness of the individuality of each twin; to assist in medical research. Operates speakers' bureau; maintains bibliography of books on twin care.

Publications: *MOTC's Notebook*, quarterly. Newsletter.

Conventions/Meetings: annual meeting.

★3037★ NATIONAL ORGANIZATION FOR WOMEN (NOW)
1000 16th St. NW, Ste. 700
Washington, DC 20036   PH: (202)331-0066
Patricia Ireland, Pres.   FX: (202)785-8576

Founded: 1966. **Members:** 280,000. **Staff:** 30. **Regional Groups:** 9. **State Groups:** 50. **Local Groups:** 800. **Languages:** English. **National.** Men and women who support "full equality for women in truly equal partnership with men." Seeks to end prejudice and discrimination against women in government, industry, the professions, churches, political parties, the judiciary, labor unions, education, science, medicine, law, religion, "and every other field of importance in American society." Promotes passage of the Equal Rights Amendment and enforcement of federal legislation prohibiting discrimination on the basis of sex. Engages in lobbying and litigation. Works to increase the number of women elected to local, county, and state offices, the House of Representatives, and the Senate. Sponsors student essay contests.

Publications: *NOW Times*, bimonthly. Newspaper.

Conventions/Meetings: annual conference (exhibits).

★3038★ NATIONAL OSTEOPATHIC WOMEN PHYSICIANS'
ASSOCIATION (NOWPA)
West Virginia School of Osteopathic
Medicine
400 N. Lee St.
Louisburg, WV 24901   PH: (304)645-6270
Marlene A. Wager D.O., Exec. Officer   FX: (304)645-4859

Founded: 1904. **Members:** 200. **Languages:** English. **National.** Professional sorority - osteopathy. **Awards:** Annual (grant). ● Periodic (scholarship). **Committees:** Education. **Formerly:** (1988) Delta Omega.

Publications: *The Alpha*, annual. Magazine.

★3039★ NATIONAL POLITICAL CONGRESS OF BLACK WOMEN
PO Box 422
Rancocas, NJ 08073
Dempsey Portia, Exec.Dir.   PH: (609)871-1500

National. Works to promote the political agenda of issues facing African American women.

★3040★ NATIONAL PRO-LIFE DEMOCRATS (NPLD)
PO Box 23467
Minneapolis, MN 55423
Mary Jo Cooley, Exec.Dir.   PH: (612)825-4639

Languages: English. **National.** Encourages pro-life Democrats to participate in the Democratic party. Provides education on becoming active in the Democratic party at the local level. Conducts workshops; develops educational materials. Compiles statistics.

★3041★ NATIONAL REPUBLICAN COALITION FOR CHOICE (NRCC)
709 2nd St. NE, Ste. 100
Washington, DC 20002   PH: (202)543-0676
Mary Dent Crisp, Natl. Chair   FX: (202)543-0676

Founded: 1989. **Members:** 4,000. **Languages:** English. **National.** Independent political committee founded to ensure a national voice for pro-choice Republicans. (Defines pro-choice as an individual who opposes governmental, political, and legislative attempts to ban abortion.) Seeks to identify, organize, and elect pro-choice Republicans to office and to promote the pro-choice position as the official position of the Republican Party. **Computer Services:** Mailing lists; data base.

Conventions/Meetings: periodic.

★3042★ NATIONAL RIGHT TO LIFE COMMITTEE (NRLC)
419 7th St. NW, Ste. 500
Washington, DC 20004
Wanda Franz Ph.D., Pres.   PH: (202)626-8800

Founded: 1973. **State Groups:** 50. **Local Groups:** 3,000. **Languages:** English. **National.** Pro-life organization that opposes abortion, euthanasia, and infanticide. Supports abortion alternative programs involving counseling and adoption. Provides ongoing public education programs on abortion, euthanasia, and infanticide. Lobbies before congressional committees; encourages passage and ratification of a constitutional amendment to protect all human life. Conducts research; compiles statistics; maintains speakers' bureau. **Libraries:** Type: reference. Holdings: books, periodicals, clippings, audio recordings, video recordings. **Committees:** National Right to Life Political Action. **Departments:** Communications; Education; Legislative; News.

Publications: *National Right to Life News*, biweekly. Newsletter.

Conventions/Meetings: annual meeting (exhibits).

★3043★ NATIONAL RIGHT TO LIFE EDUCATIONAL TRUST FUND
(NRLETF)
419 7th St. NW, Ste. 500
Washington, DC 20004   PH: (202)626-8800
David O'Steen, Exec.Dir.   FX: (202)737-9189

Languages: English. **National.** Educational branch of the National Right to Life Committee. Fosters awareness of and responsibility for human life before and after birth, particularly those whom the group feels are "vulnerable" and "disadvantaged," such as the mentally retarded and the physically handicapped. Sponsors public awareness campaigns about bioethical issues, including abortion, human experimentation, infanticide, genetic engineering, and euthanasia. Encourages research and public education on parenthood and on the prevention of birth defects and mental retardation. Promotes "enlightened care and assistance" for pregnant women, children, handicapped, mentally retarded, and aged persons with special needs. Offers seminars and conferences. Sponsors Annual speech contest. **Libraries:** Type: reference.

Publications: *Abortion: Question and Answer Series*. Monograph.

★3044★ NATIONAL SENIOR WOMEN'S TENNIS ASSOCIATION
(NSWTA)
1696 W. Calimjrna, No. B
Fresno, CA 93711
Elaine Mason, Pres.   PH: (209)432-3095

Founded: 1974. **Members:** 800. **Languages:** English. **National.** Women over 30 years of age and others interested in senior women's competitive tennis. Promotes senior women's tennis events. Sponsors a national, intersectional, team competition event. **Committees:** Team Competition.

Publications: *National Senior Women's Tennis Association Newsletter*, quarterly.

Conventions/Meetings: annual - always spring. Houston, TX, United States.

★3045★ NATIONAL SOCIETY OF THE COLONIAL DAMES OF
AMERICA (NSCDA)
2715 Q St. NW
Washington, DC 20007   PH: (202)337-2288
Mrs. John B. Watkins, Pres.   FX: (202)337-0348

Languages: English. **National.** American women who are descendan is persons who rendered civil or military service and lived in one of the British Colonies in the U.S. Provides a forum for communication and exchange among, members.

Conventions/Meetings: biennial meeting.

★3046★ NATIONAL SOCIETY COLONIAL DAMES XVII CENTURY
1300 New Hampshire Ave. NW
Washington, DC 20036
Ms. John Chenault, Pres.Gen.   PH: (202)293-1700

Founded: 1915. **Members:** 14,000. **Staff:** 2. **State Groups:** 45. **Local Groups:** 400. **Languages:** English. **National.** American women who are lineal descendants of persons who rendered civil or military service and lived in one of the British Colonies in the U.S. before 1701 as a colonist or a descendant of one. Aids in preservation of records and historical sites and fosters interest in historical colonial research. Maintains museum collection and library dealing with lineage, birth, and cemetery records and county histories. **Awards:** Periodic (scholarship). **Committees:** Colonial Research and Records; Custodian of the American Flag; Grave Markers; Heraldry and Coats of Arms; Museum; Music; National Defense; Pocahontas Fund; Restoration and Marking Colonial Sites; Scholarship; Veterans Service.

Publications: *Seventeenth Century Review*, 3/year. Newsletter.

Conventions/Meetings: annual (exhibits) - always April. Washington, DC, United States.

★3047★ NATIONAL SOCIETY, DAUGHTERS OF THE AMERICAN
COLONISTS (DAC)
2205 Massachusetts Ave. NW
Washington, DC 20008
Mrs. Robert W. Leavene, Pres.   PH: (202)667-3076

Founded: 1921. **Members:** 10,700. **State Groups:** 51. **Local Groups:** 332. **Languages:** English. **National.** Women descended from men and women who gave civil or military service to the Colonies prior to the Revolutionary War. **Libraries:** Type: reference.   **Awards:** Periodic (scholarship). **Committees:** Army, Navy, Coast Guard, Air Force, and Merchant Marine Acadamy Honor Cadets; Colonial and Oencalogical Records; Colonial Heritage; Flag and Banner Service; Memorials and Marking Historic Spots; National Defense; Patriotic Education; Veterans Service.

Publications: *Colonial Courier*, 3/year. Newsletter. ● *Directory*, annual. ● Also publishes handbook.

Conventions/Meetings: annual general assembly - always April. Washington, DC, United States.

★3048★ NATIONAL SOCIETY, DAUGHTERS OF THE AMERICAN
REVOLUTION (DAR)
1776 D St. NW
Washington, DC 20006-5392
Mrs. Donald S. Blair, Pres.Gen.   PH: (202)628-1776

Founded: 1890. **Members:** 204,000. **Staff:** 150. **Local Groups:** 3,152. **Languages:** English. **National.** Women descendants of Revolutionary War patriots. Conducts historical, educational, and patriotic activities. Maintains Americana museum and documentary collections antedating 1830; organizes Junior American Citizens Clubs for schoolchildren; maintains two schools in the South and supports others; founded National Society of the Children of the American Revolution; initiated American History Month (February) and Constitution Week. **Libraries:** Type: reference.   Subjects: genealogical and historical research. **Awards:** Periodic Good Citizenship (recognition). Recipient: school children. ● ROTC medals. Recipient: graduating cadets. ● Periodic (scholarship). Recipient: Nursing student. ● Annual American History (scholarship). **Committees:** American Heritage; American History Month; American Indians; Americanism and DAR Manual for Citizenship; Children of the American Revolution; Conservation; Constitution Week; DAR Good Citizens; DAR Museum; DAR Service for Veteran-Patients; Ethics; Flag of the United States of America; Genealogical Records; Honor Roll; Insignia; Junior American Citizens; Lineage Research; Motion Picture, Radio, and Television; National Defense Committee of the Daughters of the American Revolution (see separate entry); Public Relations; Units Overseas.

Publications: *Daughters of the American Revolution*, 10/year. Magazine. Covers association activities; includes information on genealogy, the American Revolutionary period, and current national defense issues. **ISSN:** 0011-7013. **Circulation:** 45,000. **Advertising:** accepted. **Also Cited As:** *DAR Magazine.* ● *Directory of Committees,* annual. ● *Proceedings,* annual. Bulletin. ● *Manual For Citizenship.* Book.

Conventions/Meetings: annual congress - always April.

★3049★ NATIONAL SOCIETY, DAUGHTERS OF THE BRITISH
EMPIRE IN THE UNITED STATES OF AMERICA (DBE)
839 Elm Way
Edmonds, WA 98020
Mrs. Ingvard Kvinge, Pres.   PH: (206)774-4041

Founded: 1909. **Members:** 5,000. **Regional Groups:** 4. **State Groups:** 32. **Local Groups:** 271. **Languages:** English. **National.** Women of British or British Commonwealth birth, or who are naturalized subjects of Britain or a Commonwealth country; women with proven British or British Commonwealth ancestry; wives of men born in Britain or the British Commonwealth. Maintains retirement homes for both men and women.

Publications: *National Society, Daughters of the British Empire in the United States of America—Yearbook,* annual. Booklet. **Circulation:** 400. **Advertising:** not accepted.

Conventions/Meetings: annual meeting.

★3050★ NATIONAL SOCIETY DAUGHTERS OF FOUNDERS AND
PATRIOTS OF AMERICA (DFPA)
Park Lane Bldg., Ste. 300-05
2025 I St. NW
Washington, DC 20006
Mrs. James Earl Haynes Jr., Pres.

Founded: 1898. **Members:** 2,250. **State Groups:** 53. **Languages:** English. **National.** Women who are lineal descendants, in the male line of either parent, from an ancestor who settled in any of the colonies between May 13, 1607 and May 13, 1687, and whose intermediate ancestors in the same line gave military service or assistance to the colonies during the American Revolution. Restores records of the 13 original colonies. Places lineage books in libraries throughout the U.S. **Libraries:** Type: reference; not open to the public.   **Awards:** Annual Shadow-Box Award for utstanding contribution to education. **Committees:** Genealogical Records; Historical Education; Lineage Books, DFPA Gazette; Military Education; Restoration Projects; Special Awards and National President's Project.

Publications: *Yearbook-Directory of Chapter Officers,* annual. ● *Gazette,* periodic. Newsletter.

Conventions/Meetings: semiannual congress - always April and October. Washington, DC, United States.

★3051★ NATIONAL SOCIETY DAUGHTERS OF UTAH PIONEERS
(NSDUP)
300 N. Main St.
Salt Lake City, UT 84103-1699
Louise C. Green, Pres.   PH: (801)538-1050

Founded: 1901. **Members:** 24,000. **Staff:** 30. **Regional Groups:** 175. **Local Groups:** 1,200. **Languages:** English. **National.** Female descendants of Utah pioneers. Publishes the histories of Utah pioneers; places historical markers; preserves pioneer documents, relics, and craftsmanship. Maintains Pioneer Memorial Museum and Carriage House in Salt Lake City. Operates speakers' bureau. Conducts lectures. **Libraries:** Type: reference.
  Computer Services: Data base, membership information. **Committees:** Documents Preservation; History; Marker; Museum Artifacts; Relics.

Publications: *Historical Brochure,* monthly. Booklet. ● *Legacy,* quarterly. Newsletter. ● *An Enduring Legacy.* Monograph. ● *Chronicles of Courage.* Monograph.

Conventions/Meetings: annual meeting - always September. Salt Lake City, UT, United States. ● annual seminar - always June. ●.

★3052★ NATIONAL SOCIETY, UNITED STATES DAUGHTERS OF
1812
45 Indian Trail
Sanford, NC 27330
Mrs. George E. Lundeen, Pres.   PH: (919)499-2292

Founded: 1892. **Members:** 4,600. **State Groups:** 38. **Local Groups:** 144. **Languages:** English. **National.** Women descendants of those who rendered civil, military, or naval service during the years 1784-1815. Promotes patriotism and seeks to increase knowledge of American history by preserving documents and relics, marking historic spots, recording family histories and traditions, and celebrating patriotic anniversaries. Operates biographical archives. Conducts speakers' bureau; operates children's services and charitable program; maintains museum; compiles statistics. **Libraries:** Type: reference. Holdings: 400. Subjects: genealogy and history.
  Committees: American Merchant Marine; Bacone Flora Adams Darling Daughters; Lineage and Historical Records; Location of 1812 Graves; Mountain Schools; National Defense; Restoration of Constellation School of the Ozarks; Star Spangled Banner Flag House; Veterans' Rehabilitation.

Publications: *Newsletter,* semiannual. Includes membership list and obituaries. **Advertising:** not accepted. ● *Ancestors Index.* Book. ● *Roster,* periodic. Directory.

Conventions/Meetings: annual conference - always April. Washington, DC, United States.

★3053★ NATIONAL SOCIETY WOMEN DESCENDANTS OF THE
ANCIENT AND HONORABLE ARTILLERY COMPANY (DAH)
9027 S. Damen Ave.
Chicago, IL 60620
Mrs. Luther D. Swanstrom, Pres.   PH: (312)238-0423

Founded: 1927. **Members:** 1,150. **Languages:** English. **National.** Women of lineal descent from members of the Ancient and Honorable Artillery Company (1637-1774) or from members of the General Court (Boston) of 1638. Compiles genealogical data. **Awards:** Periodic (scholarship). Recipient: history students at Hillside School for Boys.

Publications: *Yearbook,* annual. Directory.

Conventions/Meetings: annual congress - Washington, DC, United States.

★3054★ NATIONAL SORORITY OF PHI DELTA KAPPA
8233 S. Martin Luther King Dr.
Chicago, IL 60619
Edna Murray, Exec.Sec.   PH: (312)783-7379

Founded: 1923. **Members:** 5,000. **Regional Groups:** 5. **Languages:** English. **Multinational.** Women who teach or who hold administrative positions in education. Conducts educational conferences (Teach-A-Rama), reading and study centers for youth, youth guidance programs. Awards three lifetime memberships annually to members of the National Association for the Advancement of Colored People; offers tutorial programs. **Libraries:** Type: lending.   Subjects: children's books. **Awards:** Periodic (scholarship). **Computer Services:** Mailing lists. **Committees:** Assault on Illiteracy; Education and Human Rights; History; International Project; Legal Defense Fund; Legislative Affairs; National Council of Negro Women; National Urban League; Wire Service and Schomburg Center for Research and Black Culture.

Publications: *Bulletin,* quarterly. ● *Directory,* annual. ● *Krinon,* annual. Magazine.

Conventions/Meetings: biennial meeting (exhibits).

★3055★ NATIONAL TRANSSEXUAL - TRANSVESTITE FEMINIZATION
UNION (NATTFU)
PO Box 297
Peru, IL 61354
Jean Stevens, Dir.   PH: (815)223-6971

Founded: 1992. **Members:** 250. **Staff:** 3. **Languages:** English. **National.**
Assists transsexuals and transvestites in obtaining the services of plastic
surgeons and physicians for cosmetic surgery and hormone therapy.

Conventions/Meetings: periodic meeting - 1995 June.

★3056★ NATIONAL UNION OF ERITREAN WOMEN - NORTH
AMERICA (NUEW)
PO Box 631
New York, NY 10025   PH: (212)678-1977
Saba Issayas   FX: (212)870-2736

Founded: 1979. **Regional Groups:** 7. **State Groups:** 20. **Languages:**
English. **National.** Women of Eritrean descent in North America. Works to
increase public knowledge of Eritrean women and to promote members'
interests. Conducts fundraising activities.

Publications: *Voice of Eritrean Women* (in English). Newsletter.

Conventions/Meetings: biennial congress.

★3057★ NATIONAL UNITED WOMEN'S SOCIETIES OF THE
ADORATION OF THE MOST BLESSED SACRAMENT (NUWSAMBS)
1127 Freida St.
Dickson City, PA 18519
Ceil D. Lallo, Pres.   PH: (717)489-4364

Founded: 1933. **Members:** 5,695. **Languages:** English. **National.** Women,
16 years and older, affiliated with the Polish National Catholic Church of
America and Canada. Fosters and promotes Christian perfection through
personal, family, and community development. Plans to establish library of
historical data, Polish prose and poetry, and women's magazines. Sponsors
charitable programs.

Publications: *Polka*, quarterly. Magazine.

Conventions/Meetings: semiannual meeting.

★3058★ NATIONAL WOMAN ABUSE PREVENTION PROJECT
(NWAPP)
1112 16th St. NW, Ste. 920
Washington, DC 20036   PH: (202)857-0216
Mary Pat Brygger, Dir.   FX: (202)659-5597

Founded: 1986. **Staff:** 5. **Budget:** US$300,000. **Languages:** English.
National. Works to prevent domestic violence and improve services offered
to battered women. Seeks to increase public awareness of, and sensitivity to,
domestic violence. Conducts educational programs; operates speakers'
bureau. **Libraries:** Type: reference.

Publications: *Exchange*, quarterly. Newsletter. Includes model program
highlights and resource reviews. **Circulation:** 2,500. **Advertising:** not accepted.

★3059★ NATIONAL WOMAN'S CHRISTIAN TEMPERANCE UNION
(WCTU)
1730 Chicago Ave.
Evanston, IL 60201
Rachel B. Kelly, Pres.   PH: (708)864-1396

Founded: 1874. **Members:** 50,000. **Staff:** 19. **Budget:** US$360,000. **State
Groups:** 48. **Local Groups:** 4,000. **Languages:** English. **National.** Nonpartisan, interdenominational Christian women dedicated to educate America's
youth about the harmful effects of alcohol, narcotic drugs, and tobacco on
the human body and American society. Seeks to build sentiment for total
abstinence through teaching the relation of alcohol to the mental, moral,

social, spiritual and physical well-being of the individual and the nation.
Promotes essay, poster, and medal contests as well as intercollegiate
oratorical contests on alcohol and related problems; produces films and
filmstrips on temperance for use in schools and churches; sponsors total
abstinence training camps for children and youth; makes available research
materials to professionals and students; conducts philanthropic activities.
Research and educational programs deal with such topics as alcohol and
traffic accidents; consumer expenditures; teenage drinking; per capita
consumption of alcohol; economic aspects; tobacco and health; gambling;
and narcotics. Sponsors Youth's Temperance Council (ages 13-29) and
Loyal Temperance Legion (ages 6-12). Maintains Frances E. Willard Home as
a museum. **Libraries:** Type: reference.   Subjects: alcohol,
narcotics, tobacco, gambling, and prohibition. **Departments:** Christian Outreach; Education; Home Protection; Legislation/Citizenship; Projection Methods; Public Relations; Social Service.

Publications: *Directory*, annual. ● *Monthly Promoter*. Newsletter. Contains
excerpts of new literature. ● *The Union Signal*, monthly. Magazine. Includes
consumer and Legislative updates and annual index. **ISSN:** 0041-7033.
Circulation: 5,000. ● *The Young Crusader*, monthly. Magazine. For children.
ISSN: 0162-9808. **Circulation:** 2,500.

Conventions/Meetings: annual meeting - always August.

★3060★ NATIONAL WOMAN'S PARTY (NWP)
Sewall-Belmont House
144 Constitution Ave. NE
Washington, DC 20002
Sharon Griffith, Exec.Dir.   PH: (202)546-1210

Founded: 1913. **State Groups:** 8. **Languages:** English. **National.** Strives to
raise the status of women. Directs attention toward equal rights matters;
advocates ratification of the Equal Rights Amendment. Maintains NWP Equal
Rights and Suffrage Art Gallery and Museum in the Sewall-Belmont House in
Washington, DC, a designated national landmark filled with memorabilia of
suffrage and ERA.

Publications: *Equal Rights*, quarterly. Newsletter. ● *Answers to Questions
about the ERA*. Booklet.

Conventions/Meetings: biennial meeting.

★3061★ NATIONAL WOMAN'S RELIEF CORPS, AUXILIARY TO THE
GRAND ARMY OF THE REPUBLIC
629 S. 7th
Springfield, IL 62703
Lurene I. Wentworth, Treas.-Sec.   PH: (217)522-4373

Founded: 1883. **Members:** 12,000. **State Groups:** 33. **Local Groups:** 530.
Languages: English. **National.** Patriotic women over age 13 who are citizens
of the U.S., of good moral character, and are interested in perpetuating the
principles of fraternity, charity, and loyalty for which the Grand Army of the
Republic stood. Members are not required to be blood relatives of Civil War
veterans. Original purpose was to urge the teaching of patriotism and the
Pledge of Allegiance to the flag in private and public schools. Supports
volunteer participation in treatment and rehabilitation programs for patients at
Veterans Administration hospitals. Finances loan funds aat universities,
annual gifts to honor students at at universitites. Promotes Americanism and
patriotic education; cooperates with agencies serving the foreign-born; and
sponsors national essay contest on patriotic topics. Maintains Grand Army of
the Republic Memorial Museum. Has established patriotic and historical
memorials and markers throughout the U.S. and has planted thousands of
trees as "living memorials" to the Grand Army of the Republic. Promotes
child welfare and sponsors a Junior Corps for girls ages 6 to 16. **Awards:**
Periodic (grant). **Committees:** Americanization; Child Welfare; Civil Defense;
Historian and Founders Day; Junior Advisory; Narcotics Prevention and
Education; Radio and Television; Red Cross; Southern Memorial; State
Hospital; Veterans Administration Volunteer Service.

Publications: *General Orders*, bimonthly. Newsletter. ● *Journal of the National Convention*, annual. ● *Roster*, annual. Directory.

★3062★ NATIONAL WOMEN BOWLING WRITERS ASSOCIATION
(NWBW)
8061 Wallace Rd.
Baltimore, MD 21222
Theresa Ray, Sec.   PH: (410)284-6884

Founded: 1948. **Members:** 914. **Languages:** English. **National.** Professional and nonprofessional women writers. Seeks to: promote the sport of bowling; foster communication and exchange of information among members; recognize outstanding publications by members; examine problems common to members. Sponsors writing and photography competitions. Operates charitable program. **Committees:** Arts and Crafts; Courtesy; Exchange Mart; Historian; Knows for News; Luncheon; Special Awards; Writing and Photography Contests.

Publications: *Knows for News*, 5/year. **Advertising:** not accepted. ● *Publicity Guide*. Book.

Conventions/Meetings: annual congress - always April.

★3063★ NATIONAL WOMEN STUDENT'S COALITION (NWSC)
c/o USSA
815 15th St. NW, Ste. 838
Washington, DC 20005   PH: (202)347-8772
Sobrina Smith, Co-Chair   FX: (202)393-5886

Founded: 1978. **Languages:** English. **National.** A subsidiary of the United States Student Association whose members are all women. Lobbies for women students' issues at the national level; acts as a network among members to accomplish such lobbying.

Publications: *Affirmative Action*. Book. ● *Violence Against Women Act*. Book.

Conventions/Meetings: semiannual meeting.

★3064★ NATIONAL WOMEN'S CONFERENCE COMMITTEE (NWCC)
1000 Vermont Ave. NW, Ste. 300
Washington, DC 20005-5605
Dr. Elizabeth A. Abramowitz, Co-Chwm.   PH: (202)842-2790

Members: 470. **State Groups:** 14. **Languages:** English. **National.** Established by a mandate from the first National Women's Conference held in Houston, TX in 1977. Designed to represent and sustain grass roots involvement in women's equality. Purpose is to mobilize support for the National Plan of Action resulting from the conference addressing the need for legal, economic, and social changes to ensure equality. Maintains speakers' bureau. **Task Forces:** Decade of Women; ERA.

Publications: *NWCC Newsletter*, semiannual. ● *Facts and Action Guide*. Booklet.

Conventions/Meetings: annual meeting. ● periodic workshop. ● periodic seminar.

★3065★ NATIONAL WOMEN'S ECONOMIC ALLIANCE FOUNDATION
(NWEAF)
1440 New York Ave. NW, Ste. 300   PH: (202)393-5257
Washington, DC 20005   FX: (202)639-8685
Patricia Harrison, Pres.   TX: 756546

Founded: 1983. **Members:** 750. **Languages:** English. **National.** Executive-level women and men. Promotes dialogue among men and women in industry, business, and government. Focuses on enhancins women's professional, economic, and career status and how to address these issues within the framework of the free enterprise system. Conducts research programs and leadership seminars; offers placement service; maintains

biographical archives. **Awards:** . **Computer Services:** Data base, women on corporate boards.

Publications: *NWEA Outlook*, semiannual. Newsletter. ● *Policy Papers*, periodic. Newsletter. ● *Women Directors of the Top 1000 Corp.s*, annual. Directory. Women who serve on corporte boards of Fortune 1000 comp anies. ● *America's New Women Entrepreneurs*. Book.

Conventions/Meetings: annual meeting.

★3066★ NATIONAL WOMEN'S HEALTH NETWORK (NWHN)
1325 G St. NW
Washington, DC 20005   PH: (202)347-1140
Beverly Baker, Exec.Dir.   FX: (202)347-1140

Founded: 1976. **Members:** 15,000. **Staff:** 5. **Local Groups:** 500. **Languages:** English. **National.** Individual consumers, organizations, and health centers. Represents the women's health movement. Monitors federal health policy as it affects women; testifies before Congress and federal agencies. Supports feminist health projects. Sponsors the Women's Health Clearinghouse, a national resource file on all aspects of women's health care. Operates speakers' bureau. **Committees:** AIDS; Cancer; FDA Monitoring; Health Law and Regulation; National Health Plan; Occupational and Environmental Health; Older Women's Health; Reproductive Rights; Rural Health.

Publications: *National Women's Health Network*, bimonthly. Newsletter. Provides health information and medical alerts for wo men. **ISSN:** 8755-867X. **Circulation:** 1,500. **Advertising:** not accepted. ● *Newsalerts*, periodic. Newsletter.

Conventions/Meetings: annual meeting.

★3067★ NATIONAL WOMEN'S HISTORY PROJECT (NWHP)
7738 Bell Rd.
Windsor, CA 95492   PH: (707)838-6000
Molly MacGregor, Dir.   FX: (707)838-0478

Founded: 1977. **Staff:** 8. **Budget:** US$1,000,000. **Languages:** English. **National.** Encourages multicultural study of women to reclaim contributions and impact of all groups of women and to persuade constructive and expansive social change. Focuses on the rich and inspiring heritage of women's contributions. Sponsors Annual National Women's History Month. Maintains archive for National Women's History Month. Conducts workshops and educational training sessions introducing women into curricula and offers educational consulting for teachers, teacher trainers, administrators, and workplace organizers. Sponsors Women's History Network. Operates speakers' bureau.

Publications: *Women's History Network Directory*, semiannual. Listing of network participants. Includes a brief biograph ical sketch and/or a description of women's history activities. **Circulation:** 800. **Advertising:** not accepted. ● *Women's History Network News*, quarterly. Covers educational resources, commemorative holidays, traveling exhibits, and NWHP activities. Includes calendar of events and news members. **Circulation:** 800. **Advertising:** not accepted. ● *Women's History Resource Catalog*, annual. Includes books, films, records, posters, and program planning guides on women's history. Also includes subject index. **Circulation:** 300,000. **Advertising:** accepted.

Conventions/Meetings: semiannual conference.

★3068★ NATIONAL WOMEN'S LAW CENTER (NWLC)
1616 P St. NW
Washington, DC 20036
Nancy Duff Campbell, Co-Pres.   PH: (202)328-5160

Founded: 1972. **Staff:** 18. **Languages:** English. **National.** Works to guarantee equality for women under the law and to seek protection and advancement of their legal rights and issues at all levels. Areas of interest include employment, education, health, income security, tax reform, reproductive rights, child support enforcement, dependent care, and the family. Successful projects have included: obtaining a back-pay ruling on sex and race discrimination for employees of a major bank; securing court order that government must enforce laws prohibiting sex discrimination in schools; litigating to establish women's statutory and constitutional rights and ensure enforcement of those rights; securing enforcement of state child support laws without regard to family income. Conducts research on current and proposed policies and regulations to evaluate their impact on women's rights and determines the legality and constitutionality of practices and policies affecting women.

Publications: *Sex Discrimination in Education.* Book. ● *Dependent Care Tax Provisions in The States.* Book. ● *Title 1X: A practical Guide to Achieving Sex Equity in Education.* Book.

★3069★ NATIONAL WOMEN'S MARTIAL ARTS FEDERATION
(NWMAF)
PO Box 4688
Corpus Christi, TX 78469-4688
Melanie Fine, Treas.   PH: (512)855-6975

Founded: 1972. **Members:** 550. **Membership Dues:** US$12 annual. **Regional Groups:** 13. **Languages:** English. **National.** Female martial artists. Promotes excellence in martial arts. Encourages "the widest range of women" to train in the spirit of building individual and collective strength. Sponsors competitions, educational, and charitable programs. Maintains biographical archives. **Awards:** Periodic Lifetime Achievement.

Publications: *NWMAF Newsletter,* quarterly. Includes articles and features on female maritial artists, and news about upcoming events. **Advertising:** accepted. **Alternate Formats:** online. ● *Directory,* periodic.

Conventions/Meetings: annual meeting (exhibits). ● periodic workshop. ● periodic regional meeting.

★3070★ NATIONAL WOMEN'S PARTY
144 Constitution Ave. NE
Washington, DC 20002
Mary Eastwood, President   PH: (202)546-1210

Founded: 1913. **Members:** 2,500. **Regional Groups:** 5. **Languages:** English. **National.** Women whose primary political goal is the ratification of the Equal Rights Amendment. Supports and promotes other legislation and political actions relevant to women's issues such as domestic violence, pay equity, and sexual harassment.

Publications: *Equal Rights* (in English).

★3071★ NATIONAL WOMEN'S STUDIES ASSOCIATION (NWSA)
University of Maryland
College Park, MD 20742-1325
Deborah Louis, Dir.   PH: (301)405-5573

Founded: 1977. **Members:** 4,000. **Budget:** US$550,000. **Regional Groups:** 12. **Languages:** English. **National.** Teachers, students, community activists, and interested individuals; academic and community-based programs, projects, and groups interested in feminist education. Works to further the social, political, and professional development of women's studies programs. Supports feminist causes; lobbies for women's studies at the elementary, secondary, and college level; encourages the development of a network for distributing information on women's studies; cooperates with women's projects in communities; Compiles statistics. Conducts conferences to address topics such as: new developments and controversies in feminist research and theory in the humanities, social sciences, and sciences; curricular development; political and legal strategies; intersection of race and gender; international women's studies. **Awards:** Periodic (scholarship). ● Periodic Best manuscript in women's studies (monetary). **Computer Services:** Mailing lists, women's studies programs. **Projects:** Inclusion/Empowerment of Under-represented Constituencies; Women's Studies Archival. **Committees:** African - American Women; Aging and

Ageism; Community ollege; Disability; Jewish Women; Lesbian; Poor and Working Class Women; Women's Centers/Services.

Publications: *Biannual Women's Studies Program Directory,* periodic. ● *NWSA Journal,* quarterly. **Price:** US$21/year for individual members; US$32/year for individual nonmembers; US$40/year for member groups; US$80/year for nonmember groups.. **Advertising:** accepted. ● *NWSAction,* periodic. Newsletter. Contains calendar of events, conference reports, fellowship and employment opportunity listings, association news, and resources listings. **Circulation:** 4,000. **Advertising:** not accepted. ● *Liberal Learning and The Women's Studies Major.* Book.

Conventions/Meetings: annual conference (exhibits).

★3072★ NATIVE AMERICAN WOMEN'S HEALTH EDUCATION
RESOURCE CENTER
PO Box 572
Lake Andes, SD 57356-0572
Charon Asetoyer, Director   PH: (605)487-7072

Languages: English. **National.** Promotes education and health awareness among Native American women. Seeks to reduce the occurance of fetal alcohol syndrome.

★3073★ NATIVE DAUGHTERS OF THE GOLDEN WEST (NDGW)
543 Baker St.
San Francisco, CA 94117
Karen Perazzo, Exec.Sec.   PH: (415)563-9091

Founded: 1886. **Members:** 13,500. **Staff:** 10. **Languages:** English. **National.** Native born Californian women. Works to promote the history of the State of California, venerate California pioneers, promote child welfare programs, assist in marking and restoring historic landmarks, and participate in civic affairs. Maintains museum and historical collection. **Libraries:** Type: reference. **Awards:** Annual (scholarship).

Publications: *Star,* bimonthly. Newsletter. ● *Proceedings.* Booklet.

Conventions/Meetings: annual meeting - always June.

★3074★ NAVY MOTHERS' CLUBS OF AMERICA (NMCA)
1718 Spruce St.
Philadelphia, PA 19103
Peggy Rizzo, Cmdr.   PH: (215)732-1566

Founded: 1930. **Members:** 3,000. **State Groups:** 27. **Local Groups:** 185. **Languages:** English. **National.** Mothers of present or former servicemen and women in the active or reserve branches of the Navy, Marines, or Coast Guard. Conducts welfare activities; visits veterans' and naval hospitals; sponsors social programs for servicemen.

Publications: *Navy Mothers' News,* bimonthly. Newsletter.

Conventions/Meetings: biennial meeting. ● biennial regional meeting.

★3075★ NAVY WIFELINE ASSOCIATION (NWA)
Washington Navy Yard, Bldg. 172
Washington, DC 20374   PH: (202)433-2333
Peggy Mauz, Chwm.   FX: (202)433-2639

Founded: 1965. **Languages:** English. **National.** Spouses of both officers and enlisted men in the Navy, Marine Corps, and Coast Guard. Serves as a clearinghouse for information in an effort to better educate members on the importance of their spouses' careers. Fosters a sense of belonging among spouses of naval personnel by serving as a point of contact to help them combat the problems encountered due to separation from loved ones and constantly changing environments. Operates Family Ombudsman Program, which functions as a liaison between command family members and Navy, Marine Corps, and Coast Guard officials. Maintains Navy Family Service Center, which provides information and referral, counseling, family programs, and hospitality kits to active duty and retired Navy personnel and their families. Provides child care services.

Publications: *Navy Family Lifeline*, quarterly. Magazine. Includes articles from Navy wives worldwide. ● *Social Customs and Traditions of The National Services*. Book. ● *Guidelines for The Spouses of Commanding Officers and Executive Officers*. Book.

★3076★ NAVY WIVES CLUBS OF AMERICA (NWCA)
c/o Nancy Perry
149 Whitney St.
Auburn, ME 04210
Nancy Perry, Pres.

Founded: 1936. **Members:** 1,383. **Regional Groups:** 5. **Local Groups:** 83. **Languages:** English. **National.** Spouses of all enlisted persons in the Navy, Marine Corps, and Coast Guard, as well as their retired and active reserve components. Members participate in community projects and charitable programs. **Awards:** Annual President's Theme. ● Periodic (scholarship). Recipient: Childrenof Navy, Marine Corps, and Coast Guard enlisted personnel.

Publications: *Mailing Directory*, periodic. ● *Monthly Mimeo*. Bulletin. ● *Operating Manual*. Book.

Conventions/Meetings: annual conference - always October.

★3077★ NETWORK OF ENTREPRENEURIAL WOMEN (NEW)
PO Box 1100
Falls Church, VA 22041
Barbara Ragsdale, President   PH: (703)435-4449

Founded: 1984. **Members:** 200. **Languages:** English. **Local.** Business women promoting and supporting women in business. Coordinates a network of contacts for business women. Organizes social and informational gatherings.

Publications: *NEW Trends* (in English). Newsletter.

★3078★ NETWORK OF GAY AND LESBIAN ALUMNI/AE
        ASSOCIATIONS (NetGALA)
PO Box 15141
Washington, DC 20003

Founded: 1985. **Members:** 500. **Budget:** US$5,000. **Regional Groups:** 3. **Languages:** English. **National.** Provides leadership and support to gay, lesbian, and bisexual alum groups. Works to create a greater understanding between academic institutions and gay and lesbian graduates, students, faculty, and staff. Acts as a clearinghouse for information and ideas in the gay and lesbian community. Provides professional and social network. Assists in organizing new gay and lesbian alum associations. Sponsors charitable and educational programs. Compiles statistics. Offers referral and placement service. **Computer Services:** Mailing lists. **Alternate name:** NetGALA.

Publications: *NetGALA News*, quarterly. Newsletter. **Advertising:** accepted. ● *Directory*, periodic.

Conventions/Meetings: annual conference.

★3079★ NETWORK FOR PROFESSIONAL WOMEN (NPW)
c/o JoAnne P. Smith
216 Main St.
Hartford, CT 06103   PH: (203)727-1988
JoAnne P. Smith, Pres.   FX: (203)727-9623

Founded: 1979. **Staff:** 3. **Languages:** English. **National.** Seeks educate and motivate professional women in all facets of their lives. Sponsors seminars and workshops on topics including management of credit, employment networking, IRAs, and reentering the work force.

Conventions/Meetings: annual women's conference conference.

★3080★ NETWORKING PROJECT FOR DISABLED WOMEN AND
        GIRLS (NPDWG)
c/o YWCA of City of New York
610 Lexington Ave.
New York, NY 10022
Angela Perez, Dir.   PH: (212)735-9767

Founded: 1984. **Staff:** 5. **Languages:** English. **National.** A project of the Young Women's Christian Association of New York City. Purpose is to increase the educational, social, and career aspirations of adolescent girls with disabilities by linking them to successful, disabled role models. Provides support groups; offers advocacy training, pre-employment skills development, and one-to-one mentoring. Organizes visits to the role model's workplace. Currently operates in the New York City area and is providing technical assistance to facilitate replication at several sites throughout the country.

Publications: *Book*. books, and videotapes.

Conventions/Meetings: periodic meeting.

★3081★ NEW WAYS TO WORK
149 9th St.
San Francisco, CA 94103
Barney Olmstad, Co-Dir.   PH: (415)552-1000

Founded: 1972. **National.** Works to assist women in alternative career development programs such as job sharing, permanent part-time status, and flex time programs.

★3082★ NINETY-NINES, INTERNATIONAL WOMEN PILOTS
Will Rogers Airport
PO Box 59965
Oklahoma City, OK 73159   PH: (405)685-7969
Loretta Jean Gragg, Exec.Dir.   FX: (405)685-7985

Founded: 1929. **Members:** 6,900. **Budget:** US$400,000. **Languages:** English. **Multinational.** Women pilots united to foster a better understanding of aviation. Encourages cross-country flying; provides consulting service and gives indoctrination flights; flies missions for charitable assistance programs; endorses air races. Develops programs and courses for schools and youth organizations and teaches ground school subjects. Participates in flying competitions. Maintains resource center, biographical archives, and a 700 volume library with a display area dedicated to the preservation of women's achievements in aviation. Bestows Amelia Earhart Memorial Scholarship Award, entitling winners to advanced flight training or courses in specialized branches of aviation; awards Amelia Earhart Research Scholar Grant to a specialized, professional scholar. Operates placement service. Conducts seminar on safety education, lecture on personal aviation experience, and charitable event. Compiles statistics. **Computer Services:** Data base, information on women in aviation careers; data base, membership listing. **Committees:** Aerospace Archives Librarian; Airmarking; Audio Visual Education; Flying Activities; Historian; NIFA Award; Public Relations; Safety Education; Scrapbook; NIFA Award; Public Relations; Safety Education.

Publications: *Ninety-Nine News*, 10/year. **Circulation:** 7,000. **Advertising:** accepted. ● *Ninety-Nines, International Women Pilots—Membership Directory*, annual. **Circulation:** 7,000. ● *History of the Ninety-Nine—Sixty and Counting*. ● Also publishes brochures.

Conventions/Meetings: annual meeting, Business. (exhibits).

★3083★ NON-TRADITIONAL EMPLOYMENT FOR WOMEN
243 W. 20th St.
New York, NY 10011
Lola Snyder, Dir.   PH: (212)627-6252

Founded: 1978. **National.** Promotes women's blue-collar career development such as construction and factory work. Offers placement services and technical assistance. Works to increase the number of women in trade occupations.

★3084★ NORTH AMERICAN INDIAN WOMEN'S ASSOCIATION
(NAIWA)
9602 Maestor's Ln.
Gaithersburg, MD 20879
Ann French, Contact   PH: (301)330-0397

Founded: 1970. **Regional Groups:** 6. **Local Groups:** 19. **Languages:** English. **National.** Women, 18 years and older, who are members of federally recognized tribes. Seeks to foster the general well-being of Indian people through unity of purpose. Promotes inter-tribal communication, awareness of the Native American culture, betterment of family life, health, and education, and strengthening of communication among Native Americans.

Conventions/Meetings: annual conference - always June.

★3085★ NORTH AMERICAN NETWORK OF WOMEN RUNNERS
(NANWR)
PO Box 719
Bala Cynwyd, PA 19004
Phoebe B. Jones, Dir.   PH: (215)668-9886

Founded: 1979. **Members:** 500. **Staff:** 8. **State Groups:** 10. **Languages:** English. **National.** Women runners, fitness participants, racers, health professionals, women in sports, and women concerned about opportunities for health, fitness, and sport. Dedicated to winning the financial resources that will make athletic careers, physical fitness, and good health accessible to women internationally. Holds low-cost women's workouts with child care in various sports through community, school, and business facilities.

Publications: *Newsletter*, quarterly.

Conventions/Meetings: biennial conference.

★3086★ NOW LEGAL DEFENSE AND EDUCATION FUND (NOW
LDEF)
99 Hudson St., 12th Fl.
New York, NY 10013   PH: (212)925-6635
Helen Neuborne, Exec.Dir.   FX: (212)226-1066

Founded: 1970. **Staff:** 25. **Languages:** English. **National.** Functions as an educational and litigating sister group to the National Organization for Women to provide legal assistance to women and to educate the public on gender discrimination and other equal rights issues. Purpose is to combat, by legal action and educational and community-based projects, discrimination based on race, sex, religion, or national origin. Conducts research; compiles and publishes facts and statistics concerning the legal, educational, and economic situation of women. Sponsors Women's Media Project, Project on Equal Education Rights, National Judicial Education Program to Promote Equality for Women and Men in the Courts, Women's Economic Rights Project, and Family Law Project. **Programs:** Information and Referral Service; Legal Intern.

Publications: *State by State Guide to Women's Legal Rights*. Book. ● *Facts on Reproductive Rights*. Book.

Conventions/Meetings: annual meeting.

★3087★ OFF OUR BACKS
2423 18th St. NW
Washington, DC 20009
Amy Hamilton, Office Coordinator   PH: (202)234-8072

Founded: 1970. **Members:** 22,000. **Staff:** 12. **Budget:** US$80,000. **Languages:** English. **Multinational.** Radical feminists. Aims to raise awareness of women's rights. Conducts research on women's issues as they pertain to the modern women's movement.

Publications: *Off Our Backs* (in English), monthly. Journal.

★3088★ OLDER WOMEN'S LEAGUE (OWL)
666 11th St. NW, Ste. 700
Washington, DC 20001   PH: (202)783-6686
Joan A. Kuriansky, Exec.Dir.   FX: (202)638-2356

Founded: 1980. **Members:** 21,000. **Staff:** 11. **Budget:** US$700,000. **State Groups:** 2. **Local Groups:** 120. **Languages:** English. **National.** Middle-aged and older women; persons of any age who support issues of concern to mid-life and older women. Primary issues include access to health care insurance, support for family caregivers, reform of social security, access to jobs and pensions for older women, effects of budget cuts on women, and maintaining self-sufficiency throughout life. Operates speakers' bureau; prepares educational materials; compiles statistics.

Publications: *OWL OBSERVER*, bimonthly. Newsletter. Membership activities. **Advertising:** not accepted. ● *Status Report*, annual. Booklet. ● *Older Women and Job Discrimination*. Book. ● *Model State Bills*. Book. ● *A Matter of Life and Death*. Videos.

Conventions/Meetings: biennial meeting.

★3089★ ONE, INCORPORATED (OI)
3340 Country Club Dr.
Los Angeles, CA 90019
W. Dorr Legg, Sec.-Treas.   PH: (213)735-5252

Founded: 1952. **Budget:** US$90,000. **Languages:** English. **National.** Corporate trustees. Provides group therapy, individual counseling, and referrals to gays and lesbians. Offers some programs for transsexuals and transvestites. Provides college-level courses, lectures, and panels under state-authorized M.A. and Ph.D. degree program (ONE Institute of Homophile Studies). Sponsors placement service; participates with public and community committees. Compiles statistics and bibliographies; maintains biographical archives; operates speakers' bureau. **Libraries:** Type: reference. Holdings: 22,000; periodicals, books, archival material, audio recordings. **Committees:** Audiovisual; Editorial; News Bureau.

Publications: *ONE Calendar*, 9-10/year. Bulletin. ● *ONEletter*, monthly. Newsletter. **Advertising:** accepted.

Conventions/Meetings: annual meeting. ● periodic seminar.

★3090★ OPERATION RESCUE (OR)
PO Box 1180   PH: (607)723-4012
Binghamton, NY 13902   FX: (607)723-4265

Founded: 1987. **Languages:** English. **National.** Coalition of pro-life pastors and laypeople of all faiths. Organizes rescues/sit-ins at abortion clinics to block patient entry and: "save the lives of innocent children"; stop the exploitation of mothers from the "violence" of abortion; "call America to repent for allowing 25 million children to be slaughtered since 1973"; "rescue children and mothers in a way that produces political change."

★3091★ ORDER OF THE DAUGHTERS OF THE KING (DOK)
PO Box 2196
Marietta, GA 30061-2196   PH: (404)419-8580
Elizabeth A. Hart, Pres.   FX: (404)419-0686

Founded: 1885. **Members:** 12,000. **Regional Groups:** 51. **Languages:** English. **National.** Lay order for women in the Episcopal church (and churches in communion with the Episcopal church or sharing the historic Episcopate) who have taken vows of prayer and service for the spread of Christ's Kingdom. Supports domestic and overseas missionaries. **Awards:** Periodic (scholarship). **Alternate name:** Daughters of the King.

Publications: *The Royal Cross*, quarterly. Newsletter.

Conventions/Meetings: periodic National retreat meeting

★3092★ ORDER OF THE GOLDEN CHAIN (OGC)
584 Bloomfield Ave., Apt. 10-B
West Caldwell, NJ 07006
Freda R. Jayson, Grand Sec.   PH: (201)226-8555

Founded: 1929. **Members:** 2,000. **Local Groups:** 10. **Languages:** English. **National.** Female relatives of Masons and Master Masons. Supports cancer and leukemia research and programs for learning disabilities.

Conventions/Meetings: annual meeting.

★3093★ ORGANIZATION OF CHINESE AMERICAN WOMEN (OCAW)
1300 N St. NW, Ste. 100
Washington, DC 20005   PH: (202)638-0330
Pauline W. Tsui, Exec.Dir.   FX: (202)638-2196

Founded: 1977. **Members:** 2,000. **Languages:** English. **National.** Advances the cause of Chinese American women in the U.S. and fosters public awareness of their special needs and concerns. Seeks to integrate Chinese American women into the mainstream of women's activities and programs. Addresses issues such as: equal employment opportunities at both the professional and nonprofessional levels; overcoming stereotypes; racial and sexual discrimination and restrictive traditional beliefs; assistance to poverty-stricken recent immigrants; access to leadership and policymaking positions. Develops training models for Chinese and Asian American women. Conducts training and job placement for class participants, widening teenage women's career choices, and networking for Chinese American women. **Programs:** Communication; Cultural Events; Research; Technical Assistance; Women to Women's Exchange.

Publications: *OCAW Speaks*, quarterly. Newsletter.

Conventions/Meetings: biennial conference. ● periodic banquet.

★3094★ ORGANIZATION OF PAN ASIAN AMERICAN WOMEN (PANASIA)
PO Box 39128
Washington, DC 20016
Nguyen Minh Chau, Pres.

Founded: 1976. **Members:** 100. **Languages:** English. **National.** To provide a voice for the concerns of Asian Pacific-American (APA) women and to encourage their full participation in all aspects of American society. Seeks to: promote an accurate and realistic image of APA women in America; develop the leadership skills and increase the occupational mobility of these women; maintain a national communications network. Produces legislative updates on national issues of concern to Asian Pacific Americans. Sponsors workshops and lectures; maintains speakers' bureau.

Publications: *Membership Directory*, annual. ● *Pan Asia News*, periodic. Newsletter. ● *Pan Asan Women: A Vital Force*. Book.

★3095★ ORGANIZATION OF WOMEN ARCHITECTS AND DESIGN PROFESSIONALS (OWA)
PO Box 26570
San Francisco, CA 94126   PH: (415)550-6051

Founded: 1972. **Members:** 200. **Languages:** English. **National.** Women architects and other design professionals. Functions as a support and informational network. Organizes meetings and discussions on architectural issues. Offers career development assistance.

Publications: *OWA Newsletter* (in English).

★3096★ OUT/LOOK FOUNDATION
540 Castro St.
San Francisco, CA 94114   PH: (415)626-1955
Jeffrey Escoffier, Dir.   FX: (415)626-3334

Founded: 1988. **Staff:** 6. **Budget:** US$450,000. **Languages:** English. **National.** Promotes public debate on gay/lesbian social and cultural issues in the community. Sponsors educational programs.

Publications: *Out/Look*, quarterly. Journal. **ISSN:** 0089-7733. **Circulation:** 15,000. **Advertising:** not accepted.

Conventions/Meetings: annual OutWrite National Lesbian and Gay Writer's Conference (exhibits).

★3097★ PAN AMERICAN LIAISON COMMITTEE OF WOMEN'S ORGANIZATIONS (PALCO)
3203 Beech St. NW
Washington, DC 20015
Ruth Donaldson, Pres.   PH: (202)362-3274

Founded: 1944. **Members:** 200. **Multinational.** Individuals and women's organizations in Western Hemisphere countries. Encourages closer friendship and understanding through cultural, educational, charitable, scientific, and literary projects and activities. Organizes training courses in leadership development; conducts workshops on the Laubach method of training literacy teachers and seminars on Pan-Americanism and parliamentary procedure. Awards scholarships; gives financial support to small, local self-help initiatives.

Publications: *Newsletter*, monthly. ● *Roster*, biennial.

★3098★ PAN AMERICAN WOMEN'S ASSOCIATION (PAWA)
c/o Frances R. Grant
310 W. End Ave., Apt. 16C
New York, NY 10023
Frances R. Grant, Pres.   PH: (212)362-0710

Founded: 1930. **Languages:** English. **Multinational.** Women united to foster greater inter-American understanding. Promotes common action for the well-being of the people of the Western Hemisphere through cultural and educational exchange. Organizes music, art, dance, and student programs; sponsors periodic panel discussions.

★3099★ PAN PACIFIC AND SOUTHEAST ASIA WOMEN'S ASSOCIATION OF THE U.S.A. (PPSEAWA-USA)
Box 1531, Madison Square Sta.
New York, NY 10159
Ann Allen, Pres.   PH: (212)228-5307

Founded: 1928. **Members:** 350. **Budget:** US$50,000. **Local Groups:** 5. **Languages:** English. **Multinational.** Seeks to strengthen peaceful ties by fostering international understanding and friendship among the women of Asia and the Pacific and women of the U.S.A. Promotes cooperation among women of these regions for the study and improvement of social, economic, and cultural conditions. Engages in studies on Asian and Pacific affairs; offers friendship, hospitality, and assistance to Asian and Pacific area women; presents programs of educational and social interest, dealing with the customs and cultures of Asian and Pacific countries; Conducts lectures, panels, and workshops.

Publications: *USA Newsletter*, semiannual. Informs members about association activities. **Advertising:** not accepted. ● *International Bulletin*, semiannual. Provides information of significant activites in member countries and interest areas.

Conventions/Meetings: annual meeting. ● triennial conference - 1994 Aug., Nuku Alofa, Tonga.

★3100★ PANEL OF AMERICAN WOMEN (PAW)
205 19th St. NE, Apt. 108
Canton, OH 44714
Nancy Boylan, Exec. Officer   PH: (216)453-6160

Founded: 1957. **Members:** 150. **Regional Groups:** 2. **Local Groups:** 14. **Languages:** English. **National.** Groups of women volunteers in cities all over the United States promoting understanding among people of all races and religions. Members present panel-type programs for church, school, and civic groups, discussing their personal experiences in confronting prejudice and discrimination. Each panel usually includes a moderator and four or five panelists representing Protestant, Catholic, Jewish, Black, Hispanic, Native American, and/or other ethnic groups, depending on the ethnic makeup of the community. The panels discuss issues affecting women and the prejudices they and their families have met in schools, housing, employment, and other situations; panels then answer questions from the audience. Also sponsors youth panels. Acts as a community resource, putting organizations in touch with agencies or providing them with resource materials.

Publications: *National Panel of American Women*, 3-4/year. Newsletter.

★3101★ PARENT CARE (PC)
9041 Colgate St.
Indianapolis, IN 46268-1210   PH: (317)872-9913
Sarah Killion, Admin.Dir.   FX: (317)872-5464

Founded: 1982. **Members:** 400. **Staff:** 1. **Languages:** English. **National.** Parents of premature and high-risk infants, perinatal professionals, parent groups, and related service organizations. Goals are to: support efforts of parents in forming and maintaining local groups; facilitate and encourage communication between local groups, parents, and perinatal professionals increase public awareness of special needs of families of premature and high risk infants. Offers educational programs; maintains speakers' bureau. **Libraries:** Type: reference. **Computer Services:** Data base, support groups; mailing lists. **Committees:** Development; Education; Policy.

Publications: *News Brief*, quarterly. Newsletter. Contains articles on neonatal intensive care. **Advertising:** accepted. ● *Parents of Prematures Resource Directory*, annual. ● *Guiding Your Infant Through Preterm Development*. Book.

Conventions/Meetings: annual conference (exhibits) - 1994 Jan., Salt Lake City, UT, United States. ● periodic regional meeting.

★3102★ PARENTS' CHOICE FOUNDATION (PCF)
PO Box 185
Newton, MA 02168   PH: (617)965-5913
Diana Huss Green, Editor-in-Chief   FX: (617)963-4516

Founded: 1978. **Languages:** English. **National.** Provides parents and professionals with a central source of information about the videos, books, toys, games, music, television programs, movies, and computer software selections made by parents, children, teachers, librarians, and other experts. **Awards:** .

Publications: *Parents' Choice*, quarterly. ● *What Kids Who Don't Like to Read, Like to Read*. Booklet.

★3103★ PARENTS AND FRIENDS OF LESBIANS AND GAYS
          FEDERATION (ParentsFLAG)
PO Box 27605
Washington, DC 20038   PH: (202)638-4200
Thomas H. Sauerman, Exec. Officer   FX: (202)638-0243

Founded: 1981. **Budget:** US$550,000. **Local Groups:** 235. **Languages:** English. **National.** Selfhelp and educational organization that provides support and referrals for parents of local gay group members in 235 cities across North America and abroad. Offers emotional support for parents and children trying to keep family bonds intact. Has sponsored national educational efforts directed toward schools, professional groups, and other parents' organizations, and worked for legislative protection of gay rights.

Publications: *PFLAG Pole Newsletter*, bimonthly. Covers regional and national news. ● *About Our Children*. Booklet. ● *Can We Understand?*. Booklet. ● *Is Homosexuality a Sin?*. Booklet.

Conventions/Meetings: annual meeting.

★3104★ PARENTS HELPING PARENTS (PHP)
535 Race St., Ste. 140
San Jose, CA 95126
Florene M. Poyadue R.N., Exec.Dir.   PH: (408)288-5010

Founded: 1976. **Members:** 3,380. **Staff:** 10. **Budget:** US$486,000. **Regional Groups:** 3. **Languages:** English. **National.** Parents, professionals, lay counselors, families, and friends committed to alleviating the problems, hardships, and concerns of families with children having special needs, such as physical, mental, emotional, or learning disabilities; intensive nursery care; preemies; long-term, chronic, or terminal illness due to accident, birth defect, or illness. Helps children with special needs receive the care, services, education, love, hope, respect, and acceptance they need. Offers education, support, information, and training for parents to decrease isolation and increase a sense of personal control. Provides a forum for the discussion of financial, social, and emotional needs, ideas, and experiences. Conducts workshops for professionals on communicating with individuals with disabilities and their families and assistance in psychosocial care of patients. Sponsors the Family Friends program, which matches volunteers 55 and older with chronically ill and disabled children 12 and younger to provide support and respite for parents, growth for the child, and an inspiring job opportunity for the senior citizen. Keeps parents abreast of legislation laws affecting education for disabled children. Offers: parent instruction and enhancement; behavior management training; peer counseling and training; early intervention workshops; individual education planning; guidance sessions. **Libraries:** Type: reference. Holdings: 500. Subjects: disabled children. **Awards:** Periodic Valley of Hearts. **Computer Services:** Mailing lists. **Divisions:** Autistic; Cleft Lip/Palate; General; Handicaps Understanding and Group Support; Intensive Care Nursery Parents; Learning Disabled Network; Parents of Down Syndrome; Parents of Near Drownings; Residential Placement Network; Sickle Cell Community Network. **Programs:** Family Friends Respite; Infant Massage; Newborn Gift; Siblings of Disabled Children; Visiting Parent.

Publications: *Special Addition*, bimonthly. Newsletter. Includes medical and legislative updates, division highlights, association news, and calendar of events. ● *Visiting Parents*. Book. ● *Communicating With Parents of Disabled*. Book. ● *Steps to Starting Self Help*. Book.

Conventions/Meetings: annual meeting (exhibits) - always October. San Jose, CA, United States.

★3105★ PARENTS WITHOUT PARTNERS (PWP)
8807 Colesville Rd.   PH: (301)588-9354
Silver Spring, MD 20910   TF: (800)637-7974
C. Nelson, Contact   FX: (301)588-9216

Founded: 1957. **Members:** 112,000. **Staff:** 15. **Budget:** US$2,000,000. **Regional Groups:** 90. **Local Groups:** 750. **Languages:** English. **National.** Custodial and noncustodial parents who are single by reason of widowhood, divorce, separation, or otherwise. To promote the study of and to alleviate the problems of single parents in relation to the welfare and upbringing of their children and the acceptance into the general social order of single parents and their children. Participates in research of single parent topics. Operates Single Parent Clearinghouse. Compiles statistics; sponsors competitions; holds International Family Talent Exhibit. **Libraries:** Type: reference. Holdings: 500. Subjects: divorce, death, single parenting, and custody. **Awards:** Annual (scholarship). **Committees:** Family and Youth; International Youth Council; Legislative Affairs; Programs and Education; Public Relations; Research and Development; SOS (Community Services).

Publications: *Directory of Chapters*, annual. ● *The Single Parent*, bimonthly. Newsletter. **Advertising:** accepted.

Conventions/Meetings: annual meeting (exhibits) - always July.

★3106★ PATHFINDER INTERNATIONAL (PI)
9 Galen St., Ste. 217
Watertown, MA 02172   PH: (617)924-7200
Daniel E. Pellegrom, Pres.   FX: (617)924-3833

Founded: 1957. **Staff:** 115. **Budget:** US$20,000,000. **Languages:** English. **Multinational.** Established to find, demonstrate, and promote new and more efficient family planning programs in developing countries. Objectives are to: introduce and expand the availability of effective family planning services; improve the welfare of families in developing countries; assist developing countries in implementing population policies favorable to national development. Conducts activities with a concern for upholding human rights, enhancing the status and role of women, and respecting the views of family planning clients.

Publications: *Pathways*, quarterly. Newsletter.

★3107★ PEACE LINKS
747 8th St. SE
Washington, DC 20003
Carol Williams, Dir.   PH: (202)544-0805

National. Women working to redirect national policies in the United States away from nuclear weapons and war into peaceful ways of resolving conflicts. Strives to redirect more of the United States' resources toward human needs. Conducts a letter-writing exchange between Americans and individuals in the former Soviet Union.

★3108★ PEO SISTERHOOD
3700 Grand Ave.
Des Moines, IA 50312   PH: (515)255-3153
Deborah Cowan, CAO   FX: (515)255-3820

Founded: 1869. **Members:** 247,600. **Staff:** 39. **State Groups:** 50. **Local Groups:** 5,640. **Languages:** English. **National.** International women's organization seeking to further opportunities for higher education for women. Has established International Peace Scholarship Fund, Educational Loan Fund, Program for Continuing Education, and PEO Scholar Awards. Maintains Cottey Junior College for Women, Nevada, MO.

Publications: *Directory of Presidents*, annual. ● *PEO Record*, 10/year. Newsletter. **ISSN:** 0746-5130.

Conventions/Meetings: biennial meeting - 1993 Sept. 17 - 19, Atlanta, GA, United States; 1995, Denver, CO, United States; 1997, Seattle, WA, United States; 1999, Baltimore, MD, United States.

★3109★ PEOPLE FOR LIFE (PFL)
3375 N. Dousman
Milwaukee, WI 53212
Pam Cira, Chairperson   PH: (414)332-3423

Founded: 1984. **Languages:** English. **National.** A grass roots, pro-life organization. Provides counseling for anyone experiencing problems following an abortion, adoption placement, or miscarriage; matches counselor with similar experience to counselee. Facilitates postadoption support group for women who have placed their child up for adoption or are considering such a placement. Provides training for counselors. Sponsors seminars. Compiles statistics. **Committees:** Public Relations; Speakers' Bureau; Statistics.

Publications: *Annual Statistics*. Journal. ● *Counselor*, monthly. Newsletter. Organization activities newsletter. Includes calendar of events.

★3110★ PEP
PO Box 6306
Captain Cook, HI 96704   PH: (808)929-9696
Ryam Nearing, Pres.   FX: (808)929-9831

Founded: 1984. **Members:** 600. **Membership Dues:** Supporting, US$30 annual; Patron, US$60 annual. **Languages:** English. **National.** Promotes polyfidelity, an equalitarian form of group marriage. Provides a forum for exchange between members. Works to increase public awareness through media campaign and educational programs. Maintains speakers' bureau.

Publications: *Loving More Journal*, quarterly. **Advertising:** accepted. **Also Cited As:** *PEPTALK*. ● *Loving More: The Polyfidelity Primer*. Book.

Conventions/Meetings: annual meeting (exhibits).

★3111★ PHARMACISTS FOR LIFE (PFL)
PO Box 130
Ingomar, PA 15127   PH: (412)364-3422
Bogomir M. Kuhar Pharm., Pres.   TF: (800)227-8359
    FX: (412)364-5265

Founded: 1984. **Languages:** English. **Multinational.** Pharmacists and interested groups and individuals. Seeks to educate pharmacists, other medical professionals, and the public about the "abortion holocaust." Defends the right to life from conception to natural death, regardless of biological stage, dependency, or residence. Provides medical supplies and vitamins to women and crisis pregnancy centers. Provides children's services; sponsors charitable, educational, and research programs. Maintains speakers' bureau. Compiles statistics. Offers financial, legal, and medical referrals. **Libraries:** Type: reference.

Publications: *Beginnings*, bimonthly. Newsletter. Contains book and literature reviews, guest analyses and editor ials, and news on current events. **Advertising:** accepted. ● *Can Cancer Pain be Relieved?*. Book. ● *IUD: Device of Death*. Book. ● *Norplant: A New Abortifacient*. Book. ● *Pharmacists Code of Ethics*. Book.

Conventions/Meetings: annual meeting (exhibits).

★3112★ PHI EPSILON PHI
PO Box 4096
Burlingame, CA 94011-4096
Bernice O'Leary, Exec.Sec.   PH: (415)347-1765

Founded: 1937. **Members:** 600. **Languages:** English. **National.** Social and educational sorority. Conducts charitable program for the American cancer Society. **Committees:** Philanthropy.

Publications: *Circumference Newsletter*, quarterly.

Conventions/Meetings: annual meeting.

★3113★ PHI MU
3558 Habersham at Northlake
Tucker, GA 30084
Lana Lewis, Exec.Dir.   PH: (404)496-5582

Founded: 1852. **Members:** 100,000. **Staff:** 15. **Languages:** English. **National.** Social sorority sponsors charitable and educational activities; offers placement service. Conducts competitions.

Publications: *Aglaia*, quarterly. Magazine. **Circulation:** 100,000. ● *Newsletter*, periodic. ● *Directory*, periodic.

Conventions/Meetings: biennial meeting.

★3114★ PHI SIGMA SIGMA
23123 State Rd. 7, Ste. 250
Boca Raton, FL 33428   PH: (407)451-4415
Dianne Macey, Exec. Officer   FX: (407)451-4576

Founded: 1913. **Members:** 31,957. **Languages:** English. **National.** Social sorority. **Awards:** .

Publications: *Sphinx*, quarterly. Newsletter.

Conventions/Meetings: annual meeting - always August.

★3115★ PHYSICIANS FOR CHOICE (PFC)
c/o Planned Parenthood Federation of
  America
810 7th Ave.
New York, NY 10019   PH: (212)541-7800
Laurie Novick, Coordinator   FX: (212)261-4352

Founded: 1981. **Members:** 3,000. **Languages:** English. **National.** Physicians who believe in preserving the right of all women to decide when or whether to bear a child. Conducts a variety of activities to educate legislators and the public on the health benefits of reproductive freedom. Testifies at congressional hearings; circulates petitions; lobbies legislators. Maintains speakers' bureau.

★3116★ PI ALPHA KAPPA
c/o Mary Jo McCary
3201 Wisconsin, Apt. 114
Vicksburg, MS 39180
Mary Jo McCary, Exec. Officer   PH: (601)636-7236

Founded: 1947. **Members:** 156. **Languages:** English. **National.** Women 18 years of age and older united for the appreciation of music, art, and literature. Sorority is not college affiliated.

Publications: *Keynote*, quarterly. Newsletter.

Conventions/Meetings: biennial meeting.

★3117★ PI OMICRON NATIONAL SORORITY
3001 S. Fairfield Ave.
Ft. Wayne, IN 46807
Veda E. Moore, Exec.Sec.   PH: (219)456-1926

Founded: 1928. **Members:** 767. **Staff:** 1. **Languages:** English. **National.** Purposes are to: provide the opportunity for cultural growth through adult education; sponsor philanthropic projects; lend assistance for worthy and charitable causes. **Awards:** Annual (scholarship). **Divisions:** Cities' Councils; District; State.

Publications: *The Pharos*, 3/year. Newsletter.

Conventions/Meetings: biennial meeting - always July.

★3118★ PLANNED PARENTHOOD FEDERATION OF AMERICA (PPFA)
810 7th Ave.
New York, NY 10019   PH: (212)541-7800
David J. Andrews, Pres.   FX: (212)245-1845

Founded: 1916. **Staff:** 10,068. **Budget:** US$405,000,000. **Languages:** English. **National.** Organizations providing leadership in: making effective means of voluntary fertility regulation, including contraception, abortion, sterilization, and infertility services, available and fully accessible to all as a central element of reproductive health; stimulating and sponsoring relevant biomedical, socioeconomic, and demographic research; developing appropriate information, education, and training programs to increase knowledge about human reproduction and sexuality. Supports and assists efforts to achieve similar goals worldwide. Operates 900 centers that provide medically supervised reproductive health services and educational programs. **Libraries:** Type: reference. Holdings: 5,000. Subjects: contraception, abortion, sterilization, family planning, and population. **Awards:** Annual PPFA Margaret Sanger Award. ● Annual PPFA Maggie Awards for Media Excellence. ● Annual Arthur and Edith Wippman Scientific Research Award. **Alternate name::** Planned Parenthood, Planned Parenthood/World Population.

Publications: *Annual Report*.

Conventions/Meetings: annual meeting (exhibits) - always fall. 1993 Nov. 3 - 7, Los Angeles, CA, United States; 1994 Oct. 5 - 9, Atlanta, GA, United States.

★3119★ POLISH WOMEN'S ALLIANCE OF AMERICA (PWAA)
205 S. Northwest Hwy.
Park Ridge, IL 60068
Helen Wojcik, Pres.   PH: (708)692-2247

Founded: 1898. **Members:** 65,000. **Staff:** 36. **State Groups:** 17. **Local Groups:** 758. **Languages:** English. **Multinational.** Fraternal benefit life insurance society administered by women. Supports and contributes to charitable and relief foundations in the U.S. and abroad. **Libraries:** Type: reference. Holdings: 7,500. Subjects: Polish, English, and American history and culture. **Committees:** Civic and Welfare; Cultural and Scholarship; Old Age Assistance; Youth Conference.

Publications: *Glos Polek* (in English and Polish), bimonthly. **Also Cited As:** *The Polish Women's Voice*.

Conventions/Meetings: quadrennial meeting.

★3120★ POPULATION ACTION INTERNATIONAL
1120 19th St. NW, Ste. 550
Washington, DC 20036

Languages: English. **Multinational.** Disseminates information on population control. Works to improve the health of women and children.

★3121★ POPULATION COMMUNICATIONS INTERNATIONAL
777 United Nations Plaza
New York, NY 10017

Languages: English. **Multinational.** Works to enable women to control the number and spacing of their children. Disseminates family planning information to developing nations through radio and television soap operas.

Publications: *International Dateline* (in Spanish and English), monthly. Bulletin. includes insert on government organizations.

★3122★ POSTPARTUM SUPPORT, INTERNATIONAL (PSI)
927 N. Kellogg Ave.
Santa Barbara, CA 93111
Jane Honikman, Pres.   PH: (805)967-7636

Founded: 1987. **Members:** 200. **Membership Dues:** Individual, US$30 annual; Group, US$45 annual; Professional Organization, US$50 annual. **Languages:** English. **Multinational.** Promotes public awareness about the mental health issues of childbearing. Encourages research and the formation of support groups; addresses legal and insurance coverage issues. Provides educational programs. **Libraries:** Type: reference. Holdings: books, audio recordings, video recordings. Subjects: maternal mental health.

Publications: *PSI News*, quarterly. Newsletter.

Conventions/Meetings: annual conference (exhibits).

★3123★ PREGNANCY AND INFANT LOSS CENTER (PILC)
1421 E. Wayzata Blvd., No. 30
Wayzata, MN 55391   PH: (612)473-9372

Founded: 1983. **Members:** 850. **Staff:** 2. **Budget:** US$98,000. **Languages:** English. **National.** Parents who have suffered a miscarriage, stillbirth, or infant death; concerned health care professionals and volunteers. Seeks to increase public awareness and establish a network of support for families affected by perinatal death. Provides referral services for parents who wish to contact support groups, counselors, or other couples who have also experienced a perinatal death. Offers assistance to speakers and workshop directors seeking to contact churches, schools, and service organizations interested in conducting perinatal bereavement assistance programs. Produces educational materials dealing with funeral arrangements, guidelines for the friends and families of bereaved parents, high-risk pregnancies, and the grief of surviving siblings . Offers perinatal bereavement seminars and consulting services. Operates telephone help-line. Maintains speakers' bureau. Conducts program on grief and loss. Sponsors Annual Pregnancy and Infant Loss Awareness Month in October; distributes information packets. Compiles statistics. **Libraries:** Type: reference. Subjects: perinatal bereavement.

Publications: *Loving Arms*, quarterly. Newsletter. Features articles, poems, and resources on miscarriage, stillbirth, and infant death. **Circulation:** 2,500. **Advertising:** not accepted.

Conventions/Meetings: annual, includes workshop and exhibits (exhibits) - always April. Minneapolis, MN, United States.

★3124★ PREGNANCY AND INFANT LOSS SUPPORT
St. Joseph's Health Center
300 1st Capitol Dr.
St. Charles, MO 63301
Catherine Lammert, Exec.Dir.   PH: (314)947-6164

Founded: 1977. **Members:** 10,000. **Staff:** 2. **Regional Groups:** 280. **State Groups:** 55. **Local Groups:** 3. **Languages:** English. **Multinational.** Parents who have suffered the loss of a child through miscarriage, stillbirth, or early infant death; supporters. Purposes are: to provide comfort and support to the bereaved parents; to continue reassurance and care beyond the hospital stay; to encourage the physical and emotional health of the parents and siblings. Makes presentations accompanied by films. Assists with formation of local groups. Local group activities include conducting support meetings with speakers, providing lists of addresses and phone numbers to make resources readily available, developing keepsake kits, and facilitating parent-to-parent support. Sponsors presentations on grief. Plans to offer computerized services. **Libraries:** Type: reference. Subjects: grief, newborn death, and adoption. **Committees:** Education; Fundraising; Outreach. **Formerly:** (1991) SHARE.

Publications: *International Perinatal Support Groups Listing*, periodic. Directory. ● *SHARE Newsletter*, bimonthly. Concerned with bereavement especially following miscarriage, ectopic pregnancy, stillbirth, or newborn death. Includes listing of books and resources. **Circulation:** 2,000. **Advertising:** accepted. ● *Bittersweet.hellogoodbye: a Resource for Planning Farewell Rituals when a Baby Dies.* Book. ● *Thumpy's Story.* Videos. perinatal grief.

★3125★ PRESBYTERIAN WOMEN (PW)
100 Witherspoon St.   PH: (502)569-5365
Louisville, KY 40202   TF: (800)872-3283
Gladys Strachan, Exec.Dir.   FX: (502)569-5018

Founded: 1988. **Members:** 400,000. **Staff:** 14. **Budget:** US$5,000,000. **Regional Groups:** 187. **Local Groups:** 10,000. **Languages:** English. **National.** Purposes are to promote the Presbyterian church and its teachings and to provide a forum for Presbyterian women. Administers to the needs of individuals through missions worldwide; defends the rights of those who are economically and politically powerless; makes political and social commitments to issues involving justice, peace, freedom, and world hunger; examines topics such as apartheid, child abandonment, rape, divorce, and displaced women. Participates in Presbyterian educational ministry and the training of church leaders. Offers economic justice consultations; organizes overseas study seminars and leadership and training events; conducts local, regional, and national workshops. Maintains speakers' bureau and biographical archives; offers charitable program; compiles statistics. **Libraries:** Type: reference. Holdings: 0. **Awards:** Annual Women of faith. **Committees:** Enabler; Leadership Development; Mission; Spiritual Growth.

Publications: *Crosswinds*, monthly. Newsletter. Provides updates and information for members. ● *Horizons*, bimonthly. Magazine. Includes book reviews, Washington Watch, and information on reg ional groups and leaders. **ISSN:** 0010-5163. ● *Women's Ministry Unit Newsletter*, semiannual. ● *Etchings of Diversity.* Book.

Conventions/Meetings: triennial meeting - next 1994. ● quadrennial Eco-Justice Consultation - 1996.

★3126★ PRESBYTERIANS PRO-LIFE (PPL)
PO Box 19290
Minneapolis, MN 55419

Languages: English. **National.** Lay and clergy members of the Presbyterian Church (USA) who are opposed to abortion. Works to protect the rights of human life from conception until natural death. Opposes abortion, infanticide, and euthanasia. PPL believes that a "return to the Biblical teaching concerning the Sacred value of the family is essential to recovering respect for the sacred valvue of individual human lives.".

★3127★ PRIESTS FOR EQUALITY (PFE)
PO Box 5243
West Hyattsville, MD 20782
Rev. Joseph A. Dearborn, Sec.   PH: (301)779-9298

Founded: 1975. **Members:** 2,300. **Staff:** 1. **Languages:** English. **National.** Catholic priests seeking to achieve full equality for women both in the Catholic church and in society. Believes that women can and should be ordained as priests; that women and men are "equally precious to a loving Creator, equally bearing the image of that Creator, equally called to develop his or her human rights." Engages in sociological studies and surveys. Sponsors research studies, reports, and other activities designed to raise the consciousness of individuals and strengthen their commitment to equality.

Publications: *Newsletter*, quarterly.

★3128★ PRO-CHOICE DEFENSE LEAGUE (PCDL)
131 Fulton Ave.
Hempstead, NY 11550
Bill Baird, Dir.   PH: (516)538-2626

Founded: 1984. **Members:** 300. **Languages:** English. **National.** Individuals seeking to protect reproductive freedom of choice. Serves as a clearinghouse of information on reproductive rights. Sponsors public education programs and workshops; conducts training sessions for abortion clinic operators on methods of securing facilities against violence and harassment.

Publications: *Newsletter*, periodic.

Conventions/Meetings: periodic meeting.

★3129★ PRO-LIFE ACTION LEAGUE (PLAL)
6160 N. Cicero, No. 600
Chicago, IL 60646   PH: (312)777-2900
Joseph M. Scheidler, Exec.Dir.   FX: (312)777-3061

Founded: 1980. **Members:** 12,000. **Staff:** 6. **Budget:** US$200,000. **Languages:** English. **National.** Individuals, including doctors, lawyers, business leaders, and students, who are pro-life. Purpose is "to stop abortions now, through effective, legal, nonviolent means" and to lay the groundwork for outlawing all abortions through a constitutional amendment. Conducts demonstrations and picketing against abortion clinics and pro-abortion agencies; appears on radio and television talk shows and demands equal media time to counter pro-abortion views; engages in lobbying. Sponsors seminars for community organizations; lectures student groups; holds workshops; trains volunteers to counsel women in front of clinics. Compiles statistics. **Libraries:** Type: reference. Holdings: 1,000; books, audio recordings, video recordings, clippings. Subjects: pro-life issues. **Awards:** Annual National protector. **Committees:** Public Demonstration; Public Protest; Street Counselors. **Departments:** Public Relations; Publicity. **Committees:** . **Departments:** .

Publications: *Bulletin*, periodic. ● *Pro-Life Action News*, quarterly. Newsletter. ● *Closed: 99 Ways to Stop Abortion.* Book. ● *Videos.* Preventing abortion.

Conventions/Meetings: annual conference.

★3130★ PRO-LIFE DIRECT ACTION LEAGUE (PDAL)
PO Box 11881
St. Louis, MO 63105
Ann L. O'Brien, Pres.   PH: (314)863-1022

Founded: 1984. Languages: English. National. Opposes legalized abortion and promotes adherence to the "sanctity of life ethic." Group believes that this ethic is an integral part of Christian morality, and that abortion for any reason is in opposition to it; also believes that "law which deprives individuals of their basic human rights" is not valid, and that breaking such statutes is a Christian duty. Conducts sit-ins and other forms of nonviolent protest near abortion clinics. Maintains speakers' bureau. Holds seminars and training meetings.

Publications: Direct Action News, monthly. Newsletter.

★3131★ PROFESSIONAL WOMEN IN CONSTRUCTION (PWC)
342 Madison Ave., Rm. 451
New York, NY 10173   PH: (212)687-0610
Lenore Janis, Pres.   FX: (212)490-1213

Founded: 1980. Members: 500. Regional Groups: 2. Languages: English. National. Management-level women in construction and allied industries; owners, suppliers, architects, engineers, field personnel, office personnel, and bonding/surety personnel. Provides a forum for exchange of ideas and promotion of political and legislative action, education, and job opportunities for women in construction and related fields; forms liaisons with other trade and professional groups; develops research programs. Strives to reform abuses and to assure justice and equity within the construction industry. Sponsors mini-workshops. Maintains Action Line which provides members with current information on pertinent legislation and on the association's activities. Awards: . Task Forces: Architects/Engineers; Management Field Personnel; Management Office Personnel; Owners; Suppliers; Surety/Insurance.

Publications: Calendar of Events, monthly. Bulletin. • Newsletter, quarterly.

Conventions/Meetings: annual meeting. • monthly dinner.

★3132★ PROFESSIONAL WOMEN PHOTOGRAPHERS (PWP)
c/o Photographics Unlimited
17 W. 17th St., No. 14
New York, NY 10011
Mariette Allen, Chwm.   PH: (212)255-9678

Founded: 1975. Members: 500. Languages: English. National. Women professional photographers; other interested individuals. Conducts charitable, educational, and artistic activities to stimulate public interest in, support for, and appreciation of photographic art (particularly members' works). Encourages professional development of photographers. Has participated in New York City's first art parade and has sponsored The Me Generation, a traveling group exhibition. Maintains speakers' bureau. Conducts group shows and projects. Computer Services: Mailing lists.

Publications: PWP Newsletter, 5/year. Includes meeting schedule and selected biographies. Circulation: 400. Advertising: accepted.

Conventions/Meetings: monthly meeting.

★3133★ PROFESSIONAL WOMEN SINGERS ASSOCIATION (PWSA)
PO Box 884
Planetarium Sta.
New York, NY 10024
Sandra VanCleve, President   PH: (212)969-0590

Founded: 1982. Members: 60. Languages: English. National. Works to advance the careers of professional women singers and promote musical quality. Provides information on professional job opportunities for women singers. Organizes community concerts. Awards: Periodic (grant).

Conventions/Meetings: bimonthly executive committee meeting.

★3134★ PROFESSIONAL WOMEN'S APPRAISAL ASSOCIATION (PWAA)
8383 E. Evans Rd.
Scottsdale, AZ 85260   PH: (602)998-4422
Deborah S. Johnson, Exec.Dir.   FX: (602)998-8022

Founded: 1986. Members: 650. Budget: US$60,000. Languages: English. National. Women appraisers in government agencies and national banks; independent professional appraisers. Goal is to provide a support system for women real estate appraisers. Offers continuing education classes in appraisal trends, technical methods, and legislation regarding the appraisal industry. Conducts research.

Conventions/Meetings: annual conference (exhibits).

★3135★ PROGRAM FOR APPROPRIATE TECHNOLOGY IN HEALTH
4 Nickerson St.
Seattle, WA 98109

Languages: English. Multinational. Works to provide contraceptive technology to developing countries. Disseminates information on pregnancy, child birth, and spacing of children. Seeks to erradicate harmful traditions, including female circumcision. Conducts feasiblity studies.

★3136★ PROJECT PRIESTHOOD (PP)
c/o Women's Ordination Conf.
PO Box 2693
Fairfax, VA 22031   PH: (703)352-1006
Ruth Fitzpatrick, Coordinator   FX: (703)352-5181

Founded: 1976. Members: 500. Staff: 1. Languages: English. National. Women who believe themselves called to the Roman Catholic priesthood. Aim is to create solidarity among participants and to promote the women's ordination movement. Conducts research programs; compiles statistics. Computer Services: Data base.

Publications: We Are Called, periodic. Newsletter.

★3137★ PROJECT SAFE RUN (PSR)
PO Box 22234
Eugene, OR 97402
Shelley Reecher, Founder   PH: (503)345-8086

Founded: 1981. Languages: English. National. Works to enable women to walk or jog safely by themselves. Trains dogs to accompany and protect solitary woman joggers. Dogs are maintained at local chapter houses, from which they can be checked out by women interested in using this service.

★3138★ PROUTIST UNIVERSAL WOMEN (PUW)
PO Box 114
Northampton, MA 01061
Jody Wright, Pres.   PH: (413)586-3488

Founded: 1961. Members: 10,000. Regional Groups: 4. Local Groups: 30. Languages: English. National. Women and girls. Purpose is to enhance the dignity of women through economic independence, cultural renaissance, and lasting social change based on neo-humanism and a universal spiritual outlook. Encourages adherence to ideals outlined in PROUT, the Progressive Utilization Theory, which stresses decentralized economics, world government, and universalism. Sponsors classes, seminars, and a two-month training session in social and spiritual philosophy and organization. Organizes grass roots social service projects and fundraising events to benefit developing countries.

Publications: Rising Sun Newsletter, monthly. • Tara: Journal of the Women's Prout Movement, quarterly. Circulation: 10,000. Advertising: not accepted.

Conventions/Meetings: semiannual conference.

★3139★ PUBLIC LEADERSHIP EDUCATION NETWORK (PLEN)
1001 Connecticut Ave. NW, Ste. 925
Washington, DC 20036
Marianne Alexander, Dir.   PH: (202)872-1585

Founded: 1978. **Members:** 17. **Staff:** 2. **Languages:** English. **National.** A consortium of women's colleges working together to educate women for public leadership positions. Sponsors public policy internships in Washington, D.C.

Publications: *PLEN Newsletter*, semiannual. **Circulation:** 1,000. **Advertising:** not accepted. ● *Lerning to Lead*. Book. ● *Wingspread Report: Educating Women for Leadeship*. Book.

Conventions/Meetings: annual meeting - always March. ● annual women in public policy seminar. ● periodic women and congress seminar.

★3140★ RADICAL WOMEN (RW)
523-A Valencia St.
San Francisco, CA 94110
Nancy Reiko Kato, Organizer   PH: (415)864-1278

Founded: 1967. **Local Groups:** 9. **Languages:** English. **National.** Women with a socialist-feminist political orientation who believe that women's leadership is decisive for basic social change. Works toward reform in the areas of reproductive rights, child care, affirmative action, divorce, police brutality, rape, women of color, lesbians, and working women. Opposes efforts of conservative anti-feminist groups.

Conventions/Meetings: annual conference.

★3141★ REDSTOCKINGS OF THE WOMEN'S LIBERATION MOVEMENT
290 9th Ave., No. 2G
New York, NY 10001
Marisa Figueiredo, Sec.   PH: (212)568-1834

National. Originally founded by veteran members of the 1960s women's rights movement. Works to advance the agenda of women and equal rights in the United States. Develops teach-ins, learn-ins, speak-ins, and consciousness raising groups.

★3142★ REFORMED CHURCH WOMEN (RCW)
475 Riverside Dr., Rm. 1825
New York, NY 10027
Diana Paulsen, Exec.Dir.   PH: (212)870-2844

Founded: 1864. **Members:** 25,000. **Languages:** English. **National.** Women of the Reformed Church in America dedicated to promoting fellowship for spiritual growth among members. Provides opportunities and avenues of service for community involvement in areas of concern such as the homeless and hungry. Encourages theological contemplation. Sponsors Footsteps Program which allows women to serve at missions. Conducts leadership seminars.

Publications: *Reformed Church Women News*, quarterly. Newsletter. ● *Resource Guide*, quarterly. Directory.

Conventions/Meetings: triennial general assembly.

★3143★ REFUGEE WOMEN IN DEVELOPMENT (RefWID)
810 1st St. NE, Ste. 300
Washington, DC 20002
Sima Wali, Dir.   PH: (202)289-1104

Founded: 1981. **Members:** 1,200. **Staff:** 2. **Budget:** US$200,000. **Languages:** English. **National.** Refugee women who have resettled in the U.S. Seeks to enable Third World refugee women to attain social and economic independence and security through acculturation, economic security, ethnic preservation, and emotional support. Focuses on low-income working-age refugee women with limited skills and those suffering escape trauma. Sponsors education and research programs; advocates improvements in

programs and services for refugee women. Develops program models, training curricula, and community involvement approaches. Programs included leadership development, human rights/protection, and international representation. Priorities include conducting training in domestic violence prevention and intervention; developing practical programs models for leadership development and coalition building; carrying out education and advocacy with refugee and mainstream organizations, policymakers, and the general public.

Publications: *Understanding Family Violence Within U.S. Refugee Communities: A Training Manual*. Book. ● *The Production and Marketing of Ethnic Handcrafts in The U.S.*. Book. ● *Leadership Development Motel for Refugee Women: A Replication Guide*. Book.

★3144★ RELIGIOUS COALITION FOR ABORTION RIGHTS (RCAR)
100 Maryland Ave. NE, Ste. 307
Washington, DC 20002
Ann Thompson Cook, Exec.Dir.   PH: (202)543-7032

Founded: 1973. **Members:** 36. **Staff:** 9. **State Groups:** 25. **Languages:** English. **National.** Religious organizations. Seeks to encourage and coordinate religious support for: safeguarding the legal option of abortion; ensuring the right of individuals to make decisions concerning abortion in accordance with their conscience and responsible medical practices; opposing efforts to deny these rights through constitutional amendment, or federal or state legislation. Educates on the diversity of religious beliefs about abortion and the connection between reproductive and religious freedom. Monitors developments in Congress and state legislatures. Alerts members and individuals on both state and national levels.

Publications: *Common Ground - Different Planes*, quarterly. Newsletter. addresses healthcare issues particular to women of color. ● *Legislative Update*, periodic. Bulletin. ● *Religious Coalition for Abortion Rights Newsletter*, periodic. **Circulation:** 60,000. **Advertising:** not accepted. ● *Abortion and the Holocaust: Twisting the Language*. Booklet. ● *Judaism and Abortion*. Booklet. ● *Personhood, the Bible, and the Abortion debase*. Booklet.

Conventions/Meetings: annual conference.

★3145★ RELIGIOUS NETWORK FOR EQUALITY FOR WOMEN (RNEW)
475 Riverside Dr., Rm. 812-A
New York, NY 10115   PH: (212)870-2995
Dr. Zelle W. Andrews, Coordinator   FX: (212)870-2338

Founded: 1976. **Members:** 42. **Staff:** 2. **Budget:** US$98,000. **Languages:** English. **National.** Interreligious coalition of faith groups committed to legal and economic justice for women. Engages in education and advocacy programs on behalf of women's rights, especially for the poor. Provides economic literacy program to educate women about the economic system. Lobbies for national legislation on civil rights and economic reform. Participates in the campaign to ratify the United Nations Convention on the Elimination of Discrimination Against Women.

Publications: *RNEW Update*, 3/year. Newsletter. ● *Learning Economics*. Book.

Conventions/Meetings: 3/year meeting.

★3146★ REPUBLICAN WOMEN OF CAPITOL HILL (RWCH)
160B Longworth House Office Bldg.
Washington, DC 20515
Maxine Dean, Pres.   PH: (202)225-4176

Founded: 1963. **Members:** 250. **Languages:** English. **National.** Social club for female employees of Republican representatives on Capitol Hill, Republican National Committee, or in the administration; associate members are women who have worked for one of the above. Provides members with the opportunity to establish contacts and meet influential leaders in Washington, DC. Arranges speakers including ambassadors, White House staff members, and congressional representatives. Sponsors Annual fashion show, Christmas bazaar, and embassy parties. **Committees:** Historian; Social; Publicity.

Publications: *Trunk Line*, monthly. Newsletter.

Conventions/Meetings: monthly luncheon.

★3147★ REPUBLICANS FOR CHOICE (RFC)
1315 Duke St., Ste. 201
Alexandria, VA 22314
Ann Stone, Chm.
PH: (703)836-8907
FX: (703)519-8843

Founded: 1990. **Staff:** 5. **Languages:** English. **National.** Republicans who support a woman's right to choose abortion. Seeks to change the Republican party platform to reflect the views of pro-choice party members. Supports pro-choice Republican candidates at all levels in primaries and general elections. Maintains the Republicans for Choice Emergency Task Force to counteract pro-life pressure at the state level.

★3148★ RESOLVE, INC.
1310 Broadway
Somerville, MA 02144-1731
Diane D. Arenson, Exec.Dir.
PH: (617)623-1156
FX: (617)623-0252

Founded: 1973. **Members:** 25,000. **Membership Dues:** Individual, US$35 annual; Professional, US$60 annual. **Staff:** 13. **Budget:** US$450,000. **Local Groups:** 54. **Languages:** English. **National.** Persons with problems of infertility and associated professionals who work with infertile couples, such as adoption workers, doctors, and counselors. Offers information, referral, and support to persons with problems of infertility. Maintains speakers' bureau; operates telephone helpline.

Publications: *Resolve National Newsletter*, quarterly. Provides information on medical, emotional, and legislative issues, and upcoming conferences. Includes book reviews and research report. **Circulation:** 13,000.

Conventions/Meetings: annual conference. ● periodic regional meeting.

★3149★ RESOLVE THROUGH SHARING (RTS)
La Crosse Lutheran Hospital
1910 South Ave.
La Crosse, WI 54601
Brenda Morgan, Admin.
PH: (608)791-4747

Founded: 1981. **Languages:** English. **National.** A perinatal bereavement program based in more than 1000 hospitals. Addresses the individual needs of parents who have experienced miscarriages, ectopic pregnancies, stillbirths, or newborn deaths. Offers bereavement counseling courses for health care professional and support materials and services to family members.

Publications: *Counselor Connection*, quarterly. Newsletter.

Conventions/Meetings: biennial conference - 1995.

★3150★ RE'UTH WOMEN'S SOCIAL SERVICE (WSSI)
130 E. 59th St., Ste. 900
New York, NY 10022
Rosa Strygier, Pres.
PH: (212)836-1570
FX: (212)836-1114

Founded: 1951. **Members:** 1,500. **Languages:** English. **National.** Raises funds for hospitals and homes for the aged in Israel by means of subscription social functions.

Publications: *Journal*, annual.

★3151★ ROADWORK
1375 Harvard St. NW
Washington, DC 20009
Amy Horowitz, Exec. Dir.
PH: (202)234-9308

Founded: 1978. **Languages:** English. **National.** Women of diverse cultural

backgrounds. Provides opportunities and venues for women to express themselves and their cultures through arts and crafts.

★3152★ ROCKETTE ALUMNAE ASSOCIATION (RAA)
c/o Fern Weizner
908 N. Broadway
Yonkers, NY 10701
Fern Weizner, Pres.
PH: (914)423-3636

Founded: 1955. **Members:** 340. **Languages:** English. **National.** Former members of the Radio City Music Hall dance troupe, the Rockettes, united for social and philanthropic causes. **Awards:** Periodic Russell Market (scholarship). Recipient: dance students at the Juliard school of Music.

Publications: *Journal*, annual. ● *Newsletter*, 5/year.

Conventions/Meetings: 5/year meeting. ● annual luncheon - always spring.

★3153★ ROSARY FOR LIFE ORGANIZATION (RFL)
PO Box 40213
Memphis, TN 38174
Patrick V. Benedict, DIR.
PH: (901)725-5937

Founded: 1988. **Languages:** English. **National.** Promotes praying the Rosary as a means of "saving the lives of unborn babies." Assists in planning and conducting peaceful prayer demonstrations in front of abortion facilities for "pregnant mothers, abortionists and their supporters, and preborn babies who are routinely killed by surgical abortion as well as abortifacients such as the intrauterine device (IUD) and the so-called birth control pill." Supplies information and guidelines on how to coordinate a Rosary Novena for Life in local communities.

Publications: *Rosary for Life Newsletter*, periodic. ● *Rosary for Life Planning Manual*. Book.

★3154★ ROUNDTABLE FOR WOMEN FOOD-BEVERAGE-HOSPITALITY (RWFBH)
145 W. 1st St., Ste. A
Tustin, CA 92680
Beverly Totman-Ham, Contact

Founded: 1983. **Members:** 1,000. **Staff:** 3. **Budget:** US$150,000. **Regional Groups:** 5. **Languages:** English. **National.** Women in the food and food service industries; persons providing services to these areas. Promotes advancement and success of women in the food industry. Acts as clearinghouse for food service, business, educational, and career information. Holds roundtables to clarify issues and promote entrepreneurial opportunities; provides practical counseling service for members entering, reentering, or advancing in the industry. Promotes recognition of products and services; maintains speakers' bureau; conducts seminars. Operates job bank; compiles industry statistics. Plans include a hot line to provide information and counseling concerning food service entrepreneurship, and professional certification. **Awards:** Annual Pacesetter. **Computer Services:** Data base.

Publications: *Pacesetter Journal*, periodic. ● *Roundtable Journal*, periodic. ● *RWF Membership Directory*, annual. Includes listing of services offered. **Circulation:** 2,000. **Advertising:** accepted. ● *RWF News*, quarterly. Newsletter.

★3155★ ROYAL NEIGHBORS OF AMERICA (RNA)
230 16th St.
Rock Island, IL 61201
Delores Ghys, Supreme Oracle
PH: (309)788-4561
TF: (800)747-4762

Founded: 1895. **Members:** 159,982. **Staff:** 712. **State Groups:** 42. **Local Groups:** 1,975. **Languages:** English. **National.** Fraternal life insurance society administered by women that insures men, women, and children. Sponsors Orphan Benefit program and provides a home for aged members. Maintains Help to Hear and Dogs for the Deaf projects to aid the hearing disabled. Conducts educational and charitable programs. **Libraries:** Type: reference. Holdings: 1,000. **Awards:** Periodic (scholarship).

Publications: *Field News*, monthly. Newsletter. ● *Office News*, monthly. Newsletter. ● *Royal Neighbor*, monthly. Magazine. **ISSN:** 0035-905X. **Circulation:** 150,000. **Advertising:** not accepted.

Conventions/Meetings: annual conference.

★3156★ RURAL AMERICAN WOMEN (RAW)
50002 Old Jeanerette Rd.
New Iberia, LA 70560
Judy Voehringer, Pres.   PH: (318)367-3277

Founded: 1977. **Members:** 1,024. **Staff:** 4. **Languages:** English. **National**. Federation of individuals and affiliated organizations making up an ethnically, geographically, and economically diverse group of rural American women. Seeks to organize rural women of America to work together, develop their individual capabilities, contribute to the welfare of their families, improve their communities, tackle a broad range of issues in rural America, and give visibility to the contributions of rural women to our society. Believes rural women to be catalysts both for rekindling certain traditional values of which they feel the country has lost sight and for bringing about changes in the conditions of rural life. Offers rural community leadership training sessions and conducts food and energy workshops; provides home business aid. Maintains speakers' bureau.

Publications: *News Journal of Rural American Women*, bimonthly. ● *Annotated Bibliography on Rural Women*. Book.

★3157★ RUSSIAN ORTHODOX CATHOLIC WOMEN'S MUTUAL AID SOCIETY
975 Greentree Rd.
Pittsburgh, PA 15220
Martha Lomakin, Sec.-Treas.   PH: (412)922-6664

Founded: 1907. **Members:** 1,789. **Local Groups:** 42. **Languages:** English. **National**. Fraternal benefit life insurance society administered by women for persons of Russian Orthodox faith. Contributes donations to Russian Orthodox seminaries, "Patient in Need" civic organizations, Penn State Slavic Folk Festival, March of Dimes Birth Defects Foundation children's hospitals, and churches. **Awards:** Periodic Make a wish (scholarship).

Publications: *Newsletter*, semiannual.

Conventions/Meetings: quadrennial meeting - next 1994. ● annual meeting - Pittsburgh, PA, United States.

★3158★ RV-ING WOMEN
PO Box 82606
Kenmore, WA 98028
Lovern Root King, Contact   TF: (800)333-9992

Founded: 1991. **Members:** 4,000. **Staff:** 8. **Languages:** English. **Multinational**. Women in the United States, Canada, Mexico, Germany, and South Africa. Provides a network and forum for women interested in the recreational vehicle (RV) lifestyle. Conducts educational programs on RV maintenance and safety and social activities in various regions of the United States. **Computer Services:** Information services, travel routing program.

Publications: *Directory*, annual. ● *RVing Women*, bimonthly. Newsletter.

★3159★ SAGARIS
10 2nd St. NE, No. 100
Minneapolis, MN 55413
Linda J. Harness, Admin.   PH: (612)379-2640

Founded: 1974. **Members:** 7. **Languages:** English. **National**. Feminist therapy collective. Offers psychotherapy to men, women, their partners, children, and families on issues including job problems, relationship problems, low self-esteem, and expression of anger or sadness. Offers consultation to

organizations experiencing structural or interpersonal tensions. Sponsors workshops, short lecture series, and training in a feminist approach to therapy.

★3160★ SAKHI FOR SOUTH ASIAN WOMEN
PO Box 1428, Cathedral Sta.
New York, NY 10025
Anannya Bhattacharjee, Exec.   PH: (212)866-6591
   Coordinator   FX: (212)714-9153

Founded: 1989. **Members:** 30. **Staff:** 2. **Budget:** US$165,000. **Languages:** English, Hindi, Urdu, Punjabi, Gujarati, Bengali, Malayalam, Tamil, Kannada. **National**. Works to eradicate domestic violence among South Asian immigrant women. Aims to empower South Asian women so that they may resist violence and exploitation. Maintains that education and awareness are the keys to eliminating domestic violence. Offers workshops and presentations, vocational training, shelter, and social services for abused women. Provides referrals and advocacy for victims of domestic violence. Conducts research on domestic violence among South Asian immigrant communities. **Libraries:** Type: reference.   Subjects: issues concerning women immigrants.

Publications: *Bulletin* (in English), monthly.

Conventions/Meetings: monthly meeting. ● weekly board meeting.

★3161★ SALVADORAN WOMEN'S ASSOCIATION (AMES)
PO Box 40311
San Francisco, CA 94140   PH: (415)552-5015

Languages: English. **National**. Seeks to enhance women's living conditions in El Salvador. Works to: establish education programs; upgrade medical care; and improve sanitation.

★3162★ SAVE A BABY (SB)
PO Box 101
Orinda, CA 94563
Dr. James Fiatarone, Founder & Dir.   PH: (415)648-6436

Founded: 1973. **Languages:** English. **National**. Persons opposed to abortion. Purpose is to inform the public about the physical and emotional circumstances surrounding abortion and about what the group calls the sanctity of life and the threats posed by the anti-life and abortion-killing mentalities today. Encourages women to continue their pregnancies; offers counseling and coordinates assistance for women choosing to have their babies. Collects and distributes baby and maternity clothes and other supplies to women in need; broadcasts television and radio programs; sponsors anti-abortion programs and speeches for groups and organizations. Operates CARE-avan, an international humanitarian program in which volunteers provide medical and educational assistance and materials to needy people. Maintains speakers' bureau.

Publications: *Save A Baby*. Booklet. ● *Going Gentle*. Booklet.

★3163★ SAVE THE CHILDREN FEDERATION
48 Wilton Rd.
Westport, CT 06880

Languages: English. **Multinational**. Works to improve health, education, and economic status of women and children. Believes that meeting women's needs is a prerequisite to meeting the needs of children. Assists women in the attainment of credit. Conducts research and disseminates information on the nutritional status of children.

Publications: *Already I feel the Change*. Book. ● *Women's Voices in Four Countries*. Book. ● *Handbook for the Development of Savings Groups and Women's Business Skills*. Booklet.

★3164★ SCREEN ACTORS GUILD - WOMEN'S COMMITTEE
1515 Broadway, 44th Fl.
New York, NY 10036   PH: (212)944-1030

Languages: English. **National.** Supports and promotes women in the film industry. Works for equal employment opportunity. Seeks to improve the role of women in film production and to establish a new image of women in films.

★3165★ SEAMLESS GARMENT NETWORK (SGN)
c/o Carol Crossed
109 Pickwick Dr.
Rochester, NY 14618
Rose Evans, Sec.   PH: (716)442-8497

Founded: 1987. **Members:** 70. **Languages:** English. **National.** Organizations advocating a pro-life stand and peace. Promotes the protection of life which the group feels is threatened by war, abortion, the arms race, poverty, the death penalty, and euthanasia. Believes that these issues are linked under a "consistent ethic of life" and that individuals promoting these causes should "work together in a spirit of peace, justice, and reconciliation." The organization's name is derived from speeches by Cardinal Joseph Bernardin which alluded to pro-life work as being like Christ's seamless garment. Operates speakers' bureau. **Libraries:** Type: reference.

Publications: *Consistent Ethic Resources*, periodic. Directory. Organizations, speakers, and publications. **Advertising:** not accepted.

Conventions/Meetings: annual board meeting - always spring.

★3166★ SECRETARIAT FOR FAMILY, LAITY, WOMEN, AND YOUTH
(SFLWY)
3211 4th St. NE
Washington, DC 20017   PH: (202)541-3040
Dolores R. Leckey, Exec.Dir.   FX: (202)541-3088

Languages: English. **National.** Division of the National Conference of Catholic Bishops. Works to provide service in the areas of Laity, marriage and family, women in church and society, and youth. Develops national policy in these area for the body of bishops.

Publications: *Newsletter*, quarterly. **Advertising:** not accepted.

★3167★ SECTION ON WOMEN IN LEGAL EDUCATION OF THE AALS
c/o Association of American Law
   Schools
1201 Connecticut Ave. NW, Ste. 800
Washington, DC 20036
Mary Becker, Chair   PH: (202)296-8851

Languages: English. **National.** Women law professors. Section of the Association of American Law Schools assisting women lawyers in teaching and scholarship. Provides information on the integration of women and women's concerns into the legal profession; makes recommendations on matters concerning the administration of law schools, the status of women in legal education, and improvement of law school curricula. Promotes communication of ideas and interests among members.

Publications: *Newsletter*, semiannual.

Conventions/Meetings: annual meeting (exhibits). ● periodic conference.

★3168★ SECTION FOR WOMEN IN PUBLIC ADMINISTRATION
(SWPA)
1120 G St. NW
Washington, DC 20005   PH: (202)393-7878

Founded: 1971. **Languages:** English. **National.** Established by the American Society for Public Administration to initiate action programs appropriate to the needs and concerns of women in public administration. Promotes equal educational and employment opportunities for women in public service, and full participation and recognition of women in all areas of government. Develops strategies for implementation of ASPA policies of interest to women in public administration; recommends qualified women to elective and appointive ASPA governmental leadership positions; acts as forum for communication among professional and laypeople interested in the professional development of women in public administration. **Awards:** Periodic Joan Fiss Bishop Memorial. ● Periodic (grant).

Publications: *Bridging the Gap*, semiannual. Newsletter. ● *Membership Directory*, periodic.

Conventions/Meetings: annual conference (exhibits).

★3169★ SELF HELP FOR EQUAL RIGHTS (SHER)
Box 105
Garret Park Post Office
Garret Park, MD 20896
Billie Mackey, President

Founded: 1972. **Languages:** English. **National.** Investigates sex discrimination, sexual harassment, and other women's issues; provides informational programs on such issues. Organizes and coordinates a network, a support group, and social gatherings for women. Offers financial assistance to women pursuing "meritorious discrimination cases."

★3170★ SENIOR ACTION IN A GAY ENVIRONMENT (SAGE)
208 W. 13th St.
New York, NY 10011   PH: (212)741-2247
Arlene Kochman, Exec.Dir.   FX: (212)366-1947

Founded: 1977. **Members:** 4,000. **Staff:** 7. **Budget:** US$526,000. **Languages:** English. **National.** Trained volunteers including social workers, doctors, lawyers, psychologists, gerontologists, and others dedicated to meeting the needs of older gays and lesbians and ending the isolation that has kept them separate from each other, other gays, and from the larger community. Provides: information and referral in areas of legal matters, home care and long-term facilities, and social service agencies; personal visits; social activities to reduce loneliness, rebuild relationships, and establish supportive connections with the gay and lesbian community. Provides in-service training for agency members and institutions serving older gays. Educates professionals and the public with regard to lesbian and gay aging. Sponsors AIDS Service Program for the Elderly. Conducts weekly workshops and training programs for volunteers and social service agencies interested in issues of lesbian and gay aging. Maintains speakers bureau; sponsors oral history project; conducts research programs; compiles statistics. **Committees:** Assessors; Communications; Friendly Visiting; Group Activities; History Project; Office Volunteers; Social Services; Third World Outreach.

Publications: *SAGE Bulletin*, monthly. ● *SAGE News*, semiannual. Newsletter. **Circulation:** 12,000.

Conventions/Meetings: monthly meeting. ● monthly dinner.

★3171★ SERVICE EMPLOYEES INTERNATIONAL UNION - WOMEN'S
PROGRAM
1313 L St. NW
Washington, DC 20005
Pat Thomas, Contact   PH: (202)898-3365

Languages: English. **National.** Supports and promotes the interests of women working in service industries. Investigates and makes recommendations on women's issues.

★3172★ SHELTER OUR SISTERS IN ISRAEL (SOSI)
PO Box 4527
New York, NY 10185
Thelma Peskin Halpern, Exec. Dir.

National. Provides assistance to abused women in Israel. Works to raise funds for shelters and other support services. Strives to prevent violence, emotional and physical breakdown, suicide, and murder in the family.

Disseminates information concerning battered women and their families. Organizes Friends of SOSI in Jewish communities internationally.

★3173★ SIGMA DELTA EPSILON, GRADUATE WOMEN IN SCIENCE
(SDE/GWIS)
111 E. Wacker Dr., Ste. 200
Chicago, IL 60601-9298
Edna R. Bernstein, Sec.
PH: (312)616-0800
FX: (312)616-0223

Founded: 1921. **Members:** 1,500. **Budget:** US$31,000. **Languages:** English. **National.** Professional organization - graduate women, science. Fosters research in science and seeks to increase the participation of women in science. Works to: improve science and mathematics education for women; encourage women with science degrees to enter the workforce; support study of the history of women in science; cooperate with organizations with similar goals; make use of the media to publicize the accomplishments of women in science. Sponsors competitions conducts fundraising activities. **Awards:** Periodic Eloise Gerry Fellowship. ● Periodic (scholarship). **Committees:** Fellowships; Liaison with Women in Science Societies; Program Development. **Formerly:** (1977) Sigma Delta Epsilon.

Publications: *Bulletin*, bimonthly. ● *Membership List*, biennial. Directory.

Conventions/Meetings: annual meeting - always summer.

★3174★ SIGMA DELTA TAU
401 Pennsylvania Pkwy., Ste. 110
Indianapolis, IN 46280
Ann Stringer Braly, Exec.Dir.
PH: (317)846-7747
FX: (317)575-5562

Founded: 1917. **Members:** 35,000. **Languages:** English. **National.** Social sorority. Presents awards and scholarships. Offers career networking for alumnae, placement services, and educational loans. Maintains charitable program. Supports the National Committee for the Prevention of Child Abuse Sponsors workshops.

Publications: *Bulletin*, monthly. ● *The Torch*, semiannual. Newsletter. ● *70th Anniveersary Alumnae Directory*.

Conventions/Meetings: biennial meeting - 1994. ● periodic conference.

★3175★ SIGMA GAMMA RHO SORORITY
8800 S. Stony Island Ave.
Chicago, IL 60617
Bonita M. Herring, Exec.Sec.
PH: (312)873-9000

Founded: 1922. **National.** Works for the development of the African American community. Encourages educational opportunities for African American youth. Promotes human rights legislation. Supports economic development in the African American community. Emphasizes strengthening of the family through programs that address quality education, adequate child care, elimination of domestic violence, reduction in teenage pregnancies, and comprehensive health care.

★3176★ SIGMA KAPPA
8733 Founders Rd.
Indianapolis, IN 46268
Cindy Garrett, Exec.Dir.
PH: (317)872-3275
FX: (317)872-0716

Founded: 1874. **Members:** 96,000. **Staff:** 12. **Languages:** English. **National.** Social sorority.

Publications: *Harris Directory*, quinquennial. ● *Sigma Kappa Triangle*, quarterly. Magazine.

Conventions/Meetings: biennial meeting (exhibits).

★3177★ SIGMA SIGMA SIGMA
Box 466
Woodstock, VA 22664
Jayne E. Kozminski, Exec.Dir.
PH: (703)459-4212
FX: (703)459-2361

Founded: 1898. **Members:** 60,000. **Staff:** 19. **Languages:** English. **National.** Service sorority. Conducts philanthropic play therapy project for children at University of North Carolina Hospital (Chapel Hill, NC) and Children's Medical Center, (Dallas, TX). Maintains Sigma Sigma Sigma Education Foundation. Sponsors leadership schools. **Departments:** Alumnae; Collegiate; Philanthropy; Treasury.

Publications: *The Triangle*, 3/year. Newsletter.

Conventions/Meetings: triennial meeting.

★3178★ SINGLE MOTHERS BY CHOICE (SMC)
PO Box 1642, Gracie Square Sta.
New York, NY 10028
Jane Mattes, Chairperson
PH: (212)988-0993

Founded: 1981. **Members:** 1,000. **State Groups:** 10. **Languages:** English. **National.** Primarily single professional women in their 30s and 40s who have either decided to have or are considering having children outside of marriage; also welcomes women who are considering adoption as single parents (does not include mothers who are widowed or divorced). Provides support for single mothers; disseminates information to women who choose to be single parents. Sponsors workshops and play groups for children. Offers the opportunity for single women to discuss the problems and benefits of being a single parent. Maintains resource files and speakers' bureau; conducts research programs. **Computer Services:** Data base; information services. **Committees:** Information.

Publications: *SMC Newsletter*, 20/year.

Conventions/Meetings: periodic meeting. ● periodic seminar. ● periodic workshop.

★3179★ SINGLE PARENT RESOURCE CENTER
141 W. 28th St., Ste. 302
New York, NY 10001
Suzanne Jones, Exec.Dir.
PH: (212)947-0221

Founded: 1981. **Languages:** English. **National.** Purpose is to establish a network of local single parent groups so that such groups will have a collective political voice. Is currently in the process of identifying existing single parent organizations.

★3180★ SISTERS IN CRIME
PO Box 442124
Lawrence, KS 66044-8933
M. Beth Wasson, Exec.Sec.
PH: (913)842-1325

Founded: 1986. **Members:** 1,600. **Membership Dues:** U.S. and Canada., US$20; international., US$25. **Languages:** English. **National.** Women writers, readers, editors, literary agents, booksellers, librarians and others interested in mystery writing. Aims to: eliminate discrimination against women mystery writers; educate publishers and the public on female authors; publicize members' work; and foster mutual support among members. Studies images of women in crime fiction.

Publications: *Newsletter* (in English), semiannual. ● *Books in Print Catalogue*, semiannual. ● *Membership Directory* (in English), periodic. ● *Shameless Promotion for Brazen Hussies* (in English). Booklet.

Conventions/Meetings: annual meeting.

★3181★ SISTERS OF MERCY OF THE AMERICAS
8300 Colesville Rd., Ste. 300
Silver Spring, MD 20910   PH: (301)587-0423
Amyith Hoey, Councillor   FX: (301)587-0533

Languages: English. **National.** Christian women participating in community service activities. Works to improve living conditions of the underprivileged.

★3182★ SLOVENIAN WOMEN'S UNION (SWU)
431 N. Chicago St.
Joliet, IL 60432
Olga Ancel, Sec.   PH: (815)727-1926

Founded: 1926. **Members:** 10,000. **Staff:** 2. **State Groups:** 106. **Local Groups:** 1. **Languages:** English. **National.** Membership is composed primarily of Christian women and children of Slovenian ancestry. Conducts research programs; sponsors competitions. Maintains biographical archives and Slovenian Women's Union Heritage Museum in Joliet, IL. **Committees:** Cultural Heritage; Scholarship; Sports; Youth Activities.

Publications: *ZARJA - The Dawn*, monthly. Magazine. Includes calendar of events, chapter news, and obituaries. **ISSN:** 0044-1848. **Circulation:** 6,400. **Advertising:** accepted. ● *From Here to Slovenia.* Book. ● *Footsteps Thru Time.* Book.

Conventions/Meetings: quadrennial. ● next 1995.

★3183★ SOCIETAS DOCTA (SOD)
2207 Glynnwood Dr.
Savannah, GA 31404
Dr. Abbie W. Jordan, Founder & Dir.   PH: (912)354-4634

Founded: 1987. **Members:** 40. **Staff:** 3. **Budget:** US$4,000. **Languages:** English. **National.** Minority women who have earned a doctorate degree from an established, accredited institution. Seeks to motivate minority women doctorates. Conducts mentoring program. **Computer Services:** Mailing lists.

Publications: *Alert*, annual. Newsletter.

Conventions/Meetings: annual conference

★3184★ SOCIETY FOR THE ADVANCEMENT OF WOMEN'S HEALTH
  RESEARCH
1601 Connecticut Ave. NW, Ste. 801
Washington, DC 20009
Joanne Howes, Director   PH: (202)328-2200

National. Women in health and medical sciences who work for the abolishment of inequities in health research on women.

★3185★ SOCIETY FOR ASSISTED REPRODUCTIVE TECHNOLOGY
  (SART)
c/o American Fertility Society
1209 Montgomery Hwy.
Birmingham, AL 35216-2809   PH: (205)978-5000
Mary Fasshauer, Contact   FX: (205)978-5005

Members: 140. **Languages:** English. **National.** Institutions conducting assisted reproductive procudures. Works to extend knowledge of human in vitro fertilization techniques. Conducts educational programs; gathers and disseminates information.

Conventions/Meetings: annual convention, in conjunction with American fertility Society. ● annual meeting.

★3186★ SOCIETY FOR GYNECOLOGIC INVESTIGATION (SGI)
409 12th St. SW
Washington, DC 20024   PH: (202)863-2544
Ava Tayman, Dir.   FX: (202)544-0453

Founded: 1953. **Members:** 600. **Languages:** English. **National.** Present and former faculty members of institutions interested or engaged in fundamental gynecologic research. Purpose is to stimulate, encourage, assist, and conduct gynecologic research.

Publications: *Gynecologic Investigation*, semiannual. Published as a section of the *American Journal of Obstetrics and Gynecology*.

Conventions/Meetings: annual convention - always March.

★3187★ SOCIETY FOR MENSTRUAL CYCLE RESEARCH (SMCR)
10559 N. 104th Pl.
Scottsdale, AZ 85258
Mary Anna Friederich M.D., Sec.-Treas.   PH: (602)451-9731

Founded: 1979. **Members:** 100. **Languages:** English. **National.** Physicians, nurses, endocrinologists, geneticists, physiologists, psychologists, sociologists, researchers, educators, students, and others interested in the health needs of women as related to the menstrual cycle. Goals are: to identify research priorities, recommend research strategies, and promote interdisciplinary research on the menstrual cycle; to establish a communication network for facilitating interdisciplinary dialogue on menstrual cycle events; to disseminate information and promote discussion of issues among public groups.

Publications: *Membership Roster*, periodic. Directory. ● *Newsletter*, quarterly. ● *Changing Perspectives on Menopause.* Book. ● *Menstrual Health in Women's Lives.* Book.

Conventions/Meetings: biennial conference.

★3188★ SOCIETY OF MILITARY WIDOWS (SMW)
5535 Hempstead Way
Springfield, VA 22151   PH: (703)750-1342
Maj.Gen. J. C. Pennington USA, Contact   FX: (703)354-4380

Founded: 1968. **Members:** 6,500. **Local Groups:** 30. **Languages:** English. **National.** Widows of deceased career or active duty military personnel; affiliate members are persons who support the society's goals. Seeks to obtain equity for military widows under the Survivor Benefit Plan and to educate the public concerning the problems and needs of military widows. Monitors federal legislation affecting military widows; provides members with fact sheets on changes in survivor benefits. Has introduced bills before Congress and testified before congressional committees. Conducts surveys. Local chapters maintain the Reach Out To Help Program, a support system for the newly widowed, and sponsor social and educational activities.

Conventions/Meetings: annual conference.

★3189★ SOCIETY OF OUR LADY OF THE WAY (SOLW)
147 Dorado Terr.
San Francisco, CA 94112
Blanche McNamara, Unit Dir.   PH: (415)585-3319

Founded: 1936. **Members:** 275. **Languages:** English. **National.** A secular society of laywomen who devote themselves by vow to the apostolate. Aims to Christianize the world and witness to Christ while living a secular life. Maintains archives. **Libraries:** Type: reference.

Publications: *Witness*, semiannual. Newsletter.

★3190★ SOCIETY OF PERINATAL OBSTETRICIANS (SPO)
409 12th St. SW
Washington, DC 20024-2188   PH: (202)863-2476
Pat Stahr, Exec.Dir.   FX: (202)554-0453

Founded: 1977. **Members:** 1,262. **Languages:** English. **National.** Obstetricians and gynecologists specializing in maternal-fetal medicine. Works to improve perinatal care through promotion and expansion of education in obstetrical perinatology. Provides a forum for exchange among members.

Publications: *American Journal of Obstetrics and Gynecology*, periodic.

Conventions/Meetings: annual clinical meeting meeting.

★3191★ SOCIETY OF REPRODUCTIVE ENDOCRINOLOGISTS (SRE)
c/o American Fertility Society
1209 Montgomery Hwy.
Birmingham, AL 35216-2809 PH: (205)978-5000
Mary Fasshauer, Contact FX: (205)978-5005

Members: 420. **Languages:** English. **National.** Medical doctors with American Board of Obstetrics and Gynecology certification as reproductive endocrinologists. Works to extend knowledge of human reproduction and endocrinology; makes available to members continuing education programs. Conducts seminars.

Conventions/Meetings: annual convention, in conjunction with the American fertility Society.

★3192★ SOCIETY FOR REPRODUCTIVE SURGEONS (SRE)
c/o American Fertility Society
1209 Montgomery Hwy.
Birmingham, AL 35216-2809 PH: (205)978-5000
Mary Fasshauer, Contact FX: (205)978-5005

Members: 450. **Languages:** English. **National.** Reproductive surgeons. Gathers and disseminates information on reproductive surgery; conducts continuing education programs for members. Makes available referrals list.

Conventions/Meetings: annual convention, in conjunction with the American Fertility Society. ● annual meeting.

★3193★ SOCIETY FOR THE STUDY OF BREAST DISEASE (SSBD)
Sammons Tower
3409 Worth
Dallas, TX 75246 PH: (214)821-2962
Gerorg N. Peters M.D., Sec. FX: (214)827-7032

Founded: 1976. **Members:** 250. **Languages:** English. **National.** Physicians and nurses, primarily those engaged in the fields of obstetrics and gynecology, surgery, radiology, family practice, and medical and radiation oncology. Seeks to further the study of diseases of the breast and to inform physicians and other health care professionals of developments in the diagnosis and treatment of breast cancer and benign diseases of the breast. Serves as a forum for discussion among members. Encourages research pertaining to breast disease.

Publications: *Breast Disease - An International Journal*, quarterly. ● *Newsletter*, periodic.

Conventions/Meetings: annual meeting.

★3194★ SOCIETY FOR THE STUDY OF WOMEN IN LEGAL HISTORY
(WLH)
c/o Nancy S. Erickson
619 Carroll St.
Brooklyn, NY 11215
Nancy S. Erickson, Founder PH: (718)783-8162

Founded: 1979. **Members:** 250. **Languages:** English. **National.** Teachers of law, legal history, history, and women's studies. Encourages research into the status, rights, and responsibilities of women under the law throughout history, especially, but not restricted to, American history. Sponsors seminars.

Publications: *Newsletter*, periodic.

Conventions/Meetings: annual luncheon.

★3195★ SOCIETY OF WOMEN ENGINEERS (SWE)
345 E. 47th St., Rm. 305
New York, NY 10017 PH: (212)705-7855
B. J. Harrod, Acting Exec.Dir. FX: (212)319-0947

Founded: 1950. **Members:** 15,000. **Budget:** US$500,000. **Local Groups:** 67. **Languages:** English. **National.** Educational service society of women engineers; membership is also open to men. Supplies information on the achievements of women engineers and the opportunities available to them; assists women engineers in preparing for return to active work following temporary retirement. Serves as an informational center on women in engineering. Administers several certificate and scholarship programs. Offers tours, professional workshops, and career guidance; conducts surveys. Compiles statistics; maintains archives. **Awards:** Periodic (grant). ● Periodic (scholarship). **Committees:** Achievement; Career Guidance; Continuing Development; Industrial Support; Publicity; Resource; Strategic Planning; Student Activities.

Publications: *U.S. Woman Engineer*, bimonthly. Journal. **ISSN:** 0272-7838. **Circulation:** 15,000. **Advertising:** accepted. ● *Career guidance*. Booklet. ● *Profile of the Women Engineer*. Book.

Conventions/Meetings: annual student conference (exhibits) - always June. 1994, Pittsburgh, PA, United States; 1995, Boston, MT, United States.

★3196★ SOCIETY FOR WOMEN IN PLASTICS (SWP)
PO Box 775
Sterling Heights, MI 48078-0775 PH: (313)949-0440
Elaine Wallace, Pres. FX: (313)949-8460

Founded: 1979. **Members:** 138. **Languages:** English. **National.** Women with education or employment experience in the field of plastics or related businesses. Promotes knowledge of the plastics industry. Conducts plant tours; operates speakers' bureau.

Publications: *Dimensions*, monthly. Newsletter. **Advertising:** not accepted.

Conventions/Meetings: monthly convention.

★3197★ SOCIOLOGISTS FOR WOMEN IN SOCIETY (SWS)
American Sociological Association PH: (202)833-3410
1722 N St. NW FX: (202)785-0146
Washington, DC 20036 E-Mail: BITNET:
Dr. Carla Howery, Pres. CBH@GWUVM

Founded: 1970. **Members:** 1,500. **Local Groups:** 20. **Languages:** English. **National.** Female professional sociologists, female students of sociology, and others interested in the purposes of the organization. Dedicated to: maximizing the effectiveness of and professional opportunities for women in sociology; exploring the contributions which sociology can, does, and should make to the investigation of and improvement in the status of women in society. Acts as watchdog of the American Sociological Association to ensure that it does not ignore the special needs of women in the profession. Has organized a job market service to bring potential jobs and applicants together; established a discrimination committee offering advice and organizational support for women who pursue cases charging sex discrimination; has aided women to establish social, professional, and intellectual contacts with each other. Conducts workshops and seminars at meetings of sociological societies. **Awards:** Periodic Cheryl Miller Lecturer Award. **Computer Services:** Mailing lists. **Committees:** Career Development; Discrimination; Job Market; Social Issues.

Publications: *Directory*, annual. ● *Gender & Society*, quarterly. Journal. Includes articles, research reports and book reviews. **ISSN:** 0891-2432. **Advertising:** accepted. ● *Network News*, quarterly. Newsletter. Includes articles, letters to Editor, columns, minutes of meetings, and job announcements. **Advertising:** accepted. ● *Directory*, periodic. membership information. ● *The Social Construction of Gender*. Book.

Conventions/Meetings: convention, in conjunction with the American Sociological Association - 1994 Aug. 5 - 9, Los Angeles, CA, United States; 1995

Aug. 9 - 13, Washington, DC, United States; 1996 Aug. 10 - 14, Chicago, IL, United States. ● annual meeting.

★3198★ SOUTHERN BAPTIST CONVENTION - WOMEN'S MISSIONARY UNION
PO Box 830010
Birmingham, AL 35283-0010
June Whitlow, Assoc.Exec.Dir.   PH: (205)991-8100

National. Baptist women working to provide support to girls and women. Conducts mission programs.

★3199★ SOUTHERN BAPTIST WOMEN IN MINISTRY/FOLIO (SBWM/ FOLIO)
2800 Frankfort Ave.
Louisville, KY 40206   PH: (502)896-4425

Founded: 1983. **Members:** 300. **Staff:** 2. **State Groups:** 10. **Languages:** English. **National.** Ordained and unordained female Baptist ministers; students of the Baptist ministry; interested individuals. Promotes the image of women as ministers within the Southern Baptist Convention. Fosters support and communication among members. Conducts educational and research programs. Offers placement service; maintains speakers' bureau and biographical archives. **Libraries:** Type: reference.

Publications: *Folio*, quarterly. Newsletter. Includes news and features pertaining to women ministers. **Circulation:** 4,000. **Advertising:** not accepted.

Conventions/Meetings: annual meeting - always May.

★3200★ STANTON FOUNDATION (KCSF)
PO Box 603
Seneca Falls, NY 13148
Mary Ellen Snyder, Pres.   PH: (315)568-8486

Founded: 1978. **Regional Groups:** 1. **Local Groups:** 1. **Languages:** English. **National.** Participants include educators and activists from Seneca Falls and central New York who work to interpret the works of Elizabeth Cady Stanton (1815-1902), the suffragist responsible for the first women's rights convention held in 1848. Supports the Women's Rights National Historical Park in Seneca Falls, NY. Has purchased the home of Stanton and donated it to the National Park Service in 1982. Has administered national design competition for architectural restoration of the Wesleyan Chapel, site of the first convention; has produced video documentary about the chapel. Sponsors lectures, forums, and artistic presentations that relate the history of women's rights activities to contemporary concerns. **Committees:** Corinne Guntzel Research Grant in Women's Studies; Education; Park Support.

Publications: *Newsletter*, San. Includes information on foundation activities, book reviews, and reprints of lectures. **Advertising:** not accepted. ● *Seneca Falls, 1848: All Men and Women are Created Equal*. Book. ● *The Weslyan Chapel: Birthplace of Women's Rights*. Videos. ● *Newsletter*. Includes information on foundation activities, book reviews, and reprints of Lectures.

Conventions/Meetings: meeting - 3/year. Seneca Falls, NY, United States.

★3201★ STATION JOAN'S INTERNATIONAL ALLIANCE U.S. SECTION (SJIA-USA)
2131 N. 37th St.
Milwaukee, WI 53208
C. Virginia Finn, Pres.   PH: (414)444-0976

Founded: 1965. **Languages:** English. **National.** Objectives are to secure legal and de facto equality between women and men in society, church, and state. Has worked for the passage of the Equal Rights Amendment since 1966. The International Alliance, founded in 1911, has worked with the United Nations (and earlier with the League of Nations) for: the abolition of child and forced marriages and slavery traffic and traffic in persons; the political rights of women; equal access to education and vocational training

and economic opportunities; family law; elimination of discrimination against women. In the church, the alliance has petitioned for lay men and women observers and women auditors at the Second Vatican Council, for the revision of the nuptial liturgy, revision of those canons of the code that adversely affect women, and admission of women to the diaconate and priesthood on the same terms and under the same conditions as men. Seeks dialogue with bishops regarding the status of women in the church. Maintains speakers' bureau. **Libraries:** Type: reference. **Committees:** ERA; Public Relations and Press; Sexist Language and Readings in the Liturgy.

Publications: *Catholic Citizen*, semiannual. Newsletter. **Advertising:** not accepted. **Also Cited As:** *Alleanza* and *L'Alliance*. ● *President's Newsletter*, periodic.

Conventions/Meetings: biennial convention.

★3202★ STUNTWOMEN'S ASSOCIATION OF MOTION PICTURES (SAMP)
5215 Lankershim Blvd., Ste. 8
North Hollywood, CA 91601
Mary Peters, Pres.   PH: (213)462-1605

Founded: 1968. **Members:** 21. **Languages:** English. **National.** Stunt actresses and stunt coordinators who belong to the Screen Actors Guild and/or to the American Federation of Television and Radio Artists.

Conventions/Meetings: monthly meeting.

★3203★ SUPREME CALDRON, DAUGHTERS OF MOKANNA (D of M)
4240 Vernon NW
Canton, OH 44709
Ruby Kalkman, Supreme Rodeval Sec.   PH: (216)492-4484

Founded: 1919. **Members:** 4,822. **Staff:** 3. **Local Groups:** 36. **Languages:** English. **National.** Fraternal Masonic order for women relatives of Supreme Council, Mystic Order Veiled Prophets of Enchanted Reulm members. Sponsors competitions for singing groups and drill teams.

Publications: *Roster*, quinquennial. Directory. ● *Supreme Caldron, Daughters of Mokanna—Proceedings*, annual. Booklet. **Advertising:** not accepted.

Conventions/Meetings: annual convention - always September. Toledo, OH, United States.

★3204★ SUPREME LADIES AUXILIARY KNIGHTS OF STATION JOHN (SLAKSJ)
1606 Otis NE
Washington, DC 20018
Iris L. Nelson, Supreme Sec.   PH: (202)526-5322

Founded: 1900. **Members:** 14,521. **Staff:** 4. **Languages:** English. **Multinational.** Fraternal society of Catholic women. Sponsors competitions; provides children's services; conducts charitable and educational programs. **Committees:** Legislative; Military; Mission; Sports.

Publications: *Convention Proceedings*, biennial. Booklet. ● *Grand*, annual. State proceedings.

Conventions/Meetings: biennial meeting.

★3205★ SUPREME LODGE OF THE DANISH SISTERHOOD OF AMERICA (DSA)
c/o Lorraine Zembinski
2916 N. 121 St.
Milwaukee, WI 53222
Lorraine Zembinski, Pres.

Founded: 1883. **Members:** 4,000. **Staff:** 7. **Local Groups:** 77. **Languages:** English. **National.** Women of, or related to those of, Danish birth or descent or those married to men of Danish descent; individuals interested in the Danish heritage. **Awards:** Periodic (scholarship).

Publications: *Danish Sisterhood News*, monthly. Newsletter. Includes national and lodge information. **Circulation:** 4,000. **Advertising:** not accepted.

Conventions/Meetings: quadrennial convention.

★3206★ SUPREME SHRINE OF THE ORDER OF THE WHITE SHRINE OF JERUSALEM (SSOWSJ)
107 E. New Haven Ave.
Melbourne, FL 32901   PH: (407)952-5323
Helen R. Piechulis, Sec.   FX: (407)728-0011

Founded: 1894. **Members:** 69,000. **Staff:** 2. **Local Groups:** 650. **Languages:** English. **National.** Primarily women relatives of Master Masons; Master Masons are also members. Provides charitable aid to those who are unable to obtain it through other channels. **Computer Services:** Mailing lists.

Publications: *Appendix*, annual. Directory. ● *Official Letter*, semiannual. Newsletter. ● *Proceedings*, annual. Booklet. ● *Supreme Herald*, quarterly. Bulletin. **Circulation:** 6,000. **Advertising:** not accepted.

Conventions/Meetings: annual conference - always May. 1994 May, St. Paul, MN, United States; 1995 May, Reno, NV, United States.

★3207★ SUPREME TEMPLE ORDER PYTHIAN SISTERS (STOPS)
PO Box 1257
Anaconda, MT 59711
Wenonah Jones, Supreme Sec.   PH: (406)563-6433

Founded: 1888. **Members:** 22,000. **Staff:** 3. **State Groups:** 43. **Local Groups:** 647. **Languages:** English. **National.** Women's auxiliary of the Supreme Lodge Knights of Pythias. Donates to many projects benefitting blood drives, retarded citizens, and patients suffering from cancer, cystic fibrosis, polio, cerebral palsy, and heart and kidney ailments.

Publications: *Pythian International*, 4/year. Newsletter.

Conventions/Meetings: biennial meeting.

★3208★ SWEDISH WOMEN'S EDUCATIONAL ASSOCIATION INTERNATIONAL (SWEA)
PO Box 2585
7414 Herschel Ave., No. 001
La Jolla, CA 92038-2585   PH: (619)459-8435
Boel Alkdal, Admin.   FX: (619)597-4111

Founded: 1979. **Members:** 4,500. **Languages:** English. **Multinational.** Women aged 18 and over who are fluent in the Swedish language and interested in preserving and promoting Swedish culture and tradition. Conducts public relations activities on behalf of Sweden. **Awards:** Periodic (scholarship).

Publications: *Directory*, annual. ● *SWEA Forum*, 2/year. Journal.

Conventions/Meetings: annual conference.

★3209★ TANGENT GROUP (TG)
115 Monroe St.
Bossier City, LA 71111
Don Slater, Founder   PH: (318)742-4709

Founded: 1965. **Members:** 200. **Languages:** English. **National.** Supports the Homosexual Information Center by donations of money and time. Conducts charitable programs; maintains speakers' bureau. **Committees:** Fight Exclusion of Homosexuals from the Armed Forces. **Alternate name:** Tangents.

Conventions/Meetings: annual - always July. Los Angeles, CA, United States.

★3210★ TAU BETA SIGMA
PO Box 849
Stillwater, OK 74076   PH: (405)372-2333
          TF: (800)543-6505
David E. Solomon, Exec.Dir.   FX: (405)372-2363

Founded: 1946. **Regional Groups:** 6. **Local Groups:** 129. **Languages:** English. **National.** Honorary sorority - band. Presents awards.

Publications: *Convention Proceedings*, biennial. Booklet. ● *Directory of Active Chapters*, annual. ● *The Podium*, semiannual. Newsletter.

Conventions/Meetings: biennial convention.

★3211★ TAU GAMMA DELTA
c/o Ernestine Belfield
3152 Greenfield Dr.
Rocky Mount, NC 27804
Ernestine Belfield, Pres.   PH: (919)443-6786

Founded: 1942. **Members:** 1,500. **Regional Groups:** 4. **Local Groups:** 60. **Languages:** English. **National.** Service sorority - women in business and the professions. Sponsors Tauettes, for girls ages 13-18, to "help instill good character" and expose them to "the finer cultures"; also sponsors Taugadette, an Annual arts program to promote young artists ages 19-35. Maintains hall of fame; compiles statistics. **Awards:** Periodic (scholarship). **Committees:** National Service; Social Action.

Publications: *Roster*, annual. Directory. ● *The Star*, semiannual. Newsletter.

Conventions/Meetings: annual convention - always August.

★3212★ THETA PHI ALPHA
312 Joslin Ave.
Cincinnati, OH 45220
Lisa Amlung, Contact   PH: (513)221-7188

Founded: 1912. **Members:** 10,000. **Languages:** English. **National.** Social sorority. Sponsors Annual Founders Day; conducts fundraising projects for charitable organizations. **Awards:** Periodic (scholarship). **Committees:** Float Building; Garment; Greek Week; Historian; Memoirs; Publicity; Social Spirit.

Publications: *The Compass of Theta Phi Alpha*, quarterly. ● *Newsletter*.

Conventions/Meetings: biennial convention.

★3213★ THEY HELP EACH OTHER SPIRITUALLY (THEOS)
1301 Clark Bldg.
717 Liberty Ave.
Pittsburgh, PA 15222
Sue Rumbaugh, Exec. Dir.   PH: (412)471-7779

Languages: English. **National.** Fosters communication and exchange among widows and widowers. Organizes local support groups in the United States and Canada.

Publications: *THEOS* (in English), periodic. Magazine. ● Also publishes books.

★3214★ TRADE UNION WOMEN OF AFRICAN HERITAGE (TUWAH)
530 W. 23rd St., Ste. 4051
New York, NY 10011
Thelma Dailey, Pres.   PH: (212)547-5696

Founded: 1969. **Staff:** 1. **Languages:** English. **National.** Black women union members. Supports various causes of ethnic working women; participates in community activities; conducts alternative school programs. Maintains Global Women of African Heritage, Maverick Center for Self Development, and Leaders of the 21st Century. Operates speakers' bureau; compiles statistics; conducts research programs.

Publications: *The Ethnic Woman*, periodic. Magazine. **Circulation:** 3,000.

Advertising: accepted. ● *Newsletter*, periodic. ● *Third World Women*, semiannual.

Conventions/Meetings: annual convention.

★3215★ TRADESWOMEN, INC.
PO Box 40664
San Francisco, CA 94140
Kai Douglas, Contact   PH: (415)821-7334

Founded: 1979. **Members:** 1,000. **Languages:** English. **National.** Women who work in nontraditional, blue-collar occupations including construction, transportation, and industrial work; women who seek to enter these fields or who support the right of others to do so. Serves as a network for women in the trades. Conducts social gatherings and local and regional forums and workshops on topics such as: health and safety on the job; racism and sexism in the trades; sexual harassment; working within unions. Makes available children's services; maintains speakers' bureau. Compiles statistics. **Libraries:** Type: reference.

Publications: *Trade Trax*, monthly. Newsletter. **Advertising:** accepted. ● *Tradeswomen*, quarterly. Magazine. Features news on finding a job, contracting, networking, and tools; legislation and legal cases. Includes book and movie reviews. **ISSN:** 0739-344X. **Circulation:** 1,500. **Advertising:** accepted. ● *What Are Journey Sisters*. Booklet.

Conventions/Meetings: periodic regional meeting.

★3216★ TRANSNATIONAL FAMILY RESEARCH INSTITUTE
8307 Whitman Dr.
Bethesda, MD 20817

Languages: English. **Multinational.** Works to increase awareness and acceptance of family planning throughout the world. Conducts research on abortion and other health-related issues involving women.

Publications: *Abortion Research Notes*, periodic. Journal.

★3217★ TRIKONE
Box 21354
San Jose, CA 95151
Arvind Kumar, Pres.   PH: (408)270-8776

Founded: 1985. **Languages:** English. **Multinational.** Participants are gay and lesbian persons living in southern Asia or of southern Asian descent and their friends. Support group for gay or lesbian persons from southern Asia. Seeks to help participants come to terms with their sexual orientation. Networks with homosexual groups around the world. Is compiling material for a gay/lesbian archives to document the history of homosexuality in the area. **Formerly:** (1987) Trikon.

Publications: *Trikone: Gay and Lesbian South Asians*, quarterly. Newsletter. includes penfriends section. **Advertising:** not accepted. **Also Cited As:** *Trikon*.

★3218★ TURKISH WOMEN'S LEAGUE OF AMERICA (TWLA)
821 United Nations Plaza, 2nd Fl.
New York, NY 10017
Ayten Sandikcioglu, Pres.   PH: (212)682-8525

Founded: 1958. **Members:** 300. **Languages:** English. **Multinational.** Turkish women united to promote equality and justice for women. Organizes cultural and recreational activities to foster better understanding between the people of Turkey and the U.S; brings together Turkic-speaking people in the U.S; works to educate Turkish-Americans about their human and civil rights in the U.S. Operates Ataturk School, which offers courses in Turkish language, history, music, and folk dancing; sponsors workshops and seminars for high school teachers.

Publications: *News Bulletin*, 10/year.

Conventions/Meetings: annual convention - always June.

★3219★ UKRAINIAN NATIONAL WOMEN'S LEAGUE OF AMERICA (UNWLA)
108 2nd Ave.
New York, NY 10003
Maria Savchak, Pres.   PH: (212)533-4646

Founded: 1925. **Members:** 5,000. **Regional Groups:** 9. **Local Groups:** 119. **Languages:** English. **National.** Women of Ukrainian birth or descent living in the United States. Presents literary awards for works dealing with Ukrainian history and historical fiction. Sponsors prekindergarten for children ages three to five. Founded the Ukrainian Museum in New York City in 1976. Offers pen pal program for children and adults. **Awards:** Periodic (scholarship). **Committees:** Arts and Museum; Culture; Education; Public Relations; Welfare.

Publications: *Our Life* (in English and Ukrainian), monthly. Magazine.

Conventions/Meetings: triennial convention.

★3220★ UNION OF PALESTINIAN WOMEN'S ASSOCIATION IN NORTH AMERICA (UPWA)
PO Box 29110   PH: (312)436-6060
Chicago, IL 60629   FX: (312)436-6460

Founded: 1986. **Local Groups:** 26. **Languages:** English. **National.** Promotes national and social self-determination and independence for Palestine. Encourages unity among Palestinian women; supports the women's movement worldwide. Works to raise social consciousness and develop women's self-reliance and leadership skills. Conducts educational programs in an effort to preserve Palestinian culture, heritage, and identity. Sponsors campaigns demanding release of Palestinian women political prisoners. Operates family sponsorship program and clothing collection and distribution program; assists Palestinian cooperatives. Offers counseling and support services.

Publications: *Voice of Palestinian Women*, periodic. Newsletter. ● *UPWA Bulletin*, periodic.

★3221★ UNION OF POLISH WOMEN IN AMERICA (UPWA)
2636-38 E. Allegheny Ave.
Philadelphia, PA 19134-5185
Eleanor Schol, Adm.Sec.   PH: (215)425-3807

Founded: 1920. **Members:** 9,379. **Staff:** 4. **Regional Groups:** 3. **Local Groups:** 65. **Languages:** English. **National.** Fraternal benefit life insurance society of women, men, boys, and girls. Presents awards for essays. Conducts charitable and cultural activities; sponsors folk dances, glee clubs, baton groups, and exhibits; provides student loans. **Awards:** Periodic (scholarship).

Publications: *Gwiazda*, weekly. Newsletter. **Also Cited As:** *Polish Star*.

Conventions/Meetings: quadrennial convention. ● annual conference. ● quadrennial convention.

★3222★ UNITARIAN UNIVERSALIST WOMEN'S FEDERATION (UUWF)
25 Beacon St.
Boston, MA 02108   PH: (617)742-2100
Mairi Maeks, Exec.Dir.   FX: (617)367-3237

Founded: 1963. **Members:** 6,000. **Staff:** 10. **Local Groups:** 300. **Languages:** English. **National.** Federation of women's groups and individual members in local Unitarian Universalist Churches in the U.S. and Canada. Works for human rights for all, especially rights of women. Promotes: Supreme Court decision in favor of abortion; quality in childcare centers; concern for the family; action on clergy sexual misconduct; prevention of violence against women; work for and with the aging; work in area of women and religion. Sponsors volunteer representatives in Washington, DC. Holds personal growth workshops; operates speakers' bureau. **Awards:** Annual Ministry to Women.

Publications: *Federation Communicator*, 5/year. Newsletter.

Conventions/Meetings: biennial convention.

★3223★ UNITED AUTO WORKERS - WOMEN'S COMMITTEE
505 8th Ave., 14th Fl.
New York, NY 10018
Beverley Gans, Contact   PH: (212)736-6270

National. Promotes the interests of women working in the United States auto industry. Seeks to activate and educate women within the UAW. Supports reproductive rights for women.

★3224★ UNITED CHURCH OF CHRIST COORDINATING CENTER
FOR WOMEN IN CHURCH AND SOCIETY (CCW)
700 Prospect Ave.
Cleveland, OH 44115   PH: (216)736-2150
Mary Sue Gast, Contact   FX: (216)736-2156

Founded: 1980. **Budget:** US$495,000. **Languages:** English. **National**. Works to eliminate sexism in the church and society. Promotes advocacy for women's concerns through cooperative projects with United Church of Christ agencies; cooperates in projects by helping to establish a network to respond to legislation affecting women. Promotes consciousness-raising by contributing to other United Church of Christ publications. Recognizes the contributions of lay women. Provides speakers; conducts workshops. **Libraries:** Type: reference. Holdings: 200. Subjects: women's issues, theology, economics, and employment. **Awards:** Biennial Antoinette Brown. Recipient: Award to clergy women.

Publications: *Common Lot*, quarterly. Journal. ● *Mom's Morning Out*. Book.

Conventions/Meetings: biennial general assembly.

★3225★ UNITED DAUGHTERS OF THE CONFEDERACY (UDC)
328 N Blvd.
Richmond, VA 23220-4057
Mrs. Dan Bragg Cook, Pres.Gen.   PH: (804)355-1636

Founded: 1894. **Members:** 25,000. **Staff:** 4. **Local Groups:** 1,000. **Languages:** English. **National**. Women descendants of Confederate veterans of the Civil War. **Libraries:** Type: reference.   Subjects: American Civil War. **Committees:** Benevolent; Children of the Confederacy; Education; History; Memorial; Patriotic; Southern Literature; Southern Poets.

Publications: *United Daughters of the Confederacy Magazine*, 11/year. **Circulation:** 9,500. **Advertising:** accepted.

Conventions/Meetings: annual convention - always November. 1994, Richmond, VA, United States; 1995, LA, United States; 1996, Richmond, VA, United States.

★3226★ UNITED METHODIST CHURCH - GENERAL COMMISSION
ON THE STATUS AND ROLE OF WOMEN
1200 Davis St.
Evanston, IL 60201
Kioyoko Kasai Fujiu, Gen.Sec.   PH: (708)869-7330

Founded: 1972. **National**. Fosters awareness of women's issues and problems throughout the Methodist church. Ensures inclusiveness of women in church power and policy-making at all levels. Encourages women to take leadership role in the church mission and ministry throughout leadership training sessions.

★3227★ UNITED METHODIST CHURCH - WOMEN'S DIVISION
c/o United Methodist Church
475 Riverside Dr., 15th Fl.
New York, NY 10115
Mary Kercherval Short, Exec.Sec.   PH: (212)870-3752

National. Acts as an advocate for oppresses dispossessed women. Works to build a supportive community · of women and foster the growth of Christianity.

★3228★ UNITED NATIONS DEVELOPMENT FUND FOR WOMEN
(UNIFEM)
304 E. 45th St., 6th Fl.   PH: (212)906-6400
New York, NY 10017   CBL: UNDEVPRO NEW
Sharon Capeling-Alakija, Dir.   YORK

Founded: 1976. **Staff:** 18. **Budget:** US$6,000,000. **Regional Groups:** 5. **Languages:** English, French, Spanish. **Multinational**. Autonomous fund operating in association with the United Nations Development Programme and created by the U.N. General Assembly following the International Women's Year, 1975. Provides technical and financial support to educational programs in developing countries that benefit rural women or underprivileged women in urban areas. Funds numerous projects including: training in food preservation; training of child care workers; promotion and training of rural women in income-raising group activities; case studies. Organizes workshops to build skills in management of small-scale industries. Areas of interest include revolving loan funds, energy resource development, and community self-help activities for low-income women.

Publications: *Development Review*, semiannual. ● *Information Booklets*, periodic. ● *A Guide to Community Revolving Loan Funds*. Book. ● Also publishes and occasional papers.

Conventions/Meetings: semiannual intergovernmental committee meeting.

★3229★ UNITED NATIONS INTERNATIONAL RESEARCH AND
TRAINING INSTITUTE FOR THE ADVANCEMENT OF WOMEN
(INSTRAW)
(Instituto Internacional de Investigacion y Capacitacion de las
Naciones Unidas para la Promocion de la Mujer)
EPS No. A-314
PO Box 52-4121
Miami, FL 33152-4121
Eleni Stamiris, Deputy Dir.

Founded: 1980. **Staff:** 40. **Budget:** US$2,837,000. **Languages:** English, French, Spanish. **Multinational**. Conducts information gathering, research, and training activities to help women overcome obstacles and constraints to their full and effective participation in development processes, particularly in developing nations. Advocates establishment of a development process more responsive to women's concerns. Works to enhance the efforts of women, as well as those of the international community, in moving toward a new and more equitable international order. Provides advisory services and sponsors fellowship and internship programs. Maintains documentation center; compiles statistics. **Computer Services:** Data base, bibliographic information and rosters of development experts and in stitutions; mailing lists. **Divisions:** Information, Documentation, and Communication; Research and Training.

Publications: *INSTRAW News* (in English, French, and Spanish), semiannual. ● Also publishes case studies, conference papers, research and technical reports, and position papers.

Conventions/Meetings: annual board meeting. ● periodic seminar.

★3230★ UNITED NATIONS WOMEN'S GUILD (UNWG)
1 United Nations Plaza, Rm. DC-1-550
New York, NY 10017
Elsa Wurfl, Pres.   PH: (212)963-4149

Founded: 1948. **Languages:** English. **Multinational**. Women employees of the United Nations ; wives of those employed by the U.N. and its specialized agencies; individuals who contribute services to the guild. Goal is to send direct aid to underprivileged children worldwide. Members suggest projects involving institutions that provide assistance to young victims of poverty, disease, and war. Works with sister groups offering suggestions for projects or requesting aid in supporting their own local projects. Sponsors fundraising projects.

Publications: *Directory*, annual. ● *Newsletter*, annual. ● *History of UNWG*.

Conventions/Meetings: annual - always February, New York.

★3231★ UNITED ORDER TRUE SISTERS (UOTS)
212 5th Ave, No. 1307
New York, NY 10010   PH: (212)679-6790

Founded: 1846. **Members:** 12,000. **Staff:** 1. **National Groups:** 45. **Languages:** English. **National.** Charitable organization administered by women that offers personal service to indigent cancer and AIDS patients. Sends children with cancer to camp.

Publications: *Echo*, quarterly. Newsletter.

Conventions/Meetings: biennial.

★3232★ UNITED PRESBYTERIAN CHURCH - USA WOMEN'S UNIT
100 Witherspoon St.
Louisville, KY 402020
Rev. Mary J. Kuhns, Contact

National. Promotes justic for women in the Presbyterian church by providing opportunities for women of all ages and races to participate in and hold leadership positions. Conducts research on the status of women. Develops and implements strategies for addressing concerns of women throughout the church. Works for the fair representation of women in the church structure.

★3233★ U.S. COALITION FOR LIFE (USCL)
Box 315
Export, PA 15632
Randy V. Engel, Dir.   PH: (412)327-7379

Founded: 1972. **Languages:** English. **National.** Pro-life, anti-abortion organizations, hospitals, and government and health agencies. Research organization and clearinghouse on population control activities such as abortion, genetic engineering, and government family planning. Issues mailings on pro-life legislation. Maintains international reprint service. Aids in the development of research programs. **Committees:** Education; Inter-Liaison; Research.

Publications: *Pro-Life Reporter*, quarterly. Newsletter.

Conventions/Meetings: periodic seminar.

★3234★ UNITED STATES DELEGATION FOR FRIENDSHIP AMONG
   WOMEN
2219 Caroline Ln.
South St. Paul, MN 55075
Mary Pomeroy, Sec.-Treas.   PH: (612)455-5620

Founded: 1970. **National.** Promotes cultural exchange and understanding among women leaders of the world. Supports cultural and peaceful co-existence among peoples of the world.

★3235★ UNITED STATES WOMEN'S CURLING ASSOCIATION
   (USWCA)
4114 N. 53rd St.
Omaha, NE 68104
Luella M. Ansorge, Reference Chwm.   PH: (402)453-6574

Founded: 1947. **Members:** 3,400. **Budget:** US$50,000. **Local Groups:** 72. **Languages:** English. **National.** Women amateur curlers. Maintains archive of association competition, awards, and administrative records.

Publications: *North American Curling News*, bimonthly. Newsletter. Contains results of national competition, sites and dates of upcoming Bonspiels, and minutes of executive directors' meetings. **Advertising:** accepted. ● *Roster of USWCA*, annual. Directory. ● *Booklet.* Handbook of rules and regulations. ● *Some Aspects of Curling.* Booklet.

Conventions/Meetings: semiannual convention. ● U.S. Women's National Bonspiel and Annual U.S. Senior Women's Bonspiel. ● periodic competition.

★3236★ UNITED STATES WOMEN'S LACROSSE ASSOCIATION
   (USWLA)
45 Maple Ave.
Hamilton, NY 13346   PH: (315)824-2480
Susanna McVaugh, Exec.Sec.   FX: (315)824-4533

Founded: 1931. **Members:** 2,500. **Budget:** US$100,000. **Local Groups:** 60. **Languages:** English. **National.** Promotes the sport of lacrosse for women. Establishes rules for competition; trains umpires; conducts seminars and clinics. **Awards:** Annual Beth Allen (recognition). **Committees:** Accreditation; Camps; Clinics; Collegiate Coaches; Fundraising; High School and College All-American; Loan Kits; Manual Revision; Memorial Fund; National Tournament; Rules; Safety; Stick Repair; Tours; Umpiring; Youth LaCrosse.

Publications: *Directory*, annual. ● *U.S. Women's Lacrosse Association— Newsletter*, 5/year. Includes calendar of events. **Advertising:** not accepted.

Conventions/Meetings: annual convention - always May. ● annual competition.

★3237★ UNITED STATES WOMEN'S TRACK COACHES
   ASSOCIATION (USWTCA)
c/o Karen Dennis
Michigan State University
Women's Athletic Dept.
East Lansing, MI 48824
Karen Dennis, Pres.   PH: (517)353-9299

Founded: 1967. **Members:** 100. **Languages:** English. **National.** A subcommittee of the Athletics Congress/USA. Track coaches interested in women's track and field. To provide information and serve as a forum for the discussion of issues involving women's track and field. Plans to compile statistics and develop awards program.

Publications: *Membership Directory*, periodic. ● *Newsletter*, quarterly.

Conventions/Meetings: annual convention - always December.

★3238★ UNIVERSAL MASONIC ORDER OF THE EASTERN STAR
   (UMOES)
PO Box 1067
South Orange, NJ 07079
Dorothy West, P.R. Coordinator   PH: (201)763-1780

Founded: 1960. **Members:** 2,400. **Languages:** English. **National.** Women dedicated to community service, especially programs assisting battered women. Promotes love and harmony of global sisterhood. Provides financial and public relations support to charitable organizations. **Awards:** Periodic (scholarship). ● Periodic (grant).

Conventions/Meetings: annual - always July. ● annual convention - always November.

★3239★ VALUE OF LIFE COMMITTEE (VOLCOM)
637 Cambridge St.
Brighton, MA 02135
Marianne Rea-Luthin, Pres.   PH: (617)787-4400

Founded: 1970. **Staff:** 2. **Languages:** English. **National.** Fosters respect for human life from fertilization to natural death and educates and informs the public on all issues concerning life. Maintains speakers' bureau. **Libraries:** Type: reference. Holdings: 650; clippings, books, periodicals. Subjects: abortion, euthanasia, ethics, and genetics. **Committees:** Educational.

Conventions/Meetings: annual - always October.

★3240★ VICTIMS OF CHOICE (VOC)
PO Box 6268
Vacaville, CA 95696-6268
Nola Jones-Noboa, Exec. Officer   PH: (707)448-6015

Founded: 1985. **Languages:** English. **National.** Christian, pro-life, grassroots organization. Provides training and assistance to individuals who counsel women suffering from various types of ''maternal loss'' including those who are dealing with the consequences of negative abortion experiences, or ''post-abortion syndrome''. Provides materials to churches, crisis pregnancy centers, and other pro-life organizations. Coordinates a national hotline and referral system for counselors. Seeks to educate the public on the ''negative effects of abortion''. Conducts press conferences, provides speakers to rallies, and offers testimony before local, state, and national legislatures. Sponsors an annual, national ''Memorial Day of Mourning'', in which women who have had abortions engage in a march and ''funeral''. Distributes information packets, brochures, bumper stickers, and buttons.

Conventions/Meetings: annual convention.

★3241★ VIETNAM WOMEN'S MEMORIAL PROJECT (VWMP)
2001 S St. NW, Ste. 302
Washington, DC 20009
Diane Carlson Evans, Chair & Founder
PH: (202)328-7253
FX: (202)986-3636

Founded: 1984. **Languages:** English. **National.** Works to identify and document women who served during the Vietnam War, and promotes the placing of a memorial in Washington, DC to honor their service. Educates the public regarding the contributions of women during the Vietnam War; maintains speakers' bureau.

★3242★ VOTERS FOR CHOICE/FRIENDS OF FAMILY PLANNING
(VFC)
2604 Connecticut Ave.
Washington, DC 20008
Julie Burton, Exec.Dir.
PH: (202)588-5200
FX: (202)822-6644

Founded: 1984. **Languages:** English. **National.** Independent, bi-partisan political committee. Seeks election and reelection of candidates to federal and state office who support the pro-choice position concerning abortion. Provides technical assistance and consulting services for favored candidates; offers direct financial contributions and services.

Publications: *Winning With Choice.*

★3243★ WAGES DUE LESBIANS (WDL)
PO Box 11795
Philadelphia, PA 19101
PH: (215)668-9886
FX: (215)664-8556

Founded: 1975. **Languages:** English. **National.** Campaigns for wages for housework performed by lesbian women. Defends lesbian mothers' custody of their children. Promotes lesbian women's contributions to civil, welfare, labor, anti-rape, peace, and ecological movements.

Publications: *Policing the Bedroom and How To Refuse It* (in English). Book.

★3244★ WAGES FOR HOUSEWORK CAMPAIGN - UNITED STATES
PO Box 86681
Los Angeles, CA 90086-0681
Phoebe Jones Schellenberg, Contact
PH: (213)221-1698

Founded: 1972. **National.** Works for ''the compensation of unwaged work women do, to be paid by dismantlking the military-industrial complex.'' Compensation includes welfare, benefits, higher wages, Social Security, and child care.

★3245★ WAVES NATIONAL (WN)
72 Meeting Hill Rd.
Hillsborough, NH 03244
Jane Gefvert, Pres.
PH: (603)464-5073

Founded: 1979. **Members:** 7,000. **Budget:** US$45,000. **Local Groups:** 129. **Languages:** English. **National.** Women who have served on active duty in the U.S. Navy and can show proof of service and an honorable discharge; women who are currently on active duty or who have retired from duty in the U.S. Navy, Naval Reserve, Fleet Reserve, or Coast Guard. Encourages

principles of patriotism and loyalty to God, country, and family among former WAVES (Women Accepted for Volunteer Emergency Service) who have served since World War II, and other women who have served in the Navy. Provides a network of support and assistance and an opportunity for locating, communicating, and associating with former WAVES; serves as a medium of exchange between its local units. Maintains collection of pictures, newspaper clippings, and military uniforms. Makes available World War II memorabilia to museums. Operates biographical archives. **Formerly:** (1986) Waves National Corp.

Publications: *White Caps*, bimonthly. Newsletter. Membership activities. **Circulation:** 6,700. **Advertising:** not accepted.

Conventions/Meetings: biennial convention - 1994 Aug. 29 - Sept. 3. ● biennial conference.

★3246★ WE ARE AWARE
PO Box 242
Bedford, MA 01730-0242
Nancy Bittle, President
PH: (508)443-5404

Founded: 1990. **Budget:** US$6,000. **Languages:** English. **National.** Seeks to reduce rape and violence against women by teaching women about effective self-protection. Stresses the concepts of choice and empowerment, with the philosophy that individuals should be armed with courage, determination, spirit, and knowledge, whether or not one is armed with anything else. Advocates self-protection methods incorporating a range of weapons, recognizing that firearms are not the solution for every situation. Makes referrals and acts as information clearinghouse. Offers courses taught by certified instructors in the use of firearms, temporarily disabling aerosols, and in general personal protection. Operates speakers' bureau. (AWARE stands for Arming Women Against Rape and Endangerment and Advancing Women's Armed Rights through Education.).

Publications: *Newsletter*, quarterly. **Advertising:** accepted.

★3247★ WESTERN WOMEN PROFESSIONAL BOWLERS (WWPB)
8523 Lindley Ave.
Northridge, CA 91325
Miss Pat Rossler, Pres.
PH: (818)886-9197

Founded: 1965. **Members:** 176. **Staff:** 3. **Languages:** English. **National.** Adult women with a bowling average of 175 or higher in 60 or more games. Objectives are to: provide an organization in which women bowlers may participate as tournament competitors and as involved members; develop support among women bowlers for national, state, and local competitions; promote an interest in competitive participation among women bowlers; encourage good fellowship and sportsmanship, thereby creating a desirable public image to promote and elevate bowling as a whole. Conducts 12-15 tournaments per year. Maintains collection of program books. **Awards:** Annual WWPB Bowler of the Year. ● Annual WWPB Rookie of the Year. ● Periodic Merle Matthews Distinguished Service. **Committees:** Good Cheer; Pennants and Banner.

Publications: *Code of Operations*, annual. Booklet. ● *Program Book*, annual. ● *Squad Room*, 12-15/year. Newsletter. Circulated after each tournament. ● *Tournament Guide for Hosting Centers*. Book.

Conventions/Meetings: annual convention - always January.

★3248★ WHIRLY-GIRLS (INTERNATIONAL WOMEN HELICOPTER PILOTS)
PO Box 584840
Houston, TX 77058-8484
Colleen Nevius, Exec.Dir.
PH: (713)474-3932

Founded: 1955. **Members:** 790. **Languages:** English. **Multinational.** Women helicopter pilots. Stimulates interest among women in rotary-wing aircraft. Members serve as standby pilots for search and rescue work. **Awards:** Annual (scholarship). Recipient: aspiring helicopter pilots.

Publications: *Membership List*, periodic. ● *Newsletter*, quarterly.

Conventions/Meetings: annual conference (exhibits). ● annual dinner, Presents awards..

★3249★ WIDER OPPORTUNITIES FOR WOMEN (WOW)
1325 G St. NW, Lower Level
Washington, DC 20005
Cynthia Marano, Exec.Dir.
PH: (202)638-3143
FX: (202)638-4885

Founded: 1964. **Membership Dues:** US$55 annual. **Staff:** 15. **Budget:** US$1,000,000. **Regional Groups:** 500. **Local Groups:** 500. **Languages:** English. **National**. To expand employment opportunities for women through information, employment training, technical assistance, and advocacy. Works to overcome barriers to women's employment and economic equity, including occupational segregation, sex stereotypic education and training, discrimination in employment practices and wages. Sponsors Women's Work Force Network, a national network of 500 women's employment programs and advocates. The network monitors current policies to increase the priority given to employment needs of women; provides information to congressional staffs to clarify the impact of various legislative proposals on women; issues public policy alerts and informational materials when relevant federal policy is being proposed or undergoing revision; conducts investigative projects to assess how legislative programs are implemented and their impact on women. Offers technical assistance to education institutions, government agencies, and private industry on programs to increase women's participation in non-traditional employment and training. Maintains National Commission on Working Women and Industry Advisory Council. **Awards:** Annual Women at Work.

Publications: *Women at Work*, quarterly. Newsletter. ● *A More Promising Future: Strategics to Improve the Workplace*. Book. ● *Growing Up in Prime Time: An Analysis of Adolescent Girls on Television*. Book.

Conventions/Meetings: periodic convention. ● periodic regional meeting. ● periodic workshop.

★3250★ WIDOWED PERSONS SERVICE (WPS)
c/o American Association of Retired
   Persons
601 E St. NW
Washinton, DC 20049
Ruth J.L. Richard, Manager
PH: (202)434-2260

Languages: English. **National**. Offers emotional and legal support to recently widowed women. Fosters the development of similar organizations. Conducts professional training programs for counsellors.

Publications: *Insights* (in English), periodic. Newsletter.

Conventions/Meetings: annual conference. ● periodic regional meeting - 10/ year.

★3251★ WIDOWS OF WORLD WAR I (WWWI)
324 Gregory SW
Burleson, TX 76068
Helen Green, Pres.
PH: (817)295-1658

Founded: 1946. **Members:** 4,000. **State Groups:** 4. **Local Groups:** 47. **Languages:** English. **National**. Widows of veterans of World War I. Works to obtain better legislation for widows of World War I. **Committees:** Americanism; Hospital and rehabilitation; Legislation; Publicity.

Publications: *Bulletin*, quarterly. ● *Newsletters to Chapters*, monthly.

Conventions/Meetings: annual convention - usually April.

★3252★ THE WOMAN ACTIVIST (TWA)
2310 Barbour Rd.
Falls Church, VA 22043-2940
Flora Crater, Pres.
PH: (703)573-8716

Founded: 1975. **Languages:** English. **National**. Nonprofit consulting firm specializing in service on issues of political concern to women. Activities include research, program development, issue analysis, report writing, and statistics compilation. Rates members of Congress on women's issues and compares voting patterns of congressmen and congresswomen on civil and social rights issues. Compiles Woman Activist Mailing List of political feminists. **Libraries:** Type: reference. Holdings: books. Subjects: feminism.

Publications: *The Woman Activist*, 10/year.

★3253★ WOMAN'S EDUCATION AND LEADERSHIP FORUM (WELF)
1825 I St. NW, Ste. 400
Washington, DC 20006
Patricia Brockbank, Exec. Officer
PH: (202)223-2908
FX: (202)429-9574

Founded: 1986. **Languages:** English. **National**. Seeks to empower women to achieve self-sufficiency, confident decision-making, and personal and professional success skills to meet the challenges and demands in the "changing world." Believes that self-confidence, knowledge, and skills are the only means that can ensure an individual's success and that an individual's success is essential to our nation's success. Sponsors state-by-state day-long conferences providing a woman-to-woman network and support system.

★3254★ WOMAN'S HOME AND FOREIGN MISSION SOCIETY
   (WHFMS)
PO Box 23152
Charlotte, NC 28212
Beatrice Moore, Pres.
PH: (704)545-6161
FX: (704)753-0712

Founded: 1897. **Members:** 2,750. **Staff:** 2. **Regional Groups:** 5. **Local Groups:** 225. **Languages:** English. **National**. Administered by the Department of Women's Ministries of the Advent Christian Church. Christian women. Seeks to: unite members for action; encourage spiritual growth; involve women in evangelism and provide them with fellowship, mission education, and service opportunities. Works to provide leadership training and revitalize and increase the ministry potential of local member groups. Provides a means whereby members may share information and ideas. Raises funds to support worldwide Advent Christian ministries and field operations. Supports and encourages growth of children's groups in local ministries. Operates speakers' bureau. Holds training seminars and workshops. **Computer Services:** Data base, information on organizational presidents and children's group leaders. **Projects:** Christmas in October.

Publications: *Advent Christian News*, monthly. Newsletter. ● *Advent Christian Witness*, 10/year. Bulletin. ● *Prayer and Praise*, monthly. Bulletin.

Conventions/Meetings: triennial convention. ● periodic regional meeting.

★3255★ WOMAN'S MISSIONARY UNION (WMU)
PO Box 830010
Birmingham, AL 35283-0010
Dellanna W. O'Brien, Exec.Dir.
PH: (205)991-8100
FX: (205)991-4990

Founded: 1888. **Members:** 1,200,728. **Staff:** 150. **Budget:** US$14,000,000. **State Groups:** 38. **Languages:** English. **National**. Female members of churches that are part of the Southern Baptist Convention. Purposes are to teach, support, and promote individual involvement in missions. **Libraries:** Type:. Holdings: 0. Subjects: Missions, international studies, and religious doctrine. **Awards:** Periodic (scholarship). Recipient: missionaries and their children.

Publications: *Accent*, monthly. Bulletin. ● *Aware*, quarterly. Newsletter. ● *Contempo*, monthly. Bulletin. ● *Dimension*, quarterly. Bulletin. ● *Discovery*, monthly. Bulletin. ● *Nuestra Tarea*, monthly. Bulletin. ● *Royal Service*, monthly. Bulletin. • *Share*, quarterly. Bulletin. • *Start*, quarterly. Bulletin. • *Year Book*, annual.

Conventions/Meetings: annual meeting - 1994 June 12 - 14, Orlando, FL, United States; 1995 June 20 - 22, Atlanta, GA, United States.

★**3256**★ WOMAN'S NATIONAL AUXILIARY CONVENTION OF FREE
   WILL BAPTISTS (WNACFWB)
PO Box 5002
5233 Mt. View Rd.
Antioch, TN 37011-5002
Mary R. Wisehart, Exec.Sec.-Treas.   PH: (615)731-6812
                                          FX: (615)731-0049
Founded: 1935. **Members:** 10,223. **Staff:** 4. **Budget:** US$184,000. **Regional Groups:** 3. **State Groups:** 23. **Local Groups:** 1,500. **Languages:** English. **National.** Provides opportunities for women to fulfill their role in the family, church, and community. Encourages involvement in prayer, study, and action through participation in local auxiliaries. Assists young people in making a commitment to Christianity. Contributes to the needs of missions; maintains a missionary provision closet with sheets, towels, and other household items for working missionaries; and participates in mission activities. Encourages the formation of local auxiliaries. Conducts district, state, and national workshops and seminars. Provides loans to qualified Christian students attending the Free Will Baptist College in Nashville, TN. Sponsors biennial retreat and creative writing contest. Maintains archives. **Libraries:** Type: reference.

Publications: *Co-Laborer*, bimonthly. Magazine. • *Sparks into Flame: A History of WNAC*. Book.

Conventions/Meetings: annual conference - 1994 July 18 - 19, Little Rock, AR, United States; 1995 July 17 - 20, Charlotte, NC, United States. • biennial retreat - 1994 Sept..

★**3257**★ WOMAN'S NATIONAL DEMOCRATIC CLUB (WNDC)
1526 New Hampshire Ave. NW   PH: (202)232-7363
Washington, DC 20036   FX: (202)986-2791
Founded: 1922. **Members:** 2,000. **Budget:** US$1,300,000. **Languages:** English. **National.** Women democratic party members concerned with analyzing educational, social, and political issues to effect an informed democratic opinion. Purposes are to: study the processes of democracy and procedures of government; render educational and social services to the community; educate members in political science, economics, and the arts. Activities include travel events and panel discussions. Maintains Public Policy Committee composed of task force committees on subjects such as foreign policy, the economy, social security, education, energy, the environment, and human rights. **Libraries:** Type: reference.   Subjects: history.
Awards: Periodic Outstanding Democratic Woman.

Publications: *WNDC Calendar Notes*, monthly. Bulletin. • *WNDC Membership Directory*, semiannual. • *WNDC News*, monthly. Newsletter. **Advertising:** not accepted.

Conventions/Meetings: annual - always June. Washington, DC, United States. • weekly luncheon, with speaker. • periodic dinner.

★**3258**★ WOMAN'S ORGANIZATION OF THE NATIONAL
   ASSOCIATION OF RETAIL DRUGGISTS (WONARD)
205 Daingerfield Rd.
Alexandria, VA 22314
Vivian Przondo, Contact   PH: (703)683-8200
Founded: 1905. **Members:** 600. **Regional Groups:** 5. **Languages:** English. **National.** Women and female relatives of men in the pharmaceutical business. Objective is to unite the families of persons interested in all aspects of the pharmaceutical profession. Promotes legislation for the betterment of the retail drug and pharmacy business. Conducts charitable program. **Awards:** Periodic (scholarship). **Committees:** Consumer Education; Legislation.

Publications: *WONARD Newsletter*, quarterly. Reports on legislation, education, and association activities. **Circulation:** 500.

Conventions/Meetings: annual trade exposition.

★**3259**★ WOMAN'S PROJECT
2224 Main St.
Little Rock, AR 72206   PH: (501)372-5113
Janet Perkins, Dir.   FX: (501)372-0009
Founded: 1981. **Members:** 400. **Staff:** 5. **Budget:** US$180,000. **Languages:** English. **National.** Organization is committed to: the elimination of sexism and racism, particularly violence against women, children, and people of color; women's economic issues, especially those affecting low-income women; social justice issues such as sexism, racism, homophobia, ageism, "ableism," classism, and anti-Semitism. Offers educational programs. **Libraries:** Type: reference.

Publications: *Transformation*, bimonthly. Newsletter. Contains commentary and analysis on women's and social issues; book reviews. **Circulation:** 2,500.

★**3260**★ WOMEN IN AEROSPACE (WIA)
6352 Rolling Mill Pl., No. 102
Springfield, VA 22152   PH: (703)644-7875
Susan Brand, Pres.   FX: (703)866-3526
Founded: 1985. **Members:** 300. **Languages:** English. **National.** Women and men working in aerospace and related fields; allied organizations and businesses. Seeks to increase women's visibility as aerospace professionals and to expand their opportunities for career advancement. Goals are to: provide a forum for exchange of ideas and information among members and recognition of outstanding women in the field; assist members in meeting and maintaining contact with peers and key players in the profession; establish a positive public attitude toward the role of women as leaders in aerospace and related fields; influence the legislative process as it affects the industry; educate organization members about current issues in aerospace; encourage students to develop interests and abilities in the field. Maintains speakers bureau.

Publications: *Newsletter*, quarterly. • *WIA Membership Directory*, annual.

Conventions/Meetings: annual reception - always September. • monthly meeting.

★**3261**★ WOMEN AGAINST MILITARY MADNESS (WAMM)
3255 Hennepin Ave. S
Minneapolis, MN 55408   PH: (612)827-5364
Lucia Wilkes, Co-Dir.   FX: (612)827-6433
Founded: 1982. **Members:** 3,000. **Membership Dues:** Individual, US$30 annual; Household, US$40 annual; Sustainer, US$100 annual. **Staff:** 3. **Budget:** US$100,000. **Languages:** English. **National.** Women seeking to bring an end to "systems perpetuating militarism and injustice." Supports higher priority of social concerns such as poverty and hunger. Conducts children's services and educational, charitable, and research programs. Operates speakers' bureau. **Libraries:** Type:. Holdings: books, video recordings, periodicals. Subjects: disarmament, social issues, and women. **Committees:** Anti-Racism; Media Watch; Mothers' Network; Economic Justice; Police Accountability.

Publications: *WAMM Newsletter*, monthly. **Advertising:** accepted. • *Empowerment of People for Peace*. Booklet.

Conventions/Meetings: annual convention - always January. • periodic meeting.

★3262★ WOMEN AGAINST PORNOGRAPHY (WAP)
PO Box 845
Times Square Sta.
New York, NY 10036-0845
Mark Rose, Exec. Officer   PH: (212)307-5055

Founded: 1979. Members: 10,000. Languages: English. National. Feminist organization founded by author Susan Brownmiller. Seeks to change public opinion about pornography so that Americans no longer view it as socially acceptable or sexually liberating. Offers tours of New York's Times Square district, which the group considers "the porn capital of the country," to women and men of all ages and backgrounds. The tour is intended to show firsthand that "the essence of pornography is about the degradation, objectification, and brutalization of women." Also offers adult and high school slide shows/lectures which show how pornographic imagery pervades popular culture. Offers referral service to victims of sexual abuse and sexual exploitation. Maintains speakers' bureau and biographical archives; compiles statistics; organizes protests.   Computer Services: Mailing lists. Committees: Home Video Games; Mass Transit Ads; Media (Film and Music); Newsreport; Slide Show; WAP/ZAP (Advertising). Task Forces: Pornography and Sexual Abuse.

Publications: Women Against Pornography—Newsreport, 2-4/year. Newsletter. Profiles feminist anti-pornography movements and events throughout the world. Discusses current and proposed pornography legislation, and reviews art. Circulation: 10,000.

★3263★ WOMEN AGAINST RAPE (WAR)
Box 02084
Columbus, OH 43202   PH: (614)291-9751

Founded: 1972. Members: 60. Staff: 3. Budget: US$90,000. Local Groups: 1. Languages: English. National. Works toward the prevention of rape. Sponsors crisis intervention services including a rape crisis hotline for support and referrals and rape survivor support groups. Also offers rape prevention training including self-defense classes for women. Maintains speakers' bureau.

Publications: W.A.R. Newsletter, semiannual. Includes current information on rape issues and calendar of events. Circulation: 5,000. Advertising: not accepted.

★3264★ WOMEN IN AGRIBUSINESS (WIA)
PO Box 10241
Kansas City, MO 64111
Dolores Emily, Pres.

Founded: 1985. Members: 400. Languages: English. National. Women working in agribusiness. Provides a forum for the discussion of ideas and information related to agribusiness. Offers placement, networking, and peer/ mentor support services.

Publications: Women in Agribusiness, quarterly. Bulletin. Advertising: not accepted.

★3265★ WOMEN AND AIDS RESOURCE NETWORK (WARN)
c/o Washington Square Church
135 W. 4th St.
New York, NY 10012   PH: (212)475-6713

Founded: 1987. Languages: English. National. Works to increase public awareness of the risk of AIDS among women and children. Provides medical, educational, and counseling services. Offers informational and educational materials; disseminates information about AIDS. Researches AIDS and issues relevant to women.

★3266★ WOMEN AIRFORCE SERVICE PILOTS WORLD WAR II
  (WASPWWII)
Texas Woman's University
Blagg-Huey Library
PO Box 23715
Denton, TX 76204-1715   PH: (817)898-2665
Dawn Letson, Archivist   FX: (817)898-3726

Founded: 1946. Members: 850. Membership Dues: US$15 annual; Lifetime, US$100 annual. Languages: English. National. Women who graduated from or trained in the U.S. Army Air Corps between 1942 and 1944; military pilots of the Women Auxiliary Ferrying Squadron. Offers friendship and assistance to female pilots who flew together from training bases in Houston or Sweetwater, TX and army air bases throughout the U.S. Provides information to students conducting research on the history of the WASPWWII. Assists local WASP groups in organizing exhibits in schools and museums. Maintains biographical archives of old clippings, publications, and scrapbooks. Libraries: Type: reference.

Publications: Newsletter, semiannual. ● WASP News, quarterly. Magazine. ● WASP Roster, biennial. Directory.

Conventions/Meetings: biennial meeting - 1994, Washington, DC, United States.

★3267★ WOMEN IN THE ARTS FOUNDATION (WIA)
1175 York Ave., Apt. 2G
New York, NY 10021
Roberta Crown, Exec. Coordinator   PH: (212)751-1915

Founded: 1971. Members: 300. Membership Dues: Individual, US$40 annual; Supporting, US$75 annual. Languages: English. National. Women artists and women interested in the arts. Works to overcome discrimination against women artists, arrange exhibits of the work of women artists, and protest the underrepresentation of women artists in museums and galleries. Conducts specialized education programs, compiles statistics, and sponsors competitions. Maintains archives.

Publications: Women in the Arts Newsletter, 3-4/year. Includes book reviews, calendar of events, exhibit announcements, and lists of employment opportunities. Circulation: 400. Advertising: accepted.

Conventions/Meetings: monthly meeting.

★3268★ WOMEN ASSOCIATED WITH CROSSDRESSERS
  COMMUNICATION NETWORK (WACS)
Box 17
Bulverde, TX 78163-0017
C. Phillips

Founded: 1989. Membership Dues: US$12 annual. Staff: 2. Languages: English. National. Promotes communication among women involved with crossdressers. Operates speakers' bureau; provides children's services; Conducts research, charitable, and educational programs. Libraries: Type: not open to the public; reference. Holdings: books, periodicals, clippings. Subjects: crossdressing.

Publications: WACS, quarterly. Newsletter. Circulation: 250.

★3269★ WOMEN BAND DIRECTORS NATIONAL ASSOCIATION
  (WBDNA)
345 Overlook Dr.
West Lafayette, IN 47906
Gladys Stone Wright, Sec. & Founder   PH: (317)463-1738

Founded: 1969. Members: 380. Staff: 1. Regional Groups: 6. Languages: English. National. Women band directors. Objectives are: to develop a comprehensive program of musical and educational benefit to women band directors and their subjects; to work with administrators to provide the best music education program possible; to provide for equality of women in the profession; to establish a common meeting ground for an exchange of ideas, methods, and problems peculiar to women band directors. Encourages young women entering the instrumental musical field; recognizes the obligations of the school band to school and community, and encourages reciprocal support. Maintains hall of fame and biographical archives. Compiles statistics. **Awards:** Periodic International Golden Rose. Recipient: female musician. ● Periodic Silver Baton. Recipient: outstanding educator. ● Periodic (scholarship).

Publications: *Newsletter*, quarterly. ● *WBDNA Directory*, annual. ● *The Woman Conductor*, quarterly. Journal. Reports on career improvement, conducting techniques, and association news. Features employment opportunities. **Circulation:** 500. **Advertising:** accepted. ● *Women of the Podium*, periodic. Directory. Biographical information.

Conventions/Meetings: annual convention (exhibits). ● periodic competition.

★3270★ WOMEN IN BROADCAST TECHNOLOGY (WBT)
2435 Spaulding St.
Berkeley, CA 94703
Susan Elisabeth, Contact   PH: (510)540-8640

Founded: 1983. **Members:** 50. **Languages:** English. **National.** Women employed in broadcast-related technology fields; media students; interested individuals. Functions as a networking support group for women equipment operators and technicians in the television, radio, cable, video, and film industries.

Publications: *Informational Flyer*, periodic. Bulletin. ● *Newsletter*, periodic. ● *Resources*, periodic. Directory. ● *Women in Broadcast Technology Directory*, annual.

★3271★ WOMEN IN CABLE (WIC)
c/o P.M. Haeger & Assocs.
500 N. Michigan Ave., Ste. 1400
Chicago, IL 60611   PH: (312)661-1700
Pamela V. Williams, Exec.Dir.   FX: (312)661-0769

Founded: 1979. **Members:** 2,200. **Staff:** 5. **Local Groups:** 20. **Languages:** English. **National.** Individuals engaged in professional activity in cable television and related industries and disciplines. Encourages a high standard of professional business conduct; provides ongoing exchange of experience and opinions. Focuses attention on broadening the sphere in which women can contribute to the industry; highlights achievements of members. Provides speakers' bureau.

Publications: *Membership Directory*, annual. ● *Newsletter*, bimonthly.

Conventions/Meetings: annual National Cable Management Conference.

★3272★ WOMEN IN CELL BIOLOGY (WICB)
University of Miami, RM. 124
Dept. of Anatomy and Cell Biology
1600 NW 10th Ave.
Miami, FL 33101   PH: (305)547-5643
Dr. Mary Lou King, Chwm.   FX: (305)480-2770

Members: 800. **Budget:** US$1,500. **Languages:** English. **National.** Sponsored by the American Society of Cell Biology. Serves as a forum for the discussion of various women's issues.

Publications: *How to Get a Job.* ● *Directory*, periodic. membership list. ● *How to Get a Post-Doc.* Book. ● *Alternate Careers in Cell Biology.* Book.

Conventions/Meetings: annual convention (exhibits).

★3273★ WOMEN CHURCH CONVERGENCE (WCC)
c/o Loretto Staff Office
590 E. Lockwood Ave.
St. Louis, MO 63119
Sr. Virginia Williams, Contact   PH: (314)962-8112

Founded: 1977. **Members:** 2,000. **Languages:** English. **National.** National

Catholic organizations concerned with the empowerment of women in society and the church. Seeks to create a political base that will bring a "gospel perspective" to issues of racism, classism, and sexism in the institutional church. Works to make women aware of the Catholic church's stance on these issues.

Conventions/Meetings: quadrennial conference. ● semiannual meeting.

★3274★ WOMEN OF THE CHURCH OF GOD (WCG)
1303 E. 5th St.
Anderson, IN 46012
Doris Dale, Exec.Sec.-Treas.   PH: (317)642-0256

Founded: 1932. **Members:** 46,000. **Staff:** 4. **Budget:** US$2,000,300. **State Groups:** 57. **Local Groups:** 2,000. **Languages:** English. **National.** Female members of churches affiliated with the Church of God who are interested in individual stewardship and promotion of missions in the United States and abroad. Local groups meet at least monthly for Bible study, fellowship, and educational programs. Raises funds for mission work.

Publications: *Church of God Missions*, 11/year. Newsletter.

Conventions/Meetings: annual conference - always June. Anderson, IN, United States. ● quadrennial convention - 1994 Sept. 15 - 18, Kissimmee, FL, United States.

★3275★ WOMEN OF COLOR PARTNERSHIP PROGRAM (WOCPP)
100 Maryland Ave. NE, Ste. 307
Washington, DC 20002   PH: (202)543-7032
Elizabeth Castro, Dir.   FX: (202)543-7820

Founded: 1985. **Languages:** English. **National.** A division of the Religious Coalition for Abortion Rights. Educates women about reproductive health issues such as accessibility and cost of health care, role of the church, male responsibility, sterilization, and medical abuse of women. Conducts forums and workshops. Maintains speakers' bureau.

Publications: *Common Ground - Different Planes*, semiannual. Newsletter.

★3276★ WOMEN IN COMMUNICATIONS, INC. (WICI)
2101 Wilson Blvd., Ste. 417
Arlington, VA 22201
Susan Lowell Butler, Exec.VP   PH: (703)528-4200

Founded: 1909. **Members:** 12,000. **Languages:** English. **National.** Women working in journalism and communications. Offers placement service; compiles statistics. **Awards:** Periodic National Clarion. ● Periodic Vanguard. Recipient: companies who hire and promote women equally with men. **Committees:** Freedom of Information; Professional Development; Progress of Women in Communications. **Formerly:** (1972) Theta Sigma Phi.

Publications: *Leading Change*, periodic. Newsletter. ● *Membership and Resource Directory*, biennial. ● *The Professional Communicator*, 5/year. ● *Careers in Communications.* Booklet.

Conventions/Meetings: annual conference.

★3277★ WOMEN IN COMMUNITY SERVICE (WICS)
1900 N. Beauregard St., Ste. 103   PH: (703)671-0500
Alexandria, VA 22311   TF: (800)562-2677
Ruth C. Herman, Exec.Dir.   FX: (703)671-4489

Founded: 1964. **Staff:** 150. **Budget:** US$3,500,000. **Languages:** English. **National.** Service coalition of five organizations: Church Women United; National Council of Catholic Women; National Council of Jewish Women; National Council of Negro Women; American GI Forum Women. Combines resources and efforts to coordinate programs of community welfare in the U.S. with special emphasis on services to young women. Creates and identifies employment opportunities; trains and supports individuals so they can take advantage of those opportunities. Recruits, screens, and provides support service before, during, and after Job Corps training to poor young women. **Awards:** Annual Rosa Parks Award.

Publications: *The Story of WICS*. Book. ● *This is WICS*, semiannual. Newsletter.

Conventions/Meetings: annual convention.

★3278★ WOMEN CONSTRUCTION OWNERS AND EXECUTIVES, U.S.A.
6802 Industrial Dr., Ste. 112
Beltsville, MD 20705
Rebecca Llewellyn, Exec. Officer   TF: (800)788-3548

Founded: 1983. **Members:** 360. **Membership Dues:** individual, US$150 annual; corporate, US$200 annual. **Staff:** 1. **Budget:** US$100,000. **State Groups:** 11. **Local Groups:** 6. **Languages:** English. **National.** Promotes the interests of female construction owners and executives. Maintains library on construction law, legislation, and certification information.

Publications: *The Turning Point*, monthly. Magazine. **Circulation:** 1,000. **Advertising:** not accepted.

Conventions/Meetings: semiannual convention (exhibits).

★3279★ WOMEN IN CRISIS (WIC)
133 W. 21st St., 11th Fl.
New York, NY 10011
Mari DaSilza, Dir.   PH: (212)242-4880

Founded: 1979. **Staff:** 2. **Languages:** English. **National.** National conference participants concerned with the plight of "women in crisis," including victims of sexual discrimination and poverty, battered wives, rape and incest victims, women offenders, and female drug abusers and alcoholics. Focuses efforts on women and work, mental health, women in leadership positions, drugs and alcohol, and justice. Seeks to create a network of professionals in these areas.   **Committees:** Alcohol; Drugs; Justice Task Forces; Mental Health.

Conventions/Meetings: annual conference.

★3280★ WOMEN EDUCATORS (WE)
University of Toledo
Department of Education
SM 356
Toledo, OH 43636-3390
Dr. Renee Martin, Chair   PH: (419)537-4337

Founded: 1973. **Members:** 300. **Languages:** English. **National.** Educational researchers and educators in institutions of higher education, school systems, government units, and private research organizations. Promotes equal opportunity for women in educational research. Received grant from the Women's Educational Equity Act Program for a Project on Sex Stereotyping in Education. **Awards:** Annual Research on Women in Education. ● Periodic Sex-Affirmative Curriculum Materials.

Publications: *Annual Awards Report*. ● *Newsletter*, periodic. ● *Handbook for Achieving Sex Equity Through Education*. ● *Sex Equity Handbook for Scholars*.

Conventions/Meetings: annual convention (exhibits).

★3281★ WOMEN EMPLOYED (WE)
22 W. Monroe, Ste. 1400
Chicago, IL 60603   PH: (312)782-3902
Anne Ladky, Exec.Dir.   FX: (312)782-5249

Founded: 1973. **Members:** 1,800. **Languages:** English. **National.** Working women and women seeking employment. Helps women improve their jobs and employment opportunities. Conducts advocacy efforts on issues including pay equity, parental leave, and nontraditional jobs for women. Offers career development services that include seminars, counseling, and network-ing opportunities. Monitors government enforcement of equal opportunity laws. Conducts public education programs on issues concerning working women. Sponsors Women Employed Institute (see separate entry). **Divisions:** Career Development Network.

Publications: *Women Employed News*, quarterly. Newsletter. **Circulation:** 1,800. ● *Directory of Work/Family Benefits Offered by Chicago-Area Employers*. ● *Occupation Segregation: Economic Crisis for Women*. Book. ● *Workers and Families: Recommended Employee Policies*. Book.

Conventions/Meetings: annual conference - always April or May. Chicago, IL, United States.

★3282★ WOMEN EMPLOYED INSTITUTE (WEI)
22 W. Monroe, Ste. 1400
Chicago, IL 60603   PH: (312)782-3902
Anne Ladky, Exec.Dir.   FX: (312)782-5249

Founded: 1973. **Languages:** English. **National.** Research and education division of Women Employed (see separate entry) devoted to promoting economic equity for women. Analyzes government programs and employer policies; develops recommendations for public and corporate policy to promote equal opportunity. Sponsors advocacy programs to increase women's accessibility to vocational education and training for higher paying, nontraditional jobs. Develops model employment awareness/readiness programs for disadvantaged women. Conducts research projects; compiles statistics on women's economic status.

Publications: *Directory of Work/Family Benefits Offered by Chicago-Area Employers*.

★3283★ WOMEN AND EMPLOYMENT (WE)
601 Delaware Ave.
Charleston, WV 25302   PH: (304)345-1298
Pam Curry, Exec.Dir.   FX: (304)342-0641

Founded: 1979. **Members:** 1,450. **Budget:** US$350,000. **State Groups:** 2. **Languages:** English. **National.** Seeks to improve the economic position and quality of life for women, especially low-income and minority women. Works to provide access to job training and employment options to women. Supports self-employed women and small business owners by offering training and technical assistance and information. Advocates women's legal right to employment, training, education, and credit. Seeks to inform the public on economic issues related to women. Cooperates with national and international organizations on issues relating to employment and economic justice for women. Maintains speakers' bureau. Compiles statistics; conducts research. **Libraries:** Type: reference. **Programs:** Community Economic Development; Community Resource Development; Employment Resources; Micro/Small Business Development; Non-Traditional Jobs Advocacy; Community Resource Development; Employment Resources; Micro/Small Business Development.

Publications: *Women & Employment News*, quarterly. Includes association activities and information on economic and employment issues relating to women.

Conventions/Meetings: annual conference. ● quarterly, programs.

★3284★ WOMEN IN ENDOCRINOLOGY
Northwestern University
Department of Neurobiology and
   Physiology
Hogan Hall, Rm. 2-120
2153 Sheridan Rd.
Evanston, IL 60208
Meena B. Schwartz, President   PH: (708)491-5767

National. Women endocrinologists in the United States. Promotes the involvement of women in the study of endocrinology.

★3285★ WOMEN IN ENGINEERING PROGRAM ADVOCATES NETWORK (WEPAN)
WEPAN Member Services
Purdue University
Women in Engineering Programs
CIVL Bldg. - G293
West Lafayette, IN 47907
Cathy Deno, Founder
PH: (317)494-5387
E-Mail:
wiep@ecn.purdue.edu

Founded: 1990. **Members:** 239. **Membership Dues:** individual, US$30; institution, US$200; corporate, US$500; endowing corporate, US$1,000. **Languages:** English. **National.** Encourages young women to pursue engineering careers. Initiates women in engineering prorams at colleges and universities.

Publications: *Directory*, periodic. College and university programs for women in engineering. ● *Booklet*, periodic. Conference proceedings.

★3286★ WOMEN EXECUTIVES IN PUBLIC RELATIONS (WEPR)
PO Box 609
Westport, CT 06881
Frances Gallogly, Admin.
PH: (203)226-4917

Founded: 1946. **Members:** 110. **Staff:** 1. **Languages:** English. **National.** Women and men senior-level executives in public relations (membership by invitation). Purposes are to: provide a support network for women in public relations; cooperate for mutual advancement and broaden professional knowledge; foster equality of opportunity, management development, training, promotion, and remuneration in public relations. Offers internships to college students majoring in communications. **Awards:** Periodic (grant). ● Periodic (scholarship). **Formerly:** (1971) Committee on Women in Public Relations.

Publications: *Network*, quarterly. Newsletter. **Circulation:** 150. **Advertising:** not accepted.

★3287★ WOMEN EXPLOITED BY ABORTION (WEBA)
Rte. 1, Box 821
Venus, TX 76084
Kathy Walker, Pres.
PH: (214)366-3600

Founded: 1982. **Members:** 90,000. **Staff:** 6. **Regional Groups:** 8. **State Groups:** 45. **Local Groups:** 300. **Languages:** English. **National.** Christian-oriented organization of women who have had abortions and regret their action; associate members are concerned individuals who have not had abortions. Provides support and counseling for women suffering from emotional and physical problems as a result of their abortions. Offers counseling to pregnant women considering abortion; refers women who decide to have their babies to other groups that assist needy expectant mothers. Seeks to reeducate society about abortion and the effect it has on women. Provides speakers for pro-life groups, schools, churches, seminars, and television and radio programs. Conducts research; compiles statistics. **Libraries:** Type: reference.

Publications: *Reconciler*, bimonthly. Newsletter. Newsletter covering pro-life and post-abortion issues. **Advertising:** accepted. **Alternate Formats:** online. ● *Before You Make the Decision*. Booklet. ● *Joy Comes in the Mourning*. Booklet. ● *Surviving Abortion*. Booklet.

★3288★ WOMEN FOR FAITH AND FAMILY
PO Box 8326
St. Louis, MO 63132
Helen Hull Hitchcock, Dir.
PH: (314)863-8385
FX: (314)863-8385

Founded: 1984. **Staff:** 10. **Languages:** English. **National.** Catholic women. Assists orthodox Catholic women in ''their effort to provide witness to their faith, both to their families, and to the world.'' Aids women in understanding the Catholic faith and developing fellowship; serves as an information clearinghouse for women seeking guidance. Provides speakers' bureau. **Libraries:** Type: reference. Holdings: books, periodicals, clippings, archival

material. **Awards:** Annual Women for Faith and Family Award. Recipient: outstanding Roman Catholic religious or lay person.

Publications: *Voices*, quarterly. Newsletter. **Circulation:** 6,000. **Advertising:** not accepted.

Conventions/Meetings: annual conference (exhibits).

★3289★ WOMEN IN FILM (WIF)
6464 Sunset Blvd., Ste. 530
Hollywood, CA 90028
Billie Beasley-Jenkins, Contact
PH: (213)463-6040
FX: (213)463-0963

Founded: 1973. **Members:** 1,500. **Budget:** US$500,000. **Languages:** English. **National.** Purpose is to support women in the film and television industry and to serve as a network for information on qualified women in the entertainment field. Sponsors screenings and discussions of pertinent issues. Conducts workshops featuring lectures and discussions on such areas as directing, producing, contract negotiation, writing, production development, acting, and technical crafts. Works to improve the image and increase participation of women in the industry. Provides speakers' bureau. Maintains Women in Film Foundation, which offers financial assistance to women for education, research, and/or completion of film projects and bestows grants for the employment of trainees as interns with major studios and independent film companies. **Awards:** Periodic Crystal.

Publications: *WIF Directory*, annual. ● *WIF Reel News*, monthly. Newsletter.

Conventions/Meetings: annual Women In Film Festival - always fall. ● annual luncheon - always June.

★3290★ WOMEN IN FILM AND VIDEO
PO Box 19272
20th St. Sta.
Washington, DC 20036
Betty Kotcher, President
PH: (202)436-6372

Members: 444. **Regional Groups:** 8. **Languages:** English. **National.** Promotes and supports women in film and video industries. Organizes and coordinates cultural, educational, and professional activities for women. Offers networking opportunities. Recognizes and awards women's contributions to the industry.

Publications: *Women in Film and Video Newsletter* (in English).

★3291★ WOMEN IN THE FIRE SERVICE (WFS)
PO Box 5446
Madison, WI 53705
Terese M. Floren, Exec.Dir.
PH: (608)233-4768
FX: (608)233-4768

Founded: 1983. **Members:** 900. **Staff:** 1. **Languages:** English. **National.** Women working in fire service, including career and volunteer firefighters, emergency medical technicians and paramedics, inspectors and arson investigators, fire safety educators, and administrators; women interested in careers in fire service; interested men. Provides support and advocacy for women in fire service; promotes professional development of members in an effort to make women more effective firefighters. Collects and disseminates information on issues affecting women in fire service; maintains resource bank on issues such as recruitment, physical agility testing, promotional testing, fitness training, firefighting techniques, and maternity leave. Offers guidance in decisions concerning sexual harassment, sexual discrimination, and other issues. Supports and facilitates the development of local groups. Maintains speakers' bureau; compiles statistics; conducts charitable and educational programs. **Awards:** Periodic (scholarship).

Publications: *Firework*, monthly. Newsletter. ● *WFS Quarterly*. Journal. Focuses on gender integration of fire service. **Circulation:** 200. **Advertising:** accepted.

Conventions/Meetings: biennial conference (exhibits)

★3292★ WOMEN AND FOUNDATIONS-CORPORATE PHILANTHROPY (WAF/CP)
322 8th Ave., Rm. 702
New York, NY 10001

PH: (212)463-9934
FX: (212)463-9417

Founded: 1977. **Members:** 600. **Staff:** 4. **Budget:** US$300,000. **Languages:** English. **National.** Staff and trustees of grant-making organizations. Seeks to increase the amount of money for programs on behalf of women and girls and to enhance the status of women as decision-makers within private philanthropy. Builds regional networks of women and men in philanthropy; conducts research on grant-making patterns in the funding of programs; disseminates information to promote thoughtful decision-making with regard to the funding of programs that meet the needs of women.

Publications: *Annual Report.* ● *Newsletter,* 3/year. ● *Papers,* 1-2/year. Journal.

★3293★ WOMEN IN GOVERNMENT RELATIONS (WGR)
1325 Massachusetts Ave. NW, Ste. 510
Washington, DC 20005-4171
Cynthia Lebrun-Yaffe, Pres.

PH: (202)347-5432
FX: (202)347-5434

Founded: 1975. **Members:** 750. **Staff:** 2. **Budget:** US$265,000. **Languages:** English. **National.** Professional women and men who have legislative or regulatory responsibilities involving federal, state, and local governmental bodies; members represent corporations, trade associations, the executive and legislative branches of government, and nonprofit organizations. Promotes the professional status of women; provides a forum for discussion of issues of national importance with political and business leaders; gives members the opportunity to develop contacts in the government relations field. Conducts workshops and educational seminars on improving communications skills, establishing professional credentials, achieving career objectives, and developing management techniques. Maintains speakers' bureau and job bank for government Sponsors Women in Government Relations LEADER Foundation. **Awards:** Annual Distinguished Member. **Committees:** Career Services; Executive Branch Liaison; Congressional Relations; Foreign Relations; Professional Development; Public Relations; Regulatory Relations; Skills Development; State Liaison. **Task Forces:** Budget & Tax; Education; Banking and Financial Services; Energy; Environment; Grassroots Lobbying; Health Services; Industrial Relations; International Trade; PACs and Politics; Telecommunications; Transportation.

Publications: *Annual Report.* ● *Membership Directory,* annual. ● *Women in Government Relations,* bimonthly. Newsletter. **Circulation:** 1,000. **Advertising:** accepted.

Conventions/Meetings: annual conference.

★3294★ WOMEN IN GOVERNMENT RELATIONS LEADER FOUNDATION
American Paper Institute
1250 Connecticut Ave. NW, Ste. 210
Washington, DC 20038
Patricia Hill, Contact

PH: (202)463-2581

Founded: 1979. **Languages:** English. **National.** Seeks to provide women with management opportunities in business and government relations through leadership, education, advancement, development, endowment, and research (LEADER). Sponsors proposals and projects to enhance corporate management skills and increase knowledge. Provides resources, techniques, methods, information, and training opportunities not otherwise available to women. Maintains a central resource on career development programs related to business/government relations; sponsors internship programs and career seminars. Offers fellowships to professional women in the field of government relations. **Committees:** Career Seminar; Intern Program; Success Strategies for Contemporary Women.

★3295★ WOMEN GROCERS OF AMERICA (WGA)
1825 Samuel Morse Dr.
Reston, VA 22090
Thomas K. Zavcha, Pres.

PH: (703)437-5300

Founded: 1983. **Members:** 200. **Languages:** English. **National.** Serves as information and advisory arm to National Grocers Association. Supports and recognizes women in the food distribution industry and assists in the educational and professional needs of its members. Objectives include: organizing food donation programs for the needy; testifying before Congress on issues concerning the operations of independent retail groceries; coordinating programs with educational institutions that promote careers in the food distribution industry.

Publications: *Exchange,* 3/year. Newsletter.

Conventions/Meetings: annual convention.

★3296★ WOMEN FOR GUATEMALA (WG)
2119 S. Bennett St.
Seattle, WA 98108-1910
Patricia Ortiz, Coordinator

Founded: 1982. **Staff:** 2. **Budget:** US$35,000. **Languages:** English. **Multinational.** Women working to improve life for Guatemalan women. Disseminates information to women in the U.S. on issues relating to the socioeconomic conditions, human rights, politics, and culture of Guatemalan women and children. Seeks to: broaden awareness and understanding among North American women of the complexity of Guatemalan women's situation; establish linkages between Guatemalan and North American women. Sponsors tours and exhibitions. Conducts charitable programs; maintains speakers' bureau; compiles statistics.

★3297★ WOMEN AND HEALTH ROUNDTABLE (WHR)
1000 Connecticut Ave. NW, Ste. 9
Washington, DC 20036
Lori Cooper, Co-Chwm.

Founded: 1976. **Languages:** English. **National.** A monthly forum on women's health issues for representatives of health-related and women's organizations, consumer groups, and federal agencies. Monitors and attempts to improve federal and state health policies' responsiveness to women's health priorities. Exchanges information on policy developments, learns of new issues through informal briefings, and develops common strategies for accomplishing legislative or executive agency objectives. Disseminates information to universities, medical schools, health systems agencies, and women's health advocates.

Publications: *Roundtable Report,* 11/year. Newsletter. Lists employment opportunities, conferences, and resources. **Circulation:** 150. **Advertising:** not accepted.

Conventions/Meetings: convention - 10/year. Washington, DC, United States.

★3298★ WOMEN HELPING WOMEN (WHW)
c/o Ruth Kvalheim
525 N. VanBuren St.
Stoughton, WI 53589
Ruth Kvalheim, Pres.

PH: (608)873-3747

Founded: 1978. **Staff:** 1. **Regional Groups:** 5. **Languages:** English. **National.** Women who are divorced, in the process of divorce, or considering divorce, with emphasis on those women over age 40 and married for 20 or more years. Offers mutual support and exchange of ideas for those going through the divorce procedure. Meets weekly to share practical and emotional concerns. Offers local seminars on divorce-related topics.

★3299★ WOMEN IN HOUSING AND FINANCE (WHF)
655 15th St. NW, Ste. 300
Washington, DC 20005   PH: (202)639-4999

Founded: 1979. **Members:** 276. **Local Groups:** 1. **Languages:** English. **National.** Professionals employed in the fields of housing or finance. Purpose is to provide women finance professionals with the opportunity for continued professional development through interaction with others with similar interests. Promotes educational development of women in housing and finance; provides members with services and benefits to help them attain higher levels of expertise. Sponsors social events for members; holds receptions for congressional and regulatory leaders; provides speakers from federal agencies, Congress, and the private sector. Sponsors career development workshops. Activities are concentrated in the Washington, DC area.

Publications: *Newsletter*, 10/year. ● *Women in Housing and Finance—Membership Directory*, annual.

Conventions/Meetings: annual - always June. Washington, DC, United States. ● monthly luncheon.

★3300★ WOMEN IN INFORMATION PROCESSING (WIP)
Lock Box 39173
Washington, DC 20016
Janice H. Miller, Pres.   PH: (202)328-6161

Founded: 1979. **Members:** 4,827. **Staff:** 3. **Regional Groups:** 5. **Languages:** English. **Multinational.** Women who are professionals in computer fields, office automation, robotics, telecommunications, artificial intelligence, and related disciplines. Seeks to: advance the industry by helping women benefit from opportunities created by automation; attract additional qualified women; aid women in building professional contacts. Sponsors product demonstrations and exhibits. Offers speakers' bureau, career counseling, resume guidance, and discussions. Compiles statistics; offers group rate medical insurance. **Awards:** Annual Meritorious Achievement. ● Periodic (scholarship).

Publications: *Forumnet*, quarterly. Newsletter. ● *Salary and Perception Survey*, annual. Bulletin.

Conventions/Meetings: annual, teleconference. ● monthly seminar.

★3301★ WOMEN, INK.
777 United Nations Plaza, 3rd Fl.
New York, NY 10017
Marilyn Carr, Contact

Multinational. Fosters women's development worldwide. Markets and distributes women and development resource materials published by the United Nations Development Fund (UNIFEM) and similar worldwide organizations.

★3302★ WOMEN AND INTERNATIONAL DEVELOPMENT (WID)
Michigan State University
202 CIP
East Lansing, MI 48824
Rita Gallin, Director   PH: (517)353-5040

Founded: 1978. **Languages:** English. **Multinational.** Researches the needs of women in developing countries. Investigates the social, economic, and political status of women. Seeks to increase public awareness of developing women's interests. Disseminates information.

Publications: *Working Papers on Women in International Development* (in English). ● *WID Forum Series* (in English). ● *WID* (in English). Bulletin.

★3303★ WOMEN FOR INTERNATIONAL PEACE AND ARBITRATION
PO Box 9619
Glendale, CA 91226   PH: (818)240-7014
Juana Conrad, President   FX: (818)568-1439

Languages: English. **Multinational.** Women dedicated to the cause of world peace. Sponsors educational programs; disseminates information.

★3304★ WOMEN IN INTERNATIONAL SECURITY (WIIS)
c/o Center for International Security
    Studies
University of Maryland - College Park
School of Public Affairs
College Park, MD 20742   PH: (301)403-8109
Frances G. Burwell, Exec.Dir.   FX: (301)403-8107

Founded: 1987. **Staff:** 2. **Languages:** English. **Multinational.** A project of the Center for International Security Studies. Provides a forum for professional and social contact between women working on international development issues in the military, academia, research and business organizations, and governmental and nonprofit groups. Acts as a nonpartisan network and professional development program. Serves as a clearinghouse for information for and about women, especially those working on international and foreign policy issues. Sponsors panel discussions. Maintains speakers' bureau. **Computer Services:** Data base.

Publications: *WIIS Words*, periodic. Newsletter. Includes information on seminars and speakers. ● *Internships in Foreign and Defense Policy*. Directory.

★3305★ WOMEN INVOLVED IN FARM ECONOMICS (WIFE)
Box 191
Hingham, MT 59528   PH: (406)397-3311
Elaine Stuhr, Pres.   FX: (406)397-3311

Founded: 1976. **Budget:** US$90,000. **State Groups:** 22. **Local Groups:** 180. **Languages:** English. **National.** Committed to improving profitability in production agriculture through educational, legislative, and cooperative programs. Promotes public and governmental awareness of the importance of agriculture in the American economy; maintains that agriculture is the most vital renewable industry and that economic prosperity in the United States is dependent upon economic prosperity in agriculture. Upholds the "family farm" concept for the production of food and fiber in the U.S. Works with governmental agencies and Congress to promote stability in the agricultural industry. Encourages communication regarding agricultural issues. Cooperates with other agricultural organizations and commodity groups in an effort to provide a unified voice for the industry. Conducts educational activities including Ag in the Classroom program, seminars, and workshops. Sponsors National Ag Day promotions. Maintains archives. **Committees:** Education; Energy; Farm Credit; Labor; Natural Resources; Public Relations; Resolutions; Safety; Taxation; Trade; Transportation.

Publications: *Directory and Policy Summaries*, annual. **Advertising:** not accepted. ● *Wifeline*, monthly. Newsletter. Includes editorials and reports on commodities. **Circulation:** 4,000. **Advertising:** not accepted.

Conventions/Meetings: annual convention - always November. 1993 Nov., Bozeman, MT, United States. ● annual legislative conference - always June. Washington, DC, United States.

★3306★ WOMEN JUDGES' FUND FOR JUSTICE (WJFJ)
733 15th St. NW, Ste. 700
Washington, DC 20005   PH: (202)783-2073
Marilyn Nejelski, Exec. Officer   FX: (202)783-0930

Founded: 1980. **Languages:** English. **National.** Women judges committed to strengthening the role of women in the American judicial system. Primary goals are to: increase the number of women judges at all levels of the federal and state judiciary; minimize gender bias in the judicial system through support of special task forces, development of educational materials, and provision of training for male and female judges; increase the effectiveness of women judges through provision of education and other support programs. Has developed a curriculum on the judicial selection process and candidate skills. Provides assistance in developing and funding education programs of the National Association of Women Judges. Sponsors institutes.

Publications: *Operating a Task Force on Gender Bias in the Courts: A Manual for Action.* Book. ● *Learning From the New Jersey Task Force on Women in the Courts.* Book. ● *Planning for Evaluation: Guidelines for Task Forces on Gender.* Book.

★3307★ WOMEN LIFE UNDERWRITERS CONFEDERATION (WLUC)
1126 S. 70th St., Ste. 5106
Milwaukee, WI 53214
Liane L. Gonzalez, Exec. Officer
PH: (800)776-3008
FX: (414)475-2585

Founded: 1987. **Members:** 1,500. **Staff:** 1. **Budget:** US$100,000. **Local Groups:** 30. **Languages:** English. **National.** Life and health underwriters. Objectives are to: advance the life insurance field; inform women members of opportunities in the profession; develop educational opportunities; provide peer support and sales motivational techniques; act as a forum for exchange of sales ideas and industry news. Encourages development of local chapters. Maintains speakers' bureau. **Committees:** Education; Mentor.

Publications: *Roster,* annual. Directory. ● *WLUC News,* monthly. Newsletter. Available to members only. **Advertising:** accepted.

Conventions/Meetings: annual convention - 1994, San Antonio, TX, United States.

★3308★ WOMEN MAKE MOVIES (WMM)
462 Broadway
New York, NY 10013
Debra S. Zimmerman, Dir.
PH: (212)925-0606
FX: (212)925-2052

Founded: 1972. **Members:** 400. **Staff:** 13. **Budget:** US$750,000. **Languages:** English. **National.** Individuals devoted to the development of a strong multicultural feminist media that accurately reflects the lives of women. Aim is the universal distribution of woman-made productions that encourage audiences to explore the changing and diverse roles women play in our society. Conducts sale or rental of films and videos made by women about issues important to women; filmmakers are available to attend screenings and to speak with audiences about the films and making process. Distributes more than 300 films and videotapes on topics such as health, gender equity, and cultural identity. **Libraries:** Type: reference.

Publications: *News from Women Who Make Movies,* periodic. Newsletter.

★3309★ WOMEN IN MANAGEMENT (WIM)
2 N. Riverside Plaza, Ste. 2400
Chicago, IL 60606
Patricia Kelps, Admin.
PH: (312)263-3636
FX: (312)263-0923

Founded: 1976. **Members:** 1,700. **Staff:** 2. **Budget:** US$75,000. **Languages:** English. **National.** Support network of women in professional and management positions that facilitates the exchange of experience and ideas. Promotes self-growth in management; provides speakers who are successful in management; sponsors workshops and special interest groups to discuss problems and share job experiences. **Committees:** Career Development; Film; Hospitality; Speakers Bureau; Special Events.

Publications: *Memorandum,* quarterly. Newsletter. ● *WIM National Newsletter,* quarterly. Includes chapter contacts. ● *Women in Management—National Directory,* annual. **Advertising:** accepted.

Conventions/Meetings: annual convention - always June.

★3310★ WOMEN MARINES ASSOCIATION (WMA)
140 Merengo, No. 605
Forest Park, IL 60130
Helen H. Laukes, Pres.
PH: (708)366-6408

Founded: 1960. **Members:** 3,200. **State Groups:** 79. **Languages:** English. **National.** Women in the U.S. Marine Corps or the U.S. Marine Reserve, or those who have been discharged under honorable conditions; those separated or retired from the U.S. Marine Corps. Perpetuates comradeship among members and promotes the welfare of all women of the Marine Corps; encourages responsible civic leadership and citizenship; fosters patriotism in American youth through education; provides entertainment, care, and assistance to hospitalized veterans. Maintains charitable program. Sponsors competitions. Member of Navy-Marine Corps Council; Marine Corps Council. **Awards:** Periodic Molly Marine. Recipient: women graduates of the recruit training program. **Committees:** MCJROTC; VAVS.

Publications: *WMA Announcements,* quarterly. Newsletter. Includes information on membership, scholarships, chapters, and current leadership of the association and the Marine Corps. **Advertising:** accepted. ● *Women Marines Association—Membership Directory,* biennial. Includes application forms and scholarship information. **Circulation:** 3,200. **Advertising:** accepted.

Conventions/Meetings: biennial convention - 1994 Sept. 4 - 12, Orlando, FL, United States; 1996, San Antonio, TX, United States.

★3311★ WOMEN AND MATHEMATICS EDUCATION (WME)
Mt. Holyoke College
302 Shattuck Hall
South Hadley, MA 01075
Charlene Morrow, Exec. Officer
PH: (413)538-2608

Founded: 1978. **Members:** 500. **Languages:** English. **National.** Individuals concerned with promoting the mathematical education of girls and women. Serves as a clearinghouse for ideas and resources in the area of women and mathematics. Establishes communications for networks focusing on doctoral students, elementary and secondary school teachers, and teacher educators. Encourages research in the area of women and mathematics, especially research that isolates factors contributing to the dropout rate of women in mathematics. Emphasizes the need for elementary and secondary school programs that help reverse the trend of avoidance of mathematics by females. Maintains speakers' bureau. **Awards:** Dora Helen Skypek. **Computer Services:** Mailing lists.

Publications: *Women and Mathematics,* annual. Directory. Resource list. ● *Women and Mathematics Education,* 3/year. Newsletter. Supplies information on conferences, institutes, programs, and meetings significant to members. **Circulation:** 500.

Conventions/Meetings: annual convention.

★3312★ WOMEN IN MILITARY SERVICE MEMORIAL FOUNDATION
5510 Columbia Pike, Ste. 302
Arlington, VA 22204
Willma L. Vaught, President
TF: (800)222-2294

Languages: English. **National.** Works to raise awareness of women's contributions to military activities. Conducts fund-raisers for the construction of a memorial to all women who have served in the military.

Publications: *Newsletter* (in English), 3/year.

★3313★ WOMEN IN MINING NATIONAL (WIM)
1801 Broadway St., Ste. 400
Denver, CO 80202
Patricia A. Kemper, Pres.
PH: (303)298-1535

Founded: 1972. **Members:** 500. **Membership Dues:** Individual, US$25 annual; Sustaining, US$50 annual. **Budget:** US$10,000. **Regional Groups:** 2. **State Groups:** 4. **Local Groups:** 2. **Languages:** English. **National.** Women employed or interested in the mineral resource industry. Provides technical education and scientific programs fostering public awareness of economic and technical interrelationships between mineral production and the national economy. Monitors and participates in related legislative activities. Conducts field trips and seminars; holds legislative receptions; participates in career days at local public schools. Encourages the growth of additional chapters. Sponsors competitions; maintains hall of fame. **Awards:** Annual (scholarship). **Committees:** Education; Public Relations.

Publications: *National Quarterly.* Journal. **Advertising:** not accepted. ● *Women in Mining National—Membership Directory,* annual. ● *Women in Mining—National Quarterly.* Newsletter. Covers legislative issues and national and chapter activities of the association. Includes calendar of events. **Circulation:** 750. ● *Mineral Activity.* Booklet.

Conventions/Meetings: annual conference (exhibits) - 1994 Apr. 20 - 23, San Francisco, CA, United States. ● monthly meeting, with speakers..

★3314★ WOMEN IN MINISTRY PROJECT
475 Riverside Dr., Rm. 704
New York, NY 10115
Liz Vendesi, Director   PH: (212)870-2144

National. Promotes the involvement of women in ministry projects in the United States. Conducts charitable programs.

★3315★ WOMEN IN MUNICIPAL GOVERNMENT (WIMG)
National League of Cities
1301 Pennsylvania Ave. NW
Washington, DC 20004   PH: (202)626-3000
Kathryn Shane McCarty, Coordinator   FX: (202)626-3043

Founded: 1974. **Members:** 400. **Languages:** English. **National.** Women who are elected and appointed city officials including mayors, council members, and commissioners. Seeks to: encourage active participation of women officials in the organizational and policy-making processes and programs of the National League of Cities and state municipal leagues; identify qualified women for service in the NLC and other national positions; promote issues of interest to women and the status of women in the nation's cities.

Publications: *Constituency Report,* quarterly. Newsletter.

Conventions/Meetings: semiannual, seminars and programs - 1993 Dec. 4 - 8, Orlando, FL, United States.

★3316★ WOMEN OF THE NATIONAL AGRICULTURAL AVIATION ASSOCIATION (WNAAA)
Rt. 1, Box 475
Greenwood, MS 38930   PH: (601)455-3000
Dorothy Kimmel, Pres.   FX: (601)455-1611

Founded: 1976. **Members:** 1,000. **Languages:** English. **National.** Wives of members of the National Agricultural Aviation Association. Assists NAAA members with public relations and recreational activities. Sponsors educational programs. Provides scholarship program for children or grandchildren of agricultural aviators.

Conventions/Meetings: annual convention, in conjunction with NAAA (exhibits) - always December.

★3317★ WOMEN OF NATIONS
PO Box 40309
St. Paul, MN 55104   PH: (612)222-5830

Membership Dues: US$1. **Languages:** English. **National.** Provides support services to battered Native American women in the United States.

★3318★ WOMEN ORGANIZED TO RESPOND TO LIFE-THREATENING DISEASES (WORLD)
PO Box 11535
Oakland, CA 94611
Rebecca Denison, Exec.Dir.   PH: (510)658-6930

Founded: 1991. **Languages:** English. **National.** Individuals infected or affected by the HIV virus. Offers support and information to women suffering from AIDS and HIV. Acts as a clearinghouse for information about women and AIDS.

Publications: *WORLD,* monthly. Newsletter. **Circulation:** 2,500. **Advertising:** not accepted.

★3319★ WOMEN ORGANIZING WOMEN
PO Box 1652
New Haven, CT 06507-1652
Barbara Pearce, Treas.   PH: (203)281-3400

National. Political action committee of women working to involve women in politics and government in the United States. Promotes feminist agendas within the U.S. government.

★3320★ WOMEN OUTDOORS (WO)
55 Talbot Ave.
Medford, MA 02155
Diana Weidenbacker, Pres.

Founded: 1980. **Members:** 700. **State Groups:** 27. **Languages:** English. **National.** Women whose vocation or interests include outdoor activity. Purpose is to maintain a network for women with a common interest in the outdoors. Encourages and holds professional training programs in development of leadership qualities and outdoor skills among women; promotes an ethic of care and respect for the environment. Conducts leadership development workshops. **Libraries:** Type: reference.   Subjects: women's adventure travel. **Awards:** Periodic (scholarship).

Publications: *Women Outdoors,* quarterly. Magazine. **Advertising:** accepted. ● *Bibliography of Women's Travel and Adventure Literature.* Booklet. ● *Getting a Job Out There.* Booklet. ● *Low Impact Use.* Booklet. ● *Female Hygiene in the Backwoods.* Booklet.

Conventions/Meetings: annual conference (exhibits).

★3321★ WOMEN IN PRODUCTION (WIP)
347 5th Ave., No. 1008
New York, NY 10016-5010   PH: (212)481-7793
Karen Koopman Stone CAE, Exec.Dir.   FX: (212)481-7969

Founded: 1977. **Members:** 702. **Budget:** US$120,000. **Languages:** English. **National.** Persons involved in all phases of print and graphics, including those working in magazine and book publishing, agency production and print manufacturing, print-related vending and buying, and advertising production. To improve job performance by sharing information with each other and with suppliers of printing services. Acts as a network of contacts for those in the printing professions; offers assistance to persons with production problems. Sponsors competitions, charitable program, and placement service; maintains speakers' bureau. Compiles statistics. Conducts seminars and educational tours of printing and printing-related facilities. **Awards:** Periodic (scholarship). **Committees:** Design; Education; Employment; Production; Special Projects.

Publications: *Women in Production,* bimonthly. Newsletter. ● *WIP Roster,* annual. Directory.

Conventions/Meetings: annual conference.

★3322★ WOMEN IN PSYCHOLOGY FOR LEGISLATIVE ACTION
436 N. Bedford Dr., No. 404
Beverly Hills, CA 90210
Gerry Simmons, Contact   PH: (213)458-1405

National. Women psychologists. Political action committee working for the involvement of women in politics and government. Promotes legislation assisting women in the United States and their development.

★3323★ WOMEN FOR RACIAL AND ECONOMIC EQUALITY (WREE)
198 Broadway, Rm. 606
New York, NY 10038
Rudean Leinaeng, Chair   PH: (212)385-1103

Founded: 1975. **Members:** 1,000. **Membership Dues:** US$20 annual. **Budget:** US$30,000. **Local Groups:** 8. **Languages:** English. **National**. Multiracial and multinational group of working and working class women. Purposes include: to end race and sex discrimination in hiring, pay, and promotion practices; to support quality integrated public education and federally funded comprehensive child care; to promote peace and solidarity with women of all countries; to work for passage of the Women's Bill of Rights, a program of legislative demands that guarantees economic independence and social equality. Lobbies for equal employment, education, child care, and health issues. Conducts community education and action campaigns, conferences, seminars, forums, leadership training, and research projects. Maintains speakers' bureau. **Awards:** Annual Fannielou Hamer. **Task Forces:** Affirmative Action; United Nations Collective.

Publications: *WREE-View of Women*, quarterly. Newsletter. Reports on racism, affirmative action, child care, the environment, housing, and other issues. Includes book reviews. **ISSN:** 0892-3116. **Circulation:** 5,000. **Advertising:** accepted. ● *Facts About U.S. Women*. Book.

Conventions/Meetings: periodic convention (exhibits).

★3324★ WOMEN REFUSING TO ACCEPT TENANT HARASSMENT
   (WRATH)
607 Elmira Rd., Ste. 299
Vacaville, CA 95687   PH: (707)449-1122

Founded: 1991. **Languages:** English. **National**. Works to promote awareness of and end sexual harassment by landlords. Offers information, resources, and support for women who have been sexually harassed by their landlords; seeks to educate those who are in a position to prevent this type of harassment, including property owners, landlords, and property management companies. Plans to compile a list of resources and legal contacts for women seeking legal recourse; also plans to conduct informational workshops.

Publications: *What Is Sexual Harassment in Housing?*. Booklet.

★3325★ WOMEN IN SALES ASSOCIATION (WIS)
8 Madison Ave.
PO Box M
Valhalla, NY 10595   PH: (914)946-3802
Marie T. Rossi, Chwm.   FX: (914)946-3633

Founded: 1979. **Members:** 500. **Staff:** 5. **Regional Groups:** 3. **Languages:** English. **National**. Professional saleswomen. Promotes professional development of women in sales. Provides opportunity to establish business contacts, and to share information and ideas. Conducts work sessions on topics including personal communication skills and use of audiovisual aids in sales presentations; provides speakers on topics fundamental to sales skills; sponsors career guidance workshops and position referral service. Provides discounts to members on relevant publications; offers financial planning advice. **Awards:** Periodic Women in Sales (recognition).

Publications: *Membership Directory*, periodic. ● *Sales Leader*, quarterly. Newsletter. Promotes the professional development of women in sales. Includes position referral service. **Circulation:** 1,000.

Conventions/Meetings: annual conference (exhibits).

★3326★ WOMEN IN SCHOLARLY PUBLISHING (WISP)
University Press of Kansas
2501 W. 15th St.
Lawrence, KS 66049-8350   PH: (913)864-4155
Susan Schott, Contact   FX: (913)864-4586

Founded: 1979. **Members:** 300. **Languages:** English. **National**. Women involved in scholarly publishing and men who support the organization's goals. Promotes professional development and advancement, management skills, and opportunities for women in scholarly publishing. Concerns include career development, job sharing information, surveys of salaries and job opportunities for women, and practical workshops or other training opportunities. Provides a forum and network for communication among women in presses throughout the U.S. Sponsors educational workshops, programs, and seminars, in conjunction with the Association of American University Presses Compiles statistics. **Computer Services:** Mailing lists.

Publications: *WISP Newsletter*, quarterly. Includes association news, columns on benefit issues, calendar of events, and job openings; lists award recipients.

Conventions/Meetings: annual conference - always June.

★3327★ WOMEN IN SHOW BUSINESS (WiSB)
PO Box 2535
North Hollywood, CA 91610   PH: (310)271-3415
Scherr Lillico, Exec.V.P.   FX: (818)994-6181

Founded: 1961. **Members:** 150. **Languages:** English. **National**. Women employed in the entertainment industry and allied fields. Raises funds to pay for reconstructive and restorative surgery for poor children who are not eligible for state or federal aid and/or insurance coverage. Also provides for equipment, supplies, therapy, counseling, training services, prosthetics, and other materials.

Publications: *Newsletter*, monthly.

Conventions/Meetings: annual Celebrity Benefit Ball.

★3328★ WOMEN FOR SOBRIETY (WFS)
PO Box 618
Quakertown, PA 18951   PH: (215)536-8026
Dr. Jean Kirkpatrick, Exec.Dir.   TF: (800)333-1606

Founded: 1975. **Members:** 5,000. **Staff:** 5. **Local Groups:** 450. **Languages:** English. **National**. Self-help groups of women alcoholics who use a program "based on abstinence, comprised of thirteen acceptance statements that, when accepted and used, will provide each woman with a new way of life through a new way of thinking.starts with coping first but then moves on to overcoming and a whole change in the approach to each day." Recognizes differences between male and female alcoholics in the method of successful recovery. Small groups organize and meet independently. Maintains speakers' bureau.

Publications: *Newsletter*, monthly. ● *Sobering Thoughts*, monthly. Newsletter. Contains book reviews, calendar of events, and research updates. **Circulation:** 3,000.

Conventions/Meetings: annual conference. ● periodic seminar. ● periodic workshop.

★3329★ WOMEN STRIKE FOR PEACE (WSP)
105 2nd St. NE
Washington, DC 20002
Ethel Taylor, Coordinator   PH: (202)543-2660

Founded: 1961. **Members:** 5,000. **Budget:** US$60,000. **Local Groups:** 10. **Languages:** English. **National**. A movement and membership organization focusing on peace activism in the form of national campaigns, grass roots activities, and lobbying. Concentrates on disarmament, anti-interventionism, and mobilizing public opinion in the U.S. against current nuclear war-fighting plans. Local branches exercise autonomy in developing programs and adapting national action to local communities.

Publications: *Women Strike for Peace—Legislative Alert*, monthly. Newsletter. Informs readers of actions taken by the United States and other countries on disarmament and other foreign policy issues. **Circulation:** 5,000.

Conventions/Meetings: annual conference.

★3330★ WOMEN ON THEIR OWN (WOTO)
PO Box 1026
Willingboro, NJ 08046
Maxine Karelitz, Exec.Dir.   PH: (609)871-1499

Founded: 1982. **Languages:** English. **National.** Participants are single, divorced, separated, or widowed women raising children on their own. Links participants together to help each other. Offers support and advocacy; provides referrals. Conducts workshops and Maintains speakers' bureau. Makes available small, interest-free loans. Assists other organizations serving the same population.

Publications: *Directory*, periodic. ● *Newsletter*, periodic. **Advertising:** accepted.

Conventions/Meetings: periodic workshop. ● periodic seminar.

★3331★ WOMEN IN TRANSITION (WIT)
125 S. 9th St., Ste. 502
Philadelphia, PA 19107
Roberta L. Hacker, Exec.Dir.
PH: (215)922-7177
FX: (215)922-7686

Founded: 1971. **Staff:** 18. **Budget:** US$490,000. **Languages:** English. **National.** Offers services to women experiencing difficulties or distress in their lives. Facilitates selfhelp support groups for abused women and women recovering from substance abuse problems. Provides outreach, assessment, and referrals to women with drug and/or alcohol addiction; makes available individual, and family counseling. Trains facilitators for selfhelp support groups. Offers consultation and training to mental health and social service agency personnel. Maintains speakers' bureau. **Telecommunication Services:** Phone referral system, crisis counseling, information and resource referrals: (212)922-7500.

Publications: *Annual Report*. ● *Volunteer Newsletter*, periodic. ● *Facilitator's Guide to Working with Separated and Divorced Women*. Book. ● *Child Support: How You Can Obtain and Enforce Support Orders*. Book.

★3332★ WOMEN WELCOME WOMEN
63 High Noon Rd.
Weston, CT 06883
Betty Sobel, Coord.   PH: (203)227-9493

Founded: 1984. **Membership Dues:** US$25 annual. **Languages:** French, German, Italian, Spanish, Dutch, English. **Multinational.** Women from all ages and backgrounds worldwide. Fosters international friendship among women from different countries; coordinates members' travel and visits with other members.

Conventions/Meetings: annual meeting.

★3333★ WOMEN ON WHEELS (WOW)
PO Box 5147
Topeka, KS 66605
Kathryn Greenwood, Exec.Dir.
PH: (913)267-3779
TF: (800)322-1969

Founded: 1982. **Members:** 1,500. **Staff:** 3. **Local Groups:** 37. **Languages:** English. **National.** Women motorcyclists. Goals are to unite women motorcyclists and to gain recognition from the motorcycle industry concerning the needs of female consumers. Activities include compilation of statistics and participation in motorcycle events. Plans to organize rallies, interchapter social affairs, fashion activities, and fundraising for public service projects.
Computer Services: Mailing lists.

Publications: *Membership Directory*, annual. ● *Women on Wheels*, bimonthly. Magazine.

Conventions/Meetings: annual convention, national rally and exhibits. (exhibits). ● monthly meeting.

★3334★ WOMEN IN THE WIND (WITW)
PO Box 8392
Toledo, OH 43605
Becky Brown, Founder

Founded: 1979. **Members:** 450. **Staff:** 3. **Local Groups:** 34. **Languages:** English. **National.** Women motorcyclists and enthusiasts united to promote a positive image of women motorcyclists. Educates members on motorcycle safety and maintenance. Conducts charitable programs.

Publications: *Shootin' the Breeze*, 9/year. Newsletter. Contains membership activities news and calendar of events. **Circulation:** 550.

Conventions/Meetings: semiannual conference.

★3335★ WOMEN ON WINE (WOW)
6110 Sunset Ranch Dr.
Riverside, CA 92506-4621
Barbara Mader Ivey, Dir.   PH: (714)784-3096

Founded: 1981. **Members:** 1,000. **Languages:** English. **National.** Female and male consumers of wine and wine trade members. Seeks to educate the wine consumer and to recognize and encourage contributions of women to the wine trade. Maintains speakers' bureau. **Awards:** Periodic (scholarship). Recipient: ecology students.

Publications: *Women on Wine National News*, quarterly. Membership newsletter on activities in the wine industry. Includes regional news and calendar of events. **Advertising:** accepted. ● *WOW Chapter Flyer*, monthly. Bulletin.

Conventions/Meetings: periodic conference. ● monthly meeting. ● periodic competition.

★3336★ WOMEN TO THE WORLD (WW)
1730 N. Lynn St., Ste. 500
Arlington, VA 22209
Margaret F. Cudney, Pres.
PH: (703)243-9500
FX: (703)243-1681

Founded: 1987. **Languages:** English. **Multinational.** Assists women in developing countries in areas of: project design and management training for health programs; sanitation; education; agriculture; economic programs. Conducts cross-cultural exchange projects.

★3337★ WOMEN WORLD WAR VETERANS (WWWV)
Morgan Hotel
237 Madison Ave.
New York, NY 10016
Dorothy Frooks, Cmdr.   PH: (212)684-6728

Founded: 1919. **Languages:** English. **National.** Honorably discharged women who served in the Navy, Army, Coast Guard, Marine Corps, and Air Force during World Wars I and II.

Conventions/Meetings: annual convention, in conjunction with American Legion.

★3338★ WOMEN'S ACTION ALLIANCE (WAA)
370 Lexington Ave., Ste. 603
New York, NY 10017
Shazia Z. Rafi, Exec.Dir.
PH: (212)532-8330
FX: (212)779-2846

Founded: 1971. **Staff:** 14. **Languages:** English. **National.** Develops educational programs and services to assist women and women's organizations in achieving full equality for women. Maintains the Information Services Program, which provides information and referrals and disseminates publications on women's issues and programs to individuals and organizations. Administers the Women's Centers Program, which offers assistance in building networks among women's groups and has initiated projects including the Women's Centers and AIDS Project and the Women's Alcohol and Drug Education Project. Also conducts Sex Equity in Education Program and the Computer Equity Training Project, which seeks to remediate girls' pattern of "computer avoidance" in the middle years by developing school strategies. Maintains profiles of national and professional women's groups and materials on program planning, organizational development, and fundraising. Maintains speakers' bureau. **Libraries:** Type:. Holdings: 3,000; books, periodicals. Subjects: Children, education, and women's issues. **Computer Services:** Mailing lists. **Telecommunication Services:** Phone referral system. **Projects:** Teen-Age Pregnancy Prevention.

Publications: *Alliance Quarterly.* Newsletter. Includes calendar of events. • *Equal Play,* semiannual. Journal. Information for educators, parents, and others on nonsexist child raising and education of young children. Includes book reviews. • *Women's Action Alliance Catalog,* periodic. Directory. • *Women's Action Almanac,* periodic. Directory. • *The Neuter Computer.* Book. • *Does Your Daughter Say "No, Thanks" to the Computer?.* Book.

★3339★ WOMEN'S ACTION COALITION
High School for the Humanities
351 W. 18th St.
New York, NY 10011   PH: (212)967-7711

National. Women working for direct action on issues affecting the rights of all women. Promotes pay equity, fair representation in government, and an end to homophobia, racism, religious prejudice, and violence against women. Supports women's rights to health care, child care, and reproductive freedom. Organizes and participates in demonstrations and rallies for equal rights.

★3340★ WOMEN'S ACTION FOR NEW DIRECTIONS (WAND)
PO Box B
Arlington, MA 02174   PH: (617)643-6740
Marjorie Smith, Contact   FX: (617)643-6744

Founded: 1980. **Members:** 10,000. **Staff:** 7. **Budget:** US$223,046. **Regional Groups:** 35. **Languages:** English. **National.** Women's initiative uniting women and men in an effort to halt and reverse the nuclear arms race and redirect spending to meet domestic needs. Objectives are: to raise public awareness about nuclear issues; to support grass roots organizing for educational and political activities across the country; to monitor legislative activities that have an impact on nuclear weapons policy; to organize congressional district lobbying networks to be mobilized before key nuclear weapons votes. Offers workshops, fact sheets, and publications on the issues of nuclear arms and effective organizing and lobbying. Compiles statistics. Has established WAND Education Fund. **Libraries:** Type: reference. Holdings: audio recordings, video recordings, books. Subjects: nuclear war, civil defense, and nuclear weapons.

Publications: *WAND Bulletin,* quarterly. • *Organizing for Nuclear Disarmament.* Booklet. • *Grassroots Fundraising Manual.* Book.

Conventions/Meetings: semiannual convention.

★3341★ WOMEN'S AFRICA COMMITTEE OF THE AFRICAN-AMERICAN INSTITUTE (WACAAI)
c/o African-Amer. Institute
833 United Nations Plaza
New York, NY 10017
Warren Ruppel, Sec.-Treas.   PH: (212)949-5666

Founded: 1959. **Languages:** English. **Multinational.** Volunteer organization of African and American women. Members seek to become better acquainted through social, educational, and cultural activities.

Conventions/Meetings: monthly meeting.

★3342★ WOMEN'S AGLOW FELLOWSHIP INTERNATIONAL (WAFI)
PO Box 1548   PH: (206)775-7282
Lynnwood, WA 98046-1548   TF: (800)755-2456
Jane Hansen, Pres.   FX: (206)778-9615

Founded: 1967. **Membership Dues:** US$25 annual. **Staff:** 52. **Local Groups:** 2,600. **Languages:** English. **Multinational.** People in approximately 100 countries providing support, education, training, and ministry opportunities to "lead women to Jesus Christ and provide opportunity for Christian women to grow in their faith and minister to others.".

Publications: *Connection,* quarterly. Newsletter. • *Lost in the Money Maze?.* Book. • *Inside A Woman.* Book.

Conventions/Meetings: biennial conference, international. • annual conference, national - 1993 Oct. 7 - 10, Phoenix, AZ, United States.

★3343★ WOMEN'S ALL-STAR ASSOCIATION (WASA)
29 Garey Dr.
Chappaqua, NY 10514
Pearl Keller, Exec.Dir.   PH: (914)241-0365

Founded: 1971. **Members:** 450. **Staff:** 6. **Languages:** English. **National.** Amateur and professional women bowlers aged 17 and older with established minimum averages of 170 for one season in a sanctioned bowling league. Formed to provide tournaments for members and promote women bowlers and their accomplishments. Maintains hall of fame and seniors group. Compiles statistics and updates and maintains historical records. **Awards:** Annual Rookie of the Year. • Annual Sportsman of the Year. • Periodic (monetary). **Committees:** Awards; Hall of Fame; Legislative.

Publications: *Newsletter,* 14/year. • *Directory,* periodic.

Conventions/Meetings: annual meeting - always December.

★3344★ WOMEN'S ALLIANCE FOR THEOLOGY, ETHICS AND RITUAL (WATER)
8035 13th St., Stes. 1, 3, & 5
Silver Spring, MD 20910   PH: (301)589-2509
Mary E. Hunt, Co-Dir.   FX: (301)589-3150

Founded: 1983. **Members:** 3,000. **Staff:** 3. **Budget:** US$90,000. **Languages:** English. **Multinational.** Participants include ministers, members of religious communities, and individuals seeking spiritual renewal from a feminist and liberation perspective. Promotes religious education inclusive of women's experiences and viewpoints of spirituality. Offers programs including Women Crossing Worlds, which unites women of the U.S. and Latin America for the purpose of sharing feminist theology and fostering international solidarity. Also offers special liturgies and rituals and counseling. Sponsors study groups. Provides consulting services; operates speakers' bureau. **Libraries:** Type: reference. Holdings: 1,500. **Computer Services:** Mailing lists.

Publications: *Waterwheel,* quarterly. Newsletter. **ISSN:** 0898-6606. **Advertising:** not accepted. • *Women Crossing Worlds,* periodic. Directory. • *Fierce Tenderness - A Feminist Theology of Friendship.* Book.

Conventions/Meetings: periodic conference, includes workshops, seminars, and lectures..

★3345★ WOMEN'S ALTERNATIVE ECONOMICS NETWORK (WAEN)
1405 E. 3rd St.
Winston-Salem, NC 27101
Anne Lennon, Contact   PH: (919)370-4330

National. Women working to develop new economic strategies to eradicate poverty and achieve an improved standard of living. Seeks to enhance women's economic and political status.

Conventions/Meetings: biennial convention.

★3346★ WOMEN'S AMERICAN ORT
315 Park Ave. S
New York, NY 10010
Tehila Elpern, Exec.Dir.
PH: (212)505-7700
FX: (212)674-3057

Founded: 1927. **Members:** 100,000. **Staff:** 65. **State Groups:** 80. **Local Groups:** 1,000. **Languages:** English. **Multinational.** American Jewish women's organization supporting the Organization for Rehabilitation Through Training network of over 800 vocational and technical training installations in 32 countries. Seeks to end anti-Semitism and ensure democracy and pluralism in the U.S; Promotes women's rights and issues. Promotes quality public and upgraded vocational education in the U.S. and national literacy campaign. Operates technical institutes throughout the U.S. **Awards:** Periodic Beverly Minkoff.

Publications: *Women's American ORT Reporter*, quarterly. Magazine. **ISSN:** 0043-7514. **Circulation:** 155,000. **Advertising:** accepted.

Conventions/Meetings: biennial convention (exhibits) - 1993 Oct., Miami Beach, FL, United States. ● biennial conference - next 1994.

★3347★ WOMEN'S AQUATIC NETWORK (WAN)
PO Box 4993
Washington, DC 20008
Nancy Daves, Chwm.

Founded: 1983. **Budget:** US$5,000. **Languages:** English. **National.** Women and institutions concerned with fresh water and marine affairs; persons involved in all areas/sectors related to aquatic affairs. Focuses on policy issues related to marine and aquatic topics; promotes the importance of women taking an active part in this field. Serves as information clearinghouse. Maintains speakers' bureau.

Publications: *Directory*, periodic. ● *Women's Aquatic Network—Newsletter*, monthly. Membership activities newsletter covering issues of concern to the marine community. Includes calendar of events and employment opportunities. **Circulation:** 400. **Advertising:** accepted.

Conventions/Meetings: monthly convention.

★3348★ WOMEN'S ARMY CORPS VETERANS ASSOCIATION (WACVA)
1340 Bayonne Ave.
Whiting, NJ 08759
Martha A. LaMort, Pres.
PH: (908)350-8176

Founded: 1947. **Members:** 5,000. **Budget:** US$30,000. **Local Groups:** 60. **Languages:** English. **National.** Veterans of the United States Women's Army Corps and Women's Army Auxiliary Corps, women soldiers and officers of the line who are on a tour of active duty with, or have been honorably discharged from, the United States Army, and women who have served honorably or are serving in the United States Reserve or Army National Guard. Seeks "to be of service to all veterans and the communities in which we live and promote justice, tolerance, peace and goodwill." Conducts hospital and community service programs. Supports the Women's Army Corps Museum at Ft. McClellan, AL. Has assisted in the establishment of Women's Army Corps Veterans Redwood Memorial Grove in Big Basin Redwoods State Park, CA. Raises funds for Women's Memorial in Washington, DC. Conducts charitable projects. **Awards:** Annual Edith Nourse Rogers (scholarship). ● Periodic Dallas Athene. Recipient: ROTC cadets. **Committees:** Community Projects; Hospital.

Publications: *The Channel*, 10/year. Newsletter. Membership activities; includes directory listing national and chapter officers. **Circulation:** 4,100. **Advertising:** not accepted. ● *The Yearbook*, annual. Directory.

Conventions/Meetings: annual convention - always August. 1994, Boston, MA, United States.

★3349★ WOMEN'S ASSOCIATION FOR THE DEFENSE OF FOUR FREEDOMS FOR UKRAINE (WADFFU)
136 2nd Ave.
New York, NY 10003
Dasha Procyk, Pres.
PH: (716)882-2010
(716)260-2494

Founded: 1967. **Regional Groups:** 4. **State Groups:** 25. **Local Groups:** 4. **Languages:** English. **Multinational.** American women of Ukrainian descent whose objectives are: to promote human and national rights in the Ukraine; to disseminate information and educate people on the plight of Ukrainians; to support efforts of Ukrainians to secure basic rights of freedom of speech, freedom of conscience, freedom from fear, and freedom from want. Encourages participation in legislative activities denouncing repression and supporting full implementation of the Helsinki Final Act, Human Rights Provision. Conducts charitable program.

Publications: *Between Death and Life*. Book.

Conventions/Meetings: triennial convention. ● annual conference. ● periodic competition.

★3350★ WOMEN'S AUXILIARY TO THE MILITARY ORDER OF THE COOTIE (WAMOC)
PO Box 809
Bryan, OH 43506
Patricia Fritch, Treas.
PH: (419)636-3686

Founded: 1961. **Members:** 17,022. **State Groups:** 40. **Local Groups:** 595. **Languages:** English. **National.** Women who are members of the Ladies Auxiliary to the Veterans of Foreign Wars of the U.S.A. Activities include volunteer work in VA hospitals and local hospitals, rest homes, and mental institutions. **Awards:** Periodic (scholarship). **Committees:** Hospital; VFW National Home Christmas Party.

Publications: *Bulletin*, monthly. ● *General Orders*, monthly. Published within *Cootie Courier*.

Conventions/Meetings: annual - always August.

★3351★ WOMEN'S BASKETBALL COACHES ASSOCIATION (WBCA)
46B Lodgeville Hwy.
Lilburn, GA 30247
Betty Jaynes, Exec.Dir.
PH: (404)279-8027
FX: (404)248-0451

Founded: 1981. **Members:** 3,000. **Staff:** 5. **Budget:** US$500,000. **Languages:** English. **National.** Head basketball coaches, assistants, athletic directors, officials, media personnel, organizations lending financial support to the association, and others interested in women's basketball. Purposes are to foster amateur sports competitions at both national and international levels, and to promote a reputable image of women's basketball by developing the game. Works to refine rules, regulations, and procedures that will enhance athletic leadership, sportsmanship, and women's participation in basketball. Encourages education and development of members and players; promotes health and welfare of participants in the sport. Sponsors eight national clinics in the fall and a Coaching Certification Program. **Awards:** Periodic All-America. ● Annual Coach of the Year. ● Annual Player of the Year. **Computer Services:** Mailing lists. **Committees:** Ethics and Eligibility.

Publications: *Backboard*, bimonthly. Bulletin. ● *Fast Break Alert*, monthly. Newsletter. ● *Coaching Women's Basketball*. Book.

Conventions/Meetings: annual convention (exhibits).

★3352★ WOMEN'S BRANCH, UNION OF ORTHODOX JEWISH CONGREGATIONS OF AMERICA
156 5th Ave., Rm. 1006
New York, NY 10010
Deborah Turk, President
PH: (516)431-1933

Languages: English. **National.** Fosters friendship and solidarity among Orthodox Jewish women. Promotes strict adherence to the Torah and Talmud in daily life.

★3353★ THE WOMEN'S BUILDING (TWB)
3543 18th St.
San Francisco, CA 94121   PH: (415)431-1180
Josefina Velasquez, Exec. Dir.   FX: (415)861-8969

Founded: 1979. **Staff:** 3. **Budget:** US$450,000. **Languages:** Spanish, English. **National.** Seeks to improve the social and economic status of women. Operates a community center. Represents the interests of women; offers assistance to women. Provides binlingual services and referrals in the following areas: job listings and resource information, housing, education, and support groups. Conducts AIDS education and awareness program for women and youth, as well as an AIDS support group. **Committees:** Crafts Fair; Development; Program; Multicultural.

★3354★ WOMEN'S CAMPAIGN FUND (WCF)
120 Maryland Ave. NE
Washington, DC 20002   PH: (202)544-4484
Jane Danowitz, Exec.Dir.   FX: (202)544-4517

Founded: 1974. **Members:** 23,000. **Staff:** 7. **Budget:** US$650,000. **Languages:** English. **National.** Contributors to the fund. Purpose is to foster and support the election of qualified, progressive women to public offices. To achieve this aim, the WCF raises funds; makes direct cash contributions to the campaigns of endorsed candidates; provides campaign counsel and services (media, field organization, and polling) to candidates; recruits and develops progressive candidates; stimulates support for WCF-endorsed candidates by other groups and individuals; promotes public awareness of the need for more women in public office.

★3355★ WOMEN'S CAUCUS FOR ART (WCA)
Moore Coll. of Art
20th The Parkway
Philadelphia, PA 19103
Essie Karp, Exec.Dir.   PH: (215)854-0922

Founded: 1972. **Members:** 3,500. **Budget:** US$100,000. **State Groups:** 35. **Languages:** English. **National.** Professional women in visual art fields: artists, critics, art historians, museum and gallery professionals, arts administrators, educators and students, and collectors of art. Objectives are to: increase recognition for contemporary and historical achievements of women in art; ensure equal opportunity for employment, art commissions, and research grants; encourage professionalism and shared information among women in art; stimulate and publicize research and publications on women in the visual arts. Conducts workshops, periodic affirmative action research, and statistical surveys. **Awards:** Annual (recognition). Recipient: women in the visual arts. **Committees:** Affirmative Action; Exhibitions; Honors; Networking. **Formerly:** (1974) Women's Caucus of the College Art Association.

Publications: *Chapter Newsletter*, periodic. ● *WCA Honor Awards: Honor Awards for Outstanding Achievement in the Visual Arts*, annual. Directory. Catalog containing biographies of women artists and their works honored at the caucus' national conference. ● *WCA National Directory*, biennial. Lists WCA membership. ● *Women's Caucus for Art—National Update*, quarterly. Newsletter. Covers national and chapter news. Includes calendar of events and lists employment opportunities and exhibitions.

Conventions/Meetings: annual conference - always February. ● periodic regional meeting.

★3356★ WOMEN'S CAUCUS OF THE ENDOCRINE SOCIETY (WE)
University of Maryland School of
    Medicine
Department of Physiology
655 W. Baltimore St.
Baltimore, MD 21201
Phyllis Wise, Sec.-Treas.   PH: (410)328-3851

Founded: 1975. **Members:** 850. **Languages:** English. **National.** Promotes the professional advancement of women endocrinologists. Maintains biographical archives; compiles statistics.

Publications: *Letter to Membership*, periodic. Newsletter.

Conventions/Meetings: annual convention. ● annual meeting, with leadership symposium. ● periodic workshop. ● periodic seminar.

★3357★ WOMEN'S CAUCUS FOR POLITICAL SCIENCE (WCPS)
Emory University
Department of Political Science
Atlanta, GA 30322   PH: (404)727-6572
Karen O'Connor, President   FX: (404)874-6925

Founded: 1969. **Members:** 900. **Regional Groups:** 5. **Languages:** English. **National.** Women professionally trained in political science. Purposes are to: upgrade the status of women in the profession of political science; promote equal opportunities for women political scientists for graduate admission, financial assistance in such schools, and in employment, promotion, and tenure. Advances candidates for consideration for APSA offices and committees. **Committees:** Affirmative Action; APSA Liaison; Assessment of Progress; Editorial Review; Promotion of Professional Standards; Women's Platform.

Publications: *WCPS Quarterly*. Newsletter. Includes information about the association and employment opportunities. **Advertising:** accepted. ● *Women's Caucus for Political Science Membership Directory*, biennial. Lists names, addresses, job title, and field of study. **Circulation:** 1,200. **Advertising:** not accepted.

Conventions/Meetings: annual conference, in conjunction with APSA (exhibits). ● periodic workshop.

★3358★ WOMEN'S CIRCLE SUPPORT SERVICES
Agency Village
Box 689
Sisseton, SD 57262   PH: (605)698-4129

Languages: English. **National.** Offers assistance to Native American victims of domestic violence and sexual assault throughout the United States. Addresses the effects of chemical dependency.

★3359★ WOMEN'S CLASSICAL CAUCUS (WCC)
5 Chester Dr.
Rye, NY 10580   PH: (914)698-8798
Prof. Barbara McManus, Treas.   (914)632-5300

Founded: 1972. **Members:** 500. **Membership Dues:** students, US$3 annual; individual and institution, US$10 annual. **Languages:** English. **National.** Ancient historians, archaeologists, art historians, and classicists. Works to support the professional status of women in the classics and related fields, and facilitates research on women in the areas of archaeology, ancient history, and ancient literature. Makes available outlines for courses on Women in Antiquity and syllabi for other courses. **Computer Services:** Mailing lists.

Publications: *WCC Newsletter*, semiannual.

Conventions/Meetings: annual conference, in conjunction with American Philological Association and Archaeological Institute of American (exhibits) - always December.

★3360★ WOMEN'S COLLEGE COALITION (WCC)
1090 Vermont Ave. NW, 3rd Fl.
Washington, DC 20005   PH: (202)789-2556
Jadwiga S. Sebrechts, Dir.   FX: (202)842-4032

Founded: 1972. **Members:** 63. **Staff:** 2. **Budget:** US$150,000. **Languages:** English. **National.** Women's colleges concerned with their roles in supporting the intellectual, professional, and personal development of women. Raises public awareness of women's colleges and the educational needs of women. Disseminates information to the press, educational researchers, women's colleges, and the general public. Conducts and supports research on women's colleges.

Publications: *A Profile of Women's College Presidents*. Book. ● *A Study of the Learning Environment at Women's Colleges*. Book. ● *Alumnae Giving at Women's Colleges: A Ten Year Study*. Book.

Conventions/Meetings: annual congress.

★3361★ WOMEN'S COMMISSION FOR REFUGEE WOMEN AND CHILDREN
c/o International Rescue Committee
386 Park Ave. S
New York, NY 10016
Mary Anne Schwalbe, Director
PH: (212)679-0010
FX: (212)689-3459

Founded: 1989. **Languages:** English. **National.** Works to defend and protect women's rights. Lobbies the U.S. State Department, United Nations officials, and governments regarding the interests of refugee women and children. Disseminates information to raise international awareness of the challenges facing refugee women and children. Encourages women's participation in development programs.

★3362★ WOMEN'S COUNCIL ON ENERGY AND THE ENVIRONMENT (WCEE)
PO Box 33211
Washington, DC 20033
Maureen Healy, Contact
FX: (202)328-5002

Founded: 1981. **Members:** 200. **Budget:** US$10,000. **Languages:** English. **National.** Individuals, primarily women, who work for the federal government, consulting firms, private industry, and the environmental community and are involved in educating the public about national policy issues. Works to facilitate networking among members on public issues, particularly those concerning energy and the environment. Promotes the professional development of women interested in energy and environmental issues. Advocates informed decision-making on such issues by business and government officials. Maintains speakers' bureau. Sponsors public programs that include roundtable and panel discussions and lectures. **Committees:** Activities; Professional Opportunities.

Publications: *Membership Directory*, annual. ● *WCEE Newsletter*, monthly.

Conventions/Meetings: annual seminar.

★3363★ WOMEN'S COUNCIL OF REALTORS (WCR)
430 N. Michigan Ave.
Chicago, IL 60611
Catherine M. Collins, Exec.V.Pres.
PH: (312)329-8483
FX: (312)329-3290

Founded: 1938. **Members:** 18,000. **Staff:** 10. **Budget:** US$1,400,000. **Regional Groups:** 12. **State Groups:** 38. **Local Groups:** 325. **Languages:** English. **National.** Women real estate brokers and salespeople. Provides opportunity for real estate professionals to participate at local, state, and national levels. Makes programs available for personal and career growth. Encourages increased productivity, financial security, and the development of leadership skills among members. Offers courses in leadership training, and referral and relocation business. Maintains speakers' bureau and resource bank.

Publications: *Women's Council of Realtors—Communique*, 10/year. Newsletter. Newsletter. **ISSN:** 0199-9028. **Circulation:** 18,000. ● *Women's Council on Realtors—Referral Roster*, annual. Membership directory. **Circulation:** 18,000. **Advertising:** accepted.

Conventions/Meetings: annual convention - 1993 Nov. 10 - 14, Miami, FL, United States; 1994 Nov. 3 - 8, Anaheim, CA, United States; 1995 Nov. 9 - 14, Atlanta, GA, United States.

★3364★ WOMEN'S DIRECT RESPONSE GROUP (WDRG)
224 7th St.
Garden City, NY 11530
Phyllis L. Kusel, Pres.
PH: (516)746-6700

Founded: 1970. **Members:** 600. **Budget:** US$110,000. **Regional Groups:** 4. **Languages:** English. **National.** Direct marketing professionals. Seeks to: advance the interests and influence of women in the direct response industry; provide for communication and career education; assist in advancement of personal career objectives; serve as professional network to develop business contacts and foster mutual goals. Maintains career talent bank. Sponsors summer internship program. Distributes information. **Awards:** Annual Direct Marketing Woman of the Year. **Committees:** Advertising Sales; Education; Programming; Publicity; Research.

Publications: *Women's Direct Response Group—Membership Roster*, annual. Directory. **Circulation:** 600. **Advertising:** accepted. ● *Women's Direct Response Group—Newsletter*, quarterly. Membership activities with information on career developments. Includes calendar of events and profiles of new members. **Circulation:** 700. **Advertising:** accepted.

Conventions/Meetings: annual meeting - always June. ● monthly luncheon. ● periodic seminar. ● periodic workshop.

★3365★ WOMEN'S DISTANCE COMMITTEE (WDC)
1750 Whittier Ave., No. 14
Costa Mesa, CA 92627
Karen Hunsaker, Chwm.
PH: (714)646-9832

Founded: 1977. **Members:** 10. **Languages:** English. **National.** Women and men who promote distance running for women. Encourages women's running nationally and internationally, for exercise and in preparation for the Olympics. Sponsors seminars and clinics at races or club meetings. Compiles statistics.

Publications: *Running Women - The First Steps*. Booklet.

Conventions/Meetings: annual convention.

★3366★ WOMEN'S DIVISION OF THE BOARD OF GLOBAL MINISTRIES OF THE UNITED METHODIST CHURCH
475 Riverside Dr., Rm. 1504
New York, NY 10115
Joyce D. Sohl, Exec. Officer
PH: (212)870-3752
FX: (212)870-3736

Founded: 1940. **Members:** 1,200,000. **Staff:** 39. **Budget:** US$22,000,000. **Languages:** English. **National.** Women members of the United Methodist Church united to promote spiritual growth and leadership development among women worldwide. Makes available financial support to ministries and social programs benefitting women, children, and youth.

Publications: *Response*, monthly. Magazine.

Conventions/Meetings: quadrennial general assembly - 1994, Cincinnati, OH, United States.

★3367★ WOMEN'S DRUG RESEARCH PROJECT (WDR)
Univ. of Michigan
School of Social Work
1065 Frieze Bldg.
Ann Arbor, MI 48109-1285
Beth G. Reed, Coord.
PH: (313)763-5958

Founded: 1973. **Languages:** English. **National.** Has investigated differences in the needs and problems of men and women entering drug abuse treatment programs. Studied two outpatient methadone programs and two residential therapeutic communities, which were established to gather new information about women addicts, their needs, and possible methods for meeting those needs. Also collected data from 20 programs in five cities for studies on treatment organization and psychosocial characteristics of addicts.

★3368★ WOMEN'S ECONOMIC RIGHTS PROJECT (WERP)
c/o NOW Legal Defense and Educ. Fund
99 Hudson St., 12th Fl.
New York, NY 10013   PH: (212)925-6635
Deborah Ellis, Legal Dir.   FX: (212)226-1066

Staff: 2. **Languages:** English. **National.** A project of the NOW Legal Defense and Education Fund Legal Program. Participants include feminist attorneys involved in employment litigation or constitutional law. Seeks to aid women in attaining economic equality with men. Conducts public educational programs.

★3369★ WOMEN'S ECONOMIC ROUND TABLE (WERT)
866 United Nations Plaza, Ste. 4052
New York, NY 10017   PH: (212)759-4360
Dr. Amelia Augustus, Pres.   FX: (212)666-1625

Founded: 1978. **Members:** 500. **Budget:** US$100,000. **Languages:** English. **National.** Business women and men who question economic policymakers in a public forum; economists, business executives, and unionists. To consolidate the voice of women in the formation of national economic policy and decisions. Conducts seminars; sponsors round tables to clarify national economic issues and make economic policy leaders accessible to members and the public; examines national and international economic issues; acts as resource center for the media and business and other institutions seeking experts and executives. Educates women on how to maintain control over the economic power they hold and stresses the importance of doing so. **Awards:** Periodic Maria and Sidney E. Rolfe Award.

Conventions/Meetings: convention - 8-12/year.

★3370★ WOMEN'S FOREIGN POLICY COUNCIL
845 3rd Ave., 15th Fl.
New York, NY 10022
Mim Kelber, Co-Chairman   PH: (212)759-7982

Languages: English. **National.** Encourages women's involvement in international politics. Seeks to raise awareness of women's issues. Disseminates information.

★3371★ WOMEN'S HEALTH ACTION AND MOBILIZATION (WHAM!)
PO Box 733
New York, NY 10009   PH: (212)713-5966

Founded: 1989. **Members:** 3,000. **Local Groups:** 5. **Languages:** English. **National.** Direct action group committed to demanding, securing, and defending absolute reproductive freedom and quality health care for all women. Maintains a speakers' bureau and offers educational programs. **Libraries:** Type: reference. Holdings: 0; periodicals, clippings, audio recordings, video recordings, archival material. Subjects: women's health.

Publications: *Contact Sheet*, weekly. Bulletin. ● *Frontlines*. Newsletter. quarterly. **Circulation:** 3,000.

★3372★ WOMEN'S HISTORY NETWORK (WHN)
7738 Bell Rd.
Windsor, CA 95492   PH: (707)838-6000
Mary Ruthsdotter, Co-Dir.   FX: (707)838-0478

Founded: 1983. **Members:** 500. **Languages:** English. **National.** A project of the National Women's History Project. Coordinates the recognition and celebration of the contributions of women in U.S. history. Furnishes information, materials, referrals, technical assistance, and support services to aid those who seek to recognize and promote women's achievements and possibilities. Develops, discovers, and collects ideas and resources for women's history activities for educators, historians, community organizers, workplace activists, and unaffiliated individuals. Maintains a women's history performers bureau and biographical archives.

Publications: *Network News*, quarterly. Newsletter. ● *Network Participant Directory*, semiannual.

★3373★ WOMEN'S HOME AND OVERSEAS MISSIONARY SOCIETY
c/o Department of Overseas Missions
  AME, Zion Church
475 Riverside Dr., Rm. 1910
New York, NY 10115
Mrs. Alcestis Coleman, President   PH: (212)870-2952

Founded: 1880. **Members:** 800,000. **Languages:** English. **Multinational.** Women working to educate people worldwide about Christianity. Promotes and supports Christians abroad and organizes activities to assist spiritual growth. Conducts humanitarian, economic, and political projects intended to aid people in a Christian context. Investigates and offers assistance with drug abuse, domestic violence. and minority issues.

Publications: *Missionary Seer* (in English).

★3374★ WOMEN'S INDEPENDENT LABEL DISTRIBUTION NETWORK
  (WILD)
1712 E. Michigan Ave.
Lansing, MI 48912
Terry Grant, Exec. Officer   PH: (517)484-1712

Founded: 1979. **Members:** 8. **Languages:** English. **National.** Independent record distributors affiliated with the women's music industry. Disseminates information to improve distribution and women's business abilities. Holds annual roundtables and seminars on sales, bookkeeping, marketing, advertising, time management, cost analysis, and promotion.

Publications: *Newsletter*, monthly.

Conventions/Meetings: annual conference - always May.

★3375★ WOMEN'S INFORMATION BANK (WIB)
3918 W St. NW
Washington, DC 20007   PH: (202)338-8163
Barbara Sylvester, Pres.   FX: (202)337-9096

Founded: 1970. **Languages:** English. **National.** Informal network of individuals who aid women seeking business partners and start-up capital, freelance work opportunities, short-term housing and home exchanges in Washington and other major cities, travel partners, and employment and educational opportunities. Operates Global Women's Network, which helps women travelers locate individuals with similar interests in several American cities. **Libraries:** Type: reference. **Telecommunication Services:** Electronic bulletin board.

Publications: *Thinking Woman*, periodic. Newsletter.

★3376★ WOMEN'S INFORMATION EXCHANGE (WIE)
PO Box 68
Jenner, CA 95450   PH: (707)632-5763
Jill Lippitt, Exec. Officer   FX: (707)632-5589

Founded: 1980. **Staff:** 3. **Languages:** English. **National.** Feminist women computer specialists who believe that computer technology may be used to support the efforts of women and women's organizations nationwide. Promotes networking and communication between women and women's organizations. Provides speakers on such topics as gender-based learning differences, office automation, and women and technology. **Computer Services:** Data base, women's service providers, including health centers, women's centers, and women's studies programs.

★3377★ WOMEN'S INITIATIVE OF THE AMERICAN ASSOCIATION OF
  RETIRED PERSONS (AARP)
1909 K St. NW
Washington, DC 20049

Languages: English. **National.** Women 50 years of age or older, working or retired. Seeks to improve every aspect of living for older women. Disseminates information.

Publications: *Network News* (in English), periodic. Newsletter. Issues involving midlife and older women.

★3378★ WOMEN'S INSTITUTE (WI)
5225 Pooks Hill Rd., Ste. 1718-N
Bethesda, MD 20814
Rita Z. Johnston, Pres.   PH: (301)530-9192

Founded: 1975. **Languages:** English. **National.** Serves as a vehicle for the development and presentation of programs on special problems and major issues of concern to women. Provides an educational and political forum for women's roles in economic, family, political and social life on a local, national, and international level. Conducts research. **Libraries:** Type: reference.
     Awards: Periodic Myra E. Barrar Journalism Award. Recipient: Feminist journalism student at the American University in Washington, DC.

Publications: *Winds of Change: Korean Women in America.*

Conventions/Meetings: annual board meeting. ● annual meeting.

★3379★ WOMEN'S INSTITUTE FOR FREEDOM OF THE PRESS
(WIFP)
3306 Ross Pl. NW
Washington, DC 20008
Dr. Martha Leslie Allen, Dir.   PH: (202)966-7783

Founded: 1972. **Languages:** English. **National.** Women concerned with the expansion of women's outreach in media. Believes that through establishing an independent two-level women's communication system (initially, women raising issues among themselves in their own media, and secondly women working in male-dominated media raising these issues for wider debate and discussion) and increasing women's media outreach to equal that of men, ''oppression, wherever it exists'' will decline. Conducts research programs on theory of communications; disseminates information. **Libraries:** Type: reference. Holdings: periodicals. Subjects: women's movement.

Publications: *Syllabus Sourcebook on Media and Women.* Directory. ● *Strategy to Equalize Media Outreach.* Book.

★3380★ WOMEN'S INSTITUTE FOR HOUSING AND ECONOMIC
DEVELOPMENT
179 South St.
Boston, MA 02111   PH: (617)423-2296

Languages: English. **National.** Promotes the development of low-income women and their children in the United States. Provides assistance to women, women's and community groups regradless of race, nationality, class, political affiliation, or religion. Works to advance the status of women by providing a variety of real estate, business development, public education, and community programs. Conducts workshops and training sessions; disseminates information.

Publications: *A Development Primer.* Booklet. Housing and business ventures. ● *Manual on Transitional Housing.* Book. Planning operational concerns in development. ● *Taking Action: A Comprehensive Approach to Housing Women and Children in Massachusetts.* Book. Design and financing issues in developing housing and related services for low-income women and children.

★3381★ WOMEN'S INTERART CENTER (WIC)
549 W. 52nd St.
New York, NY 10019
Margot Lewitin, Artistic Dir.   PH: (212)246-1050

Founded: 1969. **Members:** 250. **Budget:** US$310,000. **Languages:** English. **National.** Professional women artists (painters, sculptors, actors, poets, photographers, filmmakers, video artists, writers, ceramists, and serigraphers). Offers opportunities for members to practice their crafts or explore new ones; exchange ideas; meet and work with other artists. Encourages members to explore new areas of expertise. Activities include film and video

festival, panels, lectures, demonstrations, and workshops. Facilities include a theatre and a gallery which house events such as poetry readings, theatrical performances, painting, sculpture and photography exhibitions, and seminars and lectures. Maintains video documentary archives of women visual artists and a Fine Arts Museum.

Publications: *Interart News*, quarterly. Newsletter.

★3382★ WOMEN'S INTERNATIONAL BOWLING CONGRESS (WIBC)
5301 S. 76th St.
Greendale, WI 53129-1191   PH: (414)421-9000
Sandra Shirk, COO   FX: (414)421-4420

Founded: 1916. **Members:** 2,800,000. **Staff:** 101. **Budget:** US$7,000,000. **State Groups:** 54. **Local Groups:** 2,784. **Languages:** English. **Multinational.** Women bowlers of American tenpins. Sanctions bowling for women and associations in 20 countries. Provides uniform qualifications, rules, and regulations to govern WIBC sanctioned teams, leagues, and tournaments. Conducts leadership training seminars and lane inspectors' workshops; sponsors Annual championship, Queens, and Queens Pro Am tournaments; bestows awards. Maintains hall of fame, museum, and biographical archives; compiles statistics. Supports BVL Fund to aid persons in Veterans Administration hospitals. Cosponsors Young American Bowling Alliance as well as collegiate and senior league programs and National Senior and National Mixed Tournaments. **Computer Services:** Mailing lists. **Sections:** Championship Tournament; Field Service; Tournament Sanctions; Field Service; Public Relations; Rules.

Publications: *Annual Report.* ● *Media Guide*, annual. **Also Cited As:** *Tournament and Record Guide.* ● *WIBC News*, monthly. Includes tournament results and calendar of events. ● *WIBC Playing Rules and Bylaws Book*, annual. **Circulation:** 250,000. **Advertising:** accepted. ● *Woman Bowler Magazine*, 8/year. ● *Tournament Program.* Booklet. ● *Bowlers Guide.* Book. ● Also publishes instruction and record brochure, handbooks, pamphlets, and printed forms.

Conventions/Meetings: annual conference - 1993, Baton Rouge, LA, United States; 1994, Salt Lake City, UT, United States; 1995, Tucson, AZ, United States.

★3383★ WOMEN'S INTERNATIONAL LEAGUE FOR PEACE AND
FREEDOM - UNITED STATES SECTION (WILPF-US)
                         PH: (215)563-7110
                         FX: (215)864-2022
1213 Race St.   E-Mail: PEACENET:
Philadelphia, PA 19107-1691   WILPFNATL and
Mary Zepernick, Pres.   WILPFLEGIS

Founded: 1915. **Members:** 15,000. **Staff:** 12. **Budget:** US$520,000. **Regional Groups:** 4. **State Groups:** 33. **Local Groups:** 110. **Languages:** English. **Multinational.** Women working, through nonviolent means, to: eliminate U.S. economic and military intervention abroad, discrimination on any basis, and governmental surveillance and repression; establish total universal disarmament and unconditional amnesty for war resisters; improve and ensure civil rights; promote peace education in schools and communities; establish ''an economy that puts people before profits.'' Sponsors committee of educators and parents studying ways to teach peaceful attitudes in social relationships. Conducts research and seminar/training programs. U.S. section is one of 28 sections of the Women's International League for Peace and Freedom in Geneva, Switzerland. **Awards:** Periodic Jane Adams Children's Book. Recipient: children's author that promotes international friendship and understanding. **Committees:** Central America; Chemical Weapons; Civil Liberties; Disarmament; Economics; Europe; Federal Budget; Feminist Task Force; Labor; Middle East; Nuclear Power; Peace Education; Racism; Southeast Asia; Southern Africa; United Nations. **Former Project:** Comprehensive Test Ban Campaign, Women Poll Project.

Publications: *Pax et Libertas*, quarterly. Newsletter. **Circulation:** 20,000. **Advertising:** not accepted. ● *Peace and Freedom*, bimonthly. Journal. Organization's activities. Includes book reviews and legislative news. **Circu-**

lation: 20,000. **Advertising:** accepted. **Alternate Formats:** microform. ● *Program and Legislative Action*, bimonthly. Newsletter. ● *The Women's Budget*. Book. ● *Women for All Seasons*. Book.

Conventions/Meetings: biennial congress, national. ● biennial congress, international.

★3384★ WOMEN'S INTERNATIONAL NETWORK (WIN)
187 Grant St.
Lexington, MA 02173
Fran P. Hosken, Coordinator/Editor
PH: (617)862-9431
FX: (617)862-9431

Founded: 1975. **Staff:** 2. **Languages:** English. **Multinational.** Goal is to encourage cooperation and communication between women of all backgrounds, beliefs, nationalities, and age groups through the compilation and dissemination of information on women's development. Participants voluntarily contribute news and information on women and health, environment, media, violence, female genital mutilation, and United Nations events of concern to women. The network's Women and International Affairs Clearinghouse surveys career opportunities for women interested in working in international and development agencies. Conducts research on women's health and on women's development throughout the world. **Libraries:** Type: reference.

Publications: *WIN News*, quarterly. Journal providing information on women and women's groups worldwide. **ISSN:** 0145-7985. **Advertising:** accepted. ● *Hosken Report: Genital and Sexual Mutilations of Females* (in English, French, and Spanish). *Action Guide*, and *The Childbirth Picture Book*, including flip charts and color slides.

★3385★ WOMEN'S INTERNATIONAL POLICY ACTION COMMITTEE
ON ENVIRONMENT AND DEVELOPMENT (IPAC)
IPAC Secretariat
c/o Women's Foreign Policy Council
845 3rd Ave., 15th Fl.
New York, NY 10022
PH: (212)759-7982
FX: (212)759-8647

Multinational. Women working to control development and preserve the natural environment.

★3386★ WOMEN'S INTERNATIONAL PROFESSIONAL TENNIS
COUNCIL (WIPTC)
100 Park Ave., 2nd Fl.
New York, NY 10017
Jane G. Brown, Mng.Dir.
PH: (212)878-2250
TX: 422609

Founded: 1975. **Members:** 27. **Languages:** English. **Multinational.** Goal is to sanction, administer, and promote women's professional tennis throughout the world. Sponsors tournaments worldwide.

Publications: *Virginia Slims World Championship Series Rules and Regulations*.

Conventions/Meetings: quarterly meeting, in conjuction with Grand Slam tennis events and Women's Series Tournaments.

★3387★ WOMEN'S INTERNATIONAL PUBLIC HEALTH NETWORK
7100 Oak Forest Ln.
Bethesda, MD 20817
Naomi Baumslag, President
PH: (301)469-9210

Founded: 1986. **Multinational.** Umbrella organization of women's groups in health-related areas that seeks to improve the nutrition, health, and status of women worldwide. Supports grassroots women's health projects with funds and medical equipment.

★3388★ WOMEN'S INTERNATIONAL RESOURCE EXCHANGE (WIRE)
122 W 27th St., 10th Fl.
New York, NY 10001
Sybil Wong, Admin.
PH: (212)741-2955

Founded: 1981. **Staff:** 1. **Languages:** English. **Multinational.** Collective whose objectives are to: confront sexism, racism, and classism; develop an understanding and global perspective of women's struggles and gains; provide low-cost information on the status of Third World women.

Publications: *Resistance, War and Liberation: Women of Southern Africa*. Book. ● *Nicaragua Women: Unlearning the Alphabet of Submission*. Book. ● *Voices of Women: Poetry by and About Third World Women*. Book.

★3389★ WOMEN'S INTERNATIONAL SURFING ASSOCIATION (WISA)
30202 Silver Spur Rd.
PO Box 512
San Juan Capistrano, CA 92693
Mary Lou Drummy, Pres.
PH: (714)493-2591

Founded: 1975. **Members:** 95. **Languages:** English. **Multinational.** Promotes the sport of surfing and the development of quality competition for amateur and professional women surfers of all ages. Sponsors surfing instructionals; presents slide and movie shows for school groups; conducts public relations work; supports beach preservation efforts; sponsors competitions.

Publications: *Membership List*, semiannual. Directory. ● *Women in Waves*, semiannual. Newsletter.

Conventions/Meetings: monthly meeting.

★3390★ WOMEN'S ISSUES, STATUS, AND EDUCATION (WISE)
Meredith Coll
3800 Hillsborough St.
Raleigh, NC 27607-5298
Mary Johnson, Dir.
PH: (919)829-8353
FX: (919)829-2828

Founded: 1983. **Members:** 100. **Languages:** English. **National.** Women members of the American Association for Adult and Continuing Education. Purposes are: to plan and implement activities that will enhance opportunities for women in adult education; to increase channels of communication within the organization, with appropriate subdivisions of the parent organization and with other organizations; to identify needs and concerns of women in the field. Conducts research and reports activities on the status of women in adult education.

Publications: *Minutes of Meeting*, annual. Bulletin. ● *Newsletter*, 1-2/year.

Conventions/Meetings: annual conference, in conjunction with AAACE (exhibits).

★3391★ WOMEN'S JEWELRY ASSOCIATION (WJA)
1111 2nd Ave.
New Hyde Park, NY 11040
Tina Segal, Pres.
PH: (516)326-1369

Founded: 1983. **Members:** 700. **Staff:** 1. **Languages:** English. **National.** Women involved in jewelry design, manufacture, retail, and advertising; men may join as associate members. Aims to: enhance the status of women in the jewelry industry; make known the contribution of women to the industry; provide a network for women involved with fine jewelry. Maintains hall of fame; offers placement services. **Awards:** Periodic (scholarship). **Computer Services:** Data base, membership information. **Committees:** Publicity; Fundraising; Hospitality; Job Opportunities.

Publications: *Jewelry Association Newsletter*, semiannual.

Conventions/Meetings: semiannual - always February and July. New York, NY, United States.

★3392★ WOMEN'S LAW FUND (WLF)
57 E. Washington St.
Chagrin Falls, OH 44022　　　　　PH: (216)247-6167
Nancy Krammer, Exec. Officer　　　(216)431-4850

Founded: 1972. **Languages:** English. **National.** Purpose is to eradicate sex-based discrimination in education, employment, government benefits, and housing by providing legal assistance to individuals who have administrative charges pending before state and federal governmental agencies. Provides representation in court proceedings. Conducts lectures, speeches, and conferences; provides technical assistance to professionals and others; promotes full participation of women in American life by securing and protecting their Constitutional rights.

★3393★ WOMEN'S LAW PROJECT (WLP)
125 S. 9th St., Ste. 401
Philadelphia, PA 19107　　　　　PH: (215)928-9801
Carol Tracy, Exec.Dir.　　　　　　FX: (215)928-9848

Founded: 1974. **Staff:** 6. **Budget:** US$350,000. **Languages:** English. **National.** Nonprofit feminist law firm working to challenge sex discrimination in the law and in legal and social institutions through litigation, public education, research and writing, representation of women's groups, and individual counseling. Conducts test case and class action litigation in the areas of family law, education, employment, prison reform, reproductive rights, and sex-based insurance rates. Maintains speakers' bureau. **Telecommunication Services:** Phone referral system, information on women's legal rights and community education programs.

Publications: *Child Support Handbook: How You Can Obtain Child Support Orders in Philadelphia.* ● *Women's Rights and the Law.* Book.

★3394★ WOMEN'S LEAGUE FOR CONSERVATIVE JUDAISM (WLCJ)
48 E. 74th St.
New York, NY 10021　　　　　　PH: (212)628-1600
Bernice Balter, Exec.Dir.　　　　FX: (212)772-3507

Founded: 1918. **Members:** 150,000. **Staff:** 19. **Budget:** US$800,000. **Regional Groups:** 28. **Local Groups:** 750. **Languages:** English. **National.** Composed of Sisterhoods affiliated with the Conservative movement, dedicated to the perpetuation of traditional Judaism and the translation of its ideals into practice. Purposes are: to guide its affiliates in local, national, and international activities, making them aware of their civic responsibilities; to foster Jewish education through study courses, Jewish Family Living Institutes and through the establishment of Synagogue and Sisterhood libraries. **Committees:** Adult Education; Canadian Public Affairs; Community Service; Creative Handicrafts; Field Service; Israel Affairs; Jewish Family Living; Judaica Shop; Music; Program; Public Relations; Services to the Disabled; Singles; Social Action; Training Services; United Nations; Youth/School Liaison.

Publications: *Ba' Olam*, bimonthly. Newsletter. Provides news and commentary on world affairs. **Advertising:** not accepted. ● *Report*, biennial. Booklet. **Circulation:** 2,000. **Advertising:** not accepted. **Also Cited As:** *Convention Handbook.* ● *Calendar Diary*, annual. Book. Lists Hebrew and English dates and holidays. Includes prayers and readings. **Circulation:** 18,000. **Advertising:** not accepted. ● *Outlook*, quarterly. Magazine. Covers programs of social action, health, education, history and culture, and Jewish lifestyles. **ISSN:** 0043-7557. **Circulation:** 130,000. **Advertising:** accepted. ● *Hebrew Word Guide: Building Your Vocabulary.* Book. ● *Doorway to Understanding.* Book.

Conventions/Meetings: biennial (exhibits) - always November. ● biennial World Affairs Conference - always fall. ● biennial conference.

★3395★ WOMEN'S LEAGUE FOR ISRAEL (WLI)
160 E. 56th St.
New York, NY 10022
Trudy Miner, Pres.　　　　　　PH: (212)838-1997

Founded: 1928. **Members:** 5,000. **Staff:** 6. **Local Groups:** 45. **Languages:**

English. **Multinational.** Women interested in the redevelopment of Israel and in supporting educational, vocational, and social service programs for residents and newcomers. Maintains homes in Haifa, Jerusalem, Tel Aviv, and Nathanya, Israel and a vocational and rehabilitation center. Built women's dormitory, cafeteria, and student center at Hebrew University in Jerusalem, Israel, and two dormitories for women on Mount Scopus. **Awards:** Annual Freedom Cup.

Publications: *Bulletin*, quarterly. ● *Women's League for Israel—Newsletter*, 3/year. **Circulation:** 4,500. **Advertising:** not accepted.

Conventions/Meetings: annual congress - 1994. ● triennial conference.

★3396★ WOMEN'S LEGAL DEFENSE FUND (WLDF)
1875 Connecticut Ave. NW, Ste. 710
Washington, DC 20009　　　　　PH: (202)986-2600
Judith Lichtman, Pres.　　　　　FX: (202)986-2539

Founded: 1971. **Members:** 1,800. **Staff:** 18. **Budget:** US$1,100,000. **Languages:** English. **National.** Attorneys, administrators, publicists, and secretaries. Purpose is to secure equal rights for women through litigation, advocacy and monitoring, legal counseling and information, and public education. Works for women's rights in family law, employment, education, and other areas. Maintains speakers' bureau. **Committees:** Counseling on Domestic Relations; Counseling on Employment Discrimination; Litigation Screening.

Publications: *WLDF News*, semiannual. Newsletter. Reports on women's legal rights in the areas of employment and family law, including Supreme Court decisions and legislative developments. **ISSN:** 0736-9433. **Circulation:** 2,000. **Advertising:** not accepted.

Conventions/Meetings: annual luncheon.

★3397★ WOMEN'S MEDIA PROJECT (WMP)
1333 H St. NW, 11th Fl.
Washington, DC 20005
Rosanna Landis, Contact　　　　PH: (202)682-0940

Founded: 1979. **Budget:** US$250,000. **Languages:** English. **National.** A project of the NOW Legal Defense and Education Fund (see separate entry). Feminist activists united to eliminate sex role stereotyping of women and men in the media and to increase the participation of women and minorities in broadcasting. Purposes are to: conduct public education campaigns with up-to-date information on issues that affect women; guide individuals and groups in developing effective dialogues with local broadcasters and publishers through community action campaigns; monitor compliance with equal employment legislation in the communications industry; encourage development and distribution of quality television and radio programming that offers realistic and contemporary images of women. Identifies programming promoting equality between women and men. Conducts research in broadcast employment. **Formerly:** (1987) Media Project.

Publications: *Women's Media Campaign Workbook*, annual. ● Also publishes research reports.

★3398★ WOMEN'S MISSIONARY COUNCIL OF THE CHRISTIAN METHODIST EPISCOPAL CHURCH (WMCCMEC)
623 San Fernando Ave.
Berkeley, CA 94707
Dr. Sylvia Faulk, Pres.

Founded: 1918. **Members:** 129,000. **Staff:** 5. **Regional Groups:** 37. **Languages:** English. **National.** Women members of the Christian Methodist Episcopal church. Seeks to: discover and share the mission of the church; promote cooperation, fellowship, and mutual counsel concerning the spiritual life and religious activities of the church; encourage Bible study and assist in spreading the Gospel; research and answer society's needs in order to develop programs and resources that will respond to that need. Conducts educational and charitable programs. **Awards:** Periodic Helena B. Cobb (scholarship). **Commissions:** Christian Social Relations; Communications; Education; History. **Divisions:** Service and Outreach; Structure. **Programs:** Aid to Ministers' Widows; The Black Family and Child Advocacy; Christian Social Relations; Ecumenical Relations; Educational Services and Scholarship Aid; Literature and Publications; Marches and Convocations; Missionary Education; Overseas Missions; Personal Stewardship; Projects for Our Colleges; The Relief of Hunger; Spiritual Development; Status of Women.

Publications: *The Missionary Messenger*, monthly. Newsletter. **Advertising:** not accepted.

Conventions/Meetings: quadrennial general assembly.

★3399★ WOMEN'S MISSIONARY AND SERVICE COMMISSION OF THE MENNONITE CHURCH (WMSCMC)
421 S. 2nd St., Ste. 600
Elkhart, IN 46516-3243   PH: (219)294-7131
Marian B. Hostetler, Exec.Sec.   FX: (219)294-8669

Founded: 1915. **Staff:** 3. **Budget:** US$118,000. **Regional Groups:** 21. **Local Groups:** 500. **Languages:** English. **National.** Encourages spiritual growth in women through prayer, Bible study, and community service. Operates speakers' bureau. **Awards:** Periodic (scholarship). Recipient: Mennonite women for graduate and undergraduate studies. **Divisions:** Business and Professional Women; Family Life; Literature; Peace and Social Concerns.

Publications: *Resource Packet*, annual. In conjunction with Women in Mission of the General Conference Mennonite Church. Includes devotional lessons, brochures, and audio-visual materials. **Circulation:** 1,500. **Advertising:** not accepted. ● *Voice*, 11/year. Magazine. Features inspirational growth articles, service project opportunities, and chapter updates. **Circulation:** 21,000. **Advertising:** not accepted. ● *Mennonite Women*. Book. ● *Books Abroad and at Home*. Booklet.

Conventions/Meetings: biennial general assembly - 1995 July 25 - 30, Wichita, KS, United States.

★3400★ WOMEN'S MISSIONARY SOCIETY, AME CHURCH (WMS)
1134 11th St. NW
Washington, DC 20001   PH: (202)371-8886
Delores L. Kennedy Williams, Pres.   FX: (202)371-8820

Founded: 1944. **Members:** 800,000. **Languages:** English. **National.** Women members of the African Methodist Episcopal Church. Seeks to: "help each woman and youth grow in the knowledge and experience of God through his son Jesus Christ; seek fellowship with women in other lands; make possible opportunities and resources to meet the changing needs and concerns of women and youth through intensive training, recruitment, and Christian witnessing; offer a fellowship so strong, a message so convincingly interpreted and imparted, and an enthusiasm so contagious, that the Gospel through us will be at work in the world so that we will be able to draw humankind into the fellowship of love." Sponsors administrative retreats, health institutes, international exchanges, missionaries, leadership training programs, and educational programs for religious leaders. Operates womens information bureau; compiles statistics; maintains biographical archives. Organizes charitable activities; offers children's services. Sponsors competitions. **Awards:** Periodic Handy-Simmons (scholarship). **Divisions:** Young People's. **Committees:** Christian Social Relations; Creative Arts; Family Life; Research on the Status of the Black Woman.

Publications: *Missionary Magazine*, 9/year. ● *President's Newsletter*, quarterly. ● *Young People's Division Newsletter*, quarterly. ● *Inspirational Preparatory Workbook*. ● *Women's Missionary Society Handbook*.

Conventions/Meetings: annual convention - 1994 Jan. 30 - Feb. 2. ● quadrennial general assembly. ● periodic conference.

★3401★ WOMEN'S MOTORCYCLIST FOUNDATION (WMF)
7 Lent Ave.
LeRoy, NY 14482-1009
Sue Slate, Contact   PH: (716)768-6054

Founded: 1984. **Staff:** 2. **Budget:** US$28,000. **Languages:** English. **National.** Information and service organization for women motorcyclists. Organizes biennial festival. Offers networking opportunities.

Publications: *Chrome Rose's Review*, semiannual. Newsletter. Contains travel information and maintenance tips. **Circulation:** 200. **Advertising:** not accepted.

★3402★ WOMEN'S NATIONAL BOOK ASSOCIATION (WNBA)
160 5th Ave., Rm. 604
New York, NY 10010   PH: (212)675-7805
Sandra K. Paul, Exec. Officer   FX: (212)989-7542

Founded: 1917. **Members:** 1,000. **Local Groups:** 8. **Languages:** English. **National.** Women and men professionally engaged in all phases of book publishing; booksellers, editors, authors, and librarians. Encourages professional networking in order to facilitate exchange of information. Sponsors sessions on the book industry at meetings of related professional associations. Maintains archives at Columbia University, New York City. **Awards:** Periodic Lucile Michaels Pannell Award for creative use of books with children. **Committees:** Education for Publishing.

Publications: *The Bookwoman*, 3/year. Covers association activities and women's issues in the publishing industry; includes book reviews and member profiles. **ISSN:** 0163-1128.

★3403★ WOMEN'S NATIONAL REPUBLICAN CLUB (WNRC)
3 W. 51st St.
New York, NY 10019   PH: (212)582-5454
Mrs. Lila Prounis, Exec. Officer   FX: (212)977-8972

Founded: 1921. **Members:** 1,300. **Staff:** 50. **Languages:** English. **National.** Women interested in promoting the programs of the Republican Party and creating interest in political participation. Conducts educational, cultural, social, and political programs. Maintains the Henrietta Wells Livermore School of Politics, which provides political training and education on city, state, national, and international affairs. Operates speakers' bureau. **Libraries:** Type: reference. **Awards:** Annual Republican Woman of the Year. ● Periodic Distinguished Political Service Award. **Committees:** Arts; Calvin Coolidge Memorial Library; Henrietta Wells Livermore School of Politics; International Affairs; Juniors; Public Relations; Special Events.

Publications: *Guidon*, monthly. Newsletter. **Advertising:** not accepted.

Conventions/Meetings: semiannual convention - always January and April.

★3404★ WOMEN'S ORDINATION CONFERENCE (WOC)
PO Box 2693
Fairfax, VA 22031   PH: (703)352-1006
Ruth Fitzpatrick, Coordinator   FX: (703)352-5181

Founded: 1975. **Members:** 3,500. **Staff:** 2. **Local Groups:** 100. **Languages:** English. **National.** Roman Catholic women and men, lay and ordained, who believe that women have the right to participate fully in church life, including the priestly ministry. Plans to continue prayer, support, networking, and lobbying until sexism is removed from the process of priestly ordination and from the structures and understandings of the Roman Catholic church. Conducts research; compiles documentation. Maintains national speakers' bureau and archives. Sponsors specialized education and research programs.

Publications: *New Women/New Church*, bimonthly. Newsletter. **ISSN:** 1043-2221. **Circulation:** 4,000. **Advertising:** not accepted. ● *Liberating Liturgies*. Book.

Conventions/Meetings: annual meeting - Washington, DC, United States.

★3405★ WOMEN'S OVERSEAS SERVICE LEAGUE (WOSL)
1850 Englewood SE
Grand Rapids, MI 49506
Bernice R. Couzynse, Pres.

Founded: 1921. **Members:** 1,250. **Staff:** 4. **Local Groups:** 44. **Languages:** English. **National**. Women who served overseas with the armed services, American Red Cross, Salvation Army, or other service organizations, or with any agency approved by the U.S. government to work with the armed forces during World Wars I and II, Korean conflict, Vietnam, Persian Gulf, or aftermath; women of the U.S. Armed Forces or her allies. Carries on patriotic activities, services to disabled veterans, and aid to members in need. **Committees:** International Relations; Patriotic; Public Relations; Service; Patriotic; Public Relations; Service.

Publications: *Carry On*, quarterly. Newsletter.

Conventions/Meetings: annual convention - 1994 July, Indianapolis, IN, United States.

★3406★ WOMEN'S PEACE INITIATIVE (WPI)
1531 44th St. NW
Washington, DC 20007
Dr. Jancis Long, Coordinator   PH: (202)333-0235

Founded: 1984. **Members:** 2,000. **Staff:** 1. **Languages:** English. **National**. Women seeking an end to the arms race. Participates in local and national lobbying; provides educational materials concerning congressional bills; networks with other peace groups. Supports a comprehensive test ban treaty and a halt to specific weapon systems.

★3407★ WOMEN'S PEACE NETWORK (WPN)
121 W 27th St., Ste. 301
New York, NY 10001
Vivian Stromberg, Co-Chairman   PH: (212)254-1925

Languages: English. **National**. Promotes international understanding and nuclear disarmament. Conducts research; disseminates information.

★3408★ WOMEN'S PRISON ASSOCIATION (WPA)
110 2nd Ave.
New York, NY 10003   PH: (212)674-1163
Ann L. Jacobs, Exec.Dir.   FX: (212)677-1981

Founded: 1844. **Staff:** 35. **Budget:** US$1,200,000. **Languages:** English. **National**. Service agency that aids women who have been in conflict with the law. Promotes alternatives to incarceration; sponsors transitional programs for women being released from prison.

★3409★ WOMEN'S PROFESSIONAL RACQUETBALL ASSOCIATION (WPRA)
153 S. 15th St.
Souderton, PA 18964   PH: (215)723-7356
Molly O'Brien, Exec.Dir.   FX: (215)723-7163

Founded: 1979. **Members:** 500. **Budget:** US$200,000. **Languages:** English. **National**. Individuals interested in women's racquetball. Promotes the participation of women in sports. Organizes and implements a professional racquetball tour for women. Oversees all aspects of sanctioned tournaments; encourages communication among members regarding the rules of the game; provides a public relations service for women's racquetball. Compiles statistics; sponsors charitable program.

Publications: *Women in Racquetball Newsletter*, bimonthly. Features profiles of players from across the country; includes tournament updates, professional rankings, and calendar of events. **Advertising:** accepted. ● *WPRA Handbook*, biennial. Booklet. ● *WPRA Official Tour Program*, annual. Booklet.

Conventions/Meetings: annual competition. ● periodic seminar.

★3410★ WOMEN'S PROFESSIONAL RODEO ASSOCIATION (WPRA)
Rt. 5, Box 698
Blanchard, OK 73010
Lydia Moore, Sec.-Treas.   PH: (405)485-2277

Founded: 1948. **Members:** 2,000. **Staff:** 1. **Languages:** English. **National**. To produce and compete in All Professional Girl Rodeos and Barrel Races in rodeo sanctioned by the Professional Rodeo Cowboys Association. Conducts seminars and clinics on fundamentals of horsemanship and rodeo events. Operates National Cowgirl Hall of Fame. **Libraries:** Type: reference.
          Awards: Periodic (monetary). Recipient: barrel racing and rodeo champions.

Publications: *Newsletter*, monthly. ● *Reference Book*, annual. Directory. ● *Rule Book*, annual. Booklet.

Conventions/Meetings: annual convention - always January. Denver, CO, United States.

★3411★ WOMEN'S RESEARCH AND EDUCATION INSTITUTE (WREI)
1700 18th St. NW, Ste. 400
Washington, DC 20009   PH: (202)328-7070
Betty Parsons Dooley, Exec.Dir.   FX: (202)328-3514

Founded: 1977. **Staff:** 5. **Languages:** English. **National**. Nonpartisan policy research organization. Provides information to policymakers, legislators, women's research centers, and the media concerning issues of importance to women and families. Sponsors Congressional Fellowships on Women and Public Policy. Conducts research projects on women's access to health care and women in the military. **Awards:** Annual American Woman. **Committees:** Long-Term Research Advisory. **Formerly:** (1980) Congresswomen's Caucus Corp..

Publications: *Annual Report on the Status of Women*. Booklet. ● *Directory of Women's Research and Policy Centers*, biennial. ● *The American Woman*, biennial. Journal.

Conventions/Meetings: periodic conference - Washington, DC, United States.

★3412★ WOMEN'S RIGHTS COMMITTEE (WRC)
c/o Human Rights Department
555 New Jersey Ave. NW
Washington, DC 20001
Barbara Van Blake, Dir.   PH: (202)879-4400

Founded: 1970. **Languages:** English. **National**. Carries out policy resolutions of the American Federation of Teachers in the area of women's rights. Encourages programs on the local level that implement these policies; works with other feminist groups with the same views. Conducts research and education programs; maintains speakers' bureau; compiles statistics.

Publications: *Action*, weekly. Bulletin. ● *American Educator*, quarterly. Magazine. ● *American Teacher*, monthly. Newsletter.

Conventions/Meetings: biennial convention. ● annual conference.

★3413★ WOMEN'S RIGHTS PROJECT (WRP)
c/o American Civil Liberties Union
132 W. 43rd St.
New York, NY 10036
Isabelle Katz Pinzler, Dir.   PH: (212)944-9800

Founded: 1972. **Languages:** English. **National**. Strives to end sex discrimination in the U.S. through major class-action litigation in precedent-setting cases usually referred through affiliates. Emphasis is on sex discrimination in education and in the work place.

Conventions/Meetings: biennial convention, in conjunction with the American Civil Liberties Union.

★3414★ WOMEN'S RIGHTS PROJECT OF HUMAN RIGHTS WATCH
485 5th Ave.
New York, NY 10017
Dorothy Q. Thomas, Director

Founded: 1990. **Multinational.** Monitors violence against women and gender discrimination throughout the world.

★3415★ WOMEN'S SPIRITUALITY FORUM (WSF)
PO Box 11363
Oakland, CA 94611
Z. Budapest, Pres.   PH: (510)420-1454

Founded: 1971. **Staff:** 2. **Budget:** US$30,000. **Languages:** English. **National.** Seeks to bring women's spirituality into the mainstream and feminist awareness. Promotes "the female side of one's concept of god, natural laws, and the empowerment of women." Conducts classes, workshops, and Sunday lecture series on topics such as women's spirituality, feminist history, craft skills, women's mysteries, European shamanism, women's holy days, and "the presence of the Goddess in everyday life." Performs rituals, rites of passage, blessings, memorials, and other community services. Conducts telephone inquiries and referrals; maintains speakers' bureau. **Computer Services:** Mailing lists.

Publications: *Callisto*, 3-4/year. Newsletter. Contains schedules of classes, workshops, retreats, rituals, festivals, and lecture series. **Circulation:** 10,000. **Advertising:** not accepted.

Conventions/Meetings: annual Halloween Sacred Dance. ● Winter Solstice Yulefest - Berkeley, CA, United States.

★3416★ WOMEN'S SPORTS FOUNDATION (WSF)
342 Madison Ave., Ste. 728   PH: (212)972-9170
New York, NY 10173   TF: (800)227-3988
Dr. Donna Lopiano, Exec.Dir.   FX: (212)949-8024

Founded: 1974. **Members:** 300,000. **Staff:** 8. **Budget:** US$1,000,000. **Languages:** English. **National.** Encourages and supports the participation of women in sports activities for their health, enjoyment, and mental development; educates the public about athletic opportunities and the value of sports for women. Activities include: conducting sports-related seminars and symposia; developing educational guides; providing internship program; supporting the enforcement of the Title IX amendments of the 1972 Equal Education Act and the Amateur Sports Act. Sponsors an information and resource clearinghouse on women's sports and fitness. Presents awards for outstanding contributions and achievements in women's sports. Maintains International Women's Sports Hall of Fame. Maintains biographical archives; compiles statistics. **Awards:** Periodic (grant).

Publications: *College Scholarship Guide*, annual. Directory. ● *The Woman's Sports Experience*, quarterly. Newsletter. ● *A Woman's Guide to Coaching*. Book. ● *Aspire Higher: Careers in Sports for Women*. Book. ● *The Winning Combination: Girls and Sports*. Book.

Conventions/Meetings: annual convention (exhibits).

★3417★ WOMEN'S STUDENT ASSOCIATION (WSA)
c/o Hebrew Union Coll.
Jewish Inst. of Religion
1 W. 4th St.
New York, NY 10012
Paula Feldstein, Chairperson   PH: (212)674-5300

Members: 35. **Regional Groups:** 2. **Languages:** English. **National.** Female rabbinic, cantorial, and education students and rabbis. Acts as an educational, political action, and support group for women in the rabbinate and cantorate. Holds seminars and topical discussions with speakers.

Conventions/Meetings: annual conference.

★3418★ WOMEN'S TENNIS ASSOCIATION (WTA)
133 1st St. NE
St. Petersburg, FL 33701   PH: (813)895-5000
Gerard Smith, CEO & Exec.Dir.   FX: (813)894-1982

Founded: 1973. **Members:** 450. **Staff:** 32. **Budget:** US$2,000,000. **Languages:** English. **National.** Professional women tennis players. Purpose is to represent members with regard to professional tournaments.

Publications: *Getting Started*, annual. Newsletter. ● *Inside Women's Tennis*, monthly. Magazine. ● *Media Guide*, annual. Directory. ● *Players Handbook*, annual. ● *Tournament Guide*, annual. Directory.

Conventions/Meetings: annual convention.

★3419★ WOMEN'S TRANSPORTATION SEMINAR-NATIONAL (WTSN)
1 Walnut St.
Boston, MA 02108-2616
Helen Hall, Exec.Sec.

Founded: 1977. **Members:** 2,500. **Staff:** 1. **Budget:** US$200,000. **Local Groups:** 24. **Languages:** English. **National.** Male and female transportation professionals. Assists women interested in transportation; advances the knowledge and training of transportation professionals; encourages communication among members of the transportation industry. Provides a neutral forum for business leaders and government executives to discuss transportation initiatives. Serves as vehicle for network development. Conducts seminars on career planning and management skills; sponsors legislative forums to provide members with the opportunity to hear congressional staff express views on upcoming transportation bills. Sponsors roundtable to allow members to discuss developments with transportation specialists. Makes benefits discounts available to members. **Awards:** Annual (scholarship). Recipient: outstanding female college and graduate students majoring in transportation. **Committees:** Chapter Development; Corporate Relations; Cultural Diversity; Job Bank; Legal; Minority Recruitment; Newsletter; Professional Development; Public Relations; Racial; Recognitions; Scholarship.

Publications: *Women's Transportation Seminar—National Membership Directory*, annual. **Circulation:** 2,500. ● *WTS National Newsletter*, bimonthly. Covers current transportation issues, board meetings, and association activities. **Circulation:** 2,500.

Conventions/Meetings: annual conference (exhibits).

★3420★ WOMEN'S WORLD BANKING (WWB)
8 W. 40th St., 10th Fl.
New York, NY 10018   PH: (212)768-8513
Nancy Berry, Pres.   FX: (212)768-8519

Founded: 1980. **Staff:** 15. **Languages:** English, French, Spanish. **Multinational.** Network of banks and other financial institutions. Assists in securing financing for women with no credit and/or financial history. Encourages governments and financial institutions to change laws restricting women in private enterprise in Third World nations. Encourages private enterprise among women.

Publications: *What Works* (in English, French, and Spanish), 6-8/year. Newsletter. **Advertising:** not accepted. ● *Women at Work* (in English), periodic. **Advertising:** not accepted.

★3421★ WOODSWOMEN
25 W. Diamond Lake Rd.   PH: (612)822-3809
Minneapolis, MN 55419   TF: (800)279-0559
Denise Mitten, Dir.   FX: (800)279-0559

Founded: 1977. **Members:** 800. **Staff:** 5. **Budget:** US$300,000. **Regional Groups:** 4. **Languages:** English. **National.** Women who share an interest in outdoor activities including mountaineering, canoeing, and backpacking. Encourages members' sense of adventure and independence; sponsors educational programs in leadership training and the history of outdoorswomen; conducts wilderness trips. Provides children's services and educational programs. Maintains speakers' bureau and biographical archives; compiles statistics.

Publications: *International Women's Climbing Directory*, biennial. ● *Woodswomen Membership Directory*, annual. ● *Woodswomen News*, quarterly. Newsletter. Contains articles about outdoor trips, an adventure travel directory, and a trip calendar listing. **Circulation:** 10,000. **Advertising:** not accepted.

★3422★ WORLD FEDERATION OF ESTONIAN WOMEN'S CLUBS IN EXILE (WFEWCE)
c/o Mrs. Juta Kurman
68-50 Juno St.
Forest Hills, NY 11375
Mrs. Juta Kurman, Pres.   PH: (718)261-9618

Founded: 1966. **Members:** 1,000. **Staff:** 5. **Budget:** US$500. **Regional Groups:** 14. **State Groups:** 4. **Local Groups:** 3. **Languages:** English, Estonian. **Multinational.** Women's clubs and individuals in Australia, Canada, Germany, Sweden, and the United States. Seeks to preserve Estonian language and ethnic culture; supported the development of an independent Estonia. Conducts charitable programs; maintains biographical archives and speakers' bureau; compiles statistics. Operates archive of local Estonian newspapers and bulletins. **Libraries:** Type: reference.
Subjects: Estonian, Baltic, and American literature.

Publications: *Shawl of Haapsalu*. Circulars and letters.

Conventions/Meetings: annual.

★3423★ WORLD FEDERATION OF HEALTH AGENCIES FOR THE ADVANCEMENT OF VOLUNTARY SURGICAL CONTRACEPTION (WFHAAVSC)
79 Madison Ave., 7th Fl.   PH: (212)561-8095
New York, NY 10016-7802   FX: (212)599-0959
Ms. N. Lynn Bakamjian, Exec.Dir. TX: 425604 ASVUI

Founded: 1975. **Members:** 200. **Staff:** 5. **Budget:** US$450,000. **Languages:** English. **Multinational.** Individual experts; national, regional, and local leadership groups. Fosters the inclusion of voluntary surgical contraception as a choice within basic health services and seeks to advance the understanding of issues involved. Promotes high quality health care and advocates the inclusion of procedures such as tubal ligation, vasectomy, and some nonpermanent, but long-lasting methods in family planning and basic medical programs worldwide. Serves as liaison among members and other international health and population organizations; maintains communications network. Encourages worldwide examination and comparison of educational, legal, professional, scientific, and social issues in the field; develops and disseminates policies and guidelines on pertinent issues; establishes standards for data collection, education, equipment maintenance, medical surveillance, training, and other services. Maintains speakers' bureau.
Committees: Information and Education; International Expert; Legal; Scientific; Statistics; Training.

Publications: *Communique Newsletter* (in Arabic, French, and Spanish), periodic. ● *Communique Newsletter* (in English), annual. ● *Safe & Voluntary Surgical Contraception*. Book.

Conventions/Meetings: biennial general assembly.

★3424★ WORLD FEDERATION OF METHODIST WOMEN, NORTH AMERICA AREA (WFMWNAA)
623 San Fernanco Ave.
Berkeley, CA 94707   PH: (510)526-5536
Dr. Sylvia Faulk, Pres.   FX: (510)528-9842

Founded: 1939. **Languages:** English. **National.** A division of World Federation of Methodist Women. Methodist women representing the United Methodist Church, Methodist Church in the Caribbean and the Americas, Christian Methodist Episcopal Church, African Methodist Episcopal Church,

and African Methodist Episcopal Zion Church. Conducts evangelistic activities; sponsors healing ministries. Seeks an end to discrimination against women worldwide; supports the passage of legislation to prevent child abuse. Examines issues concerning women in the Third World. Promotes the development of literacy training and translation programs. Encourages the establishment of counseling and educational programs on family issues such as food production, malnutrition, hygiene, and family planning. Conducts charitable programs.

Publications: *Tree of Life*, monthly. Newsletter. **Advertising:** not accepted.

Conventions/Meetings: quinquennial seminar. ● periodic regional meeting.

★3425★ WORLD WOMEN FOR ANIMAL RIGHTS/EMPOWERMENT VEGETARIAN ACTIVIST COLLECTIVE
c/o Connie Salamone
616 6th St., No. 2
Brooklyn, NY 11215
Connie Salamone, Dir.   PH: (718)788-1362

Founded: 1982. **Languages:** English. **National.** Individuals interested in the preservation and conservation of animals and the environment. Promotes animal rights through the dissemination of information and promotional materials. Seeks to heighten women's "sensitivity to nature and ecology" through feminism. Conducts research; offers student intern program. Maintains archive of 4000 slides. **Formerly:** American Vegetarian Association.

★3426★ WORLD WOMEN IN THE ENVIRONMENT
1331 H St. NW, Ste. 903
Washington, DC 20005
Meliss Dann, Exec.Dir.   PH: (202)347-1514

Multinational. Worldwide network of women concerned about environmental management and protection. Strives to educate the public and policy makers about the "vital linkages between women, natural resources, and sustainable development."

★3427★ WORLD'S WOMAN'S CHRISTIAN TEMPERANCE UNION - UNITED STATES
c/o Mrs. Winifred L. Nelson
1730 Chicago Ave.
Evanston, IL 60201
Mrs. Winifred L. Nelson, Sec.

National. Women working to educate children and adults on the "evils of alcohol, tobacco, and narcotic drugs." Conducts drug abuse seminars and workshops for youth; sponsors professional training programs for counselors.

★3428★ WORLDWIDE MARRIAGE ENCOUNTER (WWME)
1908 E. Highland, No. A
San Bernardino, CA 92404
Don and Rita Kainz, Exec. Team   PH: (714)881-3456
Members   FX: (714)881-3531

Founded: 1952. **Budget:** US$400,000. **Regional Groups:** 16. **Languages:** English. **National.** Conducts weekend events to help Catholic married couples examine their relationship with each other and with God; guidance is given by three married couples and a priest.

Publications: *Matrimony*, quarterly. Newsletter.

Conventions/Meetings: biennial convention.

★3429★ WORLDWIDE NETWORK (WorldWIDE)
1331 H St. NW, Ste. 903
Washington, DC 20005
Waafas Ofosu-Amaah, Mgr. Dir.   PH: (202)347-1514
                                 FX: (202)347-1524

Founded: 1982. **Members:** 3,400. **Staff:** 4. **Languages:** English. **National.** Women and men interested in environmental protection. Promotes strengthening the role of women in the development and implementation of environmental and natural resource policies. Educates and promotes communication among members concerning the consequences of decisions affecting the environment, especially the contamination and destruction of ecological systems. Encourages members to include environmental and natural resource management activities in their lives; seeks to educate policymakers about problems of women and the environment and to foster increased inclusion of women and their perspectives in the development and implementation of policies and programs. Keeps members informed of environmental projects and women's activities in related areas. Encourages women to serve as agents of change on environmental issues. **Councils:** International Advisory.

Publications: *Follow-Up Special Reports*, quarterly. Newsletter. ● *WorldWIDE Directory of Women in Environment*, annual. ● *WorldWIDE News*, bimonthly. Bulletin. ● *Women and Environment: An Analytical Review*. Book. ● *The Global Assembly Green Book*.

Conventions/Meetings: periodic Global Assembly of Women on Environment general assembly. ● periodic regional meeting.

★3430★ WORLDWIDE: WORLD WOMEN IN THE ENVIRONMENT
1331 H St. NW, Ste. 903
Washington, DC 20005   PH: (202)347-1514
Waafas Ofosu-Amaah, Director   FX: (202)347-1524

Founded: 1981. **Members:** 7,500. **Staff:** 5. **Budget:** US$300,000. **Languages:** English. **Multinational.** Women interested in environmental issues. Works to inform women on a worldwide basis about environmental and development issues pertaining to their communities. Encourages women to become involved in environmental management. Fosters organizational skills and enhances leadership abilities. Conducts forums to deal with environmental issues on community or national levels. **Libraries:** Type:. Holdings: 0. Subjects: Worldwide environmental and development issues. **Computer Services:** Data base, sources of information and materials on environmental and development topics.

Publications: *Global Assembly of Women and the Environment, vol. I and II.* ● *WorldWIDE News*, bimonthly. Newsletter. Features information on individuals, events, projects, studies and reports, organizations and policies pertaining to the environment. ● *WorldWIDE Directory of Women in Environment*, annual. A listing of names, addresses, interests, and expertise of women who participate in WorldWIDE international network.

Conventions/Meetings: monthly meeting - Washington DC, United States.

★3431★ Y-ME NATIONAL ORGANIZATION FOR BREAST CANCER
INFORMATION AND SUPPORT (Y-ME)
18220 Harwood Ave.   PH: (708)799-8338
Homewood, IL 60430   TF: (800)221-2141
Sharon Green, Exec.Dir.   FX: (708)799-5937

Founded: 1978. **Members:** 2,000. **Staff:** 10. **Budget:** US$400,000. **Languages:** English. **National.** Purpose is to provide peer support and information to women who have or suspect they have breast cancer. Activities include presurgical counseling and referral service, inservice programs for health professionals, hot line volunteer training, and technical assistance. Offers seminars and workshops to organizations and businesses on all aspects of breast disease (in English and Spanish). Administers the Deborah David Dewar Fund and the Billie Klein Memorial Fund. **Libraries:** Type: reference.   **Telecommunication Services:** Phone referral system, (708)799-8338. **Committees:** Educational; Fund Raising; Medical Advisory; Planned Giving.

Publications: *Breast Cancer Bibliography*, annual. Book. ● *Y-ME Hotline*, bimonthly. Newsletter. ● *Guidelines for Breast Cancer Support Groups*. Booklet.

Conventions/Meetings: annual luncheon, with benefit fashion show. ● semiannual conference. ● monthly meeting.

★3432★ YOUNG WOMEN OF THE CHURCH OF JESUS CHRIST OF
LATTER-DAY SAINTS (YW)
76 N. Main
Salt Lake City, UT 84150   PH: (801)240-2141
Janette C. Hales, Pres.   FX: (801)240-5458

Founded: 1869. **Members:** 480,000. **Staff:** 5. **Languages:** English. **National.** Girls between the ages of 12 and 18. Seeks to strengthen the spiritual life of young women through Christian values and experiences. Reinforces the values of faith, divine nature, individual worth, knowledge, choice and accountability, good works, and integrity. Works to develop leadership attributes in young women through service in the community. **Awards:** Periodic Young Womanhood Medallion (recognition).

★3433★ YOUNG WOMEN'S CHRISTIAN ASSOCIATION OF THE
UNITED STATES OF AMERICA (YWCA-USA)
726 Broadway
New York, NY 10003   PH: (212)614-2700
Gwendolyn Calvert Baker, Exec.Dir.   FX: (212)677-9716

Founded: 1858. **Members:** 2,000,000. **Staff:** 21,000. **Regional Groups:** 3. **Local Groups:** 446. **Languages:** English. **National.** Women and girls over 12 years of age and their families who participate in service programs of health education, recreation, clubs and classes, and counseling and assistance to girls and women in the areas of employment, education, human sexuality, self improvement, voluntarism, citizenship, emotional and physical health, and juvenile justice. Seeks to make contributions to peace, justice, freedom, and dignity for all people; works toward the empowerment of women and the elimination of racism. Conducts international advocacy program on human rights and on peace and development. Sponsors national advocacy programs on: international peace and justice; economic and social justice; improved environmental quality; individual rights and liberties. Local units include 366 community YWCA's, 39 student associations, 112 YWCA residences/shelters, and 24 resident camps. Men and boys participate in YWCA activities as associates or registrants. Maintains archives; compiles statistics. **Libraries:** Type:. Holdings: 8,000; books, periodicals, clippings. Subjects: contemporary American women. **Awards:** Periodic Tribute to Women in Industry. **Divisions:** Business Support Services; Communications/Public Relations; Data Center/ Research; Executive Office; Field Services; Finance; Financial Development; Leadership Development; MIS; National Personnel Services; National Support; Program Services; Services to Student Associations; Public Policy; Racial Justice; World Relations.

Publications: *Young Women's Christian Association of the U.S.A.*, annual. Booklet. **Advertising:** not accepted. ● *Young Women's Christian Association of the U.S.A.*, triennial. Directory. **Advertising:** not accepted. ● *YWCA Interchange*, quarterly. Newsletter. Covers national and local YWCA news. **Circulation:** 22,000. **Advertising:** not accepted.

Conventions/Meetings: triennial convention - next 1994.

★3434★ ZETA PHI BETA
1734 New Hampshire Ave. NW
Washington, DC 20009   PH: (202)387-3103
Linda Thompson, Exec.Dir.   FX: (202)232-4593

Founded: 1920. **Members:** 75,000. **Regional Groups:** 8. **Languages:** English. **National.** Service and social sorority. Maintains Zeta Phi Beta Sorority Educational Foundation. Maintains speakers' bureau and charitable program; sponsors competitions. **Awards:** Periodic (scholarship). **Committees:** Economic Empowerment; Education; Substance Abuse Prevention.

Publications: *Archon*, semiannual. Journal. Includes listing of employment opportunies. **Advertising:** not accepted. ● *Membership Directory*, annual. ● *National President's Newsletter*, quarterly.

Conventions/Meetings: biennial convention (exhibits).

★3435★ ZETA TAU ALPHA
3330 Founders Rd.
Indianapolis, IN 46268
Deb Ensor, Exec.Dir.   PH: (317)872-0540

Founded: 1898. **Members:** 122,000. **Languages:** English. **National**. Social sorority. **Awards:** Periodic (scholarship).

Publications: *Themis*, quarterly. Newsletter.

Conventions/Meetings: biennial convention.

Alphabetic Name Index

Organizations are listed alphabetically by the official name of the organization. Official name citations are followed, in parentheses, by the city and country in which the organization is located. National language name translations and former/alternate names of organizations are also listed alphabetically. Index numbers refer to entry numbers, not to page numbers. A star (★) before an entry number signifies that the name is not listed separately, but is mentioned or described within the entry indicated by the entry number.

B

C

Alphabetic Name Index

Alphabetic Name Index

Alphabetic Name Index

E

Alphabetic Name Index

J

N

W

XYZ

Alphabetic Name Index

Organizations' Activities Index

Organizations are listed alphabetically by the official name of the organization under applicable bolded subject term references. *"See"* and *"See Also"* italicized citations refer the user to related bolded subject terms listed in the index. Index numbers refer to entry numbers, not to page numbers.

Organizations' Activities Index

Organizations' Activities Index

Organizations' Activities Index

Organizations' Activities Index

Families

Organizations' Activities Index

Feminism (See Also **Equal Rights; Women's Studies**)

Organizations' Activities Index

Organizations are listed alphabetically under each applicable subject term

Organizations' Activities Index

Organizations are listed alphabetically under each applicable subject term

Organizations' Activities Index

Organizations' Activities Index

American Psychological Association - Women's Program
(Washington, DC, USA)............................**2527**
Association for Women in Psychology (Philadelphia, PA, USA)........**2581**
Women in Psychology for Legislative Action (Beverly Hills, CA,
USA)..**3322**

Publishing — *See* Business and Management

Rape (*See Also* Sexual Abuse)
American Rape Prevention Association (Orinda, CA, USA)..............**2529**
American Women's Self-Defense Association (Lindenhurst, NY,
USA)..**2549**
Anti-Rape Campaign, A Women's Collective (Panaji, GD, India)........**550**
Asociacion Asistencia a Mujeres Violadas (Madrid, Spain)...........**2093**
Canadian Association of Sexual Assault Centres (Vancouver, BC,
Canada)..**2305**
Casa Pensamiento de Mujer (Aibonito, PR, USA)....................**2620**
Centro de Ayuda a Victimas de Violacion (San Juan, Puerto
Rico)..**998**
Comision para la Investigacion de Malos Tratos a las Mujeres
(Madrid, Spain).......................................**2130**
Forum Against the Oppression of Women (Bombay, MH, India)........**576**
Gabriela Commission on Violence Against Women (Quezon City,
Philippines)..**815**
Korea Rape Crisis Center (Seoul, Republic of Korea)................**662**
National Clearinghouse on Marital and Date Rape (Berkeley, CA,
USA)..**2979**
National Coalition Against Sexual Assault (Washington, DC, USA).....**2983**
National Collective of Rape Crisis and Related Groups of
Aotearoa (Palmerston North, New Zealand)................**733**
Northern Ireland Rape Crisis Association - Rape and Incest Line
(Belfast, AT, Northern Ireland)..........................**2019**
Project Safe Run (Eugene, OR, USA)............................**3137**
Rape Crisis National Office (Wellington, New Zealand)..............**757**
Rape Crisis Society of Trinidad and Tobago (Port of Spain,
Trinidad and Tobago)...................................**1064**
Stree Adhar Kendra (Pune, MH, India)...........................**616**
Victims Advocates (Christchurch, New Zealand)...................**763**
We Are AWARE (Bedford, MA, USA)...........................**3246**
Women Against Rape (Columbus, OH, USA)......................**3263**
Women Against Rape - Britain (London, England)..................**1726**
Women in Crisis (New York, NY, USA)...........................**3279**

Recreation — *See* Sports and Recreation

Refugees
Australian National Consultative Committee on Refugee Women
(Camperdown, NW, Australia)...........................**410**
Refugee Women in Development (Washington, DC, USA)............**3143**
Women's Commission for Refugee Women and Children (New
York, NY, USA)......................................**3361**

Religion and Theology (*See Also* Catholic; Jewish)
African Methodist Episcopal Church - Women's Missionary
Society (Washington, DC, USA).........................**2422**
All India Council of Christian Women (Madras, TN, India)...........**545**
American Academy of Religion - Women's Caucus (St. Louis,
MO, USA)..**2445**
American Atheist Women (Austin, TX, USA).......................**2466**
American Baptist Women's Ministries (Valley Forge, PA, USA)........**2467**
American Humanist Association - Feminist Caucus (San Jose,
CA, USA)..**2496**
American Society of Church History - Women in Theology and
Church History (Philadelphia, PA, USA)...................**2534**
Anglican Church Women (Andros, Bahamas)......................**925**
Anglican Women's Fellowship (Cape Town, Republic of South
Africa)..**243**
Archconfraternity of Christian Mothers (Pittsburgh, PA, USA)........**2555**
Asian Christian Center for Women Studies (Manila, Philippines)......**807**
Association of Anglican Women (Palmerston North, New Zealand)......**704**
Association de l'Eglise Evangelique Reformee du Burkina
(Ouagadougou, Burkina Faso)...........................**31**
Association of Presbyterian Women (Christchurch, New Zealand)......**705**
Association of Theologically Trained Women of India (Kerala,
India)...**553**
Australian Church Women (Burnie, TA, Australia)..................**406**
Baha'i International Community (New York, NY, USA)...............**2590**
Baha'i National Women's Committee (London, England)..............**1607**
Baha'i Women's Association of Guam (Agana, Guam)................**522**

Baha'i Women's Committee (Palmerston North, New Zealand)..........**707**
Baha'i Women's Committee of Northern Ireland (Magheramorne,
LR, Northern Ireland)..................................**2002**
Baptist Women's League of Sri Lanka (Dehiwela, Sri Lanka)..........**853**
Baptist Women's Ministries (Dunedin, New Zealand)................**708**
Baptist World Alliance - Women's Department (McLean, VA,
USA)..**2592**
Barbados Conference of Moravian Women's Fellowship (St.
Thomas, Barbados)....................................**931**
Black Women in Church and Society (Atlanta, GA, USA).............**2602**
Buddhist Churches of America Federation of Buddhist Women's
Associations (San Francisco, CA, USA)...................**2614**
Campus Ministry Women (Ann Arbor, MI, USA)...................**2618**
Caribbean Church Women - Antigua (St. John's, Antigua-
Barbuda)..**918**
Caribbean Church Women - Jamaica (Kingston, Jamaica).............**982**
Caribbean Church Women - Trinidad and Tobago (Port of Spain,
Trinidad and Tobago)..................................**1035**
Christian Conference of Asia - Women's Division (Singapore,
Singapore)...**841**
Christian Women Fellowship (Kampala, Uganda)...................**330**
Christian Women's Club of Guam (Agana, Guam)..................**524**
Christian Women's Fellowship of the Associated Churches of
Christ (Wanganui, New Zealand).........................**712**
Church of Scotland Women's Guild (Edinburgh, Scotland)...........**2072**
Church Women in Kenya (Nairobi, Kenya)........................**104**
Church Women United (New York, NY, USA).....................**2643**
Church Women United - Trinidad and Tobago (Mount Lambert,
Trinidad and Tobago)..................................**1037**
Circles of Exchange (Seattle, WA, USA).........................**2644**
Comite Evangelico Pro-Ayuda al Desarrollo - Programa Pastoral
de la Mujer (Managua, Nicaragua)........................**1312**
Commission of the Status and Role of Women (Evanston, IL,
USA)..**2659**
Commission for the Status of Women - Australian Council of
Churches (Sydney, NW, Australia).......................**417**
Concerned Women for America (Washington, DC, USA)..............**2680**
Ecumenical Celebrations (New York, NY, USA)....................**2719**
Ecumenical Women's Group (Mendoza, Argentina).................**1095**
Eglise Methodiste Libre au Rwanda (Kigali, Rwanda)...............**218**
Emunah Women of Canada (Montreal, PQ, Canada)................**2326**
Episcopal Women's Caucus (Laurel, MD, USA)....................**2723**
European Baptist Women's Union (Budapest, Hungary)..............**1888**
Evangelical and Ecumenical Women's Caucus (Hadley, NY, USA)......**2730**
Evangelischer Frauenbund der Schweiz (Zurich, Switzerland)..........**2181**
Federacion Femenina Evangelica Metodista Argentina (Buenos
Aires, Argentina).....................................**1100**
Federacion de Mujeres Metodistas (Panama, Panama)...............**1328**
Federation of Methodist Women in Bolivia (La Paz, Bolivia)..........**1129**
Federation of Methodist Women Norway (Oslo, Norway)............**2034**
Formacion y Participacion de la Mujer en el Autodesarrollo
Comunitario (Alajuela, Costa Rica)......................**1231**
General Commission on the Status and Role of Women
(Evanston, IL, USA)...................................**2769**
Gereformeerde Vrouwenbond (Baarn, Netherlands)................**1971**
Grace of God Movement for the Women of the World (Los
Angeles, CA, USA)...................................**2778**
Grail Movement (Loveland, OH, USA)...........................**2779**
Hindu Women's Organization of Trinidad and Tobago
(Woodbrook, Trinidad and Tobago)......................**1044**
Hindu Women's Society (Colombo, Sri Lanka)....................**857**
History of Women Religious (Los Angeles, CA, USA)...............**2789**
Home and Family Association (Dar es Salaam, United Republic
of Tanzania)...**299**
Iniciativa de Mujeres Cristianas (San Salvador, El Salvador)..........**1264**
Institute of Women Today (Chicago, IL, USA)....................**2804**
International Association of Liberal Religious Women
(Wemeldinge, Netherlands).............................**1972**
International Association of Ministers Wives and Ministers
Widows (Chesapeake, VA, USA).........................**2814**
International Association of Women Ministers (Stroudsburg, PA,
USA)..**2818**
International Christian Women's Fellowship (Indianapolis, IN, USA).....**2823**

Reproductive Medicine (See Also Obstetrics and Gynecology)

Organizations' Activities Index

Science (See Also Social Sciences)

Society for Canadian Women in Science and Technology
(Vancouver, BC, Canada)....................2366
Society of Women Engineers (New York, NY, USA)..............3195
Women in Cell Biology (Miami, FL, USA)....................3272
Women in Engineering Centre (London, England)..............1730
Women in Engineering Program Advocates Network (West
Lafayette, IN, USA)....................3285
Women in Information Processing (Washington, DC, USA).......3300
Women Inventors Project (Etobicoke, ON, Canada)............2375
Women in Physics (London, England)....................1738
Women in Science and Engineering (Mississauga, ON, Canada)......2376
Women in Science Enquiry Network (Glebe, NW, Australia)......458
Women's Aquatic Network (Washington, DC, USA)..............3347
Women's Engineering Society (London, England)..............1751
Women's Initiatives for Successful Entrepreneurship (London, ON,
Canada)....................2384

Self-Help
Fat Lip Readers Theater (Oakland, CA, USA)..............2736
Homosexuals Anonymous Fellowship Services (Reading, PA,
USA)....................2792
Largesse (New Haven, CT, USA)....................2886
Women for Sobriety (Quakertown, PA, USA)..............3328
Women in Transition (Philadelphia, PA, USA)..............3331
Women Who Love Too Much (Downsview, ON, Canada)..........2380

Service Clubs
Amigas Sefaradies de NA'AMAT (Buenos Aires, Argentina)......1085
Association of Wa-Tan-Ye Clubs (Mason City, IA, USA)........2575
Association of Women's Forum Clubs of Australia (Sorrento, QL,
Australia)....................405
British NA'AMAT (Leeds, WY, England)....................1612
Co-Ette Club (Detroit, MI, USA)....................2647
Elisheva Group NA'AMAT (Melbourne, VI, Australia)..........2745
Federation of Woman's Exchanges (Memphis, TN, USA)........2770
General Federation of Women's Clubs (Washington, DC, USA).......2770
Jaycees Women's League (Port of Spain, Trinidad and Tobago).......1047
Legion of Young Polish Women (Chicago, IL, USA)............2894
NA'AMAT Canada (Montreal, PQ, Canada)..............2347
NA'AMAT Femmes Pionnieres (Paris, France)..............1814
NA'AMAT Hungary (Budapest, Hungary)....................1889
NA'AMAT Pioneiras (Sao Paolo, SP, Brazil)..............1154
NA'AMAT Pioneras (Buenos Aires, Argentina)..............1104
NA'AMAT Pioneras (Montevideo, Uruguay)..............1369
NA'AMAT Pioneras (Collondesa, DF, Mexico)..............2403
NA'AMAT Pioneras Grupo Shalom Mane Prutzchi (Lima, Peru).......1353
NA'AMAT Union des Femmes Pionieres (Brussels, Belgium).......1545
National Association of Colored Women's Clubs (Washington,
DC, USA)....................2942
National Association of Negro Business and Professional
Women's Clubs (Washington, DC, USA)....................2953
National Association for Women in Careers (Chicago, IL, USA).......2958
National Federation of Business and Professional Women's Clubs
of the Republic Ireland (Dublin, Ireland)..............1904
Orah Group NA'AMAT (Hawthorn, VI, Australia)..............443
Quota International - Australia (Manly, NW, Australia)..........446
Soroptimist Club - Trinidad and Tobago (St. Clair, Trinidad and
Tobago)....................1067
Soroptimist Foundation of Canada (Calgary, AB, Canada).......2367
Soroptimist International (Lome, Togo)....................319
Soroptimist International of Europe (Geneva, Switzerland).......2196
Soroptimist International of Great Britain and Ireland (Stockport,
CH, England)....................1713
Soroptimist International of Guam (Agana, Guam)............533
Soroptimist International of Israel (Tel Aviv, Israel)..........2267
Soroptimist International of New Zealand (Wellington, New
Zealand)....................762
Soroptimist International of Northern Ireland (Lurgan, AM,
Northern Ireland)....................2023
Soroptimist International - Portugal (Lisbon, Portugal)..........2068
Soroptimist International of the South West Pacific (Sydney, NW,
Australia)....................449
Soroptimist International of Uganda (Kampala, Uganda)..........344
South African Council of Soroptimist Clubs (Durban, Republic of
South Africa)....................265

Unie van Soroptimistenclubs in Nederland, Suriname en de
Nederlandse Antillen (Amsterdam, Netherlands)..............1983
Union of Jewish Women (Harare, Zimbabwe)..............388
Union Luxembourgeoise du Soroptimist International (Fentange/
Plateau, Luxembourg)....................1963
Women in Show Business (North Hollywood, CA, USA)..........3327
Zonta International - Australia (Attadale, WA, Australia)..........470
Zonta International - Netherlands (Velp, Netherlands)..........1997
Zonta International-New Zealand (Auckland, New Zealand).......781

Sexual Abuse (See Also Rape)
Centro de Apoyo para Mujeres Violadas (Mexico City, DF,
Mexico)....................2392
Coalition of Asian Sisters Against Sexual Exploitation (New York,
NY, USA)....................2650
Comision para la Investigacion de Malos Tratos a las Mujeres
(Madrid, Spain)....................2130
Female Circumcision Project (Cairo, Egypt)..............64
Foundation for Women (Bangkok, Thailand)..............887
Medusa - Landelijk Bureau Ontwikkeling Beleid & Hulpverlening
Seksueel Geweld (Utrecht, Netherlands)..............1975
National Collective of Rape Crisis and Related Groups of
Aotearoa (Palmerston North, New Zealand)..............733
Sanctuary (London, England)....................1710
Victims Advocates (Christchurch, New Zealand)..............763
Werkgroep Partner van een Slachtoffer van Seksueel Geweid
(Aalst, Belgium)....................1565
Women Against Sexual Violence by Public Health Workers
(Nijmegen, Netherlands)....................1988
Women in Crisis (New York, NY, USA)....................3279
Women's Centre of Nigeria (Eket, RV, Nigeria)..............210
Women's Circle Support Services (Sisseton, SD, USA)..........3358
Women's Protection League (New Delhi, DH, India)..........635

Sexual Freedom
PEP (Captain Cook, HI, USA)....................3110
Sexuality Information and Resources Clearing House (Ottawa,
ON, Canada)....................2363
Women Associated with Crossdressers Communication Network
(Bulverde, TX, USA)....................3268

Sexual Harassment
American Federation of State, County and Municipal Employees -
Women's Rights Department (Washington, DC, USA)..............2484
American Federation of Teachers - Women's Rights Committee
(Washington, DC, USA)....................2485
Association for the Sexually Harassed (Philadelphia, PA, USA).......2572
Canadian Association Against Sexual Harassment in Higher
Education (Victoria, BC, Canada)....................2304
European Association Against Violence Against Women at Work
(Paris, France)....................1799
Friends of Women Foundation (Bangkok, Thailand)..............888
National Union of Civil and Public Servants: Women's Advisory
Committee (London, England)....................1692
Self Help for Equal Rights (Garret Park, MD, USA)..........3169
Vimochana (Bangalore, KA, India)....................624
Women in Crisis (New York, NY, USA)....................3279
Women Refusing to Accept Tenant Harassment (Vacaville, CA,
USA)....................3324

Single Mothers (See Also Mothers; Parenting; Child Care)
Association des Maisons d'Acceuil (Brussels, Belgium)..........1506
Cherish (Dublin, Ireland)....................1896
Federation Suisse des Familles Monoparentales (Zurich,
Switzerland)....................2182
Fundacion Accion Ya (San Jose, Costa Rica)..............1232
Gingerbread-Northern Ireland (Belfast, AT, Northern Ireland).......2009
Mothers Without Custody (Houston, TX, USA)..............2928
National Council for the Single Mother and Her Child (Melbourne,
VI, Australia)....................434
National Service for Women (Santiago, Chile)..............1186
Only Mama (Moscow, Russia)....................1437
Parents Without Partners (Silver Spring, MD, USA)..........3105
Scottish Council for Single Parents (Edinburgh, Scotland).......2081
Single Mothers By Choice (New York, NY, USA)..............3178
Single Parent Resource Center (New York, NY, USA)..........3179
Solo Parents New Zealand (Wainuiomata, New Zealand).......761

Organizations are listed alphabetically under each applicable subject term

461

Organizations' Activities Index

Women's International Motorcycle Association (Upper Hutt, New Zealand)......774

Women's International Professional Tennis Council (New York, NY, USA)......3386

Women's International Surfing Association (San Juan Capistrano, CA, USA)......3389

Women's League of Health and Beauty (London, England)......1763

Women's Motorcyclist Foundation (LeRoy, NY, USA)......3401

Women's Professional Racquetball Association (Souderton, PA, USA)......3409

Women's Professional Rodeo Association (Blanchard, OK, USA)......3410

Women's Sports Foundation (New York, NY, USA)......3416

Women's Sports Foundation (London, England)......1770

Women's Tennis Association (St. Petersburg, FL, USA)......3418

Womensport Australia (Adelaide, SA, Australia)......467

Woodswomen (Minneapolis, MN, USA)......3421

Substance Abuse (See Also Temperance)

Foundation for Women and the Use of Medication (Eindhoven, Netherlands)......1969

International Advisory Council for Homosexual Men and Women in Alcoholics Anonymous (Washington, DC, USA)......2812

Women in Crisis (New York, NY, USA)......3279

Women for Sobriety (Quakertown, PA, USA)......3328

Women of the World Against Drugs (Moscow, Russia)......1482

Women's Drug Research Project (Ann Arbor, MI, USA)......3367

Temperance (See Also Substance Abuse)

Australian National Woman's Christian Temperance Union (Gordon, NW, Australia)......411

Finnish White Ribbon Association (Helsinki, Finland)......1780

German Women's Organization for Alcohol Free Culture (Egelsbach, Germany)......1849

National British Women's Total Abstinence Union (London, England)......1684

National Woman's Christian Temperance Union (Evanston, IL, USA)......3059

New Zealand Women's Christian Temperance Union (Cambridge, New Zealand)......752

Philippine Woman's Christian Temperance Union (Quezon City, Philippines)......831

Schweizerischer Bund Abstinenter Frauen (Winterthur, Switzerland)......2193

White Ribbon, Norwegian Woman's Christian Temperance Union (Oslo, Norway)......2039

Women for Sobriety (Dunedin, New Zealand)......770

Women's Christian Temperance Union - Republic of South Africa (Cape Town, Republic of South Africa)......279

Women's Temperance Union of Sri Lanka (Colombo, Sri Lanka)......874

World's Woman's Christian Temperance Union (Birmingham, WM, England)......1774

World's Woman's Christian Temperance Union - Australia (Belmont, VI, Australia)......468

World's Woman's Christian Temperance Union - Bermuda (Hamilton, Bermuda)......947

World's Woman's Christian Temperance Union - Japan (Tokyo, Japan)......657

World's Woman's Christian Temperance Union - Korea (Seoul, Republic of Korea)......672

World's Woman's Christian Temperance Union - United States (Evanston, IL, USA)......3427

Transportation — See Business and Management

Umbrella Organizations

Advocates for Community Based Training and Education for Women (Toronto, ON, Canada)......2295

All-China Women's Federation (Beijing, People's Republic of China)......497

All Pakistan Women's Association (Karachi, Pakistan)......784

ASEAN Confederation of Women's Organizations (Bangkok, Thailand)......883

Association des Femmes Camerounaises (Yaounde, Cameroon)......37

Association des Femmes Ivoiriennes (Abidjan, Cote d'Ivoire)......57

Association des Femmes du Niger (Niamey, Niger)......180

Association of Hungarian Women (Budapest, Hungary)......1887

Association des Maisons d'Acceuil (Brussels, Belgium)......1506

Association of Women of Zimbabwe (Marlborough, Zimbabwe)......382

Association of Women's Organizations in Jamaica (Kingston, Jamaica)......981

Belize National Women's Commission (Belize City, Belize)......1110

Bond van Vormings - en Ontwikkelingsorganisties - Inventarisatie Vormingswerk met Vrouwen (Louvain, Belgium)......1509

Botswana Council for Women (Gaborone, Botswana)......23

Bund Osterreichischer Frauenvereine (Vienna, Austria)......1492

Caribbean Family Planning Affiliation (St. Johns, Antigua-Barbuda)......919

Coalition of Australia Participating Organisation of Women (Kingston, AC, Australia)......416

Coalition of Leading Women's Organizations (New York, NY, USA)......2653

Conseil des Femmes Libanaises (Beirut, Lebanon)......2284

Conseil National des Femmes Belges (Brussels, Belgium)......1519

Conseil National des Femmes Francaises (Paris, France)......1795

Conseil National des Femmes Hellenes (Athens, Greece)......1867

Conseil National des Femmes Luxembourgeoises (Luxembourg, Luxembourg)......1953

Consejo de Mujeres de la Republica Argentina (Buenos Aires, Argentina)......1094

Consejo Nacional de Mujeres de Bolivia (La Paz, Bolivia)......1126

Consejo Nacional de Mujeres de Colombia (Bogota, Colombia)......1198

Consejo Nacional de Mujeres de Espana (Barcelona, Spain)......2133

Consejo Nacional de Mujeres de Mexico (Mexico City, DF, Mexico)......2397

Consejo Nacional de Mujeres del Paraguay (Asuncion, Paraguay)......1337

Consejo Nacional de Mujeres del Peru (Lima, Peru)......1348

Consejo Nacional de Mujeres de la Republica Dominicana (Santo Domingo, Dominican Republic)......964

Consejo Nacional de Mujeres del Uruguay (Montevideo, Uruguay)......1364

Conselho Nacional de Mulheres do Brazil (Copacabana, RJ, Brazil)......1148

Consiglio Nazionale delle Donne Italiane (Milan, Italy)......1914

Cook Islands National Council of Women (Rarotonga, Cook Islands)......513

Coordinadora Organizaciones de Mujeres Memch '83 (Santiago, Chile)......1172

Coordinadora de Organizaciones No Gubernamentales de Mujeres (Caracas, Venezuela)......1376

Council of Women in the Bahamas (Nassau, Bahamas)......927

Council of Women's Associations (Rangoon, Myanmar)......692

Council of Women's Organizations in Israel (Jerusalem, Israel)......2259

Deutscher Frauenring (Bad Nauheim, Germany)......1831

Dominica National Council of Women (Roseau, Dominica)......952

Elliniko Diktio Gynekon Evropis (Athens, Greece)......1868

European Association for the Development of Information and Training of Women (Brussels, Belgium)......1521

European Centre of the International Council of Women (Schifflange, Luxembourg)......1954

European Network of Women (Brussels, Belgium)......1525

European Union of Women (Munich, Germany)......1841

Evangelischer Frauenbund der Schweiz (Zurich, Switzerland)......2181

Family Planning International Assistance (Nairobi, Kenya)......109

Fatupaepae Tokelau (Apia, Western Samoa)......912

Federation of Asian Women's Associations (Manila, Philippines)......814

Federation of Business and Professional Women's Associations (Karachi, Pakistan)......789

Federation of Cuban Women (Havana, Cuba)......950

Federation des Femmes Burkinabe (Ouaga, Burkina Faso)......33

Federation of Greek Women (Athens, Greece)......1871

Federation of Japanese Women's Organizations (Tokyo, Japan)......649

Federation of Jewish Women's Organizations (New York, NY, USA)......2743

Federation Nationale des Associations des Femmes du Benin (Cotonou, Benin)......15

Federation Nationale des Femmes Luxembourgeoises (Luxembourg, Luxembourg)......1956

Federation of Organizations for Professional Women (Washington, DC, USA)......2744

Federation of Women's Associations - Turkey (Ankara, Turkey)......2218

Fiji National Council of Women (Suva, Fiji)......516

Gambia National Women's Bureau (Banjul, Gambia)......77

Gambia Women's Federation (Banjul, Gambia)......78

General Arab Women Federation (Baghdad, Iraq)......2256

Organizations' Activities Index

Unions

Widows

Women of Color (*See Also* African American; Asian American; Hispanic American; Native Women)

Organizations' Activities Index

Women's Studies

Organizations' Activities Index